The West Legal Studies Series

Your options keep growing with West Legal Studies

Each year our list continues to offer you more options for every area of the law to meet your course or on-the-job reference requirements. We now have over 140 titles from which to choose in the following areas:

Accounting and Financials for the Law Office
Administrative Law
Alternative Dispute Resolution
Bankruptcy
Business Organizations/Corporations
Civil Litigation and Procedure
CLA Exam Preparation
Computer in the Law Office
Contract Law
Criminal Law and Procedure
Document Preparation
Elder Law
Employment Law
Environmental Law
Ethics
Evidence Law
Family Law

Intellectual Property
Interviewing and Investigation
Introduction to Law
Introduction to Paralegalism
Law Office Management
Law Office Procedures
Legal Nurse Consulting
Legal Research, Writing, and Analysis
Legal Terminology
Paralegal Employment
Product Liability
Real Estate Law
Reference Materials
Social Security
Sports Law
Torts and Personal Injury Law
Wills, Trusts, and Estate Administration

You will find unparalleled, practical support

Each book is augmented by instructor and student supplements to ensure the best learning experience possible. We also offer custom publishing and other benefits such as West's Student Achievement Award. In addition, our sales representatives are ready to provide you with dependable service.

We want to hear from you

Our best contributions for improving the quality of our books and instructional materials is feedback from the people who use them. If you have a question, concern, or observation about any of our materials, or you have a product proposal or manuscript, we want to hear from you. Please contact your local representative or write us at the following address:

West Legal Studies, 5 Maxwell Drive, Clifton Park, NY 12065-2919

For additional information point your browser at
www.westlegalstudies.com

THOMSON

DELMAR LEARNING

Introduction to Law

Introduction to Law

FOURTH EDITION

Beth Walston-Dunham

THOMSON

DELMAR LEARNING

Australia Canada Mexico Singapore Spain United Kingdom United States

THOMSON

DELMAR LEARNING

WEST LEGAL STUDIES

Introduction to Law, Fourth Edition
by Beth Walston-Dunham

Vice President, Career Education Strategic Business Unit:
Dawn Gerrain

Director of Editorial:
Sherry Gomoll

Acquisitions Editor:
Pamela Fuller

Senior Developmental Editor:
Melissa Riveglia

Editorial Assistant:
Sarah Duncan

Director of Production:
Wendy A. Troeger

Production Manager:
Carolyn Miller

Production Editor:
Matthew J. Williams

Director of Marketing:
Donna J. Lewis

Channel Manager:
Wendy E. Mapstone

Cover Image:
Getty Images

Cover Design:
Dutton & Sherman Design

Library of Congress Cataloging-in-Publication Data
Walston-Dunham, Beth.
    Introduction to law / Beth Walston-Dunham.--4th ed.
       p. cm.
Includes bibliographical references and index.
    ISBN 1-4018-3462-0
  1. Law--United States. I. Title.
    KF385.W35 2003
    349.73--dc21
                                        2003051666

For Bobby

Thank you for introducing me to what's important again.

CONTENTS

CHAPTER   5

The Legal Professional   111

CHAPTER   6

The Law of Ethics   137

CHAPTER   7

Substantive and Procedural Issues   165

CHAPTER   8

Jurisdiction   207

TABLE OF CASES

PREFACE

The purpose of this book is not to answer all of one's questions about the law but to generate questions. The goal of this book as an introductory text is to create an awareness and appreciation for the effect that law has on virtually every facet of life and society. The chapters guide the student from a basic introduction of the rationale behind the structure of the American system of government to a discussion of each major area of law in the legal system. Regardless of the initial reason for picking up this book, the intended outcome of reading it remains the same: to gain a better understanding of not only how but also why law is such an integral part of our professional and personal lives and to gain some sense of the order and stability law provides while remaining adaptive to the ever-changing face of American society.

This text is aimed at the student who is studying law for the first time. Each chapter is designed to introduce the student to fundamental legal concepts and principles. Chapters 1 to 6 provide an introduction to the American legal system, the manner in which law is created and administered, and certain considerations that affect legal disputes. The remaining chapters (Chapters 7 to 16) concentrate on different areas of law by exploring basic principles and terminology. The areas covered include property, business, estates, tort, family, contract, and criminal law and procedure. Chapter 5 addresses the roles of legal professionals and their support staff. Throughout the text, and specifically in Chapter 6, discussion is given to the ethical considerations that affect legal professionals and subjects of law.

CHANGES TO THE FOURTH EDITION

The fourth edition of *Introduction to Law* is an updated version of the prior texts. In this edition, new cases are included to reflect the current trends of the courts in the areas of law presented. Sections have been added to introduce the student to the basic concepts and principals of growing areas of practice. The employment section of the chapter on torts has been expanded to touch on actions based on nonphysical injuries such as sexual harassment. Finally, new assignments and applications reflect the changes in the text and law. They will provide more opportunity for the student to analytically process the information. The intent of these changes is to provide the student with the opportunity to obtain an understanding at an introductory level of the current state of the American legal system.

CHAPTER FORMAT

Recent case law has been incorporated to provide a better view of the current position of courts across the nation. Chapter features include the following:

- Chapter objectives open each chapter to focus students' attention on the main elements the student will learn.
- Hypothetical applications are interspersed through each chapter to illustrate chapter concepts. Points for Discussion follow the applications and provide a springboard for class discussion.
- Longer edited cases, most new to this edition, are followed by questions that encourage students to consider the major issues in each case.
- Assignments throughout each chapter test students' knowledge by asking them to apply the chapter material.
- Key terms are set in **boldface** type and defined in the margin where they first appear within the chapter. Also, for easy review, each chapter ends with a list of the key terms found in the chapter.
- Ethical Considerations and Ethical Circumstances in each chapter provide insight to the legal issues presented.
- A chapter summary ends each chapter with a brief review of the main points covered.
- Review questions follow the chapter material, which allow students yet another opportunity to review the chapter content.
- Relevant Links and Internet Assignments connect the text material to the most current resources.

SUPPORT MATERIAL

This fourth edition is accompanied by a support package that will assist students in learning and aid instructors in teaching:

- An **Instructor's Manual** and **Test Bank** by Beth Walston-Dunham accompanies this edition and has been greatly expanded to incorporate all changes in the text and to provide comprehensive teaching support. It includes such items as sample syllabi, a lecture key consisting of a synopsis of all major concepts, answers to all applications, information to guide classroom discussion in the Points for Discussion following applications, assignment and review questions, and answers. Also included are case briefs for all cases found in the text. A comprehensive test bank provides 480 objective test questions and answers. The test bank consists of questions that have already been successfully class tested.

- **On-line Resources™**—the On-line Resource™ provides students with additional support materials in the form of reality based examples, review questions and relevant terminology. The On-line Resource™ can be found at *www.westlegalstudies.com* in the On-line Resource™ section of the Web Site.

- **Web page**—Come visit our website at *www.westlegalstudies.com* where you will find valuable information such as hot links and sample materials to download, as well as other West Legal Studies products.
- **WESTLAW®**—West's on-line computerized legal research system offers students "hands-on" experience with a system commonly used in law offices. Qualified adopters can receive ten free hours of WESTLAW®. WESTLAW® can be accessed with Macintosh and IBM PC and compatibles. A modem is required.
- **Strategies and Tips for Paralegal Educators,** a pamphlet by Anita Tebbe of Johnson County Community College, provides teaching strategies specifically designed for paralegal educators. A copy of this pamphlet is available to each adopter. Quantities for distribution to adjunct instructors are available for purchase at a minimal price. A coupon on the pamphlet provides ordering information.
- **Survival Guide for Paralegal Students,** a pamphlet by Kathleen Mercer Reed and Bradene Moore covers practical and basic information to help students make the most of their paralegal courses. Topics covered include choosing courses of study and note-taking skills.
- **West's Paralegal Video Library**—West Legal Studies is pleased to offer the following videos at no charge to qualified adopters:
  - *The Drama of the Law II: Paralegal Issues Video*
    ISBN: 0-314-07088-5
  - *"I Never Said I Was a Lawyer"*
    Paralegal Ethics Video
    ISBN: 0-314-08049-x
  - *The Making of a Case Video*
    ISBN: 0-314-07300-0
  - *ABA Mock Trial Video—Anatomy of a Trial: A Contracts Case*
    ISBN: 0-314-07343-4
  - *ABA Mock Trial Video—Product Liability*
    ISBN: 0-314-07342-6
  - *Arguments to the United States Supreme Court Video*
    ISBN: 0-314-07070-2
- **Court TV Videos**— West Legal Studies is pleased to offer the following videos from Court TV for a minimal fee:
  - *New York v. Ferguson—Murder on the 5:33: The Trial of Colin Ferguson*
    ISBN: 0-7668-1098-4
  - *Ohio v. Alfieri*
    ISBN: 0-7668-1099-2
  - *Flynn v. Goldman Sachs—Fired on Wall Street: A Case of Sex Discrimination?*
    ISBN: 0-7668-1096-8
  - *Dodd v. Dodd—Religion and Child Custody in Conflict*
    ISBN: 0-7668-1094-1
  - *In Re Custody of Baby Girl Clausen—Child of Mine: The Fight for Baby Jessica*
    ISBN: 0-7668-1097-6
  - *Fentress v. Eli Lilly & Co., et al—Prozac on Trial*
    ISBN: 0-7668-1095-x

- *Garcia v. Garcia—Fighting over Jerry's Money*
  ISBN: 0-7668-0264-7
- *Hall v. Hall—Irretrievably Broken—A Divorce Lawyer Goes to Court*
  ISBN: 0-7668-0196-9
- *Maglica v. Maglica—Broken Hearts, Broken Commitments*
  ISBN: 0-7668-0867-x
- *Northside Partners v. Page and New Kids on the Block—New Kids in Court:
  Is Their Hit Song a Copy?*
  ISBN: 0-7668-9426-7

Please note the internet resources are of a time-sensitive nature and URL addresses may often change or be deleted.

Contact us at westlegalstudies@delmar.com

ACKNOWLEDGMENTS

Thanks and appreciation are extended to the manuscript reviewers, instructors, and others who provided invaluable suggestions and support in the preparation of the fourth edition:

Cynthia Baker Lauber
Community College of Aurora
Aurora, CO

Deborah Howard
University of Evansville
Evansville, IN

Kristine Mullendore
Grand Valley State University
Grand Rapids, MI

Diane Pevar
Manor College
Jenkintown, PA

Melody Schroer
Maryville University
St. Louis, MO

Paula Sinopoli
Mississippi Gulf Coast Community College
Gulfport, MS

I would like to thank Steven Skaggs for his valuable input in the creation of these materials.

Beth Walston-Dunham

CHAPTER 1

The Historical Basis and Current Structure of the American Legal System

CHAPTER OBJECTIVES

After reading this chapter, you should be able to:

- Distinguish the positivist, naturalist, and sociological theories.

- Explain the role of the political theories in the present system of American government.

- Discuss the weaknesses of the Articles of Confederation.

- Describe the function of each branch of government under the Constitution.

- Explain the differences between legislative, judicial, and administrative law.

- Distinguish the traditional and modern balance of application of laws.

- List the hierarchy of law and explain the exception to the rule of the hierarchy.

THE HISTORICAL BASIS OF AMERICAN LAW

Before the Government

The American legal system was not developed hastily. The first settlers in the New World had no intention of creating an entirely new legal system. Rather, for more than a century, these people clung to the methods of law and order that they or their ancestors had known in Europe, predominately in England. Not only did the colonists adhere to many of the laws of England, but they also accepted and sanctioned the prevailing attitudes toward religion under which people were charged and punished by the government for committing acts regarded as sinful and thus illegal. However, as the American population grew, the British and other European governments increased their efforts to establish a formal and permanent influence in America. These attempts included establishment of all aspects of the foreign governments in the colonies. Although the colonists were willing to adopt many legal principles from England, they were not interested in adopting a governmental structure that they felt was not responsive to the will of the people, especially since this was the very structure they had sought to avoid by coming to America.

During the revolutionary era, the colonists realized that they had to establish some form of permanent governmental structure if they were to avoid rule by another country. The present-day structure derives from a combination of factors that influenced those responsible for establishing the American government. The founders' foresight is evidenced by many of the laws and procedures they established that are still in place over two centuries later.

Initially, the colonists' primary legal concern was to deter and punish criminal acts as a means of maintaining order. The founders sought to prosecute and punish those who committed crimes against the morals of the predominantly religious population. Since what was considered morally and religiously right was usually determined by members of the aristocracy, it is no coincidence that the aristocrats were rarely found guilty of immoral or criminal acts. The focus of law in early American society thus was an attempt by the aristocracy to impress its perception of right and wrong upon the working classes and to punish those who the wealthy and powerful perceived to be improper or sinful.

naturalist theory
Philosophy that all persons know inherently the difference between right and wrong.

The original system of justice in America was a simplistic theory of right and wrong. For some time, the colonists saw no need for written statutes, because this theory, also known as the **naturalist theory,**[1] was based on the belief that all persons were born with the ability to distinguish the difference between right and wrong and the knowledge of the responsibility to act in the proper manner. However, the population increased, industry advanced and expanded, cultures mixed, and vast numbers of individuals with different opinions of right and wrong came together in communities. These developments made a justice system predicated on simple aristocratic beliefs of right and wrong obsolete. The people required a more detailed legal system that included written legal principles applicable to a myriad of circumstances and the entire population.

Almost simultaneously with the increase in population and industry came direct attempts by other nations to control the colonies. Initially, each colony fought this control as an individual government without ties to the other colonies; but the colonists quickly realized that if any of the colonies were to succeed against the attempts of the British and others to take control, the colonies must become unified.

The Results of the Revolution

At the time of the Revolution, the colonies came together and issued their Declaration of Independence. To enforce such a document was not an easy task for a largely unsophisticated, poorly armed, and disorganized band of citizens who were matched against Great Britain's army and navy. Nevertheless, the people succeeded and formed a central government made up of individual states.

This new government was guided by a document known as the Articles of Confederation. The Constitution was not passed until 11 years later in September 1787. The Articles bore little resemblance to the current Constitution. Under the Articles, each state sent delegates as members of Congress who then nominated and elected a president among themselves. The delegates passed laws, acted as judges in disputes among the states, negotiated treaties, and served as the government for the new nation. The duties assigned the president were to preside over sessions of Congress and act as an ambassador to, and receive representatives of, other governments. All legal disputes with respect to individuals continued to be dealt with by each state's own system of justice.

In a short time, the colonists considered the Articles of Confederation and Congress largely ineffective. The national government had no "enforcement power": it had no judges, no jails, and no way to force collection of the monies each state was supposed to contribute. Moreover, there was no money or organization to support a national army. Nor was there a staff of government employees to operate the government when Congress was not in session. The president was only the head of a small group of delegates, not the leader of the nation. Clearly, if such a nation was to succeed, a much more organized system would have to be created.

Interestingly, the first real issue in creating a permanent government was whether to allow the states to continue in existence. Several delegates, including some from the South, believed that the individual states should be abolished and that all people and all legal issues should be governed by a central authority. Recall that in history, small states within a country often ended up in conflict with one another. In this instance, however, the idea failed to gain popular support as the settlers were fiercely independent and sought to preserve as much personal freedom from government as possible. In the end, a government of separate state governments and a national government with specific functions was created. The states were left intact because they could respond effectively and quickly to the needs of their citizens and the individual state economies. Keep in mind that mass transit and communication were virtually nonexistent and a distant national government was seen as being uninformed and uninvolved on matters of local concern. The national government was formed to protect the fundamental rights of all citizens and ensure that the state governments would not prohibit individual rights. The national government would also handle national issues such as interstate commerce, Indian affairs and immigration, and international issues such as treaties for trade and nonaggression.

Establishment of branches of government.   Once the issue of statehood was decided, the Constitutional Congress convened in Philadelphia to create a structure for the new federal government. The Constitutional Congress drafted the Constitution, which clearly defined the powers and limitations of the national and state governments with respect to each other and to individual citizens. The members of the Constitutional Congress agreed that there would be three distinct branches of government, each with separate duties and all with the obligation to cooperate with and monitor the other branches to ensure that no one branch obtained too much power.

The first branch of government created by the Constitutional Congress was the legislative branch, to be called Congress. Congress would be elected by the people (directly for the House of Representatives, indirectly for the Senate, which was elected by the state legislatures until the Seventeenth Amendment was ratified in 1913). Congress would retain the sole authority to make statutory law. In this way, the people as a whole would always have significant influence in making the laws that all persons were required to follow. As delegated by the Constitution, only Congress, and no other branch, has the power to create statutory law. In the past, when any other governmental source attempted to create statutory law, the law was struck down as being in violation of what is known as the delegation doctrine. The delegation doctrine is based on the legal principle that Congress cannot delegate or give away its authority to make statutory law. The doctrine has been applied most often in the creation of regulatory law by administrative agencies under the executive branch. Chapter 4, which covers administrative law specifically, discusses the delegation doctrine more fully.

The second branch of government created was the executive branch. The president heads the executive branch at the national level, while each state executive branch is headed by a governor. Under the Constitution, the president is elected indirectly by the people through the electoral college. Each state is entitled to appoint a number of electors equal to the state's total number of senators and representatives to Congress. A person cannot serve as both a member of Congress and an elector. Each state legislature determines the manner in which the electors are appointed. The electors vote and elect the president by a majority. Generally, the electoral vote reflects the popular vote. In the event there is no one person with a majority, the House of Representatives is responsible for electing the president. The details of the electoral process can be found in Article II of the Constitution (Appendix A). Chapter 4 further discusses the executive branch.

The president has power to approve or reject acts of Congress; however, the power is not absolute, and the president cannot deny the authority of Congress to enact law if it is in fact the will of the majority that such law be enacted.

Rejection by the president of a law enacted by Congress is known as the veto power and can be overridden by a significant majority of Congress. The president also has several important functions with respect to foreign affairs and has the ultimate duty to enforce the laws of the United States. Consequently, federal law enforcement agencies are considered part of the executive branch. A similar structure is in place at the state level between the governor and state law enforcement personnel. The various powers and functions of the executive branch are discussed further in Chapter 4.

Finally, the Constitutional Convention determined that a third and separate branch of government was needed to serve as mediator of disputes. Thus, the judicial branch was established. The judiciary has the authority to interpret laws and protect the Constitution from violation by Congress, the president, or the states. Although the Constitution vests the ultimate authority to enforce laws in the president, in practice, the judiciary also assists in enforcement when the courts apply law to specific cases.

The Bill of Rights. The three separate but related branches of government were designed to offer protection from a small number of persons gaining power over the entire population. By independent operation of the branches but with the power of the branches to influence one another, the people are better protected from one branch obtaining too much power or using its power unwisely. Through this system of checks and balances, each branch can use its specially designated powers to make sure the other branches act within their constitutionally prescribed limits.

In addition to framing the Constitution, Congress, with the approval of the people, subsequently passed the Bill of Rights, which protects essential fundamental human freedoms. The Bill of Rights protects all citizens from government infringement on those matters presumed to be inherently personal and a matter of choice for all human beings. The following rights are specifically protected:

- Freedom of speech, religion, and press; peaceable assembly; petitions for governmental change.
- Right to bear arms.
- Freedom from unreasonable invasion of home by the government for purposes of search and seizure of persons or property.
- Right to have an independent judicial magistrate determine if probable cause exists before a search or arrest warrant can be issued.
- Right not to be tried twice for the same crime.
- Right not to have persons or property seized without due process.
- Right to a speedy and public trial.
- Right to an impartial jury in the jurisdiction where the alleged crime occurred.
- Freedom from forced self-incrimination.
- Right to counsel in criminal prosecutions.
- Right of the accused to know of the crime alleged.
- Right of the accused to confront the witnesses for the prosecution.
- Right not to be subjected to excessive bail.

◆ Freedom from cruel or unusual punishment.

◆ Right of the states to govern on matters not addressed in the Constitution or its amendments.

The Bill of Rights establishes the standards of fundamental fairness by which the government must deal with its citizens. The standards of fairness established by the Bill of Rights have been and continue to be protected by the U.S. Supreme Court.

Additional individual rights.   In recent years, the Supreme Court has been increasingly asked to resolve issues that determine the rights of persons to be free from governmental intrusion into their private lives. Issues have ranged from abortion to the rights of law enforcement to search and seize persons and evidence of criminal activity. Frequently, news reports will discuss opinions of the Supreme Court that define the boundaries between the government obligations and individual freedoms with respect to the Bill of Rights. From time to time, additional language regarding these freedoms has been added through amendments to the Constitution as Congress and the people have deemed appropriate.

Not only were the Constitution and its amendments documents created over 200 years ago to establish a new government, but they are also the foundations of present-day law. Every time Congress passes a statute, the executive branch enforces the law, or the judiciary interprets law to be applicable to a situation or an individual, such action must be taken in accordance with the requirements of the Constitution and its amendments. All law created in this country must be consistent with, and embody the spirit of, the rights guaranteed in the Constitution and its amendments. The Constitution and its amendments continue to be responsible for giving definition to the rights of citizens and government alike. In recent years, the courts have used the Constitution and its amendments to prevent police from invading the privacy of individuals without a warrant, to allow people the right to publicly express their religious and political beliefs, and to encourage the public to take an active role in government through elections, petitions, and peaceful protests.

Assignment 1.1

> Identify which right from the Bill of Rights protects each of the following items.
>
> 1. Burning the flag as a formal protest against actions of the U.S. government.
> 2. Refusal to testify in a criminal case brought against oneself.
> 3. Right to be free prior to conviction and pending trial in a criminal case.
> 4. Right to believe in a religion that does not acknowledge the traditional Christian role of God and Jesus.

5. Right to refuse entry to one's home to police or government officials under ordinary circumstances.
6. Right to publish antigovernment sentiments in newspapers and magazines.
7. Right, under reasonable circumstances, to own a gun.
8. Right to own real property that the government cannot seize for government use without proper justification and payment.
9. Right to refuse use of personal property by armed forces.
10. Right to have criminal charges either prosecuted or dropped in a reasonable time.

Assignment 1.2

1. Following 9/11/01, a large number of individuals of Middle Eastern descent were picked up and detained for periods ranging from a few days to months. How does this correspond to the right to be free from unreasonable search and seizure?
2. Identify another situation when one's constitutional right might be outweighed by the need for public safety/interests.

The Influence of Political Theories

The functioning of the branches of government and the manner in which issues between government and citizens are decided are the product of distinct philosophies that have influenced the American legal system since its inception. As Congress structured the new government, the naturalist theory became inadequate to deal with the complexity of legal issues that arose. As a result, other theories regarding the establishment of an orderly society were incorporated into the U.S. system of government and law. One influential theory was the **positivist theory,** which proposes that a government should have a single entity to determine what is right and wrong as a matter of law.[2] The law cannot be questioned or challenged. If a law is violated, punishment will automatically follow. This theory is evident in the court of last resort—the U.S. Supreme Court. Short of a constitutional amendment, the decisions of the Supreme Court are not subject to any other authority.

Another political theory of law that has become an integral part of American law is rooted in social consciousness. This sociological view suggests that people as a group determine what is and is not acceptable, based on the needs of society at the time. **Sociological theory** holds that the law is in a constant state of change and adjusts accordingly to the needs of society. Society as a whole decides what is right and what is wrong.[3] In conjunction with the naturalist theory, the positivist and sociological theories provide the components for a successful and durable

positivist theory
Political belief that there should be a superior governmental entity that is not subject to question or challenge.

sociological theory
Doctrine that follows the principle that government should adapt laws to reflect the current needs and beliefs of society.

government. Today the majority of law is created by representatives elected to Congress by the population. If citizens believe a law is wrong, they can lobby to have it changed. If they believe their elected representatives are not enacting laws that embody the beliefs of the people, they can elect new legislators. If the legislature passes a law that appears to violate the Constitution, citizens can challenge the law in the courts that have the power to resolve the issue by upholding the statute or invalidating it as unconstitutional.

Balance as the Key to Success

In some respects, the U.S. government is a product of each of the three philosophies previously discussed. The naturalist theory is reflected in the language of the Constitution and the Bill of Rights, which (especially the Bill of Rights) state what was and continues to be considered fundamentally fair. The Constitution and the Bill of Rights also contain statements indicative of the positivist idea of an ultimate authority that interprets the laws and decides in what circumstances they apply and how they should be enforced. The ultimate rule has been embodied in the judiciary. Although laws can be challenged, in such cases, the Supreme Court is generally the final authority on legal issues. A decision by this court can be affected only by a congressional constitutional enactment or in a decision wherein the Court revises a previous position (both are relatively rare occurrences). The Supreme Court helps ensure that the laws are applied consistently to all people. The duty of the Court is to guarantee that each individual's rights will be protected against government, persons, or entities that might violate those rights.

The sociological theory plays an important role in our governmental structure, because society can influence the government and laws in a number of ways. The people have the right to periodically elect representatives to Congress and to select the president. They even have the right to approve or reject constitutional amendments and certain other laws. If society's needs change, the flexible system of government allows passage of laws or election of representatives who will enact laws suited to the changing times or both. Evidence of this can be seen in any governmental election. Senators and representatives are elected by a majority who share similar political beliefs. Theoretically, the members of Congress elected by the majority represent the beliefs of the people with regard to the law.

As a practical matter, citizens have more frequent personal contact with the judicial branch than with any other branch of government. Judges hear everything from traffic cases to domestic disputes to claims that Congress has exceeded the limits of its authority by passing laws that are in violation of the Constitution. Since the beginning of the current system of government, courts have continually faced the task of balancing competing interests. These interests might be called the **traditional balance** and the **modern balance,** both of which judges employ when determining legal claims.

The traditional balance arose from the very heart of our governmental system. The people no longer wanted strictly positivist rule from a single source but wanted to have input into the laws by which they had to live. However, not everyone agrees as to what the law should be in a given situation. Under majority

traditional balance

Goal of the judiciary to allow maximum personal freedom without detracting from the welfare of the general public.

modern balance

Goal of lawmaking authorities to balance the need for consistency and stability against the need for a flexible and adaptive government.

rule, laws are enacted based on what the majority thinks is necessary to protect the rights of the public as a whole. Some individuals, however, maintain that they have a valid right to disobey a particular law or that the law as written does not apply to their particular situation. In that case, the judiciary must examine the broadly written laws and apply them to individual circumstances. The challenge facing every judge is to enforce the laws to the extent necessary to protect the rights of the public while permitting the greatest amount of personal freedom possible for the individual. Simply stated, the traditional balance equals The Rights of the People versus The Rights of the Individual.

APPLICATION 1.1

Tamika Gotsis is a retailer for exotic birds. She has a peacock-breeding facility at her home, which is situated on approximately 3 acres. Most of her birds are shipped around the world. The town nearby decides to annex the area and create a new subdivision of upscale homes to attract people from a large city 30 miles away and thereby boost the local economy. As individuals begin moving into the homes, they realize that peacocks and peahens are extremely vocal animals, especially at night. The once rural property is now within city limits and subject to zoning laws. The city informs Tamika that she must move the birds to another location. Tamika takes the position that she has an established business and the right to continue it in the location where it has always been. The court must consider Tamika's rights versus those of public interest and, in particular, the adjacent neighbors.

Realistically, Tamika would probably lose her case. Not only are the interests of other citizens at issue, but also the significant boost to economy of the entire local community. Tamika's business is not of the type that she would lose a great deal of walk-in business if she were forced to relocate.

Point for Discussion
- What if Tamika's business was a raceway that attracted top-level racers from around the country and fans from around the state for weekend races (also quite noisy events)?

Initially, judges had only to balance individual freedoms against the good of the nation as a whole. But over the course of time, American society became increasingly complex. People from many different cultures, races, and religions came to this country in large numbers. The industrial revolution reached full force, followed by the age of advanced technology. The government withstood a civil war, two world wars, and numerous conflicts with other countries of different political structures. Many other governments and societies have crumbled under much less stress. The longevity of the American government is largely the result of the willingness of the judiciary and the other branches of government to develop and employ the modern balance in conjunction with the traditional balance.

The modern balance is a very delicate one. In essence, it is the need to enforce existing legal principles based on the Constitution versus the need to adopt legal principles more reflective of current society. To write laws that would envision all the potential situations and changes in society for hundreds of years to come is an impossible task. Thus, the judiciary, with the help of the executive branch and Congress, must be able to recognize those situations where modifications in the existing system were warranted. This balance has been accomplished without ever disturbing the fundamental structure set forth in the Constitution. Indeed, the modern balance is the ability to enforce law consistently while retaining enough flexibility to adapt to changes in societal standards.

APPLICATION 1.2

For more than 100 years, the law of State X has been that a person could not sue and recover for the emotional injury suffered by merely witnessing injury to a family member. Nancy Du Four watched as a drunken motorist appeared to deliberately run down and kill her child who was walking on the sidewalk in front of her home. Nancy sued the driver for the death of her child and for the emotional trauma of witnessing this accident, which cost her thousands of dollars in psychiatric services to help her deal with the memory of the accident. The court must determine whether it should (to promote consistency in the law) follow the law established in the 1900s that witnesses cannot recover or allow for the first time—and thereby establish new precedent—a bystander to recover for the trauma incurred by witnessing injury to a family member. The court must evaluate what the majority of present-day society would deem appropriate.

The law in State A has been clear for 200 years that the natural father of an illegitimate child had no rights with regard to placement for adoption of the child at birth. Burt Donovan is a 22-year-old father of one child, but is not married to the mother of the child. The birth mother has indicated her intention to place the child for adoption. Burt wants very much to have custody of the child and has filed a petition to prevent the adoption. The court is faced with the issue of following the existing law, which would preclude Burt from stopping the adoption, or changing the legal precedent to allow Burt to seek legal rights of paternity including custody. The court must make its decision based on societal changes with respect to the role of the father in American culture and the differences in the approach to constitutional rights regarding parenting.

Point for Discussion

◆   Explain how and why you think each issue should be resolved.

THE MODERN LEGAL SYSTEM

The present U.S. government that enacts and administers federal law in the United States is far more sophisticated and much larger than the first government that took office under the Constitution in 1789. The first government was a single Congress of senators and representatives from the 13 colonies (the Senate with two senators elected by each state legislature and the House of Representatives with members proportionate to the population of each state), a president whose role was still not well defined beyond basic duties listed in Article II of the Constitution, and a single court to serve as the judiciary for an entire nation.

Today, that same Congress includes senators and representatives elected by the population of each of the 50 states. The presidency has developed into a complicated office that not only represents this country in foreign affairs but also oversees the administrative agencies of government and approves or rejects all acts of Congress. The federal judiciary has grown to include three separate levels: the Supreme Court, 13 U.S. Circuit Courts of Appeals, and more than 90 U.S. District Courts. Interestingly, all three branches still follow the same basic purposes outlined in the Constitution. The manner in which each of these branches operates today is discussed in greater detail in subsequent chapters.

The Sources of Law

The primary source of all law in this country is the U.S. Constitution. Added to that are the state constitutions for each of the 50 states. From these flow the other sources of law. A common misconception is that legislatures—either state or federal (Congress)—are the source of all laws. In reality, legislatures are only one source of law. Law, also known as a **legal standard** or legal principle, comes in different forms and from different sources. It can apply to people in general, a particular group of citizens, or a specific person or entity such as a corporation.

legal standard
Legal principle, point of law. May appear in the form of statutory, judicial, or administrative law.

Each branch of government plays an active role in creating the law of the nation. In addition, each state has a system of government similar to the federal structure, and law at the state level is created in much the same way as at the federal level. The distinction is that state governments are responsible for dealing with those issues not addressed by the U.S. Constitution. The following discussion examines the sources of law as well as their relationship to each other and the hierarchy of law.

Statutory law.   As just noted, the most familiar law is **statutory** (legislative) **law.** Such laws are enacted by a state legislature or by Congress.[4] If a state legislature enacts a law, all persons and entities present in the state must obey it. If Congress enacts a federal law, all persons in the nation are required to follow it. (Chapter 3 addresses the manner in which legislative laws are created.) Once approved by the legislature, a statute will generally continue indefinitely as law until either the legislature repeals (deactivates) it or the high court of the state or federal government rules it unconstitutional. Federal laws must be consistent with the U.S. Constitution, whereas state laws must be in accordance with both the state and the federal

statutory law
A statute. Law created by the legislature.

FIGURE 1.1

Vermont Statute
(T.9 § 4452 on
p 1–23A)

VERMONT STATUTES ANNOTATED
TITLE NINE. COMMERCE AND TRADE
PART 7. LANDLORD AND TENANT
CHAPTER 137. RESIDENTIAL RENTAL AGREEMENTS

§ 4452. Exclusions

Unless created to avoid the application of this chapter, this chapter does not apply to:

(1) occupancy at a public or private institution, operated for the purpose of providing medical, geriatric, educational, counseling, religious or similar service;

(2) occupancy under a contract of sale of a dwelling unit or the property of which it is a part, if the occupant is the purchaser or a person who succeeds to the interest of the purchaser;

(3) occupancy by a member of a fraternal, social or religious organization in the portion of a building operated for the benefit of the organization;

(4) transient occupancy in a hotel, motel, or lodging during the time the occupancy is subject to a tax levied under chapter 225 of Title 32;

(5) occupancy by the owner of a condominium unit or the holder of a proprietary lease in a co-operative;

(6) rental of a mobile home lot governed by chapter 153 of Title 10.

constitutions. Similarly, no state constitution can conflict with the U.S. Constitution.[5] The provision of the U.S. Constitution declaring that federal laws take precedence over conflicting state laws is known as the supremacy clause.

The language of statutes is fairly broad. Such language is necessary because the legislature wants to include as many potential situations as possible when it sets down a legal standard of what is right and what is wrong. However, if a court determines that a law is written so vaguely that citizens cannot determine exactly what is and is not acceptable conduct, the law will not be upheld as valid. The Constitution guarantees the right to fair notice of what is considered illegal conduct. Thus, courts have stricken statutes for being unconstitutional because of overly broad language.[6] The legislature has a particularly difficult but necessary task in establishing laws that apply to all intended persons and situations but that are also specific enough to warn an individual of what is required in a particular situation. Figure 1.1 is an example of statutory law.

CASE

SUPREME COURT OF THE UNITED STATES

JOHN ASHCROFT, ATTORNEY GENERAL, PETITIONER,

V.

AMERICAN CIVIL LIBERTIES UNION ET AL.

122 S.Ct. 1700
Argued Nov. 28, 2001.
Decided May 13, 2002.

This case presents the narrow question whether the Child Online Protection Act's (COPA or Act) use of "community standards" to identify "material that is harmful to minors" violates the First Amendment. We hold that this aspect of COPA does not render the statute facially unconstitutional.

"The Internet . . . offer[s] a forum for a true diversity of political discourse, unique opportunities for cultural development, and myriad avenues for intellectual activity." 47 U.S.C. § 230(a)(3) (1994 ed., Supp. V). While "surfing" the World Wide Web, the primary method of remote information retrieval on the Internet today, individuals can access material about topics ranging from aardvarks to Zoroastrianism. One can use the Web to read thousands of newspapers published around the globe, purchase tickets for a matinee at the neighborhood movie theater, or follow the progress of any Major League Baseball team on a pitch-by-pitch basis.

The Web also contains a wide array of sexually explicit material, including hardcore pornography. See, e.g., *American Civil Liberties Union v. Reno*, 31 F.Supp.2d 473, 484 (E.D.Pa.1999). In 1998, for instance, there were approximately 28,000 adult sites promoting pornography on the Web. Because "[n]avigating the Web is relatively straightforward," *Reno v. American Civil Liberties Union*, 521 U.S. 844, 852, 117 S.Ct. 2329, 138 L.Ed.2d 874 (1997), and access to the Internet is widely available in homes, schools, and libraries across the country, children may discover this pornographic material either by deliberately accessing pornographic Web sites or by stumbling upon them. See 31 F.Supp.2d, at 476 ("A child with minimal knowledge of a computer, the ability to operate a browser, and the skill to type a few simple words may be able to access sexual images and content over the World Wide Web").

When this litigation commenced in 1998, "[a]pproximately 70.2 million people of all ages use[d] the Internet in the United States." App. 171. It is now estimated that 115.2 million Americans use the Internet at least once a month and 176.5 million Americans have Internet access either at home or at work. See More Americans Online, *New York Times*, Nov. 19, 2001, p. C7.

Congress first attempted to protect children from exposure to pornographic material on the Internet by enacting the Communications Decency Act of 1996(CDA), 110 Stat. 133. The CDA prohibited the knowing transmission over the Internet of obscene or indecent messages to any recipient under 18 years of age. See 47 U.S.C. § 223(a). It also forbade any individual from knowingly sending over or displaying on the Internet certain "patently offensive" material in a manner available to persons under 18 years of age. See § 223(d). The prohibition specifically

extended to "any comment, request, suggestion, proposal, image, or other communication that, in context, depict [ed] or describ[ed], in terms patently offensive as measured by contemporary community standards, sexual or excretory activities or organs." § 223(d)(1).

The CDA provided two affirmative defenses to those prosecuted under the statute. The first protected individuals who took "good faith, reasonable, effective, and appropriate actions" to restrict minors from accessing obscene, indecent, and patently offensive material over the Internet. See § 223(e)(5)(A). The second shielded those who restricted minors from accessing such material "by requiring use of a verified credit card, debit account, adult access code, or adult personal identification number." § 223(e)(5)(B).

Notwithstanding these affirmative defenses, in *Reno v. American Civil Liberties Union*, we held that the CDA's regulation of indecent transmissions, see § 223(a), and the display of patently offensive material, see § 223(d), ran afoul of the First Amendment. We concluded that "the CDA lack[ed] the precision that the First Amendment requires when a statute regulates the content of speech" because, "[i]n order to deny minors access to potentially harmful speech, the CDA effectively suppress[ed] a large amount of speech that adults ha[d] a constitutional right to receive and to address to one another." 521 U.S., at 874, 117 S.Ct. 2329.

Our holding was based on three crucial considerations. First, "existing technology did not include any effective method for a sender to prevent minors from obtaining access to its communications on the Internet without also denying access to adults." *Id.*, at 876, 117 S.Ct. 2329. Second, "[t]he breadth of the CDA's coverage [was] wholly unprecedented." *Id.*, at 877, 117 S.Ct. 2329. "Its open-ended prohibitions embrace[d]," not only commercial speech or commercial entities, but also "all nonprofit entities and individuals posting indecent messages or displaying them on their own computers in the presence of minors." *Ibid.* In addition, because the CDA did not define the terms "indecent" and "patently offensive," the statute "cover[ed] large amounts of nonpornographic material with serious educational or other value."

Ibid. As a result, regulated subject matter under the CDA extended to "discussions about prison rape or safe sexual practices, artistic images that include nude subjects, and arguably the card catalog of the Carnegie Library." *Id.*, at 878, 117 S.Ct. 2329. Third, we found that neither affirmative defense set forth in the CDA "constitute[d] the sort of 'narrow tailoring' that [would] save an otherwise patently invalid unconstitutional provision." *Id.*, at 882, 117 S.Ct. 2329. Consequently, only the CDA's ban on the knowing transmission of obscene messages survived scrutiny because obscene speech enjoys no First Amendment protection. See *id.*, at 883, 117 S.Ct. 2329.

After our decision in *Reno v. American Civil Liberties Union*, Congress explored other avenues for restricting minors' access to pornographic material on the Internet. In particular, Congress passed and the President signed into law the Child Online Protection Act, 112 Stat. 2681-736 (codified in 47 U.S.C. § 231 (1994 ed., Supp. V)). COPA prohibits any person from "knowingly and with knowledge of the character of the material, in interstate or foreign commerce by means of the World Wide Web, mak[ing] any communication for commercial purposes that is available to any minor and that includes any material that is harmful to minors." 47 U.S.C. § 231(a)(1).

Apparently responding to our objections to the breadth of the CDA's coverage, Congress limited the scope of COPA's coverage in at least three ways. First, while the CDA applied to communications over the Internet as a whole, including, for example, e-mail messages, COPA applies only to material displayed on the World Wide Web. Second, unlike the CDA, COPA covers only communications made "for commercial purposes." And third, while the CDA prohibited "indecent" and "patently offensive" communications, COPA restricts only the narrower category of "material that is harmful to minors." *Ibid.*

The statute provides that "[a] person shall be considered to make a communication for commercial purposes only if such person is engaged in the business of making such communications." 47 U.S.C. § 231(e)(2)(A) (1994 ed., Supp. V). COPA then defines the term "engaged in the business" to mean a person:

"who makes a communication, or offers to make a communication, by means of the World Wide Web, that includes any material that is harmful to minors, devotes time, attention, or labor to such activities, as a regular course of such person's trade or business, with the objective of earning a profit as a result of such activities (although it is not necessary that the person make a profit or that the making or offering to make such communications be the person's sole or principal business or source of income)." § 231(e)(2)(B).

Drawing on the three-part test for obscenity set forth in *Miller v. California*, 413 U.S. 15, 93 S.Ct. 2607, 37 L.Ed.2d 419 (1973), COPA defines "material that is harmful to minors" as

"any communication, picture, image, graphic image file, article, recording, writing, or other matter of any kind that is obscene or that—
"(A) the average person, applying contemporary community standards, would find, taking the material as a whole and with respect to minors, is designed to appeal to, or is designed to pander to, the prurient interest;
"(B) depicts, describes, or represents, in a manner patently offensive with respect to minors, an actual or simulated sexual act or sexual contact, an actual or simulated normal or perverted sexual act, or a lewd exhibition of the genitals or post-pubescent female breast; and
"(C) taken as a whole, lacks serious literary, artistic, political, or scientific value for minors." 47 U.S.C. § 231(e)(6).

Like the CDA, COPA also provides affirmative defenses to those subject to prosecution under the statute. An individual may qualify for a defense if he, "in good faith, has restricted access by minors to material that is harmful to minors—(A) by requiring the use of a credit card, debit account, adult access code, or adult personal identification number, (B) by accepting a digital certificate that verifies age; or (C) by any other reasonable measures that are feasible under available technology." § 231(c)(1). Persons violating COPA are subject to both civil and criminal sanctions. A civil penalty of up to $50,000 may be imposed for each violation of the statute. Criminal penalties consist of up to six months in prison and/or a maximum fine of $50,000. An additional fine of $50,000 may be imposed for any intentional violation of the statute. § 231(a).

One month before COPA was scheduled to go into effect, respondents filed a lawsuit challenging the constitutionality of the statute in the United States District Court for the Eastern District of Pennsylvania. Respondents are a diverse group of organizations, most of which maintain their own Web sites. While the vast majority of content on their Web sites is available for free, respondents all derive income from their sites. Some, for example, sell advertising that is displayed on their Web sites, while others either sell goods directly over their sites or charge artists for the privilege of posting material. 31 F.Supp.2d, at 487. All respondents either post or have members that post sexually oriented material on the Web. *Id.*, at 480. Respondents' Web sites contain "resources on obstetrics, gynecology, and sexual health; visual art and poetry; resources designed for gays and lesbians; information about books and stock photographic images offered for sale; and online magazines." *Id.*, at 484.

In their complaint, respondents alleged that, although they believed that the material on their Web sites was valuable for adults, they feared that they would be prosecuted under COPA because some of that material "could be construed as 'harmful to minors' in some communities." App. 63. Respondents' facial challenge claimed, *inter alia*, that COPA violated adults' rights under the First and Fifth Amendments because it (1) "create[d] an effective ban on constitutionally protected speech by and to adults"; (2) "[was] not the least restrictive means of accomplishing any compelling governmental purpose"; and (3) "[was] substantially overbroad." [FN5]*Id.*, at 100-101.

The District Court granted respondents' motion for a preliminary injunction, barring the Government from enforcing the Act until the merits of respondents' claims could be adjudicated. 31 F.Supp.2d, at 499. Focusing on respondents' claim that COPA abridged the free speech rights of adults, the District Court concluded that respondents had

established a likelihood of success on the merits. *Id.*, at 498. The District Court reasoned that because COPA constitutes content-based regulation of sexual expression protected by the First Amendment, the statute, under this Court's precedents, was "presumptively invalid" and "subject to strict scrutiny." *Id.*, at 493. The District Court then held that respondents were likely to establish at trial that COPA could not withstand such scrutiny because, among other reasons, it was not apparent that COPA was the least restrictive means of preventing minors from accessing "harmful to minors" material. *Id.*, at 497.

The Attorney General of the United States appealed the District Court's ruling. *American Civil Liberties Union v. Reno*, 217 F.3d 162 (C.A.3 2000). The United States Court of Appeals for the Third Circuit affirmed. Rather than reviewing the District Court's "holding that COPA was not likely to succeed in surviving strict scrutiny analysis," the Court of Appeals based its decision entirely on a ground that was not relied upon below and that wa "virtually ignored by the parties and the amicus in their respective briefs." *Id.*, at 173-174. The Court of Appeals concluded that COPA's use of "contemporary community standards" to identify material that is harmful to minors rendered the statute substantially overbroad. Because "Web publishers are without any means to limit access to their sites based on the geographic location of particular Internet users," the Court of Appeals reasoned that COPA would require "any material that might be deemed harmful by the most puritan of communities in any state" to be placed behind an age or credit card verification system. *Id.*, at 175.

Hypothesizing that this step would require Web publishers to shield "vast amounts of material," *ibid.*, the Court of Appeals was "persuaded that this aspect of COPA, without reference to its other provisions, must lead inexorably to a holding of a likelihood of unconstitutionality of the entire COPA statute." *Id.*, at 174.

We granted the Attorney General's petition for certiorari, 532 U.S. 1037, 121 S.Ct. 1997, 149 L.Ed.2d 1001 (2001), to review the Court of Appeals' determination that COPA likely violates the First Amendment because it relies, in part, on community

CASE

standards to identify material that is harmful to minors, and now vacate the Court of Appeals' judgment.

The First Amendment states that "Congress shall make no law . . . abridging the freedom of speech." This provision embodies "[o]ur profound national commitment to the free exchange of ideas." *Harte-Hanks Communications, Inc. v. Connaughton*, 491 U.S. 657, 686, 109 S.Ct. 2678, 105 L.Ed.2d 562 (1989). "[A]s a general matter, 'the First Amendment means that government has no power to restrict expression because of its message, its ideas, its subject matter, or its content.'" *Bolger v. Youngs Drug Products Corp.*, 463 U.S. 60, 65, 103 S.Ct. 2875, 77 L.Ed.2d 469 (1983) (quoting *Police Dept. of Chicago v. Mosley*, 408 U.S. 92, 95, 92 S.Ct. 2286, 33 L.Ed.2d 212 [1972]). However, this principle, like other First Amendment principles, is not absolute. Cf. *Hustler Magazine v. Falwell*, 485 U.S. 46, 56, 108 S.Ct. 876, 99 L.Ed.2d 41 (1988).

Obscene speech, for example, has long been held to fall outside the purview of the First Amendment. See, e.g., *Roth v. United States*, 354 U.S. 476, 484-485, 77 S.Ct. 1304, 1 L.Ed.2d 1498 (1957). But this Court struggled in the past to define obscenity in a manner that did not impose an impermissible burden on protected speech. See *Interstate Circuit, Inc. v. Dallas*, 390 U.S. 676, 704, 88 S.Ct. 1298, 20 L.Ed.2d 225 (1968) (Harlan, J., concurring in part and dissenting in part) (referring to the "intractable obscenity problem"); see also *Miller v. California*, 413 U.S., at 20-23, 93 S.Ct. 2607 (reviewing "the somewhat tortured history of th[is] Court's obscenity decisions"). The difficulty resulted from the belief that "in the area of freedom of speech and press the courts must always remain sensitive to any infringement on genuinely serious literary, artistic, political, or scientific expression." *Id.*, at 22-23, 93 S.Ct. 2607.

Ending over a decade of turmoil, this Court in *Miller* set forth the governing three-part test for assessing whether material is obscene and thus unprotected by the First Amendment: "(a) [W]hether 'the average person, *applying contemporary community standards'* would find that the work, taken as a whole, appeals to the prurient interest; (b) whether the work depicts or describes, in a patently offensive way, sexual conduct specifically defined by the applicable state law; and (c) whether the work, taken

as a whole, lacks serious literary, artistic, political, or scientific value." *Id.*, at 24, 93 S.Ct. 2607 (internal citations omitted; emphasis added).

Miller adopted the use of "community standards" from *Roth*, which repudiated an earlier approach for assessing objectionable material. Beginning in the 19th century, English courts and some American courts allowed material to be evaluated from the perspective of particularly sensitive persons. See, e.g., *Queen v. Hicklin* (1868) L.R. 3 Q.B. 360, 1868 WL 9940; see also *Roth*, 354 U.S., at 488-489, and n. 25, 77 S.Ct. 1304 (listing relevant cases). But in *Roth*, this Court held that this sensitive person standard was "unconstitutionally restrictive of the freedoms of speech and press" and approved a standard requiring that material be judged from the perspective of "the average person, applying contemporary community standards." *Id.*, at 489, 77 S.Ct. 1304. The Court preserved the use of community standards in formulating the *Miller* test, explaining that they furnish a valuable First Amendment safeguard: "[T]he primary concern . . . is to be certain that . . . [material] will be judged by its impact on an average person, rather than a particularly susceptible or sensitive person—or indeed a totally insensitive one." *Miller*, 413 U.S., at 33, 93 S.Ct. 2607 (internal quotation marks omitted); see also *Hamling v. United States*, 418 U.S. 87, 107, 94 S.Ct. 2887, 41 L.Ed.2d 590 (1974) (emphasizing that the principal purpose of the community standards criterion "is to assure that the material is judged neither on the basis of each juror's personal opinion, nor by its effect on a particularly sensitive or insensitive person or group").

The Court of Appeals, however, concluded that this Court's prior community standards jurisprudence "has no applicability to the Internet and the Web" because "Web publishers are currently without the ability to control the geographic scope of the recipients of their communications." 217 F.3d, at 180. We therefore must decide whether this technological limitation renders COPA's reliance on community standards constitutionally infirm.

In addressing this question, the parties first dispute the nature of the community standards that jurors will be instructed to apply when assessing, in prosecutions under COPA, whether works appeal to the prurient interest of minors and are patently offensive with respect to minors. Respondents contend that jurors will evaluate material using "local community standards," Brief for Respondents 40, while petitioner maintains that jurors will not consider the community standards of any particular geographic area, but rather will be "instructed to consider the standards of the adult community as a whole, without geographic specification." Brief for Petitioner 38.

In the context of this case, which involves a facial challenge to a statute that has never been enforced, we do not think it prudent to engage in speculation as to whether certain hypothetical jury instructions would or would not be consistent with COPA, and deciding this case does not require us to do so. It is sufficient to note that community standards need not be defined by reference to a precise geographic area. See *Jenkins v. Georgia,* 418 U.S. 153, 157, 94 S.Ct. 2750, 41 L.Ed.2d 642 (1974) ("A State may choose to define an obscenity offense in terms of 'contemporary community standards' as defined in *Miller* without further specification . . . or it may choose to define the standards in more precise geographic terms, as was done by California in *Miller*"). Absent geographic specification, a juror applying community standards will inevitably draw upon personal "knowledge of the community or vicinage from which he comes." *Hamling, supra,* at 105, 94 S.Ct. 2887. Petitioner concedes the latter point, see Reply Brief for Petitioner 3-4, and admits that, even if jurors were instructed under COPA to apply the standards of the adult population as a whole, the variance in community standards across the country could still cause juries in different locations to reach inconsistent conclusions as to whether a particular work is "harmful to minors." Brief for Petitioner 39.

Because juries would apply different standards across the country, and Web publishers currently lack the ability to limit access to their sites on a geographic basis, the Court of Appeals feared that COPA's "community standards" component would effectively force all speakers on the Web to abide by the "most puritan" community's standards. 217 F.3d, at 175. And such a requirement, the Court of Appeals concluded, "imposes an overreaching burden and

restriction on constitutionally protected speech." *Id.,* at 177.

In evaluating the constitutionality of the CDA, this Court expressed a similar concern over that statute's use of community standards to identify patently offensive material on the Internet. We noted that "the 'community standards' criterion as applied to the Internet means that any communication available to a nationwide audience will be judged by the standards of the community most likely to be offended by the message." *Reno,* 521 U.S., at 877-878, 117 S.Ct. 2329. The Court of Appeals below relied heavily on this observation, stating that it was "not persuaded that the Supreme Court's concern with respect to the 'community standards' criterion has been sufficiently remedied by Congress in COPA." 217 F.3d, at 174.

The CDA's use of community standards to identify patently offensive material, however, was particularly problematic in light of that statute's unprecedented breadth and vagueness. The statute covered communications depicting or describing "sexual or excretory activities or organs" that were "patently offensive as measured by contemporary community standards"—a standard somewhat similar to the second prong of *Miller's* three-prong test. But the CDA did not include any limiting terms resembling *Miller's* additional two prongs. See *Reno,* 521 U.S., at 873, 117 S.Ct. 2329. It neither contained any requirement that restricted material appeal to the prurient interest nor excluded from the scope of its coverage works with serious literary, artistic, political, or scientific value. *Ibid.* The tremendous breadth of the CDA magnified the impact caused by differences in community standards across the country, restricting Web publishers from openly displaying a significant amount of material that would have constituted protected speech in some communities across the country but run afoul of community standards in others.

COPA, by contrast, does not appear to suffer from the same flaw because it applies to significantly less material than did the CDA and defines the harmful-to-minors material restricted by the statute in a manner parallel to the *Miller* definition of obscenity. See *supra,* at 1705, 1707. To fall within the scope of COPA, works must not only "depic[t], describ[e], or represen[t], in a manner patently offensive with respect to minors," particular sexual acts or parts of the anatomy, they must also be designed to appeal to the prurient interest of minors and "taken as a whole, lac[k] serious literary, artistic, political, or scientific value for minors." 47 U.S.C. § 231(e)(6).

These additional two restrictions substantially limit the amount of material covered by the statute. Material appeals to the prurient interest, for instance, only if it is in some sense erotic. Cf. *Erznoznik v. Jacksonville*, 422 U.S. 205, 213, and n. 10, 95 S.Ct. 2268, 45 L.Ed.2d 125 (1975). Of even more significance, however, is COPA's exclusion of material with serious value for minors. See 47 U.S.C. § 231(e)(6)(C). In *Reno*, we emphasized that the serious value "requirement is particularly important because, unlike the 'patently offensive' and 'prurient interest' criteria, it is not judged by contemporary community standards." 521 U.S., at 873, 117 S.Ct. 2329 (citing *Pope v. Illinois*, 481 U.S. 497, 500, 107 S.Ct. 1918, 95 L.Ed.2d 439 [1987]). This is because "the value of [a] work [does not] vary from community to community based on the degree of local acceptance it has won." *Id.*, at 500,107 S.Ct. 1918. Rather, the relevant question is "whether a reasonable person would find . . . value in the material, taken as a whole." *Id.*, at 501, 107 S.Ct. 1918. Thus, the serious value requirement "allows appellate courts to impose some limitations and regularity on the definition by setting, *as a matter of law*, a national floor for socially redeeming value." *Reno, supra*, at 873, 117 S.Ct. 2329 (emphasis added), a safeguard nowhere present in the CDA.

When the scope of an obscenity statute's coverage is sufficiently narrowed by a "serious value" prong and a "prurient interest" prong, we have held that requiring a speaker disseminating material to a national audience to observe varying community standards does not violate the First Amendment. In *Hamling v. United States*, 418 U.S. 87, 94 S.Ct. 2887, 41 L.Ed.2d 590 (1974), this Court considered the constitutionality of applying community standards to the determination of whether material is obscene under 18 U.S.C. § 1461, the federal statute prohibiting the mailing of obscene material. Although this statute does not define obscenity, the petitioners in *Hamling* were tried and convicted

under the definition of obscenity set forth in *Book Named "John Cleland's Memoirs of a Woman of Pleasure" v. Attorney General of Mass.*, 383 U.S. 413, 86 S.Ct. 975, 16 L.Ed.2d 1 (1966), which included both a "prurient interest" requirement and a requirement that prohibited material be "'utterly without redeeming social value.'" *Hamling, supra*, at 99, 94 S.Ct. 2887 (quoting *Memoirs, supra*, at 418, 86 S.Ct. 975).

Like respondents here, the dissenting opinion in *Hamling* argued that it was unconstitutional for a federal statute to rely on community standards to regulate speech. Justice Brennan maintained that "[n]ational distributors choosing to send their products in interstate travels [would] be forced to cope with the community standards of every hamlet into which their goods [might] wander." 418 U.S., at 144, 94 S.Ct. 2887. As a result, he claimed that the inevitable result of this situation would be "debilitating self-censorship that abridges the First Amendment rights of the people." *Ibid.*

This Court, however, rejected Justice Brennan's argument that the federal mail statute unconstitutionally compelled speakers choosing to distribute materials on a national basis to tailor their messages to the least tolerant community: "The fact that distributors of allegedly obscene materials may be subjected to varying community standards in the various federal judicial districts into which they transmit the materials does not render a federal statute unconstitutional." *Id.*, at 106, 94 S.Ct. 2887.

Fifteen years later, *Hamling's* holding was reaffirmed in *Sable Communications of Cal., Inc. v. FCC*, 492 U.S. 115, 109 S.Ct. 2829, 106 L.Ed.2d 93 (1989). *Sable* addressed the constitutionality of 47 U.S.C. § 223(b) (1982 ed., Supp. V), a statutory provision prohibiting the use of telephones to make obscene or indecent communications for commercial purposes. The petitioner in that case, a "dial-a-porn" operator, challenged, in part, that portion of the statute banning obscene phone messages. Like respondents here, the "dial-a-porn" operator argued that reliance on community standards to identify obscene material impermissibly compelled "message senders . . . to tailor all their messages to the least tolerant community." 492 U.S., at 124, 109 S.Ct. 2829. Relying on *Hamling*, however, this Court once again rebuffed this attack on the use of community standards in a federal statute of national scope: "There is no constitutional barrier under *Miller* to prohibiting communications that are obscene in some communities under local standards even though they are not obscene in others. *If Sable's audience is comprised of different communities with different local standards, Sable ultimately bears the burden of complying with the prohibition on obscene messages.*" 492 U.S., at 125-126, 109 S.Ct. 2829 (emphasis added).

The Court of Appeals below concluded that *Hamling* and *Sable* "are easily distinguished from the present case" because in both of those cases "the defendants had the ability to control the distribution of controversial material with respect to the geographic communities into which they released it" whereas "Web publishers have no such comparable control." 217 F.3d, at 175-176. In neither *Hamling* nor *Sable*, however, was the speaker's ability to target the release of material into particular geographic areas integral to the legal analysis. In *Hamling*, the ability to limit the distribution of material to targeted communities was not mentioned, let alone relied upon, and in *Sable*, a dial-a-porn operator's ability to screen incoming calls from particular areas was referenced only as a supplemental point, see 492 U.S., at 125, 109 S.Ct. 2829. In the latter case, this Court made no effort to evaluate how burdensome it would have been for dial-a-porn operators to tailor their messages to callers from thousands of different communities across the Nation, instead concluding that the burden of complying with the statute rested with those companies. See *id.*, at 126, 109 S.Ct. 2829.

While Justice KENNEDY and Justice STEVENS question the applicability of this Court's community standards jurisprudence to the Internet, we do not believe that the medium's "unique characteristics" justify adopting a different approach than that set forth in *Hamling* and *Sable*. If a publisher chooses to send its material into a particular community, this Court's jurisprudence teaches that it is the publisher's responsibility to abide by that community's standards. The publisher's burden does not change simply because it decides to distribute its material to every community in the Nation. See *Sable, supra*, at 125–126, 109 S.Ct. 2829 . . . but nonetheless utilizes a medium that transmits its speech from

coast to coast. If a publisher wishes for its material to be judged only by the standards of particular communities, then it need only take the simple step of utilizing a medium that enables it to target the release of its material into those communities.

Respondents offer no other grounds upon which to distinguish this case from *Hamling* and *Sable*. While those cases involved obscenity rather than material that is harmful to minors, we have no reason to believe that the practical effect of varying community standards under COPA, given the statute's definition of "material that is harmful to minors," is significantly greater than the practical effect of varying community standards under federal obscenity statutes. It is noteworthy, for example, that respondents fail to point out even a single exhibit in the record as to which coverage under COPA would depend upon which community in the country evaluated the material. As a result, if we were to hold COPA unconstitutional *because of* its use of community standards, federal obscenity statutes would likely also be unconstitutional as applied to the Web, a result in substantial tension with our prior suggestion that the application of the CDA to obscene speech was constitutional. See *Reno*, 521 U.S., at 877, n. 44, 882-883, 117 S.Ct. 2329.

Respondents argue that COPA is "unconstitutionally overbroad" because it will require Web publishers to shield some material behind age verification screens that could be displayed openly in many communities across the Nation if Web speakers were able to limit access to their sites on a geographic basis. Brief for Respondents 33-34. "[T]o prevail in a facial challenge," however, "it is not enough for a plaintiff to show 'some' overbreadth." *Reno, supra*, at 896, 117 S.Ct. 2329 (O'CONNOR, J., concurring in judgment in part and dissenting in part). Rather, "the overbreadth of a statute must not only be real, but substantial as well." *Broadrick v. Oklahoma*, 413 U.S. 601, 615, 93 S.Ct. 2908, 37 L.Ed.2d 830 (1973). At this stage of the litigation, respondents have failed to satisfy this burden, at least solely as a result of COPA's reliance on community standards. Because Congress has narrowed the range of content restricted by COPA in a manner analogous to *Miller's* definition of obscenity, we conclude, consistent with our holdings in *Hamling* and *Sable*, that any variance caused by the

CASE

statute's reliance on community standards is not substantial enough to violate the First Amendment.

The scope of our decision today is quite limited. We hold only that COPA's reliance on community standards to identify "material that is harmful to minors" does not *by itself* render the statute substantially overbroad for purposes of the First Amendment. We do not express any view as to whether COPA suffers from substantial overbreadth for other reasons, whether the statute is unconstitutionally vague, or whether the District Court correctly concluded that the statute likely will not survive strict scrutiny analysis once adjudication of the case is completed below. While respondents urge us to resolve these questions at this time, prudence dictates allowing the Court of Appeals to first examine these difficult issues.

Petitioner does not ask us to vacate the preliminary injunction entered by the District Court, and in any event, we could not do so without addressing matters yet to be considered by the Court of Appeals. As a result, the Government remains enjoined from enforcing COPA absent further action by the Court of Appeals or the District Court.

For the foregoing reasons, we vacate the judgment of the Court of Appeals and remand the case for further proceedings.

It is so ordered.

Case Review Question
Ashcroft v. ACLU, 122 S.Ct. 1700, 152 L.Ed.2d. 771 (2002).
How is the COPA statute significantly different from the CDA statute?

judicial law
Opinions that have the effect of law and that are issued by members of the judiciary in legal disputes.

Judicial law.   A second type of law is **judicial law**. The judiciary interprets law from other sources but also on occasion creates legal standards. Judges may consider a statute and determine whether it was meant to apply to the circumstances of a particular case. Persons in similar situations may then look to the judge's decision to guide their own conduct. Furthermore, the legislature cannot possibly enact laws to apply to every conceivable circumstance. Therefore, when no law exists, judges are responsible for making law or extending decisions of judges in previous similar cases.

The tradition of judges looking to previous rulings in similar past cases is an integral part of the American system of justice. The continuation of existing legal standards is the stability element in the modern balance. This process is commonly referred to as **stare decisis** (literally, "let the decision stand"). The doctrine of stare decisis basically holds that following the same legal principles in similar cases gives our legal system consistency. People can look to the past for guidance in what to expect from the courts in the future. The wisdom of past judges is utilized to achieve fair and consistent treatment of persons involved in similar cases.

stare decisis
"Let the decision stand." Method used by the judiciary when applying precedent to current situations.

precedent
Existing legal standards to which courts look for guidance when making a determination of a legal issue.

When a court applies stare decisis and follows the same type of ruling as issued in a previous similar case, it is following a **precedent**—a previously established legal standard. Courts generally attempt to apply stare decisis with respect to precedents unless the prior case is too dissimilar in facts or issues or unless societal standards have changed since the precedent was established, making the former legal principle of the precedent impractical. In such a case, the court does not employ stare decisis but rules on the case based on new societal standards and establishes a new precedent for future reference. Chapter 2 presents more information on the way in which precedents are created.

CASE

COURT OF APPEALS OF MINNESOTA.

CHANCELLOR MANOR, APPELLANT,

V.

JUDY GALES, ET AL., RESPONDENTS.

Aug. 27, 2002.

Opinion

HALBROOKS, JUDGE.

Appellant challenges the dismissal of its eviction action against respondents, arguing that the trial court erred in finding that appellant did not suffer an adverse financial effect from its repeated disputes with respondents so as to warrant eviction under the Department of Housing and Urban Development guidelines. Because we conclude that the administrative costs incurred by appellant constitute an adverse financial effect, we reverse and remand.

Facts

Appellant Chancellor Manor owns an apartment building in Burnsville and rents to respondents Judy Gales and Rasheda Gales through a Department of Housing and Urban Development (HUD) subsidized program. Appellant has filed at least 68 late-rent notices and 8 prior unlawful detainer/eviction actions against respondents since October 1992. Respondents always eventually paid the rent due and the penalties and other costs that appellant could recover under the law. Appellant often worked out special arrangements with respondent Judy Gales to help her avoid missing work and incurring legal fees.

Appellant filed the latest eviction action on October 25, 2001, after respondents failed to pay rent for September and October. Appellant instructed respondents to vacate the premises by November 30, pursuant to a HUD provision in the lease permitting eviction for repeated minor lease violations that have an adverse financial impact on the program. After receiving this notice, respondents paid rent for September, October, and November. Respondents also tendered rent for December, but appellant rejected the December payment because it wanted respondents to vacate the apartment by November 30. Appellant denied respondents' internal appeal.

Wendy Howell, site manager at respondents' building, testified on behalf of the appellant at a bench trial. Howell testified that filing a late-rent notice involves filling out the required paperwork and then copying, filing, and mailing the forms. She stated that the steps to file an eviction action include preparation of the eviction forms by the home office, driving to the home office to pick up the forms, filing them at the courthouse, serving the documents on the subject-residents, and re-filing them at the courthouse. Howell estimated that the eviction-notice process takes approximately three hours, not including any time spent in the ensuing court proceedings. She also testified that respondents paid all the late fees and court costs that they owed, but that appellant paid its own attorney fees.

The trial court acknowledged that respondents had paid their rent late many times in the past, but found that appellant had recovered all its costs allowed under the law. While recognizing that appellant incurred attorney fees from these disputes, the trial court concluded that appellant could have avoided fees by having one of its employees represent it in these actions. As a result, the court dismissed the case on the ground that appellant failed to prove that it had suffered an adverse financial effect from respondents' late payments. This appeal follows.

Issue

Did the trial court err in finding that appellant did not suffer an adverse financial effect in its repeated disputes with respondents?

Analysis

Appellant argues that the trial court erred in finding no adverse final effect when the record shows the considerable time and expense incurred due to respondents' repeated violations. Appellant contends that its costs above and beyond those that it can legally recover constitute an adverse financial effect. Respondents claim that the record supports the trial court's findings because appellant recovered all those costs to which it is legally entitled and because the law permits respondents to redeem the property by paying the rent and costs due. Respondents also argue that appellant is estopped from acting on respondents' late payments because it failed to follow through with prior threats to do so.

HUD regulations apply to all participants in HUD-subsidized housing programs. These regulations outline the conditions under which landlords may evict tenants. *Oak Glen of Edina v. Brewington*, 642 N.W.2d 481, 485 (Minn.App.2002). The relevant regulation, also incorporated into respondents' lease, permits a landlord to evict a tenant for material noncompliance with the rental agreement. 24 C.F.R. § 247.3(c) (2001). Material noncompliance is defined, in relevant part, as:

> (2) Repeated minor violations of the rental agreement that:
> (i) Disrupt the livability of the project,
> (ii) Adversely affect the health or safety of any person or the right of any tenant to the quiet enjoyment of the leased premises and related project facilities,
> (iii) Interfere with the management of the project, or
> (iv) Have an *adverse financial effect* on the project.

"Minor violations" include paying rent late. It is undisputed that respondents' late payments constituted repeated minor violations.

We find no cases or other authority, including the HUD Handbook, that address the scope of "adverse financial effect" as applied to HUD housing. We briefly touched on the issue in *Oak Glen*. In that case, the tenant paid her rent late on 17 occasions in five years and the landlord sought to evict her under the HUD regulation set out above. We concluded that the late payments constituted repeated minor violations, but declined to address whether the late payments had an adverse financial effect warranting eviction because the parties had not presented that issue to the district court. As a result, the question of whether such administrative costs amount to an "adverse financial effect" is an issue of first impression.

Plainly read, the regulation is unqualified and contains no minimum amount necessary to constitute "adverse financial effect." Nor does the common definition of "adverse" imply a particular threshold. Because there is no qualification or threshold, we interpret "adverse financial effect" to refer to all those effects that adversely impact the program. As a result, we conclude that the administrative costs resulting from preparing more than 70 late-rent and eviction notices create an adverse financial effect that is sufficient to meet the HUD standard. Several reasons compel us to adopt the plain meaning of the term.

First, this court construes words according to their common usage before resorting to interpretative devices. Because this regulation can be plainly read to encompass any and all adverse financial effect, we need not employ judicial construction to discern its meaning.

Second, the Minnesota Supreme Court has rejected our prior attempt to read equitable standards into HUD regulations when the regulation is carefully crafted and addresses all the concerns intended. *See Lor*, 591 N.W.2d at 703-04. In *Lor*, a HUD regulation gave public-housing authorities (PHAs) discretion to develop eviction policies that protect other tenants and the greater public while permitting managers to consider individual circumstances. When Lor's landlord attempted to evict her for her son's violation of its policy, the trial court examined not only whether the policy had been violated, but also whether Lor could have known about the violation and whether Lor would suffer severe hardship if evicted. We agreed with the trial court that it had discretion to look beyond the issue of whether the tenant violated the landlord's policies and consider the equitable circumstances surrounding the eviction. The Minnesota Supreme Court reversed, holding that the HUD regulations plainly vest the PHAs, not the courts, with the authority to develop eviction standards. The court reasoned that,

> [i]n light of HUD's careful crafting of the PHA role in eviction decisions, HUD would likely have spelled out any additional supervisory responsibilities it wished courts to take.

Id. at 704.

Likewise, the HUD eviction regulation here is detailed and thorough, and in fact defines other terms such as "drug-related criminal activity" and "material noncompliance." *See* 24 C.F.R. § 247.2 (2001). Thus, we must assume that HUD would have further defined "adverse financial effect" had it intended to impose a threshold financial requirement.

Finally, the United States Supreme Court also followed the plain meaning of a HUD-related statute when it was asked to read in a qualification in *Dep't of Hous. and Urban Dev. v. Rucker*, _____ U.S. _____, _____, 122 S.Ct. 1230, 1233, 152 L.Ed.2d 258 (2002). In *Rucker*, a tenant asked the Court to read 42 U.S.C. § 1437d(*l*)(6) (1994 & Supp. V 1999), a HUD-related statute permitting eviction if any member or any guest of the tenant's household engaged in drug-related criminal activity, to mean that grounds for eviction existed only when the tenant had knowledge of the criminal activity. *Id.* at _____ _____, 122 S.Ct. at 1232-33. The Court refused to qualify the provision with a "knowledge" requirement when Congress did not do so. *Id.* at _____, 122 S.Ct. at 1233. Similarly, the regulation here does not qualify the meaning of "adverse financial effect" and thus we must refrain from adopting anything but the plain meaning of the language.

Because the plain reading of the regulation contains no qualification or threshold for "adverse financial effect," the trial court erred when it failed to find that appellant's administrative costs meet the standard. The trial court's error is two-fold. First, the trial court made no findings regarding appellant's administrative costs, despite ample evidence of the costs incurred. Howell's testimony regarding the time involved with filing more than 70 late-rent and eviction notices certainly satisfies any accepted meaning of "adverse financial effect." Second, the trial court premised its holding on the belief that appellant suffered no adverse financial effect because it recovered all the costs to which the law entitles it. But the HUD regulation is concerned with the costs incurred, not merely with the costs that go uncompensated. Thus, although a landlord may recover all the costs allowed under the law, it is possible, as happened here, that a landlord will suffer costs beyond those for which the law compensates it.

We decline to address respondents' arguments regarding redemption and estoppel because those claims were not presented to the trial court. But we note that an estoppel defense does not apply where, as here, the landlord refuses to accept the final rent payment. *See Oak Glen*, 642 N.W.2d at 487 (stating that a landlord need only refuse the final payment to protect itself against a claim of waiver).

Decision

Because the administrative costs that appellant suffered from respondents' filing more than 70 late-rent and eviction notices constitute an "adverse financial effect," the trial court erred in dismissing appellant's eviction action.

Reversed and remanded.

Case Review Question

Manor v. Gales, 649 N.W.2d 892 (2002).
Would the result likely change if the only costs associated with collection of late rent was the time of the landlord in repeatedly asking for the rent in person and by phone?

Over the years, countless disputes have arisen that required a decision of law for resolution. The legal issues involved in such cases are not considered significant or common enough to require a legislative act, and the courts are left to issue rulings to resolve the disputes. In this way, the judiciary frequently serves as a valuable bridge between the people and the legislature when it interprets statutory legal standards in very specific circumstances or creates legal standards where none exist. For example, José Martinez intends to repair his roof. José is seriously injured when the ladder he is climbing collapses. José wants the ladder company to pay for his injuries, but there is no statute that requires ladder companies to pay for injuries caused by faulty ladders. The court, however, may look to prior cases that require manufacturers to be careful in the design and construction of products. Relying on precedent such as those prior cases, the court can apply stare decisis and require the ladder company to pay for José's injuries.

Judicial law has indirectly provided guidance to the state and federal legislatures as to the type of laws needed to be enacted. A perfect example of this involves the advent of the automobile. At first, many people were skeptical, and certainly most people never envisioned that motor-driven vehicles would become such an essential part of life. However, as more and more automobiles were placed on the roads, accidents happened, the need for roadways and traffic control developed, an overwhelming source of jobs was discovered, and mass transit became a reality. For the first time in history, the world became very mobile with unlimited travel that was convenient and fast. Rules were needed so that people could make, sell, and buy vehicles efficiently and travel in them in safety and comfort.

Until the issues of automobile travel and its accompanying disputes became so significant as to warrant legislation, the judiciary handled them. As the number of automobiles and related legal issues increased, the legislature stepped in and established broad legal standards for the manufacture, sale, and operation of motor vehicles.

Administrative law.   Although the legislature attempts to arrive at legal principles that apply to all persons, the judiciary deals with individual circumstances. Over the years, however, it became increasingly clear that an additional source of law that could tailor rules for specific groups of citizens or subjects was necessary. In many sectors of our society and economy, large numbers of people or areas of commerce need specific guidelines. Such an area is the air transportation industry, which is overseen by the Federal Aviation Administration (FAA). It is impractical for Congress or even state legislatures to attempt to deal with all of the questions raised by this massive industry. At the same time, it would be unduly burdensome and increase the likelihood of inconsistent decisions from different judges in different areas if the judiciary had to handle all cases that arose. The response to dilemmas of this sort has been the advent of **administrative law.**

administrative law

Regulations and decisions that explain and detail statutes. Such regulations and decisions are issued by administrative agencies.

The Constitution gives the duty for enforcement of law to the executive branch. Therefore, the executive branch has the primary responsibility to determine when a law has been violated or whether the law is even applicable to a particular situation. Administrative agencies are overseen by the executive branch with direct influence by the Congress and the judiciary. At the federal level, the president is assisted by administrative agencies in carrying out the law enacted by Congress.

Administrative law primarily consists of two elements: administrative regulations (sometimes called rules) and administrative decisions. Administrative agencies issue regulations or rules that more specifically define the broadly written statutes. Administrative decisions issued for very specific cases have the same effect of law as judicial or legislative law. These cases usually involve persons or entities that challenge the authority of the agency to issue or enforce a particular regulation.

Administrative law is an extension of statutory law established by Congress. Failure to obey administrative law can result in penalties or even criminal prosecution. Figure 1.2 shows an example of administrative law.

Administrative law is quite complex and is discussed further in Chapter 4.

The Hierarchy of Law

Although the sources of American law are the legislature, the judiciary, and the executive branch, they are all interrelated. If the sources of law were completely independent, the potential for deadlock would exist if the sources conflicted with regard to the law.

FIGURE 1.2   24 C.F.R. § 247.3 Entitlement of Tenants to Occupy

CODE OF FEDERAL REGULATIONS
TITLE 24—HOUSING AND URBAN DEVELOPMENT
SUBTITLE B—REGULATIONS RELATING TO HOUSING
AND URBAN DEVELOPMENT CHAPTER II—OFFICE
OF ASSISTANT SECRETARY FOR
HOUSING—FEDERAL HOUSING
COMMISSIONER, DEPARTMENT OF HOUSING AND
URBAN DEVELOPMENT SUBCHAPTER B—
MORTGAGE AND LOAN INSURANCE PROGRAMS
UNDER NATIONAL HOUSING
ACT AND OTHER AUTHORITIES PART 247—
EVICTIONS FROM CERTAIN SUBSIDIZED AND
HUD-OWNED PROJECTS SUBPART A—SUBSIDIZED
PROJECTS
Current through September 17, 2002; 67 FR 58678

§ 247.3 Entitlement of tenants to occupancy.

(a)   General. The landlord may not terminate any tenancy in a subsidized project except upon the following grounds:

(1)   Material noncompliance with the rental agreement,

(2)   Material failure to carry out obligations under any state landlord and tenant act,

(3)   Criminal activity by a covered person in accordance with sections 5.858 and 5.859, or alcohol abuse by a covered person in accordance with section 5.860. If necessary, criminal records can be obtained for lease enforcement purposes under section 5.903(d)(3).

(4)   Other good cause.

No termination by a landlord under paragraph (a)(1) or (2) of this section shall be valid to the extent it is based upon a rental agreement or a provision of state law permitting termination of a tenancy without good cause. No termination shall be valid unless it is in accordance with the provisions of § 247.4.

(b)   Notice of good cause. The conduct of a tenant cannot be deemed other good cause under § 247.3(a)(4) unless the landlord has given the tenant prior notice that said conduct shall henceforth constitute a basis for termination of occupancy. Said notice shall be served on the tenant in the same manner as that provided for termination notices in § 247.4(b).

(c)   Material noncompliance. The term "material noncompliance with the rental agreement" includes:

(1)   One or more substantial violations of the rental agreement;

(2)   Repeated minor violations of the rental agreement that:

(i)   Disrupt the livability of the project,

(ii)   Adversely affect the health or safety of any person or the right of any tenant to the quiet enjoyment of the leased premises and related project facilities,

(iii)   Interfere with the management of the project, or

(iv)   Have an adverse financial effect on the project;

(3)   If the tenant:

(i)   Fails to supply on time all required information on the income and composition, or eligibility factors, of the tenant household, as provided in 24 CFR part 5; or

(ii)   Knowingly provides incomplete or inaccurate information as required under these provisions; and

(4)   Non-payment of rent or any other financial obligation due under the rental agreement (including any portion thereof) beyond any grace period permitted under State law, except that the payment of rent or any other financial obligation due under the rental agreement after the due date; but within the grace period permitted under State law, constitutes a minor violation.

American law is governed by a distinct hierarchy. First in the hierarchy is the U.S. Constitution. Although technically the Constitution and its amendments are statutory law, they are considered superior to all other law, since they established the governmental structure and the process for creating all other law. One concept that has remained consistent throughout the legal history of this country is that all branches of state and federal government and all persons in the United States must function within the parameters of the U.S. Constitution. If at any time the will of the people is in conflict with the Constitution, the Constitution can be amended through the proper process, which is designed to guarantee that the amendment does in fact reflect the will of the majority. Chapter 3 discusses further the process for amendment of the Constitution.

Next in the hierarchy of laws are the legislative (statutory) acts of Congress. Statutes have greater weight than judicial or administrative law, since statutes are enacted by Congress and state legislatures, which are composed of people elected by the people. Thus, statutes are most likely to represent the laws intended for and desired by the majority.

The judiciary has the authority to interpret legislation and to fill in gray areas where the law is unclear or nonexistent. The judiciary is also obligated to ensure that the law is consistent with the Constitution. We might think of the judiciary as the protectors of the Constitution. In any case when the judiciary determines that the law does not meet the requirements of the Constitution, it has the authority to declare the law invalid and thereby supersede the ordinarily superior statutory law. Constitutionality is the only basis for judicial rather than statutory law controlling an issue. A prime example of this would be a law that is vague or overbroad. Such a law is unconstitutional because it would not provide fair and clear notice to persons of what is illegal conduct. Such notice is a requirement of the Constitution and its amendments. Thus, the court would have the authority to strike down the statute and dismiss charges against anyone who is alleged to have violated the statute.

Last in the hierarchy is administrative law. Administrative agencies assist Congress by issuing regulations and decisions that clarify and aid in the enforcement of statutes. However, Congress has the right to eliminate an agency or regulations that are inconsistent with legislative objectives. The judiciary also has the authority to overrule actions of an agency when such actions are unconstitutional. The authority of the judiciary to overrule and invalidate law is not exercised lightly or frequently. The courts generally defer to the Congress unless there is a clear constitutional violation.

Assignment 1.3

Examine the following situations and determine which source of law would most appropriately deal with each situation.

1. New legal standards need to be created to govern security measures taken by private airports over private planes and pilots.

2. A person charged with driving under the influence on a public thoroughfare claims that she was on private property at the time of the observation by the officer and subsequent arrest.
3. An individual arrested for speeding on a city street says in his situation the law does not apply because he was on horseback.

Ethical Considerations

The very heart of the American legal system depends on honor and integrity. It is essential for the government to work as intended, and for the representatives of that governmental structure to act in an ethical manner. Knowing, however, that individuals are fallible and subject to the temptations of power and greed, the framers of the Constitution created a government based on a system of checks and balances that prevents any one person or group of persons from gaining too much power over the government or the population.

Ethical Circumstance

In the early part of the twentieth century, the United States suffered through two world wars and an economic depression of epic proportion. Through the end of the depression years and throughout World War II, President Franklin D. Roosevelt led the nation. Although the process was complicated and involved the input of many people, Roosevelt was largely credited with ending the depression and bringing the war near its conclusion. He died shortly before the end of World War II. Prior to his unexpected death, however, was a great deal of support for a third term of office for Roosevelt as president. So close on the heels of the rise of Hitler to power in Germany, many feared that the executive branch was gaining far too much power here. Thus, in 1951, the Twenty-First Amendment to the Constitution was ratified, precluding any president from seeking a third term of office by election. This effectively defeated the power of any individual—whether pure in intent or unscrupulous—from gaining such a stronghold in the executive branch of government.

CHAPTER SUMMARY

This chapter has introduced you to the origins and development of the American legal system. The system began as a singular governmental structure under the Articles of Confederation, which were found to be ineffective and were replaced by the Constitution and the Bill of Rights. Under the Constitution, the government comprises three separate but interrelated branches designed to provide effective government of, by, and for the people: the judiciary, the executive branch, and the legislature (Congress). The Bill of Rights and subsequent constitutional amendments serve as the framework for the protection of individual rights and establish boundaries between areas subject to state and federal law.

The method of law followed in the United States is actually a combination of three theories. The naturalist theory believes that people know the difference between right and wrong and should be held accountable for any wrong conduct that results in injuries to another party. The positivist theory is represented by the principle that the supreme authority of a jurisdiction is the final decision in legal matters. Appeals may be made to the highest authority, but beyond this, decisions are not subject to challenge or question. The sociological theory tempers American law by providing for changes in the law when they are in the best interest of society as a whole.

The three branches of government are the three sources of law: the legislature (statutes), the executive branch (administrative actions from administrative agencies created by Congress but overseen by the executive branch on a day-to-day basis), and the judiciary (judicial opinions). The legislative body issues broadly written laws that must be adhered to by all persons. Administrative agencies give definition to and enforce statutory law. Judicial law interprets statutory law for specific individual circumstances.

In all law—but most apparent in judicial law—are the balances that enable the American system to function so efficiently. Under the traditional balance, government strives to maintain maximum personal freedom while protecting the interests of society as a whole. The modern balance aims toward following existing legal standards to provide stability to the government and give clear guidance to citizens while responding with flexibility to changes in societal standards.

One constant is that the Constitution is the supreme law of the land. Ordinarily, statutes have priority over judicial opinions and administrative law. However, if the judiciary finds a statute or administrative law to be unconstitutional, it has the right to invalidate the statute or administrative law and to rule on the case based on judicial precedent or other applicable statutory or administrative law. No law, under any circumstance, can be enforced if it is in conflict with the Constitution. If society demands such a law be held valid, the Constitution must be amended.

The following chapters give much attention to the various branches of government and should be fully understood before proceeding to subsequent chapters that refer to the sources commonly responsible for establishing legal standards in particular subjects of law. Further, it is helpful in a more practical sense to understand where law originates as well as the law's place in the hierarchy. Such understanding enables one in a real-life situation to assess much more clearly one's position with regard to the law.

CHAPTER TERMS

administrative law
judicial law
legal standard
modern balance

naturalist theory
positivist theory
precedent
sociological theory

stare decisis
statutory law
traditional balance

REVIEW QUESTIONS

1. What was the structure of the U.S. government under the Articles of Confederation?
2. What political theories influenced the structure of the U.S. government?
3. How does the U.S. Constitution guarantee that power will not fall into the hands of one person?
4. Explain how each political theory appears in present-day government.
5. The flexibility and stability elements of the modern balance express what goals of the judiciary?

6. The individual elements and the elements of the people as a whole of the traditional balance represent what goals of the judiciary?

7. Explain the difference between stare decisis and precedent.

8. Give two characteristics of each type of legal standard: statute; case; regulation. (An example of a characteristic would be the source of the legal standard.)

9. What is the only situation in which judicial decision is more powerful than a statute?

10. Why does the executive branch have the power to create administrative law through administrative agencies?

RELEVANT LINKS

Government Guide Main (links to local, state, federal government offices)
www.governmentguide.com

FirstGov (links to branches of federal government)
www.firstgov.com

INTERNET ASSIGNMENT 1.1

Locate the official government website for each branch of state government where you live.

NOTES

1. William Statsky, *Legal Thesaurus/Dictionary* (St. Paul: West, 1982).
2. Id.
3. Statsky, *Legal Thesaurus/Dictionary.*
4. Statsky, *Legal Thesaurus/Dictionary.*

5. *Gonzalez v. Automatic Emp. Credit Union,* 419 U.S. 90, 95 S.Ct. 289, 42 L.Ed.2d 249 (1974).
6. *Schware v. Board of Bar Examiners,* 353 U.S. 232, 77 S.Ct. 752, 1 L.Ed.2d 796 (1957).

 For additional resources, please visit our Web site at www.westlegalstudies.com

CHAPTER 2

The Courts

CHAPTER OBJECTIVES

After reading this chapter, you should be able to:

- Discuss the characteristics unique to judicial law.

- Explain the twofold purpose of judicial law.

- Discuss the process of legal analysis.

- Apply the process of case analysis to a judicial opinion.

- Describe the structure of the federal court system.

- Describe the role of each primary level of federal courts.

- Describe the present-day function of the U.S. Supreme Court.

- Describe the two general types of state court structures.

- Discuss the types of cases generally considered by the U.S. Supreme Court.

As explained in Chapter 1, American law comes from one of three sources: legislative, judicial, or executive/administrative. This chapter focuses on the law established by the judicial branch of government, giving consideration to the manner in which the federal and state court systems are structured as well as how they function with each other. In addition, the chapter addresses the method of analyzing past judicial law for present and future application.

THE PURPOSE AND EFFECT OF JUDICIAL LAW

Characteristics of Judicial Law

All elements of the legal system are equally necessary. The executive branch monitors the conduct of Congress and, through executive supervision of administrative agencies, establishes regulations for specific industries and specialized groups. Congress, through legislation, sets down statutory law that guides the conduct of all the people. The judiciary reviews the acts of Congress and the executive branch but, more importantly, serves as a forum for the people. Because every situation is different in some respect, judges are expected to have the knowledge and objectivity to examine individual situations and determine the legal standards that should apply and how. Everyone can have access to the governmental system through the judicial branch, which is designed to provide fairness and enforcement of rights of all persons.

The only avenue by which people can seek individual resolution of personal legal issues is the judicial branch. The court is the only forum in which a person can present information supporting a legal position and obtain court approval and enforced legal action. Legislatures enact laws to govern all people in a variety of circumstances. The executive branch, through administrative law, further defines and enforces legislative law. But the judiciary considers the situations of individuals on a case-by-case basis and attempts to apply the most appropriate law and reach the result that is most fair under the Constitution. In this way, the courts are the most responsive branch of government to the individual. The judicial branch is the only governmental authority with the power to create law for an individual situation when none exists. The legislative and executive branches are more indirect reflections of the needs of society as a whole. However, these branches are also necessary to establish legal standards that the people can, in most cases, follow without the need for judicial intervention.

Clarification of the Law

By necessity, statutes are written in general terms that apply to everyone. As a result, it is unclear many times whether a statute encompasses a very specific situation. This is where the assistance of the judiciary becomes essential. Judges are expected to have sufficient knowledge and training to evaluate statutes and determine whether they apply to a specific situation. In the event a judge finds a statute inapplicable, another statute or legal principle from a prior case can be applied. In doing so, the judge is performing one of the primary functions of the judiciary: to clarify the law as it applies to specific circumstances.

These interpretations of statutory or administrative law occur anytime a statute or administrative regulation or decision is an issue in a case. If, for example, someone challenges a speeding ticket, the government must prove that the statute of maximum miles per hour was violated. The judge must review the statute and the facts of the case. The judge must then determine whether under the facts the law applies and whether the law was violated. This is one example of a judicial interpretation of a statute.

APPLICATION 2.1

Roman owns a house that has been in his family for four generations. He was born in the house, as was his father, grandfather, and great grand-father. Over the past century what was originally rural farmland has developed to the point that the house is now in the center of a large city. The local government wants to locate the new police station at a more central location and the proposed site includes the property where Roman's house is located. Roman opposes the sale of his home because he knows it would be demolished. The local government files an action in court to force the sale of the property based on the allegation that the public interest outweighs the private interest. The court must consider the statutes and constitutional provisions that protect private property interests and determine whether there are other reasonable alternatives for the city, the value of maintaining the historical residence, and the rights of Roman. If the determination is made that public interest in a centrally located facility, assuming no other reasonable sites are available, outweighs Roman's private interests, then the proper statutory guidelines must be followed to value the property, compensate Roman, and complete the sale.

Point for Discussion
- If the Bill of Rights protects property rights of citizens from unreasonable seizure, how can certain statutes permit the government to effectively seize private property?

As the preceding application illustrates, most cases have much more complicated facts than the broad language of a statute addresses. There seem always to be specific questions that are not clearly answered by the statute and to which the judge must at this point establish answers. This is done by looking to the purpose of the statute and the intent of the legislature in passing the statute. Judges also look at how past similar cases were treated in the courts. Although no two cases are exactly alike, a judge may apply the same ruling in cases that have striking similarities. Such similarities may be in the facts of the case, in the legal issues involved, or in both. Finally, judges are required to draw on their knowledge and experience to establish what is considered to be a logical and fair interpretation of the statute.

In cases when no applicable statute exists, a judge is required to establish the law. This may be done by looking to case law (the precedents of past similar cases) and applying the principle of stare decisis. In the situation when no prior judicial precedent exists whatsoever, a judge must create one. This is known as common law, a term that has carried over from medieval times when judges created law for the common man. Technically, common law is defined as a newly established legal principle, whereas case law is the application of stare decisis (carryforward of a prior legal principle). In actual practice, the terms *common law* and *case law* have come to be used interchangeably. The basic concept is that the terms represent judicially created law. In some instances, such law may be a specific interpretation and definition of a statute, whereas in other cases, it refers to the creation or continuation of a legal principle where no statutory language applied. Still another case might call for the creation of a legal standard when no applicable law exists.

Case law significantly benefits the general public. Individuals can look at existing case law in relation to their own situations. By comparing established precedents, persons involved in lawsuits can often predict with some certainty the likely outcome of their case. In so doing, through a process known as legal analysis, they can make intelligent decisions about whether to pursue, settle, or dismiss a dispute. It is also a very useful method to determine the best course of action for avoiding a dispute. (Legal analysis is discussed in more detail later in the chapter.)

Assignment 2.1

Examine the following situations. Evaluate and determine whether each situation represents a court's application of a statute, creation of common law, or application of stare decisis. Explain your answer.

1. A man stops to help a motorist stranded on the side of the highway. The man does not turn off the ignition of his car, which is parked in front of the disabled vehicle. The other motorist is run down and killed when the car of the man stopping to assist slips out of gear and rolls backward. The family of the man killed sues the man who stopped to help for wrongful death. A judge determines that the prior knowledge of the man that the transmission of his vehicle was unreliable is sufficient to impose responsibility for the death despite no legal precedent for such a circumstance.

2. A farmer allows hunters to hunt and camp on his property through the fall and winter seasons for a fee. He does not inform the hunters that the ground of the fields has been treated with chemicals. A hunter suffers severe chemical burns on his hands when gathering kindling for a fire. Although no similar cases of this nature are on record, a judge holds that the farmer had a duty to warn persons invited onto the property of any dangers not readily

visible according to other past cases involving invitees on private property and existing conditions that could cause harm.

3. A golfer plays on a course near a major river where bald eagles are known to fish. The golfer hits an errant shot. The golf ball strikes and kills a bald eagle that is in flight. The golfer is arrested and ultimately convicted for killing a bald eagle, which is a violation of federal law.

Protection of the Law

A second function of the judiciary is to protect and uphold law that is consistent with the Constitution. To provide such protection, the judiciary has the duty to impose legal liability when legal principles are violated. For example, when one person crashes into another person's car, the court would require the driver at fault to accept responsibility and pay for the damage to the innocent driver's vehicle and any other related damages. In a criminal situation, the police may arrest individuals who allegedly commit crimes, but it is up to the judge to determine whether allegations of such violations are true and to see that violators are penalized or make restitution for their actions or both. Essentially, when one person injures the rights, person, or property of another, the court must determine whether the law has been violated and what an appropriate compensation or penalty for the injury would be.

APPLICATION 2.2

Macias attends a professional ice hockey game. During one of the breaks between periods in the game, a local radio station promoting its programs selects persons from the audience to take part in a game for prizes on the ice. Macias is chosen to be in the game. While walking across the ice she falls and suffers a compound fracture of her right arm. She is a professional musician and as a result of her injuries is off work for nearly 4 months. Macias sues the facility for her injuries. The facility claims it has no responsibility because the radio station was the one conducting the game. The court must answer the following questions:

1. Is the facility responsible for the acts of others who are paying for use of the facility for promotional events?
2. Did the facility act or fail to act in a way that caused or contributed to the circumstances of the injury?
3. Did any action or nonaction of the facility violate an existing legal principle?
4. If the facility is found to be at fault, what should be done to remedy the situation?

To answer these questions the court must first look to cases and statutes that address the situation. The court must then determine the result that would be indicated when the legal principles of those cases and statutes are applied to the present situation. The court would then issue a verdict.

Point for Discussion

- Would the case be substantially different if Macias had entered the ice to retrieve something she dropped over the rail rather than being invited to participate in a game? If so, how would it change the consideration of the court?

THE STRUCTURE OF THE JUDICIAL SYSTEM

federal court

A court that is part of the U.S. court system that has limited authority and hears only cases involving the U.S. government, federal laws, or appropriate cases of diversity of citizenship.

state court

A court that is a part of the judicial branch in the state in which it is located. Typically, state courts hear cases involving state law.

trial court

A court that has authority to hear the evidence of the parties and render a verdict.

appellate court

A court that reviews the actions of a trial court and determines whether an error has been committed that requires corrective action.

Originally, the U.S. Constitution provided for a single **federal court**. Congress was also given the authority to create new courts as needed.[1] Similarly, each state was responsible for establishing **state courts** to address the needs of its population. In the 200 plus years since the U.S. Supreme Court was created, literally thousands of state and federal courts have been added to the judicial systems to handle the ever-increasing number of legal claims of both individuals and government.

Trial Versus Appellate Courts

The present federal and state court systems consist of two basic types of courts: trial and appellate. The **trial court** is the court in which the case is presented to the judge or jury. In the trial court, each party follows certain required procedures to prepare the evidence for a fair and complete presentation. The judge and, in many cases, a jury hear the evidence to support the claims of both sides of the dispute. This is the opportunity for both parties in a lawsuit to present their version of what occurred to produce the legal dispute. At the trial court level testimony is given under oath, other types of evidence such as documents are presented, and each party has the opportunity to address the judge and/or jury deciding the case. When this is completed, a verdict is then given declaring whether the defendant is at fault for violation of a legal standard. In the event there is a finding of fault, a penalty may be assessed and the defendant may be ordered to compensate those injured by the violation of legal standards.

A court that hears trials is known as a court of original jurisdiction.[2] This is where the case is determined for the first time (originates). If a party believes the trial court verdict is the result of failure to properly follow legal requirements for the proceedings, then that party may choose to appeal the verdict. Examples include failure to observe a technical requirement of procedural rules, failure to allow or improper permission to introduce certain evidence, or anything else that might be considered a flaw in the trial process that affects the outcome of the case. When a case is brought on appeal, the judges of an **appellate court** will review part or all of the trial court's proceedings. An appellate court has authority superior to that of a trial court and has the power to change the trial court's verdict. Often, appellate courts consist of several judges who review cases as a panel. By utilizing multiple reviewers, there is less chance that mistakes will be made in the review of an application of law to a particular case. This type of judicial authority is known as appellate jurisdiction.[3] Quite often, panels of three judges will review a particular case. However, in very important cases, the entire group of appellate judges may review a case collectively. In such a situation, the decision the judges render is considered to be *en banc*.[4]

An important distinction between trial and appellate courts is the actual purpose of each court. It is the duty of the trial court to determine the applicable law, hear the evidence, and render a verdict, whereas it is the duty of the appellate court to only review what took place in the trial court and determine whether the law was correctly applied to the evidence presented. Appellate courts generally do not hear new evidence such as testimony of witnesses. Nor do appellate courts issue new verdicts. Rather, they affirm (approve) or reverse (reject) the trial (lower) court verdict. If the appellate court reverses the decision of the trial court, it also generally issues instructions as to the next stage of the proceedings, such as to order a new trial. Regardless if the court is part of a state system or the federal system, the distinction between trial and appellate court is essentially the same. More information regarding the actual proceedings in trial and appellate courts can be found in the chapters that discuss civil and criminal procedure.

The Federal Court System

The federal court system started with a single court, now known as the U.S. Supreme Court. Over time, Congress added several courts to the federal judicial branch. Currently, the federal court system comprises three levels (see Figure 2.1), each of which functions totally independent of state court systems, just as each state judicial branch functions independent of the other states.

An easy way to distinguish a federal court from a state court is by the court's name. All federal courts will have the words *United States* or *U.S.* in the title. No state court may include this language as part of its name. Of the three levels of federal courts, the trial courts—where the vast majority of federal cases originate—are known as the U.S. District Courts. Generally, the U.S. District Courts are used as trial courts. However, in limited circumstances, a federal case can be initially heard by an administrative hearing officer with the executive branch and appealed to the U.S. District Court. In such an instance, the U.S. District Court takes on appellate authority rather than its usual original jurisdiction. Also, there are very specific types of cases that may be initially filed for trial at the appellate level and bypass the U.S. District Court altogether. This is not a common occurrence, however. Typically, the appellate level is reserved for parties who wish to challenge the decision of the U.S. District Court. Such an appeal is made to the next level, which is the U.S. Court of Appeals. Following such an appeal, a party who is still dissatisfied with the result of the case may seek appellate review by the U.S. Supreme Court.

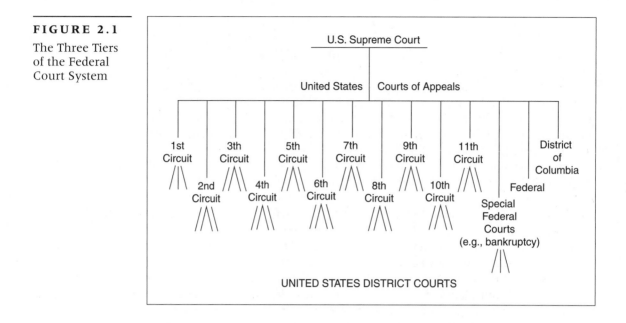

The U.S. District Courts

Perhaps the busiest courts within the federal court system are the trial courts, known as the U.S. District Courts. Currently, there are over 90 such courts. Congress has increased the number of these courts when warranted by the number of cases filed and tried in the federal system. When the burden becomes too heavy for one court, Congress creates an additional court to handle part of the load.

The various U.S. District Courts are separated by geographical boundaries. Legal disputes over federal law that occur or have connections to the court within the court's physical boundaries are subject to the authority of the U.S. District Court. For example, if an individual violated a federal law in Montana, the U.S. District Court for the District of Montana would try the case.

For convenience and to facilitate understanding by the population, state lines have been used as district boundary lines. However, there is no connection between state court authority and federal court authority because of the setting of such boundaries. Courts simply use the same imaginary line to separate themselves from other courts. State and federal courts remain distinct even though a state court or U.S. District Court authority does not exceed the geographical boundaries of the state in which the court is located.

Some states with substantial population and litigation have more than one U.S. District Court divided by county lines (for convenience) within the state. For example, the state of Illinois has three U.S. District Courts: the Northern District, the Central District, and the Southern District. A district that covers a wide geographical area may be subdivided into divisions, which operate as branches of a district court, with buildings in each division as a means of making the court more accessible to the citizens.

Special Federal Courts

Although the vast majority of cases are brought to and decided through the U.S. District Courts and the U.S. Courts of Appeals, other federal courts are set up for the express purpose of handling specific types of cases. Specified types of claims made against the U.S. government must be filed with the U.S. Court of Claims. Claims involving federal taxation are tried in the U.S. Tax Court. The Court of International Trade hears disputes involving international trade agreements. The U.S. Court of Military Appeals offers a final review of military tribunal actions. These claims involve very specific and often a complex series of legal standards. Additionally, the cases are often quite involved and drawn out. Thus, the dedication of specific courts and a judiciary that is specially selected based on experience and training for these types of matters creates a more appropriate environment for the fair disposition of these cases.

The U.S. Courts of Appeals

A party to a lawsuit who is dissatisfied with a U.S. District Court decision may appeal to the U.S. Court of Appeals designated to hear cases appealed from the particular U.S. District Court where the case originated.[5] For example, someone who wanted to appeal a case from a U.S. District Court of Iowa would file the appeal with the 8th U.S. Circuit Court of Appeals. By requiring the appeals from each U.S. District Court to go to a specific U.S. Court of Appeals, parties are prevented from shopping for the appellate court that appears most favorable to their point of view. This system of pairing specific trial courts with a particular appellate court allows the appellate courts to create legal standards to be consistently followed by the designated U.S. District Courts subject to the appellate court's authority.

The U.S. Courts of Appeals in the federal court system are intermediate level appellate courts. Review at this level resolves cases that would otherwise be appealed to the U.S. Supreme Court, thus lessening the burden on the high court. U.S. Courts of Appeals were originally established to make appellate review faster, easier, and more accessible to parties in litigation. Over the years, as the number of cases filed has increased, so has the activity of these courts, which today are an essential element of the federal court structure.

Because of the tremendous number of cases filed and appealed in the federal court system, there are multiple U.S. Courts of Appeals, known as circuit courts. Currently there are 13 courts of appeal: 11 courts that are located across the country and identified by number (e.g., 1st U.S. Circuit Court of Appeals); the U.S. Circuit Court of Appeals for the District of Columbia, which hears cases originating in the U.S. District Court for the District of Columbia; and the U.S. Federal Court of Appeals, which hears cases from special federal courts such as the U.S. Court of Claims and the U.S. Court of International Trade.

The U.S. Courts of Appeals are the courts most responsible for establishing legal standards. These courts publish many more decisions than the U.S. District Courts or the U.S. Supreme Court. And while the U.S. Supreme Court opinions control in any situation, the limited number of opinions limits the amount of legal standards established by the high court. Thus, when one is looking for precedent on a federal issue, a likely source would be the published opinions of the U.S. Courts of Appeals. Further, since these courts are superior authorities to the U.S. District Courts, a precedent from such an appellate court would be more persuasive than one from a trial court.

Like the U.S. District Court, the physical limits of authority of each U.S. Court of Appeals are defined by geographical boundaries. For the sake of convenience rather than any connection with the states, the 11 circuits are divided by the boundary lines of several states. These boundaries delineate the area of authority of a particular circuit court of appeals over the U.S. District Courts contained within the area. For example, the U.S. 5th Circuit Court of Appeals has authority over all appeals from U.S. District Courts located within Texas, Louisiana, and Mississippi. Similarly, the 8th circuit governs U.S. District Courts located in North Dakota, South Dakota, Nebraska, Minnesota, Iowa, Missouri, and Arkansas.

Each circuit court of appeals is responsible for handling the appeals coming from the federal courts within the geographical boundaries of the circuit. These boundaries are determined by Congress and are altered periodically to adjust the flow of cases more equitably. As with the U.S. District Courts, when the burden of cases becomes too heavy for a U.S. Circuit Court of Appeals, Congress has the authority to create a new court or redefine the boundaries of the circuit. Figure 2.2 indicates the boundaries of the U.S. Circuit Courts of Appeals and the U.S. District Courts.

No U.S. Court of Appeals has authority over any other. Each court functions independently and is accountable only to the U.S. Supreme Court. Frequently, different U.S. Courts of Appeals decide the same issue differently. When this occurs, the Supreme Court may accept one or more of these cases and decide what exactly the legal standard shall be. This eliminates any inconsistency that may arise among the rulings of the various circuits.

The U.S. Supreme Court

The U.S. Supreme Court is the final authority on all matters of federal jurisdiction in the American legal system.[6] It has the authority to review actions of Congress, the president, and the state governments. However, this authority is not limitless. Our legal system is based on the Constitution, and if the Court wants to take any action superior to one of the other branches of government, it must do so on constitutional grounds. In other words, the Court cannot overrule Congress or the president unless the legislative or executive branch has in some way violated or exceeded the authority granted to the branch by the Constitution and that action has been challenged in the courts.

The primary function of the Supreme Court is one of review. The Supreme Court reviews cases from the federal courts and, in some instances, from the highest state courts that have constitutional issues or that include the government as a party.[7] The key element in the authority of the Supreme Court is that there must be a federal issue at stake either in the form of the parties involved or in the constitutionality of state or federal law.

FIGURE 2.2   U.S. Circuit Courts of Appeals and U.S. District Courts

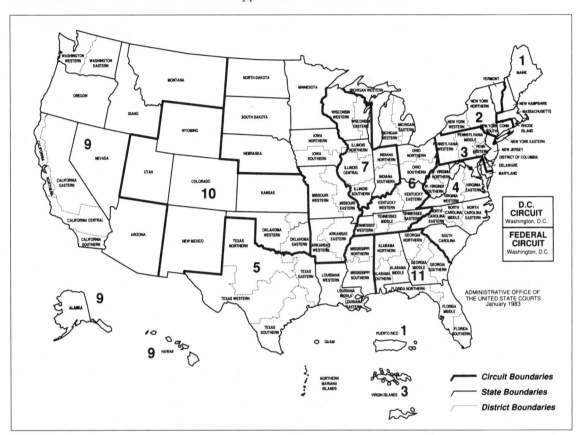

The Supreme Court has limited original jurisdiction.[8] Cases involving original jurisdiction are not appealed but rather are filed in court for the very first time at the level of the U.S. Supreme Court. Original jurisdiction is limited to only the types of situations listed in Article III of the Constitution.[9]

The U.S. Supreme Court has two common methods of obtaining review.[10] The first is by right. Certain types of cases are automatically entitled to review by the Supreme Court if the party so desires. The Court will review the case as long as the procedural rules for filing the appeal meet compliances.

The second and more common method is known as certiorari (sir-shore-are-ee), which describes the authority of the Court to accept a number of cases for review where there is no right, but where it would serve the interests of justice to have the Court make a final and ultimate determination of a legal standard. Well over 1,000 petitions for certiorari are filed with the Supreme Court each year. However, since the Court can consider only a limited number within its term, it often selects those cases that contain major issues that have been decided differently in various courts and require a final decision to settle the matter permanently.

Another significant factor in the determination of whether to grant certiorari of cases is when the decision offered for review involves constitutional rights. An ultimate goal of the Court is to ensure that the Constitution will be applied fairly for all persons. When the Court declines to accept a petition for certiorari, the practical effect is that it accepts and indirectly affirms the decision of the U.S. Court of Appeals. Finally, a U.S. Court of Appeals may "certify a question," in which case the appeals court may specifically request that the Supreme Court resolve a pertinent issue on which the various U.S. Courts of Appeals are divided.

THE STATE COURT SYSTEM

Totally independent of the federal courts are the state court systems for each of the 50 states. Each state government has legislative, executive, and judicial branches, which in many ways parallel the federal government. Every state has a judicial system to provide a forum for the resolution of disputes among persons and entities within the state. Such disputes must involve acts or occurrences that are controlled by state rather than federal law. The law may be case law or state legislative law. Federal courts and state courts are independent of and not subject to the authority of one another. (The exception is that all courts of the nation are subject to the U.S. Supreme Court.) No state court is bound by the authority of a court from a different state. Nor is a court obligated to follow the rulings of an equivalent court. Like the U.S. Courts of Appeals, state courts have equal authority. If a state court system has an intermediate appellate level of several courts, the opinions of these courts would not be binding on one another. Rather, only the lower trial courts within the purview of authority of the particular appellate court would be bound.

The states utilize two basic judicial structures: three-tiered and two-tiered systems. The three-tiered system is comparable to that of the federal system. The three tiers are a court of last resort (the highest court of the state), an intermediate appellate court level, and a trial court level. Heavily populated states may have several appellate courts similar to the numerous U.S. Circuit Courts of Appeals in the federal system. The trial courts include courts for civil and criminal trials, matters of domestic relations disputes, probate, juvenile, small claims, magistrates, and justices of the peace.

Approximately half the states employ the three-tiered system. The other states use a two-tiered system consisting of only one appellate (supreme) court and the various trial courts. However, because of the increase in litigation, more states are considering the three-tiered system. In the two-tiered system, appeals from the trial court are taken directly to the high court of the state, placing the total burden on a single group of judges. In the three-tiered system, appeals are first taken to the intermediate appellate court in the same manner as applied in the federal system. A party who wants further review may then appeal to the highest court of the state. However, most appeals end after the first review, as the likelihood of a reversal declines dramatically with each appeal.

The terms *district court* and *circuit court* are used in some states in the same way as in the federal system. Other states reverse these titles. The circuit court is the trial court, and the district court is the appellate court. Some states use other names entirely to describe their courts. Persons not trained in the structure of the legal system can be misled as to the importance of a judicial opinion by attaching more weight to the decision than is warranted simply because of the name of the court that rendered the opinion. What matters is that each state has a trial court level and an appellate court level and the decisions carry lesser weight in descending order from the highest appellate level to the lowest trial court.

Since the trial courts of the states handle more cases than any other level of state or federal court in the American legal system, they must be organized to process the multitude of cases filed each year. Most often, state courts will divide the time of the various judges by the type of case filed. For example, certain judges will devote their attention to domestic relations (divorce, custody, support, adoption, etc.), while other judges will hear only criminal cases. These various divisions operate together to create the trial court level. In addition, the trial courts within a particular state (usually at least one per county) are divided into geographical regions, usually bounded by county borders. Each court is responsible for the legal rights of persons and the legal issues arising from occurrences within the borders of the court's authority. By having a court within each county, the people are guaranteed reasonable access to the courts.

Figure 2.3 shows a three-tiered state court system. (A two-tiered system would eliminate the intermediate level of appellate courts.)

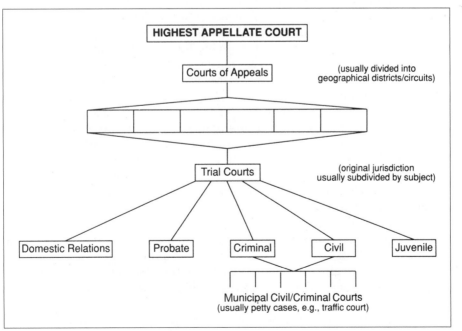

FIGURE 2.3
Three-tiered State Court System

A two-tier court system is the same as the system pictured above, but with the intermediate level court of appeals deleted.

THE PROCESS OF LEGAL ANALYSIS

Analytical ability is present in every fact of life. It is the skill of applying past experiences to current or foreseen circumstances to determine the probable outcome. This skill begins to develop in childhood. For example, if Billy refuses to wear a coat to school on a chilly day and is cold on the way to and from school, in the future, he will know the experience was unpleasant and on the next cold day will wear a coat to prevent it from happening again. As knowledge accumulates, this ability to examine how situations develop and resolve becomes more refined and guides our present and future conduct. For attorneys, the skill lies in the ability to analyze past similar situations handled within the legal system and use them to predict the likely outcome of a present case. Because no two situations are exactly alike and legal issues are not as simplistic as dressing for the weather, **legal analysis** is performed at a much more complex level. It is necessary to identify all of the relevant similarities and differences of facts, the law of the jurisdiction, the parties, and the apparent attitudes of the judge and potential jury. Each of these must be evaluated in terms of their significance and impact on the likelihood of a similar result in the present case. Analytical skill also is directly supported by the training and skill required to locate and identify all relevant facts and law in a particular case.

legal analysis
The process of examining precedent in detail in order to predict its effect on future similar circumstances.

It is rare that both legal research and investigation/discovery of facts produce little or no result. On the contrary, it is more often the case that attorneys must sift through a great wealth of information and either retain the facts as significant or discard them as unimportant or inapplicable. This process in and of itself is legal analysis at the base level. Next, the more complicated task of evaluation (analysis) of the applicability and significance of what remains becomes the focus. Finally comes the crucial point when the lawyer determines the likely outcome of the case by applying the existing legal principles now analyzed in terms of the present case. This determination guides the case in terms of settlement, trial tactics and strategies, and even whether to appeal unsatisfactory results.

Legal analysis is the cornerstone of the American judicial system. Legal professionals, judges, lawyers, and paralegals all utilize the process in their daily work. Legal analysis allows the judge to resolve a dispute consistent with the modern balance and allows the lawyer to advise the client as to the appropriate course of conduct based on past experiences of similarly situated persons. It enables the paralegal to know what information will be necessary to interview a client and prepare legal documents.

Legal analysis is performed with respect to statutes, administrative law, and cases. The process of analyzing different types of law varies somewhat, because the format between law generated for the general public and legal standards applied to specific parties is different. However, the desired effect is the same— to determine the applicability or nonapplicability of the legal standard to the case at hand.

Legal analysis is predominantly the domain of legal professionals and lawyers in particular. The paralegals, legal investigators, and entire support staff of the attorney as well as those professions directly affected by law (e.g., tax law accountants) routinely engage in some level of legal analysis. The nonprofessional also derives significant benefit from the process of legal analysis in the application of legal standards through contact with attorneys and even the media.

By looking to established legal precedents, the paralegal and support staff can develop a sense of how various types of cases typically proceed, which also enables them to anticipate and deal with common procedural issues. In knowing what was and was not acceptable when engaged in discovery and investigation based on past cases, the legal support professional can perform these tasks much more efficiently and effectively. Human beings are basically analytical creatures who learn by experience and example. While traditional methods of education are necessary, lessons are truly learned and then applied in a variety of other circumstances when they are experienced or, at the very least, observed in a realistic setting. It is one thing to read a principle of law such as the definition of negligence, but that principle becomes much clearer when a judicial opinion is read that demonstrates how negligence occurs in a real-life situation. As the legal support professional gains more and more knowledge of legal principles through practice, the skills of the professional can become highly developed.

Of the various methods of legal analysis, case analysis is the specific method of legal analysis of past judicial opinions and their impact on a current situation. The similarities and differences between the past cases and the current situation give insight with regard to whether the outcome should be similar in the present

APPLICATION 2.3

Suzanne is a paralegal student who accepts a part-time position with a law firm to gain experience. Part of her duties include basic client interviews in divorce cases. She begins with a checklist of standard questions but does not know how to proceed when matters come up in the interview that are not referenced in the questionnaire. Suzanne asks one of the more experienced paralegals in the firm if she can sit in while he interviews clients. She watches how the interviews proceed and asks questions of the paralegal about why certain matters are investigated more fully and others are not. As a result, Suzanne becomes very adept at interviewing clients and extracting the right information without wasting time and energy on matters that will not have significant relevance later in the case.

Point for Discussion
◆   What is the problem with confining the interview to the questionnaire?

Assignment 2.2

> Explain in the following situations how legal analysis could help.
>
> 1. A new client comes to see an attorney. The client complains that a contractor building a house a block away dug a basement that affected a natural levy and now the client's basement floods every time it rains. Is there a case? The client has no connection to the contractor and the houses in between are not being affected.
> 2. A young attorney is hired directly out of law school. The position requires him to prepare cases for trial in a firm that specializes in personal injury. The attorney has never had a course in this area of law specifically other than a general course on civil cases in the first year of law school. He needs to know what evidence is needed and what documents are routinely used in these types of cases.

case. Because case analysis is used so extensively, an organized system for publishing and arranging the cases is necessary so that cases on specific topics or from particular courts can be easily accessed.

Legal Analysis of Case Law (Judicial Opinions)

Although judicial opinions are discussed in greater detail in subsequent chapters, a brief introduction will be given here for the purposes of illustration.

Published cases are predominantly appellate for quite practical reasons. First, since trial courts are generally the lowest level of judicial authority, a trial court opinion need not be followed by a judge in a subsequent case. Appellate court opinions, on the other hand, must be followed by those trial courts that are subordinate to the authority of the appellate court that issued the opinion. Appellate decisions also are usually rendered by a panel of appellate judges whose collective wisdom is respected by the legal community. Such opinions are infrequently overturned by higher appellate courts and thus provide a stable basis for comparison of the state legal standard to a present situation. A second reason for the limited number of published trial court opinions is cost effectiveness. Literally hundreds of thousands of trials take place annually in this country. It would not be reasonable to publish all of the opinions supporting the outcome of these cases when they are of such limited authority.

Judicial opinions are published chronologically, as they are handed down by the courts, in a series of books. That is to say that the published opinions of a jurisdiction and sometimes more than one, are published in the same book series as they are issued. Each new volume in the publication is numbered consecutively and contains the most recently issued opinions. When there is a change in how the information is presented, such as introductory materials in advance of each published case, the changes are signaled by a new series of the same publication, for example, Pacific Reporter, Pacific Reporter 2nd Series, Pacific Reporter 3rd Series. With each new series, the numbering of volumes starts over as well. For example, the last book of the first series may be volume 311; the next book to be issued, if a new series is beginning, would be volume 1 of the second series rather than volume 312. This series and volume renumbering signals a change in the format of the material within, but not a change in the chronological publication of opinions as they come down from the court or courts for whom the reporter is published.

The usefulness of published cases is immeasurable. By having access to opinions the courts have issued in the past, the parties can often determine with great accuracy the outcome of current disputes. Judges look to published cases to determine the appropriate legal standards and the manner in which the standards should be applied. In addition, it is not uncommon for parties or their lawyers to examine the published cases before taking any action whatsoever. Such examination often guides the conduct of an individual or business in matters that do not involve imminent legal action. Rather, these legal standards may be consulted in an attempt to avoid finding oneself in the very circumstances that have prompted lawsuits in the past.

When reading judicial opinions for the first time, they may appear to be long and drawn out with many difficult terms and obscure references, and they may not seem to make clear sense. However, with some basic skills and practice, reading and analyzing a case may become second nature. It is possible to read an opinion and mentally analyze it simultaneously. Throughout this text a number of cases are included for illustration of the various legal principles under discussion. Although these cases are edited somewhat to facilitate ease of comprehension, all of the essential elements of the original are represented. Reading the judicial opinions in the text serves two functions. First, they are real-life demonstrations of the subject matter of the various chapters. Second, reading them provides the opportunity to develop basic legal analytical skills. Even those who do not anticipate a career in the legal profession can benefit from the ability to read and understand legal principles as law impacts all facets of personal and professional life.

Regardless of the judge or jurisdiction from which an opinion is derived, nearly all complete judicial opinions contain the same essential elements. This consistency allows not only a thorough understanding of the opinion and reasoning behind it, but also an easy comparison to other similar legal issues that arise. Because the process of legal analysis allows consistency in the application of legal standards in similar cases, it is necessary that a regular pattern of information and reasoning be included.

The initial step in analyzing the meaning of a case is to know the elements of a judicial opinion. Note first that various methods are available for analyzing a case. Additionally, note that the elements are sometimes broken down differently and given different titles. Do not be discouraged or confused by this. No matter the titles or number of elements a person assigns to a case analysis, the summary should contain the same basic information. The information is just packaged differently. Below is one method of analyzing a case. The analysis can be renamed or reorganized in any fashion but will still contain the same elements.

Virtually everyone who performs case analysis consistently uses the term *case briefing*. The legal profession employs many types of briefs. The term *case brief* describes a synopsis of a judicial opinion. A common purpose of a case brief is to facilitate a determination of the effects of a previously issued judicial opinion on a current situation. To accurately make such a determination, one must examine each aspect of the case and decide whether the case is sufficiently similar to the present situation to create a likelihood that the same legal standards would be applied in the same way today.

CASE

SUPERIOR COURT OF NEW JERSEY, APPELLATE DIVISION.

GAYNELL GAC (A/K/A GAYNELL CICCARELLI), PLAINTIFF-RESPONDENT,

V.

PAUL LUDWIG GAC, DEFENDANT-APPELLANT.

351 N. J. Super, 54
796 A2d 951(2002).

I

The parties were married in 1971. Two children were born of the marriage, Justin and Alyssa. Justin was eight and Alyssa was five when the parties separated in 1983. The parties were divorced in 1987. While the judgment required defendant to pay $225 per month in child support, it was silent concerning the obligations of the parties toward the college expenses of the children.

It is undisputed that the marriage was a stormy one. During the divorce proceedings, the Family Part ordered Dr. Mathias Hagovsky to perform a psychological evaluation of the family. Plaintiff recounted in her interview with Hagovsky that the marriage was punctuated by defendant's abusive and threatening acts. She asserted that defendant "physically abused her in [the presence] of the children." This allegation was corroborated by Justin who told Hagovsky that he "had seen

violence and bitter exchanges between his parents." Hagovsky found that Justin was "traumatized" by these experiences, "convinced that his father would not change," and felt "no safety in contact with [defendant]," fearing that defendant "could hurt someone." Alyssa harbored similar feelings toward defendant. While convinced that her mother "want[ed] her to [visit] with [defendant]," she felt "nervous" about that prospect and "despite her best intentions," was unable "to tell her father how she really felt." Defendant admitted to Hagovsky that he "ha[d] a terrible temper in the past which affect[ed] his wife and children." While "frustrated" by his children's negative feelings toward him, defendant conceded that "there was a good deal of rage and face-to-face screaming to which the children were often exposed."

These experiences had a profound effect on the parties and both children. Dr. Hagovsky observed:

Essentially, both children and their mother have allied themselves in a very effective manner against the father to the point where considerable fear and trauma exists even at the possibility of contact between them. At the moment, this fear is real to the children and to Mrs. Gac as well, and is unlikely to be effectively assuaged even with direct, psychotherapeutic intervention.

In effect, these three have divested themselves emotionally from their husband and father to the point where productive contact is literally impossible.

Formal statements of availability at any time should they wish access should be made including an opportunity for him to write or perhaps even call on special occasions; a chance to send occasional gifts to the children should also be made available. Emphasis should be placed on Mr. Gac's development of this "one way" relationship until such times as the children develop their own need to respond to him.

The Family Part followed Hagovsky's recommendation and did not order visitation between defendant and the children. Although defendant sought to develop a relationship with the children, these efforts proved wholly unavailing. Defendant followed the advice of Dr. Hagovsky and pursued the "one way" relationship recommended, but neither Justin nor Alyssa ever responded. To the contrary, at age sixteen Alyssa made it clear that she did not consider defendant to be her father and she did not want to see him. She reiterated that sentiment at age twenty-two.

During the period between 1987 and 1994 defendant sent postcards, packages, holiday cards, and monthly or bi-weekly letters to the children. He did not telephone the children, because he was told that they did not want to speak with him. With the exception of returning the written cards and letters to defendant with a note, which read: "we don't want to hear from you. We don't want anything to do with you," Alyssa did not respond to her father's communications. These communications stopped in 1994 when Alyssa moved with her maternal grandparents and plaintiff to Vermont. Plaintiff did not provide defendant with her telephone number or address when she moved with the children.

In 1994, when Justin was nineteen and Alyssa was sixteen, defendant moved to reduce temporarily his child support payments, because he was unemployed and his unemployment benefits were about to expire. He also sought to establish family mediation, and to require plaintiff to send monthly reports and photographs of the children. On August 5, 1994, the Family Part judge denied, without prejudice, defendant's motion for family mediation. The judge granted defendant's request for monthly reports, which were to begin on September 1, 1994. Additionally, the judge reserved decision on defendant's motion to reduce child support until documents were received and the court could conduct a hearing. The court did not conduct that hearing because defendant subsequently obtained employment.

Defendant continued to make the $225 monthly child support payments until May 2000. On July 11, 2000, after Alyssa graduated college, defendant filed a motion to terminate his child support obligations for both children. At that time, Justin was twenty-five years old and Alyssa was twenty-two years old. Plaintiff opposed that motion and cross-moved for reimbursement of Alyssa's college tuition. The record does not reveal whether the court heard arguments on that motion.

On August 25, 2000, the Family Part entered an order terminating defendant's child support obligations as of July 11, 2000. The judge also ordered that defendant pay fifty percent of the loans Alyssa incurred pursuing her undergraduate degree. The order required plaintiff to provide proof of Alyssa's loans, excluding those from family members. The record does not reveal whether a statement of reasons accompanied that order. Nor does the order state whether the judge placed his reasons on the record.

Thereafter, plaintiff submitted a statement to the Family Part indicating the principal amount of Alyssa's non-family member student loans as $62,818 with interest of $7912. On October 2, 2000, the judge entered an order requiring defendant to pay $35,000 of Alyssa's student loans. The judge also ordered the matter stayed while the parties pursued further discovery. The preprinted language of the order states that the court conducted a hearing, but the record does not indicate whether the parties actually appeared. Also, neither the record nor the order reveals whether a statement of reasons accompanied the October 5, 2000, order. To the contrary, the record discloses that hearings were conducted on December 21, 2000, and May 2, 2001, *after* the court entered the order requiring defendant to reimburse his estranged daughter for her college tuition.

Much of the hearings that were ultimately conducted were devoted to defendant's claim that he has been totally rejected by both Justin and

Alyssa. That fact is not in dispute. Alyssa explained that she wanted nothing to do with defendant. She testified that her "earliest memories [were] of [her] father and mother fighting." She recalled a great deal of "violence." Alyssa recounted that Justin was "very protective of [her] and [would] take [her] to places in the house where [she] could not see or hear the fighting." Alyssa vividly remembered her "father pulling [her] mother's hair and screaming [at her]." She "observed" several incidents in which her mother was "screaming in pain."

At the hearing, defendant testified as to his social and financial status. Defendant remarried in 1989. A daughter was born, who was six years old at the time of the hearings. Defendant also has two stepchildren. Between 1987 and the early 1990's defendant held various jobs where he earned six dollars per hour. In the early 1990's he enrolled in paramedic training school. Defendant stated that he paid part of the $6800 tuition with a $3000 loan from his father-in-law, and made $2800 in installment payments. Additionally, his stepdaughter, who was paying her own way through college at that time, loaned him $1000 of her scholarship money to pay the balance of the tuition. Then, in 1995 defendant began working as a firefighter in Philadelphia. At that time he earned approximately $23,000 a year. Defendant estimated his annual salary for the past four years as follows: 1997—$32,000; 1998—$38,000; 1999—$42,000; and 2000—$50,000.

Defendant was required to reside in Philadelphia as a condition of his employment. Initially he rented a room, but later purchased a 700 square foot "row house" for $27,000. The monthly mortgage payment on that house is $290.83. The outstanding balance of that mortgage is approximately $25,000. Defendant primarily resides with his current wife in a house in Barnegat. His current wife purchased the house in 1991 for $150,000. A mortgage in the principal amount of $120,000, with monthly payments of $1400, remains on that house.

Plaintiff testified as to her financial status. After the parties separated, she and the children resided with plaintiff's parents in New Jersey. Plaintiff returned to college and began teaching school in New Jersey. Sometime in 1992 plaintiff filed for food stamps. In 1995, she filed a bankruptcy petition. Also in 1995, plaintiff suffered an injury that prevented her from working. She received $200 in weekly disability benefits. Plaintiff currently earns $200 a week as a part-time teacher in Vermont where she continues to reside with her parents.

On June 4, 2002, the Family Part judge issued a letter opinion in which he reinstated his prior order requiring defendant to pay $35,000 of Alyssa's student loans. Although the judge referred to *Newburgh v. Arrigo*, 88 *N.J.* 529, 443 *A.*2d 1031, he focused his attention on only two of the twelve factors described in that opinion. The judge characterized as "irrelevant" the fact that Alyssa had totally rejected defendant's efforts to establish a "mutually affectionate" relationship, noting that it was "futile" to "try [and] fix blame." The judge found that defendant's position as a firefighter provided a sufficient financial basis to require him to contribute one-half of Alyssa's loans plus interest if he is to make that payment in installments.

It is against that backdrop that we review the Family Part's order.

We begin our analysis by reciting well-settled principles. By virtue of statute, *N.J.S.A.* 9:2–4, and case law, *Grotsky v. Grotsky*, 58 *N.J.* 354, 356, 277 *A.*2d 535 (1971), parents are equally charged with their children's care, nurture, education and welfare. In general, this obligation terminates upon the emancipation of the child.

Emancipation can occur upon the child's marriage, by court order, or by attainment of an appropriate age. A rebuttable presumption against emancipation exists prior to attaining the age of majority. Parents are thus not ordinarily under a duty to support children after the age of majority.

However, "in appropriate circumstances, the privilege of parenthood carries with it the duty to assure a necessary education for [the] children." *Newburgh v. Arrigo*, 88 *N.J.* at 543, 443 *A.*2d 1031. The concept of what constitutes a "necessary education" has changed considerably in recent years. In *Khalaf v. Khalaf*, 58 *N.J.* 63, 275 *A.*2d 132 (1971), our Supreme Court observed that "[w]hile a 'common public school and high school education' may have been sufficient in an earlier time, . . . the trend has been toward greater education."

This subject was covered at length by the Court in *Newburgh v. Arrigo*, 88 *N.J.* 529, 443 *A*.2d 1031. There, the Court observed that "[i]n the past, a college education was reserved for the elite, but the vital impulse of egalitarianism has inspired the creation of a wide variety of educational institutions that provide postsecondary education for practically everyone." While the cost of a college education has vastly increased over the years, "[s]tate, county and community colleges, as well as some private colleges and vocational schools provide educational opportunities at reasonable costs." Emphasizing the emerging need for post-secondary education, the Court stated that "[i]n general, financially capable parents should contribute to the higher education of children who are qualified students" and "[i]n appropriate circumstances, parental responsibility includes the duty to assure children of a college and even of a post-graduate education such as law school." Justice Pollock, writing for the Court, enunciated specific standards and guidelines to be applied:

> In evaluating the claim for contribution toward the cost of higher education, courts should consider all relevant factors, including (1) whether the parent, if still living with the child, would have contributed toward the costs of the requested higher education; (2) the effect of the background values and goals of the parent on the reasonableness of the expectation of the child for higher education; (3) the amount of the contribution sought by the child for the cost of higher education; (4) the ability of the parent to pay that cost; (5) the relationship of the requested contribution to the kind of school or course of study sought by the child; (6) the financial resources of both parents; (7) the commitment to and aptitude of the child for the requested education; (8) the financial resources of the child, including assets owned individually or held in custodianship or trust; (9) the ability of the child to earn income during the school year or on vacation; (10) the availability of financial aid in the form of college grants and loans; (11) the child's relationship to the paying parent, including mutual affection and shared

goals as well as responsiveness to parental advice and guidance; and (12) the relationship of the education requested to any prior training and to the overall long-range goals of the child. [*Id.* at 545, 443 *A*.2d 1031].

As we noted earlier, the Family Part judge in this case referred to only two of the factors set forth in *Newburgh*. One factor—the relationship between defendant and Alyssa and her responsiveness to parental advice and guidance—the judge found to be irrelevant. The second factor—the financial resources of the parties—the judge in highly conclusory language determined that defendant had the ability to shoulder one-half of Alyssa's student loans. The judge ignored all of the other factors described by the Court in *Newburgh* that come to bear in determining whether a parent should be required to contribute to a child's college expenses. Among other circumstances, the judge should have considered the fact that: (1) defendant was excluded from participating in decisions pertaining to Alyssa's college education, (2) plaintiff and Alyssa chose a relatively expensive private college rather than available New Jersey or Vermont institutions, (3) Alyssa apparently did not seek summer employment during several of the years she attended college, (4) there may have been additional grants available that would have defrayed a portion of Alyssa's college expenses, and (5) plaintiff did not seek reimbursement of Alyssa's student loans during the years these obligations were incurred, thus possibly impairing defendant's ability to make sound financial judgments.

The judge's failure to consider the full set of applicable standards and guidelines and to render specific findings regarding these criteria undermines our confidence in the ultimate conclusion he reached.

We emphasize, however, that we do not reject as out of hand the judge's conclusion that defendant should retroactively bear the obligation to pay a portion of Alyssa's student loans. While the judge should consider the fact that Alyssa has rebuffed defendant's attempt to establish a relationship, that undisputed fact, standing alone, does not necessarily eradicate the parental obligation to make appropriate

CASE

contributions for college education. In *Moss v. Nedas*, 289 *N.J.Super*. 352, 674 *A*.2d 174 (App.Div.1996), we considered the question whether a non-custodial father is obligated to reimburse his estranged daughter for any part of the student loans she incurred where she neither advised her father of her decision to attend college nor sought his advice and guidance on the subject. There, the trial judge terminated the father's obligation to contribute to the college expenses of his daughter. *Id*. at 353, 674 *A*.2d 174. Considering "the absence of any meaningful" father-daughter relationship, the judge found it inappropriate to compel the father to contribute to his daughter's college expenses." *Id*. at 360, 674 *A*.2d 174. We sustained that conclusion, finding that the judge had properly applied the *Newburgh* factors. *Id*. at 353, 674 *A*.2d 174.

We do not read *Moss* as holding that a child's rejection of a parent's attempt to establish a mutually affectionate relationship invariably eradicates the parent's obligation to contribute to the child's college education. In this case, for example, a judge could reasonably find from the evidence that defendant's abusive conduct during the marriage so traumatized the children as to render nugatory any real possibility of a rapprochement. In that event, it would not be reasonable to penalize Alyssa for the defendant's misconduct. Nor would it be reasonable to reward defendant by removing his financial obligation to contribute to his daughter's college costs. There are indeed circumstances where a child's conduct may make the enforcement of the right to contribution inequitable, but here it is claimed that it was the defendant himself who was the architect of his own misfortune.

Unfortunately, the Family Part judge made no finding, one way or the other, respecting this issue. To the contrary, the judge specifically disavowed any attempt to determine the truth or falsity of the allegations concerning violence and abuse or the psychological sequelae that allegedly followed.

We are thus constrained to reverse the order entered and remand the matter for further consideration. The parties should be afforded the opportunity to supplement the record with additional relevant testimony and material. The Family Part judge is to apply the *Newburgh* criteria and to make explicit findings of fact and conclusions of law. We do not retain jurisdiction.

Case Review Question

Gaynell GAC v. Ludwig GAC, 351 N.J.Super. 54, 796 A.2d 951 (2002).
Would the outcome likely change if the child attended a local community college rather than an expensive private university?

Case Brief

Facts: Parties divorce after violent marriage. No visitation was recommended and none occurred. Father attempted remote communication through letters but it was entirely one-sided and after several years this stopped because he did not have a current address for the minor children. After minor children achieved majority and youngest child graduated college, the father sought to terminate child support obligations. The court ordered that the child support should terminate but ordered the father to pay $35,000 toward the college debts of the youngest child.

Issue: Whether the trial court abused its discretion when it retroactively awarded one-half of the college debt of the youngest child to be paid by the father with whom the child had no contact since early minority.

Law: *Newburgh v. Arrigo*, 88 N.J. 529, 443 *A*.2d 1031 (1982). Numerous factors should be considered when a determination is made regarding continued support beyond a child's minority for the purposes of postsecondary education.

Rule: While courts often recognize the need for divorced parents to continue support of their children during college education, several factors must be considered. In this case, the trial court neglected to consider the large majority of these factors including the fact that the father had no contact with the child and no voice in the type of education, education expenses, and consequently no ability to consider his potential responsibility for these expenses when making decisions regarding his own financial status.

Reversed.

The following paragraphs describe the elements of a case. While judicial opinions may be lengthy, the case brief is usually not, since a brief's purpose is to identify only those points that were pivotal in the decision and consequently would be considered in a similar case. Therefore, when analyzing a case, no matter what element is being examined, one should focus only on those statements that directly affected the final decision.

The Facts

Since case law is the application of a prior judicial determination to a similar situation, the first step in preparing a case brief is to identify the key facts. In many situations, such identification will control whether the legal principles of a previous case would be applicable to another situation.

A case brief contains two types of facts: occurrence facts and legal (sometimes called procedural) facts. Both are important to the brief for different reasons, both are generally present in the opinion in full detail, and both should be edited in the case brief to include only those facts, either occurrence or legal, that had a direct impact on the result in the case. Facts to be excluded from the case brief include those that provide a backdrop for the case and help to fill in details of the occurrence and legal proceedings but do not directly impact the outcome.

Occurrence facts are the details of the circumstances that initially gave rise to the lawsuit. The amount of such information that is included in the opinion depends largely on the particular writing style of the judge, who is the author. However, most opinions contain a substantial amount of factual information based on what has been disclosed by the parties, which creates a clear representation of the setting of the case, development of legal issues, and circumstances of the various parties to the suit.

Although background information is helpful to thoroughly understand the intricacies of a judicial opinion, it is not necessary to include all factual details in a case brief. When editing an opinion for the composition of a brief, keep in mind that only the most essential facts should be included. Two questions can be asked about each fact when deciding whether to include that fact in a brief: (1) Will exclusion of the fact from the brief prevent the reader from understanding the general premise of the case? (2) Was the fact pivotal in the outcome of the case?

The legal facts consist of what took place once litigation began and then chronicle the progression of the lawsuit. A number of these facts may be recited in the opinion to show case development; however, the only real legal facts usually necessary in a case brief are those that tie directly into the basis for the appeal, which ultimately prompted the ruling and consequent judicial opinion. When first learning to read and analyze judicial opinions, there is a temptation to assume that the appeal is based on an allegedly improper finding of liability or innocence. Appeals are almost never so simply stated. Rather, there must be a legally objectionable basis for how the improper result originated. Examples include exclusion or inclusion of evidence objected to by one of the parties, improper jury instructions, and so forth. When preparing a case brief, the important legal facts to include are those surrounding the alleged error that created the basis for the appeal.

There are, of course, exceptions to the rule as to when less than absolutely vital information should be included. Such cases occur when otherwise ordinary information has an impact as the result of the particular circumstances of the case. With occurrence facts, an example might be the time of day in a case involving an auto accident, when visibility is an issue, or a date in a contract case. Similarly, a pretrial motion might be a relevant legal fact to include if the subject of that motion ultimately becomes an issue at trial or causes the case to be dismissed before trial. Although such information is more often than not a backdrop for the case, if it might influence other facts or legal issues, then it should be included.

◆ APPLICATION 2.4

A lawsuit that ultimately produced an appeal and published judicial opinion arose from the following facts reported in the opinion:

A man was hired to come to work at a small manufacturing plant of about 40 employees. During the first week on the job, the man was told he had to go to a shop area for the new employee "weighing in" ceremony. The man was then told to hold on to a bench while he was "measured." He did so and while numerous other employees looked on, a coworker came from behind and struck the man across the backside with a 2 × 4 piece of lumber. The employees all laughed and told the man he was now "officially" an employee of the plant. The man suffered severe bruising and a broken tailbone as a result of the incident. He filed suit against the employer. The owners of the plant claimed no knowledge of this practice of initiating new employees and further claimed that since it occurred during the lunch break, they were not responsible for the acts of the other employees. Additional evidence included the fact that employees were not allowed to leave the site on breaks and that the shop manager was present at the "weighing in" ceremony. A jury awarded the man a judgment against the company for $3,560 in medical and related expenses, and punitive damages in the amount of $1,000,000.

In a case brief, the facts may include: A new hire at a manufacturer was subjected to an "initiation" by other employees on company property during a lunch break, that resulted in serious injuries. Present at the initiation was a member of management of the company. The company defended it did not have knowledge and was further not liable as the occurrence took place when employees were not on the clock. The verdict was in favor of the plaintiff for medical expenses of $3,560 and punitive damages of $1,000,000.

Point for Discussion
◆   Why is it relevant that one of the people present was the shop manager?

The Legal Issue

Identifying the issue in the opinion is quite often one of the most difficult tasks for someone just beginning legal analysis. As with legal facts, the assumption tends to be that the legal issue is the question of guilt or liability of the defendant. In the case of a published judicial opinion, this is almost never the issue. As discussed, the appellate courts that publish the vast majority of judicial opinions do not serve the same function as trial courts. While the ultimate legal issue in a trial court is usually one of guilt or innocence, in the appellate court, and consequently the published opinion, the issue is almost always whether something inappropriate occurred in the trial court that in turn prevented the proper finding on the issue of guilt or innocence. Most often the question turns on whether the trial court judge or jury properly applied one or more legal principles to the evidence before the court.

The authority of a trial court is not one with clearly defined boundaries, because the law itself is not black and white. The law instead considers the relevant factors in an individual circumstance. Because no two cases are exactly alike, there must be some room for the court to consider and apply the law it interprets for a given situation. Likewise, no two juries are identical in makeup or in the way they interpret evidence. Because the American legal system places such high value on the ability to have questions decided by one's fellow citizens, a significant respect is also afforded the reasoning on a jury as to why a particular verdict is reached. Consequently, both judges and juries are given a certain degree of discretion in their roles. The appellate court examines whether this grant of discretion has been abused in such a way that the result in the case is clearly and unequivocally contrary to the existing principles of law and whether any justification exists for the deviation. Therefore, when conducting legal analysis of a judicial opinion, the task is to identify what serious breach of discretion is asserted by the appellant, that is, the party seeking to have the trial court action reviewed and changed.

The goal of case analysis is to identify why the appellate court ultimately agreed or disagreed with the trial court. This result rests on the question considered by the appellate court. One method that can be helpful to the less experienced in the identification of the legal issue is to read the opinion and then complete the following statement:

The appellant alleges the trial court erred (abused its discretion) when_____.

or

The question before the court is_____.

Very often, one of these statements or a similar one will appear in the opinion itself. Without exception; the judicial opinion will make some reference to the legal issue either as part of the recitation of the legal facts or in a discussion of the task before the appellate court. It might read, for example, "The defendant sought a new trial and subsequently filed this appeal asserting the jury ignored the manifest weight of the evidence;" or "The question that lies before this court is whether the trial court abused its discretion when it granted summary judgment on the finding that no reasonable issue existed as to the defendant's liability."

The Law

The third step in case analysis is to determine the authority upon which the court's decision was based. Since judges always search for guidance from existing legal standards, if there are no such standards, the judge looks to the beliefs of society and the fundamentals of right and wrong as viewed by society. Often the latter are determined by looking to the opinions of legal scholars and other noted authorities on a subject. In any event, the decision in a case will be based on some existing statement of law or wisdom. The court uses such a statement as authority and applies it to the occurrence and legal facts of the case to determine the answer to the issue before the court.

Most often the court will use an established legal standard as authority. However, sometimes the judge applies an opinion of a scholar, but this is private opinion and not law. However, by incorporating such opinion into the judicial opinion, the private opinion becomes the legal standard in that court. Consequently, the use of the term *law* describes the authority adopted and applied by a judge as the guiding legal standard in deciding a case.

In a case brief, one should indicate the source of the "law" (legal principle) used to determine a case. Just as importantly, the actual principle should be stated. It is not helpful to know one without the other. When analyzing the effects of a case, it is necessary to know not only the source but also the content of the legal standard. When identifying the law for use in a case brief, the student should seek out those principles that address the issue at hand. The following excerpt from a judicial opinion that responds to the issue in that opinion is an example of legal authority:

> *Issue*: Can a person be convicted of assisting in a robbery when there is evidence that the person's life was threatened in order to coerce assistance?

> *Law*: "When a party is forced, under threat of serious harm, to perform an illegal act, then that party cannot be held accountable for committing a criminal act." *People of the State of Maine v. Jezbera*, 402 A.2d 777 (Maine Sup. Ct. 1980).

The quoted material is the legal standard. The information that follows is the source. Specifically given is the name of the case, the volume number, the name of the reporter series where the opinion is published, and the page number where the case begins. The information in parentheses indicates the court that decided the case and the year of the opinion.

If you looked up *Atlantic Reports*, 2d Series, at a library, located volume 402, and opened it to page 777, you would see the case of *Maine v. Jezbera*. You would also find information indicating that this opinion was handed down by the Supreme Court of Maine in 1980.

The Rule

Judicial opinions do not merely state the law (both principle and its source) and then follow with a blanket statement of the case's winner. Rather, the court will give some explanation regarding why or how the legal standard applies to the facts and issue of the case. In a case brief, such information is essential. It is impossible to predict the effects of a case without understanding the reasoning of the court in the judicial opinion. Unless this information is included in the case analysis (brief), one could not determine whether the same legal standards would apply in the present situation to the present facts and issue.

Once the facts, issue, law, and rule have been determined, the case brief can be used to compare the case with other situations of similar facts and issue. Similarities and differences should be identified. One should then determine whether the similarities are strong enough to create a likelihood that the same legal standards would be applied in the same way in the other situation. This can be done in large part by examining the rule of the case. One must ask just how and why the previous court applied the particular legal standard to the case. If the case is briefed for purposes of comparison to another situation, then the next issue to explore is the likelihood that the law would be applied in the same way under the facts and issue of the other situation.

What follows are two judicial opinions. A case brief has been provided after the first opinion.

CASE

MISSOURI COURT OF APPEALS, WESTERN DISTRICT.

MARGO L. ROGERS, RESPONDENT,

V.

RICHARD K. ROGERS, APPELLANT.

Sept. 17, 2002.
2002 W. L. 310 55412
(MoApp WD)

I. Factual and Procedural Background
Richard and Margo Rogers' marriage was dissolved on September 23, 1997. As part of the original decree, the parties were awarded joint legal custody of the parties' minor children, Sara Anne Rogers (born September 25, 1977) and Amy

Christine Rogers (born April 4, 1979). Ms. Rogers was designated as the primary physical custodian of the children, and Mr. Rogers was ordered to pay child support in the amount of $555.00 per child, per month ($1,100.00 a month).

In August of 1999, the trial court entered a judgment modifying the child support requirements of Mr. Rogers. This judgment declared Sara Rogers as an emancipated adult under § 452.340.5, and it set the child support for Amy Rogers at $630.00 per month effective May 1, 1999. Beginning in September 1999, the disbursement of these payments was to be paid in the following fashion: $420.00 to Ms. Rogers and $210.00 directly to Amy Rogers.

Mr. Rogers paid child support on a regular basis until May 2000, when his employment terminated. After Ms. Rogers filed a contempt action for his failure to make these payments, Mr. Rogers paid the child support in arrears, which totaled $1,680.00.

◆ **CASE**

On January 30, 2001, Mr. Rogers filed the instant action, seeking to abate his child support obligations in their entirety. In addition, Mr. Rogers sought a reimbursement of child support payments that he had already made because he contended that both of the children failed to comply with the child support eligibility requirements of § 452.340.5 by failing to provide him with regular transcripts of their progress in school. Also, on two occasions, Amy failed to take twelve credits per semester as required by § 452.340.5. Accordingly, Mr. Rogers argued that this abatement and reimbursement was mandated by law.

This matter went to trial on August 16, 2001, in the circuit court of Cass County. At trial, both Mr. and Ms. Rogers testified, as well as their daughter, Amy Rogers.

The trial court ruled that, as of August 2000, Amy Rogers was ineligible to receive child support payments after September 1, 2000, "for failure to comply with the provisions of Chapter 452, with respect to furnishing schedule and transcripts." Moreover, it reaffirmed the circuit court's prior ruling, based on agreement by the parties, that Sara Rogers was emancipated on May 1, 1999. Because it was found by the trial court that Mr. Rogers was "current" on his child support obligations, it was held that he was not required to make any further child support payments.

However, the trial court denied Mr. Rogers' other requested relief, to reimburse previously made child support payments. In issuing this ruling, the trial court found that Mr. Rogers' evidence at trial went unrefuted demonstrating that he "was not furnished transcripts, grades of courses earned, or other information concerning the progress of the two daughters in college." Notwithstanding this fact, the trial court denied his request for any reimbursement of child support payments, reasoning that it "finds it to be inequitable to revert back for the length of time [Mr. Rogers] requests."

Mr. Rogers brings two points on appeal, Point One dealing with Amy Rogers and Point Two dealing with Sara Rogers. Because similar arguments are raised in both points, they will be treated as one for ease of analysis. In making his argument on appeal, it is Mr. Rogers' contention that the trial court erred in refusing his requested relief of ordering Ms. Rogers to refund child support payments previously made by him because the children failed to follow the provisions of § 452.340.5 that require a college student to satisfy reporting requirements to be eligible to receive child support payments. Absent such compliance with the statute, it is Mr. Rogers' contention that a college student becomes "statutorily disqualified" and, therefore, is ineligible for child support payments. In this case, it is argued that his children failed to follow these provisions by failing to provide college transcripts to him, and also because Amy Rogers failed to take at least twelve hours of college credit on two occasions. Accordingly, as a matter of law, Mr. Rogers argues that such unauthorized child support payments must be refunded to him.

II. Standard of Review

The parties on appeal agree that the governing standard of review is the one set out by the Supreme Court in *Murphy v. Carron*, 536 S.W.2d 30, 32 (Mo. banc 1976). Under that standard, the trial court's judgment will be affirmed by this court unless there is no substantial evidence to support it, it is against the weight of the evidence, or it erroneously declares the law or applies the law. *Id.*

III. Legal Analysis

It is Mr. Rogers' argument on appeal that his daughters, Amy and Sara, violated the mandatory provisions of receiving child support as it pertains to the eligibility of children who are college students (§ 452.340.5), and, therefore, these child support payments previously made by Mr. Rogers must be refunded as a matter of law. Section 452.340.5 states, in pertinent part, that:

> If the child is enrolled in an institution of vocational or higher education not later than October first following graduation from a secondary school or completion of a graduation equivalence degree program and so long as the child enrolls for and completes at least twelve hours of credit each semester, not including the

summer semester, at an institution of vocational or higher education and achieves grades sufficient to reenroll at such institution, the parental support obligation shall continue until the child completes his or her education, or until the child reaches the age of twenty-two, which ever first occurs. To remain eligible for such continued parental support, at the beginning of each semester the child shall submit to each parent a transcript or similar official document provided by the institution of vocational or higher education which includes the courses the child is enrolled in and has completed for each term, the grades and credits received for each such course, and an official document from the institution listing the courses which the child is enrolled in for the upcoming term and the number of credits for each such course.

The trial court, in its judgment in this matter, made the factual finding that both Sara and Amy Rogers did not comply with § 452.340.5 because they failed to supply their father with their college transcripts. Therefore, the central question is whether the trial court erred in holding that, although these terms of the statute were violated by his children, Mr. Rogers has no legal right to be reimbursed for these child support funds already dispersed by him.

The child support statutory scheme in Missouri does provide for returning of monies to a parent who has made payments to an "emancipated" child under § 452.370.4. This provision of the statute provides as follows:

Unless otherwise agreed in writing or expressly provided in the judgment, provisions for the support of a child are terminated by emancipation of the child. The parent entitled to receive child support shall have the duty to notify the parent obligated to pay support of the child's emancipation and failing to do so, the parent entitled to receive child support shall be liable to the parent obligated to pay support for child support paid following emancipation of a minor child.

Accordingly, this case turns on whether the children's undisputed non- compliance with § 452.340.5 rises to the level of legally "emancipating" them under § 452.370.4. If so, a reimbursement is required by law. *In re Marriage of Hammerschmidt*, 48 S.W.3d 614, 619 (Mo.App. E.D.2001).

In arguing that child support funds already paid by him must be reimbursed as a matter of law, Mr. Rogers brings two, somewhat distinct, legal theories. Mr. Rogers argues that in fact. "both girls became emancipated on September 23, 1997," and therefore, he is eligible for reimbursement under § 452.370.4. Furthermore, Mr. Rogers contends that his children's failure "to supply respondent with transcripts . . . [as] required by Section 452.340.5 RSMo statutorily disqualifies [his children] from parental support from the appellant." As Mr. Rogers points out, "for the child to *continue* receiving child support, the statute requires the child to provide each parent with a [college] transcript." *Morton v. Myers*, 21 S.W.3d 99, 106 (Mo.App. W.D.2000) (emphasis added) (quoting *In re Marriage of Kohring*, 999 S.W.2d 228, 233 [Mo. banc 1999]); *see also Lyons v. Sloop*, 40 S.W.3d 1, 7 (Mo.App. W.D.2001).

But in this case, we are dealing with the unique situation where a parent *has already made the child support payments in question*, and instead of petitioning to a court to be relieved of a debt or future payment (as was done in each of the aforementioned cases), Mr. Phillips sought the unique relief of having payments, already disbursed by him, reimbursed. Section 452.340.5 does not contain a reimbursement provision for child support funds; one must turn to § 452.370.4 for this type of relief. Accordingly, because the circuit court has already terminated any past or future child support obligations of Mr. Rogers under § 452.340.5, the sole issue presented for review today is whether such reporting non-compliance by his children allows for a reimbursement under § 452.370.4. To resolve that issue, we must determine, as previously stated, whether this reporting non-compliance of the children legally "emancipated" them under § 452.370.4. *See generally Hammerschmidt*, 48 S.W.3d at 618.

In *In re Marriage of Hammerschmidt*, father filed for reimbursement of child support from ex-wife

CASE

under § 452.370.4. *Id.* at 616. In granting the motion, it was held by the Eastern District that, "as a matter of law [the child] was emancipated . . . having previously reached the age of eighteen, he stopped attending and progressing toward the completion of a secondary education program by withdrawing from school." *Id.* at 618. Accordingly, the court found that the mother had "the responsibility to repay to the noncustodial parent all child support paid after the actual date of emancipation." *Id.* at 619.

But *Hammerschmidt* is distinct from today's case. In *Hammerschmidt*, it was clear, as a matter of law, that the child in question was "emancipated" through the child's failure to successfully earn class credits while attending school, coupled with his subsequent withdrawal from school. *Id.* at 618. In our case, the same cannot be said for the Rogers children. The trial court concluded, and the record on appeal so reflects, that both attended secondary school in the fashion required by § 452.340.5. Accordingly, the distinction between the child's conduct in *Hammerschmidt* and our case is stark. Failing to attend school and receive class credit is distinct and different from failing to give a parent transcripts of the child's educational progress. Simply put, it is this court's opinion that the latter, by itself, does not "emancipate" a child under § 452.370.4. *Cf. Kohring*, 999 S.W.2d at 234 (holding that "[d]espite daughter's failure to comply with the statute [by failing to provide father with school transcript], father is not relieved of future payments for daughter's educational expenses"). [FN5] Because the children were not "emancipated" during the time in question, Mr. Rogers cannot, as a matter of law, be eligible for a reimbursement under § 452.370.4.

We appreciate that the legislature provided this reporting requirement in the statute so that the non-custodial parent can insure that their children are using these child support payments to actually obtain a college education. However, as previously stated, it is also the duty of the custodial parent under § 452.370.4 to insure that the non-custodial parent is given notice when the child is "emancipated" by the child's failure to meet the minimum requirements of attending college under the statute. *Hammerschmidt*, 48 S.W.3d at 618-19. Accordingly, a parent who has not been provided with the requisite transcripts, and who later learns that his children have failed to use these funds for college, has a legal recourse for reimbursement under § 452.370.4. Finally, we encourage parents obligated to pay child support to insure (by diligently asking their children, and, if necessary, petitioning the appropriate court of law) that their children provide them with college transcripts as required by the statute. It is only through this process that parents can insure that their child support payments have been appropriately used for educational purposes in the past, and determine "whether the non-custodial parent is still required to support his or her child through college." *Lyons*, 40 S.W.3d at 7.

In this case, though, because the Rogers children were not "emancipated" during the time period in question (having attended college as required under § 452.340.5), Mr. Rogers is not eligible for a reimbursement under § 452.370.4.

IV. Conclusion

Based on our review of the record, we cannot conclude that the trial court erred. Accordingly, the trial court's judgment is affirmed.

Case Review Question

Rogers v. Rogers, 2002 WL 31055412 (MoApp WD 2002).

Would the result likely be different if there were no communication such as in *Manor v. Gale*?

Assignment 2.3

> Prepare a case brief for *Rogers v. Rogers*.

Statutory and Administrative Analysis

Unlike the case brief, which requires the synopsis of a factual occurrence as well as legal issues, the statutory analysis and administrative legal analysis procedure is much more straightforward. Statutes and administrative regulations are more broadly written and do not generally provide detailed discussions of exact case scenarios. A statute will only be applied when its various conditions or elements are satisfied. Because statutes are written to apply to the entire public rather than specific individuals, the language and description of legal standards is generally quite different from the judicial opinion.

When examining a statute, the first step is to break it down into specific elements. Great care should be used in evaluating the effect of each word in a statute to determine whether all conditions *must* be met, as opposed to whether different ones can satisfy the statute alternatively. See Figure 2.4.

FIGURE 2.4   3 V.A.M.S. § 4522.340

VERNON'S ANNOTATED MISSOURI STATUTES
TITLE XXX. DOMESTIC RELATIONS
CHAPTER 452. DISSOLUTION OF MARRIAGE, DIVORCE, ALIMONY AND SEPARATE MAINTENANCE
DISSOLUTION OF MARRIAGE

452.340. Child support—relevant factors—abatement and termination—change of custody—college expenses—guidelines and use thereof—retroactive support

1. In a proceeding for dissolution of marriage, legal separation or child support, the court may order either or both parents owing a duty of support to a child of the marriage to pay an amount reasonable or necessary for the support of the child, including an award retroactive to the date of filing the petition, without regard to marital misconduct, after considering all relevant factors including:

 (1) The financial needs and resources of the child;

 (2) The financial resources and needs of the parents;

 (3) The standard of living the child would have enjoyed had the marriage not been dissolved;

 (4) The physical and emotional condition of the child, and the child's educational needs;

 (5) The child's physical and legal custody arrangements, including the amount of time the child spends with each parent and the reasonable expenses associated with the custody or visitation arrangements; and

 (6) The reasonable work-related child care expenses of each parent.

2. The obligation of the parent ordered to make support payments shall abate, in whole or in part, for such periods of time in excess of thirty consecutive days that the other parent has voluntarily relinquished physical custody of a child to the parent ordered to pay child support, notwithstanding any periods of visitation or temporary physical and legal or physical or legal custody pursuant to a judgment of dissolution or legal separation or any modification thereof. In a IV-D case, the division of child support enforcement may determine the amount of the abatement pursuant to this subsection for any child support order and shall record the amount of abatement in the automated child support system record established pursuant to chapter 454, RSMo. If the case is not a IV-D case and upon court order, the circuit clerk shall record the amount of abatement in the automated child support system record established in chapter 454, RSMo.

3. Unless the circumstances of the child manifestly dictate otherwise and the court specifically so provides, the obligation of a parent to make child support payments shall terminate when the child:

FIGURE 2.4   3 V.A.M.S. § 4522.340   (*continued*)

(1) Dies;

(2) Marries;

(3) Enters active duty in the military;

(4) Becomes self-supporting, provided that the custodial parent has relinquished the child from parental control by express or implied consent;

(5) Reaches age eighteen, unless the provisions of subsection 4 or 5 of this section apply; or

(6) Reaches age twenty-two, unless the provisions of the child support order specifically extend the parental support order past the child's twenty-second birthday for reasons provided by subsection 4 of this section.

4. If the child is physically or mentally incapacitated from supporting himself and insolvent and unmarried, the court may extend the parental support obligation past the child's eighteenth birthday.

5. If when a child reaches age eighteen, the child is enrolled in and attending a secondary school program of instruction, the parental support obligation shall continue, if the child continues to attend and progresses toward completion of said program, until the child completes such program or reaches age twenty-one, whichever first occurs. If the child is enrolled in an institution of vocational or higher education not later than October first following graduation from a secondary school or completion of a graduation equivalence degree program and so long as the child enrolls for and completes at least twelve hours of credit each semester, not including the summer semester, at an institution of vocational or higher education and achieves grades sufficient to reenroll at such institution, the parental support obligation shall continue until the child completes his or her education, or until the child reaches the age of twenty-two, whichever first occurs. To remain eligible for such continued parental support, at the beginning of each semester the child shall submit to each parent a transcript or similar official document provided by the institution of vocational or higher education which includes the courses the child is enrolled in and has completed for each term, the grades and credits received for each such course, and an official document from the institution listing the courses which the child is enrolled in for the upcoming term and the number of credits for each such course. If the circumstances of the child manifestly dictate, the court may waive the October first deadline for enrollment required by this subsection. If the child is enrolled in such an institution, the child or parent obligated to pay support may petition the court to amend the order to direct the obligated parent to make the payments directly to the child. As used in this section, an "institution of vocational education" means any postsecondary training or schooling for which the student is assessed a fee and attends classes regularly. "Higher education" means any junior college, community college, college, or university at which the child attends classes regularly. A child who has been diagnosed with a learning disability, or whose physical disability or diagnosed health problem limits the child's ability to carry the number of credit hours prescribed in this subsection, shall remain eligible for child support so long as such child is enrolled in and attending an institution of vocational or higher education, and the child continues to meet the other requirements of this subsection. A child who is employed at least fifteen hours per week during the semester may take as few as nine credit hours per semester and remain eligible for child support so long as all other requirements of this subsection are complied with.

6. The court shall consider ordering a parent to waive the right to claim the tax dependency exemption for a child enrolled in an institution of vocational or higher education in favor of the other parent if the application of state and federal tax laws and eligibility for financial aid will make an award of the exemption to the other parent appropriate.

7. The general assembly finds and declares that it is the public policy of this state that frequent, continuing and meaningful contact with both parents after the parents have separated or dissolved their marriage is in the best interest of the child except for cases where the court specifically finds that such contact is not in the best interest of the child. In order to effectuate this public policy, a court with jurisdiction shall enforce visitation, custody and child support orders in the same manner. A court with jurisdiction may abate, in whole or in part, any past or future obligation of support and may transfer the physical and legal or physical or legal custody of one or more children if it finds that a parent has, without good cause, failed to provide visitation or physical and legal or physical or legal custody to the other parent pursuant to the terms of a judgment of dissolution, legal separation or modifications thereof. The court shall also award, if requested and for good cause shown, reasonable expenses, attorney's fees and court costs incurred by the prevailing party.

FIGURE 2.4   3 V.A.M.S. § 4522.340   (*Continued*)

8. The Missouri supreme court shall have in effect a rule establishing guidelines by which any award of child support shall be made in any judicial or administrative proceeding. Said guidelines shall contain specific, descriptive and numeric criteria which will result in a computation of the support obligation. The guidelines shall address how the amount of child support shall be calculated when an award of joint physical custody results in the child or children spending substantially equal time with both parents. Not later than October 1, 1998, the Missouri supreme court shall publish child support guidelines and specifically list and explain the relevant factors and assumptions that were used to calculate the child support guidelines. Any rule made pursuant to this subsection shall be reviewed by the promulgating body not less than once every three years to ensure that its application results in the determination of appropriate child support award amounts.

9. There shall be a rebuttable presumption, in any judicial or administrative proceeding for the award of child support, that the amount of the award which would result from the application of the guidelines established pursuant to subsection 8 of this section is the correct amount of child support to be awarded. A written finding or specific finding on the record in a judicial or administrative proceeding that the application of the guidelines would be unjust or inappropriate in a particular case, after considering all relevant factors, including the factors set out in subsection 1 of this section, is required if requested by a party and shall be sufficient to rebut the presumption in the case. The written finding or specific finding on the record shall detail the specific relevant factors that required a deviation from the application of the guidelines.

10. Pursuant to this or any other chapter, when a court determines the amount owed by a parent for support provided to a child by another person, other than a parent, prior to the date of filing of a petition requesting support, or when the director of the division of child support enforcement establishes the amount of state debt due pursuant to subdivision (2) of subsection 1 of section 454.465, RSMo, the court or director shall use the guidelines established pursuant to subsection 8 of this section. The amount of child support resulting from the application of the guidelines shall be applied retroactively for a period prior to the establishment of a support order and the length of the period of retroactivity shall be left to the discretion of the court or director. There shall be a rebuttable presumption that the amount resulting from application of the guidelines under subsection 8 of this section constitutes the amount owed by the parent for the period prior to the date of the filing of the petition for support or the period for which state debt is being established. In applying the guidelines to determine a retroactive support amount, when information as to average monthly income is available, the court or director may use the average monthly income of the noncustodial parent, as averaged over the period of retroactivity, in determining the amount of presumed child support owed for the period of retroactivity. The court or director may enter a different amount in a particular case upon finding, after consideration of all relevant factors, including the factors set out in subsection 1 of this section, that there is sufficient cause to rebut the presumed amount.

11. The obligation of a parent to make child support payments may be terminated as follows:

   (1) Provided that the child support order contains the child's date of birth, the obligation shall be deemed terminated without further judicial or administrative process when the child reaches age twenty-two if the child support order does not specifically require payment of child support beyond age twenty-two for reasons provided by subsection 4 of this section;

   (2) The obligation shall be deemed terminated without further judicial or administrative process when the parent receiving child support furnishes a sworn statement or affidavit notifying the obligor parent of the child's emancipation in accordance with the requirements of subsection 4 of section 452.370, and a copy of such sworn statement or affidavit is filed with the court which entered the order establishing the child support obligation, or the division of child support enforcement;

   (3) The obligation shall be deemed terminated without further judicial or administrative process, when the parent paying child support files a sworn statement or affidavit with the court which entered the order establishing the child support obligation, or the division of child support enforcement, stating that the child is emancipated and reciting the factual basis for such statement; which statement or affidavit is served by the court or division on the child support obligee; and which is either acknowledged and affirmed by the child support obligee in writing, or which is not responded to in writing within thirty days of receipt by the child support obligee;

FIGURE 2.4   3 V.A.M.S. § 4522.340   (*Continued*)

---

(4) The obligation shall be terminated as provided by this subdivision by the court which entered the order establishing the child support obligation, or the division of child support enforcement, when the parent paying child
support files a sworn statement or affidavit with the court which entered the order establishing the child support
obligation, or the division of child support enforcement, stating that the child is emancipated and reciting the factual basis for such statement; and which statement or affidavit is served by the court or division on the child support obligee. If the obligee denies the statement or affidavit, the court or division shall thereupon treat the sworn
statement or affidavit as a motion to modify the support obligation pursuant to section 452.370 or section
454.496, RSMo, and shall proceed to hear and adjudicate such motion as provided by law; provided that the
court may require the payment of a deposit as security for court costs and any accrued court costs, as provided
by law, in relation to such motion to modify.

12. The court may enter a judgment terminating child support pursuant to subdivisions (1) to (3) of subsection 11 of
this section without necessity of a court appearance by either party. The clerk of the court shall mail a copy of a
judgment terminating child support entered pursuant to subsection 11 of this section on both the obligor and
obligee parents. The supreme court may promulgate uniform forms for sworn statements and affidavits to terminate orders of child support obligations for use pursuant to subsection 11 of this section and subsection 4 of section 452.370.

The specific elements of a statute are rarely given in a laundry list format.
Rather, they are written most often in a narrative form. Often a single sentence
includes multiple elements that must be satisfied for the statute to apply and to
indicate a result. Consequently, great care must be taken in reading the statute
and identifying the exact meaning of each statutory requirement based on the
language used.

Assignment 2.4

Examine and evaluate the statute in Figure 2.4 and break into the applicable components.

Application of Legal Analysis

The evaluation of legal authorities is only one part of the process of legal analysis. Once authorities have been considered and summarized appropriately, the
second stage can begin. This involves the comparison of the legal precedent and
the current case. The effective legal professional considers not only those
authorities who support the position taken, but also those who discount it. The
latter can be useful in predicting and preparing for the opposition.

When considering applicable authorities, the key is to compare and distinguish. With respect to judicial opinions, the information contained within the case
brief should be closely compared with the current facts and issues. A similarity in
legal issues is obviously necessary, but equally important is the fact comparison.
A case that is too dissimilar in facts can be easily distinguished as inapplicable.
Although no two cases are exactly alike, it is important to seek out those cases

involving similar fact patterns with respect to the pivotal facts of the current situation. Any facts that are not present or mentioned, or that are dissimilar, must be considered in terms of the importance they played or might play in affecting the outcome of the present case. Legal standards should also be compared in terms of their applicability to the present case and the degree of influence the authority, the precedent, and its cited legal standards would have on the court in the current lawsuit if one is pending or anticipated. Ultimately, a decision must be reached as to whether the present case is likely to have a similar or different outcome.

As mentioned, statutory analysis also requires more than synthesizing the language of the statute. It is important to closely examine all the facts of the present case to determine whether they are addressed in the current statute. If they are not, a determination must be made as to the overall applicability of the statute to the case. If it does apply, what result does the analysis indicate? If it does not appear to apply due to the absence of facts that satisfy the elements, then be prepared to explain how the statute can be distinguished from the present case.

Ethical Considerations

All legal professionals have an obligation to present all applicable legal standards to the court in a case. As a result, any positive or negative principles determined in the process of legal analysis must be revealed. Although in some instances this might appear to be self-defeating, it is necessary to meet the ultimate goals of the American legal system, which is fairness and consistency to all in the application of laws.

Ethical Circumstance

A paralegal is conducting research for a case that is being considered in court the following day. Toward the end of the day, the paralegal receives a routine e-mail update from the highest appellate court of the state. The update indicates that a decision that day by the high court would severely and negatively impact the case, that heretofore was quite strong. The paralegal informs the attorney. The attorney is faced with the ethical decision of whether to bring up the recent change in the law at the hearing and almost certainly lose, or take the chance that the judge and opposition are unaware of it and win the case for his client.

CHAPTER SUMMARY

This chapter has explored the judicial branch of the American legal system. The judicial system has several unique characteristics. The judicial branch of government deals with specific cases on an individual and direct basis. It has the authority to overrule an act of the legislature or the executive branch if the act violates the Constitution. When a dispute arises and no statutory law exists, the judicial branch has power to create law and provide an immediate resolution to the dispute.

The judicial system is set up to clarify and protect the law. The courts must determine whether a broadly written statute or existing precedent applies to an individual circumstance. The courts also have the duty to uphold the U.S. Constitution and to see that the other branches of state and federal government honor the Constitution.

Because state and federal governments operate independently, each has its own judicial system to interpret and apply law. As long as the states establish and apply only law that is consistent with the Constitution of the United States, they are free to enact and enforce any law that is necessary for an orderly society.

The federal judicial system consists of three tiers. The U.S. District Courts, where cases are generally filed and trials are held, occupy the lowest tier. The next level is made up of the U.S. Courts of Appeals, which determine whether any error was committed by the U.S. District Court (trial court) in its determination of the dispute. Finally, the U.S. Supreme Court issues the final statement on disputes that claim that the Constitution has been violated. The states follow a similar type of structure, with approximately half incorporating the three-tiered system and the remaining half incorporating a two-tiered system by combining the functions of the court of appeals and the supreme court.

Many appellate (and some trial) judicial opinions are published for future reference. They contain certain information that allows an adequate comparison between the opinion and a case presently before a court. This information includes relevant facts, the actual issue in the dispute, the authority used to determine the dispute, and the manner in which the authority was applied.

Chapter 3 examines the legislative system in some detail. Chapter 4 addresses the functions of the executive branch. It is important to keep in mind that each branch of government has an effect on the law in a distinct way that complements the other two branches.

CHAPTER TERMS

appellate court	legal analysis	trial court
federal court	state court	

REVIEW QUESTIONS

1. What is a key element in the Supreme Court's authority?
2. What happens when a case has no applicable statute to guide the outcome?
3. What is the difference between common law and case law?
4. What is the significance of common law and case law?
5. How does the judiciary uphold law that is consistent with the Constitution?
6. Why are published cases predominately from appellate courts?
7. Why is a panel of judges used for appellate cases?
8. What is an easy method to distinguish between a state and federal court?
9. What are the differences between a trial and appellate court?
10. What is the first step in analyzing a statute?

RELEVANT LINKS

United States Supreme Court
www.supremecourtsus.gov

Federal Courts
www.uscourts.gov

INTERNET ASSIGNMENT 2.1

Identify the internet address for the U.S. District Court and state trial court which would have authority over matters happening where you live.

NOTES

1. *Black's Law Dictionary* (St. Paul: West, 1979).
2. Opinion of the Justices, 280 Ala. 653, 197 So.2d 456 (1967).
3. William Statsky, *Legal Thesaurus/Dictionary* (St. Paul: West, 1982).
4. Id.
5. *Black's Law Dictionary.*
6. 28 U.S.C. Rules of the Supreme Court, Rule 9.
7. Id.
8. Id., at Rule 10.
9. 28 U.S.C. Rules of Appellate Procedure, Rule 1,3.
10. Id., at Rules 3 and 4.

 For additional resources, please visit our Web site at www.westlegalstudies.com

CHAPTER 3

Legislation

CHAPTER OBJECTIVES

After reading this chapter, you should be able to:

- Distinguish statutory law from judicial law.

- Describe the method of election of members to both houses of Congress.

- Describe the process of legislation.

- Discuss the effect of the presidential veto power on legislation.

- Discuss the publication process of new legislation.

- Describe the role of the lobbyist.

- Describe the role of the judiciary with respect to statutory law.

THE LEGISLATIVE BRANCH

A primary source of U.S. law is legislation enacted by the federal legislative branch known as the Congress. (Since the legislative process at the state level is generally similar to the federal process, this chapter focuses on legislation by the U.S. Congress.) Although the judicial and executive branches make significant contributions to law in the American legal system, often they are responding to actions already taken by the legislature. A primary responsibility of the judicial branch is to interpret and apply the laws. According to the Constitution, the executive branch has the general task to faithfully execute the Constitution and the laws passed by Congress.

The authority of Congress is stated with specificity in Article I of the Constitution. Congress has the power to raise, through taxation, revenues that are used to support governmental functions. Congress also has the authority to determine the manner in which these revenues are to be spent. Another major power of Congress—and the subject of much legislation—is the authority to regulate commerce. This authority generally extends to all aspects of production, sale, and transfer of interstate commerce. Any commerce that is totally contained within a state and any other subject not addressed in the Constitution are the exclusive subject of state law. Congress also has the authority to raise and support armies and to declare and support wars.

Perhaps the most significant power of the Congress is the authority to establish such law as is necessary and proper to achieve congressional objectives. This broad authority vests in Congress the power to pass virtually any legislation that (1) is constitutional, (2) will facilitate the orderly operation of the government, and (3) will protect the constitutional rights of the citizens in such matters as health, safety, welfare, and personal freedoms. Congress has allowed for the creation of administrative agencies (see Chapter 4) to assist in the delivery of legal rights of the people.

The legislative branch at the federal level is a bicameral system (a two-part body), as provided for in Article I of the Constitution. The House of Representatives consists of persons elected based on the population in geographical districts. This component of the legislature guarantees that all people are represented whether they live in a heavily populated area or a small, rural district. The Senate comprises two senators from each state elected by the voters of the state. The body of the Senate guarantees that all states are represented equally regardless of size, population, or economical strength.

representative

A person elected to the House of Representatives, which is designed to ensure equal representation of all citizens.

The members of the House of Representatives are elected every two years. A **representative** must be at least 25 years old, have been a U.S. citizen for at least seven years, and reside in the state that he or she is representing. The number of representatives for each state is based on the decennial census of the population. Invariably, with each census, as population moves and increases, the number of representatives for each state varies. However, the Constitution guarantees that there be at least one representative for each state.

The members of the Senate are elected to six-year terms. The elections of **senators** from the various states are staggered so that every two years one-third of the seats in the Senate come up for election. A U.S. senator must be at least 30 years old, a citizen of the United States for nine years, and a resident of the state he or she is elected to represent.

The Senate and the House of Representatives function on a separate but related basis. To avoid duplicity of work, there are joint committees comprising members from both houses who work together to draft laws that will meet approval by the entire Congress. Although many laws proceed individually through the houses for passage or defeat, to enact law, approval is required by a majority of both houses.

senator
A person elected to the Senate, which is designed to ensure equal representation of all states.

Assignment 3.1

Answer the following questions by referring to the U.S. Constitution in Appendix A. Indicate the section of the Constitution in which you find the answer.

1. Can legislative law be passed by the executive or judicial branch as well as by Congress?
2. Under what circumstances can a member of Congress be arrested while Congress is in session?
3. Who is the president of the Senate?
4. What is the length of term of a member of the House of Representatives?
5. How many votes does each member of the Senate have?
6. Has Congress ever been prevented from limiting immigration into the United States?
7. When can the president of the Senate vote on an issue?
8. If a member of the House of Representatives dies in office, how is the position filled until the next election?
9. What is required to expel a member of Congress?
10. Who in government has the actual authority to declare war?

THE PURPOSE OF LEGISLATION

In general, legislation serves three purposes, and the particular purpose a statute serves strongly influences the statute's content and scope. A primary purpose of the American democratic system of government is to provide laws that will protect society from what is unsafe for or unacceptable to the majority of citizens. Generally, statutes serve to protect the citizens as a whole from unnecessary physical, social, and financial dangers. Law as a protective measure began with the original 10 amendments to the Constitution, known as the Bill of Rights. From the very start, specific laws were established to protect the people from unnecessary governmental influence or intrusion into their private lives. The Bill of Rights ensures people the right to live freely and to comment and produce change when laws are established or enforced unfairly. Unfortunately, it was some time before all races as well as women were identified as persons who were entitled to these basic rights. Also with the passage of time came additional constitutional amendments and statutes designed to provide protection from dangers that would interfere with other fundamental personal rights. In the latter half of the twentieth century, numerous laws were passed to ensure that the rights of all persons are protected regardless of a variety of characteristics that might otherwise be used to differentiate them from the general population.

The protection of fundamental rights as put forth in the amendments to the Constitution is not the only way legislation protects the public. Many other laws serve another type of protective purpose. Any statute that sets out the type of conduct required of individuals protects the public from improper conduct by others. For example, something as simple as the statutes that govern motor vehicles serves an invaluable protective purpose. Without such laws, persons could drive as they pleased, and untold injuries and deaths could occur.

Many different types of laws serve a protective purpose. Laws that make it an offense to manufacture, sell, or distribute illegal drugs attempt to protect our society from an influence that can produce physical, financial, and social harm. Laws that ensure compensation to workers who are injured on the job protect such workers from being left physically disabled without funds to pay for adequate medical care. These statutes protect citizens not only from invasion of personal rights but also from injury to personal property.

Laws that serve as a protective measure come in a variety of forms and address many subjects that affect the order and members of society. There is, however, a common thread in all laws that serve a protective purpose. Protective laws are designed to set forth what people are entitled to expect as citizens of this country. Protective laws do exactly what their name implies: They protect what are considered to be the rights of the people to a safe and reasonable environment in which to live and work.

Legislative laws (statutes) can also serve a remedial purpose. A remedial statute is one that creates an alternative action or a means to enforce a right. This type of statute corrects existing law or remedies an existing grievance.[1] As this definition indicates, remedial statutes are designed to cure something that has already gone wrong or caused injury. Occasionally, a remedial statute is one that supersedes a previous statute that was unfair or poorly drafted and resulted in injury or invasion of personal rights or property interests. One example of an extremely important remedial law is the Thirteenth Amendment, which states in part:

AMENDMENT XIII, Section 1. Neither slavery nor involuntary servitude, except as a punishment for crime whereof the party shall have been duly convicted, shall exist within the United States, or any place subject to their jurisdiction.

With the ratification of this amendment to the Constitution, all previous decisions of courts and state and federal legislatures that permitted slavery were overruled. The amendment was the method of correcting laws that the majority of the people believed were wrong, unfair, and injurious to a large element of our society.

Another example of remedial legislation is the repeal of prohibition. Congress initially believed that the majority of the people wanted to be protected from the negative results associated with alcohol. With the Eighteenth Amendment, intoxicating liquor was outlawed. However, it became apparent in a very short time that this was not the opinion of the majority. Consequently, prohibition was repealed, and the sale of intoxicating liquor was legalized again by passage of the Twenty-first Amendment.

Remedial law is not always in the form of a constitutional amendment. More often, remedial laws are federal or state laws that are used to adjust law to the needs of the society. (They would fall under the heading of sociological theory, discussed in Chapter 1.) Familiar examples of such statutes are state workers' compensation laws. Every state has enacted laws that provide that an employer will be responsible for costs associated with the injuries of an employee if the injuries occur while the employee is performing duties of employment. Before these laws, many people injured on the job lost their income at the time of the injury. They could not pay their medical bills, and some were forced into poverty. Employees were left with no alternative but to file a formal lawsuit against their employers. Some verdicts were significant enough to put the employer out of business altogether. Those employers who remained in business were rarely willing to allow the employee to return to work after suit was filed.

The burden on individuals and the economy was increasingly great. The response was to pass workers' compensation laws in every state. Under such laws, the employee's medical bills are covered. In addition, if disputes arise between the employee and the employer (and/or the employer's insurance company) as to how much money is necessary to compensate the employee for the injury, the law contains a legislative provision for a hearing process. The employee's medical bills can be paid, the employee is entitled to a living allowance while off work, the courts rarely become involved, and usually the employee can return to the job after recovery. With the advent of these laws, many employers took out insurance to cover the costs of medical and financial assistance to injured employees.

Workers' compensation laws are examples of both protective and remedial statutes. On the one hand, a statute may set out the rights that citizens are entitled to enjoy. At the same time, a statute may correct a situation that was dealt with ineffectively by the legal system or change a law that is considered unfair by the majority.

A third purpose that legislation serves is to ensure that protective and remedial statutes are available and applied to all citizens in the same way.[2] Such laws are known as procedural laws. Subsequent chapters on civil and criminal procedure discuss the need and actual application of procedural laws. For now, we will deal with procedural laws only in terms of the purpose they serve.

If it were not for procedural laws, citizens would have no effective way of enforcing the rights to which they are entitled. Procedural laws give specific directions on everything from how to initiate a lawsuit to how a trial is to be conducted. They even explain how to get a bill introduced to the legislature for consideration as law. Occasionally, people complain that the procedural laws are too numerous and that the legal system is more concerned with procedures than with resolving issues. In reality, our legal system guarantees all citizens the right to be heard. Consequently, hundreds of thousands of lawsuits are filed every year. All people in the nation have the right to submit their disputes to state and federal legislators, judges, and members of the executive branches of government. Given the size of their task, the procedural laws are extremely efficient.

Procedural laws are not designed solely to deal with great numbers of people. Rather, their true purpose is to ensure that everyone can enjoy the same basic rights in the legal system. All persons are entitled to have their case heard by a judicial officer. All are entitled to voice their opinion to elected delegates in Congress. All persons affected by law are entitled to dispute that law. The procedural laws make it possible for the orderly expression of rights to occur in a fair setting and provide for fair treatment to all parties in a dispute. Without procedural laws, there would be no clear, consistent, and fair method of seeking assistance from or input to the legal system.

Assignment 3.2

> Examine the statutory language in Figure 3.1 and determine whether the purpose of each statute is protective, procedural, or remedial.

THE LEGISLATIVE PROCESS

Each state has a somewhat different method of enacting statutes. With the exception of a few procedural details, the basic legislative process has remained the same in the federal government since 1787, when the U.S. Constitution was enacted. Article I, Section 7, of the Constitution is quite specific regarding this (see Appendix A).

The Path from Concept to Law

bill
Proposed law presented to the legislature for consideration.

When a proposed law is introduced to the legislature, it is called a **bill.** The Constitution requires that revenue-raising bills be initially introduced in the House of Representatives. Other bills may be initiated in either house of Congress. A bill is sponsored by a legislator who introduces it. When a bill is formally proposed as legislation, it is registered and assigned a number. Often, the bill is also known by the name of the legislators who introduce it, for example, the Graham Rudman Act. Officially, however, the statute is referenced in publications by its assigned number. As the bill progresses through the legislative

FIGURE 3.1 Statutory Excerpts

INDIANA RULES OF TRIAL PROCEDURE

II. COMMENCEMENT OF ACTION; SERVICE OF PROCESS, PLEADINGS, MOTIONS AND ORDERS

TRIAL RULE 4. PROCESS

(A) JURISDICTION Over Parties or Persons—In General. The court acquires JURISDICTION over a party or person who under these RULES commences or joins in the action, is served with summons or enters an appearance, or who is subjected to the power of the court under any other law.

(B) Preparation of Summons and Praecipe. Contemporaneously with the filing of the complaint or equivalent pleading, the person seeking SERVICE or his attorney shall promptly prepare and furnish to the clerk as many copies of the complaint and summons as are necessary. The clerk shall examine, date, sign, and affix his seal to the summons and thereupon issue and deliver the papers to the appropriate person for SERVICE. Affidavits, requests, and any other information relating to the summons and its SERVICE as required or permitted by these RULES shall be included in a praecipe attached to or entered upon the summons. Such praecipe shall be deemed to be a part of the summons for purposes of these RULES. Separate or additional summons shall, as provided by these RULES, be issued by the clerk at any time upon proper request of the person seeking SERVICE or his attorney.

(C) Form of Summons. The summons shall contain:

(1) The name and address of the person on whom the SERVICE is to be effected;

(2) The name of the court and the cause number assigned to the case;

(3) The title of the case as shown by the complaint, but, if there are multiple parties, the title may be shortened to include only the first named plaintiff and defendant with an appropriate indication that there are additional parties;

(4) The name, address, and telephone number of the attorney for the person seeking SERVICE;

(5) The time within which these RULES require the person being served to respond, and a clear statement that in case of his failure to do so, judgment by default may be rendered against him for the relief demanded in the complaint. The summons may also contain any additional information which will facilitate proper SERVICE.

(D) Designation of Manner of SERVICE. The person seeking SERVICE or his attorney may designate the manner of SERVICE upon the summons. If not so designated, the clerk shall cause SERVICE to be made by mail or other public means provided the mailing address of the person to be served is indicated in the summons or can be determined. If a mailing address is not furnished or cannot be determined or if SERVICE by mail or other public means is returned without acceptance, the complaint and summons shall promptly be delivered to the sheriff or his deputy who, unless otherwise directed, shall serve the summons.

(E) Summons and Complaint Served Together—Exceptions. The summons and complaint shall be served together unless otherwise ordered by the court. When SERVICE of summons is made by publication, the complaint shall not be published. When JURISDICTION over a party is dependent upon SERVICE of PROCESS by publication or by his appearance, summons and complaint shall be deemed to have been served at the end of the day of last required publication in the case of SERVICE by publication, and at the time of appearance in JURISDICTION acquired by appearance. Whenever the summons and complaint are not served or published together, the summons shall contain the full, unabbreviated title of the case.

ARKANSAS CODE

15-4-502. Articles of incorporation—Contents.:

(a) The articles of incorporation shall state:

(1) The name of the corporation, which name shall include the name of the city, town, or county and the words "industrial development," and the word "corporation," "incorporated," "inc.," or "company." The name shall be such as to distinguish it from any other corporation organized and existing under the laws of this state;

(2) The purpose for which the corporation is formed;

(3) The names and addresses of the incorporators who shall serve as directors and manage the affairs of the corporation until its first annual meeting of members or until their successors are elected and qualified;

(4) The number of directors, not less than three (3), to be elected at the annual meetings of members;

(5) The address of its principal office and the name and address of its agent upon whom process may be served;

(6) The period of duration of the corporation, which may be perpetual;

(7) The terms and conditions upon which persons shall be admitted to membership in the corporation, but if expressly so stated, the determination of such matters may be reserved to the directors by the bylaws;

(8) Any provisions, not inconsistent with law, which the incorporators may choose to insert for the regulation of the business and the conduct of the affairs of the corporation.

(b) It shall not be necessary to set forth in the articles of incorporation any of the corporate powers enumerated in this act.

process, it carries the same number for identification until it is voted into law, defeated, or dies in session. The latter occurs when a bill is introduced but fails to be acted upon during the legislative term of Congress.

Once a bill has been introduced, it is assigned to the appropriate committee of legislators for consideration of its contents and its potential ramifications as law. Congress has created a number of such continuing committees to study the need for legislation and proposed laws in specific areas of government, commerce, and other appropriate legislative subjects. At times, the bill will be revised while in committee with necessary additions or deletions to make it a complete and effective statute. After committee hearings, the bill is presented to the originating body of Congress (House of Representatives or Senate) for a vote by the legislators. The bill must pass by a majority vote before it can be sent to the corresponding body for consideration. Prior to a vote, the bill is discussed and debated by Congress. At this time, changes may be made in the language of the bill. Often such changes are necessary to gain the approval of a sufficient number of legislators to pass the bill.

If a bill succeeds by a majority vote in the body of Congress where it began, it moves on to the corresponding body. For example, if a bill is introduced in the House of Representatives and passes by a majority vote, the final version is then submitted to the Senate. If the bill passes by a majority in the corresponding body of Congress, it is forwarded to the president for approval or disapproval (either direct or implied).

veto

Presidential power to invalidate a law passed by a majority of Congress (two-thirds majority of each house is needed to override a veto).

Once a bill has been submitted to the president, the **veto** power of the president may be exercised. The veto is a key element in the system of checks and balances. As mentioned in Chapter 1, each branch of government has a method to influence the other branches. Such a mechanism is designed to prevent one branch from obtaining too much power or acting in a way that is inconsistent with the Constitution. According to Article I of the U.S. Constitution, each bill that has received a majority vote in both houses of Congress shall be presented to the president. After the president receives a bill, under the Constitution, the bill must be acted upon within 10 days, excluding Sundays.[3] If nothing is done during this time and Congress is still in session, the bill automatically becomes law. If Congress is not in session, it becomes a pocket veto. If the president signs the bill, it becomes law on the date indicated by Congress. If the president returns the bill with no objections to the house where it originated, the bill is vetoed (rejected). Once a bill has been vetoed, a second vote can be taken. If each body of Congress approves the bill by at least a two-thirds majority (rather than by the originally required simple majority), the bill becomes law regardless of the presidential veto. Figure 3.2 illustrates this legislative process. Another type of bill has the sole purpose of repealing an existing law. Nevertheless, even this type of bill is assigned a number and, if passed, is published in place of the law it reverses.

Constitutional Amendments

The process of passing a constitutional amendment is substantially similar to the process of passing a bill. Because the Constitution is the ultimate law of the land, an amendment must pass both houses by a two-thirds majority rather than the

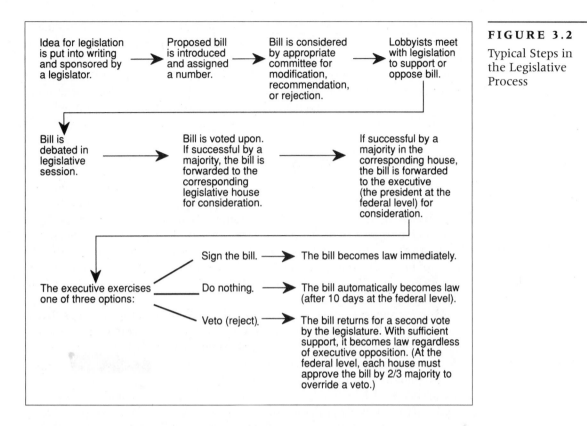

FIGURE 3.2

Typical Steps in the Legislative Process

typical simple majority. The amendment must then be approved by three-fourths of the state legislatures before it is ratified and becomes part of the Constitution. By placing such stringent requirements on constitutional amendments, it is extremely difficult to pass law that is not representative of the will of the people.

The Function of Lobbyists

Throughout the legislative process, **lobbyists** make numerous contacts with the legislators. Lobbyists are individuals who represent groups of citizens or industries that have a special interest in certain bills. If a proposed bill is going to substantially affect certain interests, groups often hire persons to lobby with the legislators to attempt to persuade them to vote in a particular way on the bill. The term originates from the early days of our government when such persons would actually wait in the lobby of the buildings of Congress to speak with legislators.

Critics of lobbyists say that a few people unduly influence legislators who are supposed to represent the majority of the people. Proponents argue, however, that lobbyists in fact represent those people who stand to be directly affected by the legislation and that lobbying is a practical and effective method by which citizens' groups and industry can voice their opinions to legislators.

Lobbyists are generally very well educated in the subject of the legislation and the legislation's potential effects on the private sector. The lobbyist can often give insight to legislators about the strengths and weaknesses of proposed legislation.

lobbyist
Individual hired to meet with legislators regarding proposed laws.

In turn, the legislators receive information with which to amend a bill and make a final decision on whether to support it. Without lobbyists, it would be up to legislators and their support staffs to research and learn about the subject of every bill introduced to Congress. Besides attending sessions of Congress and committee meetings and communicating with their home-state voters, legislators would find it virtually impossible to make informed decisions on all bills presented for a vote.

Public Hearings and Sessions

Another method of information gathering by Congress is through attending frequent public hearings at which citizens may appear and voice their opinions and concerns about contemplated or pending actions by Congress. Public hearings enable Congress to hear firsthand the voice of the people it was elected to represent. Although it would not be feasible to allow all interested persons to speak out on every item of proposed legislation, public hearings and direct contact between constituents and their legislators are effective tools to convey the general opinion of the public.

session law

Law passed during a particular session of Congress.

Congress meets several months of each year to consider proposed laws. These meetings are called sessions. Each annual session is numbered consecutively (e.g., 85th Congress). After a full session of Congress has been concluded, all laws passed during the session take on the collective name of **session law.**[4] Session laws are published in the *Statutes at Large*. Each session law is assigned a public law number, which represents the session of Congress in which the law was passed and the chronological order of the law in relation to other laws passed during the same session. For example, Public Law 92–397 would be the 397th law proposed during the 92nd session of Congress. Each session law is identified by its public law number until it can be incorporated into the publication of all statutes (organized by subject) currently in effect. This process of incorporating the public law into the existing law code is known as **codification.**

codification

Process of incorporating newly passed legislation into the existing law code.

Publication of Legislation

All federal laws currently in effect are published in a multivolume set. Because laws are constantly being added, deleted, or modified, it is difficult to keep them organized in a single permanent set of books. Usually these collections of existing laws are known as Revised Statutes or Codes. The U.S. (federal) laws are officially published in the United States Code (commonly referred to as U.S.C.).

The U.S.C. is located in multiple-bound volumes, and the method by which the volumes are organized enables the statutes to remain current in light of constant change. First, all laws are divided by basic subject. For example, virtually all laws pertaining to banking institutions are located in one section in the statutes, known as a title (e.g., "Banking"). (This is similar to chapters in the text you are now reading. Each chapter deals with a different subject and bears a name that indicates the subject addressed in that part of the text.) Second, all subjects are arranged in alphabetical order. Third, each law within a title (subject) is assigned a section number, allowing for future revision of the organization of the laws.

If one law exists and is later amended, the amendment is assigned the same number as the previous law. For example, Title 21, Section 1316, can be amended and the new language of Section 1316 printed where the prior language previously appeared. If an additional law is passed on a general subject (title) and that particular law is new to the subject, it is assigned a new section number that is not assigned to any other law on the subject. For example, assume Section 1316 is the last law to appear in Title 21. If a new law is passed, it might be assigned Section 1317. Consequently, the subject of law will lead one to the correct title (grouping of laws on a particular topic). Each title contains a table of contents listing specific sections (laws) of the title and descriptive headings for each section. The statutes also have an extensive subject index, making them even more accessible.

As stated previously, the U.S. Code takes up numerous volumes. It would be impractical to publish an entirely new set after every session of Congress to incorporate information from laws that are newly passed, amended, or repealed. For this reason, supplements are used between publications of the bound volumes. After each session of Congress, the session laws are codified (given their permanent title and section numbers) and published in supplemental volumes to the Code. Usually, these volumes are paperback books located within the back cover (called pocket parts) or next to the hardbound volume where the codified law will eventually appear. Supplements are published annually to incorporate changes from the most recent session of Congress and all past sessions that have occurred since the last bound publication. If an existing law cannot be found in the bound Code, it is probably located in the corresponding supplement. Periodically, newly bound editions are published that incorporate all prior supplements, and the process of supplementation starts again.

With regard to publication of federal statutes, and in many states, two types of publications are commonly used. The first, just discussed, is the Code. The second is an annotated statute. Such collections are no different in terms of the included text of the statutes, supplements, and organization by subject and number. However, an annotated statute has an added feature. Following the text of each statute are annotations—very brief (usually one sentence) descriptions of judicial opinions that interpret the particular statute. For the person doing legal research, annotated statutes are especially helpful. Annotated statutes not only give the language of the law but also provide information about any attempts by the judiciary to apply the law. Because statutes are necessarily broad, judicial interpretations often give insight as to the true purpose of the statute.

LEGISLATION AND JUDICIAL REVIEW

Many times, parties will disagree with a court on one of two common issues relating to statutory interpretation. The first issue is whether a statute should even be applied to the particular situation. The second is how the statute should be applied to the specific circumstances of the case. Since the court system acts as an interpreter of the law, it is up to the court to make these determinations based on legal analysis. Statutes must therefore be analyzed in terms of their effect on a situation in much the same way case law is analyzed. There is, however, a striking difference: Statutes are broadly written and generally do not include discussions of exact case scenarios. Consequently, the process of legal analysis of a statute must be somewhat modified. When examining a statute, one should first break it down into each element that must be satisfied for the statute to apply. Second, one needs to compare each element to the facts of the particular case. If all elements are substantially met, the likelihood is very strong that the statute would be considered applicable. This method of legal analysis differs in that there are no specific case facts to compare. However, the analysis still requires a close comparison of the statute and current situation as well as a deduction as to the likely outcome of the situation if the statute is applied.

APPLICATION 3.1

Consuela was employed in a bakery. The bakery owner provided her with a hand mixer, which had a sharp blade surrounded by a plastic housing. As instructed by the bakery owner, the mixer should be submerged into a container at all times when the motor is engaged. On one occasion, Consuela was mixing two different bowls of cake batter. She did not turn off the mixer when she moved between bowls. Suddenly, the mixer blade came loose and struck her, causing serious injuries. Shortly thereafter, the bakery owner fired Consuela. She claimed the firing was in violation of a statute that prohibits termination of employees on the basis they had filed a workers' compensation claim for a job-related injury. The bakery owner claimed Consuela was fired because she had a long history of not doing her job as instructed. The judge must examine the workers' compensation statute and the facts of the case, and determine the true reason for the termination. Then the judge must find whether the statute was violated by the employer.

Point for Discussion
◆ Would the case likely be treated differently if Consuela was on probation at the time the injury occurred for her poor work habits?

Assignment 3.3

Examine the statute in Figure 3.3 and break it down into elements that must be satisfied.

Determine whether the statute in Figure 3.3 should apply to the following situation. Explain your answer.

SITUATION: Rita was employed by Acme Company. She had been reprimanded several times for violation of various company policies. Other employees filed written requests not to have to work with her. On October 9, Rita was injured on the job (three days before her annual performance evaluation). On October 12, she was terminated. Rita claims retaliatory discharge based on her injury and pending workers' compensation claim.

In most situations, the job of the court regarding legislation is limited to deciding which laws are relevant to the facts and how the laws apply to a particular situation. On occasion, however, the courts are called upon to protect constitutional guarantees from violation by a statute.

Legislatures do not intentionally violate the Constitution when they pass laws. Sometimes it is not apparent until a law is actually put into effect that the law violates the constitutional rights of a citizen. If a citizen's rights are violated and the citizen brings a claim to the courts, the court has the authority to overrule the statute in favor of protecting the person's constitutional guarantees. This is the only circumstance under which a court can invalidate action of the legislature. The U.S. Supreme Court has this authority over the Congress, as does the high court of each state over the state's legislative body. Such overruling rarely occurs, but when it does occur, the law is rendered ineffective and is no longer applied to the citizen.

A final role of the courts with respect to the legislature is a quasi-advisory role. From time to time, the courts will indirectly express an opinion through the language of case law as to what the law should be; however, it is not within the court's authority to write laws that will apply as legislation to all of the people. The courts can rule only on situations before them involving particular citizens; but because of its continuous personal contact with the citizens, the court is often in a position to assess the needs of the individual. Therefore, the courts will periodically issue opinions on specific cases that include messages to Congress. The courts can thus act as a bridge between the people and the legislators without exceeding their authority or purpose.

FIGURE 3.3

Florida Statute Workers' Comp Law Regarding Retaliatory Discharge

---

WEST'S FLORIDA STATUTES ANNOTATED
TITLE XXXI. LABOR
CHAPTER 440. WORKERS' COMPENSATION

440.205. Coercion of employees

No employer shall discharge, threaten to discharge, intimidate, or coerce any employee by reason of such employee's valid claim for compensation or attempt to claim compensation under the Workers' Compensation Law.

CASE

**SUPREME COURT
OF APPEALS OF
WEST VIRGINIA.**

**MICHAEL
BUTCHER,
PETITIONER
BELOW,
APPELLANT,**

V.

**JOE E. MILLER,
COMMISSIONER,
WEST VIRGINIA**

**DIVISION OF
MOTOR VEHICLES,**

**RESPONDENT
BELOW, APPELLEE.**

2002WL 1271005 (W.Va.)
Submitted: May 21, 2002.
Filed: June 7, 2002.

This appeal was filed by Michael Butcher, appellant/petitioner below (hereinafter referred to as "Mr. Butcher"), from a ruling by the Circuit Court of Wetzel County affirming an administrative decision to suspend Mr. Butcher's driver's license. Mr. Butcher's driver's license was suspended by Joe E. Miller, Commissioner of the West Virginia Division of Motor Vehicles, appellee/respondent below (hereinafter "the Commissioner"), as a result of Mr. Butcher's refusal to take a designated chemical breath test to determine whether he was driving while impaired. Mr. Butcher contends that he was not properly informed that his driving license would be suspended should he refuse to take the designated chemical breath test. After reviewing the briefs and record in this case and listening to oral arguments, we reverse the circuit court's order.

I. Factual and Procedural History

During the late evening hours of December 14, 1996, officer S.G. Kastigar, a deputy sheriff of Wetzel County, stopped a vehicle driven by Mr. Butcher. Deputy Kastigar stopped the car because Mr. Butcher was driving, at night, without headlights. During the stop, deputy Kastigar noticed signs that indicated Mr. Butcher had been drinking. Deputy Kastigar

administered three field sobriety tests to Mr. Butcher. He failed all three tests. When deputy Kastigar asked Mr. Butcher to take a chemical breath test, he refused. Deputy Kastigar then read to Mr. Butcher a standard implied consent statement, thereby informing him that should he refuse to take the chemical breath test his driver's license "may" be suspended for a period of at least a year and up to life. Nevertheless, Mr. Butcher again refused to take the chemical breath test. Deputy Kastigar subsequently arrested Mr. Butcher for second offense driving under the influence.

After the arrest, deputy Kastigar forwarded to the Commissioner a report indicating Mr. Butcher had been arrested for driving under the influence. The report also stated that he refused to take a chemical breath test. On December 27, 1996, the Commissioner issued an order notifying Mr. Butcher that his driver's license was revoked because of his refusal to take the chemical breath test. The order informed Mr. Butcher that he was entitled to have an administrative hearing to contest the revocation. Mr. Butcher contested the revocation. A hearing was held on April 8, 1997. Following the hearing, the Commissioner found that the evidence established that Mr. Butcher had refused the chemical breath test. Consequently, the Commissioner issued a final order on December 2, 1997, revoking Mr. Butcher's driver's license for 10 years.

On December 30, 1997, Mr. Butcher appealed the Commissioner's final order to the circuit court. On June 30, 2000, the circuit court filed an order affirming the Commissioner's final order. Mr. Butcher filed a motion for reconsideration on July 6, 2000. The circuit court filed an order on June 6, 2001, denying the motion for reconsideration. Thereafter, this appeal was filed.

II. Standard of Review

The issue presented in this case requires an analysis of our DUI statutes. We have held that "[w]here the issue on an appeal from the circuit court is clearly a question of law or involving an interpretation of a statute, we apply a *de novo* standard of review." Syl.

pt. l, *Chrystal R.M. v. Charlie A.L.*, 194 W. Va. 138, 459 S.E.2d 415 (1995). Moreover, "[e]videntiary findings made at an administrative hearing should not be reversed unless they are clearly wrong." Syl. pt. l, *Francis O. Day Co., Inc. v. Director, Div. of Envtl. Prot.*, 191 W.Va. 134, 443 S.E.2d 602 (1994).

III. Discussion

Mr. Butcher contends that deputy Kastigar informed him that his driver's license "may" be suspended for refusing to take the chemical breath test. Mr. Butcher asserts that this warning was erroneous because under W.Va.Code § 17C-5-7(a) (2000), he should have been informed that the revocation of his driver's license for refusing to take the chemical breath test was mandatory. This Court has held that "[w]hen interpreting a legislatively created law, we typically afford the statute a construction that is consistent with the Legislature's intent." *Coordinating Council for Indep. Living, Inc. v. Palmer*, 209 W.Va. 274, 281, 546 S.E.2d 454, 461 (2001). *See also* Syl. pt. 1, *Smith v. State Workmen's Comp. Comm'r*, 159 W.Va. 108, 219 S.E.2d 361 (1975) ("The primary object in construing a statute is to ascertain and give effect to the intent of the Legislature."). We have also indicated that "[a] statutory provision which is clear and unambiguous and plainly expresses the legislative intent will not be interpreted by the courts but will be given full force and effect." Syl. pt. 2, *State v. Epperly*, 135 W.Va. 877, 65 S.E.2d 488 (1951). However, "[a] statute that is ambiguous must be construed before it can be applied." Syl. pt. l, *Farley v. Buckalew*, 186 W.Va. 693, 414 S.E.2d 454 (1992).

The pertinent language in W.Va.Code § 17C-5-7(a) provides that an officer attempting to perform a chemical breath test must inform the driver "that his refusal to submit to the secondary test finally designated *will* result in the revocation of his license to operate a motor vehicle in this state for a period of at least one year and up to life."

Mr. Butcher argues that the word "will," as used in W.Va.Code § 17C-5-7(a), implies a definite suspension. Therefore, he was incorrectly advised by deputy Kastigar's use of the word "may," as "may" implies a discretionary suspension. Several cases from other jurisdictions have been cited by Mr. Butcher as

support for his position. For example, in *State v. Huber*, 540 N.E.2d 140 (Ind.App.Ct.1989), the defendant refused to take a chemical breath test after the arresting officer warned him that his driver's license "may" be suspended. The defendant's driver's license was suspended; however, a trial court ordered the license restored because the arresting officer failed to use the word "will" when advising the defendant, as required by statute, regarding the suspension of his license. The Indiana Court of Appeals upheld the trial court's decision. In doing so, the court stated: "The phrase 'may be suspended' connotes discretionary action. Thus the advisement failed to convey the strong likelihood that suspension of driving privileges would follow Huber's refusal to submit to a breathalyser test." *Huber*, 540 N.E.2d at 142. *See also Graves v. Commonwealth*, 112 Pa.Cmwlth. 390, 535 A.2d 707 (Pa.1988) (reversing suspension because officer used the word "could" instead of "will"); *Mairs v. Department of Licensing*, 70 Wash. App. 541, 854 P.2d 665 (Wash.Ct.App.1993) (reversing suspension because officer used the word "probably" instead of "will"); *Welch v. State*, 13 Wash.App. 591, 536 P.2d 172 (Wash.Ct.App.1975) (reversing suspension because officer used the word "could" instead of "will").

Conversely, the Commissioner argues that deputy Kastigar's warning "substantially" complied with the requirements of the statute and therefore the suspension of Mr. Butcher's driving license should not be disturbed. A few cases were cited by the Commissioner to support its "substantial" compliance argument. For example, in *Commonwealth Dep't of Pub. Safety v. Tuemler*, 526 S.W.2d 305 (Ky.Ct.App.1975), a driver had his license suspended for refusing to take a breathalyser test. The driver argued that the arresting officer informed him that "chances" were he would lose his license for refusing to take the test. The driver contended that this warning was misleading, because suspension was automatic. The appellate court ruled that the warning "substantially apprised [the driver] of the consequences of refusing to take the test." *Tuemler*, 526 S.W.2d at 306. The appellate court also noted that "revocation is not necessarily 'automatic,' but is subject to an administrative hearing[.]" *Id.* The appellate court reinstated the suspension.

CASE

In another case cited by the Commissioner, *In re Olien*, 387 N.W.2d 262 (S.D. 1985), a driver had his license revoked after refusing a blood test. The driver contended on appeal that the officer misled him by stating that refusal to take the blood test "can" result in revocation of his license. The applicable statute required warning that a license revocation "shall" be imposed. The Supreme Court of South Dakota acknowledged that the statute was not literally complied with by the arresting officer. However, the court affirmed the revocation after finding "the officer's advice substantially complied with [the statute.]" *Olien*, 387 N.W.2d at 264.

We are not persuaded by the "substantial" compliance authorities cited by the Commissioner. The pertinent language of W.Va.Code § 17C-5-7(a) is clear and unambiguous. "[A] statute which is clear and unambiguous should be applied by the courts and not construed or interpreted." *Carper v. Kanawha Banking & Trust Co.*, 157 W.Va. 477, 517, 207 S.E.2d 897, 921 (1974) (citation omitted). Under the statute, an officer making a DUI arrest must inform the arrestee that a refusal to submit to a chemical breath test "will" result in a license suspension.

Here, Mr. Butcher was never informed that his license "will" be suspended for refusing to take the chemical breath test. Instead, Mr. Butcher was erroneously told that his license "may" be suspended. Our cases have held that "[t]he word 'may' generally . . . connotes discretion." *State v. Hedrick*, 204 W.Va. 547, 552, 514 S.E.2d 397, 402 (1999) (citations omitted). No discretion existed. Mr. Butcher's license was automatically suspended when the Commissioner received the report from deputy Kastigar. We are unable to determine from the record what course Mr. Butcher would have taken had he been properly advised of the consequences of his refusal to take the chemical breath test. As Mr. Butcher was unable to make an intelligent decision because of the erroneous warning given to him, we reverse the circuit court's order.

IV. Conclusion

Mr. Butcher's driver's license was suspended as a result of his being given an inaccurate and misleading warning regarding the consequences of his refusal to take a chemical breath test. Therefore, we reverse the circuit court's affirmance of the suspension. We further order that Mr. Butcher's driver's license be restored.

Reversed.

Case Review Question
Butcher v. Miller, 2002 WL 1271005 (W.Va.)
Would the result have likely changed if the defendant had caused a fatal accident prior to his arrest? Why or why not?

Ethical Considerations

Legislators are particularly concerned with ethical issues. Because an elected official is required to represent the interests of the people, it is important that legislators avoid the appearance of improper influence by private interests. Extensive ethical rules are imposed on all legislators and their staffs. In addition are ethical committees, which review alleged violations of ethical rules by legislators. A pronouncement by a committee that a legislator has violated ethical rules can result in formal disciplinary action and irreparable damage to the legislator's political career.

Although previously some legislators openly disregarded the rules of ethics, that trend has largely reversed. With the advent of mass media, a legislator's constituents are informed almost immediately of any alleged improprieties. Consequently, the responsibility to act ethically and loyally to the office held is greater than ever.

Ethical issues are not new to U.S. government. In the revolutionary era, Thomas Paine made the noted remark, "These are the times that try men's souls." This commentary on the obligation to do what is right demonstrates that ethics are part of the very fabric of the American legal system.

Ethical Circumstance

Congresswoman X is an elected official from an urban population. While she represents tens of thousands of constituents, she is seldom in contact with the individuals. However, at fundraisers for election and re-election, she becomes very familiar with a number of wealthy business owners. These people in large part provide the necessary financial base for her campaign. They also employ thousands of the citizens she represents. Would it be acceptable for her to then give the majority of her time in Congress to pursue issues of interest to these business owners even if the decisions would result in higher taxes for the individual citizens? Why or why not?

CHAPTER SUMMARY

As with every branch of government, the legislative branch has a specific and necessary purpose. However, like the other branches, the legislature cannot function effectively without the influence of the other branches and the people. With the assistance of these branches, the legislature is able to enact laws that reflect the opinion of the majority regarding what our society should be.

The lawmaking authority of the Congress includes the power to tax, raise and support armies, declare and support war, regulate interstate commerce, and enact laws that are necessary and proper to carry out its powers and objectives.

The legislature is able to adjust to changing times while keeping in sight those basic guarantees of the Constitution. When the legislature fails in this effort, the judiciary has the authority to act on a statute to prevent violation of a citizen's constitutional guarantees. Such adaptability helps to serve the various purposes of legislation, such as indicating what will be considered unacceptable conduct, protecting citizens from injury or damage to property, and providing remedies for those citizens when injury or damage does occur. Further, because of the enormous complexity of the legal system and the number of litigants, procedural laws are designed to process claims as efficiently as possible.

A primary reason for the tremendous adaptability of legislation lies in the method in which legislation is created. Citizens elect delegates (senators and representatives), who propose laws (bills) that, when approved by the majority of the delegates, become law. The citizens are thus represented, and laws can be enacted as necessary with little procedural difficulty.

Safeguards exist against the enactment of laws that are not in the best interests of the people or that violate the Constitution. An important safeguard is the president's veto power. Before a vetoed bill can become law, the bill requires approval by a much higher percentage of Congress than initially required. Presumably, this reflects a desire by a significant majority of the people to enact the law. The judicial branch has limited power to override statutory law. This exception to the general rule of superiority of statutory over judicial law takes place when the judiciary determines the statutory law to be in violation of the Constitution.

CHAPTER TERMS

bill   representative   session law
codification   senator   veto
lobbyist

REVIEW QUESTIONS

1. How do the House of Representatives and the Senate avoid duplicity of work?
2. What is the purpose of remedial statutes?
3. What can happen when a bill is passed by Congress and sent to the president?
4. Who are lobbyists and what is their function?
5. What is the purpose of procedural law?
6. What challenges are typically made to the statutes in a particular case?
7. What is the quasi-advisory role?
8. What is the purpose of protective laws?
9. How is a veto overridden?
10. Where do revenue-raising bills originate and why?

RELEVANT LINKS

United States Congress
www.Congress.com

Government Guide to Legislative Branch
www.governmentguide.com/officials

INTERNET ASSIGNMENT 3.1

Locate the website for your representatives in the U.S. Congress and U.S. Senate.

NOTES

1. William Statsky, *Legal Thesaurus/Dictionary* (St. Paul: West, 1982).
2. *Litsinger Sign Co. v. American Sign Co.* 11 Ohio St. 2dl, 227 N.E.2d 609 (1967).
3. Article I, U.S. Constitution.
4. Statsky, *Legal Thesaurus/Dictionary*.

 For additional resources, please visit our Web site at www.westlegalstudies.com

CHAPTER **4**

The Executive Branch and Administrative Authority

CHAPTER OBJECTIVES

After reading this chapter, you should be able to:

- Describe how the members of the electoral college are selected.

- Describe the process of the electoral college and discuss the effect of the Twelfth Amendment on the process.

- List the duties of the president.

- Describe the delegation doctrine.

- Identify the steps in the creation of an administrative agency.

- Discuss the function and purpose of an administrative agency.

- Identify the requirements of an administrative agency when proposing and issuing a new regulation.

- Describe the considerations of a court in the review of an administrative agency action.

- Discuss the purpose and nature of the Administrative Procedure Act.

THE EXECUTIVE BRANCH

Article II of the U.S. Constitution establishes the executive branch as a fundamental element in our system of government. Consequently, the executive branch plays an important role in our legal system. Section 1 of Article II specifies the manner in which the president and vice president shall be elected and the term of office of the president and the vice president. Section 1 also contains provisions in case a president does not complete a term, specifies who may run for president, and describes the timing and method of elections. Sections 2 and 3 address the authority and responsibilities of the president. Section 4 of Article II lists the offenses for which a president, vice president, or other officer of the U.S. government can be removed from office. Review the text of Article II, Section 1.*

Changes in the Electoral Process

In 1804, Section 1 of Article II was amended by passage of the Twelfth Amendment, which slightly altered the process of the electoral ballot and election of the president by the House of Representatives in the event no majority was achieved by the electoral college. Perhaps the most significant change was the method of selection of the vice president. Under the original Constitution, the person having the greatest number of votes in the House of Representatives (assuming no majority was reached in the electorate) would assume the position of president. Following this, the person with the greatest number of votes in the electoral college (other than the person elected president) would be the vice president. If there was no one person with a majority, then the Senate would elect a vice president in a manner similar to the election of the president. See Figure 4.1.

An obvious difficulty with the original process was that the person with the second greatest number of votes in the electorate would automatically become vice president. This person could very likely have been the president's strongest political opponent, which would make administration of government very difficult, given the opposing views of the two. By having both the president and the vice president go through a second election process (in the event no majority was reached in the electoral college), such a result could be avoided. With the 1804 amendment, the result of a failed majority in the electoral college would be two elections. The House of Representatives would elect the president. However, rather than an automatic appointment of vice president, that person would be elected by the Senate. While the possibility still exists for election of officials with contradictory views, at least some thought could be given to the most positive combination of personalities.

The 2000 presidential election was the closest test applied in recent history to the constitutional provisions. Because the electoral college is made up of delegates from each of the states, these delegates rely heavily on the popular

*Note irregularities in spelling, grammar, and punctuation are reflective of the original form of the Constitution.

FIGURE 4.1   Article II, Section 1

Section 1. The executive Power shall be vested in a President of the United States of America. He shall hold his Office during the Term of four Years, and, together with the Vice-President, chosen for the same Term, be elected, as follows

Each State shall appoint, in such Manner as the Legislature thereof may direct, a Number of Electors, equal to the whole Number of Senators and Representatives to which the State may be entitled in the Congress: but no Senator or Representative, or Person holding an Office of Trust or Profit under the United States, shall be appointed an Elector.

[The Electors shall meet in their respective States, and vote by Ballot for two Persons, of whom one at least shall not be an Inhabitant of the same State with themselves. And they shall make a List of all the Persons voted for, and of the Number of Votes for each; which List they shall sign and certify, and transmit sealed to the Seat of the Government of the United States, directed to the President of the Senate [who] shall, in the Presence of the Senate and House of Representatives, open all the Certificates, and the Votes shall then be counted. The Person having the greatest Number of Votes shall be the President, if such Number be a Majority of the whole Number of Electors appointed; and if there be more than one who have such Majority, and have an equal Number of Votes, then the House of Representatives shall immediately chuse by Ballot one of them for President; and if no Person have a Majority, then from the five highest on the List the said House shall in like Manner chuse the President. But in chusing the President, the Votes shall be taken by States, the Representation from each State having one Vote; A quorum for this Purpose shall consist of a Member or Members from two-thirds of the States, and a Majority of all the States shall be necessary to a Choice. In every Case, after the Choice of the President, the Person having the greater Number of Votes of the Electors shall be the Vice President. But if there should remain two or more who have equal Votes, the Senate shall chuse from them by Ballot the Vice-President.]

The Congress may determine the Time of chusing the Electors, and the Day on which they shall give their Votes; which Day shall be the same throughout the United States.

No person except a natural born Citizen, or a Citizen of the United States, at the time of the Adoption of this Constitution, shall be eligible to the Office of President; neither shall any Person be eligible to that Office who shall not have attained to the Age of thirty-five Years, and been fourteen Years a Resident within the United States.

In Case of the Removal of the President from Office, or of his Death, Resignation, or Inability to discharge the Powers and Duties of the said Office, the same shall devolve on the Vice President, and the Congress may by Law provide for the Case of Removal, Death, Resignation or Inability, both of the President and Vice President, declaring what Officer shall then act as President, and such Officer shall act accordingly, until the Disability be removed, or a President shall be elected.

The President shall, at stated Times, receive for his Services, a Compensation, which shall neither be increased nor diminished during the Period for which he shall have been elected, and he shall not receive within that Period any other Emolument from the United States, or any of them.

Before he enter on the Execution of his Office, he shall take the following Oath or Affirmation: — "I do solemnly swear (or affirm) that I will faithfully execute the Office of President of the United States, and will to the best of my Ability, preserve, protect and defend the Constitution of the United States."

vote as the indicator of the direction in which their electoral votes should be cast. In 2000, the popular vote was the closest election in history. Additionally, the results in some areas, particularly Florida, did not reflect the number of people registered with the various parties. Added to a variety of issues about the actual voting process, recounts, and so forth, was a great concern over the accuracy of the numbers reported as the results of the popular vote. Although many called for a variety of measures to reassess the vote, the U.S. Supreme Court held that the vote would stand. This decision then paved the way for the electoral college, which followed the popular vote. However, doubt remains as to whether President George Walker Bush was the actual winner. This controversy demonstrates in the most powerful way the importance of the vote of each individual and the necessity for the utmost care in the voting process by election officials.

CASE

**SUPREME COURT
OF THE UNITED
STATES**

**GEORGE W. BUSH,
ET AL.,
PETITIONERS,**

V.

**ALBERT GORE, JR.,
ET AL.**

148 L.Ed. 2d 388,
121 S.Ct. 525
Dec. 12, 2000.

On December 8, 2000, the Supreme Court of Florida ordered that the Circuit Court of Leon County tabulate by hand 9,000 ballots in Miami-Dade County. It also ordered the inclusion in the certified vote totals of 215 votes identified in Palm Beach County and 168 votes identified in Miami-Dade County for Vice President Albert Gore, Jr., and Senator Joseph Lieberman, Democratic candidates for President and Vice President. The State Supreme Court noted that petitioner, George W. Bush asserted that the net gain for Vice President Gore in Palm Beach County was 176 votes, and directed the Circuit Court to resolve that dispute on remand. *Gore v. Harris*, 772 So.2d 1243, 1248, n. 6. The court further held that relief would require manual recounts in all Florida counties where so-called "undervotes" had not been subject to manual tabulation. The court ordered all manual recounts to begin at once. Governor Bush and Richard Cheney, Republican candidates for President and Vice President, filed an emergency application for a stay of this mandate. On December 9, we granted the application, treated the application as a petition for a writ of certiorari, and granted certiorari.

On November 8, 2000, the day following the Presidential election, the Florida Division of Elections reported that petitioner Bush had received 2,909,135 votes, and respondent Gore had received 2,907,351 votes, a margin of 1,784 for Governor Bush. Because Governor Bush's margin of victory was less than "one-half of a percent . . . of the votes cast," an automatic machine recount was conducted under § 102.141(4) of the election code, the results of which showed Governor Bush still winning the

race but by a diminished margin. Vice President Gore then sought manual recounts in Volusia, Palm Beach, Broward, and Miami-Dade Counties, pursuant to Florida's election protest provisions. Fla. Stat. Ann. § 102.166 (Supp.2001). A dispute arose concerning the deadline for local county canvassing boards to submit their returns to the Secretary of State (Secretary). The Secretary declined to waive the November 14 deadline imposed by statute. §§ 102.111, 102.112. The Florida Supreme Court, however, set the deadline at November 26. We granted certiorari and vacated the Florida Supreme Court's decision, finding considerable uncertainty as to the grounds on which it was based. *Bush I*, 531 U.S., at 78, 121 S.Ct. 471. On December 11, the Florida Supreme Court issued a decision on remand reinstating that date. 772 So.2d at 1273–1290.

On November 26, the Florida Elections Canvassing Commission certified the results of the election and declared Governor Bush the winner of Florida's 25 electoral votes. On November 27, Vice President Gore, pursuant to Florida's contest provisions, filed a complaint in Leon County Circuit Court contesting the certification. Fla. Stat. Ann. § 102.168 (Supp.2001). He sought relief pursuant to § 102.168(3)(c), which provides that "[r]eceipt of a number of illegal votes or rejection of a number of legal votes sufficient to change or place in doubt the result of the election" shall be grounds for a contest. The Circuit Court denied relief, stating that Vice President Gore failed to meet his burden of proof. He appealed to the First District Court of Appeal, which certified the matter to the Florida Supreme Court.

Accepting jurisdiction, the Florida Supreme Court affirmed in part and reversed in part. *Gore v. Harris*, 772 So.2d. 1243 (2000) The court held that the Circuit Court had been correct to reject Vice President Gore's challenge to the results certified in Nassau County and his challenge to the Palm Beach County Canvassing Board's determination that 3,300 ballots cast in that county were not, in the statutory phrase, "legal votes."

The Supreme Court held that Vice President Gore had satisfied his burden of proof under § 102.168(3)(c) with respect to his challenge to Miami-Dade County's failure to tabulate, by manual count, 9,000 ballots on which the machines had failed to detect a vote for President ("undervotes"). *Id.*, at 1256. Noting the closeness of the election, the court explained that "[o]n this record, there can be no question that there are legal votes within the 9,000 uncounted votes sufficient to place the results of this election in doubt." *Id.*, at 1261. A "legal vote," as determined by the Supreme Court, is "one in which there is a 'clear indication of the intent of the voter.'" *Id.*, at 1257. The court therefore ordered a hand recount of the 9,000 ballots in Miami-Dade County. Observing that the contest provisions vest broad discretion in the circuit judge to "provide any relief appropriate under such circumstances," § 102.168(8), the Supreme Court further held that the Circuit Court could order "the Supervisor of Elections and the Canvassing Boards, as well as the necessary public officials, in all counties that have not conducted a manual recount or tabulation of the undervotes . . . to do so forthwith, said tabulation to take place in the individual counties where the ballots are located." *Id.*, at 1262.

The Supreme Court also determined that both Palm Beach County and Miami-Dade County, in their earlier manual recounts, had identified a net gain of 215 and 168 legal votes for Vice President Gore. *Id.*, at 1260. Rejecting the Circuit Court's conclusion that Palm Beach County lacked the authority to include the 215 net votes submitted past the November 26 deadline, the Supreme Court explained that the deadline was not intended to exclude votes identified after that date through ongoing manual recounts. As to Miami-Dade County, the court concluded that although the 168 votes identified were the result of a partial recount, they were "legal votes [that] could change the outcome of the election." *Ibid.* The Supreme Court therefore directed the Circuit Court to include those totals in the certified results, subject to resolution of the actual vote total from the Miami-Dade partial recount.

The petition presents the following questions: whether the Florida Supreme Court established new standards for resolving Presidential election contests, thereby violating Art. II, § 1, cl. 2, of the United States Constitution and failing to comply with 3 U.S.C. § 5, and whether the use of standardless manual recounts violates the Equal Protection and Due Process Clauses. With respect to the equal protection question, we find a violation of the Equal Protection Clause.

The closeness of this election, and the multitude of legal challenges which have followed in its wake, have brought into sharp focus a common, if heretofore unnoticed, phenomenon. Nationwide statistics reveal that an estimated 2% of ballots cast do not register a vote for President for whatever reason, including deliberately choosing no candidate at all or some voter error, such as voting for two candidates or insufficiently marking a ballot. In certifying election results, the votes eligible for inclusion in the certification are the votes meeting the properly established legal requirements.

This case has shown that punchcard balloting machines can produce an unfortunate number of ballots which are not punched in a clean, complete way by the voter. After the current counting, it is likely legislative bodies nationwide will examine ways to improve the mechanisms and machinery for voting.

The individual citizen has no federal constitutional right to vote for electors for the President of the United States unless and until the state legislature chooses a statewide election as the means to implement its power to appoint members of the Electoral College. U.S. Const., Art. II, § 1. This is the source for the statement in *McPherson v. Blacker*, 146 U.S. 1, 35, 13 S.Ct. 3, 36 L.Ed. 869 (1892), that the state legislature's power to select the manner for appointing electors is plenary; it may, if it so chooses, select the electors itself, which indeed was the manner used by state legislatures in several States for many years after the framing of our Constitution. *Id.*, at 28–33, 13 S.Ct. 3. History has now favored the voter, and in each of the several States the citizens themselves vote for Presidential electors. When the state legislature vests the right to vote for President in its people, the right to vote as the legislature has prescribed is fundamental; and one source of its fundamental nature lies in the equal weight accorded to each vote and the equal dignity owed to each voter. The State, of course, after granting the franchise in the special context of Article II, can take back the power to appoint electors. See *id.*, at 35, 13 S.Ct. 3

CASE

(" '[T]here is no doubt of the right of the legislature to resume the power at any time, for it can neither be taken away nor abdicated'") (quoting S.Rep. No. 395, 43d Cong., 1 st Sess. 9 (1874)).

The right to vote is protected in more than the initial allocation of the franchise. Equal protection applies as well to the manner of its exercise. Having once granted the right to vote on equal terms, the State may not, by later arbitrary and disparate treatment, value one person's vote over that of another. See, *e.g., Harper v. Virginia Bd. of Elections,* 383 U.S. 663, 665, 86 S.Ct. 1079, 16 L.Ed.2d 169 (1966) ("[O]nce the franchise is granted to the electorate, lines may not be drawn which are inconsistent with the Equal Protection Clause of the Fourteenth Amendment"). It must be remembered that "the right of suffrage can be denied by a debasement or dilution of the weight of a citizen's vote just as effectively as by wholly prohibiting the free exercise of the franchise." *Reynolds v. Sims,* 377 U.S. 533, 555, 84 S.Ct. 1362, 12 L.Ed.2d 506 (1964).

There is no difference between the two sides of the present controversy on these basic propositions. Respondents say that the very purpose of vindicating the right to vote justifies the recount procedures now at issue. The question before us, however, is whether the recount procedures the Florida Supreme Court has adopted are consistent with its obligation to avoid arbitrary and disparate treatment of the members of its electorate.

Much of the controversy seems to revolve around ballot cards designed to be perforated by a stylus but which, either through error or deliberate omission, have not been perforated with sufficient precision for a machine to register the perforations. In some cases a piece of the card—a chad—is hanging, say, by two corners. In other cases there is no separation at all, just an indentation.

The Florida Supreme Court has ordered that the intent of the voter be discerned from such ballots. For purposes of resolving the equal protection challenge, it is not necessary to decide whether the Florida Supreme Court had the authority under the legislative scheme for resolving election disputes to define what a legal vote is and to mandate a manual recount implementing that definition. The recount mechanisms implemented in response to the

decisions of the Florida Supreme Court do not satisfy the minimum requirement for nonarbitrary treatment of voters necessary to secure the fundamental right. Florida's basic command for the count of legally cast votes is to consider the "intent of the voter." 772 So.2d, at 1262. This is unobjectionable as an abstract proposition and a starting principle. The problem inheres in the absence of specific standards to ensure its equal application. The formulation of uniform rules to determine intent based on these recurring circumstances is practicable and, we conclude, necessary.

The law does not refrain from searching for the intent of the actor in a multitude of circumstances; and in some cases the general command to ascertain intent is not susceptible to much further refinement. In this instance, however, the question is not whether to believe a witness but how to interpret the marks or holes or scratches on an inanimate object, a piece of cardboard or paper which, it is said, might not have registered as a vote during the machine count. The factfinder confronts a thing, not a person. The search for intent can be confined by specific rules designed to ensure uniform treatment.

The want of those rules here has led to unequal evaluation of ballots in various respects. See *id.,* at 1267 (Wells, C.J., dissenting) ("Should a county canvassing board count or not count a 'dimpled chad' where the voter is able to successfully dislodge the chad in every other contest on that ballot? Here, the county canvassing boards disagree"). As seems to have been acknowledged at oral argument, the standards for accepting or rejecting contested ballots might vary not only from county to county but indeed within a single county from one recount team to another.

The record provides some examples. A monitor in Miami-Dade County testified at trial that he observed that three members of the county canvassing board applied different standards in defining a legal vote. 3 Tr. 497, 499 (Dec. 3, 2000). And testimony at trial also revealed that at least one county changed its evaluative standards during the counting process. Palm Beach County, for example, began the process with a 1990 guideline which precluded counting completely attached chads, switched to a rule that considered a vote to be legal if any light could be seen through a chad, changed back to the 1990 rule, and then abandoned any pretense of a *per se* rule, only to have a court order that the country consider dimpled chads legal. This is not a process with sufficient guarantees of equal treatment.

An early case in our one-person, one-vote jurisprudence arose when a State accorded arbitrary and disparate treatment to voters in its different counties. *Gray v. Sanders*, 372 U.S. 368, 83 S.Ct. 801, 9 L.Ed.2d 821 (1963). The Court found a constitutional violation. We relied on these principles in the context of the Presidential selection process in *Moore v. Ogilvie*, 394 U.S. 814, 89 S.Ct. 1493, 23 L.Ed.2d 1 (1969), where we invalidated a county-based procedure that diluted the influence of citizens in larger counties in the nominating process. There we observed that "[t]he idea that one group can be granted greater voting strength than another is hostile to the one man, one vote basis of our representative government." *Id.*, at 819, 89 S.Ct. 1493.

The State Supreme Court ratified this uneven treatment. It mandated that the recount totals from two counties, Miami-Dade and Palm Beach, be included in the certified total. The court also appeared to hold *sub silentio* that the recount totals from Broward Country, which were not completed until after the original November 14 certification by the Secretary, were to be considered part of the new certified vote totals even though the county certification was not contested by Vice President Gore. Yet each of the counties used varying standards to determine what was a legal vote. Broward County used a more forgiving standard than Palm Beach County, and uncovered almost three times as many new votes, a result markedly disproportionate to the difference in population between the counties.

In addition, the recounts in these three counties were not limited to so-called undervotes but extended to all of the ballots. The distinction has real consequences. A manual recount of all ballots identifies not only those ballots which show no vote but also those which contain more than one, the so-called overvotes. Neither category will be counted by the machine. This is not a trivial concern. At oral argument, respondents estimated

there are as many as 110,000 overvotes statewide. As a result, the citizen whose ballot was not read by a machine because he failed to vote for a candidate in a way readable by a machine may still have his vote counted in a manual recount; on the other hand, the citizen who marks two candidates in a way discernible by the machine will not have the same opportunity to have his vote count, even if a manual examination of the ballot would reveal the requisite indicia of intent. Furthermore, the citizen who marks two candidates, only one of which is discernible by the machine, will have his vote counted even though it should have been read as an invalid ballot. The State Supreme Court's inclusion of vote counts based on these variant standards exemplifies concerns with the remedial processes that were under way.

That brings the analysis to yet a further equal protection problem. The votes certified by the court included a partial total from one county, Miami-Dade. The Florida Supreme Court's decision thus gives no assurance that the recounts included in a final certification must be complete. Indeed, it is respondents' submission that it would be consistent with the rules of the recount procedures to include whatever partial counts are done by the time of final certification, and we interpret the Florida Supreme Court's decision to permit this. See 772 So.2d, at 1261–1262, n. 21 (noting "practical difficulties" may control outcome of election, but certifying partial Miami-Dade total nonetheless). This accommodation no doubt results from the truncated contest period established by the Florida Supreme Court in *Palm Beach County Canvassing Bd. v. Harris*, at respondents own urging. The press of time does not diminish the constitutional concern. A desire for speed is not a general excuse for ignoring equal protection guarantees.

In addition to these difficulties the actual process by which the votes were to be counted under the Florida Supreme Court's decision raises further concerns. That order did not specify who would recount the ballots. The county canvassing boards were forced to pull together ad hoc teams of judges from various Circuits who had no previous training in handling and interpreting ballots. Furthermore,

CASE

while others were permitted to observe, they were prohibited from objecting during the recount.

The recount process, in its features here described, is inconsistent with the minimum procedures necessary to protect the fundamental right of each voter in the special instance of a statewide recount under the authority of a single state judicial officer. Our consideration is limited to the present circumstances, for the problem of equal protection in election processes generally presents many complexities.

The question before the Court is not whether local entities, in the exercise of their expertise, may develop different systems for implementing elections. Instead, we are presented with a situation where a state court with the power to assure uniformity has ordered a statewide recount with minimal procedural safeguards. When a court orders a statewide remedy, there must be at least some assurance that the rudimentary requirements of equal treatment and fundamental fairness are satisfied.

Given the Court's assessment that the recount process underway was probably being conducted in an unconstitutional manner, the Court stayed the order directing the recount so it could hear this case and render an expedited decision. The contest provision, as it was mandated by the State Supreme Court, is not well calculated to sustain the confidence that all citizens must have in the outcome of elections. The State has not shown that its procedures include the necessary safeguards. The problem, for instance, of the estimated 110,000 overvotes has not been addressed, although Chief Justice Wells called attention to the concern in his dissenting opinion. See 772 So.2d, at 1264, n. 26.

Upon due consideration of the difficulties identified to this point, it is obvious that the recount cannot be conducted in compliance with the requirements of equal protection and due process without substantial additional work. It would require not only the adoption (after opportunity for argument) of adequate statewide standards for determining what is a legal vote, and practicable procedures to implement them, but also orderly judicial review of any disputed matters that might arise. In addition, the Secretary has advised that the recount of only a portion of the ballots requires that the vote tabulation equipment be used to screen out undervotes, a function for which the machines were not designed. If a recount of overvotes were also required, perhaps even a second screening would be necessary. Use of the equipment for this purpose, and any new software developed for it, would have to be evaluated for accuracy by the Secretary, as required by Fla. Stat. Ann. § 101.015 (Supp.2001).

The Supreme Court of Florida has said that the legislature intended the State's electors to "participat[e] fully in the federal electoral process," as provided in 3 U.S.C. § 5.772 So.2d, at 1289; see also *Palm Beach County Canvassing Bd. v. Harris*, 772 So.2d 1220, 1237 (Fla.2000). That statute, in turn, requires that any controversy or contest that is designed to lead to a conclusive selection of electors be completed by December 12. That date is upon us, and there is no recount procedure in place under the State Supreme Court's order that comports with minimal constitutional standards. Because it is evident that any recount seeking to meet the December 12 date will be unconstitutional for the reasons we have discussed, we reverse the judgment of the Supreme Court of Florida ordering a recount to proceed.

Seven Justices of the Court agree that there are constitutional problems with the recount ordered by the Florida Supreme Court that demand a remedy. The only disagreement is as to the remedy. Because the Florida Supreme Court has said that the Florida Legislature intended to obtain the safe-harbor benefits of 3 U.S.C. § 5, Justice BREYER's proposed remedy—remanding to the Florida Supreme Court for its ordering of a constitutionally proper contest until December 18-contemplates action in violation of the Florida Election Code, and hence could not be part of an "appropriate" order authorized by Fla. Stat. Ann. § 102.168(8) (Supp. 2001).

None are more conscious of the vital limits on judicial authority than are the Members of this Court, and none stand more in admiration of the Constitution's design to leave the selection of the President to the people, through their legislatures, and to the political sphere. When contending parties invoke the process of the courts, however, it becomes our unsought responsibility to resolve the federal and constitutional issues the judicial system has been forced to confront.

The judgment of the Supreme Court of Florida is reversed, and the case is remanded for further proceedings not inconsistent with this opinion.

Pursuant to this Court's Rule 45.2, the Clerk is directed to issue the mandate in this case forthwith.

It is so ordered.

Case Review Question

Bush et al. v. Gore, 121 S.Ct. 525, 148 L.Ed.2d 388, 531 U.S. 98 (2000).

Would the result have likely been different if there were no statutory cutoff date for ending election disputes? If so, what would the result have likely been?

Powers and Authority of the President

Sections 2 and 3 of Article II describe the powers and obligations of the office of the president. Each of these sections of Article II is still influential in the daily operation of government. Frequently, questions arise regarding the proper use of power by the branches of government and the effectiveness of the system as detailed in the Constitution. A closer look at these two sections may be helpful at this point. See Figure 4.2.

The powers described in these sections indicate that the president has the basic authority to negotiate treaties, appoint judges and other government officers, convene the Congress, grant pardons or reprieves, appoint ambassadors and heads of departments (the Cabinet), and command the armed forces. Specifically, the president exercises great latitude in establishing, maintaining, or ending foreign relations with other countries. On occasion, this authority

FIGURE 4.2   Article II, Sections 2 & 3

Section 2. The President shall be Commander in Chief of the Army and Navy of the United States, and of the Militia of the several States, when called into the actual Service of the United States; he may require the Opinion in writing, of the principal Officer in each of the executive Departments, upon any subject relating to the Duties of their respective Offices, and he shall have Power to Grant Reprieves and Pardons for Offenses against the United States, except in Cases of Impeachment.

He shall have Power, by and with the Advice and Consent of the Senate, to make Treaties, provided two-thirds of the Senators present concur; and he shall nominate, and by and with the Advice and Consent of the Senate, shall appoint Ambassadors, other public Ministers and Consuls, Judges of the supreme Court, and all other Officers of the United States, whose Appointments are not herein otherwise provided for, and which shall be established by Law; but the Congress may by Law vest the Appointment of such inferior Officers, as they think proper, in the President alone, in the Courts of Law, or in the Heads of Departments.

The President shall have Power to fill up all Vacancies that may happen during the Recess of the Senate, by granting Commissions which shall expire at the End of their next Session.

Section 3. He shall from time to time give to the Congress Information of the State of the Union, and recommend to their Consideration such Measures as he shall judge necessary and expedient; he may, on extraordinary Occasions, convene both Houses, or either of them, and in Case of Disagreement between them, with Respect to the Time of Adjournment, he may adjourn them to such Time as he shall think proper; he shall receive Ambassadors and other public Ministers; he shall take Care that the Laws be faithfully executed, and shall Commission all the Officers of the United States.

covers military actions as well. Under current statutes, however, the president must report to the Congress on military actions, since the power to declare war is vested in the Congress under the Constitution.

In addition, the president is vested with the enforcement power over the laws. Consequently, federal law enforcement organizations are overseen by the executive branch. The president also appoints the attorney general, who serves as counsel for the executive branch on matters of enforcement.

The bulk of the powers of the president derives from one small portion of one sentence near the end of Article II, Section 3:"... he shall take Care that the Laws be faithfully executed. ... " This statement has been expanded to create the executive authority to oversee administrative law, one of the principal sources of law in the United States.

The president cannot create administrative law directly but is responsible for supervising the activities of federal administrative agencies. A similar process occurs at the state level between the state executive branch (office of the governor) and the state administrative agencies. The creation and the operation of an administrative agency are discussed in the following sections.

Assignment 4.1

> Create a chart that details the two methods of presidential and vice presidential elections before and after the 1804 amendment.

The Role of the President, Then and Now

Originally, the role of the president was similar to a head of state in other developed nations. Most often in monarchies, the head of state was primarily a ceremonial position. Duties included serving as a physical representative of the nation, to provide a central figure behind which citizens could unite and with whom other nations could identify. One significant duty was the negotiation of treaties with other nations; however, with limited travel capabilities, no form of rapid or mass communication, and a largely rural population separated from other countries by ocean on three sides, the early presidents had few demands placed upon them, in comparison with presidents in more recent times.

During the Civil War, the very fabric of the nation was torn and a primary postwar objective was to bring the nation together both for the sake of the citizens and as a signal to other nations that the United States was not weakened and subject to intrusion. At about the same time, methods of transportation were advancing with railroads extending throughout the country and maritime travel taking place both on the rivers and the oceans. Telegraph lines also made communication to most localities possible. These advancements and the need to unify the nation caused a change in the direction of the presidency. The primarily ceremonial role was left behind and the president became increasingly involved in communicating with and representing the people of the nation with respect to other branches of our own government and other nations.

During the twentieth century the role of the president changed dramatically. Two world wars and an unprecedented economic depression all within a span of 45 years was a tremendous strain on the nation. The president worked with the other branches of government to keep the nation strong and independent. The technological advancements and immense increase in population through births and immigration required extensive legislation and governmental supervision to protect a largely uneducated public. The result was the creation of numerous administrative agencies within the executive branch of government. It became the responsibility of the president to oversee such agencies in addition to the duties already undertaken. As time passed, the trend continued and by the end of the twentieth century, the president was as involved with the actual representation of the population as any other element of government.

ADMINISTRATIVE AGENCIES

Role of the Administrative Agency

An **administrative agency** has a unique and constantly growing place in the role of government in American society. The population of the country is so large, the geographical area so great and varied, and the system of government so complex that it is essential to have government officials who can respond to the specific needs of the many facets of society. When Congress passes a statute, the law must be written broadly enough to encompass all situations it is designed to address. However, that same law must be specific enough to allow people to know whether their actions are in compliance with or in violation of the law. Hence the need for the administrative agency, whose basic role is to act as liaison between the Congress and the people. The administrative agency explains what Congress means in particular statutory language, clarifies and defines terms, and ultimately, under the supervision of the executive branch, enforces the law. (See Figure 4.3 for a diagram of the federal government structure and placement of administrative offices.)

administrative agency
Government office created by the legislature and overseen by the executive branch. The purpose of such agencies is to apply certain specified laws created by the legislature.

Clarify what Congress said + enforce those laws

The responsibility of the president to carry out and enforce the laws passed by Congress is immense. With the assistance of administrative agencies, individuals can have personal access to government. Congress first passes laws that enable the creation of an administrative agency and then passes additional statutes that must be enforced. The president staffs and oversees the administrative agency as it clarifies, defines, and enforces the statutes passed by Congress. Many of these agencies are controlled by the 14 departments of the executive branch (e.g., the Department of Justice controls the FBI; the Treasury Department controls the IRS), although some federal agencies are not part of a specific department. The heads of the executive departments serve as members of the president's cabinet (e.g., the secretary of defense and the attorney general).

Although the day-to-day operation of an administrative agency is largely within the control of the executive branch, an agency is ultimately created by the Congress. Article I, Section 8, paragraph 18, of the Constitution provides as follows:

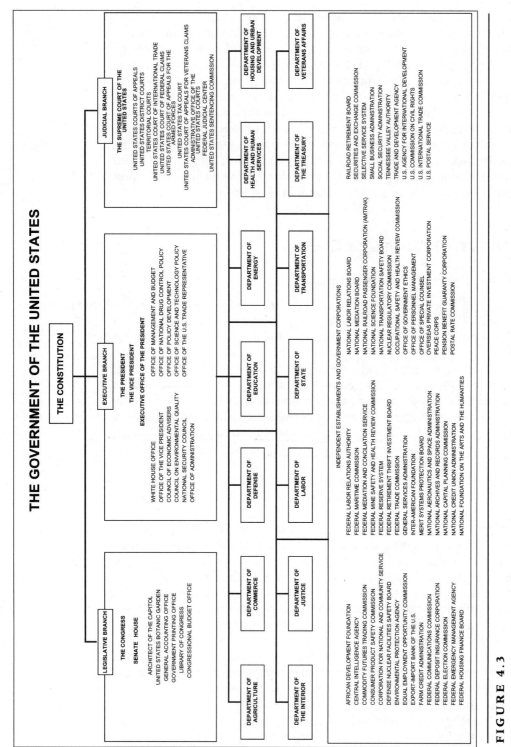

FIGURE 4.3

Chart of Federal Government structure, U.S. Government Manual, 1997 (Washington D.C.) U.S. Government Printing Office (1997)

The Congress shall have power . . . To make all Laws which shall be necessary and proper for carrying into Execution the foregoing Powers, and all other Powers vested by this Constitution in the Government of the United States, or in any Department or Officer thereof.

From this statement, Congress has drawn its authority to make laws. This statement has also been interpreted to permit Congress to enact laws that allow government agencies to clarify the laws through regulations and administrative decisions. The president's power to appoint federal officers allows the executive branch to staff the agencies. The executive duty to see that the laws are faithfully executed vests in the president the authority to oversee the agencies as they enforce the laws passed by the Congress.

Administrative agencies have been a part of the American legal system since the 1800s, since agencies can perform many legal functions that Congress, for practical reasons, cannot effectively accomplish. Administrative agencies offer several advantages, including the following:

1. They can deal with large groups of citizens or entire industries.
2. They have the ability to respond quickly to rapidly changing needs of industries or citizens.
3. Their staff members are more knowledgeable about the specifics of an industry or a group of citizens than the legislature or the judiciary.
4. They can provide consistent and fair standards for citizens and industries.

Agencies touch virtually every part of American life. Anyone who is employed is affected by agencies such as the Social Security Administration and Occupational Safety and Health Administration (OSHA), as well as labor laws and immigration laws. Purchases of property may be affected by the Environmental Protection Agency and whether part of the land is subject to its rules and regulations. Other areas under agency direction include banking, civil rights, investments, travel, consumer transactions, retirement, and emergency aid for areas hit by natural disaster. See Figure 4.4 for a partial list of federal agencies and their common acronyms.

An example of an area in which an administrative agency has been particularly effective is social security, administered by the Social Security Administration. All working people in the United States pay into a social security fund, from which payments are made to persons who retire or become disabled. Given the number of persons who have worked in this country since the establishment of social security in 1935, the task of collecting and distributing the funds is incomprehensible. But such a task can be carried out most effectively by an administrative agency such as the Social Security Administration rather than Congress. This agency establishes rules for eligibility and procedures to receive funds, payment of legally required contributions by workers, cost of living increases, and other matters that are necessary to administer the funds but do not require an elected body to perform them.

FIGURE 4.4

Common
Acronyms for
Federal Agencies

Note: The following is a partial list of existing federal agencies.
CIA—Central Intelligence Agency
CPSC—Consumer Products Safety Commission
DHHS—Department of Health and Human Services
DOD—Department of Defense
DOJ—Department of Justice
DOT—Department of Transportation
EEOC—Equal Employment Opportunity Commission
EPA—Environmental Protection Agency
FAA—Federal Aviation Administration
FBI—Federal Bureau of Investigation
FCC—Federal Communications Commission
FDA—Food and Drug Administration
FERC—Federal Energy Regulatory Commission
FRB—Federal Reserve Board
FTC—Federal Trade Commission
HUD—Department of Housing and Urban Development
ICC—Interstate Commerce Commission
INS—Immigration and Naturalization Service
IRS—Internal Revenue Service
NHTSA—National Highway and Traffic Safety Administration
NLRB—National Labor Relations Board
NRC—Nuclear Regulatory Commission
NSC—National Security Council
OSHA—Occupational Safety and Health Administration
SEC—Securities Exchange Commission
SSA—Social Security Administration
USDA—United States Department of Agriculture

The Creation of an Administrative Agency

In many areas, an administrative agency is the most effective way to deal knowledgeably, efficiently, and equitably with many legal issues on an individual basis. The following paragraphs examine the basic process for creating an administrative agency in today's legal system. Be aware that many additional details must be dealt with in the actual agency creation process.

Before an agency comes into existence, Congress must pass a resolution saying that an agency is necessary to carry out the goals of certain legislation. Congress must determine that no more effective way to implement the goals exists and that the goals of the legislation must be enforced. Congress then passes what is commonly referred to as an **enabling act**—a statute that expresses the goals of Congress on a particular subject of legislation.

An example is the enabling act that ultimately provided for the creation of the Environmental Protection Agency (EPA), which carries out and enforces legislation passed by Congress to protect, enhance, or correct problems in the environment. When the National Environmental Policy Act (NEPA) was passed as an enabling act in 1969, it was the first major environmental protection law enacted by Congress. Shortly thereafter, President Nixon issued an executive order calling for the creation of an agency to carry out the goals of the NEPA.

enabling act
Congressional enactment that creates the authority in the executive to organize and oversee an administrative agency by establishing specific legislative goals and objectives.

The executive order is a form of procedural law that implements the enabling act. Although executive orders have the weight of law, they are issued by presidents, or at their direction, and only affect administrative agencies or functions.

The acts that permit the creation of administrative agencies have been a great source of controversy for Congress over the years. In effect, by creating an administrative agency, Congress is relinquishing some of its lawmaking authority. Early on, the delegation of authority to make rules with the effect of law was strictly prohibited by the U.S. Supreme Court.[1] As time passed and the needs of the country grew, the Court relaxed its position somewhat to permit administrative agencies to play a larger role in the legislative process. Although they have never been allowed to "create law," agencies are permitted to create regulations to promote efficient, responsive, and effective government.

Through cases that come before them, the courts have continued to monitor Congress and the executive branch very closely with respect to the creation and operation of administrative agencies. The chief concern of the courts with respect to the creation of administrative agencies is that the delegation doctrine not be violated. The **delegation doctrine** is based on the premise that Congress cannot be permitted to give away any of its actual lawmaking power.[2] Rather, Congress can only give up or delegate the authority to clarify and enforce laws passed. The delegation of the authority to clarify and enforce laws is permissible even if it means that the agency must enact additional law in the form of rules and regulations as needed to clarify or enforce the original laws of Congress. An agency to which Congress has delegated authority is not free to make original laws of its own. All agency law must serve the functions of clarification and enforcement.

delegation doctrine
Principle that Congress may not assign its authority to create statutory law nor may any other government entity assume such authority.

Periodically, a person or entity affected adversely by an agency rule or regulation will challenge that the agency went beyond the objectives of clarification and enforcement of statutory law. The challenge is that the agency exceeded its authority and created new law. This alleged violation of the delegation doctrine is then reviewed—typically first at the agency level and then in the courts. In some instances such reviews have proceeded to the U.S. Supreme Court, which has in turn developed certain standards to contain the work of agencies within their purpose.

Through its interpretations of the delegation doctrine, the Supreme Court has established several major criteria that must be followed in the creation and operation of any administrative agency. The authority delegated by Congress must not allow nonlegislative bodies to enact major laws. Therefore, the Court requires any act that enables the creation of an administrative agency to be clear in its purpose with definable limits.[3] In this way, an agency is prevented from enacting regulations in areas other than those it was created to administer.

If it appears from the language of the enabling act that Congress did not clearly state as its purpose an "intelligible principle to which the [agency must][3] conform," the enabling act can be struck down as being unconstitutionally overboard.[4] The reasoning is that if a law is so broad that an agency is limitless in the extent of law that it can create, Congress has delegated its original lawmaking authority rather than the authority to clarify and enforce the laws. This violates the Constitution, which vests the authority to create statutes solely in the Congress.

A second major criterion of the delegation doctrine is that the agency's enforcement of the law must be accomplished fairly and openly.[5] If the enabling act and subsequent statutes enacted by Congress do not give some guidance to the president and the administrative agencies under the president's supervision in the manner of enforcing the law, the delegation doctrine has been violated. Under the Constitution, the people are entitled to know what the law is and how it will be enforced against persons who do not obey it. Since laws created by Congress must meet this standard, obviously any agency to which Congress gives the power to enforce the laws must also meet it. If an agency fails to create regulations that provide for the fair and open administration of laws, the president and the agency have not received proper guidance from Congress. Once again, the enabling act will be considered to be too vague or overboard and therefore inconsistent with the Constitution.[6]

Agency officers.   Finally, Article II of the Constitution states that the president should appoint government officers. With respect to agencies, officers are persons who will be responsible for the enforcement of the law. Agency staff members cannot be employed in any profession or industry that the agency oversees, since that would not constitute fair and unbiased administration of the law. Further, according to the Constitution, the laws are to be enforced by the government and not by the private sector. This particular situation came to the attention of the U.S. Supreme Court in 1936. In *Carter v. Carter Coal Company*,[7] many of the regulations for the coal industry were discovered to have been created by committees of persons employed at high levels in the industry. The Court found that this was an improper method of enforcing laws. The president may, however, ask persons who are experts in their field to leave private industry to come to work in the agency.

In summary, the passage of an enabling act and the creation of an agency must be done in a manner that at the very least meets the following criteria:

1. The goals of the statutes must be clear, and the statutes must have definable limits.
2. The methods the agency uses to enforce the statutes must be fair and open to all members of the public.
3. The enforcement of the statutes must be accomplished by officers of the government, not by persons with private interests.

Agencies Today

During the 1930s, the number of agencies increased dramatically. Agencies were part of the New Deal era, which sought to aid the country in its economic recovery from the Great Depression. Congress increased its use of administrative agencies and cooperated with the president in using them to deal quickly with the problems of the nation. Some people believed, however, that the agencies were not acting properly and within the bounds of their authority. In large part, the delegation doctrine was refined during and shortly after this time.

In the years that followed, the courts became more involved in reviewing the efforts of the executive branch to oversee agencies, and the delegation doctrine imposed more stringent requirements upon the manner in which agencies could be created and operated. Congress responded in 1946 with the **Administrative Procedure Act (APA)**, which was to be used in addition to each agency's enabling act. The APA included the elements necessary to satisfy the requirements of the delegation doctrine. Since that time, the APA has been modified and improved on several occasions to ensure that agencies are in compliance with the criteria the courts have established under the delegation doctrine. Thus, the APA together with the enabling act provides for the creation of an agency as well as for the agency's fair and efficient operation.

Administrative Procedure Act (APA)
Congressional enactment applied to all federal administrative agencies that requires agencies to follow certain procedures in the issuance of administrative law.

The Operation of an Administrative Agency

Once an agency is staffed, its employees are responsible for organizing its administration and addressing the subject or industry that the statutes affect. An agency is permitted a virtual free rein in its methods of internal operations and management as long as it is well organized and efficient. Such organization and efficiency will vary among agencies. An agency such as the Federal Aviation Administration, which oversees public air travel, does not require the same type of staffing, organization, and procedures as the Internal Revenue Service, which administers the tax laws for both individuals and businesses.

The type of agency that is created influences not only the manner in which the agency is organized but also the agency's basic functions. Some of the more common responsibilities of agencies include enforcing federal statutes through prosecution; negotiating settlements of claims made against government entities; testing, inspecting, and monitoring industries; recalling, seizing, or suspending products or activities that violate federal laws; and advising the public of the legal effect of the law. These various functions are performed through information collection, investigation, issuance of regulations, and administrative hearings.

When an agency must collect information or conduct an investigation to meet the goals and purpose of its enabling act, it is permitted to obtain information from the public and industry. However, this information must be voluntary and obtained in a manner that does not infringe upon individuals' rights to privacy under the Constitution. In addition, individuals cannot be compelled to testify at agency hearings about any information that might result in criminal prosecution against them, just as they cannot be compelled to incriminate themselves before the judiciary or the legislature.

Authority of Administrative Agencies

The most prominent function of administrative agencies is their authority to issue regulations. **Administrative regulations** must be required to achieve the goals of the enabling act or any other federal laws that the agency has the responsibility to enforce. Thus, all regulations must be derivative of legislation formerly enacted by Congress. If an agency holds a hearing and determines that a regulation has been violated, then the agency may impose sanctions on the violator.

administrative regulation
Form of administrative law, a regulation defines, clarifies, or enforces a statutory objective.

Assignment 4.2

Determine whether the administrative regulation in Figure 4.5 applies to the following situation:

SITUATION: You attended a community college where you received student loans in 1995 and 1996. Three years later, in 1999, you defaulted (stopped payment) on the loan and declared bankruptcy. However, the bankruptcy court would not discharge the student loan debt. In 2000, you resumed payment and completed payment in 2001. You want to resume your education at State U. Are you eligible for a student loan?

If an agency wishes to issue rules, it must follow a specific procedure set forth in the APA. Additionally, some enabling acts dictate the precise steps an agency must take when establishing and publishing regulations for the public. These formal rulemaking procedures often require public hearings, the opportunity for testimony, and other input from the public before any regulations are put into force. However, most agencies are also allowed to promulgate rules through an informal process governed by a series of detailed requirements set forth in the APA. Most agencies must adhere to the following procedures when passing rules that will have an impact upon the public, an industry, or a subject that the agency regulates:

1. The agency must give advance notice to the public of the basic terms of the rules it proposes to enact. At the federal level, this must be done in the *Federal Register*, a daily publication that includes information about the actions of federal administrative agencies.
2. The agency must give the public the opportunity to participate in the agency decision by submitting comments, ideas, and suggestions regarding the proposed rules.
3. After consideration of the public comment, the agency must issue, with the final rule, a general statement of the basis and purpose of the administrative agency supporting the rule.[8]

After all the requirements of the APA have been satisfied, the agency issues its formal regulations and publishes them first in the *Federal Register* and then in the **Code of Federal Regulations (CFR)**, where all existing regulations are located. Each agency is assigned a title similar to a title in the Code. Each regulation is assigned a specific section number and is placed with the other regulations of that agency under its proper title. Like the Code, an index of the regulations within a title is included.

Code of Federal Regulations (CFR)
Publication that contains all current administrative regulations.

The APA requires agencies to review their regulations periodically to evaluate their effectiveness and necessity.[9] In addition, the APA gives citizens certain rights with respect to agencies. Citizens have the right of access to agency information that pertains to the public and a right to information the agency has about them personally. Business entities or individuals who believe that a regulation has an unfair and adverse effect may have their complaint heard by the agency. If they do not receive satisfaction, they may have the right to have the issue heard by a judge in the judicial branch of the government.

FIGURE 4.5   Regulation

CODE OF FEDERAL REGULATIONS
TITLE 34–EDUCATION

§ 682.201 Eligible borrowers.

(a) Student borrower. A student is eligible to receive a GSLP loan, and an independent undergraduate student or a graduate or professional student is eligible to receive a PLUS Program loan, if the student—

(1) Is enrolled or accepted for enrollment on at least a half-time basis at a participating school, and meets the requirements of paragraph (c) of this section;

(2) Provides his or her social security number;

(3) Authorizes the school in writing to pay directly to the lender that portion of any refund of school charges that is allocable to the loan, in accordance with 34 CFR Part 668;

(4) Meets the qualifications pertaining to citizenship and residency status, set forth in paragraph (d) of this section;

(5) Meets the qualifications concerning defaults and overpayments, set forth in paragraphs (e) and (f) of this section;

(6) Complies with the requirements pertaining to registration with the Selective Service, set forth in 34 CFR Part 668;

(7) Complies with the requirements for submission of a Statement of Educational Purpose, set forth in § 682.203; and

(8) In the case of an undergraduate student who seeks a GSLP loan for the cost of attendance at a school that participates in the Pell Grant Program, receives a preliminary or final determination from the school of the student's eligibility or ineligibility for a Pell Grant.

(b) Parent borrower. A parent is eligible to receive a PLUS Program loan if the parent—

(1) Is borrowing to pay for the educational costs of a dependent undergraduate student who meets all of the qualifications set forth in paragraphs (a) (1) through (6) of this section;

(2) Provides his or her social security number;

(3) Meets the qualifications pertaining to citizenship and residency status set forth in paragraph (d) of this section;

(4) Meets the qualifications concerning defaults and overpayments set forth in paragraphs (e) and (f) of this section; and

(5) Complies with the requirements for submission of a Statement of Educational Purpose set forth in § 682.203.

(c) Enrollment status. To be eligible as a student or a borrower under the GSLP or the PLUS Program, a student must—

(1) If currently enrolled, be maintaining satisfactory progress, as determined by the school;

(2) If enrolled or accepted for enrollment in a foreign school, be a national of the United States; and

(3) If enrolled in a flight school program at a vocational school or an institution of higher education, meet the additional requirements set forth in paragraph (g) of this section.

(d) Citizenship and residency status. Each borrower, and each student for whom a parent is borrowing, must be—

(1) A national of the United States;

(2) A permanent resident of the United States and must provide evidence from the Immigration and Naturalization Service of that status;

(3) In the United States for other than a temporary purpose and must provide evidence from the Immigration and Naturalization Service of intent to become a citizen or permanent resident;

(4) A permanent resident of the Trust Territory of the Pacific Islands or the Northern Mariana Islands; or

(5) A citizen of the Marshall Islands, the Federated States of Micronesia, or the Republic of Palau.

(e) Effect of default on eligibility.

(1) Except as provided in paragraph (e)(2) of this section, a person is ineligible to be a borrower under the GSLP or PLUS Program if that person, or the student for whom a parent is borrowing, is in default on any loan made under any title IV student financial assistance program identified in 34 CFR Part 668. For loans made under the National Direct Student Loan Program, the term "default" is defined in 34 CFR Part 674.

(2) If a borrower, or student for whom a parent is borrowing, is in default, as set forth in paragraph (e)(1) of this section, the borrower may receive a GSLP or PLUS Program loan only if the person who is in default has made satisfactory arrangements with the holder of the loan to repay the defaulted loan.

(3) The school may rely on the borrower's or student's written statement that he or she is not in default, unless the school has information to the contrary.

(4) The Secretary does not consider either a loan that is discharged in bankruptcy or a defaulted loan that is paid-in-full after default to be in default for purposes of this section. . . .

exhaustion of remedies

The requirement that anyone having a dispute with an administrative agency must first follow all available procedures to resolve the dispute within the agency before taking the issue before the judiciary.

Frequently, citizens who challenge the authority of an agency to promulgate rules or to use a particular method to enforce an agency regulation are required to exhaust their remedies. This means that before they can turn to the courts, they must first pursue all opportunities to have the issue resolved by dealing directly with the agency. This may involve formal claims, hearings, or appeals at various levels of the agency structure. Exceptions to this requirement of **exhaustion of remedies** occur in limited circumstances. For example, an individual may turn to the courts first when it is apparent that there is little or no chance that the matter can be resolved by the agency or if time is an important factor and irreparable damage will be done if the citizen must wait to file a claim in the judicial system. As a general rule, however, a citizen must exhaust any possible remedies at the agency level before bringing the issue before the courts.

If the judicial system does become involved in a dispute between a citizen and an agency, it will consider several factors. First, the court must determine whether the agency's authority was clearly defined and whether the agency's action exceeded the limits of the agency's authority under the delegation doctrine. Second, the agency must have followed proper statutory procedures according to the enabling act, the APA, and any other relevant statutes. Finally, the court must consider whether the agency's action was conducted fairly and openly and whether it violates any constitutional rights of the citizen. If all of these requirements are satisfied in the agency's favor, the court will not disturb the action of the agency.

Chapter 1 pointed out that a court will not invalidate laws or substitute its judgment for that of the Congress unless the Constitution has been violated. This is also true with agency law, which, although administered and enforced through the executive branch, is ultimately an extension of the Congress and is entitled to the same protection.

Earlier in this chapter we focused on the role of the executive branch and its supervision of administrative agencies. Although this role is not always obvious in agency proceedings, the president has a great responsibility and considerable influence with respect to administrative agencies. The president is responsible for keeping the agency appropriately staffed, has influence over the approval of the agency budget, and may exercise authority over the agency through the issuance of an executive order. Such orders specify the manner in which the president wants laws to be executed.

Assignment 4.3

Which of the following would be more appropriate subjects for law enacted solely by legislature?

(a) Licensure provisions for ham radio operators.
(b) Requirements that shelters for the homeless must meet to be eligible for state funds.
(c) The method by which trials are conducted.
(d) The type of safety equipment employers must provide to workers who use heavy machinery.
(e) The creation and administration of retirement plans for state employees.

Assignment 4.4

Which of the items in Assignment 4.3 would be more appropriate for supplemental law from an administrative agency?

Assignment 4.5

Create a flow chart that tracks a concept of law to creation of a regulation used to define the concept.

Ethical Considerations

As the primary elected official in government, the president takes an oath of loyalty to the people of the nation. As the leader of the United States of America, the president is the role model for ethical behavior by all other elected officials. It is the obligation of the president to enforce the laws of the nation fairly and without preference or prejudice.

As representatives of government, agency officials also are obliged to put personal issues aside and to administer the law fairly and equally. In fact, the very objective of the Human Rights Commission is to see that all persons are afforded equal legal rights and are not treated disparately because of a nonrelevant factor such as race, sex, age, or disability. The very theme of equitable treatment by government as an ethical foundation can be traced to the Declaration of Independence, which sets forth the principle that "all men are created equal."

Ethical Circumstance

In the late 1990s, President Bill Clinton faced impeachment for what amounted to claims of unethical, to the point of illegal, conduct. He had engaged in an extramarital relationship. During depositions in a lawsuit, he made statements under oath that implied the relationship had not occurred. He was faced with a moral dilemma of either admitting his conduct publicly and to his family or attempting to cover it with what many considered to be ambiguous but essentially false answers. Ultimately, Clinton made certain admissions about the relationship. The issue before Congress and other disciplinary bodies, such as various bar associations of which he was a member, was not the president's personal conduct, but whether he lied under oath. Although by today's standards this may not seem sufficient to warrant repercussions of such magnitude, the oath to be truthful in matters before the courts is a cornerstone of the American legal system and the president as much as anyone is obliged to honor this treasure.

CHAPTER SUMMARY

The executive branch has many important functions, such as foreign relations, negotiation of treaties, supervision of the armed forces, and appointment of ambassadors and heads of governmental units. One of the most important functions, and one that has a direct and immediate effect on the citizenry, is to see that the laws are faithfully executed. From this comes the power to oversee administrative agencies and to ensure that the goals of Congress are carried out.

The government operates more effectively with the use of administrative agencies. Because administrative agencies are heavily influenced by all branches of government, limits are placed on the opportunities for abuse of agency power by agency staff or by the executive or legislative branches. In addition, judicially imposed limitations on the areas that are subject to agency regulation also limit the potential for abuse.

An administrative agency can be created only by a legislative enactment. Agency authority is limited to the clarification and enforcement of statutory law. The agency is staffed and overseen by the chief executive (president or governor). In the event the executive fails to properly oversee the agency or the legislative body gives the agency too much authority, the courts have the power to invalidate agency actions.

CHAPTER TERMS

administrative agency
Administrative Procedure Act
administrative regulation

Code of Federal Regulations
delegation doctrine

enabling act
exhaustion of remedies

REVIEW QUESTIONS

1. Describe the original role of the president.
2. What are some advantages of administrative agencies?
3. What is an enabling act?
4. Who appoints top federal agency officers?
5. What is meant by exhaustion of remedies?
6. What are the basic responsibilities of the president as outlined by the Constitution?
7. What is the purpose of an administrative agency?
8. In what areas of law are administrative agencies appropriate?
9. What is the delegation doctrine?
10. Describe the minimum criteria for creation of an administrative agency.

RELEVANT LINKS

Internet Legal Resource Guide
www.ilrg.com
U.S. Government
www.governmentguide.com
U.S. Government
www.firstgov.gov

Thomas Legislative Information on the Net
http://www.thomas.loc.gov/home/legbranch/legalbranch.html

INTERNET ASSIGNMENT 4.1

Identify the U.S. senators for your state and the U.S. representatives for your district. Locate the internet address for each.

NOTES

1. *Buttfield v. Stranahan*, 192 U.S. 470, 24 S.Ct. 349, 48 L.Ed. 525 (1904).
2. Id.
3. *J. W. Hampton, Jr., & Co. v. United States*, 276 U.S. 394, 48 S.Ct. 348, 72 L.Ed. 624 (1928).
4. Id.
5. 5 U.S.C.A. § 551 et seq.
6. *Schware v. Board of Bar Examiners*, 353 U.S. 232, 77 S.Ct. 752, IL.Ed.2d 796 (1957).
7. 298 U.S. 238, 56 S.Ct. 855, 80 L.Ed.1160 (1936).
8. 5 U.S.C.A. § 551–§ 1305.
9. 5 U.S.C.A. § 551 et seq.

 For additional resources, please visit our Web site at www.westlegalstudies.com

CHAPTER 5

The Legal Professional

CHAPTER OBJECTIVES

After reading this chapter, you should be able to:

- Describe the special skills expected of a licensed attorney.

- Explain what is necessary to become a licensed attorney.

- Explain the difference between a trial judge and an appellate judge.

- Define the role of an administrative law judge.

- Discuss the evolution of the paralegal profession.

- Describe the skills of a qualified paralegal.

- Discuss the various members of the legal team and their duties.

- Explain why some nonlawyers have a limited license to engage in what would otherwise be considered the unauthorized practice of law.

WHO ARE TODAY'S LEGAL PROFESSIONALS?

As our society and culture increase in complexity, so does the legal system designed to maintain order among the population. The growth of the structure of the American legal system has resulted in the evolution of various law-related professions. Initially, the legal professions consisted primarily of judges and lawyers. These date back to the earliest beginnings of a civilized society and the imposition of laws to maintain order. Even in ancient Egypt, there were judges and counselors. Often the judges passed orders of punishment and retribution for some violation of laws set down by government leaders such as the kings and pharaohs. Counselors were employed by the aristocrats and advised them on how to remain in favor with the ruling power and with others in positions of power. Eventually, as governments became more sophisticated and the network of legal standards grew, more and more individuals sought out the advice of those who made their living by studying and explaining the law. Over time, a clerical role developed to assist the lawyers and judges in maintaining records of legal events. This was the beginning of the principles we know as precedent and the doctrine of stare decisis. These roles of legal scholars and counselors remained relatively unchanged for hundreds of years. But, similar to all aspects of society and culture, the past 200 years have been an evolution unparalleled in history. During this time, governments have become extremely complex, populations have soared, and the need for more laws than ever to maintain a sense of order and balance has resulted in a whole new industry of legal professionals. The various roles and opportunities for those instrumental to the administration of law in the United States and the world in law-related settings are virtually limitless.

In the American legal system today, those who make their careers in law consist of numerous types of judges, court clerks and employees, law clerks, court officers, lawyers, paralegals/legal assistants, legal investigators, legal secretaries, general accounting and clerical staff, and others. Most of these positions have developed during the twentieth century as a result of the great increases in population, technology, transportation, and communications systems and the complexity of government. To illustrate some of these changes, take the example of filing a court document. In 1850, the lawyer handwrote the legal document using a quill or fountain pen and bottle of ink. He then carried it to the courthouse and often presented it personally to the judge. Today, just over 150 years later, the same document would probably first be discussed by the lawyer and paralegal, and researched by the lawyer, paralegal, or law clerk. Then a form document might be accessed by computer and completed with a simple filling of blanks; or it could be dictated by machine or perhaps even spoken directly into the computer. The clerical staff would prepare the final document and format it including the required procedural details such as the captions (headings) and attorney identifications such as name, address, and license number. The document might be transmitted electronically to the parties to suit and the court or sent/taken in hard copy form to the court and appropriate parties. At the court, the document is registered, as thousands are annually, recorded into the computerized filing system, and forwarded to an assigned judge. The clerk or an assistant to the judge would then establish a time for hearing and notify all parties of such by telephone, mail, or electronic transmission such as a fax or e-mail.

The technological advances no doubt have reduced the labor involved by a few people processing a case. Efficiency has certainly improved on a dramatic scale. However, the complexity of the legal system and the sheer volume of cases filed have resulted in new opportunities for all members of professions with their basis in the American legal system. The following discussion gives insight into some of the more common members of the law-related professions and the roles they play.

Judges

Jurists, commonly called **judges,** are individuals who resolve disputes between parties who have different interpretations of the law. It is the duty of a judge to objectively evaluate the circumstances of the parties and to determine which legal standards are the most appropriate. In the jury trial system, the jury then listens to the evidence presented of the facts as each side views them. The judge presides over the proceedings to ensure that the law is applied properly and that the evidence is presented in accordance with rules of evidence and procedure. Before and often during trial, a judge issues rulings on various procedural issues such as discovery of evidence, motions of parties, selection of a jury, and how the jury is to be instructed about the case in question. The judge must also determine which laws will be applied to the facts of the case presented. The jury has the responsibility to apply the law, as determined by the judge, to the facts and reach a conclusion.

On certain occasions, judges make determinations regarding the outcome of a case without benefit of a jury. In the judicial branch, this occurs in bench trials and appellate reviews. In a bench trial, the parties waive the right to a jury and the judge makes the determination of law and applies it to the facts for a final conclusion. In an appellate review, a panel of judges reviews the findings at the trial court level and renders a determination of whether the outcome was consistent with the applicable legal principles.

Becoming a trial court or appellate judge is considered an honor and may occur in a variety of ways. Typically, when a judicial position opens, the candidates are considered based on their experience, knowledge of law, and ability to apply the law in a fair and unbiased manner. In the state court systems, some judges are appointed by the executive (governor) with approval of the legislature. Others are appointed by the senior judge or a committee of judges in the particular venue, and still others are elected. Terms of office and methods for retention or removal are just as varied. In the federal judicial system, most appointments are made by the president with approval of Congress; and with the exception of special courts, federal judicial appointments are for life. This policy has come under fire in recent years, however, as some judges have been found guilty of professional misconduct but technically had the right to retain their position.

The present-day legal system has various kinds of judges: federal and state appellate judges, trial judges, and magistrates; municipal judges and various levels of hearing officers; and administrative law judges. All have the essential duty to

jurist (judge)
Judicial officer who presides over cases in litigation within the court system.

interpret and apply the law within the boundaries of their particular role as an officer of the court. However, significant differences in the function and authority of judges lie in the distinction between trial, appellate, and administrative judges.

Trial judges.   To properly perform their duties as described herein, trial judges must maintain current knowledge of the law at all times. Because of the large volume of litigation, many courts assign trial judges to specific categories of cases, such as domestic relations, probate, or criminal. This not only creates a more organized and efficient court system, but also allows the trial judge the opportunity to develop expertise in certain areas of law. However, many less-congested courts still have judges in courts of general jurisdiction who hear cases of all types.

Changes in case law begin with the trial judge. At some point, a judge will take the position that an existing legal standard, relied upon in the past as a rule of law, is no longer appropriate. The judge may follow new statutory or administrative legal standards or indicate that societal standards dictate a change in the legal standards applicable to a situation. The judge has the option of applying existing precedent. When the case reaches conclusion, and possibly earlier in certain situations, a party dissatisfied with the result may challenge the trial court judgment before an appellate court. In some jurisdictions, including federal, a series of appeals can be taken before increasingly powerful courts. On appeal, the higher court affirms or reverses the position of the trial court and establishes the rule of law to be followed in the future. Consequently, the trial judge plays a crucial role in the establishment of legal standards.

Appellate judges.   Appellate judges review cases that have been previously ruled on in a trial court. The goal of an appellate judge is to ensure that the correct law was applied properly, fairly, and consistently. If it is the opinion of the appellate court that the lower court exceeded or improperly used its authority (abuse of discretion), the court issues a ruling as to what should occur next in the case to correct the error. The case then returns to the lower court for corrective action. If, however, the court finds that the actions in the trial court were appropriate, then the result in the lower court is affirmed. In many cases and in many jurisdictions, there are a series of courts that one can follow with subsequent appeals.

The likelihood of a reversal declines as each subsequent judge(s) considers a case and agrees with those who have previously considered the appeal. Usually, several appellate judges review a case as a panel in an appellate court. This collective wisdom reduces the possibility of error or personal bias on a legal issue. Because it is the duty of appellate judges to ensure proper, fair, and consistent application of law for a jurisdiction, the position of appellate judges requires a great deal of knowledge of legal principles. As with other legal professionals, appellate judges often have the assistance of law clerks, which are discussed later in the chapter.

Typically, the appellate panel will issue a written opinion after consideration of a case and possibly after hearing a short argument by each party. The opinion will not only give the rationale for the judgment but also indicate the support or nonsupport by each judge. If the entire membership of an appellate court—rather than a panel of a few members—issues a joint decision, such decision is known as an *en banc* opinion. Typically, such collective decisions are reserved for issues of great significance such as a change in precedent. A judge who agrees with the final result in a case but not with the supporting rationale of the other appellate judges may issue a *concurring* opinion. This explains a different reasoning used to reach the same result. A judge who disagrees with the result but is in the minority may issue a *dissenting* opinion. Concurring and dissenting opinions are valuable for the light they may shed on future cases or cases that have both significant similarities and differences. The majority opinion, however, is the controlling precedent to which lower courts generally look for guidance in future cases. The majority opinion also dictates the outcome of the particular case on appeal.

Administrative law judges.   The administrative law judge (ALJ) functions in a totally different arena from that of the appellate or trial judge. The duties of ALJs are confined to hearing cases involving the conduct of administrative agencies and the effects of that conduct on the individual or entity who challenges the agency action.

The ALJ is presumed to be an objective judicial authority who rules exclusively on issues of administrative law. The ALJ determines such issues as whether a party is subject to the authority of the agency and whether a party's conduct is in accordance with administrative rules and regulations. Typically, administrative cases are initially filed with the agency rather than in the courts. Appeals of an administrative decision are generally made to the trial court level in the judicial system. This is a limited instance when the trial court exercises appellate rather than original authority.

Each type of judicial officer plays an extremely important role in the American legal system. Whether hearing evidence at trial or reviewing another judge's application of law, the input of a judge as an objective observer with knowledge of legal standards is necessary to the effective operation of the American system of government.

Lawyers

The practice of law defined.   Although the definition of the practice of law varies from state to state, certain components of the definition are fairly standard. Most jurisdictions give the lawyer, when licensed to practice law, the generally exclusive privilege to give legal advice and to advocate with third parties on the behalf of a client's legal rights.

Legal advice and analysis.   Giving legal advice requires a special analytical ability by a lawyer. A lawyer is responsible for examining the law applicable to a situation, informing a client as to the likely outcome of the case, and often recommending the next course of action. Based on the information received, the client can choose to accept the analysis and recommendation or reject it.

A licensed attorney must use analytical ability to locate all relevant legal principles in a given circumstance, to recognize the significant facts of the case, and to determine the impact of the principles on those facts. To do this, the lawyer must be able to take each of the applicable legal principles, break them down into the necessary components, and compare them to the specific elements of the client's circumstance. Then based on the similarities and differences identified in this analysis, the lawyer must make a determination of the likely outcome of the client's case if these legal principles were to be applied by a court. Such analytical ability by a lawyer is a valued and respected skill and, because clients often determine future conduct affecting their rights based on the lawyer's recommendation, the process of giving legal advice is licensed by the state and prohibited for anyone not having a proper license.

Advocacy. The second function of a licensed attorney is advocacy, the process of representing the legal rights and interests of another person within the confines of legal proceedings in one branch of government. In business, it is not uncommon to have an agent represent one's interests in such areas as negotiations, sales, and purchases, but a license to practice law is required to represent the interests of another person in court and other legal proceedings. Many times, however, attorneys delve in nonlegal proceedings if the effect is on the legal rights of the parties, such as in contractual matters, because in the event a dispute arises, a party wishes his or her legal rights to be well protected. Because advocacy frequently has a long-term effect on practice requirements, failure to represent one's client zealously and with the degree of competence required by law can result in an action for malpractice as well as disciplinary action by a state bar association.

lawyer/attorney
Individual who has completed the necessary requirements of education and training and who has been licensed to practice law in a jurisdiction.

Becoming a licensed attorney.   Because of the increasing complexity of the American legal system, **lawyers (attorneys)** function not only as advocates for clients but also as counselors and liaisons between the lay public and the courts, legislatures, and executive branches of state and federal governments. To become a lawyer, certain graduate level coursework must be completed and standards for licensure in the state or federal area of practice must be met. Most states require that prior to licensure, the lawyer must graduate from an accredited law school following completion of an undergraduate bachelor's degree and pass a bar exam in the licensing state or in another state. The exam tests the legal knowledge and the analytical ability of the lawyer.

Typically, the law school component of a lawyer's education consists of study that, if completed in the traditional setting, would consist of three years of full-time study, although today many law schools offer part-time programs so that students may continue full-time employment while preparing for their career in law. The study for a career as an attorney consists of almost exclusively law-related courses in all general subjects of law, some specialized areas, government and court procedures, ethics, and litigation.

While historically, states often granted licenses to practice to those who demonstrated licensure in another state, known as reciprocity, the trend has been to require licensure by examination in each state of practice. This is due, at least in part, to the fact that as laws become more complex in each jurisdiction, the likelihood of variance in legal procedures and standards increases. Consequently, many states require a lawyer to demonstrate a working knowledge of the laws of that particular state prior to licensure. For example, states with unique elements of their economy, such as states with heavy oil reserves, are likely to be affected dramatically by these qualities, so a knowledge of this area of law is important to provide effective representation to a large element of the population.

Generally, there are three elements to meeting the standard of knowledge for licensure as an attorney. First is a standardized exam administered to test the knowledge of general areas of law. This is part of the bar exam in so many states that it is referred to as the "multistate." A second element tests more specific areas of law that tend to have application within the particular state. Often the multistate exam is offered on one day and the state exam on the next or preceding day. Additionally, most jurisdictions require that within a period of time before or after the state bar exam, an applicant pass a separate exam on ethics.

Once an attorney is licensed to practice in a particular state, additional considerations are expected to fully exercise the practice of law. Some states require membership in good standing in a state bar association. Certain federal courts also require specific additional requirements before an attorney is permitted to practice before them. One such example is the U.S. Courts of Appeals. Before an attorney can appear and represent a client in these courts, the attorney must first be approved. This is accomplished through the submission of an application and the endorsement of several attorneys already licensed to practice therein. As stated, the requirements may vary among jurisdictions, but the objective is the same. Each jurisdiction takes the steps considered reasonably necessary to ensure that one is not permitted to represent, defend, and protect the legal rights of another without first demonstrating a basic level of knowledge of the law, legal analysis, and governmental procedures.

When an individual undertakes the practice of law without a license, a statutory violation occurs and criminal proceedings may be instituted. In recent years, there has been an increasing awareness of this issue as a gray area has developed among lawyers and some other professions. However, the real controversy has been in drawing the line within the lawyer's own office. At what point does a subordinate staff member such as a legal assistant, legal secretary, or even law clerk stop providing support and start practicing law. Secondly, what of the freelance individuals who prepare legal forms, provide legal services, and assist persons in meeting the procedural requirements of the legal system? There has been litigation across the United States in the last decade over issues such as these. Essentially, the courts have maintained their original position: If the conduct of the individual extends in any way to giving advice, thus affecting another person's legal rights or advocacy on behalf of another's legal rights, then the practice of law has occurred. If the individual is not properly licensed, then a criminal prosecution may follow. Additionally, if the individual was in the employ of a licensed attorney, a suit for malpractice may be brought and disciplinary action can be taken against the lawyer in some circumstances.

CASE

COLUMBUS BAR ASSOCIATION

V.

SMITH ET AL.

Submitted May 22, 2002.
Decided July 31, 2002.
722 N.E.2d 637
(OH 2002).

Respondent Jack B. Smith owns respondent All Ohio Insurance Agency, Inc. ("All Ohio"), which employs respondents Gregory P. Smith and Sheila A. Smith. The Smiths operated a business known as respondent License Recovery, which is wholly owned and operated as a division of All Ohio. None of the Smiths has ever been admitted to the practice of law in Ohio or any other jurisdiction, and All Ohio and License Recovery are neither legal professional corporations nor owned or operated by any individual admitted to practice law in Ohio or any other jurisdiction.

Doing business as License Recovery, respondents obtained computerized lists identifying individuals who were subject to driver's license suspensions by the Ohio Bureau of Motor Vehicles and used these lists to solicit customers to assist in retaining their driving privileges or appealing their administrative suspensions. Respondents prepared documents, such as petitions to modify point suspensions, and provided advice and instructions for filing the documents in various Ohio courts.

In August 2000, relator, Columbus Bar Association, filed a complaint before the Board of Commissioners on the Unauthorized Practice of Law, alleging that by preparing documents and giving advice for filing the documents in Ohio courts, respondents engaged in the unauthorized practice of law. Respondents filed an answer, and the parties subsequently filed a stipulation of facts and waiver of notice of hearing. In the stipulation, respondents admitted that their preparation of documents and provision of advice for filing them constituted the practice of law.

In its final report filed March 28, 2002, the board found the facts as previously set forth and concluded that respondents had engaged in the unauthorized practice of law. The board recommended that respondents be enjoined from engaging in further activity constituting the unauthorized practice of law in Ohio and that costs be taxed to respondents.

On review of the record, we adopt the findings, conclusions, and recommendation of the board. "'The practice of law * * * embraces the preparation of pleadings and other papers incident to actions and special proceedings and the management of such actions and proceedings on behalf of clients before judges and courts.'" *Disciplinary Counsel v. Shrode*, 95 Ohio St.3d 137, 2002-Ohio-1759, 766 N.E.2d 597, at ¶6, quoting *Land Title Abstract & Trust Co. v. Dworken* (1934), 129 Ohio St. 23, 1 O.O. 313, 193 N.E. 650, paragraph one of the syllabus; see, also, *Lorain Cty. Bar Assn. v. Kennedy* (2002), 95 Ohio St.3d 116, 116-117, 766 N.E.2d 151. Moreover, "[t]he practice of law is not restricted to appearances in court; it also encompasses giving legal advice and counsel." *Cincinnati Bar Assn. v. Telford* (1999), 85 Ohio St.3d 111, 112, 707 N.E.2d 462. By preparing documents for filing in courts and giving legal advice, respondents engaged in the unauthorized practice of law.

Respondents are hereby enjoined from further actions that constitute the unauthorized practice of law. Costs are taxed to respondents.

Judgment accordingly.

MOYER, C.J.,
DOUGLAS,
RESNICK, FRANCIS
E. SWEENEY, SR.,
PFEIFER, COOK
AND LUNDBERG
STRATTON, JJ.,
CONCUR.

Case Review Question
Columbus Bar Assoc. v. Smith et al., 772 N.E.2d 637 (2002).
How is the conduct of respondents in this case different from what paralegals do?

Places of employment.   When considering the employment of attorneys, the first thing that comes to mind for most people is an office full of books and large desks, and secretaries typing away. However, today, only a percentage of attorneys are employed in the traditional law firm setting. Tens of thousands of attorneys never work in a law firm throughout their careers. Today's opportunities for individuals trained in the law are virtually limitless. Because of the complexity of society, the capability and ease of interstate and even global travel, communication, and commerce, more than ever private industry is faced with a need for competent legal advice and representation.

Many lawyers still work in the traditional setting and follow a career path that includes representation of individuals in matters of civil law. Issues concerning property rights, transfers, and possession are still common. This includes, but is not limited to, transfers of real estate interests, landlord tenant law, property rights among co-owners, and condominium law. The law of domestic relations covers a range of subjects from prenuptial agreements through divorce, custody, support and maintenance, surrogacy, and cohabitation.

Lawyers also work in probate, the law of estates and guardianships, as well as in criminal defense and other areas of general civil law such as personal injury and contracts. In addition to these private party matters, however, are numerous opportunities within the legal setting that have nothing to do with individual disputes. Virtually every type of commercial business is faced with some sort of legal concern. Health care professionals face risk management issues regarding matters of alleged malpractice. Anyone concerned with transportation of goods either interstate or international has laws to consider that govern these transactions. Insurance companies must comply with state and federal laws and enter into contractual agreements with providers of health care services or whatever type of business they insure. Banks and investment companies need legal professionals to assist in the management of retirement funds, trusts, and other assets. The explosive growth of e-commerce via the internet in the past few years has created a new realm of legal issues. As the population and technology continue to increase, so will the potential for problems that must be addressed by those with legal training and expertise.

Paralegals

The concept of the **paralegal,** or **legal assistant,** has been recognized as a formal profession in this country only during the past few decades and the development of this career path has been rapid. Although no uniformly accepted definition of a paralegal exists, certain standards have been developed and have gained wide acceptance in the United States. In recent years, a number of states have issued definitions of paralegals or legal assistants, or recognized duties for which services may be billed. Essentially, a paralegal is someone with training and knowledge in the law who should be able to perform all functions historically performed by an attorney with the exception of giving legal advice and

paralegal (legal assistant)
One with training and knowledge in legal principles/practices who supports and assists attorney in practice of law.

advocacy. In some jurisdictions, even limited advocacy may be permitted. While the typical perception of an attorney is someone who is in court all of the time, the reality is quite different. Attorneys have traditionally performed many daily functions that are now also within the parameters of the paralegal's job description. The evolving standards of competence of the paralegal clearly identify a growing place of this paraprofessional within the American legal system.

Many paralegals are still employed to conduct, in addition to true paralegal duties, a degree of work that is clerical in nature. This is waning, however, because of the economic benefits of having a trained paralegal perform paralegal functions. Because the tasks performed by a paralegal are traditionally those performed by attorneys, it has been established that a paralegal's services may be billed to clients. This principle was a major achievement in establishing paralegals as legal professionals in their own right. However, a key element that remains in paralegal functions and billing is that billed paralegal work must be performed under the supervision of a licensed attorney. Nevertheless, the paralegal continues to evolve and gain respect as a valuable member of the team comprising those who contribute to the functioning of the American legal system. Much greater detail is given in subsequent chapters as to the role and opportunities of today's qualified paralegal.

In addition to the paralegal, a number of support personnel have become recognized as integral parts of today's law office or legal department. Each position represents the performance of duties key to the orderly and efficient progression of legal matters. Although the degree of training and education necessary for the positions may vary dramatically, the role played by each is of equal importance. Much like a team on an assembly line, the legal team works together to move a case or law-related matter from inception to conclusion in such a way as to maximize efficiency, produce the best possible result, and adhere to the necessary parameters, such as procedural rules. Following is a brief description of the personnel often found within law offices and legal departments providing necessary support services to attorneys.

CASE

SUPREME COURT OF OHIO.

COLUMBUS BAR ASSOCIATION

V.

PURNELL.

760 N.E.2d 817
(Ohio 2002).

Submitted Sept. 19, 2001.
Decided Jan. 9, 2002.

PER CURIAM
Loc.R. 75.8(A)(2) of the Probate Division of the Common Pleas Court of Franklin County requires that an independent paralegal "shall be registered for each case in which the independent paralegal is performing services," identifying, *inter alia*, a supervising attorney. That attorney must sign the registration, certifying that the independent paralegal is qualified to perform the services and that the supervising attorney will supervise and be responsible for all services of the paralegal.

On September 22, 1999, respondent, Dellwin Purnell, filed an independent paralegal registration in the probate court in connection with the personal injury claim of a minor, Kyle Petersen. The form was not signed by a supervising attorney. On September 24, 1999, respondent filed an "Application to Settle a Minor's Claim" in the probate court, striking the words "attorney" and "attorney's" from the form language "reasonable attorney fee for the attorney's services" and substituting therefor the phrase "reasonable paralegal fee for the services." The application indicated that the fee would be $3,500 and that a fee agreement between respondent and the minor's parent was attached to the application. In a letter to Liberty Mutual Insurance Company, dated October 16, 1998, respondent had indicated that he was engaged to "represent Kyle Petersen in a claim for personal injuries." On January 24, 2000, the probate judge found respondent in contempt for representing himself as a paralegal without a supervising attorney.

On September 13, 2000, relator, Columbus Bar Association, filed a complaint charging respondent with the unauthorized practice of law. Respondent failed to answer, and on December 4, 2000, relator filed a motion for default. The matter was referred to the Board of Commissioners on the Unauthorized Practice of Law ("board"), which granted the motion. The board found the facts as stated and concluded that respondent's conduct constituted rendering legal services for another by a person not admitted to the practice of law in Ohio. The board recommended that respondent be prohibited from engaging in the unauthorized practice of law in the future.

On review of the record, we adopt the findings, conclusion, and recommendation of the board. A paralegal who, without the supervision of an attorney, advises and represents a claimant in a personal injury matter is engaged in the unauthorized practice of law. *Cincinnati Bar Assn. v. Cromwell* (1998), 82 Ohio St.3d 255, 695 N.E.2d 243.

Respondent is hereby enjoined from any further activities that might constitute the unauthorized practice of law. Costs are taxed to respondent.

Judgment accordingly.

MOYER, C.J.,
DOUGLAS,
RESNICK, FRANCIS
E. SWEENEY, SR.,
PFEIFER, COOK
AND LUNDBERG
STRATTON, JJ.,
CONCUR.

Case Review Question

Columbus Bar Assoc. v. Purnell, 94 Ohio St.3d 126, 760 N.E.2d 817 (2002).
Under these circumstances, would the result change if the respondent had filed the case in a different county in Ohio? Why or why not?

Law Office Administrators

A law office administrator manages the day-to-day operations of the law office or legal department as a business entity. Included in a typical administrator's duties are hiring, evaluation, and termination of staff; scheduling; overseeing billing and accounting issues; delegation of work to appropriate personnel; coordination of attorneys and support staff; and supervision of risk management issues such as conflict of interest files, court and deposition schedules, and deadlines.

Support Personnel

Often a law clerk is a law school student or recent graduate awaiting licensure who performs basic functions such as legal research and document/correspondence drafting under the supervision of an attorney. In the court system, law clerks usually assist the judge by performing legal research and providing a synopsis of the results in preparation of written judicial opinions.

Another fast growing field of employment is legal investigation. Originally, legal investigators were most often found in law firms specializing in personal injury. Their primary task was to locate witnesses and evidence in support of the client's case. As the complexity of laws and the basis for lawsuits increase, however, many firms and corporate legal departments now employ legal investigators or contract with legal/private investigation firms. Their primary function is still to collect evidence of all types in support of and opposition to a client's case, to enable the attorney to assess and follow through appropriately on the case.

During the first 75 years of the twentieth century, because of the number of legal publications and regular updates, many larger law firms and corporate legal departments had to employ individuals as law librarians to maintain the constantly growing body of information. The publications had to be maintained in an organized fashion and frequent, sometimes daily, updates had to be incorporated into the existing collection. However, as more and more legal research is performed by computer, the job of the law librarian may change somewhat from manual record keeping to maintaining a current working knowledge of computer programs, updates, and research techniques. The role of the law librarian is still essential in the large firm or corporate legal department to facilitate the work of those performing legal research.

Historically, the clerical staff in a law firm spent most of the workday typing legal documents. That duty is still a fundamental part of the job; however, the traditional role of the legal secretary has expanded to include having exceptional computer skills, the ability to coordinate the schedules of any number of attorneys from various firms for depositions and hearings, and to act as the primary contact person between the attorney and other staff members as well as clients and professionals outside the firm. The legal secretary may see that documents are properly and timely filed with the courts and provide all forms of general clerical support to the attorney, legal investigator, law clerks, and paralegals.

Even with the advent of the computer transference of information, the legal profession still ultimately relies on hard copy of all pertinent information. The legal documents, correspondence, research, memos, notices, and documentary evidence all must be maintained. Even the smallest law firm processes hundreds, perhaps thousands, of pieces of paper. This must be done in a predictably organized manner and kept current as well. For this reason, an integral position within any law firm or legal department is an individual responsible for managing the documents within the files. The person(s) with this responsibility must be extremely organized and attentive to detail. It is also important that this individual and all members of the staff understand the importance of maintaining the confidentiality of all files.

Aside from the practice of law, the ultimate truth is a law firm or legal department is a business that operates on incoming funds. To do this, it is important to track the time spent by the attorneys and other staff members who bill their time on each client's file. This information must then be integrated into the proper accounts and tracked for billing and collection. The billing clerk may also manage incoming and outgoing funds, but in large firms or corporate legal departments, this position may be expanded to a complete accounting department. Smaller firms often coordinate with an independent accountant for monthly accounting statements and tax issues.

One of the most important people in the law firm is the receptionist. Although this person does not have the authority of an attorney or administrator, he or she is often the first and last contact the client has with the law firm. As a result, the attitude, professionalism, and general appearance of the firm may be judged by the presentation of the receptionist. With respect to duties, the receptionist may schedule appointments and screen and route phone calls and appointments with clients and others who come into contact with the firm.

These are a few of the roles necessary to make the legal profession operate in an organized and efficient manner. All work is considered to be done under the ultimate supervision of the attorney, and it is the legal responsibility of the lawyer to see that each person works within the constraints of the ethical standards imposed on all licensed attorneys. As discussed in the chapter, the failure of any staff member to adhere to appropriate ethical standards can result in liability of the attorney. The absence of any of these individuals also can cause the most organized law firm to falter and even allow for mistakes that might ultimately result in liability for malpractice. Unlike many businesses, the law firm depends on support staff not only for daily operations but also for the future viability of the practice.

Assignment 5.1

> Prepare a diagram to show the placement of each of the positions in a law office structure.

Quasi Legal Professionals

In recent years, as technology and business have developed rapidly, so has the reality that other licensed professionals engage in practices that might be considered as practice's of law. For example, a certified professional accountant (CPA) might advise a client on tax matters involving federal, state, and local tax laws. A licensed real estate agent or broker might advise a client about certain laws or regulations relevant to a transfer of property. Thus far, the courts have by and large dealt with such situations on a case-by-case basis. They examine the law involved, the other subject area affected (such as accounting or property), the expectations of the party receiving information, and the extent of the advice given by the professional. Typically, if the conduct of the professional was well within the accepted industry standards of that profession and did not unreasonably affect the legal rights of the individual, a very limited ability to practice law is inferred from the professional license of the individual.

THE NEW LEGAL PROFESSIONAL—PARALEGAL

In this chapter we have briefly mentioned the position of paralegal within the law office structure. The entrance of the paralegal as a recognized member of the legal team has been a significant development in the history of the legal profession. Further explanation will be given in the discussion that follows to examine how the position evolved and what changes it has brought to the way law is practiced in the American legal system.

The Paralegal as a Member of the Legal Team

The most commonly known setting for the paralegal is perhaps the law office, where the paralegal works primarily as an extension of the licensed attorney. The paralegal may assist or even perform many functions independently, albeit ultimately under the supervision of the attorney. These include interviewing clients and witnesses, scheduling various meetings such as depositions, preparing basic legal documents, and doing legal research and writing. In many offices, especially smaller firms with more limited budgets, the paralegal sometimes also serves in a quasi clerical role. However, this is not usually the most efficient use of the paralegal's time, skills, or the attorney's resources.

The areas where the paralegal may be employed are virtually limitless. The position is recognized in the federal government and in most states. Paralegals work in numerous places, from the offices of the legislature to administrative agencies. Many are employed by the courts to assist judges, clerks of court, and other court officers. Administrative agencies make particularly extensive use of paralegals, because much of the work performed requires basic legal knowledge but not the advocacy and analytical skills of a licensed attorney. Throughout the various levels of government, the paralegal has come to be viewed as a valuable member of staff who carries out the objectives of the legal system. In the past, these roles were largely filled by attorneys, but the training and experience of a qualified paralegal is equally suitable for these positions in the majority of instances. More often than not, the team of attorneys has been replaced with a team of paralegals under the supervision of one or more attorneys.

Examples of paralegals as part of the team in a government office include administrative agencies, courts, legislatures, and any other subbranch that is involved in the creation or enforcement of legal standards. Paralegals in administrative agencies may be used to research or write rules and regulations, prepare cases for litigation, and review applications for agency action. Most of this work can be done by a highly qualified paralegal. The attorney supervises the work, is ultimately responsible for it, and completes any elements of the work that include the actual practice of law. Paralegals in the courts can work on file preparations in the office of the court clerk, assisting judges with research and preparation of orders and opinions, as well as maintaining records and files. Paralegals can be extremely useful to members of state and federal legislatures with the research and organization of legislative materials, and even drafting of legislation.

This increasing use of paralegals in what were traditionally attorney roles has not been lost on corporate America. In the past decade, as companies fought to stay current with ever-changing legal standards while keeping costs from escalating, many former corporate attorneys were replaced with paralegals. The logic is much the same as that used by the government. Much of what is accomplished on a daily basis in a corporate legal department does not require extensive legal analysis or advocacy. Corporate paralegals (under the supervision of an attorney) can prepare documents and correspondence, investigate legal issues, and perform legal research. By hiring an individual who has comparable skills in most of the necessary areas but does not have the expertise required for the practice of law, the corporate employer reaps a significant savings in overhead. This translates to the ability to hire more people for less money and thereby increases efficiency while controlling rising overhead costs.

A myriad of opportunities exist for employment of paralegals beyond the law office, government, and large corporations. Virtually every industry in existence encounters legal issues on a daily basis. Manufacturers must comply with environmental and labor regulations; service industries ranging from health care to real estate risk liability for failure to properly follow all the requirements of their profession; banks deal with various legal documents in the form of loans, trusts, and so forth every day; and all entities who have subordinate employees must adhere to applicable labor laws and regulations. As the complexity of the legal system and American society increases, so does the need for individuals who can assist in coping with the interaction of law and society.

Assignment 5.2

Identify five specific types of businesses where a paralegal might be employed and the type of work this person might perform for each business.

Development of the Paralegal Profession

The term *paralegal* or *legal assistant* is now firmly entrenched in the vocabulary of the legal profession. Similarly, the general public seems to have a basic awareness of the existence of paralegals, although, as recently as the early 1980s, the profession was still largely unknown to the public, and their role and function in today's American legal system was often misunderstood. Today, while great strides have been made, it is still common to find paralegals whose skills are underutilized. As understanding increases with demand for competent legal services at a reasonable cost, this should improve.

Various changes in American culture during the twentieth century, specifically after 1929, caused a domino effect that kept a steady and astounding pressure on technological development for the remainder of the century and beyond. During the economic depression of the 1930s, the nation was forced to restructure business, banking, employment, and commercial activities. Throughout the 1930s, as the country attempted to recover, the workforce was largely reorganized into areas of mass employment. This was facilitated by the technological development of the business of manufacturing. As more people went to work in large-scale business, many moved away from the more isolated and traditional mom-and-pop operations and farming. Simultaneous with the increase of people in the industrial workforce was the almost explosive dramatic development of the transportation industry. New and improved engines increased the speed, availability, and efficiency of rail and river carriers; the new federal interstate system enabled over-the-road trucking on a wide scale; the advent of air transportation totally changed the speed of movement of goods and widened the scope of potential customers for businesses nationwide.

On the heels of the depression came World War II. A whole new element entered the workforce in mass. As young healthy men went to war, they were replaced in the factories with women, who had almost exclusively worked in the home for all of civilized history. The demand for military supplies and equipment on an immediate and large-scale basis taxed the existing system and required constant development and innovation. Throughout the war, those left behind developed American business and technology and gained a new sense of their ability to contribute their talents outside the home. At the end of the war, the country was optimistic and businesses flourished with new and advancing technology. The predictable increase in population after the war also caused a chain reaction increase in demand for all aspects of a capital-based society. Consequently, the demand for legal services increased dramatically in areas ranging from assistance with the purchase and transfer of real estate, to an increase in representation regarding business contracts, to estate planning, and, as traditional family roles began to change, to an increased demand for legal representation in domestic relations law. These developments in such a relatively short time required more legal expertise than the profession had to give. An additional factor was the need for efficiency and the ability to offer legal services at a cost the general population could afford. By the 1960s, it was dramatically evident that a better way to deliver the services of the legal profession had to be found.

Many other professions found themselves in a similar situation and created paraprofessional positions. This was especially evident with health care providers as physician assistant, nurse practitioner, dental hygienist, and dental assistant educational programs were developed and flourished. The creation of the role of a paraprofessional seemed to be the perfect answer. Paraprofessionals were not intended to be as extensively trained, but they could deliver a number of the less technical and sophisticated services that were previously the responsibility of licensed professionals. Appropriate supervision could be used to ensure the quality of service and contain the scope of service to the appropriate levels.

For the attorney, this paraprofessional role came about in an almost incidental way. The role of paralegal was the natural evolution that merely became more focused and accelerated by the demands on the legal profession. For many years, the legal secretary had performed nonclerical roles to some extent. When clients called or came in and the attorney was not available, it was the legal secretary who answered basic questions about scheduled hearings, status of documents filed with the courts, and so on. While it was never permissible for the legal secretary to give legal advice or advocate the client's interests with third parties, the rules of conduct were much cloudier for other tasks that were formerly the exclusive domain of the lawyer. As the demand for legal services grew, the need for assistance in routine but time-consuming tasks grew as well: interviewing clients and witnesses, preparing documents, gathering information, organizing collected evidence, and even carrying out basic research assignments. As demands grew, secretaries who had the confidence of their attorney employers were delegated tasks in addition to the basic clerical role of their employment. This had already been in place to some extent, but it became a more formal arrangement for many attorneys in the 1960s. As many legal secretaries began to demonstrate an aptitude for this type of work, attorneys similarly identified the potential value. Additionally, while an attorney could not legally charge for legal services performed by a clerical person, it was conceivable that such services performed by a trained paraprofessional were billable at a rate commensurate with the level of training.

As the use of legal paraprofessionals spread, a number of developments began to occur. The dramatic increase in firms and businesses who employed paralegals demonstrated a broad consensus that there was a valuable role to be served by them within the legal system. The value was both monetary and a support to the profession of attorneys. In terms of serving the public, the concept was popular. The paralegal made the services of the legal profession more accessible and the cost more reasonable. In the relatively short time of approximately 30 years, an entirely new profession developed that came to be widely known as paralegal or legal assistant. Today, the U.S. Bureau of Labor Statistics recognizes paralegal as one of the fastest growing professional opportunities.

 **APPLICATION 5.1**

Joseph is a recent law school graduate who has started his own law practice. Currently, the business is thriving. He has more than 200 clients. However, his time at work seems to be increasing exponentially. In an average week he spends 15 to 20 hours in court plus an additional 2 hours of travel time. He has office hours to meet new clients scheduled 5 hours each week and typically they are full. He spends approximately 1.5 hours each day going through mail and dictating responses. He spends about 1 hour a day keeping up on new cases, legislation, and administrative law changes that might affect his clientele. He spends about 1 hour per week going over billing and calculating payroll for his secretary and receptionist. He spends 2 hours per day meeting with current clients to review their cases, answer requests from the opposition, and prepare for upcoming hearings. He spends about 1.5 hours each day drafting documents for pending cases, and 1 hour a day returning phone calls to clients who have questions about their cases. Currently his work week is averaging more than 60 hours. Although Joseph does not have enough work to justify the added expense of a partner or associate, his practice continues to grow and so does the commitment of time. Joseph examines his schedule and determines that a qualified paralegal could assist him in the following ways:

1. Review changes in the law and prepare summaries of anything that affects the type of cases he handles—5 hours.
2. Draft approximately 50 percent of the legal documents, possibly more—5 hours.
3. Meet with clients to obtain information and review their cases, and in some cases prepare for hearings—7 hours.
4. Review billing and payroll—1 hour.
5. Take over the information collection portion of new client meetings—3 hours.
6. Prepare return correspondence for 75 percent of the mail received—4 hours.
7. Handle 75 percent of client calls—4 hours.

It is apparent that almost immediately a qualified part-time paralegal could cut Joseph's schedule in half. This would enable him to continue to expand the practice and focus his energy on the types of things for which he was specifically trained. As the practice grows, there is room for the paralegal to increase his or her duties by another 25 percent.

Point for Discussion
◆   Why shouldn't Joseph simply hire another attorney?

Current Defining Standards of Competence

By the 1970s, a number of educational programs were appearing around the United States with the specific objective of providing training for paralegals. Initially, many of these programs were intensified courses of study ranging from several months to a year or so in duration. By the early 1980s, there were accredited academic degree programs throughout the United States. Today there are any number of alternatives to train paralegals. The original method of the on-the-job training is still applied in many communities; however, the trend has been to rely on more formal methods. The intensive and accelerated courses are still considered a successful means to train an entry level position for paralegals, but typically these courses of study are confined to the exclusive field of paralegal training and do not offer other support areas such as English or math that might be useful in a higher level position. Therefore, paralegals should strive to have adequate skills in these areas before undertaking such a program if future opportunities are to be optimized. There are also many associate and baccalaureate degrees, postbaccalaureate certificates, and even master's degrees available at colleges and universities throughout the United States that focus on paralegal and law office administration. These programs are geared toward a more comprehensive college education with focus in paralegal and related skills. In the United States, hundreds of training and education programs for paralegals are in place. It is also not uncommon to find individuals who have trained in other fields, or even former lawyers serving in the role of paralegal. The type and extent of training one pursues depends in large part on the background of the paralegal, the kind of support the paralegal wishes to provide in the workplace, and the setting in which the paralegal seeks employment and advancement.

While the methods and extent of paralegal training and education vary widely, some standards have been established to assist attorneys, paralegals, and the public in developing reasonable expectations of what job skills the qualified paralegal should possess. In reality, a number of factors influenced the need for an established set of standards and, while the standards and tools of measurement are still evolving, there are now widely accepted criteria for a qualified paralegal. Still no universally accepted, standardized method of validation exists, and without such standards virtually anyone can be a self-proclaimed paralegal. Thus, the responsibility is on the one who hires a paralegal to fully investigate the true nature and level of education and acquired skill. The strategies used to establish competence vary as widely as the methods of training—from attempts for uniform standards of competence to legal liability for damage caused by malfeasance. It should be noted that many jurisdictions do provide some sort of definition of the term *paralegal* either in statute, court rules, or case law; however, this varies by state and in some instances is considered on a case-by-case basis.

One natural method of regulation is the extension of the rules used to protect the public from incompetence and/or malfeasance by attorneys, called tort liability. The subject of tort law will be expanded upon in a later chapter. It is important to understand at this juncture that the law provides a remedy for those injured in some way by the unacceptable acts or omissions by their attorney. Rules of ethics, standards for licensure as an attorney, and well-established legal principles handed down by the courts present a clear picture of what is expected of attorneys with regard to level of skill in the various areas of law and in meeting the duty to serve their clients.

When an attorney accepts an individual as a client, this creates an obligation to represent that client within the requirements of accepted legal standards of conduct and competence. If the attorney fails to meet any of those standards, a violation of the duty toward the client occurs. If that violation is the primary cause of injury to the client, then the attorney may be held liable for the value associated with the injury. In the event a subordinate of the attorney, such as a paralegal, is actually responsible for the violation, as the employer, the attorney may still be held accountable under the theory that he or she did not properly supervise the work of the employee. For example, an attorney has an obligation to keep information provided by a client confidential. This responsibility extends to those employed by the attorney as well. The employee may also be held personally liable for any damage caused. This is true of a paralegal working under the direction of an attorney. If a paralegal is independently employed or employed on a per job basis by an attorney, such as one employed on a freelance basis, the liability could be directly assigned to the paralegal. In either situation, realistically speaking, the ultimate responsibility for performing work in a competent manner ends with the paralegal. Even if liability is assigned to the supervising attorney, the future career for the paralegal is not too promising if he or she is the ultimate cause of that liability. While the theory is that the attorney is to supervise, the reality is that even the most conscientious attorney cannot be omnipotent with regard to everything a paralegal does and says. There has to be an earned degree of trust between the attorney and the paralegal. That trust must include the paralegal's skills as well as knowledge of the limits between assisting an attorney and the actual practice of law.

Generally speaking, the paralegal cannot give legal advice or advocate the legal rights of a client with respect to third parties. These two tasks require a licensed attorney. This is important because legal advice and advocacy can cause a client or third party to act or not act in a way that directly impacts the rights of the client. Therefore, only a licensed attorney, that is, one who has demonstrated comprehensive proficiency at understanding the law and its applicability to given situations, may perform these duties. There is an exception to this rule in that some regulatory agencies permit nonattorneys to represent individuals in agency matters; however, this is very limited in scope and in the number of agencies that permit it. In the event a paralegal, or anyone else, undertakes to engage in the practice of law, such as by advocating the rights of another or giving legal advice, then two possibilities arise. First, the individual may be prosecuted by the government for practicing law without a license. Second, the individual may be sued for any damage caused by the attempted practice of law. In most jurisdictions, the requirement is that the individual must have acted as a competent attorney would have under the same circumstances. The failure to do so would then result in civil liability. In essence, if one performs the practice of law, he or she is held accountable to possess and exercise the skills of a licensed attorney. Because the line drawn between professional services and those that constitute the unauthorized practice of law is not always clearly discernible, it is advisable to use great caution when approaching it.

APPLICATION 5.2

Kishara is a paralegal working under the supervision of a new attorney at a large firm. During a trial, they decide to have a working lunch and go to a local restaurant near the courthouse. Unknown to them, a woman in the potential jurors pool is sitting at the next table. She overhears them while they discuss the case. Later that day she is selected for the jury. When it comes time for deliberations at the end of the trial, she uses the information she obtained eavesdropping and ultimately affects the outcome of the case. Kishara, as an experienced paralegal, knew she should not be discussing case specifics in such a public place. However, the attorney who is her supervisor initiated and basically dominated the conversation. The conversation of case specifics about a client in public is a clear breach of the obligation to keep matters confidential. Ultimately the truth comes out from juror interviews, and the attorney and Kishara are sued.

Point for Discussion

◆   What could Kishara have done to prevent the situation?

The obvious problem with tort liability as a sole means of policing the quality and delivery of services by the paralegal is that control is put in place after the harm is done. As a result, while tort liability can be an effective method of compensating the victims of incompetence and misconduct, it does nothing proactively to prevent these behaviors. Thus, early on in the profession of paralegal, the need was clear for some method by which attorneys and the public could identify competent and responsible paralegals.

One method used throughout the United States is approval of paralegal programs by the American Bar Association (ABA). Because attorneys are ultimately liable for the work and conduct of the paralegals they employ, the legal profession has a strong interest in creating standards by which paralegals are trained and educated. Consequently, an arm of the ABA was delegated the task of defining standards of education and applying them to the various types of formal paralegal training programs. This group also monitors adherence to the standards by those programs. ABA approval is a voluntary process and not required for any program of education. Programs may also have other types of approval by organizations that survey and rate or approve various types of educational programs and institutions at the postsecondary level. Currently, fewer than one-half of the existing paralegal programs have ABA approval, although such approval is highly regarded by the legal profession. Approval by the ABA is a rigorous process and once achieved is subject to regular review. Programs must demonstrate comprehensive training by qualified instructors. They must show an established program with definite goals, methods of achievement, and accurate measurement of student progress. The program directors are required to stay abreast of developments in the profession and to incorporate them into the programs when appropriate. Other organizations provide similar credentialization or endorsement of qualified education and training programs. Such approvals offer the legal profession and the aspiring paralegal objective standards by which to measure the quality of education and level of skill to be expected from individuals graduating from these programs.

The types of subject matter addressed in approved paralegal training/educational programs are those in which the paralegal can expect to be called upon in a supportive role to the attorney. This includes a clear understanding of the American legal system, and its function and form. There is also an expectation of practical knowledge and skills. The ideal paralegal is able to perform all tasks formerly and currently done by attorneys that do not include elements exclusive to the practice of law. The various supportive tasks in which a qualified paralegal should be trained include legal writing, basic legal research, drafting documents, interviewing clients and witnesses, investigative techniques, and any other routine matters that arise within the procession of a case. Figure 5.1 depicts duties traditionally performed by the attorney that a qualified paralegal can do understate within the scope of the profession. Note the variation in the standards and limits from jurisdiction to jurisdiction and that in some states the paralegal is permitted an even more active role.

Many practices today specialize by confining their practice to particular topics of law such as real property, estate planning, or tort law (personal injury). A great deal of overlap occurs, though, and the qualified paralegal needs at least an introductory knowledge of most basic subjects of law, including a command of relevant terminology, current legal principles, common procedures, and relevant forms and documents. The paralegal is then in a position to appreciate the potential impact of certain occurrences within a case, rather than being limited to a knowledge of how to complete a form and file it with the appropriate court/agency. A fundamental concept supporting paralegal training/education and the profession as a whole is that to provide a valuable system of support, the paralegal should have the ability to not only perform routine tasks, but also to understand the underlying reasons for them and to know when the various tasks are appropriate and why.

In addition to the tort (retroactive) and educational (proactive) forms of monitoring the quality of skill and service delivered by paralegals, methods have also developed by which practicing paralegals can measure their ability and achieve a level of acceptance within their profession. As the profession

FIGURE 5.1

Comparison of Duties of Attorneys and Paralegals*

DUTY/SKILL	Attorney	Paralegal
Legal advice and representation (client contract, settlement negotiation, depositions, trial, and all situations involving advisement or advocacy)	X	
Client interview and subsequent meetings	X	X
Legal research	X	X
Draft pleadings/motions	X	X
Obtain evidence	X	X
Interview witnesses	X	X
Draft demand letters and settlement documents	X	X
Select and prepare jury instructions	X	X
Abstract depositions	X	X
Trial notebook and general case management	X	X
Draft contracts and corporate documents	X	X

*With proper attorney supervision, the qualified paralegal can perform all of the functions indicated in the table and all other tasks required in the law office that do not involve legal advice or advocacy. Some paralegals also make excellent law office administrators, especially helpful in firms that do not employ a full-time administrator.

has evolved, paralegal organizations have developed as well, such as the National Association of Legal Assistants (NALA), one of the oldest formalized bodies that supports the paralegal profession. In addition to the local chapters throughout the United States that offer support, continuing education, and communication for paralegals, NALA offers a rigorous and respected examination to test one's paralegal skills. To be eligible for the exam, the candidate must demonstrate a background that would establish a basic knowledge of paralegal skills. These skills are then measured by the examination, and the successful candidate receives a certificate from NALA that allows the use of the designation certified legal assistant (CLA). Throughout the United States, the exam and certificate are considered authentication by many attorneys with respect to a paralegal's level of skill. The organization and certification are purely voluntary, however, and only a small percentage of the paralegals in the United States have achieved this level. There is a distinction to be made between a person with the CLA designation and one who has received a certificate of completion from a paralegal education or training program. While both are indicative of a certain level of demonstrated skill, they are by no means interchangeable titles. Several national, state, and local organizations exist with similar functions related to the promotion of professional standards of competence and acceptance for paralegals. See Relevant Links at the end of the chapter for a partial list of national organizations and their websites.

Another support organization is the National Federation of Paralegal Associations (NFPA). An original objective of NFPA, formed in 1974, was to bring together various local paralegal organizations and form a cohesive group with a collective ability to advance the paralegal career and professional standards on a national level. The organization has as members more than 60 paralegal organizations throughout the United States and more than 17,500 individual members. In 1994, the organization elected to create a comprehensive exam to validate the skills of paralegals. NFPA recommends a four-year degree, with a minimum two-year degree. The Paralegal Advanced Competency Examination (PACE) is available to paralegals with the title registered paralegal (RP). Like NALA, the NFPA organization enjoys a positive reputation in the legal community, and one who has passed the rigorous standards to achieve the title of registered paralegal is considered to have proven skills as a legal professional.

Through the years, many states have sought to establish guidelines and standards for paralegal skills, but as yet no comprehensive legislation is in place to test, regulate, and monitor this profession. However, as most service professions have developed during the last century, the government has identified a strong public interest in regulating such professions to protect an unwitting public from those who would act with less than a necessary degree of competence or integrity. Some states have enacted or modified legislation with respect to the definition of the unauthorized practice of law and placed limitations on law-related services by nonlawyers such as the preparation and sale of generic legal documents including kits to prepare wills and noncontested divorces. There is no comprehensive legislation at this stage, however, to address licensure or regulation of paralegals. In this respect the profession is still quite young. Thus, it is highly unlikely that the paralegals will see a great deal of legislation concerning the profession in the near future.

Issues that have arisen with regard to government regulation are serious. Paralegals and attorneys alike recognize the need for some sort of standard by which to measure and monitor paralegal skills and abilities. The problem lies in the wide array of backgrounds that exist in the profession. Universally, an attorney is required to meet minimum educational requirements and demonstrate a basic level of knowledge, but there are no such uniform standards for paralegals. In addition to those formally educated are thousands of job-trained paralegals and numerous laterally trained paralegals. These are individuals who entered the profession because of their technical knowledge and skill in another field. For example, a medical professional such as a nurse or an engineer can be of invaluable assistance to an attorney involved in complex litigation concerning those subject areas. The legal knowledge of such persons may be limited or nonexistent, yet, along with formally educated, degreed paralegals, they are within the same field of employment. The task of creating a system to evaluate skills relevant to the particular employment of such a wide array of professionals has led to great difficulty for governing bodies. Because of the need for regulation that is clearly identified and is generally seen to outweigh the obstacles, it can likely be expected to further develop in the coming years.

Ethical Considerations

The ethics of the legal profession are closely monitored by the media and the public in general. Although other professions have ethical duties, the legal profession is somewhat unique. Most other professionals have a duty with regard to their relationship to the client. The legal profession has this duty as well, but it extends to the representation of that client with third parties, the courts, and other elements of the government. The legal profession is the only one in which the failure to perform the duties undertaken could result in something as serious as the loss of liberty and even the death penalty. While the results in most circumstances are certainly much less serious, the degree of responsibility is not.

Ethical Circumstance

Gerry was shot by police during a robbery of a convenience store. His injuries were life threatening but he received competent medical care and survived. It is the policy of the hospital that information about the actions of anyone brought in under suspicion of criminal conduct be withheld as much as possible from medical personnel until after treatment is provided. This allows the medical staff to offer the best services without influence or emotion about what the individual may or may not have done prior to the injuries. Gerry was charged with robbery and the murder of the store clerk and two children that had interrupted the robbery when they came in to purchase candy. The children attempted to run, but Gerry shot them in the parking lot to prevent them from identifying him. A local attorney has been appointed to represent Gerry. The attorney and her paralegal are both parents of children the approximate ages of the children who were murdered. The attorney and consequently the paralegal have an ethical duty to represent and defend Gerry to the very best of their ability. Should the attorney ask to be removed from the case?

CHAPTER SUMMARY

The legal profession is one of the oldest on record. For thousands of years it remained relatively unchanged. During the twentieth century, however, it underwent a dramatic transformation that reflected similar societal and technological advances. Today the American legal system offers hundreds of different roles for those with legal background and training. Additionally, the legal profession has streamed into many other aspects of the economy. As a result, legal professionals can be found in an infinite number of settings offering support and insight with regard to the structure and function of all branches of government.

Perhaps the most significant development in the legal profession in recent history has been the advent of the paralegal. This individual bridged a wide gap between availability of basic legal services for individuals and much needed technical support for attorneys. The paralegal started as a job-trained, highly functioning clerical position. It has grown to one that often involves extensive formal education and duties once considered the exclusive domain of attorneys. The development, however, has happened so rapidly that standards are still lacking to protect the integrity of the profession and to define clear guidelines of competence.

CHAPTER TERMS

jurist (judge)   lawyer/attorney   paralegal (legal assistant)

REVIEW QUESTIONS

1. What is the difference between an administrative law judge and an appellate judge?
2. What two skills distinguish a licensed attorney?
3. What is the difference between a certified legal assistant and a registered paralegal?
4. When can someone without a license practice law?
5. Identify five distinct types of settings in which paralegals may be found.
6. How is the function of a qualified paralegal different from that of a legal secretary?
7. What is the role of the law office administrator?
8. Identify and describe two other roles in the law practice other than attorney, paralegal, legal secretary, and law office administrator.

RELEVANT LINKS

West Legal Studies
www.westlegalstudies.com
National Association of Legal Assistants (NALA)
www.nala.org
National Federation of Paralegal Associations
(NFPA)
www.paralegals.org

American Association for Paralegal Education
www.aafpe.org
American Bar Association Standing Committee/
Legal Assist.
www.abanet.org/legalassts/home.html
Legal Assistant Management Association
www.lamanet.org

INTERNET ASSIGNMENT 5.1

Using one of the resources listed above, identify
a paralegal organization in your state.

*For additional resources, please visit our Web site at
www.westlegalstudies.com*

CHAPTER 6

The Law of Ethics

CHAPTER OBJECTIVES

After reading this chapter, you should be able to:

- Explain the role of ethical standards in the American legal system.

- Discuss the attitude of the legal profession toward ethical standards.

- Describe the ethical standards applicable to various components of the legal profession.

- Distinguish between ethical canons and ethical standards.

- Explain the rationale for holding attorneys accountable for the ethical conduct of subordinates.

- Discuss major ethical requirements that are universal to all legal professionals.

HOW LAW AND ETHICS INTERRELATE

In the preceding chapters, the ethical considerations introduce the concept of law and ethics. The concept is not a new one. Throughout history, individuals with economic or governmental power are subject to the trust of those dependent upon the wise exercise of such power; and when such individuals violated that trust, the ultimate consequences have been severe. Greed, selfishness, and insensitivity to the basic needs of others have toppled many governments. Today, such scenarios still play out in some nations around the globe. In the United States, fortunately, the importance of the trust placed in those with a unique position of power to assist others is recognized and protected. Ethical considerations are not confined solely to the legal professions. Most professions that require a state authorized license will carry with that license a certain degree of duty to act responsibly with respect to the power given in association with the license. This applies to plumbers and electricians who have a legal obligation to perform their duties in accordance with approved codes and regulations. It applies to accountants, lawyers, and physicians who have the legal obligation to perform their duties within established standards and to the best of their abilities. In addition, certain professions have increased responsibilities to act with a so-called *professional responsibility*. This duty carries with it the obligation to act in what the majority would consider a morally appropriate manner—a manner that is appropriate to the high level of trust and the great personal gain or loss associated with that trust by the individual.

Legal Ethics and Their Impact on Professionals

Legal professionals are quite aware of their responsibility to the public and its seriousness. They know that individuals often place personal legal rights, and possibly a tremendous impact on one's future, entirely into their hands. This relationship of trust is a significant one. In some cases, the result has minimal effects; in others, it can mean the difference between prosperity and bankruptcy, freedom and prison, even the right to a relationship with one's own children. Often, for the client, the personal stakes in a legal dispute are high. In an increasingly complicated legal system, with a plethora of legal standards, a virtual litigation explosion, and constantly changing technology, legal professionals have an overwhelming task to effectively represent the best interests of their clients. Rules of ethics help to ensure that this responsibility is met to the very best of the ability of the legal professional and subject to minimum standards of competence and integrity.

Legal professionals are typically assertive by nature. This is a minimum requirement for success when acting as an advocate for others. Yet, while the objective of the legal professional is to provide the best possible representation for the client, the professional must also be constantly aware of the demanding ethical considerations. The obligation to act in what society would consider a morally correct manner may well affect the method in which representation is given to clients. Certain conduct is strictly prohibited. Other things may be discouraged or, alternately, demanded as part of what would be considered ethical representation. Thus, certain rules have nothing to do with the representation itself, but significantly impact how that representation is delivered.

Established legal ethical standards have a tremendous effect on the legal profession and the public as a whole. Without such standards, legal professionals would have no guideposts for those questionable situations that arise in the ordinary course of business. Because each person brings a unique culmination of experience and values to a situation, today's society is far too complex to expect that a uniform and very narrow standard of conduct would develop if the entire system were to operate on an honor system. Even in the early development of legal standards in the United States, it became apparent that there were far too many possible interpretations of appropriate behavior, and the need for formally established rules began. In a society like that of today, with such a mix of culture and background, it is not surprising that similar results are necessary for an accepted code of conduct.

Ethical Standards

Essentially, ethical standards are accepted rules that form the framework of the **fiduciary** (trust-based) relationship between the legal professional and client. Historically these formalized rules were created for lawyers, but today's paralegal associations have adopted similar rules that correspond to the duties of the paralegal with respect to the client and the supervising attorney.

fiduciary
One who is in a position of trust by another with respect to rights, person, and/or property.

The lawyer–client relationship is entirely based on trust. The client places in the lawyer and support staff trust in ability, trust in commitment to competently perform the required duties, and trust to act in the best interest of the client to the exclusion of all others. Consider the following definitions:

Ethics—Principles, moral principles, code of conduct, right and wrong, values, conscience, moral philosophy, mores, criteria.
Ethical—Legitimate, proper, aboveboard, correct, unimpeachable, principled, honorable, decent, upright, respectable.

As can be seen from these definitions, the foundation for legal ethics is quite similar to the general interpretation of ethical behavior. The American legal system, and society in general, places a high value on behavior that is considered moral, truthful, and concerned about its effects on others. The legal professional's ethical obligations have the same underlying theme; however, for the legal professional, certain acts with respect to the client have been specifically identified and a definition has been given to what actually constitutes ethical behavior. By doing this, when a situation occurs that may be somewhat questionable in terms of the legal professional's ethical duty, the stated ethical rules can provide guidance.

APPLICATION 6.1

Jason is a paralegal working at a small firm in a relatively small community. He is assigned the duty of preparing documents for a custody battle. His firm represents a young woman who is the mother of a two-year-old girl. He knows the father of the child personally, although not well. He is aware that the father of the child is alcoholic and lives with an older woman. Jason is aware of rumors that the mother of the child has a substance abuse problem and is unfit to raise her daughter. Jason has seen some behavior by the mother that would support this. The father has now filed for custody. Jason also is aware that the woman with whom the father lives is the primary caretaker of the child during the father's visitations. This woman is respected in the community, a successful business owner, and in Jason's opinion, by far the superior choice of who can best care for the child. However, Jason is in the position of assisting preparation of a case against the father and the woman, and defending the mother, about whom he has serious concerns. He does not want to accept the assignment. In a town this size, he knows he will receive many assignments throughout his career in which he will have some personal knowledge and opinions about the parties.

Point for Discussion

♦ Would the ethical issues be significantly different if Jason were the attorney?

As illustrated in the example, knowing the right thing to do is not always clear. In the application, the paralegal must consider a number of factors, including the obligation to a client of the firm, how much personal knowledge he or she has about the parties, and what the ramifications could be if he refused to accept an assignment from his superiors. Often ethical questions fall into a gray area and require close examination and a logical resolution. This can be difficult, because ethical standards inherently have an emotional quality. One's sense of right and wrong is based on personal beliefs rather than knowledge of facts. It is not a mathematical or scientific equation that can be answered with absolute certainty. Rather, it is a qualitative problem that must be transferred somehow into a quantitative sum. This requires a careful balance of all known facts and a disregard of any information that is based in pure emotion.

Assignment 6.1

Consider the following situation and explain whether there appears to be an ethical issue for the legal professional involved.

Percy and Scarlett decide to divorce after nine years of marriage. They have one child. It is an amicable split and Scarlett offers to hire an attorney to handle the matter. Because they have agreed on financial and custody/visitation issues, neither party sees the need for a second attorney to represent Percy. Scarlett's attorney asks Percy to sign a form acknowledging that the legal representation is of Scarlett and not Percy. The parties agree that Scarlett will take possession of the house and all equity in it as she will be responsible for primary custody of their child. Percy will accept responsibility for the three major credit cards of the parties. It is unspecified in the final order, but to the knowledge of everyone involved, the credit cards have a collective balance at the end of the preceding month of $1,250, and the equity in the house is about $30,000 with a balance on the mortgage of about $60,000. Ordinarily the parties would share the debt and Percy would be entitled to a significant portion of the value of the house, but he is willing to give this up voluntarily. He claims this is best for the welfare of the child and to reduce the financial strain on Scarlett. Just before the final hearing in which the divorce and its terms will become final, Scarlett proudly confides in her attorney that she has been secretly involved in a long-standing affair with another man, and that with him, she has carried out a plan diverting funds from other accounts and taking $15,000 in cash advances on the credit cards during the past two weeks, all without Percy's knowledge to increase the equity in the house to $60,000. Once the divorce is final, Percy will be left with virtually all the debt of the parties and she will walk away with most of the accumulated wealth.

Ethical Canons and Rules

Initially, rules of ethical conduct were established only for attorneys. Today, similar types of rules have been established for other legal professionals, including members of the judiciary and paralegals. Becoming a member of a certain component of a law-related profession, such as a licensed attorney, involves an underlying acceptance to be bound by the formal requirements established for ethical conduct that protect the integrity of the profession and the interests of those who are served by the profession. Failure to honor these rules can result in a variety of consequences from a formal statement of reprimand to revocation of licensure. For attorneys, the root of ethical considerations is in the form of rules promulgated by the American Bar Association (ABA). Most jurisdictions have adopted these or similar standards as conditions of licensure for attorneys. The ethical standards for attorneys consist of canons, or traits, that all attorneys should aspire to include in their work when serving clients. These are more or less the qualities of the consummate legal professional with the highest degree of integrity. Disciplinary rules are those basic requirements of conduct that, when violated, can result in formal discipline as well as civil actions for damages by parties injured as a result of the conduct. Consequently, the conduct of all legal professionals should fall within a range between the minimum requirements of the disciplinary standards and the ultimate goals of the canons. The professional career of a licensed attorney should reflect a constant compliance with disciplinary rules and evidence of a continuing effort to exemplify the ethical canons. The appendices of this textbook contain a more complete publication of common standards, although a few of those more relevant to the everyday function of lawyers and paralegals will be addressed within the context of this chapter.

◆ APPLICATION 6.2

Georgea has been employed as a legal secretary at the same law firm for 10 years. Recently, the firm accepted a case defending a man who has been charged with embezzlement. The man worked in the accounting office at a used car lot. The man is adamant to the police and his attorney that he is innocent and never took anything from the dealership where he was employed. Coincidentally, the teenage son of the man is the best friend of Georgea's son. When the man was arrested, Georgea's son informed her that his friend told him he knew his father was guilty because he had seen evidence of changed paperwork on car sales that his father kept at home. The paperwork indicated that the man was altering the numbers on car sales and pocketing the difference.

Point for Discussion
◆   Should Georgea report the information to the attorney? Should she report it to the authorities?

Four of the most common issues for attorneys and paralegals, as well as support staff, are those involving competency, confidentiality, conflict of interest, and commitment to zealous representation. Each of these is of extreme importance and has served as the basis for many lawsuits when lawyers or their staff have failed to meet the required standards. There are other standards as well, but these four affect virtually every type of legal professional and every client relationship. Each supports part of the fiduciary relationship between attorney and client that is so protected in the American legal system.

Competency.

Rule 1.1: A lawyer shall provide competent representation to the client. Competent representation requires the legal knowledge, skill, thoroughness and preparation reasonably necessary for the representation. (ABA Model Rules of Professional Conduct of 2002)

The question of **competence** is more involved than one might first surmise. Every lawyer who is licensed today must pass an examination that tests basic knowledge of legal principles. However, this does not ensure that the attorney will keep abreast of changes in the law and always apply that knowledge in client representation. That is an ethical responsibility placed on the attorney as part of the privilege of the license. Many jurisdictions have continuing education requirements to assist in this objective, but this is by no means a guarantee that competence will be exercised in every situation.

To act competently, an attorney should meet one of three basic requirements: He or she must (1) possess an adequate and current knowledge of the subject matter of the representation, (2) obtain such knowledge prior to undertaking representation, or (3) refer the matter to an attorney who has adequate and current knowledge of the subject matter. Because the law is so varied and complex, and in a constant state of change, maintaining full and current knowledge of one, much less many, areas of law can be a daunting task. Yet, this is the requirement imposed on legal professionals to ensure that the client, who places trust in the attorney, is protected.

While in theory it is quite easy for the requirement of competence to be met, in practice it is quite a different thing. After all, the practice of law is a business. A business only profits from serving its customers. If too many clients are referred to other attorneys, there will not be a practice sufficient in volume to support the attorney and staff. On the other hand, additional cases that are accepted by an attorney increase the hours needed to properly represent the clients. This may leave scarce time for education and keeping abreast of changes. Then, too, what of the subordinate staff? The attorneys and paralegals who are employed by a firm or legal department are paid to get the work done. Frequent refusals to take on assignments on the ground of lack of competence does not create a promising future for any professional. The obligation is present and serious, but as shown, the burden is significant to balance the responsibilities associated with it and client representation in general.

competence

Have adequate knowledge/skill/training to undertake specific legal representation in a matter.

CASE

SUPREME COURT OF LOUISIANA.

IN RE TYRONE C. BROWN.

813 So. 2d 325
(LA, 2002).

Attorney Disciplinary Proceedings
PER CURIAM.
This case arises from one count of formal charges filed by the Office of Disciplinary Counsel

("ODC") against respondent, Tyrone C. Brown, an attorney licensed to practice law in the State of Louisiana.

Underlying Facts
Respondent worked as an attorney for the East Baton Rouge Parish Public Defender's Office. While there, respondent met Robert C. Matthews, a convicted felon who was later pardoned, who worked as an investigator for the public

CASE

defender's office. Although Mr. Matthews was not licensed to practice law, he apparently "represented" various personal injury clients and obtained settlements on their behalf from insurance companies. Mr. Matthews was successful in his activities, and many insurance adjusters mistakenly believed he was an attorney. However, his activities later came under suspicion, and Mr. Matthews became the subject of a fraud investigation by the Louisiana State Police.

In order to continue his activities, Mr. Matthews approached respondent with a scheme whereby Mr. Matthews would act as respondent's paralegal. Respondent agreed to provide Mr. Matthews with blank, pre-signed letters of representation on respondent's letterhead, which purportedly authorized Mr. Matthews to deal with the insurance companies. Additionally, respondent provided Mr. Matthews with pre-signed letterhead stationery which was otherwise blank. Respondent agreed to pay Mr. Matthews an undetermined fee based on the amount of the fee generated by each case.

> It is noteworthy that by this time, respondent had left the public defender's office and was employed by the Attorney General's Office, where he was prohibited from having a private practice.
>
> The letter, on respondent's letterhead, stated: Dear _____
>
> This letter is intended to inform your company that I represent _____ in regard to the above-captioned personal injury loss. Either myself or Mr. Robert Matthews, who works with me, will be contacting you regarding this claim.
>
> All documentation of my client's injuries will be provided when received.
>
> If you have any problem or questions with the foregoing please contact me by phone or mail.

Disciplinary Proceedings
Formal Charges
After investigation, the ODC filed one count of formal charges against respondent, alleging his conduct violated Rules 5.3 (failure to properly supervise a non-lawyer assistant), 5.5 (assisting a person who is not a member of the bar in the unauthorized practice of law), 8.4(a) (knowingly assisting another in a violation of the Rules of Professional Conduct), and 8.4(c) (engaging in conduct involving dishonesty, fraud, deceit, or misrepresentation) of the Rules of Professional Conduct. Respondent filed an answer denying the allegations of the formal charges. A formal hearing was scheduled, but respondent failed to appear, despite receiving notice of the hearing.

Hearing Committee Recommendation
At the formal hearing, the ODC presented the testimony of Cleve Franklin, an investigator for GEICO Insurance Company. Mr. Franklin testified that his company believed Mr. Matthews was an attorney working with respondent. The ODC also presented the testimony of Trooper Kermit Smith, of the Louisiana State Police Insurance Fraud Division. Trooper Smith testified that in the course of the State Police investigation into the activities of Mr. Matthews, copies of respondent's pre-signed letterhead stationery were found in the office of Mr. Matthews. Finally, the ODC introduced a copy of respondent's deposition, taken in connection with the investigation of the disciplinary charges. During the deposition, respondent admitted that he exercised no supervision over Mr. Matthews.

> During the deposition, the following exchange took place:
>
> Q. What mechanism did you set up to supervise Mr. Matthews?
>
> A. I didn't really feel the need. I trusted him. And in terms of the cases we received, and those eight cases, I felt that if I could relay to him what he could and could not do, that he wouldn't betray that.

At the conclusion of the hearing, the hearing committee found respondent violated the professional rules as charged. The committee recommended respondent be suspended from the practice of law for a period of fourteen months.

Disciplinary Board Recommendation

The disciplinary board found the record supported the conclusion of the hearing committee that respondent violated Rules 5.3, 5.5, 8.4(a) and 8.4(c) of the Rules of Professional Conduct. It noted respondent aided Mr. Matthews in his unauthorized practice of law, and deceived clients into believing Mr. Matthews was an attorney working with him. While the board was unable to determine from the record whether any clients suffered actual injury, it found the potential for injury from respondent's actions was significant.

As aggravating factors, the board found respondent had a dishonest or selfish motive, refused to acknowledge the wrongful nature of his conduct, and had substantial experience in the practice of law, having been admitted to the bar in 1989. The board recognized respondent's lack of a prior disciplinary record as a mitigating factor.

In fashioning a sanction, the board observed that there was little jurisprudence involving violations of Rules 5.3 and 5.5. It cited *In re: Tosh*, 99-1972 (La.9/3/99), 743 So.2d 197, in which the respondent was disbarred for numerous professional violations including failure to supervise a non-lawyer employee. While the board did not find that respondent's conduct in the instant case was as egregious as in *Tosh*, it concluded a longer sanction than that recommended by the hearing committee was justified. Accordingly, the board recommended respondent be suspended for a period of two years. One member dissented, indicating disbarment should be imposed.

Neither respondent nor the ODC filed an objection in this court to the disciplinary board's recommendation; however, pursuant to Supreme Court Rule XIX, § 11(G)(1)(a), this court ordered the parties to submit written briefs within twenty days, addressing the appropriateness of the proposed sanction. The court's order particularly

directed the parties to address the applicability of *Louisiana State Bar Ass'n v. Edwins*, 540 So.2d 294 (La.1989). The ODC filed a brief, arguing in favor of disbarment; respondent filed no brief.

Discussion

The record supports the hearing committee's factual determination that respondent violated Rules 5.3, 5.5, 8.4(a) and 8.4(c) of the Rules of Professional Conduct. In particular, the undisputed evidence establishes that respondent aided Mr. Matthews in his unauthorized practice of law and that he failed to make any effort to supervise Mr. Matthews.

In *Louisiana State Bar Ass'n v. Edwins*, 540 So.2d 294, 299 (La.1989), we interpreted Disciplinary Rule 3-101(A), the predecessor to Rules 5.3 and 5.5, and explained the dangers inherent in the delegation of a lawyer's professional responsibility to non-lawyer assistants:

The condemnation of the unauthorized practice of law is designed to protect the public from legal services by persons unskilled in the law. The prohibition of lay intermediaries is intended to insure the loyalty of the lawyer to the client unimpaired by intervening and possibly conflicting interests. Cheatham, Availability of Legal Services: The Responsibility of the Individual Lawyer and of the Organized Bar, 12 UCLA Rev. 438, 439 (1965). A lawyer can employ lay secretaries, lay investigators, lay detectives, lay researchers, accountants, lay scriveners, nonlawyer draftsmen or nonlawyer researchers. In fact, he may employ nonlawyers to do any task for him except counsel clients about law matters, engage directly in the practice of law, appear in court or appear in formal proceedings as part of the judicial process, so long as it is he who takes the work and vouches for it to the client and becomes responsible to the client. ABA Comm. on Professional Ethics, Op. 316 (1967).

The facts of *Edwins* are somewhat similar to the instant case. Rallie Edwins, a Baton Rouge attorney, entered into an arrangement with a paralegal, Rob Robertson, to use Mr. Robertson's paralegal office in New Iberia as Mr. Edwin's branch law office. Mr. Robertson apparently met with a personal injury client, William Livingston, and led Mr. Livingston to believe he was an attorney. Mr. Robertson entered into an attorney-client contract with Mr. Livingston, but later advised Mr. Livingston that he would be represented by Mr. Edwins. Subsequently, Mr. Edwins was hospitalized, and he authorized Mr. Robertson to sign his name to various pleadings. Mr. Edwins admitted that he never saw Mr. Livingston's file. Subsequently, Mr. Livingston's personal injury case was settled for $9,000. Of this amount, Mr. Edwins turned over $8,000 to Mr. Robertson. This court concluded that Mr. Edwins assisted Mr. Robertson in the unauthorized practice of law:

> The respondent attorney in the present case, in our opinion, knowingly assisted the non-lawyer, Robertson, to engage in the unauthorized practice of law. Even if Edwins was unaware that Robertson had held himself out as an attorney, we are convinced that he knowingly allowed Robertson to perform the functions of a lawyer in advising prospective clients as to their claims, entering employment contracts with them, preparing and filing lawsuits, motions and briefs for them, counseling them on the advisability of the settlement of their cases, and receiving, distributing and accounting for their settlement funds. Moreover, in all of these respects Edwins delegated the exercise of his professional judgment to Robertson, adopting the non-lawyer's decisions as his own with little or no supervision by the attorney.

We are convinced further that Edwins assisted Robertson in the unauthorized practice of law with the intent to obtain a benefit for himself and the non-lawyer. Edwins allowed Robertson to hold his paralegal office out to the public as the attorney's branch law office and paid part of the expenses of its operation. Edwins clearly intended to profit and did profit from the

attorney fees that were generated by the unauthorized services performed by Robertson. Likewise, the arrangement intentionally benefitted Robertson by enabling Edwins to compensate Robertson for his work in connection with cases that Edwins may not have been able to handle without the unauthorized legal assistance of Robertson. *Id.* at 302.

As in *Edwins*, respondent in the instant case knowingly allowed Mr. Matthews to perform the functions of an attorney by giving him access to blank, pre-signed stationery from respondent's law firm. Respondent completely delegated the exercise of his professional judgment to Mr. Matthews, and, by his own admission, exercised no supervision over Mr. Matthews. In *Edwins*, the court concluded that disbarment is "the prima facie appropriate sanction for the respondent's aiding unauthorized practice violation. . . . " *Id.* at 303.

In determining an appropriate sanction, we are mindful that disciplinary proceedings are designed to maintain high standards of conduct, protect the public, preserve the integrity of the profession, and deter future misconduct. *Louisiana State Bar Ass'n v. Reis,* 513 So.2d 1173, 1177-1178 (La.1987). The discipline to be imposed depends upon the facts of each case and the seriousness of the offenses involved, considered in light of any aggravating and mitigating circumstances. *Louisiana State Bar Ass'n v. Whittington,* 459 So.2d 520, 524 (La.1984).

Considering the total abdication of respondent's duties to a non-lawyer assistant, we find the baseline sanction for respondent's misconduct is disbarment. Three aggravating factors are present: dishonest or selfish motive, refusal to acknowledge the wrongful nature of the conduct, and substantial experience in the practice of law (admitted in 1989). As a mitigating factor, respondent has no prior disciplinary record. The presence of this single mitigating factor does not justify a downward deviation from the baseline sanction. Accordingly, we will disbar respondent from the practice of law.

Decree
Upon review of the findings and recommendation of the hearing committee and the disciplinary board, and considering the record and briefs filed herein, it is ordered that the name of Tyrone C. Brown be stricken from the roll of attorneys and that his license to practice law in the State of Louisiana be revoked. All costs and expenses in the matter are assessed against respondent in accordance with

Supreme Court Rule XIX, § 10.1, with legal interest to commence thirty days from the date of finality of this court's judgment until paid.

813 So.2d 325, 2001-2863 (La. 3/22/02)

Case Review Question
In re Brown, 813 So.2d 325 (La. 2002).
Would the result likely change if the respondent was not paid for his assistance to the nonlawyer?

Confidentiality.

Rule 1.6: Confidentiality of Information
(a) A lawyer shall not reveal information relating to representation of a client unless the client consents after consultation, except for disclosures that are impliedly authorized in order to carry out the representation, and except as stated in paragraph (b)
(b) A lawyer may reveal such information to the extent the lawyer reasonably believes necessary:
(1) to prevent the client from committing a criminal act that the lawyer believes is likely to result in imminent death or substantial bodily harm; or
(2) to establish a claim or defense on behalf of the lawyer in a controversy between the lawyer and the client, to establish a defense to a criminal charge or civil claim against the lawyer based upon conduct in which the client was involved, or to respond to allegations in any proceeding concerning the lawyer's representation of the client. (1999 American Bar Association Model Rules of Professional Conduct)

The ethical requirement that is vigorously enforced is the duty to maintain client **confidentiality.** In only a handful of relationships will the courts protect private communications with total commitment. One is the attorney–client relationship. The benefits of protecting the confidentiality of such communications is seen as essential to the protection of the fundamental freedoms associated with the American legal system. Other such relationships include minister–parishioner, physician–patient, and husband–wife. These are relationships that, by their nature, often involve private matters and communications that arise from a bond of trust between the parties. They are also seen as positive relationships that should be supported in and by society and government. The refusal of government to intrude on these relationships and expose their communications to compulsory disclosure is an obvious example of the original intent of

confidentiality
The obligation to retain all communications of any sort, that occur within the attorney–client relationship as private and privileged.

the framers of the Constitution to protect individuals from unnecessary and/or unfair intrusion into private lives. The added benefit is to encourage full disclosure in highly personal relationships that can affect the legal rights of the individual, such as a client who is seeking assistance of legal counsel.

The privilege of confidential communications belongs exclusively to the party who is disclosing private information. In the attorney–client relationship, this party is the client. The privilege cannot be waived or in any way compromised by the attorney. The only exceptions occur when the client personally waives the privilege, when breach of the privilege is necessary to prevent a death or serious bodily harm, or when the client places the substance of the communication in issue and/or disclosure is necessary pursuant to court order. These exceptions are uncommon and highly scrutinized by the courts.

To qualify as an attorney–client communication, there must be a statement made verbally, nonverbally, or in a documentary form from a party who reasonably believes to be represented by the attorney and further reasonably believes the communication to be subject to the protection of the privilege. For example, the fact that one is a friend of an attorney does not create a professional relationship. Communications that take place as the product of social interaction are usually not considered privileged. Communications that take place prior to the establishment of a formal legal relationship would not be considered privileged unless those communications were made with the intent that such a relationship be formed as the result, that is, an initial consultation followed by an agreement for representation.

It is not necessary that a statement be made directly to an attorney to receive protected status as confidential. If the relationship exists, then statements made to an employee or other representative of the attorney—such as a paralegal, clerical staff, legal investigator, or another attorney connected with the primary attorney on the case—are also considered privileged. The ethical rules for attorneys require also that the attorneys take reasonable steps to see that their subordinates and associates maintain the same standards with respect to client communications. The failure to do this can have a number of negative effects. Of course, the attorney can be disciplined for inappropriate conduct that occurred with respect to a matter under his or her supervision. Another significant risk is that of a civil action for malfeasance by the client and against the attorney and/or the paralegal. In such a case, the client need only prove that confidentiality was breached. This breach, in and of itself, is considered to be damaging. There is no requirement to establish that the client suffered some personal or financial harm as the result of the breach.

It is impractical to think an attorney could or should oversee every word spoken and action taken by paralegals and other support staff. Each must monitor his or her own behavior and ensure that it meets the ethical requirements of the attorney. For this reason, it is essential that attorneys educate and impress upon their staff the importance of ethical conduct and make such behavior a key element of continued employment. When it comes to ethical behavior, the law grants little or no tolerance for laziness or neglect.

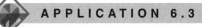

APPLICATION 6.3

Shelley is a paralegal with a law firm specializing in personal injury cases. She is assigned to interview a client to collect information regarding a pending lawsuit. During the interview, the client begins discussing other personal matters, including the fact that she has recently ended an abusive relationship but is fearful that her former boyfriend may have molested one of her children.

Point for Discussion

♦ Does the obligation to keep information confidential extend to matters beyond those for which the client is represented?

Assignment 6.2

Regarding Application 6.3, explain what Shelley should do with the information to properly handle the matter but still meet any ethical obligations.

Conflict of Interest.

Rule 1.7: Conflict of Interest: General Rule
(a) A lawyer shall not represent a client if the representation of that client will be directly adverse to another client unless:
   (1) the lawyer reasonably believes the representation will not adversely affect the relationship with the other client; and
   (2) each client consents after consultation.
(b) A lawyer shall not represent a client if the representation of that client may be materially limited by the lawyer's responsibilities to another client or to a third person, or by the lawyer's own interests, unless:
   (1) the lawyer reasonably believes the representation will not be adversely affected; and
   (2) the client consents after consultation. When representation of multiple clients in a single matter is undertaken, the consultation shall include explanation of the implications of the common representation and the advantages and risks involved. (American Bar Association Model Rules of Professional Conduct, 1999)

The issue of **conflict of interest** is a particularly difficult one for attorneys. Unlike other professions, the legal profession is based on an adversarial system. There are conflicting sides to a lawsuit and each has strategies and information that is not available to the other. Unlike the physician–patient or minister–parishioner relationship, the attorney may also have personal

conflict of interest
The actual, or appearance, of divided loyalty by one who is a fiduciary.

interests that could potentially conflict with those of the client and the duty to put the client's interests first. A wide variety of situations can present conflict of interest questions, ranging from a current or former professional relationship with an opposing party to a business opportunity in which both the attorney and the client might be involved.

All professions, including law, have a certain percentage of turnover. It is unusual in the present day for someone to accept a position and keep that same job for the remainder of his or her career. As opportunities arise, interests change, or personal conflicts develop, people change jobs. Because legal training is relatively specific, the majority of these changes take place within the same employment area, both as to type of work and geography. The potential for problems is enormous. What happens when a person leaves a job with one local firm and accepts a position with another firm that represents the opposition in a number of cases? If the first job was of long duration, the individual could have dealt with literally thousands of cases. Working at a firm with clients who are adversaries in any of these cases creates an ethical conflict of interest. The client of the former firm may be at a disadvantage because the legal professional had access to his or her file and is now employed by the opposition. Presumably, the knowledge gained as part of the fiduciary relationship could now be used against the client. To avoid this type of occurrence and unfair treatment of unsuspecting individuals, rules have been established to require certain safeguards to protect the interests of a client.

By definition, a fiduciary relationship is one of trust. The relationship between a lawyer and a client is fiduciary. As a result, the client is entitled to certain expressions of loyalty. This includes not only confidentiality, but also that their interests will be put first. Thus, when legal professionals change employment, they are not permitted to have any type of contact or to disclose any information with respect to cases that involve either the former client or their adversaries. This is commonly known as building an ethical wall. To accomplish this, firms typically maintain a cross-referenced index of clients. Essentially, they maintain an index of all their own clients and a separate index of all opposing parties. It is also helpful to have an index of all opposing counsel in various law firms and the cases they represent. Any new employee should consult this and identify all opposing parties who are or were represented by their former employer. Each of these files should be earmarked in some way to indicate that the new employee is to have no contact with the case in any capacity. Even if the employee (lawyer, paralegal, etc.) did not have contact with the client's case at the former employer, the presumption remains that the accessibility to the file creates a dangerous situation for the client. The best way to avoid problems is to avoid the file of the client at the new employer.

Another safeguard used regularly is for a legal professional to maintain an ongoing list of all client files, including names of opposition, with whom there is contact. Clients may change lawyers during the pendency of a lawsuit and it is unreasonable to expect one to remember the name of every case. A list of client files allows an easier matching of potential conflicts when there is a change in employment. Whatever method is used, the key is to maintain a clear separation from any file with which there has been the opportunity for access to the opposing position's case. Luckily, with the advent of computers, such files and cross indexes are more easily generated than the hand-typed index cards for each client, opposition, and opposing counsel file of just a few years ago.

There are exceptions to the rule on conflicts with regard to client files. For example, a client may have more than one lawsuit pending or completed in the past for which there could be a conflicting interest. However, if there is absolutely no connection with the present case, then it may be permissible for an attorney, paralegal, or other legal personnel to assist on the present case. Even in this situation, there should be a full disclosure to both sides of the case and consent before any action is taken.

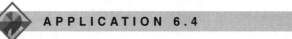

APPLICATION 6.4

Jerome is an attorney employed by Firm 1. He changes positions and goes to work for Firm 2. A few months later, one of the partners from Firm 2 dies unexpectedly. Two of the other attorneys are out of town, leaving only Jerome and another attorney (who is a single parent with a disabled child) to manage the firm. Tomorrow, depositions (testimony under oath to gather information in a lawsuit) begin in a multiparty lawsuit, which has been scheduled for six months. The depositions involve 8 witnesses and 15 attorneys from various cities. It is set to take place in a city several thousand miles away. Originally, the partner who recently died was scheduled to represent the client at the deposition. No one else in the firm is available to make the trip due to absence or personal inability to travel. Jerome is willing to go, but Firm 1 is also involved in the case, although Jerome did not work directly for that client.

Point for Discussion

◆   What are the options with respect to the depositions?

Other issues that can bring about questions of conflict of interest are when a client and lawyer or other legal professional have common business interests. Because it is presumed that the legal professional may have expertise and/or skills superior to that of the client, such relationships are to be avoided. This includes entering into business relationships with clients other than as attorney–client (e.g., co-investors) and entering into competitive business opportunities in which the client would be considered a competitor. If such an opportunity is presented, the legal professional has the obligation to pass on it until such time as it becomes clear that the client has considered and decided to disregard the opportunity. This approach ensures that the legal professional will not employ his or her professional skill to the detriment of the client. Similarly, a legal professional should generally represent a client in any matter that will result in additional benefits to the legal professional, such as preparing a will for someone in which the legal professional is named as beneficiary. A case such as this would be ripe for attack on the grounds that undue influence was exercised on the client. An exception, however, might be found if the attorney was the only surviving relative of the client and if other facts would make him or her by all indications the most likely beneficiary of the estate regardless of who prepared the will.

There are as many possibilities for conflict of interest as there are clients and attorneys. For this reason the rules are broadly written, but, the basic rule of thumb is no action should be taken that could in any way be perceived as putting the interests of oneself or another ahead of those of the client or that could be considered as disloyal or a breach of trust in any fashion.

Commitment to Zealous Representation.

> Rule 1.3: A lawyer shall act with reasonable diligence and promptness in representing a client. (ABA Model Rules of Professional Conduct, 2001)

Once a professional relationship with a client has been established, there is a duty to represent the client with complete professionalism. This requires that the best efforts of the legal professional be used in all aspects of the case. What constitutes zeal and professionalism is a somewhat open-ended question because every case is unique. However, certain steps can be taken to create and maintain a professional relationship with the client. Important considerations in any professional legal relationship include the following:

1. Communicate with clients on a regular basis to keep them abreast of the statute or changes in the matters of representation.
2. Meet all deadlines in a timely manner with respect to communications with the opposition, courts, and all legal proceedings.
3. Make sure the client understands the typical steps in the matter of representation and the time frames generally associated with each step.
4. Respond promptly and completely to all inquiries of the client, no matter how trivial they seem.
5. Provide a thorough explanation of all billing and expenditures made on behalf of the client and for which the client is responsible.
6. Consult the client in advance on all matters that affect the cost and/or potential outcome of the case.
7. Document the time, date, and nature of all communications with the client and concerning matters of representation.
8. Demonstrate an ongoing interest in the matters of representation.

These considerations take time, and in the profession of law, time is money. Each of these items also leads to ethical and effective representation and client relations. The general attitude reflected in the manner and actions of the legal professional has a direct impact on future referrals and client satisfaction. Thus, such behaviors as those listed are not only professional, ethical, and supportive of the duties of the legal professional, but they are also ultimately good public relations and marketing.

CASE

CARNIVAL CORPORATION, A/K/A CARNIVAL CRUISE LINES, INC., CURTIS J. MASE, AND MASE & SREENAN, P.A., PETITIONERS,

V.

YVONNE BEVERLY, RESPONDENT.

744 So. 2d 489
Sept. 16, 1999.
(Fl App., 1999 1st Dist).

Factual and Procedural History
In May 1995, Beverly and her family took a cruise on a Carnival ship, the Ecstasy. The ship made port in Key West, where some of the Beverly party planned to go ashore. The Beverly family sought to take the elevator down to the lower deck, where they could board a launch to shore. In the action below, Beverly alleged that a Carnival employee refused to allow her and her family to use the elevator and, instead, directed them to take the stairs. She fell on the stairs suffering significant personal injuries.

Beverly's complaint against Carnival was filed in 1995. The matter came to trial on May 28, 1998, where the events occurred which are the subject of this appeal. The record indicates that the trial was highly contentious. Even from the cold record, the animosity between the parties' attorneys is obvious. The focus of our opinion, however, is limited to the trial conduct of Mase which led to his disqualification by the trial court.

During voir dire, Mase asked a venireman if he would agree "that changes in the version of how the accident happened after an individual hires a lawyer are suspect?" Beverly's counsel objected, requesting a sidebar conference at which he argued that Mase's comment impugned the integrity of Beverly's attorneys in that Mase was implying that counsel was involved in the suborning of perjury by Beverly. Mase answered that he had not

mentioned the names of any attorneys. The trial court overruled the objection.

As the trial proceeded, in his opening statement Mase pointed out that the medical reports prepared immediately after Beverly's fall indicate that Beverly missed a step or steps and then fell. He noted that, later, Beverly's story changed and she contended she slipped on wet steps. Specifically, Mase said:

> Well, something happened between June and the next time we find a medical entry concerning Ms. Beverly. She hired a lawyer, Mr. Lassiter.
> And after she hired Mr. Lassiter, we have a new entry in the medical records. She slipped on some stairs which were wet.

There was no immediate objection. Mase continued with his opening statement, during which he was admonished several times by the trial court for presenting argument beyond what the evidence at trial would show and for "making a final argument," rather than an appropriate opening statement. During one of the several sidebar conferences, Beverly's counsel again complained that, when Mase pointed out that Beverly had given a different version of the facts after she retained counsel, Mase was resorting to unprofessional attacks on Beverly's attorneys by implying that Beverly's counsel had suborned perjury in some manner. Beverly asked the trial court to admonish Mase and warn him that he would be sanctioned if he continued. The trial court agreed that Mase's comments could be considered to mean that Beverly had been encouraged by her counsel to change her story. Mase argued that his comments were appropriate and requested leave to provide supporting authority to the court. The trial court instructed Mase that "in this phase of the trial" he was prohibited from referring to the fact that, after Beverly retained counsel, her statements varied from "the statements she gave to the shipboard doctor, to the nurses, and to the emergency-room physician." The trial court emphasized the extent of the ruling, stating that " at this point, until you

◆ **CASE**

[Mase] can give me the case law where I can read it, there will be no further mention of this."

Mase's opening statement continued, and the trial court again was required to admonish Mase for "making a final argument to the jury." Specifically, the court warned: "Mr. Mase, you're going far beyond—and I've told you, and I'm not going to tell you anymore. You can pout or whatever. Save this for your final argument. . . ." Immediately thereafter, the court said "next time, there's going to be some sanctions."

The next morning, before the trial proceedings began, the trial court brought up the matter of Beverly's motions to sanction Mase. The trial court advised that it was denying the motions made during the sidebar discussion the previous day, noting that in fact the early medical reports were different than Beverly's later explanation of the accident. The trial court found that Mase had not impugned Beverly's counsel, but advised Mase that "you're on very dangerous ground" and offered to give a curative instruction if counsel for Beverly desired. The trial court ruled that it would allow Mase's cross-examination on the subject, but reminded him that he was "on pretty dangerous ground." Mase acknowledged that he was "on the edge," and the court emphasized that "you're right on the razor's edge." Beverly's motion for a mistrial was denied.

As the trial proceeded, John Brown, Beverly's son, testified that, when he sought to use the elevator while leaving the ship for an earlier snorkeling excursion, a Carnival employee told him that he must use the stairs, rather than the elevator. On cross-examination, Mase sought to impeach Brown concerning his detailed memory of the Carnival employee's instructions, questioning him, as follows:

Q. You talked to [counsel for Beverly] before you took the stand here today, didn't you?
A. Yes, sir.
Q. You discussed what you were going to say to this jury?
A. Discussed what we was going to say?
Q. Yes, sir.

A. He just—we talked about—well I ain't never been in a courtroom—what would go on, you know, and different things.

Q. Standing out there in that hallway, he explained to you exactly what he needed for you to say to this jury, didn't he?
[COUNSEL FOR BEVERLY]: Objection Your Honor.

Another sidebar conference followed. At sidebar, Beverly moved to strike Carnival's pleadings and to hold Mase in contempt. Mase maintained that there was nothing improper about his question. Counsel for Beverly asked the record to show that Mase was standing "smirking" and moved the trial court to sanction Mase by prohibiting him from further participation in the proceedings, arguing that co-counsel for Carnival could proceed in the trial. Beverly contended that Mase had engaged in a pattern of conduct of not honoring the trial court's rulings and of continuing to impugn Beverly's counsel before the jury, and argued the "only way to stop it was to get Mase out of the case." In response, Mase accused Beverly's counsel of intentionally disrupting the proceedings by their continual objections. The trial court noted that this was the second time Mase had implied misconduct by Beverly's attorneys, and that Mase had been warned the first time during his opening statement. The court then indicated that it would disqualify Mase from further participation in the case, but would give him an opportunity to argue the issue further the next morning. At that point, Mase moved for a mistrial on the ground that Carnival was not being represented by counsel of its choosing.

The next morning, the trial court entered a mistrial on its own motion. The trial court then entered a written order disqualifying Mase from further participation in the case. In this order, the trial court made the following findings:

During opening statements defense counsel Curtis Mase made intentionally inappropriate remarks which suggested misconduct by Mr. Lassiter, one of Plaintiff's counsel. This Court strongly admonished Mr. Mase for his conduct and ordered him to refrain from any similar conduct throughout the trial.

***

[D]uring cross-examination of one of Plaintiff's fact witnesses, John Brown, Mr. Mase again intentionally suggested misconduct by Plaintiff's counsel, in direct violation of this Court's order. Mr. Lassiter moved ore tenus for Mr. Mase's disqualification from any further participation in this case and the Court granted the motion, but gave Mr. Mase an overnight opportunity to submit his case law and argument to the Court on the morning of Friday, May 29, 1998. An addendum to this order will be the official transcript of the total trial proceedings, as soon as the same is available, showing the totality of Mr. Mase's improper conduct. Plaintiff's counsel were likewise allowed to submit case law and argument in response. The Court reviewed the cases submitted and heard argument of counsel. The Court then ratified its Disqualification of Mr. Mase from any further participation in this case, and, on the Court's own motion, over the strenuous objections of the Plaintiff's [sic], declared a mistrial. The Court finds that the sole cause of the mistrial was the conduct of Mr. Mase in violating the Court's Orders and undoubtedly prejudicing the jury as a result. Plaintiff's [sic] have suffered yet another delay in their trial and needless waste of time and resources as a result. Judicial economy and resources have been squandered as well.

The same day, the trial judge granted Carnival's motion for his own disqualification. A new trial judge scheduled a hearing on Carnival's motion for reconsideration of the order of disqualification, but ruled that Mase could not participate in that hearing.

Thereafter, Carnival filed a petition for writ of prohibition in this court. This court entered an order denying prohibition, but ruled that Carnival's petition would be treated as a petition for writ of certiorari and imposed a stay on further proceedings in the lower court.

Standard of Review

A trial court's decision to sanction an attorney for trial misconduct is reviewed under an abuse of discretion standard. *See Belote v. Slye*, 206 So.2d 276 (Fla. 1st DCA 1968). Because the trial court has witnessed the actions at issue, the trial court is in the best position to determine whether it is necessary to summarily punish counsel for contemptuous conduct. *In Re Gustafson*, 650 F.2d 1017, 1023 (9th Cir.1981). Thus, appellate courts "give great deference to a trial judge's explicit determination that . . . summary procedures are necessary." *Id.*

> Rule 3.830, Fla.R.Crim.P., "is patterned after Federal Rule of Criminal Procedure 42(a)." Committee Notes, Rule 3.830, Fla.R.Crim.P., *In re Amendments to Florida Rules of Criminal Procedure*, 606 So.2d 227, 336 (Fla.1992). "Federal case law which construes a federal rule after which a Florida rule is patterned may be considered in interpreting the Florida rule . . ." *Sheradsky v. Basadre*, 452 So.2d 599, 602 (Fla. 3d DCA 1984) (citations omitted), *rev. denied*, 461 So.2d 113 (Fla.1985). Thus, when considering the summary contempt power of courts, Florida courts have frequently cited to federal authority. *See, e.g., Shelley v. District Court of Appeal*, 350 So.2d 471, 473 (Fla.1977).

Inherent Authority of Trial Court

Petitioners argue that the trial court did not possess the authority to sanction Mase by disqualification in the underlying case. We cannot agree.

The adversarial method of trial imposes dual and conflicting obligations on attorneys. *See, generally,* Nathan M. Crystal, *Limitations on Zealous Representation in an Adversarial System,* 32 Wake Forest L.Rev. 671 (1997). As an advocate, the attorney has a duty to zealously represent his or her client within the bounds of the law and rules of professional conduct. The comment to rule 4-1.3, Rules Regulating The Florida Bar, explains that [a]

CASE

lawyer . . . may take whatever lawful and ethical measures are required to vindicate a client's cause or endeavor. A lawyer should act with commitment and dedication to the interests of the client and with zeal in advocacy upon the client's behalf.

At the same time, "[a] lawyer is . . . an officer of the legal system, and a public citizen having special responsibility for the quality of justice." Preamble, Chapter 4, Rules Regulating The Florida Bar. Thus, an attorney has a duty to refrain from advocacy that undermines or interferes with the functioning of the judicial system. *See Malautea v. Suzuki Motor Co., Ltd.,* 987 F.2d 1536, 1546 (11th Cir.1993) (Judge Fay states: "An attorney's duty to a client can never outweigh his or her responsibility to see that our system of justice functions smoothly. This concept is as old as common law jurisprudence itself."); *see, e.g.,* rules 4-3.5(c) ("a lawyer shall not engage in conduct intended to disrupt a tribunal"), and 4-8.4(d) (a lawyer shall not "engage in conduct in connection with the practice of law that is prejudicial to the administration of justice, including to knowingly . . . disparage . . . witnesses . . . or other lawyers on any basis. . . ."), Rules Regulating The Florida Bar. When professional judgment does not restrain a lawyer's zealous advocacy, however, the courts must act to assure that aggressive advocacy does not frustrate or disrupt the administration of judicial proceedings. *See In Re Terry,* 128 U.S. 289, 302, 9 S.Ct. 77, 79, 32 L.Ed. 405 (1888); *Sandstrom v. State,* 309 So.2d 17 (Fla. 4th DCA 1975), *cert. dismissed,* 336 So.2d 572 (Fla.1976); *see also* Louis S. Raveson, *Advocacy and Contempt, Constitutional Limitations on the Judicial Contempt Power, Part One: The Conflict Between Advocacy and Contempt,* 65 Wash.L.Rev. 477, 539-40 (1990).

As Judge Marvin E. Aspen succinctly states: "[A]ny notion that the duty to represent a client trumps obligations of professionalism is, of course, indefensible as a matter of law." Marvin E. Aspen, *Let Us Be Officers of the Court,* A.B.A.J., July 1997 at 94. The rules of professional conduct governing Florida lawyers recognize the lawyer's professional obligation to resolve these conflicting professional obligations:

A lawyer's responsibilities as a representative of clients, an officer of the legal system, and a public citizen are usually harmonious. . . .

Difficult ethical problems may arise from a conflict between a lawyer's responsibility to a client and the lawyer's own sense of personal honor, including obligations to society and the legal profession. . . . Such issues must be resolved through the exercise of sensitive professional and moral judgment guided by the basic principles underlying the rules [of professional conduct].

Preamble, Chapter 4, Rules Regulating The Florida Bar. In balancing conflicting professional obligations, the lawyer's function includes a measure of objectivity in the implementation of legal skills, goals, or practices. . . . [O]bjectivity . . . refer[s] to a sense of impartiality in evaluating competing interests. In other words, objectivity is the ability to distance oneself from personal and client desires in order to evaluate the effect of potential actions on clients, third parties, and the legal system.

Paul C. Zacharis, *Reconciling Professionalism and Client Interests,* 36 Wm. & Mary L.Rev. 1303, 1307 (1995).

Professor Rob Atkinson urges courts to "continue, perhaps even redouble, their present efforts to maintain at least the minimum order required for the rule of law, particularly in judicial administration." Rob Atkinson, *A Dissenter's Commentary on the Professionalism Crusade,* 74 Tex.L.Rev. 259, 325 (1995). He cautions, however, that "[t]hey should be careful, however, in their efforts to police . . . incivility . . . and be wary of using highly coercive penalties in view of the dangers of chilling vigorous advocacy, and the difficulties of distinguishing conscientious activism from ill-motivated aggression." *Id.*

From the early English common law, when contempt was committed in the presence of the court while it was in session, the use of summary contempt was considered an inherent judicial power necessary to maintain order in the court and to protect the court's dignity. *See* Teresa S.

Hanger, *The Modern Status of the Rules Permitting a Judge to Punish Contempt Summarily,* 28 Wm. Mary L.Rev. 553, 554 (1987). The United States Supreme Court has recognized that summary contempt power is inherent in all courts, see *In re Terry,* 128 U.S. at 306, 9 S.Ct. 77 and the Supreme Court of Florida has determined that "the imposition of a summary contempt sanction is a proper and necessary disciplinary tool to aid a judicial tribunal in carrying out its necessary court functions. . . ." *Shelley v. District Court of Appeal,* 350 So.2d 471, 472 (Fla.1977). It is well settled that "counsel commits a direct criminal contempt when counsel, in the presence of the court, violates a direct order of the trial court relating to the conduct of court proceedings . . . ," *Vizzi v. State,* 501 So.2d 613, 619 (Fla. 3d DCA 1986), even if the order is erroneous. *Soven v. State,* 622 So.2d 1123, 1125 (Fla. 3d DCA 1993); *McQueen v. State,* 531 So.2d 1030, 1031 (Fla. 1st DCA 1988); *Rubin v. State,* 490 So.2d 1001, 1003-04 (Fla. 3d DCA 1986).

Petitioners argue that in *Burns v. Huffstetler,* 433 So.2d 964 (Fla.1993), the Florida Supreme Court established that trial courts do not possess the power to disqualify counsel as a sanction. *Burns* does explain the limits on the judiciary's use of the summary contempt sanction power to discipline an attorney. Contrary to the argument of petitioners, however, *Burns* confirms the inherent sanction authority of a court to disqualify an attorney in a case in which the attorney is found guilty of contemptuous conduct.

In *Burns,* based upon allegations that defense counsel had impeded the first degree murder trial of his client by requesting continuances on false grounds and admitting the defendant into a psychiatric hospital, the trial court found defense counsel in contempt and, as a sanction, removed him as counsel of record in the case and required him to surrender his license to practice law as an alternative to incarceration. *Id.* at 965. The disqualified attorney filed a petition for writ of prohibition, asserting that the trial court had no authority to order the surrender of his license to practice law. In granting the writ, the *Burns* court observed that "[t]here are three alternative methods

for disciplining of attorneys. . . ." *Id.* The first two methods are set forth in the Rules Regulating The Florida Bar. Those methods involve either the "traditional grievance committee—referee process," *Burns,* 433 So.2d at 965, in which an attorney is prosecuted by The Florida Bar and sanctions are imposed by the Florida Supreme Court, now governed by rules 3-3.1 through 3-7.7, Rules Regulating The Florida Bar, or a proceeding initiated by the judiciary, prosecuted by the state attorney in a trial before a circuit court judge, and subject to review by the supreme court. *Burns,* 433 So.2d at 965; *see* rule 3-7.8, Rules Regulating The Florida Bar.

The third method of discipline "is the exercise of the inherent power of the courts to impose contempt sanctions on attorneys for lesser infractions. . . ." *Burns,* 433 So.2d at 965. The *Burns* court discussed the significance of this inherent sanction power, as follows:

> [T]he imposition of a summary contempt sanction is a proper and necessary disciplinary tool to aid a judicial tribunal in carrying out its necessary court functions. . . . The contempt power is a proper and historical alternative to existing formal disciplinary proceedings. The Integration Rule of The Florida Bar, Article XI, Rule 11.14, providing for disciplinary proceedings in circuit courts, is no bar to *the use of this summary power in cases of lesser infractions* of the various rules governing the practice of law which affect the necessary operations of a court.

Id., quoting Shelley v. District Court of Appeal, 350 So.2d at 472-73 (emphasis in *Burns*). The court emphasized, however, that "[w]hen the offense is serious enough to warrant a suspension or disbarment . . . either The Florida Bar grievance process or the judicial disciplinary process must be utilized. . . ." *Id.* at 966. Thus, in *Burns,* the court held that the trial court's order requiring the surrender of an attorney's license to practice law "amounts to a suspension from the practice of law and that such a punishment may not be imposed as a sanction. . . ." *Id.; see also Gifford v. Payne,* 432 So.2d 38, 39 (Fla.1983). The court explained, however, that its "holding is not intended to

CASE

prohibit the trial court from using contempt proceedings to punish attorney misconduct in this or any other cause." *Burns,* 433 So.2d at 966. Importantly for the instant case, the court in *Burns* expressly found "no basis in this record to vacate the order removing petitioner as counsel for the criminal defendant." *Id.*

Thus, under *Burns,* it is clear that, while Florida courts lack the authority to suspend an attorney from the practice of law, they possess the inherent contempt power to sanction an attorney by the removal of that attorney as counsel in the case in which the conduct occurred. *Id.* Nevertheless, disqualification "strikes at the heart of one of the most important associational freedoms that a person may have— the right to choose one's own lawyer." *Kusch v. Ballard,* 645 So.2d 1035, 1036 (Fla. 4th DCA 1994) (Farmer, J., concurring). Accordingly, disqualification of a party's chosen counsel is a harsh and drastic sanction and an extraordinary remedy that should be resorted to sparingly. *Lee v. Gadasa Corp.,* 714 So.2d 610, 612 (Fla. 1st DCA 1998); *City of Apopka v. All Corners, Inc.,* 701 So.2d 641, 644 (Fla. 5th DCA 1997); *Pascucci v. Pascucci,* 679 So.2d 1311 (Fla. 4th DCA 1996). It is because disqualification is such an extraordinary sanction that a trial court must exercise its discretion to disqualify counsel only as a last resort to prevent further conduct in defiance of the court's order or authority. *In Re Gustafson,* 650 F.2d at 1022. Even then, the court's power should be exercised with great caution, and the court should consider the use of lesser sanctions before invoking disqualification.

Respondent's additional reliance on *Double T Corp. v. Jalis Dev., Inc.,* 682 So.2d 1160 (Fla. 5th DCA 1996) and *Tuazon v. Royal Caribbean Cruises, Ltd.,* 641 So.2d 417 (Fla. 3d DCA 1994), as authority for the trial court's general power to disqualify counsel, is misplaced. Both of these cases are distinguishable from the instant appeal because, in both cases, the trial court disqualified an attorney, not for misconduct, but for a conflict of interest related to the attorney's

possession of confidential information of an opposing party in litigation. The court's power to sanction an attorney for trial misconduct arises from the court's inherent contempt power. *See Burns v. Huffstetler,* 433 So.2d 964, 965-66 (Fla. 1983); *Shelley v. District Court of Appeal,* 350 So.2d 471, 472 (Fla. 1977). For example, the court may issue curative instructions, a reprimand, an assessment of fines, and warnings that future misconduct will subject the attorney to summary contempt proceedings and disqualification for further participation in the proceedings. *See, e.g., Koller v. Richardson-Merrell, Inc.,* 737 F.2d 1038, 1056, n. 49 (D.C.Cir. 1984).

Requirements for Use of Summary Contempt
The order on review does not expressly find Mase in contempt. Nevertheless, because the sanction assessed is necessarily founded upon the court's inherent contempt powers, we conclude that a finding of direct contempt is implicit in the instant order. Further, although the trial court possessed the authority to assess compensatory fines against Mase for civil contempt, *see Lamb v. Fowler,* 574 So.2d 262 (Fla. 1st DCA 1991), the order before us must be characterized as one based on direct criminal contempt because it provided punishment rather than coerced compliance with a court order. *See Young v. Wood-Cohan,* 727 So.2d 322, 323-24 (Fla. 4th DCA 1999); *Fredericks v. Sturgis,* 598 So.2d 94, 96-98 (Fla. 5th DCA 1992); *Anderson v. City of Wilton Manors,* 490 So.2d 1313, 1315 (Fla. 4th DCA 1986).

A court may hold a person or party in direct criminal contempt for the violation of a court order or for an act that is contemptuous on its face. *See Johnson v. Bednar,* 573 So.2d 822, 824 (Fla.1991) ("If a party can make oneself a judge of the validity of orders issued by trial courts, and by one's own disobedience set them aside, then our court's are devoid of power, and the judicial power, both federal and state, would be a mockery."); *Martin v. State,* 711 So.2d 1173, 1174-75 (Fla. 4th DCA 1998); *Lawrence v. Lawrence,* 384 So.2d 279, 280 (Fla. 4th DCA 1980). "Counsel's perception of the correctness of the trial court's ruling is no excuse for engaging in contemptuous behavior and disregarding the court's order." *Soven v. State,* 622 So.2d at 1125 (citations omitted). If counsel believes a trial court ruling is incorrect, the remedy is to challenge those rulings at the appellate level. *Id.* "[A]n aggrieved party's failure to abide by the order may be punished by contempt even if the order is ultimately found to be erroneous." *Rubin v. State,* 490 So.2d at 1003; *see also In re Weinstein,* 518 So.2d 1370, 1373-74 (Fla. 4th DCA 1988).

Prior to assessing contempt sanctions for a violation of a court order, the trial court must first have issued a clear and unambiguous order or otherwise clearly established for the record the standards of conduct required by the court. *See U.S. v. Robinson,* 922 F.2d 1531, 1534-35 (11th Cir. 1991). "One may not be held in contempt of court for violation of an order . . . which is not clear and definite so as to make the party aware of its command and direction." *Lawrence v. Lawrence,* 384 So.2d at 280; *see also Levine v. State,* 650 So.2d 666, 668 (Fla. 4th DCA 1995).

During the trial below, counsel for respondent provided Mase with a copy of The Florida Bar Trial Lawyers Section Guidelines for Professional Conduct, which was represented to have been adopted in the Fourth Judicial Circuit. Respondent argues that Mase's conduct also violated those guidelines. We note that courts have used the standards of conduct specified in local rules and civility codes as the basis for sanctions, *see In re Maurice,* 167 B.R. 114, 127 (Bankr.N.D.Il.1994), 179 B.R. 881, 882 (Bankr.N.D.Il.1995), *affd,* 69 F.3d 830, 832 (7th Cir.1995) (attorney sanctioned for, among other things, violations of Seventh Circuit Standards of Professional Conduct); *McLeod, Alexander, Powel & Apffel, P.C. v. Quarles,* 894 F.2d 1482, 1486-87 (5th Cir.1990) (sanction for violation of Texas Lawyer's Creed); *Dondi Properties Corp. v. Commerce Sav. & Loan Ass'n,* 121 F.R.D. 284, 287-88 (N.D.Tex.1988) (en banc) (adoption of standards of litigation conduct for Northern District of Texas as basis for sanctions); although the practice of enforcing aspirational professionalism or civility codes through sanctions has been criticized.

See, e.g., Green v. Green, 263 Ga. 551, 437 S.E.2d 457, 461 (1993) (J. Sears-Collins concurring); *see also* Amy R. Mashburn, *Professionalism as a Class Ideology: Civility Codes and Bar Hierarchy,* 28 Val.U.L.Rev. 657, 706 (1994). The record here, however, does not reflect that the trial court imposed or applied those guidelines below. Because these guidelines were not applied by the trial court in assessing sanctions on Mase, we do not address whether a violation of the guidelines could also be a basis for imposing sanctions.

Further, under rule 3.830, Florida Rules of Criminal Procedure, in a proceeding for direct criminal contempt, a trial court must

> inform the defendant of the accusation against the defendant and inquire as to whether the defendant has any cause to show why he or she should not be adjudged guilty of contempt by the court. . . .

"Scrupulous compliance with rule 3.830 is required because its provisions constitute the essence of due process." *Martin v. State,* 711 So.2d at 1174 (quoting *Kahn v. State,* 447 So.2d 1048 (Fla. 4th DCA 1984)). The rule assures that "[b]efore a person may be held in criminal contempt, he must be sufficiently advised of the charge so as to accord him a reasonable opportunity to meet it by way of defense or explanation." *Young v. Wood-Cohan,* 727 So.2d at 324.

In the order on review, the trial court disqualified Mase for "a direct violation of this Court's order" due to Mase's inference that Brown changed his explanation of the facts after conferring with counsel. The record reflects, however, that during the trial proceedings the trial court responded in an ambiguous and inconsistent manner to Mase's comments and examination concerning a witness's alleged change of explanation after retaining or conferring with counsel.

Initially, the trial court overruled objections concerning voir dire inquiry on the subject. Then, following several references to Beverly's change of her explanation of the accident during Mase's opening statement, the trial court instructed Mase "at this phase of the trial" not to refer to the fact

CASE

that Beverly changed her explanation after retaining counsel and warned Mase that he was "on dangerous ground," which Mase expressly acknowledged. When the trial court denied respondent's motion for sanctions, however, it seemed to change its view of Mase's statements by finding that Mase had not impugned Beverly's counsel, by expressly noting that the medical reports appeared to indicate that Beverly's explanation of the accident had changed over time, and by allowing Mase to proceed with cross-examination on the subject. During Mase's opening statement the trial court did admonish Mase and warn that sanctions would be assessed—but this warning was given for Mase's argumentative opening statement, not for his implications that Beverly changed her explanation after retaining counsel.

We readily acknowledge that the necessity of constant admonitions by the trial court for various trial conduct combined with Mase's "smirking" and "pouting," observed on the record, would disturb any judge and place serious strain on any judicial patience. Clearly, the trial judge was faced with a difficult task in the administration of this trial, and the use of sanctions certainly may well have been appropriate. Nevertheless, the trial court's position during the trial with respect to Mase's statements about Beverly changing her explanation of the accident was ambiguous and inconsistent. After allowing Mase to cross-examine on the subject, the trial court did not caution or warn Mase that he would be cited for contempt if he continued to question witnesses about alleged changes in their testimony after conferring with counsel. *See Carroll v. State,* 327 So.2d 881, 882 (Fla. 3d DCA 1976).

Thus, we find that the trial court did not issue a clear and unambiguous order or otherwise make Mase aware of the court's directions regarding trial conduct and did not provide Mase with an opportunity to show cause why he should not be held in contempt. *Lawrence. v. Lawrence,* 384 So.2d at 280; *Young v. Wood-Cohan,* 727 So.2d at 324. Accordingly, we must conclude that it was an abuse of discretion to exercise the trial court's contempt powers and impose the extraordinary sanction of disqualification for Mase's conduct.

In granting the petition for writ of certiorari, we share the concerns of other courts under similar circumstances that, even if our opinion is legally correct, it may have the effect of encouraging uncivil and unprofessional trial conduct. *See, e.g., Evanoff v. Evanoff,* 262 Ga. 303, 418 S.E.2d 62, 63 (1992) (J. Benham concurring). Our opinion, however, should not be read as condoning the lack of professionalism and civility revealed by the record of the trial below.

Based upon the foregoing analysis, we conclude that the order disqualifying Mase constitutes a material departure from the essential requirements of law. Thus, we grant the petition for writ of certiorari, and quash the order granting the motion to disqualify counsel.

PETITION GRANTED; ORDER QUASHED.

Case Review Question
Carnival Corporation v. Beverly, 744 So.2d 489 (Fla.App. 1st Dist. 1999).
How is it justice when the appellate Court agrees with the lower court's findings that the conduct was wholly inappropriate and then reverses its final order?

THE RESULT OF ETHICAL VIOLATIONS

The license to practice law, the certification granted by NALA, and the validation by NEPA are essentially earned privileges. When someone demonstrates the requisite ability and qualifications to receive the license or certification, it is done subject to certain conditions. Failure to abide by these conditions can have a variety of results.

As mentioned, a lawyer can be the subject of disciplinary action by the professional body. A lawyer, paralegal, or other members of the support staff may also be the subject of legal action in the courts initiated by injured parties. These remedies are not mutually exclusive in any way. The professional discipline of an attorney and a lawsuit against a lawyer or paralegal are seen as separate and distinct. The disciplinary action is designed to protect an unwitting public by taking action against the licensure/certification of someone who negligently or deliberately acts unethically in violation of these license/certification requirements. The focus of the lawsuit is to compensate a specifically injured party for damage caused as the result of another's unethical conduct.

In the first circumstance; anyone can lodge a complaint with the appropriate administrative body stating the facts of the alleged unethical behavior. The allegations of the complaint are investigated and a determination made as to whether action is warranted. In some circumstances, a hearing may be held to give the alleged wrongdoer the opportunity to present a response to the complaint in person. Once the merits of the complaint have been evaluated, there are a number of possible outcomes. Although each state has its own specific rules and disciplinary procedures, common outcomes are often utilized. It is possible that the authoritative body will find the complaint unfounded or the conduct insufficient to constitute a clear violation worthy of disciplinary action. Conversely, if it is found that a violation has occurred, then based on severity, willfulness, previous history of violations, and damage to the client, then a variety of forms of discipline may be imposed. These include everything from a formal reprimand to suspension or total revocation of licensure. Any negative outcome in a disciplinary action almost always results in negative publicity and a likely increase in the cost of malpractice insurance; and possibly the loss of income as the result of lost business. In some instances, the individual who is the subject of the complaint may be required to attend educational programs to raise his or her level of awareness of ethical duties.

In addition to disciplinary action, the party allegedly injured by the unethical conduct can, in many cases, file a legal action for malfeasance against the attorney and any involved support staff. The procedure would be the same as for any other type of personal injury lawsuit including a statement of the allegedly wrongful conduct by the defendant and the consequent injury to the party filing suit (plaintiff). The possible outcome would range from dismissal of the action to a monetary judgment against the defendant, payable to the plaintiff. The party or parties named could include the party who is accused of having acted unethically, and in some instances, the employer if the accused conduct is performed by a subordinate employee of one required by law to conduct business in an ethical manner.

Ethical Considerations

Ethical conduct is expected among the members of the general population, but only a handful of professions condition licensure and the practice of the profession on continued ethical conduct. The legal profession is one such entity.

The failure of a lawyer or any other individual working in the legal field to act ethically can have a number of repercussions that range from mild to the most severe, including in some cases even criminal prosecution. The duty to act ethically hinges on the fiduciary relationship with the innocent persons who place their trust, and sometimes their personal and financial well-being, in the hands of the legal professionals.

Ethical Circumstance

Simone is the beneficiary of a large inheritance. In a short time she has managed to squander nearly half of the money. In an attempt to preserve the balance, which if properly handled will support her for the rest of her life, Simone hires an attorney to create a trust fund. She trusts the attorney and asks her to manage the trust and distribute the interest earned by the investment of the money on a periodic basis. The attorney agrees. What Simone does not know is that the attorney borrows money from the trust fund now and then. In the past, the money has always been repaid within a year of the "loan." What, if anything, is wrong with the conduct of the attorney?

CHAPTER SUMMARY

The duties and obligations associated with legal ethics are present in every area of law and at every level of the law-related professions. For this reason, it should be a constant presence in the minds of legal professionals and should guide the manner in which they do their work. Keys to ethical behavior consist of acting at all times with honesty, integrity, and the clients' best interest at the forefront. Because the legal relationship to a client is a fiduciary one, the duty to honor a client's trust in matters of confidence is paramount. The privilege of confidentiality belongs to the client and typically can only be waived by the client unless a court order or planned criminal conduct is involved. In addition to confidentiality, all legal professionals, associates, and support staff are required to avoid situations in which a conflict of interest might occur. This requires that the interests of the client come first in matters of business opportunities and in matters involving employment of the legal professional. At no time may an attorney or other legal professional be in a position that might create an occasion for the breach of any other ethical duty, such as confidentiality, or result in benefit to the

professional at the expense of the client. In line with this is the obligation to undertake to perform only those duties for which the legal professional has achieved an adequate level of competence. If this cannot be accomplished, then there is an obligation to decline the representation or assistance. This level of competence requires not only training but also current knowledge in the area of concern. Thus, legal professionals are under a continuing obligation to maintain their skills and knowledge of the law. Finally, legal professionals are required to act at all times with a degree of professionalism that constitutes zealous representation of their clients. While attorneys are bound by the ABA Code of Ethics, the NALA has adopted its own code, which incorporates ABA's code by reference. All subordinate staff members and those associated with the delivery of legal services are similarly bound as a matter of reality even if not as a condition of licensure. The failure to honor legal ethical standards can result in formal disciplinary action, legal action in civil court, and long-term effects on professional employment and advancement.

CHAPTER TERMS

competence   conflict of interest   fiduciary
confidentiality   ethics

REVIEW QUESTIONS

1. Why are attorney–client communications confidential?
2. What is an ethical wall?
3. What is a conflict of interest?
4. Describe the general ethical responsibilities of a paralegal employed by an attorney.
5. Who in the law office is bound to keep attorney–client communications privileged?
6. Why are ethical codes in place for attorneys and paralegals?
7. What difficulty can arise from continuing representation in a case where there is a conflict of interest?
8. What are the potential consequences of ethical violations?
9. What is the requirement regarding competent representation?
10. When can an attorney represent as the only counsel in a case such as a dissolution of marriage?

RELEVANT LINKS

American Bar Association Center for Professional Responsibility
www.ABANET.org/cpr/home.html
NFPA Model Code of Ethics
www.paralegals.org/Development/modelcode.html

NALA Code of Ethics and Professional Responsibility
www.nala.org/stand.html
Legal Ethics Resources
www.legalethics.com

INTERNET ASSIGNMENT 6.1

Identify the site in your state that contains the ethical requirements for members of the state bar.

For additional resources, please visit our Web site at www.westlegalstudies.com

CHAPTER 7

Substantive and Procedural Issues

CHAPTER OBJECTIVES

After reading this chapter, you should be able to:

- Distinguish substantive and procedural law.

- Explain the difference in procedure between a jury trial and a bench trial.

- Discuss the function and application of an appellate court.

- Explain the purpose and method of applicability of the rules of evidence.

- List and describe each stage of a trial.

- Identify the difference between a Motion for Judgment NOV and a Motion for New Trial.

- Explain the purpose of exceptions to hearsay evidence.

- List the two functions of substantive law.

SUBSTANTIVE AND PROCEDURAL ISSUES

The body of law that has developed in this country can be organized in countless ways. Each method of organization provides a way of distinguishing one area of law from another. First, all law can be defined as substantive or procedural. In addition, law can be divided into criminal and civil law (of which contract law and tort law are types). The purpose of this chapter is to clarify the differences between substantive and procedural law and to provide an understanding of the procedural aspects of civil law. Criminal procedure is addressed in Chapter 15. Later chapters will also examine various kinds of civil and criminal substantive as well as procedural law.

The Difference Between Civil and Criminal Law

civil law
Law that governs the private rights of individuals, legal entities, and government.

Let us begin by clarifying the difference between civil and criminal law. **Civil law** governs the issues that arise between parties over private rights. Thus, a citizen who sues another for an invasion of personal rights has grounds for a civil case. An example of a civil case is an individual suing the government for invasion of private rights. Another example is a suit by one citizen against another for property damage or physical injury caused by an automobile accident. A civil case is brought by the injured party for damage to his or her personal rights, person, or property. The injured party seeks some sort of compensation (usually monetary) for the injury or damage to the person or property.

A criminal case is a suit that is brought by the government for violation or injury to public rights. Even though a crime may be perpetrated against a single victim, the public as a whole demands safety and certain conduct by all persons. An individual who violates these demands against anyone violates the rights of the public as a whole. The government enforces the rights of the public through prosecution based on criminal law, which ranges from parking violations to murder. Criminal law includes all laws designed by the legislature to maintain order and safety in our society. It carries a penalty of a fine, imprisonment, or community service, paid to the government rather than to a particular victim. A court may also order restitution (compensation) to the victim. With the exception of an order of restitution, generally any claim for damages by a victim who may have been injured by a crime must be resolved in a civil suit against the alleged criminal brought by the injured party.

compensatory damages
An award of money payable to the injured party for the reasonable cost of the injuries.

In a civil case, the penalties are quite different. For example, there is no imprisonment. Secondly, any judgment that awards money is payable to the individual whose rights were invaded and injured. The award of money should be sufficient to compensate the injured party for the reasonable cost of the injuries, thus the term **compensatory damages.** Additionally, in cases where money cannot adequately compensate but some action could, the guilty party may be ordered to act or refrain from acting in a certain way. This is called injunctive relief and, more particularly, specific performance. This type of relief is quite limited. Some jurisdictions also permit the recovery of punitive damages (also known as exemplary damages), which are additional monies that the defendant is ordered to pay as a form of punishment. The reasoning behind punitive damages is that some actions are so grossly improper that the defendant should be punished in a way that will serve as an example to others who might contemplate the same wrongful conduct.

In civil cases, procedural law takes effect when citizens bring a dispute to the legal system. In criminal law, the law enforcement agencies and prosecutors who are part of the legal system initiate a claim against a citizen. Therefore, criminal procedural law begins at the time the law enforcement personnel anticipate that they will bring a dispute into the legal system. This is addressed at great length in Chapter 15. The remainder of the discussion in this chapter is confined to issues of civil law.

APPLICATION 7.1

Jose is a businessman who travels extensively. He was on a company plane making a business trip when the plane crashed. Jose was killed but the pilot survived. Jose's wife sued the company for the wrongful death of her husband due to the negligence of the company pilot. Criminal charges were also brought against the pilot for violation of federal law when he attempted to fly the plane while under the influence of illegal substances.

The criminal trial was brought by the government to prosecute for the violations of criminal law and injury to the public safety. The civil case by Jose's wife was brought to trial to establish the responsibility of the company for the improper supervision of its pilot employee and the conduct of the pilot for negligently undertaking to fly while under the influence of drugs.

Point for Discussion

◆   Why would it be improper to determine the criminal and civil issues of a case in a single trial?

Assignment 7.1

Which of the following examples are likely to be part of a criminal action, and which would more likely be part of a civil action?

a.   Parking ticket.
b.   Legal action against a neighbor who ran over a person's mailbox backing out of the driveway.
c.   A defendant is ordered to pay a fine of $100 for throwing a rock through a window of a business.
d.   A defendant is ordered to pay $100 to replace the window of a business through which he threw a rock.

e.   A defendant is named in a lawsuit after turning over and damaging headstones in a city cemetery.

f.   A defendant is sentenced to 40 hours of community service cleaning the grounds of a cemetery after defacing headstones.

g.   A defendant is ordered to pay $1,000 for physical injuries caused to another during a fight.

h.   A defendant is sued by a family for the death of a family member as the result of the defendant's drunk driving.

i.   A defendant is ordered to return property taken from her former spouse after the property had been awarded to the spouse in a divorce proceeding.

j.   A defendant is placed in jail for 48 hours after being held in contempt of court for an outburst during a court proceeding.

SUBSTANTIVE VERSUS PROCEDURAL LAW

For hundreds of years, substantive and procedural law have coexisted. Without procedural law, substantive law could never be created. Without substantive law, there would be no need for procedural law. It remains more clear than ever that in today's complex society, substantive law and procedural law play equally important roles in our legal system.

Substantive Law

substantive law
The law that creates and resolves the issue between the parties. Legal standards that guide conduct and that are applied to determine whether conduct was legally appropriate.

Substantive law creates, defines, and regulates rights, as opposed to protective, procedural, or remedial law, which provides a method of enforcing rights.[1] It is exactly what its name implies: the body, essence, and substance that guides the conduct of citizens. It encompasses principles of right and wrong as well as the principle that wrong will result in penalty. It includes the rights and duties of citizens, and it provides the basis to resolve issues involving those rights. Every citizen has the right to live and enjoy his or her own property free from intrusion by other citizens. All members of a populous society are obligated to respect and to not interfere with the rights of others. Substantive law establishes the extent of this right and obligation to which all persons are subject.

When a person engages in conduct that has an adverse effect on another individual, an injury may occur. An innocent injured party who wants to be compensated for the damage caused by the injury may request assistance from the legal system on the basis that the injuring party acted wrongfully. Such wrongful conduct gives rise to the dispute between the two parties. The court will examine the situation to determine whether the conduct of the party alleged to be at fault was indeed wrongful by society's standards. If it was, the party will be judged and will be penalized. If it was not, the party will be judged innocent. In either situation, the court resolves the issue based on what society has determined to be right and wrong conduct between individuals and entities.

APPLICATION 7.2

The issue arises: Jane is driving her car down the street when she notices that a local department store is having a giant sale. She quickly stops to turn into the store's parking lot. Suddenly, her car is hit from behind by another car. Jane's vehicle is badly damaged. She brings suit against Tom, the driver of the other car. Jane claims that Tom was driving carelessly and that his careless (wrongful) conduct caused damage to her vehicle. Tom claims he was driving carefully but could not avoid the collision when Jane slammed on the brakes of her car.

The issue is resolved: The court will hear the evidence of both Jane and Tom in this case. If it determines that Tom was driving carelessly and could have avoided the accident, Tom will be judged liable and will have to pay for the damage to Jane's car. If the court decides that even careful driving by Tom could not have prevented the accident, Tom will be found not to be liable. In either situation, the court will apply what society has determined to be a standard (requirement) of careful conduct. The conduct of the parties is measured against this minimum level of careful conduct. If the conduct of a party does not meet this standard, the party is guilty. If the conduct of the party does meet the standard, the party is considered not liable. Thus, the existing legal standards of rightful and wrongful conduct are used to resolve the issue between parties who are in dispute.

Point for Discussion
- What occurs when no substantive law is applicable to a situation but two parties appear in court claiming conflicting rights?

Procedural Law

Procedural law prescribes a method of enforcing rights or of obtaining redress for the invasion of rights.[2] The basic function of civil procedural law is to facilitate the movement of a lawsuit through the legal system. Procedural laws are created to ensure that each party will be afforded fair and impartial treatment. Further, procedural law has its goal that judges and juries will receive only evidence that will allow them to make a fair and impartial decision.

Civil procedure can be likened to a large piece of machinery that assembles a product. It does not feel or possess opinions. The function of procedural law is to assemble all of the pieces into a complete product. The parties to the suit provide the pieces to the product at appropriate times and in the

procedural law
Law used to guide parties fairly and efficiently through the legal system.

appropriate manner. The completed product delivered from the machine is the decision that resolves the dispute. This decision is based on the pieces of information (substantive law and facts of the case) that have been fed into the machine and assembled.

In the lawsuit previously discussed, Jane and Tom became involved in litigation. The principles of law that were applied in their case to determine who should prevail, based on the most reasonable explanation of the facts, is substantive law. Procedural law also plays a part in the litigation and includes the following:

1. The time limit for bringing a lawsuit.
2. The manner in which the lawsuit is begun (e.g., by filing a complaint or petition).
3. The proper way to inform the defendant that a lawsuit has been filed.
4. The types of information that each party must release to the other party.
5. The procedure at trial.
6. The evidence that can be introduced at trial.
7. The method for appealing the decision if the losing party feels the decision was unfair.

The Common Ground

On occasion, substantive rights are affected by procedural law. Most often, when there is a conflict of law (different legal standards apply in different states) or when more than one jurisdiction has contact with the dispute, there is the potential for procedural law to affect the outcome of the suit rather than substantive law. Such a case could arise when the parties bring their action in federal court based on diversity of citizenship (discussed in Chapter 8). Another situation might involve a dispute based on a series of events that occurred in different jurisdictions and ultimately resulted in an injury.

In different jurisdictions, procedural law and conflicting substantive law may be dealt with differently. The general rule is that a court should attempt to apply its own procedural rules regardless of which substantive law applies.[3] The courts, including the U.S. Supreme Court, have continued to address issues of this nature for quite some time with no final decision.

The issue of conflicting procedural and substantive standards from varying jurisdictions arises when more than one jurisdiction (area within a court's authority) could serve as the forum for a lawsuit. The party bringing the action will no doubt select the jurisdiction whose laws most favor the claim. An example is a choice between two states based on the statute of limitations laws. The statute of limitations is a procedural law in a jurisdiction that indicates the maximum amount of time in which a lawsuit can be commenced. For example, in some states, a personal injury claim must be brought within three years. In other states, the limit is one year. Thus, if a plaintiff in one of these states with a personal injury claim decides to file a suit two years after the injury, the suit could be brought only in a state with a three-year statute of limitations. In a jurisdiction with a one-year statute of limitations, the suit would be barred after one year had passed. Because the circumstances that produce a lawsuit sometimes occur in more than one jurisdiction, there is more than one place where suit could be brought.

The conflict of the statute of limitations gave rise to the establishment of the outcome determinative test by the U.S. Supreme Court.[4] The test was originally created to be used by federal courts faced with a case based on state laws where more than one state is connected with the case or where either state law or federal law could be applied. Under this test, the court examines what would happen under each law. The goal is that the outcome should be the same whether the case is heard in federal court or state court (under state law). If the outcome of the suit would be different solely because of federal procedural rules (such as a statute of limitations that differs from the state statute of limitations), the state procedural rule should be applied. The idea is to discourage persons from filing a case in a particular court just because they have a better possibility of winning in that court when they could not win in another court that also had jurisdiction. This practice is referred to as forum shopping. Courts encourage parties to select a court because it is the best equipped to hear their claim and consider all the evidence, not because it is the best court strategically. While in reality part of diligent representation is making the best strategical moves, the courts have tried to place limits on this to the extent strategy becomes an attempt at manipulation of the outcome which is supposed to be under fair and impartial terms.

The U.S. Supreme Court has, in recent years, formed a blend of the general rule and the outcome determinative test.[5] The accepted rule now is that a court should apply its own procedural rules when possible. However, when the laws of the various jurisdictions involved are so different that it is clear the plaintiff was shopping for the court with the most favorable laws and not for the most appropriate site for the case, the outcome determinative test should be applied.

Assignment 7.2

Consider the following situation and explain why you think the case should or should not be dismissed.

Seth lives in Illinois. He is suing his former wife who lives in Missouri for fraud. Seth has been sued for the collection of the debt on a credit card he was not aware even existed. In his suit against his former wife, Seth claims she committed fraud when she applied for the card and then used it to obtain goods and services in his name. The suit is filed in Missouri where the former wife lives, where the card was allegedly obtained by her and most purchases made. In Illinois, where Seth lives, the statute of limitations for the action has expired. Seth's former wife is seeking to have the suit dismissed.

THE CREATION AND APPLICATION OF CIVIL PROCEDURE LAW

Creating Laws of Procedure

Laws of procedure, sometimes referred to as rules, are created by the authority of the legislature. Procedural law applies to all people and is created to facilitate an organized court system and to protect the constitutional guarantees to citizens. Because the laws deal with the mechanics of the court system, judges are often better equipped than the legislature to create fair and reasonable rules that provide for an efficient court system. Therefore, in many jurisdictions, the legislatures vest the courts with authority to create such laws. At the very least, the courts have input into what the procedural laws should be.

Even though they are created with the assistance of the judicial branch, procedural laws are adopted by the legislature as statutes. Thus, they can often be found in the published statutes along with the other enactments of the legislature. Although procedural rules are not published with the opinions of the judges on individual cases, interpretations of the rules often appear in judicial opinions.

Types of Procedural Law

For the sake of convenience, procedural law has been divided into several categories. A person researching the law has a much easier time finding the particular laws or rules that apply to a given case if the law is organized according to subject. Most often, a jurisdiction will divide its procedural law into the following categories:

1. Rules of civil procedure
2. Rules of criminal procedure
3. Rules of evidence
4. Rules of appellate procedure

In addition to having the power to create rules that are enacted into law for an entire jurisdiction, courts generally have the power to create local rules, which apply only to the court that creates them and to no other court. An example would be a county rules court. Although the procedural laws of a state apply to all of the state courts including county courts, each county court may enact its own local rules as well. Local rules are designed to supplement the state laws of procedure.[6]

APPLICATION 7.3

The state legislature enacts a rule of procedure that requires all petitions to have an estate probated be filed in the county where the decedent was domiciled. This would apply as a procedural law to the entire jurisdiction (state). The local court of Wier County enacts a procedural rule that requires petitions to probate an estate be filed with an information sheet that provides data on the parties filing the petition, whether there is a will, and a check for filing fees. This is an example of a local rule of procedure.

Point for Discussion
◆ Why doesn't the legislature just enact all procedural rules that are applicable to all courts for all matters of procedure and eliminate local rules?

RULES OF CIVIL PROCEDURE

The rules of civil procedure include the laws that dictate how a suit will be filed, all pretrial matters, trial proceedings (with the possible exception of rules of evidence), and posttrial issues until the case is concluded or an appeal is initiated. Most state rules of civil procedure follow or are similar to a standard model. Note, however, that each state has the right to create its own procedural rules that are followed and enforced in the state courts and that may vary from the standard rules followed in most jurisdictions.

Pretrial Proceedings

The rules of civil procedure first become relevant at the time a lawsuit is begun. This occurs by commencing an action with the filing of appropriate initial court documents and fees. In exceptional circumstances, an action may be commenced in some jurisdictions by filing documents seeking immediate court intervention to prevent irreparable damage or harm of some sort. The vast majority of cases, however, are commenced with the filing of a complaint or petition.[7]

Complaint. An action (lawsuit) is filed by the plaintiff, who presents the **complaint,** or petition (document alleging what the defendant did that was legally wrong), with appropriate filing fees (costs of processing the documents), to the clerk of the court. Traditionally, a complaint sought monetary damages and a petition sought some sort of equitable relief such as the distribution of assets in a fair manner or specific court-ordered conduct by the defendant for the benefit of the plaintiff. This dates back to a time when courts were divided into two divisions. The courts of chancery dealt with damage claims and the courts of equity dealt with other matters requiring legal action to achieve a fair result. The latter might be a breach of contract action when the plaintiff wanted the defendant to be ordered to complete the contract terms, or a case of probating and distributing the estate of a decedent. Today, courts usually have a number of subdivisions in most jurisdictions but they are more often by type of case. Preservation of the terms *complaint* for chancery type actions and *petition* for actions based in equity persists, but some blending has taken place. Each jurisdiction, however, states within the

complaint
Also known as a petition. The document that apprises the court and the defendant of the nature of the cause of action by plaintiff.

procedural rules (local or jurisdiction wide) the appropriate terminology. The important thing to remember is that either document, regardless of name, achieves the same purpose, which is to initiate a legal proceeding. For discussion purposes, the term *complaint* will be generally used in this textbook. The complaint is organized into what are usually single statements numbered and referred to as paragraphs. Each statement is either a statement of the existing law or a statement of a fact that the plaintiff alleges has occurred. When read in its entirety, the complaint should state which laws have allegedly been breached and which facts state how the law was allegedly broken. Additionally, the complaint will indicate what compensation is necessary to satisfy the plaintiff's injuries (see Figure 7.1).

Summons.   Once the lawsuit has been filed, the wheels of the judicial system begin to turn. A summons (formal legal notice of suit) is issued to the defendant in the lawsuit, and is usually accompanied by a copy of the complaint. The method of giving notice of the suit is also prescribed by procedural law. A summons indicates how long a party has to respond to the claims of the complaint. Methods of service include personal delivery to the defendant or a suitable representative and publication of the information in a newspaper where the defendant lives or is believed to live. Some states allow other methods, and as technology of communication expands, so most likely will methods of service. If the defendant does not respond to the complaint within the allowed time period, the court will accept everything alleged in the complaint as true and grant a decision in favor of the plaintiff. This is known as default judgment.

Response.   A defendant may respond to the complaint in a number of ways. Responsive pleadings have different names in different states. However, the basic methods of responding to a complaint are the same. One method is through an answer, in which the defendant responds to each item specifically alleged in the complaint. Commonly, the defendant will respond by admitting, denying, or pleading the inability to admit or deny based on lack of information. This latter claim is given in response to an allegation that is vague or cannot be answered with an admission or denial unless more information is provided by the plaintiff. Claiming a lack of knowledge is generally treated as a denial to protect the defendant from having to admit to or deny claims about which too little is known at the time. If an answer is filed, the parties move into pretrial proceedings (see Figure 7.2).

Another response to a complaint might be a Motion for a Bill of Particulars, a claim by the defendant that the complaint as it is stated cannot be answered. A Motion for a Bill of Particulars requests the court to order the plaintiff to clarify one or more allegations of the complaint by explaining or adding information. If the motion is granted, the plaintiff will be required to provide the defendant with additional information. If the motion is denied, the defendant will be ordered to answer the complaint as it stands.

FIGURE 7.1

Complaint

In the District Court
45th Judicial District
State of Tucammawa

Buzzy Jamison,
Plaintiff
vs.
Malcolm Smythe,
Defendant.

COMPLAINT

Comes now the Plaintiff Buzzy Jamison, by his attorneys Marjoram, Coburn, and McEachern, and for his cause of action against Defendant Malcolm Smythe, complains as follows:

1. On or about March the 17th, 1990, Tucammawa state highway 7098, ran in an east-west direction through Langdon County, State of Tucammawa.

2. On the aforementioned date, at approximately 3:00 a.m., Defendant Malcolm Smythe was operating a motor vehicle in a westerly direction along said highway in the vicinity of highway mile-marker 31.

3. At the aforementioned place and time, Defendant Malcolm Smythe caused his vehicle to cross the median separating east- and westbound traffic, and did then and there enter the eastbound lanes.

4. Immediately following the entry of Malcolm Smythe's westbound vehicle into the eastbound lane, said vehicle collided with the vehicle operated by Plaintiff, in an easterly direction.

5. Said collision was the direct and proximate result of one or more of the following negligent acts or omissions of Defendant Malcolm Smythe:
   a) Driving while under the influence of alcohol and/or other drugs.
   b) Driving too fast for conditions.
   c) Failure to keep a proper lookout.
   d) Failure to properly maintain his vehicle in properly marked lanes.
   e) Westbound entry into lanes limited to eastbound traffic.

6. Said collision was with such force that Plaintiff's vehicle was severely damaged.

7. Said collision further caused serious and permanent injuries to the Plaintiff which include but are not limited to the following:
   a) Injuries to the Plaintiff's head, face, and neck.
   b) Injuries to the Plaintiff's right arm.
   c) Injuries to the Plaintiff's left leg.
   d) Injuries to the Plaintiff's back.
   e) Injuries to the Plaintiff's skeletal, muscle, and nervous system.

8. Said injuries to the Plaintiff have caused great physical and emotional suffering, loss of wages, and medical expenses incurred in an attempt to be cured of said injuries. Said injuries have further caused permanent disability and disfigurement to Plaintiff, and will result in additional future lost wages, and expenses in an attempt to be cured of said injuries.

WHEREFORE, the Plaintiff prays that the Court will find the Defendant to be guilty of negligence, and further that the court will grant damages and costs to the Plaintiff as compensation for the above said injuries.

Buzzy Jamison
Attorneys Marjoram, Coburn, & McEachern
7719 Hamilton
Sequoia, Tucammawa 00000

FIGURE 7.2

Answer

In the District Court
45th Judicial District
State of Tucammawa

Buzzy Jamison,
Plaintiff
vs.
Malcolm Smythe,
Defendant.

ANSWER

Comes now the Defendant Malcolm Smythe, by his attorneys Cochran, Eastwood, and McQueen, and with respect to the allegations of the Plaintiff's Complaint answers as follows:
1. Admitted.
2. Admitted.
3. Admitted.
4. Admitted.
5. Denied.
6. Denied.
7. Denied.
8. Denied.

AFFIRMATIVE DEFENSE

Defendant further states as an affirmative Defense that he was forced into the eastbound lane as the result of a hazard in the westbound lane; and that Plaintiff, seeing the Defendant approach, failed to take any evasive action whatsoever to avoid the collision. The Plaintiff is guilty of gross negligence in failing to take steps to avoid the collision, and as a result should not be permitted to recover against the Defendant.

Malcolm Smythe
Attorneys Cochran, Eastwood, and McQueen
Success Building, Suite I
1700 Pennsylvania Ave
Sequoia, Tucammawa 00000

If the complaint is deficient in some way, a Motion to Dismiss (in some states, a similar document is known as a Demurrer) may be filed. This simply states that the complaint either does not contain facts that warrant any type of lawsuit or that the complaint is improperly stated according to procedural rules. Every lawsuit brought must be done so under a recognized legal theory also known as a cause of action. Each cause of action has specific elements that must be proven. For example, to prove someone was so negligent that he or she is legally responsible for injuries to another person as the result of that negligence, there must be evidence of certain elements that make up the legal definition of negligence. A complaint based on the legal cause of action for negligence must allege sufficient evidence of these elements in the present case. Failure to do so may result in a motion to dismiss for failure to properly state a cause of action against the defendant. Additionally, procedural rules specify the type and extent of information to be included in a complaint. Typically this will include a statement of why the court has jurisdiction over the case, the specific identity of the parties, and the alleged cause of action with sufficient supporting facts to support the elements of the legal theory as well as a claim for the relief sought, such as monetary damages. Some jurisdictions require the complaint to be specific, while others permit more general statements to suffice. It is always important to comply with the procedural rules fully when drafting a complaint. The failure to properly prepare a complaint can result in a delay of months and additional time of the parties as appearances are made in court to argue the sufficiency of the complaint and time spent amending the original document.

If a Motion to Dismiss or Demurrer is granted, the complaint can result in permanent dismissal of the lawsuit or dismissal without prejudice. This is the same as dismissal with leave to amend, which means that the plaintiff can correct the errors. Often, if this is done within a specified period of time, the suit does not need to be refiled. Dismissal with prejudice is a permanent dismissal and is rarely ordered, as the court wants to provide the parties with the full opportunity to pursue their legal rights. An example, however, might be in a case when there is no dispute that the statute of limitations has expired and with it the plaintiff's right to pursue legal remedies.

Whether a request to dismiss on any basis is granted with or without prejudice depends on the reasons supporting the motion/request. If the reason is no basis exists for any type of lawsuit, the suit may be dismissed with prejudice unless the plaintiff can demonstrate to the court that additional facts could be added to the complaint that would create the foundation for a lawsuit. If the motion is denied and the complaint is found to be proper, the defendant is ordered to file an answer to the complaint.

It is also important to note that the failure to properly serve the summons or complaint on the dismissal on the defendant can result in an action being dismissed. For example, if the summons and complaint was not served on the defendant, or an appropriate representative, or was served at an inappropriate place or time, the defendant could file a motion to dismiss. Each jurisdiction has its own procedural rules concerning the service of process that need to be followed closely.

Arbitration.   A more recent phenomenon to take a firm hold in the justice system is that of **arbitration.** Each year tens of thousands of lawsuits are filed in this country. Statistics show that the large majority end in settlement by the parties at some stage of the proceedings. To this end, the courts in all states favor any measure that relieves the already overcrowded dockets and brings the cases to conclusion sooner than would be achieved by the traditional method of litigation. As a result, all states have added a stage of either voluntary or mandatory arbitration.

At this stage, the parties agree upon or accept a court-appointed (depending on the jurisdiction) arbitrator. This person is trained not only in law but also in the art of mediating disputes. Often parties will agree that the decision of the arbitrator will be final and not subject to appeal. In some cases, the parties reserve the right to return to the courts for traditional processes in the event the arbitrator's determination is unacceptable to them.

arbitration
Third-party resolution of a legal issue that has arisen between two or more parties. Typically, parties are agreed (arbitration clause) or court ordered (compulsory) to submit evidence to arbitrator for binding decision.

When a case goes through arbitration, the parties submit their accumulated evidence and an objective arbitrator acts as a sort of judge and jury. The evidence is considered in light of applicable law and the arbitrator renders what he or she believes a fair result would be and likely what would result in the courts. The parties then take this decision, and depending on the terms of their arbitration agreement, either end the case at this stage or go forward in the courts. It is a method by which many less complicated cases can reach conclusion in a fair manner, much more quickly and with less expense than the traditional method of trial in the courts.

Similar to arbitration in this respect is mediation. Mediators specialize in working between parties in dispute to reach a settlement acceptable and reasonable to both. Mediation is seen frequently in domestic relations cases where parties are unable to agree about terms of issues such as custody, visitation, support, and other matters that continue to connect the parties after the marriage has ended. Mediation is also effective in other types of cases such as probate of estates and contract disputes. As with arbitration, the goal is to reach an acceptable and fair result without the time and expense associated with processing a case through already overcrowded courts.

Discovery.   During the period after a suit is filed and prior to trial or settlement, procedural rules guide the parties in their preparations for the ultimate conclusion of the dispute. The most significant event during this time is known as **discovery.** At this stage, the parties exchange information under strict guidelines and close supervision of the courts. A primary goal of discovery is to foster the fair exchange of information to enable the parties to clearly evaluate their positions.[8] Often, discovery will result in settlement of the case once the parties become aware of all the information pertinent to the case, since the parties may not have been aware of certain facts that would influence the outcome of the case in a trial. Discovery can be considered "show and tell" where both parties present their evidence. This practice encourages the objective assessment of the strengths and weaknesses of each side, thereby encouraging settlement. The parties may utilize several different methods of discovery.

discovery

Court-supervised exchange of evidence and other relevant information between parties to a lawsuit.

Interrogatories.   Frequently, the first step in discovery is the submission of interrogatories—written questions submitted to the opposing party in the case (see Figure 7.3). The party who receives the questions must answer them under oath and in writing. A party may object to answering questions that are irrelevant or immaterial, invade the attorney–client privilege, or violate some other procedural rule. When an objection is raised, the judge will determine whether the party must answer the questions. Many jurisdictions limit the number of interrogatories that may be sent to the opposition.

Request for production.   Often interrogatories are accompanied by another means of discovery—the request for production of documents (see Figure 7.4). This is a written request to produce documents or copies of documents. Because many of the functions of our society are dependent upon

In the District Court
45th Judicial District
State of Tucammawa

Buzzy Jamison,
Plaintiff
vs.
Malcolm Smythe,
Defendant.

INTERROGATORIES

Comes now the Plaintiff Buzzy Jamison by his attorneys Marjoram, Coburn, and McEachern and with respect to the above-named case submit the following interrogatories pursuant to Court Rule 606. Pursuant to said rule, the interrogatories below are to be answered in writing and under oath within 28 days of the date submitted.

1. With respect to the Defendant please state:
   a) All names by which the Defendant has been known.
   b) All addresses at which the Defendant has claimed residence since 1970.
   c) The names and current address of any current or former spouse.
   d) The address of Defendant's current employment, position held, and current wage rate.
   e) The Defendant's social security number.
2. State the whereabouts of the Defendant between the hours of 3:00 p.m. March 16, 1990, and 3:00 a.m. March17, 1990.
3. With respect to the time and dates listed in interrogatory number 2, state the name and address of each person, business, or other entity which provided alcohol or other drugs, by gift or sale, to the Defendant.
4. State all prescription medications and the prescribing physician's name and address for all drugs the Defendant was taking March 16–17, 1990.

Buzzy Jamison
Attorneys Majoram, Coburn, & McEachern
7719 Hamilton
Sequoia, Tucammawa 00000

Submitted to Defendant by placing the above-stated interrogatories, postage paid, in the United States Mail, on the 31st day of April 2003.

FIGURE 7.3
Interrogatories

Comes now the Defendant, in the above-captioned action, and pursuant to applicable rules of civil procedure, request that the plaintiff produce for examination, testing, sampling or copying by the defendant or agents of the following items:

1. All photographs, recordings, reports, records, documents, videotapes, notes, memoranda, accounts, books, papers, and other recorded, written, photographic or transcribed information that represent, are pertinent or related to in any manner, the allegations of the plaintiff against the defendant. The only exception to such request are the working papers and/or notes of plaintiff's attorney which would be characterized as work product of said attorney.

Marvin Henry, atty.
Winter, Somers and Snow, P.C.
Suite 260 Park Place
Canoga, State 000000

FIGURE 7.4
Request for Production

written records, it is often very helpful to review documents for insight into what actually occurred. These requests are also subject to objection based on a claim that the answers contain privileged or irrelevant information, and a judge may rule whether or not they must be complied with. Privileged information is information that was conveyed within the context of a confidential relationship, such as the attorney–client, doctor–patient, or clergy–parishioner relationship. Irrelevant information is information that is not probative or likely to produce evidence that is probative of the facts in the case.

Deposition.   One method of discovery—the deposition—applies not only to the parties in the lawsuit but also to all persons with relevant information about it. In a deposition, the attorneys ask a party or witness in the suit to respond to extensive questions about his or her knowledge of the case. Usually, depositions are taken in person and in the presence of the attorneys for each party. The entire proceeding is taken down by a stenographer court reporter who is also a notary public and asks the person deposed to swear to tell the truth (see Figure 7.5).

More often, depositions are taken on videotape. In another type of deposition, the party requesting the deposition sends written questions and the deposee is asked to answer the questions under oath and to provide a notarized statement that the responses are true and accurate to the best of his or her knowledge.

If it is anticipated that the witness will not be present at trial, the deposition may be taken for evidentiary purposes. The procedure is basically the same, but in addition to the discovering party asking questions, the other attorneys may ask questions in the same manner as they would in a trial. Both direct examination and cross-examination are conducted. If objections are made, the questions are later presented to a judge. If it is determined that the witness should respond, the answers will be given and presented to the jury.

Physical evidence.   In some cases, physical evidence is an integral part of the lawsuit. For example, if a person is injured by a tool or on private property, the condition of the tool or the property may become paramount in the lawsuit. When such physical evidence is owned or controlled by another party

---

FIGURE 7.5

Notice of
Deposition

> Pursuant to the rules of civil procedure applicable to this proceeding, the oral deposition of Defendant shall be taken before a notary public on December 12, 1994, commencing at 1:00 p.m. and continuing thereafter until such time as completed. The aforementioned deposition will be conducted at place of business of the Defendant, 401 East 1st St., Knobbe, IK 030303.
>
> Marvin Henry, atty.
> Winter, Somers and Snow, P.C.
> Suite 260 Park Place
> Canoga, State 000000

to the suit, the discovering party may file a request for inspection. This type of discovery allows a party to inspect, photograph, measure, and evaluate a particular item or place. If the party wants custody of an item or wants to subject the item to any procedures that might affect it, court approval may be required. Otherwise, in most cases, plaintiffs and defendants are entitled to reasonable inspection of items that may be produced as evidence in a trial.

Examination. A party may also request a physical or mental examination of an opposing party if such examination is relevant to the lawsuit. An example is a plaintiff who is claiming injuries as the result of alleged negligence by the defendant. In such a case, the defendant may very well be allowed to select a physician to examine the plaintiff and give an opinion as to the extent of the injuries. Another example is a custody battle by the parents of a child. If the child or one of the parents has a history of abnormal behavior, the court may allow a mental examination by a qualified specialist to determine whether the behavior has had an adverse effect on the child. However, the court may also enforce limits on the extent or nature of the examination.

Genuineness of documents. Finally, if a party discovers information from another party through discovery or through independent investigation and the information is so crucial that it could ruin the other party's case, a Motion to Admit Genuineness of Documents, or facts, may be filed, (In some jurisdictions, this is known as a Request for Admission—see Figure 7.6). Although this type of motion is not usually considered an official form of discovery, it is directly related to information discovered. It asks the party to review the facts or documents discovered and to either admit or deny the truthfulness of the content. If the truthfulness is admitted or verified, the party who filed the motion may seek an early end to the lawsuit with a Motion for Summary Judgment (the effect of which is discussed a little later). Usually, a Motion to Admit Genuineness of Documents or Facts is not submitted unless the evidence directly contradicts the core basis of the other party's case. Because most parties genuinely believe their case and have evidence to support it, these motions are not seen in the majority of lawsuits.

> Comes now the Plaintiff, by and through her attorneys as requests that the Defendant admit the genuineness and truthfulness of content of the attached document for the purposes of the above-captioned action, and further to stipulate the admission of said document into evidence in the above-captioned action.
>
> Marvin Henry, atty.
> Winter, Somers and Snow, P.C.
> Suite 260 Park Place
> Canoga, State 000000

FIGURE 7.6
Request for Admission

CASE

OLIVIERO

v.

PORTER HAYDEN COMPANY

241 N.J.SUPER. 381,
575 A.2d 50 (1990).

DEIGHAN, J. A. D.

Plaintiffs Ralph and Maria Oliviero filed an action against 19 suppliers, manufacturers and distributors of asbestos. The complaint alleged that Ralph Oliviero had contracted asbestosis from exposure to defendants' products while working as a materials technician at the American Cyanamid Company in Boundbrook between 1953 and 1982. Maria Oliviero sued per quod.

During discovery, plaintiffs answered a number of standard Middlesex Country asbestos interrogatories, as well as several supplemental interrogatories. They also submitted a witness list containing the names of 118 witnesses. Among those named on this list, which was submitted 10 days prior to trial, were Anthony Jannone, the purchasing agent for American Cyanamid, and Samuel Jannone, a laborer.

Trial commenced on February 2, 1989. At this point, plaintiffs had settled with all of the defendants except the Porter Hayden Company (Porter Hayden), Eagle Picher Industries, Inc. (Eagle Picher) and Owens-Corning Fiberglass Corporation (Owens-Corning). Pursuant to a general order on asbestos litigation issued in 1982 by the Law Division in Middlesex County, Ozzard, Wharton Klein, Mauro, Savo & Hogan of Somerville was designated as lead counsel; McCarter & English was designated as medical counsel.

On the fourth day of trial, plaintiffs' attorney called Anthony Jannone as a witness. Jannone testified about several asbestos products manufactured by Porter Hayden and Eagle Picher which had been present on American Cyanamid's premises during the term of Ralph Oliviero's employment. While defendants made several objections during the course of this testimony, they did not object to Jannone's appearance as a witness. On the next day, however, defendants moved for a mistrial on the grounds that Anthony Jannone had not been listed in plaintiffs' answers to interrogatories and had never been deposed. Counsel claimed that they had confused Anthony Jannone with Samuel Jannone, who had been listed in plaintiffs' answers to interrogatories and subsequently deposed. They argued that Anthony Jannone's testimony was severely prejudicial. Plaintiffs arguing that defendants had already heard his testimony and cross-examined him. The trial court denied this request. On appeal by plaintiffs, this court reversed and allowed Jannone to testify in the second trial. However, we instructed the Law Division to "assess reasonable costs, payable by plaintiffs counsel to the Superior Court Clerk and not to be reimbursed by plaintiffs for the waste of publicly supported judicial resources occasioned by counsel's default and the resulting mistrial order." This court also noted that:

> We view counsel's conduct as, at best, grossly negligent. We are advised defendants 'counsel have moved for costs in the trial court. Our order shall not affect the outcome of their motion.

In a subsequent motion for attorney's fees, defendants' lawyers certified the reasonable value of their services at $16,660 during the aborted first trial. Although the trial court granted their motion, it awarded only $2,400 per attorney, for a total of $9,600. In addition, it ordered plaintiffs' attorney to pay $2,346 in court costs. The court further ordered plaintiffs not to reimburse their attorney for these expenses. These decisions were formalized in orders dated March 10 and April 27, 1989.

I

Initially plaintiffs' attorneys argue that the trial court may not impose sanctions against a lawyer whose failure to comply with a discovery request causes a mistrial unless that lawyer acted in bad faith. They cite no authority to support this proposition. They submit that "this court should follow Federal Court interpretations of 28 U.S.C.A. s 1927, which authorizes sanctions against attorneys who 'unreasonably and vexatiously' complicate trial proceedings." We find that both of these proposals are clearly without merit. . . .

The discovery rules were designed to eliminate, as far as possible, concealment and surprise in the trial of law suits to the end that judgements rest upon real merits of the causes and not upon the skill and maneuvering of counsel. It necessarily follows, if such rules are to be effective, that the courts impose appropriate sanctions for violations thereof. *Evtush v. Hudson Bus Transportation Co.,* 7 N.J. 167, 173, 81 A.2D 6 (1951).

Aside from specific rules, a court has inherent power to require a party to reimburse another litigant for its litigation expenses, including counsel fees. *Vargas v. A. H. Bull Steamship Co.,* 25 N.J. 293, 296, 135 A.2D 857 (1957) ("Thus we find no error in conditioning the order of dismissal upon the payment of counsel fees. Allowance of fees under such circumstances is within the inherent power of the court; in effect, they are but reimbursement for expenses."); accord *Busik v. Levine,* 63 N.J. 351, 372, 307 A.2D 571(1973); *Crudup v. Marrero,* 57 N.J. 353, 361, 273 A.2D 16 (1971); *Trieste, Inc. II v. Gloucester Tp.,* 215 N.J.Super. 184, 188–189, 521 A.2D 864 (App.Div.1987) ("as a procedural sanction, [counsel fees are] within [the] broad constitutional power, and as such, they are within the statutory provision for costs").

Further, R. 4:23 (Failure to Make Discovery, Sanctions) specifically provides in several instances for expenses, "including attorney's fees" R. 4:23-1(c) (Motion for Order Compelling Discovery—Award of Expenses of Motion); R. 4:23-2 (Failure To Comply With Order); R. 4:23-4 (Failure of Party to Attend at Own Deposition or Comply With Demand or Respond to Requests for Inspection). Lastly, R. 1:2-4 (Sanctions: Failure to Appear; Motions and Briefs) provides: "(a) Failure to Appear. If without just excuse or because of failure to give reasonable attention to the matter, . . . an application is made for an adjournment, the court may order any one or more the following: (a) the payment by the delinquent attorney . . . applying for the adjournment of costs, in such amount as the court shall fix, to the Clerk of the County in which the action is to be tried . . .; (b) the payment by the delinquent attorney . . . applying for the adjournment of reasonable expenses, including attorney's fees, to the aggrieved party. . . ."

It is perfectly clear from the foregoing that the trial court, aside from the mandate of this court, had more than ample authority to assess sanctions and counsel fees against plaintiff's attorneys for inconveniences and expenses incurred in attending an aborted three-day trial. Plaintiffs' attorneys were undeniably negligent in preparing the case and the defendants were substantially prejudiced by counsel's conduct. Anthony Jannone was the key witness for plaintiff and testified at the first trial that the defendants Porter Hayden and Eagle Picher had supplied a large portion of the asbestos products used by American Cyanamid during the period of Oliviero's employment. In view of the fact that defendants never had an opportunity to depose Anthony Jannone, the trial court had no choice but to declare a mistrial. In determining to grant counsel fees to defense counsel, Judge Reavey awarded only $2,400 each, for a total of $9,600. In so doing, she observed

Owens-Corning settled with plaintiffs prior to this litigation and waived its right to Judge Reavey's award of $2,400. For the purposes of this appeal, defendants' attorneys were therefore awarded only $7,200 in attorneys' fees.

. . . [W]hile I appreciate the accuracy and the almost bare bones minimum application for each of those certifications appreciating the amount of effort and time and work that goes into preparation for a case of this kind, I can't award those kind of figures as far as costs of the litigation are concerned. I do think that I'm certainly authorized to, in fact, almost obligated to impose some compensation to each of these law firms for the time that they spent here that was truly a waste of time in light of the mistrial that had to be declared. . . . I find appropriate certainly the eight hour day that these trials do run figuring a little bit of time just to get to and from the courthouse. And I think $100 an hour is a reasonable compromise for their application despite the fact that I know that they're billing their clients more than that and everybody does. So again, I multiplied that out and it comes to $2,400.

◆ **CASE**

II

Plaintiffs' attorneys also argue that the trial court abused its discretion by imposing costs in favor of the Superior Court for the three days of the first aborted trial. In our mandate to the trial court, we directed that "the Law Division will assess reasonable costs payable by plaintiff's counsel to the Superior Court Clerk . . . for the waste of publicly supported judicial resources occasioned by counsel's default and resulting in a mistrial." Plaintiff's attorneys argue that the trial judge should have restricted her assessment of court costs to the statutory allowable tax costs and that actual costs are not expressly provided under the rules of court as required by R. 4:42-9(a)(7). They argue that costs over and above tax costs and costs of everyday running the court system is an expense that the State would have incurred in any event. We disagree.

As previously noted, if a party or counsel, "without just excuse" or for "failure to give reasonable attention to the matter" requires "an application . . . for an adjournment, the court may order . . . (a) the payment by the delinquent attorney . . . of costs, in such amount as the court shall fix, to the Clerk of the County in which the action is to be tried. . . ." R. 1:2-4(a).

In assessing $2,346 in court costs, Judge Reavey multiplied the three days which the first trial had taken by the estimated daily expense to the State. . . .

Affirmed.

Case Review Question

Should witnesses with vital information who are identified during a trial be excluded because they have not been named in the discovery?

Assignment 7.3

> Assume you are employed by a law firm representing one of several plaintiffs in a lawsuit against a person who was driving under the influence and struck your client's vehicle. Each of the three plaintiffs is represented by a different attorney to avoid conflict of interest issues. Your client, Sara, was driving the vehicle after leaving a birthday party at a local club. Sara was severely injured and has astronomic medical bills and no insurance. Plaintiff Lila was the owner of the car but did not drive because she had been drinking. She was not injured, but her new car was a total loss. Plaintiff Estate of Sam represents the interest of Sam, who was a passenger and was killed in the accident. The defendant is Joe, who had been club-hopping for several hours before the accident and had a blood alcohol level of 3 times the legal limit of .08.
>
> Try to identify the types of records and information you would like to obtain through discovery from the other parties in the suit and identify which type of discovery you would use to obtain the records.

motion

Formal request by a party to a lawsuit for court-ordered action/nonaction.

Motion practice.   Throughout any lawsuit, the parties communicate with the court largely through motions. A **motion** is a request by an attorney whose party seeks assistance—or a ruling—from the court on a particular issue between the parties. Motions can result in something as serious as permanent dismissal of the lawsuit. The following discussion examines some of the more

FIGURE 7.7

Motion to
Dismiss

Comes now the Defendant, Pauline McPaul, by and through her attorneys, Winter, Somers, and Snow, and moves the Court to enter an order dismissing the Complaint of Defendant. In support thereof, the Defendant states as follows:

1. On or about August 19, 1993, the Plaintiff instituted an action against the Defendant in the above-captioned court.
2. The Complaint of Plaintiff fails to state a cause of action upon which relief can be granted. Further, Plaintiff's allegations are legal conclusions and unsupported by any allegations of fact. WHEREFORE, the Defendant prays that the Court enter an order dismissing the Plaintiff's complaint, awarding Defendant costs and such other and further relief as the Court deems necessary and proper.

Respectfully submitted,

Marvin Henry, atty.
Winter, Somers and Snow, P.C.
Suite 260 Park Place
Canoga, State 000000

common motions in terms of what they request and the effect they have if granted. We have seen that motions can be used to request dismissal of suit when the complaint is deficient in some way. Motions also have many other uses through pretrial, trial, and even posttrial proceedings. Some of the more commonly sought motions are discussed here.

Motion to dismiss.   As stated earlier, this motion is used when a party believes that the facts of the case do not support a viable legal claim or that the complaint is improperly stated and does not conform to legal requirements as outlined by the rules of procedure (see Figure 7.7).

Motion to make more definite and certain.   Also called a Bill of Particulars, this document is filed by the defendant and asks that the plaintiff be required to provide more detailed information than that contained in the complaint (see Figure 7.8).

Motion to quash service of process.   This motion is filed when a plaintiff does not follow the rules of procedure for serving a summons and complaint on the defendant. If the rules are violated, the service is quashed, or rejected, and the plaintiff must attempt to serve the defendant properly.

Motion to inspect.   This motion is a discovery motion used to gain access to private property. If granted, the party is allowed to inspect the property as it pertains to evidence in the lawsuit. Examples include access to private property that was the scene of an accident and inspection of an item, such as a weapon, that was involved in an injury (see Figure 7.9).

Motion for mental/physical exam.   This motion is used when the mental or physical condition of a party or witness is relevant to the lawsuit. When granted, it allows the party to have the physician of choice examine the other party or witness and to give a report as to the person's mental or physical condition. An

> Comes now the Defendant, Pauline McPaul, by and through her attorneys, Winter, Somers, and Snow, and moves the Court to enter an order requiring Plaintiff to additional facts to support the allegations of his Complaint. In support thereof, the Defendant states as follows:
>
> 1. On October 31, 1993, Plaintiff instituted an action against the Defendant alleging breach of contract with respect to an agreement to which both Plaintiff and Defendant were parties.
> 2. That during the period 1990–1994, Plaintiff and Defendant had an ongoing business relationship, the product of which was no fewer than 70 separate contracts.
> 3. That Defendant is without information as to the specifics of the alleged breach and as a result is unable to frame a proper answer to the allegations of Plaintiff.
>
> WHEREFORE, the Defendant prays that the Court will enter an order requiring the Plaintiff to more particularly describe the specifics of the facts supporting the allegations of Plaintiff's Complaint.
>
> Respectfully submitted,
>
> Marvin Henry, atty.
> Winter, Somers and Snow, P.C.
> Suite 260 Park Place
> Canoga, State 000000

> Comes now the Plaintiff, Mortimer Vance, by and through his attorneys, Winter, Somers, and Snow, and moves the Court to enter an order permitting Plaintiff to inspect the premises under control of the Defendant. In support thereof, the Plaintiff states as follows:
>
> 1. On or about July 5, 1993, Plaintiff instituted an action in this Court against the Defendant alleging injury as the result of negligent conduct of Defendant.
> 2. Said allegations of neglect arose from an explosion that occurred on Defendant's property in which Plaintiff was seriously injured.
> 3. It is necessary for Plaintiff to inspect the aforementioned property of Defendant and site of Plaintiff's injuries for the proper preparation of Plaintiff's case.
> 4. Said inspection is appropriate pursuant to applicable rules of procedure.
>
> WHEREFORE, the Plaintiff prays the Court will enter an order permitting Plaintiff to inspect the aforementioned property of Defendant upon reasonable notice and circumstances for the purposes of discovery in the above-captioned action.
>
> Respectfully submitted,
>
> Marvin Henry, atty.
> Winter, Somers and Snow, P.C.
> Suite 260 Park Place
> Canoga, State 000000

example would occur in a personal injury claim. The defendant might want to have his or her own doctor examine the plaintiff to render an opinion as to the extent of the plaintiff's injuries (see Figure 7.10).

Motion to compel. During discovery, a party has certain time limits to respond to requests for information by the other party. When these time limits are not honored, the party expecting the information may request that the court order compliance immediately (see Figure 7.11).

Comes now the Defendant, Pauline McPaul, by and through her attorneys, Winter, Somers, and Snow, and moves the Court to enter an order requiring the Plaintiff to submit to a physical exam upon reasonable notice by a physician of Defendant's choice. In support thereof, Defendant states as follows:

1. On or about August 31, 1993, Plaintiff instituted an action against the Defendant alleging negligence and consequent physical injury.
2. That pursuant to applicable rules of civil procedure, when Plaintiff places her physical condition in issue in litigation, the Defendant has the right to reasonable examination of Plaintiff's condition and medical records.
3. To date, Plaintiff has been unwilling to voluntarily undergo physical examination by a physician agent of the Defendant.
4. Said examination is essential to preparation of Defendant's defense to the allegations of the Plaintiff.

WHEREFORE, the Defendant prays that the Court enter an order requiring the Plaintiff, under reasonable notice and circumstances, to submit to a physical examination by a physician of Defendant's choosing and to order such other relief as the Court deems necessary and proper.

Respectfully submitted,

Marvin Henry, atty.
Winter, Somers and Snow, P.C.
Suite 260 Park Place
Canoga, State 000000

FIGURE 7.10

Motion for Physical Examination

Comes now the Plaintiff, Mortimer Vance, by and through his attorneys, Winter, Somers, and Snow, and moves the Court to enter an order compelling Defendant to respond to Plaintiff's discovery. In support thereof, Plaintiff states as follows:

1. On or about January 13, 1993, Plaintiff submitted interrogations to Defendant in accordance with applicable rules of civil procedure.
2. Response from Defendant to said interrogatories was due on or about February 13, 1993.
3. Said date for response has passed, and Plaintiff has made further written requests to Defendant for compliance with this discovery. As of March 29, 1993, Defendant has failed to respond to the aforementioned interrogatories.
4. Defendant is in violation of the rules of discovery and is thwarting Plaintiff's attempts to proceed with this litigation.

WHEREFORE, the Plaintiff prays the Court to enter an order compelling the Defendant to respond to Plaintiff's interrogatories within 7 days and to order such other further and necessary relief as the Court deems proper.

Respectfully submitted,

Marvin Henry, atty.
Winter, Somers and Snow, P.C.
Suite 260 Park Place
Canoga, State 000000

FIGURE 7.11

Motion to Compel

Motion for sanctions.   This motion is used during discovery and at any other time during the proceedings when one party is of the opinion that the other party is willfully disregarding rules of procedure or orders of the court. The motion seeks punishment of the party at fault. If granted by the court, the penalty can range from being held in contempt of court to dismissal of the suit in the aggrieved party's favor.

Motion for summary judgment.   This is not a routinely filed motion. The basis of the motion is that the evidence is so overwhelmingly in favor of one party that no reasonable judge or jury could find in favor of the other party. Consequently, the party seeking the motion contends that there is no basis for a trial and the case should be determined without trial and in favor of the requesting party. The Motion for Summary Judgment is one of the most serious motions that can be filed in any lawsuit. It asks that the judge make a final decision on the issues of the suit without a trial. The decision is made solely on the basis of the evidence that exists at the time of the motion. The effect of such a motion is that the judge removes the case from the hands of the jury before it ever reaches them. Because our system of government places so much importance on the jury system, this is a very serious step for any judge to take.

When a Motion for Summary Judgment is sought, the judge must make a serious evaluation of the evidence. If the evidence is so strongly in favor of a party that a jury could only reasonably reach one decision and there is no substantial question left to be determined regarding the facts that occurred, a Motion for Summary Judgment may be granted. However, if there is any way that the jurors could reach a different conclusion as to whose version of the story is more probable, a Motion for Summary Judgment must be denied, and the case must be left to the trier of fact.[9]

Because the effect of a successful Motion for Summary Judgment is that there will be no trial in the case, such a motion must be filed before trial begins. Beyond that, when or if the motion is filed is up to the moving party. Usually, a Motion for Summary Judgment will not be filed unless there is evidence so strong that the opposing party's case is effectively defeated by the evidence. In most cases, each side has evidence that would tend to prove or disprove the case. Consequently, Motions for Summary Judgment are filed less often than other types of motions and are rarely granted (see Figure 7.12).

If a Motion for Summary Judgment by a defendant is granted, the case is dismissed with prejudice. This means that the lawsuit brought by the plaintiff will be dismissed and can never be brought again. No amendments to the complaint can be made, and the issue between the parties is permanently settled. If a Motion for Summary Judgment by a plaintiff is granted, the defendant is not entitled to a trial to present evidence in defense to the plaintiff's claims. If the plaintiff asked for a specific dollar amount of damages in the complaint, the defendant is automatically judged liable and must pay the plaintiff an appropriate amount. Sometimes the amount of damages specified in the complaint is appropriate, but other times a trial must be held to determine exactly how much the defendant should pay.

FIGURE 7.12

Motion for
Summary
Judgment

Comes now the Defendant, Pauline McPaul, by and through her attorneys, Winter, Somers, and Snow, and moves the Court to enter an order of Summary Judgment in favor of Defendant and against Plaintiff. In support thereof, the Defendant states as follows:

1. On or about August 31, 1993, Plaintiff filed an Amended Complaint against Defendant alleging that the Defendant negligently caused Plaintiff's financial injury and ultimate bankruptcy as the result of a breach of contract. Defendant filed an answer denying the allegations of the Plaintiff.

2. The parties have subsequently engaged in discovery, and the information discovered indicates that no genuine issue of fact exists to support Plaintiff's allegations.

3. Attached in support of Defendant's motion is the affidavit of Plaintiff's former employee, Alexander Grant. Said affidavit states, inter alia, that as general manager of Plaintiff's business, Mr. Grant had full knowledge of Plaintiff's financial status at the time of the alleged breach of contract.

4. Affiant further states that at the time of the alleged breach of contract by Defendant, the Plaintiff was insolvent and consulting attorneys with respect to filing bankruptcy. Shortly following the alleged breach, Plaintiff did in fact file for bankruptcy.

5. Affiant avers that if called to testify, he would affirmatively state that Plaintiff suffered no financial injury by Defendant's breach and that said breach had no bearing on Plaintiff's subsequent bankruptcy.

WHEREFORE, the Defendant prays that the Court enter a finding that no genuine issue of facts exists with respect to Plaintiff's allegations of damage proximately caused by Defendant, and further that the Court enter an order of Summary Judgment in favor of the Defendant and against the Plaintiff and such other and necessary relief as the Court deems necessary and proper.

Respectfully submitted,

Marvin Henry, atty.
Winter, Somers and Snow, P.C.
Suite 260 Park Place
Canoga, State 000000

Motion in limine.   This motion is filed in an attempt to prevent certain evidence from being presented to a jury. It is based on the contention that certain evidence would interfere with an informed and fair decision by the jury. Usually, this motion is filed when there are graphic depictions of injuries or when information duplicates other evidence. It is granted only when the information would lead a jury to unfair conclusions and when there is other sufficient means of presenting evidence of the facts to the jury (see Figure 7.13).

Motion for directed verdict.   Not to be confused with the summary judgment motion, this motion is filed after evidence has been presented to a jury (rather than before a trial has begun). However, similar to the summary judgment motion, the Motion for Directed Verdict asks that the judge make a determination that there is only one reasonable outcome to the suit and because of this, the jury should be told what its verdict will be (see Figure 7.14).

Motion for judgment notwithstanding the verdict (Non Obstante Verdicto).   Also known as Judgment NOV, this request is made after the verdict has been delivered by the jury and a party contends that the jury misconstrued the evidence and

FIGURE 7.13

Motion in Limine

> Comes now the Defendant, Pauline McPaul, by and through her attorneys, Winter, Somers, and Snow, and moves the Court to enter an order excluding certain evidence that Plaintiff has indicated it intends to submit in the trial of the above-captioned action. In support thereof, the Defendant states as follows:
>
> 1. This action involves allegations of personal injury to the Plaintiff as the result of claimed negligence of the Defendant.
> 2. Through discovery, Defendant has ascertained that Plaintiff intends to submit into evidence certain graphic photographs depicting Plaintiff's injuries.
> 3. Said photographs are immaterial in that they are not necessary to a fair and informed determination by the jury. Further, said photographs are of a nature that could inflame and prejudice the jury and prohibit the jury from making an objective finding.
> 4. Other suitable evidence of Plaintiff's injuries exist that would adequately and accurately depict the injuries for the jury's consideration.
> 5. Attached for the Court's consideration are copies of the aforementioned photographs and the alternative forms of evidence.
>
> WHEREFORE, the Defendant prays that the Court enter an order excluding from evidence the aforementioned photographs and further that the Court order Plaintiff, Plaintiff's attorneys, witnesses, and all others from any direct or indirect reference to said photographs during the proceedings of the above-captioned action.
>
> Respectfully submitted,
>
> Marvin Henry, atty.
> Winter, Somers and Snow, P.C.
> Suite 260 Park Place
> Canoga, State 000000

FIGURE 7.14

Motion for Directed Verdict

> Comes now the Defendant, Pauline McPaul, by and through her attorneys, Winter, Somers, and Snow, and moves the Court to enter a Directed Verdict in favor of Defendant and against Plaintiff. In support thereof, the Defendant states as follows:
>
> 1. Plaintiff has concluded the presentation of her case in chief and in doing so has failed to present a prima facie case that would reasonably allow a jury to find in Plaintiff's favor based on a preponderance of the evidence.
> 2. "Where the plaintiff fails to present any significant evidence in support of the elements of the alleged cause of action, a directed verdict is appropriate." *Walston v. Dunham,* 111 E.W.2d 444 (CS App. 1987).
>
> WHEREFORE, the Defendant prays that the Court will direct the jury in the above-captioned action to enter a verdict in favor of Defendant and against Plaintiff and such other relief as the Court deems necessary and proper.
>
> Respectfully submitted,
>
> Marvin Henry, atty.
> Winter, Somers and Snow, P.C.
> Suite 260 Park Place
> Canoga, State 000000

reached a result that is in conflict with the totality of the evidence. If the motion is granted, the judge will substitute his or her own verdict for the verdict of the jury. Judges rarely grant this motion, however, because it usurps the jury's function to interpret the evidence.

Motion for new trial.   This motion is sought when a party contends that something occurred during the trial that prevented the legally correct result of the lawsuit. Errors can include the wrongful exclusion of certain evidence, improper testimony by a witness, or a procedural error by the judge. Actually, anything to which a party can point that had a significant impact on the case and that the party can convince the judge was irregular or inappropriate can serve as the basis for a Motion for New Trial.

It is important to note that motions such as those for summary judgment, directed verdict, and new trial are rarely granted. When they are, the judge removes the case from the hands of a jury and substitutes his or her own legal opinion for that of several peers of the parties in the suit. Most judges are not willing to take this responsibility without compelling reasons that the jury verdict is or would not be proper under the circumstances of the case.

Assignment 7.4

> The following situations are appropriate for a motion. State the type of motion that would probably be filed for each situation.
>
> 1. Sarah is served with notice of a lawsuit. However, she is not the same person as described in the Complaint. In the suit, plaintiff claims only that Sarah's conduct in breaking a date hurt the plaintiff's feelings.
> 2. Jasper is the plaintiff in a lawsuit. Although Jasper's lawyer has called the opposition several times to request answers to interrogatories served six months ago, the defendant's counsel has yet to respond.
> 3. Corinne sued the Temple Insurance Agency for refusal to pay on an insurance policy against fire in her house (the house burned to the ground). The insurance agency has witnesses that Corinne confessed to torching her home. Also, Corinne has previously been convicted of arson.

Stages of Trial

Procedural rules help to guide the parties in assembling their evidence and presenting it at trial. Rules of evidence are examined in more detail later in the chapter. At this point, discussion will focus on the actual stages of the trial and the presentation of the evidence.

Voir dire.   The first stage of trial is generally the voir dire. During this stage, the jury that will hear the case is selected. In what is known as a bench trial, the trier of fact is the judge who hears the evidence and issues a decision. This is one option of the parties regarding the form of trial. In a bench trial, there is no jury and thus no need for the voir dire stage. If the case is to receive a jury trial, a fair and impartial jury must be selected.

Voir dire begins with a large pool of potential jurors who are brought into the courtroom. The attorneys for the parties—and sometimes the judge—ask each potential juror a number of questions, the goal of which is to determine whether a potential juror has any biases regarding the parties, attorneys, or circumstances of the case. If an attorney believes that a potential juror has a particular bias that would influence the decision in the case, the attorney has the right to challenge the juror's right to sit on the jury.

An attorney can exercise two types of challenges with regard to potential jurors: peremptory challenges and challenges for cause. Each party to a lawsuit may use a given amount of peremptory challenges, which vary in number from state to state. An attorney exercising a peremptory challenge does not have to give a reason to the court. A party has an absolute right to have the challenged juror removed from the jury. The only exception is if the removal is based on a person's status within a federally protected class, such as race.

In challenge for cause, an attorney asks that a juror be excused on the basis of a particular prejudice that was evident from the juror's answers to the questions previously asked. In challenge for cause, the opposing party can object to the challenge. Usually, the objection will state that the prospective juror did not exhibit a bias so strong that the juror could not fairly consider the case. The judge considers the challenge, any objections, and the statements of the juror and then renders a decision as to whether the juror will be excused.

When the required number of jurors has been reached, voir dire is ended. Traditionally, juries are composed of 12 persons and one or two alternates. Some states also have petit juries, usually juries of fewer people. Petit juries may be utilized in cases that are less serious but that still warrant the right to a trial by a jury of one's peers under state or federal law. Some states do not allow jury trials in very minor cases, such as traffic violations, where loss of liberty is not at stake.

CASE

HUELSMANN

v.

BERKOWITZ

210 Ill.App. 3d 806,
154 Ill. Dec. 924,
568 N.E.2d 1373
(1991).

**Justice HOWERTON
delivered the
opinion of the court.**

We affirm the judgment entered on the verdict of a St. Clair County jury that found defendant liable for medical malpractice, awarding plaintiff

$79,975.80 in actual damages, but we reverse the judgment for $15,000 in punitive damages.

We hold that the comments made during voir dire were not sufficient to cause the entire panel of veniremen to be discharged. . . .

Defendant, Dr. Wallace Berkowitz, performed a tonsillectomy on plaintiff, Florence Huelsmann.

After plaintiff returned home, she had several profuse bleeding spells.

During one middle-of-the-night spell, her husband called defendant.

According to plaintiff's husband, defendant advised plaintiff to gargle with hydrogen peroxide, but did not advise her to go directly to the hospital.

Defendant contradicted this, however, and testified that he told plaintiff's husband to take plaintiff to the hospital, and that defendant waited up two hours for the emergency room personnel to call him, but when no call came, he went back to sleep.

Defendant left on vacation the next day.

Several days later, plaintiff was taken to a hospital by her husband. A blood clot was removed from her throat and her throat was treated to prevent bleeding. She was given a shot to prevent shock and was transfused with two units of blood.

She returned home.

Again, she awoke, bleeding. This time, she went to a different hospital. She was admitted and a large ulcer was found where her tonsils once had been.

Treated, the ulcer healed and the bleeding stopped.

Post-bleeding, she was diagnosed as having a dysthymic disorder, a depression due to her profuse bleeding.

***

Defendant claims that he was denied a fair trial because of comments made by two veniremen, and because the circuit court failed to discharge the entire venire present when the comments were made.

There were two episodes of comments, and both criticized the caliber of medical care defendant had provided on other occasions.

Episode No. 1
"THE COURT: You know him as a patient of his?
JUROR: I was a patient of his.
THE COURT: You are or were?
JUROR: Sir?
THE COURT: You were?
JUROR: I was years ago.
THE COURT: What did he do for you?
JUROR: I had hemorrhaging of the nose, and I had changed doctors and had the problem corrected.
THE COURT: You say you changed doctors. You were not satisfied with his treatment?
JUROR: Right.
THE COURT: Okay. What did you feel the problem was, sir?
JUROR: I had—for no reason at all I'd start hemorrhaging and I had to go to the emergency room and they couldn't stop it. I finally had to have surgery.

THE COURT: All right. Well, let me ask you this, are you going to have a problem in this case?
JUROR: Well, I didn't have a happy experience on the first occasion, I finally had to have it taken care of with another doctor.
THE COURT: Well, the question is from personal experience with this doctor is it going to be so overwhelming that you just say, "Doc, I just don't think you did good?"
JUROR: I'd probably have trouble with that.
THE COURT: Okay. We'll excuse you. You can go back to the jury room, sir."

Episode No. 2
The second episode stands as proof that every now and again something can happen in trial that can make anyone bolt upright.

After the first episode everyone went back to their own business, the excused juror to the jury room, the court and counsel to the business of asking voir dire questions.

A panel member was being questioned. Down the box sat the others.

Suddenly, from down the box, a panel member who was not being questioned and never had been questioned, who simply had been sitting silently, announced:

"JUROR: I've been thinking, Dr. Berkowitz killed by brother."

The next words were spoken by the court.

"THE COURT: What is your name, sir?
JUROR: He was talking about Dr. Berkowitz, he let my brother die. I didn't know who it was—
THE COURT: You're Mr. who?
JUROR: Mr. (name deleted.)
THE COURT: We'll excuse you sir. You're juror number what?
JUROR: 22
THE COURT: We'll excuse you, sir.
JUROR: Sorry.
THE COURT: That's fine. Thank you."

Defendant concedes that the first episode alone would be insufficient to deprive him of a fair trial, but claims that the two incidents operating together were so prejudicial that they deprived him of a fair trial. He argues it was not enough to excuse these veniremen, and that no cautionary

CASE

instruction ever could overcome the prejudice of these incidents to him, and therefore, the only remedy was to recuse the entire venire.

The circuit court has the discretion to determine whether jurors can weigh the evidence impartially, and that determination will not be set aside unless it is against the manifest weight of the evidence. *Parson v. City of Chicago* (1983), 117 Ill.App. 3d 383, 72 Ill.Dec. 895, 453 N.E.2d 770.

In *People v. Del Vecchio* (1985), 105 Ill.2d 414, 429, 86 Ill.Dec. 461, 468, 475 N.E.2d 840, 847, veniremen heard another's personal opinion of the accused. Del Vecchio held that the jury had not been tainted. Taint would have resulted only if she who had expressed her preconceived opinion was allowed to remain on the jury.

The record does not establish that the panel members were prejudiced against the defendant, much less that prejudice was pandemic.

In this case, both the juror in episode number one and the juror in episode number two were discharged. The remaining veniremen each said they could be fair.

Trial judges, no less than trial lawyers, rely on instinct in assessing veniremen, their answers and whether they should serve as jurors. In this case, the trial judge had the opportunity to see and hear the veniremen. He concluded that the statements had not prejudiced them and was convinced that they could be fair and impartial. There is nothing in the record from which we can draw an inference that he was wrong. There is nothing in the record to show that he abused his discretion.

***

The judgment on the verdict for the plaintiff and against defendant, Wallace Berkowitz, M.D., assessing plaintiff's damages as being $79,975.80 is affirmed.

Case Review Question

Should someone who has been convicted of a crime be allowed to act as a juror in a criminal case?

Opening statements.   Following voir dire, the final jury is sworn in, and the proceedings begin. The first step in most trials is the opening statement. Usually, the party who has the burden of proof makes the first opening statement. The responding party has the option of making an opening statement at this time or of waiting until the presentation of his or her evidence. Opening statements are not to be argumentative. They are to serve as an opportunity for the attorneys to outline their evidence to the jury. Legal conclusions, arguments, and pleas for verdicts are inappropriate at this time. Opening statements are not evidence. Rather, they serve as an outline of the evidence to be presented.

Case in chief.   The case in chief is the stage of a trial during which the party with the burden of proof presents evidence to support its claim. The burden of proof previously mentioned refers to the party who must convince the jury of his or her case in order to win the suit. In a civil case, the burden of proof is generally on the plaintiff, who claims injury or damage due to the defendant's fault. The party with the burden usually presents evidence first. The standard burden of proof in most civil cases is to prove one's claim by a preponderance of the evidence. This means that the party with the burden must establish that the facts alleged in the complaint are more likely than not true. The party who does not have the burden of proof needs only to present enough evidence in opposition to prevent the burden (minimum level of evidence) from being met.

Consider the example discussed earlier in the chapter of the auto accident involving Jane and Tom. Assume the suit has commenced. Since Jane has brought the action against Tom, she is obligated to meet the burden of proof at trial. Jane claims that Tom was following too closely and caused the accident. Tom claims that Jane applied her brakes without warning to turn into a parking lot and that he could not avoid hitting her car. Jane must prove her case by a preponderance of the evidence. She must establish, with evidence, that her version of the case is more likely than not the way the accident actually occurred. In essence, the burden is on Jane to produce enough proof to convince the jury that her version is the most plausible.

Evidence for a case of this type might include photographs of the scene and the vehicles as well as expert opinions about skid marks on the road or other indicators of the speed and direction of the vehicles. The party with the burden of proof must meet an additional step known as presenting a prima facie case. Translated literally, *prima facie* means "on the face." In effect, a prima facie case is what the party with the burden must prove. The evidence brought at trial must be sufficient to establish each of the facts alleged in the complaint (the face of the claim) and to support the legal claims of the complaint. If there is not evidence to support each allegation of the complaint, a prima facie case has not been established.

If a prima facie case is not established, the claims of the complaint have not been proven. At this point, the party responding to the claims can make a Motion for a Directed Verdict, which requests the court to instruct the jury that there is no need to present a defense because the allegations of the complaint have not been proven. If the motion is granted, the judge directs the jury to render a verdict against the party with the burden of proof.

Most parties with the burden of proof attempt to establish a much stronger case than one that is merely prima facie. The evidence presented must withstand contradictory evidence presented by the defense and still prevail as the most likely explanation of the circumstances that created the dispute. Realistically, a prima facie case is usually not enough to win the case.

Defense.   After the party (usually the plaintiff) with the burden of proof has presented all of his or her evidence and made a prima facie case, that party will rest. At this point, the responding party—usually the defendant—will present his or her case. If the defense did not make an opening statement at the beginning of the trial, the opportunity to make one at this time is available. The opening statement is followed by the presentation of the defendant's evidence.

In the presentation of evidence, the defendant has no initial burden to meet. Rather, a burden occurs only if the plaintiff establishes a prima facie case. At this point, the burden shifts, and the defendant must present enough evidence in response to the plaintiff's evidence to create a question in the minds of the jury that the plaintiff's version is not the most likely version of the facts.

After the defendant has concluded the presentation of evidence, the plaintiff may request permission to reopen his or her case. This may be allowed when the plaintiff has evidence that will respond to some evidence introduced by the defendant. However, it is not permissible to present entirely new evidence that the plaintiff may have forgotten or otherwise failed to include in the original presentation of evidence. The plaintiff is permitted only to respond to the evidence of the defendant. The defendant may then be permitted to introduce rebuttal evidence.

Closing argument. After both parties have concluded the presentation of evidence, the attorneys for the plaintiff and the defendant are allowed the opportunity to make closing arguments, also known as summations. In some jurisdictions, the defense presents its summation first and the plaintiff or prosecution gets the last word. In other jurisdictions, the plaintiff or prosecutor goes first and then gets a few moments of rebuttal to respond to the defendant's summation. At this stage, each attorney summarizes all of the evidence and attempts to persuade the jury of the most plausible explanation for the course of events that led to the lawsuit. Here the attorneys employ their advocacy skills and persuasive tactics to convince the jury in favor of their client.

Instructions and deliberation. After the closing arguments, the judge will read instructions to the jury. These instructions explain the law that applies to the case as well as the burden of proof and indicate what the jury is to consider as evidence. The jury is then sequestered for deliberations; that is, the jurors are secluded from all outside influences while they reach a decision. Some courts will allow the jurors to take evidence such as documents and photographs into the jury room during their deliberation. In many jurisdictions, the verdict of the jury must be unanimous in favor of one party. If a jury needs more than one

---

APPLICATION 7.4

In 1992, a nationally publicized criminal trial was held in Indiana where world champion boxer Mike Tyson was charged in an incident involving a young woman. Because of the nature of the case and parties involved, the judge sequestered the jury in a local hotel. During the trial, the hotel caught fire, and the jurors had to be moved outside and eventually to another hotel. Many jurors came into contact with persons not associated with the trial. Some concern was expressed whether a mistrial should be declared and a new trial held with new jurors because the jurors had been unsequestered and exposed to the media for a time. The judge subsequently ruled that the jury was still impartial and trial could proceed.

Point for Discussion
- What could have happened during this trial to affect juror impartiality?

day to reach a verdict, the judge will determine whether the jurors can return home for the night or whether they must be sequestered, such as in a hotel, while they are not deliberating.

Verdict.   When the jury returns with a verdict, the verdict is read to the parties. If a party requests, the judge may poll the jury. When the jury is polled, the judge asks each juror whether the verdict represents his or her opinion in the case. This is used as a safeguard to assist the court in discovering situations where jurors have been coerced by other members of the jury to change their vote to reach a verdict. If the judge discovers that a juror does not actually support and believe in the verdict, the verdict is not unanimous. This would have the effect of a hung jury where the jurors return without a verdict. In a civil suit, when a jury cannot reach a decision that the plaintiff's case is more likely than not true, the burden of proof has not been met, and the defendant prevails.

Assignment 7.5

Identify at which stage of pretrial or trial proceedings the following is most likely to occur.

a. Motion for Summary Judgment.
b. Testimony by the plaintiff in his or her behalf.
c. Evidence of the defendant's blood alcohol level at the time of the accident that allegedly caused plaintiff's injuries.
d. Evidence that the plaintiff already suffered from certain injuries at the time of the accident which plaintiff now claims were caused by the accident.
e. A description of the evidence by counsel for plaintiff.
f. A statement by counsel for the defendant that alleges the plaintiff is a malingerer and not to be believed.
g. Statement by the judge that the evidence is almost totally in favor of the plaintiff's case and the jury should find as such.
h. Questions to potential jurors.
i. Explanation to jurors of the law as it applies to the facts of the case.
j. Discussion by jurors of the evidence presented.

Rules of Evidence

The gathering and introduction of the various types of evidence are subject to many specific rules, but the rules of relevance and materiality apply to all evidence. Such rules are necessary to ensure that the evidence in any legal action is fair and proper. Evidence that is relevant and material and meets the requirements of more specific rules may be included in the trial and presented to the trier of fact.

relevant evidence
Evidence that tends to establish an essential fact in the dispute.

Relevant evidence. **Relevant evidence** is that which tends to establish some basic element of the dispute.[10] Both sides in a lawsuit are allowed to introduce evidence that will tend to prove that their version of the story is true. For example, in the lawsuit involving Jane and Tom, evidence Jane introduced that Tom has been fired from every job he ever held would not be relevant. Such evidence has nothing to do with the accident or the driving ability of either party. However, if Tom introduced evidence that Jane has been in six accidents in which her car was rear-ended under similar circumstances, the evidence might very well be relevant.

material evidence
Evidence necessary to a fair and informed decision by the trier of fact.

Material evidence. **Material evidence** is that which is considered necessary to a fair and informed determination of the dispute.[11] The same information from 20 different witnesses may not be material. In most cases, a few of these witnesses could establish the facts just as well as 20 could. Additionally, evidence that may inform the court but is so extreme that it might prevent a jury from being fair could be considered immaterial. An example would be grotesque photographs of an injury. Although the jury needs to be informed about the extent of the injuries, often the jurors can be more fair if they consider medical reports rather than extremely graphic photographs. Often the basis for a Motion in Limine will be materiality.

Hearsay. A rule of evidence that is employed in nearly every trial is that of hearsay. Entire volumes have been written about hearsay, defined as follows:

> An out-of-court statement offered to prove the truth of the matter asserted.
> Federal Rules of Civil Procedure

Hearsay follows the reasoning that everything said, written, or otherwise communicated in everyday life is not necessarily true. Therefore, such information should usually not be admitted as evidence in a trial where all other evidence is considered to be reliable and true. Hearsay evidence is testimony by a witness who repeats something that was communicated outside the trial by someone not under oath. Further, to be hearsay, the content of the communication must be offered as evidence of the truth. If it is offered only to show the ability to communicate, it would not be considered hearsay.

Because some statements are made under circumstances that are very reliable and promote only truthful communication, there are exceptions to the hearsay rule. Such information, which would otherwise be considered to be hearsay, is reliable enough in its truthfulness to warrant introduction as evidence in the trial. An example is a person's statement that is directly contrary to the person's own best interest, such as an admission of guilt. Ordinarily, individuals do not confess to acts for which they are not responsible. If there is evidence that a party or a witness made such a statement, the information may be admitted as an exception to hearsay.

When someone has an experience and makes an immediate statement about it, the statement may be considered an exception to hearsay. Statements made in circumstances where there was not time to formulate the best legal answer are highly reliable. Thus, spontaneous statements may be admitted.

Other exceptions include regularly maintained business records, statements made to physicians, and original documents. While there are many additional exceptions, it is important to remember that evidence of communication made out of court must have a high degree of reliability for truth before it will be admitted as an exception to hearsay.

APPLICATION 7.5

A widow brings a lawsuit for the pain and suffering and subsequent death of her husband after a motorcycle accident allegedly caused by the defendant. The defendant denies causing the accident and further alleges that the man died instantly; thus, no pain or suffering was involved. If the widow introduces a statement made by her husband at the scene, such statement may be introduced to show the man was alive and did indeed suffer pain from his injuries. Whether the content of the statement will be admitted—if it was relevant to the suit—depends on whether it is hearsay evidence.

Point for Discussion
- Why do you think the statement of the husband is
  a. Relevant or irrelevant?
  b. Material or immaterial?
  c. Hearsay, nonhearsay, or hearsay subject to an exception to the rule?

Privilege.   Another important aspect of evidentiary law involves privilege. Generally, a person cannot be required to testify about confidential communications, including communications made in a physician–patient, attorney–client, clergy–parishioner, husband–wife, or any other relationship that the court determines should be protected. With respect to the husband–wife privilege, some exceptions have been made in recent years, especially in the area of criminal law (see Chapter 16). Other exceptions to privilege occur when the party claiming the privilege has placed the very content of the communication in issue. For example, if a person is involved in a personal injury lawsuit, the privilege to withhold confidential medical records about the injury is waived.

Other evidence.   Numerous specific rules of evidence exist regarding such areas as opinion, habit, and personal background of a rape victim. Even when evidence is relevant, material, not hearsay, and not privileged, it may still be objected to on the basis of one of the more specific rules. Assembling and presenting admissible evidence is one of the most crucial elements of trial, if not the most crucial element. Consequently, anyone involved in litigation must be fully aware of the rules of evidence.

Rules of Appellate Procedure

Appellate procedure is largely governed by the appellate system in a jurisdiction. As discussed in Chapter 2, there are two types of appellate jurisdictional structures. One involves appeal directly to the highest court of the jurisdiction, whereas the other involves review by an intermediate court of appeals. If a jurisdiction involves an intermediate court of appeals, such as the federal judicial system's circuit courts of appeals, special rules must be created to guide a case through this level prior to reaching the highest court.

The appellate court generally reviews only what has occurred procedurally in the lower court. Such review may encompass what took place before, during, or after the trial. Most often, appellate courts refuse to hear or consider any new evidence in a case. This does not mean that the court will only hear what was admitted at trial. Rather, it will hear all evidence that was offered, irrespective of whether the trial court admitted or refused the evidence. The appellate court will not hear evidence that was available but was not presented to the trial court.[12] Appellate court decisions are usually confined to the issue of whether an error was made in the trial court. Further, the error must be serious enough to warrant intervention by the appellate court. Consequently, an appellate court will not exchange its opinion of right or wrong or guilt or innocence for that of the trier of fact. It will only consider whether the opinion of the trier of fact was based on a fair presentation of the case according to the requirements of substantive and procedural law.

APPLICATION 7.6

Marcus contests the will of his mother which left a large estate entirely to her husband of three months. Marcus claims that the man unduly influenced his mother and caused her to execute the will shortly before she died unexpectedly from causes never fully determined. The jury held there was insufficient evidence to invalidate the will and ordered distribution of the entire estate to the husband. Marcus appealed on the basis that evidence excluded as hearsay was in fact subject to exceptions to the hearsay rule and should have been admitted into evidence for the jury's consideration.

The appellate court is not faced with the decision regarding whether to uphold or invalidate the will. Rather, the only function of the court is to determine whether the evidence was improperly excluded. If such a finding is made, the case will go back to the trial court for further consideration and likely a new trial will be ordered.

Point for Discussion
♦   Why do appellate courts remand cases back to trial courts for further action rather than just correcting the errors based on their own judgment?

The appeals process is started by notice to the courts and all other parties from the appealing party (known as the appellant), who claims that something improper has taken place. The party who defends against the appeal and claims that the procedure has been proper is the appellee.

Once the courts and other parties have been given notice, several events must occur. The order and time for these events may vary from jurisdiction to jurisdiction. Generally, the appellant is responsible for having the trial court records of the case prepared and sent to the appellate court. These records enable the appellate court to review the entire history of the case, including the alleged error by the trial court. The records consist of all legal documents (commonly called pleadings and motions) filed with the court by the parties. Also included will be court orders in the case and transcribed statements of the parties, attorneys, witnesses, and the judge during court hearings.

FIGURE 7.15   Steps in a Civil Suit

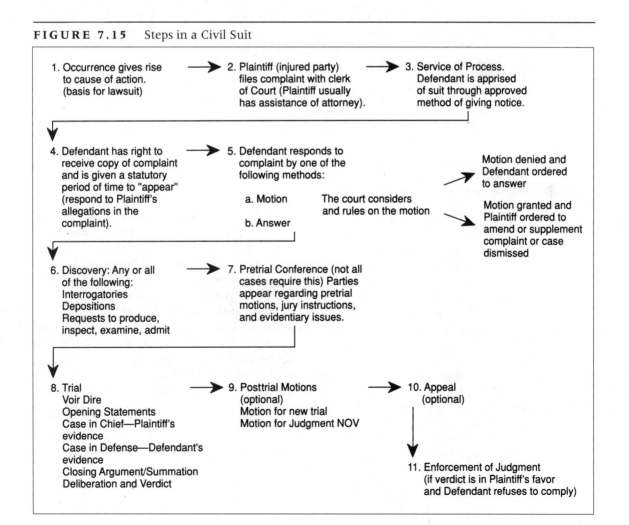

In addition to submitting the court records, the appellant as well as the appellee may submit appellate briefs—detailed explanations of the case and the law applicable to the case of the particular party—to the reviewing court. The briefs set forth the facts of the case, the issues that arose in the lower court, and the result of the case. The briefs also suggest applicable law to the appellate court that supports the position of the party with respect to the issue. The appellate court's duty is to select the law that best applies to the situation.

In many appellate cases, the courts permit attorneys for the parties to present oral arguments of the briefs. At this stage, each attorney presents the brief and answers questions by the appellate court about the brief's content. The court may ask the attorneys to explain why they think a particular point of law is applicable to the present case. In addition, the attorneys may respond to the points raised in their adversary's brief.

The appellate court will consider the case and render a written opinion. The court may affirm (approve) the proceedings of the lower court, or it may reverse the lower court and remand the case to the trial court with an order for new or different proceedings to be conducted. Occasionally, the appellate court will hold that the lower court erred to the point that the proceedings should not even have been held. In such situations, the case is dismissed entirely.

Figure 7.15 shows the steps in a civil suit from occurrence of incident giving rise to a lawsuit to appeal and enforcement of judgment.

Ethical Considerations

Discussion frequently takes place about the ethical obligations of legal professionals. Individuals whose ethical duties do not attract much attention, however, are jurors. From the time an individual is selected for a pool of potential jurors, ethical requirements apply. Even potential jurors are asked to take an oath to consider and answer questions of the parties, counsel, and the court in an honest and forthright manner. The duty of a juror is a serious one. The legal rights of total strangers have been entrusted to the juror on the premise that the juror will listen to the evidence objectively and apply only the law and not personal bias to the evidence when reaching a verdict.

Although a somewhat rare occurrence, it is not unheard of for a verdict to be reversed on appeal on the basis of discovered information that a juror considered information not presented as evidence or allowed personal bias to direct the verdict in a lawsuit. Although courts are reluctant to tamper with the sanctity of the jury process, it is necessary to monitor the process as any other aspect of the legal system for unethical conduct by those who are in such a position of trust.

Question
Can you think of a situation when a juror might act unethically?

ETHICAL CIRCUMSTANCE

In a rural county, the only physician was sued for malpractice. In the months prior to trial, the physician let it be well known that if he were found liable, he intended to close his practice and move to a more urban setting. At trial, despite compelling evidence of professional neglect of a patient that ultimately resulted in death, the physician was found not responsible. Upon interviewing the jurors after trial, it was discovered that three of the jurors had lied during voir dire and were in fact longtime patients of the physician and that they had harassed and bullied the other jurors into finding the physician not responsible for the death of the patient. In this particular case, the jurors violated their ethical obligations and their oath. Although none were prosecuted, the verdict was overturned and the case ordered to be retried in a remote community where no patients of the physician resided.

CHAPTER SUMMARY

Procedural law is never constant. Every jurisdiction creates procedural law to conform to the needs of its particular judicial structure and its population. Then, as society changes, these needs change, and the rules must be altered. In spite of these constant changes, it would be impossible for a legal system as complex and as heavily used as the American legal system to function without some type of procedural standards. In reality, the procedural laws enable any citizen in this country to utilize the court system to obtain answers to legal questions and redress for legal wrongs.

The various types of procedural law address the various stages of litigation. Rules of civil procedure often deal with the pretrial phase of a lawsuit, including the important stage of discovery. Rules of evidence give the court and the parties direction as to what types of information would be appropriate for a jury to reach a fair and intelligent verdict. Rules of appellate procedure guide the parties through the appellate process to have a case properly reviewed by a higher court.

In any lawsuit, once the procedural concerns have been dealt with, the court is free to address the heart of the issue between the parties in dispute. The substantive law guides the judiciary in doing so. The facts are examined, the true issue is identified, and the law is applied to the circumstances to make the determination of which party should prevail. In fact, if more persons would look to these legal standards before taking action, the results would be apparent, and a great number of legal disputes could be avoided. But as long as people fail to inquire as to the law or disagree as to its meaning, disputes will continue, and procedural law will facilitate the application of substantive law in the determination of these disputes.

As a case proceeds through the steps of trial, a jury is selected through a process called voir dire. Next, the attorneys make opening statements, which describe the evidence they intend to present. The plaintiff presents evidence first in a stage known as the case in chief. The defense responds with evidence that weakens or contradicts the case of the plaintiff. After all the evidence has been introduced, the attorneys summarize the evidence presented in a light most favorable to their client. Following this, the jury is instructed on the law and deliberates until it reaches a verdict.

Throughout the entire litigation process, the attorneys communicate requests to the court in the form of motions. These formal requests seek everything from information about the evidence of the opposing party to dismissal of the case against the opposition or even a new trial entirely. The process of motion practice provides an efficient and effective method of resolving issues that arise during litigation and cannot be resolved by the parties.

CHAPTER TERMS

arbitration

civil law

compensatory damages

complaint

discovery

material evidence

motion

procedural law

relevant evidence

substantive law

REVIEW QUESTIONS

1. When are punitive damages awarded?
2. When is a Motion to Dismiss usually granted?
3. What is the burden of proof on a plaintiff in a common civil case?
4. How are opening statements different from closing arguments?
5. What is voir dire and why is it conducted in jury trials?
6. What is the difference between discovery and investigation?
7. What is the purpose of discovery and investigation?
8. What is the difference between material evidence and relevant evidence?
9. Why is pure hearsay (when not subject to an exception) inadmissible?
10. What is summary judgment and when is it granted?

RELEVANT LINKS

Federal Rules of Civil Procedure
www.cornell.edu/rules/frcp/overview.html

Substantive Law Research
http//law.emory.edu/law/refdesk/country/

INTERNET ASSIGNMENT 7.1

Locate the site for your state government that provides access to the procedural rules for state courts.

NOTES

1. William Statsky, *Legal Thesaurus/Dictionary* (St. Paul: West, 1982).

2. Id.

3. *Erie R. Co. v. T Tompkins*, 304 U.S. 64, 58 S.Ct. 817, 82 L.Ed. 1188 (1938).

4. *Guaranty Trust Co. of N.Y. v. York*, 326 U.S. 99, 65 S.Ct. 1464, 89 L.Ed. 2079 (1945).

5. *Hanna v. Plumer*, 380 U.S. 460, 85 S.Ct. 1136, 14 L.Ed. 2d 8 (1965).

6. Federal Rules of Civil Procedure, Rule 1.

7. Id. at Rule 3.

8. *Stastny v. Tachovsky*, 178 Neb. 109, 132 N.W. 2d 317 (1964).

9. Federal Rules of Civil Procedure, Rule 56.

10. Federal Rules of Evidence, 28 U.S.C.A.

11. Id.

12. *In re Edinger's Estate*, 136 N.W.2d 114 (N.D. 1965).

 For additional resources, please visit our Web site at www.westlegalstudies.com

CHAPTER 8

Jurisdiction

CHAPTER OBJECTIVES

After reading this chapter, you should be able to:

- Distinguish in personam, in rem, and quasi in rem jurisdiction.

- Describe subject matter jurisdiction.

- Identify the conditions to establish federal jurisdiction.

- Discuss the circumstances of removal and remand of a case based on federal jurisdiction.

- List the possible domiciles of a corporation.

- Explain how the domicile of a corporation is determined.

- Discuss the doctrine of forum non conveniens.

- List the factors used to make a forum non conveniens determination.

Jurisdiction plays a significant role in the American legal system. It is a necessary element of all lawsuits. Until a court has determined that it has proper jurisdiction, a case will not be allowed to proceed. In essence, jurisdiction is the authority of a court to pass judgment over a specific type of case and each party to the suit. The formal definition is as follows:

> 1. The power of a court to decide a matter in controversy. 2. The geographic area over which a particular court has authority.[1]

The first definition of jurisdiction can be quite complex. It is based on the principle that a court should not have authority to pass and enforce judgment or sentences over persons or issues with which the court has absolutely no connection. The court has the duty to uphold the rights of those within its boundaries and not to spend time interpreting cases that do not affect the citizens or property within those boundaries. Because the authority of the court is related to all of the parties to the lawsuit and all the incidents that ultimately produced the suit, the decision of exactly which court has jurisdiction can be a complicated process.

The judiciary and the legislatures have created various rules to help courts determine when they have authority over persons and issues associated with a particular lawsuit. Jurisdiction has been broken down into several categories, each of which represents subtypes of the general concept of court authority. Each type of jurisdiction addresses a particular aspect of the court's authority over a case.

TYPES OF JURISDICTION

There are a number of elements to consider when making the determination of whether a court has authority to hear a case. The various considerations are represented by the different types of jurisdiction. In any lawsuit, the court must have jurisdiction over the parties as well as over the dispute. This not only allows the court to determine who wins but also gives the court authority to enforce the verdict.

Subject Matter Jurisdiction

subject matter jurisdiction
Authority of a court to determine the actual issue between the parties.

Subject matter jurisdiction is just what its name implies. It is the authority of a court over the actual dispute between the parties. This jurisdiction is concerned with the relationship of the court to the dispute.[2]

Persons cannot create this type of jurisdiction by an agreement as to which court will have authority to hear their case. Nor can this type of jurisdiction be created because a party fails to object if a case is improperly brought in a particular court. Rather, subject matter jurisdiction is an issue that each court must identify before any case proceeds.

APPLICATION 8.1

Santos was in Ohio and chartered a private plane to Chicago. The plane was registered in Illinois and the pilot, Marco, was a resident of Illinois. Over Indiana, the plane crash-landed. Santos suffered severe injuries. He sued the pilot claiming his negligence caused both the plane to crash and his injuries. Marco defends claiming Santos had been drinking heavily during the flight and grabbed the controls causing the plane to crash.

If Santos were to bring suit against Marco in Kentucky, the Kentucky court would have no subject matter jurisdiction, because of the lack of connection between the accident and the state of Kentucky. The citizens of the state could not possibly benefit from having the case decided there. Even if Marco did not object—or perhaps even agreed to the suit in Kentucky—the court would still not have subject matter jurisdiction. The state of Kentucky would be burdened with another lawsuit and the costs of processing it through a trial. The citizens of Kentucky would be delayed in their own access to the courts. Subject matter jurisdiction would not exist for these reasons. The courts with subject matter jurisdiction would be Indiana, Ohio, or Illinois, where the parties resided or the accident occurred.

Point for Discussion
◆   Would the result be different if the plane crossed over Kentucky during the flight but before the accident occurred?

The citizens of a jurisdiction as a whole must have some interest in a lawsuit before the court will have subject matter jurisdiction to hear the case. Stated another way, the laws of the jurisdiction must be promoted by the determination of the case. A primary obligation of the judiciary is to apply the laws of a jurisdiction for the benefit of the people. Therefore, applying laws of another jurisdiction, when not even one citizen would be affected, would be a misuse of the court's authority. To achieve subject matter jurisdiction, many states require that the circumstances giving rise to the dispute occur in the state or that a party reside in the state. This general rule has exceptions, and when determining the jurisdiction over a particular action, the appropriate state law should be consulted.

Assignment 8.1

Examine each of the following situations and determine which court(s) has subject matter jurisdiction. (At this point, assume there are no other rules regarding jurisdiction and no issue subject to federal jurisdiction.) Be prepared to discuss your answer.

1. Sydney is cycling across the country. He is a resident of New Jersey. In New York, Sharon is driving along the highway when she fails to see Sydney on the roadside and strikes him with her car. Sharon is a resident of New Jersey as well.
2. Terry buys a DVD player while on vacation in California. Back at home in Oklahoma, the DVD player does not work. Terry mails the DVD player back to California for repair or replacement by the store where it was purchased. The store claims never to have received the player and refuses to replace it. Terry sent it by standard mail and has no tracking record to prove the store received it, but she claims the store received it and kept it.

In addition to the broad notion of subject matter jurisdiction is a more particular application. State and federal jurisdictions have several judges and, in fact, several courts to hear all of the cases. Chapter 2 discussed the many federal courts. In addition, the states have a court in each county, known as trial courts of general jurisdiction. These courts can hear at trial any type of case and parties over which they have authority. For matters of convenience and efficiency, many trial courts are divided into subclasses by the type of case or issue being addressed. Trial courts are also often called courts of **original jurisdiction.**

original jurisdiction

Authority of a court to determine the rights and obligations of the parties in a lawsuit (e.g., trial court).

The following is an example of divisions within a trial court: One judge will hear criminal cases; another, domestic disputes; and yet another, major trials on contract and tort claims. The subject matter authority of the judges within each of these subdivided courts is limited by the type of case the judges are assigned to hear. Consequently, a judge assigned to the domestic relations court would not ordinarily have authority to hear a major breach of contract claim. This type of authority is based on the idea of organization of the courts, and is not considered a true form of jurisdiction.

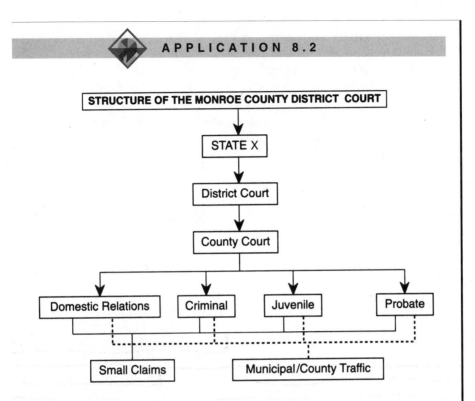

APPLICATION 8.2

STRUCTURE OF THE MONROE COUNTY DISTRICT COURT

STATE X

District Court

County Court

Domestic Relations — Criminal — Juvenile — Probate

Small Claims

Municipal/County Traffic

The following is an example of how a court structure, as diagrammed herein, might function:

- District Court. Hears all major civil cases with a value assessed at greater than $20,000 and not otherwise assigned to a court by subject matter.
- County Court. Hears all civil cases with a value between $2,500.01 and $19,999.99 and not otherwise assigned to a court by subject matter.
- Domestic Relations. Hears all matters involving divorce, annulment, alimony (spousal maintenance), child support, child custody, and child visitation, regardless of the dollar value of the case.
- Criminal. Hears all matters involving criminal charges, with the exception of misdemeanor traffic charges and cases involving juveniles as defendants.
- Juvenile. Hears all cases in which juveniles are charged criminally.

- Probate. Hears all cases regarding the estate (property) of decedents, minors, and incompetents (persons legally determined to be incapable of managing their own affairs).
- Small Claims. Hears all civil cases of a value of $2,500.00 or less.
- Municipal/County Traffic. Hears all cases involving charges of traffic violations of the municipalities of the county, or county ordinances that are misdemeanor (penalty of less than one year incarceration or fine of less than $1,000) in nature.

Point for Discussion
- Why would it be beneficial to have the same judge(s) hear all cases involving a particular area of law, such as domestic relations?

Occasionally, a dispute between two parties is not confined to a single issue. When several claims arise from the same occurrence, a court that has subject matter jurisdiction will also usually have **ancillary jurisdiction**—the authority to hear related claims that the court generally would not have the power to hear if they were in a separate case. Similar to this is **pendent jurisdiction**—the authority of a federal court presented with a federal claim to also hear claims based on state law that arise out of the same set of circumstances that produced the federal claim. Allowing courts to hear such matters prevents duplicity of trials in state and federal courts.

Jurisdiction in Personam (Personal Jurisdiction)

Assume for the purposes of the following discussion that a suit has been filed in a court that has subject matter jurisdiction. The court has the authority to determine who will prevail in the lawsuit. However, the court must still have jurisdiction over the parties to enforce any judgment or ruling it might render in the lawsuit. The court can obtain such authority over the parties in any of three methods.

The first method of authority is **in personam jurisdiction**—the authority of the court over the person.[3] This type of authority gives the court the power to compel the person to appear in court and answer questions or claims of a party to the lawsuit. It also includes the power to seize all assets of the person or even to impose a jail sentence.

Domicile.   A court may obtain in personam jurisdiction over an individual in several ways. The most common is domicile—the place where one intends to make a permanent residence and has actual residence (even if periodic). A person is presumed to be subject to the authority of a court if that person

ancillary jurisdiction

Authority of a court over issues in a case that is subject to the court's authority on other grounds.

pendent jurisdiction

Authority of a federal court, presented with a federal claim, to also determine interrelated claims based on state law.

in personam (personal) jurisdiction

Authority of a court to render and enforce rulings over a particular individual and the individual's property.

lives in the geographical jurisdiction. The key to domicile is intent. Although a person may have residences in many states, the domicile is considered to be the primary residence. The domicile may be shown by examples of a strong connection to the jurisdiction, such as paying income taxes in a particular jurisdiction, registering to vote, obtaining a driver's license, or living in that residence more than any other place during the year. The greater the number of elements such as those mentioned, the more likely a certain jurisdiction will be considered one's domicile. A person can have only one domicile.

Consent (waiver).   The court may have authority over an individual who is not domiciled in a jurisdiction. Personal jurisdiction can be obtained by consent of the individual either voluntarily or by waiver. If a person agrees to be subjected to the authority of the court, the lawsuit may be filed with that court, assuming, of course, that subject matter jurisdiction exists. An example of this may be two persons who are separated and want to file for divorce. If the parties reside in different states, one may agree to be subject to the in personam authority of the state where the other resides and where the parties resided when living together. If a suit is filed against a person over whom the court has no personal jurisdiction and that party does not object at the onset of the lawsuit, the right to object is waived. When a person fails to object to a court's authority over him or her, it is presumed that the person agrees to the exercise of authority. Such authority is in personam jurisdiction by waiver.

Long-arm statutes.   Finally, all states have what are known as **long-arm statutes,**[4] which refer to the authority of a court over a nonresident because of contacts within a state. Under these laws, the person, or business entity, need not live in the jurisdiction or consent to court authority. Rather, one's acts are considered to contain implied consent. The theory is that if one accepts the benefits of a jurisdiction and subsequently injures a party within the jurisdiction, the courts of the jurisdiction have the right to impose responsibility for wrongdoing. Thus, the court has a "long arm" that will reach into other jurisdictions and draw the individual or entity back.

The circumstances that trigger long-arm jurisdiction statutes vary from state to state. One circumstance used in many states is with regard to the operation of a motor vehicle. The reasoning is that if a person accepts the benefits of driving on a highway system within a jurisdiction, the person should also accept responsibility for any damage caused while driving. Another example involves persons who do business with parties in a jurisdiction. By accepting the financial benefits of doing business, the persons also must answer to injury claims as a result of doing business. Such claims may cover contract actions or any other type of injury that may occur. Each jurisdiction applies specific considerations to determine whether someone was actually "doing business" within the state (see Figure 8.1).

long-arm statute
Authority of a court to impose in personam jurisdiction over persons beyond the geographical boundaries of the court (allowed only in statutorily specified circumstances).

The non residence motor statue

FIGURE 8.1

Indiana Trial Rule
4.4(f)(1)

INDIANA RULES OF TRIAL PROCEDURE
II. COMMENCEMENT OF ACTION; SERVICE OF PROCESS, PLEADINGS,
MOTIONS AND ORDERS

TRIAL RULE 4.4 SERVICE UPON PERSONS IN ACTIONS FOR ACTS DONE IN THIS
STATE OR HAVING AN EFFECT IN THIS STATE

(A) Acts Serving as a Basis for JURISDICTION. Any person or organization that is a non-resident of this state, a resident of this state who has left the state, or a person whose residence is unknown, submits to the JURISDICTION of the courts of this state as to any action arising from the following acts committed by him or his agent.

(1) doing any business in this state;

(2) causing personal injury or property damage by an act or omission done within this state;

(3) causing personal injury or property damage in this state by an occurrence, act or omission done outside this state if he regularly does or solicits business or engages in any other persistent course of conduct, or derives substantial revenue or benefit from goods, materials, or SERVICES used, consumed, or rendered in this state;

(4) having supplied or contracted to supply SERVICES rendered or to be rendered or goods or materials furnished or to be furnished in this state;

(5) owning, using, or possessing any real property or an interest in real property within this state;

(6) contracting to insure or act as surety for or on behalf of any person, property or risk located within this state at the time the contract was made; or

(7) living in the marital relationship within the state notwithstanding subsequent departure from the state, as to all obligations for alimony, custody, child support, or property settlement, if the other party to the marital relationship continues to reside in the state.

(B) Manner of SERVICE. A person subject to the JURISDICTION of the courts of this state under this RULE may be served with summons:

(1) As provided by RULES 4.1 (SERVICE on individuals), 4.5 (SERVICE upon resident who cannot be found or served within the state), 4.6 (SERVICE upon organizations), 4.9 (in rem actions); or

(2) The person shall be deemed to have appointed the Secretary of State as his agent upon whom SERVICE of summons may be made as provided in RULE 4.10. . . .

Assignment 8.2

For each of the following situations, state whether there would be in personam jurisdiction and, if so, whether it is because of domicile, consent, or long arm.

1. Midori, a California resident, was driving on a state highway in Utah when she knocked over a mile marker post with her car.

2. Max, a Pennsylvania resident, was sued by Agnes, a New York resident, in a Pennsylvania court.

3. John, a traveling salesman, routinely sold his goods in the state of Florida. Although John had no residence in Florida, he was sued there when a widget he had sold exploded and injured someone.

4. Mike and Blair entered a contract. Before the contract was completed, they became involved in a dispute over what the terms of the contract actually meant. Mike and Blair decided that a suit

> would be filed in Arizona, where Blair resided permanently, even though Mike's only residence was in New Mexico.
>
> 5. Marge sued Ken in Wisconsin. Marge's only home is in Illinois. Ken has a summer cabin on a lake in Illinois but lives primarily in Wisconsin. The suit is over a fight the two had in Wisconsin, when Ken struck Marge and injured her.

CASE

AGRICREDIT ACCEPTANCE COMPANY,

L.L.C., D/B/A AGRICREDIT ACCEPTANCE COMPANY, A DELAWARE LIMITED LIABILITY COMPANY, PLAINTIFF-APPELLEE,

v.

GOFORTH TRACTOR, INC., LYNN GOFORTH, AND ETHEL GOFORTH, DEFENDANTS-APPELLANTS.

2002 WL 1973195
Aug. 28, 2002.

MILLER, J.

Goforth Tractor, Inc. (hereinafter "Goforth Tractor"), Lynn Goforth, and Ethel Goforth appeal, following grant of interlocutory appeal, from the trial court's ruling denying their motion to dismiss for lack of personal jurisdiction. They contend (1) the evidence fails to establish sufficient minimum contacts between them and the State of Iowa, (2) Ethel was not timely served and has no connection to the agreements being sued upon, and (3) pursuant to the fiduciary-shield doctrine, no contacts between Goforth Tractor and plaintiff Agricredit Acceptance Company, L.L.P., can be weighed against Lynn or Ethel. We affirm in part, reverse in part, and remand to the trial court for further proceedings.

I. Background Facts.
Agricredit Acceptance Company, L.L.C., d/b/a Agricredit Acceptance Company (hereinafter

"Agricredit"), is a Delaware limited liability company that provides financing for sales of farm equipment. Its North American headquarters are located in Des Moines, Iowa. Agricredit has more than 300 agricultural equipment dealers in forty-eight states that seek financing of equipment sales from Agricredit at its Des Moines headquarters.

Goforth Tractor is a Virginia corporation located in Max Meadows, Virginia, where its president, Lynn Goforth, resides. On July 8, 1986, Lynn Goforth, as president of Goforth Tractor, signed a retail financing agreement establishing terms and conditions regarding assignment by Goforth Tractor, and acceptance by Agricredit, of retail installment contracts relating to the sale or lease by Goforth Tractor of agricultural and industrial equipment to Goforth Tractor's retail customers. To induce Agricredit to extend retail financing facilities to Goforth Tractor, on July 8, 1986, Lynn Goforth also signed a personal guarantee regarding Goforth Tractor's liabilities to Agricredit. On August 21, 1986, Ethel Goforth, of Olin, North Carolina, Lynn's mother, who was then apparently the secretary and treasurer of Goforth Tractor, signed a personal guarantee regarding the liabilities of Goforth Supply, Inc. (hereinafter "Goforth Supply"), a North Carolina corporation, to Agricredit.

Lynn and Ethel have never resided in Iowa, nor do they own any property in this state. They have never been physically present in this state except for a personal trip in 1957.

On September 2, 1986, Agricredit accepted in Des Moines the retail financing agreement that was

CASE

signed by Lynn for Goforth Tractor on July 8, 1986. On December 22, 1992, Lynn Goforth, as president of Goforth Tractor, signed a recourse supplement to the 1986 retail financing agreement. It was accepted by Agricredit in Des Moines on January 7, 1993.

In November 1992 Wyle Maloyed entered into a lease agreement and a lease agreement purchase option supplement with Goforth Tractor. Goforth Tractor then assigned the lease agreement to Agricredit at its office in Des Moines. In August 1996, Maloyed entered into a retail installment contract and security agreement with Goforth Tractor. Goforth Tractor again assigned the retail installment contract and security agreement to Agricredit at its head office in Des Moines. In February 1998, Agricredit renewed and refinanced Maloyed's retail installment contract and lease. Agricredit has terminated Goforth Tractor as an authorized Agricredit dealer.

Agricredit filed suit against Goforth Tractor, Lynn, and Ethel (collectively "defendants") in June 2000 seeking the balance due under the financing agreements issued to Goforth Tractor and Maloyed. The defendants filed a motion to dismiss for lack of personal jurisdiction. The district court denied the motion, concluding that the defendants had sufficient minimum contacts with the State of Iowa. It also determined that Lynn's acceptance of service on behalf of Ethel, together with Agricredit's act of re-serving her personally, cured any defect in the service of process on her. It found the defendants were not immunized from personal jurisdiction under the fiduciary shield doctrine. The defendants appeal.

II. Scope and Standards of Review.
When reviewing a ruling on a motion to dismiss for lack of personal jurisdiction, the district court's factual findings have the effect of a jury verdict, and they are subject to challenge only if not supported by substantial evidence. *All Tech Inc. v. Power Prod. Co.,* 581 N.W.2d 202, 203 (Iowa Ct.App.1998). We are not bound by the court's application of legal principles or its conclusions of law. *Id.* Allegations of a petition other than those that go to the merits of a claim may be contradicted by affidavits, testimony, and other

evidence. *Martin v. Ju-Li Corp.,* 332 N.W.2D 871, 873 (Iowa 1983). Allegations that go to the merits of a claim, however, are taken as true and are not subject to contradiction in a proceeding on a motion to dismiss for lack of personal jurisdiction. *Id.* The plaintiff has the burden to sustain the requisite jurisdiction, but when the plaintiff has established a prima facie case for jurisdiction the defendant has the burden to produce evidene to rebut or overcome it. Bankers Trust Co. v. Fidata Trust Co., 452 N.W.2d 411, 414 (Iowa 1990).

III. Minimum Contacts.
Under the Due Process Clause of the Fourteenth Amendment to the United States Constitution, personal jurisdiction exists over a nonresident defendant only when that defendant has "certain minimum contacts with [the forum state] such that the maintenance of the suit [in Iowa] does not offend 'traditional notions of fair play and substantial justice.'" *Universal Coops., Inc. v. Tasco, Inc.,* 300 N.W.2d 139, 143 (Iowa 1981) (quoting *Int'l Shoe Co. v. Washington,* 326 U.S. 310, 316, 66 S.Ct. 154, 158, 90 L.Ed. 95, 102 [1945]). These minimum contacts must be such that there is a sufficient connection between the defendant and forum state so as to make it fair to force the defendant to defend the action in that state. *In re Marriage of Wallick,* 524 N.W.2d 153, 157 (Iowa 1994). The critical focus is on the relationship between the defendant, the forum, and the litigation. *Meyers v. Kallestead,* 476 N.W.2d 65, 67 (Iowa 1991) (citing *Rush v. Savchuk,* 444 U.S 320, 327, 100 S.Ct. 571, 576, 62 L.Ed.2d 516, 524 [1980]). In analyzing due proces principles, we ordinarily consider five factors:

1. the quantity of the contacts;
2. the nature and quality of the contacts;
3. the source and connection of the cause of action with those contacts;
4. the interest of the forum state; and
5. the convenience of the parties.

Hodges v. Hodges, 572 N.W.Sd 549, 552 (Iowa 1997).

The defendants would have us focus on the creation of the contract between the parties in 1986 to analyze whether they have had sufficient minimum contacts with Iowa. We note that a contract alone cannot automatically establish sufficient contacts. *Cascade Lumber Co. v. Edward Rose Bldg. Co.*, 596 N.W.2d 90, 92 (Iowa 1999) (citation omitted). However, in this case, as in *Cascade,* the initial contract developed into a contractual relationship which lasted several years and involved continuing contacts. *See id.* at 92-93. Therefore, we look at the ongoing relationship between the defendants, Iowa, and the litigation to determine whether the defendants had sufficient minimum contacts with this state.

A. Goforth Tractor.

We first consider whether the assertion of personal jurisdiction over Goforth Tractor offends the dictates of the Due Process Clause. Goforth Tractor has had multiple contacts with Iowa. Agricredit accepted the parties' 1986 agreement in Des Moines, and accepted the 1992 recourse supplement in Des Moines. Goforth Tractor communicated with Agricredit via phone calls, mailings, and faxes numerous times during the years of its relationship with Agricredit. The contracts being sued upon were submitted by Goforth Tractor to Agricredit in Des Moines for the approval of financing. In fact, Goforth Tractor submitted numerous applications to Agricredit in Des Moines. From 1993 to the termination of the parties' relationship, Goforth Tractor submitted more than fifty retail installment contracts and/or leases to Agricredit in Des Moines for financing. The total amount financed by Agricredit on behalf of Goforth Tractor during that time period was approximately $744,611. Although records for the period from 1986 to 1993 were not readily available, Agricredit indicated it financed numerous other retail installment contracts and/or leases for Goforth Tractor's customers during that period.

Agricredit maintained a dealer reserve account for Goforth Tractor's benefit in Des Moines. This account was comprised of one percent of the total scheduled payments due under each retail installment contract and/or lease issued to Goforth Tractor's customers. Agricredit maintained for and forwarded to Goforth Tractor a retail finance ledger statement, which included information regarding the current balance of the reserve account. Agricredit also prepared and provided periodic reports for Goforth at its headquarters in Des Moines. These reports provided information regarding the current status of the retail contracts and/or leases, including the original amount financed, the total owing, the payoff amount, the account balance as of a particular date, and any past due indebtedness. In evaluating these contacts, we conclude the first three factors weigh heavily in favor of finding that Goforth Tractor had sufficient minimum contacts with Iowa such that it could expect to be haled into an Iowa courtroom.

We also conclude the last two factors weigh at least minimally in favor of personal jurisdiction over Goforth Tractor in Iowa. The State of Iowa has a strong interest in protecting its residents from damage as a result of breaches of contractual duties by nonresident defendants. *Berkley Int'l Co. v. Devine*, 289 N.W.2d 600, 605 (Iowa 1980). Furthermore, the convenience of the parties weighs in favor of jurisdiction in Iowa as well. Agricredit expects to call numerous witnesses from its headquarters in Des Moines and it appears reasonably possible that following dismissal of this lawsuit as against Ethel Goforth as ordered below Lynn Goforth may be the only material witness for the two remaining defendants. We conclude the trial court did not err in overruling the defendants' motion to dismiss as to Goforth Tractor for lack of personal jurisdiction.

B. Lynn Goforth.

We next consider whether Iowa may exercise personal jurisdiction over Lynn. He signed a personal guarantee in which he

> absolutely and unconditionally personally [guaranteed] the due and punctual payment to Agricredit Acceptance Corporation . . . of the liabilities which [Goforth Tractor] has incurred or is under or may incur or be under to [Agricredit], whether arising from dealings between [Agricredit] and [Goforth Tractor] or from other dealings by which [Agricredit] may become in any manner whatever a creditor of [Goforth Tractor]. . . .

CASE

In an absolute guaranty, liability is imposed upon the guarantor immediately upon default of the principal debtor regardless of whether the guarantor has received notice of the default. *Williams v. Clark,* 417 N.W.2d 247, 251 (Iowa Ct.App.1987). A guaranty is absolute unless its terms contain a condition precedent to the guarantor's liability. *Id.* There is no condition precedent in the guarantee here. Furthermore, according to the allegations in the petition, allegations which go to the merits and must for present purposes be accepted as true, Goforth Tractor owes Agricredit $26,529.22 which Agricredit has demanded from Goforth Tractor to no avail. Thus, liability was imposed upon Lynn immediately upon Goforth Tractor's default.

The question remains whether Iowa has personal jurisdiction over Lynn as the guarantor of Goforth Tractor. We note that Lynn was the president of Goforth Tractor. He signed the guarantee agreement with the purpose of inducing Agricredit to extend retail financing facilities to Goforth Tractor. The guarantee was ongoing. He became personally obligated to pay Goforth Tractor's liabilities to Agricredit. Therefore, he created substantial, ongoing connections between himself and the State of Iowa. We conclude that Lynn had sufficient contacts with the State of Iowa such that he would reasonably expect to be haled into the courts of this state. *See Hager v. Doubletree,* 440 N.W.2d 603, 606-09 (Iowa 1989) (holding that nonresident personal guarantors of nonresident incorporated insurance agencies, who were principal officers in their companies and signed guaranty agreements to induce a resident corporation to do business with them, created substantial, ongoing connections between themselves and the State of Iowa, and were therefore subject to the jurisdiction of the State of Iowa). *But cf. Bankers Leasing Co. v. Eagle Valley Environmentalists, Inc.,* 387 N.W.2d 380, 383 (Iowa Ct.App.1986) (finding personal guaranty alone was not sufficient to vest Iowa with personal jurisdiction over nonresident guarantor where he was not guarantor of Iowa corporation nor did he engage in tortious wrongdoing, and his guaranty was for a corporate purpose as opposed to a personal purpose).

C. Ethel Goforth.

Last, we consider whether Ethel had sufficient minimum contacts such that Iowa may exercise personal jurisdiction over her. Agricredit's petition alleged Ethel executed a personal guarantee in favor Agricredit on or about August 21, 1986, and incorporated by reference an attached guarantee. Agricredit relies on that guarantee, and "numerous contacts between and among Goforth Tractor, Inc. and Lynn and Ethel Goforth and representatives of Agricredit at its North American headquarters in Polk County, Iowa," as the contacts justifying personal jurisdiction of Ethel in this case. Ethel did execute a personal guarantee in favor of Agricredit. However, as shown by the plaintiff's own petition as well as Ethel's affidavit, it guaranteed payment of the liabilities of Goforth Supply, a North Carolina corporation, not Goforth Tractor, the Virginia corporation involved in this lawsuit. Further, Agricredit's allegation of "numerous contacts" between Ethel and the other defendants on the one hand and Agricredit on the other does not claim that any contacts by Ethel were in her individual capacity rather than a corporate capacity, and no substantial evidence indicates that any such contacts were in her individual capacity. We conclude Agricredit has not met its burden of making a prima facie showing that Ethel had personal, individual contacts with the State of Iowa sufficient to establish jurisdiction of her person. We reverse the trial court as to her.

IV. Fiduciary Shield Doctrine

The defendants argue that pursuant to the fiduciary shield doctrine, no contacts between Goforth Tractor and Agricredit can be weighed against Ethel or Lynn. Because we have already determined Iowa does not have personal jurisdiction over Ethel, we analyze only whether the fiduciary shield doctrine applies to Lynn.

We conclude that Lynn is subject to the jurisdiction of the State of Iowa by virtue of his acts as guarantor, and not as a corporate officer of Goforth Tractor. Pursuant to the fiduciary shield doctrine, a nonresident corporate agent is not individually subject to the forum state's in personam jurisdiction if that individual's only contact with the state is by virtue of his acts as a fiduciary of the corporation. *State ex rel. Miller v. Internal Energy Mgmt. Corp.,* 324 N.W.2d 707, 711-12 (Iowa 1982). Status as a corporate employee does not insulate from personal jurisdiction, however. *Whalen v. Connelly,* 545 N.W.2d 284, 295 (Iowa 1996) (citing *Calder v. Jones,* 465 U.S. 783, 790, 104 S.Ct. 1482, 1487, 79 L.Ed.2d 804, 813 [1984]). Each defendant's contacts with the forum state are assessed individually. *Id.* (citing *Calder v. Jones,* 465 U.S. at 790, 104 S.Ct. at 1487, 79 L.Ed.2d at 813). Because we find Lynn is subject to the jurisdiction of Iowa based on his personal guarantee and not on any action as a fiduciary of Goforth Tractor, his status as an employee of Goforth Tractor does not insulate him from the jurisdiction of the courts of this state.

V. Conclusion.

We conclude the State of Iowa has personal jurisdiction over Goforth Tractor and Lynn Goforth. We determine Ethel Goforth has not been shown to have sufficient minimum contacts such that Iowa may exercise personal jurisdiction over her. Accordingly, we affirm the trial court's ruling in part, reverse in part, and remand for dismissal of Agricredit's claim as against Ethel Goforth and for further proceedings.

Case Review Question

Agricredit Acceptance Company v. Goforth Tractor, Inc., 2002 WL 1973195 (Iowa App. 2002).

Assume someone bought a product over the internet from a company in another state and then failed to pay. Could the purchaser be sued in the state where the internet company was located based on this case?

In Rem and Quasi in Rem Jurisdictions

In rem and **quasi in rem jurisdictions** refer to the authority of a court to affect property or a person's rights over property. A suit in rem is begun by naming the actual property as a defendant in the court of the state where the property is located. The party claiming ownership defends his or her rights over the property. In fact, if a suit is brought in rem, all persons who have an interest in the property must defend that interest. Because the authority is over the actual property, there is no need for personal jurisdiction over persons who claim it.

in rem jurisdiction

Authority of a court over a specific item of property regardless of who claims the property or an interest in it.

quasi in rem jurisdiction

Authority of a court over a person's interest in certain property.

APPLICATION 8.3

John purchases a houseboat in Florida. He makes the purchase by phone after receiving information and photos regarding the boat via internet. When he arrives in Florida to take possession of the boat, it is occupied by a family who claims to also have bought the boat from the same owner who sold the boat to John. The choices available to John are to sue the boat in rem to have the rights of each person claiming ownership determined. If the other owner family is properly served notice of the action and does not appear to defend the members' interest, they may lose rights to the property.

Points for Discussion
1. What court(s) would probably have subject matter jurisdiction?
2. Why is in personam jurisdiction less appropriate for this situation?

The distinction between in rem and quasi in rem turns on the property owners who are affected. In an action in rem, all persons claiming ownership or some other type of interest in the property may be affected and therefore must defend their interest.[5] In an action based on quasi in rem, only the interests of the person or persons identified in the suit and who claim rights to the property are affected.[6]

Quasi in rem may be a way to obtain jurisdiction over the property interests of a person when in personam jurisdiction cannot be achieved. Assume a person is subject to the court's authority but cannot be located. Or, perhaps the person appears at trial and a judgment is rendered against the person, but the person seemingly has no assets in that state. In the first instance, the plaintiff can file an action on the basis of quasi in rem jurisdiction to attach any of the property of the missing person in the state where the property is located. In the latter situation, a suit that claims quasi in rem jurisdiction can be brought in any state where assets exist for the purpose of satisfying the judgment rendered in another jurisdiction.

In rem and quasi in rem actions are brought much less frequently than actions based on in personam jurisdiction. The primary reason is that if a suit is brought in personam and is won, virtually all of the assets of the defendant can be used to satisfy the judgment. In an action based on property, no matter how great a judgment, only the value of the property named or the degree of interest in the property can be used to satisfy the judgment. Therefore, if the injuries or rights one seeks to protect are greater than the value of the property, it is wiser to seek in personam jurisdiction.

◆ APPLICATION 8.4

Suzanne and Gerry lived together for several years. When they split, Gerry gave no forwarding address. He also left Suzanne with a number of debts they had incurred jointly. Suzanne sues Gerry for breach of contract and wins. She sues a motor home that Gerry owned jointly and equally with his brother, Greg. Anyone claiming an interest in the motor home, including Gerry, Greg, or a creditor, must appear to defend that interest. If Suzanne wins, she can receive only the value of Gerry's interest in the motor home; but she can then petition to have the motor home sold if Gerry does not appear to pay the amount or Greg cannot pay the amount of Gerry's interest to obtain sole ownership.

Point for Discussion

◆   Why wouldn't Suzanne want to try to collect from all of Gerry's personal assets under the theory of in personam?

Assignment 8.3

Examine the following situations and determine whether each suit was brought in personam, in rem, or quasi in rem.

1. Partners Joy, Bob, and Bud were equal owners of a golf driving range. In his divorce settlement, Bob was ordered to pay $10,000 to his ex-wife Shirley. When Bob refused to pay, Shirley filed another suit to collect and was awarded the entire driving range.
2. Same situation as question 1, except Shirley is now equal partners with Joy and Bud.
3. Maxine sued Vince for damages he allegedly caused in a car accident. Maxine prevails and collects her judgment by seizing Vince's vacation cabin, boat, and gun collection.

FEDERAL JURISDICTION

As pointed out in earlier chapters, the federal and state court systems operate independently. Although similar in many respects, each system has its own substantive and procedural law, and each has its own system of appeals. The opportunity to present a case in a federal court is most often the result of those situations where (1) a federal law or the Constitution is involved, (2) the United States is a party, or (3) there is complete diversity of citizenship and a controversy valued in excess of $75,000. The following sections describe each of these situations.

Bankruptcy

↖ *More than that*

As always, the federal court where the case is filed must have subject matter jurisdiction. If it does not, the case must be transferred to the federal court or the state court where such jurisdiction exists. If the suit is brought against a citizen of the United States, automatic in personam jurisdiction exists, since citizenship implies domicile in this country.

Subject matter jurisdiction in the federal courts can be established only in specific circumstances. The courts are careful to avoid unnecessary interference with the authority of state court systems and simultaneously burden federal courts with the time and expense of processing claims related to a state's own laws and citizens.

Federal Question

One type of federal jurisdiction is known as a **federal question,** which occurs when a primary issue in the dispute is based on federal law. Such law can include regulations of federal administrative agencies, federal laws, or elements of the Constitution or its amendments. For this type of jurisdiction to exist, the issue that arises out of federal law must be considered by the court to be a substantial issue in the case, for example, a claim that a police officer violated the civil rights of a minority citizen by using unnecessary force.

federal question
Authority of a federal court to hear a case on the basis of the Constitution and other federal law.

If it appears that a party has created a federal question by adding an issue of federal law to the suit when it was unnecessary or when it was not an inherent part of the claim, the court will not take the case.[7] The conspiring in such a tactic by a plaintiff and a defendant is referred to as collusion. As a result, no federal jurisdiction will exist. Similarly, a defendant cannot create a federal question in a countersuit—and thereby create federal jurisdiction by simply alleging application of a federal law in the answer to the plaintiff's lawsuit—unless the lawsuit is actually based on or affected by a federal law.

APPLICATION 8.5

Farmer A and Farmer B are involved in a boundary dispute. Neither wants to have the case heard in the local court. Farmer A and the local judge have never gotten along. Farmer B is sponsored by a corporation, and local people (who would constitute the jury) have a strong dislike for big business. Farmer A and Farmer B decide that in addition to their filing the boundary dispute, Farmer A will claim that the applicable law in the case is unconstitutional. Such claim will create a federal question, the case can be heard in the U.S. District Court, and the local judge and jury will be avoided. If a court finds that there is no reasonable basis for the claim of unconstitutionality and that the two parties were in collusion, the case will be dismissed from the federal court.

Points for Discussion
If Farmer B doesn't agree to a claim of unconstitutionality:

1. Is there still collusion?
2. Is there still federal jurisdiction?

A pendent claim exists when there are separate issues based on federal and state law filed in the same lawsuit in federal court. In such a situation, the federal court has pendent jurisdiction. The federal court will usually not order that the case be split into two cases but rather may exercise pendent jurisdiction and hear the federal and state issues. When this is done, the federal court will follow principles of state law in determining the state issues and will apply federal law when determining the federal issues.

The case of pendent jurisdiction occurs frequently in federal courts. As legal disputes in our society become more and more complex and many issues must be decided, the likelihood increases that some of the issues will arise out of state law and others will arise from federal law. It would be far too expensive and time consuming for the parties and the courts to try all of the issues separately. Exercising pendent jurisdiction has become the solution to this problem. However, if the state and federal issues are totally distinct, the judge may order that the claims be severed and tried in separate courts. This prevents parties from combining claims for the sole purpose of having them heard in a court that may be perceived as more favorable to the case.

Distinguished from pendent authority is **concurrent jurisdiction,** which occurs when more than one federal court or federal and state courts have subject matter jurisdiction over a case. The case may have solely federal or state issues, but because of the domicile of the parties or the occurrence of several parts of the claim in different jurisdictions, more than one court finds itself with the authority to determine the issues. In such a situation, the case may be filed by the plaintiff in any court with subject matter jurisdiction. However, the case *may* be subject to transfer under forum non conveniens (see subsequent discussion).

concurrent jurisdiction
Situation in which more than one court has authority to hear a particular case.

The United States as a Party

An obvious type of federal jurisdiction exists when the United States has been named as a party to the suit. Since the federal courts are a branch of the federal government, when the U.S. government is sued, the suit must be filed in federal court. Such a suit might involve an employee, officer, or elected official of the federal government or a federal agency.

The U.S. government traditionally followed the English doctrine of sovereign immunity: The sovereign (the government entity) is immune from claims by the citizens; that is, the government may not be sued. The United States has made some exceptions to this rule. A handful of statutes have set forth specific instances in which the government may be liable for physical or financial injuries to a citizen. If a suit is brought against the United States, it must be done in accordance with these statutes.[8] Each requirement of the statutes must be met. Often this includes first making a claim to the appropriate administrative agency. If no satisfaction is received, a claim may then be filed in the courts. If there is no statutory provision for the type of claim an individual wishes to make, no suit can be filed against the United States.

Diversity of Citizenship

A much-used method of achieving federal jurisdiction is through diversity of citizenship. This basis for jurisdiction was developed because juries and judges in a state court system are drawn from that particular state. As a consequence, it is possible that a party to the suit who is from another state will not receive fair or adequate treatment. In today's mobile society, this possibility is less of a threat than 200 years ago when there were great rivalries among the states. However, as a safeguard, the federal courts still accept cases of substantial value that involve parties from different states. From time to time, Congress amends the amount in controversy between parties that serves as the minimum for a case involving diversity of citizenship. The basis for this is to prevent use of the federal courts for matters that are not considered substantial in terms of dollar value.

Diversity of citizenship means that all parties to the lawsuit must have citizenship in different states than an opposing party. Thus, all plaintiffs must reside in different states than all defendants. It is acceptable if the plaintiff resides in one state or several states; the same is true of defendants. But there can be no common state between any plaintiff and any defendant. Diversity among parties must be complete.

APPLICATION 8.6

1. Jeff, the plaintiff, is domiciled in South Carolina, while Jack, the defendant, is domiciled in North Carolina. Thus, there is complete diversity of the state citizenship between the plaintiff and the defendant, and Jeff may sue Jack in federal court.
2. Jeff sues Jack and Molly in federal court. Jeff and Molly are domiciled in South Carolina, while Jack is domiciled in North Carolina. There would be no federal jurisdiction in this situation, because a plaintiff and one of the defendants are domiciled in the same state. Thus, diversity is not complete.

A simple method to determine whether diversity exists is to make a table with two columns. In one column, list the states of domicile of all the plaintiffs; in the second column, list the states of domicile of each defendant (see accompanying diagram). If any state appears in both columns, there is no diversity. Conversely, if no state appears in both columns, the first condition of diversity jurisdiction is satisfied. Like federal question jurisdiction, diversity cannot be created by collusion of the parties. Simply put, a party cannot represent domicile in a state different from the defendant for the purpose of creating jurisdiction. Domicile must be the intended permanent residence.

SITUATION 1		SITUATION 2	
PLAINTIFF	**DEFENDANT**	**PLAINTIFF**	**DEFENDANTS**
SC	NC	SC	SC
			NC

Points for Discussion

1. Regarding situation 1, assume Jeff has all relevant connections, including longest annual residence in North Carolina, except that he claims South Carolina as his domicile for purposes of paying federal income tax. Is the result different? Explain your answer.
2. Regarding situation 2, what if Jack and Molly were domiciled in South Carolina and Jeff was domiciled in North Carolina? Would the result be different?

A second aspect of citizenship diversity is required for federal jurisdiction to apply. The claim must allege damages of more than the statutorily required amount. It does not matter whether a single claim or several claims in the same suit exceed the minimum amount. It is necessary only that the claim be valued at more than the minimum. Generally, this is not a problem. However, if it is discovered that the claim could never be considered as reasonably worth the statutory minimum, the federal court will dismiss the case. If a jury should return a verdict of less than the statutory minimum, federal jurisdiction is not defeated. It must only be shown that the claim could reasonably have been considered as worth that much. Thus, it is important that a party claiming jurisdiction by diversity of citizenship be able to establish not only that the diversity is complete but also that the claim is reasonably worth more than the statutory minimum.

Two exceptions exist to a claim of federal jurisdiction based on diversity of citizenship: domestic relations and probate cases. The law governing domestic relations (divorce, adoption, custody, support, alimony, and other related issues) is so specific from state to state that the federal courts will not generally become involved in these issues. The same applies to the law of probate, which includes distribution of estates of deceased persons and management of estates of minors and adults who are legally disabled. The federal government will not determine the rights of parties in these actions. The only exception is that after the case has been determined, if the requirements of diversity are met, the federal court may exercise jurisdiction to interpret or enforce the decrees of the state court.

Assignment 8.4

Examine the following situations and determine whether federal jurisdiction applies to each and, if so, what type.

1. Marjoram Industries sues Two Suns Networking Corporation. Marjoram claims that Two Suns has created a monopoly of the industry and effectively prevented new companies from starting or growing beyond a local level. Marjoram's claims are based on laws passed by the U.S. Congress that encourage new industry and growth and prohibit one company from gaining so much power that new industry cannot be developed.
2. Brad sues Beth. Beth is domiciled in Texas. Brad claims domicile in Arizona where he lives year-round. However, he owns property in Texas and claims residence there for tax purposes, as Texas has no state income tax. He maintains a Texas driver's license and has bank accounts in Texas and Arizona. He is not a registered voter.
3. O sues the state where he is domiciled. He claims the local police failed to properly conduct an investigation. As a result, O was arrested and held for three months in a local jail on child

molestation charges, while he proved his innocence. Following his release, O found evidence that the police had clear knowledge of his innocence almost immediately after his arrest and failed to disclose it or drop the charges while they searched for the real criminal. O claims his constitutional rights were violated.

4. Tyrone sues Amanda, Ben, and Austin. Tyrone and Ben are domiciled in the same state. Amanda and Austin are both domiciled in another state where they share an apartment.

Removal and Remand

What happens when there is concurrent jurisdiction between the state and federal courts but the plaintiff brings the action in state court? Or, if there is no federal jurisdiction at the outset of the lawsuit but developments cause it to arise? Examples include amendments of claims to add federal question issues and change of domicile of a party, thereby creating diversity. The defendant is not totally at the mercy of the plaintiff's choice of forum. When federal jurisdiction exists or arises in a state court action, the defendant may seek to have the case brought before the federal courts.

The Congress has passed the following law:

Title 28 United States Code Section 1441: Actions Removable Generally.

(a) Except as otherwise expressly provided by Act of Congress, any civil action brought in a State court of which the district courts of the United States have original jurisdiction, may be removed by the defendant or the defendants, to the district court of the United States for the district and division embracing the place where such action is pending.

(b) Any civil action of which the district courts have original jurisdiction founded on a claim or right arising under the Constitution, treaties or laws of the United States shall be removable without regard to the citizenship or residence of the parties. Any other such action shall be removable only if none of the parties in interest properly joined and served as defendants is a citizen of the State in which such action is brought.

(c) Whenever a separate and independent claim or cause of action which would be removable if sued upon alone, is joined with one or more otherwise nonremovable claims or causes of action, the entire case may be removed and the district court may determine all issues therein, or, in its discretion, may remand all matters not otherwise within its original jurisdiction.

Translated, the basic thrust of this statute is that if the federal court would also have jurisdiction to hear a case, the defendant can remove the case from the state and into federal court (see Figure 8.2). When this occurs, the case is actually transferred from the state to the federal system. The procedure for removal is quite specific:

a) A defendant has only thirty days from the date the defendant should be aware there is federal jurisdiction to file for removal. If federal jurisdiction

FIGURE 8.2
Petition to
Remove

IN THE UNITED STATES DISTRICT COURT
DISTRICT OF MONTE VISTA

MATHIAS SNYDER,   ]
Plaintiff   ]
                                         ]
vs.   ]   Docket No. 94-321
                                         ]   Judge David Madde
                                         ]
BILL BOON,   ]
Defendant   ]

PETITION TO REMOVE

Comes now the Defendant, Bill Boon, by and through his attorneys, Smart, Steel, and Harper, and petitions this court to remove the above-captioned case from the state court where it is pending and to accept said case into this court for further proceedings. In support of his petition, the Defendant states as follows:

1. On or about June 1, 1993, the Plaintiff instituted an action against Defendant in the District Court of Diamond County, State A, which case is assigned state Docket number 93-1010.

2. Since the commencement of Plaintiff's action against Defendant, diversity of citizenship has occurred when Plaintiff's domicile changed on or about August 31, 1993, from State A to State B.

3. Plaintiff's complaint alleges damages due from Defendant in an amount in excess of $50,000.

4. The current circumstances of the pending case satisfy all requirements of diversity of citizenship, and consequently, this court is vested with the authority to remove said case pursuant to the Federal Rules of Civil Procedure.

WHEREFORE, Defendant prays that this court will grant said petition and cause the aforementioned case to be removed from the state court where it is currently pending and to be filed in this court for further proceedings.

Respectfully submitted,

Sam Harper
Attorney for Defendant Bill Boon
Smart, Steel, and Harper
1 Empire Drive
Union City, UN 11190

exists from the outset, the suit must be filed within thirty days of the defendant being served with the suit. If something occurs during the suit that establishes federal jurisdiction, the defendant has thirty days from knowledge of that event to seek removal. An example of the latter would be if a party moved his or her domicile and there was diversity of citizenship.

b) To start the removal proceedings the defendant must file a Petition for Removal in the federal court. The Petition must be filed in the federal court whose geographical boundaries include the location of the state court. The Petition must state all of the facts of the case that indicate there is federal jurisdiction. The Petition must be verified. This means that the defendant must swear in writing that all of the information in the Petition is true and accurate. Also, all pleadings (legal documents) that have been filed in the case in state court must be attached to the Petition. A copy of the Petition must be sent to all parties.

c) In addition to the Petition, the defendant must file a bond with the federal court. This is a sort of insurance policy that the removal is properly based on actual federal jurisdiction over the case. A fee or promise of a fee is given to the court as bond. If the case remains in the federal court, then the defendant is entitled to have the bond returned. If it turns out that the case was removed improperly, then the defendant forfeits the amount of the bond to the court. d) Once the Petition for Removal is filed, all proceedings in the state court stop. All future hearings, motions, and the trial will be conducted in the federal court. The state court loses authority over the case. Removal is automatic, and it cannot be prevented from happening by objections from the plaintiff.

A plaintiff who believes that a case was improperly removed may file a Motion to Remand—a motion filed with the federal court that asks the court to review the case and make a determination of whether federal jurisdiction actually exists (see Figure 8.3). If the court finds that it does not, the case will be

FIGURE 8.3
Petition to Remand

IN THE UNITED STATES DISTRICT COURT
DISTRICT OF MONTE VISTA

MATHIAS SNYDER,   ]
Plaintiff   ]
vs.   ]   Docket No. 94-321
                         ]   Judge David Madden
BILL BOON,   ]
Defendant   ]

PETITION TO REMAND

Comes now the Plaintiff, Mathias Snyder, by and through his attorneys, Hayford, Stanley, and Jackson and petitions this court to remand the above-captioned case to the state court where it was originally filed, for all further proceedings. In support of his petition, the Plaintiff states as follows:

1. On or about September 30, 1993, the Defendant filed a Petition to Remove the above-captioned case on the basis of diversity of citizenship and subject to the Federal Rules of Civil Procedure.

2. In said petition, the Defendant represented to this Court that the Plaintiff's domicile had changed to State B.

3. The Plaintiff has a temporary residence in State B for the purpose of attending State University during the months of August through May 1994.

4. At no time has the Plaintiff had the intent to adopt State B as his domicile and further has maintained all domiciliary ties with State A.

5. Defendant's petition is unfounded as both Plaintiff and Defendant continue to reside in State A. Therefore, diversity of citizenship does not exist between the parties to this action.

WHEREFORE, the Plaintiff prays that his petition to Remand be granted and that the above- captioned action be permitted to resume proceedings in the District Court where it originated.

Respectfully submitted,

Michael J. George
Attorney for Plaintiff Mathias Snyder
Firm of Hayford, Stanley, and Jackson
311 Lagoon Lane
Harristown, UN 11115

remanded; that is, the case is sent back to the state court. The federal court will take no further action in a case after it is remanded. If a Motion to Remand fails, the case remains in the federal court.

Regardless of whether a case is filed in federal court by a plaintiff or removed by a defendant, the court will not entertain a case where federal jurisdiction is based on collusion. (Recall that collusion occurs when one or more of the parties to the lawsuit conspire to create the appearance of federal jurisdiction.) For example, if a party changes domicile for the sole purpose of creating diversity of citizenship, such action is treated as an attempt to falsely allege the existence of federal jurisdiction, and the action will be remanded. Thus, the reason for federal jurisdiction must be a sincere and real part of the dispute.

OTHER JURISDICTIONAL CONSIDERATIONS

Corporations

As discussed, the domicile of individuals is important for purposes of determining proper state jurisdiction, the existence of federal jurisdiction cases, and venue. Ordinarily, the law treats a corporation as a person (recall that a person can have only one domicile). This can create a particular problem when a corporation has a continuing business in several states. As a result, special rules have been developed to determine the domicile of a corporation.

Example – Gateway

The state in which a corporation has filed its articles of incorporation is presumed to be the corporation's domicile. A corporation that does regular business in a state other than where it was incorporated is required to register as a foreign corporation. In doing so, the corporation must appoint someone in that state who will accept notice on behalf of the corporation of lawsuits filed in the state courts. This person is known as the registered agent and may be someone in an office of the corporation or some other individual, so long as it is clearly designated who will accept legal documents. Many states designate or require their secretary of state to accept legal documents on behalf of any corporation registered to conduct business within the state.

For purposes of federal jurisdiction, a problem arises in determining diversity of citizenship. A corporation is not considered to be domiciled in every state where it does business. If this were so, it would be virtually impossible for large corporations to ever be subject to federal jurisdiction by way of diversity. In a determination of diversity, a corporation is considered to have dual citizenship, or domiciles. A corporation is considered to be domiciled in the state of incorporation as well as in the state where the corporation's central business is conducted. If the operations are diffuse, the court will apply the nerve center test, which examines the location of the administration of the corporation. An example is the corporate headquarters. Once the domiciles of a corporation have been identified, a determination can be made as to whether diversity exists with opposing parties.

CASE

ALBERTS v. MACK TRUCKS, INC.

540 N.E.2d 1268
(Ind.App.1989).

GARRARD, Presiding Justice.

Delos K. Alberts (Alberts) appeals an order of the Jasper Circuit Court granting Mack Trucks, Inc.'s (Mack Trucks') and National Seating Company's (NSC's) motions to dismiss for lack of personal jurisdiction. We affirm in part and reverse in part.

Alberts alleges in his complaint that he was injured on May 14, 1985, while driving a Mack Truck and sitting in a seat manufactured by NSC. The incident occurred in Illinois when Alberts's truck hit a bump in the road which caused his seat to thrust him into the roof of his truck cab. Alberts is an Indiana resident employed at the Lafayette, Indiana, terminal of the LCL Transit Company, a Wisconsin corporation.

In response to Alberts's complaint both Mack Trucks and NSC filed motions to dismiss pursuant to Indiana Rules of Procedure, Trial Rule 12(B)(2). An unrecorded hearing was held on these motions in the court's chambers. Prior to the filing of its motion, NSC mailed interrogatories to Alberts's counsel.

Alberts then filed a motion for leave to file amended complaint, which was granted. The motions to dismiss of Mack Trucks and NSC were also granted in the same order. Subsequently, Alberts filed a motion to set aside dismissal without prejudice. After a hearing, Alberts's motion was denied by the court. Alberts next attempted to file a second verified amended complaint; however, this was not allowed by the trial court.

Thereafter, Alberts filed his motion to correct errors. Attached to the motion was the sworn affidavit of the attorney who represented Alberts at the hearing on his motion to dismiss.

Alberts's motion was denied. He now appeals raising . . . [the issue] for our review [of whether] the trial court erred in granting Mack Trucks' motion to dismiss.

Alberts . . . argues that the trial court abused its discretion in failing to find in personam jurisdiction over Mack Trucks. We agree.

His first contention, that the trial court erroneously overlooked arguments by counsel, we have already rejected.

Alberts secondly contends that the trial court misconstrued *World-Wide Volkswagon v. Woodson* (1980), 444 U.S. 286, 100 S.Ct. 559, 62 L.Ed.2d 490 when it found, based on that case, that Indiana did not have jurisdiction over Mack Trucks, Inc. Mack Trucks's brief alternatively argues that World-Wide Volkswagon supports the trial court's holding.

However, a discussion of World-Wide Volkswagon is premature. It is first necessary to consider the burden of proof in jurisdictional matters. In Indiana, jurisdiction is presumed and need not be alleged. TR 8(A). A party challenging jurisdiction must establish it by a preponderance of the evidence unless lack of jurisdiction is apparent on the fact of the complaint. *Mid-States Aircraft Engines v. Mize Co.* (1984), Ind. App., 467 N.E.2D 1242, 1247. *See also Town of Eaton v. Rickert* (1968), 251 Ind. 219, 240 N.E.2D 821.

Mack Trucks argues that it should not be required to carry the burden of proof and cites *Reames v. Dollar Savings Association* (1988), Ind. App., 519 N.E.2D 175, 176 as support for its position. In Reames the first district did state that:

> The burden of proving the existence of personal jurisdiction is on the party claiming personal jurisdiction if challenged, as in this case by a motion to dismiss. *Nu-Way Systems v. Belmont Marketing, Inc.* (7th Cir. 1980), 635 F. 2d 617, 619, n. 2.

The cited footnote states:

> Nu-Way also argues that the district court committed reversible error by allocating to it the burden of proof on the personal jurisdiction question contrary to Trial Rule 8(C) of the Indiana Rules of Trial Procedure, which places the burden of proof on the moving party.

However, despite ambivalent phraseology, the district judge did not actually shift the burden of proof. In essence he ruled that Nu-Way had failed to show 'a basis' for the exercise of in personam jurisdiction and had failed to contradict any of the facts in the record, which standing uncontradicted, were insufficient to establish the requisite 'minimum contacts' with Indiana as required by *International Shoe Co. v. Washington,* 326 U.S. 310, 66 S.Ct. 154, 90 L.Ed. 95. Any presumption of jurisdiction under Trial Rule 8(C) is of course rebuttable. Moreover, in another recent Indiana diversity case Chief Judge Steckler held the burden of proof to show personal jurisdiction based on the Indiana long-arm provision is on the plaintiff if challenged, as here, by a motion to dismiss. *Oddi v. Mariner-Denver, Inc.,* 461 F. Supp. 306, 310 (S.D.Ind.1978).

Nu-Way Systems v. Belmont Marketing, Inc., supra. However, *Oddi v. Mariner-Denver, Inc., supra,* is a diversity action and therefore distinguishable from the present case. In that sense, federal courts are courts of limited jurisdiction whereas the court in the present case is a court of general jurisdiction. Oddi is not inconsistent with our Supreme Court's holding in *Town of Eaton v. Rickert, supra,* 240 N.E.2d at 824:

> In the case of a court of general jurisdiction, such as a circuit court of this state, the record need not affirmatively show such jurisdiction, although such a showing is necessary in a court of inferior or limited jurisdiction. The burden is on the party attacking jurisdiction to make a proper showing in a court of general jurisdiction.

Furthermore, Indiana law is consistent with Nu-Way because there the lower court ruled that Nu-Way had failed to show "a basis" for the exercise of in personam jurisdiction. Similarly, in Indiana, the party challenging jurisdiction does not have the burden of proof where the face of the complaint fails to reveal a basis for jurisdiction.

In the present case, Alberts alleges jurisdiction over Mack Trucks on the face of the complaint. The complaint alleges that "The Defendant, Mack

Trucks, Inc., is a corporation doing business in the State of Indiana." Pursuant to Indiana's long arm statute, T.R. 4.4, "doing business in the State of Indiana" is a basis for the exercise of jurisdiction over Mack Truck by an Indiana court.

Therefore, it was Mack Trucks's initial burden to at least go forward with evidence to establish that Indiana courts did not have jurisdiction. Mack Trucks produced no evidence at the hearing on the motion to dismiss to carry this burden.

We recognize that there may be due process implications under World-Wide Volkswagon concerning where the ultimate burden of proving jurisdiction rests. However, in the present case that issue need not be reached because no evidence as to jurisdiction was presented by Mack Trucks (or by Alberts) at the hearing on its motion to dismiss. Since no evidence was presented, Mack Trucks did not meet its initial burden of going forward with the evidence. Therefore, the trial court erred in granting Mack Trucks's motion to dismiss.

Alberts next argues that the trial court erred in granting NSC's motion to dismiss. He first claims the trial court erred in finding that NSC did not waive jurisdiction by sending to Alberts's counsel interrogatories which sought to generate a defense on the merits. A party who is not otherwise subject to the personal jurisdiction of the court may, nevertheless, submit himself to the court's jurisdiction. *State v. Omega Painting, Inc.* (1984), Ind.App., 463 N.E.2D 287, 291. Alberts argues that by sending interrogatories to his counsel, Mack Trucks submitted itself to the Indiana court's jurisdiction. In *Omega Painting, supra,* 463 N.E.2D at 293, we held:

> While the State could have properly preserved the question of jurisdiction in its answer and then proceeded with a defense on the merits, by filing its interrogatories prior to the assertion of the defense, the State has waived the jurisdictional issue.

* * *

Alberts finally argues that the trial court erred in not allowing the plaintiff to file his verified second amended complaint as a matter of right after Mack

CASE

Trucks's and NSC's motions to dismiss were granted. He argues that this was in error because TR 6(C)(2) allows a plaintiff to file a verified amended complaint as a matter of right. We disagree. TR 6 concerns the time limits for taking appropriate action. Subsection (C)(2) merely provides that if the court grants a Rule 12 motion and corrective action is allowed, it shall be taken within ten days. The pleading in question was Alberts's second amended complaint. Since the dismissal was granted pursuant to TR 12(B)(2), the automatic right to plead over where a TR 12(B)(6) motion is granted had no application. Pursuant to TR 15(A) Alberts was required to secure leave of court to again amend his complaint:

(A) Amendments. A party may amend his pleading once as a matter of course at any time before a responsive pleading is served or, if the pleading is one to which no responsive pleading is permitted, and the action has not been placed upon the trial calendar, he may so amend it at any time within thirty [30] days after it is served. Otherwise a party may amend his pleading only by leave of court or by written consent of the adverse party; and leave shall be given when justice so requires. A party shall plead in response to the original pleading or within twenty [20] days after service of the amended pleading, whichever period may be the longer, unless the court otherwise orders. (emphasis added)

Since Alberts did not ask for leave to file his verified second amended complaint, the court did not err in denying Alberts' motion. *Sekerez v. Gary Redevelopment Commission* (1973), 157 Ind. App. 654, 301 N. E. 2d 372.

Affirmed in part and Reversed in part.
STATON and BAKER, JJ., concur.

Case Review Question
Is a bus company that routinely travels through a state, without stopping, doing business in that state?

Venue

If jurisdiction exists, all courts within a system, such as all federal district courts, have authority to hear a case. An additional requirement, however, is that the case must be brought in the proper venue—the specific court within a judicial system where a case is brought. Venue is the court where the case should be tried according to the law of procedure. Although each type of federal jurisdiction has its own rules regarding what constitutes proper venue, it can be safely said that proper venue will always have some relationship to the domicile of the parties or the subject of the lawsuit.

Typically, the proper venue is the court within whose geographical boundaries all defendants (and/or sometimes all plaintiffs) are domiciled or where the lawsuit arose. In state systems, the proper venue would be the trial court at the county level. In the federal system, it would be the particular district court within whose boundaries one of the jurisdictional elements exists.

Frequently, the media will feature a news story about a request for a change of venue in a much-publicized case. While the courts have the authority to hear cases over which there is proper jurisdiction and venue, they also have discretion to decline venue when a case could not be fairly heard. This discretion also extends to cases where there is concurrent jurisdiction with other courts and another court would be more suitable. The process of declining jurisdiction in such a case is known as forum non conveniens (discussed in the following section).

[handwritten margin note: Different courts in the same jurisdiction]

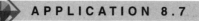

APPLICATION 8.7

Jason is 14 years old. His family is quite wealthy and lives on an estate with its own firing range. Jason is an expert marksman. One day, to demonstrate his marksmanship to a group of friends, Jason takes aim and systematically shoots six hunting dogs on a neighboring estate. The owners of the dogs file suit against Jason and his family. The publicity around the case is enormous. Jason and his family's attorney seek a change of venue to a court in another part of the state.

Point for Discussion

♦   How is venue different from jurisdiction?

Forum Non Conveniens

When more than one jurisdiction has authority to hear a case, the plaintiff is usually given the choice of where the lawsuit will be conducted. Literally translated, the term *forum non conveniens* means "an inconvenient forum", and refers to the situation in which a court, for all practical purposes, is nonconvenient when compared with other courts that also have jurisdiction to hear a case. In such a situation, the court has the discretion to use its own judgment and determine whether the case should be dismissed, with permission granted to the plaintiff to file suit in another jurisdiction.

The courts are hesitant to disturb the right of the plaintiff to choose the forum. However, if it appears that another court is in a much better position to decide the case, the first court may decline to exercise its jurisdiction based on forum non conveniens.

The issue of forum non conveniens is usually brought to the attention of the court by the defendant. The most common scenario is a defendant believes that the plaintiff filed a suit in a particular jurisdiction for no other reason than to obtain the most favorable result. For example, such motions often appear in jurisdictions where jury verdicts are reported to be unusually high in certain types of cases. Whatever the plaintiff's reason for filing suit in a jurisdiction, the court will not question it—that is, until a motion is made to the court based on forum non conveniens. When such a motion is filed, the court compares all courts with jurisdiction over the case.

The consideration of the court in such an issue is commonly referred to as an unequal balancing test.[9] The court presumes that the plaintiff's right to choose the forum will be honored unless the defendant shows that another court would be a far more appropriate place to have the trial. In making this determination, the court considers several factors:

1. The residence of the parties.
2. The location of the witnesses.
3. The location of the evidence.

4. The site of the occurrence (in cases when a judge wants a jury to see the site and when the site is accessible).
5. The docket of the two courts. (Where could the trial be held sooner?)
6. The interest of the citizens of the current jurisdiction in having the case heard. (Will the case help settle an issue of undecided law in the state?)
7. The state law to be applied.

If the balance of these facts strongly favors the defendant's suggested forum, it will be considered to outweigh the important right of the plaintiff to choose the forum. Although it occurs less frequently, the court may also invoke forum non conveniens on its own motion. In either situation, the same test is applied. If the test establishes a significantly more appropriate forum, the case will be dismissed in the original court, and the order of dismissal will indicate where the case should be filed.

ESTABLISHING JURISDICTION

To summarize, in establishing the appropriate jurisdiction, the court would ask the following questions:

1. Where did the actual basis for a lawsuit occur? What state? What county? What federal district?
2. Who are the plaintiffs?
3. Who are the defendants?
4. Are any of the parties corporations? If so, what is the state of incorporation? What is the nerve center of the corporation?
5. Does the suit involve federal law? If so, is the law subject to the authority of a special federal district court (e.g., U.S. District Court of Claims)?
6. Will any officer or branch of the U.S. government be named as a party?
7. Does any plaintiff share a common state of domicile with any party? If not, is the amount in controversy greater than the statutory minimum?
8. Is property the basis for jurisdiction? If so, where is it located?
9. Does any one court have **exclusive jurisdiction?**
10. What are the possible venues?
11. If there is concurrent jurisdiction, is there one court with significantly more contacts to the case than another?

exclusive jurisdiction

Authority of a court to hear a case, which authority is superior to authority of all other courts.

◆ APPLICATION 8.8

An accident occurs between a truck and a family vehicle. The truck is owned by a corporation with businesses in Ohio and Pennsylvania. The truck driver is from Ohio. The corporation is incorporated in Delaware but is headquartered in Pennsylvania. The family members in the vehicle include a grandmother domiciled in New Jersey and a mother and daughter domiciled in Connecticut. The accident occurs in New York. The family sues the corporation.

Points for Discussion
1. Is there federal jurisdiction?
2. What states have jurisdiction? (Assume subject matter jurisdiction requires the incident or the residents of all defendants to be in the state of suit.)

Ethical Considerations

Jurisdictional issues are often raised in response to questions about the truthfulness of parties regarding domicile, place of injury, etc. The very doctrine that disallows collusion was developed in response to parties who conspired to circumvent the purpose of procedural laws. It is extremely important that parties to suit understand that their ethical obligations are not limited to telling the truth when on the stand, but that these obligations commence with the very first representations to the court about matters as seemingly trivial as one's intended place of permanent residence. The procedural laws pertaining to jurisdiction are firmly embedded and well founded in the rationale of procedural law, and all those taking advantage of the benefits of the legal system are commensurately obligated to follow the system's standards.

Question
What might a person seek to gain by misrepresenting his or her domicile to obtain jurisdiction in a particular court?

Ethical Circumstance

Joe works for a boat company that hauls barges up and down the Mississippi River. While at work, he is seriously injured. A federal law allows maritime workers to file suit in state or federal court and not be subject to workers' compensation laws. Joe's lawyer plans to file a lawsuit against his employer for providing faulty equipment to the employees. The jury verdicts in County X have a history of averaging 3 times as much from those in County Y just 100 miles downstream. One choice for jurisdiction is to file where the accident occurred. Joe has told his lawyer that he is almost certain the boats had passed into County Y when the accident occurred. The lawyer knows if the claim is that the accident occurred in County X and the case is filed there, the outcome for Joe and his lawyer is likely to be much greater. The boat was in constant motion, so there is little evidence beyond Joe's own recollection as to where the accident occurred. To file the suit in County X would effectively result in Joe's lying under oath.

CHAPTER SUMMARY

Jurisdiction truly opens the doors of the legal system to those persons who have need of the system's benefits. Jurisdiction should always be the first consideration of persons who consider seeking judicial review of an issue and of the court to whom the issue is brought. Parties should be aware that even though a court has jurisdiction, it may decline to hear the case entirely. The ultimate function of the courts with respect to jurisdiction is to have the dispute between parties decided by the most appropriate law and in the appropriate court.

Jurisdiction must exist over the issue (subject matter) and the litigants (in personam) or their property or property interests (in rem, quasi in rem). In federal courts, the jurisdiction must be based on either a federal law, the fact that the United States is a party to the suit, or diversity of citizenship and a controversy valued at more than the statutory minimum. With regard to diversity, corporations may have residence in more than one state.

Clearly, no lawsuit can proceed until all jurisdictional questions have been addressed.

CHAPTER TERMS

ancillary jurisdiction	in personam (personal)	original jurisdiction
concurrent jurisdiction	jurisdiction	pendent jurisdiction
exclusive jurisdiction	in rem jurisdiction	quasi in rem jurisdiction
federal question	long-arm statute	subject matter jurisdiction

REVIEW QUESTIONS

1. Why are courts required to have subject matter jurisdiction?
2. What is personal jurisdiction?
3. Why do states have long-arm jurisdiction statutes?
4. What are the most common bases for federal jurisdiction?
5. What process is used to move a case from state to federal court (describe the steps involved)?
6. What process is used to move a case from federal to state court (describe the steps involved)?
7. What is concurrent jurisdiction?
8. What is collusion?
9. Where is a corporation considered to be domiciled for purposes of jurisdiction?
10. What determines domicile for an individual?

RELEVANT LINKS

Law and Borders—The Rise of Law in Cyberspace, 48 Stanford Law Review 1367 (1996). www.cli.org/X00225_LBFIN.html

Chicago—Kent College of Law Cyber Jurisdiction www.kentlaw.educ/cyber
LII—Law—About Jurisdiction www.law.cornell.educ/topics/jurisdictio

INTERNET ASSIGNMENT 8.1

Locate an article (other than the one listed in Relevant Links) that discusses jurisdictional issues in cyberspace.

NOTES

1. William Statsky, *Legal Thesaurus/Dictionary* (St. Paul: West, 1982).
2. *Lowry v. Semke,* 571 P.2d 858 (1977).
3. *Estate of Portnoy v. Cessna Aircraft Co.,* 603 F.Supp. 285 (S.D.Miss. 1985).
4. *Black's Law Dictionary,* 5th ed. (St. Paul: West, 1979).
5. *T.J.K. v. N.B.,* 237 So.2d 592 (Fla.App. 1970).
6. *Atlas Garage & Custom Builders Inc. v. Hurley,* 167 Conn. 248, 355 A.2d 286 (1974).
7. Federal Rules of Civil Procedure, 28 U.S.C.A.
8. Id.
9. 10 A.L.R. Fed. 352.

For additional resources, please visit our Web site at www.westlegalstudies.com

CHAPTER 9

The Law of Contracts

CHAPTER OBJECTIVES

After reading this chapter, you should be able to:

- Identify the elements of a valid offer to contract.

- Differentiate between a unilateral and bilateral contract.

- Distinguish fraud in fact and fraud in the inducement.

- List the defenses to alleged breach of contract.

- Distinguish compensatory damages, liquidated damages, and specific performance.

- Explain the purpose of the statute of frauds.

- Discuss the application of assignment and delegation in a contract.

- Discuss the remedies available to one who has entered a contract with a mistaken understanding of the terms of the agreement.

Contract law is based on the principle established in most societies that people should be secure in the knowledge that promises will be honored and are legally enforceable when made between persons in order to provide each party with some type of benefit. This principle has evolved and developed over the years into one of the most precise areas of the law. Because so many of the transactions among individuals involve some type of reliance on one another, contract law has pervaded virtually all aspects of society. Consequently, other areas of law are frequently affected by principles of contract law.

contract

A legally binding agreement that obligates two or more parties to do something they were not already obligated to do or refrain from doing something to which they were legally entitled.

Because each situation is unique, the law of contracts continues to change. Rarely does anyone go through a day of his or her life without becoming involved in or receiving benefits from a **contract.** The food we eat is usually produced, shipped, bought, and sold through contractual agreements. The same applies to clothing. Even the utilities in our homes, such as heat, water, and cooling, are received through contractual agreements to provide and pay.

As technology grows and society changes, the potential for contractual agreements (and disputes) grows. This chapter discusses the basic and settled principles of contract law. Apart from slight variations or modifications in each of the states, these principles continue to be the accepted standards by which persons who enter contractual agreements should guide their conduct. Typically, when new situations arise, the essential principles of contract law are modified or adapted to reach a result that is fair and consistent with precedent when possible.

The leading authorities on contract law have defined a **contractual agreement** as:

contractual agreement

A promise or set of promises for the breach of which the law provides a remedy and the performance of which the law recognizes a duty.

> A promise or a set of promises for the breach of which the law provides a remedy, or the performance of which the law recognizes a duty.[1] (Statsky, *Legal Thesaurus/Dictionary.* West, 1982)

In essence, this means that if parties make a promise or promises to one another, those parties are obligated to perform (complete) the terms of the promise(s). Consequently, in the event a party fails to complete the obligations of a promise, the party who is injured by not receiving that to which he or she is entitled by the promise will have recourse in the courts against the party who broke the promise. For example, a person who borrows money from a bank promises to repay the money. If that person fails to repay the money, the bank can go to court and attempt to collect the money that is owed.

ELEMENTS OF A VALID CONTRACT

Every valid contract has certain characteristics. If any of them are absent, the enforceability of the agreement comes into question. Essentially, every contract must have parties who provide some act or benefit that the other party does not otherwise have the legal right to receive. Specifically, all contracts must involve (1) at least two parties, (2) parties who have legal capacity, (3) a manifestation of assent by all parties to the contract, and (4) consideration that supports a legal and enforceable promise.[2] The following discussion addresses each of these elements in greater detail.

At Least Two Parties

A person cannot enter into a contractual agreement with oneself. This issue has generally arisen in situations when a person who has a partial ownership interest in a business also attempts to make an agreement with the business to provide it with certain benefits. An example is a lawyer who is also a CPA who contracts with his or her own incorporated law firm to provide accounting services to the firm.

The rule traditionally has been that a person with an ownership interest in a business cannot contract to render services that are part of the primary purpose of the business. Generally, such services are deemed part of the responsibility of the owner. In recent times, however, exceptions to this rule have been made, especially when the services contracted for are not ordinary duties of an owner.[3] The preceding example would be such a case. Although the attorney/CPA would ordinarily be required to render the skills of an attorney, maintenance of accounting records for the firm probably would not be considered part of the duties of an attorney for the firm. Such services would not be within the ordinary expectations of the business toward any particular owner. Thus, the attorney very likely could contract as an individual to provide these services to the law firm as separate entity. Consequently, two distinct legal entities—the attorney/CPA as (1) an individual and as (2) a member of the total firm—are parties to the contract.

Typically, the contractual requirement of at least two parties is the most easily met when establishing the elements of a contract in a given circumstance. However, this remains a basic element of contract law.

Parties Who Have Legal Capacity

In contract law, legal capacity means that a person is an adult (based on the age defined by state statute) and has mental competence (which simply means that the person has not been declared by any court to be incapable of managing his or her own affairs). The law is relatively settled that only competent adults can be bound by the terms of contracts. An issue arises, then, when a party without **contractual capacity** enters into a contract.

Age. The age requirement is forthright. The parties to the contract must be of the age of majority according to the law of the state governing the contract at the time the agreement is entered. A simple determination of the beginning of the agreement and the date of birth of the parties is the only information necessary. However, a question may arise if there is a dispute as to the state whose law will govern the contract. This comes into question when the parties or the subject of the agreement involve more than one state. For example, an 18-year-old goes into State X where the age of majority is 18 and contracts to purchase a car. However, the state of domicile of the 18-year-old (State Y) considers the age of

contractual capacity

The ability to enter into and be bound by a legal contract, which ability is not diminished by age of minority or adjudicated incompetence.

majority as 20. If the 18-year-old buyer defaults on the payments, does the law of State X or State Y control? If the applicable state law is that of X, there is an enforceable contract. If the law of State Y is applied, there was no capacity and thus no valid contract between the parties.

Usually, to avoid such issues, a written contract will indicate by agreement the law of the state that will apply in the event of a contractual dispute. When there is no written agreement, the court will determine the law of the state to be applied. As you can see, this determination can substantially affect the suit. This is why most written contracts include an agreement as to the state law to be applied in the event of a dispute.

Mental capacity. The issue of mental capacity is somewhat more complicated. Technically, lack of mental capacity only considers persons who have been legally adjudicated (by order of the court) to be without the ability to manage their own affairs. However, what of the case when someone is quite obviously severely mentally challenged? Generally, the law that only adjudicated incompetents lack capacity will be upheld. Most individuals are given a minimal amount of responsibility to avoid contracting with someone who is obviously mentally challenged to the degree this person's ability to complete a contract is in question.

Many people may appear to be outside the normal range of behavior. This does not mean they are without the ability to manage their own affairs. Many famous and wealthy individuals have been notorious for "odd" behavior. Yet, their behavior did not prevent them from amassing great fortunes. Conversely, some of the most notorious and vicious criminals of our time functioned in society relatively unnoticed for years. The law cannot be based on subjective individual perceptions of sane or insane behavior. Thus, anyone who has not been declared incompetent by a court is responsible for any contractual agreements to which he or she is a party regardless of his or her actual mental abilities.

APPLICATION 9.1

Gary is a severely retarded adult. He lives with his elderly mother who suffers from chronic illness. Their combined disability income qualifies them for a small home loan. They purchase a home and live there together for many years. Gary receives a preapproved credit card offer in the mail. He understands enough of the brochure to realize if he signs the form and returns it, he will receive a credit card. He does not understand the payment and interest obligations. He only realizes that he has seen people pay for things in stores with credit cards. He receives the credit card and begins making purchases. He does this for several months and runs up bills of several thousand dollars before the card is suspended for nonpayment. Gary does not understand the statements and throws them away when they arrive. Eventually, collection agencies begin calling the house. With accumulated interest and late fees, Gary owes in excess of $10,000. Gary has never been legally adjudicated as incapacitated despite a finding by social security that he is disabled. Because Gary's name is on the house, the collection agency can take a judgment for the debt and place a lien against the house.

Point for Discussion

◆   Would the outcome differ if Gary had been legally adjudicated as incapacitated?

Contracts with persons without capacity.   Traditionally, if a person with capacity entered a contract with a person without legal capacity, the person without capacity could choose whether to complete the terms of the contract. The other party to the contract was virtually at the mercy of the person without capacity. The party without capacity could disaffirm or withdraw from the contract at any time. It did not matter that the party with capacity had already performed all obligations under the contract. The minor or incapacitated person could accept the benefits of that performance without further obligation. The reasoning behind this was that because the party was legally incapable of being a party to a contract, a contract could not be enforced against the person.

The inherent unfairness of this situation caused the courts and some legislatures to set forth legal standards that would protect parties with capacity who entered in good faith into a contract with a minor or incapacitated person. This was done under the theory of restitution,[4] which is based on the principle of fairness. With respect to contracts, the theory basically states that if one person accepts or takes a benefit from another who was not obligated to provide that benefit, some sort of payment should be made.

In addition to enacting the law of contracts, many states have enacted statutes, and many courts have issued decisions that follow the theory of restitution. Such legal standards provide a remedy to those who have entered contractual agreements with parties who do not have capacity. However, these legal standards often limit the recovery from the minor or incapacitated person. Commonly, such limitations involve the amount of liability of the minor or incapacitated person. Such amount will be the reasonable value of the goods or services received rather than the amount contracted for. An example is a contract between a minor and a competent adult to purchase a car. Although the minor enters a contract to purchase a car for $8,000, if the minor fails to complete payment, the car owner may be able to recover only the actual value of the car under the theory of restitution. If a court determines that the car is worth only $4,000, that amount is all that could be recovered from the minor. Additionally, the law of several states regarding the liability of minors and incompetents is that restitution can be claimed only for items considered to be necessary to life, such as food and shelter.[5]

As a consequence of the law of contracts and the law of restitution, the person with capacity usually requires the minor or incompetent to have an additional party enter the contract in his or her behalf. For example, a competent adult might cosign a loan with a minor. Then, if the minor breaches the contract, the contract can be enforced against the adult who cosigned. (Note that competent persons may also be required to have a cosigner as a condition of the contract for other reasons, such as to guarantee good credit.)

Assignment 9.1

Identify which of the following parties could be bound by contract.

1. Marcel is 15 years old. His father is out of town and Marcel agreed to sell the family's tractor for $2,000 to a neighboring farmer. Marcel accepted the money and the neighbor took the tractor. Marcel did not know the tractor is an antique and worth much more.
2. Two weeks ago, Louise ordered a new vehicle with all of the options available. She agreed to pay in cash, the price asked by the dealer and signed the appropriate papers. Yesterday it was discovered that Louise suffers from a large brain tumor, which has impaired her thinking and reasoning significantly.
3. Cindy was out of town on a camping trip when her babysitter, Maxine, took Cindy's son into an orthodontist. The orthodontist recommended braces for the child (at a cost of $4,000) and Maxine agreed. The orthodontist placed braces on the child. Cindy refused to pay and is now being sued for the cost of the braces.
4. Ronnie is 21 years old and a severe diabetic. When his sugar level is low he often makes irrational decisions. On one such occasion, he signed the papers to finance a $10,000 stereo. Ronnie is unemployed and lives with his parents. The stereo store wants either Ronnie or his parents to comply with the agreement.

Manifestation of Assent by All Parties

In all contracts, each party to the agreement must signify acceptance of the terms in some way. This requirement to manifest or demonstrate a willingness to be bound by the contract is essential. Otherwise, it would be possible for persons to claim a contract existed where one party did not even have notice of a contract or the intention to enter one. The following discussion explores several issues relevant to the manifestation of assent: (1) the objective standard that must be met to prove there was assent, (2) circumstances that may affect the termination of whether there was assent, and (3) methods of creating a situation for assent to a contract by the parties.

Objective standard.   Whether someone has manifested assent to a contract is measured by an objective standard. There is a great difference between objectivity and subjectivity. When one is objective, no personal bias plays a role in one's perceptions. However, when one is subjective, personal bias greatly influences one's perceptions. For example, if an individual were named as a defendant in a lawsuit, he or she would probably have very strong feelings about his or her innocence. This view of the lawsuit would be quite subjective. However, if a person were to stop someone on the street and tell them about the lawsuit, the perceptions would be objective if the listener knew no one involved in the suit and was unfamiliar with the suit's details.

As discussed in Chapter 7, during the voir dire stage, the parties in a suit attempt to select jurors who have no personal experience or beliefs that would prevent an objective consideration of the evidence as it applies to the parties. Similarly, in contract law, as a fundamental part of determining whether all the elements of a contract were present, the judge and jury have the duty to determine whether there was mutual assent by all parties to the agreement.

The objective standard requires that a third person observing the transaction would perceive that the parties agreed to the terms of the contract and intended to be legally bound by those terms. The parties do not need to say or do any particular thing. Rather, only their conduct needs to indicate agreement to the terms of the contract.[6] The existence of subjective intent claimed or denied by a party is not relevant for the purposes of determining whether a contract existed. For example, the jury will not consider the claim of a party that the party's conduct, even though it may appear to indicate intent, was not what the party meant.

APPLICATION 9.2

Fernando promises Antonio $15 if he does not speak for three hours. Antonio nods but does not say anything. He continues to remain silent for the next three hours. His nod and continued silence would indicate to an observer that Antonio had accepted the terms of the contract.

Point for Discussion

◆   What if Fernando claims that he meant that Antonio would have to verbally agree before the contract would begin?

Circumstances.   Following are situations that will *not* give rise to the creation of a valid and enforceable contract:

1. Agreements made in jest or as jokes.
2. Negotiations prior to the creation of an actual contract.

3. Promises or indications of future gifts in exchange for another's promise or performance.
4. Promises for what a person is already legally obligated to do.

Agreements made in jest.   With respect to the first situation, persons cannot be held to agreements that have been made in jest. If such agreements were enforced, everyone would have to be on guard against saying things in conversations that could later be construed as a contractual promise. An example is an individual who says in idle conversation that he or she would sell a second person a house for 50 cents. However, cases of this type are usually more realistic. Often a very real offer and acceptance will be made. However, one party will claim that the other party should have known that there was no real intent and that the discussion was just that and not the establishment of contractual terms.

A primary legal obstacle to enforcing contracts when there are circumstances indicating jest is the inability to prove that the party meant to be bound by the agreement. Normally, persons talking in jest have no real intent to form a contract. Therefore, when attempting to enforce a contract under such circumstances, it would be necessary to show that an objective observer would conclude that the parties actually intended to be bound by their statements or conduct regardless of the jovial manner of their discussion. In the preceding example, it would be necessary to show that the seller really intended to convey the house for only 50 cents. In nearly all cases, this would be quite difficult to prove. However, if someone at a party said to another guest, "I've always loved your house. If you ever wanted to sell it, I'd pay you $100,000—no questions asked." The guest responds, "It's yours for $100,000." If the seller declined and attempted to avoid the purchase, the jury would have to determine whether there was real contractual intent given the general value of the house and circumstances of the conversation.

Negotiations.   For much the same reason, negotiations do not constitute contractual agreements. During negotiation, there is no real intent to make a firm commitment. Rather, the intent of parties during negotiation is to explore whether the parties can meet on a common ground. If they cannot, no contract will have been entered, and both parties are left as they started. If this were not the case, little business would ever be accomplished, since parties who engaged in an initial discussion about a contract could later be bound by that discussion.

Future gifts or performance.   With respect to the third circumstance, it may at first seem illogical to refuse enforcement of contracts for future gifts. It is certainly possible to contract for a future performance of some act. It is also necessary in every contract that a person promise something he or she is not otherwise legally obligated to do. So why is it not legal to contract for a future gift? The answer is quite simple. In legal terms, a gift has the quality of something that one is never *required* to grant. In a contract, however, if something becomes the basis of a contractual agreement, it loses its gift quality and is required to be delivered. If not delivered, there are legal consequences. Thus, it is a contradiction in terms to promise a gift (something one is not required to do) as part of a contract, where performance of the "gift" becomes a legal obligation.

Legal obligation.   Another situation of interest occurs when someone contracts to do what is already legally required. The basis of any contractual agreement must be voluntary acts by the parties. If persons promised what they were already legally obligated to do, the receiving party would not be getting anything to which he or she was not already entitled. Thus, there would be no basis for a mutual agreement. For example, Bridget and Larry enter into a contractual agreement. Under the terms of the agreement, Bridget promises to buy Larry a new car if Larry will promise not to drive above the speed limit. Under current laws, Larry already has the obligation to drive at or below the speed limit. Therefore, Bridget is receiving nothing that she would not receive in the absence of her promise., Consequently, there is no basis to support her promise in the agreement.

Elements of assent.   Before there can be assent to a contract, the parties must have come to some meeting of the minds about the terms of the contract. Frequently, an offer to enter a contract does not occur until after various types of negotiation have taken place. When one party has actually made an offer, the other party can accept or reject the offer for as long as it is in effect. The following discussion examines the stages of offer and acceptance and some particular situations that affect these stages.

Offer.   The terms *offer* and *acceptance* are commonly employed in reference to the assent by each party. The party who creates the opportunity to be bound by a contract (as opposed to negotiation) is the offeror. The party who accepts the offer is the offeree. The acceptance is the last step in the formation of a valid contract, assuming the subject of the contract constitutes appropriate consideration. (Acceptance is discussed more specifically a little later in this section.) An integral part of any offer and acceptance to contract is consideration. Simply stated, consideration is the value each party gives in exchange for the benefit he or she expects to receive. Consideration is examined later in the chapter in greater detail, not only as an element of assent but also as a necessary and integral part of any contract.

An offer can be made to enter a bilateral contract or a unilateral contract. If the offeror makes a promise and by that promise induces the offeree to make a return promise, a **bilateral contract** has been created.[7] Each party gives a promise in exchange for the other party's promise. Completion of what is promised by each party will complete the contract. An example is the promise of a car salesperson to give title to a car to a customer who promises to make monthly payments for 24 months. At this point, the two parties have entered into the contract. The purchaser must make the payments, and the salesperson must deliver title to the vehicle. When these steps are accomplished, the contract and the obligations of the parties have been satisfied, and the agreement has reached its logical end.

bilateral contract
An agreement between two or more persons in which each party promises to deliver a performance in exchange for the performance of the other.

unilateral contract

A contractual agreement in which one party makes a promise to perform upon the actual performance of another.

A **unilateral contract** is created when a promise is made in exchange for actual performance (without first making a promise of that performance).[8] Using a scenario similar to the previous example, a unilateral contract would occur if the following took place: A car salesperson promises to give title to a car to a customer in exchange for payment of $5,000 (the promise). The customer gives the salesperson $5,000 (the performance). The salesperson gives title to the car to the customer (completion of the promise). At this point, all terms of the contract have been satisfied.

When negotiations precede the contract, it is sometimes difficult to distinguish the offeror from the offeree. Usually, both parties will suggest terms for the contract. When negotiations take place, the point at which they cease to be mere negotiations—the point at which one party makes an offer that can become the basis for a contract—must be determined. Identifying when negotiations end as well as the identity of the offeror and the offeree is necessary to separate the terms of the contract from the terms of the negotiations. Only the terms of the contract will be enforceable. In the law of contracts, the following definition of an offer has been developed for use in making the determination of when the offer is made and by whom:

> . . . [the] manifestation of willingness to enter a bargain, so made as to justify another person in understanding that his assent to that bargain is invited and will conclude it.[9] (Statsky, *Legal Thesaurus/Dictionary.* West, 1982)

The question to be asked is, would a reasonable objective observer perceive the actions of a person to be those of one who is creating the opportunity for a second person to enter into a contractual relationship by doing nothing more than accepting the terms that are already clearly set forth by the first person? If so, the last person to have offered terms during the negotiations would be the offeror. The offeror is the person who identifies all significant terms of the actual contract and then promises or performs. All that needs to follow is the assent by promise or performance of the second person, who is the offeree. Additionally, the time for acceptance by the offeree must be reasonably ascertainable.[10]

Advertisements. Much of the general public shares the belief that all advertisements are offers to enter contractual agreements for the sale of goods or services. Conversely, much of the legal community believes that such advertisements do not create an offer, because certain terms of the agreement are lacking. In reality, both are partially correct and partially incorrect. Whether an advertisement is an offer must be judged on an individual basis.

As a consequence of the requirements of identity of the offeror, time for acceptance, and clearly defined consideration, most advertisements do not contain sufficient specificity to constitute an offer. Rather, they are an invitation to a buyer to make an offer after selecting specific goods or services. If, however, an advertisement indicates a particular good or service whose value can be reasonably ascertained by one who sees or hears the advertisement, the time for the contract to be accepted is clear, and the offeree is clearly identified (e.g., the first 10 customers), the advertisement may be treated as an offer, and offerees have the opportunity to accept it and form a contract.

APPLICATION 9.3

The following newspaper advertisements illustrate the differences between nonoffers and offers:

Nonoffer: "All shoes on sale! Available to the public at one low price of $19.99 while supplies last."

Offer: "All genuine snakeskin shoes on sale! Available to first twenty customers, Saturday March 18, at one low price of $19.99 per pair. One pair per customer."

Point for Discussion

♦   What is the significant difference between the two examples?

Indefinite promises.   Similar to the advertisement is the indefinite promise. Even if all the terms necessary to a contract are technically present, an indefinite promise is not an offer and cannot lead to a valid and enforceable contract. A promise is indefinite if the benefit offered by the promise (the consideration) is vague or incapable of having its value reasonably determined.[11] For example, the promise by a cat breeder of simply "a cat" in exchange for $400 would probably not be a contract. However, if the breeder promises a registered kitten from a litter of Burmese cats, the value of such a kitten is much more easily discovered than a vague description such as "a cat." If the vague language in contracts were enforceable, persons could take advantage of others who had different expectations. Much of the determination of whether a promise is indefinite is based on the circumstances and whether the other party could, in fact, identify with specificity the value of the consideration to be received.

Auctions.   When identifying the offeror and offeree in an auction, the key term is *reserve*. In an auction, all elements of the offer are usually present. The item is specific, it can be inspected and valued, and the time for acceptance is set (while the item is being bid upon). The only thing that will affect the identity of the party who makes the offer is a sale with or without reserve. If an auction is conducted with reserve, the auctioneer can reserve in advance the right to refuse a bid prior to the final sale of the particular item. In effect, this makes the auctioneer an offeree with the right to refuse an offer (bid). Therefore, until an auctioneer announces whether a bid will be accepted, the contract is not formed. In an auction without reserve, the auctioneer is an offeror upon calling for bids (acceptance) of the promise of any amount on an item. When a bid is received, the contract is established.[12] As noted earlier, the amount of the bid (promise to pay) is not a matter of legal concern.

Illusory promises.   An illusory promise is one in which the promisor retains the ability to negate the promise,[13] for example, "I may sell you my house if you promise to pay me $50,000." In reality, the owner of the house has promised nothing at all. Therefore, the person promising to pay $50,000 is receiving no consideration for that promise. There is nothing real to induce the promise.

Termination of the offer.   Until acceptance occurs, the offeror has the opportunity to retract the offer at any time. The only exception to this is when the offeree has purchased an option—a type of contract in and of itself. Generally, an offeror and offeree will enter into an agreement where the offeree has the exclusive right to accept the offer during a specific period of time. The offeree gives consideration of some type in exchange for the offeror's consideration of promising not to accept an offer from another offeree or cancel the offer during the specified time. Otherwise, the offeror may withdraw the offer at any time prior to acceptance. However, if the offer is for a unilateral contract and the offeree begins performance, the law will imply an option contract that prevents the offeror from revoking the offer during the performance by the offeree.[14]

APPLICATION 9.4

Saul and Dorothy are considering the purchase of the home they now rent. Saul and Dorothy pay the landlord $1,000 for an option contract to purchase the property. In exchange for the payment of $1,000, the landlord promises not to sell the property to anyone but Saul and Dorothy during a certain period of time.

Point for Discussion
♦   What happens to the $1,000 if Saul and Dorothy elect not to purchase the property?

Implied option contract.   Cindy contracts with Kelley to paint her house. Cindy promises to pay Kelley $500 after the house has been painted. Kelley accepts the offer by starting to paint Cindy's house. Two weeks later, when Kelley is approximately halfway finished, Cindy says she has changed her mind; she does not want the house painted and will not pay Kelley. Ordinarily, performance must be complete to accept a contract. However, in situations such as this, the law will imply an option on Kelley's part. Thus, the offer must remain open until Kelley has had the opportunity to complete the performance. The implied option contract prevents unfair results for someone who has entered into performance in a contract in good faith. When the circumstances show that a party has entered into performance in a unilateral contract and taken substantial steps toward completion, they have the option to complete the performance regardless of the desire of the other party to withdraw or cancel the offer. This places responsibility on the offeror to be certain he or she desires the contract terms prior to making the promise.

In addition to cancellation by the offeror, an offer may terminate prior to acceptance in other ways. An offer that is open for a specified time and is not accepted during that time will cease to be an offer. If no time is specified, the law will imply a reasonable time for that type of offer. If the offeree rejects the offer, the offer is no longer effective; to contract, a new offer must be made. A counteroffer by an offeree is considered a rejection of the offeror's offer and is treated as a new and different offer, thereby making the initial offeree the offeror. Finally, if the offeror or the offeree should die or lose legal capacity prior to acceptance, the offer will be terminated automatically.[15]

Acceptance. The ultimate step in creating any contract is an acceptance of the terms by the offeree. What constitutes an acceptance is at least in part dictated by the type of contract. In a bilateral contract (a promise for a promise), before the contract becomes binding, the offeree must give a promise in exchange and as consideration for the offeror's promise. At that point, both parties are obligated to fulfill their promises according to their terms.

To solidify a unilateral contract, the offeree must begin performance in response to the offeror's promise. The contract is not actually accepted until the offeree has substantially performed what was asked by the offeror. At that time, however, the offeror cannot withdraw the offer that induced the offeree to perform and is obligated to allow the offeree to finish the job. This prevents an offeror from accepting the benefits of a performance and withdrawing the offer before the performance is complete. If the offeree completes the task, the offeror must provide the promised consideration. When an offeree does not complete performance of a unilateral contract, the offeror may have to pay partial consideration for the work done if the offeree substantially performed.

The offeree must have knowledge of an offer. Acceptance cannot be the result of coincidence. If by chance or for some other reason the offeree promises or performs what the offeror seeks, there will be no contract. For a contract to exist, the offeree must be induced by the offeror's promise to give a specific promise or performance in exchange. Similarly, the consideration for each party must be something the party would not otherwise be entitled to receive. If it is not, consideration would not act as an inducement to enter the contract.

As a general rule, but subject to the following exception (discussed under "Methods of acceptance"), an offeree cannot alter, delete, or add terms to the contract when accepting. The contract must be accepted or rejected "as is." If such changes were allowed, there would really be no offer at all. In bilateral contracts (where acceptance is by making a promise), the altered or additional terms would actually be nothing more than another offer or additional negotiations of what the offeree's promise should be. More importantly, in unilateral contracts (where acceptance is by performance), allowing changes in the terms could cause the offeror to receive something very different from what he or she sought. The offeror might not want the different type of consideration. Thus, performance by the offeree would no longer be of consideration that would encourage the offeror to honor the original promise.[16] An example of the latter situation would be if someone offered to pay $15,000 for the immediate delivery of an Arabian horse. In response, an offeree ships a Shetland pony. The offeror should not be bound in this situation, because a Shetland pony was not what the offeror contracted to receive.

The exceptions to this general rule are commercial transactions between persons engaged in the sale of goods. Merchants are governed by the laws of the state designed especially for commercial transactions and commercial contractual agreements. The Uniform Commercial Code (commonly referred to as the U.C.C.) is a series of laws regarding commercial transactions that have been adopted, at least in part, by all the states. The U.C.C. governs the various practices of sales and financing by commercial businesses with one another and the general public. A variety of other subjects, such as banking and bulk transfers, are included in the code. Each subject is addressed in a separate article, similar in organization to a book chapter. Article 2 of the Uniform Commercial Code sets forth provisions for commercial transactions involving the public sale of goods by merchants. Under Article 2, it is permissible for an offeree to include additional or varied terms when accepting a written contract. However, if the offer in the contract states that such changes must be expressly approved by the original offeror, no acceptance is valid, and no contract exists until the offeror has approved of the offeree's added or varied terms.[17] Article 2 also has provisions that guide the conduct of parties who are involved in a contract and the breach of that contract occurs or is imminent. (Breach of contract pertaining to financing agreements is discussed near the end of the chapter.)

Methods of acceptance.   Generally, acceptance is effective at the time it is tendered. The exception, of course, occurs in a unilateral contract. Acceptance by the tender of performance is sufficient to create an option to continue until the performance and, consequently, the acceptance are complete. If the offer is made to a specific individual or type of individual (e.g., the first 10 customers), no one else may respond. If it is made to the general public, all who become aware of the offer are offerees and have the right to accept the contract. This is also subject to rules regarding advertisements.

In face-to-face confrontations, usually, little doubt exists as to when an acceptance becomes effective. At the moment an objective observer would perceive the offeree as tendering an acceptance of the contract terms, the contract would take effect. Often the situation is much different, however, and acceptance is communicated through a medium other than a face-to-face meeting.

A common situation occurs when an offeree accepts the terms of an offer by mail, telegraph, or electronically. As a general rule, in such cases, the acceptance is effective when posted. However, it is necessary for the offeree to do everything that is required to ensure delivery. For an offer accepted by mail, the proper address must be included, the postage prepaid, and the acceptance deposited in a valid postal receptacle or post office. In the case of telegrams, the communication must be delivered to the telegraph office and paid for in advance. More recently, the internet has become a new arena for contracts and contract law. While the same basic rules of contract law apply, the use of electronic communications to offer, accept/reject, and create contracts has benefits and disadvantages when it comes to acceptance or cancellation of an offer. On the one hand, e-mail communications provide data including the exact moment of the transmission. This eliminates most questions about whether an acceptance or cancellation took place first. However, electronic data is always subject to damage or loss by a variety of occurrences. For this reason it is still essential to maintain actual documents showing the communications and transmissions to support any claim regarding a contract. In the case of unilateral contracts, the offeror must have a reasonable basis to discover that performance has begun.[18]

At any time prior to acceptance, the offeror may revoke the offer. If this is done by mail, the offeror's revocation will generally be considered valid when received by the offeree. If an offeree mails an acceptance at approximately the same time an offeror sends a revocation, the court can use the mail carrier's date stamp to ascertain whether acceptance or revocation occurred first. If the rule was that acceptance was effective upon receipt, it would be up to the parties to convince the court when actual receipt occurred. In addition, in the case of unilateral contracts, if acceptance by performance begins and a communication is sent to inform the offeror of this, it would be unfair to require the offeree to perform at his or her own risk until such time as the acceptance reached the offeror. After all, in local transactions, the start of performance binds the offeror, and the rule should be no different for long-distance transactions.

An exception to the rules regarding acceptance conveyed by mail, telegraph, or electronic communications is the reasonableness of mail or telegraph as a means of communication. If the circumstances indicate that another method of acceptance, such as personal delivery or face-to-face acceptance, would be more reasonable, the court may find that it was improper to accept by mail, and it will be ineffective to create a contract.

Assignment 9.2

Which of the following situations describe an offer and acceptance sufficient to create a valid contract? If no contract exists, explain why.

1. Tomás promises Andy that he will take Andy's place on a blind date in exchange for $50.
2. A local dress shop advertises three "original dresses" for $100 per dress to the first three buyers on Saturday, June 12. On that date, Mariana comes into the store, says "I accept the offer for all three dresses," and hands the owner $300.
3. A local dress shop advertises three "original dresses by the designer Elaine" for $100 per dress to the first three buyers on Saturday, June 12. On that date, Mariana comes into the store, says "I accept the offer for all three dresses," and hands the owner $300.
4. Paul tells Abigail, "I may give you $50 if you promise to buy me a fabulous birthday present."

5. Colleen verbally agrees to give Joe one year of piano lessons in exchange for Joe taking her to the prom as his date.
6. Susan agrees to pay $5,000 to Mark, a government official, for top-secret information regarding government contracts that have not yet been awarded to private companies (several of whom employ Susan).

Consideration That Supports a Legal and Enforceable Promise

As stated, to constitute an offer to contract, all material terms must be present. One of these terms is consideration—the benefit received by a party in exchange for the party's promise or performance. Essentially, consideration is the element that induces a person to enter a contract.[19] The person promises or does something he or she is not obligated to do in exchange for a promise or performance he or she is not otherwise entitled to receive.

The value of the consideration for the specific contract must be determinable. This is merely to ensure that a party is getting something of value in exchange for the promise or performance. Essentially, such determination is required to prevent deception of innocent parties. The courts will not recognize a contract where the description of the consideration is vague or where the consideration's value is incapable of being measured. The courts are not usually concerned with the amount of value of a consideration or whether one party benefits more than another. That is a matter left for the parties to negotiate. The law does require, however, that a party to a contract be able to reasonably determine the value, quantity, and quality of the consideration to be received. This allows the party to make an informed decision of whether to enter the contract.

For consideration to be legally enforceable, it must be something that the law will recognize as a proper basis for a contract. Generally, this means that the consideration cannot be something that would be illegal or that would force the party to engage in illegal conduct. If, for example, one party promised another party $50 in exchange for stealing a typewriter, there would not be a valid contract. Because one party's consideration is an illegal act, the fourth element necessary to establish a contract (consideration that supports a legally enforceable promise) is not met.

In addition, the consideration must be something that is genuine. It does not matter that one party's consideration is seemingly inadequate when compared with the other party's offered consideration. The law does not concern itself with the adequacy of consideration.[20] The only exception to this would be if the consideration was represented as the real article and was actually a fake. If the consideration is a promise that turns out to be a sham in an attempt to deceive another party, it may not be treated as valid consideration, and the contract will not be enforced.

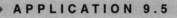

APPLICATION 9.5

A salesman approaches a potential customer about investing in a diamond mine. In exchange for the customer's contribution of $10,000, the salesman promises that the customer will be given a controlling interest in a currently producing diamond mine. The customer agrees and gives the salesman $5,000. Before paying the balance, the customer decides to investigate and finds that the diamond mine is nothing but a swamp. Because the salesman's promise was a sham, the customer cannot be forced under contract law to continue her obligation and pay the remaining $5,000.

Point for Discussion

◆   Can the customer recover the original $5,000 in investment?

CASE

COURT OF APPEALS OF WASHINGTON, DIVISION 1.

WILLIAM A. SMITH, APPELLANT, V. SOLO WATERSPORTS, INC., A WASHINGTON CORPORATION; SKI-FREE WATER SPORTS DEVELOPMENT, INC., A NEVADA CORPORATION; AND ROBIN SELLS AND JANE DOE SELLS, HUSBAND AND WIFE, AND THE MARITAL COMMUNITY COMPOSED THEREOF, RESPONDENTS.

2002 WL 1765615
(Wash. App. Div. 1)
July 29, 2002.

PER CURIAM.

On October 4, 2000, William Smith loaned $100,000 to Solo Watersports Inc. and Ski-Free Watersports Development Inc. (collectively Solo). Solo signed a promissory note providing a due date of October 25, 2000, for repayment of the loan. As additional consideration for the loan, Smith received 100,000 shares of Ski-Free common stock. Robin Sells, the president of both Ski-Free and Solo, also executed a personal guarantee on the loan.

The due date on the note passed without payment and Smith began informal efforts to collect on the loan. After assuring Smith several times that payment was forthcoming, Sells wrote a check for the amount due on November 4, 2000. After Smith learned that there were insufficient funds to honor the check, he served a notice of default on Sells on November 21, 2000. Under the terms of the note, Solo had five days to cure the default.

Still receiving no payment, Smith visited Sells' office on December 15, 2000, to collect on the loan. Although the parties disagree over what was said, it is undisputed that at that meeting, Sells issued Smith an additional 100,000 shares of Ski-Free stock.

Smith later received information on the excessive debt and the lack of financial health of Solo and Ski-Free. He also learned that since the fall of 2000, the state had been in the process of issuing a "cease and desist" order forbidding Solo

CASE

and Free Ski Inc. from distributing shares, based on numerous violations of state security laws.

On February 1, 2001, Smith sued Sells, Solo, and Ski-Free seeking to collect on the note. Smith moved for summary judgment on May 23, 2000, asserting that no genuine issues of material fact existed and that he was entitled to judgment as a matter of law.

Solo opposed summary judgment, asserting that on December 15, 2000, Sells and Smith had agreed to extend the due date for repayment. In a declaration submitted to the trial court, Sells stated that during the December 15th meeting, Smith:

> extended the due date on the Note by agreeing to forego any type of legal proceedings against [Solo] or myself to collect on the Note, with the understanding that the principal together with the interest due on the Note would be paid to William Smith upon completion of our next phase of funding. At that time, we anticipated that funding would be available to us within three to six months. As consideration for this agreement, William Smith was issued 100,000 additional shares of stock in Ski-Free Watersports Development, Inc.

Solo also submitted a copy of a letter that Sells claims was sent to Smith memorializing this agreement. The letter, dated December 15th, states in part:

> Further to our conversations in connection with your past due loan in the amount of $100,000, we are pleased to issue you share certificate #00672 as additional consideration for our outstanding indebtedness to you. We acknowledge that the loan has entered into default status, but with this additional consideration we appreciate your willingness to forgo any type of legal proceedings against, Ski-Free, SOLO or me, personally, with the understanding that the principal together with all accrued interest will be paid to you upon the completion of our next phase of funding. As discussed, this funding may be derived from

either the injection of capital from private source funding, venture capital, the offering processes that have been described in the shareholders meetings and investor newsletters or other sources that may present themselves. When this funding has been received with a minimum advance to us of at least $750,000 we will then be in a position to retire our obligation to you in full. . . . As we are continually working on the funding process and with the interest that we have garnered thus far, we anticipate and hope that funding in at least one of these categories will be available to us within the next three to six months, if not sooner.

Smith replied with his own affidavit denying there was any agreement to extend the due date on the note, and asserting that Sells paid him the 100,000 additional shares as consideration for the forbearance he had already granted. Smith also denied ever receiving the above-quoted letter. Smith also submitted the declaration of a Ski-Free employee who was present at the December 15th meeting. She stated that Sells told Smith "I promise I'll get you some of the money in a few days," but that Smith never agreed not to sue on the note. According to the employee, Sells gave Smith a certificate for additional Ski-Free shares, stating something to the effect of "this is for your patience."

The trial court granted summary judgment in Smith's favor. As to Solo's claim that the note was modified on December 15th, the trial court noted that "the subsequent agreement, as alleged, does not include all of the essential elements of a contract," because Sells' promise to pay was illusory. Solo now appeals.

Analysis

When reviewing summary judgment, we engage in the same inquiry as the trial court. We affirm if there is no genuine issue of material fact and the moving party is entitled to judgment as a matter of law.

The central issue in this case is whether Smith was entitled to payment under the promissory note as of the time of summary judgment or whether, as

Solo contends, the due date was extended by agreement. A promissory note is a simple contract to pay money. *Reid v. Cramer,* 24 Wn.App. 742, 744-45, 603 P.2d 851 (1979). Written contracts, including those that purport to forbid such modification, may be orally modified by the contracting parties. *Pacific N.W. Group A v. Pizza Blends, Inc.,* 90 Wn.App. 273, 277-78, 951 P.2d 826 (1998). Contract modification requires mutual assent in the form of an offer and acceptance on the essential terms of the modification, as well as additional consideration over and above that which supported the original contract. *Bulman v. Safeway, Inc.,* 144 Wn.2d 335, 351-52, 27 P.3d 1172 (2001): *Saluteen-Machersky v. Countrywide Funding Corp.,* 105 Wn.App. 846, 851-52, 22 P.3d 804 (2001).

Solo contends that genuine issues of fact remain over whether the parties orally modified the promissory note on December 15, 2000, to extend the time for repayment. Solo points out that additional Ski-Free shares were given to Smith on that date as consideration, and refers to Sells' affidavit and the letter that Sells purportedly sent to Smith. Based on those documents, Solo contends the note was modified so that the due date was extended until such time that Solo and Ski-Free achieved the next "phase of funding" from investors to the level of $750,000. We disagree.

Parties may modify executory contracts, including promissory notes, to extend the time for performance. But to be binding, an extension of time "must be for a definite and certain time or be capable of being made so by some future event which is sure to happen." 17A. Am.Jur.2d *Contracts* § 531 (2001): *Pavey v. Collins,* 31 Wn.2d 864, 870-71, 199 P.2d 571 (1948). Absent sufficient definiteness, a contractual promise is essentially illusory and unenforceable. An illusory promise is one that is so indefinite that it cannot be enforced, or by its terms makes performance optional or entirely discretionary on the part of the promisor. Such a promise is insufficient consideration to support enforcement of a return promise.

The time-tested case of *Stickler v. Giles* (*Stickler v. Giles,* 9 Wash. 147,37 P. 293 [1894]) demonstrates this need for definiteness with regard

to promissory notes. In that case, a borrower, who was a contractor, defaulted on a loan debt because he had fallen on hard times and did not have the funds to repay the lender. During the default period, the debtor notified the lender that he had been awarded a contract with the county, that he expected to receive his first estimate for the work between August 12th and 15th, and that he would repay the loan with agreed interest when he was paid on the contract. The lender replied that "he would wait." Our Supreme Court held that this was not a valid modification of the contract for repayment. In so holding, the Court reasoned that the time for repayment was indefinite and that the contingency for repayment—that the debtor would perform under the expected contract with the county—was entirely uncertain and dependent upon conditions which might or might not result. The Court noted that if "for any reason the work was not done to the satisfaction of the county it might refuse the estimate; or the work might be entirely abandoned and any right to payment therefore forfeited by the [lender]." *Stickler,* 9 Wash. at 149.

Here, Solo's alleged promise to pay Smith upon achieving the "next phase of funding" was similar to *Stickler* in its indefiniteness. It was entirely possible that the purported influx of funding would never occur due to any number of contingencies, including the lack of investors or their refusal to provide sufficient capital. Additionally, it was speculative whether Solo or Ski-Free would ever reach the required level of $750,000 in funding mentioned in the letter as a contingency for repayment. And as the trial court noted, achieving this level of funds was an event that was dependent upon and was largely within the control of the debtors, who could simply choose not to pursue the funding in a timely fashion. Thus, the language of the letter and Sells' affidavit reveal that the occurrence of the condition precedent to repayment was entirely uncertain and dependent upon conditions "which might or might not result." *Stickler,* 9 Wash at 149. The trial court properly granted summary judgment.

◆ **CASE**

Solo also points out the general rule that where a contract is unclear as to the time for performance, a court can impose a "reasonable time." *See Smith v. Smith,* 4 Wn.App. 608, 612, 484 P.2d 409 (1971) (where contract is silent as to the time of duration, court may imply that performance was intended to take place within a reasonable time). Solo argues that the trial court should have imposed a three to six month extension for repayment, based on Sells' statement in the December 15th letter that this was the anticipated time frame for achieving the "next phase of funding." We disagree that this was sufficient to cure the illusory promise to repay. Solo fails to cite a single case where, as here, the reasonable time proposed was based on

the mere "anticipation and hope" that the contingency for performance would occur. As discussed above, Sells' proposed three-to-six-month time frame was built upon factors that were entirely speculative and largely within the borrowers' control. Because the alleged promise to pay is illusory, the letter cannot reasonably be construed as imposing a six-month extension of the note.

We affirm.

Case Review Question

Smith v. Solo Watersports, Inc., 2002 WL 1765615 (Wash.App. Div. 1, 2002).

Would the result change if the respondent had applied for specific bank loan to pay the debt?

THIRD-PARTY INVOLVEMENT IN CONTRACTS

third-party beneficiary
One who, as the result of gift or collateral agreement, is entitled to the contractual performance owed another.

Sometimes parties will enter a contract with the intent to benefit persons who are not directly involved in the contract. Such an agreement is known as a third-party contract, and the person entitled to the contractual benefits is known as a **third-party beneficiary.** Another situation occurs when a party enters into a contract and later turns his or her contractual interest over to a third party. This latter occurrence is called assignment and delegation. Specific rules govern the rights and duties of all concerned in such situations.

Third-Party Contracts

Three types of third-party contracts exist. The third parties in these types of contracts are known as donee beneficiaries, creditor beneficiaries, and incidental beneficiaries. The donee beneficiary receives benefit from the contract as a gift from one of the promisors. The creditor beneficiary receives benefit from one promisor as satisfaction of an existing debt from the other promisor. The incidental beneficiary is not intended by the parties to benefit directly from the contract but receives the benefit as a side effect of the contract.

The various beneficiaries are distinguished in terms of their rights in satisfaction of the contract. A donee or creditor beneficiary can enforce the contract against the party obligated to provide the benefit. The creditor beneficiary can enforce the contract against the party who owes the benefit or against the party who has contracted to provide it.[21]

APPLICATION 9.6

Donee beneficiary.   Susan and Patrice enter into a contract. Susan promises to pay Patrice $50. Patrice promises to clean Beverly's (Susan's mother) house. Beverly is a donee beneficiary. Susan is the donor (party making the gift); Patrice is the obligor (party required to satisfy the gift).

Creditor beneficiary.   Matthew and Keith enter a contract. Matthew promises to clean Keith's swimming pool for three months. Keith promises to pay Local Community College, Matthew's tuition, which Matthew owes for the current semester. Local Community College is a creditor beneficiary.

Incidental beneficiary.   Lily contracts to purchase a car from Johnny's Junkers. Part of the agreement is that Johnny will put new tires on the car from J. C. Montgomery Tire Company. J. C. Montgomery is an incidental beneficiary.

Point for Discussion
- What are the significant differences between the types of beneficiaries?

The incidental beneficiary has no rights against either party to the contract, because there was never any intent to make the contract for the purpose of benefiting this party. If the contract can be satisfied without involvement of the particular beneficiary, the parties are not obligated in any way to make compensation for failure to provide the benefit. In the preceding application, if Johnny can provide tires from another source that is acceptable to Lily, J. C. Montgomery will have no rights to force Johnny to purchase the tires from the company.

Similarly, in the preceding application, Beverly could not force Susan to ensure that Patrice satisfied the contract. It was purely gratuitous, and there are no contractual rights to gifts from the donor. However, Beverly and Susan would both have the right to compel Patrice to satisfy the contract and provide the benefit (gift) to Beverly as long as Susan had met her obligations under the contract.

Assignment and Delegation

Assignment or delegation takes place when one or more parties to a contract assign rights or delegate duties under the contract to a third party. Generally, assignment or delegation is acceptable unless (1) the parties have stipulated in the contract that it is not permissible or (2) the assignment or delegation would significantly alter the duty or rights of the other party to the contract.[22]

In assignment, a party assigns the rights or benefits he or she is entitled to receive under the terms of the contract. The party to the contract is the assignor; the party receiving these rights is the assignee. If there is a complete assignment, the assignee steps into the shoes of the assignor and can enforce the contract against the remaining party to the contract. In a partial assignment, the enforcement would come from the assignor.

The following is an example of an impermissible assignment: Pak has purchased and paid for a three-year maintenance agreement for his computer with a local office supply business. After one year, Pak closes his business and assigns his rights to maintenance of his computer to another business with two computers. This would significantly increase the obligations of the remaining party to the contract (the office supply store), and the assignment would probably not be considered valid.

To delegate one's duties under a contract, the person accepting the duties (delegatee) must be able to provide an equivalent performance. In addition, the party delegating the duties (delegator) remains responsible under the contract until the duties are performed satisfactorily by the delegate.[23]

The following is an example of delegation: Pak owns a fleet of taxi cabs. He has an agreement with a local service station for routine maintenance and major repairs at a specified rate. The owner of the station in turn delegates the duties of maintenance and repair to the local high school shop class. If the class does not perform the repairs satisfactorily, the station owner, in addition to the high school class, may be held responsible.

CASE

LITTLE ROCK WASTEWATER UTILITY v. LARRY MOYER TRUCKING, INC.

321 Ark. 303, 902 S.W.2d 760 (1995).

DUDLEY, Justice.

Road widening project subcontractor brought action against sewer utility, alleging it was third-party beneficiary of sewer line relocation agreement between Highway and Transportation Department and utility, and contending that it suffered damages as result of delays caused by utility's failure to perform relocation agreement satisfactorily. The Circuit Court, Pulaski County, John Ward, J., entered judgment for subcontractor. Utility appealed, and subcontrators cross-appealed. The Supreme Court, Dudley, J., held that: (1) whether subcontractor was third-party beneficiary of sewer line with location agreement was question for jury; (2) the fact that subcontractor was not prime contractor did not preclude subcontractor from being third-party beneficiary of sewer line

relocation agreement; (3) "no damage" provision in specifications for project that applied to construction contract between project prime contractor and Department did not preclude subcontractor from recovering against utility; (4) substantial evidence supported jury's award of damages; (5) proof of anticipated profit damages suffered by subcontractor was not impermissibly speculative, and (6) it would remand action to trial court for consideration of whether to award attorney fees to subcontractor.

The Arkansas State Highway Commission decided that Baseline Road in Pulaski County should be widened from two lanes to five lanes, and it knew that appellant, Little Rock Wastewater Utility, owned sewer lines that were located where the construction would take place. In anticipation of the earthwork and construction involved in widening the road, the Commission, acting through the Arkansas Highway and Transportation Department, entered into a contract with the Little Rock Wastewater Utility to relocate Utility's sewer lines. In this agreement, dated August 12, 1988, and styled "The Relocation Agreement," Utility was to relocate its facilities when notified to do so by the Department. Upon notice, it was to act with diligence, begin the relocation work within thirty days, complete the work within

150 days thereafter "in a manner as will result in no avoidable interference or delay in the construction work," and adjust the sewer facilities as required by the construction work. After the contract was executed, Utility was given notice and started its work. By the spring of 1991, Utility had completed most of its relocation work. On March 5, 1991, the Department entered into a separate contract with Southern Pavers, Inc. to widen the roadway and surface the road. That same day, Southern Pavers, the prime contractor, entered into a subcontract with Larry Moyer Trucking, Inc. to clear and grub for widening the road and to install drainage and related facilities. The subcontractor, appellee Moyer Trucking, started its work.

In the performance of its subcontract with Southern Pavers, Moyer Trucking experienced delays. It contends the delays were caused by Utility's failure to perform its contract with the Department and that it suffered damages as a result of these delays. Moyer Trucking filed this suit in which it alleged it was a third-party beneficiary of the Relocation Agreement and it suffered damages as a result of Utility's failure to perform that agreement satisfactorily. Upon trial, a jury returned a $62,563.49 verdict in Moyer Trucking's favor. Utility appeals, and Moyer Trucking cross-appeals. We affirm on direct appeal and reverse and remand on cross-appeal.

Utility's first point on direct appeal is that there is no legal basis for Moyer Trucking's claim that it was a third-party beneficiary of the relocation contract between the Department and Utility. The presumption is that parties contract only for themselves, and a contract will not be construed as having been made for the benefit of third parties unless it clearly appears that such was the intention of the parties. *Howell v. Worth James Constr. Co.*, 259 Ark. 627, 535 S.W.2d 826 (1976). However, a contract is actionable by a third party where there is substantial evidence of a clear intention to benefit that third party. *Id.* at 629, 535 S.W.2d at 828. It is not necessary that the person be named in the contract, and if he is otherwise sufficiently described or designated, he may be one of a class of persons if the class is sufficiently described or designated. *Id.* at 630, 535 S.W.2d at 829.

We held that a provision in the contract by which the subdivision retained forty percent of the contract price as a bond for the trenching contractor evidenced its intent to be a surety for it and that the utility contractor was an intended beneficiary. *Id.* at 630, 535 S.W.2d at 829.

Both Utility and Moyer Trucking agree that Howell is the leading case on third-party beneficiary contracts in this State, but each that ends the case supports its argument in this appeal. In *Howell*, the appellee contractor, Worth James Construction Co., constructed water lines for the appellant subdivision, Tall Timber Development Corp, *Id.* at 638, 585 S.W.2d at 827. Appellant subdivision contracted separately with co-appellant, Howell, for co-appellant to do trenching. *Id.* Howell damaged the water lines during trenching, and the appellee utility contractor, Worth James, sued for damages based upon a provision in the contract between the subdivision, and the trenching contractor. *Id.*, 535 S.W.2d at 827–28. The appellant subdivision argued that the contract sued upon was for the benefit of the subdivision and the trenching contractor only. *Id.* at 629, 535 S.W.2d at 828. We held that a provision in the contract by which the subdivision retained forty percent of the contract price as a bond for the trenching contractor evidenced its intent to be a surety for it and that the utility contractor was an intended beneficiary. *Id.* at 630, 535 S.W.2d at 820.

In the case at bar, Utility argues that, since there was no retainage provision in the relocation contract, this case does not come within the ambit of Howell. The argument is not persuasive. It is not necessary that there be a retainage provision in order for there to be third-party beneficiary of a contract. Other factors may demonstrate that a third party was in the class of persons intended to be a beneficiary of the contract.

Here, the language of the Relocation Agreement shows that the relocation work to be performed by Utility was to be practically completed before the earthwork and surfacing contract would be let by the Department.

Larry Moyer, the president of appellee Moyer Trucking, testified that, when making Moyer Trucking's bid for the subcontract, he relied on the fact that Utility essentially had completed its work

CASE

and would coordinate the remaining work with the Department while construction on the roadway was in progress. Randy McNulty, president of Southern Pavers, testified that he relied on this fact when he made the primary bid and that he bid less because the relocation of the utilities would be almost complete, there would be less interference, and it would cost less to complete the construction job. Billy Morgan, superintendent for Southern Pavers, testified that he understood that the utility moving had been done before the job was started, but, as it turned out, the moving had not been done, and the work done by Moyer Trucking was significantly impaired.

In determining whether Moyer Trucking was in the class to be benefitted by the contract, the reasoning underlying cases from other jurisdictions is helpful. In *Moore Constr. Co. v. Clarksville Dep't of Elec.,* 707 S.W.2d 1 (Tenn. App. 1985), the Tennessee Court of Appeals considered the question of whether a contractor can be an intended beneficiary of a construction contract between an owner and another prime contractor for work being performed as part of the same construction project. *Id.* at 10. It held that unless the construction contracts involved clearly provide otherwise, prime contractors on construction projects involving multiple prime contractors will be considered to be intended or third-party beneficiaries of the contracts between the project's owner and other prime contractors. *Id.* The Tennessee court relied in part on a New Jersey case, *Broadway Maintenance Corp. v. Rutgers,* 90 N.J. 253, 447 A.2d 906 (1982), in which the New Jersey Supreme Court said that when parties conceived that the prime contractors would benefit from the performance of their fellow contractors, when the project could not have been finished without each contractor meeting its respective obligations, and when the obligations of others induced each contractor to undertake its job at the agreed price, the contractors could recover from each other as third-party beneficiaries of the contracts between them and the owner. *Rutgers,* 447 A.2d at 910.

Here, Utility agreed to move the sewer lines so they would not interfere with the construction work that the Department was to later undertake.

Then the Department contracted with Southern Pavers, which in turn subcontracted with Moyer Trucking to do the construction work. Thus, the trial court correctly refused to grant a directed verdict in favor of Utility and correctly allowed the third-party beneficiary issue to be submitted to the jury.

In its final argument Utility contends that the trial court erred in charging the jury about the measure of damages because (1) there was no competent evidence to support giving the instruction and (2) the instruction incorrectly stated the elements of damage. We have already reviewed the evidence, and there is no need to repeat it in addressing this point of appeal. In addition to questioning the sufficiency of that evidence, Utility argues that the damages were speculative.

When a party seeks to recover anticipated profits under a contract, he must present a reasonably complete set of figures to the jury and should not leave the jury to speculate as to whether there could have been any profits. Lost profits must be proven by evidence showing that it was reasonably certain the profits would have been made had the other party carried out its contract. Such proof is speculative when based upon such factors as projected sales when there are too many variables to make an accurate projection. *See Sumlin v. Woodson,* 211 Ark. 214, 199 S.W.2d 936 (1947). In *Kennedy Bros. Constr. Co.,* we upheld an award of profits when the appellee lost a bid from the U.S. Army Corps of Engineers because of a faulty surety bond. *Kennedy Bros.,* 282 Ark. at 546, 670 S.W.2d at 799. The figures presented to the jury were based upon the cost of the job if it had been completed within the contract time. The work was not done because the bid was lost; therefore, expert testimony was used to estimate the figures, and we held the damages were reasonably accurate. *Id.* at 547, 670 S.W.2d at 800. The loss of profit in the case at bar was based upon work already completed, and this figure was accurate enough to be submitted to a jury.

In Utility's last part of this argument, it argues, without any citation of authority and actually without any real argument, that the instruction incorrectly stated the elements of damage. We have often said that assignments of error unsupported by convincing argument or authority will not be considered on appeal, unless it is apparent without further research that they are well taken. *Mikel v. Hubbard,* 317 Ark. 125, 876 S.W.2d 558 (1994).

Case Review Question

What is the role of each member of a third-party contract?

PROBLEMS IN CREATING OR ENFORCING THE CONTRACT

Terms of the Contract

On occasion, both parties intend to enter, and believe they have entered, into a valid contractual agreement, but as they begin to fulfill their contractual obligations, it becomes apparent that they have understood and agreed to different terms. When this situation occurs, the law has developed methods of determining whose expectations will be enforced.

Generally, in the case of an innocent mistake, the court will examine each side of the contract and make a determination as to what a reasonable person would perceive the terms to be under the circumstances (use of objective standard to determine intent). If it appears that a reasonable person would have understood what the offeror intended, the offeree will be bound by the offeror's original terms. Similarly, if it is apparent that the offeror should have understood the intentions of the offeree and the terms that supported the offeree's consideration, the offeror will be bound by the offeree's interpretation of the terms of the contract.

In making this interpretation of the terms of the contract, the court will apply the plain meaning rule.[24] Simply stated, this means that in most cases the court will assume that the offeror or offeree should have used ordinary meanings and definitions when interpreting the terms of the contract. The court will, however, deviate from this rule when terms of art (terms of technical terminology or terms used in a particular trade) are used. If all parties to the contract are members of the profession or trade that utilizes this type of terminology, the common meaning of the term by members of the profession or trade will be used to determine what the offeror and offeree should have interpreted the term to mean.[25]

Assignment 9.3

Which of the following items would be valid and enforceable consideration?

1. Spouse A promises to not use illegal drugs in exchange for custody of the children in a divorce proceeding with Spouse B.
2. Spouse A promises not to move out of state for 10 years in exchange for custody of the children in a divorce proceeding with Spouse B.

Unconscionable Contracts

There are two basic types of unconscionable contracts. The first is the classic unconscionable contract, in which the innocent party had no real bargaining power or opportunity to decline. This is often based on a lack of knowledge of the true terms of the contract. The innocent party is given the terms of the contract without an opportunity to discover their real meaning and extent. For example, an unqualified person goes to the sight of a natural disaster, such as a hurricane, and takes contracts for home repairs for elderly persons at exorbitant rates. Because the homeowners are in need of immediate shelter they have little choice but to pay the price regardless of how high it may be. Effectively, the homeowners are in an untenable position. They have nowhere to go and no shelter if they do not seize the opportunity. They do so only to find that the work is unsatisfactory and greatly overpriced. In such cases, the contract may be considered unconscionable.

Another type of unconscionable contract is an adhesion contract, which is induced by duress. The innocent party enters the contract under the threat of some type of force.[26] The threat may include physical injury, financial injury, injury to reputation, or anything else that might cause significant harm to the innocent party. A perfect example is a promise to pay money in exchange for a promise not to publish information that would be damaging to a person's reputation. If a court finds that in reality a reasonable person would have no choice but to agree to the terms of the contract as a means of protecting oneself, the contract will be unconscionable because it is an adhesion contract. Sometimes the circumstances may also support criminal charges of extortion.

Unconscionability is extremely difficult to prove for several reasons. First, the courts are reluctant to judge a party's real motivation for entering a contract. Second, there is a presumption that every party should investigate the terms of a contract before agreeing to it. Finally, if the terms are for an illegal purpose, the party has the option of calling the appropriate law enforcement agencies rather than succumbing to the other party's demands. Nevertheless, occasions do occur in which a party believes there is no alternative but to enter into a contract that is unconscionable. In such instances, the court will declare the contract to be invalid.

Fraud in Contracts

Fraud is an action that can be brought in a variety of situations, one of which is contract. Specifically, two types of actions for fraud can be brought to invalidate a contract: fraud in fact and fraud in the inducement. They occur under different circumstances and, if proven, have different results.

Fraud in fact occurs when one party tricks another into signing a contract by leading the other party to believe the contract is something entirely different,[27] for example, asking for a party's signature on a receipt for merchandise when, in fact, the "receipt" not only acknowledges receipt of that merchandise but also includes a purchase contract for additional merchandise.

Fraud is difficult to prove because parties generally have a duty to examine a document before affixing their signature. However, if it can be shown that the terms were not obvious or were added later, or that some other circumstance existed that prevented the party from ascertaining that he or she was actually signing a contract, the court may find fraud in fact.

When fraud in fact is proven, the result is recision; that is, the contract is treated as if it never existed. The court will take necessary steps to restore the parties to the condition they were in prior to the contract. For example, if an innocent party has incurred obligations because of the contract, the party responsible for the fraud may be forced to pay or to do whatever is necessary to satisfy or eliminate these obligations.

The elements of fraud in the inducement are as follows:

1. A misrepresentation of a present or past fact that is false must exist.
2. The party making the misrepresentation must know that what he or she is presenting is false and, further, must intend for it to operate as an inducement to another to enter a contractual agreement.
3. The innocent party must be reasonable both in the belief that the representation is true and in the reliance on the term as an inducement to enter the contract.
4. The misrepresentation must be a material element of the contract.[28]
5. The innocent party must suffer measurable damages as a result of its reasonable reliance on the misrepresentation.

Fraud in the inducement generally occurs when one party intentionally misrepresents the amount or quality of the consideration the opposing party is to receive under the contract. For example, a party takes reasonable steps to determine the value of the consideration he or she will receive in exchange for the promise or performance and relies on the value of the consideration in making the decision to enter the contract. In reality, the consideration is worth considerably less, and fraud in the inducement has occurred.

APPLICATION 9.7

A real estate agent undertakes to sell a certain property to a young couple buying their first home. The agent encourages the couple to have the home appraised and even offers the names of qualified individuals. The couple has the home appraised, and the appraiser confirms the value of the home as originally stated by the real estate agent. In reality, the agent paid the appraiser to confirm a value that is actually much higher than what the home is worth. The couple purchases the home, only to discover that the insurance company will insure it for only half the purchase price. Assuming there have been no changes in the market or other influences on home values, this may be circumstances for an action for fraud in the inducement.

Point for Discussion

◆   What if the agent did not conspire with the appraiser but did have knowledge about a major defect in the sewer system that was not apparent to the appraiser or the purchasers?

When an action for fraud in the inducement succeeds, a court will allow a party to disaffirm the contract. This means that each party walks away from the contract. An attempt may be made to achieve fairness based on the true value of the consideration, but the parties will not be restored to their original condition.

Statute of Frauds

statute of frauds
Statutory law that specifies what contracts must be in writing before they will be enforced.

Although all states recognize oral and written contracts, it has long been established that certain types of contracts must be in writing before they are considered valid and enforceable. The concept of a **statute of frauds** originated in England. Historically, the courts established certain important matters of agreement that should be in writing to minimize doubt or difficulty in completing the agreement. Today, this theory has been followed in each state with the enactment of a similar statute that states what types of contracts must be in writing before a court will enforce them. Generally, these are substantial contracts whose terms should be clearly stated to minimize the opportunity for mistake or misinterpretation.[29] There are some variations from state to state, but most jurisdictions require the following types of contracts to be written before they become effective.

1. A promise by the executor or administrator of an estate to answer personally for the debts or obligations of the deceased.
2. A promise by one party to answer for the debts or obligations of another.
3. A promise given in exchange for a promise of marriage.
4. A promise to sell, transfer, or convey an interest in land (this may include ownership, possession, control, or any other interest).
5. A promise for the sale of goods by a merchant in which the price exceeds $500.
6. An agreement that, by its terms, cannot be completed within one year.

If a contract is not required to be written and is, in fact, oral, the existence of a contract will be judged objectively by what the conduct of the parties would indicate they meant the terms of the agreement to be. If, however, the contract falls within one of the situations covered by the state statute of frauds, it must be in writing before a court will even recognize that a contract exists.

In the following situations, determine whether the contract should be in writing to be enforceable.

1. Maya and Ella agree to split the money equally from a bank robbery in which Maya plans to demand (and receive) $10,000 and Ella agrees to drive the getaway car.
2. George promises to pay Sam $5,000 to marry George's daughter Maggie.
3. Jesse and Kenneth agree that Jesse will give Kenneth haircuts for one year in exchange for a one-time fee of $150.
4. Olivia is the 23-year-old daughter of Martin. Olivia is being threatened with a lawsuit to collect on a debt she owes a local department store. Martin phones the department store and offers to pay the amount of the debt plus an extra $100 if the store will refrain from suing Olivia. The store agrees.
5. Beau offers to sublet the house Jack is renting for the amount of the regular rent plus $25 per month. Jack agrees.

DEFENSES TO AN ALLEGATION OF BREACH OF CONTRACT

When an action for breach of contract is brought, several defenses are available that may prevent a judgment against the defendant. Many were discussed previously as defects or irregularities in the steps of creating a contract. The following discussion covers these and other defenses in the context of defenses.

Some of the more common defenses include the following:

1. Absence of one or more essential elements to create a contract.
2. Unconscionable contract.
3. Fraud.
4. Statute of frauds.
5. Accord and satisfaction.
6. Justifiable breach.
7. Impossibility/impracticability.
8. Frustration of purpose/terminated duty.

A party may allege one, several, or all of the defenses alternatively. Thus, while a jury may not find sufficient evidence to support one defense, it might be persuaded that another applies, and the plaintiff's case will fail.

One defense is known commonly as accord and satisfaction. Under this defense, the defendant claims to have performed by completing a new and different performance on which the parties agree in place of the original consideration. The "accord" amends the original agreement by substituting a new performance for the original, and the "satisfaction" is the fulfillment of the original contract by the substituted performance. For example, the defendant would claim to have satisfied the contract by painting the plaintiff's house instead of fixing the plaintiff's car, as promised in the original contract. If the defendant fails to complete the satisfaction, however, the plaintiff can sue on either of the defendant's promises.

A second type of defense is a justified breach of contract. When one party breaches a contract, the second party is excused from the completion of performance. The reasoning is that the second party did not receive the consideration that originally induced his or her own promise or performance. Therefore, if consideration fails, there is no basis for requiring the contractual agreement to continue.

In addition, some circumstances force involuntary breach of contract. When this occurs, the party who fails to perform as required by the contract will not be held liable. Most commonly, such situations are referred to as impossibility or impracticability of performance and include situations where the contract cannot be completed through no fault of the parties.[30]

APPLICATION 9.8

Chiyoko contracts with Timothy to paint her house. She promises to pay Timothy $400 per week for two weeks in exchange for Timothy's performance of painting the house completely within two weeks. After one week of painting, Chiyoko pays Timothy $400 on Friday. On Saturday, Chiyoko's house catches fire, and although a badly burned shell is left standing, the house is considered a total loss. Timothy discontinues his painting. Chiyoko sues Timothy for breach. The likely result is that Timothy would not be found guilty of breach, because his continued performance was rendered impossible or at the very least impracticable by the fire. Timothy would also probably be entitled to retain the $400 already paid as a fair exchange for the portion of the performance he actually did complete.

Point for Discussion
- What if the house hadn't been destroyed but the smoke damage was so severe it took Timothy an additional month to finish the job?

Similar to the impossibility or impracticability rule are the defenses of frustration of performance and terminated duty. Frustration of performance occurs when, through no action by the parties, the purpose of the contract is destroyed. Consequently, the duty to perform ends.[31] For example, a distributor contracts to sell liquor to a grocery store with delivery seven days per week. If the legislature passes a law prohibiting the sale of liquor on Sundays, the distributor is frustrated in performance of his or her obligations under the contract. When this occurs, the duty to perform is terminated, and there can be no action for breach of contract.

REMEDIES FOR BREACH OF CONTRACT

As the preceding examples illustrate, numerous defenses can be offered against the charge of breach of contract. However, it is up to the trier of fact to determine whether these defenses warrant a finding in favor of the defendant. When the finding is that a breach did occur and is not justified in any way, the plaintiff will be entitled to some type of remedy for the damage incurred as a result of the breach.

Breach of contract has three common remedies: compensatory damages, liquidated damages, and specific performance. Each is distinct and applies only in particular situations of breach.

The most common remedy is compensatory damages to a plaintiff who has suffered from a breach of contract. The purpose of compensatory damages is to award a sufficient amount of money to place the plaintiff in the same position he or she would be in if the contract had been fulfilled. In this way, the plaintiff is compensated for any loss or injury. Even if the injury or loss did not actually involve money, the purpose of the remedy is to enable the plaintiff to repair the damage.

Parties use a liquidated damage clause when they know that a court will have difficulty estimating actual damages in the event of breach. In a true liquidated damage clause, the parties will arrive at a fair compensation to be paid by a party in the event that party breaches the agreement. This clause will then be included in the terms of the contract (see Figure 9.1).

Liquidated damages are an alternative to compensatory damages. The court has the duty to determine whether a breach occurred and, if so, whether the liquidated damage clause of the contract was, in fact, for liquidated damages or merely a prestated penalty for breach. If the court finds that the clause is a penalty, the clause will not be enforced. The courts do not generally impose penalties set by the parties. Rather, the court will determine whether a penalty is appropriate in addition to the compensatory damages. The reasoning behind the refusal to enforce penalty clauses is quite simple. In some situations, a party does not have a defense to the breach but, for unforeseen reasons, must cease performance under the contract. Many times there are circumstances in which a party had no prior intent to breach but finds it necessary to do so. In such instances, it would not be fair to allow parties to penalize one another in excess of what would be reasonable compensation for the breach. The courts prefer to retain authority to determine appropriate circumstances for penalizing persons who breach a contract.

In the event that the seller fails to tender the property in satisfactory condition pursuant to the terms of this agreement, on the date heretofore agreed upon, the seller shall be in default of the terms of this agreement and shall pay to the buyer as liquidated damages the amount of $200 per day for each day the seller remains in default. Said liquidated damages shall serve as reasonable compensation for costs incurred as the direct and proximate result of seller's default. Provided, if seller should remain in default of this agreement for a period greater than 60 days, the buyer shall have the option of retaining liquidated damages for said period and further buyer may elect to be released from all obligations and liability associated with this agreement. In the latter event, the seller shall be similarly released from all further obligations to buyer with respect to this agreement.

FIGURE 9.1
Liquidated Damage Clause

In a very limited number of circumstances, a court will award specific performance in cases of breach. When specific performance is awarded, the party who has breached is ordered to continue performance under the contract to the best of his or her ability. Cases in equity are based on the principle that money is an insufficient remedy and fairness warrants the imposition of performance. The key to obtaining compelled performance is that the performance is so unique that the only way it can be satisfied is through the actual performance. In contract law, this equitable remedy is called specific performance. Before the court will award specific performance, the plaintiff must show that he or she has fully satisfied all obligations under the contract and that he or she has clean hands (meaning that the plaintiff has not acted in such a way as to cause the breach by the defendant, such as frustration or lack of cooperation). Another common requirement, known as "laches," is that the plaintiff must not have waited so long to raise the claim that the defendant is impaired in the ability to render performance.

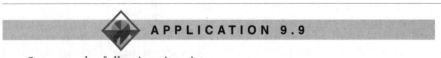

APPLICATION 9.9

Compare the following situations:

1. In October, Mrs. Sanchez contracts with a well-known artist to paint portraits of her three children as a Christmas present to Mr. Sanchez. The artist agrees to the contract but in November informs Mrs. Sanchez that he will not be completing the project because he is moving to another part of the country. Because an artist's talent is unique, money would be inadequate to compensate Mrs. Sanchez for the loss of the artist's expertise. In this situation, a court may very well award specific performance and order the artist to complete the portraits.

2. In October, Mrs. Sanchez contracts with an artist to paint portraits of her three children as a Christmas present to Mr. Sanchez. The artist agrees to the contract but in November informs Mrs. Sanchez that the portraits cannot be completed because Mrs. Sanchez has refused on numerous occasions to schedule sittings for the portraits. Although an artist's talent is unique, and money would be inadequate to compensate Mrs. Sanchez for the loss of the artist's expertise, in this situation, a court would probably not award specific performance and order the artist to complete the portraits, because Mrs. Sanchez would be seeking the specific performance with "unclean hands." The breach is directly related to Mrs. Sanchez's frustration of the artist's attempts to satisfy the contract.

Point for Discussion

◆ What is the problem with an order of specific performance of a unique talent such as that described in the application?

███████████ ## Ethical Considerations

An obligation underlying all contractual agreements is the duty to act ethically. This includes fair dealing and honesty. As seen in the preceding discussion, dishonesty regarding the terms of the contract, misrepresentations as to the consideration, and taking unfair advantage of the vulnerabilities of the other party can result in legal action against the wrongdoer. Consequently, anyone who is engaged in a contractual agreement has made an unspoken additional commitment to act in a manner that would be considered by an objective observer to be ethical. This is not to say that one contracting must put the interests of the co-contractor above one's own interests. Rather, the duty is to act in such a way that the co-contractor is not the victim of unfair advantage or dishonesty.

Questions

If you were selling your car and you knew that the tires (which are obviously worn) do not handle well in snow, do you have an ethical obligation to tell this to all prospective buyers? What if, instead, the defect were a loose electrical connection that had caught fire in the past but is not readily noticeable?

███████████ ## Ethical Circumstance

Nick is a paralegal working for a law firm. He is asked by the attorney to have a client on an existing case come in and sign a contract for representation. The file does not contain a contract from the initial meeting with the client and the attorney claims that this was somehow missed at the initial meeting. The contract, among other things, waives responsibility on the part of the lawyer for any loss of evidence left in her possession. Nick knows for a fact that the lawyer recently left her briefcase in a bar and lost several client files including that of this client. Nick also remembers the lawyer telling him that she was concerned because several Polaroid photos to be used as evidence in the case had been in the file and could not be reproduced. Should Nick ask the client to sign the contract without divulging this information?

CHAPTER SUMMARY

The law of contracts is complex and contains many intricacies not addressed here. It is also an area of law that continues to change and adapt to new situations. Therefore, it is important to remember that in addition to the basic principles set forth here, there are many, many variations of these themes that should be explored when confronted with a contractual dispute.

The best approach is always to prepare a contract with the fullest expectation that it will be litigated someday. By using this approach, many of the grounds for dispute can be prevented through clear and appropriate language and good faith compliance by the parties.

When preparing or interpreting a contract, one should be mindful that there must be two or more parties, legal capacity, assent, and consideration. Each of these elements is determined by objectively looking at the situation surrounding the creation of the contract. Further, the terms of the contract, such as time of performance, price, quantity, and identity of the offeror and offeree, must be definite. Many contracts must be in writing before a court will enforce them. Enforcement may also be denied on the basis of irregularities in the circumstances surrounding the contract such as mistake, fraud, illusory promises, frustration of purpose, or unconscionable terms. Persons with a third-party relationship to a contract,

such as beneficiaries, assignees, or delegatees, may also have certain rights or obligations with respect to the contract that must always be addressed.

Finally, the remedies for a broken or breached contract include money damages, recision, reformation, and, in limited cases, specific performance. The appropriateness of each of these remedies depends entirely upon the nature of the contract and the circumstances under which the contract was created. Therefore, when evaluating or creating a contract, be particularly aware of the situation that surrounds it.

CHAPTER TERMS

bilateral contract
contract
contractual agreement

contractual capacity
statute of frauds
third-party beneficiary

unilateral contract

REVIEW QUESTIONS

1. Describe capacity to contract.
2. What is the difference between an objective and subjective standard in determining the effectiveness of a contract?
3. Why are contracts for gifts unenforceable?
4. What is assignment?
5. What is delegation?
6. What is fraud in fact?
7. Why are adhesion contracts unenforceable?
8. Why are advertisements generally not considered contracts?
9. When can an offer be terminated?
10. What is the difference between a bilateral and unilateral contract?

RELEVANT LINKS

General contract law principles
Contract forms
Contract law discussion

www.freeadvice.com/law/518us.htm
www.contractsonline.net
http://resource.lawlinks.com/Content

INTERNET ASSIGNMENT 9.1

Using internet resources, locate a form contract to use for the following:
a. Purchase of an automobile.

b. Legal representation.
c. Agreement to provide personal service (e.g., home repair/remodel).

NOTES

1. William Statsky, *Legal Thesaurus/Dictionary* (St. Paul: West, 1982).
2. 17 Am.Jur.2d., Contracts, Section 10.
3. Id., Section 15.
4. Restatement (Second) of Contracts, Section 12.
5. Id.; Childres and Spritz, Status in the Law of Contracts, 47 *New York Law Review* 1 (April 1972).
6. *Kilroe v. Troast,* 117 N.H. 598, 376 A.2d 131 (1977).
7. 1 Williston on Contracts 3d ed., Section 13.
8. *Flemington National Bank & Trust Co. (N.A.) v. Domler Leasing Corp.* 65 A.D.2d 29, 410 N.Y.S.2d 75 (1978).
9. Restatement (Second) of Contracts, Section 24.
10. 17 Am.Jur.2d, Contracts, Section 31.
11. *European-American Banking Corp. v. Chock Full O'Nuts Corp.,* 109 Misc.2d 615, 442 N.Y.S.2d 715 (1981).
12. 7A C.J.S., Auctions and Auctioneers, Section 11.
13. *Schmidt v. Foster,* 380 P.2d 124 (Wyo. 1963).
14. *Mobil Oil Corp. v. Wroten,* 303 A.2d 698, aff'd 315 A.2d 728 (Del. 1973).
15. *Taylor v. Roberts,* 307 F.2d 776 (10th Cir. 1962).
16. *Honolulu Rapid Transit Co. v. Paschoal,* 51 Hawaii 19, 449 P.2d 123 (1968).
17. 17 C.J.S., Contracts, Section 43.
18. *Reserve Insurance Co. v. Duckett,* 249 Md. 108, 238 A.2d 536 (1968).
19. *Clausen & Sons Inc. v. Theo. Hamm Brewing Co.,* 395 F.2d 388 (8th Cir. 1968).
20. *Wavetek Indiana, Inc. v. K. H. Gatewood Steel Co., Inc.,* 458 N.E.2d 265 (Ind. App. 1984).
21. Id.
22. Restatement (Second) of Contracts, Section 302, et seq.
23. Id.
24. 17A C.J.S., Contracts, Section 586.
25. *Damora v. Christ-Janer,* 184 Conn. 109, 441 A.2d 61 (1981).
26. *Mitchell v. Aetna Casualty & Surety Co.,* 579 F.2d 342 (5th Cir. 1978).
27. *Christian v. Christian,* 42 N.Y.2d 63, 396 N.Y.S.2d 817, 365 N.E.2d 849 (1977).
28. See note 21. Sections 151, 152.
29. Id.
30. 17 Am.Jur.2d. Contracts, Section 400, et seq.
31. Id.

For additional resources, please visit our Web site at www.westlegalstudies.com

CHAPTER 10

Property Law

CHAPTER OBJECTIVES

After reading this chapter, you should be able to:

- Explain the concept of undivided interest.

- Distinguish tenancy in common, joint tenancy, and tenancy by the entirety.

- List the elements of adverse possession.

- Discuss the remedies to retrieve wrongfully taken or held personal property.

- Distinguish habitability and quiet enjoyment.

- Explain the concept of constructive eviction.

- Discuss the basic obligations of landlord and tenant.

The law of property in this country stems in large part from the common law principles of English property law. During the Middle Ages, the English court system created general rules for the possession, transfer, and disposition of property upon death of the owner. While many of these principles continue in the American legal system, in some ways, the states altered, modified, and, in some cases, even abolished certain rules over time to develop the statutory and common law of property in our country today. These legal changes have been the result of an effort to adapt to the changes that have occurred in society and in the types of land interests in this country that did not exist in feudal England. This chapter defines and examines the current law of property, including personal property, real property, and associated interests.

Before discussing the types of property and the rights related to the purchase, conveyance (transfer), ownership, possession, or alteration of property, we clarify the legal definition of the term *property,* which generally means the right to possess or control.[1] This meaning is different from the everyday language used to interpret property as an actual physical thing, such as a parcel of land. Consequently, in legal terms, when discussing an interest in property, the focus is on the type of right to possess, control, or own the item in question rather than on the item itself. This chapter is organized by type of area subject to property law, and within those areas, the rights associated with them are discussed.

REAL PROPERTY

real property
Land or anything permanently affixed to land and no longer movable.

Real property is land or that which is attached to the land in such a way that it is permanent, fixed, and immovable.[2] The law of real property governs all that is part of the land naturally or as a result of being artificially incorporated into the land in a permanent way. Real property includes houses, buildings, and other structures that are affixed to the property by some permanent means. An example of something that would not ordinarily be considered real property is a mobile home that has not been permanently affixed to the ground. This type of structure is considered movable and falls into the category of personal property (discussed at the end of the chapter).

The following sections discuss the types of interest or rights to real property. These interests and rights can be affected by ownership, inheritance, marital status, and terms of possession. The right to control or own property can be obtained in a number of ways, and as they are explored, it should become clear that property law is one of the most well-developed areas of law in our country.

Freehold Estates

freehold estate
An interest in real property that involves certain rights of ownership.

Traditionally, **freehold estate** has been the term used to describe ownership and interests in land.[3] This is to be distinguished from non-freehold estates, such as lease or rental agreements (discussed later in the chapter). Freehold estates involve the rights of a property owner and the conditions or limitations that might be imposed on that ownership. Several types of freehold estates exist, including single ownership, ownership by two or more persons, and certain rights of uninterfered possession without actual ownership.

Fee simple.   The most common type of ownership in America is **fee simple.**[4] Under English common law, when a man obtained property in fee simple, it meant that the man owned the property for the duration of his lifetime.[5] In other words, the man possessed a life estate (discussed next). At the end of the owner's life, the property automatically reverted back to the original owner.

fee simple
In American law, this involves absolute ownership of real property.

To own property outright on a permanent basis, the property had to be owned in fee simple absolute, which required special language in the document used to transfer the property (deed) that prevented it from reverting to the original owner. In the United States today, fee simple has an interpretation of fee simple absolute. All transfers of ownership of property are by fee simple unless otherwise stated. Such transfers are considered to be a sale of total and absolute rights over the property. In most jurisdictions, a limited term of possession/ownership must be granted by express language in the transferring document.

Life estates.   A **life estate** gives the holder the right to totally control the property for the holder's lifetime without interference. Such an estate includes the right to do all things an owner in fee simple could do, with one exception: The property cannot be disposed of (sold or given away) or treated in such a way as to ruin it for its usual purpose[6] (known as wasting). An example of wasting property would be one who had a life estate in farmland and put toxic chemicals on the land that prevented the land from being used in the future as farmland. If a life estate holder is found to be wasting the property, the life estate can be legally terminated. When the life estate ends by legal termination of the estate or death of the holder, ownership goes to the party who originally owned the property or to the person designated by the original owner to receive the property.

life estate
The right to possess and use real property for the duration of one's life with limited ownership rights.

A life estate is considered to be a type of freehold estate in and of itself, even though it does not contain the basic element of transferability. A person with a life estate cannot transfer *ownership* to someone else, but can transfer part or all of his or her *interest* in the property, if allowed by the grantor. This means that a life tenant could lease the property during the course of his or her lifetime, but such a lease would expire when the life tenant died. Thus, with the exception of limitations on transferability and the condition of not wasting the property, the life estate holder has all the rights otherwise associated with ownership. One common situation of creation of a life estate occurs when a spouse leaves a life estate in solely owned real property to the surviving party who may not otherwise have rights of inheritance over the property. When the surviving spouse dies, the estate passes completely and automatically to an heir named in the will of the spouse who originally owned the property.

APPLICATION 10.1

Dale and Larry have been life partners for many years. They have lived in the same home together for much of that time. Dale has two children by a former marriage. Dale's only significant asset consists of his sole ownership of the house he shares with Larry. When Dale finds he is terminally ill, he creates a life estate in the property and house for Larry. Upon Larry's death, the property interest would pass to Dale's children.

Point for Discussion
◆   What rights do Dale's children have during Larry's life estate?

Other estates.   Various other types of conveyances in fee (transfers of property interest) exist. Conveyances subject to reversion require that under certain conditions, the property revert back to its original owner. The effect of such estates is similar to the old definition of fee simple but occurred under different circumstances. An example is one who is buying land by paying rent along with a payment toward ownership each month. The agreement might provide that if the lessor/buyer died before the property was paid for, all interests in the property would revert to the original owner.

Defeasible fees are those that end ownership upon the happening of a certain event, at which time the property would pass to another named person. While the various fee estates had great influence historically in property rights, today they rarely become an issue. Land is owned predominantly in fee simple or fee simple subject to a life estate.

The remainder interest is one type of interest that has survived the changes in property law. This interest is created automatically upon the end of another. Giving one's surviving spouse a life estate is one type of remainder interest. Unless the remainder interest is indicated on the document used to transfer title (e.g., the deed), a conveyance of property ownership is presumed to be in fee simple absolute, with total control and ownership vested in the receiving party.

Today, the law is much more equal to spouses in the distribution of property than in old English law. Under original property law, women could not own property. Even property inheritances were passed on to the woman's spouse and male children. Currently, there is no distinction between men and women on the issue of property ownership and inheritance. In the event that a spouse does not provide adequately for the surviving spouse by will, a statutory provision for what is commonly known as a **forced** (or elected) **share**[7] permits a surviving spouse to claim or elect a certain percentage of the property (real and personal) of the deceased. This claim is superior to all other heirs and prevails even if it decreases the amount received by persons designated in a will. One can generally disinherit children or anyone else by will except for a spouse. The law makes no distinction whether the surviving spouse is husband

forced share
The legal right of a surviving spouse to receive a certain percentage of the estate of a deceased spouse, superior to the terms of a will or other rights of inheritance of heirs.

or wife. The interest received is in fee simple (rather than a life estate), and surviving children are not necessary for the interest to be received. (The rights of surviving spouses are discussed in greater detail in Chapter 13.)

Assignment 10.1

Identify the interests or actions of the various parties in the following situation under the American legal system.

Josiah freely owns property upon which he has operated a wild game reserve for 40 years. The admission fees for people driving through the reserve to see the animals have provided income to his family during this time. Josiah dies and leaves the right to control the property for his lifetime to the caretaker. Upon the caretaker's death, the total ownership of the property will pass to the descendants of Josiah. The caretaker starts cutting and selling all the trees on the property and effectively wipes out the population of the wild animals through the loss of habitat.

Types of Ownership between Multiple Parties

Today it is common for more than one party to hold the title to (own) real property. The relationships of these persons and reasons for multiple ownership vary. As a result, certain types of ownership have evolved that govern the rights of these various multiple ownership arrangements. Such arrangements may be for business or personal reasons. The different types of multiple ownership of property clarify such issues as what portion of the property is possessed by each person, who has the right to sell or dispose of the property, and what should happen in the event one of the owners dies. The most commonly employed types of multiple ownership are tenancy in common, joint tenancy, and tenancy by the entirety.

Tenancy in common.   Unless otherwise stated in the purchase agreement, the type of tenancy of multiple owners is presumed to be **tenancy in common.** With this type of ownership, each owner has an undivided interest in the property,[8] meaning that each owner has an equal share in every part of the property. The undivided interest guarantees that no one owner has a better portion of the property. Each owner has a balanced interest in both the positive and negative aspects of the property as a whole. The percentage of undivided interest is equal to the percentage of ownership. For example, if one tenant owns 50 percent of the property and two remaining partners each own 25 percent of the property, the first partner is entitled to a one-half undivided interest in all the property and the other partners are each entitled to an undivided 25 percent share in the total property.

In addition to their undivided interest, tenants in common may do all things with their interest as if they owned the property entirely. The only limitation is that they cannot act in such a way as to interfere with the rights of the other

tenancy in common

A form of multiple ownership of property whereby each tenant (owner) shares with the other(s) an undivided interest in the property.

APPLICATION 10.2

Three friends decide to purchase a 25-acre tract of land together as tenants in common and use it for investment. After several years, two of the friends want to sell their portion of the property to an interested developer. The developer wants to purchase only the two-thirds of the acreage that sits atop a hill; however, each of the friends owns an equal one-third interest in the upper two-thirds of the property as well as the lower one-third portion. The lower one-third is a steep slope and is heavily wooded with vines and underbrush and of little value in and of itself. This shared interest in the best and worst attributes of the property prevents any one of the partners from being left with less than a fair share of the property.

Point for Discussion

◆   If the parties can agree on a two-thirds percentage of the land to sell to the developer, what will the relationship of the developer be with the third investor?

tenants in common. A tenant in common cannot make use of the property in a way that is inconsistent with the other tenants, nor can the tenant waste the property. A tenant who does either of these things with any part of the property is doing it with a portion of the property controlled by the other tenants.

When tenants in common (or other types of multiple ownership tenants) cannot agree on the rights and use of the property, a legal action for partition may be brought by one or more of the tenants. In a partition action, the court divides the land into individual portions and creates an individually owned portion of land for each of the parties. The effect of this is to equitably extinguish the tenancy in common and create two or more fee simple tenancies. Another

APPLICATION 10.3

In the preceding application, only two of the three tenants in common want to sell the property. If no agreement can be reached as to what portion of the property will be sold, an action for partition can be filed and a court will make a determination of how to equitably (fairly) split the property into three equal shares.

Point for Discussion

◆   If the matter resulted in partition, should the court give the upper portion of the property to the two selling owners since that is what the buyer wants to purchase and failing to do so could cause the sale to go through?

possible result in such a situation would be for a tenant to buy the interest of another tenant and thus convert the tenancy in common to a single tenancy in fee simple.

When one tenant in common voluntarily sells or conveys his or her interest in the property, the new owner becomes a tenant in common with the other tenants in common. Similarly, when one tenant in common dies, the heirs of the estate become tenants in common with the other tenants in common. Tenants in common have no rights of survivorship. The exception to this rule is when the property is owned by a partnership, in which case, when a tenant in common dies, the ownership of that tenant goes to the surviving partners rather than the tenant's heirs.

In a tenancy in common, the individual's ownership interest can be conveyed during that person's lifetime, but no more than the tenancy in common interest can be transferred. In other words, one cannot convey a type of tenancy not possessed such as joint tenancy. The rights are those of tenancy in common, so that is all that can be transferred. This will become clearer as the other types of tenancy are explored.

Joint tenancy. Joint tenancy must be specified in the instrument transferring the property (the deed). It is generally accepted that **joint tenancy** includes the **right of survivorship,**[9] that is, when one joint tenant dies, the remaining joint tenants automatically take ownership of the property. The heirs of the deceased owner have no claim or inheritance.

The right of survivorship, simply stated, means that when a party to joint tenancy dies, the interest automatically vests by operation of law in the other tenant(s). In this way, the joint tenancy among *surviving* tenants is preserved. However, technically, a new joint tenancy is created when each surviving tenant simultaneously receives an undivided right of possession from the deceased party. The previous rights of the parties remain the same, and there is usually no requirement to formally create a new joint tenancy through a new deed.

The right of survivorship restricts a party's interest from flowing naturally to the descendants. Because of this, it is necessary for a party involved in a joint tenancy to formally agree from the outset that there is the intent to create such an interest. In this way, the heirs are protected from losing an interest in property when it was not the desire of the deceased to do so.

For joint tenancy to exist, the joint tenants must establish four common points of ownership, called unities:

1. Each tenant must have received his or her interest in the property at the same moment (unity of time).
2. The interest for each must come from the same source, namely, the previous owner (unity of title).
3. Each tenant must have identical rights regarding the property, such as an equal share (unity of interest).
4. Each party must have an undivided interest in the land itself (unity of possession).

joint tenancy
A form of multiple property ownership whereby the property owners have fee simple and share four unities and each owner shares in the right of survivorship.

right of survivorship
A characteristic associated with multiple property ownership in which the ownership interest transfers automatically to surviving co-owners upon death of an owner rather than passing by will or intestate succession.

Thus, the only way to have a joint tenancy is when the multiple owners agree to it with the intent of right of survivorship among themselves and they purchase the entire property at the same time, from the same owner, in equal shares, and with an undivided right of possession. If all of the preceding occur and a state statute does not indicate otherwise, the parties also receive the right of survivorship. In some states, the statute requires that the intent for a right of survivorship be specified in the conveying instrument (usually the deed). If no such statute exists, the right is usually presumed from the words *joint tenancy* in the deed.

It should be recognized that a joint tenancy exists only so long as the four unities exist. When one party conveys his or her interest in the property to an outsider, only the remaining original joint tenants remain as joint tenants. The new owner is a tenant in common. The important effect of this is that the new tenant does not have a right of survivorship should one of the original joint tenants die.[10] Consequently, if any party conveys any right to title or interest or possession in the property, the joint tenancy as to that party is destroyed. Any conveyance to another would violate the unity of time and title, because the new recipient would obtain an interest at a different time and from a different source than the other owners. Joint tenancy is also severed when a party conveys his or her interest to other members of the original joint tenancy.

◆ APPLICATION 10.4

Burt, Jill, Jeff, and Nina are joint tenants. Burt comes into financial difficulty and decides to sell his interest in the property. He conveys his interest to Petra. The result is as follows:

Previously: Burt, Jill, Jeff, and Nina owned the property as joint tenants.

Now: Jill, Jeff, and Nina are joint tenants with one another. Petra is a tenant in common with Jill, Jeff, and Nina.

Effect: Under the old situation, if any joint tenant dies, the other three split the interest of the deceased. Under the new situation, if Petra dies, his interest passes to his heirs. If Jill, Jeff, or Nina dies, the interest of the deceased is split between the remaining joint tenants but not with Petra.

Point for Discussion
◆   How would the tenancy be affected if all of the tenants were originally tenants in common?

The basic rights of joint tenants are similar to those of tenancy in common. The joint tenant can use and possess the property in any way that does not waste the property or interfere with the rights of the other joint tenants. However, a joint tenant cannot successfully devise (give) his or her interest to heirs in a will. Such conveyance would take place after the owner's death, which would violate the right of survivorship. Therefore, a bequest in a will does not sever the joint tenancy and will not be honored if a right of survivorship exists in the joint tenancy. When the right of survivorship does exist, it occurs by operation of law; that is, it is automatic upon the death of a joint tenant as a matter of law, and the wishes of the tenant expressed in a subsequently probated will are not considered. Consequently, if a joint tenant wants to sever the joint tenancy, such severing must be done prior to death by legal conveyance of one or more of the unity interests to another.

 CASE

BRADFORD V. DUMOND

675 A.2d. 957 (1996).

WATHEN, CHIEF JUSTICE.

Defendant Danny G. Dumond appeals from a judgment of the Superior Court (Cumberland County, Brodrick, J.) in an action to partition real estate. The court granted plaintiff Laura H. Bradford one-half of the two parcels of real estate owned in common by the parties. The court adjusted the final division to reflect mortgage payments made by defendant and acts of conversion committed by defendant. On appeal defendant argues that (1) the court erred in ruling that the parties owned equal shares of both parcels of real estate, (2) the court erred in finding defendant liable for conversion of plaintiff's personal property, (3) the court erred in assessing damages for conversion, and (4) the court abused its discretion in limiting defense counsel's cross-examination of plaintiff on the issue of damages. Because the court erred with respect to one parcel of real estate, we vacate in part.

The facts presented at trial may be summarized as follows: The parties started dating in 1983. In August 1984, plaintiff moved in with defendant in a rented camp in Standish. Plaintiff and defendant talked about getting married and started planning their future, including purchasing property together. Plaintiff began to work without pay at a steel yard owned and operated by defendant. Plaintiff and defendant

commingled their funds extensively and paid their personal and household expenses primarily with funds from the business.

In August of 1986, the couple purchased a house and a parcel of land abutting the steel yard. ("The Scarborough Property"). The deed conveyed the property to both defendant and plaintiff as joint tenants. The down payment of $35,000 was provided by defendant. The taxes, mortgage payments and insurance payments for the property were paid with funds from his business. Plaintiff performed all of the maintenance and upkeep on the property, including landscaping, while working full-time at the steel yard without pay.

In the spring of 1987, plaintiff began to receive $150 per week for her services at the steel yard. Plaintiff testified that this amount did not accurately represent the value of her services and in fact the funds were deposited in a joint account and used to pay joint expenses.

In January 1983, the couple purchased a camp and a lot of land in Standish. The deed conveyed the property to the parties as tenants in common. Plaintiff provided $8,000 for the down payment. Defendant provided between $30,000 and $40,000 for the remainder of the down payment and closing costs.

Subsequent payments for taxes, mortgage, and insurance were paid from the steel yard account. Plaintiff performed all of the maintenance and upkeep on this property as well while continuing to work at the steel yard.

The trial testimony on this figure was conflicting, and the trial court did not make a specific finding on this amount.

Problems developed in the relationship and plaintiff moved out permanently in January 1990. She packed a few belongings and drove her Ford Bronco (which she claimed was a gift from defendant, although it was registered in the name of his business) to Maryland to stay with relatives. A week later, plaintiff reported that the Bronco had been stolen; it was later located in defendant's possession. When plaintiff moved back to Maine and inquired about retrieving the rest of her personal property and items the couple jointly owned, defendant threatened to harm her physically if she returned to either property.

After 1990, defendant retained exclusive possession of the two properties and collected rent from a tenant on the Standish property. He has paid all taxes, insurance, and mortgage payments since that time. In addition, he has paid off the outstanding mortgages on both properties.

Plaintiff commenced this action seeking division of the real estate and damages for conversion of her personal property. After a nonjury trial, the Superior Court ruled in favor of plaintiff on all claims. The court found plaintiff's version of the events more credible than defendant's and concluded that the parties had agreed and intended to be joint owners of both parcels.

The court then considered each party's contribution in order to fairly and equitably partition the real estate. The court declined to consider defendant's initial contributions towards the purchase of either property, as the court considered both properties to be held in JOINT TENANCY. Although it found that defendant paid all mortgage, tax, and insurance payments, the court offset defendant's contribution with plaintiff's undercompensated services for the business, her services in maintaining both properties, and the fact that defendant enjoyed sole possession of the properties for the period after the breakup and collected rental income which was not shared with plaintiff. Finding the properties equal in value, the court granted the Standish property to defendant and the Scarborough property to plaintiff. The court granted defendant a lien on the Scarborough property for the amount of $58,066, representing defendant's prepayment of plaintiff's half of the outstanding mortgages. This lien was reduced by $17,295, representing the value of the personal property that the court found had been wrongfully converted by defendant. From this judgment, defendant appeals.

I. Initial Contributions Towards Purchase of Jointly Owned Properties.

The issue of a proper accounting for the down payment made by defendant in purchasing each parcel of real estate is confused by the parties' failure to differentiate between a JOINT TENANCY and a tenancy in common.

The pleadings, the pretrial memoranda, and the exhibits accurately reflect that the Scarborough property was held in a JOINT TENANCY and the Standish property was held in a tenancy in common. Throughout the trial, however, the parties used the loose phrase "joint ownership." As a result, in its judgment the court treated both parcels as though they were held in JOINT TENANCY and, despite the parties' differing views on the treatment of defendant's initial contribution, the court was never disabused of its mistaken belief. Although the trial judge is not to be faulted, the error is obvious and the judgment is tainted by the parties' failure to distinguish between the two forms of joint ownership.

In general, joint tenants own equal undivided shares even though their initial contributions may have been unequal. That result is a consequence of the right of ownership that attaches to a JOINT TENANCY. Tenants in common, on the other hand, are presumed to own equal shares, but this presumption may be overcome by evidence, such as evidence of unequal initial contributions, establishing an intention to have unequal shares. Thus it is evident that the court erred in failing to consider defendant's initial contribution to the Standish property, held as a tenancy in common. Because this results in the necessity for vacating only a part of the judgment, we proceed to consider the remaining issues.

In addition, defendant argues the court erroneously refused to consider the initial payments he made in purchasing the Scarborough property. Even though this property was held in

JOINT TENANCY, defendant argues that *Boulette v. Boulette,* 627 A.2d 1017(Me.1993), cited by the trial court, is inapplicable because that case dealt with the creation of a JOINT TENANCY after the acquisition of the property. Defendant argues that where, as here, the purchase money for the property was extended simultaneously with the creation of the JOINT TENANCY, the joint tenant who extended the purchase money should be credited that amount on partition.

Defendant's argument is contrary to the very purpose of JOINT TENANCY. In Boulette, we stated:

> [A]s joint tenants, the parties initially held an undivided one-half interest in the property. The division of property held in JOINT TENANCY should take into account all equities growing out of that relationship. Contributions of the parties to the property prior to the JOINT TENANCY, however, are not equities growing out of the JOINT TENANCY relationship. To allow the consideration of contributions preceding the JOINT TENANCY would defeat joint ownership.

Boulette v. Boulette, 627 A.2d 1017, 1018 (Me.1993). *See also Lalime v. Lalime,* 629 A.2d 59 (Me.1993) (where husband deeded his own property to himself and his wife in JOINT TENANCY, the rules of ownership unique to JOINT TENANCY would apply regardless of husband's assertion that the transfer was solely for the purpose of securing a loan and was not intended as a 'true' JOINT TENANCY).

Although it is true that in *Boulette* we did not specifically deal with a simultaneous contribution and creation of a JOINT TENANCY, this issue has been settled in Maine for over half a century. In *Greenberg v. Greenberg,* 141 Me. 320, 323–24, 43 A.2d 841, 842 (Me.1945),we held that the joint tenants owned an equal, undivided share of the property, even when one joint tenant supplied 100% of the purchase price and simultaneously had the land deeded to himself and another as joint tenants.

II. Co-tenant's Contributions Towards the Properties. Defendant next argues that the court erred in finding that, after purchase, both parties had contributed equally to the properties. Specifically, defendant argues that plaintiff's performance of housekeeping and maintenance duties should not be considered as a contribution. Defendant also argues that the court erred in finding that plaintiff was undercompensated for the services she provided at the steel yard.

The court's findings as to the value of each parties' contributions are findings of fact. "Findings of fact shall not be set aside unless clearly erroneous, and due regard shall be given to the opportunity of the trial court to judge the credibility of the witnesses." M.R.Civ.P. 52(a)(1995). We will not disturb the court's determination of the monetary value of plaintiff's services, as it is supported by competent evidence in the record. The record also supports the finding that plaintiff's maintenance of the properties was in furtherance of the parties' agreement concerning both properties.

Judgment vacated in part. Remanded for further proceedings consistent with the opinion herein.

All concurring.

Case Review Question

What must occur differently in the creation of a tenancy in common as opposed to a joint tenancy?

Tenancy by the entirety. The last and least common type of tenancy is **tenancy by the entirety,** held by husband and wife. Many states no longer recognize this tenancy as different from joint tenancy, and those that do, often require it to be specified in the deed. This type of tenancy includes the presence of the four unities. In addition, the unity of person (that the tenants be husband and wife) is necessary. Tenancy by the entirety also has the right of survivorship: when one spouse dies, the other receives the property as the sole owner in fee simple.

tenancy by the entirety

A form of multiple ownership of property between spouses that includes the characteristics of joint tenancy, including the right of survivorship.

Tenancy by the entirety cannot be conveyed, because of the unity of person requirement. Any conveyance by one spouse would result in a tenancy in common between the remaining spouse and new purchaser. The interest of a tenant by the entirety also cannot be conveyed by a will to another person. Nor is the interest of one of the tenants subject to claims of nonjoint creditors. By operation of law, when one spouse dies and there is a tenancy by the entirety, the surviving spouse automatically receives the entire share of the property. Thus, because the property has already been transferred, there is nothing to pass under the terms of the will.

Assignment 10.2

In the following situation, indicate (a) what type of tenancy exists, (b) whether the tenancy changes, (c) when a change occurs, if one does, and (d) what is the resulting tenancy.

1. Suelin, Karl, and Dinah form an equal partnership, and together they buy a parcel of property from Charles. They are going to use the property as an agricultural investment and hire someone to farm it. They agree that if one of them should die, the others should receive the deceased partner's interest so that the partnership can continue. Karl, however, puts in his will that upon his death, his dear daughter Camille will inherit his share.

2. José and his brother Juan purchase a parcel of land. They grow Christmas trees on it until José becomes too ill to continue his share of the work. José then sells his interest in the land to Ricardo.

3. Tori and Marty are married. They want to share everything completely and equally. Consequently, they buy a lot from Michael upon which to build their dream house. During the construction, Tori and Marty divorce each other. They agree, however, to remain owners of the property until the market improves and they can sell the house.

4. On January 1, four brothers purchase a piece of property as a group from their sister. Each brother agrees that the property will be used as a place to build an ice cream stand and that each will work an equal amount and receive an equal share of profits. Subsequently, the youngest brother joins the Army and sells his interest to a neighbor.

Air and Subsurface Rights

Since the early days of property principles in common law, it has been held that the ownership of property extends below the property to the center of the earth and above the property to the top of the sky.[11] With respect to moving waters, when a nonnavigable stream flows on property, the owner possesses the bed of the stream but not the water flowing on it, because that water is not a permanent part of the land. Navigable streams are part of the public domain, and ownership of property adjacent to them generally extends to the shore.[12]

As population and technology have grown, these concepts have been altered slightly, but remarkably, the basic principle still holds true. While an owner possesses all of the property to the very heights, the public necessity of flight cannot be abridged, and it overrides the right to control the entire sky above one's property. Similarly, while an owner is entitled to control a streambed on the property, the course of the bed cannot be changed so as to substantially alter the flow of water across another's property, since such change could flood the adjacent land or deprive the owners downstream of the use of the water.

The owner has the right, consistent with these rights above and below the land, to sell or lease these portions of property (except that which is controlled for public use). For example, the owner of a condominium on the twelfth floor of a high rise actually owns the air space occupied by that condominium. However, the owner is not entitled to alter the construction of the air space because—as with moving land or water—such change would invade another's right over his or her own property. Similarly, one who owns the land can sell the rights to property below the land's surface, for example, sell mineral rights to another and allow the person to set up a drill to obtain oil or other deposits from beneath the land.

Incorporeal Interests

In the law of property, the term *incorporeal interests* describes rights or privileges associated with ownership of real property. One such right that is highly protected is the right of quiet enjoyment. It is presumed that the right to possess real property automatically includes the right to such possession and use free from interference by others. When someone invades another's property, he or she is, in effect, invading the right of quiet enjoyment. A corresponding area of incorporeal interests deals with the law of easements—legal rights of nonowners to affect the use of the owner's real property. Essentially, this area of law permits the holder of the easement a limited right of interference with the property otherwise protected by the right of quiet enjoyment. The law of easements is fairly complex and is only briefly introduced here.

Easements. An easement is a right of one other than the owner to affect the property owned. In simpler terms, it is a limited legal right to invade the right of possession and quiet enjoyment of a property owner.[13] The property that is affected is sometimes referred to as the servient tenement (it serves someone other than its owner). The party with the right to affect use of someone else's property is known as the dominant tenement (it dominates the servient owner). An easement is not a right to possess part or all of the servient tenement. Rather, it is the limited right to use or control the use of the servient tenement. This is often only a portion of the property. If an easement is *in gross,* the dominant tenement is the right of a specific person or group to use the servient tenement and this right cannot usually be transferred (although some commercial or business easements in gross are transferrable). If an easement is *appurtenant,* the dominant tenement is a specific parcel of land whose owner has the right to use the servient tenement, and this right passes to each new owner of the dominant tenement.

An easement is an interest associated with real property and is therefore subject to the statute of frauds, which, as noted in Chapter 9, requires that certain legal transactions be in writing before a court will enforce them. Among them is the transfer of any interest in real property. If real property or an easement affecting it is conveyed, conveyance must be done in writing to be effective. Therefore, the voluntary creation or continuation of an easement must be in writing before a court will enforce it.

An easement can be created in several ways. Two common methods are easement by necessity and easement by conveyance. An easement of necessity (implication by circumstances) can be created when no other reasonable alternative exists to satisfy the rights of others. Because all property is adjacent to other property, it is somewhat common for the use of one's property to interfere with another's. An easement created by necessity may be without the consent of the owner but, unless agreed to by the owner, must be recognized by a court before it can be enforced. Easement by conveyance occurs when a party voluntarily grants an easement affecting his or her property. Often this is an easement in gross and done in exchange for compensation of some type, such as the right to drill for oil on another's land. Finally, an easement can be created by prescription when a landowner acquiesces to someone else's use of his or her land without permission for a certain period of time. A prescriptive easement is similar to adverse possession, which is discussed later in the chapter.

Easements are classified in two ways. The first is known as an affirmative easement, which occurs when the party holding the dominant tenement has the right to enter onto the servient tenement for a particular purpose.[14] This could be having the right to cross the land of another party to reach your own property when no other reasonable means of reaching it exists.

APPLICATION 10.5

A farmer is converting farmland into land to be developed for a subdivision. The first lot to be developed is at the rear of the property. At this point in development, the only access to the property is to cross a lot at the front of the property until roads have been installed, which is not planned for three years. Consequently, a court would be likely to grant the owner of the lot to be developed an easement of necessity across the front lot, giving the right to cross a very specific portion of the front lot for ingress and egress until the road is installed.

Point for Discussion

◆   Why do you think that the owner's right of quiet enjoyment is not considered superior to a nonowner's right of access across private land?

The other type of easement is known as a negative easement—the right to prevent certain uses of property by the owner of the servient tenement because these uses would adversely affect the rights of the dominant tenement.[15]

APPLICATION 10.6

A homeowner wants to build a greenhouse at the rear of his yard. Because of trees and so forth, the best place for the greenhouse is the southwest corner of the yard. However, before digging the footings to place the concrete floor for the greenhouse, the homeowner contacts the utility company to locate any underground lines. The homeowner is informed that the lines run directly through the location of the proposed greenhouse and that the utility company owns an easement that prohibits the homeowner from erecting any structure that might prevent access to the lines for maintenance.

Point for Discussion

♦   Why doesn't the utility company have to buy the land it occupies with lines?

Assignment 10.3

With respect to the following situations identify (a) the servient and dominant tenement and (b) whether the easement is affirmative or negative.

1. Landowner X has property that is bordered on the west by a major waterway and is bordered on the north, east, and south by the property of Landowner M. Landowner X uses a roadway across M's property to reach his own.
2. Jules has the right to come onto Anne's property and mine for gold.
3. Ichiro has the right to electricity in his house even though the lines would have to cross his neighbor's farmland.

CASE

SUPREME COURT OF MISSISSIPPI.

PRENTIES B. DIECK

V.

PRESTON D. LANDRY, SR. AND DIANNE M. SCHEIB.

796 So. 2d 1004

Aug. 9, 2001.
Rehearing Denied
Oct. 18, 2001.

Prenties B. Dieck appeals the finding of the Pearl River County Chancery Court that a prescriptive

CASE

easement existed across his property for ingress and egress purposes benefitting Preston D. Landry, Sr., and Dianne M. Scheib. Upon a thorough review of the trial transcript and accompanying exhibits, we narrow Dieck's assignments of error and address the dispositive issue regarding whether Landry and Scheib effectively proved that a prescriptive easement existed across Dieck's property.

Prenties Dieck owns approximately two acres of property in Pearl River County, Mississippi. A twenty-two foot wide, three hundred forty foot long strip of this property, known at times as Toro Lane, serves as the basis for the underlying conflict in this appeal. All of the parties involved own neighboring property located between Meadow Lane on the west and Amigo Lane on the south. Additional neighboring landowners, not made party to this litigation, own property within the area that effectively landlocks Landry and Scheib from access to either Meadow Lane or Amigo Lane. The disputed strip of property (Passageway) runs along the southern border of Dieck's property from Meadow Lane east to Scheib's property line. This small, one large, gravel passageway serves as the northern border to Landry's property. Both Dieck and Landry share a common eastern border with Scheib.

Landry acquired his property in December of 1968. When Landry purchased this piece of property, there was access over and across the land in question via the existing passageway, although it was not as well defined as it is today. In fact, testimony given at trial by Huey Smith confirmed that the passageway was first cut and used by landlocked property owners as early as 1962. Robert A. Lee further testified that he lived on property adjacent to the passageway and used it to access his land from 1966 through 1967. From 1968 through February 1999, Landry had unrestricted access over the property in question. In March of 1969, George Livermore, Sr. and George Livermore, Jr. bought the property which contains the passageway. Landry never asked for nor received permission to continue use of the passageway, assuming that he had access to his property from Meadow Lane through his earlier

purchase. In July, of 1986, Dieck purchased the portion of the Livermore property containing the passageway.

Shortly thereafter, in June of 1987, Scheib purchased the property slightly further down the passageway from the Landry property. Scheib acquired the property and house from Ralph Lowery, who obtained the land from the Adams family. Michael Adams testified that he and his family lived on the property and used the passageway from October of 1980 until Lowery bought the land in July of 1986.

In 1987, Dieck approached Scheib and her now deceased husband claiming that the passageway belonged to him. He told them that they would have to find other access to their property. The Scheibs responded that they would look into the matter. Dieck also confronted Landry about his use of the passageway. Over the next several years, Landry and Scheib continued to use the passageway unabated. In 1991, Scheib requested the county place a fresh load of gravel on the passageway and grade it, and the county complied. This action enraged Dieck who renewed his conversations with Landry and Scheib in an effort to have them find alternate access to their land. That same year, Dieck sent a letter to each party telling them that he planned to re-fence his property, including the disputed passageway. Despite this admonition, Dieck did nothing to restrict Landry or Scheib's access to their property.

Dieck hired an attorney to explore alternative routes to the landlocked property and conduct meetings with Landry and Scheib, but these efforts failed for lack of enthusiasm among those involved. Landry and Scheib maintained that they already had access over Dieck's property and no other route was necessary. Finally, in February of 1999, Dieck built a fence across the passageway physically blocking access to Landry and Scheib's property.

Standard of Review
This Court will not disturb the factual findings of a chancellor unless such findings are manifestly

wrong or clearly erroneous. *Denson v. George,* 642 So.2d 909, 913 (Miss.1994). When substantial evidence exists in the record to support the chancellor's findings of fact, those findings must be affirmed here. *Id.* However, questions of law will be reviewed do novo. *Holliman v. Charles L. Cherry & Assocs., Inc.,* 569 So.2d 1139, 1145 (Miss 1990).

Legal analysis

Landry and Scheib argued successfully at trial that they obtained a prescriptive easement over the passageway. Dieck submitted that Landry and Scheib used the passageway with his permission and the permission of his predecessor in title, thus negating any claim to a prescriptive easement because of our well-settled law that permission cannot ripen into easement by prescription. *Sharp v. White,* 749 So.2d 41, 42 (Miss.1999)(citing *Dethlefs v. Beau Maison Dev. Corp.,* 511 So.2d 112, 117(Miss.1987)). In order to establish an easement by prescription, the claimant has the burden of proving that the use of the land is (1) open, notorious and visible; (2) hostile; (3) under claim of ownership; (4) exclusive; (5) peaceful; and (6) continuous and uninterrupted for ten years. *Myers v. Blair,* 611 So.2d 969, 971 (Miss. 1992). To determine whether these elements were satisfied, we review the evidence presented to support each.

(1) Open, notorious and visible

A litany of testimony was presented by all involved parties and their respective witnesses that Landry and Scheib used the road in question on an almost daily basis for access to their home. Dieck was on actual notice of its use when he purchased his property. Further testimony was presented that the road was used at times by school buses, delivery trucks and other private and commercial vehicles. At times, the passageway appeared on assorted county maps denominated as Toro Lane. In fact, both Landry and Scheib had their mail delivered to mailboxes on the passageway when it was known as Toro Lane. Dieck later had the county reassess the nature of the passageway and mail delivery was stopped. It is impossible to classify this use as anything other than open, notorious and visible.

(2) Hostile

Much of the argument at trial and on appeal concerns whether the use of the passageway by Landry and Scheib can be classified as permissive. As the trial court noted, there is no evidence that Landry or Scheib ever requested permission to use the passageway. Rather, they simply used it without regard to permissive considerations. George Livermore testified in an effort to clarify the permissive character of the passageway. The Livermores acquired their property after Landry, who used the passageway for ingress and egress purposes. It is clear from the testimony that Livermore and Landry never discussed the use of the passageway. It is equally clear, however, that Landry's use of the passageway was hostile to the Livermores' estate. For example, while there is uniform agreement that the passageway is not a public road, the evidence presented at trial regarding it's use by the public delivering services to Landry and Scheib operates as a further reflection on its hostile use to Dieck's claims.

On one occasion, Livermore stated that if Landry angered him, Landry would have to use a pogo stick to get to his property. That one statement, over the span of these many years, was the only conversation mentioned at trial that related to the permissive use of the passageway. It is impossible to impute a clear meaning to it as its context was not thoroughly outlined in the record. In any event, no one took it seriously, including Livermore. Livermore never attempted to limit or end Landry's use of the passageway and the testimony at trial was clear that neither Landry nor Scheib understood their use to be permissive from Livermore or his predecessor in title.

When trying to establish the elements of a prescriptive easement, requiring a litigant to prove a lack of permission existed is unreasonable because the law typically frowns upon requiring a party to prove a negative. *Morris v. W.R. Fairchild* Constr. Co., 792 So.2d 282, 284 (Miss.Ct.App.2001)(See *United States v. Denver & Rio Grande* R.R., 191 U.S. 84, 92, 24 S.Ct. 33, 48 L.Ed. 106 (1903)).

CASE

(3) Under claim of ownership

Both Landry and Scheib operated under a claim of ownership in regard to the passageway. When Landry purchased his property, the passageway was in use and had been used by previous tenants. No mention of the passageway was made by the attorney who participated in the real estate closing because it was the only way to access the land. When Landry purchased landlocked property, an easement by necessity arose. An easement by necessity arises by implied grant when a part of a commonly-owned tract of land is severed in such a way that either portion of the property has been rendered inaccessible except by passing over the other portion or by trespassing on the lands of another. *Huggins v. Wright,* 774 So.2d 408, 410 (Miss. 2000)(citing *Taylor v. Hays,* 551 So.2d 906, 908 (Miss.1989)). An easement by necessity requires no written conveyance because it is a vested right for successive holders of the dominant tenement and remains binding on successive holders of the servient tenement. Huggins, 774 So.2d at 411. *See also Broadhead v. Terpening,* 611 So.2d 949, 954 (Miss.1992) (holding that the owner of the larger tract cannot create a landlocked parcel by conveying an interior portion, so easement is conveyed whether described or not when the dominant estate is deeded; easements by necessity run with the land and are deeded with each conveyance regardless of description). An identical situation arose when Scheib purchased her property. Additionally, Landry and Scheib had the county come out and work on the passageway in 1986 and 1993 and times in between to maintain its effectiveness as an access route to Meadow Lane. Landry and Scheib clearly operated under a claim of ownership.

(4) Exclusive

Scheib's property currently serves as her full-time residence, and Landry formerly resided on his property. Landry and Scheib made exclusive use of passageway by having the postal services deliver their mail to 8 Toro Lane and 15 Toro Lane, respectively, at various points prior to this action. They further utilized the passageway by having

other county and business vehicles such as the water company and telephone company access their property for private land use purposes.

(5) Peaceful

Other than the expected arguments and disagreements associated with a property dispute that arises among neighbors, little evidence was presented that anyone breached the peace in their use of passageway.

(6) Continuous and uninterrupted for ten years

Landry used the passageway continuously and uninterrupted from the date of his purchase in 1968 until February of 1999. Scheib used the passageway continuously and uninterrupted from the date of purchase in 1986 until February of 1999. By either standard, the ten year limitations period expired before Dieck erected his fence across the passageway. In *Logan v. McGee,* we held that

> a prescriptive right to an easement is equivalent to a deed conveying such right, and that proper acquisition of the right is presumed from adverse and continuous enjoyment of a right-of-way for the ten year statutory period. If an easement by prescription is equivalent to the conveyance of such right by deed, then it follows that such an easement will run will the land. In *Browder v. Graham,* 204 Miss. 773, 38 So.2d 188(1948), Browder purchased a dominant tenement and it was ruled that 'the conveyance to him of the dominant tenement carried with it the appurtenant easement.' The acquisition of an easement by adverse user for the statutory time is no less efficacious than a deed (properly drawn and delivered) in investing such user with full rights to use, enjoy, own and convey such an easement.

Logan v. McGee, 320 So.2d 792, 793 (Miss.1975) (citations omitted). Even if Landry's and Scheib's individual periods of time spent adversely possessing the passageway were insufficient to meet the limitations requirement, we have applied the doctrine of tacking for landowners in privity to easements by prescription. *See Rutland v. Stewart,*

630 So.2d 996, 999 (Miss. 1994). The statutory time period was met in each case.

Conclusion

Finding that all of the elements necessary to establish an easement were proven convincingly at trial, we affirm the judgment of the chancery court.

AFFIRMED.

Case Review Question

Dieck v. Landry, 796 So.2d. 1004 (Miss. 2001). Would the result change if the property was bordered by a navigable waterway and access could be obtained by boat?

Buyers' and Sellers' Rights

Persons who have not previously been involved in the sale of real property are not aware of the many issues that must be addressed before such a sale is completed. The sale generally includes not only the buyer and the seller but also a broker, a mortgagor, a financier, and an attorney, as well as others who play a necessary role in completing the transaction.

Documents associated with the sale of property include the following:

1. Purchase agreement (seller agrees not to sell to another; buyer pays earnest money as a deposit) (see Figure 10.1).
2. Mortgage or financing agreement (agreement between buyer and party financing the sale for repayment).
3. Deed (used to record the transfer of title).
4. Required government forms (used to make necessary records of property transfers within a state).
5. Required inspections (often required by government and also customary for parties to produce certificates of inspection of the property, such as a termite certificate, and to ensure the property is structurally sound).
6. Escrow agreement (written agreement between buyer and seller as to who—usually an independent party—will hold the earnest money deposit during the completion of the transaction).
7. Buyer and seller agreements (often called contract for deed, used when the seller finances the sale and turns over the deed to the property when the buyer has completed payment).
8. Title policy (an insurance policy from a title company that guarantees that it has searched the chain of title to the property, that no other claims to the property are superior to the prospective buyer, and that the seller has the right to convey the title).

Although it is generally true that conveyances of title to real property must be in writing under the statute of frauds, an exception is recognized in some jurisdictions. Under the doctrine of part performance, if a substantial portion of the purchase price has been paid and actual possession of the property has been turned over, the transaction will be enforced.[16] The court infers from the actions of the parties that the parties intended the conveyance of the property, and the

FIGURE 10.1

Purchase
Agreement

THIS IS A BINDING CONTRACT, IF NOT UNDERSTOOD
SEEK COMPETENT LEGAL ADVICE.

The undersigned BUYERS agree to purchase and the undersigned OWNERS agree to sell the real estate and all improvements located at _____

Upon the following terms:

$_____ shall be Earnest Money evidenced by personal check to be deposited upon acceptance of this offer as deposit on the purchase price. Said Earnest Money shall be deposited in escrow in an interest-bearing account at _____ Bank and shall not be subject to withdrawal prior to closing unless this Contract should become null and void and for failure of one or more of the conditions of sale set forth in this Agreement. Upon closing, said Earnest Money shall be paid directly to OWNERS. In the event this contract fails due to any fault, neglect, or intentional breach by BUYERS, said _____ Earnest Money and all interest accrued thereon shall be paid directly to OWNERS. In the event this contract fails due to any fault, neglect, or intentional breach by OWNERS, said Earnest Money and all interest accrued thereon shall be paid directly to BUYERS.

$_____ Balance due on the specified date of closing, upon delivery of Warranty Deed conveying merchantable title free and clear of liens and encumbrances except easements, restrictions, and covenants of record, and which have been made known to BUYERS.

$_____ :Purchase Price.

This sale is contingent upon BUYERS obtaining a home mortgage at a fixed rate of _____% plus one point or less, for a term of no less than 3 years amortized over 30 years. Loan to be applied for within 10 days and approved within 30 days. Appraisal to be equal to or greater than the purchase price. BUYERS and OWNERS agree to pay in equal shares costs of closing, including but not limited to title insurance and recording fees. Closing to be on May 30, 2004.

Upon acceptance of the terms by OWNERS, the Earnest Money shall be applied as part payment on the purchase price but shall be held in escrow prior to closing as stated above. If this offer is rejected by the OWNERS, or if title to said premises is not merchantable or cannot be made so within sixty (60) days after written notice is delivered to OWNERS stating the defects, or if no effort is made to make the said property merchantable by OWNERS, this contract shall be null and void and all earnest money shall be refunded to BUYERS who shall have no further claim against the OWNERS. If this sale is not consummated within 30 days of the closing date stated above, time being of the essence, because of neglect or failure on the part of the BUYERS to comply with the terms and conditions herein agreed to, then all Earnest Money shall be forfeited and this Contract shall be of no further binding effect. But such forfeiture shall not release BUYERS from any liability for the fulfillment of this Contract of sale if OWNERS shall, within 30 days after BUYERS have defaulted, give BUYERS written notice by certified mail of their intention to sue.

The property is to be conveyed by good and sufficient Warranty Deed and insured Title Policy, in an amount equal to the purchase price, showing merchantable title free and clear of all liens and encumbrances except easements, or restrictions of record, or those which the purchaser agrees to assume as part of the purchase price as herein set forth. OWNERS shall pay all costs and expenses necessary to convey title in fee simple.

OWNERS shall maintain fire and extended coverage insurance on the premises until the date of closing. In the event the premises shall be destroyed or damaged prior to closing, BUYERS shall have the option to accept the insurance settlement and complete the transaction or to declare this Contract void, and thereupon all deposits made hereunder shall be refunded to the BUYERS. BUYERS shall make said election within seven (7) days after receipt of written notice of the injury to the property.

Real estate taxes, utilities, and sewer charges due, if any, shall be prorated as of the date of closing or the date of possession, whichever is later, taxes to be prorated on the last known tax bill which buyers agree to assume and pay accordingly.

BUYERS have personally inspected the property and are accepting it in its present condition, with the exception of any contingencies listed. OWNERS agree to maintain the heating, sewer, plumbing, and electrical systems and any built-in appliances and equipment in normal working order and to maintain the grounds and to deliver the property in the same condition as at the time of inspection by BUYERS.

OWNERS hereby warrant that prior to the execution of this instrument, neither they nor their agent has received any notice issued by any city, village, or other governmental authority, of a dwelling code violation upon the premises herein described.

It is understood and agreed that only the personal property listed below is included in the sale: all built-in appliances, water softener, all ceiling fans, computerized temperature monitor and sensors, custom-made draperies, 2 garage door openers with remote controls, retractable clothesline.

OWNERS agree that any personal property left upon the premises after delivery of possession has been abandoned by OWNERS and becomes the property of BUYERS. OWNERS agree to leave premises in a clean condition, free of all litter and debris.

In the event OWNERS shall remove any personal property included in this Contract, or any improvements, OWNER(s) shall pay BUYERS in an amount equal to the replacement or repair cost of the item or items so removed or damaged.

OWNERS agree to vacate the premises prior to closing and shall pay a rent from the date of closing the sum of $_____ per month in advance for each month or portion thereof OWNERS remain in possession of the premises.

OWNERS to provide a termite certificate showing no active infestation.

This agreement shall be binding upon the parties hereto, their heirs, executors, administrators, and assigns.

This sale is subject to the terms and conditions set forth in this agreement.

We, the BUYERS, hereby agree to purchase the above-described property on the terms above and agree to pay the price of $176,000 for said property.

Dated: _____

Buyer: _____

Buyer: _____

We, the OWNERS, hereby approve the above sales agreement and agree to sell the above described real estate for $ _____

Dated: _____

Accepted by Owner _____

Accepted by Owner _____

Dated: _____

Accepted by Buyer _____

Accepted by Buyer _____

FIGURE 10.1

Purchase Agreement *(Continued)*

court will require the parties to complete the transaction. The courts are divided on this issue, and in many states, a written agreement is required to enforce completion of a real property transaction.

Even when a written agreement exists, the problem often arises as to responsibility for the property during the completion of the purchase requirements. The numerous documents and other transactions associated with the purchase of property are not prepared overnight. Often, a sale of property takes two to six months to complete. During this time, what happens if the property is partially or totally destroyed? What if the property is discovered to have a claim on it? What if the seller wastes the property? These are all issues that have arisen in the past.

While there is some variation among the courts, general principles have been established. Generally, if something occurs during a pending sale that partially or totally destroys the property through no fault of the seller, the liability for the loss is on the buyer.[17] An example is a house that is destroyed by fire and the house is the only real asset of the property. The seller may require the buyer to complete the sale. If the property is only partially destroyed and repair is feasible, the seller is given a reasonable amount of time to adequately repair, and the buyer may be held to the purchase agreement. Because the buyer bears some risk of loss, the buyer may also insure the property to the extent of the risk, even though title has not yet passed.

A minority of jurisdictions place on the seller the cost of loss due to a casualty. However, the most common occurrence is that the purchase agreement will specify who bears the risk of loss. If it is the buyer, the buyer has a valid interest that can be insured even though title to the land has not yet been formally passed.

If some defect or irregularity in the title is discovered, the seller is given a reasonable amount of time to cure the defect and is generally allowed to use part of the purchase price to do so.[18] If, for example, there is a government lien on the property for back taxes, the seller would be allowed a reasonable amount of time to raise the money to satisfy the tax debt or would be allowed to accept the purchase price and pay the debt before conveying title. Ordinarily, the purchase price and title are conveyed simultaneously.

All sellers are under a general duty to care for the property and prevent it from waste during the time necessary to complete the sale. In the sale of real property with dwellings on it, a seller is also under a duty to convey the property in habitable condition (generally interpreted to mean safe for occupancy and having access to utilities).

Not all duties, however, are on the seller. The courts do apply the theory of caveat emptor—"let the buyer beware."[19] Under this theory, a purchaser of property has the limited duty to reasonably investigate and discover defects in the property. Failure to do so can result in the court's refusal to rescind the purchase agreement or require the owner to repair the defect. If, for example, a buyer notices an air-conditioning unit outside the house, he or she should not assume that the unit works properly. Questions regarding the working order and age of all appliances and portions of the house that might require replacement or repair should be asked. Then, if the seller makes representations that turn out to be false, the buyer may have recourse in actions for breach of an express warranty or fraud.[20] Any of the generally accepted duties of buyer and seller can be altered by agreement.

Adverse Possession

Not all real property is obtained by purchase or gift. The law has created a method by which a party can gain good title to land simply by using the land. The theory of adverse possession is recognized as a means of obtaining title to property without consent or voluntary transfer by the owner when certain conditions are met. The reasoning behind adverse possession is that the government encourages the productive use of land, and if the owner does not productively use the land and does not protect the right to possess owned property, the law will recognize ownership in one who will.

While every state has a statute setting the requirements, the following elements are usually needed to prove title by adverse possession:[21]

+ Open and notorious possession.
+ Continuous possession.
+ Exclusive possession.
+ Adequate duration of possession.

Open possession requires that the person seeking title by adverse possession actually possess the property. This does not mean that the person must spend the days walking the boundaries. However, the adverse possessor must act in such a way that others, including an alert property owner, would perceive such actions as those of one exercising control over the entire property. An example is farming a large acreage or building a permanent home on the property.

Continuous possession is designed to prevent transients and squatters from claiming title to the property. The law does not propose to vest title in anyone who wants the property. Rather, it gives title to persons who show an ongoing concern for the property. Therefore, it is necessary to exercise control or possession of the property in a way that is perceived as continuous. Abandonment for a significant time will prevent this element from being proven.

Exclusive possession is necessary to show that the person claiming title by adverse possession acted in a way to exclude others from possessing the property. Until all the elements are sufficiently met, this does not apply to the original owner. The true owner of the property who becomes aware of someone else possessing the property can retrieve it. However, after the statutory period, the adverse possessor has the right to exclude others from the property, for example, by erecting No Trespassing signs.

The final element requires the adverse possessor to do all of the preceding for a specified period of time. Statutes vary on the length of time, but generally, the provision requires possession for a period of 5 to 20 years. The reasoning is that possession should be for a period of time that not only demonstrates a continuing intent to utilize the land but also gives the true owner every opportunity to reclaim his or her property.

Many states as well as the federal government do not permit claims of adverse possession over their land. Those that allow such claims do so only in specified areas. For example, national parks are not subject to claims of adverse possession. Preservation of these large areas of protected wilderness takes precedence over any needs or rights of private individuals.

Adverse possession can be established even though a series of different persons actually possessed the property during the specified period of time. When this occurs, it is called tacking and is allowed only under certain circumstances. When a statute permits tacking, it usually requires succeeding owners to be descendants/heirs, a spouse, or someone who was voluntarily granted possession during the life of the first adverse possessor.[22]

The law gives every chance to the original owner to retain the rights of title to the property. However, when there is a total failure to utilize property for a significant period of time and there is a party who would make beneficial use of the property, adverse possession takes effect.

CASE

STOKES V. KUMMER

85 Wash. App. 682, 936
P.2d 4 (1997).

SCHULTHEIS,
JUDGE.

The court denied Duane Stokes, Sandra Baker, Terril Johnson and B. G. Knight's claim for ejectment and quieted title to three parcels of land used by brothers Terril Kummer, Arlan Kummer and Kevin Kummer for dry land wheat farming, based on their adverse possession of the fields for more than 10 years. The court also granted the brothers a 75-foot easement across Mr. Stokes's and Ms. Baker's property, for access between two of the fields. On appeal, Mr. Stokes, Ms. Baker and Mr. Knight contend the Kummers' use of field 2 was permissive at its inception, negating the element of hostility required to demonstrate adverse possession. Mr. Johnson contends the Kummers conceded his superior title in 1982 by not contesting an easement he granted to others and did not prove adverse possession for a sufficient period thereafter. All of the appellants contend biennial cropping of agricultural land is insufficient use to establish title by adverse possession. We affirm.

The property at issue in this case is in a fairly desolate part of Kittitas County, accessible only by a gravel county road. The region is rocky and arid, covered mostly with sagebrush and tumbleweeds. There are pockets or hummocks of soil, however, that are suitable for dry land wheat farming. Aerial photographs show the three fields at issue have been cultivated since at least 1954. Sometime during or before October 1971 the quarter section where these fields are located, the northeast one-quarter of Section 33, Township 17 North, Range 18 East, Willamette Meridian, and the quarter section immediately west, the northwest one-quarter of Section 33, Township 17 North, Range 18 East, Willamette Meridian, were divided into tracts of roughly 20 acres each. The platted subdivision, known as the Valley View Ranch tracts, was not recorded. Nor was it surveyed, permanently staked or fenced. The appellants each own a Valley View Ranch tract underlying the three wheat fields that the Kummer brothers have been farming since 1976. See the field survey map attached as an appendix.

It is unclear from the record when Lawrence Hall began growing winter wheat in the area, but in 1953 he leased from Agnes C. Meagher "all that certain crop land owned by [her] and lying within a certain fenced area" in the northeast one-quarter of Section 33 to grow wheat. The lease was for four years, from October 1, 1953, to October 1, 1957. Mary Hall married Lawrence Hall in 1956, and in 1957 moved to the old homestead house on his property south of Umptanum Road and west of Durr Road. Mrs. Hall said that when she moved out to the property, Mr. Hall was farming the same fields across the road (Umptanum Road) that the Kummer brothers later farmed. Mr. Hall originally farmed some of the property north of the road for Estil Wright under a crop share agreement, but later bought that property.

On January 28, 1976, the Kummer brothers bought out the Halls. They acquired title to 2,540 acres, including that part of the northeast one-quarter of Section 33 lying south and east of Umptanum Road, and most of the northwest one-quarter of Section 34, which borders the Valley View Ranch tracts on the east. Mr. Hall drove them around the various fields on the property and also gave the Kummers a 1954 aerial photograph of the area. It shows numerous wheat fields, which are irregularly spaced and shaped due to uneven topography and soil.

In March 1976 the Kummers moved onto the property and began farming the same areas Mr. Hall had farmed, including the three fields just north of Umptanum Road. There were no fences, posts or other markers suggesting the northeast one-quarter of Section 33 had been divided into parcels. The Kummers have continuously harvested wheat from all their fields every other year, beginning in 1976—except one year in the early 1980s when they participated in a federal program and ended up harvesting in an odd year, 1981. During crop years they reseed the fields if necessary early in the season, spray later for weeds, harvest the wheat with a combine, and, when soil moisture permits, plow the stubble under in the fall. During the intervening fallow years, they plow, cultivate, fertilize and seed the fields. Every year the Kummers post the perimeters of their wheat fields against trespassing and hunting, and they regularly tell people to get off the land during hunting season.

Meanwhile, S & S Enterprises, Inc., was selling Valley View Ranch tracts. Duane Stokes acquired tract 40 in August 1988 by quitclaim deed from his parents, who had bought it in approximately 1972. When Mr. Stokes first visited the property in fall 1973, he observed most of it was sagebrush, but there was evidence the northern part had been farmed. It looked substantially the same when he next visited in fall 1980—he saw wheat stubble on the northern end. When he last visited in fall 1991 it looked the same, "like somebody had plowed the field."

Sandra Baker (nee Burchfield) acquired tract 41 in June 1973 by deed from S & S Enterprises, after her brother assigned her his interest under a 1971 purchase contract. She first visited the property shortly after she acquired it and was thoroughly unimpressed. It was dry, arid and rocky, covered with sagebrush and tumbleweeds. She visited the property again in the early 1980s, twice in one year, but she only looked at the tract from the road. She did not walk the property and could not see the northern part of it. She did the same thing once more later in the 1980s. Every visit was during winter. Until the lawsuit, she had never seen the north end of the property where the wheat fields extend onto it.

B.G. Knight acquired tract 36 in the 1970s from Melvin and Emma Orness, who deeded the tract to him in January 1980 in fulfillment of his contract with them and their 1971 purchase contract. He saw only a picture of the property when he bought it and it was apparent from the picture that it had been farmed. He learned about the Valley View Ranch tracts from Alex Varunok, a close friend and fellow Boeing employee, who had bought tracts 34 and 35.

In 1978, Mr. Varunok approached the Kummer brothers and told them they were farming on property north of Umptanum Road that did not belong to them. He showed them a deed and a map.

After some discussion and correspondence between Terril Kummer and Mr. Varunok, they reached a lease agreement. On May 7, 1978, Mr. Varunok signed a handwritten "farm lease/share agreement," apparently drafted by him, in which Kevin Kummer agrees to farm tracts 35 and 36, belonging to Mr. Knight and Mr. Varunok, and to provide 25 percent of the gross proceeds of the 1978 and 1979 crops and thereafter 33 1/3 percent. Mr. Knight signed on May 8 and Kevin Kummer signed on May 17 at the request of his brother Terril. Terril Kummer then returned the signed lease agreement to Mr. Varunok with a note advising him that they normally harvest wheat every other year, so the next crop after 1978 would likely be 1980.

On November 20, 1978, Terril Kummer sent Mr. Varunok a note and a check for $1,035. In August 1979 Terril Kummer sent Mr. Varunok a letter and newspaper article explaining they had had serious crop damage from grasshoppers. On November 1, 1981, Terril Kummer sent Mr. Varunok a note and a check for $1,810.90. In June 1983, the Kummers bought tracts 34 and 35 from Mr. Varunok. They continued farming field 2 as they always had, believing they now owned the tracts underlying it.

Mr. Knight received his share of the 1978 and 1981 lease payments from Mr. Varunok. He never met or talked with any of the Kummer brothers. Though he did not receive any payments after 1981, he did not ask Mr. Varunok about it. When Mr. Knight visited his property in winter 1982 or 1983, he noticed it had obviously been farmed in wheat because there was wheat stubble on part of it and sagebrush on part. Mr. Knight visited his property probably once more in the 1980s and again in about 1991, both times in the winter. He said he assumed somebody would send him money if the Kummers farmed his property, and since he was not receiving any money, he concluded they must not be farming it. Mr. Knight did not try to contact the Kummers until approximately 1991 or 1992, when he learned from a Realtor that his property was being farmed. At that time, he was unable to locate a telephone number for the Kummer brothers and did not pursue the matter further.

CASE

Finally, Mr. Johnson acquired tract 39 in December 1990 by quitclaim deed from his parents, who had bought it in September 1975 from the original purchasers, Derwin and Avis Lisk. Mr. Johnson first saw the property in 1975 just before the Lisks transferred it to his parents, and at that time, part of it was a wheat field, early fallow or stubble. Tract 39 is divided roughly into western and eastern halves by a road that provides access from Umptanum Road to the north. The road was not shown on the unrecorded plat map, but it was there when the Johnsons bought the tract and Milo England had been using it to get to his property ever since he bought his acreage in summer 1976.

Mr. England remembered the fields on either side of the road had been farmed when he moved there, and that the Kummers had farmed both fields since 1976. In fact, they crossed the road to get from one field to the other and when they did not raise their tractor attachments high enough they disturbed the already rough road surface. In October 1982, Mr. England contacted the Johnsons, after determining from county records that they owned tract 39, and asked if they knew their property was being farmed. They apparently did not. Terry Johnson visited the property and ascertained it was being farmed by the Kummers. He met with Mr. England and Earl and Lorna Lyon, who also used the road to get to their property, and on behalf of his parents gave them a recorded, handwritten easement to use the road.

Mr. Johnson also met with at least two of the Kummer brothers. He advised them he was giving the Englands and the Lyons an easement and discussed the Kummers' farming of his property. According to Mr. Johnson, he insisted the Kummers sign a written lease with him and agree to pay something for the crops they had taken in previous years, or he would not give them permission to continue farming. No agreement was reached, but the Kummers continued farming as they always had. Mr. Johnson returned in January or February 1987, and once again in winter 1990. Both times the property was just as it was when he first saw it in 1975. He did not contact Mr. England or the Kummers after October 1982.

The tract owners, all of whom live west of the Cascade Mountains, joined in this ejectment suit. The Kummers were served on January 12, 1994, and the summons and complaint were filed on March 18. They answered, and counterclaimed to quiet title in themselves under the doctrine of adverse possession. After a two-day bench trial in February 1995, the court quieted title to the three wheat fields in the Kummers and granted them a 75-foot easement across tracts 40 and 41 for access between fields 1 and 2. The tract owners appeal.

Adverse Possession
In order to establish a claim of adverse possession, there must be possession that is (1) open and notorious, (2) actual and uninterrupted, (3) exclusive, and (4) hostile, all for a period of 10 years. *ITT Rayonier, Inc. v. Bell,* 112 Wash.2d 754, 757, 774 P.2d 6 (1989); RCW 4.16.020. Because the presumption of possession is in the holder of legal title, the party claiming adverse possession has the burden of establishing each element. *ITT Rayonier,* 112 Wash.2d at 757, 774 P.2d 6. Adverse possession is a mixed question of law and fact. Whether essential facts exist is for the trier of fact; but whether the facts, as found, constitute adverse possession is for the court to determine as a matter of law.

Field 2
Tract owners Mr. Stokes, Mr. Knight and Ms. Baker contend the Kummers farmed field 2, covering much of the Knight tract and a small portion of the Baker and Stokes tracts, after they received permission to do so under the May 1978 lease agreement. They assert permissive use is not hostile and does not commence the running of the prescriptive period. They argue the permissive use of this wheat field could not ripen into a prescriptive right unless the Kummers made a distinct and positive assertion of a right hostile to the owners.

As the Kummers point out, and the court found, Mr. Stokes and Ms. Baker were not privy to the lease and could not gain any benefit from it. The Kummers established they adversely possessed those parts of tracts 40 (Stokes) and 41 (Baker) that they and their predecessor Mr. Hall had farmed continuously from the 1950s into the 1990s, including the prescriptive easement granted by the court.

With respect to Mr. Knight, use of his property was not permissive at its inception, though it may have been from mid-1978 to mid-1983. The lease does not make it clear that Mr. Knight was the Kummers' landlord for any specific property, or that he owned one of the tracts outright. The court found the statutory period began running at the latest in June 1983, when the Kummers bought tracts 34 and 35 from Mr. Varunok.

> The tract owners assign error to the finding that the Kummers thought they were buying the 40 acres covered by the Varunok and Knight lease. The finding is supported by the evidence, although it is not necessary for a determination of adverse possession since it is irrelevant whether they appropriated the land knowingly or by mistake. *Chaplin,* 100 Wash.2d at 860, 676 P.2d 431.

As the court pointed out in its memorandum decision, the assertion that the Kummers never repudiated the lease is without merit. Apart from questions whether it was ever valid or whether it terminated with Mr. Varunok's sale of his tracts, the sale itself signaled a significant change in the parties' relationship. Mr. Varunok had handled all aspects of the lease arrangement, including paying Mr. Knight his share; Mr. Knight had never even spoken with any of the Kummer brothers. When Mr. Varunok advised Mr. Knight he was selling out, Mr. Knight was put on notice he would have to make different arrangements regarding the lease, which, as previously noted, did not specify his interest in any event. He did nothing. That fall, when he did not receive a lease payment, he again did nothing. He did nothing until this suit was commenced in January 1994 by service on the Kummers, and by then it was too late.

Possession is hostile when one holds property as his own, whether under mistaken belief or willfully. Here, after they bought the two tracts upon which they thought their wheat field was located, the

Kummers no longer made lease payments because they held the property as their own. They continued to farm it openly and they kept the proceeds from the crops. The Kummers' actions were of such open, notorious and hostile character that Mr. Knight would have known they were farming his land, had he looked or inquired.

Fields 1 and 3

Mr. Johnson contends the Kummers did not prove adverse possession for the requisite 10 years. First, he argues they did not establish tacking because Mr. Hall farmed the property under a 1953 lease and Mrs. Hall recalled he farmed some property north of Umptanum Road under a verbal agreement with another landowner. There was no evidence that Mr. Hall's occupancy was anything other than permissive; thus, if there was adverse possession it could not have begun before 1976.

The evidence establishes Mr. Hall farmed both fields from 1957 to 1976, but it does not establish he did so under a lease or with other permission. The property descriptions in the 1953 lease and Mrs. Hall's deposition testimony are too vague to determine what property was covered. The evidence also does not establish Mr. Hall possessed the property adversely, except that the Johnsons never gave anyone permission to farm tract 39. Under these circumstances, the earliest the prescriptive period could begin was September 1975, when the Johnsons acquired their interest.

Second, Mr. Johnson argues the Kummers deferred to and acknowledged the superior title of Mr. Johnson to the tract 39 wheat fields in October 1982 when they permitted him to grant and record an easement to Mr. England and the Lyons.

From 1976 when they acquired their property from the Halls, the Kummers' use of fields 1 and 3 was open, notorious and hostile. By at least October 1982, Mr. Johnson had actual notice they were farming his land. He confronted them and told them he owned the property, wanted payment for crops already harvested, and would not allow them to continue farming his land unless they executed a written lease. Had the Kummers stopped farming, Mr. Johnson's actions would

CASE

have interrupted their possession and restarted the prescriptive period. But they did not. They continued farming the fields just as if they owned them, not in a manner indicating recognition of or subordination to Mr. Johnson.

Mr. Johnson's grant of the easement was nothing more than permission for the Englands and the Lyons to use an existing road to access their properties. That did not interfere with or interrupt the Kummers' use of the fields on either side of the road. The Kummers' possession of the fields was (1) exclusive, (2) actual and uninterrupted, (3) open and notorious, and (4) hostile. Because he failed to effectively assert his own ownership over the fields (as opposed to the road) for more than 10 years after acquiring actual knowledge of the Kummers' adverse possession, Mr. Johnson lost his title.

Finally, the tract owners contend adverse possession cannot occur by cultivation of open farm land for crops harvested on a biennial basis when the land lies fallow in the intervening years.

The contention is completely without merit. The use and occupancy of the property need only be of the character that a true owner would assert in view of its nature and location. *Chaplin,* 100 Wash.2d at 863, 676 P.2d 431. That requirement is easily met by the Kummers' dry land farming of these fields in precisely the same manner they farm the rest of their acreage in the area. Ample evidence, including the aerial maps and the testimony of some of these tract owners, demonstrates just how visible is the Kummers' use of the property. As the surveyor put it, when asked if he had any difficulty discerning the difference between the fields and the surrounding property: "It's either field or sagebrush."

The decision of the superior court is affirmed. SWEENEY, C.J., and BROWN, J., concur.

Case Review Question

What is meant by the term *quiet title,* and why is it used in adverse possession proceedings?

Assignment 10.4

SITUATION: Steve owns property on which he has a quick shop. He erects a large, lighted sign next to the driveway on land that actually belongs to the adjoining property owner, a fundamentalist church. The owner does not object because Steve often advertises "Church Specials" for persons who attend services at the church. After 20 years, Steve dies and his son moves into town and converts the shop into a nude dancing establishment, which he advertises on the sign. The church demands the sign be removed.

QUESTION: Does the church meet the requirements of adverse possession?

Rights and Duties of Ownership

As stated previously, ownership of property generally includes the right of possession and control free from interference of third parties. Often called the right of quiet enjoyment, this right protects the right of one to do with one's own property as one pleases. Although this right is strongly protected by the law, certain obligations accompany it.

Public or private nuisance.   The first obligation is not to use one's property in such a way that it becomes a public or private nuisance to surrounding areas. A private nuisance is a use that has a direct adverse effect on specific persons,[23] such as unreasonable noise or noxious fumes emitted from the property or any continuing conduct that is harmful or poses a danger in some way to certain persons in the area. If this conduct continues, these persons have a right of action for private nuisance. They can sue in equity to have the conduct cease, and they can sue at law for damages as a result of the nuisance.

A public nuisance is one that generally has a continuing adverse effect on the public good, welfare, or safety.[24] Conduct, even though it is entirely done on one's own property, can be considered a public nuisance if its effects extend beyond the property. An example is a manufacturing plant that pollutes a waterway or emits noxious fumes over a broad area. If such harmful conduct becomes a continuing problem, public authorities may bring an action for public nuisance at equity to stop the conduct and at law to seek compensation for damages already incurred. Generally, a private party cannot bring an action for public nuisance unless the party's injury is different from that to the general public.

Condition of property.   Basic obligations also exist regarding the condition of one's property for persons entering it. This includes trespassers, licensees, and invitees. Some states treat licensees as invitees. In other states, the obligations toward each are different. However, all are owed some degree of protection from harm even if trespassing on the property.

Trespassers.   A trespasser is one who enters onto another's property without consent of any kind by the owner. The law does not offer any special protections to persons who violate the right of quiet enjoyment belonging to a landowner. However, the landowner does owe a duty to keep the property free from unreasonable dangers that a trespasser could not be expected to discover. There is no general duty to warn or take action to protect. Rather, there is only the duty to correct conditions that would cause injury or to give notice of these conditions.[25] (The owner's rights against a trespasser are discussed in Chapter 14.)

Licensees.   Licensees are persons who enter with the permission of the landowner but are not associated with the landowner's business. For example, a person hunting on property with permission free of charge and a person attending a party are common types of licensees. In states that distinguish between licensees and invitees, the obligation of a landowner toward these persons may be slightly greater than that owed trespassers. With respect to licensees, a landowner owes a general duty to warn of dangers present on the property. The reasoning is that because they are there by consent or invitation, the landowner owes a greater duty to see to their safety. This duty is somewhat broader than the duty toward trespassers and requires additional action on the part of the landowner.[26]

Invitees.   The invitee is invited (expressly or impliedly) to the property of the owner for business purposes—for the purpose of obtaining benefit for a business or for reasons of employment. Consequently, shopkeepers and landowners have a duty to actively inspect their premises to protect their invitees from harm.[27] For example, a grocery store owner has a duty to clean up a spill in one of the aisles and to restore the aisle to a safe condition in a reasonable time. An owner who does not could be held liable for injuries to anyone who steps on the area, slips and falls, and is injured.

While the privilege of quiet enjoyment is protected, the law recognizes that there are those who would abuse the privilege, and there are always occasions of persons entering on the property of others for various reasons. Consequently, the imposing of these basic duties on the landowner places the landowner under minimal obligation in return for virtually unlimited use of the property.

Condominiums

A somewhat specialized area of law is that regarding condominiums. The concept of owning property that has both freehold and non-freehold interests is not new. Records dating to medieval Europe indicate that this type of land interest existed even then. It was not unusual at that time for a person to purchase a room, apartment, or floor of a building. The owner of the building would maintain any hallways or surrounding yard. This type of ownership occurred primarily in crowded cities, where land and entire buildings were too expensive for the majority of the population. For many reasons, including the lack of established principles setting forth responsibilities of the parties to such an arrangement, this type of property ownership saw a decline. In recent times, however, with the problem of crowded cities, fast-paced lifestyles, and rising costs of purchasing and building homes, the concept of condominiums has dramatically increased in popularity, especially in the United States.

A condominium is a freehold interest. It is an absolute ownership in the property described. The property is real in that it is inextricably attached to the land. However, it may be located far above the actual soil and has specific dimensions without traditional air and subsurface rights. A condominium, however, has some non-freehold characteristics as well. Condominium ownership usually involves collateral obligations to abide by certain rules regarding the use of the property, payment of fees for maintenance of surrounding areas, and restrictions on the sale of the property. Consequently, condominiums are a hybrid of landlord/tenant (non-freehold) estates (discussed in the following section) and ownership in fee (freehold) estates.

The owners of adjoining condominiums are considered to be owners by tenancy in common over the air and subsurface rights. They are owners in fee simple over their own particular building or portion of a building. Because of this individual/multiple ownership between persons who do not have common interests and are usually strangers, all 50 states have enacted laws to govern the establishment and running of condominium complexes.[28]

Usually, a condominium complex is established by developers who create a document known as a declaration to dedicate its use to that type of ownership. A plan created to provide for the ongoing needs of the complex allows for a committee to make decisions regarding upkeep of the property, collection of fees from the owners for standard maintenance, and enforcement of any restrictions regarding purchase or sale of the property.

While it is permissible to impose restrictions on owners regarding the sale and purchase of their condominiums, these restrictions cannot be unconstitutional or even unreasonable. The law has been clear that restrictions based on race, religion, sex, or nationality are not permitted.[29] Furthermore, a restriction that is so enforced that it effectively prevents the owner of disposing of the property may be considered unreasonable.

APPLICATION 10.7

The board of directors of a condominium complex, under a restriction, has the right to approve a prospective buyer. If the members refuse all applicants for unsound reasons, the restriction would be considered unreasonable, and the court would probably not enforce it.

Point for Discussion
◆ Why are some restrictions enforced and others not?

Because the owners of the individual units are tenants in common over the air and subsurface rights and common areas, their obligations are equal as landowners. Therefore, if a trespasser, licensee, or invitee is injured on a common area through negligence, the owners are equally liable for the injuries. Consequently, the courts do allow some restrictions so that owners can ensure that they will become tenants in common with reasonable persons.

As more people become property owners and consider that property to be their most significant asset, they have an interest in protecting the property value. For this reason, many areas now have homeowners' associations. These groups of homeowners in a particular area create an organization in which all homeowners consent to certain restrictions on their property to maintain certain standards within the community. Restrictions range from colors used on the exterior of homes, to the presence of outbuildings, types of fences, types of exterior construction, and number and types of vehicles parked on or adjacent to the property. The rationale is that by giving up some degree of the right of quiet enjoyment, the value of the property will not be reduced by other property owners who might not otherwise maintain their property in a similar manner.

Non-Freehold Estates

non-freehold estate

An interest in real property that is limited in duration and involves the right of possession but not ownership.

In addition to interests associated with freehold estates of ownership, numerous non-freehold estate interests are present in American property law. **Non-freehold estates** are those that include specific rights to possess property, control it, and even exclude the true owner. However, these estates generally are by agreement, are for a fixed time, and do not include any rights of ownership. One who possesses a non-freehold estate cannot convey ownership; nor does the party in possession have the right to waste the property, and the possessor must return the property to the true owner at the agreed time or upon proper eviction proceedings. Most often, this relationship between owner and possessor is that of landlord and tenant and is governed in part by property law and in part by contract law.

Non-freehold estates are commonly called leaseholds. The parties are generally referred to as landlord and tenant. Leaseholds may or may not be in writing, depending upon the specific nature of the agreement. Generally, agreements that will extend beyond one year must be in writing under state law according to a statute of frauds, because the agreement involves real property. Basic elements should be present for an oral or written leasehold agreement to be valid. Each party must have contractual capacity; that is, each party must have reached the age of majority and/or be considered legally competent. A clear agreement to give and accept possession of the property upon specified terms must exist. A description of the property must be included that adequately describes the exact premises of which the tenant will have possession.[30]

The terms of the agreement should be clearly understood. If the agreement contains an option to renew and the option is not formally exercised but the tenant remains in possession beyond the original term, the leasehold becomes one at will. This and other types of leaseholds and tenancies are discussed subsequently. It is important, however, to first understand the rights and obligations of a landlord and tenant.

Rights and obligations of landlord and tenant. The landlord and tenant each have basic rights and obligations associated with non-freehold property interests (see Figure 10.2). The landlord has the duty to turn over the property free from latent (not reasonably discoverable) defects or dangers and to ensure that the property is habitable.[31] Although the definition of habitability varies from state to state, it is presumed to be that which is absolutely necessary to make a premises one on which persons can reasonably be expected to live. Typically, habitable property has access to electricity, hot water, shelter from the elements, and, in some states, heat. If the landlord fails to provide these things or fails to continue them during the term of the agreement, the warranty of habitability is violated and the landlord is presumed to have breached the terms of the lease agreement.

In contrast, the tenant is responsible to prevent waste from occurring on the property, to discover patent (reasonably obvious) defects or dangers, and to make ordinary repairs.[32] If a significant patent defect exists or occurs, the tenant is obligated to notify the landlord and to give the landlord a reasonable opportunity

FIGURE 10.2

Landlord and
Tenant Law

Excerpts from VERMONT STATUTES ANNOTATED
TITLE NINE. COMMERCE AND TRADE
PART 7. LANDLORD AND TENANT
CHAPTER 137. RESIDENTIAL RENTAL AGREEMENTS

§ 4455. Tenant obligations; payment of rent

(a) Rent is payable without demand or notice at the time and place agreed upon by the parties.

(b) An increase in rent shall take effect on the first day of the rental period following no less than 60 days' actual notice to the tenant.

§ 4456. Tenant obligations; use and maintenance of dwelling unit

(a) The tenant shall not create or contribute to the noncompliance of the dwelling unit with applicable provisions of building, housing and health regulations.

(b) The tenant shall conduct himself or herself and require other persons on the premises with the tenant's consent to conduct themselves in a manner that will not disturb other tenants' peaceful enjoyment of the premises.

(c) The tenant shall not deliberately or negligently destroy, deface, damage or remove any part of the premises or its fixtures, mechanical systems or furnishings or deliberately or negligently permit any person to do so.

(d) Unless inconsistent with a written rental agreement or otherwise provided by law, a tenant may terminate a tenancy by actual notice given to the landlord at least one rental payment period prior to the termination date specified in the notice.

(e) If a tenant acts in violation of this section, the landlord is entitled to recover damages, costs and reasonable attorney's fees, and the violation shall be grounds for termination under section 4467(b) of this title.

§ 4457. Landlord obligations; habitability

(a) Warranty of habitability. In any residential rental agreement, the landlord shall be deemed to covenant and warrant to deliver over and maintain, throughout the period of the tenancy, premises that are safe, clean and fit for human habitation and which comply with the requirements of applicable building, housing and health regulations.

(b) Waiver. No rental agreement shall contain any provision by which the tenant waives the protections of the implied warranty of habitability. Any such waiver shall be deemed contrary to public policy and shall be unenforceable and void.

(c) Heat and water. As part of the implied warranty of habitability, the landlord shall ensure that the dwelling unit has heating facilities which are capable of safely providing a reasonable amount of heat. Every landlord who provides heat as part of the rental agreement shall at all times supply a reasonable amount of heat to the dwelling unit. The landlord shall provide an adequate amount of water to each dwelling unit properly connected with hot and cold water lines. The hot water lines shall be connected with supplied water-heating facilities which are capable of heating sufficient water to permit an adequate amount to be drawn. This subsection shall not apply to a dwelling unit intended and rented for summer occupancy or as a hunting camp.

◆ APPLICATION 10.8

Jane rents a house for $500 per month. She does not have a signed lease agreement but has been renting the property for two years. Recently, the furnace went out. The landlord replaced it, but informed Jane on the date rent was due that effective the following month the rent will increase by $200 per month for a period of six months to pay for the furnace. Jane continues to pay $500 per month as originally agreed. The week after Jane fails to pay the additional $200, the landlord has the water to the house disconnected. The landlord has violated the agreement between the parties by breaching the warranty of habitability.

Point for Discussion

◆   What would have been the appropriate measure for the landlord when Jane failed to pay the increase in rent?

to repair it. If the defect does not affect habitability, such as a clogged sink, the tenant is generally responsible for the repair, and in many states, any costs of having the sink cleared would be the responsibility of the tenant.

The tenant is bound by the terms of the agreement and is expected to pay the rent and to give reasonable notice when vacating the property, commonly referred to as quitting the property. The tenant has the right to quiet enjoyment.

If either party substantially fails to meet his or her responsibilities, such failure may be treated as a breach, and the innocent party has the right to terminate the agreement. A landlord's failure to meet the required obligations is termed *constructive eviction*.[33] In other words, the tenant is left in a position where he or she has no reasonable choice but to vacate the premises.

The landlord does not necessarily have to *intentionally* fail to meet his or her legal responsibilities. In cases where the property is so damaged by fire or otherwise damaged that it becomes uninhabitable, the tenant is constructively evicted. Many times, the lease agreement will allow the landlord a reasonable time to repair the premises before the lease agreement will be terminated. It is important to carefully read the lease (as all legal documents should be read!) to determine just what the obligations of the parties are with respect to damage to the property and continuation of the agreement. If the lease is effectively terminated by a constructive eviction, the question of whether the tenant is able to recover any advance deposits depends on the terms of the agreement between the parties and whether the damage was the fault of the tenant.

Regardless of who initially breached the agreement, many states impose on both parties a duty to mitigate any damage caused by the premature end of the landlord–tenant relationship. *Mitigation of damages* is the term used when one is required to lessen or minimize the damage when possible. This prevents persons from adding to their damages to increase the amount of monetary recovery in a lawsuit. In the event the property is significantly damaged, the landlord is often required to make every reasonable effort to repair the premises and restore habitability. Further, if a tenant vacates or abandons the property, the landlord must make reasonable attempts to rent the property. The landlord cannot merely let the property stand empty and seek to collect the balance of the rent from the tenant.

The tenant also is responsible for mitigating damages. A tenant who is forced to move on grounds of constructive eviction must make reasonable efforts to minimize the cost of the move and damage to any personal property before recovering compensation from the landlord. The tenant who played a role in creating the condition that forced the constructive eviction probably has no recourse against the landlord.

CASE

APPELLATE DIVISION, SUPERIOR COURT,

HERB W. HYATT, PLAINTIFF AND RESPONDENT, V. NORA TEDESCO, DEFENDANT AND APPELLANT.

117 Cal. Rptr. 2d 921
Jan. 31, 2002.

Memorandum Judgment
Defendant and tenant Nora Tedesco (hereinafter appellant) timely appeals the judgement entered in favor of plaintiff and landlord Herb W. Hyatt (hereinafter plaintiff) following an unlawful detainer court trial.

On September 20, 2000, plaintiff filed an unlawful detainer action against appellant seeking possession of the premises, forfeiture of the agreement, past due rent and damages on the theory of nonpayment of rent.

On September 25, 2000, appellant filed her answer to the complaint. In her answer, appellant, among other things not germane to this appeal, denied the monthly rent amount as stated in the complaint, the amount of rent that was due and owing, and set forth the affirmative defense of breach of warranty of habitability. Appellant specifically alleged that the following conditions existed in the premises: leaking roof, missing bathtub tiles, windows not secure from the elements due to rotten frames, holes in the carpeting, cracks in the walls, security bars without release latches, water damage throughout the

house to the walls and carpets, and plumbing that does not adequately drain.

A court trial was held on October 17, 2000, wherein plaintiff, appellant, and Rocco Spinelli testified. Plaintiff's testimony established a prima facie case for relief under an unlawful detainer cause of action. Additionally, in his case-in-chief, plaintiff testified about matters raised by appellant in her answer to the complaint. According to plaintiff, the conditions that appellant complained of did not exist when he acquired the property in 1995. Plaintiff had the roof of the premises repaired in December 1999. It was not until appellant filed her answer to the complaint that plaintiff became aware of appellant's complaints. Appellant did not mention the condition of the premises when plaintiff spoke with appellant about the September rent or when appellant mailed plaintiff the September rent after expiration of the period stated in the three-day notice. After receipt of appellant's answer, plaintiff had the roof and the interior of the premises repaired.

According to the engrossed statement on appeal, appellant testified that the following conditions existed in the premises during September 2000: "the carpet was torn and dirty throughout the property, there were leaks around some of the windows[,] that the bathtub overflow valve leaked badly which had caused the sub-flooring under the tub to deteriorate, and that the thermostat for the heater did not work properly." Additionally, appellant testified that the roof to the premises had leaked during the entire term of her tenancy and, as a result, personal property had been damaged. It was appellant's contention that even though she provided plaintiff with both written and oral notice of the conditions that

CASE

existed at the premises, plaintiff had failed to make repairs with the exception of "restoring hot water to the property." In support of her testimony, appellant offered a series of exhibits which were received into evidence. Seven of the exhibits were letters from appellant to plaintiff for the time period starting on March 14, 1996, and ending on March 15, 2000, wherein appellant complained in each letter about the roof leaking when it rains, and other conditions in the apartment. The exhibits also included a series of photographs depicting the roof; water damage inside the closet, bathroom and bedroom; the bathroom with a portion of the wall exposed, crack in the sink and bathtub overflow valve; exterior window frames; carpeting worn or missing to the extent that the floorboards are visible; and pictures taken from underneath the house that include missing floorboards underneath the bathtub.

In rebuttal, plaintiff denied receiving letters from appellant concerning the premises, and reiterated his lack of knowledge as to appellant's complaints regarding the condition of the premises until receipt of her answer to the complaint. Plaintiff added that he had not been inside the premises since 1995 and did not have a key to the residence. To support his testimony, plaintiff offered some exhibits including before-and-after photographs of repairs he had undertaken upon learning of appellant's complaints.

The trial court specifically found that "the premises had conditions requiring repairs by the plaintiff during September 2000, that plaintiff had been aware of those conditions and had failed to correct them." The trial court also found that although the conditions requiring correction affected the habitability of the premises, the conditions were not "substantial" under Code of Civil Procedure section 1174.2. Nevertheless, the trial court concluded that the existence of the conditions entitled appellant to a rent reduction in the amount of $200 for the month of September. Finally the trial court entered judgment for plaintiff for possession of the premises, rent in the reduced amount of $629, damages of $70, and costs of $119.

The issue presented by this appeal is whether the trial court misapplied the law when it entered judgment for the plaintiff after finding a nonsubstantial breach of the warranty of habitability that justified a $200 reduction in the tenant's rent.

Preliminarily, this court must determine the proper standard for reviewing the trial court's conclusion that the conditions which existed at the premises were not "substantial" within the meaning of Code of Civil Procedure section 1174.2.

The decisive evidence regarding the condition of the premises, with a few exceptions, was not contested by plaintiff. Plaintiff primarily relied upon lack of knowledge of the defects in response to appellant's breach of warranty of habitability defense. In fact, plaintiff submitted his own set of before- and-after photographs to demonstrate his efforts to correct the problems.

When the facts of a case are undisputed, appellate courts are confronted with a question of law and are not bound by the findings of the trial court. (*Mole-Richardson v. Franchise Tax Board* (1990) 220 Cal.App.3d 889, 894, 269 Cal.Rptr. 662.) Thus, we are required to independently determine whether the trial court was correct in finding that the breach was not substantial under Code of Civil Procedure section 1174.2. Alternatively, applying the substantial evidence standard, the trial court's finding that the conditions existing in the apartment were not substantial is not supported by the evidence.

The California Supreme *Court in Green v. Superior Court* (1974) 10 Cal.3d 616, 639, 111 Cal.Rptr. 704, 517 P.2d 1168, held that a tenant who successfully proves that the landlord has breached the warranty of habitability is entitled not only to maintain possession of the premises but also to a reduction of rent corresponding to the reduced value of the premises. The *Green* court further held that a tenant is not entitled to a reduction in rent for minor violations that do not materially affect a tenant's health and safety. (*Id.* at p. 638, 111 Cal.Rptr. 704, 517 P.2d 1168.)

The *Green* decision is codified in Code of Civil Procedure section 1174.2. Under this statutory scheme, when a tenant raises breach of the warranty of habitability as an affirmative defense in an unlawful detainer case, the trial court is required to determine whether a substantial breach has occurred. If the court finds proof of a substantial breach, the court is then mandated to do the following: reduce the rent to reflect the breach; give the tenant the right to possession conditioned upon the tenant paying the reduced rental rate; order that the rent remain reduced until the repairs are made; and award costs and attorney fees to the tenant if permitted under the law and the contract between the parties. The trial court may also order the landlord to make repairs. If the tenant fails to pay rent in the amount ordered and within the time period set by the court, the trial court is then required to award possession and to issue judgment for the landlord. (Code Civ. Proc., § 1174.2, subd. (a).) The landlord is also entitled to possession and judgment in his favor if the court determines that there has been no substantial breach of Civil Code section 1941 or the warranty of habitability. (Code Civ. Proc., § 1174.2, subd. (b).) "Substantial breach" is defined to mean the "failure of the landlord to comply with applicable building and housing code standards which materially affect health and safety." (Code Civ. Proc., § 1174.2, subd. (c).)

Civil Code section 1941.1 defines a dwelling as untenantable for human occupancy "if it substantially lacks . . . ¶(a) Effective waterproofing and weather protection of roof and exterior walls, including unbroken windows and doors. (b) Plumbing . . . ¶maintained in good working order¶. . . . ¶(d) Heating facilities . . . maintained in good working order¶. . . . ¶(h) Floors . . . maintained in good repair."

Appellant has requested that this court take judicial notice of the legislative history of Code of Civil Procedure section 1174.2 in order to establish that it was the legislative intent that a tenant would not be entitled to a reduction of rent unless the landlord's breach of the warranty of habitability was substantial or material. Appellant's request for judicial notice is denied on the ground

that, under the general principles of statutory construction, judicial notice of the legislative intent would be inappropriate. In interpreting a statute, a reviewing court is first guided by the language of the statute. If the language is clear and unambiguous, there is no need to examine the legislative intent. It is only when the words of the statute are ambiguous that we look to the legislative intent.(*In re Luke W.* (2001)88 Cal.App.4th 650, 655, 105 Cal.Rptr.2d 905; *People v. Mom* (2000) 80 Cal.App.4th 1217, 1221, 96 Cal.Rptr.2d 172.)

Here the words of the statute are clear and unambiguous, a tenant is entitled to a reduction of rent only upon a showing of a substantial breach of the warranty of habitability or of Civil Code section 1941. As previously stated, the evidence was undisputed that the premises were not properly waterproofed from the outside elements, that the roof leaked to the extent that the rain damaged the inside walls of the property, portions of the wall were not waterproofed, that portions of the wall were visible in the bathroom, and that the thermostat was inoperative. These conditions are clearly visible in the photographs entered into evidence at the trial. Furthermore, these conditions are not merely cosmetic or aesthetic, but affect the health and safety of the tenant.

Appellant, having prevailed on her affirmative defense, was entitled pursuant to Code of Civil Procedure section 1174.2, subdivision (a) to possession of the premises and a conditional judgment in her favor.

The judgment is reversed. Appellant to recover costs on appeal.

Case Review Question

Hyatt v. Tedesco, 96 Cal.App.4th Supp. 62, 117 Cal.Rptr.2d 921(Cal.App. 2002). How would the case likely change, or would it, if the landlord could establish by clear and convincing evidence that the photos of the property were not taken until after the action was instituted against the defendant?

Assignment 10.5

For each of the following situations, identify the circumstances that represent the terms listed (terms may be used more than once).

- Mitigate.
- Habitability.
- Ordinary repairs.
- Latent defect.
- Patent defect.
- Constructive eviction.

Situation 1   Brad is walking along the front porch of his second-floor apartment to the stairs leading to the ground level. Two of the boards give way, and Brad falls through the porch to the ground. Brad's landlord refuses to repair the property, saying such repairs are Brad's responsibility.

Situation 2   Liz signed a lease for an apartment being built as part of a new complex. She signed the lease based on seeing a model apartment. On February 1, Liz picked up the keys to the new apartment at the realtor's office. The next morning, she arrived with her belongings. The only running water in the apartment was in the bathroom. Several electrical outlets were unfinished, with raw wires hanging out of the wall. The back door was completely blocked by construction debris. The kitchen countertops were missing entirely. Liz refused to move in and demanded that the landlord immediately return her $500 deposit and the two months' rent she had paid in advance. The landlord refused. Further, the landlord made no attempts to rent the apartment between February 1 and May 1, when Liz brought the landlord to court to recover the money.

Types of leasehold.   The type of leasehold is determined by the length of the lease, which will dictate whether the lease must be in writing under the statute of frauds. Generally, leases that are intended to extend beyond the period of one year and those that contain the option to purchase the leased property are required to be in writing. Shorter and less restrictive leases may be based on an oral agreement. However, it is always best to have the agreement in writing and signed by the parties to avoid future disputes as to the exact original terms of the agreement. (Figure 10.3 is a sample lease.)

Month-to-month tenancy.   Also called periodic tenancies, month-to-month tenancies are the least restrictive. The agreement between the parties is effective for one month. Unless otherwise stated, the month is presumed to begin on the first day and end on the last day of the calendar month following the date of the agreement. This type of lease automatically renews each month thereafter

FIGURE 10.3
Sample Lease

RESIDENCE LIFE
CONTRACT

NAME _____   SOCIAL SECURITY NUMBER_____
HOME (mailing) ADDRESS: _____   DATE OF BIRTH_____
_____   STATUS:
_____   1st year_____   2nd year_____
HOME TELEPHONE NUMBER _____   3rd year_____   4th year _____
PARENT'S NAMES: FATHER _____   MOTHER _____
_____

Resident hall occupancy shall be subject to all rules and regulations of the College, including those stated in the Student Handbook. A copy of the Student Handbook is available from the Student Services Office.

GENERAL REGULATIONS

The same obedience to the laws of the land and the conduct rules of the College expected of students generally is also expected of students as residence hall residents, visitors or guests. Therefore, acts contrary to federal, state or local laws constitute violations of residence hall rules. Recognition of the personal and property rights of others is expected of residence hall occupants, visitors and guests. Interference with the rights of other occupants to the use of their rooms for study or sleep constitutes violation of residence hall rules. Room-to-room canvassing and unauthorized defacing or permanently altering residence hall facilities is prohibited. Only these electrical devices may be used: coffee pots, self-contained popcorn poppers, hair dryers and electric blankets. See Handbook for further information on residence hall regulations.

Date _____

_____
Signature of Student

_____
Dean of Students

until one of the parties chooses to terminate it by giving the other party reasonable notice. The states have statutes indicating what reasonable notice is. In most cases, it is the equivalent of a one-month term and would therefore be one month. Generally, notice must be given on or before the first day of a term.

◆ **APPLICATION 10.9**

Assume an agreement automatically renews on the first day of each month. The tenant must give notice to quit on or before the first day of the term. If the tenant gives notice on or shortly before March 1, he or she can end the tenancy on March 31. If, however, the tenant gives notice on March 15, the tenancy will not end on March 31, and the tenant's responsibilities will continue until April 30.

Point for Discussion
♦   What do you think is the purpose of required notice to terminate?

Year-to-year tenancy.   The law is basically the same for agreements to lease on a year-to-year basis. Such agreements that will extend for more than one year are required to be in writing under the statute of frauds. This type of lease may renew each year unless otherwise stated, or it may require formal renewal, depending upon the terms of the agreement by the parties. The reasonable time to end a year-to-year lease is often specified in a state statute or in the agreement between the parties. A common number is three or six months. Many states have laws that limit the length of extended leases. Usually this is not a problem for landlords and tenants, because the limitation is often 100 years.

A tenant who remains in possession of the property beyond the agreed term without exercising an option to do so or without automatic renewal has no legal right to remain on the premises. Such persons are considered tenants at sufferance and can be evicted without notice. However, state statutes generally prescribe the procedure for eviction. The law does not permit "self-help." In other words, a person cannot be physically, forcibly removed from the premises by the property owner. The eviction must go through a court, and often, when physical eviction is ordered, it is overseen by law enforcement officers.

Tenancy at will.   An additional type of tenant is a tenant at will—one who enters or remains on the property with no certain terms of agreement. Consent of the owner is sufficient. Tenancy at will continues indefinitely and has no fixed term on which it will end. The amount of notice to end such a tenancy is usually set

Assignment 10.6

Examine the following lease provision and then answer the questions.

The lease term will begin on January 1, 2004, and will end on December 31, 2004. The tenant will pay lease payments of $800 payable in advance on the first day of each month commencing January 1, 2004, for a total lease payment of $9,600. This lease may be terminated by either party giving written notice to the other at least thirty (30) days prior to the expiration of the original or any renewal term thereof. Failure to give such notice shall constitute an automatic renewal of this lease for an additional term of the same duration at a lease amount subject to a three (3) percent increase over and above the lease amount of the immediately preceding term.

1. What type of leasehold exists?
2. On or before what date should notice be given to renew or vacate?
3. If the term is renewed the second year, when will that term end, what will be the amount of rent due, and what is the latest date to cancel the lease at the end of the second year?

by statute. Often reasonable notice is considered to be one month. This type of tenancy and tenancy at sufferance are the least desirable for the tenant because he or she may be required to vacate with very little or no notice.

Fixtures

Fixtures are articles of personal property that have become firmly attached to real property; they do not include houses and buildings. Fixtures are actually considered to be part of the real property in some respects because they have none of the characteristics of personal property, such as being ordinarily movable. Fixtures are those items of personal property that are affixed to the real property in such a way that they cannot be easily moved without damage to the real property, but are capable of being moved. Common examples of fixtures are items that have been physically incorporated into the structure but are removable, such as lighting and bathroom fixtures. Typically, fixtures are conveyed when the property is conveyed.

fixture
An item of personal property that has been affixed to real property for a specific purpose and in a semipermanent manner.

Disputes have arisen in the past as to what is and is not a fixture when the buyer and seller both want the personal property that is claimed to be a fixture. Generally, to determine whether something is a fixture, four things are considered: (1) intent, (2) mode of annexation, (3) adaptation, and (4) damage that will result if the object is removed (significant damage to the building indicates a fixture). Intent means the original intent of the party who attached the personal property to the real property.[34] If intent was to make the item a permanent attachment, the law would tend to consider the property to be a fixture. The mode of annexation is the actual method of attaching the fixture to the real property. Personal property that was attached in such a way that it cannot be removed without altering or damaging the real property has taken on the characteristic of a fixture. Finally, adaptation involves the function of the personal property. If the property has become attached in a way that it serves to benefit the real property in some functional way, it would be considered a fixture. The function need not be necessary, but it must directly enhance or benefit the property in some way other than its mere presence.

A special type of fixture is known as a trade fixture—an item of personal property attached to the real property for the purpose of benefiting the particular trade or business of the party who is responsible for attachment of the fixture.[35] For example, a man opening a dry-cleaning business would buy or lease property and install very specialized equipment. When he terminates ownership or possession, the presumption would be that the equipment he installed is a trade fixture and would not be conveyed with the real property, but would be removed by the owner of the trade fixture. Often, it is necessary to attach such items to the real property for practical purposes. In this example, however, because the equipment is necessary for the owner's livelihood, the owner is allowed to remove it when leaving the property. The owner of trade fixtures, however, has a duty to restore the real property substantially to the condition it was in before the trade fixtures were installed.

Assignment 10.7

Identify the following as a fixture, trade fixture, or personal property.

1. Popcorn machine at a movie theater.
2. Chandelier that is attached by screwing two wire nuts over the wires for the electrical connection at the base of the fixture.
3. Custom lighted sign for a restaurant erected in a concrete footing on a leased property.
4. Hot tub at a residence that has been built into an existing deck.
5. Storage shed that rests on a concrete slab.
6. Display light fixtures that a lighting store has wired and installed into the ceiling of a leased property.
7. Refrigerator located in a corner that has a custom wood door front made to match the cabinetry of a kitchen.
8. Walkin freezer installed in specially insulated walls for an ice cream shop at a leased property.

PERSONAL PROPERTY

personal property
Movable items that are not land or items permanently affixed to land. Personal property includes tangible (physical) and intangible items, such as rights of ownership in property held by others (e.g., bank accounts or ownership in legal entities such as stock). It does not include the rights to bring legal action against others, commonly known as a chose in action.

Personal property includes money, goods, and movable, tangible items.[36] Legally, personal property can be sold, lent, given, lost, stolen, abandoned, or altered. Personal property does not include land or, generally, items permanently attached to land such as permanent buildings, known as real property. Nor does it ordinarily include personal rights to certain intangible interests, such as the right to bring an action at law or equity (commonly called a chose in action). For example, if a person's car was damaged in an accident, the person could not sell the right to sue the person who caused the damage. Examples of intangible items that are considered to be personal property are patents and goodwill of a business, which are rights that are indirectly associated with movables.

Bailment

Bailment takes place when one party having possession of personal property (the bailor) temporarily delivers possession of the property to another party (the bailee). The delivery is made for a specific purpose and/or as part of a contract, with the understanding that the property will be cared for and returned to the original party upon demand.[37]

Specifically, the elements of a bailment are as follows:

1. Personal property.
2. Transferred by a party with the right to possession.
3. To a second party for a specific purpose and/or as part of the terms of a contract.

4. That the property will be protected.
5. That the original party has the right to reclaim the property.
6. In some cases, an additional element requires compensation in return for some act pertaining to the property.

States often have statutes that address bailment. Examples are safe deposit boxes and vehicle parking services (garages or valet parking). In the absence of statutes, general principles of common law principles of bailment apply.

Types of bailment.   Bailments generally fall into one of two categories. The type of bailment depends on the rights and duties of the bailee.

Gratuitous bailment.   Gratuitous bailment occurs when one party is benefited by the bailment without obligation or benefit to the other.[38] An example of sole benefit of bailor is free storage of winter clothing by a dry cleaners. Allowing the use of one's property by another without expecting compensation, such as lending a lawnmower, is an example of bailment that benefits only the bailee. In either situation, the bailee (party receiving the property) has the duty to exercise ordinary care to protect the bailed property. Ordinary care includes reasonable precautions under the circumstances.

Mutual benefit bailment.   A bailment for hire or compensation (payment of some type) is the most frequent kind of bailment. Such bailment encompasses all occurrences of a temporary nature where one party promises to pay some sort of compensation in return for a second party's safekeeping of personal property that belongs to the first party. In turn, the receiving party will return the property upon demand or at a time provided for by contract in exchange for the compensation.[39] Additional terms of the bailment may require the performance of some duty other than safekeeping of the property. Often, bailments include the duty to clean or repair property for compensation. An example is giving one's watch to a jeweler for repair. The jeweler is responsible for the care as well as the repair of the watch in exchange for compensation by the owner.

Whether property has been bailed is based upon the giving party's demonstrated intent to divide the rights of possession and ownership.[40] For example, leaving a vehicle in someone else's care is not considered a bailment unless the keys are turned over, since without keys to a vehicle, the receiving party cannot exercise the control over the car associated with the right of possession. If the car is parked but the owner retains the keys, the relationship is one of a lease or license dependent upon the terms and duration. The owner leases or has a license to use the space in which to park the car but retains possession of the car at all times through the car's keys. In bailment, the owner retains the title and right to ownership of the property but temporarily gives up the right to exercise possession.

When faced with a decision of whether a bailment exists and, if so, what type of bailment exists, a court will examine the relationship of the parties and determine the reasonable expectations under the circumstances. For example, if the court finds, based on the circumstances, that the two parties are close friends and often exchange property with each other, it is likely the court will find the reasonable expectation to be a gratuitous bailment, with no duty beyond ordinary care and no requirement of compensation.

Generally, the duty of a bailee is only to possess and protect the bailment from damage unless other conditions are specified by an agreement between the parties. Such an agreement can be inferred from the circumstances, and in cases of a bailment for mutual benefit, the duty to care for the bailed property is greater than in a gratuitous bailment. For example, taking a coat to a dry cleaners implies that the bailor wants the coat cleaned and that the bailee will clean it in addition to holding it in safekeeping for the bailor. A compensated bailor is expected to take greater steps than mere ordinary care to protect the property. The compensation is, at least in part, for the ensured well-being of the property.

Lost and Mislaid Property

Lost property is property that is separated from its owner involuntarily and accidentally,[41] whereas mislaid property is property that is intentionally left in a place and later forgotten.[42] Most states have statutes as well as common law principles that govern the rights and obligations of the finder of lost or mislaid property. Regarding the statutory law, some jurisdictions treat the finder of lost or mislaid property as a constructive bailee for benefit of bailor.[43] In such cases, it is implied that the finder is holding the property for its true owner. The bailee has a duty to care for the property until it is recovered and, depending on the statute, may or may not have the right to receive compensation for costs of the care of the property. If a statute permits recovery of compensation, the duties will be those of a bailee for hire, which are somewhat greater than those of a gratuitous bailee.

Other jurisdictions do not consider lost or mislaid property to be a bailment. In such states, the finder has the right to claim possession and ownership. In the case of lost property, claims to the property may be made by the finder wherever the property is found.[44] In contrast, mislaid property belongs to the owner of the premises where it is located (this party is not always the finder of the property,[45] since the mislaid property was intentionally left on the premises belonging to the owner). The exception to this is the concept of treasure trove.[46] When items of great monetary value are found, they may be claimed by the finder regardless of whether they were lost or mislaid. For treasure trove to apply, the item must usually be cash or its equivalent (e.g., coins, gold, or bullion). In any event, a person who finds personal property having value should always consult the law of his or her jurisdiction to determine rights and obligations with respect to the property.

Abandoned Property

If property has been abandoned, it must be shown that the owner gave up possession with the intent to give up dominion, control, and title to the property.[47] If so, the finder can take over possession and be declared its owner so long as the intent to dominate, control, and exercise title is continuously shown. For example, one cannot come across an item such as a piece of jewelry on the beach and ignore it and later try to claim ownership as the first finder with rights superior to another who also found it and identified it as valuable. It must be apparent to others that one intends to make the property one's own.

Confused Property

An additional aspect of property whose ownership is unclear deals with items that become confused with other similar items. An example is money. If several persons put their money in the same place and a party alleges that a certain portion of a sum of money is actually that person's property alone and that party is responsible for its becoming confused with the other money, the burden of proof is on the party claiming right to a specific portion to establish what amount of money actually belongs to that party. In cases where the items become confused and the proof cannot be established as to particular rights, the value of the confused items is shared equally by those who can establish that they are entitled to any share.[48]

Actions to Recover Property or Its Value

Many legal disputes over property arise when there is disagreement over the rights of possession or ownership. In cases dealing with persons who claim to have somehow lost possession of their property, there are several legal alternatives to regain the property. Of course, if the property was stolen, criminal laws apply. If a contract existed between the original and subsequent possessor regarding the property, an action for breach of contract may exist. In addition, other civil actions provide methods to regain wrongfully obtained property, or at least its value.

Conversion. Conversion is the basis for an action when one party receives possession of the property of another and wrongfully holds the property.[49] This can occur in one of two ways. In the first instance, a party may seize control of property without permission. In the second, and more common, instance, a party may refuse to return property that was previously bailed.

In the case of a bailment that becomes a conversion, there may also be a cause of action for the tort of negligence or for breach of contract if either element can be proven. (A further discussion of negligence and breach of contract is presented in Chapters 11 and 9, respectively.) The owner is also permitted to allege a lawsuit based on conversion that requires only proof of wrongful possession of the property by another and that the intent of the other party is to exercise control and to exclude the owner from rightful possession and ownership of the property. If the owner proves conversion, the property may be recovered; or if the property has been altered or disposed of, its value may be recovered. If the property is returned, the owner may also recover the fair market value of the use of the property during the time he or she was deprived of it. In many cases where conversion is applicable, there may also be a criminal action available to punish the party responsible for taking the property.

Trespass to chattels (personal property).   This type of action for return of property occurs when a party substantially interferes with another's possession or ownership of property. The primary difference between conversion and trespass to chattels is that in trespass to chattels, there is no need to show intent of the second party to exercise control of the property. It is only necessary to show that the second party dispossessed the first party of his or her property permanently or for a substantial period of time.[50]

As in the action for conversion, the party claiming trespass can claim the fair market value of the property. If the property was ultimately returned, a claim can still be made for the fair market value of its use during the period the true owner was denied access to the property.

Assignment 10.8

> Read the following information and identify the nature of the property in the possession of Virgil and what, if any, action might be taken by the housemates to retrieve the property or its value.
>
> Virgil is a member of a college fraternity. He resides in a house shared by several members of the fraternity. Virgil and two other housemates stay in the house through the summer. Four other students graduate and move out. Four additional students leave for the summer with the intent to return in the fall. Throughout the summer, Virgil finds a number of personal items around the house. He takes a stereo left by one of the students gone for the summer to a girlfriend's house and installs it with the intent to leave it there. He uses the house petty cash fund to pay for food for a party. This fund was something all housemates contributed to in equal shares each month to cover the costs of household supplies for cleaning, paper products, and condiments. He takes the sheets from the bed of one of the graduating students and a poster from another and puts them in his own room. While cleaning out the house and garage, he locates an electric scooter that one of the graduating students had been unable to locate before moving. He also finds about $10 in change in the couches in the house.

Replevin.   Some jurisdictions still provide for the common law action of replevin, developed in England and still a recognized cause of action in many states. The purpose of an action in replevin is to regain possession of the actual property that was wrongfully taken, and not its value. This type of equity action is based on a claim that money damages are insufficient to remedy the wrong.[51]

To bring an action for replevin, it is necessary to prove the following:

1. Plaintiff has right to immediate possession, providing plaintiff and defendant do not both have right to immediate possession.
2. Property in issue must be personal property.
3. Property must be unlawfully possessed and detained by defendant at the time the action is commenced. (The defendant need not have unlawfully taken the property.)

◆ **APPLICATION 10.10**

Otis owns a prize-winning champion bloodline hound. Emily is hired to groom the hound and refuses to return it.

    a. If Emily intends to make herself the owner of the hound and benefit from that ownership, Otis would have an action for conversion against her.

    b. If Emily deliberately allows the hound to run away, Otis would have an action for trespass to chattels.

    c. If the hound was a longtime family pet and mere money could not replace its worth to Otis and his family, Otis could have an action for replevin on the theory that money cannot adequately compensate the loss.

Point for Discussion

◆   What type of legal relationship originally existed between Otis and Emily?

Assignment 10.9

Create a factual setting that is an example of each of the following:

a.   Gratuitous bailment.
b.   Lost property.
c.   Mislaid property.
d.   Confused property.
e.   Property subject to an action for conversion.
f.   Property subject to an action for trespass to chattels.
g.   Property subject to an action for replevin.

▬▬▬ **Ethical Considerations**

Pervasive throughout property law are ethical principles. Because most property agreements are contractual in nature, the same ethical concepts of honesty and fair dealing apply to property transactions as to other types of contracts. In addition, some aspects of property lease or ownership involve long-term relationships between the interested parties. As a result, the parties have an ongoing duty to consider the legal and ethical expectations of the other when taking action with respect to the property. A landlord should make defects in rental property known to a tenant. Additionally, the landlord has the obligation not only legally but also as a matter of business ethics to keep the property habitable. One who sells property to another makes certain representations about the condition of the property. Failure to do this in an honest manner not only can have legal implications but also reflects on the seller's ethical standards and may, in fact, affect future transactions. Ethics in property—and in all activities, for that matter—not only involve moral standards of the individual but also have a direct effect on professional interactions in society.

Question

If a property seller knows of a significant defect in property but the buyer does not ask about it, does the property seller (owner) have an *ethical* (not necessarily legal) obligation to tell the buyer about the defect?

Ethical Circumstance

Max Broader is a jeweler. A woman comes in with a diamond bracelet and asks that Max repair it. He originally sold the bracelet to the woman and knows it to be worth well over $2,500. He has done much business with the woman over the years and does not issue her a receipt for the bracelet. He simply tells her the bracelet will be ready the following week. The next day, Max reads in the newspaper that the woman suffered a stroke, causing a car accident shortly after leaving his store. The article reports that the woman recalls nothing of the entire day of the accident. He waits and no one from the family comes to claim the bracelet. He assumes they are unaware she left it with him. Consider Max's legal and ethical obligations.

CHAPTER SUMMARY

Property law is a very complex area and is still changing today. It is important to remember that principles of property law may vary somewhat from state to state. Consequently, it is necessary to examine the laws of a particular state before evaluating the rights or obligations with respect to personal or real property. This chapter has discussed basic principles as they have developed until now. However, as changes continue to occur, it is necessary to keep abreast of modifications of the law of property.

A final note to remember in all property transactions is that each of the areas discussed in the text, when relevant, should be thoroughly addressed in clear and written terms in any document that represents the property interests of owners and others with an interest or rights in the property. Most legal disputes

occur as the result of misunderstandings at the time of the transactions. Such misunderstandings can be avoided through prudent consideration of all pertinent issues by each party.

The basic tenets of property law are that real property involves all land and items so attached to the land that they are immovable. Personal property includes those movable items in which ownership can be readily transferred and actual possession exchanged. Fixtures are those items of personal property that have been affixed to real property in such a way that they cannot be removed without damage to the real property.

Interests in personal property can be affected by bailment or by losing, mislaying, or abandoning the property by the owner. Nonowners can obtain the property by sale, conversion, or trespass or by finding it. Real property interests can be affected by sale, inheritance, devise, easements, trespass, or adverse possession. The remedy for one whose property or interest in it has been altered depends upon the type of property and the manner in which the property was affected. In some cases, the original owner may actually lose his or her interest in the property if care is not taken to protect it.

REVIEW QUESTIONS

1. How is real property different from personal property?
2. What is a fixture?
3. Describe an easement.
4. What is the right of survivorship?
5. Distinguish abandoned property from lost property.
6. What is a warranty of habitability?
7. What is adverse possession and why is it permitted?
8. What is constructive eviction?
9. Distinguish a mutual benefit bailment from a gratuitous benefit in terms of legal rights and responsibilities.
10. What is a non-freehold estate?

CHAPTER TERMS

fee simple
fixture
forced share
freehold estate

joint tenancy
life estate
non-freehold estate
personal property

real property
right of survivorship
tenancy by the entirety
tenancy in common

RELEVANT LINKS

Real Property, Probate and Trust Law Journal
www.abanet.org/rppt/journal.html
RentLaw.com
www. rentlaw.com

Personal Property Law
www.hg.org.perprop.html
Findlaw for Students
www.stu.findlaw.com/journals

INTERNET ASSIGNMENT 10.1

Using the internet, locate a form lease agreement.

NOTES

1. Statsky, *Legal Thesaurus/Dictionary* (St. Paul: West, 1982).
2. Id.
3. Boyer, *Survey of the Law of Property,* 3rd ed. (St. Paul: West, 1981), p. 12.
4. Id.
5. Id.
6. Id.
7. Id.

8. *Wagman v. Carmel,* 601 F.Supp 1012, 1015 (E.D.Pa. 1985).

9. *Bouska v. Bouska,* 159 Kan. 276, 153 P.2d 923 (1944).

10. *Daniel v. Wright,* 352 F.Supp. 1, 3 (D.D.C. 1972).

11. 63 Am.Jur.2d, Property.

12. *Sneed v. Weber,* 307 S.W.2d 681, 690 (Mo.App. 1958).

13. Powell & Rohan, *Powell on Property:* Matthew Bender (1968); Restatement of the Law of Property Sec. 404, American Law Institute.

14. *Putnam v. Dickinson,* 142 N.W.2d 111, 124 (N.D. 1966).

15. *Huggins v. Castle Estates, Inc.* 36 N.Y.2d 427, 369 N.Y.S. 2d 80, 330 N.E.2d 48, 51 (1975).

16. 40 Annot., 27 A.L.R. 2d 444.

17. Annot., 36 A.L.R.4th 544.

18. 8 American Jurisprudence Sec. 2, Bailments.

19. Ch. 12, Torts, Infra.

20. Annot. A.L.R. 3d 1294.

21. See note 18, page 239.

22. *Carpenter v. Coles,* 75 Minn. 9, 77 N.W. 424 (1898); *Thomas v. Mrkonich,* 247 Minn. 481, 78 N.W.2d 386 (1956).

23. See note 34, Sec. 1014[2] Annot. 96 A.L.R.3d Sec. 1014[2].

24. See note 23, Sec. 865.6[4][c][ii][B].

25. Id.

26. *Thacker v. J.C. Penney Co.,* 254 F.2d 672, 676 (8th Cir. 1958).

27. Id.

28. *Paul v. Traders & General Ins. Co.,* 127 So.2d 801, 802, (La.App. 1961).

29. See note 23, Sec. 633.33.

30. Id.; 42 U.S.C.A. § 2000a et seq.

31. Rose, *Landlord & Tenants:* (Transactions Books, 1973), p. 14.

32. Id., pp. 38–41.

33. Id.

34. Annot. 96 A.L.R.3d 1155.

35. See note 16, page 512.

36. Id.

37. *Ralston Steel Car Co. v. Ralston,* 112 Ohio St. 306, 147 N.E. 513 (1925).

38. See note 18.

39. Id. See note 18.

40. Id.

41. *United States Fire Ins. Co. v. Paramount Fur Services, Inc.,* 168 Ohio St. 431, 156 N.E.2d 121 (1959).

42. *Favorite v. Miller,* 176 Conn. 310, 407 A.2d 974 (1978).

43. *Paset v. Old Orchard Bank & Trust Co.,* 62 Ill.App.3d 534, 19 Ill.Dec. 389, 393, 378, N.E.2d 1264, 1268 (1978).

44. 8 American Jurisprudence, Sec. 62, Bailments.

45. See note 8.

46. See note 8.

47. *Schley v. Couch,* 155 Tex. 195, 284 S.W.d 2d 333, 335 (1955).

48. See note 7.

49. Annot., 39 A.L.R. 553.

50. 63 American Jurisprudence Sec. 14, Property.

51. *Ready-Mix Concrete Co. v. Rape,* 98 Ga.App. 503, 106 S.E.2d 429, 435 (1958).

For additional resources, please visit our Web site at www.westlegalstudies.com

CHAPTER 11

Torts

CHAPTER OBJECTIVES

After reading this chapter, you should be able to:

- Distinguish negligence from intentional torts.
- Distinguish negligence from strict liability.
- Explain the applicability of respondent superior in tort cases.
- List the defenses to claims of negligence.
- Discuss the applicability of the doctrine of last clear chance.

- List the types of action for defamation.
- List the elements of negligence.
- List the requirements for application of res ipsa loquiter.
- Distinguish the torts of assault and battery.
- Describe employment discrimination.

Tort law encompasses a wide range of subjects, including most subjects of law not directly related to contract principles (see Chapter 9) or criminal law(see Chapter 14). An exploration of some of these subjects may be the best way to explain or define the place of torts in the American legal system.

WHAT IS A TORT?

Legal authorities have been unable to agree on a single definition of a tort, although most would accept the following:

> A civil (as opposed to criminal) wrong (other than a breach of contract) that has caused harm to person or property.[1] (Statsky, *Legal Thesaurus/Dictionary*. West, 1982)

This definition cannot begin to encompass everything that constitutes the law of torts in this country. Fittingly, it concentrates on what is not a tort.

By definition, tort law involves only civil matters, including disputes between individual citizens and businesses or governments (state or federal) over private or proprietary rights. In other words, the parties in a tort case are involved in a dispute over rights of an individual's person or property or the property of the government. Tort law does not include criminal matters (matters in which the government acts against a party charged with a crime that injures the public good and, in many cases, specific citizens). Criminal law encompasses cases ranging from speeding in a vehicle to murder in the first degree. Tort claims that involve the government are actions regarding the value of property owned by the government or actions involving disputes between government officials and private citizens over private rights, for example, a car accident involving a government official driving a government vehicle and a private citizen driving his or her private vehicle. Dependent upon fault for the accident, one party might sue the other for personal injuries and property damage to the vehicle. This particular action would not encompass any criminal charges that might arise from the accident. Such charges would be dealt with in a separate criminal case.

A tort does not include breach of contract. Although contract actions are included in the definition of civil law, the elements of a lawsuit in tort are different from the elements of a case in contract. Contract actions occur when two or more parties voluntarily enter into a legal relationship with certain rights and obligations and subsequently a dispute arises as to the nature or extent of those rights or obligations. In contrast, a tort arises when a party infringes on the rights of another person (or government) when there was no permission or agreement to do so and causes harm as a result of that infringement. This does not mean, however, that the parties were never involved in a relationship. Rather, it means that the action (tort) committed by one party was without permission or approval of the other party irrespective of the parties' relationship.

The formal definition of a tort indicates that some harm must occur. This is an important element of the definition. No matter how seriously one party may infringe upon the rights of another party, unless there is a verifiable harm that requires some form of compensation to repair it, there is no action in tort.

The individual circumstances of a situation have a great influence on the viability of a lawsuit. In an attempt to provide a better understanding of tort law and the role circumstances play in it, the following sections explore the development of tort law and some specific types of torts that are commonly litigated in this country.

THE DEVELOPMENT OF TORT LAW

Like much of the law in the majority of U.S. jurisdictions, the American concept of tort law began in England. During the Middle Ages, the royal government instituted what came to be known as forms of action.[2] These forms were similar to modern laws that state the types of lawsuits that can and cannot be brought by a citizen. When someone had a grievance against another, the injured party was required to file a complaint stating the facts and, specifically, which form of action (law) allowed him or her to bring the lawsuit. The forms were very limited and vague as to the types of conduct allowed as the basis for a lawsuit. Thus, it was often difficult to know whether one had a successful legal claim against another.

Trespass and Trespass on the Case

Two of the most commonly employed forms of action were trespass and trespass on the case.[3] To avoid confusion, it is important to note that during the Middle Ages the word *trespass* meant "wrong" rather than its current meaning of intrusion into another's property. The difference between trespass and trespass on the case was at first quite simple. A lawsuit based on trespass meant that the alleged guilty party had acted in such a way that the party bringing the lawsuit was directly injured because of the wrongful conduct. Trespass on the case, on the other hand, was appropriate when the injury was indirect. Consider the following scenarios:

1. A farmer is building a new fence for his pasture. He takes the old fence posts and throws them alongside the adjacent road. Just as he throws a large post, a horse and rider round the bend and are struck and injured by the post.
2. A farmer is building a new fence for his pasture. He takes the old fence posts and throws them alongside the adjacent road. Some of the posts actually land in the road. That night as a neighbor is returning home in the dark, he trips over a fence post and lands unconscious in the ditch by the road.

Scenario 1 illustrates an action of trespass, whereas scenario 2 is an action of trespass on the case. The difference is that the injury in the second example did not result directly from the farmer's throwing the post. Rather, the injury occurred as an indirect result. The direct result of the farmer's action was the post landing in the road creating a dangerous condition, and as a further (or indirect) result of that, the neighbor was injured.

Through the years, lawsuits were filed on this type of basis in both England and America. It became increasingly difficult, however, to distinguish between trespass and trespass on the case. In addition, insufficient attention was being paid to whether the act was intentional. In response, the courts and lawmaking authorities attempted to define the terms, but the confusion continued.

Liability of Parties

In the early 1800s, several things happened that led to the development of tort law as it exists in the United States today. At that time, the law in effect made certain persons dealing with the public liable (responsible) for injuries caused by them.[4] For example, doctors and smiths (metal workers) were automatically considered to be liable as a matter of contract with their customers. Others, such as innkeepers and carriers (stagecoaches and the like), were liable by legislative statutes for failure to provide adequately for the safety of their customers. As the populations of urban areas increased, carriage accidents among private citizens rose dramatically, as did injuries from employment as the industrial revolution got under way. These developments led the American courts in the 1820s to accept the action of negligence as a basis for liability.[5] Negligence applied to all persons, including parties not previously included by contract or law, in disputes over injuries received as the result of a person's failure to act carefully in the interest of others.

Shortly after the emergence of negligence as a legal concept, the courts began to develop and refine related bases for liability, such as the actions for intentional torts and, later, strict liability. Hand in hand with these came the creation of legal defenses for conduct that would otherwise be considered improper.

Increase in Tort Claims

In recent years, the term *litigation explosion* has become commonplace. With the increase in technology, industry, and population, the number of lawsuits has increased dramatically. While property and contract suits are prevalent, much of the focus of law has been on the increasingly large number of tort claims filed each year. A primary reason for the attention given to these claims are the effects of such claims on the economy as a whole. Many actions in tort are defended by insurance companies that insure the defendant, for example, automobile insurance that covers claims that the insured person caused damage with the insured automobile. Claims of professional liability, premises liability (home or business owners), and so on, all contribute to the suits in which the cost of defending a lawsuit is borne by the insurance company. The chain reaction is that as costs for the insurance company increase, costs of insurance premiums go up. As these increases are passed on in costs to consumers they contribute to overall inflation.

In response to this "explosion," many legislatures have adopted laws that place restrictions on the amounts that can be awarded in certain types of tort claims and sometimes even on the circumstances under which certain tort claims can be filed. With the increased amount of litigation in tort law has come a refinement of many tort concepts into well-established doctrines. Although many of these doctrines are examined later in the chapter, keep in mind that as society changes and evolves, so does its law.

TERMINOLOGY IN TORTS

It is helpful at this point to examine certain essential terms frequently encountered in the law of torts. The following list, though not exhaustive, provides an initial explanation of some of the more commonly employed terminology in torts.

- *Negligence.* The term **negligence** is the basis for those causes of action among parties who claim (1) that a legal duty was owed by another; (2) that by failing to engage in reasonable conduct (of a standard that would prevent the harm), that duty was violated or breached; and (3) that as a proximate result of that breach, the complaining party was significantly injured. Specifically, the elements that must be proven by facts introduced to the court to sustain a cause of action in negligence are (1) duty, (2) the standard of care, (3) breach of the standard, and (4) damage proximately caused by the breach.

- *Reasonable conduct.* Throughout the law of negligence, conduct of the alleged wrongdoer is measured against the standard of reasonableness (what would have been proper). Most often, the actions or omissions of a party accused of negligence are measured against what the conduct of a reasonable person would have been. The conduct of a reasonable person varies with the circumstances of each case. However, this person is always presumed to be one who would act with care and attention to all details that affect the situation. **Reasonable conduct** requires the actor to evaluate the surroundings, all benefits, and all risks and to respond in the most careful manner. This measurement of the reasonableness of the alleged liable person does not usually take into account the mental state of the actor. It does, however, take into account the intelligence, age, experience, and physical conditions over which the actor has no control.

- *Foreseeability.* In negligence, one cannot be held responsible for an injury caused as a result of one's conduct unless the risk of that injury was apparent (foreseeable). Foreseeability is determined by a finding of whether the risk of harm was known to the actor by constructive knowledge. This finding is generally based on what the actor knew or, by reasonable examination of the situation, should have known. Foreseeability plays a key role in determining what the reasonable standard of care should have been. A person must be able to foresee an occurrence before he or she can be held responsible for it.

- *Proximate cause.* The necessary relationship between a breach of a duty and claimed damage in a negligence action is **proximate cause.** To sustain an action for negligence, the injured party must prove that the injuries occurred as a consequence of the breach of the duty by the actor both as a matter of fact and as a matter of law.

negligence
An act or failure to act toward another when (1) a duty was owed to the other person; (2) the act or failure to act was less than a reasonable person would have done under the circumstances; (3) the act or failure to act was the direct cause of injury to the other person; and (4) the injury resulted in measurable financial, physical, or emotional damage to the other person.

reasonable conduct
That action or nonaction that is appropriate under the circumstances when all risks and benefits are taken into account.

proximate cause
The direct cause that is sufficient to produce a result. There can be no other intervening force that occurs independently and prior to the result that is also sufficient to produce the result.

intentional tort

An act that the actor knows or should know, with substantial certainty, will cause harm to another.

strict liability

Liability without fault. Applied in situations where the intention or neglect of the party is immaterial. The mere performance of the act will result in liability.

◆ *Intentional tort.* This category of torts differs from negligence in several respects. The primary distinguishing factor is the element of intent. In an **intentional tort,** it is necessary for the actor to have the intent to engage in conduct that will, with near certainty, produce a result that invades the rights of or injures another. It is necessary not that the intent be to invade or injure but that the actor know or should know that the action will in all probability produce such an invasion or injury.

◆ *Strict liability.* A narrower (but steadily growing) area of tort law in the United States is **strict liability.** It is not concerned with fault or intent to cause injury. Rather, it is applied in situations where the actor derives some benefit from an activity that is extremely dangerous to other parties who have no control over the situation. The reasoning behind strict liability is that one who benefits from such a dangerous activity should shoulder the responsibility for injuries to innocent persons or property caused by it regardless of how carefully the actor conducts the activity.

Throughout the remainder of the chapter, additional peripheral terms will be introduced that play an important role in the various aspects of tort law. It is important to note that although these terms have general meanings accepted by most, some states have employed variations of these definitions when developing their own tort law.

NEGLIGENCE

In an action for negligence, the injured party must plead, and ultimately prove at trial, facts of an occurrence showing that each of the necessary elements existed. Only after such proof will the defendant (the party who is alleged to be at fault) be required to compensate the plaintiff for the injuries. The following elements[6] must be proven:

1. The actor (defendant) owed a *duty* to the injured party (plaintiff) to refrain from conduct that would cause injury.
2. By failing to exercise a care of a reasonable *standard,* the actor *breached* his or her duty.
3. The breach of the duty *proximately caused* an *injury* to the plaintiff.
4. The plaintiff's injuries are significant enough to be *measurable* and warrant *compensation* from the actor.

The Concept of Duty

The first element that must be proven in any negligence action is that of duty. Specifically, the injured party (plaintiff) must demonstrate that the actor (defendant) owed a duty of acting with care for the plaintiff's safety or well-being. It is commonly accepted that all persons have a general duty not to act negligently and thereby harm others around them. This general duty also includes the responsibility to act carefully for one's own safety under the circumstances.

It should be noted that there are occasions when the duty is to act rather than to refrain from acting. Therefore, failing to act—an omission—can also be a violation of a person's duty. An example of such an omission is a situation where danger to another is within a person's control and the person fails to exercise that control even though he or she has the opportunity to do so.

APPLICATION 11.1

Zoe is driving down a residential street at a speed of 40 mph in a 25 mph zone. Looking ahead she sees two children on rollerblades. She has a duty from the outset to drive within the 25 mph speed limit. Secondly, upon seeing a potentially dangerous speed, she has a further duty to reduce her speed to pass the children safely in the event they enter her lane of driving.

Point for Discussion
♦   What duty, if any, do the rollerbladers have?

Range of Possible Injury

To prove the element of duty in a negligence action, several things must be shown. The first is that the defendant owed a duty to the plaintiff who was injured. It is not necessary to show that the defendant owed a duty to this particular individual. Rather, it must be shown that the defendant knew or should have known that others within a certain range (which included the plaintiff) could be affected by his or her actions.

Two primary schools of thought have developed as to the area this range should include. One theory is often called the Zone of Danger,[7] which refers to the area that the defendant should reasonably expect or foresee his or her actions to affect. Consequently, no duty is owed, and no negligence can be shown for injuries that occur beyond the Zone of Danger. This means that usually there can be no recovery for injuries that are the result of remote or bizarre chain reaction events. Whether something is remote or not is generally determined by whether the defendant's conduct proximately caused the plaintiff's injuries. (Proximate cause is addressed in greater detail later.)

The second theory is the World-at-Large Approach,[8] which takes into account a much wider range. It requires the defendant to foresee more remote possibilities of harm to persons not in the immediate area and of injuries not as readily foreseeable to occur from his or her conduct. The defendant is expected to identify all persons in the surroundings who could reasonably be subjected to danger of injury as the result of the defendant's actions. The extent of this range also turns on a question of whether the conduct proximately caused the injury, but it allows a more indirect chain of events to be included as to what composes proximate cause.

Degree of Duty

Once it has been shown that the plaintiff was within the area that the defendant should have expected to be affected by his or her conduct, it is necessary to establish the degree of duty that is relative to the degree of risk of injury. The defendant's actions will expose the plaintiff to certain potential dangers in the range where risk exists. The defendant is responsible for those risks that foreseeably could cause significant harm. What this means is that when a party engages in conduct that may affect others in the surrounding area, that actor must act carefully so as not to allow that conduct to injure those persons in ways that can be reasonably foreseen. Thus, the lower the risk of significant injury, the less the degree of duty owed to others to protect them. An example is the floor of a grocery store. Although the store would have a duty to keep its floor reasonably clean from spills and debris, it would not be required to post a guard in each aisle to warn customers of recently mopped areas. A cautionary sign would be sufficient.

In some instances, a specific duty is imposed by statute or common law. The legislature and judiciary have identified particular situations as those in which a duty is always warranted. An example is traffic laws. With the establishment of these laws came the duty to obey the laws for the safety of others as well as oneself.

The Standard of Care

Once it has been established that a duty existed between the defendant and the plaintiff, it must then be established that the defendant violated the duty. This is accomplished by first establishing the appropriate standard of care to which the defendant should have adhered to meet the duty.

The usual test applied in negligence actions is whether the defendant, under all the circumstances, exercised ordinary (reasonable) care.[9] Whether the defendant acted with ordinary care is determined by measuring his or her conduct against what the reasonable person would have done in a similar situation. On the one hand, no two situations are alike, and each must be judged in light of its own unique circumstances. On the other hand, there are generally enough similarities to other commonly encountered situations that a determination can be made of what a reasonable person would have done.

It is important to note that the reasonable person in each case is generally presumed to have the same characteristics of age, intelligence, experience, and physical ability (or disability) as the defendant.[10] Also to be considered are (1) the underlying reason or necessity of the defendant's conduct (was it an act of great social value, such as saving a life?), (2) the surrounding physical environment, (3) any activities that were taking place, and (4) the types of people in the area (was it an area, for example, where children with disabilities were playing?).[11]

The particular mental ability or disability in matters of judgment of the defendant is generally not considered.[12] The mental ability of an intoxicated defendant is no doubt impaired, but intoxication is a voluntary condition, and liability for one's actions cannot be escaped through this method. In addition, one cannot possibly identify degrees of mental ability in all those possible negligent persons who surround him or her and then take appropriate measures of protection. Consequently, most courts have determined that the actor is in the best position to determine what is and is not safe conduct given his or her mental ability. Keep in mind that the courts can moderate this rule by considering the age, experience, intelligence, and physical condition of the defendant, which may affect the mental ability consideration. An example is a defendant who is mentally impaired. In some cases, this impairment so affects a person's intelligence that mental ability to evaluate circumstances is altered. Conversely, someone certified or serving in the capacity of a specialist or an expert in some field (e.g., a brain surgeon or bankruptcy lawyer) can be held to a higher standard of care than the average member of his or her respective profession.

After determining who the reasonable person is in a situation, the court must determine how the reasonable person would have acted. This is done while keeping in mind that the reasonable person takes into account all details of the surroundings, appreciates all foreseeable risks, and acts in the most prudent and careful manner. Once this is determined, the standard of care is established.

It should be pointed out that in some cases, standards other than ordinary care are applied. Two other standards sometimes applied are extraordinary (great) care and slight care. The standard of extraordinary care is usually applied in situations identified by the lawmaking authorities where the plaintiff is not capable of protecting himself or herself from the defendant's actions.[13] An example is common carriers such as buses, trains, and airplanes. Many jurisdictions require common carriers to act with extraordinary care for the safety of their passengers who have virtually entrusted their lives to the carrier.

Slight care is the most basic of all duties to take even the most minimal action to prevent injuries to those in the surrounding area.[14] When this most basic and minimal duty is violated, many jurisdictions permit an action in addition or as an alternative to one for negligence. If there is a standard of ordinary care in place, the plaintiff may also be permitted to sue for punitive damages for the failure to exercise even slight care. Punitive damages are used in some jurisdictions in addition to compensatory damages. Punitives—or exemplary damages, as they are sometimes called—punish the defendant and are designed to deter others from such gross carelessness. Circumstances that impose only a duty of slight care include situations such as the duty of a landowner to trespassers. Although there is not a duty to obey a standard of ordinary care to persons invading another person's property, neither can a person willingly expose others to substantial risks of danger.

Proximate Cause

Regardless of the *degree* of duty (standard of care), a duty must be shown in each case of negligence. The plaintiff must also establish that the defendant in some respect breached or failed to meet the standard of care that accompanied the duty to the plaintiff. Following this, the plaintiff has the further burden of establishing a legally recognized causal link between the breach and the plaintiff's injury.

Proximate cause is a major element of any negligence action. The plaintiff must demonstrate that the defendant's conduct proximately caused the plaintiff's injuries.[15] The issue is decided in two parts. First, it must be shown that the injuries were the result of the conduct as a matter of factual occurrence (known as cause in fact). Second, it must be shown that the injuries were caused by the conduct as a matter of law (commonly called the legal cause).

Prosser, a well-known and respected authority on tort law, has said that proximate cause is the "reasonable connection between the act or omission of the defendant and the damage which the plaintiff has suffered. . . . Legal responsibility must be limited to those causes which are so closely connected with the result and of such significance that the law is justified in imposing liability."[16]

In the test of proximate cause, the cause in fact is generally the simplest factor to establish. The plaintiff needs only to trace a chain of events, short or long, that leads directly from the defendant's conduct to the plaintiff's injuries. This is influenced somewhat by the extent of the duty of the defendant, as discussed earlier. In simple situations, where there are no intervening forces or remote circumstances, cause in fact and legal cause may be established by the same evidence.

Tests for determining proximate cause.   Two tests are commonly employed when deciding whether there has been proximate cause. Both are used in determining cause in fact. The first is often called the But For test.[17] Simply put, the question is asked, "But for the defendant's actions, would the plaintiff's injuries still have occurred?" This test is rarely applied, because a multitude of variables can contribute to the severity of an injury. Thus, the But For test is not appropriate for many situations.

The decline in the application of the But For test has been matched by the increasing use of Substantial Factor analysis,[18] which examines whether the defendant's conduct was a substantial factor in producing the plaintiff's injury.[19] If it was, irrespective of other factors that may have contributed, cause in fact has been established. Overall, substantial factor analysis seems to be a fairer method of determining cause in fact than the But For test.

APPLICATION 11.2

Caesar and Scarlett are driving two vehicles involved in a head-on collision that occurred when Scarlett crossed the centerline of the highway. Caesar's injuries are serious but not considered life-threatening. As he is being transported to the hospital, the ambulance is struck by a cement truck and pushed into a lake alongside that particular section of road. As a result, Caesar, who is strapped onto a gurney, drowns. Although Scarlett's negligence caused the accident and injuries to Caesar, the accident involving the ambulance and cement truck in front of a lake was a bizarre event and, in and of itself, was primarily responsible for the drowning of

Caesar. This is true even though, as a matter of cause in fact, Caesar's presence in the ambulance was due to the collision with Scarlett.

Point for Discussion

- Would there be legal causation if Scarlett had been driving Caesar to the hospital herself and was struck by the cement truck?

Proving proximate cause. When proximate cause becomes an issue, it can be the most disputed point in the case. Proximate cause is heavily influenced by the extent of the duty imposed by the court: the larger the area to which a defendant owes a duty, the greater the chance of a remote occurrence causing an injury to someone within that area. Consequently, such situations present a greater likelihood for an issue of proximate cause.

Sometimes an injury occurs and the cause is not easily foreseeable. In such a situation, proximate cause is not easily proven. Proximate cause is more than a chain of events from the act to the injury. It is a chain of events in which the actor should have reasonably foreseen the likelihood of injury. Proximate cause can be established in fairly remote situations, even when other forces come into play in producing the injury. However, when these remote situations are so removed that the occurrence is bizarre or considered a freak accident, proximate cause will be difficult to establish. Similarly, when an intervening force capable of producing the injury independently occurs between the moment of conduct by the defendant and the moment of injury, the proximate cause is very difficult to prove in terms of the original defendant. Again, the courts often apply the But For test or Substantial Factor analysis to determine legal cause.

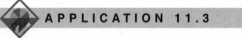 **APPLICATION 11.3**

Several children are playing around a swimming pool at a local park. The pool area is being renovated and the construction workers have removed the protective fencing. A park employee sees the children and begins chasing them away from the pool area. One child falls into the pool, which is empty, and suffers serious head injuries. Under the But For test, the park worker may or may not be considered negligent for chasing the children in a dangerous area due to the existing risk of injury with the absent fence. Under the Substantial Factor analysis, the likelihood of liability for the park worker is much greater because there is no doubt the worker contributed substantially to the factors which actually produced the injuries.

Point for Discussion

- Which test would produce a fairer result in this situation, and why?

Damage

A key element in any action for negligence is that of damage. The plaintiff must prove that he or she suffered some type of compensable injury, that is, that something happened to the plaintiff or the plaintiff's property as the proximate result of the defendant's breach of the standard of care that warrants compensation by the defendant to the plaintiff. For example, the fact that the plaintiff was delayed by the defendant's actions in and of itself is probably not sufficient. However, if the defendant's negligent conduct is the cause of a delay to the plaintiff that causes the plaintiff to suffer monetary loss (e.g., miss a flight for an important business trip), the defendant may be required to compensate the plaintiff.

Damage comes in many forms—monetary, physical, or mental/emotional. It may affect the person or the person's property. However, in a negligence action, it must be significant enough under the circumstances to warrant a monetary award as compensation.

CASE

UNITED STATES COURT OF APPEALS, SIXTH CIRCUIT.

JOE JAMES, ET AL., PLAINTIFFS-APPELLANTS, v. MEOW MEDIA, INC., Et AL., DEFENDANTS-APPELLEES.

2002 WL 1836520

Argued: Nov. 28, 2001.
Decided and Filed:
Aug. 13, 2002.

Opinion

On December 1, 1997, Michael Carneal walked into the lobby of Heath High School in Paducah, Kentucky, and shot several of his fellow students, killing three and wounding many others. The parents and estate administrators of Carneal's victims—Jessica James, Kayce Steger, and Nicole Hadley—(hereinafter collectively referred to as "James") appeal the judgment of the district court dismissing, for failing to state claims on which relief could be granted, their actions against several video game, movie production, and internet content-

Negligence

Proximate Cause

provider firms. According to James's complaint, Carneal regularly played video games, watched movies, and viewed internet sites produced by the defendant firms. These activities, James argues "desensitized" Carneal to violence and "caused" him to kill the students of Heath High School. James claims that the distribution of this material to impressionable youth like Carneal constitutes actionable negligence under Kentucky law, entitling James to recover wrongful death damages from the distributing firms. Moreover, James contends that the defendant firms purveyed defective "products," namely the content of video games, movies, and internet sites, triggering strict product liability under Kentucky law.

The defendant firms argue that they owe no duty to protect third parties from how players, watchers or viewers process the ideas and images presented in their video games, movies and internet sites. Specifically, the defendants contend that Carneal's actions were not sufficiently foreseeable to trigger the defendants' liability. Even if they were to owe such a duty to protect third parties from the consumers of their ideas and images, the defendants argue that Carneal's independent decision to kill his fellow students constitutes a superseding cause of the claimed damages and defeats the proximate cause element of James's *prima facie* case. The defendants further contend that tort liability for the non-defamatory ideas and images communicated in their respective media would raise significant First Amendment questions that ought to be avoided. Finally, the defendants note that James's theory of product liability is flawed as they have not distributed "products" under Kentucky law.

For the reasons set forth below, we affirm the district court's dismissal of James's actions.

On December 1, 1997, Michael Carneal brought a .22-caliber pistol and five shotguns into the lobby of Heath High School in Paducah, Kentucky. At the time, Carneal was a 14-year-old freshman student at the school. Upon his arrival, Carneal began shooting into a crowd of students, wounding five. His shots killed an additional three: Jessica James, Kayce Steger, and Nicole Hadley. Carneal was arrested and convicted of murdering James, Steger, and Hadley.

Subsequent investigations revealed that Carneal regularly played "Doom," "Quake," "Castle Wolfenstein," "Redneck Rampage," "Nightmare Creatures," "Mech Warrior," "Resident Evil," and "Final Fantasy," which are interactive computer games that, in various ways, all involve the player shooting virtual opponents. Carneal also possessed a video tape containing the movie, "The Basketball Diaries," in a few minutes of which the high-school-student protagonist dreams of killing his teacher and several of his fellow classmates. Investigators examined Carneal's computer and discovered that he had visited "www.persiankitty.com," which appears to catalogue and link to sites with sexually-suggestive material. It also appeared that through "www.adultkey.com," *www.adultkey.com*, a site operated by Network Authentication Systems and designed to restrict access to certain websites to viewers over certain ages, Carneal was granted age verification sufficient to visit many other pornographic sites.

The parents, who also are the estate administrators, of James, Steger, and Hadley filed this action in the United States District Court for the Western District of Kentucky. James's complaint named as defendants the companies that produce or maintain the above-mentioned movie, video games, and internet sites. James stated essentially three causes of action against the defendants. First, James alleged that the defendants had been negligent in that they either knew or should have known that the distribution of their material to Carneal and other young people created an unreasonable risk of harm to others. James alleged that exposure to the defendants' material made young people insensitive to violence and more likely to commit violent acts. But for Carneal's steady diet of the defendants' material, James contended, Carneal would not have committed his violent acts.

Second, James asserted that the video game cartridges, movie cassettes, and internet transmissions that the defendants produced and distributed were "products" for purposes of Kentucky product liability law. According to James, the violent features of the movie, games, and internet sites were product defects. The defendants, as producers and distributors of the "products," are strictly liable under Kentucky law for damages caused by such product defects.

The defendants moved to dismiss all of James's actions for failing to state any claim on which relief could be granted. *See* Fed.R.Civ.P. 12(b)(6). The district court granted the defendants' motion. The district court held that Carneal's actions were not sufficiently foreseeable to impose a duty of reasonable care on the defendants with regard to Carneal's victims. Alternatively, the district court held that even if such a duty existed, Carneal's actions constituted a superseding cause of the victims' injuries, defeating the element of proximate causation notwithstanding the defendants' negligence. With regard to James's second cause of action, the district court determined that the "thoughts, ideas and images" purveyed by the defendants' movie, video games, and internet sites were not "products" for purposes of Kentucky law and therefore the defendants could not be held strictly liable for any alleged defects.

James now appeals the district court dismissal of his negligence and product liability claims.

James contends that the defendants in this case acted negligently, perhaps in producing, but at least

◆ **CASE**

in distributing to young people, their materials. It was this negligence, according to James, that caused Carneal to undertake his violent actions and that thereby caused the deaths of the plaintiffs' daughters. In order to establish an actionable tort under Kentucky law, the plaintiff must establish that the defendant owed a duty of care to the plaintiff, that the defendant breached that duty of care, and that the *defendant's breach* was the proximate cause of the plaintiff's damages.

A.   *The Existence of a Duty of Care*

The district court held that James's allegations, even if assumed to be true, failed to establish the first element of the *prima facie* case. Specifically, the district court determined that the defendants were under no duty to protect James, Steger, and Hadley from Carneal's actions. James argues that the district court erred as a matter of Kentucky law in this regard.

The "existence of a duty of care" as an element of a tort cause of action is of relatively recent vintage. At early English common law, the existence of a duty of care was not considered as an element of an actionable tort. Then, tort law attached strict liability for any damages that resulted from "wrongful acts." Prosser on Torts § 53. The requirement that the plaintiff establish that he was owed a specific duty of care by the defendant came with the advent of negligence in place of strict liability. *See generally* Percy H. Winfield, *Duty in Tortious Negligence*, 34 Colum. L.Rev. 41 (1934). As a separate basis of liability, negligence was simply too broad, according to later English courts. Accordingly, the concept of limited duty disciplined the concept of negligence, requiring the plaintiff to establish a definite legal obligation.

At first, the limited duty of care concerned the persons to whom a defendant owed an obligation of care. *See, e.g., Shore v. Town of Stonington*, 187 Conn. 147, 444 A.2d 1379 (1982) (holding that a police officer owed no duty to protect a citizen who was killed by a drunk driver that the officer had stopped, but released). The dilemma was that it became nearly impossible categorically to demarcate the universe of people to whom a person would owe a duty to abstain from negligence. With regard to the existence of duty

between specific persons, the answer always was dependent on the circumstances.

Kentucky courts resolved this dilemma by establishing a "universal duty of care." *Grayson Fraternal Order of Eagles v. Claywell*. 736 S.W.2d 328 (Ky.1987); *M & T Chems., Inc. v. Westrick*, 525 S.W.2d 740 (Ky.1974); *Greyhound Corp. v. White*. 323 S.W.2d 578 (Ky.1958). Under the universal duty of care, "every person owes a duty to every other person to exercise ordinary care in his activities to prevent foreseeable injury." *Grayson*, 736 S.W.2d at 332. James argues that Kentucky's universal duty of care would foreclose the defendants' argument that they had no duty to protect James, Steger, and Hadley. It is clear to us, however, that Kentucky's rule of a universal duty of care simply recognizes the obvious in determining the existence of a duty of care. Of course, there are conceivable circumstances under which there would be legally enforceable duties to act without negligence between any two people. What Kentucky courts have recognized through the "universal duty of care" rule is that the existence of a duty of care is circumstantially limited: the duty is to exercise ordinary care to prevent *foreseeable* harm.

Thus, Kentucky courts have held that the determination of whether a duty of care exists is whether the harm to the plaintiff resulting from the defendant's negligence was "foreseeable." Foreseeability is an often invoked, but not terribly well defined, concept in the common law of tort. Some common law tort regimes use foreseeability as the standard for determining proximate causation. *See, e.g., Fu v. State*, 263 Neb. 848, 643 N.W.2d 659, 669 (2002); *Haliw v. City of Sterling Heights*, 464 Mich. 297, 627 N.W.2d 581, 588 (2001). *Compare Bodkin v. 5401 S.P., Inc.*, 329 Ill. App.3d 620, 263 Ill.Dec. 434, 768 N.E.2d 194, 202 (2002) (attempting to identify different forms of foreseeability for the proximate cause and the existence of a duty inquiries). Kentucky's particular use of foreseeability in the duty inquiry finds its roots in perhaps the most famous application of the foreseeability principle. In *Palsgraf v. Long Island Railroad Co.*, 248 N.Y. 339, 162 N.E. 99 (1928), then-Judge Cardozo determined that the defendant's duty is to avoid "risks reasonably to be perceived." *Id*. at 100. As every former law student remembers, the plaintiff in *Palsgraf* had bought a train ticket to travel to the Rockaways for the afternoon and was waiting on the station platform. Two men were rushing to catch a departing train, one easily hopped on board and the other struggled to pull himself onto the rear car. A conductor on the train pulled him on board, but in the process, the struggling passenger dropped onto the rails the brown-paper package he was carrying. The package was full of fireworks and exploded. The explosion overturned a large set of scales on the platform, which struck Palsgraf, and Palsgraf sued the railroad for her injuries.

Cardozo determined that the railroad simply did not owe a duty to Palsgraf to protect against *the injury that she suffered*. For Cardozo, the harm that Palsgraf suffered was not sufficiently probable that the railroad employees could have been expected to anticipate it occurring from their actions. Cardozo's reasoning, although implying that Palsgraf was the unforeseeable plaintiff, rested on the improbability of the *harm* that she suffered arising from the defendant's particular actions. *Id*. at 101. For Cardozo too, the existence of a duty of care was a creature of circumstance.

Cardozo's opinion in *Palsgraf,* while cited as the cornerstone of the American doctrine of a limited duty of care, has been criticized for its conclusory reasoning regarding whether Palsgraf's harm really was sufficiently unforeseeable. Such conclusory reasoning has been endemic in the jurisprudence of determining duty by assessing foreseeability. Courts often end up merely listing factual reasons why a particular harm, although having materialized, would have appeared particularly unlikely in advance and then simply asserting that the harm was too unlikely to be foreseeable and to create a duty to exercise due care in protecting against it. What has not emerged is any clear standard regarding what makes a projected harm too improbable to be foreseeable.

The parties in this case have argued at length over whether the foreseeability inquiry required to determine the existence of a duty of care is a pure question of law for the court or a question of fact that should generally be submitted to a jury. Under

Kentucky law, it is clear that the existence of a duty of care to the plaintiff, and its underlying foreseeability inquiry, is a pure question of law for the court. *Mullins*, 839 S.W.2d at 248 ("The question of duty presents an issue of law"); *Sheehan*, 913 S.W.2d at 6. The allocation of responsibility for determining this question to the courts, rather than to juries, reveals that the duty inquiry contains an important role for considering the policy consequences of imposing liability on a certain class of situations. Essentially, the foreseeability inquiry requires courts to determine questions inexorably tied to the ultimate question of whether the defendant was negligent. After all, the probability of the harm is a significant factor in traditional assessment of negligence. By placing the foreseeability analysis in the hands of courts, the existence of duty element of the *prima facie* case serves as a gatekeeper for the otherwise extremely broad concept of negligence.

Thus, we are called, as best we can, to implement Kentucky's duty of care analysis in this case. Our inquiry is whether the deaths of James, Steger, and Hadley were the reasonably foreseeable result of the defendants' creation and distribution of their games, movie, and internet sites. Whether an event was reasonably foreseeable is not for us to determine with the assistance of hindsight. *Mitchell v. Hadl*, 816 S.W.2d 183, 186 (Ky.1991). The mere fact that the risk may have materialized does little to resolve the foreseeability question.

Kentucky courts, in resolving foreseeability questions, have consistently inquired into the relative likelihood of the injuries produced. Of particular interest in this case are cases in which plaintiffs have sought to hold defendants liable for the actions of third parties, allegedly enabled or encouraged by the defendants. A line of cases in this vein concerns dram shops. In *Grayson*, the Kentucky Supreme Court held that an automobile accident injuring third parties was a reasonably foreseeable result of the negligent act of serving alcohol to an intoxicated individual. 736 S.W.2d at 332. In contrast, the court later held that an intoxicated patron fighting with and shooting a fellow customer was simply not a foreseeable result of continuing to serve the patron alcohol. *Isaacs v.*

◆ **CASE**

Smith, 5 S.W.3d 500, 502 (Ky.1999). According to the court, the violent fighting and shooting was so much less likely a result from the serving of alcohol than the negligent operation of a motor vehicle that it was not reasonably foreseeable. *Ibid.* Accordingly, the court held that dram shops, although negligent in serving alcohol to the obviously intoxicated, do not have a duty to protect third parties from the intentional violent acts of their intoxicated patrons. *Ibid.*

Intentional violence is less likely to result from intoxication than negligent operation of a motor vehicle. Yet, the Kentucky Supreme Court never makes clear how unlikely is too unlikely for a particular type of harm to be unforeseeable. The cases do not create a principle, portable to the context of this case, for evaluating the probability of harm.

This court has encountered this foreseeability inquiry under Kentucky law before in a situation similar to this case. In *Watters v. TSR, Inc.*, 904 F.2d 378 (6th Cir.1990), the mother of a suicide victim sued TSR for manufacturing the game "Dungeons and Dragons." The suicide victim regularly played the game. The mother contended that the game's violent content "desensitized" the victim to violence and caused him to undertake the violent act of shooting himself in the head. We held that the boy's suicide was simply not a reasonably foreseeable result of producing the game, notwithstanding its violent contest. To have held otherwise would have been "to stretch the concepts of foreseeability and ordinary care to lengths that would deprive them of all normal meaning." *Id*. at 381.

Foreseeability, however, is a slippery concept. Indeed, it could be argued that we ourselves confused it with some concept of negligence. We noted in *Watters*: "The defendant cannot be faulted, obviously, for putting its game on the market without attempting to ascertain the mental condition of each and every prospective player." *Ibid*. We almost appeared to say that the costs of acquiring such knowledge would so outweigh the social benefits that it would not be negligent to abstain from such an investigation. We can put the *foreseeability* point a little more precisely, however. It appears simply impossible to predict that these games, movie, and internet sites (alone, or in what combinations) would incite a young person to violence. Carneal's reaction to the games and movies at issue here, assuming that his violent actions were such a reaction, was simply too idiosyncratic to expect the defendants to have anticipated it. We find that it is simply too far a leap from shooting characters on a video screen (an activity undertaken by millions) to shooting people in a classroom (an activity undertaken by a handful, at most) for Carneal's actions to have been reasonably foreseeable to the manufactures of the media that Carneal played and viewed.

At first glance, our conclusion also appears to be little more than an assertion. Mental health experts could quite plausibly opine about the manner in which violent movies and video games affect viewer behavior. We need not stretch to imagine some mixture of impressionability and emotional instability that might unnaturally react with the violent content of the "Basketball Diaries" or "Doom." Of course, Carneal's reaction was not a normal reaction. Indeed, Carneal is not a normal person, but it is not utter craziness to predict that someone like Carneal is out there.

We return, however, to the Kentucky court's observation that the existence of a duty of care reflects a judicial policy judgment at bottom. From the Kentucky cases on foreseeability, we can discern two relevant policies that counsel against finding that Carneal's violent actions were the reasonably foreseeable result of defendants' distribution of games, movies, and internet material.

1. The Duty to Protect Against Intentional Criminal Actions

First, courts have held that, except under extraordinary circumstances, individuals are generally entitled to assume that third parties will not commit intentional criminal acts. *See* Restatement (Second) of Torts § 302B, cmt. d ("Normally the actor has much less reason to anticipate intentional misconduct than he has to anticipate negligence. In the ordinary case he may reasonably proceed upon the assumption that others will not interfere in a manner intended to cause harm to anyone. This is true particularly where the intentional conduct is a crime, since under ordinary circumstances it may reasonably be assumed that no one will violate the criminal law."). *See also Gaines-Tabb v. ICI Explosives USA, Inc.*, 995 F.Supp. 1304 (D.Okla.1996) (holding that fertilizer and blasting cap manufacturers were not liable for Murrah Federal Building bombing, as they were entitled to believe that third parties would not engage in intentional criminal conduct); *Henry v. Merck & Co.*, 877 F.2d 1489, 1493 (10th Cir.1989). The reasons behind this general rule are simple enough. The first reason is a probabilistic judgment that foreseeability analysis requires. Individuals generally are significantly deterred from undertaking intentional criminal conduct given the sanctions that can follow. The threatened sanctions make the third-party intentional criminal conduct sufficiently less likely that, under normal circumstances, we do not require the putative tort defendant to anticipate it. Indeed, this statistical observation explains the distinction drawn by Kentucky courts in the dram shop liability cases.

The second reason is structural. The system of criminal liability has concentrated responsibility for an intentional criminal act in the primary actor, his accomplices, and his co-conspirators. By imposing liability on those who did not endeavor to accomplish the intentional criminal undertaking, tort liability would diminish the responsibility placed on the criminal defendant. The normative message of tort law in these situations would be that the defendant is not entirely responsible for his intentional criminal act.

Does this case involve the extraordinary circumstances under which we would require the defendants to anticipate a third party's intentional criminal act? Kentucky courts have found such circumstances when the tort defendant had previously developed "a special relationship" with the victim of a third-party intentional criminal act. *See, e.g., Fryman v. Harrison*, 896 S.W.2d 908, 910 (Ky.1995) (requiring that the victim be in state custody in order to trigger governmental duty to protect her from third-party violence as a matter of Kentucky tort law). *Cf. DeShaney v. Winnebago County Dep't of Soc. Serv.*, 489 U.S. 189, 109 S.Ct. 998, 103 L.Ed.2d 249 (1989) (articulating the special relationship test to trigger a governmental duty to protect persons from private violence under the Fourteenth Amendment). This duty to protect can be triggered by placing the putative plaintiff in custody or by taking other affirmative steps that disable the plaintiff from protecting himself against third-party intentional criminal acts. Of course, a special relationship can be created by a contract between the plaintiff and the defendant. Finally, some states have imposed a duty to protect others from third-party intentional criminal acts on members of discrete professions who become aware of the third-party's intention to engage in criminal conduct against a specific person. *See Tarasoff v. Board of Regents of the Univ. of Cal.*, 17 Cal.3d 425, 131 Cal.Rptr. 14, 551 P.2d 334 (1976).

We can find nothing close to a "special relationship" in this case. The defendants did not even know James, Steger, and Hadley prior to Carneal's actions, much less take any affirmative steps that disabled them from protecting themselves.

Courts have held, under extremely limited circumstances, that individuals, notwithstanding their relationship with the victims of third-party violence, can be liable when their affirmative actions "create a high degree of risk of [the third party's] intentional misconduct." Restatement of Torts (Second) § 302B, cmt. e.H. Generally, such circumstances are limited to cases in which the defendant has given a young child access to ultra-hazardous materials such as blasting caps, *Vills v. City of Cloquet*, 119 Minn. 277, 138 N.W. 33 (1912), or firearms. *Spivey v. Sheeler*, 514 S.W.2d 667 (Ky.1974). Even in those cases, courts have relied on the third party's severely diminished capacity to handle the ultra-hazardous materials. With older third parties, courts have found liability only where defendants have vested a particular person, under circumstances that made his nefarious plans clear, with the tools that he then quickly used to commit the criminal act. *See Meers v. McDowell*, 110 Ky. 926, 62, S.W. 1013 (1901). Arguably, the defendants' games, movie, and internet sites gave Carneal the ideas and emotions, the "psychological tools," to commit three murders.

CASE

However, this case lacks such crucial features of our jurisprudence in this area. First, the defendants in this case had no idea Carneal even existed, much less the particular idiosyncracies of Carneal that made their products particularly dangerous in his hands. In every case that this court has discovered in which defendants have been held liable for negligently creating an unreasonably high risk of third-party criminal conduct, the defendants have been specifically aware of the peculiar tendency of a particular person to commit a criminal act with the defendants' materials.

Second, no court has ever held that ideas and images can constitute the tools for a criminal act under this narrow exception. Beyond their intangibility, such ideas and images are at least one step removed from the implements that can be used in the criminal act itself. In the cases supporting this exception, the item that the defendant has given to the third-party criminal actor has been the direct instrument of harm.

B. Proximate Causation

Even if this court were to find that the defendants owed a duty to protect James, Steger, and Hadley from Carneal's violent actions, the plaintiffs likely have not alleged sufficient facts to establish the third element of a *prima facie* tort case: proximate causation. The defendants argue that even if they were negligent, Carneal's intentional, violent actions constitute a superseding cause of the plaintiffs' damages and sever the defendants liability for the deaths of Carneal's victims. Generally, a third party's criminal action that directly causes all of the damages will break the chain of causation.

Yet, Kentucky courts have held that an intervening third-party criminal act will be a superseding cause breaking the chain of causation if the act was reasonably foreseeable. *See, e.g., Britton v. Wooten*, 817 S.W.2d 443, 449-50 (Ky.1991). In *Britton*, the plaintiff had been injured by a fire in his leased store. The fire started when trash piled next to the building by the landlord was ignited by an arsonist. The court held that the arsonist's intervening act was not a superseding cause of the fire because the act was

a reasonably foreseeable result of the landlord's piling of flammable material next to the building. *Ibid.*

The court reached the question of causation in *Britton* because of the landlord's well established duty of care to protect its tenants from injury. *See, e.g., Waldon v. Housing Auth. of Paducah*, 854 S.W.2d 777, 779 (Ky.Ct.App.1991) (holding landlord liable for failing to protect tenant from being shot by a third-party intruder). As we have noted above, the duty of the media defendants in this case is far from as firmly established. Outside of the landlord-tenant context, Kentucky courts are far more likely to determine that an intervening criminal act is a superseding cause. *See Briscoe v. Amazing Prod. Inc.*, 23 S.W.3d 228, 229-30 (Ky.Ct.App.2000). Compare *House v. Kellerman*, 519 S.W.2d 380 (Ky.1974) (confronting the question of superseding cause in the context of the well established duty of driver to protect his passenger). In *Briscoe*, the plaintiff was injured by a third party who battered her by spraying corrosive drain cleaner in her face. The plaintiff contended that the manufacturer of the drain cleaner was negligent and should have anticipated that it could be used as a weapon. The court held that batteror's reaction to and use of drain cleaner as a weapon was sufficiently unforeseeable to constitute a superseding cause. *Briscoe*, 23 S.W.3d at 230.

A similar analysis is applicable here. Our determination regarding the idiosyncratic nature of Carneal's reaction to the defendants' media would likely compel us to hold that his action constitutes a superseding cause. We, however, need not reach this question because we have determined that the defendants did not owe a duty to protect the decedents.

James also contends that the district court erred in dismissing his products liability claims. In his complaint, James alleged that the defendants' video games, movie, and internet transmissions constitute "products," and their violent content "product defects." Under Kentucky law, manufacturers, distributors, and retailers of "products" are strictly liable for damages caused by "defects" in those products. *Clark v. Hauck Mfg. Co.*, 910 S.W.2d 247, 250(Ky.1995); Restatement (Second) of Torts § 402A. If this theory of liability were to apply, James's failure to establish a duty to exercise ordinary care to prevent the victims' injuries (See Part III.A) would be irrelevant. Under strict liability, James would only be required to establish causation.

James's theory of product liability in this case is deeply flawed. First, and something none of the parties have mentioned, the "consumers or ultimate users" of the alleged products are not the ones claiming physical harm in this case. Restatement (Second) of Torts § 402A. Carneal was the person who "consumed" or "used" the video games, movie, and internet sites. Allegedly because of Carneal's consumption of the products, he killed the victims in this case. In early products liability law, courts had required privity between the final retailer of the product and the injured plaintiff for strict liability to attach. Eventually, courts broadened the class of plaintiffs who could avail themselves of strict liability to include those who consumed or ultimately used the product. Kentucky courts, but certainly not all courts, have extended the protection of products liability to "bystanders" who are injured by the product, but are not "using" or "consuming" the product. *Embs v. Pepsi-Cola Bottling Co. of Lexington*, 528 S.W.2d 703 (Ky.1975) (holding that bystander could recover on strict liability basis for injuries caused by exploding soda bottle); Restatement (Second) of Torts § 402A, n.1 (noting the split in authority regarding whether bystanders may recover on a strict liability basis). Imposing strict liability for the injuries suffered in this case would be an extension of Kentucky's bystander jurisprudence, as the decedents were not directly injured by the products themselves, but by Carneal's reaction to the products.

We place this open question of Kentucky law aside as the parties apparently have. James has failed to demonstrate a prior requirement, that the video games, movies, and internet sites are "products" for purposes of strict liability. This was the basis on which the district court dismissed James's products liability claims, holding that the video games, movie, and internet transmissions were not "products," at least in the sense that James sought to attach liability to them.

This court has already substantially resolved the question of Kentucky law presented. In *Watters v. TSR*, 904 F.2d 378 (6th Cir.1990), this court held that "words and pictures" contained in a board game could not constitute "products" for purposes of maintaining a strict liability action. We cannot find any intervening Kentucky authority that persuades us that *Watters* no longer correctly states Kentucky law. James's theory of liability, that the ideas conveyed by the video games, movie cassettes and internet transmissions, caused Carneal to kill his victims, attempts to attach product liability in a nearly identical way.

James argues that, at least in this case, we are not just dealing with "words and pictures." Carneal, of course, had video game cartridges and movie cassettes. James argues that the test for determining wether an item is a product for purposes of Kentucky law is whether it is "tangible," and that the cartridges and cassettes are "tangible." As for the internet sites, James points us to a court that has held that "electricity" is a "product" for purposes of strict liability under Kentucky law. *See C.G. Bryant v. Tri-County Elec. Membership Corp.*, 844 F.Supp. 347, 352 (W.D.Ky.1994). Internet sites are nothing more than communicative electrical pulses, James contends. James argues that there is no relevant difference between the internet transmissions and the electricity.

And of course James is partially correct. Certainly if a video cassette exploded and injured its user, we would hold it a "product" and its producer strictly liable for the user's physical damages. In this case, however, James is arguing that the words and images purveyed on the tangible cassettes, cartridges, and perhaps even the electrical pulses through the internet, caused Carneal to snap and to effect the deaths of the victims. When dealing with ideas and images, courts have been willing to separate the sense in which the tangible containers of those ideas are products from their communicative element for purposes of strict liability. *See, e.g., Winter v. G.P. Putnam's Sons*, 938 F.2d 1033, 1036 (9th Cir.1991); *Jones v. J.B. Lippincott Co.*, 694 F.Supp. 1216, 1217-18 (D.Md.1988). We find these decisions well reasoned. The video game cartridges, movie cassette, and internet transmissions are not sufficiently "tangible" to constitute products in the sense of their communicative content.

For all the foregoing reasons we AFFIRM the district court's dismissal of all James's claims.

CASE

Case Review Question

James v. Meow Media, Inc., 2002 WL 1836520 (6th Cir. [Ky.] 2002).

Would the result be different if the individual who shot the children claimed he was acting out one of the video games he'd been playing?

Res Ipsa Loquitur

"The thing speaks for itself" is the traditional translation of the Latin term *res ipsa loquitur*.[20] This doctrine has been applied for many years in cases of negligence involving very special circumstances. A plaintiff may claim the doctrine to ease the burden of proof in a case of negligence only when he or she can prove that (1) the occurrence was of a type that would not happen without negligence, (2) the instrument producing the injury during the occurrence was exclusively in the control of the defendant, and (3) the plaintiff did not contribute to the injury.[21]

Res ipsa loquitur is used in cases where the evidence that would disclose how the defendant was negligent is not available to the plaintiff. Such cases arise where the plaintiff or his or her witnesses have no opportunity to determine precisely which conduct produced the injury. To prevent unwarranted claims of negligence, however, the plaintiff must prove the three elements noted previously.

Although the doctrine of res ipsa loquitur is limited in its application, in appropriate cases, the plaintiff can use it to prove negligence where a cause of action might not otherwise be available for the simple reason that the plaintiff does not have access to information in the defendant's control or because there were no witnesses to the injury. It should be realized, however, that with broadening rules of discovery of information by parties, the doctrine is declining steadily.

APPLICATION 11.4

Jennifer purchases a jar of jelly. Inside the cap is a plastic seal over the top of the jar. Jennifer breaks the seal and uses the jelly to make a sandwich. As she bites into the sandwich, she immediately feels a sharp pain in her mouth. Upon examination, she finds that the jelly contains ground glass. She brings a lawsuit against the manufacturer of the jelly on the basis of res ipsa loquitur. Jennifer has no access to evidence or witnesses concerning the actual cause of negligence. In an ordinary case, she could not prove the defendant's negligence was the cause of her injuries. Under an application of res ipsa loquitur, she need only prove that the injury would not ordinarily occur without negligence, that the instrument causing injury (the jar of jelly) was in the exclusive control of the defendant, and that she did not contribute to the cause of her injuries.

Point for Discussion

♦   Would the case be treated any differently if there had been no protective seal on the product?

CASE

HOLZHAUER v. SAKS & CO.

346 MD 328, 697 A.2d 89 (1997).

CHASANOW, Judge.

The United States District Court for the District of Maryland has certified the following three questions to this Court pursuant to the Maryland Uniform Certification of Questions of Law Act, Maryland Code (1974, 1995 Repl.Vol., 1996 Supp.), Courts & Judicial Proceedings Article, ss 12-601 through 12-613, and Maryland Rule 8-305.

1. Do Appellant's allegations with respect to negligence amount to a waiver of RES IPSA LOQUITUR, as in *Dover Elevator Co. v. Swann*, 334 Md. 231, 638 A.2d 762(1994)?
2. If not, does the doctrine of RES IPSA LOQUITUR apply under the facts thus far alleged in the instant case?
3. If the doctrine of RES IPSA LOQUITUR does apply, is there any reason, including the views expressed by the Court of Appeals in Dover, why the facts of this case require a different approach than that in *Beach v. Woodward & Lothrop, Inc.*, 18 Md.App. 645, 308 A.2d 439 (1973) (Where the escalator "stop[ped]and start[ed]up with a jerk")?

We answer the first two questions in the negative. Our decision regarding question number two renders question number three moot.

The facts of the case are not disputed. On February 24, 1994, Appellant, Eugene Holzhauer, was shopping in the Saks Fifth Avenue department store in Owings Mills Mall. Appellant injured his right shoulder when the escalator upon which he was riding, with his hand on the railing, came to a sudden stop, causing him to stumble down ten to twelve steps in a twisting motion. Appellant filed suit in the United States District Court for the District of Maryland against Saks & Co., the owner of the escalator, and Montgomery Elevator Company, the organization hired to service and maintain the escalator (collectively "Appellees"). Appellant alleged that Appellees were negligent in:

The suit was originally instituted in the Circuit Court for Baltimore County, but it was removed to the United States District Court for the District of Maryland based on the parties' diversity of citizenship. 28 U.S.C. s 1441.

a. "[M]aintain[ing] as a part of such escalator and the operating mechanism thereof, old, loose, worn, frayed, and antiquated parts, apparatus and equipment;

b. [F]ail[ing] to install in such escalator as a part of the operating mechanism thereof, a proper device to prevent said escalator from suddenly stopping when in use. . . ;

c. [P]ermitt[ing]such escalator and the working parts thereof to be and remain in a condition of disrepair for an unreasonable length of time;

d. [F]ail[ing]to inspect such escalator in a proper manner and at proper intervals;

e. [F]ail[ing]to warn plaintiff of the dangers connected with the escalator and to provide to plaintiff any protection from such dangers."

Appellant alleged, additionally, that Montgomery Elevator Company "negligently installed and maintained the escalator and failed to properly maintain, inspect and repair the escalator."

The following additional information was revealed during discovery. The parties do not know what caused the escalator to stop on February 24, 1994. The escalator had been inspected by the Maryland Department of Licensing and Regulation, Division of Labor and Industry Safety Inspection Unit in June of 1993. The escalator had not malfunctioned between the time of the inspection and the time of Appellant's injury, and it has not malfunctioned since Appellant's injury. On the day of the incident, the escalator remained stopped until a store employee restarted it with a key, at which time the escalator immediately began to run properly. Upon restarting, the escalator made no

CASE

unusual movements or noises, and it did not require any repairs. Montgomery Elevator Company, in fact, was not informed of the events that occurred on February 24 until this suit was instituted.

The escalator was turned on and off daily, using a key, at the opening and closing of business by Saks & Co.'s Building Engineer or by a member of its Security Department. Any individual can also cause the escalator to stop by pushing one of the emergency stop buttons located at the top and bottom of the escalator, respectively. Once stopped, the escalator will not run again until it is started with a key.

Appellant has offered no additional evidence to support the allegations of negligence in his complaint, and it appears that he does not intend to offer expert testimony in the field of escalator maintenance, operations, or repair. The only expert witness listed on Appellant's Designation of Expert Witnesses is Dr. Steven Friedman, a medical doctor. Furthermore, in his Response to [Saks & Co's] Motion for Summary Judgment, Appellant states that "[he] is not offering any direct evidence or expert testimony, other than evidence of the event itself. He is not attempting to prove how or why the escalator stopped suddenly, only that it did."

Appellees filed Motions for Summary Judgment at the close of discovery, arguing that Appellant failed to produce evidence sufficient to sustain his burden of proof at trial. The Honorable Frank A. Kaufman initially granted the Appellees' Motions for Summary Judgment in a one sentence memorandum stating: "For reasons which this Court will shortly set forth in a more detailed document, to be filed in this case, this Court will enter summary judgment for defendants." When Judge Kaufman began to write the opinion in support of his ruling, however, he concluded that he could not continue without the answers to the three questions certified to this Court. Judge Kaufman has denied Appellees' Motions for Summary Judgment, and he will reconsider them once this Court has announced its decision.

The United States District Court seems to suggest by its phrasing of question number one that *Dover Elevator Co. v. Swann*, 334 Md. 231, 638

A.2d 762 (1994), stands for the proposition that the pleading of specific acts of negligence will preclude a plaintiff from relying on the doctrine of RES IPSA LOQUITUR. This is not so. Dover did not concern the mere pleading of acts of negligence; rather it dealt with a plaintiff's attempt to establish specific grounds of negligence at trial. We held, in that case, that one of the reasons why the plaintiff was prohibited from relying on res ipsa was because he proffered direct evidence of negligence at trial. Dover, 334 Md. at 237, 638 A.2d at 765 ("[N]umerous Maryland cases have explained that a plaintiff's 'attempt to establish specific grounds of alleged negligence precludes recourse to the doctrine of RES IPSA LOQUITUR.'") (quoting *Smith v. Bernfeld*, 226 Md. 400, 409, 174 A.2d 53, 57 (1961)).

In Dover, David Swann was injured when he entered an elevator car, the floor of which was approximately one foot below the floor outside of the elevator. 334 Md. at 234, 638 A.2d at 764. He sued three defendants, one of which was Dover, the company that manufactured, installed, and maintained the elevator at issue. *Id*. Swann alleged in his Complaint that the defendants negligently designed, manufactured, installed, and maintained the elevator. *Dover*, 334 Md. at 234–35, 638 A.2d at 764. These pleadings, however, were not the reason that Swann was precluded from relying on res ipsa. Rather than ask the jury to draw an inference of defendant's negligence from the mere fact that the elevator misleveled, Swann had an engineer/elevator consultant testify at trial that the elevator misleveled because the elevator's contacts were "burned" and that Dover was negligent in, inter alia, cleaning rather than replacing the burned contacts. *Dover*, 334 Md. at 244, 638 A.2d at 769.

We held that, under the circumstances," the doctrine of RES IPSA LOQUITUR was inapplicable to the evidence before the jury . . . "*Dover*, 334 Md. at 262, 638 A.2d at 777. The purpose of res ipsa, we explained, is to afford a plaintiff the opportunity to present a prima facie case when direct evidence of the cause of an accident is not available or is available solely to the defendant.

Dover, 334 Md. at 237, 638 A.2d at 765. Direct evidence of the specific cause of his injuries was available to Swann, however, and he proffered that direct evidence to the jury in the form of an expert opinion. Thus, one of the reasons we held res ipsa to be inapplicable was because the expert "purport[ed] to furnish a sufficiently complete explanation of the specific causes of [the elevator's] misleveling, which . . . preclude[d] plaintiff's reliance on RES IPSA LOQUITUR."*Dover*, 334 Md. at 239, 638 A.2d at 766.

Unlike the petitioner in *Dover*, Appellant in the present case has not had the chance to proffer direct evidence as to the specific cause of his injuries. Thus far, he has only pleaded specific acts of negligence. This Court discussed the impact that pleading specific acts of negligence has on a claim of RES IPSA LOQUITUR in *Joffre v. Canada Dry Ginger Ale, Inc.*, 222 Md. 1, 158 A.2d 631(1960). In that case, a woman in a delicatessen was cut in the leg by a piece of glass when a Canada Dry soda bottle shattered. *Joffre*, 222 Md. at 3, 158 A.2d at 632. Appellant sued the Canada Dry bottler and the delicatessen. *Id.* Appellant alleged that the bottler "was negligent in" placing on the market . . . a product designed for purchase in the original package without making that package safe against reasonably-to-be-anticipated variations in temperature and hazards of handling, and that the bottle was defective or the pressure within it excessive." *Id.* She alleged that the delicatessen "was negligent in failing to so locate and guard the bottle as to prevent injury to customers, knowing it might explode." *Id.* The judge directed a verdict for both defendants at the close of the plaintiff's evidence, and Appellant argued on appeal that summary judgment was improper and that she was entitled to submit her claim to the jury under the theory of RES IPSA LOQUITUR. *Id.* The delicatessen argued that Appellant was precluded from relying on that theory because she had pleaded specific acts of negligence. *Joffre*, 222 Md. at 3-4, 158 A.2d at 632.

This Court stated that the delicatessen's argument had previously been rejected in

Maryland. *Id.* (citing State for Use of *Parr v. Board of County Com'rs of Prince George's County*, 207 Md. 91, 103-04, 113 A.2d 397, 402-03 (1955)). We explained that "'[t]he doctrine RES IPSA LOQUITUR is not a rule of pleading. It relates to burden of proof and sufficiency of evidence.'"*Joffre*, 222 Md. at 6, 158 A.2d at 634 whether a party will be precluded from relying on the doctrine of RES IPSA LOQUITUR turns upon the evidence produced by the party and whether that evidence satisfies the three essential components of RES IPSA LOQUITUR; whether specific allegations of negligence have been pleaded is of no moment. We answer the first certified question in the negative.

Appellant cannot satisfy the three essential components of RES IPSA LOQUITUR, however, and, for that reason, he may not rely on the doctrine in the present case. Three elements must be proven in order to create an inference of negligence on the part of a defendant: (1) a casualty of a kind that does not ordinarily occur absent negligence, (2) that was caused by an instrumentality exclusively in the defendant's control, and (3) that was not caused by an act or omission of the plaintiff. *Dover*, 334 Md. at 236–37, 638 A.2d at 765. Appellant cannot satisfy the first two criteria.

In order to rely on RES IPSA LOQUITUR, Appellant must first prove that the accident would not have occurred in the absence of Appellees' negligence.

"[T]he doctrine of RES IPSA LOQUITUR is applicable only when the facts and surrounding circumstances tend to show that the injury was the result of some condition or act which ordinarily does not happen if those who have the control or management thereof exercise proper care. It does not apply where it can be said from ordinary experience that the accident might have happened without the fault of the defendant."

Greeley v. Baltimore Transit Co., 180 Md. 10, 12–13, 22 A.2d 460, 461(1941). Appellant cannot satisfy this requirement because the evidence and inferences fairly deducible from the evidence indicate that, in addition to the possibility that Appellees were negligent, there is an equally likely explanation for the escalator's abrupt stop.

CASE

For safety reasons, the escalator in question was equipped with two emergency stop buttons, located at the top and bottom of the escalator, respectively. When either button is pushed, if the escalator is functioning as intended, the escalator will stop. The buttons are safety devices designed to stop the escalator quickly should a hand, foot, or article of clothing become caught; thus, ready accessibility to the buttons is only sensible. We cannot say that the escalator would not stop in the absence of Appellees' negligence because the escalator would also stop whenever any person pushed one of the emergency stop buttons.

The record is silent as to whether anyone did, in fact, push one of the stop buttons, but this is of little concern. The facts need not show that a stop button definitely was pushed to preclude reliance on res ipsa; they need only show that something other than Appellees' negligence was just as likely to cause the escalator to stop. The fact that the escalator had never malfunctioned before the day in question, and has not malfunctioned since, makes it equally likely, if not slightly more likely, that the escalator did not malfunction on the day in question but, rather, that it stopped because somebody intentionally or unintentionally pushed an emergency stop button.

Appellant also cannot rely on RES IPSA LOQUITUR in the present case because he cannot satisfy the second essential component of the doctrine, that the injury-causing instrumentality be in the exclusive control of the defendant.

"The element of control has an important bearing as negativing the hypothesis of an intervening cause beyond the defendant's control, and also as tending to show affirmatively that the cause was one within the power of the defendant to prevent by the exercise of care. Thus it has been held that the inference is not permissible where . . . the opportunity for interference by others weakens the probability that the injury is attributable to the defendant's act or omission."(Citations omitted).

Lee v. Housing Auth. of Baltimore, 203 Md. 453, 462, 101 A.2d 832, 836 (1954). This Court has often held res ipsa to be inapplicable when the opportunity for third-party interference prevented a finding that the defendant maintained exclusive control of the injury-causing instrumentality. *See, e.g., Joffre*, 222 Md. at 8-10, 158 A.2d at 635-36 (holding defendant's control not exclusive where customers had access to soda bottles for approximately two months before one bottle inexplicably shattered); *Williams v. McCrory's Stores Corp.*, 203 Md. 598, 604-05, 102 A.2d 253, 256 (1954) (holding defendant's control not exclusive where thousands of customers had access to revolving stools every week).

In the present case, we must necessarily conclude that Appellant is unable to satisfy the second essential component of res ipsa. Hundreds of Saks & Co.'s customers have unlimited access to the emergency stop buttons each day. If the escalator's two emergency stop buttons are readily accessible to all persons in the vicinity and any customer can cause the escalator to stop simply by pressing one of the buttons, then it is impossible to establish that the escalator was in Appellee's exclusive control.

In *Trigg v. J.C. Penney Company*, 307 F.Supp. 1092 (D.N.M.1969), the United States District Court for the District of New Mexico held res ipsa inapplicable to facts very similar to those in the present case. In that case, the plaintiff was injured when the escalator upon which he was riding, in a department store, stopped suddenly. *Trigg*, 307 F.Supp. at 1092. The escalator was equipped with emergency stop buttons. *Trigg*, 307 F.Supp. at 1093. Although there was no evidence that anyone had pushed the button on the day that the plaintiff was injured, the court concluded that the "plaintiffs failed to prove . . . two crucial elements of the doctrine of RES IPSA LOQUITUR. There is no showing that the instrumentality was within the exclusive control of the defendant. Anyone could push one of [the emergency stop buttons] causing the escalator to stop. This conclusion necessarily leads the court to find that the second element has also not been proved. If anyone could stop the escalator by pressing the button, either intentionally or unintentionally, the accident is not one that ordinarily would not have happened in the absence of negligence on the part of the defendant."

Id.

There is yet a third reason that res ipsa is inapplicable to the case sub judice. We have, for many years, held that res ipsa is only applicable when "the circumstances attendant upon an accident are themselves of such a character as to justify a jury in inferring negligence as the cause of that accident." *Benedick v. Potts*, 88 Md. 52, 55, 40 A. 1067, 1068 (1898). This is the case when "the common knowledge of jurors [is] sufficient to support an inference or finding of negligence on the part of" a defendant. *Meda v. Brown*, 318 Md. 418, 428, 569 A.2d 202, 207 (1990); any person who regularly uses stairs knows that they rarely collapse beneath one's feet. *See Blankenship v. Wagner*, 261 Md. 37, 273 A.2d 412 (1971). The plaintiffs were permitted to rely on res ipsa because lay jurors possess the background knowledge necessary to decide whether these events ordinarily occur in the absence of someone's negligence. *See also Strasburger v. Vogel*, 103 Md. 85, 63 A. 202 (1906) (explaining that res ipsa would be proper where brick from defendant's chimney fell onto the head of an infant on the sidewalk below if defendant had not presented evidence of an intervening cause).

In some cases, however, "because of the complexity of the subject matter, expert testimony is required to establish negligence and causation." *Meda*, 318 Md. at 428, 569 A.2d at 207. For example, *Orkin*, supra, addressed the applicability of res ipsa in a medical malpractice case. In that case, the plaintiff sustained an injury to her median, ulnar, and radial nerves on her right side during surgery to repair a perforated ulcer. The plaintiff was under general anesthesia while her surgery was being performed, and she "could not 'ascribe a particular negligent act to any defendant.'" *Orkin*, 318 Md. at 432, 569 A.2d at 209. She proffered proof that her injury was one that usually does not occur absent negligence through the testimony of a neurologist.

The trial court granted summary judgment in favor of the defendants, and the plaintiff appealed, arguing that she should have been permitted to present her case to a jury under the theory of RES IPSA LOQUITUR.

Although this Court held that the trial court erred in granting the defendants' motion for summary judgment, and, therefore, remanded the case to the circuit court, we explained that the plaintiff should not be permitted to rely on RES IPSA LOQUITUR on remand. We stated that a case involving complex issues of fact, for which expert testimony is required, is not a proper case for RES IPSA LOQUITUR.

"This is not an 'obvious injury' case. Resolution of the issues of negligence and causation involved in a case of this kind necessarily requires knowledge of complicated matters, including human anatomy, medical science, operative procedures, areas of patient responsibility, and standards of care. Complex issues of the type generated by a case of this kind should not be resolved by laymen without expert assistance. RES IPSA LOQUITUR does not apply under these circumstances. *Meda v. Brown*, [318 Md. 418, 569 A.2d 202]."

We quoted this language with approval in *Dover*, where we held RES IPSA LOQUITUR to be inapplicable in a case involving the misleveling of an elevator, in part, because the common knowledge of jurors was insufficient to support an inference that the misleveling was caused by the defendant's negligence. *Dover*, 334 Md. at 254, 256, 638 A.2d at 773-74. An elevator "may experience problems absent anyone's negligence," and, thus, we explained that "[w]ithout [an expert's] opinion that the misleveling was [most likely] caused by negligence, an inference that this elevator did not mislevel or experience other problems absent someone's negligence may be unjustified." *Dover*, 334 Md. at 255, 638 A.2d at 774.

"'Mechanical, electrical, and electronic devices fail or malfunction routinely—some more routinely than others. A speck of dust, a change in temperature, misuse, an accidental unforeseen trauma—many things can cause these devices to malfunction. To allow an inference that the malfunction is due to someone's negligence when the precise cause

CASE

cannot be satisfactorily established appears . . . to be unwarranted.'"

Dover, 334 Md. at 255, 638 A.2d at 774. Thus, in cases concerning the malfunction of complex machinery, an expert is required to testify that the malfunction is of a sort that would not occur absent some negligence.

When an expert raises an inference of a defendant's negligence, however, a plaintiff must necessarily be precluded from relying on RES IPSA LOQUITUR. "If expert testimony is used to raise an inference that the accident could not happen had there been no negligence, then it is the expert witness, not an application of the traditional RES IPSA LOQUITUR doctrine, that raises the inference." *Dover*, 334 Md. at 254, 638 A.2d at 773. In such a case, the jury is not asked or permitted to draw an inference unaided by expert testimony. *Meda*, 318 Md. at 425, 428, 569 A.2d at 205, 207. Instead, the jury's function is to decide whether the expert's inference that a defendant was negligent is credible.

In the present case, Appellant has declined to present expert testimony. In doing so he has, perhaps, "confused the question of whether an inference may be drawn by an expert with that of whether an inference may be drawn by a layman." *Meda*, 318 Md. at 428, 569 A.2d at 206. It is not the presence of expert testimony that, if presented, would prevent a jury in the present case from drawing an inference of Appellees' negligence, rather, it is the complex and technical issue presented by the facts of this case. Like the elevator in *Dover*, an escalator is a complex machine. Leaving aside the presence of any emergency stop buttons, whether an escalator is likely to stop abruptly in the absence of someone's negligence is a question that laymen cannot answer based on common knowledge. The answer requires knowledge of "complicated matters" such as mechanics, electricity, circuits, engineering, and metallurgy. RES IPSA LOQUITUR does not apply under these circumstances.

For all of the foregoing reasons, we answer the second certified question in the negative. We are called upon to answer the third certified question only if the doctrine of RES IPSA LOQUITUR applies to the present case. We have stated that the doctrine does not apply.

In sum, we answer the first certified question in the negative; the allegations in Appellant's Complaint with respect to negligence do not amount to a waiver of RES IPSA LOQUITUR. We also answer the second certified question in the negative; res ipsa does not apply to the facts of the instant case because Appellant cannot prove that the event would not occur in the absence of Appellees' negligence. In addition, Appellant cannot prove that the escalator was in Appellees' exclusive control. Finally, because of the complex and technical nature of the issue presented in this case, lay jurors would not be permitted to draw an inference of negligence without the aid of expert testimony, negating the very definition of RES IPSA LOQUITUR.

Case Review Question
What are the factual elements of res ipsa loquitur in this case?

Assignment 11.1

In the following fact situations, identify which facts would support a claim of negligence by determining the following:

◆ Who owes the duty?
◆ To whom is the duty owed?
◆ What is the duty?

- How is the duty breached?
- How does the breach cause injury in fact and in law?
- What is the damage?

1. The state highway department sprays pesticides along a roadside on a very windy day. Adjacent to the roadside is an elementary school playground. The wind blows some of the pesticides across the playground where children are having gym class and many of them become violently ill and one child requires hospitalization.
2. Two golfers are playing on a busy golf course. One of the golfers puts his ball on the tee and hits toward the green. His golf ball strikes the golfer ahead who has not yet finished the hole. The struck golfer dies from the blow to the head by the golf ball traveling an estimated 90 mph.

STRICT LIABILITY

Strict liability is a much narrower area of tort law, but it is also one of the fastest growing areas of civil law. Traditionally, strict liability was applied in cases of extremely dangerous activities. This area of law grew out of the law of negligence, to be used in special circumstances. Specifically, strict liability was developed for use in cases of persons who obtained some personal or financial benefit from an activity that could not be made safe and from which the innocent public could not protect itself. Originally, strict liability was applied in cases where a person dealt with dangerous animals or was involved in other activities that could greatly injure members of the public who were in no position to protect themselves, for example, persons who used explosives, such as construction or demolition crews.

Fault, carelessness, or intent is not an issue in actions for strict liability, because no matter how carefully an activity might be conducted or an animal might be guarded, it is a near certainty that if the danger escapes into a public area, innocent bystanders will be harmed. It is further reasoned that the persons in control of the activity or animal benefit from it and it is only reasonable that they should bear the costs of harm.

More recently, strict liability has been the primary basis of litigation against manufacturers of products. Consumers (users) of products have no means of knowing how the product was designed and what aspects of it could cause injury. The manufacturer who designed the product, however, is well aware of the product's defects or dangerous aspects, and if the defect is not corrected or if a proper warning of the dangers is not given, the manufacturer has placed in commerce a dangerous instrument that is likely to injure innocent persons. This is a basis for liability of the manufacturer who ultimately benefits most from the sale of such products.

CASE

IRVINE

v.

RARE FELINE BREEDING CENTER INC.

1997 WL 564203 (685 N.E.2d 120).

JUDITH S. PROFFITT, Judge

CHEZEM

Appellant-Plaintiff, Scott Irvine ("Irvine"), appeals an order denying his motion for partial summary judgment. We affirm.

Issues

The parties raise various issues which we restate as:

  I. Whether STRICT LIABILITY is the law in Indiana WILD animal cases;

 II. Whether any exceptions or defenses to STRICT LIABILITY should be recognized; and,

III. Whether a genuine issue of material fact exists regarding either Irvine's status or any available defenses.

Facts and Procedural History

For the past thirty years, Mosella Schaffer ("Schaffer") has lived on a fifty acre farm in Hamilton County, Indiana where she has raised and maintained exotic ANIMALS. These ANIMALS have included zebras, llamas, camels, kangaroos, and, beginning in 1970, Siberian tigers. Although her original intent was to breed and sell the ANIMALS, she soon found it difficult to part with many of them.

In 1993, Scott Bullington ("Bullington") was renting a room in the garage area of Schaffer's house. Aware of his friend Irvine's interest in WILD ANIMALS, Bullington informed Irvine of Schaffer's farm and the ANIMALS she kept there. Irvine, then in his late twenties, began to stop by and see the ANIMALS as per Schaffer's open invitation. Over the next two years, Irvine visited Schaffer's farm several dozen times. During these visits, people would occasionally pet the tigers through a fence.

On the afternoon of December 2, 1995, Irvine arrived at Schaffer's home to see Bullington. The two men drank alcohol and watched television until early evening when Bullington announced that he had to leave to attend his employer's Christmas party. Because Irvine had consumed a substantial amount of alcohol, Bullington told Irvine he could stay over night on the couch. Some time after Bullington had left, Irvine exited Bullington's apartment, walked to the front of Schaffer's property and visited with the llamas and zebras. As he was doing so, Schaffer drove up, stopped her car, had a brief, friendly conversation with Irvine, and went into her house.

Around 8:00 p.m., Irvine decided to visit the tigers before going to sleep. Thus, he went through Schaffer's garage, proceeded through the utility room, continued through the sun room, and ended up in the back yard. Irvine then approached the wire caging, as he and others had done in the past, placed a couple fingers inside the enclosure, and attempted to pet a male tiger. As he was scratching the male tiger, a female tiger made some commotion, which caused Irvine to look away from the male tiger. At that moment, the male tiger pulled Irvine's arm through the two inch by six inch opening of the wire fence.

Upon hearing Irvine's shouts, Schaffer came out of her house, banged an object against the fence, and freed Irvine. Schaffer immediately drove Irvine to the hospital. Irvine was treated and admitted to the hospital. Later, he was transferred to another hospital, and underwent six surgeries during a thirteen day hospital stay. Further surgeries are indicated though Irvine is uninsured.

On May 30, 1996, Irvine filed a complaint against Schaffer containing four counts: negligence, STRICT LIABILITY, nuisance, and punitives. On September 6, 1996, Irvine filed his motion for partial summary judgment on the basis that incurred risk and assumption of risk are not valid defenses to a STRICT LIABILITY WILD animal claim, on the basis that assumption of risk is not available in a non-contract case, and on the basis that the defense of open and obvious is not available in an animal liability case. Schaffer filed a response on January 14, 1997. Irvine filed a reply on January 21, 1997. The trial court denied Irvine's motion for summary judgment on the STRICT LIABILITY count, denied summary judgment on the issue of assumption of risk, and granted summary judgment on the issue of open and obvious. The trial court granted Irvine's petition to certify three issues for interlocutory appeal: (1) whether incurred risk or other defenses are available in a STRICT LIABILITY animal case; (2) whether Irvine was an invitee as a matter of law; and (3) whether the defense of assumption of risk is available in a noncontractual case. We accepted jurisdiction of the interlocutory appeal.

Discussion and Decision

Irvine first argues that Indiana has historically adhered to strict tort liability in WILD animal cases. He further argues that when the Indiana Comparative Fault Act (Ind.Code s 34–4–33–1 et seq., the "Act") was adopted, it did not change the law in WILD animal cases. Moreover, he claims that no exceptions to STRICT LIABILITY in WILD animal cases have ever been applied in Indiana. He also argues that even if his status is somehow relevant, he was clearly an invitee. Thus, he asserts that the trial court should not have denied his summary judgment on the STRICT LIABILITY issue. In contrast, Schaffer argues that Indiana has not adopted, and should not adopt, STRICT LIABILITY animal cases. . . .

Upon review of the grant or denial of a summary judgment motion, we apply the same legal judgment is appropriate only when there are no genuine issues of material fact and the moving party is entitled to judgment as a matter of law. Ind.Trial Rule 56(C); *North Snow Bay, Inc. v. Hamilton,* 657 N.E.2d 420, 422 (IND.CT.APP.1995). On review, we may not search the entire record to support the judgment, but may only consider that which had been specifically designated to the trial court. *Id.* The party appealing the trial court's grant or denial of

summary judgment has the burden of persuading this court that the trial court's decision was erroneous. *Id.*

I. Liability in a WILD Animal Case

We first address whether STRICT LIABILITY is the common law rule for WILD animal cases in Indiana. The parties have not cited and we have not found a case specifically applying STRICT LIABILITY to a true WILD animal case in Indiana. However, the basic rule has been frequently stated in various contexts. *Holt v. Myers,* 93 N.E. 31 (Ind.Ct.App.1910) (mentioning WILD animal STRICT LIABILITY rule although case dealt with vicious dog). Accordingly, we have little difficulty concluding that Indiana's common law recognized the STRICT LIABILITY rule for WILD animal cases—despite the fact that previously, Indiana courts have not had the opportunity to apply the rule.

We next address the issue of whether the adoption of the Act changed the common law rule of STRICT LIABILITY in WILD animal cases. "We presume the legislature does not intend by the enactment of a statute to make any change in the common law beyond what it declares, either in express terms or by unmistakable implication." An abrogation of the common law will be implied (1) where a statute is enacted which undertakes to cover the entire subject treated and was clearly designed as a substitute for the common law; or, (2) where the two laws are so repugnant that both in reason may not stand. *Id.* "As a statute in derogation of the existing common law, the Act must be strictly construed." *Indianapolis Power & Light Co. v. Brad Snodgrass, Inc.,* 578 N.E.2d 669, 673 (Ind.1991).

The Act, enacted in 1983 and effective in 1985, "governs any action based on fault [.]" Ind.Code s 34–4–33–1. STRICT LIABILITY, by definition, is liability without fault. Thus, the Act would seem to be inapplicable to a STRICT LIABILITY action. The legislative history lends further support for this conclusion. The original version of Ind.Code s 34–4–33–2 provided that "Fault," for purposes of the Act, "include[d] any act or omission that

◆ CASE

[was] negligent, willful, wanton, reckless, or intentional toward the person or property of others, or that subject[ed] a person to strict tort liability, but [did] not include an intentional act. The term also include[d] breach of warranty, unreasonable assumption of risk not constituting an enforceable express consent, incurred risk, misuse of a product for which the defendant otherwise would be liable, and unreasonable failure to avoid injury or to mitigate damages." (Emphasis added).

By the time of its effective date, that same section had been changed to its current form: "'[f]ault' includes any act or omission that is negligent, willful, wanton, reckless, or intentional toward the person or property of others. The term also includes unreasonable assumption of risk not constituting an enforceable express consent, incurred risk, and unreasonable failure to avoid injury or to mitigate damages." Ind.Code s 34–4–33–2. The current form includes no reference to STRICT LIABILITY. Narrowly construing the Act, we conclude that it does not explicitly apply to a STRICT LIABILITY claim. *See Templin v. Fobes*, 617 N.E.2d 541, 544 n. 1 (Ind.1993) (products liability case in which our Supreme Court noted, "practical problems arise, at least in part, because of the operation of Indiana's Comparative Fault Act, which would apply in Templins' negligence claims against Fobes but not in the Templins' STRICT LIABILITY claim against Rockwood.").

II. Exceptions or Defenses

Having concluded that the Act has not changed common law STRICT LIABILITY in WILD animal cases, we next address Irvine's contention that no exceptions to STRICT LIABILITY in WILD animal cases have ever been applied in this state. While we agree with Irvine's contention, this fact is of no surprise in view of the lack of any true WILD animal cases in Indiana. As this is an issue of first impression, we look to the reason behind the STRICT LIABILITY WILD animal rule and consult other sources as necessary.

We have previously set out the rationale for imposing STRICT LIABILITY against owners for injuries caused by an attack by a naturally ferocious or DANGEROUS animal. *See Hardin v. Christy*, 462 N.E.2d 256, 259, 262 (Ind.Ct.App.1984). STRICT LIABILITY is appropriately placed:

upon those who, even with proper care, expose the community to the risk of a very DANGEROUS thing. . . . The kind of "DANGEROUS animal" that will subject the keeper to STRICT LIABILITY . . . must pose some kind of an abnormal risk to the particular community where the animal is kept; hence, the keeper is engaged in an activity that subjects those in the vicinity, including those who come onto his property, to an abnormal risk . . . The possessor of a WILD animal is strictly liable for physical harm done to the person of another . . . if that harm results from a DANGEROUS propensity that is characteristic of WILD ANIMALS of that class. Thus, STRICT LIABILITY has been imposed on keepers of lions and tigers, bears, elephants, wolves, monkeys, and other similar ANIMALS. No member of such a species, however domesticated, can ever be regarded as safe, and liability does not rest upon any experience with the particular animal.

Although having done so in an asbestos case and using slightly different terms, Judge Posner concisely set out the rationale for the WILD animal STRICT LIABILITY rule using the following hypothetical:

[k]eeping a tiger in one's backyard would be an example of an abnormally hazardous activity. The hazard is such, relative to the value of the activity, that we desire not just that the owner take all due care that the tiger not escape, but that he consider seriously the possibility of getting rid of the tiger altogether; and we give him an incentive to consider this course of action by declining to make the exercise of due care a defense to a suit based on an injury caused by the tiger—in other words, by making him strictly liable for any such injury.

G.J. Leasing Co. v. Union Electric Co., 54 F.3d 379, 386 (7th CIR.1995).

With the rationale for the rule in mind, we analyze whether any exceptions or defenses to the STRICT LIABILITY WILD animal rule are appropriate. Like the sources previously cited, the Restatement provides:

(1) A possessor of a WILD animal is subject to liability to another for harm done by the animal to the other, his person, land or chattels, although the possessor has exercised the utmost care to confine the animal, or otherwise prevent it from doing harm.

(2) This liability is limited to harm that results from a DANGEROUS propensity that is characteristic of WILD ANIMALS of the particular class, or of which the possessor knows or has reason to know.

Restatement (Second) of Torts s 507 (1977). However, because the general rule in s 507 is "subject to a number of exceptions and qualifications, which are too numerous to state in a single Section," s 507 should be read together with s 508, s 510, s 511, s 512, s 515, and s 517. Restatement, supra cmt. a, s 507. Thus, we look to those other sections to help flesh out the Restatement's rule.

Section 510(a) provides: "The possessor of a WILD animal . . . is subject to STRICT LIABILITY for the resulting harm, although it would not have occurred but for the unexpectable . . . innocent, negligent or reckless conduct of a third person." However, "[a] possessor of land is not subject to STRICT LIABILITY to one who intentionally or negligently trespasses upon the land, for harm done to him by a WILD animal . . . that the possessor keeps on the land, even though the trespasser has no reason to know that the animal is kept there." Restatement, supra s 511. Invitees and licensees are dealt with in s 513, which states: "The possessor of a WILD animal . . . who keeps it upon land in his possession, is subject to STRICT LIABILITY to persons coming upon the land in the exercise of a privilege whether derived from his consent to their entry or otherwise." Yet, if the invitee or licensee "knows that the DANGEROUS animal is permitted to run at large or has escaped from control they may be barred from recovery if they choose to act upon the possessor's consent or to exercise any other privilege and thus expose themselves to the risk of being harmed by the animal. (See s 515)." Restatement, supra, cmt. a, s 513.

Section 515(2), in turn, provides: "The plaintiff's contributory negligence in knowingly and unreasonably subjecting himself to the risk that a WILD animal . . . will do harm to his person . . . is a defense to the STRICT LIABILITY." Comment c. to s 515(2) explains:

Although one harmed by a WILD . . . animal that has escaped from control of its possessor or harborer is not barred from recovery because he has not exercised ordinary care to observe the presence of the animal or to escape from its attack, he is barred if he intentionally and unreasonably subjects himself to the risk of harm by the animal. Thus one who without any necessity for so doing that is commensurate with the risk involved knowingly puts himself in reach of an animal that is effectively chained or otherwise confined cannot recover against the possessor or harborer of the animal. So, too, although a licensee or an invitee upon land of another upon which he knows that WILD . . . ANIMALS are kept under the possessor's control does not take the risk that they will escape and harm him, he does nonetheless take the risk of harm by the ANIMALS that he knows are roaming at large, so that he will to a reasonable certainty encounter them if he avails himself of the invitation or permission held out to him by the possessor of the land. (Emphasis added).

Comment d. to s 515(2) states: "This kind of contributory negligence, which consists of voluntarily and unreasonably encountering a known danger, is frequently called either contributory negligence or assumption of risk, or both."

Section 515(3) provides: "The plaintiff's assumption of the risk of harm from the animal is a defense to the STRICT LIABILITY." The comment to s 515(3) states that "one employed as a lion tamer in a circus may be barred from recovery by his assumption of the risk when he is clawed by a lion. In the same manner, one who voluntarily teases and provokes a chained bear, or goes within reach of a vicious dog, is barred from recovery if he does so with knowledge of the danger." (Emphases added).

As indicated by the extensive quotations above, the Restatement clearly recognizes exceptions or defenses to WILD animal STRICT LIABILITY. *Prosser and Keeton* also agree that defenses are available to a STRICT LIABILITY WILD animal claim. "[C]ontributory negligence by way of knowingly and unreasonably subjecting oneself to a risk of harm from an abnormally DANGEROUS animal will constitute a defense" to a STRICT LIABILITY claim. *Prosser and Keeton,* supra s 79, at 565. "Thus, a plaintiff who

CASE

voluntarily and unreasonably comes within reach of an animal which he knows to be DANGEROUS, . . . has no cause of action when it attacks him." Id. at 566.

Because we agree with the rationale of the exceptions and/or defenses set out in the Restatement, and because we find it to be in keeping with Indiana's recent policy regarding allocation of fault, we adopt the Restatement's approach in WILD animal cases.

B. Defenses

In adopting the Restatement's view that incurred risk/assumed risk may be a defense to a STRICT LIABILITY WILD animal claim, we must next examine whether genuine issues of material fact exist regarding a defense in Irvine's case. Incurred risk requires a mental state of venturousness and a conscious, deliberate and intentional embarkation upon the course of conduct with knowledge of the circumstances. *Perdue Farms, Inc. v. Pryor,* — N.E.2d -, 63S01–9509-CV-172, (Ind. July 22, 1997), slip op. at 7. In other contexts, we have stated that the defense of incurred risk is generally a question of fact, and the party asserting it bears the burden of proving it by a preponderance of

evidence. *Schooley v. Ingersoll Rand Inc.,* 631 N.E.2d 932, 939 (Ind.Ct.App.1994).

Here, the parties designated conflicting evidence regarding whether Irvine knowingly and unreasonably put himself within reach of a WILD animal that was effectively chained or otherwise confined. There was evidence that around the time of the accident, Irvine had been volunteering at the Indianapolis Zoo and had been told not to have contact with tigers. Moreover, there was evidence that Irvine was aware of a prior incident wherein the tiger which injured him grabbed another man's thumb. However, there was other evidence tending to indicate that Schaffer and others had petted the tiger safely in the past. Also, there was evidence that Irvine may have been rather intoxicated on the night in question. In view of the conflicting evidence and inferences, summary judgment was properly denied on the issue of whether a defense was appropriate in this case.

Affirmed.

Case Review Question
Why is strict liability allegedly applicable in this case as opposed to a case of gross negligence?

INTENTIONAL TORTS

The third major category of torts is a tort where the primary element is intent. This is an action where the defendant has manifested an intent to bring about a particular result and, as a consequence, the plaintiff was injured. It must be shown that the defendant acted voluntarily, even with the knowledge that the act would almost certainly bring about the injury. In some instances, the injury itself is the desired result, but it need not be to constitute an intentional tort. It must only be shown that the defendant knew or should have known with substantial certainty that his or her action would bring about the injury.[22]

Intentional tort differs from the concept of degree of duty in negligence, because in an intentional tort, the risk is so great it can be counted upon to produce the injury. If the actor commits the action anyway, such action constitutes an intentional tort against the injured party. A major distinction between gross negligence and intentional tort is that in an intentional tort, mere knowledge and appreciation of a danger are insufficient. As stated, there must be evidence of voluntary conduct in light of the knowledge and appreciation of the danger. In addition, the risk of harm must be a near certainty rather than a likelihood.

Several types of intentional torts provide a basis for liability. Some of the more common types are discussed here to demonstrate the basis for the more commonly litigated actions. (Figure 11.1 lists the elements of these and other torts.)

Assault

Assault is commonly considered to be a physical attack of some sort, but in tort law, its meaning is quite different. To prove an act of assault, it must be shown that the actor engaged in physical conduct, that may or may not have been accompanied by words, that placed the plaintiff in *apprehension of immediate and harmful* contact.[23] By definition, the tort of assault involves no physical contact, only the threat of such contact. A plaintiff cannot claim assault when the threatening act consisted only of words unless under circumstances that could create a reasonable perception of imminent harm. Nor is an assault committed when a threat is made for some future point in time. The basis for an assault action is that the threat of immediate physical harm produces such fear, and/or a reaction, that it actually injures the plaintiff. For example, if I threaten to beat you up at the park the next time I see you there, no assault has occurred, because you have no realistic fear. You can avoid the attack by avoiding the park. However, if I am in the park with you and tell you that I am going to beat you up, your response may be such fear of an imminent harmful contact that the fear causes injury (e.g., heart attack), and consequently, an assault has occurred.

Battery

The tort of battery is perhaps the most litigated intentional tort, because it includes all unpermitted physical contact that results in harm. Battery encompasses physical attacks, medical treatment without consent, and every other conceivable act that results in physical contact between two parties as long as (1) there is the intent to make physical contact; (2) there is no consent to such contact; (3) the contact occurs to the person or to anything that is so closely attached that it is considered part of the person (e.g., clothing); and (4) the contact results in injury to the person.[24]

Battery encompasses much more than a physical fight between two persons. In fact, in recent years, battery has been the basis for medical malpractice claims, including such actions as leaving foreign objects (sponges or instruments) in a patient's body or performing a procedure to which the patient had not previously consented.

The Emergency Rule is an exception or defense to actions for battery.[25] The rule states that unpermitted physical contact (including medical treatment) may be allowed if a medical or other emergency exists that prevents the person from making a decision as to whether to permit the contact. For example, if an unconscious patient suffers heart failure during an operation, doctors are permitted to perform additional measures to save the patient's life even though the patient never consented to such procedures.

FIGURE 11.1   Torts and Related Causes of Action: The Elements

The Cause of Action	Its Elements
1. Abuse of Process	i. Use of civil or criminal proceedings ii. Improper or ulterior purpose
2. Alienation of Affections	i. Intent to diminish the material relationship between spouses ii. Affirmative conduct iii. Affections between spouses are in fact alienated iv. Causation

3. Assault (Civil)	i. Act
	ii. Intent to cause either:
	   a. an imminent harmful or offensive contact, or
	   b. an apprehension of an imminent harmful or offensive contact
	iii. Apprehension of an imminent harmful or offensive contact
	   to the plaintiff's person
	iv. Causation

4. Battery (Civil)	i. Act
	ii. Intent to cause either:
	   a. an imminent harmful or offensive contact, or
	   b. an apprehension of an imminent harmful or offensive contact
	iii. Harmful or offensive contact with the plaintiff's person
	iv. Causation

5. Civil Rights Violation	i. A person acting under color of state law ii. Deprives someone of a federal right
6. Conversion	i. Personal property (chattel) ii. Plaintiff is in possession of the chattel or is entitled to immediate possession iii. Intent to exercise dominion or control over the chattel iv. Serious interference with plaintiff's possession v. Causation
7. Criminal Conversation	Defendant has sexual relations with the plaintiff's spouse (adultery)

Defamation (two torts)
8. Libel
	i. Written defamatory statement by the defendant
	ii. Of and concerning the plaintiff
	iii. Publication of the statement
	iv. Damages
	   a. In some state, special damages never have to be proven in a libel case
	   b. In other states, only libel on its face does not require special damages.
	      In these states, libel per quod requires special damages
	v. Causation

9. Slander	i. Oral defamatory statement by the defendant
	ii. Of and concerning the plaintiff
	iii. Publication of the statement
	iv. Damages:
	   a. Special damages are not required if the slander is slander per se
	   b. Special damages must be proven if the slander is not slander per se
	v. Causation

FIGURE 11.1   Torts and Related Causes of Action: The Elements *(Continued)*

The cause of Action	Its Elements
10. Disparagement	i. False statement of fact ii. Disparaging the plaintiff's business or property iii. Publication iv. Intent v. Special damages vi. Causation

11. Enticement of a Child or Abduction of a Child	i. Intent to interfere with a parent's custody over his or her child
	ii. Affirmative conduct by the defendant:
	    a. to abduct or force the child from the parent's custody, or
	    b. to entice or encourage the child to leave the parent, or
	    c. to harbor the child and encourage him or her to stay away from the parent's custody
	iii. The child leaves the custody of the parent
	iv. Causation

12. Enticement of Spouse	i. Intent to diminish the marital relationship between the spouses
	ii. Affirmative conduct by the defendant:
	    a. to entice or encourage the spouse to leave the plaintiff's home, or
	    b. to harbor the spouse and encourage him or her to stay away from the plaintiff's home
	iii. The spouse leaves the plaintiff's home
	iv. Causation

13. False Imprisonment	i. An act that completely confines the plaintiff within fixed boundaries set by the defendant ii. Intent to confine plaintiff or a third person iii. Causation of the confinement iv. Plaintiff was either conscious of the confinement or suffered actual harm by it
14. Intentional Infliction of Emotional Distress	i. An act of extreme or outrageous conduct ii. Intent to cause severe emotional distress iii. Severe emotional distress is suffered iv. Causation
15. Interference with Contract Relations	i. An existing contract ii. Interference with the contract by defendant iii. Intent iv. Damages v. Causation
16. Interference with Prospective Advantage	i. Reasonable expectation of an economic advantage ii. Interference with this expectation iii. Intent iv. Damages v. Causation
Invasion of Privacy (four torts) 17. Appropriation	i. The use of the plaintiff's name, likeness, or personality ii. For the benefit of the defendant

FIGURE 11.1 Torts and Related Causes of Action: The Elements   *(Continued)*

18. False Light	i. Publicity ii. Placing the plaintiff in a false light iii. Highly offensive to a reasonable person
19. Intrusion	i. An act of intrusion into a person's private affairs or concerns ii. Highly offensive to a reasonable person
20. Public Disclosure of Private Fact	i. Publicity ii. Concerning the private life of the plaintiff iii. Highly offensive to a reasonable person
21. Malicious Prosecution	i. Initiation or procurement of the initiation of criminal proceedings ii. Without probable cause iii. With malice iv. The criminal proceedings terminate in favor of the accused
22. Misrepresentation	i. Statement of fact ii. Statement is false iii. Scienter (intent to mislead) iv. Justifiable reliance v. Actual damages
23. Negligence	i. Duty ii. Breach of duty iii. Proximate cause iv. Damage
Nuisance (two torts) 24. Private Nuisance	An unreasonable interference with the use and enjoyment of private land
25. Public Nuisance	An unreasonable interference with a right that is common to the general public
26. Prima Facie Tort	i. Infliction of harm ii. Intent to do harm (malice) iii. Special damages iv. Causation
27. Seduction	The defendant has sexual relations with the plaintiff's daughter, with or without consent.

28. Strict Liability for Harm Caused by Animals	Domestic Animals:
	  i. Owner has reason to know the animal has a specific propensity to cause harm.
	  ii. Harm caused by the animal was due to that specific propensity
	Wild Animals:
	  i. Keeping a wild animal
	  ii. Causes harm

29. Strict Liability for Abnormally Dangerous Conditions or Activities	i. Existence of an abnormally dangerous condition or activity ii. Knowledge of the condition or activity iii. Damages iv. Causation

FIGURE 11.1 Torts and Related Causes of Action: The Elements *(Continued)*

The Cause of Action	Its Elements
30. Strict Liability in Tort	i. Seller ii. A defective product that is unreasonably dangerous to person or property iii. User or consumer iv. Physical harm (damages) v. Causation
31. Trespass to Chattels	i. Personal property (chattel) ii. Plaintiff is in possession of the chattel or is entitled to immediate possession iii. Intent to dispossess or to intermeddle with the chattel iv. Dispossession or intermeddling v. Causation
32. Trespass to Land	i. An act ii. Intrusion on land iii. In possession of another iv. Intent to intrude v. Causation of the intrusion
Warranty (three causes of action) 33. Breach of Express Warranty	i. A statement of fact that is false ii. Made with the intent or expectation that the statement will reach the plaintiff iii. Reliance on the statement by the plaintiff iv. Damage v. Causation
34. Breach of Implied Warranty of Fitness for a Particular Purpose	i. Sale of goods ii. Seller has reason to know the buyer's particular purpose in buying the goods iii. Seller has reason to know that the buyer is relying on the seller's skill or judgment in buying the goods iv. The goods are not fit for the particular purpose v. Damage vi Causation
35. Breach of Implied Warranty of Merchantability	i. Sale of goods ii. By a merchant of goods of that kind iii. The goods are not merchantable iv. Damage v. Causation

Note: From Statsky, W. *Torts: Personal Injury Litigation* (New York: Delmar, 2001).

CASE

SUDUL v. CITY OF HAMTRAMCK

221 Mich.App. 455, 502 N.W.2d 478 (1997).

CORRIGAN, Judge.

Defendants were not accorded a fair trial because the error regarding assault and battery by gross

CASE

negligence pervaded the jury instructions and rendered the other special verdicts unsound. We reverse and remand for further proceedings consistent with this opinion.

We specifically agree with the discussion in the dissent/concurrence regarding the nonexistence of a tort called "assault and battery by gross negligence." We especially also hold that an individual employee's intentional torts are not shielded by our governmental immunity statute, a proposition that too frequently is mired in confusion. Nonetheless, we disagree with the position taken in the dissent/concurrence on two grounds.

I. Effect of Defective Jury Instructions on Integrity of Special Verdicts

We part company with the position taken in the dissent/concurrence with respect to the scope of the reversal. While we accept the utility of special verdicts in saving sound portions of a verdict, we nonetheless vacate all the special verdicts in this case because the flaws in the jury instructions regarding assault and battery by gross negligence tainted the entire verdict.

Justice Otis Smith observed in *Sahr v. Bierd,* 354 Mich. 353, 365, 92 N.W.2d 467 (1958), quoting Sunderland, Verdicts, General and Special, 29 Yale LJ 253, 259 (1920):

"The special verdict compels detailed consideration. But above all it enables the public, the parties and the court to see what the jury really has done. The general verdict is either all wrong or all right, because it is an inseparable and inscrutable unit. A single error completely destroys it. But the special verdict enables errors to be localized so that the sound portions of the verdict may be saved and only the unsound portions be subject to redetermination through a new trial."

We cannot say that the special verdicts concerning excessive force, grossly negligent infliction of emotional distress, and the various derivative claims were unaffected by the instructional error. The instructional error was not harmless.

After being instructed incorrectly that defendants could be held responsible for assault and battery if they were grossly negligent, the jury

retired to deliberate. Three hours later, the jurors posed several questions to the court. They first inquired whether excessive force constituted assault and battery. The court, with the agreement of counsel, replied that it did. The court's answer that excessive force was the same as assault and battery reinforced the original error that defendants could be liable for assault and battery by an act of gross negligence.

The court earlier had instructed the jury:

Gross negligence is defined in our state by statute, and it is defined as conduct so reckless as to demonstrate a substantial lack of concern for whether an injury results. The same statute states— grants immunity from tort liability to police officers performing their duty, provided that the police officers' actions are not grossly negligent. This means that the officers are not liable to plaintiffs for assault, battery or excessive force unless you find that their actions were grossly negligent.

The court then gave the correct definitions of assault and battery as set forth in SJI2d 115.01 and 115.02. The court further instructed the jury that the City of Hamtramck may be liable where if you find that the plaintiffs have been subjected to excessive force in plaintiff's arrest and excessive force was done pursuant to a governmental custom, policy, or practice.

The court also merged the concepts of gross negligence and assault and battery in its instructions regarding compensatory and future damages:

If you decide that the plaintiffs, Anthony and Bernard Sudul, are entitled to damages, it is your duty to determine the amount of money which reasonably, fairly, and adequately compensate[s] each of them for the elements of damage which you decide has resulted from the assault, battery and excessive force by the defendants' grossly negligent conduct and/or from the violation of plaintiffs' federal constitutional rights by each police officer or the city, taking into the account the nature and extent of the injury.

If you decide that the plaintiffs, Anthony and Bernard Sudul, are entitled to damages in the future, it is your duty to determine the amount of money which reasonably, fairly and adequately compensates each of them for each of the elements of damage in the future which you decide has resulted from the assault/battery and excessive force by the defendants' grossly negligent conduct and/or from the violation of plaintiffs' federal constitutional rights by each of the police officers or the city, taking into account the nature and extent of the injury.

The verdict form asked specifically whether the officers assaulted plaintiff Anthony Sudul by an act of gross negligence or battered plaintiff Anthony Sudul by an act of gross negligence. As noted, defendants specifically objected on the very ground on which they have here prevailed—that the tort of assault and battery by gross negligence does not exist.

It is critical to us that this misinstructed jury nevertheless returned verdicts of no cause of action for three of the five individual defendant police officers involved in Anthony Sudul's arrest. The jury found only Officers David Donnell and William Robinson, who pushed Sudul to the ground to handcuff him after he resisted arrest, liable with respect to the claims of grossly negligent assault and battery and excessive force.

We cannot conclude that the instructions as a whole, some correct and some incorrect, clearly apprised the jury of the governing law and protected defendants' rights. The court improperly defined assault and battery, then equated it with excessive force and gross negligence. Where a court gives conflicting instructions, one of which is erroneous, we generally presume that the jury followed the erroneous instruction. *Kirby v. Larson*, 400 Mich. 585, 606-607, 256 N.W.2d 400 (1977). Indeed, the jury's subsequent intelligent questions reflected its attempt to understand and follow the court's confusing instructions. The court's instructions permitted the jury to find liability without the requisite finding of intent for assault and battery, then merged a charge of assault and battery with the definition of excessive force in response to the jury's explicit question regarding the nature of those torts.

The author of the dissent/concurrence would also recognize a novel tort of grossly negligent infliction of emotional distress, not recognized previously in any reported case. Our Supreme Court has yet to recognize formally the tort of intentional infliction of emotional distress. We doubt that the Supreme Court would recognize such grossly negligent emotional distress where the shocking and outrageous event that the child bystander witnessed may well have been nothing more than a lawful arrest involving the use of reasonable force. On this record, we have serious reservations regarding the correct application of law to facts. These defendants are as entitled as any litigant to deliberations by a jury that has been instructed correctly concerning the law. The instructional error is manifest, is not isolated, and is not harmless. In our view, failure to reverse all the verdicts affected by the defect is inconsistent with substantial justice. *Id.*

At various points during trial, both plaintiffs' counsel and the court erroneously stated that the officers could be held liable for their subjective "bad faith" in the use of excessive force, a standard repudiated nearly five years earlier in *Graham v. Connor*, 490 U.S. 386, 109 S.Ct. 1865, 104 L.Ed.2d 443 (1989). Instead, the excessive force claim should have been analyzed under an objective reasonableness standard. In our view, the trial court improperly collapsed the excessive force and the assault and battery claims, despite the fact that they involve distinct harms, *Garner v. Michigan State Univ.*, 185 Mich.App. 750, 764, 462 N.W.2d 832 (1990), and failed in its duty to provide clear guidance with regard to the governing law. This result was manifestly unjust, regardless of whether defendant specifically objected.

Reversed and remanded for further proceedings consistent with this opinion. We do not retain jurisdiction.

Case Review Question

How does gross negligence vary from ordinary negligence?

False Imprisonment

False imprisonment occurs when a party (not necessarily a law enforcement agency) creates boundaries for another party, with the intent that the other party be confined within those boundaries. It requires also that the second party is aware of the confinement, does not consent to it, and perceives no reasonable means of escape.[26] False imprisonment has been the basis for lawsuits ranging from false arrests by law enforcement officers to kidnapping and even unwarranted detention in stores by store security and personnel.

The boundaries in a false imprisonment action need not be actual walls. It is only necessary to show that through physical barriers, conduct, or words, the injured party reasonably believed his or her liberty was restricted.[27] There is also no requirement of actual damages. The loss of liberty is considered to be an injury in and of itself, although there are often other more tangible injuries as well.

It is important to understand that an action for false imprisonment cannot be brought if the defendant was exercising a privilege when detaining the plaintiff. For example, security officers and law enforcement agencies are given a wide latitude in detaining persons suspected of criminal activity. Even if the persons are innocent, public policy requires that investigation of reasonable suspicions be allowed. If the suspicions are wholly unfounded, however, or if the investigation or detention is for an unreasonable period of time, the privilege may not apply. This most often becomes an issue in cases when store security guards detain customers on suspicion of shoplifting. If the suspicion, the detainment, and treatment of the customer are reasonable, there would probably be no grounds for an action of false imprisonment.

 CASE

SUPREME COURT OF VIRGINIA.

CARLOTTA JURY

V.

GIANT OF MARYLAND, INC., ET AL.

254 Va.235, 491 S.E.2d 718
Sep. 12, 1997.

LACY, Justice.

In this appeal we consider whether Code § 18.2-105 provides a merchant absolute immunity from civil liability for assault and battery, negligence, and intentional infliction of emotional distress alleged to have occurred during the detention of a customer suspected of shoplifting.

On January 23, 1993, 46-year-old Carlotta Jury went to a Giant Food store in Annandale, Virginia, to exchange a prescription for her niece and purchase some other items. She left two of her children, ages three and ten, in her car. After exchanging the prescription and selecting some batteries and hair ties, she returned to the front of the store, ready to check out. At that point, a man who did not identify himself approached her, grabbed her arm, and told her to accompany him. When she refused, he hit her in the chest, causing her to fall backward into the aisle between the cash registers. As Jury attempted to catch her breath, the man continued to lean over her and tried to jerk her up by pulling on her arm. Another unidentified man approached and, along with the first man, took Jury to a storage area in the back of the store. The first man twisted Jury's arm behind her back and shoved her while walking her to the back of the store. Jury later discovered that the first man who approached her was Arthur Bridcott, a security guard for the Giant Food store, and the second man was James Parker, manager of the store.

As the three reached the back of the store, one of the men kicked Jury in the back of the leg, knocking her to the floor. Her face fell in a pile of dirt, and the men were "scrounging" her face in the dirt. Jury tried to ask what was going on, but they told her to "[s]hut up," "[y]ou're a thief," and "[w]e're taking care of this and we're going to take care of you." The men called Jury crude and obscene names and subjected her to similarly crude and obscene remarks and gestures. Parker, the manager, picked Jury up off the floor by her hair, pulling some of it out of her head, and "stomped" on her foot. The men refused to allow her to use the restroom, and when she tried to tell them that her children were in the car and she was worried about them, the men responded "we'll take care of that or Social Services will."

Jury was detained in the back of the store for approximately one hour. The security guard, Bridcott, told Jury that they would let her go if she provided a written confession and if she would not come back to the store. She refused, stating that she had done nothing wrong. Parker asked Bridcott what merchandise Jury had concealed, and Bridcott responded that Jury had taken possession of batteries and hair ties. The men handcuffed Jury and summoned the police. Jury was arrested and escorted to the police station. She was released later that evening and went to the hospital the next day. At the hospital, Jury was treated, x-rayed, bandaged, given medication and a neck collar, and advised to see an orthopedic doctor.

Jury was subsequently convicted of concealment of merchandise in the general district court. That conviction was reversed on appeal to the circuit court.

Jury filed a motion for judgment alleging assault and battery, negligence, and intentional infliction of emotional distress, against Giant of Maryland, Inc. and its employees involved in Jury's detention at the Giant Food store (collectively "Giant"). She sought recovery for injuries she sustained during her detention. Prior to trial, Giant's motion for summary judgment on the assault and battery and negligence claims was granted and the claims were dismissed based on the trial court's determination that §18.2-105 granted Giant immunity from civil liability for these claims.

Following Jury's presentation of evidence on her intentional infliction of emotional distress claim, the trial court granted Giant's motion to strike, holding that § 18.2-105 also provided Giant with immunity from civil liability base on this claim. We awarded Jury an appeal and, because we concur with Jury's assertion that §18.2-105 does not provide a merchant with absolute immunity, we will reverse the judgment of the trial court and remand the case for further proceedings.

Code § 18.2-105 provides in pertinent part that: [a] merchant, agent or employee of the merchant, who causes the arrest or detention of any person . . . shall not be held civilly liable for unlawful detention, if such detention does not exceed one hour, slander, malicious prosecution, false imprisonment, false arrest, or assault and battery of the person so arrested or detained . . . provided that . . . the merchant, agent or employee . . . had at the time of such arrest or detention probable cause to believe that the person had shoplifted or committed willful concealment of goods or merchandise.

We construed this statute in *F.B.C. Stores, Inc. v. Duncan,* 214 Va. 246, 198 S.E.2d 595 (1973), as encompasing "virtually all of the intentional torts to person recognized at common law" and determined that the "scope" of the immunity "intended by the General Assembly was very broad." *Id.* at 249, 198 S.E.2d at 598. We also, however, reaffirmed the principle that, in construing statutes, "courts presume that the legislature never intends application of the statute to work irrational consequences." *Id.* at 249-50,198 S.E.2d at 598.

Construing this statute to provide absolute immunity as the trial court has done, and as Giant urges here, requires the conclusion that the General Assembly intended to shield a merchant, its agents or employees, from any and all types of assaults and batteries. Under this construction, a merchant would not be civilly liable for breaking a suspected shoplifter's legs or for other extreme

CASE

assaultive actions taken to detain a suspected shoplifter. We cannot ascribe such an intent to the General Assembly.

Because we have concluded that the immunity granted by § 18.2-105 is not absolute, we must determine the scope of that immunity. We are again guided by *Duncan.* In that case, we stated that the statute represented the General Assembly's attempt to "strike a balance between one man's property rights and another man's personal rights." Id. at 251, 198 S.E.2d at 599. The statute "enlarged" a merchant's rights to protect his property, but did not enlarge them "infinitely," and diminished, but did not extinguish, "the litigable rights of the public."

As applied to the issue in this case, we conclude that the balance between personal and property rights in § 18.2-105 is achieved by providing immunity from civil liability based on a wide range of torts, but not extending such immunity in circumstances in which the tort is committed in a willful, wanton or otherwise unreasonable or excessive manner. Under our construction, merchants, their agents or employees are shielded from civil liability for actions reasonably necessary to protect the owners' property rights by detaining

suspected shoplifters. But, individuals retain their "litigable rights" in the circumstances just noted. This construction of the statute is also consistent with the limitations imposed on other legislative grants of immunity from civil liability. *See e.g.,* §§ 8.01-220.1:1, -225, -225.1, -226.2, -226.3; 22.1-303.1; 54.1-2502, -2907, -2908, -2922, -2923, -2924.

In light of our construction of the statute, we conclude that dismissing Jury's motion for judgment on the basis that § 18.2-105 provided Giant with absolute immunity from the claims asserted by Jury was error. Accordingly, we will reverse the judgment of the trial court and remand the case for further proceedings, consistent with this opinion.

Reversed and remanded.

Case Review Question
Jury v. Giant of Maryland, Inc., 254 Va. 235, 491 S.E.2d 718 (1997).

Under the statute, was the detention proper other than the physical assault, such as leaving the suspect's children unattended in the parking lot? Why or why not?

Trespass

Trespass is the intentional invasion of property rights. It occurs when someone personally or through his or her property enters the land of another or permits such an invasion to continue when another takes control of the property.[28] An example of the latter occurs if you sell your house to someone but leave your car parked in the backyard. This is an invasion of the purchaser's right to the property.

It is not necessary that the actor have the intent to commit a trespass or even the knowledge that he or she is doing so. It is enough that the actor intends to commit the invasive act and, as a result of the commission of that act, a trespass occurs. Such a case often occurs when hunters are on publicly owned land and unknowingly enter onto private property. Even though they believe they are still on public land, they have violated a property interest. Violation of this right of landowners to quiet enjoyment free from intrusion is enough to bring an action for trespass. If the trespasser causes damage to persons or property, he or she is liable for that as well.

Fraud

The intentional tort of fraud is perhaps the most commonly claimed tort in business and financial dealings. Fraud is not easily proven, however, because the injured party must be able to show that he or she did not have the opportunity to detect any misdealing. The elements required to prove an action for fraud are numerous. It must be shown that (1) the defendant made a material (significant) representation to the plaintiff that was untrue, (2) the defendant knew the statement was untrue or that his or her failure to ascertain its truth was reckless, (3) some affirmative conduct by the defendant indicates the intent to have the plaintiff rely on the statement, and (4) the plaintiff reasonably relied on the statement and as a proximate result was injured by it.[29]

APPLICATION 11.5

Caroline decides to open her own produce stand. She spends $5,000 to purchase a used tractor to assist in growing the produce. The owner of the tractor claims that it was her husband's who is deceased and he used it only for the family garden a few times each year for a period of several years. She claims the tractor is in excellent working condition. Almost immediately after purchase, Caroline experiences problems with the tractor. Upon taking it to a dealer for repair she finds out that the tractor has had engine problems and numerous repairs and that it was purchased only a few months earlier from that same dealer for $1,000 due to its poor condition. Caroline would likely have an action for fraud.

Point for Discussion

- Would a different result occur if instead of a tractor, the item purchased was a nonmotorized lawn mower? Why or why not?

Defamation

Defamation is the combined name for two types of intentional torts: libel and slander. Libel is an action for injuries that occur as the result of a written communication to a third party.[30] Slander is the appropriate action when the injuries occur as the result of an oral communication.[31]

In both types of actions, it is necessary to show that the defendant actor made a communication to a third party about the plaintiff that caused other third persons to have a lowered opinion of the plaintiff or be discouraged from associating with him or her.[32] This communication must be made by the speaker with the intent that the receiving party perceive it as directed to himself or herself. For example, giving a written statement about someone to a secretary for the sole purpose of having it typed is not a communication of libel. Communicating the statement to the secretary with the intent that he or she believe it or giving the message to another party would constitute a communication of libel.

A different standard of defamation requirements exists with respect to public figures. Persons who place themselves in the public light are inviting comment or publicity under the constitutional rights of free speech. Nevertheless, there are limits to what can be said publicly about another. If it can be shown that a statement was made with actual malice (knowledge that the statement was false or reckless disregard for its truth or falsity), even a public figure can maintain an action for defamation.[33]

Some defenses are peculiar to actions based upon defamation. First, the truth is always a defense. If a truthful statement is made about another, no matter how damaging, no action for defamation can be brought. Another defense is known as privilege. Since certain communications are deemed to serve the public interest, someone's opinion may be exempt from an action for defamation. For example, an employer who fires an employee for suspected drug use is privileged with respect to reporting this information to government agencies, such as unemployment agencies. Generally, if a terminated employee seeks unemployment compensation, the employer will be asked the reasons for termination. The employer may not be able to prove the absolute truth of this statement about a former employee. If the suspicions were reasonable, however, the employer is permitted to give the information to government agencies who will keep it confidential. Privilege applies whenever public policy requires communication between the private sector and the government.

Emotional Distress

Emotional distress is often called the catchall tort. A plaintiff can plead it as a negligence action or as an intentional tort. Frequently, when it is difficult to prove the necessary elements of a specific intentional tort, emotional distress is used as the cause of action. It can also accompany an intentional tort as a separate and independent action.

Jurisdictions are divided on the issue of whether an actual physical contact must accompany the emotional injury. But to prove an action for intentional infliction of emotional distress, it must be shown that the actor intentionally engaged in conduct so outrageous that the actor knew or should have known that its likely result would be a mental or emotional disturbance to the plaintiff of such a magnitude that it could produce a resulting physical injury, for example, falsely or mistakenly informing a new mother that her baby was stillborn. Such a severe blow to one in an already weakened condition could likely have physical effects.

Emotional distress can also be brought as the basis of negligence. This generally occurs when the conduct was unquestionably unreasonable, but proving the intent (under the definition of an intentional tort) of the actor is difficult. This type of action is based on conduct so extremely reckless that it is considered unreasonable.

Some jurisdictions also acknowledge a separate action for negligent infliction of emotional distress. The requirements are those of an action in negligence with a damage requirement of emotional distress as previously defined.

Special Damages Awarded for Intentional Torts

Many of the intentional torts discussed here may also be the basis for a separate criminal prosecution. However, the action for an intentional tort is a dispute that is purely between the private parties, and no imprisonment or fines are imposed. If proven, however, because of the element of intent, civil actions for intentional torts often result in more severe money judgments than in cases of negligence based on careless conduct. In addition, when a jurisdiction permits, punitive damages are often awarded to the plaintiff in addition to the ordinary compensatory damages. This occurs because the courts want to send a message that conduct intentionally resulting in harm to another will be dealt with severely.

Assignment 11.2

Examine the following situations and indicate whether an intentional tort was committed and, if so, what type of intentional tort occurred.

a. A woman suffering road rage waves her fist at an oncoming driver stopped at an intersection and threatens the unborn child of the oncoming driver.

b. A woman suffering from road rage drives so closely to another car that the driver veers out of the way to avoid an anticipated accident and slams the car into a ditch.

c. A carnival worker leaves when a storm breaks out for an hour with two people trapped in a car at the top of a ferris wheel.

d. As a prank, a teenager calls a neighbor lady and tells her that he is calling from the hospital and that her son has been critically injured in a car wreck. The neighbor lady, while racing to the hospital, is seriously injured when her car is involved in an accident as the result of her running a red light.

e. The owner of a bait shop near a large state park sells fishing licenses. He also advertises that hiking permits are for sale and are now required for anyone on foot within the park boundaries. There is no such law.

PRODUCT LIABILITY

Product liability is not a specific body of tort law such as negligence, strict liability, or intentional torts. Rather, it describes a subject of a tort action that may be based on any one of the major tort theories. The common denominator is that the action involves a product that has been placed in commerce. The number of variety of commercial products has grown to such proportions that an entire area of law has been developed to establish precedent for disputes that arise out of the sale and use of products. Each year, several million injuries result from use of manufactured products. It is not surprising that the number of lawsuits in this area has grown accordingly.

Causes of Action

Some of the legal standards that have been established include causes of action in products cases and standards of care. For example, the commonly encountered causes of action in product liability cases include the following:

* Breach of express warranty.
* Breach of implied warranty of fitness for a particular purpose.
* Breach of implied warranty of merchantability.
* Negligence.
* Deceit.
* Strict liability.

It is apparent that many of the causes of action resemble ordinary tort actions. In reality, product liability actions are derived from basic tort law. However, to accommodate the unique position of the consumer/injured party and manufacturer, certain modifications have been made. Also note that res ipsa loquitur is commonly employed in product liability cases, since quite often the plaintiff has no opportunity to discover the exact action of the defendant that produced the danger in the product.

Specific legal standards regarding the standard of care in product liability cases include the idea that a manufacturer is presumed to be an expert on the product and therefore must manufacture the product with the same care as someone with extensive knowledge about the product and its potential dangers. A manufacturer who does not have such knowledge or does not utilize it to make reasonably sure that the product is safe can be held accountable for injuries caused by the product.

Defenses

Defenses in product liability cases are similar to those found in other areas of negligence. Additionally, a manufacturer may also claim as a defense extreme misuse of the product. It is established that manufacturers must foresee a certain degree of misuse of a product. However, if the consumer significantly modifies the product or uses it in a manner that the manufacturer could not have been reasonably expected to foresee, the manufacturer will not be held liable for any injuries.

APPLICATION 11.6

Drucilla has taken up woodworking to make and sell crafts. She has no training and so decides to teach herself to use the tools of the trade. She purchases a special power saw. The instructions clearly state that safety glasses should be worn at all times when operating the saw. Because Drucilla does not read the instructions, she does not wear glasses. A piece of wood flies from the saw during operation and blinds her in one eye.

Point for Discussion:
- What is the significance of Drucilla's failure to read the instructions?

Statute of Limitations

One area of difficulty in product liability law involves the statute of limitations. Typically, the statute of limitations begins to run at the time the plaintiff knows or should know he or she has a cause of action. This was found to create a problem in the area of product liability because many times, the injury did not occur until many years after the product was manufactured. Consequently, the defendant manufacturer was at a tremendous disadvantage. Much of the evidence and many of the witnesses with knowledge about the product design and creation were no longer available. In response, many state legislatures enacted what are known as statutes of repose, which place an absolute limit from the time of manufacture in which an action can be brought. For example, in a state with a statute of repose of 15 years, no product liability action can be brought more than 15 years after the manufacture of the product or when the statute of limitations runs out, whichever is first.

The unique characteristics of commercial products that are distributed (often in mass quantities) and that remain in use for many years have necessitated the development of special rules of law. With these precedents, manufacturers and consumers alike have a better awareness of their rights with respect to the sale, purchase, and use of products.

CASE

DISTRICT COURT OF APPEAL OF FLORIDA, FOURTH DISTRICT.

MARITZA SCHEMAN- GONZALEZ, ETC. ET AL., APPELLANTS,

v.

SABER MANUFACTURING COMPANY; TITAN INTERNATIONAL, INC.; MICHELIN NORTH AMERICA, INC., ETC., ET AL., APPELLEES.

816 So.2d 1133.
April 10, 2002.

Rehearing Denied
June 5, 2002.

STONE, J.

David Rodriguez suffered fatal injuries when he attempted to mount a 16 inch Michelin tire onto a 16.5 inch Saber-Titan wheel. The plaintiffs, referred to herein as "Gonzalez," appeal summary judgments entered against them in this wrongful death lawsuit against Titan International, Inc. ("Titan"), and Michelin North America, Inc. ("Michelin"). We reverse.

Titan designed and manufactured the wheel rim. The multi-count complaint alleged that Titan was liable for the negligent design of the wheel and for failing to warn customers and users that the 16.5 inch wheel would accept a 16 inch tire, but would explode when it was mounted. The complaint further alleged that these dangers were not apparent to, or known by, Rodriguez.

The rim, and a component disc within the rim manufactured by a third party, Saber, are collectively referred to throughout the proceedings as the "subject wheel."

Gonzalez charged Titan with:

a. negligent design consisting of inadequate markings to distinguish the 16.5 inch wheel from a 16 inch wheel such that "a reasonable user would recognize the size of the wheel. . . ."

b. negligent design consisting of failure to include warnings as to the danger of mismatching the wheel with 16 inch tires.

c. negligent design in that the 16.5 inch wheel readily accepts the 16 inch tire but is likely to explode on inflation because it cannot be properly seated on the wheel; furthermore, the absence of adequate warning compounds the danger.

d. negligent design of the 16.5 inch wheel similar to a 16 inch wheel which similarity "lure[s]" reasonable users into thinking that the proper wheel is in use when the 16.5 inch wheel accepts the 16 inch tire.

e. failure to warn customers and users that the wheel readily accepts a 16 inch tire and the dangers, including explosion of the tire, when mounting the smaller tire on the wheel.

f. failure to warn of the danger of removing the tire and wheel assembly from the tire changer while the tire is not fully inflated.

As to Michelin, it was alleged that Michelin negligently manufactured the subject tire and that it knew or should have known that the tire was defective and unreasonably dangerous.

Gonzalez charged Michelin with:

a. negligent design consisting of inadequate markings to distinguish the 16 inch tire from other tires, including a 16.5 inch tire such that "a reasonable user would recognize the size of the tire. . . ."

b. negligent design consisting of failure to include warnings as to the danger of mismatching the tire with a 16.5 inch wheel.

c. negligent design in that the 16 inch tire can be readily mounted on and accepted by a 16.5 inch wheel but is likely to explode on inflation because the tire cannot be properly seated on the wheel; furthermore, the absence of adequate warning compounds the danger.

d. negligent design of the 16 inch tire similar to a 16.5 inch tire which similarity "lure[s]" reasonable users into thinking that the proper tire is in use when the 16.5 inch wheel accepts the 16 inch tire.

e. negligent design and manufacture of the tire bead which fails at pressures below the rated tire pressures.

f. failure to warn customers and users that the tire readily accepts a 16.5 inch wheel and the dangers, including explosion of the tire, when mounting the smaller tire on the wheel.

g. failure to warn of the danger of removing the tire and wheel assembly from the tire changer while the tire is not fully inflated.

The grounds upon which Titan moved for summary judgment were that, as a component part manufacturer, it was not responsible for any defect in the wheel assembly and had no duty to warn end-users of potential dangers. Further, Rodriguez knew of the risk. Michelin adopted the grounds asserted in Titan's motion.

In granting summary judgment, the trial court considered several depositions which included testimony that Rodriguez was employed as a "helper" at an auto repair business and tire work was not his responsibility. However, there was also testimony that Rodriguez did help change tires after being taught to do so by Williams, his co-worker. Williams claimed to have warned Rodriguez he could injure himself if he mounted a tire on the wrong size of wheel. There was other testimony that Rodriguez was aware of this danger.

Michael Brock, the corporate officer of the employer, testified that Rodriguez was not charged with changing tires and was only responsible for stacking the tires and cleaning up. Brock acknowledged, however, that Rodriguez may have used the tire changing machine without his knowledge. In fact, Chris Ellison, a former manager, confirmed that he had witnessed Rodriguez changing tires on occasion.

The record reflects that Saber Manufacturing Company manufactured the wheel and that Titan supplied the rims. A former Saber operations manager stated that Saber began putting a warning label on the 16.5 inch rims regarding mismatch problems with 16 inch tires, but was unable to recall exactly when this practice began, only that it was probably instituted before the wheel in question was manufactured. He also stated that the tire manufacturers generally place a warning on the tire regarding the dangers of mounting the 16 inch tire on a 16.5 inch wheel.

Titan filed the affidavit of Michael Borrelli, a private investigator, who stated that he had inspected the wheel in question and was able to read the markings, including the 16.5 inch size in at least three places on the wheel. He was also able to clearly observe a marking on both the inboard and outboard sidewalls of the tire, which stated, "MOUNT ONLY ON APPROVED 16 INCH RIMS."

Gonzalez filed the affidavits of two experts in opposition to the motions for summary judgment.

According to Laughery, one of the experts, the similarity of the two wheels in size and appearance causes tire busters to rely on negative feedback as an indication that the tire they are mounting is not the correct size. However, in the case of the 16.5 inch wheel and 16 inch tire, because there is often no difficulty in placing the 16 inch tire on the 16.5 inch rim, there may be no "feedback" to indicate a mismatch.

Laughery stated that studies show the 16 inch tire has a 5-degree bead contour and the 16.5 tire has a 15-degree bead contour. As a result, a 16 inch tire placed on a 16.5 inch rim will not seat properly and will explode when inflated. However, the flange of the rim is virtually the same diameter for the 16 and 16.5 inch rim. Hence, "the task of placing a 16 inch tire on 16.5 inch rim is no more or less difficult than on a 16 inch rim."

Laughery concluded that the markings involved in this case were insufficient to warn tire mounters of the danger of mounting a 16 inch tire onto a 16.5 inch wheel. The study used by Laughery also concluded that limited warning labels, informing the user to match the tire and wheel size, even if they warned of the risk of serious injury, were inadequate. The only label he viewed as adequate was one that specifically explained that a 16 inch tire could be easily passed over the 16.5 inch rim flange but will not seat and will explode on inflation.

CASE

Gonzalez's second expert, Milner, testified that design defects in the Saber/Titan 16.5 inch wheel and the bead in the Michelin 16 inch tire caused the explosion which killed Rodriguez. Milner also confirmed that the 16 inch tire will initially be accepted onto the 16.5 inch rim, but will not seat and will eventually explode. He further noted that the 16.5 inch rim wheel is the only passenger or light truck wheel in the United States that is capable of accepting a tire which does not match its size.

Milner concluded that the subject rim is defective because it is configured to accept the 16 inch tire readily and this rim design violates the principle that if the wheel accepts the tire, it is the appropriate size. He also stated that the size markings on the tire and rim are inconspicuous and are inadequate to warn tire mounters of the danger of a mismatch. He further concluded that defective design and lack of proper warnings caused the fatal injuries.

Milner also referred to conclusions that the 16.5 inch rim could easily be redesigned to eliminate the hazard of inadvertent mismatches and that the design of the tire could be modified to use an alternative almost fail-proof bead grommet design which would have prevented the subject accident. We note, however, Milner cautioned that strengthening the tire bead grommets might otherwise compromise the integrity of the tire.

In light of the aforementioned evidence, the trial court entered summary judgment against Gonzalez. The court found that as a component part manufacturer of a part which was not inherently dangerous, Titan owed no duty to warn end users of the dangers of the wheel subsequently assembled by Saber. The court found there was no genuine issue of material fact as to whether Rodriguez knew of the importance of matching tire and wheel sizes and the dangers in mismatching tires and wheels. Therefore, Titan had no duty to warn Rodriguez, who was aware of the danger.

The court also found that none of the evidence was sufficient to show that a lack of warning regarding mismatching the 16 inch tire with the 16.5 inch rim caused Rodriguez's injuries and death. Further, the court found that there could be "no showing of proximate causation where an experienced mechanic read and did not heed the warnings while attempting to inflate a 16 inch tire on a 16.5 inch wheel."

Of significance to the trial court was the absence of eyewitnesses to the explosion who could testify as to how the accident occurred. From these facts, the court concluded that Rodriguez's negligence alone was the legal cause of the injuries. Further, the court found that Laughery's affidavit regarding the adequacy of warnings could not withstand the *Frye* test and would be inadmissible at trial. Although the court ruled Milner's testimony with respect to the defective wheel and rim design admissible under the *Frye* test, it found that, as an expert in engineering, Milner was not qualified to testify regarding the adequacy of warnings and, as such, that portion of his testimony was inadmissible *Frye v. United States,* 293 F. 1013 (D.C. Cir.1923).

As to Michelin, the order repeated the finding that there could be no showing of proximate causation where Rodriguez did not heed the warnings. The trial judge reiterated his findings regarding the inadmissibility of Laughery's testimony. With regard to Milner's testimony, the trial judge found that his testimony as to the bead grommet design satisfied the *Fyre* test but would be inadmissible because his opinion was merely conclusory, speculative and not supported by portions of the studies submitted as part of Milner's affidavit. The trial judge further found, as he had in the Titan order, that the testimony regarding the adequacy of the warnings would be inadmissible as beyond Milner's expertise.

Initially, we note that, regardless of whether portions of the testimony of Laughery and Milner may ultimately be excluded, there is no reason to exclude the factual background testimony regarding the 16/16.5 inch tire/rim mismatch phenomenon, a fact which is also discussed in several reported and unreported cases. *See, e.g., Richards v. Michelin Tire Corp.,* 21 F.3d 1048 (11th Cir.1994), *Shepherd v. Michelin Tire Corp.,* 6 F.Supp. 2d 1307(N.D.Ala.1997); *Freitas v. Michelin Tire Corp.,* No. CIV.3:94CV1812(DJS) (D.Conn. March 2, 2000).

The trial court erred in granting summary judgment in this case. Summary judgments should be granted with caution in negligence cases. *Moore v. Morris,* 475 So.2d 666, 668 (Fla. 1985); *Holl v. Talcott,* 191 So.2d 40, 46 (Fla.1966). As such, where evidence is conflicting, raises any issue of material fact, or permits different reasonable inferences, summary judgment should be denied. *See id.*

We conclude that Michelin and Titan have failed to establish the absence of genuine issue of fact as to the need to warn and whether Rodriguez knew or should have known of the danger. Although there is testimony that Rodriguez knew of the dangers of mismatching tires and wheels, generally, there is no proof that he knew of the danger involved in attempting to mount a 16 inch tire onto a 16.5 inch rim or that the tire would be initially accepted onto the wheel but the beads would not seat. As such, there remains a significant question as to whether Rodriguez was aware of the particular danger involved.

Here, we deem the *Restatement (Third) of Torts: Products Liability* (1998), instructive. It states that a product is defective in design "when the foreseeable risks of harm posed by the product could have been reduced or avoided by the adoption of a reasonable alternative design" and its omission "renders the product not reasonably safe." *Id.* at § 2(b). Additionally, a product is considered defective "when the foreseeable risks of harm posed by the product could have been reduced or avoided by the provision of reasonable instructions or warnings" and their omission "renders the product not reasonably safe." *Id.* at § 2(c); *see also Warren v. K-Mart Corp.,* 765 So.2d 235, 237-38 (Fla. 1st DCA 2000).

Unless the danger is obvious or known, a manufacturer has a duty to warn where its product is inherently dangerous or has dangerous propensities. *Am. Cyanamid Co. v. Roy,* 466 So.2d 1079, 1082 (Fla. 4th DCA 1984); *Brito v. County of Palm Beach,* 753 So.2d 109, 112 (Fla. 4th DCA 1998); *see, e.g., Cohen v. Gen. Motors Corp., Cadillac Div.,* 427 So.2d 389, 391 (Fla. 4th DCA 1983); *Perez v. Nat'l Presto Indus., Inc.,* 431 So.2d 667, 669 (Fla. 3d DCA 1983).

This court has recognized that,"[t]o warn adequately, the product label must make apparent the potential harmful consequences. The warning should be of such intensity as to cause a reasonable man to exercise for his won safety caution commensurate with the potential danger."*American Cyanamid,* 466 So.2d at 1082. In addition, "[a] warning should contain some wording directed to the significant dangers arising from failure to use the product in the prescribe manner, such as the risk of serious injury or death." *Brito,* 753 So.2d at 112. Furthermore, as is the case when considering whether the injured party knew of the danger, the sufficiency and reasonableness of a manufacturer's warnings are questions of fact which are best left to the jury unless the warnings are accurate, clear, and unambiguous. *Id.; see also Salozzo v. Wagner Spray Tech Corp.,* 578 So.2d 393, 394 (Fla. 3d DCA 1991); *Marchant v. Dayton Tire & Rubber Co.,* 836 F.2d 695, 701(1st Cir.1988); *see generally Vega v. City of Pompano Beach,* 551 So.2d 594 (Fla 4th DCA 1989).

In *Brito,* we concluded that the suggestion that only a qualified person install the wheel was merely an instruction, rather than a warning because it failed to inform consumers of the possible risk of death occurring with certain tire and wheel combinations. 753 So.2d at 112; *see also Brown v. Glade and Grove Supply, Inc.,* 647 So.2d 1033, 1035-36 (Fla. 4th DCA 1994) ("advising a user to operate a tractor with the lock-out pins in place is an instruction, not a warning"). Similarly, in this case, the warning on the tire instructed the user to mount a 16 inch tire only on a 16 inch rim but gave no hint as to the possibility of serious injury or death or of the particular hazard regarding the 16 inch tire/16.5 inch rim mismatch. As the adequacy of the tire warning must be left to the jury, it follows that the sufficiency of the wheel/rim label, which included only size markings, must be similarly resolved.

An issue of fact also remains as to proximate cause whether Rodriguez's injuries were more likely than not caused by the conduct of one or both defendants. In *Brito,* this court, having found that the manufacturer's duty to warn and the adequacy of the warning were questions for the jury, noted that the question of proximate cause is also for the jury unless the facts are "so clear that reasonable people could not differ." 753 So.2d at 113. In *Brito,* the court noted

CASE

that while the evidence strongly suggested that no warning would have stopped the decedent from placing the dangerous wheels on his Jeep, an issue of fact remained as to the failure to warn claim and, as such, the plaintiff was entitled to present the jury with that possibility. *Id.* Similarly, in this case, even if Gonzalez cannot prove that better warnings would have been noticed, read, or obeyed by Rodriguez, they were entitled to have the jury consider the possibility that the warning was inadequate to inform Rodriguez of the particular danger.

We further note that the only fair inference in this case is that Rodriguez was fatally injured in an explosion when he attempted to mount a 16 inch tire on a 16.5 inch wheel and that such a mismatch can cause an explosion. Therefore, viewing the evidence in a light most favorable to Gonzalez, there is evidence that the tire/wheel mismatch caused the injury. We have considered *Wong v. Crown Equipment Corp.*, 676 So.2d 981 (Fla. 3d DCA 1996), and *Adkins v. Economy Engineering Co.*, 495 So.2d 247 (Fla. 2d DCA 1986), and deem them distinguishable, as in each there was, in fact, no evidence of the cause of injury.

Rodriguez's own negligence is, if any, a matter of comparative negligence. We recognize that on appropriate facts, a trial court may determine that the plaintiff's negligence was the sole cause of his or her own injury. *See Standard Havens Prods., Inc. v. Benitez*, 648 So.2d 1192 (Fla.1994); *see also; Lopez v. Southern Coatings, Inc.*, 580 So.2d 864 (Fla. 3d DCA 1991); *Ashby Div. of Consol. Aluminum Corp. v. Dobkin*, 458 So.2d 335 (Fla. 3d DCA 1984). However, still unresolved is the issue that Rodriguez may have assumed he had a match if the tire was initially accepted onto the wheel, the exact danger claimed in the complaint. Therefore, even if Rodriguez was negligent, a question of fact remains as to whether that failure was the sole proximate cause of his injuries.

Further, while no one actually witnessed the explosion in this case, there were eyewitnesses to Rodriguez's actions immediately prior thereto, such that the cause of the explosion could be reasonably inferred. A summary judgment is not required simply because a plaintiff lacks eyewitnesses to an accident. *See Javits v. RSMO*

Independence Mgmt. Consultants, Inc., 738 So.2d 521, 522 (Fla. 4th DCA 1999); *Bianchi v. Garber,* 528 So.2d 969, 970 (Fla. 4th DCA 1988). Thus, the trial court's reliance on this fact is misplaced.

We conclude that there are questions of fact as to whether Michelin and Titan were required to warn Rodriguez of this particular danger, whether the warning that existed was adequate to apprise him of the danger, and whether the lack of adequate warning proximately caused Rodriguez's fatal injuries.

There is also a genuine issue of fact regarding the design defect claim against Michelin. The trial court did not consider Milner's opinion of the design defect, apparently because it recognized contrary views expressed in a study attached to his affidavit. However, the record reflects that Milner did not rely on that study as support for his conclusions regarding the tire bead grommet design defeat and, as such, his testimony on that point may be admissible.

With respect to Titan, as manufacturer of only a component part of the wheel, we note that liability of a component part manufacturer for a defective product is recognized under some circumstances. *See Favors v. Firestone*, 309 So.2d 69, 71 (Fla. 4th DCA 1975).

Although the supplier of component parts is not liable where it is simply following plans and specifications, a supplier may be subject to liability for injury caused by a product into which the component is integrated where:

(a) [t]he component is defective in itself . . . and the defect causes harm; or
(b) (1) [t]he seller or distributor of the component substantially participates in the integration of the component into the design of the product; and
   (2) [t]he integration of the component causes the product to be defective . . . ; and
   (3) [t]he defect in the product causes the harm.

Restatement (Third) of Torts: Products Liability § 5p. 140 (1997).

Accordingly, Titan, as a component part manufacturer, could be responsible if its rim was itself defective, or if the allegedly defective rim was essentially unchanged when integrated into the final unit. In light of Milner's testimony, there is a genuine issue of fact as to the defective nature of the rim.

We recognize that where a product is reasonably safe, the fact that there may be a better alternative design is not grounds for product liability. *See Husky Indus., Inc. v. Black,* 434 So.2d 988 (Fla. 4th DCA 1983). However, while a manufacturer has no duty to make a product accident proof, *see id.,* users are still protected, under the restatement reasoning, from products "fraught with unexpected dangers." *Royal v. Black & Decker Mfg. Co.,* 205 So.2d 307 (Fla. 3d DCA 1967); *Mendez v. Honda Motor Co.,* 738 F.Supp.481 (S.D.Fla. 1990). There also appears to be a disputed fact question as to whether the rim was altered in any fashion when incorporated into the wheel.

Considering the issues in favor of Gonzalez, as is required, we reverse and remand for further proceedings. We deem all other issues raised to be *Frye* issues which remain to be addressed at the time of trial.

Case Review Question
Scheman-Gonzalez v. Saber Mfg. Co., 816 So.2d 1133 (Fla.App.4th Dist., 2002).
Would the outcome have likely been different if the size difference between the tire and rim was much greater—such as several inches? Why or why not?

EMPLOYMENT AND TORTS

Tort law has had a significant influence in the area of employment. It concerns not only the actions by or against third parties but also the relationship between the employer and the employee. All states have certain statutes and case law governing the employment relationship and indicating when actions for tort based upon it are permitted. Certain exceptions to these statutes also give rise to actions in tort.

Employer–Employee Relationship

Under a long-established rule of law in this country commonly known as "respondeat superior,"[34] a superior may be held responsible for injuries caused by his or her employee. Generally, an injured third party has the right to elect to sue the employer if the third party can demonstrate that the employee was a regular employee and not an independent contractor (someone who works on a per-job basis, such as a plumber who goes to someone's office to repair a leaky faucet) and that the injury was caused by the employee while acting within the scope of his or her employment. Simply stated, the latter means that the employee is acting subject to the ultimate supervision of the employer. The employee does not need to be engaged in a regular job duty as long as he or she is engaged in a task that benefits the employer in some direct manner. Generally, employers are not responsible for occurrences while the employee is going to or from work. However, a different rule would apply if the employee were running an errand for the employer (even though it may not be a part of his or her regular duties to do so).

Ordinarily, employers will not be held responsible for intentional torts committed by an employee. An intentional tort requires that the actor knew or should have known with substantial certainty that the act would produce the injury. An employer cannot be held responsible for such intentional acts over which he or she has no control. If this were permitted, employees could escape responsibility for acts that the employer neither benefited from nor condoned. The exception to this rule takes place when the intentional tort is considered to be within the scope of the employee's duties. Security guards are a common example. Often, such personnel are required to restrain customers physically or compel them to leave the premises. In such a situation, the actions of the employee are presumed to be directed by the employer. Therefore, any injuries resulting from the guard's conduct could result in liability of the employer.

Statutes Governing the Employment Relationships That Affect Tort Actions

The federal government and every state has enacted a variety of legal standards pertaining to the workplace. These include statutes, case law and administrative regulations regarding the physical environment of the workplace, discrimination laws to place all qualified applicants and employees on an equal footing, laws designed to prevent superiors from using their authority to wrongfully manipulate the conduct of workers on nonwork-related matters, and laws to protect those injured in the performance of job duties.

The federal Occupational Safety and Health Administration (OSHA) is a branch of the United States Department of Labor. Each state also has a similar agency. The purpose of these agencies is to establish and enforce standards that provide a safe work environment regardless of the type of industry; however, given the infinite number of variables in the workplace it is impossible to anticipate every conceivable danger. As a result, other laws are in place to deal with employee injuries. In fact, this is one of the most heavily legislated and regulated aspects of employment law.

In the late eighteenth and early nineteenth centuries, mass production and the growth of machinery in the workplace resulted in large numbers of individuals going to work in factories rather than in the traditional small craftsman shops and farming. Many of these individuals were untrained and working conditions were sometimes brutal. The result was a significant number of injuries in the workplace. With disabling injuries, many workers had little alternative but to file tort actions against their own employers for damages. The length of time for such a process was often significant, and the hardship on the families of these employees was immense. At the same time, employers were suffering the blows of large jury awards for employee injuries when cases finally did come to trial. Insurance was usually available but often cost-prohibitive. Also, once an employee sued the employer, the animosity created by that suit effectively ended any chance of returning to work. Both sides were losing and the legislatures responded with workers' compensation laws during the mid-1900s.

Although the details of workers' compensation laws vary from state to state, the underlying principle is the same.[35] The statutes provide a basis for compensation to employees who are injured while performing job-related duties; but the statutes also place limitations on the extent to which an employer may be held financially liable. Workers' compensation laws in each state have fairly well-defined methods to calculate limits of compensation for various injuries. This in turn enables employers to predict with some degree of certainty what their liability will be in the event of injury. With such limits, insurers are then able to provide insurance to employers at a more reasonable cost without risking huge monetary awards by juries.

A second and major benefit of workers' compensation laws is that they typically are not based on findings of fault or negligence by the employer. This aids the injured employee who could not recover without proof of tortious conduct of the employer. The employer is presumed to have the benefit of the employee's presence on the job and contribution toward the making of profits. To bear the cost of injuries on the job, even accidental ones, seemed only fair.

One major development in the latter half of the twentieth century with respect to workers' compensation statutes had to do with job security. Employers quickly discovered that the fewer claims against them, the lower the cost of workers' compensation insurance. Many employers subsequently engaged in a kind of subversive tactic to inhibit injured employees from filing actions for workers' compensation benefits. Some employers fired employees who filed claims; others simply did not have a job available for the injured employees when they were ready to return to work. This practice quickly gained the attention of the courts and legislatures and was rightly condemned. The employers were found to be *chilling* the rights of employees to pursue the rights given to them as a matter of law. As a matter of public policy, the right to pursue statutory rights has always been protected. Now states have statutes that make it illegal to fire an injured employee for filing a workers' compensation claim.[36] If such an employee is in fact terminated, the employer must be able to establish totally independent grounds for the termination or be subject to a tort action by the employee for wrongful discharge. This provides the injured employees the opportunity to seek reasonable compensation for their injuries and for wages lost from time not working without fear of losing employment. Ultimately, the workers' compensation laws have reduced the number and expense of lawsuits between employers and employees, have encouraged employers to provide a safer working environment, and have directly contributed to the flow of industry and commerce in this country.

Employer Liability Laws

Certain circumstances, however, are exempt from otherwise applicable workers' compensation laws. For example, if an employer places an employee in a position of great danger and this action demonstrates a clear disregard for the safety of the employee, many states permit an avoidance of the workers' compensation laws in favor of an unlimited action for tort. In addition, certain types of employment that have been historically considered extremely dangerous with a high probability of serious injury or death of one's worklife are subject to federal employer liability laws. These laws preceded workers' compensation laws and are limited primarily to the railroad and maritime industries.

Although each law has specific provisions, an employer liability law will generally permit a civil action by an employee against an employer for injuries received within the scope of employment. It must be shown, however, that both parties are subject to the statute and that the employer was somehow negligent. This differs from the no-fault standard of workers' compensation laws. In addition to federal employer liability laws, a number of states also have state employer liability laws for specified areas of employment. The federal laws do not necessarily apply to employees of the federal government. Rather, they are laws passed by the national government that apply to an entire industry that operates on an interstate basis.

Originally, employer liability laws were enacted to provide protection to a class of workers who were engaged in a hazardous occupation where serious injuries or fatalities were frequent, and where the workers were often disadvantaged economically and educationally. The reasoning behind such laws was to provide protection to employees whose education and ability to seek other types of employment were frequently limited—even more so after a serious injury. The injuries that commonly occurred in these industries were so serious that the employees were often prevented, through this combination of factors, from ever working again, thus leaving them and their families with no means of support other than government assistance. Consequently, legislatures enacted statutes to ease somewhat the burden of proving civil suits against employers and at the same time to remove the limitations of recovery under the workers' compensation statutes. Although the statutes usually require the proof of negligence, they make the proof easier to establish.

Discrimination Issues

It has only been during the past 100 years that employers have been charged with the responsibility to be fair to all persons in the manner in which they are hired, supervised, and terminated. Employers have long been subject to liability for injuries to employees or third parties that arose incident to employment. In the more recent past, the focus has been just as great on the injuries that affect the psychosocial and economic aspects of employment. Today, state and federal government legislatures and agencies have established minimum legal standards for employers regarding hiring, termination, and providing a suitable work environment. Although some common law liability remains, the majority of actions are based in alleged statutory violations of legislation designed to make the workplace more fair and appropriate to all employees.

A few major strides from 1850 to 1950 for minorities and women laid the foundation for the sweeping changes that were to come in the second half of the twentieth century. The social movements of the 1960s brought about a greater awareness of the rights of minorities, women, individuals with physical impairments, and other Americans who received disparate treatment in the workplace. Case after case established that many employers would not hire individuals with certain characteristics or would treat them differently from other employees. As a result, legislation and regulations were passed to protect various classes of people. These laws were designed to keep employers from discriminating against employees for possessing characteristics that had nothing to do with their ability to adequately perform the duties of employment. Such characteristics include gender, race, religion, and age. Similar restrictions apply for individuals who are physically impaired. If an employer is found to treat an employee differently, refuse to hire someone, or use as a cause for termination one or more of the characteristics of the protected classes, the employer is subject to scrutiny under federal law. If it is determined that the employer violated the legal standards by using improper reasons for hiring, termination, or discipline, then the employer may be subject to a variety of penalties.

Another area of employment law that has grown tremendously is the psychological safety of the work environment. Just as federal agencies such as OSHA strive to protect the employee from physical dangers on the job, the branches of state and federal government are now focused on protecting the employee from unnecessary psychological and emotional dangers on the job as well. One such example is sexual harassment. If an employee can demonstrate that an employer participated or acquiesced in a course of conduct that subjected the employee to an environment that was reasonably perceived as hostile because of differential treatment based on the gender or sexual preference of the employee, the employee may have a basis for legal action against the employer. This imposes on the employer the responsibility to monitor the conduct of all employees and to be responsive to complaints in a continuing effort to maintain a workplace that encourages fair and professional treatment of each employee by the employer and coworkers alike.

Although all states have workers' compensation laws in effect, some injuries or, actually, causes of injury are exempt from these statutes. Such a case may occur when an employer willfully or deliberately places an employee in great danger and that danger results in injury to the employee. Such willful or deliberate misconduct is often an exception to workers' compensation laws, and the employee has the opportunity to file a civil action for damages against the employer.[37] Although this action imposes the requirement of proving the wrongful conduct, there is no limitation on the amount of damages that can be claimed.

TORT DEFENSES

In response to the many theories of liability in tort, defenses for conduct have been developed. These defenses are used to justify the defendant's actions or to expose the plaintiff's own part in the occurrence that produced the injury. Even today, these defenses are developing and changing. Although they vary slightly among jurisdictions, the underlying principles are substantially the same.

Contributory and Comparative Negligence

Contributory negligence is a well-known defense in this country. At one time, it was highly popular but is now experiencing a decline in popularity. In the past, the courts applied this defense when a defendant could prove that the

contributory negligence
The doctrine that maintains a plaintiff who, in any way, contributes to his or her injury cannot recover from a negligent defendant.

plaintiff contributed to his or her own injury by some form of negligent conduct. For example, in a car accident, while the defendant was driving under the influence of alcohol, the plaintiff may have been speeding on a dark and rainy night. The plaintiff was also acting negligently and contributed to the cause of the accident. When a court applies the defense of contributory negligence, the plaintiff cannot recover any damages from the defendant. The rationale for this defense is that one should not ultimately receive compensation for injuries caused by one's own wrongdoing.[38]

comparative negligence

Degree of plaintiff's own negligent conduct that was responsible for plaintiff's injury.

The defense of contributory negligence has declined in popularity for several reasons. As society has become increasingly complex, so have the causes of injuries. No longer are causes of injuries simply determined. In addition, a growing body of thought reasoned that although plaintiffs should not recover for their own misconduct, neither should defendants be relieved of liability for theirs. Accordingly, the theory of comparative negligence was developed. In **comparative negligence,** the degree of negligence of each party is assigned a percentage of the fault for the occurrence.[39] The jury arrives at such a calculation and reduces the judgment for the plaintiff by the percentage that the plaintiff contributed to his or her own injury.

Some jurisdictions apply pure comparative negligence where a plaintiff who the jury finds to be 99 percent at fault recovers only 1 percent of the damages. However, many jurisdictions apply modified comparative negligence, which prevents any recovery if a plaintiff was the significant cause of the injury, that is, was more than 50 percent at fault. In some states, a combination of contributory and comparative negligence applies. If a plaintiff is grossly negligent, contributory negligence will apply. Otherwise, comparative negligence will apply.[40]

Comparative negligence responds to negligence of the plaintiff without relieving the defendant of liability for his or her own misconduct. A steady trend by jurisdictions in this country has been to adopt the theory of comparative negligence in some form and abandon the traditional theory of contributory negligence.

Assumption of Risk

assumption of risk

Defense to negligence on the basis that the plaintiff knew of, appreciated, and voluntarily encountered the danger of defendant's conduct.

The defense of **assumption of risk** is also seeing some decline in response to the growth of comparative negligence. Traditionally, a defendant could prevent recovery by a plaintiff if the defendant could prove that the plaintiff was aware of the risk of danger, appreciated the seriousness of the risk, and voluntarily exposed himself or herself to the risk.[41] As with the application of comparative negligence, the recovery would not be barred but would be modified.

Many jurisdictions still accept assumption of risk as a defense to establish the degree to which the plaintiff was responsible for his or her own injury. An example of assumption of risk is a person attending a car race who sits at the edge of the racetrack. It is easily foreseeable that a car traveling at high speed could lose control and strike the onlooker. If the onlooker nevertheless remains in this position of danger, it may well be held that he or she assumed the risk of the danger.

Last Clear Chance

Another defense still widely used is the doctrine of **last clear chance** which, in reality, is a defense to a defense. When a defendant claims a defense such as contributory negligence that would bar recovery by a plaintiff, the plaintiff may respond with a claim of last clear chance. The doctrine states that even though a plaintiff contributed to endangering himself or herself, the defendant had the last clear opportunity to avoid the occurrence and prevent the plaintiff's injury but failed to do so.[42] An example is the preceding driving case. Even though the plaintiff was speeding in bad weather, if the defendant could have swerved at the last second and did not, the plaintiff could still recover for the defendant's failure to take advantage of the last clear chance to avoid the occurrence.

last clear chance
Defense of plaintiff responding to defenses of allegedly negligent defendant, in which plaintiff claims defendant had the last opportunity to avoid plaintiff's injury irrespective of plaintiff's own negligence.

Intentional Tort Defenses

Defenses raised in response to claims of intentional tort include the charge that not all of the elements were satisfied as well as consent, privilege, immunity, and various procedural defenses.

Although the first defense—that not all elements were satisfied—may be raised as a defense in any type of tort action, it is very appropriate in an intentional tort case. By definition, the elements of intentional torts tend to be quite specific. Thus, it is usually much easier to establish the absence of a specific event than it is to establish that the defendant's conduct met the reasonable standard of care under the circumstances in a negligence action.

Similarly, the defenses of consent, privilege, immunity, and involuntary conduct are seen most often in intentional tort suits. The defense of consent consists of proof by the defendant that the plaintiff in fact consented to or agreed overtly or by implication to the defendant's action. For example, a plaintiff might sue a defendant for battery that allegedly occurred when the defendant physician operated on the plaintiff. The defendant could claim that the plaintiff, by subjecting himself to the surgery, consented to procedures that the defendant deemed appropriate during surgery.

The defense of privilege is quite different from that of consent. Whereas in consent, the focus is on the conduct of the plaintiff toward the defendant, in privilege, the view is taken that regardless of the plaintiff's agreement or protestations, the defendant had a special legal right to act. For example, a plaintiff attempts to collect unemployment and is denied because the defendant (plaintiff's former employer) informed the Labor Department that the plaintiff was fired for drug use on the job. The plaintiff cannot successfully sue the defendant for defamation, because the employer has a privileged relationship with the government. By protecting employers, the government has the benefit of full disclosure and can therefore deny benefits to someone who is guilty of criminal activity. A variety of situations exist in which a party has a privileged relationship, and any tortious activity resulting from that privileged relationship cannot be prosecuted by a plaintiff. Another common privilege is that of self-defense. Depending on the circumstances, a person has the right to use reasonable or necessary force to defend himself or herself, and can even use force to defend someone else if that person was entitled to use self-defense. Limited force can also be used to defend property, but not if it would result in a breach of the peace, and the privilege never extends to the use of deadly force to defend property.

Like privilege, immunity gives protection to otherwise guilty defendants. The most common example is that of sovereign immunity. Historically, no lawsuit could be brought against the government for the torts committed by government servants. This was inherently unfair. However, to totally lift this ban could result in enough lawsuits against the government to bankrupt it. Consequently, federal and state legislatures have enacted laws that allow suits against the government in limited circumstances and in accordance with strict procedural rules. In this way, the government is accountable for its torts but is not at risk of being victimized by a litigation explosion of its own.

Assignment 11.3

> Examine each of the following fact situations and explain what major tort defense, if any, would apply.
>
> a. Desiree, a former teacher and now full-time homemaker, is running for a position on the school board of a large school district. The day before the election she opens the newspaper only to discover her own obituary. Desiree sues the newspaper when she loses the election.
> b. The same as above only instead of an obituary, Desiree reads an article that names her as the owner of an adult book/video store. In reality, the owner of the store has the same name as Desiree only with a slightly different spelling of the last name.
> c. Gerard is walking through a local zoo when an angry bear breaks out of its exhibit and attacks him. Gerard had been previously taunting the bear with food. Gerard sues the zoo for his injuries.
> d. The same as above only instead of taunting the bear before the breakout, Gerard throws food at the bear after it escapes the exhibit.

DAMAGES IN TORT ACTIONS

In the successful tort action, the trier of fact is faced with the task of awarding damages. In all actions at law, damages are monetary. The amount depends on a myriad of factors as well as the law of the jurisdiction. Some legislatures have enacted law that precludes anything but strictly compensatory damages; others allow punitive damages, prejudgment interest, and attorney's fees. The purpose here is to distinguish the types of damage that are possible if permitted legally by law of the jurisdiction.

DAMAGE	PURPOSE
Compensatory	To compensate the plaintiff for injury.
Specials	Those items of compensatory damage that can be specifically calculated, e.g. medical bills.
Generals	Those items of compensatory damage that must be estimated as to monetary value, e.g., pain and suffering, loss of reputation.
Punitive (also known as exemplary damages	To punish defendant and to deter defendant and others from future similar conduct.
Nominal	Allowed in other than negligence (in which actual damage is an element that must be proven) for commission of a tort by defendant but for which no actual loss by plaintiff is proven.

Typically, the award to the plaintiff will consist of compensatory damages. The types of damage that support an award of compensatory damage include property damage, physical injury, lost wages, and more abstract notions such as pain and suffering, shortened life expectancy, loss of consortium (elements of the marital relationship), and emotional distress. If proven, all are acceptable bases for compensation. In those jurisdictions where punitives are permitted, they may be awarded in especially egregious cases where the defendant's conduct was particularly reckless.

Ethical Considerations

The importance of ethics is obvious in such areas of law as contract, property, and business. At first glance, it is not so obvious in tort law. However, the requirement for ethical conduct is especially important in torts, since in these cases, juries are required to consider intangible factors such as pain, suffering, lost future wages, disability, and disfigurement. All of these factors contain built-in emotional triggers. For the unethical person, such cases provide an opportunity to manipulate and take advantage of a situation to the detriment of another. Early in the chapter, the litigation explosion was mentioned. In addition to this "explosion," a great deal of publicity has focused on some lawyers and plaintiffs who file frivolous claims in the hope of monetary gain. The response of many legislatures has been to enact statutes that penalize anyone found guilty of filing an unfounded claim. In turn, lawyers and their clients alike have been put on notice to carefully evaluate a situation before proceeding with a formal lawsuit.

Question
Assume you are a lawyer and a client comes to you with what appears to be an attempt to obtain money from a proposed defendant through an obviously unfounded claim of injury. What should you do?

Ethical Circumstance

You are a paralegal working in a civil litigation firm. During your collection of evidence in the investigation of a pending case, you discover the client has filed the exact type of suit with the same facts and injuries filed by another firm in a neighboring jurisdiction. Even the dates of the alleged injuries are similar. The client claims to have fallen and been injured in a retail store, with no alleged witnesses to either instance. Should the client be confronted about the situation or should it be assumed the client is just accident prone?

CHAPTER SUMMARY

The law of torts is growing and changing on a day-to-day basis. The courts are constantly being presented with variations on the basic principles. Legislatures in every state are considering additional statutes that will affect tort law. As a result, it is a challenge to keep current on these changes and the way that they affect our lives both personally and professionally.

Some constants remain in tort law, especially the recognized areas of tort. Negligence is the appropriate claim when one party has a duty to act with a certain degree of care toward another party and that duty is breached. For a negligence claim to succeed, it must be shown that the breach was the legal and factual cause of an injury and that the injury is of a type and extent that is compensable.

When a party's conduct goes beyond mere disregard for potentially dangerous circumstances and involves actions that are nearly certain to result in significant injury to another, an intentional tort has been committed. Although the knowledge of the actor may be more difficult to prove in such cases, when it is accomplished, the penalties are often more severe.

Finally, there are certain extremely dangerous situations in which no amount of care can prevent injury to innocent bystanders. In such instances, the party that produces the situation and benefits from it will be held responsible for the injuries. This is totally irrespective of whether that party knew of or took steps to avoid the injury. The cost of the benefit is responsibility for the injury as a matter of strict liability.

These principles have remained basically constant, although the manner and circumstances in which they are applied have changed. In addition, defenses to tort law continue to evolve and develop into principles that will produce the fairest result for all concerned. This is evidenced by the shift from the absolute defense of contributory negligence to the defense of comparative negligence, which apportions fault between the parties.

CHAPTER TERMS

assumption of risk	intentional tort	proximate cause
comparative negligence	last clear chance	reasonable conduct
contributory negligence	negligence	strict liability

REVIEW QUESTIONS

1. How does negligence differ from an intentional tort?
2. When is an employer liable for the acts of an employee?
3. Under what circumstances is assumption of risk applied?
4. Which party claims last clear chance?
5. What are the types of defamation actions?
6. How have workers' compensation laws affected tort actions?
7. When can res ipsa loquitur be applied?
8. What types of claims involve strict liability?
9. How do the torts of assault and battery differ?
10. How does a claim of strict liability differ from a claim for negligence?

RELEVANT LINKS

American Tort Reform Association
www.atra.org
Tort Law at Megalaw.com
www.megalaw.com

A Guide to Tort Law
www.hg.org/torts.html

INTERNET ASSIGNMENT 11.1

Using internet resources, identify whether your state has a statute that disallows frivolous lawsuits (claims determined to be unfounded).

NOTES

1. William Statsky, *Legal Thesaurus/Dictionary* (St. Paul: West, 1986).
2. Prosser, *Handbook on Torts* (St. Paul: West, 1971), Chapter 2, Section 7.
3. Id.
4. Id.
5. Id.
6. Id. at Chapter 5, Section 30.
7. *Palsgraf v. Long Island R. R. Co.,* 248 N.Y. 339, 162 N.E. 99 (N.Y. 1928).
8. Id., see dissent of Justice Andrews.
9. 65 C.J.S., Negligence, Section 10 (1955); (1987 supp.).
10. 65 C.J.S., Negligence, Section 11 (1955); (1987 supp.).
11. See note 9, supra.
12. See note 10, supra.
13. Id.
14. Id.
15. Id.
16. Prosser, *Handbook on Torts,* Chapter 7, Section 41.
17. Id.
18. Id.
19. William Statsky, *Torts: Personal Injury Litigation* (St. Paul: West, 1982), p. 364.
20. Id.
21. Annot., 23 A.L.R.3rd 1083.
22. Prosser, *Handbook on Torts,* Chapter 5, Section 31.
23. American Law Institute, Restatement of the Law on Torts II, Section 21(1), 1976.

24. Id., Section 13; *Mason v. Cohn,* 108 Misc.2d 674, 438 N.Y.S.2d 462 (1981).
25. Statsky, *Torts: Personal Injury Litigation,* p. 415.
26. See note 23, Section 35; *Cimino v. Rosen,* 193 Neb. 162, 225 N.W.2d 567 (1975).
27. Id.
28. See note 23, Section 217; *Guin v. City of Riviera Beach, Fla.,* 388 So.2d 604 (Fla.App. 1980).
29. See note 23, Sections 525–552.
30. See note 23, Sections 558–559.
31. Id.
32. Id.
33. Id.; *New York Times v. Sullivan,* 376 U.S. 254, 84 S.Ct. 710, 11 L.Ed.2d 686 (1964).
34. See note 23, Section 46.
35. 81 Am.Jur., Workers' Compensation, Section 1; 315.
36. Annot., 32 A.L.R.4th 1221.
37. Annot., 96 A.L.R.3rd 1064.
38. Id.
39. Id.
40. See note 23, Section 479; *Ortego v. State Farm Mutual Auto Ins. Co.,* 295 So.2d 593 (La.App. 1974).
41. See note 23, Section 496; *Parr v. Hamnes,* 303 Minn. 333, 228 N.W.2d 234 (1975).
42. Prosser, *Handbook on Torts.*

For additional resources, please visit our Web site at www.westlegalstudies.com

CHAPTER 12

The Law of Business

After reading this chapter, you should be able to:

- Discuss the role of agency in partnerships and corporations.

- Distinguish actual and apparent authority.

- Distinguish by characteristic the business forms of partnership, corporation, and sole proprietorship.

- List the determining factors for the existence of a partnership.

- Discuss limited partnerships' unique characteristics and describe the steps to create a corporation.

- Discuss a corporate promoter's role.

- Explain the rationale behind the doctrine of piercing the corporate veil.

- Describe the process of dissolution of a corporation.

TABLE 12.1

Business Organizations

Characteristic	Sole Proprietorship	General Partnership	Limited Partnership	Corporation
Number of Owners	1	2+	2+	1+
Life	Limited	Limited	Limited	Unlimited
Liability	Unlimited personal	Unlimited personal	General— Unlimited personal Limited— Limited personal	Limited personal
Control	Complete	Shared	General— Shared Limited— None of day-to-day	Limited to policy changes
Income	All personal	All personal	All personal	Only dividends personal
Legal Status	None	Very limited	Very limited	Separate entity

This chapter focuses on the major categories of business entities: sole proprietorships, general and limited partnerships, and corporations (see Table 12.1). In addition, the law of agency is discussed within the context of business organizations.

The way a business entity is organized will dictate who receives the income of the business, who is liable for debts or judgments against the business, and who in the business has the authority to make decisions regarding the operation of the business. In addition, the law of agency governs such issues as who is permitted to represent the business in dealings with other entities and the methods and procedures for such dealings.

This chapter contains references to certain model laws that have been adopted by all or a majority of the states. These laws, often known as uniform acts, are precisely what the name implies. They are designed for adoption by all the states so that every state will treat a particular business entity or transaction in substantially the same way. With interstate transactions becoming more frequent, these laws provide for fair and consistent treatment of business no matter where it is transacted. In the law of business, one of the most frequently employed uniform laws is the U.C.C.

The U.C.C. has been adopted, at least in part, by every state. It contains a series of laws that detail the legal rights and obligations of parties to formal business transactions. The adoption of this code has eliminated many of the inconsistencies in the way legal disputes over common transactions were dealt with in the various state courts.

AGENCY

An **agency** is formally defined as

> A relationship in which one person acts for another or represents another by the latter's authority.[1] (Statsky, *Legal Thesaurus/Dictionary*. West, 1982)

The person who gives authority to another to act in his or her behalf is the principal; the person who receives authority to act on behalf of another is the agent. An example of a typical agency relationship is a retail company and its sales force. As agents, these salespersons have the authority to act on behalf of the retail company (who is their principal) to sell the company's products.

◆ APPLICATION 12.1

Sara is employed as a clerk at Darell's, a shoe store at a local mall. Part of her job duties include waiting on customers and handling their purchases by accepting payment in exchange for shoes and accessories in the store. Sara is the agent and Darell is the principal. Sara's conduct is on behalf of and in place of Darell.

Point for Discussion

◆ Assume Sara and Darell are partners and take turns working the store. Would Sara still be Darell's agent when she is working?

Creation of the Agency Relationship

Before an agency can be created, the principal must have the legal capacity to authorize such a relationship;[2] that is, the principal must have the ability to enter into a contract. Specifically, the principal must be over the age of majority in the jurisdiction (usually 18 or 21) and must be legally competent. A declaration of legal incompetence means that the court has found that a person is not capable of managing his or her own affairs. If the principal is a business entity such as a corporation or partnership, it should be organized in such a way that it is recognized as that type of business entity by the laws of the state.

Conversely, it is not necessary for an agent to have contractual authority.[3] Conceivably, a principal could appoint a minor or a person who has been declared legally incompetent to act as an agent. In agency, it is still possible for such a person to have authority to deal in the affairs of a principal. Most jurisdictions, however, do impose minimum levels of competence for an agent. Generally, persons who are virtually totally deficient in mental ability (insane) will not be considered part of a valid principal–agent relationship.

agency
When one party known as the agent acts on behalf of another party known as the principal. In a valid agency relationship, the agent can legally bind the principal.

APPLICATION 12.2

Josh, age 21, decides to start repairing cars as a business. He pays Raffi and Mary Pat to wash and detail the cars as an additional part of the business. Raffi and Mary Pat are both 17 years old. Josh is the principal. Raffi and Mary Pat are agents doing work on Josh's behalf. It is not necessary that Raffi and Mary Pat have contractual capacity as agents, because they are not ultimately responsible for work contracted with Josh's business.

Point for Discussion

♦   If Josh is also 17 years old, does the legal relationship between the three (Josh, Raffi, and Mary Pat) change?

Assignment 12.1

Identify if an agency exists and, if so, the principal, agent, and whether the agency is employment related.

1.   Mike signs for a package that is delivered for his roommate Nick.
2.   Jim asks Fran to watch his house while he is on vacation.
3.   Ashley and Hope are partners in a bakery business.
4.   Duane is a delivery man for Dorothy's flower shop.
5.   As a favor to his friend Dorothy, Duane picks up flowers for her flower shop that were ordered and paid for in advance by her.

Agent's Duties

The agent has several duties toward the principal. First is the duty of a fiduciary. The agent owes complete loyalty to the interests of the principal, including protecting those interests and any confidential communications regarding them.[4] If the agent acts on behalf of another or even on his or her own behalf in a way that is in conflict with the principal's interest, the agent has violated the fiduciary duty.

Second, every agent owes the principal a duty to act with reasonable care to protect the assets and interests of the principal. An agent who is in possession of property belonging to the principal must take reasonable steps to protect the property. An agent with confidential knowledge regarding the interests of the principal must act reasonably not to allow this information to be exploited. Failure to do either of these things would constitute a breach of the agent's duty of reasonable care.[5]

Finally, the agent owes the principal a certain degree of obedience. Within the principal–agent relationship, the principal can, to a reasonable extent, direct the actions of the agent in accomplishing the purpose of the agency.[6] For example, if the agency involves the sale of the principal's product, the principal may, to a reasonable extent, dictate the sales methods used by the agents. If an agent deviates substantially from the directions of the principal, the agent has breached the duty of obedience.

If an agent does breach one of the duties owed to a principal, several things may occur. First, the responsibility of the principal to be bound to third parties by the agent's acts may be affected. The principal may also have an action at law against the agent to recover any damage suffered as a result of the breach. If the agent was paid for the services rendered, the principal may sue for damages incurred directly as a result of the breach of one or more of the duties.

Whether an agent is paid for services rendered or performs the services as a gratuitous gesture, the principal may sue the agent in tort for the breach of reasonable care of property or the failure to make reasonable efforts to accomplish the purpose of the agency. Specifically, the principal could sue the agent for negligently or intentionally failing to perform the duties of an agent.

If the agent breaches the fiduciary duty and profits from dealing on his or her own behalf rather than on behalf of the principal, the principal may recover all of the profits accumulated through the agent's self-dealing. This is allowed to prevent agents from profiting at the expense of the principal.

Principal's Duties

Just as binding are the duties of the principal toward the agent. Unless the agent has agreed to act gratuitously, every principal owes an agent a duty of reasonable compensation for the services performed on behalf of the principal.[7] In addition, an agent is entitled to reimbursement by the principal for reasonable expenses incurred in achieving the objective of the agency.[8] This duty of reimbursement also extends to losses the agent may suffer while engaged in the agency relationship. Finally, a principal has the duty to cooperate in allowing the agent to complete his or her assigned tasks.

An exception to the duty of compensation and reimbursement occurs when the loss is incurred through the fault of the agent. For example, if an agent traveling on behalf of the principal's business is in an automobile accident, the principal could be held responsible for the agent's property loss, such as damage to the car, as well as for the agent's medical costs for treatment of injuries. If, however, the accident is caused by the agent's careless driving, the principal would have no liability for the agent's losses. (Note that this does not relieve the principal of liability for injuries caused to third persons by the agent's conduct.)

If the principal fails or refuses to honor any of these duties, the agent is entitled to bring an action at law against the principal for breach of contract. In addition, the agent may be entitled to impose a possessory lien on property of the principal that the agent holds. For example, if an agent is in possession of property of the principal and the principal does not pay the agent due compensation for work performed, the agent often has the option of holding the property until the principal complies with the duty of compensation or reimbursement.

Types of Authority

Assuming that both parties have the requisite capacity and are aware of the duties of each, four general types of authority can be exercised: actual authority, apparent authority, inherent authority, and authority by ratification. They are distinguished by the kind of authority given to the agent and the manner in which it is given. Each is created in a different way and imposes different degrees of responsibility on the parties.

Actual authority.   For actual authority to exist, the element of consent must be present.[9] The principal and the agent must both speak or act in a way that manifests agreement to the relationship. In addition, the principal must have legal capacity. The agency is not required to serve a purpose that will benefit both the principal and the agent. It is entirely possible for an agency to exist in which the agent receives no consideration for representing the principal.

Usually, a written agreement regarding the agency relationship is not required. Words or actions of the two parties are enough to establish that an agency exists between them. Some states, however, have an exception to this, that is, if a purpose of the agency is to grant authority to the agent to enter into written contracts on behalf of the principal. In this situation, the agent must have written evidence of authority from the principal. This rule is known as the equal dignities rule.[10] If a contract must be in writing under the statute of frauds (the statute in each jurisdiction that states which contracts must be in writing to be valid), it is only logical that the grant of authority to enter into the contract on behalf of another should also be in writing.

An agency based on actual authority is created solely by the principal and agent through agreement and is not based on what a third party perceives as the relationship between the principal and the agent. Actual authority includes two subcategories that indicate the way in which the agency was created and, to some degree, the extent of the agent's authority.

Actual express authority.   Actual express authority occurs when the principal gives to the agent an overt verbal or written communication stating the nature of the authority.[11] The principal need not put specific limits on the authority, such as time or degree, although this is desirable. If no limits are placed on the agent and a question arises as to whether the agent exceeded the authority, the court will limit the authority to what would be usual and customary under the circumstances.[12]

An example of express authority is the relationship between the owner and the sales staff at an automobile dealership. The owner (principal) gives actual express authority to the sales personnel to negotiate for the sale of cars in the inventory of the business. The authority of the agents would not ordinarily extend to the point of giving the cars away or selling the property where the business is located.

Actual implied authority.   Actual implied authority takes effect when the principal acts in such a way that the agent reasonably believes that the authority to act for the principal has been granted.[13] In limited situations, implied authority can occur in conjunction with express authority. The agent who has express authority to accomplish certain objectives for the principal also has the principal's implied authority to do whatever is reasonably necessary to accomplish the objectives. For example, a housekeeper who is authorized to manage a household, clean the house, and prepare meals would generally also have implied authority to purchase necessary cleaning supplies and groceries on behalf of the principal.

It is also considered reasonable for an agent with express authority in a particular type of business to employ customs and methods generally used in that type of business. For example, a construction company (principal) gives express authority to an agent to submit bids for building contracts. If the customs or methods used in the bidding include negotiating first with subcontractors, it is implied that the agent has the authority to engage in such negotiations to be competitive and to obtain contracts for the principal.

A type of actual implied authority that is independent from actual express authority is called implied authority by acquiescence. It takes place when the principal has not given an agent the express authority to do certain acts on behalf of the principal.[14] Nevertheless, the agent does act, and the principal does not interfere or object and accepts any benefit that results from the agent's actions. When this type of conduct occurs, the agent is presumed to have implied authority to continue acting on behalf of the principal, and the principal will be bound by the acts of the agent that are consistent with previous actions agreed to or acquiesced to by the principal.

APPLICATION 12.3

Char is a paralegal working for attorney Shelley. Periodically, Shelley will ask Char to access an internet law subscription service to research cases. The service charges by the number of minutes used to locate legal information. Char begins to use the service from time to time in support of her work. If Shelley poses no objection, Char would be considered to have actual implied authority to incur the charges with the subscription service.

Point for Discussion
♦ Could Shelley claim she had told Char to stop using the service and thereby avoid being bound by the contractual obligation to pay for it?

Actual authority (express or implied) can be terminated. The simplest means of terminating an agency is to make the termination part of the original agency agreement. When the agency is created, the principal states when it will end. Often this is based on a certain date or the happening of a specified event. For example, if the agent is hired to obtain a certain construction contract, the agency will end when the contract is awarded to a construction company.

More complicated are agencies that end because of unforeseen circumstances. If something occurs that effectively prevents the purpose of the agency from being accomplished, a court will often find that the agency terminated at that point. If the agent continues on after the occurrence, a court may hold the agent entirely responsible for any contracts or obligations incurred. Examples of circumstances that would automatically terminate an agency include the loss or destruction of items necessary to the purpose of the agency (a fire that destroys the equipment of the construction company); a drastic change in business conditions (the opening of a new highway that diverts all traffic away from the dairy); a change in relevant laws; potential bankruptcy of the principal or agent if it is relevant to the purpose of the agency; death of the principal or agent; total loss of capacity of the agent; loss of capacity by the principal; or, if the principal is a business entity, dissolution of the entity. In addition, if an agent takes action that is adverse to the principal or the principal's purpose in hiring the agent, the agency will automatically terminate. With respect to the last method, however, if a contract is involved, there may still be liability for breach of contract.

Apparent authority.   Apparent authority, also known as ostensible authority, is created through the acts of the principal and the perception of these acts by third parties.[15] Generally, a third party cannot conclude that an agency agreement exists based solely on the acts and assertions of the agent. The general rule regarding apparent authority is that if a principal acts in such a way that third parties would reasonably believe an agency relationship exists, the third parties can rely on and deal with the agent, and the principal will be bound by such dealings.[16]

First, assume an agent represents to a third party that he or she has the authority to act for the principal. If the principal knows of this and does not tell the third party differently, the third party is justified in believing the agent has the authority. Apparent authority can also be created if the principal acts in such a way or makes statements that would reasonably lead the third party to believe the agent has authority. In such a case, if the third party and the agent make an agreement, regardless of whether the agent in fact has authority, the principal will be bound to the terms of the agreement.

APPLICATION 12.4

Corey is hired as the assistant manager of a retail store. A letter is sent to suppliers informing them that Corey has purchasing authority. Corey is frequently asked to order inventory for the store and the manager arranges payment to the third parties. A few months later, Corey orders a large amount of inventory and has it delivered to a new location claiming the store is opening a new branch. In reality, he has been fired and takes the inventory ordered and leaves town with the intent of opening up his own shop elsewhere. The bill is sent, as usual, to the retail store where he had been employed. No communication was made of his termination to the suppliers. Based on the prior communication, the suppliers are reasonable in their belief that Corey had apparent authority to make the purchases.

Point for Discussion

◆   If the manager had sent a communication stating Corey had been
    terminated, would the wholesalers have been reasonable in
    believing Corey had apparent authority?

A principal can be held responsible for an agent whose authority has previously been terminated if the principal does not make the termination known
to parties who previously did business with the agent. This is known as lingering apparent authority.[17] If the principal does not make such notification, third
parties are reasonable in believing that the agency still exists. As a consequence,
the principal will continue to be held responsible for the agent's actions. An
exception to this rule is the death or incompetency of the principal, in which
case, no notice need be given to third parties. The agent's authority automatically ceases, and the principal's estate will not be bound to any agreements
entered into after the death or declaration of incompetence of the principal.

Inherent authority.   In certain limited situations, a principal will be held
responsible for the acts of an agent even though nothing has occurred to give
the agent actual or apparent authority. This is called inherent authority, which
is based on a balance of the interests of the principal and innocent third parties.
Inherent authority is often imposed when an agent has actual or apparent
authority to do one thing and does another.

Two circumstances in which the courts will impose inherent authority are
respondeat superior and similar conduct. Under respondeat superior,[18] a
principal is held liable for the acts of an employee even when the specific act
complained of was not authorized. For example, a delivery truck driver crashes
the truck into another vehicle. The employer (principal) authorized deliveries,
not automobile accidents. Nevertheless, the principal is liable because the accident took place while the driver (agent) was performing an authorized act.

The theory of similar conduct is based on the concept that a principal should
be held responsible for actions that are so similar to the authorized acts that third
parties would not be expected to know the difference. Refer to the earlier example
of a construction company that hires an agent to submit bids for building contracts.
If the agent is represented to have authority to bid and then modifies the bid
slightly, a third party would be justified in believing the agent had this type of
authority. Consequently, if a principal wants to place precise limits on the authority of an agent, such limitations should be clearly conveyed to any third parties.

Ratification.   Ordinarily, if no agency relationship exists but someone represents agency authority to a third party, who then relies on the representation
and deals with the agent, the principal will not be bound. However, if the principal becomes aware of the representation after the fact and agrees to it, agency
by ratification exists. In essence, the principal agrees to the agency after the

agent has already acted on behalf of the principal.[19] If the principal does not agree, no agency exists, and the principal is not bound by the acts of the agent.

This theory is distinct from the other possible theories of agency that may apply in similar situations, such as actual implied authority or respondeat superior if the agent's acts were similar or closely related to those for which authority had been granted. If the principal ratifies the actions of the agent, normally that ratification is retroactive. For example, if the purported agent enters into a contract on behalf of the purported principal, the contract will be in effect from the day it was entered, not the day the principal ratified it. If the contract is one that must be completed in a certain period of time, this may be quite significant.

An exception to the time element of ratification occurs when the principal did not have legal capacity at the time of the agent's actions. Thus, if the principal gains capacity (e.g., reaches the age of majority) on or before the date of ratification, the agency and acts of the agent become effective as of the date of ratification.

A principal cannot ratify only part of the agent's actions. If the principal accepts any part of the agent's actions, all of the agent's actions must be accepted.[20] To do otherwise would be unfair to the third party, who is already in peril because of reliance on the agent who did not really have authority.

A final requirement of the entire agreement is knowledge of material facts. The principal must have access to knowledge of all facts that affect the transaction entered into by the agent before the principal ratifies them. To do otherwise would be to lead a principal blindly into an agreement that may not serve his or her best interest.

Respondeat Superior

The requirements for an action of respondeat superior based on an agency are generally the same as those based on employment. First it must be shown that there was a master–servant relationship,[21] that is, a relationship that had a clearly defined authority figure and a person to carry out the directions from the authority. This may be either an employer–employee or a principal–agent relationship. A partner in a partnership is an example of a principal–agent relationship that does not involve an employer and an employee. The partnership as a business entity has authority to give direction. The partners as individuals carry out these directions. Thus, the partnership would be the principal, and the partners would be the agents. Partners are not considered employees of the partnership, however.

The second requirement of respondeat superior is that the agent acts within the scope of the agency. Specifically, this means that the act of the agent who injured the third party must have been committed while the agent was engaged in performance of the purpose of the agency.[22] An example is an agent who is running an errand for a principal and causes an auto accident on the way. A third person who is injured in the accident could have an action against the principal as well as the agent, because the agent was involved in carrying out the purpose of the agency at the time of the accident.

It is not relevant that the principal did not authorize the specific act of the agent that precipitated the injury to a third person. It is only necessary that the action be reasonably required for the completion of the agency and/or be of the same general nature as the conduct authorized. Thus, an agent who takes a slightly different route from that directed by the principal would still be considered to be acting within the scope of the agency.

An exception to a principal's responsibility for an agent under respondeat superior occurs when the agent deviates substantially from the instructions of the principal or when the agent is engaged in conduct that ultimately serves the agent rather than the principal.[23] In most jurisdictions, the doctrine does not apply to incidents that result from the agent's smoking while driving. For example, assume an agent who is a smoker is driving to a certain location for a principal. While handling, lighting, or disposing of a cigarette, the agent is inattentive to the road and causes an accident. The agent—not the principal— would be responsible for injuries to any third parties. Examples of deviation from the purpose include picking up hitchhikers, making personal stops, changing routes for personal purposes, and driving while intoxicated. Generally, any activity that substantially departs from the purpose of the agency and benefits the agent more than the principal will be considered sufficient to relieve the principal of liability.

An additional exception to a principal's liability for the acts of an agent is an intentional tort. A principal will not be responsible for injuries to third parties if the injuries were caused intentionally by the agent.[24] The reasoning behind this is that all persons should be responsible for their own intentional acts. A principal may be held responsible for intentional acts, however, if it is the general nature of the principal's business to engage in such acts and the agent's intentional acts further the purpose of the agency. A commonly used example is a bouncer in a bar. It is customary for bouncers to employ physical force against unruly patrons. Because this serves the purpose of the principal and is done with the principal's consent, the principal can be held liable for injuries caused by the agent.

Assignment 12.2

In each of the following situations, determine whether there is an agency relationship and, if so, whether it involves (a) actual express authority, (b) actual implied authority, (c) apparent authority, (d) inherent authority, or (e) authority by ratification. Explain your answers.

1. Jean is at a local amusement park to purchase season passes for her family. While she is there, she is identified as the one-millionth customer in the history of the park and is offered five free passes (enough for her family) and a one-time opportunity to purchase additional season passes at half the normal rate. She purchases season passes on behalf of her sister's family at a cost of $200. The sister repays Jean for the passes.
2. Matt, age 12, mows lawns for extra money. He hires 14-year-old Andrew to mow while Matt goes on his family vacation. Andrew does not mow the lawns.

3. Zoe is a professional housepainter and has developed a large business over a period of several years. She hires Marcus to paint houses for her as well. Marcus paints on one side of town while Zoe completes the contracted jobs on the other side of town.
4. The same situation as in 3, except Zoe permits Marcus to bid jobs on her behalf. From time to time Marcus also accepts contracts to paint that come in his area. Zoe does not complain and Marcus continues to do this as Zoe's employee.
5. The same situation as in 3, except Zoe adds Marcus to her name as having authority to purchase paints at a local paint store.

SOLE PROPRIETORSHIPS

The sole proprietorship is the simplest of all forms of business entities. The entire ownership of the business is vested in one individual. Consequently, it is unnecessary to have an agreement that indicates who has authority in the business, how profits and losses will be shared, or who is responsible for debts or judgments against the business. A sole proprietorship may employ any number of employees, but as long as the employees do not take part in ownership decisions or have the right or obligation to share in profits and losses, the business remains individually owned.

Sole proprietorships were once the most common form of business. Although they are still popular, many sole proprietorships are changing their legal status, usually to that of a corporation even if it is a corporation with only one shareholder. The reasons for this vary, but two reasons in particular are making the sole proprietorship less and less attractive to entrepreneurs. First, an individual operating a sole proprietorship must claim all profits of the business as personal income. A corporation, however, pays taxes on its own income, and the shareholders pay taxes only on the actual income they receive from the business. Often the tax liability for the individual is much less as a shareholder than as a sole proprietor. For example, if nearly all profits are reinvested in a corporation, the shareholders would not pay personal income tax on these profits; and if an individual has several sources of income, heavy profits from a sole proprietorship could increase personal income so that the owner is placed in a much higher tax bracket.

A second reason for the decline of sole proprietorships is judgment liability. When an outside party sues a sole proprietorship and wins, the judgment can be enforced against the individual owner, including all of the owner's personal assets. For example, if a person who is injured while in the shop of a sole proprietor sues and wins, the judgment can be collected from the business and from the personal assets of the individual owner, such as houses, cars, and bank accounts. Although businesses often have insurance and business assets, these may be insufficient to satisfy the judgment. Consequently, personal assets are pursued. In the case of corporations, the shareholders are vulnerable only to the amount of their previous investment in the business. With the increasing number of lawsuits against and among businesses, many sole proprietors are left with no choice but to incorporate in order to protect their own personal and real property.

PARTNERSHIPS

The Nature of Partnerships

A **partnership** is defined as follows:

> A voluntary contract between two or more competent persons to place their resources or services, or both, in a business or enterprise, with the understanding that there shall be a proportional sharing of the profits and losses.[25] (Statsky, *Legal Thesaurus/Dictionary.* West, 1982)

Most often an issue in partnership is resolved through the law of contracts and agency. Over time, however, some rules specific to partnership law have been developed. In addition, the Uniform Partnership Act, a model law adopted by a majority of the states, outlines procedures for the creation, operation, and termination of a partnership. Because the Uniform Partnership Act has been adopted as law by a majority of the states, the principles discussed here are consistent with the act's principles.

partnership
An agreement of two or more parties to engage in business or enterprise with profits and losses shared among all parties.

Characteristics of a Partnership

In a partnership, each partner is the agent of the partnership and represents the other partners. This authority allows one partner to legally bind the partnership and, ultimately, personal assets of the partners in contractual agreements. Generally, a partner's personal assets are not protected from being applied to pay debts of the business. The liability for debts of the partnership is joint and several among the partners.[26] If there is a determination that the partnership owes a debt that exceeds the worth of the partnership assets, any individual partner (as several individuals) or all partners (as joint individuals) together may be forced to pay the debt. An obligation does not have to be divided among the partners equally. Thus, a partner who is particularly wealthy has the greatest risk of being forced to pay partnership debts after the business assets have been applied. If, however, one partner is required to satisfy a large portion of the debt, the act permits that partner to require the other partners to reimburse a share of the payment that was made, assuming that the other partners have the financial ability to reimburse that share of debt. Therefore, a major concern before one enters a partnership is the personal financial stability of the other partners.

Generally, in a partnership, the partners share profits and losses equally. The exception would be if the partners had a written agreement that provided for a different distribution, such as 70/30, which could be the case if one partner had more invested in the business. The partnership is required to file tax returns for recordkeeping purposes only, since any actual taxes are paid personally by the partners based on the income they receive from the partnership. Similarly, if the partnership has an annual financial loss, the partners can claim their proportionate share of the loss against their total annual income on their personal returns in accordance with federal and state tax laws.

Each state has its own rules of procedure that indicate the manner in which a partnership is sued. Some states require that the name of the partnership as well as the names of the partners be included in the suit. Other states require only that one or the other be named.

Limited Partnerships

limited partnership
Partnership of two or more persons in which the limited partners can be held liable for partnership debts only to the extent of their investment and cannot take part in the general management and operation of the partnership business.

A special type of partnership, known as a **limited partnership,** can be used to protect the personal assets of a partner from liability and to provide other benefits with respect to investments and taxes. The Revised Uniform Limited Partnership Act, another model law adopted by a majority of the states as a statute, sets forth the specific rights, liabilities, and means of creating and dissolving a limited partnership. Generally, in a limited partnership, a limited partner is held liable only for the amount of his or her investment or promised investment in the partnership.[27] In this sense, a limited partner is similar to a corporate shareholder. The cost to a limited partner, however, is the loss of all control or influence in the operation of the partnership.

A limited partner can have no input into the operation of the business of the partnership. A limited partner cannot work for the partnership. Finally, the limited partner's name cannot be used in the partnership name. If any of these rules are broken, a limited partner may be treated as a general partner and be subject to joint and several liability.[28] Because limited partners cannot contribute services to the partnership, as a practical necessity, the partnership also must have general partners who operate the business of the partnership. Although these general partners manage the continuing business of the partnership, their personal assets are at risk as well.

The Relationship of Partners

Partners have a fiduciary obligation to each other. A fiduciary relationship is one in which there is a particular trust between the parties. In a partnership, each partner is trusted to place the interest of the partnership above personal interest. Therefore, any partner who makes a profit in a business venture of the type the partnership would ordinarily be involved in owes that profit to the partnership.

The partnership should decide in advance whether a partner is to be compensated for work done in the partnership. A partner is not entitled to payment for services rendered as an employee, but is only entitled to a share of the profits or losses, as are the other partners. The exception is when a partner or partners are winding up the partnership business after the death of another partner. In that case, it is proper to provide reasonable compensation to the survivors for their services in closing the partnership accounts.

Partners are entitled to receive payment for monies they have expended in the ordinary business of the partnership.[29] Thus, it is not necessary to have partnership approval for payment of every expense. If the expense is one that would reasonably be incurred in the operation of the business, a partner generally has the right either to obligate the partnership for payment or to receive reimbursement if he or she makes payment personally on the partnership's behalf.

If a dispute arises among parties to a partnership, certain legal actions are permitted. Specifically, a partner may sue the partnership for an accounting of partnership assets and liabilities when one or more of the following instances[30] occur:

1. The partnership is winding up business.
2. A partner has been improperly excluded from activity in the partnership.
3. There is a reasonable basis to suspect a partner has made personal profit at the expense of the partnership.

Other than in these instances, a partner is generally not permitted to sue a partnership, because as an individual, the partner would be the plaintiff, but as a member of the partnership, he or she would be the defendant. The law does not permit persons to sue themselves, even in different capacities.

Partnership Property

Partnerships are generally allowed to own personal property or real property in the name of the partnership. Financing for such purchases, however, is still sometimes required to be in the names of the partners, because if it becomes necessary to sue the partners for repayment, the original loan documents clearly state who the partners were.

Although partners have individual rights to the partnership's income, they cannot claim an individual interest in the partnership's assets (such as vehicles or office supplies) unless otherwise agreed. Occasionally, a conflict arises regarding whether property belongs to the partnership or to a particular partner individually. When this happens, a court will look to the following[31] before making a finding as to true ownership:

1. Was the property acquired with partnership funds?
2. Has the partnership made use of the property?
3. Does the partnership have legal title to the property?
4. Is the property of a type that would be used in the business of the partnership?
5. Has the partnership taken any steps to maintain or improve the condition of the property?
6. Is the property recorded in the books of the partnership as an asset?

If the answers to these questions strongly indicate that the partnership was the rightful owner of the property, all partners will be held responsible for any obligations with respect to the property. Likewise, if the property should suddenly increase in value, the partners will be joint owners of the property for that purpose as well.

The Life of a Partnership

Creation.   A partnership is an entity that must be created by agreement of those who will be responsible for its existence. The agreement is covered by the law of contracts. An example is the contractual requirement of capacity. If a person without capacity attempts to enter a partnership agreement, the law would not recognize the person's role as partner, and the person would have no liability for partnership debts. Thus, it is in the best interest of potential partners to ascertain in advance the legal capacity of one another.

In some states, the statute of frauds does not require that a partnership contract be in writing. Oral agreements are permissible as long as the conduct of the parties is clear enough to permit inference of the agreement.

Recognition.   Several factors must be considered to determine whether a partnership actually exists and should be legally recognized as such. The following questions are most often considered:

1. Do the alleged partners have some type of joint title to real or personal property?
2. Do the alleged partners operate under a single name?
3. Do the alleged partners all share in the profits and losses of the business?
4. How much money and time does each alleged partner invest in the business?

Since none of these factors independently establishes a partnership, all of them are considered jointly. If it is determined that most of them indicate an agreement between the parties to act as a partnership, the likely result is that the law will recognize a partnership.[32]

A partnership may also be established under the principle of partnership by estoppel. This occurs when one party allows a second party to represent himself or herself as a partnership to outsiders. If the outsider relies on the representation, the original party may be held responsible for the acts of the second party. The first party is precluded from denying the existence of a partnership after allowing another to represent to outsiders that such a relationship, in fact, existed.[33]

Partnership Dealings with Third Parties

Generally, every partner in a partnership has authority to act as an agent of the partnership. The partnership entity acts as the principal. A general principle of partnership is that a partner has apparent authority.[34] A partner may transfer title to property held in the partnership name or obligate the partnership in business agreements or purchases that relate to the business of the partnership. If, however, the transaction is one that would not ordinarily be encountered in the business of the partnership, a partner must have actual authority from the partnership before he or she can make a binding agreement with third parties.

In addition to having joint and several liability for contract obligations, a partnership may also be held responsible to third parties for wrongful acts of the partners or partnership employees. For example, if a partner or partnership employee negligently injures another while engaged in the business of the partnership, the partnership may be held liable for the injuries.[35]

The liability of partners in such a situation can be claimed in one of two ways. Some jurisdictions take the position that liability is joint and that every partner must be sued for the injuries. Many other jurisdictions have made the liability joint and several, which means that all the partners or an individual partner may be sued. As in contract situations, however, if an individual partner must satisfy the entire debt of the partnership, that partner may require the other partners to contribute toward reimbursement for payment of the judgment.[36]

CASE

Douglas HILLME,
Respondent, v.
Brent CHASTAIN
and C & H Custom
Cabinets,

Inc., a Missouri
Corporation,
Appellants.
75 S.W.3d 315.
May 14, 2002.

ROBERT S. BARNEY,
Chief Judge.

Appellant, Brent Chastain, ("Chastain") appeals from the First Amended Judgment and Order Appointing Special Master rendered by the Circuit Court of Laclede County after a bench trial. The trial court found that a partnership existed between Chastain and Respondent, Douglas Hillme ("Hillme"), ordered an accounting and appointed a special master to assist in the process. In his sole point on appeal, Chastain maintains there was insufficient evidence supporting the trial court's judgment finding that a partnership existed between himself and Hillme.

> The trial court found that that part of its judgment, as amended, with respect to the finding of the existence of a partnership, was final for purposes of appeal per Rule 74.01(b).

See Rule 74.01(b), Missouri Court Rules (2001). Appellant, C & H Custom Cabinets, Inc., originally brought a third-party action against Hillme alleging that Hillme was indebted to the corporation. However, C & H Custom Cabinets, Inc., is not involved in the appeal of this particular claim.

"Appellate review of a judgment in a court-tried case is that established in *Murphy v. Carron,* 536 S.W.2d 30, 32 (Mo. banc 1976)." *Eul v. Beard,* 47 S.W.3d 424, 425 (Mo.App.2001) We must affirm the trial court's judgment unless there is no substantial evidence to support it, it is against the weight of the evidence, or it erroneously declares or applies the law. *Id.* at 426, *Murphy,* 536 S.W.2d 30 at 32. "The appellate court reviews the evidence in the light most favorable to the prevailing party, giving it the benefit of all reasonable inferences and disregarding the other party's evidence except as it supports the judgment." *Meyer v. Lofgren,* 949 S.W.2d 80, 82 (Mo.App.1997). "It does not weigh the evidence and must give due deference to the trial judge in determining the credibility of witnesses." *Id.*

A partnership is statutorily defined as "an association of two or more persons to carry on as co-owners a business for profit." § 358.060.1. [FN2] Statutory rules applicable in determining the existence of a partnership are set forth in § 358.070. Statutory references are to RSMo 1994.

◆ CASE

A partnership has also been judicially defined, as "a contract of two or more competent persons to place their money, effects, labor and skill, or some or all of them, in lawful commerce of business and to divide the profits and bear the loss in certain proportions." *Meyer,* 949 S.W.2d at 82 (quoting *Kielhafner v. Kielhafner,* 639 S.W.2d 288, 289 (Mo.App.1982)).

The partnership agreement may be written, expressed orally, or implied from the acts and conduct of the parties. *Morrison v. Labor & Indus. Relations Comm'n.* 23 S.W.3d 902, 908 (Mo.App. 2000). The intent of the parties is the primary factor for determining whether such a relationship exists. *Binkley v. Palmer,* 10 S.W.3d 166, 169 (Mo.App.1999). The required intent necessary to find a partnership existed "is not the intent to form a partnership, but the intent to enter a relationship which in law constitutes a partnership." *Meyer,* 949 S.W.2d at 82.

At trial, Hillme had the burden of proving the existence of a partnership by clear, cogent, and convincing evidence. *Morrison,* 23 S.W.3d at 907-08. The "clear, cogent, and convincing" evidentiary standard simply means that the trial court should be *"clearly convinced* of the affirmative of the proposition to be proved." *Grissum v. Ressman,* 505 S.W.2d 81, 86 (Mo.1974). "This does not mean that there may not be contrary evidence." *Id.*

A partnership agreement may be implied from conduct and circumstances of the parties and the parties are not required to know all the legal implications of a partnership. *Grissum,* 505 S.W.2d at 86. Partnership property that is held only in an individual name does not affect the partnership status. *Id.* at 87. The filing or non-filing of a partnership income tax return is not sufficient alone to prove or disprove the existence of a partnership. *Brotherton v. Kissinger,* 550 S.W.2d 904, 907-08 (Mo.App.1977). A voice in the management of the partnership business, a share of the profits of the partnership business, and a corresponding risk of loss and liability to partnership creditors are all indications of a partnership. *Arnold v. Erkmann,* 934 S.W.2d 621, 630 (Mo.App.1996).

Viewed in a light most favorable to the judgment of the trial court as we must, *Meyer,* 949 S.W.2d at 82, the record shows that Chastain and Hillme had each worked for a period of time at Classic Cabinets, a cabinet making shop. Hillme had worked there for about four years and had eight or nine years experience in cabinet making. He was in charge of the "specialty items, the mantles, the bookcases [and] gun cabinets." Chastain had also worked for the same concern and for the most part performed staining, finishing and installation work. Chastain testified that he had built cabinets on his own several years before and had worked in construction for ten years. Early in 1997, Hillme and Chastain discussed going into business together as cabinetmakers. They also had similar discussions with Chastain's spouse and Hillme's fiance at Chastain's home.

Classic Cabinets later changed its name to Classic Woodworks.

In April of 1997, Chastain and Hillme made the decision to go into business together. Hillme testified that they both agreed to divide the workload, profit, expenses, and losses equally, that is on a "50/50" basis. No written partnership agreement was executed. Each drew a flat and equal amount of pay each week. According to Hillme, any money left over they agreed to let accumulate in the partnership account.

Chastain quit his job prior to Hillme terminating his employment. Hillme wrote a check for the purchase of plywood and Chastain also contributed monies for the venture. Chastain rented a building and purchased some woodworking equipment. He also negotiated the rent for the building. Both spent time cleaning the building and prepared to move into the building. Hillme purchased furnace parts to heat the building. Both contributed tools and equipment to the business. A business insurance policy was obtained. The parties named the business "C & H Custom Cabinets." The "C" stood for Chastain's last name and the "H" stood for Hillme's last name. Both had input as to the layout of the business cards, the building sign, and Yellow Pages advertisement. Each advertisement, including the business cards, set out each one's full name and home telephone number.

The record further shows that Chastain holds a bachelor's degree in accounting. They agreed that Chastain would handle the accounting and bookkeeping matters for their business. During the day-to-day operation, Chastain ran errands and applied stain and finish to cabinets. Hillme's time was generally spent building the cabinets. Chastain was also in charge of paying bills and scheduling installations. Neither one worked any set hours and the order in which work was to be done and by whom was settled by them as the need arose.

A checking account for the business was opened at "Central Bank." The name shown on their checks was "C & H Cabinets." It was Hillme's understanding that as business partners, they were both owners of the jointly-held account at the bank. Both issued checks from the account and each carried the concern's checkbook on occasion.

Title to the checking account went through several changes while they were working together during the period of mid-1997 through mid-1999. As best we glean, initially and unbeknownst to Hillme, the checking account was titled in Chastain's name doing business as C & H Custom Cabinets. Nevertheless, Hillme and Chastain's wife were given authorization to sign checks on the account. A year and a half later, again unbeknownst to Hillme, the account was changed to reflect that owners of the account were Chastain and his spouse. Hillme was not named as an account owner. Then in 1998 the account was made "payable on death" to Hillme. In time, Hillme was removed all together from the concern's checking account. Hillme testified that he remembered signing a "different" account card from the bank, but recalled Chastain telling him that the bank had made a mistake.

In 1997, Chastain and Hillme decided their business required a cargo trailer for hauling cabinets to the installation site. They discussed the purchase and both went to a vehicle dealer to select one. According to Hillme, it was his understanding that the cargo trailer was to be paid out of the partnership account. A bank loan was initially obtained for the purchase of the

cargo trailer. Both Chastain and Hillme personally signed the note for the loan. Unbeknownst to Hillme title to the cargo trailer was placed in Chastain's name only. To the question, "Did you agree with Mr. Chastain that the title of this trailer would be issued in his own name, rather [than]the two of you as partners?", Hillme answered, "No." Hillme also stated that it was not until after his lawsuit had commenced that he had found out how the title to the cargo trailer was held.

Hillme further testified that in October 1998, a 1994 Dodge pickup truck was purchased. Hillme related that funds generated by the partnership were used for this purpose and be understood that the vehicle was to be a partnership vehicle. According to Hillme, Chastain informed him that once the 1994 pickup truck was paid for, the partnership would buy Hillme a pickup truck. However, the pickup truck was not titled in the name of the business. Rather, it was titled in Chastain's name. Once again, Hillme testified it was only after the lawsuit was filed that he first learned that the pickup truck was titled solely in Chastain's name.

According to Hillme, Chastain showed him the business records for 1997 and gave Hillme tax documents for the 1997 tax year so that Hillme could file his individual return. Each of the parties claimed half of the business expenses, such as utilities, and each claimed half of the gross income. Neither one filed an IRS partnership Form K-1.

At trial, Chastain variously claimed that Hillme was a subcontractor and then an employee Chastain's lawyer described Hillme as an independent contractor. Significantly, Chastain's 1997 tax return did not show that he had paid Hillme either as an employee or as contract laborer. Indeed, as previously set out, for the tax year involved, Chastain split the expenses of the business with Hillme. Later, Hillme received Form 1099s from Chastain for the tax years 1998 and 1999. Hillme testified, however, that the Form 1099s held no particular significance to him.

According to Hillme, in early 1999 Chastain informed him that he would incorporate the business for tax purposes, but assured him that it

CASE

would not affect their agreement. They had a limited discussion regarding the incorporation. Hillme testified that Chastain informed him that they needed to incorporate their business because of possible tax savings.

In time, the parties disagreed over Chastain's plans to build a new shop building at a cost of twenty to twenty-five thousand dollars. Hillme felt it was unwise to borrow the money for the building at that time. Because of this disagreement, Chastain built the building himself out of his personal funds.

Eventually, further disagreements over management caused Hillme to open his own cabinetmaking business some time in 1999. By then Hillme had become aware of Chastain's claims that they were not partners.

In his sole point on appeal, Chastain maintains the trial court erred in finding that a partnership existed between himself and Hillme because there was insufficient evidence to support the trial court's ruling. Chastain asserts that Hillme failed to demonstrate the necessary elements of partnership, such as, co-ownership of business assets, mutual rights of control of the business, an agreement in fact, and the right to share in profits and duty to share in losses. We disagree.

As previously related, the intent of the parties is the primary factor in determining whether a partnership exists. *Binkley,* 10 S.W.3d at 169. It is apparent that the trial court found Hillme's testimony to be more credible that that of Chastain. *Meyer,* 949 S.W.2d at 82.

While each evidentiary factor standing alone may not evince a partnership, it is clear that the combination of the following probative factors is supportive of the trial court's conclusion that a partnership was created by Chastain and Hillme in 1997.

The factors we note are the following: The name of the business was based on each party's last name. All of the advertising included each party's name and home telephone number. The day-to-day operation of the business relied on each one's specialized skills—Hillme's greater experience in cabinet making and Chastain's accounting and management skills. Each party co-signed the note for the cargo trailer. A joint checking account was originally established using the name of the business. Both parties were authorized to issue checks on the account. At one point Hillme was named a "payable at death" beneficiary of the business checking account. Additionally, Hillme had a voice in the management of the partnership. This is evidenced by his "veto" of using partnership assets for the construction of an additional shop building. Furthermore, during the first year of the partnership in 1997, each divided equally the income and expenses generated through the business. Although Chastain testified that this sharing of expenses for tax year 1997 was a "gift," it is apparent the trial court was not persuaded of the efficacy of this assertion.

We cannot say that the trial court erred in finding that a partnership existed between Chastain and Hillme. Sufficient evidence in the record supports the trial court's judgment. *Grissum,* 505 S.W.2d at 88. Point denied.

The trial court's judgment is affirmed.

Case Review Question
Hillme 75 S.W.3d 315 (2002).
Would the outcome differ if there was evidence that the plaintiff was aware assets and bank accounts were in the name of the defendant and that he should have filed a partnership tax return?

Termination or Dissolution

Any change in the partners of a partnership will result in the dissolution of that partnership.[37] Thus, when a partner dies, declares bankruptcy, sells his or her interest in the partnership, or withdraws, the partnership is dissolved. This does not mean that the partnership will cease to do business. The business of the partnership may be terminated or a new partnership begun. In addition, if the previously lawful business of the partnership becomes illegal, the partnership is dissolved and business must cease.

When a partnership is dissolved, third parties who have done business with the partnership are entitled to notice. This prevents partners from wrongfully representing apparent authority and binding the members of a dissolved partnership to third parties. All partners have the right to act as agents of the partnership and perform such duties as are required to conclude existing business obligations and concerns. However, a partner who has declared bankruptcy is no longer considered to be an active partner and cannot act on behalf of the partnership. The dissolving partnership is not allowed to engage in any new business, such as entering contracts or taking new orders.

Any partnership assets that remain after all creditors have been paid in full are distributed according to a specific procedure. First, any partner who has loaned money to the partnership, over and above investment in the partnership, will be repaid. Second, all partners are repaid the amount of their contribution or investment in the partnership. Any cash that still remains is distributed among the partners on a pro rata basis. If one partner contributed 50 percent and two other partners contributed 25 percent each of the capital for the partnership, the funds will be distributed in a 2:1:1 ratio. The first partner will receive 50 percent of the remaining funds, and the other two will each receive 25 percent of the funds.

More often, after paying the creditors, a partnership's assets are insufficient to repay all the partners for their investment. In such cases, the shortage is also distributed on a pro rata basis. To follow the preceding example, the 50 percent contributor would absorb 50 percent of the shortage, and the other two partners would each be responsible for 25 percent of the shortage.

Assignment 12.3

Examine the following situation and develop a plan for dissolving the partnership and distributing the assets by percentage.

Michael, Macy, and Miranda created a partnership to open a restaurant. Each put in $8,000 in cash and Michael also contributed the land. All worked equally in the business. After 18 years they have decided to retire. The area where the restaurant operated is in decline and they feel it would be more lucrative to liquidate than attempt to sell the operation to a new owner. The restaurant has the following fair market value assets: land $18,000; building (added in the first year of the partnership) $41,000; equipment and fixtures $9,000. Following are the debts of the partnership: mortgage on the building $12,000; various vendors $3,500; utilities, advertising, and other incidental expenses not yet paid $6,000.

CORPORATIONS

corporation

Entity legally recognized as independent of its owners, known as shareholders. A corporation can sue or be sued in its own name regarding its own rights and liabilities.

Legal advantages make the **corporation** one of the most common forms of business. In addition, because a corporation is created purely by statute, the legislatures have been free to create different subtypes of corporations to suit the needs of different types of businesses. Nevertheless, most corporations share standard characteristics, many of which have been embodied in the Model Business Corporation Act (see Appendix B).

Corporate Characteristics

A legal person.   Under the law, a corporation is recognized as a person. It can be taxed and held responsible for its acts for the purposes of lawsuits. Generally in the past, however, a corporation was not considered to be capable of committing crimes. When criminal conduct occurred, the individuals who actually committed the crime were held responsible.[38] This outlook has been changing. More and more statutes permit corporations and their agents to be convicted of criminal acts. Although a corporation cannot be imprisoned, it can be fined or dissolved as a penalty for illegal conduct. In addition, the acting individual can be held criminally responsible.

Life.   Generally, the life of a corporation goes on indefinitely as long as the requirements of the statutes that permitted its creation are met. The statutes that set forth the ways in which a corporation must be created often establish annual obligations that must be met for the corporation to continue to exist. Often these obligations include such things as payment of an annual fee for continued registration with the state as a recognized corporation and annual reports describing the activities of the corporation during the preceding year.

Limited liability.   Perhaps the greatest advantage of a corporation is that individuals who invest in it have limited exposure for losses. Ordinarily, a person who invests in a corporation is called a shareholder. In return for the investment, a shareholder is given shares of stock in the corporation. The shares represent a percentage of ownership. The greater the investment, the greater the percentage of ownership. If the corporation does well, the shareholder's ownership becomes more valuable in terms of the price of the shares or the distribution of profits. If the corporation does badly or a large monetary judgment is rendered against it as the result of a lawsuit, the shareholders usually stand to lose only the amount of their original investment.[39] Thus, the corporation differs from most other types of business entities in which the owners are responsible for the entire judgment irrespective of whether it exceeds their investment.

Ownership versus control.   A corporation may have many thousands of shareholders. Often the persons who are in a position to invest are not the persons who are best qualified to run the corporation. Therefore, for this and other

APPLICATION 12.5

George has a net worth of $350 million. He owns stock in ABC Corporation. He purchased the stock at par value (company-stated value) for $2 million, representing approximately 10 percent of the value of the company at the time of purchase. The value of the company has now gone into the negative and the debts of the company exceed the value by approximately $4 million. If the company declares bankruptcy and assets are sold to pay creditors, George is not responsible (nor are any of the other similarly situated shareholders) beyond what he has invested in the company, due to the limited liability of corporations.

Point for Discussion
◆   What would the liability of George be if he were a 10 percent owner in a partnership with the same values?

practical reasons, another characteristic common only to corporations is that management of the business is separate from ownership. When a corporation is created, a board of directors is appointed that oversees the general operation of the corporation and the officers of the corporation who supervise day-to-day activities. This method of separating the management from ownership protects the interests of shareholders who do not wish to be involved in management. It is not necessary for members of the board of directors or the officers to have any ownership interest in the corporation.

Sale of ownership.   Unlike other types of businesses, ownership (represented by shares of stock) in a corporation can be freely transferred by sale or gift with virtually no effect on the corporation. This allows the investors the opportunity to profit from their investments, and because management and ownership are separated, the corporation can continue operating uninterrupted.

Limits on operation.   When a corporation is formed, the reasons for the corporation and other information are set forth in a document called the **articles of incorporation,** or charter. These documents generally contain the name and purpose of the corporation; the number of shares to be issued and their value per share to the corporation; the voting rights of shareholders; and provisions for the election, removal, or appointment of board members or officers. The basic rules of operation and the methods to be used in carrying out the corporate purpose and in governing the corporation are set forth in **bylaws.** These charter documents can generally be changed only with the consent of the shareholders. The officers and board of a corporation cannot depart from what is set forth in the bylaws and articles of incorporation in any substantial manner without prior approval.

articles of incorporation
Document filed with the state at the time of incorporation that states the purpose of the corporation and defines the corporate structure.

bylaws
Document of a corporation that details the methods of operation, such as officers and duties, chain of command, and general corporate procedures.

Creating a Corporation

promoter

One who is hired as a fiduciary to recruit investors in a proposed corporation.

Promoters.   For some businesses, a corporation is formed by **promoters**— persons who are often initial incorporators and shareholders. A promoter's primary duty is to obtain sufficient funding (capitalization) for the corporation and ensure that all the formalities required by the statute for incorporation are satisfied. In some jurisdictions, promoters are personally liable for the contracts they make on behalf of the corporation unless and until the corporation agrees to substitute itself for the promoter in the contract (known as a *novation*). If more than one promoter is involved in forming a corporation, each has a fiduciary duty to the other and cannot act in his or her own self-interest if it will harm the interests of the other promoters.

The promoters also have a fiduciary duty to the corporation and its shareholders.[40] They cannot use secret corporate information for their personal benefit or gain. If a promoter does use secret information for self-profit, the corporation and its shareholders can file suit to reclaim that profit. If, however, the promoter fully discloses the information to the corporation and the corporation or interested shareholders who would be affected approve, the promoter may use the information to obtain all possible profits.

APPLICATION 12.6

Assume a promoter who is forming a corporation (an art gallery) becomes aware of an opportunity to purchase a rare painting at a bargain price. As long as the promoter gives the shareholders notice of this opportunity and the shareholders either decline to make the purchase or give the promoter approval to make the purchase personally, the promoter may buy the painting and sell it for the highest available profit. However, if the promoter does not apprise the corporation of this opportunity and purchases the painting as a personal investment, the corporation can file suit to claim any profits from the investment.

Point for Discussion
◆   Would the situation be any different if the promoter was planning to sell the painting to the gallery?

Statutory requirements.   All states have some type of statutory law to govern the creation, operation, and dissolution of corporate entities. A majority of the states have enacted the Model Business Corporation Act (see Appendix B), a series of laws that address all legal aspects of corporate existence. The act includes provisions for everything from establishing a corporate name to the proper procedures for dissolution. By establishing the same basic statutory provisions in most states, the process of handling legal disputes over corporate statutes is much easier to accomplish. The following is an example of a provision of the Model Business Corporation Act (MBCA):

Sec. 32 **Quorum of Shareholders**

Unless otherwise provided in the articles of incorporation, a majority of the shares entitled to vote, represented in person or by proxy, shall constitute a quorum at a meeting of shareholders, but in no event shall a quorum consist of less than one-third of the shares entitled to vote at the meeting. If a quorum is present, the affirmative vote of the majority of the shares represented at the meeting and entitled to vote on the subject matter shall be the act of the shareholders, unless the vote of a greater number or voting by classes is required by this act or the articles of incorporation or bylaws.

Assignment 12.4

> You are the officer of a corporation. A number of important issues are on the agenda for the upcoming shareholders meeting. You are concerned that insufficient shareholders will vote to legally pass on any of the issues. Analyze the preceding statutory language. Break it down into the basic components and outline the exact requirements to bind the corporation on any of the issues voted upon at the meeting.

Some of the most important statutory requirements of the MBCA or any statutory law with respect to corporations are those that provide for the creation of a corporation. Typically, this is accomplished through a number of steps, including the drafting of certain documents. The articles of incorporation and bylaws must be drafted and signed by the incorporators. Necessary documents and fees must be submitted to the secretary of state or other designated person where the business is incorporated. When the incorporators have complied properly with these formalities, the secretary of state will grant a certificate of incorporation.

The mere drafting of these documents does not establish a corporation. All other statutory requirements of the particular state must be met for the corporation to be recognized by the state as a corporation doing business in that state. Until these requirements are met, the corporation will not be entitled to the benefits generally afforded to corporations, such as limited liability. But when an outside party makes a claim against an alleged corporation in court, the court may find that a corporation exists for the purposes of the dispute even though the state has not previously recognized it.

Each state also has statutes that explain the procedure for the formation of a professional corporation (sometimes referred to as a PC). The states use various names for this entity, but the concept is basically the same. A professional corporation allows a member or members of a certain profession such as law, medicine, dentistry, or accounting to form a business that has many of the legal advantages of a corporation.[41] These corporations often do not have actual shares of stock, and when they do, the shares are usually held entirely by the professional members.

Types of Corporate Status

A de jure corporation (corporation by law) is created by meeting each requirement of relevant statutes that provide for corporation formation and maintenance. These statutes usually require that incorporators have legal capacity and submit articles of incorporation and bylaws. When all of the provisions for incorporation have been satisfied, the state issues a certificate of incorporation that is generally valid as long as the corporation continues to satisfy the statutes.

On occasion, incorporators attempt to satisfy the statutes but are not successful. In some cases, the law will recognize the organization as a de facto corporation (corporation by fact or actions). The shareholders of a business that is recognized as a de facto corporation are protected in liability the same as de jure corporation shareholders would be.

To establish a de facto corporation, there must be evidence that the incorporators made a good faith attempt to comply with the state laws regarding incorporation and continuance of corporations and that the business has been conducted as if it were a corporation. It must also be shown that the corporation was represented as such and not as another type of business entity and that outside persons dealt with the business as if it were a corporation.[42] When all such evidence exists, the court may recognize the entity as a de facto corporation and allow it to claim all of the privileges of a de jure corporation.

Corporation by estoppel (preclusion from denial of corporate existence) comes into play in one of two ways. In the first, a person or persons hold a business out as a corporation to the public and deal with the public as a corporation but later attempt to deny that the corporation ever existed.[43] The second occurs when outsiders deal with a business as a corporation with knowledge that it is not a proper corporation. Then, when a dispute arises between the two, the outsiders attempt to deny that a corporation exists and claim that the owners should be personally liable.[44] In either instance, the courts will often treat the business as a corporation by estoppel and apply the law as if it were a real corporation. The rationale is that people should not be able to derive all of the benefits from acting as or dealing with a corporation while avoiding the obligations of one.

Personal, Close Corporations, and Limited Liability Companies

The Internal Revenue Service (IRS) designates the common general corporation as a C-corporation, which includes certain subtypes. The most common forms of small corporations are the S-corporations, professional corporations, and limited liability companies. Each of these provides some degree of limitation on personal liability for corporate acts, but each allows the income of the corporation to flow through directly to the owners for tax purposes. With a general corporation, profits are taxed at a corporate rate and separate from the owners. Any distribution of profits to the owner shareholders is in the form of dividends. These are then considered personal income of the recipient for the purpose of income tax. The smaller personal corporations pay tax only once, as all of the income of the corporation is considered income of the owners. Depending on the nature of the business, its size, its profitability, the number of owners, and their own personal tax status, the most attractive corporate form may be general or personal.

The more personal and close corporations are totally created and overseen through statutory law just as the general corporation. Specific statutes prescribe the necessary steps to create, maintain, and dissolve such corporations. Historically, the S-corporations were used for small operations of several individuals in virtually any type of legal business who sought to limit the exposure to liability they might have in a partnership. The professional corporation was created for licensed professionals whose business was to provide services rather than ordinary types of commercial business. This corporate form continues to be common among licensed professionals such as physicians, attorneys, accountants, and other similarly situated independent service providers. However, the limitation of liability will not protect the professional for his or her own personal malfeasance in the delivery of professional services.

The newest corporate form, the limited liability company (LLC), is rapidly growing in acceptance and has been recognized by statute in a majority of jurisdictions. Typically, the professional corporation statutes require all shareholders to be members of a common profession. Under the LLC, individuals who are not members of the profession that is the basis for the business may be owners. For example, a physician may enter into an LLC with an attorney in which the physician provides medical services as the primary business of the corporation, and the attorney is responsible for other issues such as the management of the business. In this type of company, most often the shareholders are subject to personal liability only for their own personal conduct. Thus, in this example, the attorney would not ordinarily be held accountable for the medical malpractice of the physician. Therefore, if an action were brought against the LLC for matters related to property ownership or business dealings, any judgment could only be recovered from assets of the business and not the owners. However, if a judgment for malfeasance were obtained against the business for the professional actions of an owner engaged in the primary focus of the business, the professional found culpable would also be subject to personal liability.

Piercing the Corporate Veil

A court will sometimes ignore the corporate structure of a de jure corporation and hold all or some of the shareholders, officers, and directors responsible for the acts of the corporation. Thus, the court ignores the wall of protection from exposure to liability that shareholders usually enjoy as owners of a corporation. This is called piercing the corporate veil and happens when a court finds that the members of a corporation have improperly used corporate status.

Generally, a corporation may be subject to piercing of the corporate veil in three instances: (1) when it is necessary to prevent fraud, (2) when there is inadequate capitalization, and (3) when the corporation refuses to recognize the formalities necessary to a de jure corporation.

Prevention of fraud.   In the case of the prevention of attempted fraud, the veil will be pierced only when it can be shown that a person or persons formed the corporation in a direct attempt to avoid legal obligations to creditors or others with legal rights. Usually, such debts were incurred through the corporation but the funds were used in ways to benefit the shareholders personally. This is not the same as protecting the shareholders from obligations incurred as the result of the ordinary business of the corporation. If the obligations were originally intended to benefit the business of the corporation or were the result of doing business of the corporation, the corporation will be responsible for the obligations, and the shareholders will continue to be protected.

Inadequate capitalization.   In the case of inadequate capitalization, the point at which the corporate veil will be pierced is not as clear. Although it is true that shareholders are generally responsible only for the amount invested in the corporation, it is also true that the original corporate structure must provide for investment that is adequate to allow the corporate purpose to be achieved. For example, a family who wanted to form a corporation to operate a shoe store would have to invest enough money to purchase inventory, fixtures, and a place for the store to operate. In addition, a sufficient amount of the profits of an ongoing corporation must be reinvested to enable the corporation to continue until such time as the shareholders agree to dissolve it. If this is not done, the corporation is destined for failure, and the evidence indicates there was never a true intent to form a legal corporation for the purpose of doing legitimate business.[45]

Refusal to recognize corporate formalities.   Finally, the corporate status of a corporation that refuses to recognize corporate formalities will be ignored, and the shareholders will be held individually responsible as if they were partners in an ordinary business venture. One basis for piercing the corporate veil because of lack of corporate formality is to claim alter ego. Specifically, this means that the corporation has no true purpose of its own but is simply a tool of another organization. While a corporation may be properly created and actually engage in the business stated as its purpose, a close examination will reveal that the business is merely a front for another business. In determining whether a business is an alter ego corporation, a court may consider whether the business shares employees, funds, equipment, and any other element usually used exclusively by a business entity.

One type of alter ego corporation involves very small or close corporations, which generally consist of only a few shareholders, all of whom are often active in the business of the corporation. The problem arises when the shareholders begin to treat the property of the corporation as personal property. For example, the shareholders may use corporate funds to pay private debts, fail to keep separate corporate accounting records, or take or use corporate funds or property without following proper procedures. If the shareholders are engaging in such activities, a court is likely to find that the corporation has not had a true corporate existence.[46]

Another situation in which the alter ego theory may be applied involves parent and subsidiary corporations. It is entirely legal for one corporation to totally own and control another corporation. However, unless both corporations operate independently, comply separately with the legal corporate formalities, and represent themselves to the public as separate and distinct, the courts may consider them to be a single corporation, with one corporation acting as the alter ego of the other.[47] In that event, the parent or owning company, which usually has the greater assets, can be held liable for the debts of the subsidiary.

A situation that is encountered less frequently but is nevertheless a basis for the alter ego theory is that of joint ownership. If a shareholder has a major interest in more than one corporation and strongly influences the policies and actions of the various corporations so that they become mere common tools for the manipulation of the business of this shareholder, the corporations may be considered alter ego corporations and be held liable for the actions of one another.

Liability of parties.   When a corporation, large or small, consistently engages in any such conduct, the court is likely to find that the intent of the parties was not to carry on the business as a corporation. In addition, if it is found that the conduct of the shareholders, officers, or directors has resulted in injustice to outside persons, the court may refuse to recognize the corporate status. This forces the shareholders to be individually responsible to injured outsiders for the damage that resulted from the injuries.

When the court does ignore the corporate structure and holds the shareholders liable, it does not necessarily follow that all shareholders will have to bear the losses of the business. If a corporation consists of many shareholders, only those who actively engaged in the wrongful conduct will be held responsible.[48] Innocent shareholders who did not take part in the management of the corporation will not ordinarily be held responsible for the acts of the persons in control.

Claims resulting in piercing of the veil.   Certain types of claims most commonly result in piercing of the corporate veil. One type is tort claims, made by persons whose person or property has been injured by some negligent or intentional act of the corporation. Usually, such persons had no business dealings with the corporation. If the corporate veil could not be pierced, those who have been unjustly injured could be placed in a position of suing a corporation that is nothing more than a shell with no assets against which to file a claim. For example, assume that a person is involved in a car accident with a bus. Assume also that the bus company has no assets and does no business other than renting three old buses for charters. Assume further that the bus company carries no insurance on the buses. If it can be shown that the owners of the bus company acted in one of the ways previously discussed, it would be unfair to force the injured person to bear the total cost of the injuries while the owners continued to profit from the business of the bus company.

A second instance of piercing the corporate veil occurs in contract claims. In such situations, a party has business dealings with the corporation, only to find out later that the corporation was a sham. In most cases, the courts will find that the outsider had an opportunity to investigate the credibility of the corporation before doing business with it. If the situation did not lend itself to this, however, and would have appeared proper to reasonable persons, the corporate veil will be pierced. For example, if a seemingly credible advertisement appears in the media and persons respond to it only to find later that they have been swindled, the corporate veil might be pierced.

Assignment 12.5

> Consider the following facts, then create an argument why someone suing Perkins Corporation should not be permitted to pierce the corporate veil and reach the assets of Cruisair Industries.
>
> The Perkins Corporation manufactures components for airplanes. The sole shareholder in the Perkins Corporation is airplane manufacturing giant Cruisair Industries. Cruisair is a separate corporation but has bank accounts that automatically transfer necessary operating funds to Perkins when needed. Similarly, at the end of each calendar quarter, all funds over and above a set amount in Perkins accounts automatically transfer into the Cruisair accounts. When either corporation suffers employee turnover, employees are lent from the other company to fill the void until the position is filled. Employees of both companies also share the same benefits package and retirement plan. The employee handbooks are identical with the exception of the title page stating the company name. Cruisair employees conduct employee reviews and award raises and promotions to Perkins employees.

  CASE

LEVINE v. ALPHA ANESTHESIA, INC.

145 Or.App. 549, 931 P.2d 812 (1997).

EDMONDS, Judge.

Plaintiff seeks to hold defendant Treibick, the sole shareholder, director and president of defendant corporation, personally liable for damages awarded to plaintiff following her successful action against another corporation for breach of her employment contract. Plaintiff appeals from a judgment entered after the trial court granted Treibick's motion for summary judgment. ORCP 47. We reverse.

Defendant Alpha Anesthesia, Inc., was dismissed on appeal.

We review the record in the light most favorable to plaintiff. Treibick, an anesthesiologist, is the sole shareholder, director and president of two corporations. In 1985, he incorporated Alpha Anesthesia, Inc. (AAI), a Massachusetts corporation, for the purpose of managing the anesthesia departments of small hospitals in the eastern United States. As part of its business, AAI contracted with anesthesiologists and certified registered nurse anesthesiologists (CRNA) to provide services to the hospitals.

In 1989, AAI entered into a contract with Josephine Memorial Hospital (JMH) in Grants Pass to provide similar services. AAI also contracted with Dr. Genskow, an anesthesiologist, to provide services to JMH pursuant to its agreement with JMH. As a part of that agreement, Genskow agreed not to compete with AAI in Josephine County for 18 months in the event that his contract with AAI was terminated. In 1990, defendant incorporated Anesthesia Affiliates of Oregon, Inc., (AAO), in order to provide services to JMH and also in the hope that a local corporation would attract new business in the western United States. In December 1990, AAI assigned the AAI/JMH contract to AAO, but in 1991 JMH terminated the assigned contract.

The record does not disclose when in 1991 AAO's contract with JMH was terminated.

Also in 1991, Genskow sued AAI to resolve disputes regarding his contract with AAI and his ability to practice medicine at JMH. In part to settle that law suit, AAI and AAO entered into a contract with Genskow on September 9, 1992. That contract provided, in part:

"2.01 AAI and AAO shall assign, transfer and sell to Dr. Genskow, effective as of the Closing, their right and interest in the intangible assets of their business of arranging anesthesia coverage for [JMH], specifically consisting of their rights to engage persons to perform anesthesia services at [JMH] who previously had performed such services under arrangements with AAI or AAO and the benefit of any non-competition covenants such persons may have executed in favor of AAI or AAO. In consideration of said transfer and sale, Dr. Genskow shall pay AAI the amount of $25,000.

"2.02 AAI and AAO each agrees that, for a period of three (3) years following the Closing, it shall not, either directly or indirectly, establish, engage in, own, manage, operate, join, control, or finance or participate in the ownership, management, operation or control of, an

anesthesia department or an anesthesia medical practice in Josephine County, Oregon. In consideration for these covenants not to compete, Dr. Genskow shall pay AAI the amount of $175,000."

In the agreement, Genskow also released AAI, AAO and their stockholders and officers from all claims arising from their previous relationship.

Plaintiff is a CRNA. In 1990, AAO contracted with plaintiff for her to provide CRNA services to JMH. In March 1991, plaintiff was injured while working and filed a workers' compensation claim against AAO. AAO and plaintiff settled the workers' compensation claim, and, in a document dated October 7, 1992, plaintiff released AAO from liability for that claim. AAO also terminated plaintiff's employment in May 1991.

Plaintiff sued AAO for breach of her employment contract in March 1993 and was awarded judgments for damages and attorney fees in 1994. AAO failed to satisfy the judgment. In this action, plaintiff seeks to hold Treibick personally liable for the 1994 judgments against AAO, alleging that as the sole shareholder, director and president of both AAI and AAO, he improperly caused the proceeds from the AAI/AAO/Genskow contract to be paid to AAI in order to avoid payment of any obligations to plaintiff under AAO's contract with her.

Because there is no transcript of oral argument on the motion for summary judgment, our ability to determine what was argued below is limited to the parties' written memoranda submitted to the trial court. On appeal, plaintiff also seeks to "pierce the corporate veil"on the ground that AAO was undercapitalized at inception. Plaintiff failed to raise this issue to the trial court. Therefore, we will not consider that argument on appeal. *Finney v. Bransom,* 143 Or.App. 154, 159, 924 P.2d 319 (1996).

Pursuant to ORCP 47, Treibick moved for summary judgment. He argued that the $200,000 was paid by Genskow to AAI because AAO was no longer in business after the AAO/JMH contract had been terminated by JMH in 1991 and that there is no evidence that AAO conveyed anything of value to Genskow. Plaintiff responded:

CASE

"By defendant's own affidavit, there is evidence that defendant controls both corporations and that AAI, AAO and [defendant] shifted capital, liabilities, and receivables back and forth at the whim and pleasure of [defendant]. It is also apparent that the $200,000 receivable [from the AAI/AAO/Genskow contract] should belong to AAO. If that $200,000 was still a part of AAO's capital account, plaintiff's judgment would be satisfied." (Emphasis supplied.)

Summary judgment is appropriate only if there is not genuine issue as to any material fact and the moving party is entitled to judgment as a matter of law. ORCP 47 C; *Jones v. General Motors Corp.,* 139 Or.App. 244, 911 P.2d 1243, rev. allowed 323 Or. 483, 8 P.2d 847 (1996). To preclude summary judgment, plaintiff must offer evidence that raises a genuine issue of material fact in support of her argument that Treibick is personally liable for AAO's corporate debt. A genuine issue of material fact exists if an objectively reasonable juror could find for plaintiff.

As a general rule, the corporate form will not be disregarded solely because all of the stock of the corporation is owned by one person who also exercises control of the corporation. *Amfac Foods v. Int'l Systems,* 294 Or. 94, 107, 654 P.2d 1092 (1982). To pierce the corporate veil for purposes of personal shareholder liability where actual control by the shareholder exists, improper conduct by the shareholder must be demonstrated. Also, a plaintiff must prove a relationship between the shareholder's misconduct and the plaintiff's injury. *Id.* at 111, 654 P.2d 1092.

In this case, it is uncontroverted that Treibick exercises actual control of both AAI and AAO. We turn first to the question of whether there is evidence in the summary judgment record that his conduct was improper. Even though AAO no longer has its contract with JMH, it was a party to the contract with Genskow. The AAI/AAO/Genskow contract refers to contract rights held by AAO to engage persons who had previously provided services to it and assigns those rights to Genskow. Also, AAO agrees in the contract not to compete with Genskow for a period of three years. Those are interests that are separate from the terminated contract with JMH. In exchange for those interests, AAO received no consideration. The fact that AAO conveyed interests of apparent value under the agreement gives rise to a reasonable inference that they have value. Based on this record, an objectively reasonable juror could find that the compensation due AAO for the interests that it conveyed to Genskow was funneled to AAI.

Also, there is evidence that workers' compensation claim settlement negotiations were conducted between March 1991, the date of plaintiff's injury, and October 7, 1992. Plaintiff's employment contract was breached within that same time period. AAO, by Treibick as president, signed the AAI/AAO/Genskow contract on September 9, 1992. An objectively reasonable jury could find that Treibick knew at that time that AAO had exposure under its contract with plaintiff and that he diverted monies owed to AAO under the Genskow contract to AAI in order to render AAO judgment-proof. Such a finding would satisfy the "improper conduct" element of the Amfac test and also establish the requisite relationship between the "improper conduct" and plaintiff's damage. We conclude that, because of those issues of fact, the trial court erred by granting summary judgment to Treibick.

Reversed and remanded.

Case Review Question

When is it appropriate to disregard the personal liability protection of corporate status?

Corporate Stock

As stated earlier, a person who invests in a corporation owns a percentage of the corporation. This ownership is evidenced by shares of stock. The articles of incorporation state specifically how many shares will be issued. The total number of shares represents the total ownership of the corporation. The corporation will also usually give the shares a stated or par value, that is, the amount the corporation considers the shares to be worth.

Normally, the greater the investment, the greater the number of shares one possesses; and the greater the number of shares, the greater the percentage of ownership or control. As the corporation's profitability increases, however, so does the public value of having an ownership interest. Therefore, in times of great earnings by the corporation, the shares increase in public value, and an investor may have to spend large amounts to obtain only a few shares. The investor hopes, of course, that the shares will increase even more in value so they can be sold to the next investor at a profit. The corporation continues to value the shares at the stated value.

Types of stock.   Corporations have different classes of stock. All corporations have common stock. Corporations may also choose to issue preferred stock, which is usually entitled to higher and more frequent dividends and thus may be more marketable.

Some corporations issue what is called cumulative preferred stock. This type of stock accumulates rights to dividends. In the event there is not enough money in one year to declare a dividend, the dividend right of the preferred stock is added to the next year. When a dividend is finally declared, the preferred shareholders are entitled to payment of back dividends before any dividend can be declared on common stock.

Stock rights.   Certain rights are acquired along with some types of stock. If, for example, a shareholder purchases voting stock, in addition to having ownership interest, the shareholder receives the right to cast one vote for each share of stock. Voting is usually done annually to elect new directors and to approve major changes, such as an amendment to the articles of incorporation.

Some shares also have certain provisions regarding dividends. When the board of directors determines that a corporation is profitable, it may declare a dividend after reinvesting a reasonable amount of the profits. When a dividend is declared, the money assigned to the dividend is split among the shareholders, based on the type and number of shares owned. Preferred stock usually has a higher value than common stock and is entitled to dividends first. If sufficient funds are left, a dividend for common stock may then be paid. Ordinarily, dividends are paid in cash, but some may be given in the form of additional stock or some product of the corporation.

Also to be considered are liquidation rights, the rights of shareholders to receive the value of assets of the corporation in the event of dissolution. Preferred shareholders may have the first right to receive these assets up to the value of their stock. Common shareholders are apportioned remaining assets toward their investment. Regardless of how much a shareholder may have paid for stock, only the par or stated value is paid. This is what the corporation originally indicated each share of preferred and common stock would be worth.

Some corporations will sell stock with preemptive rights. This means that when a corporation decides to issue additional stock, the shareholders with pre-emptive rights are given an opportunity to purchase the shares of new stock based on their percentage of ownership before the shares are offered for sale to the public. Such rights are a sort of reward for investors who have previously contributed to the corporation. Additionally, they allow an investor to maintain the same percentage of ownership.

Stock subscriptions.   A corporation may sell subscriptions to stock when it is formed or after its formation when approved by the directors. Generally, a stock subscription is an agreement between the corporation and a subscriber for the stock to purchase a certain number of shares at a certain price. A corporation that has not yet been formed accepts such agreements at the time of incorporation when shares are authorized and issued. Generally, persons who offer to purchase subscriptions do not have a contract with the corporation until the board of directors accepts the subscription; instead, the subscribers have an option that the board may accept or reject.[49]

If a corporation accepts a stock subscription and the subscriber defaults and does not pay for the stock, the corporation has all of the remedies that are available in the case a breached contract, including an action against the subscriber for the value of the stock under the subscription agreement.[50]

Stock subscriptions are especially helpful to promising new corporations. The corporation receives adequate capitalization from the investors, and in return, the investors obtain the opportunity to purchase large amounts of stock at a price that is usually lower than the cost on the open market. Thus, if the prospects for a new corporation are hopeful, subscribers have an opportunity to buy more shares.

The Securities and Exchange Commission.   The courts have addressed issues such as improper profits and other illegal behavior by corporations, but significant issues with respect to the buying, selling, and trading of stock resulted in the creation of the Securities and Exchange Commission (SEC). Following the stock market crash of 1929, the Securities and Exchange Act of 1934 established the SEC to oversee the stock market system in the United States. The SEC administers laws of Congress and issues regulations with respect to major transactions of stock, corporate ownership, and management. The goal of the SEC is to see that corporations and major corporate shareholders do not take advantage of unwary minor shareholders or vulnerable corporations.

As mentioned earlier, a person who owns a controlling interest in a corporation has certain influence in corporate operations and opportunities. Under SEC rules, a shareholder who possesses 10 percent or more of the corporate stock is considered to have certain responsibilities.[51] The SEC further considers a 10 percent shareholder to owe a fiduciary duty to the corporation and its shareholders. Officers and directors have an even greater fiduciary duty to the shareholders.[52]

When a controlling shareholder sells the controlling interest in a corporation, the fiduciary duty requires that the stock not be transferred to someone who would injure the corporation. Therefore, before selling a controlling interest, the shareholder has the duty to investigate the interested purchaser. If this is not done, or if the interest is sold to someone the shareholder should know will injure the corporation to obtain personal gain (sometimes called "looting"), the shareholder may be personally liable for any damage to the corporation or other shareholders.[53]

In addition, a controlling shareholder, officer, or director who purchases controlling stock and sells that stock within a six-month period must disclose and return any profits to the corporation. This prevents the use of inside information for personal gain that will injure the corporation. The minority shareholders and the public are thus not at a disadvantage. It would be unfair to allow persons with access to information that may affect the value of the stock to avoid losses or to obtain huge profits while other shareholders or the public who lack the information lose or at least do not have the same opportunity to improve their investment. The key to legal stock transactions is disclosure. If major shareholders fully disclose their actions and adhere to the other requirements of the SEC, the corporation, its shareholders, and the public are protected.

The Corporate Existence

As stated earlier, the first board of directors of a corporation is responsible for complying with all of the statutory formalities, including preparation of the articles of incorporation and bylaws. Generally, the officers of the corporation will be responsible for daily management and administrative decisions, while long-range decisions about the policies of the corporation are made by the board.

Shareholders also have limited input into the operations of the corporation. They usually vote on major changes in the direction of the corporation and elect new board members when a term ends or a vacancy occurs. Shareholders also generally have the right to remove a director with or without reason. Examples of justifications for removal include mismanagement of the corporation or negligent risking of the shareholders' investments.

In smaller corporations, the officers, board of directors, and shareholders are often all the same people. In large corporations, however, many shareholders never even meet the board or the officers. Voting at annual meetings may be conducted by mail, and the shareholders make decisions on the basis of annual reports of the progress of the business and other printed materials provided by the corporation.

Shareholders who are dissatisfied with the job a particular director is doing may vote against the reelection of the director or vote to remove the director during a term of office. Each state has statutes that indicate when and how this may be accomplished. Each state's statutes also contain provisions that dictate the minimum number of meetings each corporation must have with shareholders annually. Statutes also provide for the type, timing, and method of notice that must be given to each shareholder before a meeting, and the procedure for voting by mail if a shareholder cannot attend a meeting.

Voting by Shareholders

Fixed rules exist with regard to which shareholders are entitled to vote on a corporate matter. Because stocks are continually sold and transferred on the stock market, a corporation's shareholders may change every day. Statutes specify a record date, the date by which one must own stock in a corporation prior to a shareholders' meeting to be eligible to vote on corporate changes. The board of directors then includes this time frame, or an even longer one, in the bylaws of the corporation when stating the amount of notice of a meeting that will be given to shareholders. Only persons whose names appear as shareholders in corporate records on the record date are entitled to vote at the annual meeting.[54]

If a shareholder cannot attend a meeting or does not vote by mail, the vote may be made by proxy, the written consent of one person to vote on behalf of another. It is also legal for a group of persons to request other shareholders to give their proxies so that votes can be accumulated on a certain issue. With respect to public corporations, this is strictly controlled by the SEC and must follow specific guidelines. A proxy can be solicited only if the shareholders are given an accurate description of the matter to be voted on and are allowed to vote for or against the issue on appropriate proxy forms. This enables the persons soliciting the proxies to determine in advance how many votes they have secured in favor of a given issue. Statutes require that at least a majority of the issued shares be voted. An amendment to the articles of incorporation may require more than a mere majority. Generally, every share is entitled to at least one vote. However, the articles of incorporation may allow for the issuance of shares without the right to vote, such as some preferred shares.

In a corporation with a very large number of shareholders, persons owning only one or a few shares would not have the opportunity to have much influence over decisions, because other persons own a great many shares. Under the method of cumulative voting, each share is entitled to one vote, and when several different issues are to be decided, each shareholder will cast one vote for every share on every issue. For example, if three new directors are to be elected and a person owns one share, that person will cast three votes total (one share vote for each issue). If a shareholder has five shares and three issues are up for vote, the shareholder has the right to cast a total of fifteen votes (5×3). If cumulative voting is permitted, the shareholder can apportion the votes in any way he or she wants. Shareholders can also add their votes together to increase voting power.

Some states allow what are commonly called voting trusts and pooling agreements. In a voting trust, several shareholders give their proxies to one person who is known as the trustee, who votes on the issues. The advantage of a voting trust is that the weight of shares on a single issue is greater.[55] The disadvantage is that the trustee votes on all issues in the manner most advantageous to the group. This may not always be perceived as what is most advantageous to an individual.

A pooling agreement is somewhat similar to a voting trust. The goal here is to concentrate the votes on an issue. In a pooling agreement, the members of the pool agree that they each will vote in the way that the majority of the members of the pool indicate.[56] Generally, in a pooling agreement, a vote per share will be cast for or against each issue. Also, a written contract states what persons are involved in the agreement.

Rights of Shareholders

In most states, all shareholders, by virtue of their ownership interest in the corporation incorporated there, are entitled to certain rights in the corporation in addition to voting rights. Shareholders ordinarily have the right to inspect the corporate records upon reasonable notice and at a reasonable time.[57] Although shareholders do not ordinarily have input into the day-to-day management and operations of the corporation, they are entitled to observe them to some extent. The rationale is that they will be better informed about their investment and will be able to make intelligent decisions when voting on corporate issues or selling their stock. In addition, limited inspection is not seen as unnecessary interference with the business of the corporation. Historically, shareholders were given the right to inspect only if they could show a proper purpose. In response, most states have now enacted statutes that do away with the requirement of proper purpose.

The right to inspect corporate records is subject to limitation. Generally, inspection must be done during a time and subject to conditions set out in the corporate bylaws. This permits shareholders to inspect and also allows the corporation to avoid unreasonable interruptions of its operations. If a state statute permits such inspections and a corporation refuses or through its bylaws makes it virtually impossible to inspect, the corporation and the officers who refuse inspection may be subject to legal penalties in the event the shareholder sues the corporation. In addition, a shareholder has the alternative of bringing an action against the corporation.

In addition to having the right of inspection, shareholders have privileges that are specified in the articles of incorporation for the particular type of stock they own. As stated earlier, these privileges may be liquidation, voting, and dividends. Finally, shareholders have the right to sue persons involved with the corporation when they have mismanaged the corporation.

Corporate Actions

Two types of actions can be brought against persons who have a fiduciary relationship to the corporation. The first is a direct action by shareholders, generally brought against officers of the corporation. If it becomes apparent that an officer has placed self-interest or the interest of a third party above the interest of the corporation in business dealings, the fiduciary duty has been breached. If this breach results in direct injury to the shareholders, such as the loss of their investment, the shareholders may maintain a direct suit against the officers.[58] It is only necessary for the shareholders who bring the suit to have been damaged and not for them to have been shareholders at the time of the wrongful conduct. If the shareholders are successful in such a suit, they may be awarded damages.

The second type of action is called a derivative action. This can be brought only by persons who were shareholders at the time of the wrongdoing and throughout the duration of the suit. Such shareholders act on behalf of the corporation against officers or others who owed a fiduciary duty to the corporation. It must be shown that the duty was breached and as a result the business of the corporation was damaged.[59] Any damages that are awarded are payable to the corporation.

Assignment 12.6

Identify the types of corporate status reflected in the following fact situations.

1. James and Darius start a corporation and run it successfully for a number of years. However, Darius neglects to pay the corporate registration fee of $75 for two years. All other matters of corporate status are observed.
2. James and Darius observe all of the visible signs of corporate status in their advertising, business dealings, and so on, but in reality, they never filed articles of incorporation. When the business is sued, they claim the defense that the defendant corporation does not even exist.
3. James and Darius legally incorporate their business and continue to meet all statutory requirements. When the corporation is sued, they claim the corporation is without assets and cannot pay any judgment. (If they are found to be a corporation, what would be an alternative for the plaintiff?)

Dissolution of the Corporation

As stated at the outset of this discussion, the life of a corporation is created by statute. It ends in the same manner. As long as the corporation complies with statutory requirements, the secretary of state will continue to recognize the business as a corporate entity. A corporation may dissolve, however, on grounds that include failure to comply with legal requirements or the action of shareholders or creditors. It may also dissolve by voluntary assent of the board of directors and, when necessary, of the shareholders. Although each state has specific requirements for dissolution, the items discussed in the following paragraphs are generally common to all state statutes.

When a corporation decides to dissolve voluntarily, several things must be accomplished prior to the dissolution. Before a formal voluntary dissolution takes effect, the following[60] are generally required.

1. The shareholders consent to the dissolution.
2. Notice is given to creditors.

3. All assets are sold.
4. No suits are pending against the corporation.
5. Debts are paid, and the remaining cash is distributed to shareholders.

Although court proceedings are usually not required in a voluntary dissolution, the corporation is usually required by statute to file documents that indicate the intent to dissolve the corporation. With the exception of what is required for the sale of assets and payment of debts, the corporation must stop doing business. After all business is completed, articles of liquidation are filed with the secretary of state. If all requirements have been complied with, a certificate of dissolution is issued.[61]

Involuntary dissolution of a corporation may come about in one of several ways. Persons who have legal authority to request an involuntary dissolution in court are the attorney general of the state, shareholders, and creditors. When an outside party is attempting to force the cessation of business, the grounds for involuntary dissolution are limited and specific.

The attorney general of the state may bring an action to dissolve a corporation when the corporation fails to appoint a registered agent to accept service (delivery) of legal documents, when the corporation exceeds or abuses its authority as stated in the articles of incorporation, or when the corporation was created through fraud.[62] Frequently, statutes provide that the attorney general must file a complaint in the courts requesting an order of involuntary dissolution. The corporation may respond to the complaint, and the court will make a determination as to the validity of the allegations.

Shareholders are entitled to bring an action to dissolve the corporation when the conduct of the directors seriously threatens the shareholders' well-being. Examples of such activities include mismanagement, fraud, deadlock on corporate decisions, wasting of corporate assets, and illegal conduct. Generally, the courts will look to the actions of the directors and, in some cases, the controlling shareholders to determine whether the directors' conduct is likely to cause irreparable injury to the shareholders.[63]

Creditors are the most limited in their ability to cause the involuntary dissolution of a corporation. In most cases, this can be accomplished only when the creditor has an actual legal judgment against the corporation and the corporation is unable to pay the debt, or when the debt has not been declared by a court but the corporation admits the existence of the debt and its inability to pay.[64]

Bankruptcy

Every business venture is not a success. Neither is every personal financial situation. In some instances the debt to profit or income ratio becomes so extreme, the only reasonable alternative is to abandon the current endeavor. Bankruptcy laws have been developed over the years to provide a variety of options and protections to both debtors and creditors.

A common misconception is that when bankruptcy is declared, the creditors lose all hope of collection. In reality, the effect of bankruptcy in many respects can be a positive result. Several different forms of bankruptcy will be discussed in this section. The forms of bankruptcy depend on either the nature of the entity or the person seeking relief, and on the type of relief sought. However, a few characteristics are common to all forms.

Initially, when a petition is made to the bankruptcy courts, an immediate "stay" is granted. The stay prohibits further attempts at collection and effectively freezes the financial activity of the debtor. To ensure fairness, the debtor is required to list all creditors with the court and provide notice of the filing of the bankruptcy petition to those creditors. By doing so, not only is the debtor protected from further collection attempts, but the creditors are also protected because they are advised of the financial situation of the debtor and have the opportunity to discontinue further extensions of credit.

Generally, following the filing of a bankruptcy petition, a series of hearings are conducted to allow input by the debtor and creditors so that the court may make an informed finding regarding whether the bankruptcy petition filed is an appropriate form of relief for the debtor and creditors. Ultimately, an order is rendered by the court which details the rights of the debtor and creditors with respect to repayment or discharge of debts.

The two primary forms of bankruptcy are reorganization and liquidation. The first, reorganization, allows an entity or person protection from collection while a plan for repayment of all debts is developed and implemented. Sometimes, the amount and time of payment is different from that originally agreed upon by the debtor and creditor. However, the creditor does receive repayment of either the total debt or an accepted amount. The law also imposes limits as to how long repayment under the plan may take.

Liquidation is the absolute discharge of debt. In this type of bankruptcy, the assets of the debtor (subject to some exceptions) are liquidated or converted to cash. The court prioritizes the debts and begins the process of repayment. What are known as secured debts have the highest priority. Secured debts are those for which there is a written pledge of collateral such as a car or house. If the amount of liquidated assets is not sufficient to cover the total amount of debt, those at the bottom of the priority list are discharged, meaning that these creditors must accept that they will never receive payment for the amount owed and thus write it off as a bad debt. Just as certain assets cannot be seized and liquidated in a bankruptcy, there are also certain debts that cannot ordinarily be discharged. These are listed in the statutes and are only included in the discharged debts in extreme circumstances, and in some cases not at all.

When discussing the different types of bankruptcy, various references are made to the term *chapter*. The term in this case refers to the chapter in the bankruptcy statutes that deals with the particular type of entity or person in bankruptcy or the specific type of relief sought. For example, Chapter 7 of the federal bankruptcy statutes is the chapter that provides for the liquidation of assets and discharge of debts. Chapter 13 provides for a reorganization plan by the individual and Chapter 11 provides for reorganization by most corporations and partnerships. Various other chapters provide for relief to farmers and highly regulated industries such as insurance companies.

When the individual or company wants to continue attempting repayment, there is a form of relief sometimes used by creditors known as involuntary bankruptcy. This type of bankruptcy occurs when a number of creditors of a single debtor cooperatively file a petition asking the court to declare a stay and impose bankruptcy. At first the question may arise, why would a creditor seek bankruptcy and possibly foreclose the chance of full repayment? The answer is quite simple: If the debtor shows an established pattern of accumulating debt beyond the value of assets, the creditors may want to put a halt to the increasing debt and thereby protect their chances of at least a partial repayment.

Bankruptcy has been a part of American law for more than 100 years. The laws continue to evolve in an attempt to provide fairness to both creditors and debtors. Consequently, bankruptcy is an area of law that is subject to frequent changes and variations.

Ethical Considerations

Members of the business community are required to honor a code of proprietary behavior in addition to the required ethical behavior of all legal professionals. The core of any business is the relationship of the business with customers, whether they be other businesses or members of the general public. To maintain an ongoing customer relationship—or for that matter to encourage new customers—it is essential that a business follow certain practices that incorporate fairness and honesty. The failure to do so results in bad customer relations and often bad publicity.

While some transactions are open to scrutiny—thus making unethical conduct easy to detect—other activities are not so visible. Many times, such situations are dealt with through administrative agencies, such as the Securities and Exchange Commission (SEC), to protect an unwary public from unethical persons. However, the ultimate responsibility for enforcing ethics is within the business arena. Companies do not want to be known for unethical practices or be associated with companies committing such practices. Consequently, ethical behavior in the workplace is an increasing concern, not only at an academic level but also in the real world of work.

Question
If you are one of four partners in a business and have knowledge that the other three partners routinely engage in unethical conduct that could result in injury to an unwary customer, realistically, what are your options?

Ethical Circumstance

Sharon is a recent business school graduate and is hired as an assistant to the head of a large stock brokerage firm. She undergoes a number of background checks and is subject to intense security clearance before being hired. She begins her new position and quickly finds that she has access to highly sensitive materials regarding business mergers and acquisitions. She quietly feeds this information to her stepsister who buys and sells small quantities of stocks over a period of time. After 10 years, Sharon and her sister have amassed wealth of some $20 million as the result of her use of confidential information. The conduct of Sharon is unethical even though the information is not stolen or gained through illegal means, because she uses a position of trust between her employer and clients to her own advantage and places herself in a highly advantageous position not available to the general public.

CHAPTER SUMMARY

This chapter has discussed the unique characteristics and similarities of various types of businesses. Sole proprietorships involve a single owner, with all profits considered personal income of that owner. The life of the business is limited to the time in which the individual owner operates the sole proprietorship. Similarly, partnership profits are considered to be the personal income of the partners, and the life of the partnership is limited in much the same way as that of the sole proprietorship. The liability of a sole proprietorship and of a partnership is personal, subject to the exception of limited partnerships. In exchange for liability limited to the extent of investment, the limited partner gives up the privilege of input in management decisions for the business. The corporation has unlimited life, regardless of any change in the owners. Liability is limited to the investment. Management decisions are made by the officers and directors, who may or may not be shareholders.

All of the forms of business typically involve the use of agency in which persons (agents) represent the fiduciary interests of other individuals or businesses (principals) for a specific purpose. Under the law of agency, the principal may be bound by the acts of the agent. Under the theory of respondeat superior, the principal may be held legally responsible for any actions by the agent that injure other parties, so long as the actions are within the scope of the agency relationship.

CHAPTER TERMS

agency
articles of incorporation
bylaws

corporation
limited partnership
partnership

promoter

REVIEW QUESTIONS

1. What role does agency play in a partnership? In a corporation?
2. How does actual authority differ from apparent authority?
3. When is respondeat superior applicable? When is it inapplicable?
4. How does a partnership differ from a sole proprietorship?
5. How does a partnership differ from a corporation?
6. What elements are examined to determine whether a partnership exists?
7. What must be done to create a corporation?
8. When can the personal assets of shareholders in a corporation be reached by someone suing the corporation?
9. What is a promoter?
10. How is a corporation dissolved?

RELEVANT LINKS

Newsletter for Securities and Exchange
Commission
www.SEClaw.com
General questions on business law
www.aolwebcenters/law/bus

Business law, legal research
www.findlaw.com

INTERNET ASSIGNMENT 12.1

Using internet resources, identify the contact
source in state government to register the name
of a new corporation.

NOTES

1. William Statsky, *Legal Thesaurus/Dictionary* (St. Paul: West, 1982).
2. 3 Am.Jur.2d, Agency, Sections 9–16.
3. Id.
4. *Sim v. Edenborn,* 242 U.S. 131, 37 S.Ct. 36, 61 L.Ed. 199 (1916).
5. 3 Am.Jur.2d, Agency, Sections 222–224.
6. Id., Section 218.
7. *Consolidated Oil & Gas, Inc. v. Roberts,* 162 Colo. 149, 425 P.2d 282.
8. *Lauderdale v. Peace Baptist Church,* 246 Ala. 178, 19 So.2d 538 (1944).
9. 3 Am.Jur.2d, Agency, Section 73.
10. *McGirr v. Gulf Oil Corp.,* 41 Cal.App.3d 246, 115 Cal.Rptr. 902 (2d. Dist. 1974).
11. *Elliott v. Mutual Life Insurance Co.,*185 Okl. 289, 91 P.2d 746 (1939).
12. 3 Am.Jur.2d, Agency, Section 77.
13. *Bronson's Ex'r v. Chappell,* 79 U.S. (12 Wall.) 681, 20 L.Ed. 436 (1871).
14. 3 Am.Jur.2d, Agency, Section 75.
15. *Cavic v. Grand Bahama Dev. Co.,* 701 F.2d 879 (11th Cir. 1983).
16. Id.
17. *Pfliger v. Peavey Co.,* 310 N.W.2d 742 (N.D. 1981).
18. *Shafer v. Bull,* 233 Md. 68, 194 A.2d 788 (1963).
19. 3 Am.Jur.2d, Agency, Section 185.
20. Id., Section 280.
21. Id.
22. *Pacific Tel. & Tel. Co. v. White,* 104 F.2d 923 (9th Cir. 1939).
23. 3 Am.Jur.2d, Agency, Section 280.
24. *Friedman v. New York Telephone Co.,* 256 N.Y. 392, 176 N.E. 543 (1931).
25. Uniform Partnership Act.
26. Id., Section 15.
27. Uniform Limited Partnership Act, Section 7.
28. Id., Section 4, 5, 7.
29. Id., Section 18(b).
30. Id., Section 22.
31. *In re Belle Isle Farm,* 76 B.R. 85, 88 (Bkrtcy. Va. 1987).
32. Uniform Limited Partnership Act, Section 7.
33. Uniform Partnership Act, Section 16.
34. Id., Section 9.
35. Id., Section 13.
36. C.J.S., Partnership, Section 95.
37. Uniform Partnership Act, Section 29.
38. Model Business Corporation Act, Section 4.
39. Id., Section 25.
40. 18 Am.Jur.2d, Corporations, Section 104.
41. Model Business Corporation Act, Section 37.
42. *Lamkin v. Baldwin & Lamkin Mfg. Co.,* 72 Conn. 57, 43 A. 593 (1899).
43. *Lettinga v. Agristor Credit Corp.,* 686 F.2d 442 (6th Cir. 1982).
44. *Fitzpatrick v. Rutter,* 160 Ill. 282, 43 N.E. 392 (1896).
45. 18 Am.Jur.2d., Corporations, Section 2804.

46. Id., Sections 45, 51.
47. Id., Section 49.
48. Id., Sections 55, 61.
49. Model Business Corporation Act, Section 17.
50. Id., Section 25.
51. Id.
52. Id.
53. Id., Section 48.
54. Id., Section 30.
55. Id., Section 34.
56. Id.

57. *Guthrie v. Harkness*, 199 U.S. 148, 26 S.Ct. 4, 50 L.Ed. 130 (1905).
58. 18 Am.Jur., Corporations, Sections 2245, 2246, 2249.
59. Id., Section 2260.
60. Id., Sections 82–93.
61. Id.
62. Id., Sections 94–98, 102.
63. Id.
64. Id.

 For additional resources, please visit our Web site at www.westlegalstudies.com

CHAPTER 13

Estates and Probate

CHAPTER OBJECTIVES

After reading this chapter, you should be able to:

- Distinguish per stirpes and per capita distribution.

- List the requirements for a valid will.

- List the grounds to contest a will.

- List the steps of probate.

- Describe the obligations of the personal representative.

- Discuss the rights of a surviving spouse.

- Distinguish testate from intestate distribution.

- Describe the process of dealing with the inheritance of one alleged to be responsible for a decedent's death.

- Discuss the requirements for a valid oral will.

WHAT IS PROBATE AND ESTATE LAW?

probate
Process of paying creditors and distributing the estate of one who is deceased.

One area of law that affects many lives is that of **probate** and estates. Many people are at some point involved in the law of domestic relations, property, and business, as well as other subject areas. In today's society, very few citizens die with no assets, no debt, and no legal heirs. Those who die without debt incur costs for burial or cremation unless they donate their body to science; and rarely does a person die without a final medical expense, even if it is confined to ambulance transportation of the body. Persons who are heirs or wish to dictate how their estate will be handled after their death will be affected by the law of probate. This area of law affects every facet of society. In addition to those who stand to inherit, nearly every person or entity with whom the deceased was in some form of financial contact prior to death is affected. Popular misconceptions are that when someone dies, the person's possessions are immediately divided up among the surviving family. In reality, the legal process is more complicated. Similarly, anyone involved in some way with **guardianship** of one

guardianship
One with legal and fiduciary responsibility to care for the welfare of another as court ordered.

who is incapacitated as an adult, or a minor in need of the supervision of an adult, will likely encounter the probate division of the courts as well. When an adult is unable to manage his or her own affairs for any reason that severely limits mental capacity, there is a need to take proper legal steps to appoint someone to manage the disabled individual's affairs. The following discussion addresses such topics as the distribution of an estate when there is no will and when there is a valid will. The probate process is also explained. Although probate administration of estates is governed by state law, many of the procedures are similar in most states. This discussion is limited to those general procedures observed in most jurisdictions.

THE FUNCTION OF THE PROBATE COURTS

The probate division of the legal system is assigned the task of administrating the estates of those who are deceased and those who are under legal guardianship. In either instance, the party can no longer be responsible for his or her own legal issues and as a result the probate courts oversee these matters. The probate courts follow specific rules of procedure and well-established substantive law with respect to the processing of these cases. Unlike the typical civil litigation, a case in the probate court may or may not have adversarial parties represented by attorneys. Indeed, a case may be entirely handled by one attorney or a large number of attorneys.

The processing of the estate of someone who is deceased typically involves an attorney for the estate. Any parties who wish to contest the manner in which the estate is considered and depleted also may be represented by counsel. This might include potential heirs, creditors, or persons who wish to contest the validity of a will or the jurisdiction of the court to process the estate. In short, anyone who stands to be affected by the final accounting and distribution of the estate of someone who is deceased may elect to have an attorney enter an appearance in the case to protect his or her interests.

APPLICATION 13.1

Candy McIntosh, age 34, is struck by a bus and killed instantly. At the time of her unexpected death, she has a large number of creditors, a home, vehicle, and several bank accounts in addition to her personal possessions. She has one son from a previous relationship and a spouse from whom she is separated but not divorced. In the probate of Candy's estate, a question arises as to whether some of the alleged creditors are valid debt holders of Candy at the time of her death. Her parents and siblings are concerned that Candy's estate will be entirely depleted by creditors and that nothing will be left to use for the care and support of her 5-year-old son. The identity of the father of Candy's son is completely unknown. Those who filed appearances in the case include an attorney representing the interests of Candy's son, an attorney for Candy's estate, an attorney for her husband, and attorneys for several of the creditors. A separate case is brought to establish legal guardianship for her son.

Point for Discussion

◆ Why would there need to be a different attorney for Candy's son and the estate?

The probate courts are also responsible to act in a supervisory role for incapacitated adults and minors without parents who have full parental rights and responsibilities. At first, one might think of this as being confined primarily to orphans and persons in a physical condition so severe as to constitute a vegetative state. This makes up only a very small percentage of the persons for whom the probate court appoints and oversees guardianships. There are countless situations in the present-day society that render an individual legally or physically unable to make a legally binding decision in a manner consistent with the individual's best interest. In many such cases, the courts will assume a supervisory role for the individual through the guardianship (conservator) process. Although some jurisdictions use different terminology, the fundamental concept of helping those not in a position to help themselves remains the same.

In the case of minors, quite often the courts will intervene on a temporary or permanent basis to protect the interests of minors. Obviously, when someone is orphaned while still a minor, the courts are obliged to step in until such time as an adoption or the age of majority or legal emancipation occurs. The same situation arises when the parental rights over a minor are superseded by the courts either temporarily or permanently. This most often occurs when a child is removed from the home by a government agency for reasons such as abuse or neglect. In any event, when the government intervenes on behalf of a minor, it may supersede the rights of the parent or parents and assume responsibility for making decisions in the best interest of the minor child.

In the case of incapacitated adults, guardianship may occur in a wide variety of situations. One such example is when a youth who is mentally disabled reaches the age of majority. If the young person is not declared legally incompetent and then proceeds to enter into legally binding agreements or situations, it may be that the young person is considered liable for the terms of the agreement.

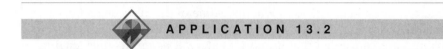

APPLICATION 13.2

Cindy is a 20-year-old woman who has a moderate mental impairment. She lives in a group home and is employed at a workshop for adults who are mentally impaired. She is unable to live independently or work in a routine job setting. Cindy's parents did not seek to have a guardianship established for her when she reached the age of majority (18 in the state where she lives). Cindy recently signed an agreement to join a video club wherein she received 20 videos of her choice in exchange for agreeing to buy 20 additional videos over the next three years at a cost of $20 per video plus $5 shipping and handling. Cindy received the free videos and passed them out on the city bus that she rides to work each day. Her parents wrote to the company about the situation, but the company refuses to disregard the agreement. They threaten collection action if the terms of the contract are not honored by Cindy.

Point for Discussion

◆   How would the situation differ if Cindy was 14 years old?

Another situation that may occur when an adult requires assistance from the courts is when a person is temporarily or permanently incapacitated due to illness or injury and did not have adequate documents in place before the occurrence to authorize such help in the event of incapacitation.

When the court is presented with a minor or an adult in need of legal supervision due to physical and/or mental condition, a petition is filed and the court establishes a form of guardianship for the individual. The terms and extent of this guardianship depend largely on the circumstances of the incapacitated individual. The court appoints a person or entity, such as a bank, to act on behalf of the incapacitated person. Additionally, if any dispute arises as to who the guardian should be or as to the terms of the guardianship, an attorney may be appointed as a guardian ad litem. The guardian ad litem should be objective to the dispute and review the circumstance in terms of the best interest of the individual at issue. The guardian ad litem then makes recommendations to the court on what he or she considers to be in the best interest of the disabled person. Issues may involve physical custody and living arrangements, health care alternatives, and management of the assets of the one who is incapacitated.

Once a guardianship has been established, the guardian is required to periodically report to the courts with respect to the guardianship and the status of the incapacitated person. The frequency of reports often depends on the age and condition of the individual as well as the size of the estate, if any, that is being overseen. In some instances the disability may resolve, or in the case of a minor returned to the full care and custody of the parents, the guardianship is discontinued. In other circumstances, the guardianship may continue under the court's supervision for the remainder of the disabled person's natural life.

CASE

SUPERIOR COURT OF PENNSYLVANIA.

ESTATE OF CAROLYN J.HAERTSCH, AN ALLEGED INCOMPETENT.

Appeal of Carolyn J.HAERTSCH. 415 Pa.Super.598.609 A.Zd 1384 Submitted Feb 6, 1992. Filed July 6, 1992.

OLSZEWSKI, Judge:

This is an appeal of an order of the Court of Common Pleas of Montgomery County dated February 7, 1991, which declared appellant, Carolyn J. Haertsch, incompetent. The order further appointed both of her parents co-guardians and established a schedule of custody and visitation. We find that the lower court did not apply the proper standard and that the evidence in the lower court failed to establish appellant incompetent. The order of the lower court is reversed and vacated. A discussion of the case follows.

Appellant is a twenty-three-year-old individual with Down syndrome. Appellant suffers from a degree of mental retardation, but has apparently been able to maintain a job and pursue many of her daily needs. Appellant's parents, Raymond and Bernadette Haertsch, were separated and subsequently divorced in 1975. Appellant lived with her father until October of 1989, when for

some reason she went to her mother's home and did not return. During 1989 both parents filed petitions to have their daughter declared incompetent and themselves declared guardian. The court appointed both parents as co-guardians and established a schedule of custody for appellant. The custody schedule involved spending half the year living with one parent and half the year with the other parent. This timely appeal followed.

We note here that no post-trial motions were filed in the lower court. We feel, however, that the appeal was properly taken. The lower court specifically provided in its order that the order was not subject to post-trial motions. Further, appellant was not represented by counsel in the lower court. We believe that in this situation the failure to file exceptions is excused. We feel that in this regard appellant is correct to refer this Court to *Storti v. Minnesota Mutual Life,* 331 Pa.Super.26, 479 A.2d 1061 (1984).

Appellant presents three issues for our consideration:

1. Did the lower court apply an erroneous standard in determining that Carolyn Haertsch is incompetent and in need of guardians of her estate and person?
2. Was the evidence sufficient to support the lower court's finding that Carolyn Haertsch is incompetent and in need of guardians of her estate and person?
3. Did the court below violate Carolyn Haertsch's due process rights under the United States Constitution by failing to appoint counsel or a

CASE

guardian *ad litem* to represent her in the incompetency and guardianship proceeding?

Since we find the lower court employed an erroneous standard and that the evidence presented below was insufficient to support a finding of incompetency, we reverse and vacate the order of the lower court.

When reviewing a competency determination, the standard of review is well settled. In regard to factual determinations, we recognize that the lower court had the opportunity to hear and observe the witnesses. We will not substitute our judgment for that of the lower court absent a clear abuse of discretion, "even though we, had we been sitting in judgment below, might have reached a contrary result, yet if the evidence is sufficient in quality and quantity to sustain the finding of incompetency such a finding should be sustained."*In re Myers' Estate,* 395 Pa. 459, 460, 150 A.2d 525,526 (1959) (citations omitted). The statute which controls the determination of incompetency provides:

An incompetent is defined as follows:

a person who, because of infirmities of old age, mental illness, mental deficiency or retardation, drug addiction or inebriety:
(1) is unable to manage his property, or is liable to dissipate it or become the victim of designing persons; or
(2) lacks sufficient capacity to make or communicate responsible decisions concerning his person.

20 Pa.C.S.A. § 5501. A statute of this nature places a great power in the court. The court has the power to place total control of a person's affairs in the hands of another. This great power creates the opportunity for great abuse. *Myers' Estate,* 395 Pa. at 460, 150 A.2d at 526. "Mental capacity and competency are to be presumed and before any person shall be deprived of the right to handle his or her own property and manage his or her affairs there must be *clear* and *convincing* proof of mental incompetency and such proof must be *preponderating.*" *Id.*

We have examined the evidence and the lower court opinion. We find that the lower court failed to apply the proper standard required under the law. Further, we find the evidence was not sufficient to establish mental incompetency.

A case to declare an adult individual mentally incompetent is not equivalent to a case to determine custody of a minor child. The question in a custody case is what custody arrangement will serve the best interests of the child. In a case to declare an adult individual an incompetent, the question is whether the alleged incompetent is indeed incompetent. With a child there is not a question of whether the child's custody must be determined. Under the law it is presumed that the child's custody must be set and, therefore, the only question is what custody arrangement will serve the best interests of the child. The case of an adult differs greatly. The adult must first be determined to be incompetent, before any determination as to what arrangement will best serve the needs of the alleged incompetent.

The trial court in this case presumed that appellant was incompetent. The trial court did not apply the above standards and determine that appellant was incompetent. Rather, a review of the trial court opinion reveals immediately that the court assumed appellant was incompetent and went on to decide what it believed to be an appropriate custody arrangement. Although appellant's mother and father had each filed a petition to have her declared incompetent, the court abused its discretion by accepting this as an acquiescence that appellant was incompetent. Appellant may very well have wished to contest whether or not she was incompetent. Since the lower court failed to apply the appropriate standard, we find that the court committed a clear abuse of discretion.

Appellant's second argument is that there was insufficient evidence presented at the trial of this matter to establish her incompetent. We agree with appellant. The evidence presented at the trail of this matter was largely related to whether appellant would do best living with her mother or her father. The entire trial court opinion is related to what living arrangement would be best for appellant. These matters are irrelevant until there has been a proper adjudication of incompetency. Our review of the record indicates that it is replete with evidence of how appellant was doing when living with each of her parents, but is lacking evidence of whether appellant is incompetent under the statutory definition. Further, all of the evidence of appellant's abilities indicates that she is not incompetent. In this situation, we feel we are required to reverse and vacate the decision of the lower court.

Appellant's third argument is that the trial court violated her due process rights under the United States Constitution by failing to appoint her counsel or a guardian *ad litem* for the trial of this matter. Since this case has been decided on a non-constitutional basis, we will not reach this constitutional issue. *Ballou v. State Ethics Commission,* 496 Pa. 127, 436 A.2d 186 (1981).

For the foregoing reasons, the order of the trial court is reversed and vacated.

Case Review Question

Estate of Haertsch, 415 Pa.Super. 598, 609 A.2d 1384 (1992).

In the present case, what steps should a court take to determine competence in future proceedings?

The law of estates affects every facet of society. Of course, there are those persons who stand to inherit when another person dies. But just as importantly, virtually every entity with whom the deceased was in financial contact prior to death is affected. Popular misconceptions are that when someone dies, the person's possessions are immediately divided up among the surviving family. In reality, the process is much more complicated. The following discussion addresses such topics as the distribution of an estate when there is no will and when there is a valid will. The probate process is also explained. Although probate (administration of estates) is governed by state law, many of the procedures are similar in most states. This discussion is limited to those general procedures observed in most jurisdictions.

INTESTATE SUCCESSION

When someone dies **intestate,** it means that the person died without leaving a known valid will. Often persons with substantial assets do not make provisions for the distribution of those assets after death. The obvious disadvantage to not leaving a valid will is that distribution by the state may not be at all what the deceased would have wished. Nevertheless, it is such a frequent occurrence that the states have designed several methods to distribute the assets of a deceased person. The manner in which this is done is called intestate succession (see Figure 13.1). Literally, this means that the state decides who will succeed to the assets of a person who dies without a valid will.

One method that is now seldom applied in laws on distribution of estates is called **per capita distribution,** discussed here for purposes of comparison. Per capita is a rather simple method. The initial task is to identify all living relatives of the deceased. The assets of the deceased that remain after probate of the estate are divided equally among the number of survivors.[1] For example, assume that two children, one grandchild, three aunts, and four cousins were left as survivors of the deceased. The entire estate would be distributed into 10 equal shares (the total number of survivors).

intestate
Dying without a valid will.

per capita distribution
Distribution of an estate in equal shares, with each person representing one share.

per stirpes distribution

Distribution of an estate in equal shares to one level or class of persons. If a member of this level or class is deceased, his or her heirs divide the share.

The second method, and the one employed by the majority of states, is known as **per stirpes distribution.** Under this method, as with per capita, all surviving relatives are identified. However, entitlement to receive any of the estate and the percentage received depend upon the proximity of the relationship.[2] For example, if children of the deceased are living but no spouse survives, the children would be entitled to the entire estate, irrespective of the fact that many cousins and siblings of the deceased may still be living, because the children are direct descendants of the deceased. If the previous example for per capita distribution were modified to leave no surviving descendants, the ascendants (aunts and possibly cousins) would receive portions of the estate. Another reason why a majority of states use per stirpes distribution is its equitable nature. In a per stirpes jurisdiction, members of a certain degree of relationship or generation will inherit equally, so that, for example, a grandchild would not inherit more than a child or other grandchild.

Assignment 13.1

> Based on the statute in Figure 13.1, identify how your own estate would proceed by intestate succession.

Each state that utilizes the per stirpes method has particular methods for determining exactly how the estate will be distributed. The common thread is that whether a person inherits depends upon the person's relationship to the deceased and how many other persons have the same relationship. Generally, the estate is distributed to descendants. If there are none, it is distributed to ascendants, such as parents, and across to siblings (brothers and sisters) and then to the descendants of the siblings. If there are no living relatives at these levels, it proceeds to ascendants such as aunts and uncles and their descendants (i.e., cousins). Depending on the limit set by the state statute, this may continue on for several degrees of family relation. The following are some of the more common rules employed based on the survivors.

If there are

(a) A surviving spouse and children all born to the surviving spouse and deceased: The spouse receives a lump sum of money and an additional percentage of the estate. The children receive the entire remaining percentage to be distributed equally.

(b) A surviving spouse and children, some or all of whom are not the children of the surviving spouse: Spouse and children receive one half of the estate each. If there is more than one child, the one half will be divided equally among the number of children.

(c) A surviving spouse, no children, surviving parents and / or siblings or children of siblings: Surviving spouse is entitled to a lump sum of cash and one half of the estate. Parents and siblings each take an equal share of the remaining one half of the estate. If a sibling is deceased but leaves children, the children each take an equal share of what would have been the sibling's share.

FIGURE 13.1   Wisconsin Statutes Annotated Chapter 852—Intestate Succession

852.01. Basic rules for intestate succession

(1) Who are heirs. The net estate of a decedent which he has not disposed of by will, whether he dies without a will, or with a will which does not completely dispose of his estate, passes to his surviving heirs as follows:

(a) To the spouse:

1. If there are no surviving issue of the decedent, or if the surviving issue are all issue of the surviving spouse and the decedent, the entire estate.

2. If there are surviving issue one or more of whom are not issue of the surviving spouse, one-half of that portion of the decedent's net estate not disposed of by will consisting of decedent's property other than marital property and other than property described under 861.02(1).

(b) To the issue, the share of the estate not passing to the spouse under part (a), or the entire estate if there is no surviving spouse; if the issue are all in the same degree of kinship to the decedent they take equally, but if they are of unequal degree then those of more remote degrees take by representation.

(c) If there is no surviving spouse or issue, to the parents.

(d) If there is no surviving spouse, issue or parent, to the brothers and sisters and the issue of any deceased brother or sister by representation.

(e) If there is no surviving spouse, issue, parent or brother or sister, to the issue of brothers and sisters; if such issue are all in the same degree of kinship to the decedent they take equally, but if they are of unequal degree then those of more remote degrees take by representation.

(f) If there is no surviving spouse, issue, parent or issue of a parent, to the grandparents.

(g) If there is no surviving spouse, issue, parent, issue of a parent, or grandparent, to the intestate's next of kin in equal degree.

(2) Requirement that heir survive decedent for a certain time. If any person who would otherwise be an heir under sub. (1) dies within 72 hours of the time of death of the decedent, the net estate not disposed of by will passes under this section as if that person had predeceased the decedent. If the time of death of the decedent or of the person who would otherwise be an heir, or the times of death of both, cannot be determined, and it cannot be established that the person who would otherwise be an heir has survived the decedent by at least 72 hours, it is presumed that the person died within 72 hours of the decedent's death. In computing time for purposes of this subsection, local standard time at the place of death of the decedent is used.

(2m) Requirement that heir not have intentionally killed the deceased. (a) If any person who would otherwise be an heir under sub. (1) has unlawfully and intentionally killed the decedent, the net estate not disposed of by will passes as if the killer had predeceased the decedent.

(b) A final judgment of conviction of unlawful and intentional killing is conclusive for purposes of this subsection.

(bg) A final adjudication of delinquency on the basis of unlawfully and intentionally killing the decedent is conclusive for purposes of this subsection.

(br) In the absence of a conviction under par. (b) or an adjudication under par. (bg), the court, on the basis of clear and convincing evidence, may determine whether the killing was unlawful and intentional for purposes of this subsection.

(c) This subsection does not affect the rights of any person who, before rights under this subsection have been adjudicated, purchases for value and without notice from the killer property that the killer would have acquired except for this subsection; but the killer is liable for the amount of the proceeds. No insurance company, bank or other obligor paying according to the terms of its policy or obligation is liable because of this subsection unless before payment it has received at its home office or principal address written notice of a claim under this subsection.

(3) Escheat. If there are no heirs of the decedent under subs. (1) and (2), the net estate escheats to the state to be added to the capital of the school fund.

(d) Surviving parents, siblings, and children of siblings: The entire estate would be distributed on the same basis as indicated in (c).

As indicated, under per stirpes, the shares are divided based on categories of *living* relatives. Thus, if siblings are alive, the shares are divided among the number of living siblings, and the siblings' children are entitled only to split a deceased sibling's share. This is different from per capita, which gives no attention to the level of the relationship but rather distributes according to the number of relations.

APPLICATION 13.3

Assume the deceased is survived by a sister, two children, an aunt, and a grandparent. Under the per capita distribution method, in the absence of a valid will, the entire estate would be distributed into five equal shares with the children of the decedent receiving the same portion of the estate as the other surviving heirs. Under per stirpes distribution in most states, the children of the decedent would receive the entire estate.

Point for Discussion
◆   How would the distribution in either situation change if there were also a surviving parent?

The per stirpes method does not search out relatives to an infinite degree to receive the estate. Rather, most states have a maximum level of relationship, such as a fifth cousin, who can inherit the estate.[3] If there are no sufficiently close relatives left surviving, the estate of the deceased goes into what is called escheat, the process by which the assets are taken over by the state. The assets become the property of the state, and no individuals are entitled to inherit.[4]

What of persons who have a partial blood relationship or relationship created by law to the deceased? As previously indicated, a spouse is considered to be a blood relative for purposes of inheritance, even though the relationship is a legal one. But what is the status of adopted children? The relationship is recognized by law. Generally, when a parent adopts a child, for all purposes of intestate succession, the child is treated as a natural child of the parent.[5] The states are divided on the status of any remaining testamentary relationship between the adopted child and the biological parents. Many states permit the child to claim inheritance from the biological parents. Other states consider the bond severed at the time of adoption and do not permit such claims. However, most states do not permit the biological parent to inherit from the adopted child in the event the parent survives the child. Any permitted inheritance in such a situation would, of course, require knowledge of the identity of the parties involved.

Siblings of half-blood relationships share only one parent with the deceased. In most states, a half-blood sibling is entitled to inherit at least some portion of the estate.[6] These states vary from a percentage inheritance to a full entitlement, as a full-blood brother or sister would receive.

If a child is born out of wedlock and subsequently makes a claim of inheritance against the father's estate, it is usually required that the father made some formal acknowledgment of the child during the father's lifetime.[7] This can be demonstrated by a legal finding of paternity or by actions of the father that would indicate the father believed the child to be his. However, with the advancement of scientific technology, it may very soon be the general rule that proof of paternity as evidence to claim inheritance can be produced after the death of the father.

A child who is born within 10 months of the death of a parent can make a claim as a posthumous heir to the estate.[8] Otherwise, all persons claiming against the estate must be alive at the time of, and for a specified period of time after, the decedent's death.[9] Consider how this latter situation could create a question.

A husband and wife are killed in an accident. The wife had two children by a previous marriage. The husband had some distant relatives (but still close enough to inherit under per stirpes). If it can be proven that the wife outlived the husband by a sufficient period of time, the wife's estate would be entitled to the entire estate of the husband. Consequently, the wife's two children (from a former marriage) would be entitled to the entire estate of their mother. If the wife did not survive the husband for a requisite period of time, the children would inherit only their mother's estate and none of their stepfather's. Ultimately, the distant relatives of the husband would inherit his entire estate by per stirpes.

Another matter that affects both intestate succession and testate succession (distribution by will) arises when the deceased was murdered. Anyone who is found by the probate court to be responsible for the death of the decedent as the result of foul play cannot inherit.[10] Many states do not even require a criminal conviction. Rather, it need only be established in probate court that the person was accused and prosecuted for the murder. Some states have a hearing in the probate court to determine whether by probate standards a murder occurred (these standards are generally less stringent than what is required for a conviction of first degree murder in a criminal prosecution).

Additionally, in some states, certain acts by a spouse prior to the death of the deceased may cause the spouse to lose rights of inheritance. Examples include adulterous conduct, abandonment for a long period of time, and other acts that indicate the spouse discarded the marital relationship. Further, a spouse who is divorced from the decedent cannot inherit by intestate succession.[11]

As this discussion has shown, intestate succession is a well-developed area of the law because of the numerous cases of death without a will. Although the law prefers creation of a will, many rules govern this process to ensure that the testator (deceased who left a will) created the will intentionally, without improper influences, and with a clear mind.

Assignment 13.2

For each of the following groups of survivors, determine who would inherit and to what percentage of the estate the heirs would be entitled based on the rules previously discussed. (Assume half-blood siblings are entitled to one-half of that entitled to a full-blood sibling.)

1. A surviving spouse and one child from a former marriage.
2. One child and one parent.

3. Two siblings, one parent, and one uncle.
4. A surviving spouse and three children (who are heirs of decedent and spouse).
5. Four siblings, two half-blood siblings, and one parent.

TESTATE SUCCESSION

Requirements of a Valid Will

Before a will can be used as the instrument to distribute an estate, it must be declared a valid will. Contrary to what may be depicted in old movies, notes written on a slip of paper immediately prior to death rarely meet the requisites of a valid will. Every state has statutes that dictate the exact procedure for the preparation of a will. If the procedure is not followed or if any significant irregularities are present, the will may be declared invalid and the estate distributed by intestate succession.

A majority of states now require that a will be in writing. Although oral wills are permitted in some states, it generally must be shown that at the time of the oral will (1) the deceased believed death to be imminent and (2) the terms of the will were declared to witnesses who would not stand to inherit.[12] The rationale for upholding oral wills by states that still honor them is that such circumstances would lend credence to the terms of the testator's oral will and thus would be truly indicative of the deceased's intent.

APPLICATION 13.4

Joe and James were life partners for approximately 30 years. Although the assets were in Joe's name, he shared everything equally with James. James did not work for the entirety of the relationship. Joe's only legal heirs were two nieces whom he had not seen or spoken with in over 35 years. During his life, Joe periodically commented that when he "went," everything would go to James. Joe died suddenly and it was only then James discovered Joe had no valid will. Without any legal inheritance rights, and without a will stating his wishes, the estate would go per stirpes to the two nieces. The fact that Joe had made verbal declarations is irrelevant, because they were not made to independent witnesses at a time Joe believed death was imminent.

Point for Discussion

♦   Would the situation change if Joe had reiterated his testamentary intentions to James within moments before death?

Oral wills are an increasingly rare occurrence. Rather, the bulk of the statutes pertain to the requirements for a valid written will. It is required that a testator sign the will with knowledge that the instrument being signed is a declaration of intent for distribution of assets upon death. Thus, if it is established that someone was tricked into signing a document without knowledge that it was a will, the document will be invalid. If the testator knows the document is a will but because of some limitation is unable to sign it, the testator can direct another to affix the signature so long as it is accomplished in the presence of the testator.[13]

It is also required that the testator have capacity to issue the will. This does not mean that the testator must have legal capacity as required in contract law. Rather, it must only be shown that the testator understood the extent and value of the estate and the effect of a will, that is, giving the estate to specified others upon death.[14]

If it is established that the testator prepared the will under some mental impairment that would prevent a full comprehension of the will's effects, the testator may be considered to not have had the requisite capacity. Additionally, if the testator prepares the terms of the will under false information, undue influence, fraud, or some other factor that would impede the ability to exercise a voluntary testamentary document, the testator would be considered to have lacked capacity. Either circumstance will result in an invalid will, and the estate will be distributed by the law of intestate succession.

Witnesses are a necessary element to any valid will.[15] It is not required that they know the contents of what they are signing. Rather, the purpose of witnesses is to establish that the document was voluntarily signed by the testator. If the testator signs the document in the presence of the witnesses and the witnesses then affix their signatures, the requirement has been met. Witnesses generally do not have to sign in the presence of one another, so long as they each were present when the testator signed the document or acknowledged the testator's signature. Thus, witnesses could sign the document at a later point in time and the requirement of witnesses to the signature would still be met.

A significant issue that arises in many will contests is the intention of the actual terms of the will. Often, a will cannot be entirely stated on one page. Thus, when there are several pages, there is the opportunity for unscrupulous individuals to insert additional terms in the will. Therefore, any will of multiple pages should indicate on each page the page number and the total number of pages. This decreases the chances of alterations. Also, many courts prefer that the testator and witnesses initial each page of the will and affix their signature to the final page of the document.

Some wills mention other documents and incorporate the terms of those documents. This is done by reference to the document and by indicating the intent that the document become part of the will. An example is a parent who, as part of the will, wants to create a trust fund for a child. The will would make reference to the documents used to create a trust fund. This type of reference to other documents is incorporation by reference.[16] The documents to which the will makes reference are incorporated into the terms of the will as if they were actually a physical part of the will. To incorporate another document by reference, it is required by statute that the document already existed at the time the will was created and that it referred to the will within its contents. This prevents persons from creating the document to serve their own purposes after the will is executed and the testator is deceased.

A testator may also place conditions on bequests received under a will. The testator may indicate an intent to grant the bequest only if the person receiving the bequest performs certain conditions. If these conditions are not met, that portion of the will is considered ineffective, and the inheritance will not occur.[17]

It is permissible for a testator to disinherit anyone but a spouse.[18] Testators can direct almost without limitation who will receive under the will as well as very specific bequests of property or money. However, by state law, a spouse is entitled to a portion of the estate unless one of the circumstances of misconduct mentioned previously exists at the time of the testator's death.

Will Codicils and Will Revocation

Many times, a person continues to live for many years after the will has been executed. During such time, circumstances may take place that alter the intent of the person with respect to the person's estate after death. Such factors as death of other family members, divorce, birth, marriage, and changed financial status influence testamentary intent. At some point, it may become necessary to alter the contents of one's will. This can be accomplished through a codicil or the execution of a new will and revocation of the old one. Which is more appropriate depends upon the extent and type of changes to be made.

A codicil is an addition to an existing will.[19] It is necessary that any codicil incorporate by reference the preexisting will. Otherwise, the codicil may be considered a complete and new will. All of the requirements necessary for a valid will are also required of a codicil, because the terms in the codicil actually become part of the will for all legal purposes. When a codicil is executed and signed, the incorporation by reference serves as a sort of reaffirmation of the terms of the original will. As a result, the date of the will is considered to be that of the codicil.[20] This is important when several wills are presented to the court, because the most recent is presumed to be the valid will reflecting the final intent of the testator.

A codicil should not contradict the terms of a previous will. If this is necessary to accomplish the objective of the testator, an entirely new will should be prepared. Often codicils are included to make new provisions for bequests when a party who would have inherited dies before the testator. Also, codicils can be used to distribute assets acquired after the original will was executed.

Will revocation becomes necessary when the intent of the testator changes with respect to the distribution of assets upon death. When a new will is executed, all prior wills are considered to be revoked and invalid, as they no longer reflect the intent of the testator.[21] Even if a testator does not execute a new will, the old will can still be revoked. If not revoked by a written document, it is often required that the testator take some steps to physically destroy or obliterate the existing will. It is not usually required that the will be totally destroyed. Rather, it need only be shown by the condition of the will and acts of the testator that destruction was intended.

In some instances, after revocation a testator will seek to have the prior will made valid again. This can occur in one of several ways. When a new will is executed, it can contain a statement that if it is declared invalid, the old will should be reinstated. This prevents automatic intestate succession if the new will is defective. Another method is for the testator to say and do acts in the presence of witnesses that clearly establish the intent that the former will be revived. A condition of this method is usually that the original will is still in existence. Assuming that a will is located and presented to the court for probate (the process of the distribution of the estate), parties still have the opportunity to challenge the contents of the will. This occurs during probate and can be based on several different grounds, as discussed in the next section.

APPLICATION 13.5

Tyranny has four children. In the past year, she has given her entire savings to her youngest child for college expenses. The amount is approximately $15,000. Tyranny's only other asset is the equity in her home which is $50,000. She executed a valid will that provides for distribution of the proceeds of the house to her three oldest children. She leaves the youngest child only the residue of her estate, stating she otherwise provided for the child during her lifetime. A short time later, Tyranny purchased a winning lottery ticket and $58,000,000 was deposited into her bank account. She called her lawyer and stated she wanted the amount split equally among the four children in a new will. The lawyer prepared the will, but Tyranny died in a car accident before it was executed. Under the present will, which is the only effective one, Tyranny's youngest child would receive all assets other than the house proceeds. While previously this only consisted of personal effects, it now includes the $58,000,000.

Point for Discussion

♦   Assume the children are the only heirs. How would the estate proceed under intestate succession? What argument could be made to invalidate the executed will?

CASE

BRITTIN v. BUCKMAN

279 Ill.App. 3d 512, 664 N.E.21d 687, 216 Il.Dec. 50 (1996).

GOLDENHERSH, Justice delivered the opinion of the court:

Respondent, Mary Ann Buckman, natural daughter of decedent, Stephen Glenn Brittin, and administrator of his estate, appeals from an order of the circuit court finding petitioners, Deborah J. Roeder, Linda Brittin, Denise Brittin, Stacie Brittin, and Laura Moore, the natural children of decedent's adopted son, William Eugene, to be decedent's legal HEIRS and reopening decedent's estate.

CASE

On appeal, respondent contends the trial court erred in finding petitioners, for purposes of INTESTATE succession, to be the legal HEIRS of decedent and in reopening decedent's estate. We affirm.

I

The facts are undisputed. The record reveals that when William Eugene was about three years of age, his mother, Estelle Willet, married the decedent, Stephen Glenn Brittin. From age three, Stephen and Estelle raised William as their son. The couple had one natural child, Mary Ann Buckman, respondent herein. Estelle Willet Brittin died on July 28, 1975. Shortly thereafter, on October 20, 1976, Stephen adopted William in an adult adoption proceeding in St. Clair County. William was 46 years old at the time of the adoption and had five children, petitioners herein. The adoption decree specifically provides that William was the child of Stephen Glenn Brittin "and for the purposes of inheritance and all other legal incidents and consequences, shall be the same as if said respondent had been born to Stephen Glenn Brittin and Estelle Willet Brittin (now deceased) in lawful wedlock." William died on May 17, 1979, predeceasing his adoptive father and leaving his five children as his descendants and HEIRS.

On February 8, 1993, Stephen died INTESTATE leaving Mary, his natural daughter, and petitioners, descendants of his adopted son, William, as his HEIRS. Decedent's INTESTATE estate was opened on March 10, 1993. The court found respondent to be the sole heir and appointed her administrator of the estate. The estate was closed on October 4, 1993, with the proceeds going to respondent. Petitioners were unaware that the administration of decedent's estate was underway without their participation until December 1993, when they learned that the estate had been closed.

On February 9, 1994, petitioners filed a petition to vacate the order of discharge and order finding heirship and to reopen the estate. Petitioners alleged in the petition that they are HEIRS of the decedent and are entitled to share in decedent's estate as the children of decedent's adopted son. After a hearing, the trial court entered its order finding petitioners legal HEIRS of decedent and reopening the estate. Respondent filed a motion to reconsider, which was denied on January 30, 1995. Respondent appeals.

II

Respondent contends that petitioners are not descendants of the decedent and may not take, by representation, their deceased father's share of the decedent's estate. Respondent acknowledges that pursuant to section 2–4(a) of the PROBATE Act (755 ILCS 5/2–4(a) (West 1992)), petitioners' father, as the adopted child of the decedent, is a descendant of his adoptive parent, and had he not predeceased decedent, he would be entitled to half of decedent's estate. However, defendant argues that the legislature, in using the term "adopted child" in section 2–4(a) of the PROBATE Act, intended to limit INTESTATE succession to the descendants of a child adopted as a minor. Respondent further asserts that the legislature did not intend to include as descendants of an "adopted child" children born to the adopted adult prior to that adult's adoption. According to respondent, because petitioners were already born at the time of decedent's adoption of their father, they are not the descendants of an "adopted child" and therefore cannot take by representation their deceased father's share of decedent's estate. We disagree.

The case before us is one of first impression and requires our consideration of the issue of whether the natural children of an adult adoptee are descendants of the adopting parent for purposes of inheritance. In considering this issue, we must consider whether the legislature, in enacting the statute granting an adopted child the status of a descendant of the adopting parent, intended to limit succession rights of the adoptee's children to the natural children of a child adopted as a minor and to exclude the natural children born to the adult adoptee prior to his adoption by the adopting parent.

The DISTRIBUTION of an INTESTATE real and personal estate of a decedent whose spouse is predeceased but who is survived by his descendants is governed by section 2–1(b) of the PROBATE Act, which provides:

"§2–1. Rules of descent and DISTRIBUTION. The INTESTATE real and personal estate of a resident decedent and the INTESTATE real estate in this State of a nonresident decedent, after all just claims against his estate are fully paid, descends and shall be distributed as follows:

(b) If there is no surviving spouse but a descendant of the decedent: the entire estate to the decedent's descendants PER STIRPES." 755 ILCS 5/2–1(b) (West 1992).

Where the decedent is survived by an adopted child, the adopted child may take a share of the INTESTATE estate as a legal heir of the decedent pursuant to section 2–4(a) of the PROBATE Act, which provides:

"§2–4. Adopted child and adopting parent.(a) An adopted child is a descendant of the adopting parent for purposes of inheritance from the adopting parent and from the lineal and collateral kindred of the adopting parent. For such purposes, an adopted child also is a descendant of both natural parents when the adopting parent is the spouse of a natural parent." 755 ILCS 5/2–4(a) (West 1992).

To determine the intent of the legislature, a court should first consider the statutory language, for its language best indicates the legislature's intent. Solich, 158 Ill.2d at 81, 196 Ill.Dec. at 657, 630 N.E.2d. "In applying plain and unambiguous language, it is not necessary for a court to search for any subtle or not readily apparent intention of the legislature." *Di Foggio v. Retirement Board of the County Employees Annuity & Benefit Fund of Cook County,* 156 Ill.2d 377, 383, 189 Ill.Dec. 753, 756, 620 N.E.2d 1070, 1073 (1993).

The Adoption Act (750 ILCS 50/1 et seq. (West 1992)) provides for the adoption of an adult as well as the adoption of minor children. Section 3 of the Adoption Act sets forth the conditions under which an adult may be adopted, stating:

"§3. Who may be adopted. A male or female adult[] may be adopted provided that such adult has resided in the home of the persons intending to adopt him at any time for more than 2 years continuously preceding the commencement of an adoption proceeding, or in the alternative that such persons are related to him within a degree set forth in the definition of a related child in Section 1 of this Act." 750 ILCS 50/3 (West 1992).

A careful review of the Adoption Act reveals no statutory distinction between an adopted adult and an adopted minor with respect to the nature of the legal relationship created between the adoptee and the adopting parent, namely, a parent–child relationship. The adoptee, regardless of his age upon adoption, attains the status of a natural child of the adopting parents. In re M.M., 156 Ill.2d 53. 62, 189 Ill.Dec. 1, 7, 619 N.E.2d 702, 708 (1993). Likewise, the Adoption Act makes no reference to the rights of an adopted child with regard to his ability to inherit from his adopting parents. Therefore, for the proper resolution of the issue before us, we must examine section 2–4(a) of the PROBATE Act.

Respondent maintains that section 2–4(a) of the PROBATE Act does not include adult adoptees because, had the legislature intended to include adopted adult children, it would have changed the word "child" to "person" so as to include all adopted persons. Respondent argues that the legislature has amended section 2–4(a) several times and has not made this change and, therefore, the legislature intended to limit inheritance to minor adopted children. We do not agree with this contention.

"Where the terms of a statute are not defined by the legislature, courts will assume that they were intended to have their ordinary and popularly understood meanings, unless doing so would defeat the perceived legislative intent." *People v. Hicks,* 101 Ill.2d 366, 371, 78 Ill.Dec. 354, 357, 462 N.E.2d 473, 476 (1984). Further, in determining the legislature's intent in using a particular term, "a reference to the subject matter and the context will ordinarily disclose the sense in which the word is used." *Bartholow v. Davies,* 276 Ill. 505, 511, 114 N.E. 1017 (1916).

"There are two meanings which may be given to the word 'child:' one an offspring or a descendant, when a person is spoken of in relation to his parents: another, a person of immature years. The word 'child,' when used with reference to the parents, ordinarily has no reference to age, but to the relation. When used without reference to the

CASE

parents, as indicating a particular individual, it usually bears the meaning of a young person of immature years." Bartholow, 276 Ill. at 511, 114 N.E. at 1019. (NOTE: Bartholow was decided prior to statutory changes allowing the adoption of adults.)

Considering the subject matter and context in which the word "child" is used in section 2–4(a), the plain language of the statute indicates that the legislature intended to use the word "child" in its relational sense; referring to the parent–child relationship between the adoptee and the adopting parent. The word "child," as used here, cannot be interpreted fairly as meaning a minor, in light of section 3 of the Adoption Act which permits adult adoptions. Moreover, there is nothing in section 2–4(a) indicating a distinction between the adoptee's status as an adult or a minor at the time of adoption with regard to the adoptee's classification as a descendant of the adopting parent. The only qualification set forth in the statute is that the adoptee be legally adopted. Nothing more is required. Accordingly, petitioner's deceased father is an adopted child of the decedent and, as such, obtained the right of succession as decedent's legal heir.

III

Respondent next asserts that the children of an adopted adult who were born before the adult's adoption are not the legal HEIRS of the decedent because they are not the children of an adopted adult. Respondent argues, therefore, that petitioners, as already-born children at the time of their father's adoption, cannot take by representation their predeceased father's share of decedent's estate. This contention is not persuasive.

As discussed above, section 2–4(a) deems all adopted children to be descendants of the adopting parent. This provision places the adopted child and the natural child in equivalent positions with respect to the child's capacity to inherit from an INTESTATE parent. Similarly, the act of adoption itself accords the adoptee the status of a natural child of the adopting parent. In re M.M., 156 Ill.2d at 62, 189 Ill.Dec. at 7, 619 N.E.2d at 708. As with natural children, the children of the adoptee, by virtue of the adoption, become the grandchildren of the adopting parent, thereby creating a grandparent–grandchild relationship.

Because section 2–4(a) deems an adopted child the descendant of the adopting parent, it logically follows that, for purposes of inheritance, the children of the adopted adult are also descendants and can take as grandchildren of the decedent. Accordingly, if the adopted child predeceases the adopting parent, leaving children, as is the case here, those children, as grandchildren of the adopting parent, are entitled to represent their deceased parent and to receive from the adopting parent's estate the share to which the adopted adult child would have been entitled to receive had he survived the adopting parent. Annotation, Adoption of Adult, 21 A.L.R.3d 1012. 1034–38, §§ 14, 16 (1968); 2 Am.Jur.2d Adoption §205, at 1132 (1994).

We believe this to be the correct reading of section 2–4(a) since section 2–4(a) does not impose any restrictions or conditions on the ability of the natural children of a predeceased adopted child to inherit from the estate of the adopting parent. Nor does the provision either expressly or impliedly state that the adopted child's children must be born subsequent to the adoption in order to be legal HEIRS of the adopting parent. Because "the plain meaning of the language used by the legislature is the safest guide in constructing any [statute]," the court cannot inject provisions not expressly included or fairly implied by the statute. *Munroe v. Brower Realty & Management Co.*, 206 Ill.App.3d 699, 706, 151 Ill.Dec. 761, 767, 565 N.E.2d 32, 38 (1990). Further, "the words of a statute must be read in light of the purposes to be served, and those words must be read to reach a common-sense result." *Munroe,* 206 Ill.App.3d at 706, 151 Ill.Dec. at 767, 565 N.E.2d at 38. Our reading of section 2–4(a) gives effect to the legislative policy of according adopted children a status of inheritance equivalent to that of natural children. With this legislative purpose in mind, we can read section 2–4(a) in no other way but as including, as descendants of the decedent, the natural children of an adopted adult. Accordingly, we find that the trial court did not err in finding petitioners to be the legal HEIRS of the decedent. As such, petitioners are entitled to represent their deceased parent, the adopted child of the decedent, and to receive the adopted child's PER STIRPES share of decedent's estate.

For the foregoing reasons, the judgment of the circuit court of Madison County is affirmed.

Affirmed.

HOPKINS, P.J., and CHAPMAN, J., concur.

Case Review Question
What distinguishes an heir from a descendant?

Assignment 13.3

In the following situations, determine whether the will should be revoked, amended with a codicil, or left as is. Give reasons for your decision.

1. Husband whose first will does not mention his wife by name but provides for "my wife" is now married to a different woman.
2. Woman who bequeaths her antique car to her neighbor Bob sells the car.
3. Mother of four children provides specific bequests to each child, but one of the children subsequently predeceases the mother.
4. A man has a valid will but before his death inherits a large sum of money.

Will Contests

Most publicity regarding probate cases is centered around will contests, when a person challenges the validity of a will. The three common grounds for will contests are mistake, duress or improper influence, and fraud. Generally, one who contests a will has the burden of proof to establish by clear and convincing evidence (less than the standard of beyond a reasonable doubt but more than a mere preponderance of the evidence) that the will is not a valid testamentary instrument properly executed by the deceased.

When a will is challenged on the basis of mistake, the challenger must allege that the testator either did not know a final will was being signed or was not aware of all of the terms and the effects of what had been included in the will.[22] When mistake is proven as to any part of a will, most courts will declare the entire instrument invalid. The reasoning is sound: if it can be shown that the testator made a significant mistake with respect to one part of the will, who is to say that other mistakes were not made as well? When the entire will is declared invalid, the estate passes by intestate succession.

The second method used to challenge a will is that of duress or improper influence. The thrust of this type of challenge is that the testator did not execute the will independently and voluntarily. In most cases, it must be shown by the contestant that the testator was convinced that there was no real intent to execute the will. Rather, the testator was so impaired that the contents of the will reflect the desires of another and that the testator would not have executed the terms of the will but for the existence of improper influences.[23]

As stated, it is the general rule that the person challenging the will has the burden of proving the duress or improper influence. There is, however, an exception to this rule. When the will is drawn up or witnessed by someone who is a fiduciary (one who is in a position of personal trust to the testator) or who stands to receive under the will, many states will presume that there was undue influence.[24] Thus, a will should always be drawn and witnessed by disinterested parties. Otherwise, no matter how sincere the testator could have been, the burden is shifted against the parties alleging the will is valid. The presumption is that there was undue influence, and the will is considered ineffective unless it can be shown by clear and convincing evidence that there was no improper influence. Because attorneys are fiduciaries, they should avoid drafting or witnessing wills in which they are beneficiaries (although most states will make an exception if the will is for a close or immediate family member).

Persons who may not draft or witness a will without the presumption of improper influence are specified in the statutes of each state. Similarly, the burden of proof (amount of evidence) needed to show that the will was properly executed is also dictated by statute. The preceding are common rules, but variations may exist in some states. Consequently, before relying on these propositions, one should always consult existing statutes in the particular state of interest.

The final reason for challenging a will is an allegation of fraud. The contestant must prove several elements before a will is considered to be ineffective on the grounds of fraud. Specifically, it must be demonstrated that (1) an identifiable person made false statements to the testator, (2) such person did so with the intent of misleading the testator by the statements, (3) the testator was in fact misled and executed a will based on the false statements, and (4) the testator would not have executed the terms of the will in the absence of reliance on the false allegations.[25]

An example of fraud is the case whereby a child (presumably an adult child) convinces a parent that another child of the parent is dead. The parent then executes a will leaving the entire estate to the child who made the false allegations. If the parent would not have executed the same will with the knowledge that the second child was living and there is no reasonable basis of determining whether the parent would have executed the will, the will was created under circumstances of fraud.

CASE

MARLENE J. ROSEN, v. MARC D. ROSEN.

2002 WL 1949690

FRANK S. MEADOW,
JUDGE TRIAL REFEREE.

This is an appeal from the denial of admission to Probate for the District of New Haven of a Will dated August 15, 1996 of Albert Rosen. On June 4, 2001, the Probate Court denied the admission on the grounds that there is insufficient evidence to admit the Will on the issue of Competence. (Exh. 7.) The reasons for the appeal are as follows:

The Will dated 8/15/96 is DENIED admission to probate. There is insufficient evidence to admit same on the issue of competence. C.G .S. 45a-250; *In re Lockwood,* 80 Conn. 513 (1902).

1. The instrument dated August 15, 1996, which was presented for probate by the proponent, was the last Will and testament of the deceased, executed in accordance with the requirements of law, when he was of the age of 73 years.
2. The deceased was of sound mind, and in possession of sufficient testamentary capacity at the time he executed the August 15, 1996, Will.
3. The deceased at the time he executed the August 15, 1996, Will was not subjected to any undue influence from outside parties.

A copy of the Will is annexed marked Exhibit A.

The defendant Marc Rosen (Marc) denies the allegations and as a Special Defense asserts that on August 15, 1996, the decedent Albert Rosen was the subject of undue influence from outside parties when he executed the Will dated August 15, 1996.

Burden of Proof
In a Will contest the proponent of the Will in this case Marlene Rosen (Marlene), the widow and named executrix under the August 15, 1996, Will has to prove the issue of testamentary capacity and due execution whereas the opponent of the Will, in this case Marc, son of the decedent and widow Marlene bears the burden to show undue influence.

In *Jackson v. Waller,* 126 Conn. 294, 301 the Court stated:

> The fundamental test of the testatrix's capacity to make a Will is her condition of mind and memory at the very time when she executed the instrument. *Nichols v. Wentz,* 78 Conn. 429, 435, 62 Atl. 620; *Sturdevant's Appeal,* 71 Conn. 392, 401, 42 Atl. 70; *Kimberly's Appeal,* 68 Conn. 428, 439, 36 Atl. 847; 1 Schouler, Wills, Executors & Administrators (6th Ed.) § 97. While in determining the question as to the mental capacity of a testator evidence is received of his conduct and condition prior and

subsequent to the point of time when it is executed, it is so admitted solely for such light as it may afford as to his capacity at that point of time and diminishes in weight as time lengthens in each direction from that point. *Canada's Appeal,* 47 Conn. 450, 463, *Cullum v. Colwell,* 85 Conn. 459, 465, 83 Atl. 695.

The burden of proof in disputes over testamentary capacity is on the party claiming under the Will (citations omitted) and that the testator has mind and memory sound enough to know and understand the business upon which he was engaged at the time of execution. (Citations omitted.) The ultimate determination whether a testor has measured up to this test is a question for the trier of fact. See *Stanton v. Grigley,* 177 Conn. 558, 564.

The defendant argues that Marlene has failed to establish that the decedent had the mental capacity because he did not know at the time (1) what his estate consisted of (2) to express how he wanted his estate distributed and (3) to read or understand the Will that was prepared for him.

The Will of August 15, 1996, was prepared by Norman Hurwitz (Hurwitz), an attorney admitted to the Connecticut Bar in 1958. Hurwitz draws about 50 to 60 Wills per year who testified he did not have any notes in his file about the assets of the decedent and if he knew the estate was larger he would have considered trusts. Hurwitz's understanding was a to draw simple mirror Wills giving all assets to each other if surviving the other by 90 days. (Exh. A.) Nothing in notes list any assets. Hurwitz was to prepare what he called viceversa documents. Hurwitz had no recollection if Rosen read his Will or not. Husband and wife coming to his office together are never separated and he discusses their issues together. Hurwitz could not testify if Rosen was able to read and had no recollection of Rosen reading his Will. Hurwitz's general practice was to give photostatic copies of the Will to his clients and he goes through the Will paragraph by paragraph. Hurwitz's only recollection of Rosen was he could ambulate and that it was obvious he had a stroke. Rosen held onto his wife's arm to walk. Hurwitz could not recall if Rosen read the Will. Hurwitz did not have

◆ CASE

a recollection whether he went over the Rosen Will paragraph by paragraph in this case. All that Hurwitz was able to testify to was his best recollection because he had no notes.

Hurwitz had other matters with the Rosens but could not recall whether it was before or after the execution of the Will. All Hurwitz's verbal conversations were with Marlene Rosen. Marlene Rosen called about drawing up the Wills. Hurwitz had nothing in his notes that Rosen had given him a prior Will he had drawn in New York in 1993. Hurwitz had business with the Rosens for about four or five years after the Will of Rosen.

Hurwitz also prepared, as he did customarily, Powers of Attorney for both the Rosens. Hurwitz testified that it was necessary for him to form an opinion as to capacity and he felt that Rosen was unable to verbally communicate with Hurwitz.

Hurwitz was unable to go through his usual procedures that he follows in drawing up Wills. In the Rosen case Hurwitz tried to make sure what Marlene Rosen was relating to him about the Rosen Will was understood by Rosen. All the Hurwitz could recall was that Rosen nodded his head as he went through the paragraphs in affirmation. When asked by Hurwitz if Rosen knew what Hurwitz was doing Rosen nodded his head affirmatively. Hurwitz could not recall if Rosen said yes or no to any paragraphs.

Marlene Rosen testified that Albert had his stroke April 23, 1996, and two weeks later he entered Rehabilitation at Gaylord and that he came home May 30, 1996. Marlene testified that Albert Rosen understood everything and knew what he wanted to say. Marlene was the executrix under the Will (Exh. 1) dated August 15, 1996. Marlene testified he had difficulty retrieving words.

Marlene had requested a copy of their Wills from their lawyer in New York, Gerald Rosenblum (Rosenblum) (Exh. B) executed March 25, 1993. Marlene stated she and Albert were upset over the Wills drawn by Rosenblum because they contained Trusts so she called Attorney Hurwitz.

Marlene said that during the time Hurwitz was reading the Will (Exh. 1) that Albert was listening. Marlene on cross-examination admitted that

Albert's stroke affected his brain. After Gaylord rehabilitation he had a speech therapist.

Marlene testified that Albert had considerable assets when they went to Attorney Hurwitz's office. He owned a home in New Haven, a condo in Florida, a gas station in New York that is the subject matter of a pending law suit in New York between the late Albert Rosen and his son Marc and a lawsuit against family partners which resulted in a substantial later settlement of monies which were distributed to Albert, Marlene and their sons. The defendant argues had Hurwitz known of the assets that it is reasonable to assume and from the testimony of Hurwitz, who had no notes to reflect any assets, that he would have prepared more than simple Wills leaving everything to Marlene. Also from Albert's bad experience with his mother's estate and lack of planning resulting in the tax consequences that Albert was unhappy with, he would have provided that information to Hurwitz. This court can only conclude from the evidence and argument that Albert did not have sufficient knowledge to know the business at hand. (See *City National Bank & Trust Co. Appeal* 518, 521.)

The testimony of Elyse Berman (Berman), the speech language pathologist who treated Rosen after his stroke, is very significant in this case. Berman testified Rosen had a lot of difficulty at the time immediately following the stroke. Berman saw Rosen for about six months after the stroke starting in November 1996 to March 1997. She agreed with the therapist report (Exh. D) that Rosen suffered from receptive and expressive aphasia. Rosen had verbal apraxia which is the loss of ability to sequence words and sentences. He had moderate defects with auditory conynelieusion, contrary to the argument of the plaintiff that he had defective hearing aids which contributed to his condition. According to Berman, Rosen had gone through the spontaneous recovery stage after a stroke and when she saw him in November 1996 he had improved somewhat. Berman testified that Rosen had difficulty with problem solving such as to affect telling of time and unscrambling letters. Both parties agreed that when Berman saw Rosen in the year 2000 for a deposition in the lawsuit between him and his son Marc that his condition at that time was too remote from the date of the execution of the Will in 1996. Rosen may have known what he wanted to say but he had difficulty getting the words out. His condition in 2000 was the same as that of 1996 through 1997 although by the year 2000 he was able to compensate. Berman testified he could not read or answer more than one-word sentences. Berman stated his answers as yes would mean no and vice versa. Rosen tried to answer correctly and the questions would have to be asked two to three times and eventually he might give correct answers. Berman testified as to Rosen's cognitive skills that he was not able to do simple arithmetic or unable to keep a check book.

Rosen was able to sign his name from long-term memory. Rosen was unable to remember one-word terms five minutes after they were said, showing he had lost his short-term memory.

Berman in her reexamination in the year 2000 makes substantially the same finding as those made in the year 1996.

Valerie J. Denny, witness to the Will who had been employed at the Hurwitz law office, did not have any recollection of Rosen. Her job is to go in and sign the document. She never speaks or asks client about the Will. Denny was unaware that Rosen had a stroke and would have made inquiry if known.

The court concludes from all the evidence adduced at trial that the proponent of the Will executed August 15, 1996, has failed to meet her burden of proof to establish that Rosen had the requisite testamentary capacity to make his Will at that time.

The court need not address the special defense of undue influence having decided the issue of testamentary capacity.

Accordingly, the appeal is dismissed and judgment is entered in favor of the opponent to the Will dated August 15, 1996.

Case Review Question
Rosen v. Rosen, 2002 WL 1949690 (Conn.Super. 2002). If the will was denied probate, why would the son appeal still claiming undue influence?

PROBATE OF ESTATES

Probate describes the process of distributing the estate of a person who is deceased. Whether the person dies intestate or **testate,** the court determines what creditors are entitled to funds from the estate and what persons are entitled to receive a share of that which remains after debts of the estate are paid.

Originally, each state developed laws of probate. These laws established formal procedures for the handling of assets, evaluation and payment of persons claiming to be creditors of the deceased, and distribution of the remaining assets to heirs and persons named in wills. With the increasing mobility of our society, it is no longer unusual for a decedent's assets to be scattered throughout several states. Laws of property generally require that real property be governed by the law where it is located. However, the law of estates often requires the probate to take place in the jurisdiction where the decedent was domiciled at the time of death. In response to these and similar potential conflicts, the Uniform Probate Code was adopted. A majority of states have adopted the code, which establishes identical probate procedures and standards in each adopting state. In the past, it was possible that under differing state laws the rights of inheritance could vary dramatically. With the Uniform Code, however, the inheritance rights are determined in the same manner irrespective of where the property of the estate is located.

testate
Dying with a valid will.

FIGURE 13.2	**Testate**	**Intestate**
Typical Steps in Probate	1. Filing of petition* (to admit will and appointment of personal representative).	1. Filing of petition (to open estate and appointment of personal representative).
	2. Notification of heirs/beneficiaries.	2. Notification of heirs.
	3. Notice to creditors.	3. Notice to creditors.
	4. Inventory of estate.	4. Inventory of estate.
	5. Hearing on creditors' claims/payment of creditors.	5. Hearing on creditors' claims/payment of creditors.
	6. Final accounting of estate.	6. Final accounting of estate.
	7. Distribution of estate to beneficiaries in accordance w/terms of will.**	7. Distribution of estate in accordance w/laws of intestate succession.
	8. Hearing on creditors' claims/payment.	

*Law varies by state regarding when a hearing on a will contest occurs.

**In some cases, bequests cannot be honored because the property did not exist in the estate or the property was sold or otherwise used to satisfy creditors or the spouse's statutory rights.

Regardless of whether a state has adopted the Uniform Probate Code, the procedure for probating an estate follows some common basic steps (see Figure 13.2). When an individual dies, state law often requires that all assets be frozen (businesses owned by the person may continue). All bank accounts, stocks, bonds, and other financial transactions in the name of the deceased must stop. These assets are frozen until such a time as the court has finally determined the status of the deceased's estate (assets and liabilities).

The first step in probate is to file with the court the appropriate documents, which generally include the original copy of the will and affidavits by the witnesses that they signed the will after witnessing the signature of the testator.[26] If there is no will, a petition is presented to the court for probate of an intestate estate.

Before going any further, challenges to the validity of the will are made and decided. Once determined, the court decides whether to probate the estate testate (with a will) or intestate (without a will) according to procedures of state law. For all practical purposes, the estates are probated in the same manner until such time as it becomes necessary to distribute the assets of the estate.

The next step in probate is to appoint someone to oversee the assets of the estate during probate. In many states, such persons are called administrators (in the case of an intestate estate) or executors (in testate cases). These persons are responsible to oversee the estate. They must inventory the assets, pay creditors (when approved by the court), and generally protect the estate until it is finally distributed. The administrator/executor is a fiduciary of the estate[27] and is under an obligation to care for the assets of the estate and not to convert them to personal use or waste them. Any breach of the duty as a fiduciary can result in criminal charges.

If the deceased is survived by a spouse or minor children, claims can be made for living allowances—sums of money that the spouse and/or children can use for daily living expenses until such time as the estate is probated.[28] Statutes give some direction and judges have discretion as to what is a suitable allowance based upon the size of the estate and the needs of the spouse and children.

In addition to allowances, certain property in which the deceased may have had an interest is exempt from probate.[29] Generally, such property includes the primary residence of the deceased (if the surviving spouses and/or minor children reside there), an automobile, apparel, home furnishings, and other personal items specified by statute. The idea is to protect the family from claims against the property by creditors. Again, these allowances are generally effective only when there is a surviving spouse or minor children, and state statutes list exactly what may be considered exempt from the estate of the deceased.

After an executor or administrator is appointed, inventory of the estate is completed, and allowances to the spouse and children are handled, it is necessary to process the claims of creditors. In modern times, it seldom occurs that a person dies totally free of obligations. Thus, each state has procedures for notifying creditors of the deceased person. Often such procedures include publication in the legal section of the classified ads of local papers and other methods designed to reasonably alert potential creditors of the pending probate of the deceased's estate.[30]

Creditors are generally given a specific amount of time to come forward with claims against the estate—often several months to provide every opportunity for claims. Creditors who seek to have obligations paid by the estate must file the appropriate forms with the court that document the amount and nature of the claim. If the administrator or executor challenges the validity of the claim, a hearing is needed to determine whether it should be paid by the estate in whole or in part.

After the deadline has passed for making claims, the court considers all requests by creditors. Arrangements are made for the payment of the claims from the assets of the estate. Occasionally, it is necessary to sell items of property to obtain enough money to pay all of the creditors. This is so even if the sale of assets depletes items that were bequeathed in a will.

Following the payment of creditors, in a testate estate, many states give the surviving spouse the option of accepting what he or she is entitled to under the will or claiming what is known as a **forced share.** This law grants an absolute minimum to a surviving spouse, generally, a significant portion of the estate. The only exception to such a case might be if the spouse had previously waived the right to claim a forced share by signing an antenuptial agreement.

forced (elected) share
Right of a spouse to receive a statutorily designated percentage of a deceased spouse's estate.

Once all creditor claims and the claim by the spouse have been addressed, the court can proceed to distribute the estate. If there is a will, the estate will be distributed according to its terms so long as the assets bequeathed (granted in the will) are still in the estate. Each state has provisions that indicate how situations are to be dealt with when a bequeathed asset is no longer part of the estate (known as *ademption*) either because the testator disposed of it before death or because sale was necessary to satisfy the claims of creditors.

Most wills also have what is known as a residuary clause, which identifies a beneficiary to receive all remaining assets in the estate after bequests have been satisfied. This can cover a major portion of the estate if a person entitled to receive property died before the testator. Another possibility that could greatly increase the residuary clause is if additional assets were acquired after the execution of the will and no codicil was prepared to distribute them.

In the case of intestate estates, the common procedure is to reduce the assets to cash or appraise their value and distribute them according to the intestate method of distribution recognized by the state. As stated, this is generally going to be by per stirpes.

Ethical Considerations

As demonstrated in the discussion of will contests, ethics plays a significant role in probate law. A person's inheritance can be directly affected by the propriety of conduct exercised with respect to the testator. Probate courts are required to consider everything from an allegedly greedy family member or friend to cases of murder. Lawyers who prepare wills are under an obligation to take the necessary steps to eliminate doubts about the capacity of the testator, and personal representatives have the responsibility to care for and protect the inventory of the estate until it can be distributed. All of the preceding responsibilities inherently require ethical conduct, including both objectivity and fiduciary duty. The failure to undertake such conduct could result in a distribution of an estate that has no resemblance to the intent of the testator.

Question

If you are a paralegal and are asked to sign as a witness to a will of a client of your firm whom you have never met, what should you ask to ethically undertake the responsibility of witness?

Ethical Circumstance

Samantha is a probate lawyer who has been in practice for 25 years. She has one sister who has not been in touch with her family in over a decade and who has virtually no relationship with any of them. Samantha has cared diligently for her parents and after the death of her father, took her mother in to live with her. Samantha's mother wishes to execute a new will leaving her entire estate to Samantha. She asks Samantha to prepare the will. If she were to do so, she would open the door to Samantha's sister for a will contest. First, it would be unethical to prepare a will in which the preparer is the only heir. This is compounded by the fact that the only other surviving heir is being disinherited in the document. Regardless of the circumstances of the relationship with the disinherited child, it would be inappropriate for Samantha to prepare the will in which she doubles her inheritance. Even while the information provided would give a slanted view against the sister, no information has been given about Samantha, the condition of her mother, or any other relevant factors.

CHAPTER SUMMARY

It is hoped that this chapter has produced a better understanding of some of the complexities of estate law. From the discussion in the chapter, it should be clear that the death of someone does not affect only the family, employers, and insurance companies. Banks and all persons or entities with whom the deceased had any financial dealings may also be drawn into the probate process. Consequently, in any aspect of business or industry, it is important to understand the legal consequences of a person's death.

When a person leaves a will, the document must have been properly written and under fair and reliable circumstances. When irregularities exist in a will or no will was left by the deceased, the law of intestate succession takes effect. While this does not always account for all of the wishes of the deceased, it does provide an equitable distribution of the property to the heirs who are presumed to be the most likely candidates for devise had the testator left a valid will. If one wants control over the distri-bution of the estate, the solution is quite sim-ple. A proper will should be executed and kept current as changes occur in the estate or the people selected to inherit.

Regardless of whether a person dies testate or intestate, the probate courts serve the function of ensuring that the debts of the estate are paid and that the remaining assets of the estate are properly distributed. This is also accomplished with the assistance of an administrator in an intestate case and an executor in a testate estate. In either case, this party keeps the estate organ-ized and intact until the final order of the probate court is issued to dissolve and close the estate.

CHAPTER TERMS

forced share
guardianship
intestate

per capita distribution
per stirpes distribution

probate
testate

REVIEW QUESTIONS

1. How is per stirpes different from per capita distribution?
2. What is required for a valid will?
3. On what grounds can a will be contested?
4. What are the major steps in probate of an estate?
5. Define the term *estate*.
6. What are the duties of an administrator or an executor?
7. Who can be disinherited in a will?
8. Who can inherit by intestate succession?
9. Who determines the inheritance of a person charged with murdering the testator?
10. Explain the common requirements of an oral will in states where such a will is per-mitted.

RELEVANT LINKS

Estate planning page
www.estateattorney.com
Estate planning basics
www.estateplanbasics.com

Estate planning
www.estateplanning.com/new/homepage.shtml

INTERNET ASSIGNMENT 13.1

Consult the law of your jurisdiction using inter-net resources and locate the per stirpes distri-bution statute.

NOTES

1. *Martin v. Beatty*, 253 Iowa 1237, 115 N.W.2d 706 (1962).
2. Id.
3. *Richard Trust Co. v. Becvar*, 440 Ohio St.2d 219, 339 N.E.2d 830 (1975).
4. *United States v. Board of Com'rs of Public Schools of Baltimore City*, 432 F.Supp. 629 (D. Md. 1977).
5. 1a C.J.S., Adoption of Children, Sections 63–65.
6. 26A C.J.S., Descent and Distribution, Section 25.
7. 3 C.J.S., Bastards, Sections 24–29.
8. Id.
9. *Debus v. Cook*, 198 Ind. 675, 154 N.E. 484 (1926).
10. *Lofton v. Lofton*, 26 N.C. App. 203, 215 S.E.2d 861 (1975).
11. *McLendon v. McLendon*, 277 Ala. 323, 169 So.2d 767 (1964).
12. 79 Am.Jur.2d., Wills, Section 289.
13. Id., at Section 321.
14. *In re Bernatzki's Estate*, 204 Kan. 131, 460 P.2d 527 (1969).
15. 71 A.L.R.3d. 877.
16. *In re Erbach's Estate*, 41 Wis.2d 335, 164 N.W.2d 238 (1969).
17. *Wright v. Benttinen*, 352 Mass. 495, 226 N.E.2d 194 (1967).
18. *Solomon v. Dunlap*, 372 So.2d 218 (Fla.App. 1st Dist. 1979).
19. *Remon v. American Sec. &Trust Co.*, 110 U.S.App. D.C. 37, 288 F.2d 849 (1961).
20. *Estate of Krukenberg*, 77 Nev. 226, 361 P.2d 537 (1961).
21. *Crosby v. Alton Ochsner Medical Foundation*, 276 So.2d 661 (Miss. 1973).
22. 79 Am.Jur.2d, Wills, Sections 415–418.
23. 36 Am.Jr.2d, Proof of Facts, Section 109.
24. Id.
25. 92 A.L.R. 784.
26. 79 Am.Jur.2d, Wills, Section 407.
27. C.J.S. Wills, Section 1262.
28. Id.
29. Id., at Section 1311.
30. Id., at Section 1288.

For additional resources, please visit our Web site at www.westlegalstudies.com

CHAPTER 14

Criminal Law

CHAPTER OBJECTIVES

After reading this chapter, you should be able to:

- Distinguish actus reus and mens rea.

- Identify the parties to crime under common law principles.

- Identify the parties to crime under the Model Penal Code.

- Explain the distinction between theft and robbery.

- Define and distinguish the types of homicide.

- Discuss the concept of corporate criminal liability.

- Distinguish justifiable and excusable conduct.

criminal law

Law created and enforced by the legislature for the health, welfare, safety, and general good of the public.

As discussed in earlier chapters, **criminal law** applies to those situations wherein public standards are violated and the public welfare is thus injured. Consequently, the government prosecutes on behalf of the people, and penalties (with the exception of restitution) are paid or served to the public. While many crimes result in injury to specific victims, such injuries are personal and are typically dealt with in civil actions, such as those for tort or breach of contract. In addition, the government may prosecute for violation of the criminal law.

In the United States today, criminal law is statutory; that is, the legislature determines what will be criminal conduct. All crimes must be stated as such by statute before the conduct described will be considered criminal. When presented with the prosecution of a defendant based on a criminal statute, the judiciary examines the particular situation to determine whether it falls within the definition of the crime specifically charged. The legislature cannot enact a statute making certain conduct criminal and provide for punishment of persons who performed the conduct before it was declared illegal.

The process of punishing someone for conduct that occurred before it was made illegal is known as an ex post facto law and is prohibited by Article I, Section 9, of the U.S. Constitution. In the United States, a primary element of all criminal laws is the concept of fair warning. Under the Constitution, this means that one must be capable of determining that conduct would be considered criminal before the fact. Allowing persons to perform some act and then making that act a criminal offense and prosecuting them for it would not be fair. This does not mean that persons must actually be aware of the criminality of their conduct but only that they could have discovered it in advance and altered their course of action had they so chosen. Thus comes the saying, "Ignorance of the law is no excuse."[1] All persons are presumed to be responsible for ascertaining the rightfulness of their actions in advance. Generally, this is not a problem, because in everyday life, right and wrong are quite apparent to persons who act in accordance with the established societal standards.

The discussion that follows examines the basic principles of criminal law that exist today in the United States. Although criminal law encompasses offenses from the most minor traffic violation to capital murder, the focus will be on the elements of more serious crimes. Further, because a majority of the states have adopted the Model Penal Code as the basis of their criminal statutes, reference will be made to the Code when appropriate. States that have not adopted the Code rely on principles and definitions created in common law as the basis for criminal statutes. Accordingly, reference will be made to the basics of common law as well. States that are described as common law jurisdictions here are states that have established their statutes on the basis of common law principles developed and adopted by the courts. Jurisdictions identified as Model Penal Code states are those that follow the principles of the Code in their criminal law.

DEFINITIONS AND CATEGORIES OF CRIME

Categories of Crime

The two basic categories of crimes are felony and misdemeanor. A **felony** is any offense punishable by death or imprisonment exceeding one year. A **misdemeanor** is a crime punishable by fine or by detention of one year or less in a jail or an institution other than a penitentiary.[2] Many states have further divided felonies and misdemeanors into subclasses, usually for the purpose of sentencing. For example, crimes that are considered Class 1 misdemeanors may carry a heavier penalty than crimes considered Class 2 misdemeanors. Once the classes are established, the various crimes are placed within a class. The definition of the criminal offense itself will indicate the elements necessary for conviction of the crime. The category and subclass will indicate to the court what sentence should be imposed.

> **felony**
> Serious crime punishable by imprisonment in excess of one year or death.

> **misdemeanor**
> Criminal offense punishable by a fine or imprisonment of less than one year.

In some cases, a mandatory sentence is required. This means that the judge has no discretion to impose or suspend a sentence. The statute prescribes exactly what the sentence must be. In the absence of a mandatory sentence, the judge is usually given a range of punishment. The judge is responsible for imposing a sentence within this range that will adequately punish the defendant for the crime committed. This range allows the judge to take the circumstances of each case into account.

Definition of Crime and the Elements of Criminal Conduct

Crime has been defined as follows:

> A positive or negative act or omission that violates the penal law of the state or federal government; any act done in violation of those duties for which an individual offender shall make satisfaction to the public.[3] (Statsky, *Legal Thesaurus/Dictionary.* West, 1982)

In more general terms, criminal conduct refers to acts that may be injurious not only to an individual but, more importantly, also to society. All persons in society should have the right to expect and enjoy certain basic privileges, including privacy, ownership of property, and physical safety. When one person invades the basic rights of another, the basic rights of society are also invaded. Therefore, criminal laws have been set up to punish and deter individuals from such actions.

Criminal law differs from civil law in several respects. Perhaps the most significant is that in criminal law, the government protects and upholds society's rights. In a civil case, *individuals* bring lawsuits to seek remedy for their personal injuries. In criminal law, the *government* prosecutes the offender to punish the person who caused the injuries. Thus, the purpose and goals of the two are distinct, although civil and criminal issues may arise from the same situation.

Included in all crimes are two basic elements: the physical conduct and the mental conduct of the perpetrator necessary for violation of a penal law. The

actus reus
Element of physical conduct necessary to commit a criminal act.

mens rea
Mental state required as an element to convict one of criminal conduct.

the action

physical conduct is called the **actus reus,** a Latin term meaning "the wrongful act."[4] All crimes require an actus reus, although in some circumstances, the wrongful conduct can be a failure to act. The mental conduct of the person is known as the **mens rea,** which means "a guilty mind or guilty purpose."[5] The state of mind element requires a certain degree of intent to commit the wrongful act or omission.

Guilty mind

Actus reus. Under the Model Penal Code, three steps are followed in establishing the actus reus.[6] First, it must be shown that actual conduct, either affirmative or by omission (failing to act when one should have acted), took place. If the criminal conduct is an omission, it must be shown that the accused was capable of acting and was obligated directly or indirectly by law to act. Secondly, if the definition of the particular crime requires a result from the criminal conduct, that result must occur to prove actus reus. For example, to charge a person with battery, the victim must have suffered some actual physical injury as the result of unpermitted physical contact. This would satisfy the requirements of prohibited conduct and a result that is necessary to prove an offense of physical battery. Finally, under some statutes, certain circumstances must exist for conduct to constitute a crime. For example, by definition, the crime of burglary involves an unlawful or unpermitted entrance onto one's property. Thus, this is a required circumstance. If someone entered the property with permission, burglary could not be established.

APPLICATION 14.1

Act: Angelina was drag-racing her vehicle with another car on a city street when she struck and killed a pedestrian in her path.

Omission: Angelina was driving down a city street when she saw two pedestrians deep in conversation step into the path of her vehicle in the middle of the block. She did not change the path of the vehicle and as a result struck and killed the pedestrians.

Both situations describe criminal conduct. The first situation resulted indirectly in the death of the pedestrian as the result of an overt act of drag-racing. The second situation was one of legally driving but failing to exercise conduct necessary to avoid an accident.

Point for Discussion
◆   Why is physical conduct alone insufficient for criminal conduct? For example, what if in the omission, Angelina did not see the pedestrians because of a glare from the sun? Would the conduct still be criminal?

Mens rea.   The definition of each crime in the statutes requires a mens rea, which means "guilty purpose, wrongful purpose, criminal intent, guilty knowledge, willfulness."[7] Mens rea describes the state of mind or the degree of intent

Common Law	
General Intent: Driving above the speed limit.	
Specific Intent: Deliberately running down a pedestrian.	

Model Penal Code	
Negligence:	Driving above the speed limit.
Recklessness:	Driving while intoxicated.
Knowledge:	Driving a car that you know has unsafe tires (pieces of tread frequently tear away at speeds over 50 mph).
Purpose:	Deliberately running down a pedestrian.

FIGURE 14.1

Examples of Intent and Act under Common Law and under the Model Penal Code

that the actor has toward accomplishing a criminal goal. Under common law, the two basic subtypes of mens rea are known as specific intent and general intent. More serious crimes often require specific intent on the part of the actor to produce the result of the crime, whereas general intent crimes require a basic awareness of the likely consequences of one's actions.[8] Under the Model Penal Code, the state of mind required for commission of a crime is based on degrees of knowledge that range from criminal negligence to recklessness to knowledge, with the most serious crimes requiring a criminal purpose. Figure 14.1 shows examples of intent and act under common law and under the Model Penal Code.

In common law jurisdictions, the statute for a particular crime or group of crimes will generally indicate only whether the intent required is specific or general. Specific intent requires that the actor form the actual intent to achieve the result of the crime,[9] whereas general intent only requires knowledge of the likelihood of the result of the act.[10] Similarly, a Model Penal Code jurisdiction will indicate the degree of awareness in the language of the statute.[11] Statutes with a mens rea standard of criminal negligence require only that the actor knew or should have been aware of the probability that the action would produce a criminal result.[12] The standard of recklessness requires, in addition to a general awareness, that the actor demonstrate a disregard for the consequence of the action. Criminal knowledge requires an awareness that the conduct would undoubtedly produce a criminal result. Finally, criminal purpose requires premeditated intent to act in a manner consistent with criminal activity.

Criminal law follows a theory similar to tort law regarding transferred intent. In criminal law, although an individual may intend to injure or kill one person and, in fact, injures or kills an entirely different person, the intent is transferred to the person actually injured or killed. The intent and act were present. It need not be shown that the intent and act were meant for a particular person or object.

A few excepted crimes have no requirement of mens rea. Commission of such crimes can result in conviction irrespective of general or specific intent. These are known as crimes of strict liability. Strict liability crimes have none of the ordinary intent requirements. Under criminal statute that imposes strict liability, an individual can be prosecuted on the basis of the act irrespective of the presence of general or specific intent.

Strict liability laws are often established to protect the general good of society. Crimes of strict liability generally do not require a preconceived intent to do or not do a particular act.[13] Rather, they are usually applied when someone's preventive measures could greatly reduce social or public harm.

An example of a strict liability crime is a violation of the statutory duty of persons selling liquor to sell it only to persons over the age of 21. Such persons may not intend to break the law, but when they allow minors to be served liquor, they are endangering both the minors and the public at large. Simple monitoring of the persons served could totally prevent the harm that is presumed by law to result from the sale of liquor to minors. Therefore, if the duty to take preventive measures is minimal when compared to the social value of these measures, strict liability may be imposed. In other words, failure to take the preventive measures may result in conviction regardless of whether there was general or specific intent to cause the harm. Rather, the guilt is based on the failure to prevent the harm.

Assignment 14.1

For each of the following situations, indicate whether (1) the situation describes criminal intent, (2) the intent would be considered specific or general under common law standards, and (3) the intent would be considered purpose, knowledge, recklessness, or negligence under the Model Penal Code.

1. Cliff was out with friends to celebrate their college graduation. They became very drunk. Cliff climbed a fence and then attempted to climb a tower where several power lines converged. Near the top, he threw a golf club into the wires and caused a power outage for a large section of the city. He was unable to get down and when emergency personnel succeeded, he was arrested for trespassing and various other charges.

2. Kerry moves to a new community with his beloved pot-bellied pig. He is unaware that city ordinances prohibit livestock of any kind within city limits.

3. Jolene's friend Randy asks if she will water his plants in his vegetable garden while he is out of town for three weeks. Jolene is happy to help and even fertilizes the plants she considers to be tomato plants that are not blooming. She is arrested for growing marijuana.

4. Meg and Dennis agree to live together. Without Dennis's knowledge, Meg takes out a credit card in his name. She charges over $5,000 and then moves out. One of the things charged was a vacation that Meg told Dennis was a present for him. Dennis first became aware of what Meg had done when he was contacted by credit collection agencies over the credit card debt: Meg is eventually charged with fraud.

CASE

**COURT OF
APPEALS
OF WASHINGTON,
DIVISION 1.**

**STATE OF
WASHINGTON,
RESPONDENT, v.
MICHAEL JAMES**

Mcintosh, Appellant.
2002 WL 1832904
(Wash. App.)

AUG. 12, 2002.

Appeal from Superior Court of King County; Hon.
Douglas McBroom.

Sharon J. Blackford, Carolyn K. Morikawa,
Washington Appellate Project, Seattle, WA, for
Appellant.

Prosecuting Atty King County, King County
Prosecutor/Appellate Unit, Seattle, WA, for
Respondent.

PER CURIAM

Criminal intent to commit residential burglary may
be inferred from the facts and circumstances
surrounding a defendant's conduct where the
conduct leads to the logical conclusion that the
defendant had the requisite intent. A witness saw
Michael McIntosh loitering near her car and a few
minutes later attempting to kick open the back
doors of her neighbor's house, quickly leaving the
area when he was unsuccessful. These facts
support the jury's verdict that McIntosh intended
to enter the house and commit a crime inside. We
affirm McIntosh's conviction of attempted
residential burglary.

At about 4:30 p.m. on February 4, 2001, Claudia
Pittinger was in her kitchen. She looked out of the
window and saw a man lingering near her car. The
man was wearing a very distinctive green plaid
jacket, jeans, and tennis shoes. Pittinger went into
another room, and a few minutes later heard a loud
banging. When she looked outside, she saw the
same man standing on her next door neighbor

Lorraine Hughes' back deck, kicking the deck doors.
Pittinger did not recognize the man as an associate or
friend of Hughes, and she told her roommate to call
the police. The man then left the deck and quickly
walked away from the area.

Police officer Randolph Kyburz answered the
police dispatch and found McIntosh, who
matched the suspect description, at a wooded
area near Pittinger's house. When McIntosh saw
Officer Kyburz, he seemed startled. Another
officer brought Pittinger and then her roommate
to look at McIntosh; each identified him as the
man she had seen at Hughes' house. Hughes
testified at trial that she did not know McIntosh,
and did not give him permission to come onto
her property or kick her door. McIntosh contends
that the evidence was insufficient to prove intent
to enter or to commit a crime inside the house
because he was not carrying any stolen property
or burglary tools when he was stopped, because
there was no evidence of entry or attempted
entry, and because he was not trying to hide his
identity by wearing concealing clothing or trying
to gain entry at night. But the particular facts
used to show intent, such as possession of
burglary tools or wearing concealing clothing, are
not prerequisites for a finding of intent. Any set
of facts that establishes intent is sufficient. In
reviewing a charge of insufficient evidence, we
determine whether, after viewing the evidence in
the light most favorable to the State, any rational
trier of fact could have found the essential
elements of the crime charged beyond a
reasonable doubt. A challenge to the sufficiency
of the evidence admits the truth of the State's
evidence and all reasonable inferences that arise
from it.

To prove that McIntosh was guilty of attempted
residential burglary, the State had the burden of
proving that he intended to commit the burglary
and took a substantial step toward committing it.
An individual commits residential burglary by
entering or remaining unlawfully in a dwelling
other than a vehicle with the intent to commit a
crime inside. RCW 9A.52.025(1). The trier of fact

CASE

may infer intent from all the facts and circumstances surrounding the defendant's conduct or from conduct "that plainly indicates such intent as a matter of logical probability." *State v. Bergeron,* 105 Wn.2d 1, 20, 711 P.2d 1000 (1985) (quoting *State v. Bergeron,* 38 Wn.App. 416, 419, 685 P.2d 648 (1984), aff'd, 105 Wn.2d 1 (1985)).

Brooks, 107 Wn.App. at 929.

Brooks, 107 Wn.App. at 929 (citing *State v. Lewis,* 69 Wn.2d 120, 123, 417 P.2d 618 (1966)).

The jury in this case found that McIntosh intended to enter the house and commit a crime inside. After reviewing the record, we conclude that the facts support the jury's decision. Pittinger testified that she knew her neighbors and their usual visitors well, and did not recognize McIntosh as one of them. Hughes testified that she did not know McIntosh nor did she give him permission to be on her property or kick her door. Pittinger saw McIntosh approach not the front door, as a visitor would be expected to do, but the back door, which was less open to the public view. Pittinger saw McIntosh kicking the deck doors with enough force to make a noise audible to Pittinger inside her house. The act of kicking a door leads logically to the conclusion that one is trying to open it and gain entry. Going to the back door and

trying to kick it open leads logically to the conclusion that one is trying to commit a crime inside, and is a substantial step toward that objective. In addition, McIntosh quickly left the area when he could not get the door open. These facts support the jury's verdict, and we affirm McIntosh's conviction.

McIntosh relies on several cases to argue that, because the facts in this case are different, they do not support the jury's verdict. In *State v. Bencivenga,* 137 Wn.2d 703, 974 P.2d 832 (1999), defendant was trying to pry open a locked store; in *State v. Berglund,* 65 Wn.App. 648, 829 P.2d 247 (1992), defendant broke a window and tried to pull out more glass; in *State v. West,* 18 Wn.App. 686, 571 P.2d 237 (1977), defendants were trying to pry open the back door of a store; in Bergeron, Bencivenga, and West, defendants wore clothing that concealed their identities. But these exact facts are not required to prove the crime, and the facts set out above are ample proof of the requisite intent.

Case Review Question

State v. McIntosh, 2002 WL 1832904 (Wash.App. Div. 1 2002).

Would the result likely be different if there was evidence that the defendant knew the occupant of the residence?

PARTIES TO CRIME

Usually, one thinks of a criminal as the person who actually committed the criminal act that caused injury or damage. Many times, however, persons act together to commit a crime. This may involve cooperation in the criminal act or assistance before or after the crime. In criminal law, one who assists in a crime can also be accused and convicted of criminal conduct. Since common law principles and the Model Penal Code are somewhat different on this point, they are discussed separately. The issue of cooperation in a joint enterprise, commonly referred to as conspiracy, is discussed later.

Under common law, there are four basic categories of participants in criminal conduct. Specific terms describe the various types of involvement by the principals—persons who are actually involved in the primary criminal conduct[14]—and the accessories—persons who aid the principals before or after the crime.[15] Common law defines two types of principals and two types of accessories.

Principal in the First Degree

The principal in the first degree is the party or parties who actually take part in a criminal act. It is necessary that they perform the actus reus and that they have adequate mens rea at the time they commit the crime. Under a variation of the definition, persons who can be charged as principals in the first degree include those who possess the mens rea but convince another to perform the actual physical conduct. This would include situations of coercion, threat, trickery or involve trained animals.

The person who commits the crime

Principal in the Second Degree

Principals in the second degree are persons who actually assist in the physical commission of a crime or persons whose conduct enables the principal in the first degree to commit the crime. If the conduct of a party is required to complete the crime successfully, either at the moment of the crime or immediately before or after, that person would be considered a principal in the second degree, for example, someone who makes deliveries for a dealer of illegal drugs. The person does not obtain, sell, or perhaps even use the drugs, but by assisting in the delivery of the drugs, he or she is enabling the crime to be completed.

Accessory before the Fact

Accessories before the fact are those persons who enable or aid the principal to prepare for a crime. Their conduct may consist of providing the principal a place to plan or wait until the time has arrived for the actual commission of the crime. A very famous example involved the owners of a boarding house in Washington, D.C., who supposedly knew the assassination of President Abraham Lincoln was being planned. These persons were convicted and subsequently hanged for their participation in the assassination.

Accessory after the Fact

Persons who assist in a successful escape or concealment of criminal activity are accessories after the fact. This category includes anyone who is aware of the criminal activity and aids the principal in successfully avoiding prosecution. Conduct of this type ranges from giving the principal a place to hide to rendering medical care or misleading authorities about the principal or facts of the crime. Persons who are closely related to the principal are an exception to the rule. Under common law, it was considered detrimental to family unity to prosecute someone for aiding his or her spouse or children. Therefore, these persons could not be charged as accessories. This exception is still recognized in most states. Additionally, a person charged as a principal cannot also be charged as an accessory.

Usually, the division into principals and accessories applies to felonies. In the commission of misdemeanors, all who are involved are considered equally guilty. Common law also held that accessories could not be prosecuted, convicted, and sentenced unless the principal was convicted. Today, most of the jurisdictions that apply common law rather than the Model Penal Code no longer require the conviction of the principal prior to the conviction of the accessory.

Another present-day change in these jurisdictions is that principals in the first and second degree and accessories before the fact are generally considered principals. Conduct that aids the preparations for a crime or enables a crime to be committed is considered as serious as the actual commission of the crime. Modern laws tend to grade the involvement of the principals and accessories as a way of determining the severity of punishment to be imposed. Thus, one who actually committed the crime may be graded more seriously than an assistant.

Parties to Crime under the Model Penal Code

The Model Penal Code recognizes principals, accessories, and persons who commit offenses of obstructing governmental operations.[16] The Code defines principals as persons who actually possess the mens rea and who either commit the required actus reus or control the commission of the actus reus by such means as coercion, trickery, or manipulation. Accessories are persons who agree to aid or actually aid in the completion of the crime, including actual physical assistance or mere encouragement. Persons who commit offenses of obstructing governmental operations can be prosecuted for assisting in the escape of the principal or the accessory or the concealment of the crime.

Under the Model Penal Code, it is not necessary that the principal be convicted before the accessory or the person who has obstructed governmental operations. Instead, each is judged on his or her own criminal conduct, although the seriousness of the penalty may be adjusted to reflect the amount of criminal involvement of the individual. This is done in much the same way as the trend toward grading the severity of each person's involvement under modern common law.

The primary difference between modern common law jurisdictions and Model Penal Code jurisdictions lies in terminology. With a few adjustments, the basic concepts are the same, as shown in Figure 14.2.

		Common Law	Model Penal Code
FIGURE 14.2 Basic Concepts of Modern Common Law and Model Penal Code	**Actus Reus**	Physical conduct	Physical conduct or encouragement of physical conduct
	Mens Rea	General intent Specific intent	Negligence Recklessness Purpose
	Parties	Principal 1st degree Principal 2nd degree Accessory before fact Accessory after fact	Knowledge Principal Accessory Obstructing governmental operations

Under Modern Common Law, these are also considered equal principals.

In what category would the individuals in the following situations be placed under (1) common law, (2) modern common law, and (3) the Model Penal Code, or would there be no criminal liability?

1. Chloe accepted ecstasy on a regular basis from her boyfriend Sean. She often passed some on to her friends as well. She never paid for the drug or accepted payment when she distributed it. Sean had a thriving business of selling ecstasy at Raves.

2. Same situation as above except on one occasion, of all the tablets Sean sold as ecstasy, only about half were real. The others were fake and contained no drugs whatsoever.

3. Cole informed two friends that his family would be out of town on a certain date. Cole also provided the friends with the code to the alarm system in case his friends wanted to hang out at the house. While Cole's family was gone, the friends burglarized the house and stole many valuable items.

4. Same situation as above except that Cole knew of the intent of his friends and even helped them sell the items upon his return in exchange for a portion of the proceeds.

5. Barbara and Sharon had a plan in which Barbara would distract store clerks asking lots of question about merchandise while Sharon stole in another part of the store. Sharon then used the money made from selling stolen merchandise to pay the rent on the apartment she shared with Barbara.

ELEMENTS OF SERIOUS CRIMES

The following discussion explains basic elements that must be present before an individual can be convicted of some of the more common crimes in our society. In addition to submitting the required proof of criminal conduct by the accused, the legal system must follow the criminal procedures outlined in Chapter 15. The laws and procedures are designed to avoid conviction of innocent persons based on improper or unfair evidence of criminal conduct.

Inchoate Offenses

Inchoate offenses[17] are crimes that occur prior to but facilitate or enable other crimes. Inchoate crimes include conspiracy to commit, attempts to commit, and solicitation to commit criminal acts. Each is addressed individually.

Conspiracy to commit criminal acts.   The crime of conspiracy involves the cooperation of two or more people in planning and completing a crime as a joint undertaking.[18] Conspiracy in itself is a crime distinct from the additional criminal act that is the common goal of the parties. As a result, conspiracy has its own mens rea and actus reus, and a defendant can be charged with both the completed criminal act and conspiracy to commit that act (as opposed to attempt and solicitation, which "merge" with the criminal act if it is completed).

The mens rea of conspiracy under common law requires specific intent. Each party to the conspiracy must have intent to agree with the other parties. Further, the agreement must be to accomplish something that is illegal. Regardless of whether the crime is actually committed, persons who have agreed to work toward a common goal that is illegal are guilty of conspiracy.

The actus reus is perhaps the most difficult element to establish in a prosecution for conspiracy. There is seldom any concrete evidence, such as a contract, that will establish that the persons have taken steps to agree to a common criminal goal. Generally, the jury must rely on evidence of the actions of the parties to the conspiracy. The prosecution's description of the acts of these parties must convince the jury beyond a reasonable doubt that the parties had no other purpose than to conspire to commit a criminal act. Many statutes today have extended this burden of proving actus reus beyond the common law. Today, most statutes require at least one of the parties to perform some physical act that demonstrates his or her intent to be part of a conspiracy.

Under the Model Penal Code, the elements of conspiracy are much more specific. Proof of the actus reus can be shown in one of three ways. There must be evidence that the conspirators assisted in planning, soliciting, attempting, or committing the actual criminal offense that is the goal of the conspiracy. In contrast, the mens rea of conspiracy required in the Model Penal Code is much less stringent. There need only be evidence that each person accused entered the agreement with the purpose of promoting or facilitating a goal of criminal conduct.[19]

The crime of attempt.   Under statutes in all states, an attempt to commit a crime is considered criminal. An attempt takes place when the person has the mens rea (state of mind) to commit a particular crime and indicates a willingness to complete the crime. For some reason, however, the actus reus is never completed.[20] As a consequence, the person cannot be convicted of that particular crime. It is not in the interest of society's goals, however, to condone even attempts at crime. Moreover, sometimes injuries result from a failed attempt, for example, attempted murder. A would-be murderer should not go free simply because the victim was fortunate enough to live through a violent crime designed to produce death. Consequently, if someone takes material steps toward such a crime, attempt can be charged.

The question the courts must determine in cases of attempt is, How far must an individual go toward the commission of a crime before the individual is considered guilty of actually attempting the crime? Several tests have been employed in common law. Perhaps the most frequently applied today is that of proximity. The court considers how close the defendant was to completing the crime. The closer a defendant was, the less likely he or she would have turned away before completion. Adequate proximity to completion of the crime means that it is very likely that the defendant would have completed the crime if given the opportunity. This is the point at which an attempt can be said to occur.

In a variation on this rule, the court examines the individual and determines whether that particular individual would be likely to commit the particular crime. The court may also examine whether the defendant had control over all of the necessary elements to commit the crime. Whatever specific questions are applied, the basic issue remains the same. Given sufficient opportunity, is it likely beyond a reasonable doubt that the person would have completed the crime?

Unquestionably, a person cannot be convicted of attempt if his or her actual goal was not criminal. Even if the individual believes that his or her conduct will constitute a crime, if in fact it does not, there can be no conviction of attempt. Similarly, if a person attempts to commit a crime but his or her actions in reality do not constitute a crime, there can be no conviction of attempt. However, a defendant who takes steps toward the commission of the crime and would have committed the crime except for some intervening fact or force can be convicted of attempt.

APPLICATION 14.2

Jamal decides to kill his former girlfriend. He invites her over to talk about things and offers her a drink. Jamal has laced the drink with his mother's window cleaner. He is certain this will poison the girl. The cleaner consists of vinegar and water. The girl doesn't like the taste, doesn't finish the drink, or even become sick. In this instance, no crime is committed. The conduct could not have resulted in the death of the girl as vinegar is not toxic. Assume, however, that Jamal put another household cleaner in the drink, and the girl again did not like the taste and did not finish the drink. In this instance, Jamal attempted and completed the necessary steps to adequately poison his former girlfriend to death. However, his crime was incomplete. In this situation, he could in fact be convicted of attempting the crime of murder. (An alternative charge might be assault and battery, which in fact was completed.)

Point for Discussion
- Would either outcome have changed if the girl had become very ill?

If the intended crime is completed, a person cannot be convicted of the offense of attempt as well as of the actual crime. It is considered that an attempt becomes part of the actual crime when it is complete.[21] Thus, the two are merged into one crime. The usual terminology is that the attempt is a "lesser included offense"; that is, it is included in the greater and more serious offense of the crime. If for some reason the crime cannot be proven, a person may still be charged with and, in many cases, convicted of attempt.

For the crime of attempt, the Model Penal Code requires that the actor do much more than simply prepare for criminal conduct. The actor must take what would be considered a "substantial step" toward completion of the crime. This substantial step is something that makes the crime more than a contemplation. At this point, the elements of the crime are within the control of the defendant and can be completed with the defendant's further actions.

The mens reas required of attempt under the Model Penal Code is more complex. The prosecution must show that the defendant had the intent to attempt the crime and must also prove any requirements of mens rea for commission of the crime itself. Thus, in a trial, the jury must look to the mens rea of the crime that the defendant attempted and determine whether all of the mens rea requirements were met. Then the jury must determine whether the defendant had the specific intent to actually commit the criminal act. In some situations, this may be redundant.

The Model Penal Code is somewhat more liberal than the common law regarding charges and conviction. In common law, one must be charged with attempt or the actual crime or both. If convicted of the crime, however, one cannot be convicted of attempt, and vice versa. Although the result under the Model Penal Code is the same, the required procedure is slightly different. The Code permits a person to be charged with only the crime. However, if the jury finds that the person did not complete the crime but did attempt it, the person can be convicted of attempt. There is no requirement that the individual be formally charged with attempt in addition to the charge for the actual crime.

The crime of solicitation.   Solicitation has been defined as the act of enticing, inviting, requesting, urging, or ordering someone to commit a crime.[22] It differs from conspiracy or attempt. In conspiracy, two or more persons work together to achieve a common goal of criminal conduct. The crime of attempt describes the acts under the control of an individual toward completion of a crime. Solicitation is a crime wherein an individual seeks to persuade another individual to commit a crime. The trend in common law states is to adopt the Model Penal Code view of solicitation. The Code allows conviction and punishment of one who solicits any criminal offense, no matter how minor. The traditional common law approach was to punish only solicitation of more serious offenses against society.

At common law, conviction can be had for anyone who attempts to communicate with another in such a way that the other person will be encouraged to commit a crime. It is not necessary that the other person receive the communication or commit the crime. Solicitation is based on the premise that it is wrong in and of itself to willfully encourage criminal conduct. The actus reus is any conduct that would demonstrate such encouragement.

Solicitation is considered a specific intent offense in common law. The person who solicits a crime by another must intend that the crime actually be committed. It is not required that the person who solicits understand that solicitation itself is considered criminal conduct. Rather, it need only be shown that the person knows that the conduct that is being encouraged is criminal.

The Model Penal Code definition of actus reus in solicitation is quite similar to the common law interpretation. The primary difference is that under the Model Penal Code, a person needs to intend and demonstrate the intent to communicate the encouragement. As with common law, it is not required that the intent actually be communicated to the other person.

The mens rea for solicitation in the Model Penal Code requires that the person be aware that the encouragement is for a criminal act. Further, to prosecute for solicitation, it must be proven that a person has the intent that would be required to actually commit the offense that is encouraged.

In addition to conviction for solicitation, in common law states, the accused may also be convicted of being an accessory before the fact. Under the Model Penal Code, a person cannot be convicted as an accessory or as a conspirator in addition to being convicted for solicitation.

Miscellaneous Offenses

Some crimes, though categorized in some states as felonies, by definition are distinctly inchoate in characteristics. Such acts directly enable a person to commit a crime. Like the crimes previously discussed, these acts are such an integral part of creating the opportunity for other criminal conduct that they become crimes in and of themselves. Common examples include the illegal possession of weapons or the possession of such large quantities of drugs that it is probable that the drugs will be distributed illegally. Another example of such an offense is burglary. Traditionally, burglary was an offense that consisted of forcibly entering the home of another at night with the intent of committing a felony within the residence. This definition has been somewhat modified in many states under present-day statutes. Today, definitions of burglary are much more general and often include any unpermitted entry (regardless of whether it requires force) into the property of another (regardless of whether it is the home, automobile, or other property) at any time of day with the intent to commit a felony within the property.[23] This sounds remarkably inchoate in its definition. Burglary is an act that creates the opportunity for felonious conduct.

In cases of burglary, it is no longer required that the intended felony actually occur. Society wants to discourage unpermitted entry into the property of another with additional criminal intent. Such unpermitted entry is a necessary precursor to the commission of a felony on the property. Thus, if burglary is punished, perhaps persons will be deterred from entering private property to commit felonies. In any event, such persons can be punished for any actions they take that would enable the felonious conduct.

The Model Penal Code also recognizes these offenses and punishes them. Generally, punishment for all inchoate offenses under the Model Penal Code includes a range of severity that approaches the penalty for the actual commission of the more serious offense that might follow a conspiracy, attempt, solicitation, burglary, or other inchoate offense. Consequently, the Model Penal Code does not recognize any offenses that are perhaps beyond the inchoate offense but are not quite completion of the more serious offense. Some common law states have such intermediate stages. Under the Model Penal Code, the definition of an inchoate offense includes all conduct leading to the moment the subsequent offense is actually completed.

Under common law, categories of homicide might include attempted murder, assault with intent to kill, and murder. Assault with intent to kill might describe a situation wherein a person actually inflicts deadly force on an individual but the individual survives. It is more than a mere attempt, but the actual murder was not achieved.

Under the Model Penal Code, a person may be charged with attempted murder or murder. The definition of attempt is broad enough—and the penalties allowed are severe enough—to include the situation where the accused comes within a breath of murder.

Felony Crimes

As the preceding discussion indicates, the common law jurisdictions and Model Penal Code jurisdictions regard the same basic types of conduct as criminal. The distinction between the two is generally in the way the crimes are formally defined. The following sections discuss some additional felony crimes that occur with some frequency. The definitions are based on basic principles of law, with the understanding that each state may have its own definitions and penalties.

Assault.   In a civil case, assault is considered to be action threatening an unpermitted physical contact. However, in the criminal sense, assault often includes actual physical contact and is synonymous with civil battery. Depending on the nature of the particular offense, assault is often a felony crime. Generally, an assault that is committed with a weapon or with the intent to do dangerous bodily harm or that results in serious bodily harm will be treated as a felony. When criminal laws differentiate assault from battery, assault is generally considered to be more consistent with the civil definition. Thus, criminal assault would be an act that causes fear of immediate physical harm through unpermitted physical contact.[24]

Battery.   Many times in criminal law, the terms *assault* and *battery* are interchangeable. When a distinction is made, battery is considered to be the unlawful contact with another person. Such contact can be direct or through an instrument such as a weapon.[25] Like assault, the extent of the contact and the actor's intent will often dictate whether the crime will be prosecuted as a felony or a misdemeanor.

Usually, the mens rea required for assault/battery is one of general intent. A person need only be aware that his or her conduct is likely to result in an unpermitted physical contact. Of course, if a more specific intent is present, that would also be sufficient, but the minimum requirement would be only a reasonable awareness.

Theft, robbery, and larceny.   In ordinary usage, many laypersons interchange the terms *burglary, theft,* and *robbery.* However, as previously indicated, burglary does not include the taking of another person's property, only the invasion of it. Similarly, theft and robbery are distinct terms, whereas theft and larceny are often synonymous in criminal law.

Theft.   Theft occurs when a party unlawfully obtains the property of another with the intent to dispossess that person of the property.[26] The intent required can be merely to dispossess, to convert the property to one's own uses, or to convey the property to another. As long as the intent is to deprive an owner of the use, possession, or ownership of property, the mens rea requirement is satisfied.

In many jurisdictions, the value of the property influences the severity of the punishment. The theft of more valuable property, usually in excess of a stated dollar amount, is considered grand larceny and is a felony. The theft of property that is valued below the stated dollar amount is considered to be petty (also known as *petit*) larceny and is usually considered to be a misdemeanor.

Robbery.   The most serious offense involving unlawfully taking property is robbery. To commit a robbery, one must deprive an owner of property by the use of force or threats of force. The robber must either use physical violence or demonstrate to the owner that unless the property is turned over, physical violence will be used to obtain the property.[27] Thus, robbery must be committed in the presence of the owner. If the owner were not present to perceive the force or threats, there would be no necessity for their use. Robbery includes situations where physical force or weapons are used or threatened against victims. Because robbery is considered to be a crime of violence, the penalties are generally more severe than those for larceny.

Homicide.   When a person is killed as the result of conduct or omission by another person, a homicide has been committed. If there is no legal justification or excuse for such conduct, a criminal homicide has been committed. Only criminal homicide can result in conviction and punishment. Legal justification or excuse includes situations in which the actor's conduct is considered non-criminal, generally, because the required mens rea for a criminal homicide is not present.

There are various types of homicide. Most often they are described as manslaughter and murder. Manslaughter is usually considered a less serious offense than murder because it is death caused without malice aforethought—a mental state that includes the intent to inflict deadly force. Manslaughter is further broken down into two categories: voluntary and involuntary.

Voluntary manslaughter.   Voluntary manslaughter is applicable in situations where the death of another was intentional but where special circumstances existed.[28] An example of such a case is a crime of passion, where a person loses all ability to reason as a result of extreme provocation by the deceased. It must be established that the deceased did something so outrageous to provoke the defendant that it is understandable that the defendant lost the ability to reason and, in the heat of the moment, attacked the deceased. Common situations include injury to one's family or to the marital relationship. One point is clear. The provocation must have been of a type so extraordinary that a jury could consider the defendant's conduct reasonable. This does not mean that the charges against the defendant will be dropped. Rather, it explains why the defendant is not charged with murder.

If the defendant has time to consider the action before it is taken, a charge of voluntary manslaughter would be inappropriate. The key element that separates murder from voluntary manslaughter is that in the latter case, the defendant did not have time to consider the ramifications of the actions about to be taken. In murder, there is time for someone to consider and plan the death or injury that ultimately produces death of another. Thus, the longer the period of time that elapses between the provocation and the act of killing, the more likely the charge will be murder.

Involuntary manslaughter.   Involuntary manslaughter occurs when one person is responsible for the death of another because of gross and extreme negligence or recklessness and without the intent to kill or inflict bodily harm.[29] Such conduct is considered to show total disregard for the safety or well-being of others. In some states, death caused as the result of driving while intoxicated is considered to be involuntary manslaughter. However, many states have a separate statute for this, such as vehicular or motor vehicle homicide. Another example of involuntary manslaughter is hunting in or around a populated area. When negligence and recklessness are differentiated by statute, negligence is treated as extreme carelessness, whereas recklessness involves a total disregard for others. Although both are types of involuntary manslaughter, generally the penalties are more severe for reckless homicide than for negligent homicide.

Reckless or negligent homicide may occur during the commission of another crime that is a misdemeanor (e.g., death caused by a drunk driver or as the result of reckless driving), or it may occur as the result of some careless act not intended to be criminal. The latter often includes situations that are the result of circumstance, although created by negligence (e.g., a person who target shoots in his or her backyard in a suburban area). Assume in such a case that a neighbor is hit and killed by a stray bullet. There was never any intent to commit a crime, and certainly no intent to kill the neighbor. Nevertheless, discharging deadly weapons in a populated area would be considered extremely careless.

Manslaughter under the Model Penal Code.   The Model Penal Code recognizes the same basic principles regarding manslaughter. Although it does not use the terms *voluntary* and *involuntary*, it grades the degree of the offense and the severity of the penalty in accordance with situations that are reckless or negligent. The Code places emphasis not on the actual provocation but on the actual emotional condition of the defendant at the time death was caused. If the defendant was in a mental state such that control was impossible, the death could be considered voluntary manslaughter. Under this application, there is no need to examine whether the defendant had time to cool off after the provocation. The entire question turns on the defendant's actual mental state at the time of the killing.

Murder.   As indicated previously, murder is a premeditated act committed with specific malicious intent. Contrary to what the community-used term *with malice aforethought* would suggest, the actor need not have thought out a careful plan to kill with hatred. Rather, the term describes the state of mind of a person who is aware of what he or she is doing and who can make the choice not to act. Many states that apply this common law theory or murder break up the definition by varying states of mind.

The term *degree* is often used to indicate various categories of murder. Murder in the first degree is usually the most serious felony. It often requires that the actor have the preconceived intent to kill and carry out that intent to fruition. This differs from murder in the second degree, which often describes a situation where a person intends to inflict serious physical harm on the victim and death follows. Finally, there is murder as the result of recklessness that is so great that the actor had no reasonable basis to believe that the death of another would not result from the action. The risk of death is more than substantial: It is a near certainty that a person will die from the actor's conduct.

Felony Murder Rule.   Some states employ an additional category of murder known as the Felony Murder Rule. This rule has two basic requirements: (1) The actor must be engaged in the commission of a dangerous felony, and (2) the acts pertaining to the felony must proximately cause the death of another.[30] Further, in some states, if the victim is injured but dies as a proximate result of those injuries within one year, the actor can be charged with murder, even though other circumstances may have contributed to the death.

◆ APPLICATION 14.3

Keith and Cassandra commit a string of robberies. During one of them, Cassandra stabs a store clerk in the chest. The store clerk suffers serious injuries to her lungs and airway and as a result develops chronic health problems. She is hospitalized several times during the months after the stabbing. Approximately 11 months after the initial injury, she develops pneumonia and succumbs. In recognizing jurisdictions, Cassandra can be charged with felony murder because the death of the clerk was the proximate result of the initial stabbing.

Point for Discussion
◆   Explain why the charge would be murder if the death was the result of pneumonia rather than the stabbing.

Assignment 14.3

Using the facts in Application 14.3, respond to the following:

1. What would the criminal charge be if the clerk died from the stab wounds?

2. What would the criminal charge be if the clerk died from the stab wounds after lingering in a coma for 13 months?
3. What would the criminal charge be if the clerk died from pneumonia as the result of the lung injuries if this particular bout of pneumonia did not strike until 13 months after the stabbing?

Murder under the Model Penal Code.   The Model Penal Code follows the same basic premise as common law when determining guilt in cases of murder. Murder that results from the intent to inflict fatal injuries is defined in much the same way as murder in the first degree under common law.[31] The Model Penal Code also provides for situations of serious bodily harm or great recklessness that produces death, although these two situations are considered an offense of the same severity under the Code. The primary difference is that the Model Penal Code contains no provision for the Felony Murder Rule. The reasoning is that the person should be charged with murder or manslaughter in addition to the felony rather than be charged with a combined single charge of felony and murder. It is reasoned that the actual guilt and mens rea can be more easily and fairly determined by this method.

Rape.   In recent years, the crime of rape has received a great deal of notoriety for a variety of reasons. Although the crime of rape went largely unreported in the past, changes in the roles of women in our society along with rape shield statutes have contributed to an increasing number of reports of sexual assault. Previously, it was not uncommon for the entire sexual history of the victim to be disclosed at the trial of the defendant in an attempt to show that the victim somehow encouraged the defendant's conduct. However, a majority of states have enacted rape shield statutes that prevent such information from being introduced as evidence. Women also are now coming forward with charges of acquaintance rape (date rape), which was virtually unheard of in the past. The government now recognizes that rape need not, and usually does not, occur between total strangers.

Rape (also known as a type of sexual assault in some jurisdictions) is the forcible act of sexual intercourse by a male against a female without consent of the female. It is a crime in all jurisdictions, and penalties range from a few years to life in prison, depending upon the circumstances. The act of rape or even consensual intercourse with a minor typically carries even heavier penalties. When consensual intercourse occurs between an adult and a minor (to whom the adult is not married), the crime of statutory rape has been committed. The presumption is that the minor is incapable of making a proper decision as to whether to consent to intercourse, and therefore, intercourse with a minor is criminal per se. The age at which a minor is presumed to have sufficient capacity to consent to intercourse varies among jurisdictions. In some jurisdictions, the fact that the minor lied about his or her age also is an adequate defense to the charge of statutory rape.

PUNISHMENT

Common law and the Model Penal Code have similar concepts of punishment. Under each, the general rule is that a greater degree of specific intent will result in a more severe range of punishment for the convicted defendant. With respect to the most extreme punishment—death—the Model Penal Code includes it but neither advocates nor discourages it. The provision for the death penalty is included as an acknowledgment that the death penalty is part of American criminal law at this time. The position of common law has varied on the issue of capital punishment. At this time, it is considered an acceptable form of punishment by the government for certain types of crime.

Other punishments typically include imprisonment, monetary fines, community service (time spent doing activities that benefit the community at large), and restitution (repayment to a victim for injury to his or her person or property). Whatever the punishment, one constant remains: The punishment must not be cruel or unusual for the crime committed according to the Eighth Amendment. For example, the death penalty has been determined to be cruel and unusual punishment for the crime of rape, although it is still permissible for other crimes, such as murder.

 CASE

COKER v. GEORGIA

433 U.S. 584, 97 S.Ct. 2861, 53 L.Ed.2d 982 (1977).

Mr. Justice **WHITE** announced the judgment of the Court and filed an opinion in which Mr. Justice **STEWART,** Mr. Justice **BLACKMUN,** and Mr. Justice **STEVENS,** joined.

Georgia Code Ann. § 26-2001 (1972) provides that '(a) person convicted of rape shall be punished by death or by imprisonment for life, or by imprisonment for not less than one nor more than 20 years.' (The section defines rape as having 'carnal knowledge of a female, forcibly and against her will. Carnal knowledge in rape occurs when there is any penetration of the female sex organ by the male sex organ.') Punishment is determined by a jury in a separate sentencing proceeding in which at least one of the statutory aggravating circumstances must be found before the death penalty may be imposed. Petitioner Coker was convicted of rape and sentenced to death. Both the conviction and the sentence were affirmed by the Georgia Supreme Court. Coker was granted a writ of certiorari, 429 U.S. 815, 97 S.Ct. 56, 50 L.Ed.2d 75, limited to the single claim, rejected by the Georgia court, that the punishment of death for rape violates the Eighth Amendment, which proscribes 'cruel and unusual punishments' and which must be observed by the States as well as the Federal Government. *Robinson v. California,* 370 U.S. 660, 82 S.Ct. 1417, 8 L.Ed.2d 758 (1962).

I

While serving various sentences for murder, rape, kidnapping, and aggravated assault, petitioner escaped from the Ware Correctional Institution near Waycross, Ga., on September 2, 1974. At approximately 11 o'clock that night, petitioner entered the house of Allen and Elnita Carver

CASE

through an unlocked kitchen door. Threatening the couple with a 'board,' he tied up Mr. Carver in the bathroom, obtained a knife from the kitchen, and took Mr. Carver's money and the keys to the family car. Brandishing the knife and saying 'you know what's going to happen to you if you try anything, don't you,' Coker then raped Mrs. Carver. Soon thereafter, petitioner drove away in the Carver car, taking Mrs. Carver with him. Mr. Carver, freeing himself, notified the police; and not long thereafter petitioner was apprehended. Mrs. Carver was unharmed.

Petitioner was charged with escape, armed robbery, motor vehicle theft, kidnapping, and rape. Counsel was appointed to represent him. Having been found competent to stand trial, he was tried. The jury returned a verdict of guilty, rejecting his general plea of insanity. A sentencing hearing was then conducted in accordance with the procedures dealt with at length in *Gregg v. Georgia*, 428 U.S. 153, 96 S.Ct. 2909, 49 L.Ed.2d 859 (1976), where this Court sustained the death penalty for murder when imposed pursuant to the statutory procedures.

Ga.Code § 26-3102 (Supp. 1976):

'Capital offenses; jury verdict and sentence.

'Where, upon a trial by jury, a person is convicted of an offense which may be punishable by death, a sentence of death shall not be imposed unless the jury verdict includes a finding of at least one statutory aggravating circumstance and a recommendation that such sentence be imposed. Where a statutory aggravating circumstance is found and a recommendation of death is made, the court shall sentence the defendant to death. Where a sentence of death is not recommended by the jury, the court shall sentence the defendant to imprisonment as provided by law. Unless the jury trying the case makes a finding of at least one statutory aggravating circumstance and recommends the death sentence in its verdict, the court shall not sentence the defendant to death, provided that no such finding of statutory aggravating circumstance shall be necessary in offenses of treason or aircraft

hijacking. The provisions of this section shall not affect a sentence when the case is tried without a jury or when the judge accepts a plea of guilty.'

Ga.Code § 27-2302 (Supp.1976):

Recommendation to mercy.
'In all capital cases, other than those of homicide, when the verdict is guilty, with a recommendation to mercy, it shall be legal and shall be a recommendation to the judge of imprisonment for life. Such recommendation shall be binding upon the judge.'
Ga.Code § 27-2534.1 (Supp. 1976):
'Mitigating and aggravating circumstances; death penalty. . . .

'(b) In all cases of other offenses for which the death penalty may be authorized, the judge shall consider, or he shall include in his instructions to the jury for it to consider, any mitigating circumstances or aggravating circumstances otherwise authorized by law and any of the following statutory aggravating circumstances which may be supported by the evidence:

'(1) The offense of murder, rape, armed robbery, or kidnapping was committed by a person with a prior record of conviction for a capital felony, or the offense of murder was committed by a person who has a substantial history of serious assaultive criminal convictions.

'(2) The offense of murder, rape, armed robbery, or kidnapping was committed while the offender was engaged in the commission of another capital felony, or aggravated battery, or the offense of murder was committed while the offender was engaged in the commission of burglary or arson in the first degree. . . .

'(7) The offense of murder, rape, armed robbery or kidnapping was outrageously or wantonly vile, horrible or inhuman in that it involved torture, depravity of mind, or an aggravated battery to the victim. . . .

'(c) The statutory instructions as determined by the trial judge to be warranted by the evidence shall be given in charge and in writing to the jury for its deliberation. The jury, if its verdict be a recommendation of death, shall designate in writing, signed by the foreman of the jury, the aggravating circumstance or circumstances which it found beyond a reasonable doubt. In non-jury cases the judge shall make such designation. Except in cases of treason or aircraft hijacking, unless at least one of the statutory aggravating circumstances enumerated in section 27-2534.1(b) is so found, the death penalty shall not be imposed.' Ga.Code § 27-2537 (Supp.1976):

'Review of death sentences.

'(a) Whenever the death penalty is imposed, and upon the judgment becoming final in the trial court, the sentence shall be reviewed on the record by the Supreme Court of Georgia. The clerk of the trial court, within ten days after receiving the transcript, shall transmit the entire record and transcript to the Supreme Court of Georgia together with a notice prepared by the clerk and a report prepared by the trial judge. The notice shall set forth the title and docket number of the case, the name of the defendant and the name and address of his attorney, a narrative statement of the judgment, the offense, and the punishment prescribed. The report shall be in the form of a standard questionnaire prepared and supplied by the Supreme Court of Georgia.

'(b) The Supreme Court of Georgia shall consider the punishment as well as any errors enumerated by way of appeal.

'(c) With regard to the sentence, the court shall determine:

'(1) Whether the sentence of death was imposed under the influence of passion, prejudice, or any other arbitrary factor, and

'(2) Whether, in cases other than treason or aircraft hijacking, the evidence supports the jury's or judge's finding of a statutory aggravating circumstance as enumerated in section 27-2534.1(b), and

'(3) Whether the sentence of death is excessive or disproportionate to the penalty imposed in similar cases, considering both the crime and the defendant. . . .

The jury was instructed that it could consider as aggravating circumstances whether the rape had been committed by a person with a prior record of conviction for a capital felony and whether the rape had been committed in the course of committing another capital felony, namely, the armed robbery of Allen Carver. The court also instructed, pursuant to statute, that even if aggravating circumstances were present, the death penalty need not be imposed if the jury found they were out-weighed by mitigating circumstances, that is, circumstances not constituting justification or excuse for the offense in question, 'but which, in fairness and mercy, may be considered as extenuating or reducing the degree' of moral culpability or punishment. App. 300. The jury's verdict on the rape count was death by electrocution. Both aggravating circumstances on which the court instructed were found to be present by the jury.

Furman v. Georgia, 408 U.S. 238. 92 S.Ct. 2726, 33 L.Ed.2d 346 (1972), . . . [makes] unnecessary the recanvassing of certain critical aspects of the controversy about the constitutionality of capital punishment. It is now settled that the death penalty is not invariably cruel and unusual punishment within the meaning of the Eighth Amendment; it is not inherently barbaric or an unacceptable mode of punishment for crime; neither is it always disproportionate to the crime for which it is imposed. It is also established the imposing capital punishment, at least for murder, in accordance with the procedures provided under the Georgia statutes saves the sentence from the infirmities which led the Court to invalidate the prior Georgia capital punishment statute in *Furman v. Georgia,* supra.

In sustaining the imposition of the death penalty in Gregg, however, the Court firmly embraced the holdings and dicta from prior cases, *Furman v. Georgia, supra; Robinson v. California,* 370 U.S. 660, 82 S.Ct. 1417, 8 L.Ed.2d 758 (1962); *Trop v. Dulles,* 356 U.S. 86, 78 S.Ct. 590, 2 L.Ed.2d 630 (1958); and *Weems v. United States,* 217 U.S. 349, 30 S.Ct. 544, 54 L.Ed. 793 (1910), to the effect that the Eighth Amendment bars not only those punishments that are 'barbaric' but also those that are 'excessive' in relation to the crime committed. Under *Gregg* [v.Ga. 428 U.S. 153 (1976)], a punishment is 'excessive' and unconstitutional if it (1) makes no measurable

CASE

contribution to acceptable goals of punishment and hence is nothing more than the purposeless and needless imposition of pain and suffering; or (2) is grossly out of proportion to the severity of the crime. A punishment might fail the test on either ground. Furthermore, these Eighth Amendment judgments should not be, or appear to be, merely the subjective views of individual Justices; judgment should be informed by objective factors to the maximum possible extent. To this end, attention must be given to the public attitudes concerning a particular sentence history and precedent, legislative attitudes, and the response of juries reflected in their sentencing decisions are to be consulted. In Gregg, after giving due regard to such sources, the Court's judgment was that the death penalty for deliberate murder was neither the purposeless imposition of severe punishment nor a punishment grossly disproportionate to the crime. But the court reserved the question of the constitutionality of the death penalty when imposed for other crimes. 428 U.S., at 187 n. 35, 96 S.Ct., at 2932.

III

That question, with respect to rape of an adult woman, is now before us. We have concluded that a sentence of death is grossly disproportionate and excessive punishment for the crime of rape and is therefore forbidden by the Eighth Amendment as cruel and unusual punishment, . . .

A

. . . At no time in the last 50 years have a majority of the States authorized death as a punishment for rape. In 1925, 18 States, the District of Columbia, and the Federal Government authorized capital punishment for the rape of an adult female. By 1971 just prior to the decision in *Furman v. Georgia,* that number had declined, but not substantially, to 16 States plus the Federal Government. *Furman* then invalidated most of the capital punishment statutes in this country, including the rape statutes, because, among other reasons, of the manner in which the death penalty was imposed and utilized under those laws. . . .

Georgia argues that 11 of the 16 States that authorized death for rape in 1972 attempted to comply with *Furman* by enacting arguably mandatory death penalty legislation and that it is very likely that, aside from Louisiana and North Carolina, these States simply chose to eliminate rape as a capital offense rather than to require death for each and every instance of rape. The argument is not without force; but 4 of the 16 States did not take the mandatory course and also did not continue rape of an adult woman as a capital offense. Further, as we have indicated, the legislatures of 6 of the 11 arguably mandatory States have revised their death penalty laws since Woodson and Roberts without enacting a new death penalty for rape. And this is to say nothing of 19 other States that enacted nonmandatory, post-*Furman* statutes and chose not to sentence rapists to death. . . .

It should be noted that Florida, Mississippi, and Tennessee also authorized the death penalty in *some* rape cases, but only where the victim was a child and the rapist an adult. The Tennessee statute has since been invalidated because the death sentence was mandatory. *Collins v. State,* 550 S.W.2d 643 (Tenn.1977). The upshot is that Georgia is the sole jurisdiction in the United States at the present time that authorizes a sentence of death when the rape victim is an adult woman, and only two other jurisdictions provide capital punishment when the victim is a child . . .

The current judgment with respect to the death penalty for rape is not wholly unanimous among state legislatures, but it obviously weighs very heavily on the side of rejecting capital punishment as a suitable penalty for raping an adult woman.

B

It was also observed in *Gregg* that '(t)he jury . . . is a significant and reliable objective index of contemporary values because it is so directly involved.' 428 U.S., at 181, 96 S.Ct., at 2929, and that it is thus important to look to the sentencing decisions that juries have made in the course of assessing whether capital punishment is an appropriate penalty for the crime being tried. Of course, the jury's judgment is meaningful only where the jury has an appropriate measure of choice as to whether the death penalty is to be imposed. As far as execution for rape is concerned, this is now true only in Georgia and in Florida; and in the latter State, capital punishment is authorized only for the rape of children.

According to the factual submissions in this Court, out of all rape convictions in Georgia since 1973 and that total number has not been tendered 63 cases had been reviewed by the Georgia Supreme Court as of the time of oral argument; and of these, 6 involved a death sentence, 1 of which was set aside, leaving 5 convicted rapists now under sentence of death in the State of Georgia. Georgia juries have thus sentenced rapists to death six times since 1973. This obviously is not a negligible number; and the State argues that as a practical matter juries simply reserve the extreme sanction for extreme cases of rape and that recent experience surely does not prove that jurors consider the death penalty to be a disproportionate punishment for every conceivable instance of rape, no matter how aggravated. Nevertheless, it is true that in the vast majority of cases, at least 9 out of 10, juries have not imposed the death sentence.

IV

These recent events evidencing the attitude of state legislatures and sentencing juries do not wholly determine this controversy, for the Constitution contemplates that in the end our own judgment will be brought to bear on the question of the acceptability of the death penalty under the Eighth Amendment. Nevertheless, the legislative rejection of capital punishment for rape strongly confirms our own judgment, which is that death is indeed a disproportionate penalty for the crime of raping an adult woman.

We do not discount the seriousness of rape as a crime. It is highly reprehensible, both in a moral sense and in its almost total contempt for the personal integrity and autonomy of the female victim and for the latter's privilege of choosing those with whom intimate relationships are to be established. Short of homicide, it is the 'ultimate violation of self.' It is also a violent crime because it normally involves force, or the threat of force or intimidation, to overcome the will and the capacity of the victim to resist. Rape is very often accompanied by physical injury to the female and can also inflict mental and psychological damage. Because it undermines the community's sense of security, there is public injury as well.

* * *

Rape is without doubt deserving of serious punishment; but in terms of moral depravity and of the injury to the person and to the public, it does not compare with murder, which does involve the unjustified taking of human life. Although it may be accompanied by another crime, rape by definition does not include the death of or even the serious injury to another person. The murderer kills; the rapist, if no more than that, does not. Life is over for the victim of the murderer; for the rape victim, life may not be nearly so happy as it was, but it is not over and normally is not beyond repair. We have the abiding conviction that the death penalty, which 'is unique in its severity and irrevocability,' *Gregg v. Georgia,* 428 U.S., at 187, 96 S.Ct., at 2931, is an excessive penalty for the rapist who, as such, does not take human life.

This does not end the matter; for under Georgia law, death may not be imposed for any capital offense, including rape, unless the jury or judge finds one of the statutory aggravating circumstances and then elects to impose that sentence. Ga.Code § 26-3102 (1976 Supp); *Gregg v. Georgia, supra,* 428 U.S., at 165–166, 96 S.Ct., at 2921–2922. For the rapist to be executed in Georgia, it must therefore be found not only that he committed rape but also that one or more of the following aggravating circumstances were present: (1) that the rape was committed by a person with a prior record of conviction for a capital felony; (2) that the rape was committed while the offender was engaged in the commission of another capital felony, or aggravated battery; or (3) the rape 'was outrageously or wantonly vile, horrible or inhuman in that it involved torture, depravity of mind, or aggravated battery to the victim.' (There are other aggravating circumstances provided in the statute, . . . but they are not applicable to rape.) Here, the first two of these aggravating circumstances were alleged and found by the jury.

CASE

Neither of these circumstances, nor both of them together, change our conclusion that the death sentence imposed on Coker is a disproportionate punishment for rape. Coker had prior convictions for capital felonies rape, murder, and kidnapping but these prior convictions do not change the fact that the instant crime being punished is a rape not involving the taking of life.

It is also true that the present rape occurred while Coker was committing armed robbery, a felony for which the Georgia statutes authorize the death penalty. In *Gregg v. Georgia,* the Georgia Supreme Court refused to sustain a death sentence for armed robbery because, for one reason, death had been so seldom imposed for this crime in other cases that such a sentence was excessive and could not be sustained under the statute. As it did in this case, however, the Georgia Supreme Court apparently continues to recognize armed robbery as a capital offense for the purpose of applying the aggravating-circumstances provisions of the Georgia Code. But Coker was tried for the robbery offense as well as for rape and received a separate life sentence for this crime; the jury did not deem the robbery itself deserving of the death penalty, even though accompanied by the aggravating circumstance, which was stipulated, that Coker had been convicted of a prior capital crime.

Where the accompanying capital crime is murder, it is most likely that the defendant would be tried for murder, rather than rape; and it is perhaps academic to deal with the death sentence for rape in such a circumstance. It is likewise unnecessary to consider the rape felony murder a rape accompanied by the death of the victim which was unlawfully but nonmaliciously caused by the defendant. Where the third aggravating circumstance mentioned in the text is present that the rape is particularly vile or involves torture or aggravated battery it would seem that the defendant could very likely be convicted, tried, and appropriately punished for this additional conduct.

We note finally that in Georgia a person commits murder when he unlawfully and with malice aforethought, either express or implied, causes the death of another human being. He also commits that crime when in the commission of a felony he causes the death of another human being, irrespective of malice. But even where the killing is deliberate, it is not punishable by death absent proof of aggravating circumstances. It is difficult to accept the notion, and we do not, that the rapist, with or without aggravating circumstances, should be punished more heavily than the deliberate killer as long as the rapist does not himself take the life of his victim. The judgment of the Georgia Supreme Court upholding the death sentence is reversed, and the case is remanded to that court for further proceedings not inconsistent with this opinion.

Case Review Question

Is the death penalty ever acceptable for a crime less than murder?

WHITE-COLLAR CRIME

Crime also exists in the workplace, and criminal responsibility for such crime has received increased attention in recent years. Although corporations generally are not specifically liable for criminal acts, it does not mean that liability is nonexistent. Although the corporation is considered a person under the law in terms of equality of rights, it is still a legal fiction. Because the corporation does not possess a mind, it is incapable of formulating the adequate mens rea to commit a criminal act. Only those who represent the corporation can do that. The law has come to recognize that the persons who represent the corporation are in fact the mind of the corporation and through them the corporation can be convicted of most criminal acts.

If a person is employed by a corporation and acts on its behalf, the corporation can be held responsible for those acts under the theory of respondent superior. As long as the act was performed within the scope of the person's employment and related directly to the corporation, the entity as well as the individual can be held responsible. Although a corporation cannot be imprisoned, it can be heavily fined or dissolved involuntarily.

Crimes frequently committed on behalf of corporations include tax law violations, securities law violations, burglary and theft (in the case of trade secrets), and damage to the property of competitors. All of these actions require some actual mental and physical conduct by an individual, but they directly or indirectly benefit the corporation. If it can be shown that the corporate representatives acted, encouraged these acts, or accepted the benefits of these acts, the corporation may be charged for the crime as well. In addition, the individuals may be held responsible as principals.

The Model Penal Code recognizes liability of business entities in much the same manner as the common law. The only real difference is that the Model Penal Code has a fairly narrow definition of the types of offenses for which a business entity may be held responsible. Specifically, for a business entity to be held responsible under the Code, the offense must be one that the legislature clearly intended to apply to corporations or one in which the criminal actions can be proven to be consistent with the purpose of the corporation.[32] In other cases, only the individual will be held responsible for the criminal acts.

In addition to those crimes for which a corporation or business entity might be held criminally liable, crimes can be committed against the entity by its fiduciaries. For example, a bank employee who over a period of time extracts funds from the bank for personal use has committed embezzlement, which essentially is theft of property. Other crimes include violation of securities laws to injure or destroy a competitor's business or to take unfair advantage of investors. In the 1980s, much publicity centered around Wall Street figures Michael Milken and Ivan Boesky who were convicted of obtaining huge profits in the securities market by violating securities laws designed to promote fairness among investors.

While white-collar crime often appears to be victimless because no clearly identifiable and individual injury is caused by the act, it is nevertheless a violation of law and is dealt with in much the same manner as other criminal conduct.

CASE

KARR v. STATE OF ALASKA

660 P.2d 450
(Alaska 1983).

COATS, Judge.

Diana Karr embezzled $356,000 from Meyeres' Real Estate, Inc. between November 1979 and December 1981. Karr was charged with one count of embezzlement by an employee for the money she took prior to January 1, 1980. (Former AS 11.20.280 reads: Embezzlement by employee or servant. An officer, agent, clerk, employee, or servant who embezzles or fraudulently converts to his own use, or takes or secretes with intent to embezzle or fraudulently convert to his own use,

CASE

money, property, or thing of another which may be the subject of larceny, and which has come into his possession or is under his care by virtue of his employment is guilty of embezzlement. If the property embezzled exceeds $100 in value, a person guilty of embezzlement is punishable by imprisonment in the penitentiary for not less than one year nor more than 10 years. If the property embezzled does not exceed the value of $100, a person guilty of embezzlement is punishable by imprisonment in a jail for not less than one month nor more than one year, or by a fine of not less than $25 nor more than $100.) [Karr] was charged with theft in the first degree, AS 11.46.120, for money she took after January 1, 1980, the effective date for the revised criminal code.

(AS 11.46.120 reads:

Theft in the first degree. (a) A person commits the crime of theft in the first degree if he commits theft as defined in § 100 of this chapter and the value of the property or services is $25,000 or more. (b) Theft in the first degree is a class B felony.) After Karr pled nolo contendere to these charges, Judge James R. Blair sentenced her to serve ten years with five suspended and to pay $300,000 restitution. Karr was sentenced to five years on each count, and the sentences were made consecutive to each other. The five-year sentence for embezzlement by employee was suspended, resulting in a sentence of ten years with five suspended.

Karr appeals her sentence to this court. We affirm.

Karr first contends that the sentence imposed was excessive. Karr is thirty-four years old and has no prior criminal record. She points to *Austin v. State,* 627 P.2D 657, 658 (Alaska App.1981), where we said, '[n]ormally a first offender should receive a more favorable sentence than the presumptive sentence for a second offender. It is clear this rule should be violated only in an exceptional case. Karr also argues that we should consider her offense as one crime, since her crime was charged as two offenses only because the new criminal code came into effect on January 1, 1980. Karr argues that an offender who embezzled only after

January 1, 1980 would have been charged only with one count, theft in the first degree. She contends she should not be treated differently merely because she embezzled both before and after January 1, 1980.

The record is clear that Judge Blair did not treat Karr differently because she was convicted of two counts. Essentially Karr was sentenced to ten years with five years suspended for theft in the first degree for a number of different acts of embezzlement committed over a period of over two years. Karr's sentence is not excessive under Austin because this is an exceptional case. Judge Blair classified Karr's offense as a particularly serious offense for an embezzlement. See AS 12.55.155(c)(10). Karr embezzled $356,000. The record establishes that Karr had earned a position of trust with Bud Meyeres, who owned Meyeres' Real Estate, and then used that position to embezzle. This amount was taken over a period of two years and involved numerous individual acts of embezzlement. In Karr's position she had to be aware of the effects of her embezzlement: at the time of Karr's sentencing, Meyeres was sixty-seven years old, and his real estate business was in serious financial trouble due to the embezzlement. Meyeres indicated that for the foreseeable future he will have to work hard to try to salvage his real estate business. It is unlikely that he will ever be able to retire. This is clearly an aggravated case. The presumptive sentence for a second class B felony offender is four years. Karr's actual sentence of imprisonment exceeds that by one year. In reviewing a sentence to determine whether it exceeds the presumptive sentence for a second offender under Austin, our primary focus is on the amount of imprisonment actually imposed. See *Tazruk v. State,* 655 P.2D 788 (Alaska App.1982). Judge Blair imposed the consecutive five-year suspended sentence primarily to enforce the restitution order. Karr's probation cannot be revoked for failure to make restitution if she makes a good faith effort to pay restitution but is unable to do so. See AS 12.55.051. In the event it is revoked she is entitled to another sentence appeal. Due to the seriousness of the offense, we conclude that this is an exceptional case, and the sentence of ten years with five suspended is not excessive.

The amount of money which Karr embezzled is the major distinguishing factor which separates this case from former Alaska cases in which lesser sentences were imposed for similar offenses. See *Fields v. State,* 629 P.2D 46 (Alaska 1981); *Huff v. State,* 598 P.2D 928 (Alaska 1979); *Amidon v. State,* 565 P.2D 1248 (Alaska 1977).

Karr also argues that the trial judge should not have imposed a consecutive sentence. However, Karr's total sentence did not exceed the sentence which she could have received for one count of theft in the first degree. Where a consecutive sentence is imposed but the total sentence does not exceed the sentence which could be imposed on one count, a consecutive sentence is not improper. See *Mutschler v. State,* 560 P.2D 377, 381 (Alaska 1977).

Karr next argues that the amount of restitution which Judge Blair ordered was excessive. Judge Blair acknowledged that it would be impossible for Karr to pay such a large amount of restitution. Karr argues that AS 12.55.045(a) is violated when a trial judge orders an amount of restitution which cannot be paid. AS 12.55.045(a) provides:

> The court may order a defendant convicted of an offense to make restitution as provided in this section or as otherwise authorized by law. In determining the amount and method of payment of restitution, the court shall take into account the financial resources of the defendant and the nature of the burden its payment will impose.

It is clear that it will be difficult for Karr to pay the whole $300,000 in restitution. She appears to have some assets and therefore may be able to pay some restitution now. During her period of incarceration it is unlikely that she will be able to make any restitution. It appears Judge Blair considered these factors, as well as the fact that Karr will probably have difficulty in obtaining future employment similar to her previous employment, when he predicted that full restitution would be impossible.

Due to the difficulty in predicting from this point in time what amount of restitution is reasonable for Karr to pay, we conclude that it was reasonable for Judge Blair to order a large amount of restitution. In so doing he did not violate AS 12.55.045(a). Karr does not argue that she did not steal at least this amount from Meyeres. By ordering restitution, Judge Blair can require Karr to attempt to undo some of the damage caused by her criminal acts. The court can only enforce the order to the extent that it is reasonable for Karr to make restitution. We conclude that the court did not err in ordering $300,000 restitution.

The sentence is AFFIRMED.

Case Review Question

What purpose is served by imposing a fine that can never be paid?

DEFENSES TO CHARGES OF CRIMINAL CONDUCT

For every act committed, there are explanations for why the act occurred. In cases of criminal acts, some explanations are sufficient to prevent conviction and punishment of the actor. Such explanations are known as defenses, and they are wide and varied. The following sections examine a number of defenses that accused persons frequently assert.

Common Defenses

Justifiable or excusable conduct. Traditionally, justifiable or excusable conduct was a defense that could be applied in criminal cases. In present-day law, conduct that is justifiable or excusable is not considered criminal conduct and thus does not provide a basis for arrest or prosecution. **Justifiable conduct** is

justifiable conduct

Conduct by one who, under the circumstances, is considered to be innocent of otherwise criminal behavior.

**excusable
conduct**

Conduct by one who,
under the color of
authority, is
considered to be
innocent of otherwise
criminal behavior.

an act that takes place under special circumstances such as defense of oneself or others.[33] **Excusable conduct** refers to acts that would be considered criminal but for the actor's status at the time of the act.[34] For example, when law enforcement officers or military personnel intrude onto another's property or perhaps even kill in the line of duty, their conduct that would otherwise be considered criminal is excused because they are supposedly doing so in the interest of the public welfare. Of course, this may not apply if such persons abuse their authority and commit these acts without basis.

Involuntary conduct.   A defense to charges of criminal conduct always exists in situations where the actor's conduct was not voluntary. Obviously, involuntary conduct includes acts over which the actor has no physical control.[35] Examples would include acts performed while sleeping, during seizures, or as the result of a reflex. Whether acts performed while under the influence of hypnosis or prescribed medication are voluntary is still questionable.

The key to the defense of involuntary conduct is proving that the defendant was physically incapable of forming the required mens rea prior to committing the crime. The lower the degree of requirement, such as general intent or awareness, the more difficult it is to prove the act was involuntary. (With respect to strict liability, since intent is not a consideration, involuntariness would not be a defense.)

Duress.   A similar defense is duress, in which a third party causes another person to act by exerting influence over that person. The actor has a mental choice between following or refusing the commands of the third person. If the situation is extreme, duress may be used as a defense on the basis that in reality, only one choice could be made. For example, if the actor is told to act or his or her children will be killed, duress would apply. Although the actor has technically been given an option, in practical terms, he or she has no choice. The court will examine the circumstances to determine just how reasonable a refusal to act would have been.

Mistake.   Mistake is a common defense to accusations of criminal acts. Two types of mistake can be alleged. Mistake of fact occurs when the person commits the act while reasonably believing something that was not true.[36] Many cases have been reported of persons who leave a store or other public building and drive away in what they think is their car, but in fact, their key fits an identical car belonging to someone else. Although such persons did indeed steal the automobile, they are not guilty of auto theft. They reasonably believed they were driving their own car. Thus, they made a mistake of fact. Any mistake of fact must bear directly on the intent required for the particular crime.

Mistake of law is applied much more rarely. It is appropriate only where a person actually believed that his or her conduct was lawful under one statute, despite the existence of another statute that might indicate such conduct was unlawful. An example is persons who exercise their right to avoid a search of their property by police without a proper warrant when another law gives police the right to search property in emergencies. If such persons are not aware of the emergency and deny the police entry, they are exercising a legal right. If, for example, unbeknownst to these persons, a criminal is hiding in their basement, these persons have made an honest mistake of law in protecting their rights and cannot be prosecuted for something such as obstruction of justice.

The Model Penal Code acknowledges both mistakes of fact and mistakes of law. In cases of mistake of fact, the mistake must be something that is believed and is part of the state of mind of the actor.[37] The Code, in line with common law, generally holds that ignorance of the law is no excuse. It does, however, allow certain exceptions that are similar to the common law exceptions that create a valid defense. Examples of these exceptions include (1) the actor did not have reasonable access to the law, (2) the actor reasonably believed the conduct was lawful (as in the common law example above), and (3) the actor was relying on the statement of the government or a government official. A person's lawyer's advice that conduct was permissible is not a defense. Such a statement must come from someone in a government capacity.

Entrapment.   A defense that has gained some notoriety in recent years is entrapment, which alleges that law enforcement personnel created a situation that would lead a law-abiding citizen with no prior criminal intent into criminal activity. The police must plant the idea and lead a person into criminal conduct that the person would not otherwise be predisposed to commit. This is often used in cases of prostitution and drug dealing. It is absolutely necessary for the police to do no more than accept or enhance the criminal conduct. The opportunity and intent to complete the crime must be developed by the criminal without any significant influence by the police.

The Insanity Defense

Probably the most publicized defense in criminal law is the insanity defense. While substantive as well as procedural law varies on this defense among the jurisdictions, the defense has common denominators. In all cases where insanity is raised as a defense to charges of criminal conduct, the issues are ultimately reduced to whether a mental impairment existed and whether the impairment played a role in the defendant's conduct at the time of the crime.

The insanity defense standards applied in about one-third of the states is the M'Naughten Rule, which in its original form dates back to 1843.[38] While the rule has been modified in some states, the basic tenet of the *M'Naughten* decision is that the mental impairment either (1) prevented the defendant from understanding the criminal nature and quality of the criminal act or (2) prevented the defendant from determining whether the act was legal or illegal. The difficulty with the M'Naughten Rule is that it requires a determination that the defendant was sane or insane, with no middle ground. Consequently, a majority of states have chosen other methods to determine the question of insanity as an influence on one charged with criminal conduct.

Some jurisdictions allow in place of or in addition to the M'Naughten Rule, the irresistible impulse theory. Under this premise, the defendant claims to have been unable to control his or her behavior as the result of mental impairment at the time of the alleged criminal conduct. The irresistible impulse theory rests on the basis that the defendant at the time of the crime was subjected to a sudden impulse that he or she did not have the capacity to control.

Finally, a number of states have adopted a defense standard similar to that used in federal prosecutions. In 1984, this defense was embodied in a statutory definition by the Congress:

> (a) Affirmative Defense: It is an affirmative defense to a prosecution under any Federal statute that, at the time of the commission of the acts constituting the offense, the defendant, as a result of a severe mental disease or defect, was unable to appreciate the nature and quality or the wrongfulness of his acts. Mental disease or defect does not otherwise constitute a defense.
> (b) Burden of Proof: The defendant has the burden of proving the defense of insanity by clear and convincing evidence.[39]

This statute made it more difficult to prove insanity as a defense. In the past, insanity was seen as a way to avoid prosecution for the acts of an otherwise reasonable individual. This statute requires extensive proof of mental disability. It must be shown that the disability was severe and that it prevented any ability to appreciate or understand the act itself and its consequences. An additional hurdle is that the burden is placed on the defendant. Usually, the burden is on the prosecution to show guilt beyond a reasonable doubt. Thus, any doubt created in the minds of the jury by the defense is sufficient to prevent conviction. Under the new insanity statute, however, the defendant must present clear and convincing evidence of the required elements.

The Model Penal Code is the approach the majority of the states take with regard to the insanity defense. The Code permits a defendant to raise the insanity defense, but the defense must prove that the defendant did not have the ability to "appreciate the criminality of his conduct" or "conform his conduct to the requirements of law."[40] This requirement parallels and strengthens the reasoning of the common law approach. Under this rule, the defendant has the burden of establishing that he or she had some cognitive inability to understand right from wrong and was unable to control his or her actions within legal bounds. The rule's significance is that ordinarily, the prosecution has the burden of proving the defendant guilty. However, when the insanity defense is raised, the burden is switched, and the defendant has the burden to present proof to meet the insanity defense standard of the jurisdiction.

Assignment 14.4

> Go to the subject index of the statutes for your particular state. Examine the statutes pertaining to homicide and determine whether the statute follows common law or the Model Penal Code. Then determine whether a statute or rule of evidence sets forth the requirements for pleading insanity as a defense to a crime.

Ethical Considerations

While most persons do not consider themselves to be criminals, neither do most consider themselves to be unethical. However, frequently, the same type of conduct that many engage in on a daily basis could be technically considered unethical, perhaps even criminal. For example, if you drive through a fast-food restaurant and upon arriving home discover the clerk gave you 35 cents more change than you were due, how likely is it that you will get back in your car and return the money to the restaurant? Most people would probably not return the money because of the amount of time required for such a small figure. But keeping the money is no more ethical or legal just because the amount is considered by most as insignificant. Much of the reason why criminal laws mirror ethical standards of society is the belief that violations of the standards should not be tolerated.

Question
Can you identify three situations that are not ethical but are entirely legal?

Ethical Circumstance

Caesar often traveled on company business. It was the policy of the company that anyone who also used company benefits for personal use report it and pay a portion of the expenses. Caesar was scheduled to attend a conference in Orlando, Florida. He traded his full-coach airline ticket in for a refund and used it to purchase four lower fare tickets. He also had his wife and two children stay in the hotel room reserved for him by the company. Each day, they would drop him off at the conference and use the company rental car to go to nearby Disneyworld. He did pay for the meals of his family members and admission to Disneyworld. The cost of the airfare, hotel room, and car did not change as the result of having his family along. However, he violated company policy to the extent it was not only unethical, but also could be considered theft by using company funds for personal benefits.

CHAPTER SUMMARY

This chapter has briefly examined some of the more frequently encountered crimes. The common thread that pervades all criminal conduct is that the defendant must be aware of the decision to act or not to act. This awareness may be merely that, or it may be a general intent, a specific intent, or awareness as defined by the Model Penal Code. Each statute that defines criminal conduct indicates expressly or by implication the level of awareness required. Further, the statute sets forth with some certainty the acts or omissions that constitute criminal conduct. In contrast, defenses are created largely by judicial law. In most cases, the courts have formulated what is an acceptable or unacceptable reason for what would otherwise be criminal conduct. This generally includes not only the core criminal act but also all acts that enable the crime to be committed or prevent the discovery of the crime or the actor. These ideas are present in both the common law and the Model Penal Code. The primary difference between the two is the manner in which they are applied.

It should also be noted that simply because criminal conduct occurs, conviction is not always in order. The circumstances of the crime and the motivation of the parties involved may excuse or justify the conduct, or they may defeat the necessary elements for commission of the crime, such as the absence of specific intent or insanity.

Further research into the criminal law of a particular jurisdiction should always involve an initial determination of whether the jurisdiction applies common law principles or the Model Penal Code. Once this determination has been made, the appropriate principles of mens rea and actus reus will apply. Thus, it is necessary to determine only the specifics of mens rea and actus reus that are required for the particular crime in question.

CHAPTER TERMS

actus reus	excusable conduct	justifiable conduct	misdemeanor
criminal law	felony	mens rea	

REVIEW QUESTIONS

1. What is a felony?
2. Explain the difference between actus reus and mens rea.
3. What types of acts are subject to strict criminal liability?
4. Identify the parties to crime under the Model Penal Code and under common law.
5. What is an inchoate offense?
6. What is the difference between theft and robbery?
7. What are the types of homicide, and how are they differentiated?
8. When can a corporation be held criminally liable?
9. How does justifiable conduct differ from excusable conduct?

RELEVANT LINKS

Criminal law
www.aol.com/webcenters/legal/criminal.adp

Criminal law
www.ncjrs.org

INTERNET ASSIGNMENT 14.1

Using internet resources, identify whether your jurisdiction has adopted a felony murder statute and give the location of your source of information.

NOTES

1. *Lord Fitzgerald Seaton v. Seaton*, L.R. 13 Ap.Ca. 78 (1888).
2. William Statsky, *Legal Thesaurus/Dictionary* (St. Paul: West, 1982).
3.–5. Id.
6. Model Penal Code, Section 1.13(9).
7. *In re Michael*, 423 A.2d 1180 (R.I. 1981).
8. *United States v. Sterley*, 764 F.2d 530 (8th Cir. 1985).
9. *People v. Love*, 11 Cal.App. 3d Supp.1, 168 Cal. Rptr. 591 (1980).
10. Id.
11. 95 A.L.R.3d 248.
12. *People v. Levitt*, 156 Cal.App. 3d 500, 156 Cal. Rptr. 276 (1984).
13. Model Penal Code, Section 1.13; 2.02.
14. *People v. Bargy*, 71 Mich.App. 609, 248 N.W.3d 636 (1976); State v. Furr, 292 N.C. 711, 235 S.E.2d 193 (1977).
15. Id.
16. Model Penal Code, Section 242.3; 2.06.
17. William Statsky, *Legal Thesaurus*.
18. *Manner v. State*, 387 So.2d 1014 (Fla. App. 4th Dist. 1980).
19. Model Penal Code, Section 5.03.
20. *State v. Stewart*, 537 S.W.2d 579 (Mo.App. 1976).
21. *Pinkett v. State*, 30 Md.App. 458, 352 A.2d 358 (1976).
22. William Statsky, *Legal Thesaurus*.
23. *State v. Lora*, 213 Kan. 184, 515 P.2d 1086 (1973).
24. *Anderson v. State*, 61 Md.App. 436, 487 A.2d 294 (1985).
25. Id.
26. *Wilcox v. State*, 401 So.2d 789 (Ala.Crim.App.1980).
27. *Dunn v. State*, 161 Ind.App. 586, 316 N.E.2d 834 (1974).
28. *State v. Beach*, 329 S.W.2d 712 (Mo. 1959).
29. *Callahan v. State*, 343 So.2d 551 (Ala.Crim.App. 1977).
30. *Goldsby v. State*, 226 Miss. 1, 78 So.2d 762 (1955).
31. *Wooden v. Commonwealth*, 222 Va. 758, 284 S.E.2d 811 (1981).
32. Model Penal Code, Section 210.2.
33. Model Penal Code, Section 2.07.
34. *State v. Williams*, 545 S.W.2d 342 (Mo.App. 1976).
35. *Law v. State*, 21 Md.App. 13, 318 A.2d 859 (1974).
36. Model Penal Code, Section 3.09.
37. Model Penal Code, Section 3.04.
38. Daniel M'Naughten's Case, 10 Cl. & F.200, 8 Eng.Rep. 718 (H.L. 1843).
39. 18 U.S.C.A. Section 20.
40. Model Penal Code, Section 402.

For additional resources, please visit our Web site at www.westlegalstudies.com

CHAPTER 15

Criminal Procedure

CHAPTER OBJECTIVES

After reading this chapter, you should be able to:

- Explain the purpose of selective incorporation and list the rights adopted into the definition of due process through selective incorporation.

- Explain the concept of double jeopardy and when it does not apply even though the defendant has gone to trial.

- Discuss when a defendant has the right to counsel.

- Discuss the determination of bail.

- Discuss when an arrest warrant is not required.

- Compare grand jury proceedings and preliminary hearings.

- Explain the process of arraignment.

Criminal procedure is one of the most rapidly changing areas of law in the United States today. It differs significantly from civil procedure. Of course, the obvious difference is that rules of civil procedure govern civil actions and rules of criminal procedure govern criminal prosecutions. In addition, criminal procedure comes into play long before the action is formally commenced against a defendant. Criminal procedure affects the prosecution from the moment a crime is suspected.

Criminal prosecutions take place in federal and state judicial systems, each of which has its own rules of procedure. However, all are ultimately governed by certain constitutional requirements. Through its various amendments, the U.S. Constitution protects all persons from unfair and unequal treatment during criminal prosecutions. The courts vigorously enforce the Constitution and require that all persons be treated fairly and equally. Therefore, although the rules may differ somewhat from jurisdiction to jurisdiction, the effect of the rules must be constitutionally permissible or the rules may be invalidated by the courts.

This chapter provides a limited introduction to the constitutional limitations on criminal procedure, the current status of criminal procedure, and the stages of a criminal prosecution. Keep in mind that since the law is subject to radical changes as the courts review various procedural rules and judge their constitutionality, only basic principles are discussed here, and even they may be subject to change.

CRIMINAL PROCEDURE AND THE CONSTITUTION

The Approach of the U.S. Supreme Court

Various amendments to the U.S. Constitution affect criminal rights. The Bill of Rights was adopted, in part, to protect individuals from being unfairly or unnecessarily penalized by the justice system.

The Fourth, Fifth, Eighth, and Fourteenth Amendments address virtually every aspect of criminal procedure, including but not limited to invasion of one's property for the purpose of searching for and seizure of criminal evidence, self-incrimination, and the grounds for capital offenses (where punishment can be death). The effects of these amendments on criminal procedure are discussed in subsequent sections.

The Fourteenth Amendment: Due Process

In recent years, the Fourteenth Amendment, passed in 1868, has played a controversial role in criminal procedure. The obvious interpretation is that all citizens are subject to federal law and, further, that no state may pass or interpret laws that would conflict with federal law or the specific rights listed in the amendment. For many years, this was the interpretation given by the U.S. Supreme Court.[1] In various decisions, the Court maintained that the Fourteenth Amendment guaranteed only fundamental rights necessary to justice and order. It did not interpret the amendment to mean that all states must follow with absolute certainty all other constitutional amendments when creating law. Rather, as long as their laws did not conflict with constitutional guarantees, the states were permitted to create laws in any manner they chose.

During the 1950s and 1960s, the Court's approach to the Fourteenth Amendment changed. At that time, the justices who had been appointed to the Court were, as a group, more liberal than at any time in the Court's history. In addition, there was a great deal of unrest in the United States. Many believed that the constitutional guarantees in the Bill of Rights were being ignored or violated at the state level. The result was a great many alleged discrimination claims against the state governments as well as civil disobedience by the citizens. In various parts of the country, individuals protesting against the alleged inequities of state laws engaged in riots and other actions. Protest marches were held, sit-ins were conducted, and various other measures were taken by individuals to protect what they perceived to be fundamental rights. In the South, civil rights volunteers came from various other parts of the country to help secure the freedom of blacks to vote, assemble, and be treated with equality in the way laws were applied. All around the United States, people began to stand up against local and state governments that they believed operated with indifference to the fundamental protections that were so important in the creation of the original Constitution and Bill of Rights.

Although the Supreme Court of the 1950s and 1960s was quite liberal in its thinking, it was unwilling to utilize the total integration approach.[2] This approach follows the theory that the Fourteenth Amendment effectively integrates the entire Constitution and its amendments into each state's laws. The actual result would be to replace the state constitutions with the federal Constitution or at least to add the federal Constitution and its amendments to all state constitutions. The states would have virtually no say in what rights would be afforded their citizens or how the citizens would be governed. All state laws would be virtually identical to federal laws.

Selective incorporation.   Because the Court believed this invaded too much on the ability of state citizens to govern themselves without unnecessary federal government interference, it engaged in **selective incorporation.**[3] Previously, the Court had followed the rule that only the rights specifically stated in the Fourteenth Amendment were required to be followed explicitly by the states, including the right to **due process** (fundamental fairness) in the application of law before a person's life, liberty, or property could be seized. In simpler terms, an individual could not be sentenced to death or prison or have real or personal property taken by any state or federal government unless the person was treated fairly by the government. In addition, all persons were to be treated equally in the way laws were applied. For a time, this was sufficient; however, it became increasingly apparent that state and local governments did not always take a liberal view as to what constituted fundamental fairness in the way accused persons were treated and prosecuted.

To remedy this, the Court decided to more thoroughly and clearly define the term *due process.* In the past, it had been interpreted to mean essentially that which was fundamentally fair in a system of justice. However, the Court took

selective incorporation
Process of expansion of the definition of due process to include certain guarantees enumerated in the Bill of Rights.

due process
That which is necessary to fundamental fairness in the American system of justice.

the position that the states needed further clarification of the term. Because the Congress passed the Fourteenth Amendment, which required the states to give all citizens due process, the U.S. Supreme Court had the authority to interpret the amendment and, specifically, its language of due process. As noted earlier, the Court could do this by simply stating that all rights in the Bill of Rights were included in the definition of due process. However, since this was seen as too invasive, the Court opted instead to review case by case and determine whether a certain right in the Bill of Rights should be included in the definition of due process. If the Court determined that right was included, it would state with specificity how the right was to be protected at the state level.

Over the years, the process of selective incorporation has resulted in expansion of the definition of due process to include the Fourth, Fifth, Sixth, and Eighth Amendments. One by one, cases have come to the Supreme Court, where it was determined that the circumstances of treatment of the accused did not afford the accused fundamental fairness during investigation, arrest, and prosecution.[4]

The ultimate effect of selective incorporation is quite simple. Once the Supreme Court finds that a particular right is incorporated into the Fourteenth Amendment, any state laws that would affect this right must be fair and reasonable. The Court will invalidate state laws that affect protected federal constitutional rights.

Selective incorporation has been especially relevant to laws of criminal procedure, which guide criminal prosecutions and set forth what is considered fundamental to the criminal process. These laws ultimately affect the American theory of innocence until guilt is proven beyond any reasonable doubt by controlling the manner in which the accused is treated and evidence is obtained.

The following sections discuss the amendments to the U.S. Constitution that have been selectively incorporated into the Fourteenth Amendment. The reasoning behind the incorporation of each particular amendment and the effect of the amendment's incorporation on state laws are included. It is especially helpful to examine the cases in which the Court made these decisions, because the cases provide examples that actually occurred.

The Fourth Amendment: Search and Seizure

As early as 1914, the U.S. Supreme Court first held that evidence in a federal criminal prosecution that was obtained without a proper search warrant or probable cause would be inadmissible in court.[5] This was the beginning of the exclusionary rule, under which improperly obtained evidence is excluded from trial. Consequently, no matter how damaging, such evidence cannot be used to convict someone of a crime. The Supreme Court adopted this position with regard to the federal court system's criminal prosecutions.

The idea that the Fourth Amendment should be incorporated into the Fourteenth, thereby requiring states to apply the exclusionary rule, was first addressed in 1949 in *Wolf v. Colorado*.[6] (338 U.S. 25, 69 S.Ct. 1359, 93 L. Ed. 1782). At that time, the Court examined what the states had done on their own and found that some 30 states had considered the exclusionary rule used in federal cases but had chosen not to follow the rule in state criminal prosecutions. Rather, these states decided to develop their own methods to discourage police from unreasonable practices in obtaining evidence. In *Wolf*, the Court decided that since a majority of the states had rejected the exclusionary rule and were using means other than the exclusion of evidence to prevent unlawful searches and seizures, it should not forcibly impose the requirement on the states. Thus, the Court held that the states could adequately protect the rights of their citizens without a forced application of the exclusionary rule to guarantee rights under the Fourth Amendment. Therefore, the Fourth Amendment was not at this time incorporated into the Fourteenth Amendment definition of due process. Consequently, the states were not yet required to adopt the federal position on the exclusionary rule. The effect was that as long as the state law was followed, a person's property could be searched and seized and any evidence of criminal activity used against the individual in a prosecution.

APPLICATION 15.1

Beth shares an apartment with Debbie. One night Beth's parked car is hit by a drunk driver. The police come to the apartment at 1:30 A.M. to inform her. While at the door, they notice Debbie sitting on the couch appearing glassy-eyed and lethargic. They enter the room without permission and conduct a search. They find large quantities of illegal drugs and cash among Debbie's belongings. Both Debbie and Beth are charged with drug trafficking. It is ultimately proven that Beth was unaware of Debbie's drug dealings and that the search was illegal, and the exclusionary rule applied causing all charges to be dropped. This occurred, however, only after much publicity of the arrest, dismissal of Beth from college for the semester with a total loss of tuition and credits, and the loss of Beth's job and a full scholarship from a religious organization. Under the exclusionary rule, the police are required to follow certain standards of reasonableness in searches and seizures. These are designed, in part, to determine who is actually involved in criminal activity and to avoid tainting innocent persons with a reputation of criminal conduct. Before the exclusionary rule was applied, in some states the search in the situation above would have been considered appropriate.

Point for Discussion

♦   Why would the search be considered illegal under the exclusionary rule?

Just 12 years after *Wolf v. Colorado*, the Supreme Court reconsidered the incorporation of the Fourth Amendment into the Fourteenth Amendment. In *Mapp v. Ohio*,[7] 367 U.S. 649, 81 S. Ct. 1684, 6 L.Ed. 2d 1081 (1961), the Court reversed its prior holding (an extremely rare occurrence) and held that the federally developed exclusionary rule is the most appropriate way of protecting citizens from unreasonable searches and seizures. The Court further held that for a citizen to be afforded due process in a criminal prosecution (a right guaranteed in the Fourteenth Amendment), the Fourth Amendment protections must be adhered to, including the federal method of using the exclusionary rule. Consequently, the Fourth Amendment protections should be incorporated into the definition of the Fourteenth Amendment. Further, the states should be required to follow the exclusionary rule, which is the method of choice to enforce the Fourth Amendment rule of no unreasonable search and seizure.

A large part of the reason for the Court's reversal of its position was the fact that since the *Wolf* decision, many states had tried methods other than the exclusionary rule and had failed. Many of these states then turned to the exclusionary rule on their own. The Court in *Mapp v. Ohio* affirmed this as an acceptable method of protecting citizens' rights.

Exclusionary rule.   With this decision, the Fourteenth Amendment began to be expanded to include the rights enunciated in other amendments. The results of the decision in *Mapp v. Ohio* are continuing even today. Since that time, the Court has reviewed many state laws to determine what is a reasonable search or seizure and what is unreasonable. Evidence obtained through the latter is prohibited under the exclusionary rule from being used as evidence at a trial.

Over the years, a great deal of concern has been expressed about the exclusionary rule, which was intended to deter or prevent law enforcement personnel from obtaining evidence by means that violate Fourth Amendment rights. The rationale was that individuals were not in a position to protect their rights against law enforcement agencies. Further, if these agencies were not encouraged in some way to honor the constitutional amendment against unreasonable search and seizure, our society could be reduced to a police state, which, in its most extreme form, might include random invasions of people's homes and property in search of evidence that might incriminate them.

However noble the intent of the exclusionary rule, the actual result is indisputable. When evidence is obtained in a questionable manner, the person who benefits is the accused. Although our government follows the doctrine that an accused is innocent until proven guilty, in many such cases, the evidence excluded is so strong that it would undoubtedly result in a verdict of guilty by a jury. As a consequence of applying the exclusionary rule to protect a defendant's Fourth Amendment rights, many criminals have gone free or plea bargained for greatly reduced charges.

The Supreme Court has been faced with a double bind. Without the exclusionary rule, improper searches and seizures of innocent people's property can occur. With the exclusionary rule, known criminals can go free because of a technical, minor, or innocent violation of the rule. In 1984, the Court considered this dilemma in *United States v. Leon,* 468 U.S. 817, 104 S. Ct. 3405, 82 L.Ed. 2d. 677.[8] In the *Leon* decision, the Supreme Court addressed at length the difficulty with enforcing a broad application of the exclusionary rule. The Court recognized that excluding evidence because of an improper search or seizure, no matter how small the infraction that caused it to be improper, resulted in preventing the jury from accurately determining innocence or guilt at a trial. When the exclusionary rule is applied, often the case is dismissed because little admissible evidence is available to support a conviction. At the very least, the jury is given only limited information with which to make its decision. The jurors are allowed to consider only properly obtained evidence. In fact, they generally do not know that additional evidence exists and has been excluded.

In *Leon*, the Court was faced with a situation where the police properly requested a search warrant. The judge properly reviewed the information to support the warrant and then issued the warrant. The police exercised the search warrant and found incriminating evidence. Only after the search occurred was it discovered that the warrant was improper. The police had requested a warrant on the basis of limited surveillance and the information of a person who had never before acted as an informant. Unless informants have a history of providing accurate information to law enforcement, their testimony usually requires much additional evidence before a judge will believe there is probable cause to suspect a crime and issue a search warrant. In this case, the defendant challenged the validity of the search warrant, and a higher judge found that it should never have been issued on such limited information.

The Supreme Court used the *Leon* decision to make a major exception to the exclusionary rule. Observing that the police had made every effort to follow the requirements to protect the Fourth Amendment rights of the defendant, the Court reasoned that since this was the entire goal of the exclusionary rule, it had been satisfied. The police had gone so far as to request permission of a judge to search for criminal evidence. Therefore, the goal of the rule had been met, and the citizen's rights had been protected. The Court refused to exclude the evidence (a large amount of illegal drugs), and the defendant was prosecuted. The Court stated that the exclusionary rule is designed to deter unreasonable practices by law enforcement personnel, not to remedy poor exercises of authority by judges.

The *Leon* decision is of vital importance in the law of criminal procedure. It signals that the Court has shifted toward a more conservative view of what is necessary to protect the rights of citizens. The Court currently regards certain areas as private and subject to the protection of a citizen's Fourteenth Amendment rights by requiring satisfaction of the guarantees under the Fourth Amendment.

Probable cause.   What a person considers to be private is that which cannot be searched or seized without **probable cause.** The Court has established a two-step test to be used in determining what is private property. First, it must be decided whether the person acted in such a way as to keep the property private from others. Second, it must be determined whether the person was reasonable in believing such property should be allowed to be kept private.[9]

probable cause
More than mere suspicion of criminal activity.

Before law enforcement personnel can search or seize private property, they must have probable cause to believe a crime has been committed and/or that the owner of the property has been involved in criminal activity. There must also be probable cause to believe that a search of the property will result in evidence that will assist in proving this. Further, when possible, the law enforcement agency must seek approval of the search and seizure by obtaining a warrant from a judicial officer. The basis for the warrant must be probable cause. Although it is much debated, no absolute formula has ever been developed to determine what constitutes probable cause. Rather, probable cause falls within a range that, when examined by a neutral observer, would be considered more than basic suspicion but less than evidence adequate to justify—conviction.[10]

If law enforcement personnel can support their suspicions and allegation of probable cause with outside information or other evidence that would create this degree of probability that the person or property is connected with criminal activity, a search warrant may be issued by a judge. If there is not time to request a search warrant, the officers may proceed with the search if there is probable cause to conduct it.[11] Because the officers are not considered to be as objective as a judicial officer, they are under a particularly heavy burden to show that their search was made with probable cause. To qualify as an exception to the warrant requirement, there must be an immediate danger that the property or person associated with the criminal activity will be lost unless an immediate search is conducted.

Warrants.　The type of property that may be searched has also been discussed by the courts. Generally, before a private residence can be searched, a warrant must be issued. If the property has been abandoned, a citizen has no expectation of privacy; therefore, no warrant is needed.[12] In addition, if the criminal activity or evidence can be observed by persons around or above the property, the property is considered to be in view of the public, and thus there is no expectation of privacy.[13] If an officer is lawfully upon another person's property for any reason and discovers criminal evidence in plain view, the property may be seized immediately (known as the plain view rule). Finally, if someone other than the resident has access to the residence and voluntarily allows officers entrance to the property, such entrance is treated as if permission had been given by the resident. Therefore, landlords, roommates, or guests have the power to admit police officers voluntarily to a residence for the purpose of searching for evidence of criminal activity.[14] In such situations, no warrant is necessary.

Police do need a warrant to invade private property by other than ordinary means. If, for example, a wiretap is going to be used to obtain the content of conversations in a residence or on a telephone line from a residence, a search warrant must be obtained, because the public would perceive a reasonable expectation of privacy in such a situation. However, devices that merely record the numbers called from a residence are not considered private, as the telephone company has access to this information at all times. Further, tracking devices on vehicles are permissible because the purpose is to track the vehicle in public. There can be no expectation of privacy about where one goes in public.

Vehicles.　Vehicles have created a whole new arena for questions about search and seizure. They are private property capable of concealing a great deal of other property. At the same time, they are transported in public, which means that the expectation of privacy is lower than that in a residence. The courts have held that looking into the vehicle from the outside is not a search and that if evidence of criminal activity is seen, there is no need for a warrant.[15]

If a car has been abandoned, there is no expectation of privacy. Therefore, no warrant is needed to examine the interior of the vehicle. The courts have also given officers the ability to search those areas of a car that are within reasonable reach of the owner when a stop is made.[16] The rationale is that the owner may be within reach of a weapon that could be used to assault the officers or to effect escape. The recent trend has been to approve searches of vehicles even when the suspect is no longer in the car or the car has been impounded. The basic requirement seems to be not that an emergency must exist but rather that the officer must have probable cause to believe that evidence or dangerous items may be in the car, its compartments, or containers within it or that the car is not in the possession of the police and is subject to removal from the jurisdiction. The regulation of police searches of automobiles is a rapidly evolving area of the law with many distinctions between states and federal government. Accordingly, it is important to know the law specific to your jurisdiction.

This is a brief examination of some of the areas that have been addressed by the courts in determining what constitutes a search under the Fourth Amendment. Because the amendment has been applied to the states, these rules must be followed by state as well as federal law enforcement officers. The theory is that these rules will afford citizens due process and fairness before their privacy is invaded or their property is searched or seized by the state government. The rules also help to ensure fairer criminal prosecutions by reducing the chances of improper convictions.

Arrest. The same basic warrant requirements that apply to search and seizure of property apply to arrest. In essence, an arrest is a search and seizure of the person. Thus, the person is entitled to the same fair treatment as his or her property would be afforded. Consequently, the courts prefer that arrest warrants be obtained upon a showing of probable cause before the arrest is made. Often criminal activity is discovered while it is occurring or immediately after it has occurred. In such cases, it is usually unreasonable to expect that the criminal will remain until a warrant is obtained. Therefore, most arrests are made on the basis of a probable cause determination by law enforcement officers. This determination is subject to judicial review, just as a search made without a warrant would be.

When an arrest based on probable cause has been made, the officer may search the arrested person and all areas within his or her reach.[17] The reason for this is that the arrestee may be carrying a weapon that could be used to harm the officer. If the officer recovers other evidence of criminal activity during the search, the evidence may also be seized. Even though it is not what the officer may have been searching for, it is considered to be fruits of crime. A suspect who carries evidence of criminal activity on his or her person and is subsequently lawfully arrested does not have a reasonable expectation of privacy regarding that property.

Even when a full-fledged arrest is not made, the officers are entitled to take minimum steps to protect their own safety. Occasionally, an officer will stop an individual on suspicion of some criminal activity, perhaps even a minor infraction, such as a traffic violation. Even on stopping such an individual, the officer has the right to frisk the individual for a concealed weapon if the officer has a reasonable suspicion that the suspect is armed or otherwise dangerous.[18] This is permitted to avoid disastrous circumstances that have occurred and still occur when an individual stopped for a minor infraction pulls out a weapon and kills an officer of the law.

As this far from exhaustive discussion illustrates, the law of search and seizure is quite complex. Further, this area of law changes continually as the Supreme Court seeks to mold specific rules regarding the expectation of privacy by individuals for themselves and their property. The Court must balance these expectations against what is necessary to promote law enforcement and the safety of the people as a whole. As long as this balancing continues, this area of criminal procedure will grow.

Assignment 15.1

Consider the following situations and determine whether the exclusionary rule would apply to prevent the use of seized evidence against a defendant in a criminal prosecution.

1. In a small midwestern town, Joanna shoots and kills a fellow student. There are no witnesses and no other evidence that points to Joanna other than a well-known and bitter rivalry between her and the victim. A local sheriff questions Joanna in her yard and finds her alibi suspicious. He then walks past Joanna into the house and starts searching. In the back of a kitchen cabinet he finds bloody clothes and the murder weapon with Joanna's fingerprints. Other than this, there is insufficient evidence to even charge Joanna with the crime.

2. Marty is driving erratically when he is stopped for reckless driving. The officer pats him down and looks in Marty's wallet where he finds several pills of an illegal drug.

3. Jane is a police officer in a foot pursuit of a mugger. The alleged mugger runs into a house and out the back door. Jane continues the pursuit but on her way through the house, a private residence, she sees several people sitting around a table snorting cocaine. She calls for backup and subsequently arrests the individuals in the house and seizes the cocaine.

The Fifth Amendment: Double Jeopardy, Self-Incrimination

Practically speaking, the role of the Fifth Amendment in criminal procedure has been primarily confined to the issues of double jeopardy and self-incrimination, addressed individually, as they are wholly separate rights.

Double jeopardy.   **Double jeopardy** is the right of every citizen to be tried once, and only once, for a specific crime charged. The theory is that the government should prove guilt beyond a reasonable doubt at trial. If this cannot be accomplished, the presumption of innocence is sustained and questions of guilt are dismissed. Citizens cannot be subjected to multiple trials for the same crime each time the government believes it can produce new evidence or select a more critical jury.

The rule of double jeopardy was rather easily incorporated into the Fourteenth Amendment and applied to the states. The Fourteenth Amendment clearly states that there can be no deprivation of life or liberty without due process of law. It seems quite logical that to force someone to be tried over and over again for the same crime would not be an exercise of due process of law. The very notion of fair treatment to all citizens is contrary to the thought that a citizen could be singled out and charged repeatedly with a crime until the prosecution was successful.

The courts have clearly defined the point at which double jeopardy becomes an issue. A person is not considered to be in jeopardy of loss of life or limb (in modern terms, penalty, liberty, or life) until it is a real possibility that such a result will occur. After a person is charged with a crime and until the time of trial, there is a possibility that the charges will be dropped. After the trial begins, however, it is assumed that a verdict will be reached and a penalty may ensue. Therefore, a person is not in jeopardy until such time as the jury has been sworn in.[19] In a bench trial before a judge, and without a jury, double jeopardy attaches when the first witness is sworn. At this point, the defendant can be subjected to a second trial for the charge only if the first trial results in a mistrial.

Once the verdict is reached, it is considered final. Following this, if the accused person is acquitted (found not guilty), he or she cannot be charged and tried again for the identical crime. In addition, the person generally cannot later be charged for other possible charges arising out of the same incident.[20] Thus, if the prosecution is unsuccessful in trying a person for murder, it cannot then charge the person with manslaughter or assault. If the judge dismisses the case because of a lack of evidence that would support a finding of guilty, ordinarily there can be no second prosecution.[21]

Once a trial has commenced and jeopardy has attached, the person cannot be charged and tried again with a crime, with a few exceptions. If there is a dismissal or a mistrial is called for any reason other than a lack of evidence or if the defendant appeals a guilty verdict, the charges may be reinstated and the case tried again. The Supreme Court has refused to adopt the double jeopardy right as a means of escaping conviction on technicalities. Thus, if the prosecution has sufficient evidence to uphold a conviction, the case may be retried. Further, if the defendant appealed a conviction and is granted a new trial, there is a second chance for sentencing as well. As long as the sentence is justified by the crime, a judge in a second trial may impose a stricter sentence than was given in the first trial.

The double jeopardy rule puts a burden on the prosecution to be relatively sure of its case before presenting it to a jury. However, the defendant is faced with the decision of accepting a guilty verdict or taking a chance on a potentially more severe sentence in a new trial.

double jeopardy
Being placed on trial for the same crime twice.

Self-incrimination.   Interpretations regarding what constitutes self-incrimination are much more pervasive than interpretations of double jeopardy. The primary issue has been at what point the right to refuse to give information that may be incriminating originates. Under the Fifth Amendment, no person may be forced to give information that may then be used to convict that person of a crime. For nearly the first 200 years of the amendment's history, the courts merely examined whether information had been given voluntarily; but during the past few decades, the courts have begun to give more attention to the circumstances surrounding communications with persons suspected or accused of a crime. The courts began to recognize that in some cases, a suspect or defendant might be influenced by the circumstances and in this way be compelled to give information that he or she would ordinarily withhold as his or her right not to take part in self-prosecution.

A landmark decision in this area of the law came in *Miranda v. Arizona.* 384 U.S. 497, 98 S.Ct.824, 54 L. Ed 2d 717, (1966).[22] In that decision, the Supreme Court firmly stated that every person accused of a crime must be informed at the very outset that all further communications might be used in a prosecution. The result of that decision was the adoption of the Miranda rights, now read to all persons in this country at the time of interrogation and/or arrest. All accused individuals are advised that (1) they have the right to remain silent, (2) anything they say may be used against them in a court of law, (3) they have the right to an attorney, and (4) they may have an attorney appointed if they cannot afford one.

As with double jeopardy, it was a logical step to incorporate this aspect of the Fifth Amendment into the Fourteenth Amendment and thus require the states to adhere to it in their own laws. Since it would be impossible to provide due process of law to any individuals who are forced to testify against themselves at any stage of a criminal proceeding, such individuals must be allowed the opportunity to remain silent.

At first this may appear to be contrary to the purpose of criminal justice, which is to catch and punish persons committing crimes against society. However, the Constitution is designed to protect all of the people, including those persons who may be innocent but lack the ability to act in their own best interest. Persons who are not adept at giving testimony and for whom the circumstances would imply guilt should have the right to protect their innocence with silence and not be penalized for it.

The *Miranda* decision clearly established that the right against self-incrimination originates at the moment an individual is held for interrogation or is placed under arrest, whichever occurs first. Therefore, all persons detained are placed on notice that any utterance can be used against them. Anything a suspected criminal says while in custody, even if it is not said to a police officer, may be used against him or her in a prosecution. The right against self-incrimination is the right to remain silent. It is not the right to make statements to some persons and not to others. A statement made to officers or within the confines of a police facility are considered to be voluntary statements with the exception of confidential communication to one's attorney.

If the police wish to interrogate a prisoner, the questioning must be done in the fairest of circumstances. The police must either allow an attorney to be present on behalf of the accused or demonstrate that the prisoner waived the right to have an attorney present.[23] Evidence of this waiver must be documented. It must be clear that the prisoner knew and understood the reasons for having an attorney present and intelligently chose not to have an attorney present. Further, the police cannot set up circumstances that play upon the weaknesses of the accused to the point that there is no voluntary waiver. For example, if a prisoner is known to suffer from some mental incapacity, the police may not take advantage of this to further impair the prisoner's ability to make a decision regarding counsel.

A prisoner who is willing to answer questions or give a statement or confession may do so without the presence or advice of legal counsel; however, the courts will scrutinize the record to make sure such information was given voluntarily. Therefore, the police will generally ask prisoners to sign a written statement that they know and understand their rights. A prisoner will acknowledge in the statement that he or she waives the right to remain silent and the right to counsel. Subsequently, the Supreme Court has held that if a prisoner knows of the right to counsel (following Miranda warnings) and does not request counsel, the police may interrogate. Once a prisoner requests counsel, however, the police are under a heavier burden to show that any communications outside the presence of counsel were indeed voluntary.

◆ APPLICATION 15.2

Dominic has a long criminal history. He has been in and out of prison for the last 15 years. He is uneducated and has lived most of his life on the street. He is now charged with murder. His counsel determines that Dominic would not communicate well on the stand and could well damage his own case by attempting to explain why he was present but uninvolved in the murder. In reality, Dominic was involved in a drug deal with someone else at the time and place of the murder; but he is certain that if he identifies his drug contact, he will be killed. Counsel is concerned that the admission of being involved in a drug deal at the time of the murder will influence the jury against Dominic. He has no real explanation to provide as to why he was present at the scene, so he decides not to testify.

Point for Discussion
◆ What can the jury legally infer from Dominic's failure to testify?

The *Miranda* decision was actually one of several similar cases. The Court was presented with numerous appeals on the same issue, although the facts differed somewhat from case to case. However, the Court applied its opinion in *Miranda* to each of the cases individually.

CASE

**MIRANDA v.
STATE OF
ARIZONA**

384 U.S. 436, 86
S.Ct. 1602, 16 L.Ed.2d
694 (1966).

**MR. CHIEF JUSTICE
WARREN
DELIVERED THE
OPINION OF THE
COURT.**

The cases before us raise questions which go to the roots of our concepts of American criminal jurisprudence: the restraints society must observe consistent with the federal Constitution in prosecuting individuals for crime. More specifically, we deal with the admissibility of statements obtained from an individual who is subjected to custodial police interrogation and the necessity for procedures which assure that the individual is accorded his privilege under the Fifth Amendment to the Constitution not to be compelled to incriminate himself.

We dealt with certain phases of this problem recently in *Escobedo v. State of Illinois,* 378 U.S. 478, 84 S.Ct. 1758, 12 L.Ed.2d 977 (1964). There, as in the four cases before us, law enforcement officials took the defendant into custody and interrogated him in a police station for the purpose of obtaining a confession. The police did not effectively advise him of his right to remain silent or of his right to consult with his attorney. Rather, they confronted him with an alleged accomplice who accused him of having perpetrated a murder. When the defendant denied the accusation and said 'I didn't shoot Manuel, you did it,' they handcuffed him and took him to an interrogation room. There, while handcuffed and standing, he was questioned for four hours until he confessed. During this interrogation, the police denied his request to speak to his attorney, and they prevented his retained attorney, who had come to the police station, from consulting with him. At his trial, the State, over his objection, introduced the confession against him. We held that the statements thus made were constitutionally inadmissible.

This case has been the subject of judicial interpretation and spirited legal debate since it was decided two years ago. Both state and federal courts, in assessing its implications, have arrived at varying conclusions. . . . A wealth of scholarly material has been written tracing its ramifications and underpinnings. . . . Police and prosecutor have speculated on its range and desirability. . . . We granted certiorari in these cases, 382 U.S. 924, 925, 937, 86 S.Ct. 318, 320, 395, 15 L.Ed.2d 338, 339, 348, in order further to explore some facets of the problems, thus exposed, of applying the privilege against self-incrimination to in-custody interrogation, and to give concrete constitutional guidelines for law enforcement agencies and courts to follow.

We start here, as we did in *Escobedo,* with the premise that our holding is not an innovation in our jurisprudence, but is an application of principles long recognized and applied in other settings. We have undertaken a thorough re-examination of the *Escobedo* decision and the principles it announced, and we reaffirm it. That case was but an explication of basic rights that are enshrined in our Constitution—that 'No person shall be compelled in any criminal case to be a witness against himself,' and that 'the accused shall have the Assistance of Counsel'—rights which were put in jeopardy in that case through official overbearing. These precious rights were fixed in our Constitution only after centuries of persecution and struggle. And in the words of Chief Justice Marshall, they were secured 'for ages to come, and designed to approach immortality as nearly as human institutions can approach it,' *Cohens v. Commonwealth of Virginia,* 6 Wheat. 264, 387, 5 L.Ed. 257 (1821).

* * *

Our holding will be spelled out with some specificity in the pages which follow but briefly stated it is this: the prosecution may not use statements, whether exculpatory or inculpatory, stemming from custodial interrogation of the defendant unless it demonstrates the use of procedural safeguards effective to secure the privilege against self-incrimination. By custodial interrogation, we mean questioning initiated by law enforcement officers after a person has been taken into custody or otherwise deprived of his freedom of action in any significant way. (This is what we meant in Escobedo when we spoke of an investigation which had focused on an accused.) As for the procedural safeguards to be employed, unless other fully effective means are devised to inform accused persons of their right of silence and to assure a continuous opportunity to exercise it, the following measures are required. Prior to any questioning, the person must be warned that he has a right to remain silent, that any statement he does make may be used as evidence against him, and that he has a right to the presence of an attorney, either retained or appointed. The defendant may waive effectuation of these rights, provided the waiver is made voluntarily, knowingly and intelligently. If, however, he indicates in any manner and at any stage of the process that he wishes to consult with an attorney before speaking there can be no questioning. Likewise, if the individual is alone and indicates in any manner that he does not wish to be interrogated, the police may not question him. The mere fact that he may have answered some questions or volunteered some statements on his own does not deprive him of the right to refrain from answering any further inquiries until he has consulted with an attorney and thereafter consents to be questioned.

1.

The constitutional issue we decide in each of these cases is the admissibility of statements obtained from a defendant questioned while in custody or otherwise deprived of his freedom of action in any significant way. In each, the defendant was questioned by police officers, detectives, or a prosecuting attorney in a room in which he was cut off from the outside world. In none of these cases was the defendant given a full and effective warning of his rights at the outset of the interrogation process. In all the cases, the questioning elicited oral admissions, and in three of them, signed statements as well which were admitted at their trials. They all thus share salient features—incommunicado interrogation of

individuals in a police-dominated atmosphere, resulting in self-incriminating statements without full warnings of constitutional rights.

An understanding of the nature and setting of this in-custody interrogation is essential to our decisions today. The difficulty in depicting what transpires at such interrogations stems from the fact that in this country they have largely taken place incommunicado. From extensive factual studies undertaken in the early 1930s, including the famous Wickersham Report to Congress by a Presidential Commission, it is clear that police violence and the 'third degree' flourished at that time. . . . In a series of cases decided by this Court long after these studies, the police resorted to physical brutality—beatings, hanging, whipping—and to sustained and protracted questioning incommunicado in order to extort confessions. . . . The Commission on Civil Rights in 1961 found much evidence to indicate that 'some policemen still resort to physical force to obtain confessions,' 1961 Comm'n on Civil Rights Rep., Justice, pt. 5, 17. The use of physical brutality and violence is not, unfortunately, relegated to the past or to any part of the country. Only recently in Kings County, New York, the police brutally beat, kicked and placed lighted cigarette butts on the back of a potential witness under interrogation for the purpose of securing a statement incriminating a third party. *People v. Portelli,* 15 N.Y.2d 235, 257 N.Y.S.2d 931, 205 N.E.2d 857 (1965).

* * *

Again we stress that the modern practice of in-custody interrogation is psychologically rather than physically oriented. As we have stated before, 'Since *Chambers v. State of Florida,* 309 U.S. 227, 60 S.Ct. 472, 84 L.Ed. 716, this Court has recognized that coercion can be mental as well as physical, and that the blood of the accused is not the only hallmark of an unconstitutional inquisition.' *Blackburn v. State of Alabama,* 361 U.S. 199, 206, 80 S.Ct. 274, 279, 4 L.Ed.2d 242 (1960). Interrogation still takes place in privacy. Privacy results in secrecy and this in turn results in a gap in our knowledge as to what in fact goes on in the interrogation rooms. A valuable source of

CASE

information about present police practices, however, may be found in various police manuals and texts which document procedures employed with success in the past, and which recommend various other effective tactics.

Even without employing brutality. . . . the very fact of custodial interrogation exacts a heavy toll on individual liberty and trades on the weakness of individuals. . . . Interrogation procedures may even give rise to a false confession. The most recent conspicuous example occurred in New York, in 1964, when a Negro of limited intelligence confessed to two brutal murders and a rape which he had not committed. When this was discovered, the prosecutor was reported as saying: 'Call it what you want—brain-washing, hypnosis, fright. They made him give an untrue confession. The only thing I don't believe is that Whitmore was beaten.' N.Y. Times, Jan. 28, 1965, p. 1, col. 5. In two other instances, similar events had occurred. N.Y. Times, Oct. 20, 1964, p. 22, col. 1; N.Y. Times, Aug. 25, 1965, p. 1, col. 1. In general, see Borchard, Convicting the Innocent (1932); Frank & Frank, Not Guilty (1957).

* * *

In the cases before us today, given this background, we concern ourselves primarily with this interrogation atmosphere and the evils it can bring. In No. 759, *Miranda v. Arizona,* the police arrested the defendant and took him to a special interrogation room where they secured a confession. In No. 760, *Vignera v. New York,* the defendant made oral admissions to the police after interrogation in the afternoon, and then signed an inculpatory statement upon being questioned by an assistant district attorney later the same evening. In No. 761, *Westover v. United States,* the defendant was handed over to the Federal Bureau of Investigation by local authorities after they had detained and interrogated him for a lengthy period, both at night and the following morning. After some two hours of questioning, the federal officers had obtained signed statements from the defendant. Lastly, in No. 584, *California v. Stewart,* the local police held the defendant five days in the station and interrogated him on nine separate

occasions before they secured his inculpatory statement.

In these cases, we might not find the defendants' statements to have been involuntary in traditional terms. Our concern for adequate safeguards to protect precious Fifth Amendment rights is, of course, not lessened in the slightest. In each of the cases, the defendant was thrust into an unfamiliar atmosphere and run through menacing police interrogation procedures. The potentiality for compulsion is forcefully apparent, for example, in *Miranda,* where the indigent Mexican defendant was a seriously disturbed individual with pronounced sexual fantasies, and in *Stewart,* in which the defendant was an indigent Los Angeles Negro who had dropped out of school in the sixth grade. To be sure, the records do not evince overt physical coercion or patent psychological ploys. The fact remains that in none of these cases did the officers undertake to afford appropriate safeguards at the outset of the interrogation to insure that the statements were truly the product of free choice.

It is obvious that such an interrogation environment is created for no purpose other than to subjugate the individual to the will of his examiner. This atmosphere carries its own badge of intimidation. To be sure, this is not physical intimidation, but it is equally destructive of human dignity. . . . The current practice of incommunicado interrogation is at odds with one of our Nation's most cherished principles—that the individual may not be compelled to incriminate himself. Unless adequate protective devices are employed to dispel the compulsion inherent in custodial surroundings, no statement obtained from the defendant can truly be the product of his free choice.

The question in these cases is whether the privilege is fully applicable during a period of custodial interrogation. In this Court, the privilege has consistently been accorded a liberal construction. *Albertson v. Subversive Activities Control Board,* 382 U.S. 70, 81, 86 S.Ct. 194, 200, 15 L.Ed.2d 165 (1965); *Hoffman v. United States,* 341 U.S. 479, 486, 71 S.Ct. 814, 818, 95 L.Ed.2d 1118 (1951); *Arnstein v. McCarthy,* 254 U.S. 71, 72–73, 41

S.Ct. 26, 65 L.Ed. 138 (1920); *Counselman v. Hitchcock,* 142 U.S. 547, 562, 12 S.Ct. 195, 197, 35 L.Ed. 1110 (1892). We are satisfied that all the principles embodied in the privilege apply to informal compulsion exerted by law-enforcement officers during in-custody questioning. An individual swept from familiar surroundings into police custody, surrounded by antagonistic forces, and subjected to the techniques of persuasion described above cannot be otherwise than under compulsion to speak. As a practical matter, the compulsion to speak in the isolated setting of the police station may well be greater than in courts or other official investigations, where there are often impartial observers to guard against intimidation or trickery . . .

This question, in fact, could have been taken as settled in federal courts almost 70 years ago, when, in *Bram v. United States,* 168 U.S. 532, 542, 18 S.Ct. 183, 187, 42 L.Ed. 568 (1897), this Court held:

> 'In criminal trials, in the courts of the United States, wherever a question arises whether a confession is incompetent because not voluntary, the issue is controlled by that portion of the fifth amendment commanding that no person 'shall be compelled in any criminal case to be a witness against himself.'

In *Bram,* the Court reviewed the British and American history and case law and set down the Fifth Amendment standard for compulsion which we implement today:

> 'Much of the confusion which has resulted from the effort to deduce from the adjudged cases what would be a sufficient quantum of proof to show that a confession was or was not voluntary has arisen from a misconception of the subject to which the proof must address itself. The rule is not that, in order to render a statement admissible, the proof must be adequate to establish that the particular communications contained in a statement were voluntarily made, but it must be sufficient to establish that the making of the statement was voluntary; that is

to say, that, from the causes which the law treats as legally sufficient to engender in the mind of the accused hope or fear in respect to the crime charged, the accused was not involuntarily impelled to make a statement when but for the improper influences he would have remained silent.' 168 U.S., at 549, 18 S.Ct. at 189. And see, id., at 542, 18 S.Ct. at 186.

* * *

The decisions of this Court have guaranteed the same procedural protection for the defendant whether his confession was used in a federal or state court. It is now axiomatic that the defendant's constitutional rights have been violated if his conviction is based, in whole or in part, on an involuntary confession, regardless of its truth or falsity. *Rogers v. Richmond,* 365 U.S. 534, 544, 81 S.Ct. 735, 741, 5 L.Ed.2d 760 (1961); *Siang Sung Wan v. United States,* 266 U.S. 1, 45 S.Ct. 1, 69 L.Ed. 131 (1924). This is so even if there is ample evidence aside from the confession to support the conviction, e.g., *Malinski v. People of State of New York,* 324 U.S. 401, 404, 65 S.Ct. 781, 783, 89 L.Ed. 1029 (1945); *Bram v. United States,* 168 U.S. 532, 540–542, 18 S.Ct. 183, 185–186 (1897).

Today, . . . there can be no doubt that the Fifth Amendment privilege is available outside of criminal court proceedings and serves to protect persons in all settings in which their freedom of action is curtailed in any significant way from being compelled to incriminate themselves. We have concluded that without proper safeguards the process of in-custody interrogation of persons suspected or accused of crime contains inherently compelling pressures which work to undermine the individual's will to resist and to compel him to speak where he would not otherwise do so freely. In order to combat these pressures and to permit a full opportunity to exercise the privilege against self-incrimination, the accused must be adequately and effectively apprised of his rights and the exercise of those rights must be fully honored.

* * *

At the outset, if a person in custody is to be subjected to interrogation, he must first be informed

CASE

in clear and unequivocal terms that he has the right to remain silent. For those unaware of the privilege, the warning is needed simply to make them aware of it—the threshold requirement for an intelligent decision as to its exercise. More important, such a warning is an absolute prerequisite in overcoming the inherent pressures of the interrogation atmosphere. It is not just the subnormal or woefully ignorant who succumb to an interrogator's imprecations, whether implied or expressly stated, that the interrogation will continue until a confession is obtained or that silence in the face of accusation is itself damning and will bode ill when presented to a jury. . . . Further, the warning will show the individual that his interrogators are prepared to recognize his privilege should he choose to exercise it.

The Fifth Amendment privilege is so fundamental to our system of constitutional rule and the expedient of giving an adequate warning as to the availability of the privilege so simple, we will not pause to inquire in individual cases whether the defendant was aware of his rights without a warning being given. Assessments of the knowledge the defendant possessed, based on information as to his age, education, intelligence, or prior contact with authorities, can never be more than speculation; . . . a warning is a clearcut fact. More important, whatever the background of the person interrogated, a warning at the time of the interrogation is indispensable to overcome its pressures and to insure that the individual knows he is free to exercise the privilege at that point in time.

The warning of the right to remain silent must be accompanied by the explanation that anything said can and will be used against the individual in court. This warning is needed in order to make him aware not only of the privilege, but also of the consequences of foregoing it. It is only through an awareness of these consequences that there can be any assurance of real understanding and intelligent exercise of the privilege. Moreover, this warning may serve to make the individual more acutely aware that he is faced with a phase of the adversary system—that he is not in the presence of persons acting solely in his interest.

The circumstances surrounding in-custody interrogation can operate very quickly to overbear the will of one merely made aware of his privilege by his interrogators. Therefore, the right to have counsel present at the interrogation is indispensable to the protection of the Fifth Amendment privilege under the system we delineate today. Our aim is to assure that the individual's right to choose between silence and speech remains unfettered throughout the interrogation process. A once-stated warning, delivered by those who will conduct the interrogation, cannot itself suffice to that end among those who most require knowledge of their rights. A mere warning given by the interrogators is not alone sufficient to accomplish that end. Prosecutors themselves claim that the admonishment of the right to remain silent without more 'will benefit only the recidivist and the professional.' Brief for the National District Attorneys Association as amicus curiae, p. 14. Even preliminary advice given to the accused by his own attorney can be swiftly overcome by the secret interrogation process. Cf. *Escobedo v. State of Illinois*, 378 U.S. 478, 485, n. 5, 84 S.Ct. 1758, 1762. Thus, the need for counsel to protect the Fifth Amendment privilege comprehends not merely a right to consult with counsel prior to questioning, but also to have counsel present during any questioning if the defendant so desires. The accused who does not know his rights and therefore does not make a request may be the person who most needs counsel. As the California Supreme Court has aptly put it:

'Finally, we must recognize that the imposition of the requirement for the request would discriminate against the defendant who does not know his rights. The defendant who does not ask for counsel is the very defendant who most needs counsel. We cannot penalize a defendant who, not understanding his constitutional rights, does not make the formal request and by such failure demonstrates his helplessness. To require the request would be to favor the defendant whose sophistication or status had fortuitously prompted him to make it.' *People v. Dorado,* 62 Cal.2d 338, 351, 42 Cal.Rptr. 169, 177–178, 398 P.2d 361, 369–370, (1965) (Tobriner, J.).

In *Carnley v. Cochran,* 369 U.S. 506, 513, 82 S.Ct. 884, 889, 8 L.Ed.2d 70 (1962), we stated: '(I)t is settled that where the assistance of counsel is a constitutional requisite, the right to be furnished counsel does not depend on a request.' This proposition applies with equal force in the context of providing counsel to protect an accused's Fifth Amendment privilege in the face of interrogation. *See Herman, The Supreme Court and Restrictions on Police Interrogation,* 25 Ohio St.L.J. 449, 480 (1964). Although the role of counsel at trial differs from the role during interrogation, the differences are not relevant to the question whether a request is a prerequisite.

Accordingly we hold that an individual held for interrogation must be clearly informed that he has the right to consult with a lawyer and to have the lawyer with him during interrogation under the system for protecting the privilege we delineate today. As with the warnings of the right to remain silent and that anything stated can be used in evidence against him, this warning is an absolute prerequisite to interrogation. No amount of circumstantial evidence that the person may have been aware of this right will suffice to stand in its stead. Only through such a warning is there ascertainable assurance that the accused was aware of this right.

If an individual indicates that he wishes the assistance of counsel before any interrogation occurs, the authorities cannot rationally ignore or deny his request on the basis that the individual does not have or cannot afford a retained attorney. The financial ability of the individual has no relationship to the scope of the rights involved here. The privilege against self-incrimination secured by the Constitution applies to all individuals. The need for counsel in order to protect the privilege exists for the indigent as well as the affluent. In fact, were we to limit these constitutional rights to those who can retain an attorney, our decisions today would be of little significance. The cases before us as well as the vast majority of confession cases with which we have dealt in the past involve those unable to retain counsel. . . . While authorities are not required to relieve the accused of his poverty, they have the obligation not to take advantage of indigence in the administration of justice. . . . Denial of counsel to the indigent at the time of interrogation while allowing an attorney to those who can afford one would be no more supportable by reason or logic than the similar situation at trial and on appeal struck down in *Gideon v. Wainwright,* 372 U.S. 335, 83 S.Ct. 792, 9 L.Ed.2d 799 (1963), and *Douglas v. People of State of California,* 372 U.S. 353, 83 S.Ct. 814, 9 L.Ed.2d 811 (1963).

In order fully to apprise a person interrogated of the extent of his rights under this system then, it is necessary to warn him not only that he has the right to consult with an attorney, but also that if he is indigent, a lawyer will be appointed to represent him. Without this additional warning, the admonition of the right to consult with counsel would often be understood as meaning only that he can consult with a lawyer if he has one or has the funds to obtain one. The warning of a right to counsel would be hollow if not couched in terms that would convey to the indigent—the person most often subjected to interrogation—the knowledge that he too has a right to have counsel present. . . . As with the warnings of the right to remain silent and of the general right to counsel, only by effective and express explanation to the indigent of this right can there be assurance that he was truly in a position to exercise it. . . .

Case Review Question
With the mass media communicating the "right to remain silent" in criminal situations, why is it still required for police officers to give this warning?

CASE

Supreme Court of the United States

KENNEDY D. KIRK
v.
LOUISIANA.

122 S. Ct. 2458
Decided June 24, 2002.

Police officers entered petitioner's home, where they arrested and searched him. The officers had neither an arrest warrant nor a search warrant. Without deciding whether exigent circumstances had been present, the Louisiana Court of Appeal concluded that the warrantless entry, arrest, and search did not violate the Fourth Amendment of the Federal Constitution because there had been probable cause to arrest petitioner. 00-0190 (La. App.11/15/00), 773 So. 2d 259. The court's reasoning plainly violates our holding in *Payton v. New York*, 445 U.S. 573, 590, 100 S.Ct. 1371, 63 L.Ed.2d 639 (1980), that "[a]bsent exigent circumstances," the "firm line at the entrance to the house . . . may not reasonably be crossed without a warrant." We thus grant the petition for a writ of certiorari and reverse the Court of Appeal's conclusion that the officers' actions were lawful, absent exigent circumstances. We also grant petitioner's motion for leave to proceed *in forma pauperis*.

On an evening in March 1998, police officers observed petitioner's apartment based on an anonymous citizen complaint that drug sales were occurring there. After witnessing what appeared to be several drug purchases and allowing the buyers to leave the scene, the officers stopped one of the buyers on the street outside petitioner's residence. The officers later testified that "[b]ecause the stop took place within a block of the apartment, [they] feared that evidence would be destroyed and ordered that the apartment be entered." 773 So. 2d, at 261. Thus, "[t]hey immediately knocked on the door of the apartment, arrested the defendant, searched him thereto and discovered the cocaine and the money." *Id.,* at 263. Although the officers sought and obtained a search warrant while they detained petitioner in his home, they only obtained this warrant after they had entered his home, arrested him, frisked him, found a drug vial in his underwear, and observed contraband in plain view in the apartment.

Based on these events, petitioner was charged in a Louisiana court with possession of cocaine with intent to distribute. He filed a pretrial motion to suppress evidence obtained by the police as a result of their warrantless entry, arrest, and search. After holding a suppression hearing, the trial court denied this motion. Petitioner was convicted and sentenced to 15 years at hard labor.

On direct review to the Louisiana Court of Appeal, petitioner challenged the trial court's suppression ruling. He argued that the police were not justified in entering his home without a warrant absent exigent circumstances. The Court of Appeal acknowledged petitioner's argument: "[Petitioner] makes a long argument that there were not exigent circumstances for entering the apartment without a warrant." *Id.,* at 261. The court, however, declined to decide whether exigent circumstances had been present, because "the evidence required to prove that the defendant possessed cocaine with the intent to distribute, namely the cocaine and the money, was not found in the apartment, but on his person." *Ibid.* The court concluded that because" [t]he officers had probable cause to arrest and properly searched the defendant incident thereto . . . [, t]he trial court properly denied the motion to suppress."*Id.,* at 263.

The Louisiana Supreme Court denied review by a vote of 4 to 3. In a written dissent, Chief Justice Calogero Explained:

> "The Fourth Amendment to the United States constitution has drawn a firm line at the entrance to the home, and thus, the police need both probable cause to either arrest or search and exigent circumstances to justify a nonconsensual warrantless intrusion into private premises. . . . Here, the defendant was arrested inside an apartment, without a warrant, and the state has not demonstrated that exigent circumstances were present.

Consequently, defendant's arrest was unconstitutional, and his motion to suppress should have been granted." App. to Pet. for Cert. 1-2.

We agree with Chief Justice Calogero that the Court of Appeal clearly erred by concluding that petitioner's arrest and the search "incident thereto," 773 So. 2d, at 263, were constitutionally permissible. In *Payton,* we examined whether the Fourth Amendment was violated by a state statute that authorized officers to "enter a private residence without a warrant and with force, if necessary, to make a routine felony arrest." 445 U.S., at 574, 100 S.Ct. 1371. We determined that "the reasons for upholding warrantless arrests in a public place do not apply to warrantless invasions of the privacy of the home." *Id.,* at 576, 100 S. Ct. 1371. We held that because "the Fourth Amendment has drawn a firm line at the entrance to the house . . . [, a]bsent exigent circumstances, that threshold may not reasonably be crossed without a warrant." *Id.,* at 590, 100 S. Ct. 1371. And we noted that an arrest warrant founded on probable cause, as well as a search warrant, would suffice for entry. *Id.,* at 603, 100 S. Ct. 1371.

Here, the police had neither an arrest warrant for petitioner, nor a search warrant for petitioner's apartment, when they entered his home, arrested him, and searched him. The officers testified at the suppression hearing that the reason for their actions was a fear that evidence would be destroyed, but the Louisiana Court of Appeal did not determine that such exigent circumstances were present. Rather, the court, in respondent's own words, determined "that the defendant's argument that there were no exigent circumstances to justify the warrantless entry of the apartment was irrelevant" to the constitutionality of the officers' actions. Brief in Opposition 2-3. As *Payton,* makes plain, police officers need either a warrant or probable cause plus exigent circumstances in order to make a lawful entry into a home. The Court of Appeal's ruling to the contrary, and consequent failure to assess whether exigent circumstances were present in this case, violated *Payton.*

Petitioner and respondent both dispute at length whether exigent circumstances were, in fact, present. We express no opinion on that question, nor on respondent's argument that any Fourth Amendment violation was cured because the police had an "independent source" for the recovered evidence. Brief in Opposition 8. Rather, we reverse the Court of Appeal's judgement that exigent circumstances were not required to justify the officers' conduct, and remand for further proceedings not inconsistent with this decision. *It is so ordered.*

Case Review Question
Kirk v. Louisiana, 122 S. Ct. 2458 (2002).
Why is allowing a known drug dealer to go free a better result than permitting a warrantless search of his property after observing drug activity?

The Sixth Amendment: Speedy Trial, Impartial Jury, Confrontation

Speedy trial by an impartial jury.   In the past, the Supreme Court has determined that a speedy trial is absolutely necessary to due process.[24] Therefore, a speedy trial must be included in the due process definition of the Fourteenth Amendment. However, the Court has just as adamantly refused to consider a standard test to determine whether a trial has or has not been provided quickly enough. The Court recognizes that different types of criminal cases require different amounts of preparation and investigation. Therefore, as long as the time for preparation is reasonable and trial is available, the Sixth Amendment right will have been honored.

The Court has established certain criteria for determining whether the Sixth Amendment right has been honored. When it is alleged that the right to a speedy trial has been violated, the Supreme Court has provided a four-factor test that judges may employ to determine whether the allegation is true. Judges should examine (1) the actual time of the delay from arrest to trial; (2) the reasons the government has cited as a basis for the delay; (3) whether the defendant, at any time prior to trial, requested a speedy trial; and (4) whether the delay caused any harm to the defendant. The harm can include problems for the defense, such as unavailability of witnesses after a long period of time, lengthened detention if no bail was granted, or any other detriment to the defendant that would have been avoided by a speedy trial.

The guarantee of a speedy trial takes effect only upon the actual indictment for a crime. Prior to the formal charge, the prosecution is free to investigate at length before determining that there is sufficient evidence to charge a defendant. Once this evidence has been accumulated, the prosecution is obligated to make the decision of whether to prosecute. If the decision is made not to prosecute, the investigation may continue, and charges may be brought later. It is required only that there be reason for the delay other than to impair the defendant's ability to obtain evidence to be used in defense.

Assignment 15.2

Consider the following facts and explain whether the case satisfies the requirement of a speedy trial or whether charges should be dropped for failure to provide this constitutional right.

Darren was arrested for drug possession with intent to distribute. The initial arrest occurred on August 1, 2002. At first, Darren attempted to hire counsel. However, after 30 days and 12 interviews with various attorneys, he was unable to come up with a sufficient retainer to hire any of them. He requested a public defender. On September 18, a public defender was assigned to his case and began preparations to defend Darren. Trial was set for November 1, 2002. On October 31, 2002, the child of the public defender was killed in an accident and the attorney took an indefinite leave of absence. The case was rescheduled for January 1, 2003. A new public defender was assigned the case on December 1, 2002. On January 1, the public defender requested an extension over Darren's objections due to a sudden and unusually large caseload as the result of the loss of the prior public defender from their office. The case was rescheduled for March 1, 2003. In February, the judge assigned to the case suffered a stroke. All trials were postponed for a period of 60 days to enable the court of shift case and replace the judge. The case was reset for May 1, 2003. The trial began as scheduled on May 1, 2003, but after approximately two hours, the judge (newly appointed to the bench) announced she was totally inexperienced in criminal matters and did not believe she was adequately prepared to provide a fair trial to Darren. The case was reassigned to a judge with experience adjudicating criminal cases and scheduled for August 1, 2003. During the preceding 12 months, Darren was unable to come up with sufficient bail to secure his release and as a result lost his job, home, personal property, car, and even visitation rights with his children from a previous marriage.

Right of confrontation. Also included in the Sixth Amendment (and in the definition of what constitutes due process under the Fourteenth Amendment) is the right to confront one's accusers. It is inherent in American law that before a person can be convicted on the basis of statements made by others, the person must be given the opportunity to face and challenge the statements of his or her accusers. Because not every person accused of a crime can adequately confront his or her accuser, this has been determined to be a **critical stage** in the prosecution that requires assistance of counsel. This includes pretrial procedures, such as identification and confrontation upon testimony at trial. The rationale is that the defendant should be given every opportunity to expose errors or irregularities in testimony of witnesses for the prosecution.

critical stage
Stage of a criminal proceeding in which the presumed innocence of the accused is in jeopardy and therefore the accused is entitled to representation of counsel.

◆ APPLICATION 15.3

Lee is charged with a brutal rape and severe beating of Cassandra. She was tortured, mutilated, and left for dead. Cassandra knew Lee as another worker at the company where she worked, although they had never met. Despite Cassandra's horrific experience, Lee has the right to confront her and challenge her accusations in court.

Point for Discussion
♦   In cases such as major trials involving, for example, drugs or organized crime, where the witness fears retaliation, is it appropriate to permit the witness to remain unidentified specifically to the defendant and still protect the right of confrontation?

Right to counsel. Subsequent to *Miranda*, the Court held that for protection of several necessary rights (such as the right to not incriminate or assist in the prosecution against oneself), counsel must be available at all points in a prosecution where there is opportunity for unfairness or where untrustworthy evidence may be obtained. Later decisions have identified these stages of prosecution as interrogation or questioning, identification procedures, first court appearance where action may be taken against the defendant, preliminary hearing or grand jury, arraignment, trial, sentencing, and probation revocation hearings. Various rights in addition to those in the Fifth Amendment have been interpreted to require this as part of the due process guarantee in the Fourteenth Amendment. The result has been that each state must follow these requirements in its own state laws and prosecutions.

Unless there are compelling circumstances, any accused is entitled to have an attorney present at the time a witness is asked to identify the accused as the one who committed a crime. Compelling circumstances would include situations that make it unreasonable to wait for an attorney to be present. Additionally, if a witness is shown only photographs of potential defendants, neither the defendant nor defendant's counsel has the right to be present. The right to assistance of counsel is considered to be necessary to aid the defendant in adequately responding to charges of a witness. Because there is little room for unfairness or prejudice in identifying a photograph, disallowing the presence of the defendant or counsel at this procedure is considered to do no harm to due process.

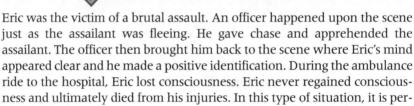

APPLICATION 15.4

Eric was the victim of a brutal assault. An officer happened upon the scene just as the assailant was fleeing. He gave chase and apprehended the assailant. The officer then brought him back to the scene where Eric's mind appeared clear and he made a positive identification. During the ambulance ride to the hospital, Eric lost consciousness. Eric never regained consciousness and ultimately died from his injuries. In this type of situation, it is permissible for the victim to make the identification at the scene. The rationale is that the circumstances make it unlikely anyone could manipulate the identification process and thereby compromise the rights of the defendant.

Point for Discussion
◆   Why shouldn't defendants be permitted to have an attorney present at identifications taking place at a crime scene?

The Supreme Court has also found that the right to assistance of counsel occurs only after the defendant has been charged with a crime and the prosecution has commenced.[25] Therefore, if a person is asked to take part in a lineup or other form of identification procedure prior to arrest, no right to assistance of counsel attaches. The point has been raised that most law enforcement agencies are encouraged to conduct identification procedures before charging the defendant and thus avoid the necessity of counsel. This is not seen as a particularly significant issue, however. First, the individual has the right to refuse to appear voluntarily in the lineup. Secondly, if the procedure is conducted in an unfair manner that unduly suggests the suspect to witnesses as the criminal, the suspect (subsequently the defendant) has the opportunity to allege this at trial. If proven, the evidence of the identification of the defendant will be inadmissible. Often, without a witness to identify the defendant as the one who committed the crime, a prosecution is unsuccessful. Therefore, police have the incentive to ensure that lineups are fairly conducted even before a defendant is formally charged with a crime.

The Eighth Amendment: Bail, Cruel and Unusual Punishment

The Eighth Amendment has also been clearly drawn into the Fourteenth Amendment definition of due process. The issues involve that of bail and freedom from cruel and unusual punishment.

Bail.   The Supreme Court has specifically addressed the issue of bail, the term used to describe release from custody during the time between arrest and conviction. Generally, the court asks for some guarantee or assurance that the defendant will not flee or commit other crimes if released. This assurance is the type or amount of bail that is required.[26] The Eighth Amendment guarantee against excessive bail has been integrated into the Fourteenth Amendment and applied to the states in an attempt to prevent the unwarranted detention and deprivation of liberty of accused persons prior to trial.

Many jurisdictions have specified amounts of bail that are predetermined for misdemeanors. In many states, if a person is charged with a traffic violation, the person's permanent driver's license will be accepted as bail. The license is then returned if the accused is found innocent or is given another penalty upon conviction. If the charges are minor, a specific dollar amount may be posted with the police to obtain release until a hearing is conducted. In other cases, the persons charged must remain in custody until they have an opportunity to appear before a judge or magistrate. Usually, this is within a matter of hours or, at most, a few days. The judge will determine what is an appropriate assurance or, in some instances, may even release the persons on their word that they will reappear at the formal hearing on the charges against them. The latter is known as being released on one's own recognizance, or O.R. In serious cases, and when there is reason to believe the accused will commit other crimes or flee the jurisdiction, the court may deny bail entirely and detain the person until trial.

The Eighth Amendment states that bail will not be excessive. A person is considered innocent until proven guilty in this country. Therefore, until proven guilty at a trial, the rationale is that accused persons should be allowed to continue their lives, earn a living, and reside with their families. Just as the circumstances vary with every case, however, so do the considerations of what would be excessive bail. For minor offenses, it is relatively assured that most persons will appear at trial. Therefore, bail may be a predetermined amount for all persons charged with those offenses. For serious crimes where the penalty upon a finding of guilt may be severe, the temptation to avoid a trial and possible sentencing by fleeing the jurisdiction is much greater. Additionally, many of the accused in these cases have criminal backgrounds. Thus, the likelihood that they will continue to commit crime while on bail is much greater.

The Eighth Amendment has been drawn into the definition of the Fourteenth Amendment on the basis of the general concept of due process.[27] The Supreme Court has reasoned that pretrial detention because bail is not allowed, or because it is so excessive that it effectively prevents an accused person from posting it, could be a deprivation of liberty without due process of law (essentially, a sentence of imprisonment prior to a trial). Thus, the factors that are considered in determining bail and the amount of bail that is required should be directly related.

The function of the courts in determining bail is to set an amount that will reasonably assure the appearance of the accused at trial.[28] If the judge determines that this cannot be assured by a sum of money and that a person should not be released on bail, the judge must make a very clear statement in the court record of reasons that support this decision.[29] The presumption is that all persons should have an opportunity to be released on bail. Therefore, this can be denied only in compelling circumstances.

The courts must consider several factors when determining bail, including but not limited to the following:

1. Past criminal history of the accused.
2. Past bail history of the accused.
3. Accused's connections to the community (such as job, family, and home).
4. Danger posed to the community by the accused.
5. Likelihood the accused will flee from the jurisdiction.

If enough of these factors or other considerations convince the court that the accused is likely to commit crimes or flee the jurisdiction, the court is justified in denying bail entirely. This does not constitute an improper violation of the individual right to due process, because the government interest in protecting the public is considered to be greater. This goes back to the traditional balance that courts try to achieve: the good of the individual versus the good of the people.

More often, the court is faced with a case that falls into a gray area. Although some factors are present that raise concern about the accused's conduct on bail release, the evidence is not sufficient to warrant holding the accused in custody until trial. In such cases, the judicial officer must make a determination of what amount of bail is reasonable to ensure that the accused will not commit crimes or flee the jurisdiction. The court must also consider what amount the accused can reasonably be expected to post as assurance that he or she will appear for trial.

In questions of bail, there is a wide berth for judicial discretion. The decision must be made on a case-by-case basis, and every individual accused presents a unique situation to the court. Therefore, for more serious crimes, there is generally no set rule for the amount of bail a court will require. The court must consider all the evidence before it on this question and exercise its best judgment. As long as a higher court can find that a determination of bail falls somewhere within a range of reasonableness, the initial determination of bail will not be altered.

Assignment 15.3

Which of the following situations, in which the defendant is charged, will likely result in (a) a hearing to determine the proper bail, or (b) an automatic predetermined amount of bail?.
Explain your answer.

1. Driving under the influence.
2. Hitchhiking on an interstate highway.
3. Murder.
4. Larceny for a theft under $500.
5. Arson and conspiracy to commit insurance fraud.
6. Driving on an expired license.
7. Trespassing.
8. Assault resulting from a bar fight.
9. Driving too fast for conditions.
10. Attempted murder and using a weapon to commit a felony.

Cruel and unusual punishment.   This guarantee of the Eighth Amendment protects all citizens from punishment deemed to be excessive or inappropriate for the crime committed according to societal standards. What defines cruel and unusual has gone through dramatic change in our nation's history consistent with the changes in our society.

Essentially, the Supreme Court has defined due process to include the protection of the Eighth Amendment with regard to the imposition of sentence. However, the Court has been somewhat reluctant to state specifics with regard to what constitutes such punishment. The Court has gone so far as to prohibit "barbaric" punishment or punishment that is excessive for the crime. Further, it has upheld the death penalty, refusing to categorize it as cruel and unusual. Part of the rationale of the Court for its position on the death penalty is that the penalty is approved by a significant majority of the states. This, in turn, supposedly reflects the belief of a majority of people that capital punishment is acceptable and appropriate. While the death penalty continues to be a topic of debate at the state level and the subject of many protests, until these laws are changed to reflect a changing society, it is unlikely that the Court will reverse its position.

Figure 15.1 lists the constitutional guarantees in the Bill of Rights and highlights those guarantees that have been included in the definition of due process.

FIGURE 15.1

Bill of Rights
Constitutional
Guarantees*

I. Establishment of religion.
Free exercise of speech.
Free exercise of press.
Peaceable assembly.
Petition of government for redress of grievances.

II. Well-regulated militia.

III. To exclude soldiers from homes in times of peace and in times of war except as prescribed by law.

IV. To be secure against unreasonable search and seizure and that no warrants shall be issued without probable cause.

V. No civilian shall be tried for capital crimes except upon grand jury indictment.
No one shall be subjected to double jeopardy.
No one shall be compelled to be a witness against himself.
No one shall be deprived of life, liberty or property without due process of law.
No private property shall be taken for public use without just compensation.

VI. Right to a speedy and public trial by an impartial jury.
To be informed of the nature and cause of the accusation.
To confront witnesses for the prosecution.
To have compulsory process to obtain witnesses in one's favor.
To have assistance of counsel in one's defense.

VII. Right to jury trial in common law actions valued greater than $20.
Jury determinations of fact are subject only to appeal in accordance with rules of common law.

VIII. No excessive bail.
No excessive fines.
No cruel and unusual punishments.

IX. No rights in the Constitution shall be used to deny other rights.

X. Powers not delegated to the U.S. or prohibited by the Constitution are reserved to the states.

*Rights affecting criminal procedure are underlined. Rights that have been integrated into the definition of due process through selective incorporation are in boldface type.

CASE

SUPREME COURT OF THE UNITED STATES

TIMOTHY STUART RING, PETITIONER, V. ARIZONA.

122 S.Ct. 2428
Argued April 22, 2002.
Decided June 24, 2002.

JUSTICE GINSBURG DELIVERED THE OPINION OF THE COURT.

This case concerns the Sixth Amendment right to a jury trial in capital prosecutions. In Arizona, following a jury adjudication of a defendant's guilt of first-degree murder, the trial judge, sitting alone, determines the presence or absence of the aggravating factors required by Arizona law for imposition of the death penalty.

In *Walton v. Arizona*, 497 U.S. 639, 110 S.Ct. 3047, 111 L.Ed.2d 511 (1990), this Court held that Arizona's sentencing scheme was compatible with the Sixth Amendment because the additional facts found by the judge qualified as sentencing considerations, not as "element[s] of the offense of capital murder." *Id.*, at 649, 110 S.Ct. 3047. Ten years later, however, we decided *Apprendi v. New Jersey,* 530 U.S. 466, 120 S. Ct. 2348, 147 L.Ed.2d 435 (2000), which held that the Sixth Amendment does not permit a defendant to be "expose[d] . . . to a penalty *exceeding* the maximum he would receive if punished according to the facts reflected in the jury verdict alone." *Id.,* at 483, 120 S.Ct. 2348. This prescription governs, *Apprendi* determined, even if the State characterizes the additional findings made by the judge as "sentencing factor[s]." *Id.,* at 492, 120 S. Ct. 2348.

Apprendi's reasoning is irreconcilable with *Walton*'s holding in this regard; and today we overrule *Walton* in relevant part. Capital defendants, no less than non-capital defendants, we conclude, are entitled to a jury determination of any fact on which the legislature conditions an increase in their maximum punishment.

At the trial of petitioner Timothy Ring for murder, armed robbery, and related charges, the prosecutor presented evidence sufficient to permit the jury to find the facts here recounted. On November 28, 1994, a Wells Fargo armored van pulled up to the Dillard's department store at Arrowhead Mall in Glendale, Arizona. T. Courier Dave Moss left the van to pick up money inside the store. When he returned, the van, and its driver, John Magoch, were gone.

Later that day, Maricopa Country Sheriff's Deputies found the van-its doors locked and its engine running-in the parking lot of a church in Sun City, Arizona. Inside the vehicle they found Magoch, dead from a single gunshot to the head. According to Wells Fargo records, more than $562,000 in cash and $271,000 in checks were missing from the van.

Prompted by an informant's tip, Glendale police sought to determine whether Ring and his friend James Greenham were involved in the robbery. The police investigation revealed that the two had made several expensive cash purchases in December 1994 and early 1995. Wiretaps were then placed on the telephones of Ring, Greenham, and a third suspect, William Ferguson.

In one recorded phone conversation, Ring told Ferguson that Ring might "cu[t] off" Greenham because "[h]e's too much of a risk": Greenham had indiscreetly flaunted a new truck in front of his ex-wife. Ring said he could cut off his associate because he held "both [Greenham's] and mine." The police engineered a local news broadcast about the robbery investigation; they included in the account several intentional inaccuracies. On hearing the broadcast

report, Ring left a message on Greenham's answering machine to "remind me to talk to you tomorrow and tell you about what was on the news tonight. Very important, and also fairly good.":

After a detective left a note on Greenham's door asking him to call, Ring told Ferguson that he was puzzled by the attention the police trained on Greenham. "[H]is house is clean," Ring said, "[m]ine, on the other hand, contains a very large bag."

On February 14, 1995, police furnished a staged reenactment of the robbery to the local news, and again included deliberate inaccuracies. Ferguson told Ring that he "laughed" when he saw the broadcast, and Ring called it "humorous." Ferguson said he was "not real worried at all now"; Ring, however, said he was "slightly concern[ed]" about the possibility that the police might eventually ask for hair samples.

Two days later, the police executed a search warrant at Ring's house, discovering a duffel bag in his garage containing more than $271,000 in cash. They also found a note with the number "575,995" on it, followed by the word "splits" and the letters "F," "Y," and "T." The prosecution asserted that "F" was Ferguson, "Y" was "Yoda" (Greenham's nickname), and "T" was Timothy Ring.

Testifying in his own defense, Ring said the money seized at his house was startup capital for a construction company he and Greenham were planning to form. Ring testified that he made his share of the money as a confidential informant for the Federal Bureau of Investigation and as a bail bondsman and gunsmith. But an FBI agent testified that Ring had been paid only $458, and other evidence showed that Ring had made no more than $8,800 as a bail bondsman.

The trial judge instructed the jury on alternative charges of premeditated murder and felony murder. The jury deadlocked on premeditated murder, with 6 of 12 jurors voting to acquit, but convicted Ring of felony murder occurring in the course of armed robbery. See Ariz.Rev.Stat. Ann. § 13-1105(A) and (B) (West 2001) ("A person commits first degree murder if . . . [a]cting either alone or with one or more other persons the person commits or attempts to commit . . . [one of several enumerated felonies] . . . and in the course of and in furtherance of the offense or immediate flight from the offense, the

CASE

person or another person causes the death of any person. . . . Homicide, as prescribed in [this provision] requires no specific mental state other than what is required for the commission of any of the enumerated felonies.").

As later summed up by the Arizona Supreme Court, "the evidence admitted at trial failed to prove, beyond a reasonable doubt, that [Ring] was a major participant in the armed robbery or that he actually murdered Magoch." 200 Ariz. 267, 280, 25 P. 3d 1139, 1152 (2001). Although clear evidence connected Ring to the robbery's proceeds, nothing submitted at trial put him at the scene of the robbery. Furthermore, "[f]or all we know from the trial evidence," the Arizona court stated, "[Ring] did not participate in, plan, or even expect the killing. This lack of evidence no doubt explains why the jury found [Ring] guilty of felony, but not premeditated, murder."

Under Arizona law, Ring could not be sentenced to death, the statutory maximum penalty for first-degree murder, unless further findings were made. The State's first-degree murder statute prescribes that the offense "is punishable by death or life imprisonment as provided by § 13-703." Ariz.Rev.Stat. Ann. § 13-1105(C) (West 2001). The cross-referenced section, § 13-703, directs the judge who presided at trial to "conduct a separate sentencing hearing to determine the existence or nonexistence of [certain enumerated] circumstances . . . for the purpose of determining the sentence to be imposed." § 13-703(C) (West Supp.2001). The statute further instructs: "The hearing shall be conducted before the court alone. The court alone shall make all factual determinations required by this section or the constitution of the United States or this state".

At the conclusion of the sentencing hearing, the judge is to determine the presence or absence of the enumerated "aggravating circumstances" and any "mitigating circumstances." The State's law authorizes the judge to sentence the defendant to death only if there is at least one aggravating circumstance and "there are no mitigating circumstances sufficiently substantial to call for leniency." § 13-703(F).

Between Ring's trial and sentencing hearing, Greenham pleaded guilty to second-degree murder and armed robbery. He stipulated to a 271/612 year sentence and agreed to cooperate with the prosecution in the cases against Ring and Ferguson.

Called by the prosecution at Ring's sentencing hearing, Greenham testified that he, Ring, and Ferguson had been planning the robbery for several weeks before it occurred. According to Greenham, Ring "had I guess taken the role as leader because he laid out all the tactics." On the day of the robbery, Greenham said, the three watched the armored van pull up to the mall. When Magoch opened the door to smoke a cigarette, Ring shot him with a rifle equipped with a homemade silencer. Greenham then pushed Magoch's body aside and drove the van away. At Ring's direction, Greenham drove to the church parking lot, where he and Ring transferred the money to Ring's truck. *Id.,* at 46, 48. Later, Greenham recalled, as the three robbers were dividing up the money, Ring upbraided him and Ferguson for "forgetting to congratulate [Ring] on [his] shot."

On cross-examination, Greenham acknowledged having previously told Ring's counsel that Ring had nothing to do with the planning or execution of the robbery. *Id.,* at 85-87. Greenham explained that he had made that prior statement only because Ring had threatened his life. *Id.,* at 87. Greenham also acknowledged that he was now testifying against Ring as "pay back" for the threats and for Ring's interference in Greenham's relationship with Greenham's ex-wife.

On October 29, 1997, the trial judge entered his "Special Verdict" sentencing Ring to death. Because Ring was convicted of felony murder, not premeditated murder, the judge recognized that Ring was eligible for the death penalty only if he was Magoch's actual killer or if he was "a major participant in the armed robbery that led to the killing and exhibited a reckless disregard or indifference for human life."

Citing Greenham's testimony at the sentencing hearing, the judge concluded that Ring "is the one who shot and killed Mr. Magoch." The judge also found that Ring was a major participant in the robbery and that armed robbery "is unquestionably a crime which carries with it a grave risk of death."

The judge then turned to the determination of aggravating and mitigating circumstances. He found two aggravating factors. First, the judge determined that Ring committed the offense in expectation of receiving something of "pecuniary value," as described in § 13-703; "[t]aking the cash from the armored car was the motive and reason for Mr.Magoch's murder and not just the result." Second, the judge found that the offense was committed "in an especially heinous, cruel or depraved manner." In support of this finding, he cited Ring's comment, as reported by Greenham at the sentencing hearing, expressing pride in his marksmanship. The judge found one nonstatutory mitigating factor. Ring's "minimal" criminal record. In his judgment, that mitigating circumstance did not "call for leniency"; he therefore sentenced Ring to death.

On appeal, Ring argued that Arizona's capital sentencing scheme violates the Sixth and Fourteenth Amendments to the U.S. Constitution because it entrusts to a judge the finding of a fact raising the defendant's maximum penalty. See *Jones v. United States,* 526 U.S. 227, 119 S.Ct. 1215, 143 L.Ed. 2d 311 (1999); The State, in response, noted that this Court had upheld Arizona's system in *Walton v. Arizona,* 497 U.S. 639, 110 S.Ct. 3047, 111 L.Ed. 2d 511 (1990), and had stated in *Apprendi* that *Walton* remained good law.

Reviewing the death sentence, the Arizona Supreme Court made two preliminary observations. *Apprendi* and *Jones,* the Arizona high court said, "raise some question about the continued viability of *Walton.*" The court then examined the *Apprendi* majority's interpretation of Arizona law and found it wanting. *Apprendi,* the Arizona court noted, described Arizona's sentencing system as one that" 'requir[es] judges, after a jury verdict holding a defendant guilty of a capital crime, to find specific aggravating factors before imposing a sentence of death,' and not as a system that 'permits a judge to determine the existence of a factor which makes a, crime a capital offense.' "200 Ariz., at 279, 25 P.3d, at 1151. Justice

O'CONNOR's *Apprendi* dissent, the Arizona court noted, squarely rejected the *Apprendi* majority's characterization of the Arizona sentencing scheme: "A defendant convicted of first-degree murder in Arizona cannot receive a death sentence unless a judge makes the factual determination that a statutory aggravating factor exists. Without that critical finding, the maximum sentence to which the defendant is exposed is life imprisonment, and not the death penalty." 200 Ariz., at 279, 25 P.3d,

After reciting this Court's divergent constructions of Arizona law in *Apprendi,* the Arizona Supreme Court described how capital sentencing in fact works in the State. The Arizona high court concluded that "the present case is precisely as described in Justice O'Connor's dissent [in *Apprendi*] Defendant's death sentence required the judge's factual findings." 200 Ariz., at 279, 25 P.3d, at 1151. Although it agreed with the *Apprendi* dissent's reading of Arizona law, the Arizona court understood that it was bound by the Supremacy Clause to apply *Walton,* which this Court had not overruled. It therefore rejected Ring's constitutional attack on the State's capital murder judicial sentencing system. 200 Ariz., at 280, 25 P.3d, at 1152.

The court agreed with Ring that the evidence was insufficient to support the aggravating circumstance of depravity, but it upheld the trial court's finding on the aggravating factor of pecuniary gain. The Arizona Supreme Court then reweighed that remaining factor against the sole mitigating circumstance (Ring's lack of a serious criminal record), and affirmed the death sentence.

We granted Ring's petition for a writ of certiorari, 534 U.S. 1103, 122 S.Ct. 865, 151 L.Ed.2d 738 (2002), to allay uncertainty in the lower courts caused by the manifest tension between *Walton* and the reasoning of *Apprendi.* ("[W]hile it appears *Apprendi* extends greater constitutional protections to noncapital, rather than capital, defendants, the Court has endorsed this precise principle, and we are in no position to second-guess that decision here."). We now reverse the judgement of the Arizona Supreme Court.

Based solely on the jury's verdict finding Ring guilty of first-degree felony murder, the maximum

CASE

punishment he could have received was life imprisonment. This was so because, in Arizona, a "death sentence may not legally be imposed . . . unless at least one aggravating factor is found to exist beyond a reasonable doubt." 200 Ariz., at 279, 25 P.3d, at 1151 (citing § 13-703). The question presented is whether that aggravating factor may be found by the judge, as Arizona law specifies, or whether the Sixth Amendment's jury trial guarantee, made applicable to the States by the Fourteenth Amendment, requires that the aggravating factor determination be entrusted to the jury.

As earlier indicated, this is not the first time we have considered the constitutionality of Arizona's capital sentencing system. In *Walton v. Arizona,* 497 U.S. 639, 110 S.Ct. 3047, 111 L.Ed.2d 511 (1990), we upheld Arizona's scheme against a charge that it violated the Sixth Amendment. The Court had previously denied a Sixth Amendment challenge to Florida's capital sentencing system, in which the jury recommends a sentence but makes no explicit findings on aggravating circumstances; we so ruled, *Walton* noted, on the ground that "the Sixth Amendment does not require that the specific findings authorizing the imposition of the sentence of death be made by the jury." 109 S.Ct. 2055, (1989). *Walton* found unavailing the attempts by the defendant-petitioner in that case to distinguish Florida's capital sentencing system from Arizona's. In neither State, according to *Walton,* were the aggravating factors "elements of the offense"; in both States, they ranked as "sentencing considerations" guiding the choice between life and death.

Walton was revisited in *Jones v. United States,* 526 U.S. 227, 119 S.Ct. 1215, 143 L.Ed.2d 311 (1999). In that case, we construed the federal carjacking statute, 18 U.S.C. § 2119 (1994 ed. and Supp. V), which, at the time of the criminal conduct at issue, provided that a person possessing a firearm who "takes a motor vehicle . . . from the person or presence of another by force and violence or by intimidation . . . shall–(1) be . . . imprisoned not more than 15 years . . . , (2) if serious bodily injury . . . results, be . . . imprisoned not more than 25 years . . . , and (3) if death results, be . . . imprisoned for any number of years up to life. . . ." The question presented in *Jones* was whether the statute "defined three distinct offenses or a single crime with a choice of three maximum penalties, two of them dependent on sentencing factors exempt from the requirements of charge and jury verdict." 526 U.S., at 229, 119 S.Ct. 1215.

The carjacking statute, we recognized, was "susceptible of [both] constructions"; we adopted the one that avoided "grave and doubtful constitutional questions." Section 2119, we held, established three separate offenses. Therefore, the facts—causation of serious bodily injury or death—necessary to trigger the escalating maximum penalties fell within the jury's province to decide. Responding to the dissenting opinion, the *Jones* Court restated succinctly the principle animating its view that the carjacking statute, if read to define a single crime, might violate the Constitution: "[U]nder the Due process Clause of the Fifth Amendment and the notice and jury trial guarantees of the Sixth Amendment, any fact (other than prior conviction) that increases the maximum penalty for a crime must be charged in an indictment, submitted to a jury, and proven beyond a reasonable doubt" *Id.*

Jones endeavored to distinguish certain capital sentencing decisions, including *Walton.*

Advancing a "careful reading of *Walton's* rationale," the *Jones* Court said: *Walton* "characterized the finding of aggravating facts falling within the traditional scope of capital sentencing as a choice between a greater and a lesser penalty, not as a process of raising the ceiling of the sentencing range available." 526 U.S., at 251, 119 S.Ct. 1215.

One year after *Jones,* the Court decided *Apprendi v. New Jersey,* 530 U.S. 466, 120 S.Ct. 2348, 147 L.Ed.2d 435 (2000). The defendant-petitioner in that case was convicted of, *inter alia,* second-degree possession of a firearm, an offense carrying a maximum penalty of ten years under New Jersey law. On the prosecutor's motion, the sentencing judge found by a preponderance of the evidence that Apprendi's crime had been motivated by racial animus. That finding triggered application of New Jersey's "hate crime enhancement," which doubled Apprendi's maximum authorized sentence. The judge sentenced Apprendi to 12 years in prison, 2 years over the maximum that would have applied but for the enhancement.

We held that Apprendi's sentence violated his right to "a jury determination that [he] is guilty of every element of the crime with which he is charged, beyond a reasonable doubt." *Id.,* at 477, 120 S.Ct. 2348.

That right attached not only to Apprendi's weapons offense but also to the "hate crime" aggravating circumstance. New Jersey, the Court observed, "threatened Apprendi with certain pains if he unlawfully possessed a weapon and with additional pains if he selected his victims with a purpose to intimidate them because of their race." *Apprendi,* 530 U.S., at 476, 120 S.Ct. 2348. "Merely using the label 'sentence enhancement' to describe the [second act] surely does not provide a principled basis for treating [the two acts] differently." *Ibid.*

The dispositive question, we said, "is one not of form, but of effect." *Id.,* at 494, 120 S.Ct. 2348. If a State makes an increase in a defendant's authorized punishment contingent on the finding of a fact, that fact—no matter how the State labels it—must be found by a jury beyond a reasonable doubt. A defendant may not be "expose [d] . . . to a penalty *exceeding* the maximum he would receive if punished according to the facts reflected in the jury verdict alone."

Walton could be reconciled with *Apprendi,* the Court finally asserted. The key distinction, according to the *Apprendi* Court, was that a conviction of first-degree murder in Arizona carried a maximum sentence of death. "[O]nce a jury has found the defendant guilty of all the elements of an offense which carries as its maximum penalty the sentence of death, it may be left to the judge to decide whether that maximum penalty, rather than a lesser one, ought to be imposed." 530 U.S., at 497, 120 S.Ct. 2348.

In an effort to reconcile its capital sentencing system with the Sixth Amendment as interpreted by *Apprendi,* Arizona first restates the *Apprendi* majority's portrayal of Arizona's system: Ring was convicted of first-degree murder, for which Arizona law specifies "death or life imprisonment" as the only sentencing options, see Ariz.Rev.Stat. Ann § 13-1105(C) (West 2001); Ring was therefore sentenced within the range of punishment authorized by the jury verdict. See Brief for Respondent 9-19. This argument overlooks *Apprendi's* instruction that "the relevant inquiry is one

not of form, but of effect." 530 U.S., at 494, 120 S.Ct. 2348. In effect, "the required finding [of an aggravated circumstance] expose[d] [Ring] to a greater punishment than that authorized by the jury's guilty verdict." The Arizona first-degree murder statute "authorizes a maximum penalty of death only in a formal sense," *Apprendi,* 530 U.S., at 541, 120 S.Ct. 2348 for it explicitly cross-references the statutory provision requiring the finding of an aggravating circumstance before imposition of the death penalty. 13-1105(C) ("First degree murder is a class 1 felony and is punishable by death or life imprisonment *as provided by* § 13-703. "If Arizona prevailed on its opening argument, *Apprendi* would be reduced to a "meaningless and formalistic" rule of statutory drafting. See 530 U.S., at 541, 120 S.Ct. 2348.

Arizona also supports the distinction relied upon in *Walton* between elements of an offense and sentencing factors. As to elevation of the maximum punishment, however, Apprendi renders the argument untenable; *Apprendi* repeatedly instructs in that context that the characterization of a fact or circumstance as an "element" or a "sentencing factor" is not determinative of the question. "who decides," judge or jury. ("[W]hen the term 'sentence enhancement' is used to describe an increase beyond the maximum authorized statutory sentence, it is the functional equivalent of an element of a greater offense than the one covered by the jury's guilty verdict."); *Id.,* at 495, 120 S.Ct. 2348 ("[M]erely because the state legislature placed its hate crime sentence enhancer within the sentencing provisions of the criminal code does not mean that the finding of a biased purpose to intimidate is not an essential element of the offense."

Even if facts increasing punishment beyond the maximum authorized by a guilty verdict standing alone ordinarily must be found by a jury, Arizona further urges, aggravating circumstances necessary to trigger a death sentence may nonetheless be reserved for judicial determination. As Arizona's counsel maintained at oral argument, there is no doubt that "[d]eath is different." States have constructed elaborate sentencing procedures in death cases, Arizona emphasizes, because of constraints we have said the Eighth Amendment places on capital sentencing.

CASE

Apart from the Eighth Amendment provenance of aggravating factors, Arizona presents "no specific reason for excepting capital defendants from the constitutional protections . . . extend[ed] to defendants generally, and none is readily apparent." The notion "that the Eighth Amendment's restriction on a state legislature's ability to define capital crimes should be compensated for by permitting States more leeway under the Fifth and Sixth Amendments in proving an aggravating fact necessary to a capital sentence . . . is without precedent in our constitutional jurisprudence."

In various settings, we have interpreted the Constitution to require the addition of an element or elements to the definition of a criminal offense in order to narrow its scope.

Arizona suggests that judicial authority over the finding of aggravating factors "may . . . be a better way to guarantee against the arbitrary imposition of the death penalty." The Sixth Amendment jury trial right, however, does not turn on the relative rationality, fairness, or efficiency of potential factfinders. Entrusting to a judge the finding of facts necessary to support a death sentence might be

"an admirably fair and efficient scheme of criminal justice designed for a society that is prepared to leave criminal justice to the State. . . . The founders of the American Republic were not prepared to leave it to the State, which is why the jury-trial guarantee was one of the least controversial provisions of the Bill of Rights. It has never been efficient; but it has always been free." *Apprendi*, 530 U.S., at 498, 120 S.Ct. .2348 (SCALIA, J., concurring).

In any event, the superiority of judicial factfinding in capital cases is far from evident. Unlike Arizona, the great majority of States responded to this Court's Eighth Amendment decisions requiring the presence of aggravating circumstances in capital cases by entrusting those determinations to the jury.

Although "'the doctrine of *stare decisis* is of fundamental importance to the rule of law[,]' . . . [o]ur precedents are not sacrosanct." *Patterson v.*

McLean Credit Union, 491 U.S. 164, 172, 109 S.Ct. 2363, 105 L.Ed.2d 132 (1989). "[W]e have overruled prior decisions the necessity and propriety of doing so has been established." 491 U.S., at 172, 109 S.Ct. 2363. We are satisfied that this is such a case.

For the reasons stated, we hold that *Walton* and *Apprendi* are irreconcilable; our Sixth Amendment jurisprudence cannot be home to both. Accordingly, we overrule *Walton* to the extent that it allows a sentencing judge, sitting without a jury, to find an aggravating circumstance necessary for imposition of the death penalty. Because Arizona's enumerated aggravating factors operate as "the functional equivalent of an element of a greater offense," *Apprendi*, 530 U.S., at 494, n. 19, 120 S.Ct. 2348, the Sixth Amendment requires that they be found by a jury.

"The guarantees of jury trial in the Federal and State Constitutions reflect a profound judgement about the way in which law should be enforced and justice administered. . . . If the defendant preferred the common-sense judgment of a jury to the more tutored but perhaps less sympathetic reaction of the single judge, he was to have it." *Duncan v. Louisiana*, 391 U.S. 145, 155-156, 88 S.Ct. 1444, 20 L.Ed.2d 491 (1968).

The right to trial by jury guaranteed by the Sixth Amendment would be senselessly diminished if it encompassed the factfinding necessary to increase a defendant's sentence by two years, but not the factfinding necessary to put him to death. We hold that the Sixth Amendment applies to both. The judgment of the Arizona Supreme Court is therefore reversed, and the case is remanded for further proceedings not inconsistent with this opinion.

It is so ordered.

Case Review Question
Ring. v. Arizona, 122 S.Ct. 2428 (2002).
Would the result change if the jury had convicted the defendant of a capital crime punishable by the death penalty, recommended imprisonment, and the judge upgraded the penalty to death based on aggravating factors?

STAGES OF CRIMINAL PROCEDURE

An understanding of the rights of accused persons in the criminal process allows a much clearer sense of the reasons for the various stages through which an accused must pass. These stages are all designed with the intent that every citizen shall have every available opportunity to have his or her conduct judged fairly without undue influence or unfair criticism. The following discussion of the actual stages of criminal procedure uses many of the examples already used in the discussion of the rights of the accused to illustrate the role these rights play in the criminal process.

Pre-Arrest

Generally, before an arrest is made and a defendant is charged with a crime, the law enforcement agencies will attempt to obtain sufficient evidence to warrant the arrest and the conviction. In fact, a standard of all arrests is that the arresting officer had probable cause to believe the suspect had committed a crime.[30] Generally, probable cause is established through introduction of evidence that connects the accused to the crime.

Right to privacy.   Many times, after or during the commission of a crime, the police look for evidence that will lead them to the person or persons who committed the crime. However, the constitutional rights guaranteed by the Fourth Amendment prevent the police from rampantly searching among members of the public and their belongings. Such searching would violate all rights of privacy and notions of fairness. The police are entitled to obtain whatever evidence exists publicly, but before they may delve into private property and dwellings, they must establish that there is probable cause to believe evidence of a crime exists there.

As indicated earlier in the chapter, items or occurrences in public view do not require probable cause, because it would be unreasonable for a person to consider such things private. Such items include things that are on private property but can be viewed from outside the property. It is also permissible to use the assistance of such items as binoculars. If the item only enhances natural ability, it is acceptable.

In addition, individuals do not have a right to privacy with regard to such matters as the phone numbers they have called. No one can reasonably expect that the phone company will not be allowed to know what numbers are called from a private telephone. Indeed, these records are necessary to the phone company's business. Therefore, since this is common knowledge to a third party, such as the phone company, individuals should not expect that no other third party could obtain the information. Thus, phone registers, which record the numbers called from a private phone, require no showing of probable cause. Nor do conversations made on public telephones. There can be no reasonable expectation of privacy in the use of public facilities.

Before the police may enter the private property of an individual, they must have probable cause to suspect a connection between the property and the crime committed. As stated earlier, the police must have more than mere suspicion. They must have access to other evidence or testimony that would indicate the likelihood of criminal activity. For example, the police may have information from informants who have had contact with the person or persons suspected of criminal activity and can provide specific information regarding their conduct (such as phone conversations about the crimes) or the exact location of criminal evidence. If the police have conducted surveillance of the persons or property and have discovered highly suspicious activities taking place, a court may find probable cause.

Search warrant.   If a court finds that there is probable cause to suspect that evidence of a crime exists in or on private property, it will issue an appropriate search warrant. Search warrants must be specific concerning the objective, location, and scope of the search.[31] If, for example, the warrant is issued to determine whether the suspects are discussing crimes on the telephone, only wiretaps on the telephones may be placed. If the warrant is issued to search the premises for evidence of a crime, only the premises can be searched, and no wiretaps would be allowed. The requirement that warrants be specific prevents unreasonable invasions of privacy by some overzealous law enforcement officers.

Plain view rule.   What happens if a search is being conducted for specific evidence and evidence of other criminal activity is discovered? This falls under the plain view rule. If police are lawfully on property (public, with consent, or with a search warrant) and discover evidence of any crime in plain view, that evidence can be used against its owners in a criminal prosecution.

Arrest warrant.   If the police can demonstrate to the court that there is enough criminal evidence to support a conviction, the court will issue an arrest warrant. When the warrant is issued, the police have the authority to take the defendant into custody and make initial criminal charges. At this point, the defendant's constitutional protection against being deprived of life or liberty without due process of law becomes a concern of law enforcement personnel.

In certain situations, no search or arrest warrant is required. In such special circumstances, police have the authority to stop, search, and, if necessary, make an arrest. If there is probable cause to believe that individuals are committing—or have in the immediate past committed—a crime, the police have the authority to stop these individuals. When the individuals are stopped, the police have the authority to pat them down and search areas within their reach to determine whether anything is available that the individuals could use to harm the officers. The police then have the option of questioning the persons and releasing them, or if probable cause exists, the persons can be placed under arrest, and the property in their immediate reach can be searched.

grand jury
A number of individuals (often more than 20) who review the evidence to determine whether the defendant could be convicted of the crime if charged and tried.

Grand jury.   Another method used in federal criminal prosecutions and some states for prosecutions of serious crimes is the **grand jury,** which consists of 20 or more citizens who, for a period of approximately six months, hear evidence of criminal activity in various cases presented by the prosecution. The duty of the grand jury is to determine whether there is enough evidence to prosecute someone for a crime. A grand jury proceeding often occurs even before an initial arrest has been made.

Much of the evidence the grand jury hears has been obtained through government investigation, the use of various search warrants, and the testimony of informants or other persons with relevant information. Suspects have no absolute right to appear at grand jury proceedings or to introduce evidence. The purpose of such proceedings is solely to determine whether enough evidence exists that a jury *could* find a person guilty of criminal conduct.

If the grand jury finds that sufficient evidence exists to formally charge an individual with a crime, it will issue an indictment ("in-dite-ment"), which gives authority to arrest and charge the individual with the crime. An indictment operates in much the same fashion as an arrest warrant issued by a judge. After apprehension, the person is taken into custody and advised of his or her rights. At that point, the stages of actual prosecution begin.

Arrest and Interrogation

Arrestee's rights.   Persons who are initially arrested must be advised of their basic rights upon arrest.[32] They must be told that they have the right to remain silent; that anything they say can and will be used against them in a court of law; that they have the right to an attorney; and that if they cannot afford an attorney, one will be appointed for them at no cost. Law enforcement agencies are making it a common practice to require all arrestees to sign a statement indicating that they have been notified of and understand their rights. These written statements have greatly reduced the number of arrestees who claim they were never advised of their rights or that the advisement came after they had incriminated themselves.

Interrogation.   After an arrest, the law enforcement officers and prosecutors may question (interrogate) the accused about the crime with which he or she is charged. Identification proceedings, such as lineups, where the victims or witnesses to the crime are asked to identify the alleged criminal from a group of persons, may also take place.

The arrestee has the right to have an attorney present to ensure that identification proceedings are not conducted in a way that would unduly influence the victims or witnesses to name the accused.[33] For example, if the police have information from a witness that the suspect was of a particular race and present a lineup of persons of other races except for the actual suspect, the witness would have no choice but to indicate the actual suspect as the criminal. Such an identification proceeding is unfair. Lineups must be conducted in such a way that they truly test the ability of the witness to identify the criminal.

Many law enforcement agencies avoid the necessity of providing attorneys for all those who are suspected of criminal activity. Instead, the police ask the individual prior to arrest to answer questions voluntarily or to take part in an identification proceeding. If the individual voluntarily complies, the police have complete consent and do not have to advise the person of his or her rights or provide counsel. The individual does, however, have the right to obtain his or her own counsel or to refuse to cooperate. An exception occurs when a grand jury issues a subpoena to the individual. In that situation, the person is required to appear to be questioned but may avoid answering on the basis of the Fifth Amendment guarantee against self-incrimination.

Confession.   A particular concern arises when an arrestee confesses to a crime. At this point, law enforcement personnel are under a particular duty to establish that the individual was not coerced in any way or misled into an involuntary confession. It must be established that the confession was given freely and without undue influence. Further, it must be shown that the individual understood the possible consequences of a confession.[34] Increasingly, law enforcement agencies are establishing that a confession was made in fair circumstances by videotaping it. This is relatively inexpensive compared to the cost of trying the issue of a confession in court. Also, when a confession is videotaped and the court can actually observe the circumstances under which it was made, a defendant is much less likely to claim that it was unfairly obtained unless such circumstances truly existed.

Bail

Shortly after arrest, the accused person is entitled to request release from custody prior to trial in exchange for bail. Bail—or bond, as it is sometimes called— is the amount paid to the court as an assurance that the suspect will not flee the jurisdiction or commit additional crimes prior to trial. It operates as an insurance policy against such conduct by the accused.

Many persons utilize the services of bail bondsmen. For a fee, the bondsman will issue a bond to the court stating that if the accused flees the jurisdiction or commits a crime while the prosecution is pending, the bondsman will be responsible for the entire amount of bail. The bondsman acts as a sort of insurance company that issues the policy for the accused. If the accused violates the terms of the bail release and flees or commits a crime, the bondsman has the right to be reimbursed by the accused.

A method utilized when larger amounts of bail are imposed is payment of 10 percent of the amount of bail. Many jurisdictions allow the accused to make this 10 percent payment. If the accused then violates the terms of the bail release, full payment is required, and the accused will be taken back into custody.

The decision of how much bail to require—or whether to grant release on bail at all—is generally left to the discretion of the judge. The judge has the duty to determine (1) what would be a reasonable amount to assure the court of the accused's good conduct and presence at future hearings and (2) what is within the means of the defendant to pay. Although these two factors are balanced against each other, the more important factor is, of course, the first.[35]

If the judge determines that no amount would be assurance that the accused will not leave the jurisdiction or commit other crimes, bail may be denied. To be justified, this usually requires substantial evidence that the accused has ignored court orders in the past or has engaged in other conduct that would indicate a likelihood that bail would be ignored.

Another option is to require no security at all in the form of bail for release. When this occurs, as previously mentioned, the person is released on his or her own recognizance. The judge makes a finding that the person's contacts to the community, such as family and work, are strong enough to prevent the person from fleeing the jurisdiction. Further, there must be evidence that the person is not likely to commit additional crimes. Release on one's own recognizance is issued most often when the charge is less serious or when it is the person's first criminal offense.

Once the issue of bail has been determined, the accused is either released or returned to the physical custody of law enforcement personnel. The next stage of prosecution is the preliminary hearing.

Preliminary Hearing and Arraignment

Shortly after arrest, a preliminary hearing is scheduled. At this time, the defendant and the prosecution appear for a decision by the judge of whether sufficient admissible evidence exists to warrant further prosecution. The prosecution introduces evidence of the defendant's guilt. The defendant has the opportunity to challenge the admissibility of this evidence under the exclusionary rule. Generally, the defendant is not allowed to introduce evidence of defense. The burden is on the prosecutor to prove that a finding of guilty is possible. The purpose of the preliminary hearing is simply to determine whether there is enough admissible evidence to meet this burden. Since no conviction can result at this stage, there is no need for a defense at this point.

If the court finds that insufficient evidence exists that would be admissible in court, the case will be dismissed and all charges will be dropped. In the event the court finds sufficient evidence to prosecute, the court will arrange an **arraignment** and schedule the case for trial. In less serious matters, the stages of bail, preliminary hearing, and arraignment may be combined into a single proceeding. In more complex cases, each side must prepare a presentation for the various issues, and the three stages are scheduled separately.

arraignment
Stage of a criminal proceeding in which the accused is formally charged.

Arraignment follows the preliminary hearing. At this stage, defendants are informed of the actual charge of which they are accused and for which they will be tried, and the charge is recorded in the court files. Often this charge is related to, but different from, the charge for which the defendant was initially arrested. This occurs because some evidence may have been excluded by the court or because additional evidence has been accumulated since the time of arrest. Either of these developments may affect the ability of the prosecution to prove guilt on a particular charge. Thus, the charge may be modified. Another possibility is that during the preliminary hearing the judge will determine that there is insufficient evidence for one charge but adequate evidence for another. In that event, the judge will order that the latter be the basis for prosecution.

During arraignment, the defendant is formally advised of the crime charged. Bail may also be reviewed by the court at this time. It may be increased, decreased, or withdrawn, with the accused placed back into custody. Most importantly, the defendant pleads on the issue of guilt at the arraignment.

Typically, a defendant pleads one of three ways. If the plea is guilty, the defendant is making an admission of responsibility for the crime committed. Thus, there is no need for a trial to prove guilt, and the procedure moves directly to sentencing. If the plea is not guilty, the court will schedule a trial date. At trial, the prosecution will attempt to prove the guilt of the defendant beyond a reasonable doubt. The third type of plea sometimes accepted by a court is nolo contendere, also known as no contest. This plea means that the defendant will not plead guilty but will raise no defense to the claims of the prosecutor. In essence, the defendant takes the position, "I am not saying I am guilty or innocent, but I will not defend myself at trial or challenge a conviction."

As a result of a nolo contendere plea, the defendant has no recorded confession of guilt, but no trial is required for a finding of guilt. Sentencing occurs immediately after this plea, just as it would upon a plea of guilty. Many times, a defendant will plead nolo contendere in a situation where someone injured by the crime may bring a civil suit against the defendant in addition to the criminal charge. If a defendant pleads nolo contendere, the injured party in a civil trial cannot introduce an admission of guilt for the act that caused the injury. Thus, it may be in the defendant's interest to plead nolo contendere in the criminal suit to increase his or her chances of success as a defendant in a civil suit.

APPLICATION 15.5

Suzette and Janet are young women at the same party. During the course of the evening they become involved in an argument that escalates into a physical fight. Suzette strikes Janet with a lamp, breaks her jaw, and causes a laceration on her face that requires plastic surgery. Suzette is charged with assault. Janet also brings a civil suit against Suzette for her injuries and related damages such as pain and suffering and disfigurement. If Suzette pleads no contest or not guilty to the charges, they cannot be admitted in the civil case even if she is convicted. However, if she pleads guilty, the criminal charge can be admitted as a legal admission of guilt for the assault.

Point for Discussion
◆   Why is the plea of no contest inadmissible?

Plea bargaining.   For a number of reasons, plea bargaining has become an integral part of the criminal process. Plea bargaining occurs when the prosecution agrees to a lesser charge or a reduced sentence in exchange for a plea of guilty by the defendant. The benefit to the defendant is that he or she will not have to stand trial and face the possibility of a more serious conviction and/or penalty. The government is saved the expense of a trial and, perhaps more importantly, is able to impose a penalty on the defendant in some degree. When the prosecution is required to go to trial, the burden of proof is so severe that there is always the possibility of acquittal.

Trial, Appeal, and Sentencing

The crucial stage of any prosecution is the trial. At this point, the trier of fact—usually the jury—will determine the guilt or innocence of the defendant based on the evidence of the prosecution. Guilt must be established beyond a reasonable doubt. In practical terms, this means that one who considers the situation logically and rationally must have no doubt that the defendant committed the crime with which he or she is charged. Guilt cannot be based on prejudice or bias or pure circumstance. There must be no other reasonable explanation than that the accused committed the crime.

This burden of proof is quite severe to ensure that innocent individuals will not be convicted because of questionable circumstances. In the American legal system, individuals are considered innocent until proven guilty. Furthermore, they cannot be compelled to testify about information that might incriminate them. Some defendants, regardless of innocence, simply are not effective witnesses in a criminal prosecution because they do not communicate well, and they do their defense more harm than good by attempting to tell their story to the trier of fact. For this reason, a defendant is not required to testify at trial. Further, a jury may not consider such a refusal to testify as evidence of guilt. The evidence of guilt must be established by the prosecutor.

If the trier of fact determines that the prosecution has met its burden, a conviction will result. If the burden is not met, the charges are dismissed, and the defendant is released from further proceedings. Upon dismissal, bail is returned to the defendant if its terms were not violated during the prosecution. Upon a conviction, bail may be returned, or it may be applied to a fine imposed as a penalty for a conviction.

After conviction, the court may sentence the defendant immediately, or sentencing may be scheduled for a later time. In some instances, a jury is asked to impose the sentence on the defendant. This usually occurs in very serious cases that require much thought and consideration of the circumstances of the crime, for example, a capital offense where the sentence could be death. The reasoning is that in such a serious matter, several of one's peers can determine just punishment as well as or better than a single judge. The prosecution and defense are both allowed to introduce evidence that will enable a fair sentence to be imposed based on all of the circumstances. Such factors include the state of mind of the defendant, such as malice or premeditation, and the extent of the criminal conduct, such as extreme violence. Other factors, such as intelligence, maturity, or likelihood of rehabilitation, may also affect sentencing.

If a defendant chooses to appeal, it is up to the trial court to determine whether the defendant will be released during the appeal. In more serious cases, the defendant is usually required to begin serving the sentence, because appeals can take a very long time. Further, after conviction and sentencing, a defendant may be very tempted to flee the jurisdiction. If an appeal is successful and the conviction is overturned, the defendant is not entitled to any compensation for time served or inconvenience caused by the prosecution of the crime. In most of these cases, a new trial is granted and the procedure starts over again. A defendant who is granted a new trial is treated as if the first trial never occurred. Therefore, the sentence can be greater or lesser if conviction is obtained a second time.

Assignment 15.4

> Evaluate the following case and diagram the likely results under the various types of pleas (guilty, not guilty, no contest).
>
> Tommy is charged with providing alcohol to minors as the result of him securing a keg of beer for his younger brother and some friends on prom night. That night, three of the teens that had consumed part of the beer died in a drunk-driving accident. The potential maximum criminal sentence for Tommy is 18 months in jail. He has been offered a plea agreement whereby if he pleads guilty, the prosecutor will recommend 6 months in the county jail and 1,000 hours of community service. A civil case has been filed by the families of the dead teens and named Tommy as a defendant.

Ethical Considerations

A common question asked of criminal defense lawyers is, "How can you represent someone that you know is guilty?" This seems to be a concept that the general public has great difficulty in reconciling as ethical behavior. However, representation of the accused is a cornerstone right guaranteed to all citizens under the U.S. Constitution. In the American system of justice, certain principles prevail. Everyone is innocent until proven guilty by evidence in a court of law—not by the media, or speculation, or circumstance, or even the accused's own lawyer. Secondly, it is not the function of a criminal defense lawyer to judge the client. Rather, it is to see that the client's defense is heard in the best light possible and to take all necessary measures to achieve a fair trial for the client. The criminal defense lawyer is assisted in this endeavor by the Bill of Rights. Consequently, the answer to the preceding question is frequently not one of the ethics of the lawyer but one of the general public. It is important to view anyone accused of criminal conduct objectively until such time as the evidence is fully reviewed. This was the goal of the framers of the Constitution who sought primarily to reverse the standard of guilty until proven innocent.

Question
Why should the standard of guilty until proven innocent be reversed?

Ethical Circumstance

Meg is a paralegal working for attorney Russel. They represent a man who claims his home and belongings were destroyed in a house fire but the insurance company refuses to pay on the allegation the fire was deliberately set. No charges have been filed. A neighbor of the man calls the office and speaks with Meg. He informs her that two days before the fire, he was home from work sick and observed the man bring his travel trailer from a nearby storage lot where he kept it and spend the better part of the day filling it with boxes of what appeared to be personal items, photos, and documents. He then returned the trailer to the storage lot. Meg gives this information to the attorney. If in fact the man was removing items of value from his house two days before it was coincidentally consumed by fire, then there is an ethical obligation to confront the man with the information and request answers. Although attorney–client privilege may prevent them from disclosing the information to the authorities, they could certainly withdraw from representation if they believe the man is attempting to commit insurance fraud and encourage him to to go to the authorities and admit his actions.

CHAPTER SUMMARY

The American legal system is committed to fairness to persons accused of criminal conduct, and every attempt is made to ensure that innocent persons are not convicted and punished. Much of the U.S. Constitution was written with this objective in mind, and it continues to be the basis for all aspects of criminal procedure.

Criminal procedure begins at the moment law enforcement authorities suspect criminal activity; often accused individuals are afforded constitutional protections before they are even aware that they are suspects. An example of such a protection is the requirement of probable cause before any search, seizure, or arrest can be made. When possible, this probable cause must be determined by a judicial officer who can view the situation more objectively than a law enforcement officer.

After arrest, the Constitution continues to influence the proceedings through its mandates regarding bail, specific charges, right to counsel, and a speedy trial. In spite of all these protections, innocent persons have still been convicted. In the majority of these cases, however, the mistaken conviction occurred as a result of misconduct by witnesses or, in some instances, prosecutors. The system, when properly applied, provides greater protection from improper convictions than perhaps any other legal system in the world.

CHAPTER TERMS

arraignment	due process	selective incorporation
critical stage	grand jury	
double jeopardy	probable cause	

REVIEW QUESTIONS

1. Selective incorporation is designed to do what?
2. Which guarantees of the Bill of Rights are currently adopted into the definition of due process?
3. What is probable cause?
4. When does double jeopardy not apply after trial has begun?
5. At what stages does a defendant have the right to counsel?
6. When can bail be denied?
7. When is an arrest warrant not necessary?
8. What is the function of a grand jury?
9. What happens when there is no grand jury?
10. What takes place at the arraignment?

RELEVANT LINKS

Criminal law
www.nolo.com/lawcenter

About the law
www.lawyers.com/common/content/
aboutlaw/crim

INTERNET ASSIGNMENT 15.1

Using internet resources, determine the penalty, if any, for refusing a breathalyzer test in an alleged driving-under-the-influence case. Trace your research steps.

NOTES

1. United States Constitution, Amendments 4, 5, 8, 14.
2. *Palko v. Connecticut,* 302 U.S. 319, 58 S.Ct. 149, 82 L.Ed. 288 (1937).
3. Id.
4. *Mapp v. Ohio,* 367 U.S. 643, 81 S.Ct. 1684, 6 L.Ed.2d 1081 (1961).
5. Id.
6. *Weeks v. United States,* 232 U.S. 383, 34 S.Ct. 341, 58 L.Ed. 652 (1914).
7. 338 U.S. 25, 69 S.Ct. 1359, 93 L.Ed. 1782 (1949).
8. See note 4.
9. 468 U.S. 897, 104 S.Ct. 3405, 82 L.Ed.2d 677 (1984).
10. *Katz v. United States,* 389 U.S. 347, 88 S.Ct. 507, 19 L.Ed.2d 576 (1967).
11. *Brinegar v. United States,* 338 U.S. 160, 69 S.Ct. 1302, 93 L.Ed. 1879 (1949).
12. *Vale v. Louisiana,* 399 U.S. 30, 90 S.Ct. 1969, 26 L.Ed.2d 409 (1970).
13. *Hester v. United States,* 265 U.S. 57, 44 S.Ct. 445, 68 L.Ed. 898 (1924).
14. *United States v. Dunn,* 480 U.S. 294, 107 S.Ct. 1134, 94 L.Ed.2d 326 (1987).
15. See note 10.
16. *New York v. Class,* 475 U.S. 106, 106 S.Ct. 960, 89 L.Ed.2d 81 (1986).

17. *New York v. Belton,* 453 U.S. 454, 101 S.Ct. 2860, 69 L.Ed.2d 768 (1981).
18. Id.
19. *Terry v. Ohio,* 392 U.S. 1, 88 S.Ct. 1868, 20 L.Ed.2d 889 (1968).
20. *Crist v. Bretz,* 437 U.S. 28, 98 S.Ct. 2156, 57 L.Ed.2d 24 (1978).
21. Id.
22. *Arizona v. Washington,* 434 U.S. 497, 98 S.Ct. 824, 54 L.Ed.2d 717 (1978).
23. 384 U.S. 436, 86 S.Ct. 1602, 16 L.Ed.2d 694 (1966).
24. *Brewer v. Williams,* 430 U.S. 387, 97 S.Ct. 1232, 51 L.Ed.2d 424 (1977).
25. *Barker v. Wingo,* 407 U.S. 514, 92 S.Ct. 2182, 33 L.Ed.2d 101 (1972).
26. Id.
27. See note 24.
28. *United States v. Salerno,* 481 U.S. 739, 107 S.Ct. 2095, 95 L.Ed.2d 697 (1987).
29. *Schilb v. Kuebel,* 404 U.S. 357, 92 S.Ct. 479, 30 L.Ed.2d 502 (1971).
30. See note 20.
31. See note 28.
32. See note 19.
33. *Marron v. United States,* 275 U.S. 192, 48 S.Ct. 74, 72 L.Ed. 231 (1927).
34. See note 23.
35. See note 24.

For additional resources, please visit our Web site at www.westlegalstudies.com

CHAPTER 16

Family Law

After reading this chapter, you should be able to:

- Explain the requirements for a valid antenuptial agreement.

- List the requirements for marriage.

- Explain the purpose of legal annulment.

- Discuss the rights of parties who cohabit without marriage.

- Discuss the function of temporary orders.

- Explain how courts determine custody issues.

- Discuss the disadvantages of joint custody.

- Explain the concept of no-fault divorce.

Family law is an area of American law that has experienced phenomenal growth in this century. Before the latter half of the twentieth century, divorce was a rare occurrence. In addition, a woman's role was perceived to be primarily that of a caretaker of the home and children, not of a worker in the public workplace. In the event of divorce, there was no question but that the husband would be solely responsible for the material needs of his wife and children. The relatively few divorces, social pressures, and the fact that the public was largely uneducated in matters of law resulted in few challenges to the fairness of court-ordered divorce settlements.

Over the years, the role of women changed in large part because of technological developments, the opening of the job market to women, and the growth of educational opportunities for women. Gradually, women began to live independently. This trend increased markedly during World War II, when for the first time, large numbers of women entered the nation's workforce. In addition, our society became more mobile as families relocated away from the traditional extended family to find jobs. These societal changes were accompanied by an increased awareness of legal rights. And for the first time, specific laws were put into place that protected the rights of victims of domestic violence. As a consequence of these developments, the option of dissolving a marriage became a more realistic choice for many. Multiple marriages in one lifetime became more likely, and as a result, more detailed laws on the total marriage relationship became necessary.

The changes in family law have ranged from defining and, in many states, abolishing common law marriage to regulating custody and visitation rights when parents live in different states. Aside from the fact that virtually everyone has some contact with family law during his or her lifetime, this area of law is having an increasing effect on the workplace. For example, some employers have the duty to report and withhold wages for payment of child support or maintenance (alimony), and job transfers or changes may be delayed while a divorced parent seeks changes in the visitation schedule or obtains court permission to remove a child from the state.

This chapter addresses the creation and dissolution of marriages and the relationships that result from terminated marriages. Its emphasis will be on the dissolution of marriages and the resulting relationships, since during a marriage, the parties are generally in accord with respect to marital concerns, such as child care and education. It is when discord occurs and cannot be resolved that the parties seek intermediary help from the legal system.

MARRIAGE AND ANNULMENT

Antenuptial (Prenuptial) Agreements

Antenuptial agreements (sometimes referred to as prenuptial agreements) are contracts entered into by parties who are going to be married. Such contracts provide for the division of property rights at the time the marital relationship between the parties ends. Originally, antenuptial agreements dealt only with property division upon the death of a spouse.

Ordinarily, one spouse cannot entirely disinherit another spouse. If no provisions are made by will, the surviving spouse can elect under a special statute (one exists in each state) to receive a percentage of the estate. In a traditional antenuptial agreement, however, each of the spouses may agree by contract not to challenge the provisions of the other spouse's will. This is often done when one spouse possesses a great deal more wealth or when one of the spouses has children from a prior marriage and seeks to protect the children's inheritance.

More recently, antenuptial agreements have taken on an entirely new meaning. In a time where dissolution occurs frequently, some parties attempt to arrange in advance for an orderly distribution of debts and assets should the marriage be dissolved. No longer are these agreements reserved only for the wealthy. Rather, they are often a reasonable alternative for spouses who each have a career and the ability to contribute financially to the relationship. Many such couples have minor children from previous relationships whose interests must be protected. For these and other reasons, an antenuptial agreement often resolves the concerns that may prevent parties from getting married at all. The agreement allows the parties to continue their relationship with one less concern. Perhaps the agreement will never be utilized, but if it is, there is some reassurance in knowing that reasonable terms were arranged when each of the parties was acting logically with fairness to the other in mind.

Requirements for an enforceable agreement.   It has taken some time for the courts and legislature to determine the requirements for an enforceable antenuptial agreement with provisions for a dissolution of the marriage. The agreement is essentially a contract and must contain the necessary elements of any contract.[1] Most states also require the agreement to be in writing pursuant to the statute of frauds. An exception to the requirement of writing occurs when one party can demonstrate that he or she has significantly altered his or her position in a detrimental manner as a direct result of reliance on the other party's promises in an oral antenuptial agreement.[2]

antenuptial agreement (prenuptial agreement)
Agreement between parties who intend to marry that typically provides for the disposition of the property rights of the parties in the event the marriage ends by death or divorce.

APPLICATION 16.1

Two young people who are friends and have dated on and off are about to graduate college. Both want to attend medical school; however, finances are a serious concern. They are aware that if they are married and both attend medical school, they would be entitled to significant financial benefits. They agree to marry and remain married while in medical school. They further agree that each will keep all assets and debts acquired individually prior to and during the marriage as separate and make no claim upon the other if the marriage should end. This agreement is put into writing and the couple marries. If there is fair and full disclosure, the contract would likely be enforceable. However, if the document were not in writing and merely an oral agreement, it would probably not be enforceable in the event one of them wanted to divorce at the conclusion of medical school. In that case, the situation would likely be treated as with any other dissolution of marriage.

Point for Discussion

◆   What would be the result if the document were in writing and in the first year of the marriage, one of the parties won the lottery of $58 million and immediately filed for divorce?

In addition to the requirement of writing, consideration must be given for the promises of each party in the antenuptial agreement. Consideration is given by each party in exchange for the promises made in the terms of the contract and is easily satisfied. Traditionally, the promise of marriage by each party has served as consideration for the other party's agreement to the terms of the antenuptial contract. Finally, a valid antenuptial agreement must be made with the free will of both parties without duress or coercion, conditional upon divorce, and not be unconscionable either when made or implemented.

Challenging an agreement.   Mutual assent to the terms of the contract has been carefully examined in most cases where such a contract has been challenged. The court is concerned that unscrupulous persons would take advantage of the position of another and persuade the other person to enter an agreement that, in the event of divorce, would be inherently unfair (known as overreaching). Examples include parties who do not disclose the full measure of their assets and liabilities and parties who accumulate assets directly from the support of their spouse but in a dissolution action allege that the support did not occur or was not substantial.

APPLICATION 16.2

A couple decides to marry. It is the second marriage for each. The wife has substantial real estate holdings. The agreement provides that all real estate held by the wife at the time of the marriage shall remain solely hers in the event of a divorce or end of the marriage. Over a period of five years, the husband systematically convinces the wife to sell off the real estate in favor of what he advises are more valuable real estate interests. After five years, he divorces the wife and claims one-half of the real estate holdings which have been purchased since the time of the marriage. Because the parties fully disclosed their financial status at the time of the marriage and entered into all of the terms of the agreement voluntarily, the husband would likely have a valid claim unless there were clear evidence of some sort of fraud. It is otherwise assumed the wife voluntarily disposed of these assets with constructive knowledge that she was also disposing of her individual property rights.

Point for Discussion

◆ Would the situation be different if the husband admitted the entire situation had been part of a long-term plan to divest the woman of her assets?

As the preceding example illustrates, it is crucial that any antenuptial agreement contain full disclosure of assets and liabilities.[3] In addition, the agreement should contain provisions for some fair and reasonable economic settlement. The parties do not usually anticipate divorce and cannot anticipate what their accumulation of wealth will be at the time of a divorce. However, they can anticipate that each will contribute to the marriage, and assets should be divided in a manner fair to each based on that contribution.

Upholding an agreement.   A difficulty in dealing with the settlement provision is that courts will often not recognize an agreement that provides for a specific financial award, since such an agreement is seen as encouraging dissolution of the marriage in an attempt to obtain a monetary settlement.[4] The courts will, however, uphold agreements that provide for a fair distribution of assets to be determined by an objective third party, such as a court, in the event the parties should cease to share marital assets. This reassures the parties that they are not being taken advantage of. Such an agreement also does not include any anticipation of divorce that the court might see as encouraging the end of a marriage. To ensure an enforceable and fair agreement, each party should seek independent legal counsel before entering into an antenuptial agreement.

Assignment 16.1

Under the following circumstances, would the antenuptial agreement be more likely to be enforced or invalidated? Why?

Marvin is 85 years old and has an estate worth approximately $400 million. He marries Rhonda who is 42. In the antenuptial agreement, Rhonda agrees to care for Marvin and attend to him for the remainder of his life. In the event the marriage ends in dissolution, Rhonda is to receive $1 million for each complete year of marriage. In the event of Marvin's death by natural causes, Rhonda is to receive $100 million regardless of the duration of the marriage. The remainder of the estate will go to his children. Rhonda has assets worth approximately $180,000 and no significant debt. All of this is disclosed in the agreement. Forty-five days after the parties marry, Marvin suffers a massive stroke and dies. His children claim the antenuptial agreement should not be enforced.

Requirements for Marriage

The process of getting married has become quite complex in the legal sense. In many states, two people wishing to marry cannot simply obtain a license at the justice of the peace and be married at the same time. Because marriage so deeply affects the lives of those involved and because many marriages do not, in fact, succeed, as well as for reasons of public health and various other concerns linked to citizen welfare, laws have been created to establish the best possible environment for the marriage. Every state has enacted laws that set forth certain requirements that must be met before a recognized marriage will exist.

Capacity and consent.   For a marriage to be valid, there must be capacity and consent.[5] As previously noted, capacity requires that the party be of legal age and not be declared legally incompetent. The party must be capable of making the decision to enter into such an agreement. Many states also have provisions for parental or court consent in the event a party to the marriage is not of legal age or has been legally determined to be incapable of appreciating the consequences and responsibilities of marriage. If there is capacity, it is also necessary that each party openly and voluntarily consent to the marriage.

Marriage license.   Each state has a licensure provision for marriages.[6] Before a legal marriage exists, the parties are directed to make application for a marriage license. The license is generally granted unless some factor exists that would prevent the marriage from being legal under state law. Examples of such factors include (1) the parties are family members who have a close blood relationship (each state indicates the degree of kinship that will prevent a valid marriage), (2) the parties are persons of the same sex (although this is a highly volatile subject of law at state and federal levels and some states give basic rights as domestic partners), (3) one or both parties lack legal capacity, and (4) one of the parties is already in an existing marriage.

Blood tests and a waiting period are also often required to obtain a marriage license. The purpose behind blood tests is twofold. First, it is presumed that each party to the marriage has the right to know whether the other carries any sexually transmitted disease that could place the party at risk. In light of the AIDS crisis in the United States, some states have amended their statutes to require an additional blood test or disclosure that would provide information regarding the presence of HIV. The second reason for blood tests is that the parties should be informed if there is a conflict between their particular blood types that may make it difficult for them to have healthy children. Although medicine has advanced to the point that most problems can be treated effectively, the parties are still presumed to be entitled to this information.

The statutes that require a waiting period (usually a matter of a few days) to discourage marriages that are entered into without sufficient thought to the consequences. Thus, requiring a brief delay between issuance of the license and the time when it can be validated by a judge or minister encourages the parties to consider the ramifications of their action.

Marriage vows.   Finally, the parties are ordinarily required to solemnize the marriage. This involves the exchange of vows (an agreement to marry) in the presence of one who is permitted to legally acknowledge the marriage.[7] Usually, this is a minister or a judge, who will then validate the license by certifying that the parties have indeed agreed to be married. At that time, the minister or judge and the parties will sign the license. Often, additional witnesses to the marriage are required to sign the license. If citizens of one state wish to marry but would not be permitted to do so in their own state, they may not simply go to another state for the purpose of marrying. Many states now have laws that declare a marriage invalid if it was entered into in another state for the purpose of avoiding the first state's laws. Thus, in some states, parties otherwise unable to legally marry can no longer cross a state line to be married. They must be able to show that they had valid reasons for conducting the marriage ceremony in another state.

Annulment

A legal **annulment** is a judicial declaration that a marriage never actually existed because the legal requirements for a valid marriage were not met.[8] This is to be distinguished from a religious annulment. The latter is granted by a church authority for reasons of, and in accordance with, religious procedures. A religious annulment has no legal meaning or effect. Accordingly, a legal annulment has no religious significance.

Legal annulments can be obtained for a variety of reasons. Whatever the basis for the annulment, one requirement is common to all. The reason that the marriage should be declared invalid must have existed at the time the parties entered into the marriage.[9] Therefore, if an annulment is sought on the basis that one or both of the parties was under the legal age or without sufficient mental capacity, the incapacity must have existed at the time the parties attempted a marriage. Other common reasons for annulment include close blood relationships, incest, or bigamy. The general rule is that an annulment may be granted if the reason for the annulment, had it been previously disclosed, would have legally prevented the parties from marrying.

If the party seeking the annulment has taken any steps toward accepting and acknowledging the marriage relationship, his or her request may be denied. The theory is that one who attempts to solemnize a marriage cannot then take the position that the marriage never existed.[10] This is very similar to the contractual defense of unclean hands, which holds that a party who helped create the circumstances for a breach of contract cannot then turn and allege that he or she has been injured because of the breach. Nevertheless, the courts may still grant an annulment if the reason is a serious one, such as bigamy or incest.

Less frequently encountered actions for annulment include actions based on frolic, duress, or fraud. If the parties married as some sort of joke or game and never truly intended a binding marriage, the court will grant an annulment. As with most contractual agreements, intent is required for a valid

annulment
Court order that restores the parties to their positions prior to the marriage. The marriage of the parties is void and treated as if it never existed. Permissible in situations where a particular legal disability prevented the marriage from becoming valid.

marriage to exist. For example, a marriage by parties who were intoxicated at the time of the marriage and did not intend to actually marry would be invalid.

If a party believes that he or she has no choice but to marry or alternatively suffer serious physical, financial, or other harm, a marriage of duress has taken place. Effectively, the party had no real choice in the matter, and the courts will likely find no real intent to marry. As a result, annulment is a very real possibility in such situations.

Annulment on the basis of fraud is one of the most difficult to establish. The party seeking the annulment must prove all of the necessary elements of fraud. In the case of marriage, the elements are (1) a misrepresentation of a fact essential to the marriage relationship must have been made, and (2) the party claiming fraud must have reasonably relied on the misrepresentation as truth when making the decision to marry. Examples of misrepresentations sufficient for an annulment based upon fraud include religious beliefs or ability to biologically parent children.

Although an annulment is a declaration that the marriage relationship never existed in the eyes of the law, it does not mean that no relationship existed. Therefore, the courts may apportion rights and duties regarding property, assets, debts, and even children as if the annulment were an action for dissolution of marriage (divorce).[11] The purpose is to return the parties to their original position before the marriage. If the parties have contributed anything to the relationship or if there are children, the court will consider the rights under the same equitable grounds used in dissolving a marital relationship. Figure 16.1 is an example of an annulment law.

Common Law Marriage

A minority of states still allow marriages created by common law. Such marital relationships are created by agreement of the parties. However, the formal requisites of license and legal solemnization by vows are not observed. Even states that do not permit the creation of common law marriages will recognize a common law marriage validly established in another state.

Generally, no public record of a common law marriage is made. Contrary to popular belief, a common law marriage is not based on the length of time two parties live together. Rather, the courts usually examine the following in determining whether such a marriage exists:

1. Did the parties hold themselves out to the public as married?
2. Did the parties cohabit?
3. Did the parties file joint tax returns?
4. Does the conduct of the parties indicate an intent to be married?

If the evidence is insufficient to establish a common law marriage or the relationship was created in a state that does not recognize common law marriage, the parties still may have legal rights under principles that deal with cohabitation (discussed in greater detail in the section that addresses non-marital relationships).

FIGURE 16.1   McKinney's Consolidated Laws of New York Annotated Domestic Relations Law Chapter 14 of the Consolidated Laws Article 9—Action to Annul a Marriage or Declare it Void

§ 140. Action for judgment declaring nullity of void marriages or annulling voidable marriage

(a) Former husband or wife living. An action to declare the nullity of a void marriage upon the ground that the former husband or wife of one of the parties was living, the former marriage being in force, may be maintained by either of the parties during the life-time of the other, or by the former husband or wife.

(b) Party under age of consent. An action to annul a marriage on the ground that one or both of the parties had not attained the age of legal consent may be maintained by the infant, or by either parent of the infant, or by the guardian of the infant's person; or the court may allow the action to be maintained by any person as the next friend of the infant. But a marriage shall not be annulled under this subdivision at the suit of a party who was of the age of legal consent when it was contracted, or by a party who for any time after he or she attained that age freely cohabited with the other party as husband or wife.

(c) Party a mentally retarded person or mentally ill person. An action to annul a marriage on the ground that one of the parties thereto was a mentally retarded person may be maintained at any time during the life-time of either party by any relative of a mentally retarded person, who has an interest to avoid the marriage. An action to annul a marriage on the ground that one of the parties thereto was a mentally ill person may be maintained at any time during the continuance of the mental illness, or, after the death of the mentally ill person in that condition, and during the life of the other party to the marriage, by any relative of the mentally ill person who has an interest to avoid the marriage. Such an action may also be maintained by the mentally ill person at any time after restoration to a sound mind; but in that case, the marriage should not be annulled if it appears that the parties freely cohabited as husband and wife after the mentally ill person was restored to a sound mind. Where one of the parties to a marriage was a mentally ill person at the time of the marriage, an action may also be maintained by the other party at any time during the continuance of the mental illness, provided the plaintiff did not know of the mental illness at the time of the marriage. Where no relative of the mentally retarded person or mentally ill person brings an action to annul the marriage and the mentally ill person is not restored to sound mind, the court may allow an action for that purpose to be maintained at any time during the life-time of both the parties to the marriage, by any person as the next friend of the mentally retarded person or mentally ill person.

(d) Physical incapacity. An action to annul a marriage on the ground that one of the parties was physically incapable of entering into the marriage state may be maintained by the injured party against the party whose incapacity is alleged; or such an action may be maintained by the party who was incapable against the other party, provided the incapable party was unaware of the incapacity at the time of marriage, or if aware of such incapacity, did not know it was incurable. Such an action can be maintained only where an incapacity continues and is incurable, and must be commenced before five years have expired since the marriage.

(e) Consent by force, duress or fraud. An action to annul a marriage on the ground that the consent of one of the parties thereto was obtained by force or duress may be maintained at any time by the party, whose consent was so obtained. An action to annul a marriage on the ground that the consent of one of the parties thereto was obtained by fraud may be maintained by the party whose consent was so obtained within the limitations of time for enforcing a civil remedy of the civil practice law and rules. Any such action may also be maintained during the life-time of the other party by the parent, or the guardian of the person of the party whose consent was so obtained, or by any relative of that party who has an interest to avoid the marriage, provided that in an action to annul a marriage on the ground of fraud the limitation prescribed in the civil practice law and rules has not run. But a marriage shall not be annulled on the ground of force or duress if it appears that, at any time before the commencement of the action, the parties thereto voluntarily cohabited as husband and wife; or on the ground of fraud, if it appears that, at any time before the commencement thereof, the parties voluntarily cohabited as husband and wife, with a full knowledge of the facts constituting the fraud.

(f) Incurable mental illness for five years. An action to annul a marriage upon the ground that one of the parties has been incurably mentally ill for a period of five years or more may be maintained by or on behalf of either of the parties to such marriage.

Assignment 16.2

> Consider the following situations. Assume that you are employed by the firm that represents one of the parties. Determine whether dissolution of marriage or legal separation would best suit the client. Then consider that you are representing the other party. Would the result change? If so, why?
>
> 1. Al and Louise have been married for 54 years. They have lived in separate parts of the house for 15 years and essentially led separate lives. Al now wants to move to a distant state and Louise does not. They have agreed on how to split their retirement income to support the two residences. Al's pension plan provides for health insurance benefits for himself and his spouse at no expense to Al. Al and Louise have no interest or intention of marrying anyone else at this point.
> 2. Craig and May have been married for 13 years. They have no children together. May has no significant assets. Craig has no current significant assets, but is the only child of a widowed mother with an estate valued at $60 million. Both Craig and May are of a religion that strongly discourages divorce when possible.

Assignment 16.3

> Prepare a chart that details the requirements for valid marriage and common law marriage (in jurisdictions where recognized).

The Marriage Relationship

Today, most states have statutes that impose an equal duty on each spouse to aid and financially support the other spouse during the marriage. Thus, no longer is it the sole duty of the husband to provide financial support for the wife. The practical result is that in the event of a dissolution, the husband may also be entitled to financial support, and in most cases, maintenance (alimony) is no longer awarded for life unless special circumstances exist. (These specifics are discussed later in the section that deals with the question of maintenance.)

During the marriage, the spouses have an ongoing duty to provide support of at least that which is necessary to meet the needs of the parties.[12] Such necessities include food, shelter, and clothing. If one party has agreed to work outside the home while the other remains at home, that party also has a duty to provide items necessary to the couple's existence. Often what is considered necessary is largely influenced by the income of the spouses and what that income enables the parties to provide.

During the marriage, most states recognize the theory of marital debt. Thus, if one spouse assumes a debt, the other spouse is equally bound. This becomes particularly important if the parties subsequently terminate their relationship. The marital debts must be apportioned fairly while taking into account the ability of each party to satisfy the claims of outside creditors. (The subject of apportionment is addressed later in the section that deals with property and debt division.)

The primary rule regarding existing marriages is the policy of nonintervention. The courts generally refuse to become involved in settling marital disputes regarding the duties of the parties.[13] When third parties such as creditors become involved and debts are not being paid, the court may declare that both parties are jointly liable. Beyond this, the courts presume that the parties are meeting their obligations of support for one another as long as they continue to live together and maintain a marital residence.

If the parties cease living together and abandon the marital relationship, the courts may become involved in dictating the legal rights of each party before and after a formal dissolution of the marriage. Most states have enacted statutes that permit awards of support during a legal separation or while a divorce is pending. Because divorces can sometimes become quite drawn out, it may be necessary to provide for the well-being of the parties (and possibly any children) during the interim.

Effects of Tort and Criminal Law on Domestic Relations

An additional factor to be considered regarding the marital relationship is the effect of a marriage on tort and criminal law. Historically, one spouse was not permitted to bring a legal action against the other spouse for injuries inflicted during the marriage. The reasoning was that marital harmony would be disturbed if the courts entertained lawsuits by spouses against one another. Slowly, the realization came about that if injuries by one spouse to another were so serious as to warrant a lawsuit, marital disharmony more than likely already existed. Further, it seemed unfair that gross negligence or intentional misconduct would be excused if it only injured a family member. Thus, most states have now abolished the doctrine of interspousal tort immunity.[14] No longer are parties who cause injury to their spouses immune from legal action.

Third-party actions against the marriage.   Other torts that affect the marital relationship include actions of third parties against the marriage. Such actions are generally quite difficult to prove, and most persons are reluctant to raise the issue. Two such torts are criminal conversation (an action by one spouse against a third party for adulterous conduct with the other spouse) and alienation of affection (an action by a spouse against a third party who has induced the other spouse to transfer his or her affections to that party).[15] Because these actions have been used as a means to threaten and as virtual extortion (blackmail), some states have abolished the statutes that permit them. In addition, as noted previously, the very nature of the actions inhibits a significant amount of actual prosecution of claims by the injured party.

Domestic violence.   Unfortunately, the occurrence of **domestic violence** (violence perpetrated by one member of a household onto another) is all too prevalent in American society and law. In 1998, the U.S. Department of Justice

domestic violence
Acts of physical violence perpetrated by one member of a household onto another member of the household.

conducted a study and concluded between partners alone (not including children and other family members) there were between 1 million and 4 million estimated annual incidents of domestic violence in the United States. In 1996, the Federal Bureau of Investigation reported that one in three female murder victims was killed by a husband or boyfriend. In 1998, another government study reported that one in five female high school students had suffered physical or sexual abuse by a partner. This does not include the number of males abused by females, child abuse, or elder abuse cases. Worse yet, it does not include the immeasurable number of cases that go unreported.

One benefit of the growing knowledge by individuals regarding their personal legal rights and the desensitization of society regarding the former shame associated with domestic violence is the increased willingness of individuals to step forward in such matters. As a result, a body of law has been developed and continues to evolve in the area of domestic violence. As recently as the mid-twentieth century, many persons aware of domestic violence in another household did not report it because the privacy of each family was considered superior to the rights of the individuals being abused. The old saying, "A man's home is his castle," was very much a reality in many communities urban and rural. However, as society became increasingly open and the awareness of the enormity of the problem became more obvious, people began to report violence, organizations began to form to assist victims, and communities came together to support those men, women, and children who found themselves in violent circumstances. As a result, state and federal government began to collect data and enact legislation to respond to the growing problem.

Many consider the actions of the legislatures, courts, and law enforcement agencies to still be in the formative stages; but there is no doubt the move is on to create legal standards designed to protect individuals against domestic violence (see Figure 16.2). While in the past such matters were dealt, at best, with things such as temporary restraining orders, the supporting laws were vague enough that these orders were difficult to enforce. Today, those laws have been elaborated and better defined to give law enforcement real authority to intervene in cases of domestic violence even when a restraining order is not in place.

Marital violence.   A rapidly changing area of criminal law that affects the family involves marital violence. More than one-half the states have now enacted statutes that permit an action of a wife for marital rape by her husband. However, many of these statutes require the parties to have been living apart at the time of the incident.[16] Additionally, because of the doctrine of nonintervention in the marital relationship, there has been little if any alternative for the spouse who has been violently abused by the other spouse. But states do have statutes permitting special intervention by police, and subsequently by the courts, where a reasonable belief exists that a spouse has committed a felony against his or her partner.

The statute in Figure 16.2 is just one example of an attempt to deal with the domestic violence issue through the legal system. In addition, many community and charitable organizations have established shelters, crisis intervention centers, hotlines, counseling, and other methods to effectively deal with the domestic

FIGURE 16.2   Family Violence Statute Connecticut General Statutes Annotated Title 46B. Family Law Chapter 815E. Marriage

§ 46b-38a. Family violence prevention and response: Definitions

For the purposes of sections 46b-38a to 46b-38f, inclusive:

(1) "Family violence" means an incident resulting in physical harm, bodily injury or assault, or an act of threatened violence that constitutes fear of imminent physical harm, bodily injury or assault between family or household members. Verbal abuse or argument shall not constitute family violence unless there is present danger and the likelihood that physical violence will occur.

(2) "Family or household member" means (A) spouses, former spouses; (B) parents and their children; (C) persons eighteen years of age or older related by blood or marriage; (D) persons sixteen years of age or older other than those persons in subparagraph (C) presently residing together or who have resided together; and (E) persons who have a child in common regardless of whether they are or have been married or have lived together at any time.

(3) "Family violence crime" means a crime as defined in section 53a-24 which, in addition to its other elements, contains as an element thereof an act of family violence to a family member and shall not include acts by parents or guardians disciplining minor children unless such acts constitute abuse.

(4) "Institutions and services" means peace officers, service providers, mandated reporters of abuse, agencies and departments that provide services to victims and families and services designed to assist victims and families. § 46b-38b. Investigation of family violence crime by peace officer. Arrest, when. Assistance to victim. Guidelines. Education and training program

(a) Whenever a peace officer determines upon speedy information that a family violence crime, as defined in subdivision (3) of section 46b-38a, has been committed within his jurisdiction, he shall arrest the person or persons suspected of its commission and charge such person or persons with the appropriate crime. The decision to arrest and charge shall not (1) be dependent on the specific consent of the victim, (2) consider the relationship of the parties or (3) be based solely on a request by the victim.

(b) No peace officer investigating an incident of family violence shall threaten, suggest or otherwise indicate the arrest of all parties for the purpose of discouraging requests for law enforcement intervention by any party. Where complaints are received from two or more opposing parties, the officer shall evaluate each complaint separately to determine whether he should seek a warrant for an arrest.

(c) No peace officer shall be held liable in any civil action regarding personal injury or injury to property brought by any party to a family violence incident for an arrest based on probable cause.

(d) It shall be the responsibility of the peace officer at the scene of a family violence incident to provide immediate assistance to the victim. Such assistance shall include but not be limited to; (1) Assisting the victim to obtain medical treatment if such is required; (2) notifying the victim of the right to file an affidavit or warrant for arrest; and (3) informing the victim of services available and referring the victim to the commission on victim services. In cases where the officer has determined that no cause exists for an arrest, assistance shall include: (A) Assistance included in subdivisions (1) to (3), inclusive, of this subsection; and (B) remaining at the scene for a reasonable time until in the reasonable judgment of the officer the likelihood of further imminent violence has been eliminated.

(e) On or before October 1, 1986, each law enforcement agency shall develop, in conjunction with the division of criminal justice, and implement specific operational guidelines for arrest policies in family violence incidents. Such guidelines shall include but not be limited to: (1) Procedures for the conduct of a criminal investigation; (2) procedures for arrest and for victim assistance by peace officers; (3) education as to what constitutes speedy information in a family violence incident; (4) procedures with respect to the provision of services to victims; and (5) such other criteria or guidelines as may be applicable to carry out the purposes of subsection (e) of section 17-38a and sections 17-38g, 46b-1, 46b-15, 46b-38a to 46b-38f, inclusive, and 54-1g.

(f) The municipal police training council, in conjunction with the division of criminal justice, shall establish an education and training program for law enforcement officers, supervisors and state's attorneys on the handling of family violence incidents. Such training shall: (1) Stress the enforcement of criminal law in family violence cases and the use of community resources and include training for peace officers at both recruit and in-service levels; (2) include: (A) The nature, extent and causes of family violence; (B) legal rights of and remedies available to victims of family violence and persons accused of family violence; (C) services and facilities available to victims and batterers; (D) legal duties imposed on police officers to make arrests and to offer protection and assistance; (E) techniques for handling incidents of family violence that minimize the likelihood of injury to the officer and promote safety of the victim.

violence that occurs in our society. As more cases are reported and the guilt often felt by victims of domestic violence is exposed as unfounded, this area of law and community support can be expected to grow dramatically in coming years.

In criminal law, certain principles affect the marriage relationship. A primary example is the testimonial privilege. Traditionally, a spouse could not testify against the other spouse during a criminal prosecution. But over time, the law has been modified, and most states now permit but cannot compel a spouse to testify against his or her partner. Because the spouse has the right to protect the confidentiality of the marriage relationship, testimony cannot be forced or ordered.

ENDING THE MARITAL RELATIONSHIP

Jurisdiction

When one or both of the parties to a marital relationship decide to end the marriage, a judicial declaration must be made before the marriage and its associated rights and duties will be terminated. The declaration must come from a court that has jurisdiction over the parties to the suit. Procedural rules in each state specify when the courts will accept jurisdiction over a marital dissolution action.

Many of the requirements in these statutes are similar throughout the states. Perhaps the most common is the requirement of residency. Although the length of residence varies, generally the states require the party commencing the action to have been a resident of the state for a specified period of time prior to initiating the action for dissolution. Parties may also obtain jurisdiction in a court if the marriage was formalized there or if the grounds for divorce occurred while the parties maintained their residence in the state (regardless of whether the time requirement has been met).[17]

When a party obtains a decree but the court does not have jurisdiction to decide matters involving the settlement of the marital estate (e.g., assets are located in another jurisdiction), the decree may be registered with a court that has jurisdiction over both of the parties and their property. That court may then proceed to determine the rights and obligations of each party. Under the U.S. Constitution, each state is obligated to give full faith and credit to the judgment of another state's decree. This means a state should honor and enforce the judgments of a court from another state.

A major jurisdictional issue in dissolution actions pertains to the authority of a court over the rights and duties concerning children of a marriage. Initially, the court that has jurisdiction to determine the rights, duties, and division of the assets of the marital estate also has authority to make findings regarding custody, visitation, and support of minor children. However, later adjustments to these findings, commonly termed modifications, may raise serious issues as to which court has authority. Fortunately, these issues have been settled in large part by the Uniform Reciprocal Enforcement of Support Act (URESA). Most states adhere to the act, which states quite specifically what courts have jurisdiction over matters concerning children of divorced parties.

Grounds for Dissolution of a Marriage

Although requirements of jurisdiction vary, the acceptable grounds for a divorce set forth by state statute are typically very similar. Although slight variations may exist, the basic premise for **dissolution of marriage** remains the same in most states. There must be sufficient evidence of some type that will establish that the marital bond is irreparably broken.

The grounds most commonly set forth in state statutes as sufficient to establish the end of the marriage relationship include, but are not limited to, the following:[18]

1. Habitual drunkenness or drug abuse.
2. Adultery.
3. Physical cruelty.
4. Mental cruelty.
5. Abandonment.
6. Insanity.

Traditionally, the party who suffered because of the existence of one or more of these grounds brought an action for divorce. He or she would be required to give evidence of the grounds, and on that basis the divorce would be granted.

More recently adopted has been the concept of no-fault divorce, the grounds for which are called irreconcilable differences. It has been recognized for many years that parties would agree to a specific grounds for a divorce as a means to expedite the end of the legal relationship when the marriage itself had come to an end sometime before. Many times, parties who no longer wish to be married have various reasons other than the statutorily stated grounds. In addition, the time and expense associated with divorce to the individuals and courts alike have increased significantly. As a result, in the past several years, every state has adopted a no-fault statute in some form. Although the requirements of proof of a broken marriage differ from state to state, the premise remains the same. It is unnecessary to claim that one party unilaterally caused the break in the marital bond. Rather, the parties have reached a point where they are no longer interested in maintaining the marital relationship.[19] For this reason, the bond is broken, and the legality of the relationship can be dissolved.

In an attempt to prevent parties from entering into a no-fault divorce when conciliation could still be achieved, many statutes impose requirements of proof that the marital bond is irreparably broken. Such requirements include lengthy separations before a no-fault divorce will be granted. Parties should be given every opportunity to evaluate the situation carefully and be sure of their decision. However, those parties who have firmly made a decision to end the marriage evade these requirements by returning to the former method of privately agreeing to one or more grounds based on fault of a party so that the divorce may be granted immediately. Thus, although the statutes have assisted many in obtaining a divorce without laying blame, abuse of statutes by giving grounds of fault continues in some states where it is much more time consuming to obtain a divorce on grounds of no-fault than on fault of a party.

dissolution of marriage
The end of the marriage relationship (also known as divorce).

Legal Separation

As previously mentioned, many times a divorce is a long and complicated process. Also, many parties do not file for divorce immediately upon separation. This may be for religious reasons, or the parties may want time to consider the possibility of reconciliation or at least the potential for agreement to the terms of the divorce. During this period, the parties remain legally obligated to each other as well as for the support of their children. As a consequence, a special area of law has developed by statute and by judicial decision that governs the rights of the parties during this period of **legal separation.**

Courts are reluctant to recognize antenuptial agreements that provide specifically for divorce. However, when a physical separation has occurred or is about to occur, the courts will consider an antenuptial or separation agreement between the parties that discusses the parties' rights and duties prior to the divorce when the marriage still exists legally but marital assets and liabilities are no longer shared. The courts will generally examine the agreement for fairness, full disclosure, and availability of legal counsel to each party.[20]

Separation agreements include such issues as custody, visitation, and support of minor children; possession of the marital residence; responsibility for payments due on marital debts; and maintenance (alimony), where appropriate. If the terms are agreeable to the parties, they may also serve as the basis for the terms in the final divorce decree for matters of convenience to the parties. However, it is important to note that legal separations have no direct connection to dissolution proceedings, and each may take place without the other.

legal separation

Legal document that establishes the property rights of the parties without effecting a dissolution of the actual marriage relationship.

Assignment 16.4

> Prepare a chart that details the differences between dissolution, annulment, common law divorce, and legal separation.

temporary restraining order

Court order that temporarily orders a party to act or refrain from acting in a particular manner until such time as the court has the opportunity to consider a more permanent ruling on the issue.

preliminary injunction

Court order that orders a party to act or refrain from acting in a particular manner for a specified period of time (often during the pendency of a legal proceeding).

Temporary Orders

Unfortunately, not all parties are willing to reach an agreement regarding property and other rights. In such instances, state statutes give a court authority to make temporary provisions during the period after commencement of a divorce but before a final decree is issued. These temporary orders provide terms that the parties must follow with respect to the marital obligations previously discussed.

In addition to issuing temporary orders, courts are often requested to issue **temporary restraining orders** and **preliminary injunctions,** granted in circumstances where the court is convinced that one spouse will injure the partner or harm, destroy, or dispose of marital property.[21] If the threat of harm is immediate, the spouse in danger of injury or harm to property can appear in court ex parte. An ex parte proceeding is conducted without giving the other party to the action the opportunity to be present and voice his or her position. Because these orders are based on one person's version of the story, the court will usually issue the order only in compelling circumstances, and such orders are usually effective for only a short period of time as an emergency measure.

APPLICATION 16.3

Chavela and Bill have been married for two years. There is a long documented history of mutual physical abuse. Bill decides to divorce Chavela. Chavela informs him that if he files for divorce, she will first cash out all of their accounts and then find him and shoot him to death before she leaves the country. Bill goes immediately to an attorney who takes him to court and, based on his testimony and police reports of past violence in the home, grants a temporary restraining order to freeze all accounts, and requires Chavela to remain 1,000 yards from Bill at all times. After 10 days, the order will expire and a new hearing will be scheduled to permit Chavela to tell her side of the story and determine whether the order should be extended.

Point for Discussion

◆   If Chavela makes the exact same claims against Bill, should she also obtain a restraining order with the same terms?

After a temporary restraining order has been issued, it is served on the party who is restrained. Even if the restrained party cannot be located, the order is effective, and if it is violated, the party can be arrested.[22] Without such a rule, parties could simply avoid being served and in the interim destroy marital property or perhaps seriously injure their spouse. Given the alternatives, the safer course seems to be to give the order effect from the time it is issued.

Temporary restraining orders are usually issued for a very short period of time. Thus, a party who can show evidence that such an order was improperly issued can have the order revoked at the earliest opportunity. When a hearing is held, however, if sufficient evidence is presented to warrant continuance of the order, a preliminary injunction will be issued that remains in effect during the pendency of the dissolution proceedings.

A preliminary injunction contains virtually the same provisions as a temporary restraining order. However, the injunction will be effective until the final divorce decree is entered. At that time, if marital property will continue to be held jointly or if the physical danger still exists, a **permanent injunction** may be issued that will remain effective until an order of the court removes it. Many times, these orders are left in force forever.

permanent injunction
Court order that permanently orders a party to act or refrain from acting in a particular manner.

APPLICATION 16.4

Saul and Sara are in the process of a bitter divorce. At the final hearing, Sara testifies that on two occasions when Saul has picked up the children for visitation, he has threatened that if she ever attempts to remarry, he will kill her. She also claims he calls at all times of the day or night and has gone through the marital residence where she lives with the children looking for clues of other men. The court grants a permanent injunction that requires Saul to not set foot on any part of the property where Sara resides and that he is to call approximately five minutes before his arrival for visitation and she will send the children to the sidewalk when he pulls up. The same terms are ordered for returning the children from visitation. He is to call and she will wait at the door to receive the children. At any other time, Saul is to remain a distance of 1,500 feet from Sara, including in public places. Saul is only permitted to contact Sara in writing except in the event of an emergency involving the children. The children are currently two and four years old. The injunction is permanent.

Point for Discussion
- If Saul has the children call their mother repeatedly during the visitation with him, would this be considered a violation of the injunction?

CUSTODY

custody (parental rights)
The rights to oversee the care, education, and rearing of a child.

Custody over minor children is perhaps one of the most litigated areas of family law, and the term is used to describe the care, control, and education of a minor child. It is effective as long as the child is a minor or is still in high school. A synonymous term used in some jurisdictions is **parental rights.** For purposes of this discussion, the term *custody* will be used. When the child reaches the age of majority under statute in the state where the child resides, custody ends, and the child is considered to be an adult.[23] Residence is determined by the child's permanent dwelling, not by where the child attends school or where the other parent whom the child visits may live. Generally, the state of residence of the custodial parent is the state of residence of the child.

Custody may not end at the age of majority for a child with mental disabilities. In cases when the child is unable to accept responsibility for his or her actions, the parent may be appointed the permanent custodian.[24]

In the event of the death of the custodial parent, the presumption is that custody will be transferred to the other parent. The exception to this is if the surviving parent is not able to provide an acceptable environment for the child. In such circumstances, stepparents, grandparents, or other interested parties who can provide a suitable environment for the child may be appointed guardian.

Fortunately, the courts rarely have to deal with such cases. However, there are quite often decisions to be made by the courts when both parents are living and willing to provide a home for the child or children. Formerly, the mother almost always received custody of the children. No longer is this the case. Courts consider numerous factors to determine who is best able to care for and attend to the needs of the children.[25]

Under what is known as the tender years doctrine, which was followed for many years but is rapidly declining in this country, the mother was presumed to be the best alternative for custody of young children of "tender years"[26] (usually children who had not reached their teens). The only way a father could overcome this presumption and have a chance for custody was to prove that the mother was unfit or, at the very least, far less able than the father to care for the children.

In recent times, many fathers have taken an increasingly active role in the upbringing of their children. Additionally, various movements throughout the country for equal rights for men have supported fathers in their quest for custody. Furthermore, it is no longer the general rule that mothers stay at home to care for the children. Many mothers work and are away from the home just as a father would be. For all of these reasons, many courts have struck down the tender years doctrine in favor of a case-by-case evaluation of who will best serve the interests and needs of the child.[27]

Who Gets Custody?

What is the standard that must be proven to obtain custody of a child? Contrary to popular belief, it is not necessary to prove that the other party is unfit as a parent. Although the evidence may establish this in some cases, it is not the standard used by most courts. Rather, the courts look at what will be in the best interests of the child. Divorce is extremely difficult for children of all ages. That is not to say it may not be a better alternative than to continue the marriage; but divorce does mean that a child's world goes through dramatic changes that require adjustment. Consequently, the court examines several areas that affect the child's life and looks to the child's particular needs. The court then looks at the environment that each parent will offer the child. The environment that is most compatible with the child's needs is the one that is in the child's best interests. Thus, each parent may offer a suitable environment, but the parent that is better suited to meet the needs of the child should prevail.

As this suggests, the standard that a parent must prove is that it is in the best interests of the child that the parent be awarded custody. The factors that a court considers in making this determination may include, but are not limited to, the following:[28]

1. The ability of the parent to care for the child personally (as opposed to extensive child care services).
2. The religion of the parent.
3. The ability of the parent to attend to any special needs of the child because of young age or disability.

4. Immoral conduct that would have a direct effect on the child (otherwise this is considered irrelevant).
5. Ability to give continuity to the child's current environment (such as home, school, and friends).
6. The availability of contact with members of the child's extended family.

None of the preceding factors is individually controlling, and the court will usually consider factors that are peculiar to each case when making its determination. The U.S. Supreme Court has determined that race or ethnic background cannot be used as the only determining factor in a custody case, although a court may consider race or ethnicity along with the other factors in a custody decision when it is relevant.[29]

An additional factor that is not controlling but may be given some weight is the desire of the child. The general rule is that a child may not be able to determine objectively what is in his or her best interests. However, as a child matures, courts are often more willing to consider the child's opinion. Many states have statutory provisions that expressly permit the judge to give weight to this factor after a child reaches a certain age.[30] Because the child is still a minor and is deemed legally incompetent to make such significant decisions, a court will rarely accept the child's wishes as the sole determining factor.

Joint Custody

Thus far, the discussion has been confined to the issue of single-parent custody, in which one parent has the primary responsibility for the care, control, and education of the child. The noncustodial parent has visitation rights but no legal right to take an active part in the decisions regarding the child's rearing.

Because the limitation on such input was unacceptable to many parents, the concept of joint custody was developed. A common misconception is that joint custody involves only shared physical custody of the child or children. Although this sometimes occurs in joint custody, it is not the primary purpose. The child may very well live permanently with one parent. Joint custody gives each parent the right to take an active part in the rearing of the child. The parents will discuss and agree upon matters of education, religion, and, in general, all major decisions that affect the child's life.[31]

A majority of states have enacted statutes that permit the courts to award joint custody. It is left to the discretion of the judges to determine on a case-by-case basis whether the circumstances are appropriate for joint custody or whether the child's interests would be better served by an award of individual custody to one parent and significant contact with the other parent.

In the best of circumstances, joint custody allows both parents to have input into all aspects of a child's upbringing. As a practical matter, however, it is often an untenable situation. Because of this, judges are often reluctant to grant joint custody unless the circumstances appear overwhelmingly in favor of it.

The problem that arises with joint custody is that in many situations it is contradictory to the divorce itself. The parties have sought a dissolution of their marriage because their relationship was one involving irreconcilable differences. Yet, in joint custody, the parties seek permission of the court to have the legal right to determine important matters, with each having an equal voice in the decision. Often the parties are so opposed to each other they are not willing to work together, even in the best interests of the child. The result is that the parties return to the same judge for mediation of their disputes on matters concerning the child. The purpose of joint custody is not achieved, the parents incur additional legal expenses, and the child is subjected to more disruption than ever. Thus, unless the parties seem to be genuinely interested and capable of working with each other, many courts are hesitant to grant joint custody.

Enforcement of Custody Orders

An increasingly common issue in child custody cases is that of court jurisdiction. With the expanding mobility of American society, it is no longer uncommon for parents to live in different states. Consequently, enforcement of child custody orders can rapidly develop into a costly and time-consuming battle for parents in conflict. In response, the Uniform Child Custody Jurisdiction Act (UCCJA) has been adopted, which sets up guidelines for determining jurisdiction and establishing cooperation among the states in the enforcement of custody orders. While not a cure, this uniform law has eliminated a great many of the problems and concerns that parents might face when they live in separate jurisdictions. Figure 16.3 gives the text of the Uniform Child Custody Jurisdiction Act.

Assignment 16.5

Bernadette has custody of her two children. Currently, their father Cole has visitation twice weekly with the children and for eight weeks during July and August. On July 1, he picks up the children and boards a plane for a city approximately 2,000 miles away where he has accepted new employment and established a residence. During the eighth week of visitation, he informs Bernadette, through his attorney, that he enrolled the children in school on July 1 (in a district that employs a year-round schedule), and that he intends to seek custody. Does he have grounds to obtain custody in the new jurisdiction under the UCCJA?

CHILD SUPPORT

Although the obligation to provide support to a spouse may end with the dissolution of the marital relationship, support of children of the marriage continues as long as the court determines it is necessary. Generally, this is for the remainder of the child's minority or until high school graduation.[32] However, judges are increasingly coming to the view that parents, when able, should also contribute toward a child's college education.[33] The theory is that the child of

FIGURE 16.3 Uniform Child Custody Jurisdiction Act

§ 1. Purposes of Act; Construction of Provisions.—

(a) The general purposes of this Act are to:

(1) avoid jurisdictional competition and conflict with courts of other states in matters of child custody which have in the past resulted in the shifting of children from state to state with harmful effects on their well-being;

(2) promote cooperation with the courts of other states to the end that a custody decree is rendered in that state which can best decide the case in the interest of the child;

(3) assure that litigation concerning the custody of a child take place ordinarily in the state with which the child and his family have the closest connection and where significant evidence concerning his care, protection, training, and personal relationships is most readily available, and that courts of this state decline the exercise of jurisdiction when the child and his family have a closer connection with another state;

(4) discourage continuing controversies over child custody in the interest of greater stability of home environment and of secure family relationships for the child;

(5) deter abductions and other unilateral removals of children undertaken to obtain custody awards;

(6) avoid re-litigation of custody decisions of other states in this state insofar as feasible;

(7) facilitate the enforcement of custody decrees of other states;

(8) promote and expand the exchange of information and other forms of mutual assistance between the courts of this state and those of other states concerned with the same child; and

(9) make uniform the law of those states which enact it.

(b) This Act shall be construed to promote the general purposes stated in this section.

§ 2. Definitions.—As used in this Act:

(1) "contestant" means a person, including a parent, who claims a right to custody or visitation rights with respect to a child;

(2) "custody determination" means a court decision and court orders and instructions providing for the custody of a child, including visitation rights; it does not include a decision relating to child support or any other monetary obligation of any person;

(3) "custody proceeding" includes proceedings in which a custody determination is one of several issues, such as an action for divorce or separation, and includes child neglect and dependency proceedings;

(4) "decree" or "custody decree" means a custody determination contained in a judicial decree or order made in a custody proceeding, and includes an initial decree and a modification decree;

(5) "home state" means the state in which the child immediately preceding the time involved lived with his parents, a parent, or a person acting as parent, for at least 6 consecutive months, and in the case of a child less than 6 months old the state in which the child lived from birth with any of the persons mentioned. Periods of temporary absence of any of the named persons are counted as part of the 6-month or other period;

(6) "initial decree" means the first custody decree concerning a particular child;

(7) "modification decree" means a custody decree which modifies or replaces a prior decree, whether made by the court which rendered the prior decree or by another court;

(8) "physical custody" means actual possession and control of a child;

(9) "person acting as parent" means a person, other than a parent, who has physical custody of a child and who has either been awarded custody by a court or claims a right to custody; and

(10) "state" means any state, territory, or possession of the United States, the Commonwealth of Puerto Rico, and the District of Columbia.

§ 3. Jurisdiction.—

(a) A court of this State which is competent to decide child custody matters has jurisdiction to make a child custody determination by initial or modification decree if:

(1) this State (i) is the home state of the child at the time of commencement of the proceeding, or (ii) had been the child's home state within 6 months before commencement of the proceeding and the child is absent from this State because of his removal or retention by a person claiming his custody or for other reasons, and a parent or person acting as parent continues to live in this State; or

(2) it is in the best interest of the child that a court of this State assume jurisdiction because (i) the child and his parents, or the child and at least one contestant, have a significant connection with this State, and (ii) there is available in this State substantial evidence concerning the child's present or future care, protection, training, and personal relationships; or

FIGURE 16.3   Uniform Child Custody Jurisdiction Act   *(Continued)*

(3) the child is physically present in this State and (i) the child has been abandoned or (ii) it is necessary in an emergency to protect the child because he has been subjected to or threatened with mistreatment or abuse or is otherwise neglected [or dependent]; or

(4) (i) it appears that no other state would have jurisdiction under prerequisites substantially in accordance with paragraphs (1), (2), or (3), or another state has declined to exercise jurisdiction on the ground that this State is the more appropriate forum to determine the custody of the child, and (ii) it is in the best interest of the child that this court assume jurisdiction.

(b) Except under paragraphs (3) and (4) of subsection (a), physical presence in this State of the child, or of the child and one of the contestants, is not alone sufficient to confer jurisdiction on a court of this State to make a child custody determination.

(c) Physical presence of the child, while desirable, is not a prerequisite for jurisdiction to determine his custody.

§ 4. Notice and Opportunity to be Heard.—Before making a decree under this Act, reasonable notice and opportunity to be heard shall be given to the contestants, any parent whose parental rights have not been previously terminated, and any person who has physical custody of the child. If any of these persons is outside this State, notice and opportunity to be heard shall be given pursuant to section 5.

§ 5. Notice to Persons Outside this State; Submission to Jurisdiction.—

(a) Notice required for the exercise of jurisdiction over a person outside this State shall be given in a manner reasonably calculated to give actual notice, and may be:

(1) by personal delivery outside this State in the manner prescribed for service of process within this State;

(2) in the manner prescribed by the law of the place in which the service is made for service of process in that place in an action in any of its courts of general jurisdiction;

(3) by any form of mail addressed to the person to be served and requesting a receipt; or

(4) as directed by the court [including publication, if other means of notification are ineffective].

(b) Notice under this section shall be served, mailed, or delivered, [or last published] at least [10, 20] days before any hearing in this State.

(c) Proof of service outside this State may be made by affidavit of the individual who made the service, or in the manner prescribed by the law of this State, the order pursuant to which the service is made, or the law of the place in which the service is made. If service is made by mail, proof may be a receipt signed by the addressee or other evidence of delivery to the addressee.

(d) Notice is not required if a person submits to the jurisdiction of the court.

§ 6. Simultaneous Proceedings in Other States.—

(a) A court of this State shall not exercise its jurisdiction under this Act if at the time of filing the petition a proceeding concerning the custody of the child was pending in a court of another state exercising jurisdiction substantially in conformity with this Act, unless the proceeding is stayed by the court of the other state because this State is a more appropriate forum or for other reasons.

(b) Before hearing the petition in a custody proceeding the court shall examine the pleadings and other information supplied by the parties under section 9 and shall consult the child custody registry established under section 16 concerning the pendency of proceedings with respect to the child in other states. If the court has reason to believe that proceedings may be pending in another state it shall direct an inquiry to the state court administrator or other appropriate official of the other state.

(c) If the court is informed during the course of the proceeding that a proceeding concerning the custody of the child was pending in another state before the court assumed jurisdiction it shall stay the proceeding and communicate with the court in which the other proceeding is pending to the end that the issue may be litigated in the more appropriate forum and that information be exchanged in accordance with sections 19 through 22. If a court of this State has made a custody decree before being informed of a pending proceeding in a court of another state it shall immediately inform that court of the fact. If the court is informed that a proceeding was commenced in another state after it assumed jurisdiction it shall likewise inform the other court to the end that the issues may be litigated in the more appropriate forum.

§ 7. Inconvenient Forum.—

(a) A court which has jurisdiction under this Act to make an initial or modification decree may decline to exercise its jurisdiction any time before making a decree if it finds that it is an inconvenient forum to make a custody determination under the circumstances of the case and that a court of another state is a more appropriate forum.

FIGURE 16.3   Uniform Child Custody Jurisdiction Act   *(Continued)*

(b) A finding of inconvenient forum may be made upon the court's own motion or upon motion of a party or a guardian ad litem or other representative of the child.

(c) In determining if it is an inconvenient forum, the court shall consider if it is in the interest of the child that another state assume jurisdiction. For this purpose it may take into account the following factors, among others:

(1) if another state is or recently was the child's home state;

(2) if another state has a closer connection with the child and his family or with the child and one or more of the contestants;

(3) if substantial evidence concerning the child's present or future care, protection, training, and personal relationships is more readily available in another state;

(4) if the parties have agreed on another forum which is no less appropriate; and

(5) if the exercise of jurisdiction by a court of this State would contravene any of the purposes stated in section 1.

(d) Before determining whether to decline or retain jurisdiction the court may communicate with a court of another state and exchange information pertinent to the assumption of jurisdiction by either court with a view to assuring that jurisdiction will be exercised by the more appropriate court and that a forum will be available to the parties.

(e) If the court finds that it is an inconvenient forum and that a court of another state is a more appropriate forum, it may dismiss the proceedings, or it may stay the proceedings upon condition that a custody proceeding be promptly commenced in another named state or upon any other conditions which may be just and proper, including the condition that a moving party stipulate his consent and submission to the jurisdiction of the other forum.

(f) The court may decline to exercise its jurisdiction under this Act if a custody determination is incidental to an action for divorce or another proceeding while retaining jurisdiction over the divorce or other proceeding.

(g) If it appears to the court that it is clearly an inappropriate forum it may require the party who commenced the proceedings to pay, in addition to the costs of the proceedings in this State, necessary travel and other expenses, including attorneys' fees, incurred by other parties or their witnesses. Payment is to be made to the clerk of the court for remittance to the proper party.

(h) Upon dismissal or stay of proceedings under this section the court shall inform the court found to be the more appropriate forum of this fact, or if the court which would have jurisdiction in the other state is not certainly known, shall transmit the information to the court administrator or other appropriate official for forwarding to the appropriate court.

(i) Any communication received from another state informing this State of a finding of inconvenient forum because a court of this State is the more appropriate forum shall be filed in the custody registry of the appropriate court. Upon assuming jurisdiction the court of this State shall inform the original court of this fact.

§ 8. Jurisdiction Declined by Reason of Conduct.—

(a) If the petitioner for an initial decree has wrongfully taken the child from another state or has engaged in similar reprehensible conduct the court may decline to exercise jurisdiction if this is just and proper under the circumstances.

(b) Unless required in the interest of the child, the court shall not exercise its jurisdiction to modify a custody decree of another state if the petitioner, without consent of the person entitled to custody, has improperly removed the child from the physical custody of the person entitled to custody or has improperly retained the child after a visit or other temporary relinquishment of physical custody. If the petitioner has violated any other provision of a custody decree of another state the court may decline to exercise its jurisdiction if this is just and proper under the circumstances.

(c) In appropriate cases a court dismissing a petition under this section may charge the petitioner with necessary travel and other expenses, including attorneys' fees, incurred by other parties or their witnesses.

§ 9. Information under Oath to be Submitted to the Court.—

(a) Every party in a custody proceeding in his first pleading or in an affidavit attached to that pleading shall give information under oath as to the child's present address, the places where the child has lived within the last 5 years, and the names and present addresses of the persons with whom the child has lived during that period. In this pleading or affidavit every party shall further declare under oath whether:

(1) he has participated (as a party, witness, or in any other capacity) in any other litigation concerning the custody of the same child in this or any other state;

(2) he has information of any custody proceeding concerning the child pending in a court of this or any other state; and

FIGURE 16.3   Uniform Child Custody Jurisdiction Act   *(Continued)*

(3) he knows of any person not a party to the proceedings who has physical custody of the child or claims to have custody or visitation rights with respect to the child.

(b) If the declaration as to any of the above items is in the affirmative the declarant shall give additional information under oath as required by the court. The court may examine the parties under oath as to details of the information furnished and as to other matters pertinent to the court's jurisdiction and the disposition of the case.

(c) Each party has a continuing duty to inform the court of any custody proceeding concerning the child in this or any other state of which he obtained information during this proceeding.

§ 10. Additional Parties.—If the court learns from information furnished by the parties pursuant to section 9 or from other sources that a person not a party to the custody proceeding has physical custody of the child or claims to have custody or visitation rights with respect to the child, it shall order that person to be joined as a party and to be duly notified of the pendency of the proceeding and of his joinder as a party. If the person joined as a party is outside this State he shall be served with process or otherwise notified in accordance with section 5.

§ 11. Appearance of Parties and the Child.—

[(a) The court may order any party to the proceeding who is in this State to appear personally before the court. If that party has physical custody of the child the court may order that he appear personally with the child.]

(b) If a party to the proceeding whose presence is desired by the court is outside this State with or without the child the court may order that the notice given under section 5 include a statement directing that party to appear personally with or without the child and declaring that failure to appear may result in a decision adverse to that party.

(c) If a party to the proceeding who is outside this State is directed to appear under subsection (b) or desires to appear personally before the court with or without the child, the court may require another party to pay to the clerk of the court travel and other necessary expenses of the party so appearing and of the child if this is just and proper under the circumstances.

§ 12. Binding Force and Res Judicata Effect of Custody Decree.—A custody decree rendered by a court of this State which had jurisdiction under section 3 binds all parties who have been served in this State or notified in accordance with section 5 or who have submitted to the jurisdiction of the court, and who have been given an opportunity to be heard. As to these parties the custody decree is conclusive as to all issues of law and fact decided and as to the custody determination made unless and until that determination is modified pursuant to law, including the provisions of this Act.

§ 13. Recognition of Out-of-State Custody Decrees.—The courts of this State shall recognize and enforce an initial or modification decree of a court of another state which had assumed jurisdiction under statutory provisions substantially in accordance with this Act or which was made under factual circumstances meeting the jurisdictional standards of the Act, so long as this decree has not been modified in accordance with jurisdictional standards substantially similar to those of this Act.

§ 14. Modification of Custody Decree of Another State.—

(a) If a court of another state has made a custody decree, a court of this State shall not modify that decree unless (1) it appears to the court of this State that the court which rendered the decree does not now have jurisdiction under jurisdictional prerequisites substantially in accordance with this Act or has declined to assume jurisdiction to modify the decree and (2) the court of this State has jurisdiction.

(b) If a court of this State is authorized under subsection (a) and section 8 to modify a custody decree of another state it shall give due consideration to the transcript of the record and other documents of all previous proceedings submitted to it in accordance with section 22.

§ 15. Filing and Enforcement of Custody Decree of Another State.—

(a) A certified copy of a custody decree of another state may be filed in the office of the clerk of any [District Court, Family Court] of this State. The clerk shall treat the decree in the same manner as a custody decree of the [District Court, Family Court] of this State. A custody decree so filed has the same effect and shall be enforced in like manner as a custody decree rendered by a court of this State.

(b) A person violating a custody decree of another state which makes it necessary to enforce the decree in this State may be required to pay necessary travel and other expenses, including attorneys' fees, incurred by the party entitled to the custody or his witnesses.

FIGURE 16.3   Uniform Child Custody Jurisdiction Act   *(Continued)*

§ 16. Registry of Out-of-State Custody Decrees and Proceedings.—The clerk of each [District Court, Family Court] shall maintain a registry in which he shall enter the following:

(1) certified copies of custody decrees of other states received for filing;

(2) communications as to the pendency of custody proceedings in other states;

(3) communications concerning a finding of inconvenient forum by a court of another state; and

(4) other communications or documents concerning custody proceedings in another state which may affect the jurisdiction of a court of this State or the disposition to be made by it in a custody proceeding.

§ 17. Certified Copies of Custody Decree.—The Clerk of the [District Court, Family Court] of this State, at the request of the court of another state or at the request of any person who is affected by or has a legitimate interest in a custody decree, shall certify and forward a copy of the decree to that court or person.

§ 18. Taking Testimony in Another State.—In addition to other procedural devices available to a party, any party to the proceeding or a guardian ad litem or other representative of the child may adduce testimony of witnesses, including parties and the child, by deposition or otherwise in another state. The court on its own motion may direct that the testimony of a person be taken in another state and may prescribe the manner in which and the terms upon which the testimony shall be taken.

§ 19. Hearings and Studies in Another State; Orders to Appear.—

(a) A court of this State may request the appropriate court of another state to hold a hearing to adduce evidence, to order a party to produce or give evidence under other procedures of that state, or to have social studies made with respect to the custody of a child involved in proceedings pending in the court of this State; and to forward to the court of this State certified copies of the transcript of the record of the hearing, the evidence otherwise adduced, or any social studies prepared in compliance with the request. The cost of the services may be assessed against the parties or, if necessary, ordered paid by the [County, State].

(b) A court of this State may request the appropriate court of another state to order a party to custody proceedings pending in the court of this State to appear in the proceedings, and if that party has physical custody of the child, to appear with the child. The request may state that travel and other necessary expenses of the party and of the child whose appearance is desired will be assessed against another party or will otherwise be paid.

§ 20. Assistance to Courts of Other States.—

(a) Upon request of the court of another state the courts of this State which are competent to hear custody matters may order a person in this State to appear at a hearing to adduce evidence or to produce or give evidence under other procedures available in this State [or may order social studies to be made for use in a custody proceeding in another state]. A certified copy of the transcript of the record of the hearing or the evidence otherwise adduced [and any social studies prepared] shall be forwarded by the clerk of the court to the requesting court.

(b) A person within this State may voluntarily give his testimony or statement in this State for use in a custody proceeding outside this State.

(c) Upon request of the court of another state a competent court of this State may order a person in this State to appear alone or with the child in a custody proceeding in another state. The court may condition compliance with the request upon assurance by the other state that state travel and other necessary expenses will be advanced or reimbursed.

§ 21. Preservation of Documents for Use in Other States.—In any custody proceeding in this State the court shall preserve the pleadings, orders and decrees, any record that has been made of its hearings, social studies, and other pertinent documents until the child reaches [18, 21] years of age. Upon appropriate request of the court of another state the court shall forward to the other court certified copies of any or all such documents.

§ 22. Request for Court Records of Another State.—If a custody decree has been rendered in another state concerning a child involved in a custody proceeding pending in a court of this State, the court of this State upon taking jurisdiction of the case shall request of the court of the other state a certified copy of the transcript of any court record and other documents mentioned in section 21.

§ 23. International Application.—The general policies of this Act extend to the international area. The provisions of this Act relating to the recognition and enforcement of custody decrees of other states apply to custody decrees and decrees involving legal institutions similar in nature to custody institutions rendered by appropriate authorities of other nations if reasonable notice and opportunity to be heard were given to all affected persons.

FIGURE 16.3   Uniform Child Custody Jurisdiction Act   *(Continued)*

[§ 24. Priority.—Upon the request of a party to a custody proceeding which raises a question of existence or exercise of jurisdiction under this Act the case shall be given calendar priority and handled expeditiously.]

§ 25. Severability.—If any provision of this Act or the application thereof to any person or circumstance is held invalid, its invalidity does not affect other provisions or applications of the Act which can be given effect without the invalid provision or application, and to this end the provisions of this Act are several.

divorced parents should be in a position similar to the child of nondivorced parents who has the benefit of family support. Additionally, support may be extended beyond a child's majority if the child has some physical or mental incapacity that prevents the child from becoming responsible for filling his or her own needs. Many states now have statutes that address issues of support during post secondary education or incapacity.

If a child marries or becomes legally emancipated before the age of majority, the child will become fully independent. As a result, the parents will no longer be legally responsible for providing support for the child. On the other hand, if a parent dies and leaves no provision for the support of the child, the child is still entitled to a share of the parent's estate for support. The exception to this occurs when the parent leaves a will in which he or she specifically disinherits the child. If this occurs, the support may, in some states, be terminated, and the child becomes the sole responsibility of the surviving parent. However, as with matters of domestic law, the particular state's law should be examined in a situation before reaching any conclusions.

There is usually little contest over the obligation to provide support. Most parties accept that they are obligated to support their natural or adopted children. The real turmoil begins when the parties attempt to determine the amount of support to be contributed. If financially able, the noncustodial parent—whether the mother or the father—is responsible for periodically paying a specified amount to the custodial parent. The money is to be used for such needs of the child as food, shelter, clothing, and medical and educational expenses.

Unless the parties agree to an amount for support, a hearing will be held to determine the financial needs of the child based on information provided by the parties and the financial ability of the noncustodial parent to contribute toward the needs of the child. With this information, the court will make a decision as to what an appropriate amount would be and how often the amount should be paid.[34]

Child Support Guidelines

When determining the amount of child support, the court considers many independent factors that influence the amount of support that it will actually order. Many states have guidelines that provide formulas for calculation or factors that should be considered, including, but not limited to, the following:

1. The number of children (of this marriage or others) for whom the parent is obligated to provide support.
2. Whether one of the parents provides health insurance for the child.
3. The net income of each parent.
4. Any special medical or educational needs of the child.
5. The standard of living the child would have enjoyed had the divorce not occurred.[35]

It is assumed that an equitable share is contributed by the custodial parent who physically provides the food, shelter, clothing, and attention to other needs of the child.

A particularly helpful statute has been adopted in recent years that establishes child support guidelines (see Figure 16.4). These guidelines have been adopted in most states and provide a formula that courts can employ to determine the appropriate amount of child support, given the financial circumstances of the parties. However, these are only guidelines, and typically, a court has the authority to override them in cases involving special considerations.

FIGURE 16.4   Nevada Revised Statutes Title 11. Domestic Relations. Chapter 125B. Obligation of Support. General Provisions

---

125B.070. Amount of payment: Definitions; review of formula by State Bar of Nevada.

1. As used in this section and NRS 125B.080, unless the context otherwise requires:

(a) "Gross monthly income" means the total amount of income from any source of a wage-earning employee or the gross income from any source of a self-employed person, after deduction of all legitimate business expenses, but without deduction for personal income taxes, contributions for retirement benefits, contributions to a pension or for any other personal expenses.

(b) "Obligation for support" means the amount determined according to the following schedule:

(1) For one child, 18 percent;

(2) For two children, 25 percent;

(3) For three children, 29 percent;

(4) For four children, 31 percent; and

(5) For each additional child, an additional 2 percent, of a parent's gross monthly income, but not more than $500 per month per child for an obligation for support determined pursuant to subparagraphs (1) to (4), inclusive, unless the court sets forth findings of fact as to the basis for a different amount pursuant to subsection 5 of NRS 125B.080.

2. On or before January 18, 1993, and on or before the third Monday in January every 4 years thereafter, the State Bar of Nevada shall review the formulas set forth in this section to determine whether any modifications are advisable and report to the legislature their findings and any proposed amendments.

125B.080. Formula for determining amount of support.

1. A court shall apply the appropriate formula set forth in paragraph (b) of subsection 1 of NRS 125B.070 to:

(a) Determine the required support in any case involving the support of children.

(b) Any request filed after July 1, 1987, to change the amount of the required support of children.

2. If the parties agree as to the amount of support required, the parties shall certify that the amount of support is consistent with the appropriate formula set forth in paragraph (b) of subsection 1 of NRS 125B.070. If the amount of support deviates from the formula, the parties must stipulate sufficient facts in accordance with subsection 9 which justify the deviation to the court, and the court shall make a written finding thereon. Any inaccuracy or falsification of financial information which results in an inappropriate award of support is grounds for a motion to modify or adjust the award.

FIGURE 16.4   Nevada Revised Statutes Title 11. Domestic Relations. Chapter 125B. Obligation of Support. General Provisions   *(Continued)*

3. If the parties disagree as to the amount of the gross monthly income of either party, the court shall determine the amount and may direct either party to furnish financial information or other records, including income tax returns for the preceding 3 years. Once a court has established an obligation for support by reference to a formula set forth in paragraph (b) of subsection 1 of NRS 125B.070, any subsequent modification or adjustment of that support must be based upon changed circumstances or as a result of a review conducted pursuant to NRS 125B.145.

4. Notwithstanding the formulas set forth in paragraph (b) of subsection 1 of NRS 125B.070, the minimum amount of support that may be awarded by a court in any case is $100 per month per child, unless the court makes a written finding that the obligor is unable to pay the minimum amount. Willful underemployment or unemployment is not a sufficient cause to deviate from the awarding of at least the minimum amount.

5. It is presumed that the basic needs of a child are met by the formulas set forth in paragraph (b) of subsection 1 of NRS 125B.070. This presumption may be rebutted by evidence proving that the needs of a particular child are not met by the applicable formula.

6. If the amount of the awarded support for a child is greater or less than the amount which would be established under the applicable formula, the court shall set forth findings of fact as to the basis for the deviation from the formula.

7. Expenses for health care which are not reimbursed, including expenses for medical, surgical, dental, orthodontic and optical expenses, must be borne equally by both parents in the absence of extraordinary circumstances.

8. If a parent who has an obligation for support is willfully underemployed or unemployed, to avoid an obligation for support of a child, that obligation must be based upon the parent's true potential earning capacity.

9. The court shall consider the following factors when adjusting the amount of support of a child upon specific findings of fact:

(a) The cost of health insurance;

(b) The cost of child care;

(c) Any special educational needs of the child;

(d) The age of the child;

(e) The responsibility of the parents for the support of others;

(f) The value of services contributed by either parent;

(g) Any public assistance paid to support the child;

(h) Any expenses reasonably related to the mother's pregnancy and confinement;

(i) The cost of transportation of the child to and from visitation if the custodial parent moved with the child from the jurisdiction of the court which ordered the support and the noncustodial parent remained;

(j) The amount of time the child spends with each parent;

(k) Any other necessary expenses for the benefit of the child; and

(l) The relative income of both parents.

Modification of Support

Once support has been awarded, it is due and payable until the child reaches the age of majority or the court orders a change in the amount of support payable. If support is being paid to a custodial parent for the care of more than one child, the noncustodial parent cannot automatically reduce the support when one of the children reaches the age of majority. Usually, a party is required to petition the court to review the original support order and modify it accordingly.

Modification of support may be granted in circumstances other than a child's reaching majority. Courts will periodically entertain petitions to modify support when there has been a substantial change in the general cost of supporting the child. If a divorce occurs when a child is very young, it may be necessary for the custodial parent to seek an increase in support at some time during the child's minority. After several years, as the child enters school, inflation and other factors may increase the cost of meeting the child's needs. It may be necessary for the custodial parent to seek an upward modification of the original order of support.

The status of the parents may change dramatically over a longer period of time. If one parent meets with long-term financial difficulty, a downward or upward modification may be in order. If the custodial parent enjoys tremendous financial gain, it may serve no purpose for the noncustodial parent to continue contributing to the child's support. The point is that many circumstances could occur that necessitate a change in the original order of support. However, most states limit the frequency with which such changes may be made and require that the circumstances that warrant such a change be substantial and long term.

Failure to Pay

If a party fails to adhere to an order of support, several things may take place. Usually, the first to occur is a legal action by the custodial parent against the parent obligated to pay support. The action is generally a request to hold the noncustodial parent in contempt of court for deliberately disobeying a court order to provide support for the minor child. In addition, many states have enacted or are considering procedures by which the licenses (drivers, business, professional, liquor, etc.) of parents failing to pay child support can be revoked. A parent who is unable to pay support on the date ordered should always attempt to modify rather than ignore the court order. In the eyes of the court, if the parent is able to pay the support but does not or is habitually late in paying, the court may enter an order of contempt.[36]

The results of a finding of contempt of court may be many and varied. The wages of the party may be garnished. The party may be fined. In extreme cases—usually where there has been ongoing contemptuous conduct—the party may be jailed for a period of time. Contrary to popular belief, a court will not deny visitation on the sole basis of failure to pay child support. Nor should a custodial parent ever expect a court to approve of deliberate denial of visitation rights based on a failure to pay support. The two issues are treated as totally separate. The reasoning of the court is that although failure to support may adversely affect a child, denial of visitation has no positive effect on the child. Rather, it only increases the adversity that the child must deal with. If a court does deny visitation, it is usually on the basis that the parent has abandoned all parental responsibility.

In the past, many actions to recover support were rendered virtually impossible because the noncustodial parent lived in another state. This made it very difficult for the court to exercise any control over the parent in terms of compelling payment of support. However, all states have now adopted the Uniform Reciprocal Enforcement of Support Act, a pact among all states to assist one another in enforcing support orders. An action may be filed in the state where the dependent resides. However, a public prosecutor in the state where the noncustodial parent resides may try the case there and enforce any orders of support or contempt. No longer can a noncustodial parent avoid support simply by moving beyond the jurisdictional and financial reach of the custodial parent.

Assignment 16.6

Consider the following situation and determine what would likely be considered when making a determination about support.

Teri and Tom were married 4 years. Teri has custody of the children. Tonya, age 3 at the time of the divorce is now 18 and attending college. Tim was age 1 at the time of the divorce and is now 16. The child support originally ordered was 45 percent of Tom's net pay. Teri agreed to this in lieu of a combination of child support and maintenance. Fourteen years later, the award was never modified. Tom now wishes to reduce the amount of child support because Tonya is a legal adult. Teri wishes to increase the amount of child support to correspond to Tom's current income. At the time of the divorce, Teri, who was not employed during the marriage, now earns an income comparable to that of Tom. However, she claims that Tonya still lives at home and thus the expenses have not decreased. She further claims that Tim is a gifted violinist and she needs additional income to afford the various lessons and supplies necessary to support his training. Tonya works part time when in school and full time during the summer, but does not contribute to the household expenses.

VISITATION

When one parent is awarded custody of the child, the noncustodial parent is usually given specific visitation rights. In some cases, the rights are characterized as reasonable visitation. However, this tends to leave the visitation to the discretion of the custodial parent in determining what is reasonable. Often the parents will dispute over this term, since what is reasonable visitation to one may be unreasonable visitation to the other. Ultimately, many parties return to court to have a judge make the determination. Therefore, the preferred choice is to set forth specific times and sometimes arrangements (when travel is involved) for visitation.

Every parent is deemed to possess a constitutional right to share the companionship of his or her child.[37] Unless the parent's conduct would endanger the child, this right cannot be abridged. However, if the parent's conduct might endanger the child, the court may limit or place conditions on the visitation. Common conditions include requiring visitation to be confined to a specific place or requiring visitation to be supervised by a third party to ensure the safety and well-being of the child. Extreme situations may result in a court's denial of visitation for a period of time to protect the welfare of the child.

Many states have statutory guidelines that judges attempt to follow to ensure each parent time and the opportunity to share special holidays and other occasions with the child. It must be understood that a visitation schedule sets forth the minimum rights of the noncustodial parent. If the two parents agree to additional or different times for visitation, this is entirely appropriate. If problems arise, however, the court will generally not enforce such agreements but will usually follow only the scheduled visitation plan.

Penalties may result in cases where a visitation schedule is set forth in a court order and the custodial parent interferes with visitation. Interference includes such things as refusing visitation, not having the children available for visitation when the noncustodial parent arrives, directly influencing the children to avoid visitation, or engaging in other conduct that interferes with the noncustodial parent's constitutional right to share companionship with the children.

When such conduct occurs, the noncustodial parent has the right to bring an action against the custodial parent for contempt of court. The allegation is generally that the custodial parent willfully ignored or interfered with a court order of visitation. A court is not likely to be tolerant of such conduct. Penalties range from monetary fines to jail sentences. In continuing and extreme cases, the court may view the conduct as adverse to the best interests of the child and may order a change of custody.

PROPERTY AND DEBT DIVISION

property settlement
Agreement as to the property rights and obligations of co-owners/co-debtors, such as parties to a marriage.

The states follow two schools of thought with respect to **property settlement** in the case of divorce. Some states are separate property states; others are community property states. The theory that a state follows will dictate the rights of the parties seeking a divorce. In cases where the parties were formally married, lived, or divorced in different states, the court will usually look to the law of the state where the parties resided when the property was acquired.

Separate Property

Separate property states take the position that all property individually owned prior to the marriage is individual property and not jointly owned marital property.[38] In addition, property acquired during the marriage through gift, inheritance, or personal earnings without contribution by the other spouse is individual property. In a divorce action, parties are awarded their individual property respectively, and the court determines how marital property should be distributed.

In a complete application of the separate property theory, a nonemployed spouse may be entitled to virtually nothing at the conclusion of the divorce. Because this effect is not fair, based on each spouse's contribution to the marital relationship, many courts have modified the rule to result in a more equitable application. While a state may still adhere to the theory of separate property, the court has a duty to equitably distribute property obtained during the marriage. Such property may have been purchased solely with the earnings of one spouse. If, however, the other spouse cared for the home and otherwise supported and enabled the first spouse to earn the money to purchase the property, such property is considered the result of a joint effort. In this way, the court can fairly consider certain property to be marital property and distribute it equally.

Community Property

Community property states take a different approach to the disposition of the property of spouses. In such states, property acquired during the marriage through personal earnings is presumed to be marital property.[39] Also included is property individually owned before the marriage that a party contributed to the marriage. When a spouse can establish that certain property was never comingled or otherwise shared with the other spouse as marital property would be, such property is not included as community property.

After the court has determined what, if any, separate property exists, it attempts to equitably divide the community property. The court considers the contribution of each partner to the marriage and then attempts to make a fairly equal division of the property. Circumstances must be rather compelling before a court is permitted to make a significantly unbalanced distribution of the parties' assets.

Pensions and Employee Benefit Programs

If a spouse was employed and received an interest in a pension or benefit plan during the marriage, under either type of property state, the other spouse may have a claim to a portion of the amount to be received under the plan. Determination of what is equitable is a perplexing problem for most courts. In many cases, the divorce occurs many years before the benefits are to be received. In addition, it is difficult to determine what an equitable share of an earned pension or benefit program would be, since the spouse has not earned the maximum pension or benefit possible. A final problem is that the parties remain somewhat bound to each other even through retirement. Many courts prefer to make a valuation of each party's interest and have one party buy out the other party's interest at the time of the dissolution. In this way, the parties' ties to each other can be completely and permanently severed, thus lessening the possibilities for future legal disputes.

It should be noted that to establish division of pension and retirement funds in a way that will be recognized by the Internal Revenue Service, a Qualified Domestic Relations Order (QDRO) must be issued (in addition to the other documents, such as property settlement agreement and Decree of Dissolution of Marriage) that details the rights and obligations of the parties with respect to these matters.

Marital Debts

The manner in which individual and marital debts are determined and distributed is substantially the same as with property. The same tests are applied to determine whether debts were incurred as part of the marital relationship or on behalf of the individual. Similarly, the courts attempt an equitable distribution of responsibility for such debts. However, debts incurred during a marriage have an additional aspect that property usually does not—the claims of third parties.

While parties may agree—or a court may determine—that certain debts are individual rather than marital, great legal expense can arise from claims of third parties that the debt is joint. For example, as long as the parties are joint owners of a credit card, any property purchased with the credit card is a joint debt. Even if a debt is taken on individually, if it is done during the marriage, there is a presumption that the debt benefited both parties.

Another facet of this problem arises when the divorce is final and responsibility for debts has been distributed equitably between the two spouses. If one spouse fails to honor the responsibility, the third party can claim and collect the debt from the other spouse. Although this may appear unfair at first, it should be remembered that the creditor was not even involved in the distribution of the debts. Therefore, the creditor is not bound by any court order as to who should bear responsibility. Since this situation arises fairly often, it is very important that all decrees contain a provision that entitles a spouse to collect reimbursement when he or she pays a debt that was to have been the responsibility of the other spouse.

CASE

DIANE E. MESSER, PLAINTIFF-APPELLEE, v. GEORGE MESSER, DEFENDANT-APPELLANT.

2002 WL 1889326
(Ohio App 2d Dist.)

BROGAN, J.

George contends that the trial court erred in invalidating the parties' antenuptial agreement. The trial court's decision was based on the nature of the parties' relationship and the lack of disclosure of assets. After reviewing the record, we find no error in the decision.

The Ohio supreme Court has held that antenuptial agreements are "valid and enforceable (1) if they have been entered into freely without fraud, duress, coercion, or overreaching; (2) if there was full disclosure, or full knowledge and understanding of the nature, value and extent of the prospective spouse's property; and (3) if the terms do not promote or encourage divorce or profiteering by divorce." *Gross v. Gross* (1984), 11 Ohio St.3d 99, 464 N.E.2d 500, paragraph two of the syllabus. Overreaching is "used in the sense of one party by artifice or cunning, or by significant disparity to understand the nature of the transaction, to outwit or cheat the other." *Id.* at 105, 464 N.E.2d 500.

The record in this case is replete with evidence of overreaching. According to the testimony, Diane and George first met when she was a child. George was a family friend. At some point, George's wife, Brenda, became paralyzed from the neck down as the result of a shooting incident (George testified that he was grabbing the gun at the time, and the shooting was accidental). Consequently, when Diane was about 14, she began coming over to help clean and take care of the couple's children. Diane and George then began having a sexual relationship when she was 15 and he was 36. Ultimately, George was given legal custody of Diane, and she moved into the house with George and Brenda. The sexual relationship continued, and resulted in Diane having an abortion when she was only 15. At the time, Diane did not want an abortion. However, George told her that if she did not get an abortion, he would tell people that she had been sleeping with every "Tom, Dick, and Harry."

Eventually, when Diane was 17 or 18, George divorced his wife. George and Diane continued to live together, and finally married in May, 1987, when Diane was 23. In the meantime, Diane had quit her high school education after eleventh grade.

George did not want to get married, as he had just gone through a nasty divorce and had lost everything. On the other hand, Diane wanted very badly to get married. About two months before the marriage, Diane signed an antenuptial agreement waiving: 1) all rights to which she might be entitled as a spouse; 2) all rights in any existing real property or any property acquired during marriage; 3) the right to any personal assets of George, including retirement funds; 4) the right to alimony; and 5) the right to custody of any children born of the marriage. George agreed to waive the right to child support. This agreement was prepared by George's attorney, and Diane was unrepresented by counsel. The agreement was preceded by two other handwritten agreements, in which Diane also promised to relinquish all rights to every article of real or personal property, except her personal belongings, and all rights to custody of any children, if George would marry her.

Although the parties dispute whether Diane read the agreement that was prepared by an attorney, and also dispute where the agreement was signed, those disputes are irrelevant. The parties also disagree about whether Diane and George both believed George was still her legal guardian at the time she signed the agreement. There is some evidence to that effect in the record, including George's deposition testimony. However, George denied this at trial. Nonetheless, in view of the history of the relationship—which was not disputed in any significant detail—there was clear evidence of overreaching on George's part.

In *Gross,* the Ohio Supreme Court stressed that on judicial review of an antenuptial agreement, the agreement "must meet the general tests of fairness as referred to previously, and must be construed within the context that by virtue of their anticipated marital status, the parties are in a fiduciary relationship to one another. The parties must act in good faith, with a high degree of fairness and disclosure of all circumstances which materially bear on the antenuptial agreement." *Id.* at 108, 464 N.E.2d 500. Obviously, a high degree of fairness did not exist here.

Furthermore, the record also supports the trial court's finding that assets were not disclosed. In this regard, *Gross,* indicates that disclosure is "satisfied either by the exhibiting of the attachment to the antenuptial agreement of a listing of the assets of the parties to the agreement, or alternatively a showing that there had been a full disclosure by other names." *Id.* at. 105. The agreement in the present case did not refer to any assets, other than a house George owned at the time, nor was any list attached to the agreement. Diane testified that she was not aware of George's other assets, including retirement funds, bank accounts, or vehicles. Similarly, George testified that at the time of the agreement, he owned a house trailer, a whole life policy of insurance through GM, a GM pension, and a vehicle. Admittedly, none of these items was disclosed in the agreement. Thus, the evidence of the record supports the trial court's finding that assets were not disclosed.

Notably, the Ohio Supreme Court has said that: "[w]hen an antenuptial agreement provides disproportionately less than the party challenging it would have received under an equitable distribution, the burden is on the one claiming the validity of the contract to show that the other party entered into it with the benefit of full knowledge or disclosure of the assets of the proponent." *Fletcher v. Fletcher,* 68 Ohio St.3d 464, 467, 628 N.E.2d 1343, 1994-Ohio-434. George clearly did not meet this burden.

In light of the preceding discussion, the second assignment of error is without merit and is overruled.

In the final assignment of error, George contends that the trial court's order requiring him to immediately pay Diane her share in the parties' real property ignores the best interests of their child. At the time of the divorce hearing, the parties had one child, Kevin, who was born on December 12, 1988. The Messers moved to their current residence (a house and about ten and a half acres) when Kevin was in kindergarten. At the hearing, George expressed a desire to keep the house and pass it on to Kevin. He also said he did not know if he would be able to obtain a loan. However, George did testify that he had checked with a bank about a loan and had been told he could borrow money. Nonetheless, George maintained that he did not think he could afford the payments. On the other hand, Diane said she needed her share of the equity, so that she could pay debts, including $3,500 in attorney fees for the divorce, a vehicle, and perhaps some schooling.

The house and land were valued at $80,000, and had an existing mortgage of about $21,389 at

CASE

the time of the hearing. After crediting George with $17,000 non-marital interest, the magistrate awarded Diane $19,130 as her share of the equity. George was ordered to try to refinance the property for purposes of paying Diane her share. If refinancing could not be obtained within sixty days, the house was to be sold.

To support his argument, George cites R.C. 3105.171(F), which states that:

"[i]n making a division of marital property and in determining whether to make and the amount of any distributive award under this section, the court shall consider all of the following factors: (1) The duration of the marriage; (2) The assets and liabilities of the spouses; (3) The desirability of awarding the family home, or the right to reside in the family home for reasonable periods of time, to the spouse with custody of the children of the marriage; (4) The liquidity of the property to be distributed; (5) The economic desirability of retaining intact an asset or an interest in an asset; (6) The tax consequences of the property division upon the respective awards to be made to each spouse; (7) The costs of sale, if it is necessary that an asset be sold to effectuate an equitable distribution of property; (8) Any division or disbursement of property made in a separation agreement that was voluntarily entered into by the spouses; (9) Any other factor that the court expressly finds to be relevant and equitable."

The factor George relies on most particularly is R.C. 3105.171 (F)(3), which deals with the desirability of awarding the marital home, or a reasonable habitation period in the home, to the party with custody of minor children. Additionally, George relies on R.C. 3105.171(J), which gives courts equitable powers to grant a spouse to use the marital dwelling for a reasonable period of time.

In divorce cases, trial courts have broad discretion to decide what property division may be equitable. *Cherry v. Cherry* (1981), 66 Ohio St.2d 348, 421 N.E. 2d 1293, paragraph two of the syllabus. We review such decisions for abuse of discretion, which means "more than an error of law or judgment; it implies that the court's attitude is unreasonable, arbitrary, or unconscionable."

Blakemore v. Blakemore (1983), 5 Ohio St.3d 217, 219, 450 N.E. 2d 1140. We are also not free to substitute our judgment for that of trial court. Instead, we are "'guided by a presumption that the findings of the trial court are correct.'" *Bauser,* 118 Ohio App. 3d 831, 836, 694 N.E. 2d 136.

In this regard, George also cites numerous out-of-state cases as evidence that courts do not abuse their discretion by delaying the sale of a home until a minor child reaches the age of majority. However, the fact that a court may not abuse its discretion by delaying sale does not mean that a court, therefore, does abuse its discretion when it divides property and orders a sale. We have said on numerous occasions that a reduced standard of living for all parties is often a regrettable byproduct of divorce. See, e.g. *Easterling v. Easterling* (April 13, 2001), Montgomery App. No. 18523, 2001 WL 369734, * 3. While this is unfortunate, the situation is not helped when parties spend significant sums of money that they do not have, in order to contest the value of limited assets. For example, the record in this case contains appraisal reports and testimony from two real property appraisers, reports from two other appraisers as to personal property, and reports of pension evaluators. However, the total value of both real and personal assets, exclusive of the pension, is not very high. Further, as we mentioned earlier, Diane has incurred at least $3,500 in attorney fees before this appeal, and one would assume that George's fees are in that range as well.

Unfortunately, the parties' only disposable assets are the house and the land. Under the circumstances of this case, we cannot find that the magistrate and trial court abused their discretion by requiring prompt payment of Diane's share of the house equity. We note that the order did not require George to leave the house; it simply said that if the house could not be refinanced, it would have to be sold. This is a scenario that occurs frequently in divorce cases. If the only source of assets is the marital home, courts do not act arbitrarily or unreasonably when they require the home to be sold. A different rule might apply in unusual circumstances, but we see no evidence of that here. Compare *Bauser,* 118 Ohio App.3d at

836, 694 N.E.2d 136 (indicating that court should not leave marital asset undivided absent evidence of particularized need to retain joint ownership). In *Bauser,* we also found that a reasonable term for a spouse to remain in the marital premises under R.C.3105.171(J), is one that is "short-term and temporary, and granted upon a showing of particularized need." *Id.* at 836, 694 N.E.2d 136. The reasons advanced by George in this case are no different than what any custodial parent might say about a desire to remain in the marital home. Although we are not unsympathetic, we cannot say that the court abused its discretion in requiring Diane to be paid for her share of the equity. Moreover, as we said, the record does not even indicate that George will have to leave the premises. To the contrary, George testified that the bank said he could borrow money. It was George's own opinion (not established by the evidence) that he did not think he could make the payments.

Based on the preceding discussion, we find no abuse of discretion in the trial court's order concerning payment of Diane's equity in the marital premises. Accordingly, the third assignment of error is without merit and its overruled.

Since all assignments of error have been overruled, the judgment of the trial court is

Affirmed.

Case Review Question
Messer v. Messer, 2002 WL 1889326 (Ohio App. 2d Dist. 2002).
What could have been done at the time of the antenuptial agreement that would have rendered it valid despite the unequal terms?

MAINTENANCE (ALIMONY OR SPOUSAL SUPPORT)

Awards of maintenance or spousal support (formerly called alimony) are becoming an increasingly rare occurrence. The reasons are numerous. Previously, in a pure application of separate property, the wife often did not receive a significant share of marital assets. Today, all states (whether they are community property or separate states) attempt to provide a more equitable distribution. In addition, women now activity participate in the workforce and have greater opportunities than ever before to become self-sufficient.

At present, a court might award maintenance to a spouse who is unable to secure employment sufficient to meet reasonable necessary expenses or to a child for whom care by one other than the parent during working hours would not be appropriate.[40] An example of the former is a spouse who has not worked for many years and, for all practical purposes, would not be able to reenter the workforce at a level that would provide independent financial support. An example of the latter is a child who suffers from physical or emotional conditions that necessitate skilled care at a cost greater than what the parent could earn if he or she were required to work full time outside the home.

As these examples suggest, the trend of the courts is to award maintenance only in compelling circumstances. Although many situations are not as clearly defined as those described, often a spouse requires some form of assistance before he or she can be restored to an independent earning capacity. For example, a spouse may have been away from the workforce but would be capable of reentering with some retraining, or the parties may have several young children who will be entering school in the reasonably near future. In such situations, short-term maintenance would be appropriate. The court may award maintenance for a specified period of time to supplement the income of the other spouse.

Today, the goal of the court is to give a spouse sufficient time and resources to prepare for financial independence. Thus, the spouse required to pay maintenance is not burdened with lifetime support of a former spouse, and the spouse receiving maintenance is not suddenly thrust into the world unequipped to provide for such basic expenses as food and shelter. Maintenance is awarded only for a period of time that is deemed reasonably sufficient to enable the receiving spouse to achieve independence.

The amount and duration of maintenance are generally left to the discretion of the court, which will consider such factors as the earning power and the reasonable needs of each party. Also considered is the amount of time necessary to prepare the spouse receiving maintenance to successfully return to the workforce.[41] If the age and educational level of this spouse effectively prevent a return to the workforce, permanent maintenance may be considered. The same is true of a situation in which the parties have an incapacitated child.

If either party dies, maintenance automatically terminates. If the intent is that the receiving party should continue to be entitled in the event of death of the payor, it should be so stipulated in the court order approving maintenance.

If the financial status of either party changes significantly during the period of maintenance payments, a modification may be requested. A formal petition must be filed with the court setting forth the reasons that would justify adjustment of the maintenance order. It is then within the discretion of the court to determine whether the modification is warranted. Significant changes in circumstances include a substantial decrease in the earning power of the payor spouse or a substantial increase in the earning power of the recipient spouse. Remarriage or cohabitation of the recipient spouse also may be considered sufficient grounds to terminate maintenance.

Failure to pay maintenance is remedied by a request to hold the wrongful party in contempt of court. The procedure and penalties are basically the same. The court will hear the petition, and penalties will ensue if grounds exist to find that a party has willfully ignored the order of maintenance.

Assignment 16.7

Examine the following situations and indicate whether a court would be likely to grant maintenance and, if so, whether maintenance would be permanent or temporary. Give reasons to support your answer.

SITUATION 1: Jamie and John have been married for 18 years. Jamie is now 38. At the time of the marriage she was a professional model who gave up her career to travel with and assist John, who was a professional golfer. Jamie did not finish high school and has few if any prospects for resuming her modeling career at this age. John has been moderately successful and has an income for the past several years in excess of $500,000 annually. Jamie has requested permanent maintenance.

SITUATION 2: Beverly is 62 and a college professor. Her husband John is 53 and previously had a business buying real estate, rehabing the property, and then selling it. His income was always intermittent and considered supplemental by the parties during the 30-year marriage and used for things such as vacations. The primary income of the parties has always been that of Beverly. At age 52, John suffered a serious heart attack and while he is able to do some things, he cannot return to his former occupation. The parties want to divorce and John has requested maintenance. Beverly wants to retire but if she does so before age 67, her income would be insufficient to support two households.

NONMARITAL RELATIONSHIPS

As previously indicated, most states do not recognize the creation of a common law marriage. Nevertheless, many couples cohabit without the formal requisites of marriage. Although they share in the acquisition of property and debts, when they decide to terminate their relationship, they do not have the specific legal rights of persons who are dissolving a legal marriage.

Although previous courts had issued decisions addressing various aspects of this particular situation, the landmark opinion was issued in *Marvin v. Marvin,*[42] in which the court fully addressed the issues associated with the dissolution of nonmarital cohabitation. Courts in several other states have cited the decision with approval and have used it as persuasive authority to adopt the position taken by the court in the *Marvin* decision.[43]

CASE

MARVIN v. MARVIN

18 Cal. 3d 660, 134 Cal.Rptr. 815, 557 P.2d 106 (1976).

En banc

1. The factual setting of this appeal.

. . . Plaintiff avers that in October of 1964 she and defendant "entered into an oral agreement" that while "that parties lived together they would combine their efforts and earnings and would share equally any and all property accumulated as a result of their efforts whether individual or combined." Furthermore, they agreed to "hold themselves out to the general public as husband and wife" and that "plaintiff would further render her services as a companion, homemaker, housekeeper and cook to . . . defendant."

CASE

Shortly thereafter, plaintiff agreed to "give up her lucrative career as an entertainer [and] singer in order to "devote her full time to defendant . . . as a companion, homemaker, housekeeper and cook"; in return defendant agreed to "provide for all of plaintiff's financial support and needs for the rest of her life."

Plaintiff alleges that she lived with defendant from October of 1964 through May of 1970 and fulfilled her obligations under the agreement. During this period the parties as a result of their efforts and earnings acquired in defendant's name substantial real and personal property, including motion picture rights worth over $1 million. In May of 1970, however, defendant compelled plaintiff to leave his household. He continued to support plaintiff until November of 1971, but thereafter refused to provide further support.

On the basis of these allegations plaintiff asserts two causes of action. The first, for declaratory relief, asks the court to determine her contract and property rights; the second seeks to impose a constructive trust upon one half of the property acquired during the course of the relationship.

Defendant demurred unsuccessfully, and then answered the complaint. Following extensive discovery and pretrial proceedings, the case came to trial. Defendant renewed his attack on the complaint by a motion to dismiss . . . .

After hearing argument the court granted defendant's motion and entered judgment for the defendant. Plaintiff moved to set aside the judgment and asked leave to amend her complaint to allege that she and defendant reaffirmed their agreement after defendant's divorce was final. The trial court denied plaintiff's motion, and she appealed from the judgment.

2. Plaintiff's complaint states a cause of action for breach of an express contract.

In *Trutalli v. Meraviglia* (1932) 215 Cal. 698, 12 P.2d. 430, we established the principle that nonmarital partners may lawfully contract concerning the ownership of property acquired during the relationship. We reaffirmed this principle in *Vallera v. Vallera* (1943) 21 Cal.2d 681, 685, 134 P.2d 761, 763, stating that "If a man and woman [who are not married] live together as husband and wife under an agreement to pool their earnings and share equally in their joint accumulations, equity will protect the interests of each in such property."

In the case before us plaintiff, basing here cause of action in contract upon these precedents, maintains that the trial court erred in denying her a trial on the merits of her contention . . . .

Numerous . . . cases have upheld enforcement of agreements between nonmarital partners in factual settings essentially indistinguishable from the present case. *In re Marriage of Foster* (1947) 42 Cal.App.3d 577, 117 Cal.Rptr. 49; . . . *Ferguson v. Schuenemann* (1959) 167 Cal.App.2d 413, 334 P.2d. 668; . . . *Ferraro v. Ferraro* (1956) 146 Cal.App.2d 849, 304 P.2d 168.

We conclude that the judicial barriers that may stand in the way of a policy based upon the fulfillment of the reasonable expectations of the parties to a nonmarital relationship should be removed. As we have explained, the courts now hold that express agreements will be enforced unless they rest on an unlawful meretricious consideration. We add that in the absence of an express agreement, the courts may look to a variety of other remedies in order to protect the parties' lawful expectations.

We do not seek to resurrect the doctrine of common law marriage, which was abolished in California by statute in 1895. (See *Norman v. Thomson* (1898) 121 Cal. 620, 628, 54 P. 143; Estate of Abate (1958) 166 Cal.App.2d 282, 292, 333 P.2d 200.) Thus we do not hold that plaintiff and defendant were 'married,' nor do we extend to plaintiff the rights which the Family Law Act grants valid or putative spouses; we hold only that she has the same rights to enforce contracts and to assert her equitable interest in property acquired through her effort as does any other unmarried person.

The courts may inquire into the conduct of the parties to determine whether that conduct demonstrates an implied contract, implied agreement of partnership or joint venture (see *Estate of Thornton* (1972) 81 Wash.2d 72, 499 P.2d 864), or some other tacit understanding between the parties . . . .Finally, a nonmarital partner may recover in quantum meruit for the reasonable value of household services rendered less the reasonable value of support received if he can show that he rendered services with the expectation of monetary reward. (See *Hill v. Estate of Westbrook,* supra, 39 Cal.2d 458, 462, 247 P.2d 19.)

Our opinion does not preclude the evolution of additional equitable remedies to protect the expectations of the parties to a nonmarital relationship in cases in which existing remedies prove inadequate; the suitability of such remedies may be determined in later cases in light of the factual setting in which they arise.

Since we have determined that plaintiff's complaint states a cause of action for breach of an express contract, and, as we have explained, can be amended to state a cause of action independent of allegations of express contract, we must conclude that the trial court erred in granting defendant a judgment on the pleadings.

Case Review Question
What if the reason the relationship broke up had been infertility?

Some courts have rejected the *Marvin* decision on the basis that it too closely resembles recognition of common law marriage, and they are not willing to adopt a position that so closely parallels it. In a time when cohabitation is a frequent occurrence, however, methods may have to be developed to determine the legal rights of the parties involved.

 CASE

JERRY HERRING, v. YVONNE DANIELS ET AL.

2002 WL 1376167(Conn.App.)

SHEA, J.

The plaintiff, Jerry Herring, appeals from the judgment of the trial court in favor of the defendant, Yvonne Daniels, in a partition action in which the plaintiff claims an equitable interest in real property owned by the defendant.

The following facts were adduced in a trial to the court. The defendant is the record titleholder of real property located at 81 Canterbury Street in Hartford. The defendant first met the plaintiff in 1981, and they had an affair that lasted for approximately six months. During that time, the plaintiff asked the defendant to cosign a $3000 loan for him, which she did. The parties resumed their relationship in 1985. In early 1987, the plaintiff moved into the house at 81 Canterbury Street and resided there on a semiregular basis until August, 1998, when the defendant obtained a restraining order against the plaintiff . . . the plaintiff did not pay any rent.

During the period in which the plaintiff was living at 81 Canterbury Street, he obtained two loans from his credit union, Hartford Firefighters Federal Credit Union, cosigned by the defendant and secured by mortgages on the defendant's real estate. The first loan was in the amount of $60,000. At the time that loan was obtained, the

CASE

defendant's property was subject to three encumbrances, a first mortgage to Northeast Savings Bank for $23,327, a second mortgage held by the mortgage brokerage Conn and Conn Company for $11,610, and a lien for $2300 in favor of the state of Connecticut. As a condition to disbursing the loan proceeds, the second mortgage to Conn and Conn Company and the state tax lien had to be paid from the gross proceeds of the loan. The plaintiff received all of the net proceeds of the loan. Beginning in February, 1987, the monthly payments on that loan were made by automatic payroll deduction from the plaintiff's paycheck.

In May 1993, the parties obtained a second loan with the Hartford Firefighters Federal Credit Union, this time in the amount of $100,000. The proceeds of that loan were used to pay off the first mortgage to Northeast Savings, an outstanding balance to Associated Financial Services for $2388.02 and the balance of the previous credit union loan. The net balance after paying those debts was approximately $60,000. Because the plaintiff was concerned that if the loan proceeds were deposited in an account under his name they would be seized to pay delinquent taxes, the defendant agreed to open a separate account in her name in which to deposit the funds. Accordingly, those proceeds were deposited in an account in the name of the defendant at Bank of Boston. Of those proceeds, the plaintiff received approximately $35,000 over the course of two months. The defendant received a $5000 cash disbursement at the time the check was deposited in the account. Although the record is unclear as to what became of the remaining $20,000, those funds apparently were dissipated as a result of various trips and gambling excursions made at the plaintiff's initiative. The payments on that loan were deducted from the plaintiff's monthly pension payments beginning on June 20, 1993. The outstanding balance on the loan at the time of the plaintiff's last regular payment, in August 1998, was $56,772.63.

In January 1999, in an attempt at reconciliation, the plaintiff moved back into the defendant's home. At that time, the plaintiff paid an additional $3500 dollars on the loan, the automatic pension deductions having been previously discontinued. Despite tentative discussions regarding marriage, the reconciliation between the parties proved unsuccessful, and in December 1999, the plaintiff was again forced to vacate the defendant's house pursuant to a restraining order.

On December 22, 1999, the plaintiff filed an amended complaint in three counts alleging an equitable interest in the property on the basis of his having resided there and assumed the mortgage payments, a contractual right based on express, verbal and implied understandings that the ownership of various assets was to be shared, and a claim for restitution based on quantum meruit.

The court found that there was insufficient evidence to support any of the claims asserted by the plaintiff and accordingly rendered judgment for the defendant. This appeal followed. Additional facts will be set forth as necessary.

The plaintiff's first claim on appeal is that the court improperly failed to find that the parties held themselves out to the public as being married, and regarded the subject premises as marital property and treated it as such. The plaintiff argues that the court was required to make such a finding as a matter of law on the basis of the court's subordinate finding that the parties were "cohabiting, unmarried lovers."

In support of his first argument, the plaintiff cites the definition, adopted by our Supreme Court in *Wolk v. Wolk,* 191 Conn. 328, 332, 464 A.2d 780 (1983), that "[c]ohabitation is a dwelling together of man and woman in the same place in the manner of husband and wife." The plaintiff apparently interprets the phrase "in the manner of husband and wife" to suggest that cohabitation is for all intents and purposes synonymous with marriage, and that cohabitation raises all of the same presumptions regarding the treatment of assets as does marriage. Such an interpretation, however, would essentially transform cohabitation into common-law marriage, contrary to the refusal of this state to recognize such relationships. "[C]ohabitation alone does not create any contractual relationship or, unlike marriage, impose other legal duties upon the parties." *Boland v. Catalano,* 202 Conn. 333, 339, 521 A.2d 142 (1987).

Rather, where the parties have established an unmarried, cohabiting relationship, it is the specific conduct of the parties within that relationship that determines their respective rights and obligations, including the treatment of their individual property. Any such finding must be determined by reference to the unique circumstances and arrangements between the parties present in each case. Those matters are questions of fact that are within the singular province of the trial court, and can only be determined by evaluating the credibility of the witnesses and weighing conflicting evidence. Accordingly, we conclude that the court was not bound as a matter of law to find that that the parties treated the subject property as a "marital asset" simply on the basis of having found that they were "unmarried, cohabiting lovers."

II

The plaintiff next claims that the court improperly found that the two mortgage loans were for the sole benefit of the plaintiff. We conclude that the evidence presented was sufficient to permit the court, as the trier of fact, reasonably to find that the loans benefited the plaintiff rather than the defendant.

It is undisputed that certain encumbrances on the defendant's property were paid out of the gross proceeds of the two loans obtained by the plaintiff in 1987 and 1993. The plaintiff argues that discharging those encumbrances provided the defendant with a benefit and, accordingly, that the court's conclusion that the loans were for the sole benefit of the plaintiff is not supported by the evidence and is clearly erroneous.

At the time that the parties renewed their relationship in 1987, but prior to obtaining the first loan, the total outstanding debt on the defendant's property was $37,237. The value

of the defendant's property at that time was $165,000. At the conclusion of the parties' dealings with each other, the debt on the defendant's property had grown to $58,000 as a result of the various loans. Thus, after fourteen years, rather than having been reduced in any significant degree, the encumbrances on the defendant's property actually increased by 64 percent. The defendant is liable on that debt as the cosigner of the loans. Such a circumstance can hardly be characterized as having conferred an advantage or benefit on the defendant.

Moreover, the court found that the monthly payments made by the plaintiff were in consideration of the defendant's assistance to him. The evidence in the record supports that finding. From the proceeds of the first loan, $13,610 of the prior encumbrances were paid out of the gross proceeds. The payments on that loan were made from February 1987, until May 1993, when the parties refinanced. When averaged over the payment period, the plaintiff's payment of the prior encumbrances amount to approximately $181 per month for the use and occupancy of the subject premises. Similarly, the payment of the $25,715 in encumbrances on the property out of the gross proceeds of the second loan, when averaged over the five years that the plaintiff continued to make payments, amounts to approximately $428 per month. In light of the plaintiff's admission that he did not pay rent while he lived in the subject premises, the court was justified in finding that this sum was paid by the plaintiff in consideration of the defendant's assistance to him. Certainly, that amount is not so large as to require the inference that it represented anything more than a reasonable rent substitute. Accordingly, we cannot say that the court's finding in that regard was clearly erroneous.

The plaintiff also claims that the court improperly treated the fact that title to the property had not, in fact, been modified to reflect the parties' joint ownership as dispositive of the issue of the parties' intent to treat the property as a shared asset. The plaintiff infers that the court accorded that particular fact undue significance because" [the court] mentioned this underlying fact twice in its [d]ecision."

We agree with the plaintiff that a failure to transfer title is not dispositive in determining the rights and interests of the parties with respect to the subject property. There is, however, no evidence in the record to suggest that the court regarded the parties' failure formally to transfer title to the subject property as dispositive. The court's findings of fact cover two and one-half pages in the memorandum of decision and include numerous facts in addition to the parties' failure to transfer title to the property. For example, the court stated in its findings that there was no credible evidence of any agreement between the parties to share the property, there was no credible evidence that the parties held themselves out to the public as husband and wife, and there was no credible evidence that the plaintiff performed maintenance and repairs on the house or that the parties had made any joint purchases of property. The plethora of operative facts cited by the court supports its conclusion regarding the intent of the parties and belies the plaintiff's suggestion that the court relied solely on any one fact as dispositive. We conclude, therefore, that the court's finding was not clearly erroneous.

The plaintiff claims that the court improperly failed to consider whether the evidence presented at trial supported a finding of an implied agreement between the parties to share equally the ownership of the subject property. The plaintiff argues that the court failed to consider whether the evidence presented showed conduct sufficient to establish an implied agreement or some other tacit understanding between the parties to share the subject property. The plaintiff argues that the court considered only whether an express contract had been proven. In support of his contention, the plaintiff cites the failure of the court to mention the case law discussed by the plaintiff and the court's failure to find that the facts in those cases proved the existence of an implied contract as a matter of law.

We agree that "[i]n the absence of an express contract, the courts should inquire into the conduct of the parties to determine whether that conduct demonstrates an implied contract, agreement of partnership or joint venture, or some other tacit understanding between the parties." (Internal quotation marks omitted.) Id., at 340-41, 521 A.2d 142. We do not agree, however, that the court failed to do so in the present case.

"An implied contract depends upon the existence of an actual agreement between the parties . . . . Whether the parties have entered into such an agreement is a question of fact." *Christensen v. Bic Corp.*, 18 Conn.App. 451, 454, 558 A.2d 273 (1989).

Although the court's memorandum of decision does not explicitly state that the proven facts failed to establish an implied agreement, the court's catalog of findings clearly addresses the absence of those circumstances that would otherwise establish the existence of an implied agreement to share the subject property. The court found that the monthly payments were made by the plaintiff in consideration of the defendant's assistance to him and, thus, were not based on an agreement, implied or otherwise, to share the property. The court also rejected the plaintiff's testimony that he performed substantial work on the property, finding that there was no credible evidence that he took care of the maintenance and repairs on the house. Finally, the court found that the plaintiff "offered no credible evidence to show that he and the defendant ever made any joint purchases of property; that he made any repairs or renovations that significantly improved the value of the defendant's property; that they shared joint bank accounts, pooled their earnings or income, filed joint tax returns or ever had signatory powers to each other's charge, bank or other accounts." Each of those findings goes directly to circumstances that would, if supported by the evidence, tend to show an implicit agreement to share assets. We conclude, therefore, that the court properly addressed the plaintiff's cause of action alleging an interest in the subject property on the basis of an implied agreement between the parties and that the court's failure to find such an agreement was not clearly erroneous.

The plaintiff also claims that the court improperly failed to find that he was entitled, under the doctrines of quantum meruit and unjust enrichment, to a share of the cash equity that had been removed from the subject property by the defendant in April and August 1999. We disagree.

The plaintiff's claim involves three mortgage loans obtained by the defendant, the first on April 23, 1999, and the second and third on August 13,1999. The first loan was for $30,000, out of which the defendant realized a net gain of $24,719. The gross amount of the second mortgage refinance loan was $82,500, and the third involved a gross balance of $16,500. The proceeds of the second loan were used to pay off the balance remaining on the $100,000 loan from the plaintiff's credit union, which was $50,375 at that time, as well as the outstanding balance on the loan of April 23, 1999. The net proceeds realized on that loan were $11,842.

For the defendant to obtain those 1999 mortgage loans, it was necessary on both occasions to obtain a release of a lis pendens that the plaintiff had placed on the subject property. The plaintiff's only role in securing those loans consisted of releasing the lis pendens. In returns for the plaintiff's release of the lien, the defendant paid him $2500.

The plaintiff argues that he is entitled to a share of the cash equity realized by those 1999 mortgage loans because he was responsible for the buildup of the equity in the property by paying down the balances of the previously obtained mortgage loans from his credit union. He also argues that he is entitled to a share of the cash equity because he was directly responsible for that equity being made available to the defendant by releasing the lis pendens on the property. We are unpersuaded.

"Plaintiffs seeking recovery for unjust enrichment must prove (1) that the defendants were benefited, (2) that the defendants unjustly did not pay the plaintiffs for the benefits, and (3) that the failure of payment was to the plaintiffs' detriment." . . . *McNeil v Riccio*, 45 Conn.App. at 475, (1997).

Accordingly, in the present case, the plaintiff was required to prove in the trial court that the defendant had received a benefit at his expense under circumstances that would otherwise make it unjust for her to retain the benefit. In part II, we concluded that the court's findings that (1) the loans from the plaintiff's credit union were obtained for the sole benefit of the plaintiff and (2) that the payment of the preexisting debts on the property from the proceeds of those loans were in consideration of the defendant's assistance to the plaintiff were not clearly erroneous. Thus, to the extent that the plaintiff made payments on those credit union loans, he did no more than fulfill his legal obligation as the beneficiary of those loans. Additionally, by the plaintiff's own admission, the defendant paid him $2500 in exchange for the release of the lis pendens. In light of those admissions and findings by the court, we cannot conclude that the court abused its discretion in failing to find that the defendant was unjustly enriched at the plaintiff's expense.

VI

The plaintiff claims finally that the court improperly considered special defenses that had been stricken. Because we already have determined that the court properly concluded that the plaintiff failed to meet his burden of proof to establish either an equitable interest in the subject property or to show a contractual right on the basis of an express or implied agreement between the parties, it is unnecessary for us to review his claim. The failure of the plaintiff to prove his case provides a ground for affirming the court's judgement independent of any alleged reliance by the court on the stricken special defenses.

The judgement is affirmed.

Case Review Question

Herring v. Daniels, 2002 WL 1376167 (Conn.App. 2002).

Would the result likely change if the plaintiff could establish the defendant had not contributed to the payment to the loans? Why or why not?

REPRODUCTIVE LAW

Paternity

An entirely new area of law that has emerged in the American legal system during the latter part of the twentieth century is the result of tremendous scientific advancements and a relaxation of cultural standards. Initially, this area developed as the shame historically associated with children born out of wedlock was overshadowed by the increasing view of society that men take responsibility for children they fathered. This was also advanced by the development of scientific means of testing for paternity. The latter developed so significantly in recent years through DNA testing that it is possible to trace ancestral lines back hundreds of years as publicized in the case of the connection between descendants of Sally Hemmings and Colonial President Thomas Jefferson. Today, paternity testing can virtually eliminate all but the true father of a child and, consequently, parental responsibilities can be placed on both mother and father.

Historically, there was no presumptive father for a child born out of wedlock. If a woman had the courage to initiate an action for paternity despite strong social pressures not to do so, the case often became focused on an issue of the credibility of the mother and alleged father. The cases were frequently notarized in newspapers as the two parties battled a finding that they were telling the truth. Even if an individual is named on the birth certificate as the father, there is no legal presumption of this fact unless the man is married to the mother at the time of the birth or openly acknowledges his paternity of the child. Any other circumstance ultimately requires a court finding of paternity.

A paternity action is initiated in the same essential manner as any other civil suit. However, many states have statutes that require specific methods of notice to the alleged father of the action. Although it is rare that a court has authority to order invasive physical procedures such as blood tests, this is one instance where, unless a man admits to paternity or accepts a finding of paternity by default, a court may order blood tests to definitively determine whether the alleged father is the biological parent of the child in question. These actions are most often filed when the mother or guardian of the child is seeking financial assistance in the form of child support. An action may also be filed by the state if the child or its mother is receiving government financial assistance such as welfare benefits. In turn, the state seeks reimbursement from the father. However, it is no longer uncommon for the action to be filed by a man who wants to resolve whether he is the father of a child, as fathers have assumed an increasingly active role in the lives of their children in recent years. By establishing parenthood, the father not only accepts the responsibilities but also gains the rights associated with parenthood, such as a right of companionship of the child and the right to oppose adoption of the child by another man or by parents who wish to adopt the child from the natural mother. In accordance with this, many states now even have registries created by statute which allow a man who believes himself to be a father to register his name and the pertinent information about the child and mother. This in turn prevents the mother from placing the child for adoption without consent until paternity is established.

◆ **APPLICATION 16.5**

Victor believes he is the natural father of a child who Oma is about to give birth. Oma has indicated to friends that she has already completed the paperwork and intends to place the baby for adoption immediately after birth. She further indicates that the identity of the father is unknown. Victor signs with a statutory registry and identifies himself as the father of Oma's unborn child. When the child is born, Oma places the child for adoption, but, in processing the paperwork, it is discovered that Victor has made a claim of paternity and the adoption is suspended while his paternity is confirmed or ruled out.

Point for Discussion
◆ Why wouldn't an objection to the adoption proceeding by Victor at the time it is initiated meet the same objective and work just as well?

Adoption

Another area of law that has seen immense growth in terms of statutory legal standards is adoption. There was a time when a child could essentially be handed over to another person or to a child care facility such as an orphanage with little or no formality. However, the exposure of baby-selling practices and other activities that did not place the best interest of the child first and ahead of any personal interests led to nationwide legislation by the states to carefully monitor the placement and adoption process. It is common now to require counseling and waiting periods for the natural parent or parents who seek to place their child for adoption. Adoptive parents are often required to go through a series of evaluations and even trial periods with the child before the adoption will be finalized regardless of whether the parties unanimously consent to the adoption.

Historically, the vast majority of adoptions were private in that the adoptive and natural parents did not know one another's identity. A trend in the latter part of the twentieth century began toward open adoptions. In this situation, the parents know of one another, they sometimes communicate, and in some cases the adoptive parents allow the natural parents to visit with the adopted child and develop some sort of relationship. Obviously, the open adoption is not something that is acceptable to all parties and the majority of adoptions are still private.

Historically, when an adoption occurred, all records with respect to the child prior to the adoption were sealed. The rationale was that a child adopted should be raised in the belief that the adoptive parents were the family, and when one placed a child for adoption he or she relinquished all rights to further contact with the child. Many times as well, because of emotional and societal pressures, the natural parent did not want to be identified. Even if an adoptive child or natural parent wanted this access, state statute prohibited such from occurring. However, with the other changes in domestic relations law in the latter twentieth century, this too has seen dramatic revision.

For a variety of reasons, adopted children and natural parents began seeking records with respect to the other party in great numbers in the 1990s. As they encountered great difficulty because of statutory prohibitions, movements began to change the laws. These movements were often supported by the medical profession as science produced more evidence of the importance of knowing one's genetic background and parental medical histories. As a result, in adoptions today, much more medical information is required at the time of an adoption. Secondly, natural parents may indicate whether they are willing to have their identities released to the adoptive child. Adoptive parents have the option of revealing their own identity and that of the adopted child to the natural parents. Once the adopted child has reached the age of majority, this decision becomes his or her own. Thus, while statutes still attempt to protect privacy and while many individuals who were party to adoptions before statutory changes still meet with the frustration of not being able to locate their natural relatives, the laws today are much more flexible in meeting the needs and desires of the individuals with respect to continued contact among natural relatives after an adoption has occurred.

CASE

SUPREME COURT OF PENNSYLVANIA.

In re ADOPTION OF R.B.F. and R.C.F. Appeal of B.A.F. and C.H.F. In re Adoption of C.C.G. and Z.C.G. Appeal of J.C.G. and J.J.G. 2002 WL 1906000 (Pa. 2002). OPINION

CHIEF JUSTICE ZAPPALA

These consolidated appeals raise the issue of whether the Adoption Act requires a legal parent to relinquish his or her parental rights in cases where a same-sex partner seeks to adopt the legal parent's child. We hold that Section 2901 of the Adoption Act, 23 Pa.C.S. § 2901, affords the trail court discretion to determine whether, under the circumstances of a particular case, cause has been shown to demonstrate why a particular statutory requirement has not been met. As Appellants'

adoption petitions were summarily dismissed, they did not have the opportunity to demonstrate cause why the relinquishment provision need not be met here. Accordingly, we vacate the orders of the Superior Court and remand to the trial courts for evidentiary hearings.

The appellants in the case of *In re: Adoption of C.C.G. and Z.C.G.,* both male, are involved in an intimate relationship and have been domestic partners since 1982. On October 24, 1991, Appellant J.J.G. adopted C.C.G. He adopted his second child, Z.C.G. on April 21, 1999. After the children were adopted, Appellant J.J.G. and his partner, Appellant J.C.G., lived together with the children as a family. On May 9, 1999, Appellants filed a petition wherein J.C.G. sought to adopt both children. The Erie County Common Pleas Court denied the adoption petition on June 18, 1999, and subsequently affirmed that order upon Appellants' request for rescission.

The *en banc* Superior Court affirmed the denial of the adoption petition, nothing that the court cannot create judicial exceptions to the requirements of the Adoption Act. *In re: Adoption of C.C.G. and Z.C.G.,* 762

A.2d 724 (Pa.Super.2000). The court held that the clear and unambiguous provisions of the Adoption Act do not permit a non-spouse to adopt a child where the legal parents have not relinquished their respective parental rights. It relied on Section 2711(d) of the Adoption Act, which states that the consenting parent of an adoptee under the age of eighteen must provide a statement relinquishing parental rights to his or her child. Appellant J.J.G., the legal parent, had attached a consent form to the adoption petition, but the phrase indicating that he intended to permanently give up his rights to his children was intentionally omitted from the form. The court held that this omission rendered the consent invalid, as it did not meet the requirements of Section 2711. It concluded that Appellant J.C.G. therefore had no legally ascertainable interest, notwithstanding the equal protection clause.

The Superior Court noted that the only exception to the unqualified consent requirement was Section 2903 of the Adoption Act, which provides that "[w]henever a parent consent to the adoption of his child *by his spouse,* the parent-child relationship between him and his child remain whether . . . he is one of the petitioners in the adoption proceeding." 23 Pa. C.S. § 2903 (emphasis added). It relied on our decision in *In re Adoption of E.M.A.,* 487 Pa. 152, 409 A 2d 10 (1979), for the proposition that Section 2903 applies solely to "stepparent" situations and has no application to unmarried persons. The court concluded that because our Commonwealth only recognizes marriages "between one man one woman," 23 Pa.C.S. § 1704, Appellant J.C.G. does not qualify as a "spouse" under Section 2903.

The Superior Court rejected Appellants' claim that the trial court was afforded when "cause has been shown" under Section 2901. The court held that "for cause shown" relates to reasons why the statutory requirements of adoption need not be met. It concluded that until the statutory requirements have been met, or cause shown as to why they need not be met, an analysis of the best interest and general welfare of the children cannot be considered. *Id.* at 729. The court further held that Appellants had failed to demonstrate cause in the instant cases and therefore their adoption petitions were properly denied.

Judge Johnson filed a dissenting statement, in which Judges Kelly and Todd joined. Judge Johnson opined that the Adoption Act permits an adoption when the children's only legal parent advocates the adoption, has joined in the petition for adoption and has retained his parental rights. He found that the majority's strict construction of Section 2711 contravenes the mandate of the Statutory Construction Act, 1 Pa.C.S. §§ 1501-1991, and is inconsistent with the Legislature's purpose in enacting Section 2711. Judge Johnson stated that the principles relied upon by the majority applied only to the involuntary termination of parental rights and that the majority failed to recognize that Section 2901 granted the trail courts discretion to grant the adoptions in the instant cases. Finally, he found that the majority's analysis erroneously focused upon the relationship between the appellants rather than the parent-child relationship.

Judge Todd filed a separate dissenting opinion, which was joined by Judges Kelly and Johnson. Judge Todd emphasized the impact of the majority's decision on the children at issue. She noted that children will not be afforded the benefits of adoption, which include: the legal protection of the children's existing familial bonds; the right to financial support from two parents; the right to inherit from two parents; and the right to obtain other available dependent benefits, such as health care insurance and Social Security benefits, from either parents. Recognizing that there have been over one hundred "second-parent" [FN4] adoptions granted in this Commonwealth in at least fourteen counties, [FN5] Judge Todd opined that the majority's decision would deny many children the legal benefits of parenthood.

The appellants in the case of *In re: Adoption of R.B.F. and R.C.F.,* both female, are also engaged in an intimate relationship and have been domestic partners since 1983. When the couple decided to raise a family. Appellant C.H.F. conceived through *in vitro* fertilization with the sperm of an anonymous donor, who retains no parental rights. C.H.F. gave to twin boys on March 11, 1997. On April 24, 1998, C.H.F. and her partner, B.A.F., filed a petition, wherein B.A.F. sought to adopt the boys. As in the companion case, C.H.F. attached a consent form to the adoption petition, which intentionally omitted the phrase indicating that she intended to permanently give up rights to the children. The Lancaster County Common Pleas Court dismissed the petition with prejudice on October 22, 1998.

A panel of the Superior Court affirmed the denial of the adoption petition. On January 21, 2000, Appellants filed an application for reargument/reconsideration, which was granted. The matter proceeded for oral argument before the *en banc* Superior Court. In a decision filed the same day as *In re: Adoption of C.C.G. and Z.C.G.*, the court affirmed the denial of the adoption petition. The analysis was nearly identical to that set forth in *C.C.G.*, and similar concurring and dissenting opinions were filed. This Court subsequently granted allowance of appeal in both case. [FN6]

We begin by recognizing that adoption is purely a statutory right, unknown at common law. *In re Adoption of E.M.A.*, 487 Pa. 152, 409 A.2d 10,11 (1979). To effect an adoption, the legislative provisions of the Adoption Act must be strictly complied with *Id.* Thus, our analysis is focused entirely on the relevant statutory provisions.

The Adoption Act provides that "[a]ny individual may be adopted, regardless of his age or residence." 23 Pa.C.S. § 2311. Similarly, "[a]ny individual may become an adopting parent." *Id.* at § 2312. Section 2701 sets forth the requisite contents of a petition for adoption filed by a prospective adoptive parent. The requirement at issue here first appears at Section 2701(7), which mandates that "all consents required by section 2711 (relating to consents necessary to adoption) are attached or the basis upon which such consents are not required." *Id,* at § 2701(7). Section 2711(a)(3) provides that consent to an adoption shall be required of the following: "The parents or surviving parent of an adoptee who has not reached the age of 18 years." *Id.* at § 2711(a)(3). Subsection (d) of Section 2711 sets forth the contents of consent and mandates, *inter alia*, that

the consent of a parent of an adoptee under 18 years of age include the following statement:

> I understand that by signing this consent I indicate my intent to permanently give up all rights to this child *Id.* at § 2711(d)(1).

An exception to this relinquishment provision appears at Section 2903, entitled "Retention of parental status," which provides as follows:

> Whenever a parent consents to the adoption of his child by his spouse, the parent-child relationship between him and his child shall remain whether or not he is one of the petitioners in the adoption proceeding. *Id.* at § 2903.

Thus, absent a qualifying provision appearing elsewhere in the Adoption Act, it is clear from a plain reading of these sections that a legal parent must relinquish his parental rights in order to consent to the adoption of his child by a non-spouse. The lower courts properly found that the spousal exception provision in Section 2903 is inapplicable to the instant cases. As noted, 23 Pa.C.S. § 1704 provides that the Commonwealth only recognizes marriage "between one man and one woman." Thus, a same-sex partner cannot be the "spouse" of the legal parent and therefore cannot attain the benefits of the spousal exception to relinquishment of parental rights necessary for a valid consent to adoption.

We addressed the aforementioned provisions in our decision in *In re Adoption of E.M.A.* There, the issue was whether a non-spouse may become an adopting parent of a biological father's child, when the biological father gives only "qualified" consent, retaining his parental rights. Our Court affirmed the denial of the adoption petition on the grounds that the consent given by the biological father did not meet the statutory requirements for adoption by a non-spouse.

We stated:

> By its express terms, section 503 [the predecessor to Section 2903] is clearly limited to adoption by the spouse of a natural parent. This statutory

provision is available only in private or family adoptions, upon the marriage or remarriage of the natural father or mother. Only in such intra-family adoption may a natural parent execute a valid consent retaining parental rights. And only in such a husband-wife relationship is the qualified consent legally sufficient for the spouse seeking to become an adopting parent.

We went on to hold that our Court has no authority to decree an adoption in the absence of the statutorily required consents. We ruled that to construe the spousal exception as applying to a non-spouse "would be unwarranted and impermissible judicial intrusion into the exclusive legislative prerogative." *Id.* Our Court rejected the appellant's contention that the spousal exception to relinquishment of parental rights is unconstitutional as applied because it discriminates against unmarried persons who wish to adopt. We held that because the Adoption Act did not preclude an unmarried person from adopting a child, it withstood constitutional scrutiny. We concluded "[i]t is appropriate and entirely reasonable for the Legislature to provide, as section [2903] does, a special type of consent available only where there is a husband-wife relationship." *Id.* at 12.

Appellants contend that *E.M.A.* is distinguishable on three grounds. First, they argue that *E.M.A.* involved only Section 2903, which they concede is not applicable in cases involving same-sex partners. Second they argue that *E.M.A.* did not involved an "intra-family adoption"and the prospective adoptive parent did not reside with the legal parent. Finally, Appellants allege that *E.M.A.* predated the Legislature's amendment of Section 2901, which they argue affords the trial court discretion to waive the statutory requirements necessary for an adoption petition upon a showing of cause.

We shall address these claims seriatim. Initially, we find that although *E.M.A.* focused upon the spousal exception to the relinquishment of parental rights provision, the decision also reinforced the proposition that the judiciary may not engraft exceptions to the statutory consent requirements of an adoption petition. Further, we discount

Appellant's characterization of the opinion as relying upon the residence of the prospective adoptive parent or the fact that the prospective adoptive parent was not part of the nuclear family. Rather, the decision was based upon the fact that the prospective adoptive parent was not the spouse of the biological parent. Thus, the Court concluded that she could not adopt the child absent relinquishment of the father's parental rights.

Appellants' final contention as to why *E.M.A.* is distinguishable, however is persuasive. It is based upon the subsequent 1982 amendment to Section 2901 of the Adoption Act. Section 2901 states in its entirely:

> § 2901.Time of entry of decree of adoption
> *Unless the court for cause shown determines otherwise,* no decree of adoption shall be entered unless the natural parent of parents' rights have been terminated, the investigation required by section 2535 (relating to investigating) has been completed the report of the intermediary has been filed pursuant to section 2533 (relating to report of intermediary) and all other legal requirements have been met. If all legal requirements have been met, the court may enter a decree of adoption at any time.

> 23. Pa. C.S. § 2901 (emphasis added).

Appellants argue that the Legislature's amendment of this provision after we decided *E.M.A.* was intended to alter that decision by affording the trial court discretion, upon cause shown, to waive a particular statutory requirement. Appellants clarify that they agree with the lower court's finding that "cause shown" is essentially an explanation as to why the statutory requirements are not met. They submit that the court can exercise its discretion in this regard by first determining the underlying purpose of the statutory requirement that the prospective adoptive parent seeks to excuse. According to Appellants, the court would then determine, upon examination of a factual showing by the petitioner, whether the purpose of the statutory requirement will otherwise be met or is irrelevant to the particular circumstances of the case.

◆ **CASE**

Appellants contend that the Superior Court erred in holding that they failed to demonstrate "cause" when they were never given an opportunity to do so. They urge our Court to remand the matter so that they may set forth a factual basis for finding that the purpose of the relinquishment provision would be fulfilled by maintaining the children's relationship with their existing parent. They assert that cause can be demonstrated in the instant cases because, "[h]ere, as in a stepparent adoption, the only means to guarantee family integrity ordinarily achieved through **termination** of existing legal parent's rights would be through **preservation** of that parent's rights." Appellants' Brief at 30 (emphasis supplied).

After careful consideration, we agree with Appellants that there is no reasonable construction of the Section 2901 "cause shown" language other than to conclude that it permits a petitioner to demonstrate why, in a particular case, he or she cannot meet the statutory requirements. Upon a showing of cause, the trial court is afforded *discretion* to determine whether the adoption petition should, nevertheless, be granted. The exercise of such discretion does not open the door to unlimited adoptions by legally unrelated adults. Such decisions will always be confined by a finding of cause and a determination of the best interests of the child in each individual case. Moreover, like other trial court decisions, findings of cause will be reviewed on appeal for an abuse of discretion.

We note that our decision is not creating a judicial exception to the requirements of the Adoption Act, but rather is applying the plain meaning of the terms employed by the Legislature. When the requisite cause is demonstrated, Section 2901 affords the trial court discretion to decree the adoption without termination of the legal parent's right pursuant to Section 2711(d). An examination of Section 2701(7), which was also amended after *E.M.A.* was decided, comports with our decision as it requires that the necessary consents under Section 2711 be attached to the adoption petition *"or the basis upon which such consents are not required."* 23 Pa.C.S. § 2701(7), (emphasis added).

Thus, contrary to our holding in *E.M.A.,* the Legislature contemplated limited circumstances where the requisite consents may not be necessary.

Furthermore, a contrary interpretation of the "cause shown" language would command an absurd result as the Adoption Act does not expressly preclude same-sex partners from adopting. *See 1* Pa.C.S. § 1922(1) (General Assembly does not intend a result that is absurd, impossible of execution or unreasonable). *See also* 23 Pa.C.S. § 2312 (stating that "any individual" can adopt). For example, the denial of Appellants' adoption petitions is premised solely upon the lack of unqualified consent by the existing legal parent. There is no language in the Adoption Act precluding two unmarried same-sex partners (or unmarried heterosexual partners) from adopting a child who had no legal parents. It is therefore absurd to prohibit their adoptions merely because their children were either the biological or adopted children of one of the partners prior to the filing of the adoption petition. It is a settled rule that in the construction of statutes an interpretation is never to be adopted that would defeat the purpose of the enactment, if any other reasonable construction can found which its language will fairly bear. *McQuiston's Adoption,* 86A.2d 205, 206 (Pa.1913).

Another example rendering absurd a contrary interpretation of Section 2901 is Appellants' and supporting *amici's* suggestion that Appellants could have filed their adoption petitions with the requisite unqualified consent of the legal parent, including the relinquishment of parental rights, and then seek to adopt their children jointly. In view of the fact that there appears to be no statutory bar to such approach, our interpretation of Section 2901 avoids such a convoluted procedure that would serve no valid purpose.

Although not directly on point, we also find support for our decision in *In re: Long,* 745 A.2d 673 (Pa.Super.2000), where the Superior Court was called upon to interpret similar "cause shown" language. There, an adoptee sought to recover information regarding her biological parents. At issue was "cause shown" language in another provision of the Adoption Act, Section 2905. Section 2905 provides that all adoption records "shall be kept in the files of the court as a permanent record thereof and withheld from inspection except on an order of court granted *upon cause shown. . . ."* 23 Pa.C.S. § 2905(a) (emphasis added).

On the record presented, the Superior Court could not determine whether the trial court made a factual finding as to whether the appellant demonstrated cause for disclosure of the adoption records as set forth in the statute. The court recognized the lack of guidance as to the meaning of the language employed in Section 2905, as well as the overriding privacy concerns of the adoption process and the Adoption Act. The court described "cause" for disclosure as a demonstration, by clear and convincing evidence, that the adoptee's need for adoption information clearly outweighed the considerations behind the statute. *Id* at 675. Accordingly, the court remanded for an evidentiary hearing at which such a determination could be made.

Presented with a similar dilemma here, we vacate the orders of the Superior Court and remand to the respective trial courts for evidentiary hearings to determine whether Appellants can demonstrate, by clear and convincing evidence, cause as to whether the purpose of Section 2711(d)'s relinquishment of parental rights requirement will be otherwise fulfilled or is unnecessary under the particular circumstances of each case.

Case Review Question

In re Adoption of R.B.F. and R.C.F., 2002 WL 1906000 (Pa. 2002).

Why didn't the appellate court grant the right to adopt instead of remanding the case back to the trial court?

Fertility and Surrogacy

A relatively new area of medicine and subsequently law is that regarding reproductive medicine. A large increase in technology in the last half of the twentieth century led to increase methods of conception as well. The development of various procedures resulted in the ability to conceive children outside the womb, insemination and fertilization of an egg by anonymous donors, and even implantation of embryos from one woman into another for the gestational period prior to birth. These procedures ultimately produced legal questions too numerous to mention. The most publicized cases, however, have dealt with parental rights when more than two individuals are involved with the conception and gestation of the child, such as when a surrogate mother gives birth and then decides she wants to keep the child. In some instances, the egg is provided by the mother and the sperm provided by the man in a married couple who wish to rear the child. In that case, the wife of the man would be an adoptive parent. Other cases involving implantation of an embryo raise the issue of whether the maternal legal rights are attached to the egg or to the woman who carries it within her body through gestation and gives birth. Question remains as to what of the anonymous sperm donor. Does he have any legal paternal rights with respect to a child produced? What of parties who have embryos frozen, then they divorce and the wife proceeds to have the embryo implanted and subsequently delivers a child? Does the natural father have obligations or rights with respect to this child he never intended to be produced? Is it even a question for courts in matters of divorce as to who should have custody of such frozen embryos, because they are truly the product and part of the physical being of both parties?

As can be seen, the legal questions arise as quickly as medical technology increases. This area of law will experience explosive growth in the coming decades.

Ethical Considerations

Legal ethics plays an important role in the law of domestic relations. It is not uncommon for only one party to retain counsel in situations involving dissolution, marital property, or interests regarding children. In such situations, the attorney is under an ethical obligation to make it clear to the other party that a lawyer cannot represent both sides of a legal issue. To do so would constitute a conflict of interest. Consequently, it is quite common that a property settlement or other document of settlement of legal issues contain a clause that identifies who is represented by the attorney.

In an uncontested dissolution of marriage where there are few matters to be determined, such as division of property, the parties may elect to use one attorney to minimize the cost. However, this does not change the position of the attorney. Ethically, the attorney can represent only one of the parties. The other party who chooses to agree to the terms presented must do so independently and without the advice or counsel of the attorney. Further, that party must always retain the right to seek legal advice on the matter from another attorney. In this way, the initial attorney cannot be considered to be attempting to represent the best interest of two parties on opposite sides of a conflict.

Ethical Circumstance

Joann and Tyrell have decided to end their marriage of 15 years. They have limited financial resources and barely generate enough income to support themselves and their three children. They have approached legal assistance organizations but most have a waiting list for services that are not considered emergencies. They contact an attorney for representation. It is clear that both have different ideas of how the issues of property rights and responsibilities, visitation, and custody should be resolved. The attorney wants to help them, but knows the cost to counsel will be unaffordable. The attorney must inform them that only one can be represented by the firm.

A much less expensive alternative to suggest is arbitration, where they agree to present both sides to an arbitrator and be bound by the arbitrator's final recommendation. Such a situation takes business away from the attorney but provides an ethical resolution. For the attorney to represent one side, knowing the other cannot afford counsel and will thus be at a disadvantage may be legal, but certainly would not be ethical.

Question
Could the attorney provide any other alternative?

CHAPTER SUMMARY

The law of domestic relations in this country has undergone radical changes in the last century. This area of law is also probably the most different from its origins, unlike areas such as contract and property law that retain many foundations in the original principles brought from England. In this century, divorce has gone from a rare and socially unacceptable occurrence, to a certainty in almost half of all marriages that occur. Dissolution of marriage and the consequent issues comprise the majority of legal principles in domestic relations law.

Assuming a marriage is legally accomplished through meeting of formal and statutory requisites, it can be ended by annulment in limited circumstances. Specifically, a condition of marriage must not have existed at the time the marriage occurred which in turn prevented it from having ever become valid. The other and much more common alternative is dissolution of marriage in which a valid marriage relationship is dissolved and the assets, debts, maintenance, and other joint issues of the parties such as child custody, support, and visitation are resolved.

Some parties elect to legally separate rather than divorce, although this is in the minority of cases. In the event of a legal separation, the marital relationship is left intact. The parties remain married for legal purposes; however, they separate their property, assets, debts, and responsibilities with respect to minor children. Historically, this was often done for parties who did not wish to continue living together but remained married due to social, cultural, and religious pressures and issues. Dissolution today is more accepted and parties most often opt for it to bring the relationship to an end and allow them to move forward in their lives independent of one another.

Parties who cohabit as if they are married are no longer considered common law spouses in the vast majority of jurisdictions. Rather, in the event the cohabitation and relationship end, the parties are left to resolve matters themselves or to pursue the issues in the courts under contract and partnership principles. This assumes, however, that the relationship was not contingent upon sexual services in which case the purpose is considered illegal and the courts will not enforce rights as if a contract or partnership existed.

CHAPTER TERMS

annulment	dissolution of marriage	preliminary injunction
antenuptial agreement	domestic violence	property settlement
(prenuptial agreement)	legal separation	temporary restraining order
custody (parental rights)	permanent injunction	

REVIEW QUESTIONS

1. Are antenuptial agreements legally enforceable?
2. What is necessary for a valid marriage?
3. When can a marriage be legally annulled?
4. What rights are available to persons who cohabit but do not marry, in the event the relationship ends?
5. How does a legal separation differ from the dissolution of a marriage?
6. What relief is available to the parties after dissolution is sought but before it is granted?
7. What standard do the courts apply when determining custody?
8. What is joint custody?
9. What is the difficulty with joint custody?
10. What are no-fault grounds for dissolution?

RELEVANT LINKS

Family law
www.aol.com/webcenters/legal/family.adp

Family law resources at About.com
www.law.about.com/msub12.html

INTERNET ASSIGNMENT 16.1

Using internet resources, identify the requirements for marriage in your jurisdiction including
waiting period, blood tests, prohibited relationships, and licensure. Trace your steps.

NOTES

1. *In re Estate of Cummings,* 493 Pa. 11, 425
   A.2d 340 (1981).
2. 81 A.L.R.3d. 453.
3. Id.
4. Mobilia, "Ante-nuptial agreements
   anticipating divorce: How effective are
   they?" 70 *Massachusetts Law Review* 82
   10 (June 1985).
5. 55 C.J.S., Marriage, Section 10.
6. Id., Sections 24, 25.
7. Id., Sections 28–31.
8. Id., Section 48.
9. *McDonald v. McDonald,* 6 Cal.2d 457, 58
   P.2d 163 (1936).
10. *Wirth v. Wirth,* 175 Misc. 342, 23 N.Y.S.2d
    289 (1940).
11. 81 A.L.R.3d. 281.
12. *Jackson v. Jackson,* 276 F.2d 501 (D.C.Cir.
    1960).
13. *Maschauer v. Downs,* 53 App.D.C. 142, 289
    Fed. 540 (1923).
14. 41 Am.Jur.2d., Husband and Wife, Section
    522.
15. Federal Rules of Evidence, 28 U.S.C.A.
    Rule 501.
16. 23 *Journal of Family Law* 454 (April
    1985).
17. 51 A.L.R.3d 223.
18. Id.
19. 24 Am.Jur.2d, Divorce and Separation,
    Section 29.
20. *Glendening v. Glendening,* 206 A.2d 824
    (D.C. App. 1965).
21. Uniform Marriage and Divorce Act,
    Section 304(b) (2).
22. 24 Am.Jur.2d., Divorce and Separation,
    Section 328.
23. 75 A.L.R.3d.
24. 48 A.L.R.4th 919.
25. Id.
26. Id.
27. 70 A.L.R.3d 262.
28. 24 Am.Jur.2d., Divorce and Separation,
    Sections 974, 975.
29. Id.
30. Id.
31. 17 A.L.R.4th 1013.
32. *Perla v. Perla,* 58 So.2d 689 (Fla. 1952).
33. Smith, "Education support obligations of
    noncustodial parents," 36 *Rutgers Law
    Review* 588 (September 1984).
34. Comment, "Battling inconsistency and
    inadequacy: Child support guidelines in
    the states," *Harvard Women's Law Journal*
    197 (Spring 1988).
35. See note 21, Section 102(5); 309.
36. 23 Am.Jur.2d, Desertion and Non-support,
    Section 128, et seq.

37. *In re J.S. & C.,*129 N.J.Super. 486, 324 A.2d 90 (1974).
38. 24 Am.Jur.2d., Divorce and Separation, Section 866.
39. Id.; 20 Am.Jur. 2d, Sections 321–370.
40. 97 A.L.R.3d 740.
41. See note 38, Section 584.
42. Monroe, "Marvin v. Marvin: Five years later," 65 *Marquette Law Review* 389 (Spring 1982).
43. *Marvin v. Marvin,* 18 Cal.3d 660, 134 Cal.Rptr. 815, 557 P.2d 106 (1976).

For additional resources, please visit our Web site at www.westlegalstudies.com

The Constitution of the United States

PREAMBLE

We the People of the United States, in Order to form a more perfect Union, establish Justice, insure domestic Tranquility, provide for the common defence, promote the general Welfare, and secure the Blessings of Liberty to ourselves and our Posterity, do ordain and establish this Constitution for the United States of America.

ARTICLE I

Section 1. All legislative Powers herein granted shall be vested in a Congress of the United States, which shall consist of a Senate and House of Representatives.

Section 2. The House of Representatives shall be composed of Members chosen every second Year by the People of the several States, and the Electors in each State shall have the Qualifications requisite for Electors of the most numerous Branch of the State Legislature.

No Person shall be a Representative who shall not have attained to the Age of twenty five Years, and been seven Years a Citizen of the United States, and who shall not, when elected, be an Inhabitant of that State in which he shall be chosen.

Representatives and direct Taxes shall be apportioned among the several States which may be included within this Union, according to their respective Numbers, which shall be determined by adding to the whole Number of free Persons, including those bound to Service for a Term of Years, and excluding Indians not taxed, three fifths of all other Persons. The actual Enumeration shall be made within three years after the first Meeting of the Congress of the United States, and within every subsequent Term of ten Years, in such Manner as they shall by Law direct. The Number of Representatives shall not exceed one for every thirty Thousand, but each State shall have at Least one Representative; and until such enumeration shall be made, the State of New Hampshire shall be entitled to chuse three, Massachusetts eight, Rhode Island and Providence Plantations one, Connecticut five, New York six, New Jersey four, Pennsylvania eight, Delaware one, Maryland six, Virginia ten, North Carolina five, South Carolina five, and Georgia three.

When vacancies happen in the Representation from any State, the Executive Authority thereof shall issue Writs of Election to fill such Vacancies.

The House of Representatives shall chuse their Speaker and other Officers; and shall have the sole Power of Impeachment.

Section 3. The Senate of the United States shall be composed of two Senators from each State, chosen by the Legislature thereof, for six Years; and each Senator shall have one Vote.

Immediately after they shall be assembled in Consequence of the first Election, they shall be divided as equally as may be into three Classes. The Seats of the Senators of the first Class shall be vacated at the Expiration of the second Year, of the second Class at the Expiration of the fourth Year, and of the third Class at the Expiration of the sixth Year, so that one third may be chosen every second Year; and if Vacancies happen by Resignation, or otherwise, during the Recess of the Legislature of any State, the Executive thereof may make temporary Appointments until the next Meeting of the Legislature, which shall then fill such Vacancies.

No Person shall be a Senator who shall not have attained to the Age of thirty Years, and been nine Years a Citizen of the United States, and who shall not, when elected, be an Inhabitant of that State for which he shall be chosen.

The Vice President of the United States shall be President of the Senate, but shall have no Vote, unless they be equally divided.

The Senate shall chuse their other Officers, and also a President pro tempore, in the Absence of the Vice President, or when he shall exercise the Office of President of the United States.

The Senate shall have the sole Power to try all Impeachments. When sitting for that Purpose, they shall be on Oath or Affirmation. When the President of the United States is tried, the Chief Justice shall preside: And no Person shall be convicted without the Concurrence of two thirds of the Members present.

Judgment in Cases of Impeachment shall not extend further than to removal from Office, and disqualification to hold and enjoy any Office of honor, Trust, or Profit under the United States: but the Party convicted shall nevertheless be liable and subject to Indictment, Trial, Judgment, and Punishment, according to Law.

Section 4. The Times, Places and Manner of holding Elections for Senators and Representatives, shall be prescribed in each State by the Legislature thereof; but the Congress may at any time by Law make or alter such Regulations, except as to the Places of chusing Senators.

The Congress shall assemble at least once in every Year, and such Meeting shall be on the first Monday in December, unless they shall by Law appoint a different Day.

Section 5. Each House shall be the Judge of the Elections, Returns, and Qualifications of its own Members, and a Majority of each shall constitute a Quorum to do Business; but a smaller Number may adjourn from day to day, and may be authorized to compel the Attendance of absent Members, in such Manner, and under such Penalties as each House may provide.

Each House may determine the Rules of its Proceedings, punish its Members for disorderly Behavior, and, with the Concurrence of two thirds, expel a Member.

Each House shall keep a Journal of its Proceedings, and from time to time publish the same, excepting such Parts as may in their Judgment require Secrecy; and the Yeas and Nays of the Members of either House on any question shall, at the Desire of one fifth of those Present, be entered on the Journal.

Neither House, during the Session of Congress, shall, without the Consent of the other, adjourn for more than three days, nor to any other Place than that in which the two Houses shall be sitting.

Section 6. The Senators and Representatives shall receive a Compensation for their Services, to be ascertained by Law, and paid out of the Treasury of the United States. They shall in all Cases, except Treason, Felony and Breach of the Peace, be privileged from Arrest during their Attendance at the Session of their respective Houses, and in going to and returning from the same; and for any Speech or Debate in either House, they shall not be questioned in any other Place.

No Senator or Representative shall, during the Time for which he was elected, be appointed to any civil Office under the Authority of the United States, which shall have been created, or the Emoluments whereof shall have been increased during such time; and no Person holding any Office under the United States, shall be a Member of either House during his Continuance in Office.

Section 7. All Bills for raising Revenue shall originate in the House of Representatives; but the Senate may propose or concur with Amendments as on other Bills.

Every Bill which shall have passed the House of Representatives and the Senate, shall, before it become a Law, be presented to the President of the United States; If he approve he shall sign it, but if not he shall return it, with his Objections to the House in which it shall have originated, who shall enter the Objections at large on their Journal, and proceed to reconsider it. If after such Reconsideration two thirds of that House shall agree to pass the Bill, it shall be sent together with the Objections, to the other House, by which it shall likewise be reconsidered, and if approved by two thirds of that House, it shall become a Law. But in all such Cases the Votes of both Houses shall be determined by Yeas and Nays, and the Names of the Persons voting for and against the Bill shall be entered on the Journal of each House respectively. If any Bill shall not be returned by the President within ten Days (Sundays excepted) after it shall have been presented to him, the Same shall be a Law, in like Manner as if he had signed it, unless the Congress by their Adjournment prevent its Return in which Case it shall not be a Law.

Every Order, Resolution, or Vote, to which the Concurrence of the Senate and House of Representatives may be necessary (except on a question of Adjournment) shall be presented to the President of the United States; and before the Same shall take Effect, shall be approved by him, or being disapproved by him, shall be repassed by two thirds of the Senate and House of Representatives, according to the Rules and Limitations prescribed in the Case of a Bill.

Section 8.   The Congress shall have Power To lay and collect Taxes, Duties, Imposts and Excises, to pay the Debts and provide for the common Defence and general Welfare of the United States; but all Duties, Imposts and Excises shall be uniform throughout the United States;

To borrow Money on the credit of the United States;

To regulate Commerce with foreign Nations, and among the several States, and with the Indian Tribes;

To establish an uniform Rule of Naturalization, and uniform Laws on the subject of Bankruptcies throughout the United States;

To coin Money, regulate the Value thereof, and of foreign Coin, and fix the Standard of Weights and Measures;

To provide for the Punishment of counterfeiting the Securities and current Coin of the United States;

To establish Post Offices and post Roads;

To promote the Progress of Science and useful Arts, by securing for limited Times to Authors and Inventors the exclusive Right to their respective Writings and Discoveries;

To constitute Tribunals inferior to the supreme Court;

To define and punish Piracies and Felonies committed on the high Seas, and Offenses against the Law of Nations;

To declare War, grant Letters of Marque and Reprisal, and make Rules concerning Captures on Land and Water;

To raise and support Armies, but no Appropriation of Money to that Use shall be for a longer Term than two Years;

To provide and maintain a Navy;

To make Rules for the Government and Regulation of the land and naval Forces;

To provide for calling forth the Militia to execute the Laws of the Union, suppress Insurrections and repel Invasions;

To provide for organizing, arming, and disciplining, the Militia, and for governing such Part of them as may be employed in the Service of the United States, reserving to the States respectively, the Appointment of the Officers, and the Authority of training the Militia according to the discipline prescribed by Congress;

To exercise exclusive Legislation in all Cases whatsoever, over such District (not exceeding ten Miles square) as may, by Cession of particular States, and the Acceptance of Congress, become the Seat of the Government of the United States, and to exercise like Authority over all Places purchased by the Consent of the Legislature of the State in which the Same shall be, for the Erection of Forts, Magazines, Arsenals, dock-Yards, and other needful Buildings;—And

To make all Laws which shall be necessary and proper for carrying into Execution the foregoing Powers, and all other Powers vested by this Constitution in the Government of the United States, or in any Department or Officer thereof.

Section 9.   The Migration or Importation of such Persons as any of the States now existing shall think proper to admit, shall not be prohibited by the Congress prior to the Year one thousand eight hundred and eight, but a Tax or duty may be imposed on such Importation, not exceeding ten dollars for each Person.

The privilege of the Writ of Habeas Corpus shall not be suspended, unless when in Cases of Rebellion or Invasion the public Safety may require it.

No Bill of Attainder or ex post facto Law shall be passed.

No Capitation, or other direct, Tax shall be laid, unless in Proportion to the Census or Enumeration herein before directed to be taken.

No Tax or Duty shall be laid on Articles exported from any State.

No Preference shall be given by any Regulation of Commerce or Revenue to the Ports of one State over those of another: nor shall Vessels bound to, or from, one State be obliged to enter, clear, or pay Duties in another.

No Money shall be drawn from the Treasury, but in Consequence of Appropriations made by Law; and a regular Statement and Account of the Receipts and Expenditures of all public Money shall be published from time to time.

No Title of Nobility shall be granted by the United States: And no Person holding any Office of Profit or Trust under them, shall, without the Consent of the Congress, accept of any present, Emolument, Office, or Title, of any kind whatever, from any King, Prince, or foreign State.

Section 10.   No State shall enter into any Treaty, Alliance, or Confederation; grant Letters of Marque and Reprisal; coin Money; emit Bills of Credit; make any Thing but gold and silver Coin a Tender in Payment of Debts; pass any Bill of Attainder, ex post facto Law, or Law impairing the Obligation of Contracts, or grant any Title of Nobility.

No State shall, without the Consent of the Congress, lay any Imposts or Duties on Imports or Exports, except what may be absolutely necessary for executing it's inspection Laws: and the net Produce of all Duties and Imposts, laid by any State on Imports or Exports, shall be for the Use of the Treasury of the United States, and all such Laws shall be subject to the Revision and Controul of the Congress.

No State shall, without the Consent of Congress, lay any Duty of Tonnage, keep Troops, or Ships of War in time of Peace, enter into any Agreement or Compact with another State, or with a foreign Power, or engage in War, unless actually invaded, or in such imminent Danger as will not admit of delay.

ARTICLE II

Section 1.   The executive Power shall be vested in a President of the United States of America. He shall hold his Office during the Term of four Years, and, together with the Vice President, chosen for the same Term, be elected, as follows:

Each State shall appoint, in such Manner as the Legislature thereof may direct, a Number of Electors, equal to the whole Number of Senators and Representatives to which the State may be entitled in the Congress; but no Senator or Representative, or Person holding an Office of Trust or Profit under the United States, shall be appointed an Elector.

The Electors shall meet in their respective States, and vote by Ballot for two Persons, of whom one at least shall not be an Inhabitant of the same State with themselves. And they shall make a List of all the Persons voted for, and of the Number of Votes for each; which List they shall sign and certify, and transmit sealed to the Seat of the Government of the United States, directed to the President of the Senate. The President of the Senate shall, in the Presence of the Senate and House of Representatives, open all the Certificates, and the Votes shall then be counted. The Person having the greatest Number of Votes shall be the President, if such Number be a Majority of the whole Number of Electors appointed; and if there be more than one who have such Majority, and have an equal Number of Votes, then the House of Representatives shall immediately chuse by Ballot one of them for President; and if no Person have a Majority, then from the five highest on the List the said House shall in like Manner chuse the President. But in chusing the President, the Votes shall be taken by States, the Representation from each State having one Vote; A quorum for this Purpose shall consist of a Member or Members from two thirds of the States, and a Majority of all the States shall be necessary to a Choice. In every Case, after the Choice of the President, the Person having the greater Number of Votes of the Electors shall be the Vice President. But if there should remain two or more who have equal Votes, the Senate shall chuse from them by Ballot the Vice President.

The Congress may determine the Time of chusing the Electors, and the Day on which they shall give their Votes; which Day shall be the same throughout the United States.

No person except a natural born Citizen, or a Citizen of the United States, at the time of the Adoption of this Constitution, shall be eligible to the Office of President; neither shall any Person be eligible to that Office who shall not have attained to the Age of thirty five Years, and been fourteen Years a Resident within the United States.

In Case of the Removal of the President from Office, or of his Death, Resignation or Inability to discharge the Powers and Duties of the said Office, the same shall devolve on the Vice President, and the Congress may by Law provide for the Case of Removal, Death, Resignation or Inability, both of the President and Vice President, declaring what Officer shall then act as President, and such Officer shall act accordingly, until the Disability be removed, or a President shall be elected.

The President shall, at stated Times, receive for his Services, a Compensation, which shall neither be increased nor diminished during the Period for which he shall have been elected, and he shall not receive within that Period any other Emolument from the United States, or any of them.

Before he enter on the Execution of his Office, he shall take the following Oath or Affirmation: "I do solemnly swear (or affirm) that I will faithfully execute the Office of President of the United States, and will to the best of my Ability, preserve, protect and defend the Constitution of the United States."

Section 2.   The President shall be Commander in Chief of the Army and Navy of the United States, and of the Militia of the several States, when called into the actual Service of the United States; he may require the Opinion, in writing, of the principal Officer in each of the executive Departments, upon any Subject relating to the Duties of their respective Offices, and he shall have Power to grant Reprieves and Pardons for Offenses against the United States, except in Cases of Impeachment.

He shall have Power, by and with the Advice and Consent of the Senate to make Treaties, provided two thirds of the Senators present concur; and he shall nominate, and by and with the Advice and Consent of the Senate, shall appoint Ambassadors, other public Ministers and Consuls, Judges of the supreme Court, and all other Officers of the United States, whose Appointments are not herein otherwise provided for, and which shall be established by Law; but the Congress may by Law vest the Appointment of such inferior Officers, as they think proper, in the President alone, in the Courts of Law, or in the Heads of Departments.

The President shall have Power to fill up all Vacancies that may happen during the Recess of the Senate, by granting Commissions which shall expire at the End of their next Session.

Section 3.   He shall from time to time give to the Congress Information of the State of the Union, and recommend to their Consideration such Measures as he shall judge necessary and expedient; he may, on extraordinary Occasions, convene both Houses, or either of them, and in Case of Disagreement between them, with Respect to the Time of Adjournment, he may adjourn them to such Time as he shall think proper; he shall receive Ambassadors and other public Ministers; he shall take Care that the Laws be faithfully executed, and shall Commission all the Officers of the United States.

Section 4.   The President, Vice President and all civil Officers of the United States, shall be removed from Office on Impeachment for, and Conviction of, Treason, Bribery, or other high Crimes and Misdemeanors.

ARTICLE III

Section 1.   The judicial Power of the United States, shall be vested in one supreme Court, and in such inferior Courts as the Congress may from time to time ordain and establish. The Judges, both of the supreme and inferior Courts, shall hold their Offices during good Behaviour, and shall, at stated Times, receive for their Services a Compensation, which shall not be diminished during their Continuance in Office.

Section 2.   The judicial Power shall extend to all Cases, in Law and Equity, arising under this Constitution, the Laws of the United States, and Treaties made, or which shall be made, under their Authority;—to all Cases affecting Ambassadors, other public Ministers and Consuls;—to all Cases of admiralty and maritime Jurisdiction;—to Controversies to which the United States shall be a Party;—to Controversies between two or more States;—between a State and Citizens of another State;—between Citizens of different States;—between Citizens of the same State claiming Lands under Grants of different States, and between a State, or the Citizens thereof, and foreign States, Citizens or Subjects.

In all Cases affecting Ambassadors, other public Ministers and Consuls, and those in which a State shall be a Party, the supreme Court shall have original Jurisdiction. In all the other Cases before mentioned, the supreme Court shall have appellate Jurisdiction, both as to Law and Fact, with such Exceptions, and under such Regulations as the Congress shall make.

The Trial of all Crimes, except in Cases of Impeachment, shall be by Jury; and such Trial shall be held in the State where the said Crimes shall have been committed; but when not committed within any State, the Trial shall be at such Place or Places as the Congress may by Law have directed.

Section 3.   Treason against the United States, shall consist only in levying War against them, or, in adhering to their Enemies, giving them Aid and Comfort. No Person shall be convicted of Treason unless on the Testimony of two Witnesses to the same overt Act, or on Confession in open Court.

The Congress shall have Power to declare the Punishment of Treason, but no Attainder of Treason shall work Corruption of Blood, or Forfeiture except during the Life of the Person attained.

ARTICLE IV

Section 1.   Full Faith and Credit shall be given in each State to the public Acts, Records, and judicial Proceedings of every other State. And the Congress may by general Laws prescribe the Manner in which such Acts, Records and Proceedings shall be proved, and the Effect thereof.

Section 2. The Citizens of each State shall be entitled to all Privileges and Immunities of Citizens in the several States.

A Person charged in any State with Treason, Felony, or other Crime, who shall flee from Justice, and be found in another State, shall on Demand of the executive Authority of the State from which he fled, be delivered up, to be removed to the State having Jurisdiction of the Crime.

No Person held to Service or Labour in one State, under the Laws thereof, escaping into another, shall, in Consequence of any Law or Regulation therein, be discharged from such Service or Labour, but shall be delivered up on Claim of the Party to whom such Service or Labour may be due.

Section 3. New States may be admitted by the Congress into this Union; but no new State shall be formed or erected within the Jurisdiction of any other State; nor any State be formed by the Junction of two or more States, or Parts of States, without the Consent of the Legislatures of the States concerned as well as of the Congress.

The Congress shall have Power to dispose of and make all needful Rules and Regulations respecting the Territory or other Property belonging to the United States; and nothing in this Constitution shall be so construed as to Prejudice any Claims of the United States, or of any particular State.

Section 4. The United States shall guarantee to every State in this Union a Republican Form of Government, and shall protect each of them against Invasion; and on Application of the Legislature, or of the Executive (when the Legislature cannot be convened) against domestic Violence.

ARTICLE V

The Congress, whenever two thirds of both Houses shall deem it necessary, shall propose Amendments to this Constitution, or, on the Application of the Legislatures of two thirds of the several States, shall call a Convention for proposing Amendments, which, in either Case, shall be valid to all Intents and Purposes, as part of this Constitution, when ratified by the Legislatures of three fourths of the several States, or by Conventions in three fourths thereof, as the one or the other Mode of Ratification may be proposed by the Congress; Provided that no Amendment which may be made prior to the Year One thousand eight hundred and eight shall in any Manner affect the first

and fourth Clauses in the Ninth Section of the first Article; and that no State, without its Consent, shall be deprived of its equal Suffrage in the Senate.

ARTICLE VI

All Debts contracted and Engagements entered into, before the Adoption of this Constitution shall be as valid against the United States under this Constitution, as under the Confederation.

This Constitution, and the Laws of the United States which shall be made in Pursuance thereof; and all Treaties made, or which shall be made, under the Authority of the United States, shall be the supreme Law of the Land; and the Judges in every State shall be bound thereby, any Thing in the Constitution or Laws of any State to the Contrary notwithstanding.

The Senators and Representatives before mentioned, and the Members of the several State Legislatures, and all executive and judicial Officers, both of the United States and of the several States, shall be bound by Oath or Affirmation, to support this Constitution; but no religious Test shall ever be required as a Qualification to any Office or public Trust under the United States.

ARTICLE VII

The Ratification of the Conventions of nine States shall be sufficient for the Establishment of this Constitution between the States so ratifying the Same.

AMENDMENT I [1791]

Congress shall make no law respecting an establishment of religion, or prohibiting the free exercise thereof; or abridging the freedom of speech, or of the press; or the right of the people peaceably to assembly, and to petition the Government for a redress of grievances.

AMENDMENT II [1791]

A well regulated Militia, being necessary to the security of a free State, the right of the people to keep and bear Arms, shall not be infringed.

AMENDMENT III [1791]

No Soldier shall, in time of peace be quartered in any house, without the consent of the Owner, nor in time of war, but in a manner to be prescribed by law.

AMENDMENT IV [1791]

The right of the people to be secure in their persons, houses, papers, and effects, against unreasonable searches and seizures, shall not be violated, and no Warrants shall issue, but upon probable cause, supported by Oath or affirmation, and particularly describing the place to be searched, and the persons or things to be seized.

AMENDMENT V [1791]

No person shall be held to answer for a capital, or otherwise infamous crime, unless on a presentment or indictment of a Grand Jury, except in cases arising in the land or naval forces, or in the Militia, when in actual service in time of War or public danger; nor shall any person be subject for the same offence to be twice put in jeopardy of life or limb; nor shall be compelled in any criminal case to be a witness against himself, nor be deprived of life, liberty, or property, without due process of law; nor shall private property be taken for public use, without just compensation.

AMENDMENT VI [1791]

In all criminal prosecutions, the accused shall enjoy the right to a speedy and public trial, by an impartial jury of the State and district wherein the crime shall have been committed, which district shall have been previously ascertained by law, and to be informed of the nature and cause of the accusation; to be confronted with the witnesses against him; to have compulsory process for obtaining witnesses in his favor, and to have the Assistance of Counsel for his defence.

AMENDMENT VII [1791]

In Suits at common law, where the value in controversy shall exceed twenty dollars, the right of trial by jury shall be preserved, and no fact tried by jury, shall be otherwise re-examined in any Court of the United States, than according to the rules of the common law.

AMENDMENT VIII [1791]

Excessive bail shall not be required, nor excessive fines imposed, nor cruel and unusual punishments inflicted.

AMENDMENT IX [1791]

The enumeration in the Constitution, of certain rights, shall not be construed to deny or disparage others retained by the people.

AMENDMENT X [1791]

The powers not delegated to the United States by the Constitution, nor prohibited by it to the States, are reserved to the States respectively, or to the people.

AMENDMENT XI [1798]

The Judicial power of the United States shall not be construed to extend to any suit in law or equity, commenced or prosecuted against one of the United States by Citizens of another State, or by Citizens or Subjects of any Foreign State.

AMENDMENT XII [1804]

The Electors shall meet in their respective states, and vote by ballot for President and Vice-President, one of whom, at least, shall not be an inhabitant of the same state with themselves; they shall name in their ballots the person voted for as President, and in distinct ballots the person voted for as Vice-President, and they shall make distinct lists of all persons voted for as President, and of all persons voted for as Vice-President, and of the number of votes for each, which lists they shall sign and certify, and transmit sealed to the seat of the government of the United States, directed to the President of the Senate;—The President of the Senate shall, in the presence of the Senate and House of Representatives, open all the certificates and the votes shall then be counted;—The person having the greatest number of votes for President, shall be the President, if such number be a majority of the whole number of Electors appointed; and if no person have such majority, then from the persons having the highest numbers not exceeding three on the list of those voted for as President, the House of Representatives shall choose immediately, by ballot, the President. But in choosing the President, the votes shall be taken by states, the representation from each state having one vote; a quorum for this purpose shall consist of a member or members from two-thirds of the states, and a majority of all states shall be necessary to a choice. And if the House of Representatives shall not choose a President whenever the right of choice shall devolve upon them, before the fourth day of March next following, then the

Vice-President shall act as President, as in the case of the death or other constitutional disability of the President.—The person having the greatest number of votes as Vice-President, shall be the Vice-President, if such number be a majority of the whole number of Electors appointed, and if no person have a majority, then from the two highest numbers on the list, the Senate shall choose the Vice-President; a quorum for the purpose shall consist of two-thirds of the whole number of Senators, and a majority of the whole number shall be necessary to a choice. But no person constitutionally ineligible to the office of President shall be eligible to that of Vice-President of the United States.

AMENDMENT XIII [1865]

Section 1.   Neither slavery nor involuntary servitude, except as a punishment for crime whereof the party shall have been duly convicted, shall exist within the United States, or any place subject to their jurisdiction.

Section 2.   Congress shall have power to enforce this article by appropriate legislation.

AMENDMENT XIV [1868]

Section 1.   All persons born or naturalized in the United States, and subject to the jurisdiction thereof, are citizens of the United States and of the State wherein they reside. No State shall make or enforce any law which shall abridge the privileges or immunities of citizens of the United States; nor shall any State deprive any person of life, liberty, or property, without due process of law; nor deny to any person within its jurisdiction the equal protection of the laws.

Section 2.   Representatives shall be apportioned among the several States according to their respective numbers, counting the whole number of persons in each State, excluding Indians not taxed. But when the right to vote at any election for the choice of electors for President and Vice President of the United States, Representatives in Congress, the Executive and Judicial officers of a State, or the members of the Legislature thereof, is denied to any of the male inhabitants of such State, being twenty-one years of age, and citizens of the United States, or in any way abridged, except for participation in rebellion, or other crime, the basis of representation therein shall be reduced in the proportion which the number of such male citizens shall bear to the whole number of male citizens twenty-one years of age in such State.

Section 3.   No person shall be a Senator or Representative in Congress, or elector of President and Vice President, or hold any office, civil or military, under the United States, or under any State, who having previously taken an oath, as a member of Congress, or as an officer of the United States, or as a member of any State legislature, or as an executive or judicial officer of any State, to support the Constitution of the United States, shall have engaged in insurrection or rebellion against the same, or given aid or comfort to the enemies thereof. But Congress may by a vote of two-thirds of each House, remove such disability.

Section 4.   The validity of the public debt of the United States, authorized by law, including debts incurred for payment of pensions and bounties for services in suppressing insurrection or rebellion, shall not be questioned. But neither the United States nor any State shall assume or pay any debt or obligation incurred in aid of insurrection or rebellion against the United States, or any claim for the loss or emancipation of any slave; but all such debts, obligations and claims shall be held illegal and void.

Section 5.   The Congress shall have power to enforce, by appropriate legislation, the provisions of this article.

AMENDMENT XV [1870]

Section 1.   The right of citizens of the United States to vote shall not be denied or abridged by the United States or by any State on account of race, color, or previous condition of servitude.

Section 2.   The Congress shall have power to enforce this article by appropriate legislation.

AMENDMENT XVI [1913]

The Congress shall have power to lay and collect taxes on incomes, from whatever source derived, without apportionment among the several States, and without regard to any census or enumeration.

AMENDMENT XVII [1913]

(1)   The Senate of the United States shall be composed of two Senators from each State, elected by the people thereof, for six years; and each Senator shall have one vote. The electors in each State shall have the qualifications requisite

for electors of the most numerous branch of the State legislatures.

(2) When vacancies happen in the representation of any State in the Senate, the executive authority of such State shall issue writs of election to fill such vacancies: *Provided,* That the legislature of any State may empower the executive thereof to make temporary appointments until the people fill the vacancies by election as the legislature may direct.

(3) This amendment shall not be so construed as to affect the election or term of any Senator chosen before it becomes valid as part of the Constitution.

AMENDMENT XVIII [1919]

Section 1. After one year from the ratification of this article the manufacture, sale, or transportation of intoxicating liquors within, the importation thereof into, or the exportation thereof from the United States and all territory subject to the jurisdiction thereof for beverage purposes is hereby prohibited.

Section 2. The Congress and the several States shall have concurrent power to enforce this article by appropriate legislation.

Section 3. This article shall be inoperative unless it shall have been ratified as an amendment to the Constitution by the legislatures of the several States, as provided in the Constitution, within seven years from the date of the submission hereof to the States by the Congress.

AMENDMENT XIX [1920]

(1) The right of citizens of the United States to vote shall not be denied or abridged by the United States or by any State on account of sex.

(2) Congress shall have power to enforce this article by appropriate legislation.

AMENDMENT XX [1933]

Section 1. The terms of the President and Vice President shall end at noon on the 20th day of January, and the terms of Senators and Representatives at noon on the 3d day of January, of the years in which such terms would have ended if this article had not been ratified; and the terms of their successors shall then begin.

Section 2. The Congress shall assemble at least once in every year, and such meeting shall begin at noon on the 3d day of January, unless they shall by law appoint a different day.

Section 3. If, at the time fixed for the beginning of the term of the President, the President elect shall have died, the Vice President elect shall become President. If the President shall not have been chosen before the time fixed for the beginning of his term, or if the President elect shall have failed to qualify, then the Vice President elect shall act as President until a President shall have qualified; and the Congress may by law provide for the case wherein neither a President elect nor a Vice President elect shall have qualified, declaring who shall then act as President, or the manner in which one who is to act shall be selected, and such person shall act accordingly until a President or Vice President shall have qualified.

Section 4. The Congress may by law provide for the case of the death of any of the persons from whom the House of Representatives may choose a President whenever the right of choice shall have devolved upon them, and for the case of the death of any of the persons from whom the Senate may choose a Vice President whenever the right of choice shall have devolved upon them.

Section 5. Sections 1 and 2 shall take effect on the 15th day of October following the ratification of this article.

Section 6. This article shall be inoperative unless it shall have been ratified as an amendment to the Constitution by the legislatures of three-fourths of the several States within seven years from the date of its submission.

AMENDMENT XXI [1933]

Section 1. The eighteenth article of amendment to the Constitution of the United States is hereby repealed.

Section 2. The transportation or importation into any State, Territory, or possession of the United States for delivery or use therein of intoxicating liquors, in violation of the laws thereof, is hereby prohibited.

Section 3. This article shall be inoperative unless it shall have been ratified as an amendment to the Constitution by conventions in the several States, as provided in the Constitution, within seven years from the date of the submission hereof to the States by the Congress.

AMENDMENT XXII [1951]

Section 1.   No person shall be elected to the office of the President more than twice, and no person who has held the office of President, or acted as President, for more than two years of a term to which some other person was elected President shall be elected to the office of President more than once. But this Article shall not apply to any person holding the office of President when this Article was proposed by the Congress, and shall not prevent any person who may be holding the office of President, or acting as President, during the term within which this Article becomes operative from holding the office of President or acting as President during the remainder of such term.

Section 2.   This article shall be inoperative unless it shall have been ratified as an amendment to the Constitution by the legislatures of three-fourths of the several States within seven years from the date of its submission to the States by the Congress.

AMENDMENT XXIII [1961]

Section 1.   The District constituting the seat of Government of the United States shall appoint in such manner as the Congress may direct:

A number of electors of President and Vice President equal to the whole number of Senators and Representatives in Congress to which the District would be entitled if it were a State, but in no event more than the least populous state; they shall be in addition to those appointed by the states, but they shall be considered, for the purposes of the election of President and Vice President, to be electors appointed by a state; and they shall meet in the District and perform such duties as provided by the twelfth article of amendment.

Section 2.   The Congress shall have power to enforce this article by appropriate legislation.

AMENDMENT XXIV [1964]

Section 1.   The right of citizens of the United States to vote in any primary or other election for President or Vice President, for electors for President or Vice President, or for Senator or Representative in Congress, shall not be denied or abridged by the United States,

or any State by reason of failure to pay any poll tax or other tax.

Section 2.   The Congress shall have power to enforce this article by appropriate legislation.

AMENDMENT XXV [1967]

Section 1.   In case of the removal of the President from office or of his death or resignation, the Vice President shall become President.

Section 2.   Whenever there is a vacancy in the office of the Vice President, the President shall nominate a Vice President who shall take office upon confirmation by a majority vote of both Houses of Congress.

Section 3.   Whenever the President transmits to the President pro tempore of the Senate and the Speaker of the House of Representatives his written declaration that he is unable to discharge the powers and duties of his office, and until he transmits to them a written declaration to the contrary, such powers and duties shall be discharged by the Vice President as Acting President.

Section 4.   Whenever the Vice President and a majority of either the principal officers of the executive departments or of such other body as Congress may by law provide, transmit to the President pro tempore of the Senate and the Speaker of the House of Representatives their written declaration that the President is unable to discharge the powers and duties of his office, the Vice President shall immediately assume the powers and duties of the office as Acting President.

Thereafter, when the President transmits to the President pro tempore of the Senate and the Speaker of the House of Representatives his written declaration that no inability exists, he shall resume the powers and duties of his office unless the Vice President and a majority of either the principal officers of the executive department or of such other body as Congress may by law provide, transmit within four days to the President pro tempore of the Senate and the Speaker of the House of Representatives their written declaration and the President is unable to discharge the powers and duties of his office. Thereupon Congress shall decide the issue, assembling within forty-eight hours for that purpose if not in session. If the Congress, within twenty-one days after receipt of the latter written declaration, or, if Congress is not in session, within twenty-one days after Congress is required to assemble, determines by two-thirds vote of both Houses that the President is unable to discharge the powers and duties of his office, the Vice President shall continue to discharge the same as Acting President; otherwise, the President shall resume the powers and duties of his office.

AMENDMENT XXVI [1971]

Section 1.   The right of citizens of the United States, who are eighteen years of age or older, to vote shall not be denied or abridged by the United States or by any State on account of age.

Section 2.   The Congress shall have power to enforce this article by appropriate legislation.

AMENDMENT XXVII [1992]

No law varying the compensation for the services of the Senators and Representatives shall take effect until an election of Representatives shall have intervened.

The Model Business Corporation Act

§ 1. Short Title*
This Act shall be known and may be cited as the ".....† Business Corporation Act."

§ 2. Definitions
As used in this Act, unless the context otherwise requires, the term:

(a) "Corporation" or "domestic corporation" means a corporation for profit subject to the provisions of this Act, except a foreign corporation.

(b) "Foreign corporation" means a corporation for profit organized under laws other than the laws of this State for a purpose or purposes for which a corporation may be organized under this Act.

(c) "Articles of incorporation" means the original or restated articles of incorporation or articles of consolidation and all amendments thereto including articles of merger.

(d) "Shares" means the units into which the proprietary interests in a corporation are divided.

(e) "Subscriber" means one who subscribes for shares in a corporation, whether before or after incorporation.

(f) "Shareholder" means one who is a holder of record of shares in a corporation. If the articles of incorporation or the by-laws so provide, the board of directors may adopt by resolution a procedure whereby a shareholder of the corporation may certify in writing to the corporation that all or a portion of the shares registered in the name of such shareholder are held for the account of a specified person or persons. The resolution shall set forth (1) the classification of shareholder who may certify, (2) the purpose or purposes for which the certification may be made, (3) the form of certification and information to be contained therein, (4) if the certification is with respect to a record date or closing of the stock transfer books within which the certification must be received by the corporation and (5) such other provisions with respect to the procedure as are deemed necessary or desirable. Upon receipt by the corporation of a certification complying with the procedure, the persons specified in the certification shall be deemed, for the purpose or purposes set forth in the certification, to be the holders of record of the number of shares specified in place of the shareholder making the certification.

(g) "Authorized shares" means the shares of all classes which the corporation is authorized to issue.

(h) "Employee" includes officers but not directors. A director may accept duties which make him also an employee.

---

*[By the Editor] The Model Business Corporation Act prepared by the Committee on Corporate Laws (Section of Corporation, Banking and Business Law) of the American Bar Association was originally patterned after the Illinois Business Corporation Act of 1933. It was first published as a complete act in 1950. In subsequent years several revisions, addenda and optional or alternative provisions were added. The Act was substantially revised and renumbered in 1969.

This Act should be distinguished from the Model Business Corporation Act promulgated in 1928 by the Commissioners on Uniform State Laws under the name "Uniform Business Corporation Act" and renamed Model Business Corporation Act in 1943. This Uniform Act was withdrawn in 1957.

The Model Business Corporation Act has been influential in the codification of corporation statutes in more than 35 states. However, there is no state that has totally adopted it in its current form. Moreover, since the Model Act itself has been substantially modified from time to time, there is considerable variation among the statutes of the states that used this Act as a model.
†Insert name of State.

(i)   "Distribution" means a direct or indirect transfer of money or other property (except its own shares) or incurrence of indebtedness, by a corporation to or for the benefit of any of its shareholders in respect of any of its shares, whether by dividend or by purchase, redemption or other acquisition of its shares, or otherwise.

§ 3. Purposes

Corporations may be organized under this Act for any lawful purpose or purposes, except for the purpose of banking or insurance.

§ 4. General Powers

Each corporation shall have power:

(a)   To have perpetual succession by its corporate name unless a limited period of duration is stated in its articles of incorporation.

(b)   To sue and be sued, complain and defend, in its corporate name.

(c)   To have a corporate seal which may be altered at pleasure, and to use the same by causing it, or a facsimile thereof, to be impressed or affixed or in any other manner reproduced.

(d)   To purchase, take, receive, lease, or otherwise acquire, own, hold, improve, use and otherwise deal in and with, real or personal property, or any interest therein, wherever situated.

(e)   To sell, convey, mortgage, pledge, lease, exchange, transfer and otherwise dispose of all or any part of its property and assets.

(f)   To lend money and use its credit to assist its employees.

(g)   To purchase, take, receive, subscribe for, or otherwise acquire, own, hold, vote, use, employ, sell, mortgage, lend, pledge, or otherwise dispose of, and otherwise use and deal in and with, shares or other interests in, or obligations of, other domestic or foreign corporations, associations, partnerships or individuals, or direct or indirect obligations of the United States or of any other government, state, territory, governmental district or municipality or of any instrumentality thereof.

(h)   To make contracts and guarantees and incur liabilities, borrow money at such rates of interest as the corporation may determine, issue its notes, bonds, and other obligations, and secure any of its obligations by mortgage or pledge of all or any of its property, franchises and income.

(i)   To lend money for its corporate purposes, invest and reinvest its funds, and take and hold real and personal property as security for the payment of funds so loaned or invested.

(j)   To conduct its business, carry on its operations and have offices and exercise the powers granted by this Act, within or without this State.

(k)   To elect or appoint officers and agents of the corporation, and define their duties and fix their compensation.

(l)   To make and alter by-laws, not inconsistent with its articles of incorporation or with the laws of this State, for the administration and regulation of the affairs of the corporation.

(m)   To make donations for the public welfare or for charitable, scientific or educational purposes.

(n)   To transact any lawful business which the board of directors shall find will be in aid of governmental policy.

(o)   To pay pensions and establish pension plans, pension trusts, profit sharing plans, stock bonus plans, stock option plans and other incentive plans for any or all of its directors, officers and employees.

(p)   To be a promoter, partner, member, associate, or manager of any partnership, joint venture, trust or other enterprise.

(q)   To have and exercise all powers necessary or convenient to effect its purposes.

§ 5. Indemnification of Directors and Officers

(a)   As used in this section:

(1)   "Director" means any person who is or was a director of the corporation and any person who, while a director of the corporation, is or was serving at the request of the corporation as a director, officer, partner, trustee, employee or agent of another foreign or domestic

corporation, partnership, joint venture, trust, other enterprise or employee benefit plan.

(2) "Corporation" includes any domestic or foreign predecessor entity of the corporation in a merger, consolidation or other transaction in which the predecessor's existence ceased upon consummation of such transaction.

(3) "Expenses" include attorneys' fees.

(4) "Official capacity" means

(A)   when used with respect to a director, the office of director in the corporation, and

(B)   when used with respect to a person other than a director, as contemplated in subsection

(i)   the elective or appointive office in the corporation held by the officer or the employment or agency relationship undertaken by the employee or agent in behalf of the corporation,

but in each case does not include service for any other foreign or domestic corporation or any partnership, joint venture, trust, other enterprise, or employee benefit plan.

(5) "Party" includes a person who was, is, or is threatened to be made, a named defendant or respondent in a proceeding.

(6) "Proceeding" means any threatened, pending or completed action, suit or proceeding, whether civil, criminal, administrative or investigative.

(b)   A corporation shall have power to indemnify any person made a party to any proceeding by reason of the fact that he is or was a director if

(1)   he conducted himself in good faith; and

(2)   he reasonably believed

(A)   in the case of conduct in his official capacity with the corporation, that his conduct was in its best interests, and

(B)   in all other cases, that his conduct was at least not opposed to its best interests; and

(3)   in the case of any criminal proceeding, he had no reasonable cause to believe his conduct was unlawful.

Indemnification may be made against judgments, penalties, fines, settlements and reasonable expenses, actually incurred by the person in connection with the proceeding; except that if the proceeding was by or in the right of the corporation, indemnification may be made only against such reasonable expenses and shall not be made in respect of any proceeding in which the person shall have been adjudged to be liable to the corporation. The termination of any proceeding by judgment, order, settlement, conviction, or upon a plea of nolo contendere or its equivalent, shall not, of itself, be determinative that the person did not meet the requisite standard of conduct set forth in this subsection (b).

(c)   A director shall not be indemnified under subsection (b) in respect of any proceeding charging improper personal benefit to him, whether or not involving action in his official capacity, in which he shall have been adjudged to be liable on the basis that personal benefit was improperly received by him.

(d)   Unless limited by the articles of incorporation,

(1)   a director who has been wholly successful, on the merits or otherwise, in the defense of any proceeding referred to in subsection (b) shall be indemnified against reasonable expenses incurred by him in connection with the proceeding; and

(2)   a court of appropriate jurisdiction, upon application of a director and such notice as the court shall require, shall have authority to order indemnification in the following circumstances:

(A)   if it determines a director is entitled to reimbursement under clause (1), the court shall order indemnification, in which case the director shall also be entitled to recover the expenses of securing such reimbursement; or

(B)   if it determines that the director is fairly and reasonably entitled to indemnification in view of all the relevant circumstances, whether or not he has met the standard of conduct set forth in subsection (b) or has been adjudged liable in the circumstances described in subsection (c), the court may order such indemnification as the court shall deem proper, except that indemnification with respect to any proceeding by or in the right of the corporation or in which liability shall have been adjudged in the circumstances described in subsection (c) shall be limited to expenses.

A court of appropriate jurisdiction may be the same court in which the proceeding involving the director's liability took place.

(e)   No indemnification under subsection (b) shall be made by the corporation unless authorized in the specific case after a determination has been made that indemnification of the director is permissible in the circumstances because he has met the standard of conduct set forth in subsection (b). Such determination shall be made:

(1) by the board of directors by a majority vote of a quorum consisting of directors not at the time parties to the proceeding; or

(2) if such a quorum cannot be obtained, then by a majority vote of a committee of the board, duly designated to act in the matter by a majority vote of the full board (in which designation directors who are parties may participate), consisting solely of two or more directors not at the time parties to the proceeding; or

(3) by special legal counsel, selected by the board of directors or a committee thereof by vote as set forth in clauses (1) or (2) of this subsection (e), or, if the requisite quorum of the full board cannot be obtained therefor and such committee cannot be established, by a majority vote of the full board (in which selection directors who are parties may participate); or

(4) by the shareholders.

Authorization of indemnification and determination as to reasonableness of expenses shall be made in the same manner as the determination that indemnification is permissible, except that if the determination that indemnification is permissible is made by special legal counsel, authorization of indemnification and determination as to reasonableness of expenses shall be made in a manner specified in clause (3) in the preceding sentence for the selection of such counsel. Shares held by directors who are parties to the proceeding shall not be voted on the subject matter under this subsection (e).

(f)   Reasonable expenses incurred by a director who is a party to a proceeding may be paid or reimbursed by the corporation in advance of the final disposition of such proceeding upon receipt by the corporation of

(1) a written affirmation by the director of his good faith belief that he has met the standard of conduct necessary for indemnification by the corporation as authorized in this section, and

(2) a written undertaking by or on behalf of the director to repay such amount if it shall ultimately be determined that he has not met such standard of conduct, and after a determination

that the facts then known to those making the determination would not preclude indemnification under this section. The undertaking required by clause (2) shall be an unlimited general obligation of the director but need not be secured and may be accepted without reference to financial ability to make repayment. Determinations and authorizations of payments under this subsection (f) shall be made in the manner specified in subsection (e).

(g)   No provision for the corporation to indemnify or to advance expenses to a director who is made a party to the proceeding, whether contained in the articles of incorporation, the by-laws, a resolution of shareholders or directors, an agreement or otherwise (except as contemplated by subsection (j)), shall be valid unless consistent with this section or, to the extent that indemnity hereunder is limited by the articles of incorporation, consistent therewith. Nothing contained in this section shall limit the corporation's power to pay or reimburse expenses incurred by a director in connection with his appearance as a witness in a proceeding at a time when he has not been made a named defendant or respondent in the proceeding.

(h)   For purposes of this section, the corporation shall be deemed to have requested a director to serve an employee benefit plan whenever the performance by him of his duties to the corporation also imposes duties on, or otherwise involves services by, him to the plan or participants or beneficiaries of the plan; excise taxes assessed on a director with respect to an employee benefit plan pursuant to applicable law shall be deemed "fines"; and action taken or omitted by him with respect to an employee benefit plan in the performance of his duties for a purpose reasonably believed by him to be in the interest of the participants and beneficiaries of the plan shall be deemed to be for a purpose which is not opposed to the best interests of the corporation.

(i)   Unless limited by the articles of incorporation,

(1) an officer of the corporation shall be indemnified as and to the same extent provided in subsection (d) for a director and shall be entitled to the same extent as a director to seek indemnification pursuant to the provisions of subsection (d);

(2) a corporation shall have the power to indemnify and to advance expenses to an officer, employee or agent of the corporation to the same extent

that it may indemnify and advance expenses to directors pursuant to this section; and

(3) a corporation, in addition, shall have the power to indemnify and to advance expenses to an officer, employee or agent who is not a director to such further extent, consistent with law, as may be provided by its articles of incorporation, by-laws, general or specific action of its board of directors, or contract.

(j) A corporation shall have power to purchase and maintain insurance on behalf of any person who is or was a director, officer, employee or agent of the corporation, or who, while a director, officer, employee or agent of the corporation, is or was serving at the request of the corporation as a director, officer, partner, trustee, employee or agent of another foreign or domestic corporation, partnership, joint venture, trust, other enterprise or employee benefit plan, against any liability asserted against him and incurred by him in any such capacity or arising out of his status as such, whether or not the corporation would have the power to indemnify him against such liability under the provisions of this section.

(k) Any indemnification of, or advance of expenses to, a director in accordance with this section, if arising out of a proceeding by or in the right of the corporation, shall be reported in writing to the shareholders with or before the notice of the next shareholders' meeting.

§ 6. Power of Corporation to Acquire Its Own Shares

A corporation shall have the power to acquire its own shares. All of its own shares acquired by a corporation shall, upon acquisition, constitute authorized but unissued shares, unless the articles of incorporation provide that they shall not be reissued, in which case the authorized shares shall be reduced by the number of shares acquired.

If the number of authorized shares is reduced by an acquisition, the corporation shall, not later than the time it files its next annual report under this Act with the Secretary of State, file a statement of cancellation showing the reduction in the authorized shares. The statement of cancellation shall be executed in duplicate by the corporation by its president or a vice president and by its secretary or an assistant secretary, and verified by one of the officers signing such statement, and shall set forth:

(a) The name of the corporation.

(b) The number of acquired shares cancelled, itemized by classes and series.

(c) The aggregate number of authorized shares, itemized by classes and series, after giving effect to such cancellation.

Duplicate originals of such statement shall be delivered to the Secretary of State. If the Secretary of State finds that such statement conforms to law, he shall, when all fees and franchise taxes have been paid as in this Act prescribed:

(1) Endorse on each of such duplicate originals the word "Filed," and the month, day and year of the filing thereof.
(2) File one of such duplicate originals in his office.
(3) Return the other duplicate original to the corporation or its representative.

§ 7. Defense of Ultra Vires

No act of a corporation and no conveyance or transfer of real or personal property to or by a corporation shall be invalid by reason of the fact that the corporation was without capacity or power to do such act or to make or receive such conveyance or transfer, but such lack of capacity or power may be asserted:

(a) In a proceeding by a shareholder against the corporation to enjoin the doing of any act or the transfer of real or personal property by or to the corporation. If the unauthorized act or transfer sought to be enjoined is being, or is to be, performed or made pursuant to a contract to which the corporation is a party, the court may, if all of the parties to the contract are parties to the proceeding and if it deems the same to be equitable, set aside and enjoin the performance of such contract, and in so doing may allow to the corporation or to the other parties to the contract, as the case may be, compensation for the loss or damage sustained by either of them which may result from the action of the court in setting aside and enjoining the performance of such contract, but anticipated profits to be derived from the performance of the contract shall not be awarded by the court as a loss or damage sustained.

(b) In a proceeding by the corporation, whether acting directly or through a receiver, trustee, or other legal representative, or through shareholders in a representative suit, against the incumbent or former officers or directors of the corporation.

(c)   In a proceeding by the Attorney General, as provided in this Act, to dissolve the corporation, or in a proceeding by the Attorney General to enjoin the corporation from the transaction of unauthorized business.

§ 8. Corporate Name

The corporate name:

(a)   Shall contain the word "corporation," "company," "incorporated" or "limited," or shall contain an abbreviation of one of such words.

(b)   Shall not contain any word or phrase which indicates or implies that it is organized for any purpose other than one or more of the purposes contained in its articles of incorporation.

(c)   Shall not be the same as, or deceptively similar to, the name of any domestic corporation existing under the laws of this State or any foreign corporation authorized to transact business in this State, or a name the exclusive right to which is, at the time, reserved in the manner provided in this Act, or the name of a corporation which has in effect a registration of its corporate name as provided in this Act, except that this provision shall not apply if the applicant files with the Secretary of State either of the following: (1) the written consent of such other corporation or holder of a reserved or registered name to use the same or deceptively similar name and one or more words are added to make such name distinguishable from such other name, or (2) a certified copy of a final decree of a court of competent jurisdiction establishing the prior right of the applicant to the use of such name in this State.

A corporation with which another corporation, domestic or foreign, is merged, or which is formed by the reorganization or consolidation of one or more domestic or foreign corporations or upon a sale, lease or other disposition to or exchange with, a domestic corporation of all or substantially all the assets of another corporation, domestic or foreign, including its name, may have the same name as that used in this State by any of such corporations if such other corporation was organized under the laws of, or is authorized to transact business in, this State.

§ 9. Reserved Name

The exclusive right to the use of a corporate name may be reserved by:

(a)   Any person intending to organize a corporation under this Act.

(b)   Any domestic corporation intending to change its name.

(c)   Any foreign corporation intending to make application for a certificate of authority to transact business in this State.

(d)   Any foreign corporation authorized to transact business in this State and intending to change its name.

(e)   Any person intending to organize a foreign corporation and intending to have such corporation make application for a certificate of authority to transact business in this State.

The reservation shall be made by filing with the Secretary of State an application to reserve a specified corporate name, executed by the applicant. If the Secretary of State finds that the name is available for corporate use, he shall reserve the same for the exclusive use of the applicant for a period of one hundred and twenty days.

The right to the exclusive use of a specified corporate name so reserved may be transferred to any other person or corporation by filing in the office of the Secretary of State a notice of such transfer, executed by the applicant for whom the name was reserved, and specifying the name and address of the transferee.

§ 10. Registered Name

Any corporation organized and existing under the laws of any state or territory of the United States may register its corporate name under this Act, provided its corporate name is not the same as, or deceptively similar to, the name of any domestic corporation existing under the laws of this State, or the name of any foreign corporation authorized to transact business in this State, or any corporate name reserved or registered under this Act.

Such registration shall be made by:

(a)   Filing with the Secretary of State (1) an application for registration executed by the corporation by an officer thereof, setting forth the name of the corporation, the state or territory under the laws of which it is incorporated, the date of its incorporation, a statement that it is carrying on or doing business, and a brief statement of the business in which it is engaged, and (2) a certificate setting forth that such corporation is in good standing under the laws of the state or territory wherein it is organized, executed by the Secretary of State of such state or territory or by such other official as may have custody of the records pertaining to corporations, and

(b)   Paying to the Secretary of State a registration fee in the amount of .... for each month, or fraction thereof, between the date of filing such application and December 31st of the calendar year in which such application is filed.

Such registration shall be effective until the close of the calendar year in which the application for registration is filed.

§ 11. Renewal of Registered Name

A corporation which has in effect a registration of its corporate name, may renew such registration from year to year by annually filing an application for renewal setting forth the facts required to be set forth in an original application for registration and a certificate of good standing as required for the original registration and by paying a fee of .... A renewal application may be filed between the first day of October and the thirty-first day of December in each year, and shall extend the registration for the following calendar year.

§ 12. Registered Office and Registered Agent

Each corporation shall have and continuously maintain in this State:

(a)   A registered office which may be, but need not be, the same as its place of business.

(b)   A registered agent, which agent may be either an individual resident in this State whose business office is identical with such registered office, or a domestic corporation, or a foreign corporation authorized to transact business in this State, having a business office identical with such registered office.

§ 13. Change of Registered Office or Registered Agent

A corporation may change its registered office or change its registered agent, or both, upon filing in the office of the Secretary of State a statement setting forth:

(a)   The name of the corporation.

(b)   The address of its then registered office.

(c)   If the address of its registered office is to be changed, the address to which the registered office is to be changed.

(d)   The name of its then registered agent.

(e)   If its registered agent is to be changed, the name of its successor registered agent.

(f)   That the address of its registered office and the address of the business office of its registered agent, as changed, will be identical.

(g)   That such change was authorized by resolution duly adopted by its board of directors.

Such statement shall be executed by the corporation by its president, or a vice president, and verified by him, and delivered to the Secretary of State. If the Secretary of State finds that such statement conforms to the provisions of this Act, he shall file such statement in his office, and upon such filing the change of address of the registered office, or the appointment of a new registered agent, or both, as the case may be, shall become effective.

Any registered agent of a corporation may resign as such agent upon filing a written notice thereof, executed in duplicate, with the Secretary of State, who shall forthwith mail a copy thereof to the corporation at its registered office. The appointment of such agent shall terminate upon the expiration of thirty days after receipt of such notice by the Secretary of State.

If a registered agent changes his or its business address to another place within the same .... ,* he or it may change such address and the address of the registered office of any corporation of which he or it is registered agent by filing a statement as required above except that it need be signed only by the registered agent and need not be responsive to (e) or (g) and must recite that a copy of the statement has been mailed to the corporation.

§ 14. Service of Process on Corporation

The registered agent so appointed by a corporation shall be an agent of such corporation upon whom any process, notice or demand required or permitted by law to be served upon the corporation may be served.

---

* Supply designation of jurisdiction, such as county, etc., in accordance with local practice.

Whenever a corporation shall fail to appoint or maintain a registered agent in this State, or whenever its registered agent cannot with reasonable diligence be found at the registered office, then the Secretary of State shall be an agent of such corporation upon whom any such process, notice, or demand may be served. Service on the Secretary of State of any such process, notice, or demand shall be made by delivering to and leaving with him, or with any clerk having charge of the corporation department of his office, duplicate copies of such process, notice or demand. In the event any such process, notice or demand is served on the Secretary of State, he shall immediately cause one of the copies thereof to be forwarded by registered mail, addressed to the corporation at its registered office. Any service so had on the Secretary of State shall be returnable in not less than thirty days.

The Secretary of State shall keep a record of all processes, notices and demands served upon him under this section, and shall record therein the time of such service and his action with reference thereto.

Nothing herein contained shall limit or affect the right to serve any process, notice or demand required or permitted by law to be served upon a corporation in any other manner now or hereafter permitted by law.

§ 15. Authorized Shares

Each corporation shall have power to create and issue the number of shares stated in its articles of incorporation. Such shares may be divided into one or more classes with such designations, preferences, limitations, and relative rights as shall be stated in the articles of incorporation. The articles of incorporation may limit or deny the voting rights of or provide special voting rights for the shares of any class to the extent not inconsistent with the provisions of this Act.

Without limiting the authority herein contained, a corporation, when so provided in its articles of incorporation, may issue shares of preferred or special classes:

(a)   Subject to the right of the corporation to redeem any of such shares at the price fixed by the articles of incorporation for the redemption thereof.

(b)   Entitling the holders thereof to cumulative, noncumulative or partially cumulative dividends.

(c)   Having preference over any other class or classes of shares as to the payment of dividends.

(d)   Having preference in the assets of the corporation over any other class or classes of shares upon the voluntary or involuntary liquidation of the corporation.

(e)   Convertible into shares of any other class or into shares of any series of the same or any other class, except a class having prior or superior rights and preferences as to dividends or distribution of assets upon liquidation.

§ 16. Issuance of Shares of Preferred or Special Classes in Series

If the articles of incorporation so provide, the shares of any preferred or special class may be divided into and issued in series. If the shares of any such class are to be issued in series, then each series shall be so designated as to distinguish the shares thereof from the shares of all other series and classes. Any or all of the series of any such class and the variations in the relative rights and preferences as between different series may be fixed and determined by the articles of incorporation, but all shares of the same class shall be identical except as to the following relative rights and preferences, as to which there may be variations between different series:

(A)   The rate of dividend.

(B)   Whether shares may be redeemed and, if so, the redemption price and the terms and conditions of redemption.

(C)   The amount payable upon shares in the event of voluntary and involuntary liquidation.

(D)   Sinking fund provisions, if any, for the redemption or purchase of shares.

(E)   The terms and conditions, if any, on which shares may be converted.

(F)   Voting rights, if any.

If the articles of incorporation shall expressly vest authority in the board of directors, then, to the extent that the articles of incorporation shall not have established series and fixed and determined the variations in the relative rights and preferences as between series, the board of directors shall have authority to divide any or all of such classes into series and, within the limitations set forth in this section and in the articles of incorporation, fix and determine the relative rights and preferences of the shares of any series so established.

In order for the board of directors to establish a series, where authority so to do is contained in the articles of incorporation, the board of directors shall adopt a resolution setting forth the designation of the series and fixing and determining the relative rights and preferences thereof, or so much thereof as shall not be fixed and determined by the articles of incorporation.

Prior to the issue of any shares of a series established by the resolution adopted by the board of directors, the corporation shall file in the office of the Secretary of State a statement setting forth:

(a)   The name of the corporation.

(b)   A copy of the resolution establishing and designating the series, and fixing and determining the relative rights and preferences thereof.

(c)   The date of adoption of such resolution.

(d)   That such resolution was duly adopted by the board of directors.

Such statement shall be executed in duplicate by the corporation by its president or a vice president and by its secretary or an assistant secretary, and verified by one of the officers signing such statement, and shall be delivered to the Secretary of State. If the Secretary of State finds that such statement conforms to law, he shall, when all franchise taxes and fees have been paid as in this Act prescribed:

(1)   Endorse on each of such duplicate originals the word "Filed," and the month, day, and year of the filing thereof.
(2)   File one of such duplicate originals in his office.
(3)   Return the other duplicate original to the corporation or its representative.

Upon the filing of such statement by the Secretary of State, the resolution establishing and designating the series and fixing and determining the relative rights and preferences thereof shall become effective and shall constitute an amendment of the articles of incorporation.

§ 17. Subscriptions for Shares

A subscription for shares of a corporation to be organized shall be irrevocable for a period of six months, unless otherwise provided by the terms of the subscription agreement or unless all of the subscribers consent to the revocation of such subscription.

Unless otherwise provided in the subscription agreement, subscriptions for shares, whether made before or after the organization of a corporation, shall be paid in full at such time, or in such installments and at such times, as shall be determined by the board of directors. Any call made by the board of directors for payment on subscriptions shall be uniform as to all shares of the same class or as to all shares of the same series, as the case may be. In case of default in the payment of any installment or call when such payment is due, the corporation may proceed to collect the amount due in the same manner as any debt due the corporation. The by-laws may prescribe other penalties for failure to pay installments or calls that may become due, but no penalty working a forfeiture of a subscription, or of the amounts paid thereon, shall be declared as against any subscriber unless the amount due thereon shall remain unpaid for a period of twenty days after written demand has been made therefor. If mailed, such written demand shall be deemed to be made when deposited in the United States mail in a sealed envelope addressed to the subscriber at his last post-office address known to the corporation, with postage thereon prepaid. In the event of the sale of any shares by reason of any forfeiture, the excess of proceeds realized over the amount due and unpaid on such shares shall be paid to the delinquent subscriber or to his legal representative.

§ 18. Issuance of Shares

Subject to any restrictions in the articles of incorporation:

(a)   Shares may be issued for such consideration as shall be authorized by the board of directors establishing a price (in money or other consideration) or a minimum price or general formula or method by which the price will be determined; and

(b)   Upon authorization by the board of directors, the corporation may issue its own shares in exchange for or in conversion of its outstanding shares, or distribute its own shares, pro rata to its shareholders or the shareholders of one or more classes or series, to effectuate stock dividends or splits, and any such transaction shall not require consideration; provided, that no such issuance of shares of any class or series shall be made to the holders of shares of any other class or series unless it is either expressly provided for in the articles of incorporation, or is authorized by an affirmative vote or the written consent of the holders of at least a majority of the outstanding shares of the class or series in which the distribution is to be made.

§ 19. Payment for Shares

The consideration for the issuance of shares may be paid, in whole or in part, in money, in other property, tangible or intangible, or in labor or services actually performed for the corporation. When payment of the consideration for which shares are to be issued shall have been received by the corporation, such shares shall be nonassessable.

Neither promissory notes nor future services shall constitute payment or part payment for the issuance of shares of a corporation.

In the absence of fraud in the transaction, the judgment of the board of directors or the shareholders, as the case may be, as to the value of the consideration received for shares shall be conclusive.

§ 20. Stock Rights and Options

Subject to any provisions in respect thereof set forth in its articles of incorporation, a corporation may create and issue, whether or not in connection with the issuance and sale of any of its shares or other securities, rights or options entitling the holders thereof to purchase from the corporation shares of any class or classes. Such rights or options shall be evidenced in such manner as the board of directors shall approve and, subject to the provisions of the articles of incorporation, shall set forth the terms upon which, the time or times within which and the price or prices at which such shares may be purchased from the corporation upon the exercise of any such right or option. If such rights or options are to be issued to directors, officers or employees as such of the corporation or of any subsidiary thereof, and not to the shareholders generally, their issuance shall be approved by the affirmative vote of the holders of a majority of the shares entitled to vote thereon or shall be authorized by and consistent with a plan approved or ratified by such a vote of shareholders. In the absence of fraud in the transaction, the judgment of the board of directors as to the adequacy of the consideration received for such rights or options shall be conclusive.

§ 21. Determination of Amount of Stated Capital

[Repealed in 1979].

§ 22. Expenses of Organization, Reorganization and Financing

The reasonable charges and expenses of organization or reorganization of a corporation, and the reasonable expenses of and compensation for the sale or underwriting of its shares, may be paid or allowed by such corporation out of the consideration received by it in payment for its shares without thereby rendering such shares assessable.

§ 23. Shares Represented by Certificates and Uncertified Shares

The shares of a corporation shall be represented by certificates or shall be uncertificated shares. Certificates shall be signed by the chairman or vice-chairman of the board of directors or the president or a vice president and by the treasurer or an assistant treasurer or the secretary or an assistant secretary of the corporation, and may be sealed with the seal of the corporation or a facsimile thereof. Any of or all the signatures upon a certificate may be a facsimile. In case any officer, transfer agent or registrar who has signed or whose facsimile signature has been placed upon such certificate shall have ceased to be such officer, transfer agent or registrar before such certificate is issued, it may be issued by the corporation with the same effect as if he were such officer, transfer agent or registrar at the date of its issue.

Every certificate representing shares issued by a corporation which is authorized to issue shares of more than one class shall set forth upon the face or back of the certificate, or shall state that the corporation will furnish to any shareholder upon request and without charge, a full statement of the designations, preferences, limitations, and relative rights of the shares of each class authorized to be issued, and if the corporation is authorized to issue any preferred or special class in series, the variations in the relative rights and preferences between the shares of each such series so far as the same have been fixed and determined and the authority of the board of directors to fix and determine the relative rights and preferences of subsequent series.

Each certificate representing shares shall state upon the face thereof:

(a)   That the corporation is organized under the laws of this State.

(b)   The name of the person to whom issued.

(c)   The number and class of shares, and the designation of the series, if any, which such certificate represents.

(d)   The par value of each share represented by such certificate, or a statement that the shares are without par value.

No certificate shall be issued for any share until such share is fully paid.

Unless otherwise provided by the articles of incorporation or by-laws, the board of directors of a corporation may provide by resolution that some or all of any or all classes and series of its shares shall be uncertificated shares, provided that such resolution shall not apply to shares represented by a certificate until such certificate is surrendered to the corporation. Without a reasonable time after the issuance or transfer of uncertificated shares, the corporation shall send to the registered owner thereof a written notice containing the information required to be set forth or stated on certificates pursuant to the second and third paragraphs of this section. Except as otherwise expressly provided by law, the rights and obligations of the holders of uncertificated shares and the rights and obligations of the holders of certificates representing shares of the same class and series shall be identical.

§ 24. Fractional Shares

A corporation may (1) issue fractions of a share, either represented by a certificate or uncertificated, (2) arrange for the disposition of fractional interests by those entitled thereto, (3) pay in money the fair value of fractions of a share as of a time when those entitled to receive such fractions are determined, or (4) issue scrip in registered or bearer form which shall entitle the holder to receive a certificate for a full share or an uncertificated full share upon the surrender of such scrip aggregating a full share. A certificate for a fractional share or an uncertificated fractional share shall, but scrip shall not unless otherwise provided therein, entitle the holder to exercise voting rights, to receive dividends thereon, and to participate in any of the assets of the corporation in the event of liquidation. The board of directors may cause scrip to be issued subject to the condition that it shall become void if not exchanged for certificates representing full shares or uncertificated full shares before a specified date, or subject to the condition that the shares for which scrip is exchangeable may be sold by the corporation and the proceeds thereof distributed to the holders of scrip, or subject to any other conditions which the board of directors may deem advisable.

§ 25. Liability of Subscribers and Shareholders

A holder of or subscriber to shares of a corporation shall be under no obligation to the corporation or its creditors with respect to such shares other than the obligation to pay to the corporation the full consideration for which such shares were issued or to be issued.

Any person becoming an assignee or transferee of shares or of a subscription for shares in good faith and without knowledge or notice that the full consideration therefor has not been paid shall not be personally liable to the corporation or its creditors for any unpaid portion of such consideration.

An executor, administrator, conservator, guardian, trustee, assignee for the benefit of creditors, or receiver shall not be personally liable to the corporation as a holder of or subscriber to shares of a corporation but the estate and funds in his hands shall be so liable.

No pledgee or other holder of shares as collateral security shall be personally liable as a shareholder.

§ 26. Shareholders' Preemptive Rights

The shareholders of a corporation shall have no preemptive right to acquire unissued shares of the corporation, or securities of the corporation convertible into or carrying a right to subscribe to or acquire shares, except to the extent, if any, that such right is provided in the articles of incorporation.

§ 26A. Shareholders' Preemptive Rights [Alternative]

Except to the extent limited or denied by this section or by the articles of incorporation, shareholders shall have a preemptive right to acquire unissued shares or securities convertible into such shares or carrying a right to subscribe to or acquire shares.

Unless otherwise provided in the articles of incorporation,

(a)   No preemptive right shall exist.

(1)   to acquire any shares issued to directors, officers or employees pursuant to approval by the affirmative vote of the holders of a majority of the shares entitled to vote thereon or when authorized by and consistent with a plan theretofore approved by such a vote of shareholders; or

(2)   to acquire any shares sold otherwise than for money.

(b)   Holders of shares of any class that is preferred or limited as to dividends or assets shall not be entitled to any preemptive right.

(c)   Holders of shares of common stock shall not be entitled to any preemptive right to shares of any class that is preferred or limited as to dividends or assets or to any obligations, unless convertible into shares of common stock or carrying a right to subscribe to or acquire shares of common stock.

(d) Holders of common stock without voting power shall have no preemptive right to shares of common stock with voting power.

(e) The preemptive right shall be only an opportunity to acquire shares or other securities under such terms and conditions as the board of directors may fix for the purpose of providing a fair and reasonable opportunity for the exercise of such right.

§ 27. By-Laws

The initial by-laws of a corporation shall be adopted by its board of directors. The power to alter, amend or repeal the by-laws or adopt new by-laws, subject to repeal or change by action of the shareholders, shall be vested in the board of directors unless reserved to the shareholders by the articles of incorporation. The by-laws may contain any provisions for the regulation and management of the affairs of the corporation not inconsistent with law or the articles of incorporation.

§ 27A. By-Laws and Other Powers in Emergency [Optional]

The board of directors of any corporation may adopt emergency by-laws, subject to repeal or change by action of the shareholders, which shall, notwithstanding any different provision elsewhere in this Act or in the articles of incorporation or by-laws, be operative during any emergency in the conduct of the business of the corporation resulting from an attack on the United States or any nuclear or atomic disaster. The emergency by-laws may make any provision that may be practical and necessary for the circumstances of the emergency, including provisions that:

(a) A meeting of the board of directors may be called by any officer or director in such manner and under such conditions as shall be prescribed in the emergency by-laws;

(b) The director or directors in attendance at the meeting, or any greater number fixed by the emergency by-laws, shall constitute a quorum; and

(c) The officers or other persons designated on a list approved by the board of directors before the emergency, all in such order of priority and subject to such

conditions, and for such period of time (not longer than reasonably necessary after the termination of the emergency) as may be provided in the emergency by-laws or in the resolution approving the list shall, to the extent required to provide a quorum at any meeting of the board of directors, be deemed directors for such meeting.

The board of directors, either before or during any such emergency, may provide, and from time to time modify, lines of succession in the event that during such an emergency any or all officers or agents of the corporation shall for any reason be rendered incapable of discharging their duties.

The board of directors, either before or during any such emergency, may, effective in the emergency, change the head office or designate several alternative head offices or regional offices, or authorize the officers so to do.

To the extent not inconsistent with any emergency by-laws so adopted, the by-laws of the corporation shall remain in effect during any such emergency and upon its termination the emergency by-laws shall cease to be operative.

Unless otherwise provided in emergency by-laws, notice of any meeting of the board of directors during any such emergency may be given only to such of the directors as it may be feasible to reach at the time and by such means as may be feasible at the time, including publication or radio.

To the extent required to constitute a quorum at any meeting of the board of directors during any such emergency, the officers of the corporation who are present shall, unless otherwise provided in emergency by-laws, be deemed, in order of rank and within the same rank in order of seniority, directors for such meeting.

No officer, director or employee acting in accordance with any emergency by-laws shall be liable except for willful misconduct. No officer, director or employee shall be liable for any action taken by him in good faith in such an emergency in furtherance of the ordinary business affairs of the corporation even though not authorized by the by-laws then in effect.

§ 28. Meetings of Shareholders

Meetings of shareholders may be held at such place within or without this State as may be stated in or fixed in accordance with the by-laws. If no other place is stated or so fixed, meetings shall be held at the registered office of the corporation.

An annual meeting of the shareholders shall be held at such time as may be stated in or fixed in accordance with the by-laws. If the annual meeting is not held within any thirteen-month period the Court of .... may, on the application of any shareholder, summarily order a meeting to be held.

Special meetings of the shareholders may be called by the board of directors, the holders of not less than one-tenth of all the shares entitled to vote at the meeting, or such other persons as may be authorized in the articles of incorporation or the by-laws.

§ 29. Notice of Shareholders' Meetings

Written notice stating the place, day and hour of the meeting and, in case of a special meeting, the purpose or purposes for which the meeting is called, shall be delivered not less than ten nor more than fifty days before the date of the meeting, either personally or by mail, by or at the direction of the president, the secretary, or the officer or persons calling the meeting, to each shareholder of record entitled to vote at such meeting. If mailed, such notice shall be deemed to be delivered when deposited in the United States mail addressed to the shareholder at his address as it appears on the stock transfer books of the corporation, with postage thereon prepaid.

§ 30. Closing of Transfer Books and Fixing Record Date

For the purpose of determining shareholders entitled to notice of or to vote at any meeting of shareholders or any adjournment thereof, or entitled to receive payment of any dividend, or in order to make a determination of shareholders for any other proper purpose, the board of directors of a corporation may provide that the stock transfer books shall be closed for a stated period but not to exceed, in any case, fifty days. If the stock transfer books shall be closed for the purpose of determining shareholders entitled to notice of or to vote at a meeting of shareholders, such books shall be closed for at least ten days immediately preceding such meeting. In lieu of closing the stock transfer books, the by-laws, or in the absence of an applicable by-law the board of directors, may fix in advance a date as the record date for any such determination of shareholders, such date in any case to be not more than fifty days and, in case of a meeting of shareholders, not less than ten days prior to the date on which the particular action, requiring such determination of shareholders, is to be taken. If the stock transfer books are not closed and no record date is fixed for the determination of shareholders entitled to notice of or to vote at a meeting of shareholders, or shareholders entitled to receive payment of a dividend, the date on which notice of the meeting is mailed or the date on which the resolution of the board of directors declaring such dividend is adopted, as the case may be, shall be the record date for such determination of shareholders. When a determination of shareholders entitled to vote at any meeting of shareholders has been made as provided in this section, such determination shall apply to any adjournment thereof.

§ 31. Voting Record

The officer or agent having charge of the stock transfer books for shares of a corporation shall make a complete record of the shareholders entitled to vote at such meeting or any adjournment thereof, arranged in alphabetical order, with the address of and the number of shares held by each. Such record shall be produced and kept open at the time and place of the meeting and shall be subject to the inspection of any shareholder during the whole time of the meeting for the purposes thereof.

Failure to comply with the requirements of this section shall not affect the validity of any action taken at such meeting.

An officer or agent having charge of the stock transfer books who shall fail to prepare the record of shareholders, or produce and keep it open for inspection at the meeting, as provided in this section, shall be liable to any shareholder suffering damage on account of such failure, to the extent of such damage.

§ 32. Quorum of Shareholders

Unless otherwise provided in the articles of incorporation, a majority of the shares entitled to vote, represented in person or by proxy, shall constitute a quorum at a meeting of shareholders, but in no event shall a quorum consist of less than one-third of the shares entitled to vote at the meeting. If a quorum is present, the affirmative vote of the majority of the shares represented at the meeting and entitled to vote on the subject matter shall be the act of the shareholders, unless the vote of a greater number or voting by classes is required by this Act or the articles of incorporation or by-laws.

§ 33. Voting of Shares

Each outstanding share, regardless of class, shall be entitled to one vote on each matter submitted to a vote at a meeting of shareholders, except as may be otherwise provided in the articles of incorporation. If the articles of incorporation provide for more or less than one vote for any share, on any matter, every reference in this Act to a majority or other proportion of shares shall refer to such a majority or other proportion of votes entitled to be cast.

Shares held by another corporation if a majority of the shares entitled to vote for the election of directors of such other corporation is held by the corporation, shall not be voted at any meeting or counted in determining the total number of outstanding shares at any given time.

A shareholder may vote either in person or by proxy executed in writing by the shareholder or by his duly authorized attorney-in-fact. No proxy shall be valid after eleven months from the date of its execution, unless otherwise provided in the proxy.

[Either of the following prefatory phrases may be inserted here: "The articles of incorporation may provide that" or "Unless the articles of incorporation otherwise provide"] . . . at each election of directors every shareholder entitled to vote at such election shall have the right to vote, in person or by proxy, the number of shares owned by him for as many persons as there are directors to be elected and for whose election he has a right to vote, or to cumulate his votes by giving one candidate as many votes as the number of such directors multiplied by the number of his shares shall equal, or by distributing such votes on the same principle among any number of such candidates.

Shares standing in the name of another corporation, domestic or foreign, may be voted by such officer, agent or proxy as the by-laws of such other corporation may prescribe, or, in the absence of such provision, as the board of directors of such other corporation may determine.

Shares held by an administrator, executor, guardian or conservator may be voted by him, either in person or by proxy, without a transfer of such shares into his name. Shares standing in the name of a trustee may be voted by him, either in person or by proxy, but no trustee shall be entitled to vote shares held by him without a transfer of such shares into his name.

Shares standing in the name of a receiver may be voted by such receiver, and shares held by or under the control of a receiver may be voted by such receiver without the transfer thereof into his name if authority so to do be contained in an appropriate order of the court by which such receiver was appointed.

A shareholder whose shares are pledged shall be entitled to vote such shares until the shares have been transferred into the name of the pledgee, and thereafter the pledgee shall be entitled to vote the shares so transferred.

On and after the date on which written notice of redemption of redeemable shares has been mailed to the holders thereof and a sum sufficient to redeem such shares has been deposited with a bank or trust company with irrevocable instruction and authority to pay the redemption price to the holders thereof upon surrender of certificates therefor, such shares shall not be entitled to vote on any matter and shall not be deemed to be outstanding shares.

§ 34. Voting Trusts and Agreements Among Shareholders

Any number of shareholders of a corporation may create a voting trust for the purpose of conferring upon a trustee or trustees the right to vote or otherwise represent their shares, for a period of not to exceed ten years, by entering into a written voting trust agreement specifying the terms and conditions of the voting trust, by depositing a counterpart of the agreement with the corporation at its registered office, and by transferring their shares to such trustee or trustees for the purposes of the agreement. Such trustee or trustees shall keep a record of the holders of voting trust certificates evidencing a beneficial interest in the voting trust, giving the names and addresses of all such holders and the number and class of the shares in respect of which the voting trust certificates held by each are issued, and shall deposit a copy of such record with the corporation at its registered office. The counterpart of the voting trust agreement and the copy of such record so deposited with the corporation shall be subject to the same right of examination by a shareholder of the corporation, in person or by agent or attorney, as are the books and records of the corporation, and such counterpart and such copy of such record shall be subject to examination by any holder of record of voting trust certificates, either in person or by agent or attorney, at any reasonable time for any proper purpose.

Agreements among shareholders regarding the voting of their shares shall be valid and enforceable in accordance with their terms. Such agreements shall not be subject to the provisions of this section regarding voting trusts.

§ 35. Board of Directors

All corporate powers shall be exercised by or under authority of, and the business and affairs of a corporation shall be managed under the direction of, a board of directors except as may be otherwise provided in this Act or the articles of incorporation. If any such provision is made in the articles of incorporation, the powers and duties conferred or imposed upon the board of directors by this Act shall be exercised or performed to such extent and by such person or persons as shall be provided in the articles of incorporation. Directors need not be residents of this State or shareholders of the corporation unless the articles of incorporation or by-laws so require. The articles of incorporation or by-laws may prescribe other qualifications for directors. The board of directors shall have authority to fix the compensation of directors unless otherwise provided in the articles of incorporation.

A director shall perform his duties as a director, including his duties as a member of any committee of the board upon which he may serve, in good faith, in a manner he reasonably believes to be in the best interests of the corporation, and with such care as an ordinarily prudent person in a like position would use under similar circumstances. In performing his duties, a director shall be entitled to rely on information, opinions, reports or statements, including financial statements and other financial data, in each case prepared or presented by:

(a)   one or more officers or employees of the corporation whom the director reasonably believes to be reliable and competent in the matters presented,

(b)   counsel, public accountants or other persons as to matters which the director reasonably believes to be within such person's professional or expert competence, or

(c)   a committee of the board upon which he does not serve, duly designated in accordance with a provision of the articles of incorporation or the by-laws, as to matters within its designated authority, which committee the director reasonably believes to merit confidence,

but he shall not be considered to be acting in good faith if he has knowledge concerning the matter in question that would cause such reliance to be unwarranted. A person who so performs his duties shall have no liability by reason of being or having been a director of the corporation.

A director of a corporation who is present at a meeting of its board of directors at which action on any corporate matter is taken shall be presumed to have assented to the action taken unless his dissent shall be entered in the minutes of the meeting or unless he shall file his written dissent to such action with the secretary of the meeting before the adjournment thereof or shall forward such dissent by registered mail to the secretary of the corporation immediately after the adjournment of the meeting. Such right to dissent shall not apply to a director who voted in favor of such action.

§ 36. Number and Election of Directors

The board of directors of a corporation shall consist of one or more members. The number of directors shall be fixed by, or in the manner provided in, the articles of incorporation or the by-laws, except as to the number constituting the initial board of directors, which number shall be fixed by the articles of incorporation. The number of directors may be increased or decreased from time to time by amendment to, or in the manner provided in, the articles of incorporation or the by-laws, but no decrease shall have the effect of shortening the term of any incumbent director. In the absence of a by-law providing for the number of directors, the number shall be the same as that provided for in the articles of incorporation. The names and addresses of the members of the first board of directors shall be stated in the articles of incorporation. Such persons shall hold office until the first annual meeting of shareholders, and until their successors shall have been elected and qualified. At the first annual meeting of shareholders and at each annual meeting thereafter the shareholders shall elect directors to hold office until the next succeeding annual meeting, except in case of the classification of directors as permitted by this Act. Each director shall hold office for the term for which he is elected and until his successor shall have been elected and qualified.

§ 37. Classification of Directors

When the board of directors shall consist of nine or more members, in lieu of electing the whole number of directors annually, the articles of incorporation may provide that the directors be divided into either two or three classes, each class to be as nearly equal in number as possible, the term of office of directors of the first class to expire at the first annual meeting of shareholders after their election, that of the second class to expire at the second annual meeting after their election, and that of the third class, if any, to expire at the third annual meeting after their election. At each annual meeting after such classification the number of directors equal to the number of the class whose term expires at the time of such meeting shall be elected to hold office until the second succeeding annual meeting, if there be two classes, or until the third succeeding annual meeting, if there be three classes. No classification of directors shall be effective prior to the first annual meeting of shareholders.

§ 38. Vacancies

Any vacancy occurring in the board of directors may be filled by the affirmative vote of a majority of the remaining directors though less than a quorum of the board of directors. A director elected to fill a vacancy shall be elected for the unexpired term of his predecessor in office. Any directorship to be filled by reason of an increase in the number of directors may be filled by the board of directors for the term of office continuing only until the next election of directors by the shareholders.

§ 39. Removal of Directors

At a meeting of shareholders called expressly for that purpose, directors may be removed in the manner provided in this section. Any director or the entire board of directors may be removed, with or without cause, by a vote of the holders of a majority of the shares then entitled to vote at an election of directors.

In the case of a corporation having cumulative voting, if less than the entire board is to be removed, no one of the directors may be removed if the votes cast against his removal would be sufficient to elect him if then cumulatively voted at an election of the entire board of directors, or, if there be classes of directors, at an election of the class of directors of which he is a part.

Whenever the holders of the shares of any class are entitled to elect one or more directors by the provisions of the articles of incorporation, the provisions of this section shall apply, in respect to the removal of a director or directors so elected, to the vote of the holders of the outstanding shares of that class and not to the vote of the outstanding shares as a whole.

§ 40. Quorum of Directors

A majority of the number of directors fixed by or in the manner provided in the by-laws or in the absence of a by-law fixing or providing for the number of directors, then of the number stated in the articles of incorporation, shall constitute a quorum for the transaction of business unless a greater number is required by the articles of incorporation or the by-laws. The act of the majority of the directors present at a meeting at which a quorum is present shall be the act of the board of directors, unless the act of a greater number is required by the articles of incorporation or the by-laws.

§ 41. Director Conflicts of Interest

No contract or other transaction between a corporation and one or more of its directors or any other corporation, firm, association or entity in which one or more of its directors are directors or officers or are financially interested, shall be either void or voidable because of such relationship or interest or because such director or directors are present at the meeting of the board of directors or a committee thereof which authorizes, approves or ratifies such contract or transaction or because his or their votes are counted for such purpose, if:

(a) the fact of such relationship or interest is disclosed or known to the board of directors or committee which authorizes, approves or ratifies the contract or transaction by a vote or consent sufficient for the purpose without counting the votes or consents of such interested directors; or

(b) the fact of such relationship or interest is disclosed or known to the shareholders entitled to vote and they authorize, approve or ratify such contract or transaction by vote or written consent; or

(c) the contract or transaction is fair and reasonable to the corporation.

Common or interested directors may be counted in determining the presence of a quorum at a meeting of the board of directors or a committee thereof which authorizes, approves or ratifies such contract or transaction.

§ 42. Executive and Other Committees

If the articles of incorporation or the by-laws so provide, the board of directors, by resolution adopted by a majority of the full board of directors, may designate from among its members an executive committee and one or more other committees each of which, to the extent provided in such resolution or in the articles of incorporation or the by-laws of the corporation, shall have and may exercise all the authority of the board of directors, except that no such committee shall have authority to (i) authorize distributions, (ii) approve or recommend to shareholders actions or proposals required by this Act to be approved by shareholders, (iii) designate candidates for the office of director, for purposes of proxy solicitation or otherwise, or fill vacancies on the board of directors or any committee thereof, (iv) amend the by-laws, (v) approve a plan of merger not requiring shareholder approval, (vi) authorize or approve the reacquisition of shares unless pursuant to a general formula or method specified by the board of directors, or (vii) authorize or approve the issuance or sale of, or any contract to issue or sell, shares or designate the terms of a series of a class of shares, provided that the board of directors, having acted regarding general authorization for the issuance or sale of shares, or any contract therefor, and, in the case of a series, the designation thereof, may, pursuant to a general formula or method specified by the board by resolution or by adoption of a stock option or other plan, authorize a committee to fix the terms of any contract for the sale of the shares and to fix the terms upon which such shares may be issued or sold, including, without limitation, the price, the dividend rate, provisions for redemption, sinking fund, conversion, voting or preferential rights, and provisions for other features of a class of shares, or a series of a class of shares, with full power in such committee to adopt any final resolution setting forth all the terms thereof and to authorize the statement of the terms of a series for filing with the Secretary of State under this Act.

Neither the designation of any such committee, the delegation thereto of authority, nor action by such committee pursuant to such authority shall alone constitute compliance by any member of the board of directors, not a member of the committee in question, with his responsibility to act in good faith, in a manner he reasonably believes to be in the best interests of the corporation, and with such care as an ordinarily prudent person in a like position would use under similar circumstances.

§ 43. Place and Notice of Directors' Meetings; Committee Meetings

Meetings of the board of directors, regular or special, may be held either within or without this State.

Regular meetings of the board of directors or any committee designated thereby may be held with or without notice as prescribed in the by-laws. Special meetings of the board of directors or any committee designated thereby shall be held upon such notice as is prescribed in the by-laws. Attendance of a director at a meeting shall constitute a waiver of notice of such meeting, except where a director attends a meeting for the express purpose of objecting to the transaction of any business because the meeting is

not lawfully called or convened. Neither the business to be transacted at, nor the purpose of, any regular or special meeting of the board of directors or any committee designated thereby need be specified in the notice or waiver of notice of such meeting unless required by the by-laws.

Except as may be otherwise restricted by the articles of incorporation or by-laws, members of the board of directors or any committee designated thereby may participate in a meeting of such board or committee by means of a conference telephone or similar communications equipment by means of which all persons participating in the meeting can hear each other at the same time and participation by such means shall constitute presence in person at a meeting.

§ 44. Action by Directors Without a Meeting

Unless otherwise provided by the articles of incorporation or by-laws, any action required by this Act to be taken at a meeting of the directors of a corporation, or any action which may be taken at a meeting of the directors or of a committee, may be taken without a meeting if a consent in writing, setting forth the action so taken, shall be signed by all of the directors, or all of the members of the committee, as the case may be. Such consent shall have the same effect as a unanimous vote.

§ 45. Distributions to Shareholders

Subject to any restrictions in the articles of incorporation, the board of directors may authorize and the corporation may make distributions, except that no distribution may be made if, after giving effect thereto, either:

(a)   the corporation would be unable to pay its debts as they become due in the usual course of its business; or

(b)   the corporation's total assets would be less than the sum of its total liabilities and (unless the articles of incorporation otherwise permit) the maximum amount that then would be payable, in any liquidation, in respect of all outstanding shares having preferential rights in liquidation.

Determinations under subparagraph (b) may be based upon (i) financial statements prepared on the basis of accounting practices and principles that are reasonable in the circumstances, or (ii) a fair valuation or other method that is reasonable in the circumstances.

In the case of a purchase, redemption or other acquisition of a corporation's shares, the effect of a distribution shall be measured as of the date money or other property is transferred or debt is incurred by the corporation, or as of the date the shareholder ceases to be a shareholder of the corporation with respect to such shares, whichever is earlier. In all other cases, the effect of a distribution shall be measured as of the date of its authorization if payment occurs 120 days or less following the date of authorization, or as of the date of payment if payment occurs more than 120 days following the date of authorization.

Indebtedness of a corporation incurred or issued to a shareholder in a distribution in accordance with this Section shall be on a parity with the indebtedness of the corporation to its general unsecured creditors except to the extent subordinated by agreement.

§ 46. Distributions from Capital Surplus
[Repealed in 1979].

§ 47. Loans to Employees and Directors
A corporation shall not lend money to or use its credit to assist its directors without authorization in the particular case by its shareholders, but may lend money to and use its credit to assist any employee of the corporation or of a subsidiary, including any such employee who is a director of the corporation, if the board of directors decides that such loan or assistance may benefit the corporation.

§ 48. Liability of Directors in Certain Cases
In addition to any other liabilities, a director who votes for or assents to any distribution contrary to the provisions of this Act or contrary to any restrictions contained in the articles of incorporation, shall, unless he complies with the standard provided in this Act for the performance of the duties of directors, be liable to the corporation, jointly and severally with all other directors so voting or assenting, for the amount of such dividend which is paid or the value of such distribution in excess of the amount of such distribution which could have been made without a violation of the provisions of this Act or the restrictions in the articles of incorporation.

Any director against whom a claim shall be asserted under or pursuant to this section for the making of a distribution and who shall be held liable thereon, shall be entitled to contribution from the shareholders who accepted or received any such distribution, knowing such distribution to have been made in violation of this Act, in proportion to the amounts received by them.

Any director against whom a claim shall be asserted under or pursuant to this section shall be entitled to contribution from any other director who voted for or assented to the action upon which the claim is asserted and who did not comply with the standard provided in this Act for the performance of the duties of directors.

§ 49. Provisions Relating to Actions by Shareholders
No action shall be brought in this State by a shareholder in the right of a domestic or foreign corporation unless the plaintiff was a holder of record of shares or of voting trust certificates therefor at the time of the transaction of which he complains, or his shares or voting trust certificates thereafter devolved upon him by operation of law from a person who was a holder of record at such time.

In any action hereafter instituted in the right of any domestic or foreign corporation by the holder or holders of record of shares of such corporation or of voting trust certificates therefor, the court having jurisdiction, upon final judgment and a finding that the action was brought without reasonable cause, may require the plaintiff or plaintiffs to pay to the parties named as defendant the reasonable expenses, including fees of attorneys, incurred by them in the defense of such action.

In any action now pending or hereafter instituted or maintained in the right of any domestic or foreign corporation by the holder or holders of record of less than five per cent of the outstanding shares of any class of such corporation or of voting trust certificates therefor, unless the shares or voting trust certificates so held have a market value in excess of twenty-five thousand dollars, the corporation in whose right such action is brought shall be entitled at any time before final judgment to require the plaintiff or plaintiffs to give security for the reasonable expenses, including fees of attorneys, that may be incurred by it in connection with such action or may be incurred by other parties named as defendant for which it may become legally liable. Market value shall be determined as of the date that the plaintiff institutes the action or, in the case of an intervenor, as of the date that he becomes a party to the action. The amount of such security may from time to time be increased or decreased, in the discretion of the court, upon showing that the security provided has or may become inadequate or is excessive. The corporation shall have recourse to such security in such amount as the court having jurisdiction shall determine upon the termination of such action, whether or not the court finds the action was brought without reasonable cause.

§ 50. Officers

The officers of a corporation shall consist of a president, one or more vice presidents as may be prescribed by the by-laws, a secretary, and a treasurer, each of whom shall be elected by the board of directors at such time and in such manner as may be prescribed by the by-laws. Such other officers and assistant officers and agents as may be deemed necessary may be elected or appointed by the board of directors or chosen in such other manner as may be prescribed by the by-laws. Any two or more offices may be held by the same person, except the offices of president and secretary.

All officers and agents of the corporation, as between themselves and the corporation, shall have such authority and perform such duties in the management of the corporation as may be provided in the by-laws, or as may be determined by resolution of the board of directors not inconsistent with the by-laws.

§ 51. Removal of Officers

Any officer or agent may be removed by the board of directors whenever in its judgment the best interests of the corporation will be served thereby, but such removal shall be without prejudice to the contract rights, if any, of the person so removed. Election or appointment of an officer or agent shall not of itself create contract rights.

§ 52. Books and Records: Financial Reports to Shareholders; Examination of Records

Each corporation shall keep correct and complete books and records of account and shall keep minutes of the proceedings of its shareholders and board of directors and shall keep at its registered office or principal place of business, or at the office of its transfer agent or registrar, a record of its shareholders, giving the names and addresses of all shareholders and the number and class of the shares held by each. Any books, records and minutes may be in written form or in any other form capable of being converted into written form within a reasonable time.

Any person who shall have been a holder of record of shares or of voting trust certificates therefor at least six months immediately preceding his demand or shall be the holder of record of, or the holder of record of voting trust certificates for, at least five percent of all the outstanding shares of the corporation, upon written demand stating the purpose thereof, shall have the right to examine, in person, or by agent or attorney, at any reasonable time or times, for any proper purpose its relevant books and records of account, minutes, and record of shareholders and to make extracts therefrom.

Any officer or agent who, or a corporation which, shall refuse to allow any such shareholder or holder of voting trust certificates, or his agent or attorney, so to examine and make extracts from its books and records of account, minutes, and record of shareholders, for any proper purpose, shall be liable to such shareholder or holder of voting trust certificates in a penalty of ten percent of the value of the shares owned by such shareholder, or in respect of which such voting trust certificates are issued, in addition to any other damages or remedy afforded him by law. It shall be a defense to any action for penalties under this section that the person suing therefor has within two years sold or offered for sale any list of shareholders or of holders of voting trust certificates for shares of such corporation or any other corporation or has aided or abetted any person in procuring any list of shareholders or of holders of voting trust certificates for any such purpose, or has improperly used any information secured through any prior examination of the books and records of account, or minutes, or record of shareholders or of holders of voting trust certificates for shares of such corporation or any other corporation, or was not acting in good faith or for a proper purpose in making his demand.

Nothing herein contained shall impair the power of any court of competent jurisdiction, upon proof by a shareholder or holder of voting trust certificates of proper purpose, irrespective of the period of time during which such shareholder or holder of voting trust certificates shall have been a shareholder of record or a holder of record of voting trust certificates, and irrespective of the number of shares held by him or represented by voting trust certificates held by him, to compel the production for examination by such shareholder or holder of voting trust certificates of the books and records of account, minutes and record of shareholders of a corporation.

Each corporation shall furnish to its shareholders annual financial statements, including at least a balance sheet as of the end of each fiscal year and a statement of income for such fiscal year, which shall be prepared on the basis of generally accepted accounting principles, if the corporation prepares financial statements for such fiscal year on that basis for any purpose, and may be consolidated statements of the corporation and one or more of its subsidiaries. The financial statements shall be mailed by the corporation to each of its shareholders within 120 days after the close of each fiscal year and, after such mailing and upon written request, shall be mailed by the corporation to any shareholder (or holder of a voting trust certificate for its shares) to whom a copy of the most recent annual financial statements has not previously been mailed. In the case of statements audited by a public accountant, each copy shall be accompanied by a report setting forth his opinion thereon; in other cases, each copy shall be accompanied by a statement of the president or the person in charge of the corporation's financial accounting records (1) stating his reasonable belief as to whether or not the financial statements were prepared in accordance with generally accepted accounting principles and, if not, describing the basis of presentation, and (2) describing any respects in which the financial statements were not prepared on a basis consistent with those prepared for the previous year.

§ 53. Incorporators

One or more persons, or a domestic or foreign corporation, may act as incorporator or incorporators of a corporation by signing and delivering in duplicate to the Secretary of State articles of incorporation for such corporation.

§ 54. Articles of Incorporation

The articles of incorporation shall set forth:

(a)   The name of the corporation.

(b)   The period of duration, which may be perpetual.

(c)   The purpose or purposes for which the corporation is organized which may be stated to be, or to include, the transaction of any or all lawful business for which corporations may be incorporated under this Act.

(d)   The aggregate number of shares which the corporation shall have authority to issue and, if such shares are to be divided into classes, the number of shares of each class.

(e)   If the shares are to be divided into classes, the designation of each class and a statement of the preferences, limitations and relative rights in respect of the shares of each class.

(f)   If the corporation is to issue the shares of any preferred or special class in series, then the designation of each series and a statement of the variations in the relative rights and preferences as between series insofar as the same are to be fixed in the articles of incorporation, and a statement of any authority to be vested in the board of directors to establish series and fix and determine the variations in the relative rights and preferences as between series.

(g)   If any preemptive right is to be granted to shareholders, the provisions therefor.

(h)   The address of its initial registered office, and the name of its initial registered agent at such address.

(i)   The number of directors constituting the initial board of directors and the names and addresses of the persons who are to serve as directors until the first annual meeting of shareholders or until their successors be elected and qualify.

(j)   The name and address of each incorporator.

In addition to provisions required therein, the articles of incorporation may also contain provisions not inconsistent with law regarding:

(1)   the direction of the management of the business and the regulation of the affairs of the corporation;

(2)   the definition, limitation and regulation of the powers of the corporation, the directors, and the shareholders, or any class of the shareholders, including restrictions on the transfer of shares;

(3)   the par value of any authorized shares or class of shares;

(4)   any provision which under this Act is required or permitted to be set forth in the by-laws.

It shall not be necessary to set forth in the articles of incorporation any of the corporate powers enumerated in this Act.

§ 55. Filing of Articles of Incorporation

Duplicate originals of the articles of incorporation shall be delivered to the Secretary of State. If the Secretary of State finds that the articles of incorporation conform to law, he shall, when all fees have been paid as in this Act prescribed:

(a) Endorse on each of such duplicate originals the word "Filed," and the month, day and year of the filing thereof.

(b) File one of such duplicate originals in his office.

(c) Issue a certificate of incorporation to which he shall affix the other duplicate original.

The certificate of incorporation, together with the duplicate original of the articles of incorporation affixed thereto by the Secretary of State, shall be returned to the incorporators or their representative.

§ 56. Effect of Issuance of Certificate of Incorporation

Upon the issuance of the certificate of incorporation, the corporate existence shall begin, and such certificate of incorporation shall be conclusive evidence that all conditions precedent required to be performed by the incorporators have been complied with and that the corporation has been incorporated under this Act, except as against this State in a proceeding to cancel or revoke the certificate of incorporation or for involuntary dissolution of the corporation.

§ 57. Organization Meeting of Directors

After the issuance of the certificate of incorporation an organization meeting of the board of directors named in the articles of incorporation shall be held, either within or without this State, at the call of a majority of the directors named in the articles of incorporation, for the purpose of adopting by-laws, electing officers and transacting such other business as may come before the meeting. The directors calling the meeting shall give at least three days' notice thereof by mail to each director so named, stating the time and place of the meeting.

§ 58. Right to Amend Articles of Incorporation

A corporation may amend its articles of incorporation, from time to time, in any and as many respects as may be desired, so long as its articles of incorporation as amended contain only such provisions as might be lawfully contained in original articles of incorporation at the time of making such amendment, and, if a change in shares or the rights of shareholders, or an exchange, reclassification or cancellation of shares or rights of shareholders is to be made, such provisions as may be necessary to effect such change, exchange, reclassification or cancellation.

In particular, and without limitation upon such general power of amendment, a corporation may amend its articles of incorporation, from time to time, so as:

(a) To change its corporate name.

(b) To change its period of duration.

(c) To change, enlarge or diminish its corporate purposes.

(d) To increase or decrease the aggregate number of shares, or shares of any class, which the corporation has authority to issue.

(e) To provide, change or eliminate any provision with respect to the par value of any shares or class of shares.

(f) To exchange, classify, reclassify or cancel all or any part of its shares, whether issued or unissued.

(g) To change the designation of all or any part of its shares, whether issued or unissued, and to change the preferences, limitations, and the relative rights in respect of all or any part of its shares, whether issued or unissued.

(h) To change the shares of any class, whether issued or unissued [sic] into a different number of shares of the same class or into the same or a different number of shares of other classes.

(i) To create new classes of shares having rights and preferences either prior and superior or subordinate and inferior to the shares of any class then authorized, whether issued or unissued.

(j) To cancel or otherwise affect the right of the holders of the shares of any class to receive dividends which have accrued but have not been declared.

(k) To divide any preferred or special class of shares, whether issued or unissued, into series and fix and determine the designations of such series and the variations in the relative rights and preferences as between the shares of such series.

(l) To authorize the board of directors to establish, out of authorized but unissued shares, series of any preferred or special class of shares and fix and determine the relative rights and preferences of the shares of any series so established.

(m)   To authorize the board of directors to fix and determine the relative rights and preferences of the authorized but unissued shares of series theretofore established in respect of which either the relative rights and preferences have not been fixed and determined or the relative rights and preferences theretofore fixed and determined are to be changed.

(n)   To revoke, diminish, or enlarge the authority of the board of directors to establish series out of authorized but unissued shares of any preferred or special class and fix and determine the relative rights and preferences of the shares of any series so established.

(o)   To limit, deny or grant to shareholders of any class the preemptive right to acquire additional shares of the corporation, whether then or thereafter authorized.

§ 59. Procedure to Amend Articles of Incorporation

Amendments to the articles of incorporation shall be made in the following manner:

(a)   The board of directors shall adopt a resolution setting forth the proposed amendment and, if shares have been issued, directing that it be submitted to a vote at a meeting of shareholders, which may be either the annual or a special meeting. If no shares have been issued, the amendment shall be adopted by resolution of the board of directors and the provisions for adoption by shareholders shall not apply. If the corporation has only one class of shares outstanding, an amendment solely to change the number of authorized shares to effectuate a split of, or stock dividend in, the corporation's own shares, or solely to do so and to change the number of authorized shares in proportion thereto, may be adopted by the board of directors; and the provisions for adoption by shareholders shall not apply, unless otherwise provided by the articles of incorporation. The resolution may incorporate the proposed amendment in restated articles of incorporation which contain a statement that except for the designated amendment the restated articles of incorporation correctly set forth without change the corresponding provisions of the articles of incorporation as theretofore amended, and that the restated articles of incorporation together with the designated amendment supersede the original articles of incorporation and all amendments thereto.

(b)   Written notice setting forth the proposed amendment or a summary of the changes to be effected thereby shall be given to each shareholder of record entitled to vote thereon within the time and in the manner provided in this Act for the giving of notice of meetings of shareholders. If the meeting be an annual meeting, the proposed amendment of such summary may be included in the notice of such annual meeting.

(c)   At such meeting a vote of the shareholders entitled to vote thereon shall be taken on the proposed amendment. The proposed amendment shall be adopted upon receiving the affirmative vote of the holders of a majority of the shares entitled to vote thereon, unless any class of shares is entitled to vote thereon as a class, in which event the proposed amendment shall be adopted upon receiving the affirmative vote of the holders of a majority of the shares of each class of shares entitled to vote thereon as a class and of the total shares entitled to vote thereon.

Any number of amendments may be submitted to the shareholders, and voted upon by them, at one meeting.

§ 60. Class Voting on Amendments

The holders of the outstanding shares of a class shall be entitled to vote as a class upon a proposed amendment, whether or not entitled to vote thereon by the provisions of the articles of incorporation, if the amendment would:

(a)   Increase or decrease the aggregate number of authorized shares of such class.

(b)   Effect an exchange, reclassification or cancellation of all or part of the shares of such class.

(c)   Effect an exchange, or create a right of exchange, of all or any part of the shares of another class into the shares of such class.

(d)   Change the designations, preferences, limitations or relative rights of the shares of such class.

(e)   Change the shares of such class into the same or a different number of shares of the same class or another class or classes.

(f)   Create a new class of shares having rights and preferences prior and superior to the shares of such class, or increase the rights and preferences or the number of authorized shares, of any class having rights and preferences prior or superior to the shares of such class.

(g)   In the case of a preferred or special class of shares, divide the shares of such class into series and fix and determine the designation of such series and the variations in the relative rights and preferences between the shares of such series, or authorize the board of directors to do so.

(h)   Limit or deny any existing preemptive rights of the shares of such class.

(i)   Cancel or otherwise affect dividends on the shares of such class which have accrued but have not been declared.

§ 61. Articles of Amendment

The articles of amendment shall be executed in duplicate by the corporation by its president or a vice president and by its secretary or an assistant secretary, and verified by one of the officers signing such articles, and shall set forth:

(a)   The name of the corporation.

(b)   The amendments so adopted.

(c)   The date of the adoption of the amendment by the shareholders, or by the board of directors where no shares have been issued.

(d)   The number of shares outstanding, and the number of shares entitled to vote thereon, and if the shares of any class are entitled to vote thereon as a class, the designation and number of outstanding shares entitled to vote thereon of each such class.

(e)   The number of shares voted for and against such amendment, respectively, and, if the shares of any class are entitled to vote thereon as a class, the number of shares of each such class voted for and against such amendment, respectively, or if no shares have been issued, a statement to that effect.

(f)   If such amendment provides for an exchange, reclassification or cancellation of issued shares, and if the manner in which the same shall be effected is not set forth in the amendment, then a statement of the manner in which the same shall be effected.

§ 62. Filing of Articles of Amendment

Duplicate originals of the articles of amendment shall be delivered to the Secretary of State. If the Secretary of State finds that the articles of amendment conform

to law, he shall, when all fees and franchise taxes have been paid as in this Act prescribed:

(a)   Endorse on each of such duplicate originals the word "Filed," and the month, day and year of the filing thereof.

(b)   File one of such duplicate originals in his office.

(c)   Issue a certificate of amendment to which he shall affix the other duplicate original.

The certificate of amendment, together with the duplicate original of the articles of amendment affixed thereto by the Secretary of State, shall be returned to the corporation or its representative.

§ 63. Effect of Certificate of Amendment

Upon the issuance of the certificate of amendment by the Secretary of State, the amendment shall become effective and the articles of incorporation shall be deemed to be amended accordingly.

No amendment shall affect any existing cause of action in favor of or against such corporation, or any pending suit to which such corporation shall be a party, or the existing rights of persons other than shareholders; and, in the event the corporate name shall be changed by amendment, no suit brought by or against such corporation under its former name shall abate for that reason.

§ 64. Restated Articles of Incorporation

A domestic corporation may at any time restate its articles of incorporation as theretofore amended, by a resolution adopted by the board of directors.

Upon the adoption of such resolution, restated articles of incorporation shall be executed in duplicate by the corporation by its president or a vice president and by its secretary or assistant secretary and verified by one of the officers signing such articles and shall set forth all of the operative provisions of the articles of incorporation as theretofore amended together with a statement that the restated articles of incorporation correctly set forth without change the corresponding provisions of the articles of incorporation as theretofore amended and that the restated articles of incorporation supersede the original articles of incorporation and all amendments thereto.

Duplicate originals of the restated articles of incorporation shall be delivered to the Secretary of State. If the Secretary of State finds that such restated articles of incorporation conform to law, he shall, when all fees and franchise taxes have been paid as in this Act prescribed:

(1) Endorse on each of such duplicate originals the word "Filed," and the month, day and year of the filing thereof.

(2) File one of such duplicate originals in his office.

(3) Issue a restated certificate of incorporation, to which he shall affix the other duplicate original.

The restated certificate of incorporation, together with the duplicate original of the restated articles of incorporation affixed thereto by the Secretary of State, shall be returned to the corporation or its representative.

Upon the issuance of the restated certificate of incorporation by the Secretary of State, the restated articles of incorporation shall become effective and shall supersede the original articles of incorporation and all amendments thereto.

§ 65. Amendment of Articles of Incorporation in Reorganization Proceedings

Whenever a plan of reorganization of a corporation has been confirmed by decree or order of a court of competent jurisdiction in proceedings for the reorganization of such corporation, pursuant to the provisions of any applicable statute of the United States relating to reorganizations of corporations, the articles of incorporation of the corporation may be amended, in the manner provided in this section, in as many respects as may be necessary to carry out the plan and put it into effect, so long as the articles of incorporation as amended contain only such provisions as might be lawfully contained in original articles of incorporation at the time of making such amendment.

In particular and without limitation upon such general power of amendment, the articles of incorporation may be amended for such purpose so as to:

(A) Change the corporate name, period of duration or corporate purposes of the corporation;

(B) Repeal, alter or amend the by-laws of the corporation;

(C) Change the aggregate number of shares or shares of any class, which the corporation has authority to issue;

(D) Change the preferences, limitations and relative rights in respect of all or any part of the shares of the corporation, and classify, reclassify or cancel all or any part thereof, whether issued or unissued;

(E) Authorize the issuance of bonds, debentures or other obligations of the corporation, whether or not convertible into shares of any class or bearing warrants or other evidences of optional rights to purchase or subscribe for shares of any class, and fix the terms and conditions thereof; and

(F) Constitute or reconstitute and classify or reclassify the board of directors of the corporation, and appoint directors and officers in place of or in addition to all or any of the directors or officers then in office.

Amendments to the articles of incorporation pursuant to this section shall be made in the following manner:

(a) Articles of amendment approved by decree or order of such court shall be executed and verified in duplicate by such person or persons as the court shall designate or appoint for the purpose, and shall set forth the name of the corporation, the amendments of the articles of incorporation approved by the court, the date of the decree or order approving the articles of amendment, the title of the proceedings in which the decree or order was entered, and a statement that such decree or order was entered by a court having jurisdiction of the proceedings for the reorganization of the corporation pursuant to the provisions of an applicable statute of the United States.

(b) Duplicate originals of the articles of amendment shall be delivered to the Secretary of State. If the Secretary of State finds that the articles of amendment conform to law, he shall, when all fees and franchise taxes have been paid as in this Act prescribed:

(1) Endorse on each of such duplicate originals the word "Filed," and the month, day and year of the filing thereof.

(2) File one of such duplicate originals in his office.

(3) Issue a certificate of amendment to which he shall affix the other duplicate original.

The certificate of amendment, together with the duplicate original of the articles of amendment affixed thereto by the Secretary of State, shall be returned to the corporation or its representative.

Upon the issuance of the certificate of amendment by the Secretary of State, the amendment shall become effective and the articles of incorporation shall be deemed to be amended accordingly, without any action thereon by the directors or shareholders of the corporation and with the same effect as if the amendments had been adopted by unanimous action of the directors and shareholders of the corporation.

§ 66. Restriction on Redemption or Purchase of Redeemable Shares

[Repealed in 1979].

§ 67. Cancellation of Redeemable Shares by Redemption or Purchase

[Repealed in 1979].

§ 68. Cancellation of Other Reacquired Shares

[Repealed in 1979].

§ 69. Reduction of Stated Capital in Certain Cases

[Repealed in 1979].

§ 70. Special Provisions Relating to Surplus and Reserves

[Repealed in 1979].

§ 71. Procedure for Merger

Any two or more domestic corporations may merge into one of such corporations pursuant to a plan of merger approved in the manner provided in this Act.

The board of directors of each corporation shall, by resolution adopted by each such board, approve a plan of merger setting forth:

(a)　The names of the corporations proposing to merge, and the name of the corporation into which they propose to merge, which is hereinafter designated as the surviving corporation.

(b)　The terms and conditions of the proposed merger.

(c)　The manner and basis of converting the shares of each corporation into shares, obligations or other securities of the surviving corporation or of any other corporation or, in whole or in part, into cash or other property.

(d)　A statement of any changes in the articles of incorporation of the surviving corporation to be effected by such merger.

(e)　Such other provisions with respect to the proposed merger as are deemed necessary or desirable.

§ 72. Procedure for Consolidation

Any two or more domestic corporations may consolidate into a new corporation pursuant to a plan of consolidation approved in the manner provided in this Act.

The board of directors of each corporation shall, by a resolution adopted by each such board, approve a plan of consolidation setting forth:

(a)　The names of the corporations proposing to consolidate, and the name of the new corporation into which they propose to consolidate, which is hereinafter designated as the new corporation.

(b)　The terms and conditions of the proposed consolidation.

(c)　The manner and basis of converting the shares of each corporation into shares, obligations or other securities of the new corporation or of any other corporation or, in whole or in part, into cash or other property.

(d)　With respect to the new corporation, all of the statements required to be set forth in articles of incorporation for corporations organized under this Act.

(e)　Such other provisions with respect to the proposed consolidation as are deemed necessary or desirable.

§ 72A. Procedure for Share Exchange

All the issued or all the outstanding shares of one or more classes of any domestic corporation may be acquired through the exchange of all such shares of such class or classes by another domestic or foreign corporation pursuant to a plan of exchange approved in the manner provided in this Act.

The board of directors of each corporation shall, by resolution adopted by each such board, approve a plan of exchange setting forth:

(a)　The name of the corporation the shares of which are proposed to be acquired by exchange and the name of the corporation to acquire the shares of such corporation in the exchange, which is hereinafter designated as the acquiring corporation.

(b)　The terms and conditions of the proposed exchange.

(c)　The manner and basis of exchanging the shares to be acquired for shares, obligations or other securities of the acquiring corporation or any other corporation, or, in whole or in part, for cash or other property.

(d)   Such other provisions with respect to the proposed exchange as are deemed necessary or desirable. The procedure authorized by this section shall not be deemed to limit the power of a corporation to acquire all or part of the shares of any class of classes of a corporation through a voluntary exchange or otherwise by agreement with the shareholders.

§ 73. Approval by Shareholders

(a)   The board of directors of each corporation in the case of a merger or consolidation, and the board of directors of the corporation the shares of which are to be acquired in the case of an exchange, upon approving such plan of merger, consolidation or exchange, shall, by resolution, direct that the plan be submitted to a vote at a meeting of its shareholders, which may be either an annual or a special meeting. Written notice shall be given to each shareholder of record, whether or not entitled to vote at such meeting, not less than twenty days before such meeting, in the manner provided in this Act for the giving of notice of meetings of shareholders, and, whether the meeting be an annual or a special meeting, shall state that the purpose or one of the purposes is to consider the proposed plan of merger, consolidation or exchange. A copy or a summary of the plan of merger, consolidation or exchange, as the case may be, shall be included in or enclosed with such notice.

(b)   At each such meeting, a vote of the shareholders shall be taken on the proposed plan. The plan shall be approved upon receiving the affirmative vote of the holders of a majority of the shares entitled to vote thereon of each such corporation, unless any class of shares of any such corporation is entitled to vote thereon as a class, in which event, as to such corporation, the plan shall be approved upon receiving the affirmative vote of the holders of a majority of the shares of each class of shares entitled to vote thereon as a class and of the total shares entitled to vote thereon. Any class of shares of any such corporation shall be entitled to vote as a class if any such plan contains any provision which, if contained in a proposed amendment to articles of incorporation, would entitle such class of shares to vote as a class and, in the case of an exchange, if the class is included in the exchange.

(c)   After such approval by a vote of the shareholders of each such corporation, and at any time prior to the filing of the articles of merger, consolidation or

exchange, the merger, consolidation or exchange may be abandoned pursuant to provisions therefor, if any, set forth in the plan.

(d)   (1)Notwithstanding the provisions of subsections (a) and (b), submission of a plan of merger to a vote at a meeting of shareholders of a surviving corporation shall not be required if:

(i)   the articles of incorporation of the surviving corporation do not differ except in name from those of the corporation before the merger,

(ii)   each holder of shares of the surviving corporation which were outstanding immediately before the effective date of the merger is to hold the same number of shares with identical rights immediately after,

(iii)   the number of voting shares outstanding immediately after the merger, plus the number of voting shares issuable on conversion of other securities issued by virtue of the terms of the merger and on exercise of rights and warrants so issued, will not exceed by more than 20 percent the number of voting shares outstanding immediately before the merger, and

(iv)   the number of participating shares outstanding immediately after the merger, plus the number of participating shares issuable on conversion of other securities issued by virtue of the terms of the merger and on exercise of rights and warrants so issued, will not exceed by more than 20 percent the number of participating shares outstanding immediately before the merger.

(2) As used in this subsection:

(i)   "voting shares" means shares which entitle their holders to vote unconditionally in elections of directors;

(ii)   "participating shares" means shares which entitle their holders to participate without limitation in distribution of earnings or surplus.

§ 74. Articles of Merger, Consolidation or Exchange

(a)   Upon receiving the approvals required by Sections 71, 72 and 73, articles of merger or articles of consolidation shall be executed in duplicate by each corporation by its president or a vice president and by its secretary or an assistant secretary, and verified by one of the officers of each corporation signing such articles, and shall set forth:

(1) The plan of merger or the plan of consolidation;

(2) As to each corporation, either (i) the number of shares outstanding, and, if the shares of any class are entitled to vote as a class, the designation and number of outstanding shares of each such class, or (ii) a statement that the vote of shareholders is not required by virtue of subsection 73(d);

(3) As to each corporation the approval of whose shareholders is required, the number of shares voted for and against such plan, respectively, and, if the shares of any class are entitled to vote as a class, the number of shares of each such class voted for and against such plan, respectively.

(b) Duplicate originals of the articles of merger, consolidation or exchange shall be delivered to the Secretary of State. If the Secretary of State finds that such articles conform to law, he shall, when all fees and franchise taxes have been paid as in this Act prescribed:

(1) Endorse on each of such duplicate originals the word "Filed," and the month, day and year of the filing thereof.

(2) File one of such duplicate originals in his office.

(3) Issue a certificate of merger, consolidation or exchange to which he shall affix the other duplicate original.

(c) The certificate of merger, consolidation or exchange together with the duplicate original of the articles affixed thereto by the Secretary of State, shall be returned to the surviving, new or acquiring corporation, as the case may be, or its representative.

§ 75. Merger of Subsidiary Corporation

Any corporation owning at least ninety per cent of the outstanding shares of each class of another corporation may merge such other corporation into itself without approval by a vote of the shareholders of either corporation. Its board of directors shall, by resolution, approve a plan of merger setting forth:

(A) The name of the subsidiary corporation and the name of the corporation owning at least ninety per cent of its shares, which is hereinafter designated as the surviving corporation.

(B) The manner and basis of converting the shares of the subsidiary corporation into shares, obligations or other securities of the surviving corporation or of any other corporation or, in whole or in part, into cash or other property.

A copy of such plan of merger shall be mailed to each shareholder of record of the subsidiary corporation.

Articles of merger shall be executed in duplicate by the surviving corporation by its president or a vice president and by its secretary or an assistant secretary, and verified by one of its officers signing such articles, and shall set forth:

(a) The plan of merger;

(b) The number of outstanding shares of each class of the subsidiary corporation and the number of such shares of each class owned by the surviving corporation; and

(c) The date of the mailing to shareholders of the subsidiary corporation of a copy of the plan of merger.

On and after the thirtieth day after the mailing of a copy of the plan of merger to shareholders of the subsidiary corporation or upon the waiver thereof by the holders of all outstanding shares duplicate originals of the articles of merger shall be delivered to the Secretary of State. If the Secretary of State finds that such articles conform to law, he shall, when all fees and franchise taxes have been paid as in this Act prescribed:

(1) Endorse on each of such duplicate originals the word "Filed," and the month, day and year of the filing thereof,

(2) File one of such duplicate originals in his office, and

(3) Issue a certificate of merger to which he shall affix the other duplicate original.

The certificate of merger, together with the duplicate original of the articles of merger affixed thereto by the Secretary of State, shall be returned to the surviving corporation or its representative.

§ 76. Effect of Merger, Consolidation or Exchange

Upon the issuance of the certificate of merger or the certificate of consolidation by the Secretary of State, the merger or consolidation shall be effected.

When such merger or consolidation has been effective:

(a) The several corporations parties to the plan of merger or consolidation shall be a single corporation, which, in the case of a merger, shall be that corporation designated in the plan of merger as the surviving corporation, and, in the case of a consolidation, shall be the new corporation provided for in the plan of consolidation.

(b)   The separate existence of all corporations parties to the plan of merger or consolidation, except the surviving or new corporation, shall cease.

(c)   Such surviving or new corporation shall have all the rights, privileges, immunities and powers and shall be subject to all the duties and liabilities of a corporation organized under this Act.

(d)   Such surviving or new corporation shall thereupon and thereafter possess all the rights, privileges, immunities, and franchises, of a public as well as of a private nature, of each of the merging or consolidating corporations; and all property, real, personal and mixed, and all debts due on whatever account, including subscriptions to shares, and all other choses in action, and all and every other interest of or belonging to or due to each of the corporations so merged or consolidated, shall be taken and deemed to be transferred to and vested in such single corporation without further act or deed; and the title to any real estate, or any interest therein, vested in any of such corporations shall not revert or be in any way impaired by reason of such merger or consolidation.

(e)   Such surviving or new corporation shall thenceforth be responsible and liable for all the liabilities and obligations of each of the corporations so merged or consolidated; and any claim existing or action or proceeding pending by or against any of such corporations may be prosecuted as if such merger or consolidation had not taken place, or such surviving or new corporation may be substituted in its place. Neither the rights of creditors nor any liens upon the property of any such corporation shall be impaired by such merger or consolidation.

(f)   In the case of a merger, the articles of incorporation of the surviving corporation shall be deemed to be amended to the extent, if any, that changes in its articles of incorporation are stated in the plan of merger; and, in the case of a consolidation, the statements set forth in the articles of consolidation and which are required or permitted to be set forth in the articles of incorporation of corporations organized under this Act shall be deemed to be the original articles of incorporation of the new corporation.

§ 77. Merger, Consolidation or Exchange of Shares Between Domestic and Foreign Corporations

One or more foreign corporations and one or more domestic corporations may be merged or consolidated in the following manner, if such merger or consolidation is permitted by the laws of the state under which each such foreign corporation is organized:

(a)   Each domestic corporation shall comply with the provisions of this Act with respect to the merger or consolidation, as the case may be, of domestic corporations and each foreign corporation shall comply with the applicable provisions of the laws of the state under which it is organized.

(b)   If the surviving or new corporation, as the case may be, is to be governed by the laws of any state other than this State, it shall comply with the provisions of this Act with respect to foreign corporations if it is to transact business in this State, and in every case it shall file with the Secretary of State of this State:

(1)   An agreement that it may be served with process in this State in any proceeding for the enforcement of any obligation of any domestic corporation which is a party to such merger or consolidation and in any proceeding for the enforcement of the rights of a dissenting shareholder of any such domestic corporation against the surviving or new corporation;

(2)   An irrevocable appointment of the Secretary of State of this State as its agent to accept service of process in any such proceeding; and

(3)   An agreement that it will promptly pay to the dissenting shareholders of any such domestic corporation the amount, if any, to which they shall be entitled under the provisions of this Act with respect to the rights of dissenting shareholders.

The effect of such merger or consolidation shall be the same as in the case of the merger or consolidation of domestic corporations, if the surviving or new corporation is to be governed by the laws of this State. If the surviving or new corporation is to be governed by the laws of any state other than this State, the effect of such merger or consolidation shall be the same as in the case of the merger or consolidation of domestic corporations except insofar as the laws of such other state provide otherwise.

At any time prior to the filing of the articles of merger or consolidation, the merger or consolidation may be abandoned pursuant to provisions therefor, if any, set forth in the plan of merger or consolidation.

§ 78. Sale of Assets in Regular Course of Business and Mortgage or Pledge of Assets

The sale, lease, exchange, or other disposition of all, or substantially all, the property and assets of a corporation in the usual and regular course of its business and the mortgage or pledge of any or all property and assets of a corporation whether or not in the usual and regular course of business may be made upon such terms and conditions and for such consideration, which may consist in whole or in part of cash or other property, including shares, obligations or other securities of any other corporation, domestic or foreign, as shall be authorized by its board of directors; and in any such case no authorization or consent of the shareholders shall be required.

§ 79. Sale of Assets Other Than in Regular Course of Business

A sale, lease, exchange, or other disposition of all, or substantially all, the property and assets, with or without the good will, of a corporation, if not in the usual and regular course of its business, may be made upon such terms and conditions and for such consideration, which may consist in whole or in part of cash or other property, including shares, obligations or other securities of any other corporation, domestic or foreign, as may be authorized in the following manner:

(a)   The board of directors shall adopt a resolution recommending such sale, lease, exchange, or other disposition and directing the submission thereof to a vote at a meeting of shareholders, which may be either an annual or a special meeting.

(b)   Written notice shall be given to each shareholder of record, whether or not entitled to vote at such meeting, not less than twenty days before such meeting, in the manner provided in this Act for the giving of notice of meetings of shareholders, and, whether the meeting be an annual or a special meeting, shall state that the purpose, or one of the purposes is to consider the proposed sale, lease, exchange, or other disposition.

(c)   At such meeting the shareholders may authorize such sale, lease, exchange, or other disposition and may fix, or may authorize the board of directors to fix, any or all of the terms and conditions thereof

and the consideration to be received by the corporation therefor. Such authorization shall require the affirmative vote of the holders of a majority of the shares of the corporation entitled to vote thereon, unless any class of shares is entitled to vote thereon as a class, in which event such authorization shall require the affirmative vote of the holders of a majority of the shares of each class of shares entitled to vote as a class thereon and of the total shares entitled to vote thereon.

(d)   After such authorization by a vote of shareholders, the board of directors nevertheless, in its discretion, may abandon such sale, lease, exchange, or other disposition of assets, subject to the rights of third parties under any contracts relating thereto, without further action or approval by shareholders.

§ 80. Right of Shareholders to Dissent and Obtain Payment for Shares

(a)   Any shareholder of a corporation shall have the right to dissent from, and to obtain payment for his shares in the event of, any of the following corporate actions:

(1)   Any plan of merger or consolidation to which the corporation is a party, except as provided in subsection (c);

(2)   Any sale or exchange of all or substantially all of the property and assets of the corporation not made in the usual or regular course of its business, including a sale in dissolution, but not including a sale pursuant to an order of a court having jurisdiction in the premises or a sale for cash on terms requiring that all or substantially all of the net proceeds of sale be distributed to the shareholders in accordance with their respective interests within one year after the date of sale;

(3)   Any plan of exchange to which the corporation is a party as the corporation the shares of which are to be acquired;

(4)   Any amendment of the articles of incorporation which materially and adversely affects the rights appurtenant to the shares of the dissenting shareholder in that it:

(i)   alters or abolishes a preferential right of such shares;

(ii)   creates, alters or abolishes a right in respect of the redemption of such shares, including a provision respecting a sinking fund for the redemption or repurchase of such shares;

(iii) alters or abolishes a preemptive right of the holder of such shares to acquire shares or other securities;

(iv) excludes or limits the right of the holder of such shares to vote on any matter, or to cumulate his votes, except as such right may be limited by dilution through the issuance of shares or other securities with similar voting rights; or

(5) Any other corporate action taken pursuant to a shareholder vote with respect to which the articles of incorporation, the bylaws, or a resolution of the board of directors directs that dissenting shareholders shall have a right to obtain payment for their shares.

(b) (1) A record holder of shares may assert dissenters' rights as to less than all of the shares registered in his name only if he dissents with respect to all the shares beneficially owned by any one person, and discloses the name and address of the person or persons on whose behalf he dissents. In that event, his rights shall be determined as if the shares as to which he has dissented and his other shares were registered in the names of different shareholders.

(2) A beneficial owner of shares who is not the record holder may assert dissenters' rights with respect to shares held on his behalf, and shall be treated as a dissenting shareholder under the terms of this section and section 81 if he submits to the corporation at the time of or before the assertion of these rights a written consent of the record holder.

(c) The right to obtain payment under this section shall not apply to the shareholders of the surviving corporation in a merger if a vote of the shareholders of such corporation is not necessary to authorize such merger.

(d) A shareholder of a corporation who has a right under this section to obtain payment for his shares shall have no right at law or in equity to attack the validity of the corporate action that gives rise to his right to obtain payment, nor to have the action set aside or rescinded, except when the corporate action is unlawful or fraudulent with regard to the complaining shareholder or to the corporation.

§ 81. Procedures for Protection of Dissenters' Rights

(a) As used in this section:

(1) "Dissenter" means a shareholder or beneficial owner who is entitled to and does assert dissenters' rights under section 80, and who has performed every act required up to the time involved for the assertion of such rights.

(2) "Corporation" means the issuer of the shares held by the dissenter before the corporate action, or the successor by merger or consolidation of that issuer.

(3) "Fair value" of shares means their value immediately before the effectuation of the corporate action to which the dissenter objects, excluding any appreciation or depreciation in anticipation of such corporate action unless such exclusion would be inequitable.

(4) "Interest" means interest from the effective date of the corporate action until the date of payment, at the average rate currently paid by the corporation on its principal bank loans, or, if none, at such rate as is fair and equitable under all the circumstances.

(b) If a proposed corporate action which would give rise to dissenters' rights under section 80(a) is submitted to a vote at a meeting of shareholders, the notice of meeting shall notify all shareholders that they have or may have a right to dissent and obtain payment for their shares by complying with the terms of this section, and shall be accompanied by a copy of sections 80 and 81 of this Act.

(c) If the proposed corporate action is submitted to a vote at a meeting of shareholders, any shareholder who wishes to dissent and obtain payment for his shares must file with the corporation, prior to the vote, a written notice of intention to demand that he be paid fair compensation for his shares if the proposed action is effectuated, and shall refrain from voting his shares in approval of such action. A shareholder who fails in either respect shall acquire no right to payment for his shares under this section or section 80.

(d) If the proposed corporate action is approved by the required vote at a meeting of shareholders, the corporation shall mail a further notice to all shareholders who gave due notice of intention to demand payment and who refrained from voting in favor of the proposed action. If the proposed corporate action is to be taken without a vote of shareholders, the corporation shall send to all shareholders who are entitled to dissent and demand payment for their shares a notice of the adoption of the plan of corporate action. The notice shall (1) state where and when a demand for payment must be sent and certificates of certificated shares must be deposited in order to obtain payment, (2) inform holders of uncertificated shares to what extent transfer of shares will be restricted from the time that demand for payment is received, (3) supply a form for demanding payment which includes a request for certification of the date on which the shareholder, or the person on whose behalf the shareholder dissents, acquired beneficial ownership of the shares, and (4) be accompanied by a copy of sections 80 and 81 of this Act. The time set for the demand and deposit shall be not less than 30 days from the mailing of the notice.

(e) A shareholder who fails to demand payment, or fails (in the case of certificated shares) to deposit certificates, as required by a notice pursuant to subsection (d) shall have no right under this section or section 80 to receive payment for his shares. If the shares are not represented by certificates, the corporation may restrict their transfer from the time of receipt of demand for payment until effectuation of the proposed corporate action, or the release of restrictions under the terms of subsection (f). The dissenter shall retain all other rights of a shareholder until these rights are modified by effectuation of the proposed corporate action.

(f) (1) Within 60 days after the date set for demanding payment and depositing certificates, if the corporation has not effectuated the proposed corporate action and remitted payment for shares pursuant to paragraph (3), it shall return any certificates that have been deposited, and release uncertificated shares from any transfer restrictions imposed by reason of the demand for payment.

(2) When uncertificated shares have been released from transfer restrictions, and deposited certificates have been returned, the corporation may at any later time send a new notice conforming to the requirements of subsection (d), with like effect.

(3) Immediately upon effectuation of the proposed corporate action, or upon receipt of demand for payment if the corporate action has already been effectuated, the corporation shall

remit to dissenters who have made demand and (if their shares are certificated) have deposited their certificates the amount which the corporation estimates to be the fair value of the shares, with interest if any has accrued. The remittance shall be accompanied by:

(i) the corporation's closing balance sheet and statement of income for a fiscal year ending not more than 16 months before the date of remittance, together with the latest available interim financial statements;
(ii) a statement of the corporation's estimate of fair value of the shares; and
(iii) a notice of the dissenter's right to demand supplemental payment, accompanied by a copy of sections 80 and 81 of this Act.

(g) (1) If the corporation fails to remit as required by subsection (f), or if the dissenter believes that the amount remitted is less than the fair value of his shares, or that the interest is not correctly determined, he may send the corporation his own estimate of the value of the shares or of the interest, and demand payment of the deficiency.

(2) If the dissenter does not file such an estimate within 30 days after the corporation's mailing of its remittance, he shall be entitled to no more than the amount remitted.

(h) (1) Within 60 days after receiving a demand for payment pursuant to subsection (g), if any such demands for payment remain unsettled, the corporation shall file in an appropriate court a petition requesting that the fair value of the shares and interest thereon be determined by the court.

(2) An appropriate court shall be a court of competent jurisdiction in the county of this state where the registered office of the corporation is located. If, in the case of a merger or consolidation or exchange of shares, the corporation is a foreign corporation without a registered office in this state, the petition shall be filed in the county where the registered office of the domestic corporation was last located.
(3) All dissenters, wherever residing, whose demands have not been settled shall be made parties to the proceeding as in an action against their shares. A copy of the petition shall be served on each such dissenter; if a dissenter is a nonresident, the copy may be served on him by

registered or certified mail or by publication as provided by law.

(4) The jurisdiction of the court shall be plenary and exclusive. The court may appoint one or more persons as appraisers to receive evidence and recommend a decision on the question of fair value. The appraisers shall have such power and authority as shall be specified in the order of their appointment or in any amendment thereof. The dissenters shall be entitled to discovery in the same manner as parties in other civil suits.

(5) All dissenters who are made parties shall be entitled to judgment for the amount by which the fair value of their shares is found to exceed the amount previously remitted, with interest.

(6) If the corporation fails to file a petition as provided in paragraph (1) of this subsection, each dissenter who made a demand and who has not already settled his claim against the corporation shall be paid by the corporation the amount demanded by him, with interest, and may sue therefor in an appropriate court.

(i) (1) The costs and expenses of any proceeding under subsection (h), including the reasonable compensation and expenses of appraisers appointed by the court, shall be determined by the court and assessed against the corporation, except that any part of the costs and expenses may be apportioned and assessed as the court may deem equitable against all or some of the dissenters who are parties and whose action in demanding supplemental payment the court finds to be arbitrary, vexatious, or not in good faith.

(2) Fees and expenses of counsel and of experts for the respective parties may be assessed as the court may deem equitable against the corporation and in favor of any or all dissenters if the corporation failed to comply substantially with the requirements of this section, and may be assessed against either the corporation or a dissenter, in favor of any other party, if the court finds that the party against whom the fees and expenses are assessed acted arbitrarily, vexatiously, or not in good faith in respect to the rights provided by this Section and Section 80.

(3) If the court finds that the services of counsel for any dissenter were of substantial benefit to other dissenters similarly situated, and should not be assessed against the corporation, it may award to these counsel reasonable fees to be paid out of the amounts awarded to the dissenters who were benefitted.

(j) (1) Notwithstanding the foregoing provisions of this section, the corporation may elect to withhold the remittance required by subsection (f) from any dissenter with respect to shares of which the dissenter (or the person on whose behalf the dissenter acts) was not the beneficial owner on the date of the first announcement to news media or to shareholders of the terms of the proposed corporate action. With respect to such shares, the corporation shall, upon effectuating the corporate action, state to each dissenter its estimate of the fair value of the shares, state the rate of interest to be used (explaining the basis thereof), and offer to pay the resulting amounts on receiving the dissenter's agreement to accept them in full satisfaction.

(2) If the dissenter believes that the amount offered is less than the fair value of the shares and interest determined according to this section, he may within 30 days after the date of mailing of the corporation's offer, mail the corporation his own estimate of fair value and interest, and demand their payment. If the dissenter fails to do so, he shall be entitled to no more than the corporation's offer.

(3) If the dissenter makes a demand as provided in paragraph (2), the provisions of subsections (h) and (i) shall apply to further proceedings on the dissenter's demand.

§ 82. Voluntary Dissolution by Incorporators

A corporation which has not commenced business and which has not issued any shares, may be voluntarily dissolved by its incorporators at any time in the following manner:

(a) Articles of dissolution shall be executed in duplicate by a majority of the incorporators, and verified by them, and shall set forth:

(1) The name of the corporation.

(2) The date of issuance of its certificate of incorporation.

(3) That none of its shares has been issued.

(4) That the corporation has not commenced business.

(5) That the amount, if any, actually paid in on subscriptions for its shares, less any part thereof disbursed for necessary expenses, has been returned to those entitled thereto.

(6) That no debts of the corporation remain unpaid.

(7) That a majority of the incorporators elect that the corporation be dissolved.

(b) Duplicate originals of the articles of dissolution shall be delivered to the Secretary of State. If the Secretary of State finds that the articles of dissolution conform to law, he shall, when all fees and franchise taxes have been paid as in this Act prescribed:

(1) Endorse on each of such duplicate originals the word "Filed," and the month, day and year of the filing thereof.

(2) File one of such duplicate originals in his office.

(3) Issue a certificate of dissolution to which he shall affix the other duplicate original.

The certificate of dissolution, together with the duplicate original of the articles of dissolution affixed thereto by the Secretary of State, shall be returned to the incorporators or their representative. Upon the issuance of such certificate of dissolution by the Secretary of State, the existence of the corporation shall cease.

§ 83. Voluntary Dissolution by Consent of Shareholders

A corporation may be voluntarily dissolved by the written consent of all of its shareholders.

Upon the execution of such written consent, a statement of intent to dissolve shall be executed in duplicate by the corporation by its president or a vice president and by its secretary or an assistant secretary, and verified by one of the officers signing such statement, which statement shall set forth:

(a) The name of the corporation.

(b) The names and respective addresses of its officers.

(c) The names and respective addresses of its directors.

(d) A copy of the written consent signed by all shareholders of the corporation.

(e) A statement that such written consent has been signed by all shareholders of the corporation or signed in their names by their attorneys thereunto duly authorized.

§ 84. Voluntary Dissolution by Act of Corporation

A corporation may be dissolved by the act of the corporation, when authorized in the following manner:

(a) The board of directors shall adopt a resolution recommending that the corporation be dissolved, and directing that the question of such dissolution be submitted to a vote at a meeting of shareholders, which may be either an annual or a special meeting.

(b) Written notice shall be given to each shareholder of record entitled to vote at such meeting within the time and in the manner provided in this Act for the giving of notice of meetings of shareholders, and, whether the meeting be an annual or special meeting, shall state that the purpose, or one of the purposes, of such meeting is to consider the advisability of dissolving the corporation.

(c) At such meeting a vote of shareholders entitled to vote thereat shall be taken on a resolution to dissolve the corporation. Such resolution shall be adopted upon receiving the affirmative vote of the holders of a majority of the shares of the corporation entitled to vote thereon, unless any class of shares is entitled to vote thereon as a class, in which event the resolution shall be adopted upon receiving the affirmative vote of the holders of a majority of the shares of each class of shares entitled to vote thereon as a class and of the total shares entitled to vote thereon.

(d) Upon the adoption of such resolution, a statement of intent to dissolve shall be executed in duplicate by the corporation by its president or a vice president and by its secretary or an assistant secretary, and verified by one of the officers signing such statement, which statement shall set forth:

(1) The name of the corporation.

(2) The names and respective addresses of its officers.

(3) The names and respective addresses of its directors.

(4) A copy of the resolution adopted by the shareholders authorizing the dissolution of the corporation.

(5) The number of shares outstanding, and, if the shares of any class are entitled to vote as a class, the designation and number of outstanding shares of each such class.

(6) The number of shares voted for and against the resolution, respectively, and, if the shares of any

class are entitled to vote as a class, the number of shares of each such class voted for and against the resolution, respectively.

§ 85. Filing of Statement of Intent to Dissolve

Duplicate originals of the statement of intent to dissolve, whether by consent of shareholders or by act of the corporation, shall be delivered to the Secretary of State. If the Secretary of State finds that such statement conforms to law, he shall, when all fees and franchise taxes have been paid as in this Act prescribed:

(a)   Endorse on each of such duplicate originals the word "Filed," and the month, day and year of the filing thereof.

(b)   File one of such duplicate originals in his office.

(c)   Return the other duplicate original to the corporation or its representative.

§ 86. Effect of Statement of Intent to Dissolve

Upon the filing by the Secretary of State of a statement of intent to dissolve, whether by consent of shareholders or by act of the corporation, the corporation shall cease to carry on its business, except insofar as may be necessary for the winding up thereof, but its corporate existence shall continue until a certificate of dissolution has been issued by the Secretary of State or until a decree dissolving the corporation has been entered by a court of competent jurisdiction as in this Act provided.

§ 87. Procedure after Filing of Statement of Intent to Dissolve

After the filing by the Secretary of State of a statement of intent to dissolve:

(a)   The corporation shall immediately cause notice thereof to be mailed to each known creditor of the corporation.

(b)   The corporation shall proceed to collect its assets, convey and dispose of such of its properties as are not to be distributed in kind to its shareholders, pay, satisfy and discharge its liabilities and obligations and do all other acts required to liquidate its business and affairs, and, after paying or adequately providing for the payment of all its obligations, distribute the remainder of its assets, either in cash or in kind,

among its shareholders according to their respective rights and interests.

(c)   The corporation, at any time during the liquidation of its business and affairs, may make application to a court of competent jurisdiction within the state and judicial subdivision in which the registered office or principal place of business of the corporation is situated, to have the liquidation continued under the supervision of the court as provided in this Act.

§ 88. Revocation of Voluntary Dissolution Proceedings by Consent of Shareholders

By the written consent of all of its shareholders, a corporation may, at any time prior to the issuance of a certificate of dissolution by the Secretary of State, revoke voluntary dissolution proceedings theretofore taken, in the following manner:

Upon the execution of such written consent, a statement of revocation of voluntary dissolution proceedings shall be executed in duplicate by the corporation by its president or a vice president and by its secretary or an assistant secretary, and verified by one of the officers signing such statement, which statement shall set forth:

(a)   The name of the corporation.

(b)   The names and respective addresses of its officers.

(c)   The names and respective addresses of its directors.

(d)   A copy of the written consent signed by all shareholders of the corporation revoking such voluntary dissolution proceedings.

(e)   That such written consent has been signed by all shareholders of the corporation or signed in their names by their attorneys thereunto duly authorized.

§ 89. Revocation of Voluntary Dissolution Proceedings by Act of Corporation

By the act of the corporation, a corporation may, at any time prior to the issuance of a certificate of dissolution by the Secretary of State, revoke voluntary dissolution proceedings theretofore taken, in the following manner:

(a)   The board of directors shall adopt a resolution recommending that the voluntary dissolution proceedings be revoked, and directing that the question of such revocation be submitted to a vote at a special meeting of shareholders.

(b)   Written notice, stating that the purpose or one of the purposes of such meeting is to consider the advisability of revoking the voluntary dissolution proceedings, shall be given to each shareholder of record entitled to vote at such meeting within the time and in the manner provided in this Act for the giving of notice of special meetings of shareholders.

(c)   At such meeting a vote of the shareholders entitled to vote thereat shall be taken on a resolution to revoke the voluntary dissolution proceedings, which shall require for its adoption the affirmative vote of the holders of a majority of the shares entitled to vote thereon.

(d)   Upon the adoption of such resolution, a statement of revocation of voluntary dissolution proceedings shall be executed in duplicate by the corporation by its president or a vice president and by its secretary or an assistant secretary, and verified by one of the officers signing such statement, which statement shall set forth:

(1)   The name of the corporation.
(2)   The names and respective addresses of its officers.
(3)   The names and respective addresses of its directors.
(4)   A copy of the resolution adopted by the shareholders revoking the voluntary dissolution proceedings.
(5)   The number of shares outstanding.
(6)   The number of shares voted for and against the resolution, respectively.

§ 90. Filing of Statement of Revocation of Voluntary Dissolution Proceedings

Duplicate originals of the statement of revocation of voluntary dissolution proceedings, whether by consent of shareholders or by act of the corporation, shall be delivered to the Secretary of State. If the Secretary of State finds that such statement conforms to law, he shall, when all fees and franchise taxes have been paid as in this Act prescribed:

(a)   Endorse on each of such duplicate originals the word "Filed," and the month, day and year of the filing thereof.

(b)   File one of such duplicate originals in his office.

(c)   Return the other duplicate original to the corporation or its representative.

§ 91. Effect of Statement of Revocation of Voluntary Dissolution Proceedings

Upon the filing by the Secretary of State of a statement of revocation of voluntary dissolution proceedings, whether by consent of shareholders or by act of the corporation, the revocation of the voluntary dissolution proceedings shall become effective and the corporation may again carry on its business.

§ 92. Articles of Dissolution

If voluntary dissolution proceedings have not been revoked, then when all debts, liabilities and obligations of the corporation have been paid and discharged, or adequate provision has been made therefor, and all of the remaining property and assets of the corporation have been distributed to its shareholders, articles of dissolution shall be executed in duplicate by the corporation by its president or a vice president and by its secretary or an assistant secretary, and verified by one of the officers signing such statement, which statement shall set forth:

(a)   The name of the corporation.

(b)   That the Secretary of State has theretofore filed a statement of intent to dissolve the corporation, and the date on which such statement was filed.

(c)   That all debts, obligations and liabilities of the corporation have been paid and discharged or that adequate provision has been made therefor.

(d)   That all the remaining property and assets of the corporation have been distributed among its shareholders in accordance with their respective rights and interests.

(e)   That there are no suits pending against the corporation in any court, or that adequate provision has been made for the satisfaction of any judgment, order or decree which may be entered against it in any pending suit.

§ 93. Filing of Articles of Dissolution

Duplicate originals of such articles of dissolution shall be delivered to the Secretary of State. If the Secretary of State finds that such articles of dissolution conform to law, he shall, when all fees and franchise taxes have been paid as in this Act prescribed:

(a)   Endorse on each of such duplicate originals the word "Filed," and the month, day and year of the filing thereof.

(b)   File one of such duplicate originals in his office.

(c)   Issue a certificate of dissolution to which he shall affix the other duplicate original.

The certificate of dissolution, together with the duplicate original of the articles of dissolution affixed thereto by the Secretary of State, shall be returned to the representative of the dissolved corporation. Upon the issuance of such certificate of dissolution the existence of the corporation shall cease, except for the purpose of suits, other proceedings and appropriate corporate action by shareholders, directors and officers as provided in this Act.

§ 94. Involuntary Dissolution

A corporation may be dissolved involuntarily by a decree of the .... court in an action filed by the Attorney General when it is established that:

(a)   The corporation has failed to file its annual report within the time required by this Act, or has failed to pay its franchise tax on or before the first day of August of the year in which such franchise tax becomes due and payable; or

(b)   The corporation procured its articles of incorporation through fraud; or

(c)   The corporation has continued to exceed or abuse the authority conferred upon it by law; or

(d)   The corporation has failed for thirty days to appoint and maintain a registered agent in this State; or

(e)   The corporation has failed for thirty days after change of its registered office or registered agent to file in the office of the Secretary of State a statement of such change.

§ 95. Notification to Attorney General

The Secretary of State, on or before the last day of December of each year, shall certify to the Attorney General the names of all corporations which have failed to file their annual reports or to pay franchise taxes in accordance with the provisions of this Act, together with the facts pertinent thereto. He shall also certify, from time to time, the names of all corporations which have given other cause for dissolution as provided in this Act, together with the facts pertinent

thereto. Whenever the Secretary of State shall certify the name of a corporation to the Attorney General as having given any cause for dissolution, the Secretary of State shall concurrently mail to the corporation at its registered office a notice that such certification has been made. Upon the receipt of such certification, the Attorney General shall file an action in the name of the State against such corporation for its dissolution. Every such certificate from the Secretary of State to the Attorney General pertaining to the failure of a corporation to file an annual report or pay a franchise tax shall be taken and received in all courts as prima facie evidence of the facts therein stated. If, before action is filed, the corporation shall file its annual report or pay its franchise tax, together with all penalties thereon, or shall appoint or maintain a registered agent as provided in this Act, or shall file with the Secretary of State the required statement of change of registered office or registered agent, such fact shall be forthwith certified by the Secretary of State to the Attorney General and he shall not file an action against such corporation for such cause. If, after action is filed, the corporation shall file its annual report or pay its franchise tax, together with all penalties thereon, or shall appoint or maintain a registered agent as provided in this Act, or shall file with the Secretary of State the required statement of change of registered office or registered agent, and shall pay the costs of such action, the action for such cause shall abate.

§ 96. Venue and Process

Every action for the involuntary dissolution of a corporation shall be commenced by the Attorney General either in the .... court of the county in which the registered office of the corporation is situated, or in the .... court of .... county. Summons shall issue and be served as in other civil actions. If process is returned not found, the Attorney General shall cause publication to be made as in other civil cases in some newspaper published in the county where the registered office of the corporation is situated, containing a notice of the pendency of such action, the title of the court, the title of the action, and the date on or after which default may be entered. The Attorney General may include in one notice the names of any number of corporations against which actions are then pending in the same court. The Attorney General shall cause a copy of such notice to be mailed to the corporation at its registered office within ten days after the first publication thereof. The certificate of the Attorney General of the mailing of such notice shall be prima facie evidence thereof. Such notice shall be published at least once each week for two successive weeks, and the first publication thereof may begin at any time after the summons has been returned. Unless a corporation shall have been served with summons, no default shall be taken against it earlier than thirty days after the first publication of such notice.

§ 97. Jurisdiction of Court to Liquidate Assets and Business of Corporation

The .... courts shall have full power to liquidate the assets and business of a corporation:

(a)   In an action by a shareholder when it is established:

(1)   That the directors are deadlocked in the management of the corporate affairs and the shareholders are unable to break the deadlock, and that irreparable injury to the corporation is being suffered or is threatened by reason thereof; or

(2)   That the acts of the directors or those in control of the corporation are illegal, oppressive or fraudulent; or

(3)   That the shareholders are deadlocked in voting power, and have failed, for a period which includes at least two consecutive annual meeting dates, to elect successors to directors whose terms have expired or would have expired upon the election of their successors; or

(4)   That the corporate assets are being misapplied or wasted.

(b)   In an action by a creditor:

(1)   Then the claim of the creditor has been reduced to judgment and an execution thereon returned unsatisfied and it is established that the corporation is insolvent; or

(2)   When the corporation has admitted in writing that the claim of the creditor is due and owing and it is established that the corporation is insolvent.

(c)   Upon application by a corporation which has filed a statement of intent to dissolve, as provided in this Act, to have its liquidation continued under the supervision of the court.

(d)   When an action has been filed by the Attorney General to dissolve a corporation and it is established that liquidation of its business and affairs should precede the entry of a decree of dissolution.

Proceedings under clause (a), (b) or (c) of this section shall be brought in the county in which the registered office or the principal office of the corporation is situated.

It shall not be necessary to make shareholders parties to any such action or proceeding unless relief is sought against them personally.

§ 98. Procedure in Liquidation of Corporation by Court

In proceedings to liquidate the assets and business of a corporation the court shall have power to issue injunctions, to appoint a receiver or receivers pendente lite, with such powers and duties as the court, from time to time, may direct, and to take such other proceedings as may be requisite to preserve the corporate assets wherever situated, and carry on the business of the corporation until a full hearing can be had.

After a hearing had upon such notice as the court may direct to be given to all parties to the proceedings and to any other parties in interest designated by the court, the court may appoint a liquidating receiver or receivers with authority to collect the assets of the corporation, including all amounts owing to the corporation by subscribers on account of any unpaid portion of the consideration for the issuance of shares. Such liquidating receiver or receivers shall have authority, subject to the order of the court, to sell, convey and dispose of all or any part of the assets of the corporation wherever situated, either at public or private sale. The assets of the corporation or the proceeds resulting from a sale, conveyance or other disposition thereof shall be applied to the expenses of such liquidation and to the payment of the liabilities and obligations of the corporation, and any remaining assets or proceeds shall be distributed among its shareholders according to their respective rights and interests. The order appointing such liquidating receiver or receivers shall state their powers and duties. Such powers and duties may be increased or diminished at any time during the proceedings.

The court shall have power to allow from time to time as expenses of the liquidation compensation to the receiver or receivers and to attorneys in the proceeding, and to direct the payment thereof out of the assets of the corporation or the proceeds of any sale or disposition of such assets.

A receiver of a corporation appointed under the provisions of this section shall have authority to sue and defend in all courts in his own name as receiver of such corporation. The court appointing such receiver shall have exclusive jurisdiction of the corporation and its property, wherever situated.

§ 99. Qualifications of Receivers

A receiver shall in all cases be a natural person or a corporation authorized to act as receiver, which corporation may be a domestic corporation or a foreign corporation authorized to transact business in this State, and shall in all cases give such bond as the court may direct with such sureties as the court may require.

§ 100. Filing of Claims in Liquidation Proceedings

In proceedings to liquidate the assets and business of a corporation the court may require all creditors of the corporation to file with the clerk of the court or with the receiver, in such form as the court may prescribe, proofs under oath of their respective claims. If the court requires the filing of claims it shall fix a date, which shall be not less than four months from the date of the order, as the last day for the filing of claims, and shall prescribe the notice that shall be given to creditors and claimants of the date so fixed. Prior to the date so fixed, the court may extend the time for the filing of claims. Creditors and claimants failing to file proofs of claim on or before the date so fixed may be barred, by order of court, from participating in the distribution of the assets of the corporation.

§ 101. Discontinuance of Liquidation Proceedings

The liquidation of the assets and business of a corporation may be discontinued at any time during the liquidation proceedings when it is established that cause for liquidation no longer exists. In such event the court shall dismiss the proceedings and direct the receiver to redeliver to the corporation all its remaining property and assets.

§ 102. Decree of Involuntary Dissolution

In proceedings to liquidate the assets and business of a corporation, when the costs and expenses of such proceedings and all debts, obligations and liabilities of the corporation shall have been paid and discharged and all of its remaining property and assets distributed to its shareholders, or in case its property and assets are not sufficient to satisfy and discharge such costs, expenses, debts and obligations, all the property and assets have been applied so far as they will go to their payment, the court shall enter a decree dissolving the corporation, whereupon the existence of the corporation shall cease.

§ 103. Filing of Decree of Dissolution

In case the court shall enter a decree dissolving a corporation, it shall be the duty of the clerk of such court to cause a certified copy of the decree to be filed with the Secretary of State. No fee shall be charged by the Secretary of State for the filing thereof.

§ 104. Deposit with State Treasurer of Amount Due Certain Shareholders

Upon the voluntary or involuntary dissolution of a corporation, the portion of the assets distributable to a creditor or shareholder who is unknown or cannot be found, or who is under disability and there is no person legally competent to receive such distributive portion, shall be reduced to cash and deposited with the State Treasurer and shall be paid over to such creditor or shareholder or to his legal representative upon proof satisfactory to the State Treasurer of his right thereto.

§ 105. Survival of Remedy after Dissolution

The dissolution of a corporation either (1) by the issuance of a certificate of dissolution by the Secretary of State, or (2) by a decree of court when the court has not liquidated the assets and business of the corporation as provided in this Act, or (3) by expiration of its period of duration, shall not take away or impair any remedy available to or against such corporation, its directors, officers, or shareholders, for any right or claim existing, or any liability incurred, prior to such dissolution if action or other proceeding thereon is commenced within two years after the date of such dissolution. Any such action or proceeding by or against the corporation may be prosecuted or defended by the corporation in its corporate name. The shareholders, directors and officers shall have power to take such corporate or other action as shall be appropriate to protect such remedy, right or claim. If such corporation was dissolved by the expiration of its period of duration, such corporation may amend its articles of incorporation at any time during such period of two years so as to extend its period of duration.

§ 106. Admission of Foreign Corporation

No foreign corporation shall have the right to transact business in this State until it shall have procured a certificate of authority so to do from the Secretary of State. No foreign corporation shall be entitled to procure a certificate of authority under this Act to transact in this State any business which a corporation organized under this Act is not permitted to transact. A foreign corporation shall not be denied a certificate of authority by reason of the fact that the laws of the state or country under which such corporation is organized governing its organization and internal affairs differ from the laws of this State, and nothing in this Act contained shall be construed to authorize this State to regulate the organization or the internal affairs of such corporation.

Without excluding other activities which may not constitute transacting business in this State, a foreign corporation shall not be considered to be transacting business in this State, for the purposes of this Act, by reason of carrying on in this State any one or more of the following activities:

(a)   Maintaining or defending any action or suit or any administrative or arbitration proceeding, or effecting the settlement thereof or the settlement of claims or disputes.

(b)   Holding meetings of its directors or shareholders or carrying on other activities concerning its internal affairs.

(c)   Maintaining bank accounts.

(d)   Maintaining offices or agencies for the transfer, exchange and registration of its securities, or appointing and maintaining trustees or depositaries with relation to its securities.

(e)   Effecting sales through independent contractors.

(f)   Soliciting or procuring orders, whether by mail or through employees or agents or otherwise, where such orders require acceptance without this State before becoming binding contracts.

(g)   Creating as borrower or lender, or acquiring, indebtedness or mortgages or other security interests in real or personal property.

(h)   Securing or collecting debts or enforcing any rights in property securing the same.

(i)   Transacting any business in interstate commerce.

(j)   Conducting an isolated transaction completed within a period of thirty days and not in the course of a number of repeated transactions of like nature.

§ 107. Powers of Foreign Corporation

A foreign corporation which shall have received a certificate of authority under this Act shall, until a certificate of revocation or of withdrawal shall have been issued as provided in this Act, enjoy the same, but no greater, rights and privileges as a domestic corporation organized for the purposes set forth in the application pursuant to which such certificate of authority is issued; and, except as in this Act otherwise provided, shall be subject to the same duties, restrictions, penalties and liabilities now or hereafter imposed upon a domestic corporation of like character.

§ 108. Corporate Name of Foreign Corporation

No certificate of authority shall be issued to a foreign corporation unless the corporate name of such corporation:

(a)   Shall contain the word "corporation," "company," "incorporated," or "limited," or shall contain an abbreviation of one of such words, or such corporation shall, for use in this State, add at the end of its name one of such words or an abbreviation thereof.

(b)   Shall not contain any word or phrase which indicates or implies that it is organized for any purpose other than one or more of the purposes contained in its articles of incorporation or that it is authorized or empowered to conduct the business of banking or insurance.

(c)   Shall not be the same as, or deceptively similar to, the name of any domestic corporation existing under the laws of this State or any foreign corporation authorized to transact business in this State, or a name the exclusive right to which is, at the time, reserved in the manner provided in this Act, or the name of a corporation which has in effect a registration of its name as provided in this Act except that this provision shall not apply if the foreign corporation applying for a certificate of authority files with the Secretary of State any one of the following:

(1)   a resolution of its board of directors adopting a fictitious name for use in transacting business in this State which fictitious name is not deceptively similar to the name of any domestic corporation or of any foreign corporation authorized to transact business in this State or to any name reserved or registered as provided in this Act, or

(2)   the written consent of such other corporation or holder of a reserved or registered name to use the same or deceptively similar name and one or more words are added to make such name distinguishable from such other name, or

(3)   a certified copy of a final decree of a court of competent jurisdiction establishing the prior right of such foreign corporation to the use of such name in this State.

§ 109. Change of Name by Foreign Corporation

Whenever a foreign corporation which is authorized to transact business in this State shall change its name to one under which a certificate of authority would not be granted to it on application therefor, the certificate of authority of such corporation shall be suspended and it shall not thereafter transact any business in this State until it has changed its name to a name which is available to it under the laws of this State or has otherwise complied with the provisions of this Act.

§ 110. Application for Certificate of Authority

A foreign corporation, in order to procure a certificate of authority to transact business in this State, shall make application therefor to the Secretary of State, which application shall set forth:

(a)   The name of the corporation and the state or county under the laws of which it is incorporated.

(b)   If the name of the corporation does not contain the word "corporation," "company," "incorporated," or "limited," or does not contain an abbreviation of one of such words, then the name of the corporation with the word or abbreviation which it elects to add thereto for use in this State.

(c)   The date of incorporation and the period of duration of the corporation.

(d)   The address of the principal office of the corporation in the state or country under the laws of which it is incorporated.

(e)   The address of the proposed registered office of the corporation in this State, and the name of its proposed registered agent in this State at such address.

(f)   The purpose or purposes of the corporation which it proposes to pursue in the transaction of business in this State.

(g)   The names and respective addresses of the directors and officers of the corporation.

(h)   A statement of the aggregate number of shares which the corporation has authority to issue, itemized by classes and series, if any, within a class.

(i)   A statement of the aggregate number of issued shares, itemized by class and by series, if any, within each class.

(j)   An estimate, expressed in dollars, of the value of all property to be owned by the corporation for the following year, wherever located, and an estimate of the value of the property of the corporation to be located within the State during such year, and an estimate, expressed in dollars of the gross amount of business which will be transacted by the corporation during such year, and an estimate of the gross amount thereof which will be transacted by the corporation at or from places of business in this State during such year.

(k)   Such additional information as may be necessary or appropriate in order to enable the Secretary of State to determine whether such corporation is entitled to a certificate of authority to transact business in this State and to determine and assess the fees and franchise taxes payable as in this Act prescribed.

Such application shall be made on forms prescribed and furnished by the Secretary of State and shall be executed in duplicate by the corporation by its president or a vice president and by its secretary or an assistant secretary, and verified by one of the officers signing such application.

§ 111. Filing of Application for Certificate of Authority

Duplicate originals of the application of the corporation for a certificate of authority shall be delivered to the Secretary of State, together with a copy of its articles of incorporation and all amendments thereto, duly authenticated by the proper officer of the state or country under the laws of which it is incorporated.

If the Secretary of State finds that such application conforms to law, he shall, when all fees and franchise taxes have been paid as in this Act prescribed:

(a)   Endorse on each of such documents the word "Filed," and the month, day and year of the filing thereof.

(b)   File in his office one of such duplicate originals of the application and the copy of the articles of incorporation and amendments thereto.

(c)   Issue a certificate of authority to transact business in this State to which he shall affix the other duplicate original application.

The certificate of authority, together with the duplicate original of the application affixed thereto by the Secretary of State, shall be returned to the corporation or its representative.

§ 112. Effect of Certificate of Authority

Upon the issuance of a certificate of authority by the Secretary of State, the corporation shall be authorized to transact business in this State for those purposes set forth in its application, subject, however, to the right of this State to suspend or to revoke such authority as provided in this Act.

§ 113. Registered Office and Registered Agent of Foreign Corporation

Each foreign corporation authorized to transact business in this State shall have and continuously maintain in this State:

(a)   A registered office which may be, but need not be, the same as its place of business in this State.

(b)   A registered agent, which agent may be either an individual resident in this State whose business office is identical with such registered office, or a domestic corporation, or a foreign corporation authorized to transact business in this State, having a business office identical with such registered office.

§ 114. Change of Registered Office or Registered Agent of Foreign Corporation

A foreign corporation authorized to transact business in this State may change its registered office or change its registered agent, or both, upon filing in the office of the Secretary of State a statement setting forth:

(a)   The name of the corporation.

(b)   The address of its then registered office.

(c)   If the address of its registered office be changed, the address to which the registered office is to be changed.

(d)   The name of its then registered agent.

(e)   If its registered agent be changed, the name of its successor registered agent.

(f)   That the address of its registered office and the address of the business office of its registered agent, as changed, will be identical.

(g)   That such change was authorized by resolution duly adopted by its board of directors.

Such statement shall be executed by the corporation by its president or a vice president, and verified by him, and delivered to the Secretary of State. If the Secretary of State finds that such statement conforms to the provisions of this Act, he shall file such statement in his office, and upon such filing the change of address of the registered office, or the appointment of a new registered agent, or both, as the case may be, shall become effective.

Any registered agent of a foreign corporation may resign as such agent upon filing a written notice thereof, executed in duplicate, with the Secretary of State, who shall forthwith mail a copy thereof to the corporation at its principal office in the state or country under the laws of which it is incorporated. The appointment of such agent shall terminate upon the expiration of thirty days after receipt of such notice by the Secretary of State.

If a registered agent changes his or its business address to another place within the same .... *, he or it may change such address and the address of the registered office of any corporation of which he or it is registered agent by filing a statement as required above except that it need be signed only by the registered agent and need not be responsive to (e) or (g) and must recite that a copy of the statement has been mailed to the corporation.

§ 115. Service of Process on Foreign Corporation

The registered agent so appointed by a foreign corporation authorized to transact business in this State shall be an agent of such corporation upon whom any process, notice or demand required or permitted by law to be served upon the corporation may be served.

Whenever a foreign corporation authorized to transact business in this State shall fail to appoint or maintain a registered agent in this State, or whenever any such registered agent cannot with reasonable diligence be found at the registered office, or whenever the certificate of authority of a foreign corporation

*Supply designation of jurisdiction, such as county, etc., in accordance with local practice.

shall be suspended or revoked, then the Secretary of State shall be an agent of such corporation upon whom any such process, notice, or demand may be served. Service on the Secretary of State of any such process, notice or demand shall be made by delivering to and leaving with him, or with any clerk having charge of the corporation department of his office, duplicate copies of such process, notice or demand. In the event any such process, notice or demand is served on the Secretary of State, he shall immediately cause one of such copies thereof to be forwarded by registered mail, addressed to the corporation at its principal office in the state or country under the laws of which it is incorporated. Any service so had on the Secretary of State shall be returnable in not less than thirty days.

The Secretary of State shall keep a record of all processes, notices and demands served upon him under this section, and shall record therein the time of such service and his action with reference thereto.

Nothing herein contained shall limit or affect the right to serve any process, notice or demand, required or permitted by law to be served upon a foreign corporation in any other manner now or hereafter permitted by law.

§ 116. Amendment to Articles of Incorporation of Foreign Corporation

Whenever the articles of incorporation of a foreign corporation authorized to transact business in this State are amended, such foreign corporation shall, within thirty days after such amendment becomes effective, file in the office of the Secretary of State a copy of such amendment duly authenticated by the proper officer of the state or country under the laws of which it is incorporated; but the filing thereof shall not of itself enlarge or alter the purpose or purposes which such corporation is authorized to pursue in the transaction of business in this State, nor authorize such corporation to transact business in this State under any other name than the name set forth in its certificate of authority.

§ 117. Merger of Foreign Corporation Authorized to Transact Business in This State

Whenever a foreign corporation authorized to transact business in this State shall be a party to a statutory merger permitted by the laws of the state or country under the laws of which it is incorporated, and such corporation shall be the surviving corporation, it shall, within thirty days after such merger becomes effective,

file with the Secretary of State a copy of the articles of merger duly authenticated by the proper officer of the state or country under the laws of which such statutory merger was effected; and it shall not be necessary for such corporation to procure either a new or amended certificate of authority to transact business in this State unless the name of such corporation be changed thereby or unless the corporation desires to pursue in this State other or additional purposes than those which it is then authorized to transact in this State.

§ 118. Amended Certificate of Authority

A foreign corporation authorized to transact business in this State shall procure an amended certificate of authority in the event it changes its corporate name, or desires to pursue in this State other or additional purposes than those set forth in its prior application for a certificate of authority, by making application therefor to the Secretary of State.

The requirements in respect to the form and contents of such application, the manner of its execution, the filing of duplicate originals thereof with the Secretary of State, the issuance of an amended certificate of authority and the effect thereof, shall be the same as in the case of an original application for a certificate of authority.

§ 119. Withdrawal of Foreign Corporation

A foreign corporation authorized to transact business in this State may withdraw from this State upon procuring from the Secretary of State a certificate of withdrawal. In order to procure such certificate of withdrawal, such foreign corporation shall deliver to the Secretary of State an application for withdrawal, which shall set forth:

(a)   The name of the corporation and the state or country under the laws of which it is incorporated.

(b)   That the corporation is not transacting business in this State.

(c)   That the corporation surrenders its authority to transact business in this State.

(d)   That the corporation revokes the authority of its registered agent in this State to accept service of process and consents that service of process in any action, suit or proceeding based upon any cause of action arising in this State during the time the corporation was authorized to transact business in this State may thereafter be made on such corporation by service thereof on the Secretary of State.

(e) A post-office address to which the Secretary of State may mail a copy of any process against the corporation that may be served on him.

(f) A statement of the aggregate number of shares which the corporation has authority to issue, itemized by class and series, if any, within each class, as of the date of such application.

(g) A statement of the aggregate number of issued shares, itemized by class and series, if any, within each class, as of the date of such application.

(h) Such additional information as may be necessary or appropriate in order to enable the Secretary of State to determine and assess any unpaid fees or franchise taxes payable by such foreign corporation as in this Act prescribed.

The application for withdrawal shall be made on forms prescribed and furnished by the Secretary of State and shall be executed by the corporation by its president or a vice president and by its secretary or an assistant secretary, and verified by one of the officers signing the application, or, if the corporation is in the hands of a receiver or trustee, shall be executed on behalf of the corporation by such receiver or trustee and verified by him.

§ 120. Filing of Application for Withdrawal

Duplicate originals of such application for withdrawal shall be delivered to the Secretary of State. If the Secretary of State finds that such application conforms to the provisions of this Act, he shall, when all fees and franchise taxes have been paid as in this Act prescribed:

(a) Endorse on each of such duplicate originals the word "Filed," and the month, day and year of the filing thereof.

(b) File one of such duplicate originals in his office.

(c) Issue a certificate of withdrawal to which he shall affix the other duplicate original.

The certificate of withdrawal, together with the duplicate original of the application for withdrawal affixed thereto by the Secretary of State, shall be returned to the corporation or its representative. Upon the issuance of such certificate of withdrawal, the authority of the corporation to transact business in this State shall cease.

§ 121. Revocation of Certificate of Authority

The certificate of authority of a foreign corporation to transact business in this State may be revoked by the Secretary of State upon the conditions prescribed in this section when:

(a) The corporation has failed to file its annual report within the time required by this Act, or has failed to pay any fees, franchise taxes or penalties prescribed by this Act when they have become due and payable; or

(b) The corporation has failed to appoint and maintain a registered agent in this State as required by this Act; or

(c) The corporation has failed, after change of its registered office or registered agent, to file in the office of the Secretary of State a statement of such change as required by this Act; or

(d) The corporation has failed to file in the office of the Secretary of State any amendment to its articles of incorporation or any articles of merger within the time prescribed by this Act; or

(e) A misrepresentation has been made of any material matter in any application, report, affidavit, or other document submitted by such corporation pursuant to this Act.

No certificate of authority of a foreign corporation shall be revoked by the Secretary of State unless (1) he shall have given the corporation not less than sixty days' notice thereof by mail addressed to its registered office in this State, and (2) the corporation shall fail prior to revocation to file such annual report, or pay such fees, franchise taxes or penalties, or file the required statement of change of registered agent or registered office, or file such articles of amendment or articles of merger, or correct such misrepresentation.

§ 122. Issuance of Certificate of Revocation

Upon revoking any such certificate of authority, the Secretary of State shall:

(a) Issue a certificate of revocation in duplicate.

(b) File one of such certificates in his office.

(c) Mail to such corporation at its registered office in this State a notice of such revocation accompanied by one of such certificates.

Upon the issuance of such certificate of revocation, the authority of the corporation to transact business in this State shall cease.

§ 123. Application to Corporations Heretofore Authorized to Transact Business in This State

Foreign corporations which are duly authorized to transact business in this State at the time this Act takes effect, for a purpose or purposes for which a corporation might secure such authority under this Act, shall, subject to the limitations set forth in their respective certificates of authority, be entitled to all the rights and privileges applicable to foreign corporations procuring certificates of authority to transact business in this State under this Act, and from the time this Act takes effect such corporations shall be subject to all the limitations, restrictions, liabilities, and duties prescribed herein for foreign corporations procuring certificates of authority to transact business in this State under this Act.

§ 124. Transacting Business Without Certificate of Authority

No foreign corporation transacting business in this State without a certificate of authority shall be permitted to maintain any action, suit or proceeding in any court of this State, until such corporation shall have obtained a certificate of authority. Nor shall any action, suit or proceeding be maintained in any court of this State by any successor or assignee of such corporation on any right, claim or demand arising out of the transaction of business by such corporation in this State, until a certificate of authority shall have been obtained by such corporation or by a corporation which has acquired all or substantially all of its assets.

The failure of a foreign corporation to obtain a certificate of authority to transact business in this State shall not impair the validity of any contract or act of such corporation, and shall not prevent such corporation from defending any action, suit or proceeding in any court of this State.

A foreign corporation which transacts business in this State without a certificate of authority shall be liable to this State, for the years or parts thereof during which it transacted business in this State without a certificate of authority, in an amount equal to all fees and franchise taxes which would have been imposed by this Act upon such corporation had it

duly applied for and received a certificate of authority to transact business in this State as required by this Act and thereafter filed all reports required by this Act, plus all penalties imposed by this Act for failure to pay such fees and franchise taxes. The Attorney General shall bring proceedings to recover all amounts due this State under the provisions of this Section.

§ 125. Annual Report of Domestic and Foreign Corporations

Each domestic corporation, and each foreign corporation authorized to transact business in this State, shall file, within the time prescribed by this Act, an annual report setting forth:

(a) The name of the corporation and the state or country under the laws of which it is incorporated.

(b) The address of the registered office of the corporation in this State, and the name of its registered agent in this State at such address, and, in case of a foreign corporation, the address of its principal office in the state or country under the laws of which it is incorporated.

(c) A brief statement of the character of the business in which the corporation is actually engaged in this State.

(d) The names and respective addresses of the directors and officers of the corporation.

(e) A statement of the aggregate number of shares which the corporation has authority to issue, itemized by class and series, if any, within each class.

(f) A statement of the aggregate number of issued shares, itemized by class and series, if any, within each class.

(g) A statement, expressed in dollars, of the value of all the property owned by the corporation, wherever located, and the value of the property of the corporation located within this State, and a statement, expressed in dollars, of the gross amount of business transacted by the corporation for the twelve months ended on the thirty-first day of December preceding the date herein provided for the filing of such report and the gross amount thereof transacted by the corporation at or from places of business in this State. If, on the thirty-first day of December preceding the time herein provided for the filing of such report, the corporation had not been in existence for a period of twelve months, or in the case of a foreign corporation had not been authorized to transact business in this State for a period of twelve months, the statement with respect to business transacted shall be furnished for the period between the date of incorporation or the date of its authorization to transact business in this State, as the case may be, and such thirty-first day of December. If all the property of the corporation is located in this State and all of its business is transacted at or from places of business in this State, then the information required by this subparagraph need not be set forth in such report.

(h) Such additional information as may be necessary or appropriate in order to enable the Secretary of State to determine and assess the proper amount of franchise taxes payable by such corporation.

Such annual report shall be made on forms prescribed and furnished by the Secretary of State, and the information therein contained shall be given as of the date of the execution of the report, except as to the information required by subparagraphs (g) and (h) which shall be given as of the close of business on the thirty-first day of December next preceding the date herein provided for the filing of such report. It shall be executed by the corporation by its president, a vice president, secretary, an assistant secretary, or treasurer, and verified by the officer executing the report, or, if the corporation is in the hands of a receiver or trustee, it shall be executed on behalf of the corporation and verified by such receiver or trustee.

§ 126. Filing of Annual Report of Domestic and Foreign Corporations

Such annual report of a domestic or foreign corporation shall be delivered to the Secretary of State between the first day of January and the first day of March of each year, except that the first annual report of a domestic or foreign corporation shall be filed between the first day of January and the first day of March of the year next succeeding the calendar year in which its certificate of incorporation or its certificate of authority, as the case may be, was issued by the Secretary of State. Proof to the satisfaction of the Secretary of State that prior to the first day of March such report was deposited in the United States mail in a sealed envelope, properly addressed, with postage prepaid, shall be deemed a compliance with this requirement. If the Secretary of State finds that such report conforms to the requirements of this Act, he shall file the same. If he finds that it does not so

conform, he shall promptly return the same to the corporation for any necessary corrections, in which event the penalties hereinafter prescribed for failure to file such report within the time hereinabove provided shall not apply, if such report is corrected to conform to the requirements of this Act and returned to the Secretary of State within thirty days from the date on which it was mailed to the corporation by the Secretary of State.

§ 127. Fees, Franchise Taxes and Charges to be Collected by Secretary of State

The Secretary of State shall charge and collect in accordance with the provisions of this Act:

(a) Fees for filing documents and issuing certificates.

(b) Miscellaneous charges.

(c) License fees.

(d) Franchise taxes.

§ 128. Fees for Filing Documents and Issuing Certificates

The Secretary of State shall charge and collect for:

(a) Filing articles of incorporation and issuing a certificate of incorporation, ... dollars.

(b) Filing articles of amendment and issuing a certificate of amendment, ... dollars.

(c) Filing restated articles of incorporation, ... dollars.

(d) Filing articles of merger or consolidation and issuing a certificate of merger or consolidation, ... dollars.

(e) Filing an application to reserve a corporate name, ... dollars.

(f) Filing a notice of transfer of a reserved corporate name, ... dollars.

(g) Filing a statement of change of address of registered office or change of registered agent or both, ... dollars.

(h) Filing a statement of the establishment of a series of shares, ... dollars.

(i) Filing a statement of intent to dissolve, ... dollars.

(j) Filing a statement of revocation of voluntary dissolution proceedings, ... dollars.

(k)   Filing articles of dissolution, ... dollars.

(l)   Filing an application of a foreign corporation for a certificate of authority to transact business in this State and issuing a certificate of authority, ... dollars.

(m)   Filing an application of a foreign corporation for an amended certificate of authority to transact business in this State and issuing an amended certificate of authority, ... dollars.

(n)   Filing a copy of an amendment to the articles of incorporation of a foreign corporation holding a certificate of authority to transact business in this State, ... dollars.

(o)   Filing a copy of articles of merger of a foreign corporation holding a certificate of authority to transact business in this State, ... dollars.

(p)   Filing an application for withdrawal of a foreign corporation and issuing a certificate of withdrawal, ... dollars.

(q)   Filing any other statement or report, except an annual report, of a domestic or foreign corporation, ... dollars.

§ 129. Miscellaneous Charges

The Secretary of State shall charge and collect:

(a)   For furnishing a certified copy of any document, instrument, or paper relating to a corporation, ... cents per page and .... dollars for the certificate and affixing the seal thereto.

(b)   At the time of any service of process on him as resident agent of a corporation, ... dollars, which amount may be recovered as taxable costs by the party to the suit or action causing such service to be made if such party prevails in the suit or action.

§ 130. License Fees Payable by Domestic Corporations

The Secretary of State shall charge and collect from each domestic corporation license fees, based upon the number of shares which it will have authority to issue or the increase in the number of shares which it will have authority to issue, at the time of:

(a)   Filing articles of incorporation;

(b)   Filing articles of amendment increasing the number of authorized shares; and

(c)   Filing articles of merger or consolidation increasing the number of authorized shares which the surviving or new corporation, if a domestic corporation, will have the authority to issue above the aggregate number of shares which the constituent domestic corporations and constituent foreign corporations authorized to transact business in this State had authority to issue.

The license fees shall be at the rate of .... cents per share up to and including the first 10,000 authorized shares, ... cents per share for each authorized share in excess of 10,000 shares up to and including 100,000 shares, and .... cents per share for each authorized share in excess of 100,000 shares.

The license fees payable on an increase in the number of authorized shares shall be imposed only on the increased number of shares, and the number of previously authorized shares shall be taken into account in determining the rate applicable to the increased number of authorized shares.

§ 131. License Fees Payable by Foreign Corporations

The Secretary of State shall charge and collect from each foreign corporation license fees, based upon the proportion represented in this State of the number of shares which it has authority to issue or the increase in the number of shares which it has authority to issue, at the time of:

(a)   Filing an application for a certificate of authority to transact business in this State;

(b)   Filing articles of amendment which increased the number of authorized shares; and

(c)   Filing articles of merger or consolidation which increased the number of authorized shares which the surviving or new corporation, if a foreign corporation, has authority to issue above the aggregate number of shares which the constituent domestic corporations and constituent foreign corporations authorized to transact business in this State had authority to issue.

The license fees shall be at the rate of .... cents per share up to and including the first 10,000 authorized shares represented in this State, ... cents per share for each authorized share in excess of 10,000 shares up to and including 100,000 shares represented in this State, and .... cents per share for each authorized share in excess of 100,000 shares represented in this State.

The license fees payable on an increase in the number of authorized shares shall be imposed only on the increased number of such shares represented in this State, and the number of previously authorized shares represented in this State shall be taken into account in determining the rate applicable to the increased number of authorized shares.

The number of authorized shares represented in this State shall be that proportion of its total authorized shares which the sum of the value of its property located in this State and the gross amount of business transacted by it at or from places of business in this State bears to the sum of the value of all of its property, wherever located, and the gross amount of its business, wherever transacted. Such proportion shall be determined from information contained in the application for a certificate of authority to transact business in this State until the filing of an annual report and thereafter from information contained in the latest annual report filed by the corporation.

§ 132. Franchise Taxes Payable by Domestic Corporations

The Secretary of State shall charge and collect from each domestic corporation an initial franchise tax at the time of filing its articles of incorporation at the rate of one-twelfth of one-half of the license fee payable by such corporation under the provisions of this Act at the time of filing its articles of incorporation, for each calendar month, or fraction thereof, between the date of the issuance of the certificate of incorporation by the Secretary of State and the first day of July of the next succeeding calendar year.

The Secretary of State shall charge and collect from each domestic corporation an annual franchise tax, payable in advance for the period from July 1 in each year to July 1 in the succeeding year, beginning July 1 in the calendar year in which such corporation is required to file its first annual report under this Act, (Alternative 1: at the rate of .... per cent of the amount represented in this State of the stated capital of the corporation, as determined in accordance with accounting practices and principles that are reasonable in the circumstances, as disclosed by the latest report filed by the corporation with the Secretary of State) (Alternative 2: at the rate of .... cents per share up to and including the first 10,000 issued and outstanding shares, and .... cents per share for each issued and outstanding share in excess of 10,000 shares up to and including 100,000 shares, and ....

cents per share for each issued and outstanding share in excess of 100,000 shares).

[If Alternative 2 is enacted, the following paragraph should be deleted.]

The amount represented in this State of the stated capital of the corporation shall be that proportion of its stated capital which the sum of the value of its property located in this State and the gross amount of business transacted by it at or from places of business in this State bears to the sum of the value of all of its property, wherever located, and the gross amount of its business, wherever transacted.

§ 133. Franchise Taxes Payable by Foreign Corporations

The Secretary of State shall charge and collect from each foreign corporation authorized to transact business in this State an initial franchise tax at the time of filing its application for a certificate of authority at the rate of one-twelfth of one-half of the license fee payable by such corporation under the provisions of this Act at the time of filing such application, for each month, or fraction thereof, between the date of the issuance of the certificate of authority by the Secretary of State and the first day of July of the next succeeding calendar year.

The Secretary of State shall charge and collect from each foreign corporation authorized to transact business in this State an annual franchise tax, payable in advance for the period from July 1 in each year to July 1 in the succeeding year, beginning July 1 in the calendar year in which such corporation is required to file its first annual report under this Act, (Alternative 1: at the rate of .... per cent of the amount represented in this State of the stated capital of the corporation, as determined in accordance with accounting practices and principles that are reasonable in the circumstances, as disclosed by the latest annual report filed by the corporation with the Secretary of State) (Alternative 2: at a rate of .... cents per share up to and including the first 10,000 issued and outstanding shares represented in this State, and .... cents per share for each issued and outstanding share in excess of 10,000 shares up to and including 100,000 shares represented in this State, and .... cents per share for each issued and outstanding share in excess of 100,000 shares represented in this State).

[If Alternative 2 is enacted, the following paragraph should be deleted.]

The amount represented in this State of the stated capital of the corporation shall be that proportion of its stated capital which the sum of the value of its property located in this State and the gross amount of business transacted by it at or from places of business in this State bears to the sum of the value of all of its property, wherever located, and the gross amount of its business, wherever transacted.

§ 134. Assessment and Collection of Annual Franchise Taxes

It shall be the duty of the Secretary of State to collect all annual franchise taxes and penalties imposed by, or assessed in accordance with, this Act.

Between the first day of March and the first day of June of each year, the Secretary of State shall assess against each corporation, domestic and foreign, required to file an annual report in such year, the franchise tax payable by it for the period from July 1 of such year to July 1 of the succeeding year in accordance with the provisions of this Act, and, if it has failed to file its annual report within the time prescribed by this Act, the penalty imposed by this Act upon such corporation for its failure so to do; and shall mail a written notice to each corporation against which such tax is assessed, addressed to such corporation at its registered office in this State, notifying the corporation (1) of the amount of franchise tax assessed against it for the ensuing year and the amount of penalty, if any, assessed against it for failure to file its annual report; (2) that objections, if any, to such assessment will be heard by the officer making the assessment on or before the fifteenth day of June of such year, upon receipt of a request from the corporation; and (3) that such tax and penalty shall be payable to the Secretary of State on the first day of July next succeeding the date of the notice. Failure to receive such notice shall not relieve the corporation of its obligation to pay the tax and any penalty assessed, or invalidate the assessment thereof.

The Secretary of State shall have power to hear and determine objections to any assessment of franchise tax at any time after such assessment and, after hearing, to change or modify any such assessment. In the event of any adjustment of franchise tax with respect to which a penalty has been assessed for failure to file an annual report, the penalty shall be adjusted in accordance with the provisions of this Act imposing such penalty.

All annual franchise taxes and all penalties for failure to file annual reports shall be due and payable on the first day of July of each year. If the annual franchise tax assessed against any corporation subject to the provisions of this Act, together with all penalties assessed thereon, shall not be paid to the Secretary of State on or before the thirty-first day of July of the year in which such tax is due and payable, the Secretary of State shall certify such fact to the Attorney General on or before the fifteenth day of November of such year, whereupon the Attorney General may institute an action against such corporation in the name of this State, in any court of competent jurisdiction, for the recovery of the amount of such franchise tax and penalties, together with the cost of suit, and prosecute the same to final judgment.

For the purpose of enforcing collection, all annual franchise taxes assessed in accordance with this Act, and all penalties assessed thereon and all interest and costs that shall accrue in connection with the collection thereof, shall be a prior and first lien on the real and personal property of the corporation from and including the first day of July of the year when such franchise taxes become due and payable until such taxes, penalties, interest, and costs shall have been paid.

§ 135. Penalties Imposed Upon Corporations

Each corporation, domestic or foreign, that fails or refuses to file its annual report for any year within the time prescribed by this Act shall be subject to a penalty of ten per cent of the amount of the franchise tax assessed against it for the period beginning July 1 of the year in which such report should have been filed. Such penalty shall be assessed by the Secretary of State at the time of the assessment of the franchise tax. If the amount of the franchise tax as originally assessed against such corporation be thereafter adjusted in accordance with the provisions of this Act, the amount of the penalty shall be likewise adjusted to ten per cent of the amount of the adjusted franchise tax. The amount of the franchise tax and the amount of the penalty shall be separately stated in any notice to the corporation with respect thereto.

If the franchise tax assessed in accordance with the provisions of this Act shall not be paid on or before the thirty-first day of July, it shall be deemed to be delinquent, and there shall be added a penalty of one per cent for each month or part of month that the same is delinquent, commencing with the month of August.

Each corporation, domestic or foreign, that fails or refuses to answer truthfully and fully within the time prescribed by this Act interrogatories propounded by the Secretary of State in accordance with the provisions of this Act, shall be deemed to be guilty of a misdemeanor and upon conviction thereof may be fined in any amount not exceeding five hundred dollars.

§ 136. Penalties Imposed Upon Officers and Directors

Each officer and director of a corporation, domestic or foreign, who fails or refuses within the time prescribed by this Act to answer truthfully and fully interrogatories propounded to him by the Secretary of State in accordance with the provisions of this Act, or who signs any articles, statement, report, application or other document filed with the Secretary of State which is known to such officer or director to be false in any material respect, shall be deemed to be guilty of a misdemeanor, and upon conviction thereof may be fined in any amount not exceeding .... dollars.

§ 137. Interrogatories by Secretary of State

The Secretary of State may propound to any corporation, domestic or foreign, subject to the provisions of this Act, and to any officer or director thereof, such interrogatories as may be reasonably necessary and proper to enable him to ascertain whether such corporation has complied with all the provisions of this Act applicable to such corporation. Such interrogatories shall be answered within thirty days after the mailing thereof, or within such additional time as shall be fixed by the Secretary of State, and the answers thereto shall be full and complete and shall be made in writing and under oath. If such interrogatories be directed to an individual they shall be answered by him, and if directed to a corporation they shall be answered by the president, vice president, secretary or assistant secretary thereof. The Secretary of State need not file any document to which such interrogatories relate until such interrogatories be answered as herein provided, and not then if the answers thereto disclose that such document is not in conformity with the provisions of this Act. The Secretary of State shall certify to the Attorney General, for such action as the Attorney General may deem appropriate, all interrogatories and answers thereto which disclose a violation of any of the provisions of this Act.

§ 138. Information Disclosed by Interrogatories

Interrogatories propounded by the Secretary of State and the answers thereto shall not be open to public inspection nor shall the Secretary of State disclose any facts or information obtained therefrom except insofar as his official duty may require the same to be made public or in the event such interrogatories or the answers thereto are required for evidence in any criminal proceedings or in any other action by this State.

§ 139. Powers of Secretary of State

The Secretary of State shall have the power and authority reasonably necessary to enable him to administer this Act efficiently and to perform the duties therein imposed upon him.

§ 140. Appeal from Secretary of State

If the Secretary of State shall fail to approve any articles of incorporation, amendment, merger, consolidation or dissolution, or any other document required by this Act to be approved by the Secretary of State before the same shall be filed in his office, he shall, within ten days after the delivery thereof to him, give written notice of his disapproval to the person or corporation, domestic or foreign, delivering the same, specifying the reasons therefor. From such disapproval such person or corporation may appeal to the .... court of the county in which the registered office of such corporation is, or is proposed to be, situated by filing with the clerk of such court a petition setting forth a copy of the articles or other document sought to be filed and a copy of the written disapproval thereof by the Secretary of State; whereupon the matter shall be tried de novo by the court, and the court shall either sustain the action of the Secretary of State or direct him to take such action as the court may deem proper.

If the Secretary of State shall revoke the certificate of authority to transact business in this State of any foreign corporation, pursuant to the provisions of this Act, such foreign corporation may likewise appeal to the .... court of the county where the registered office of such corporation in this State is situated, by filing with the clerk of such court a petition setting forth a copy of its certificate of authority to transact business in this State and a copy of the notice of revocation given by the Secretary of State; whereupon the matter shall be tried de novo by the court, and the court shall either sustain the action of the Secretary of State or direct him to take such action as the court may deem proper.

Appeals from all final orders and judgments entered by the .... court under this section in review of any ruling or decision of the Secretary of State may be taken as in other civil actions.

§ 141. Certificates and Certified Copies to be Received in Evidence

All certificates issued by the Secretary of State in accordance with the provisions of this Act, and all copies of documents filed in his office in accordance with the provisions of this Act when certified by him, shall be taken and received in all courts, public offices, and official bodies as prima facie evidence of the facts therein stated. A certificate by the Secretary of State under the great seal of this State, as to the existence or non-existence of the facts relating to corporations shall be taken and received in all courts, public offices, and official bodies as prima facie evidence of the existence or non-existence of the facts therein stated.

§ 142. Forms to be Furnished by Secretary of State

All reports required by this Act to be filed in the office of the Secretary of State shall be made on forms which shall be prescribed and furnished by the Secretary of State. Forms for all other documents to be filed in the office of the Secretary of State shall be furnished by the Secretary of State on request therefor, but the use thereof, unless otherwise specifically prescribed in this Act, shall not be mandatory.

§ 143. Greater Voting Requirements

Whenever, with respect to any action to be taken by the shareholders of a corporation, the articles of incorporation require the vote or concurrence of the holders of a greater proportion of the shares, or of any class or series thereof, than required by this Act with respect to such action, the provisions of the articles of incorporation shall control.

§ 144. Waiver of Notice

Whenever any notice is required to be given to any shareholder or director of a corporation under the provisions of this Act or under the provisions of the articles of incorporation or by-laws of the corporation, a waiver thereof in writing signed by the person or persons entitled to such notice, whether before or after the time stated therein, shall be equivalent to the giving of such notice.

§ 145. Action by Shareholders Without a Meeting

Any action required by this Act to be taken at a meeting of the shareholders of a corporation, or any action which may be taken at a meeting of the sharehold-ers, may be taken without a meeting if a consent in writing, setting forth the action so taken, shall be signed by all of the shareholders entitled to vote with respect to the subject matter thereof.

Such consent shall have the same effect as a unanimous vote of shareholders, and may be stated as such in any articles or document filed with the Secretary of State under this Act.

§ 146. Unauthorized Assumption of Corporate Powers

All persons who assume to act as a corporation with-out authority so to do shall be jointly and severally liable for all debts and liabilities incurred or arising as a result thereof.

§ 147. Application to Existing Corporations

The provisions of this Act shall apply to all existing corporations organized under any general act of this State providing for the organization of corpo-rations for a purpose or purposes for which a cor-poration might be organized under this Act, where the power has been reserved to amend, repeal or modify the act under which such corporation was organized and where such act is repealed by this Act.

§ 148. Application to Foreign and Interstate Commerce

The provisions of this Act shall apply to commerce with foreign nations and among the several states only insofar as the same may be permitted under the provisions of the Constitution of the United States.

§ 149. Reservation of Power

The .... * shall at all times have power to prescribe such regulations, provisions and limitations as it may deem advisable, which regulations, provisions and limitations shall be binding upon any and all corpo-rations subject to the provisions of this Act, and the .... * shall have power to amend, repeal or modify this Act at pleasure.

§ 150. Effect of Repeal of Prior Acts

The repeal of a prior act by this Act shall not affect any right accrued or established, or any liability or penalty incurred, under the provisions of such act, prior to the repeal thereof.

---

*Insert name of legislative body.

§ 151. Effect of Invalidity of Part of this Act

If a court of competent jurisdiction shall adjudge to be invalid or unconstitutional any clause, sentence, paragraph, section or part of this Act, such judgment or decree shall not affect, impair, invalidate or nullify the remainder of this Act, but the effect thereof shall be confined to the clause, sentence, paragraph, section or part of this Act so adjudged to be invalid or unconstitutional.

§ 152. Exclusivity of Certain Provisions [Optional]

In circumstances to which section 45 and related sections of this Act are applicable, such provisions supersede the applicability of any other statutes of this state with respect to the legality of distributions.

§ 153. Repeal of Prior Acts (Insert appropriate provisions) ....

SPECIAL COMMENTS—CLOSE CORPORATIONS

In view of the increasing importance of close corporations, both for the small family business and for the larger undertakings conducted by some small number of other corporations, this liberalizing trend has now been followed by the 1969 Amendments to the Model Act. The first sentence of section 35, providing that the business of the corporation shall be managed by a board of directors, was supplemented by a new clause "except as may be otherwise provided in the articles of incorporation." This permits the shareholders to take over and exercise the functions of the directors by appropriate provision to that effect in the articles, or to allocate functions between the directors and shareholders in such manner as may be desired. Taken with other provisions of the Model Act, which are here enumerated for convenience, this rounds out the adaptability of the Model Act for all the needs of a close corporation:

(1) By section 4*(l)* the by-laws may make any provision for the regulation of the affairs of the corporation that is not inconsistent with the articles or the laws of the incorporating state.

(2) By section 15 shares may be divided into several classes and the articles may limit or deny the voting rights of or provide special voting rights for the shares of any class to the extent not inconsistent with the Model Act. The narrow limits of this exception are revealed by section 33 which provides that each outstanding share, regardless of class, shall be entitled to one vote on each matter submitted to a vote at a meeting of the shareholders "except as may be otherwise provided in the articles of incorporation," thus expressly authorizing more than one vote per share or less than one vote per share, either generally or in respect to particular matters.

(3) By section 16 item (F) the shares of any preferred or special class may be issued in series and there may be variations between different series in numerous respects, including specifically the matter of voting rights, if any.

(4) By section 32 the articles may reduce a quorum of shareholders to not less than one-third of the shares entitled to vote, or leave the quorum at the standard of a majority or, as confirmed by section 143, increase the number to any desired point.

(5) By section 34 agreements among shareholders regarding the voting of their shares are made valid and enforceable in accordance with their terms without limitation in time. These could relate to the election or compensation of directors or officers or the creation of various types of securities for new financing or the conduct of business of various kinds or dividend policy or mergers and consolidations or other transactions without limit.

(6) The flexibility permitted by the revision of section 35 in the distribution or reallocation of authority among directors and stockholders has already been mentioned.

(7) Under section 36 the number of directors may be fixed by the by-laws at one or such greater number as may best serve the interests of the shareholders and that number may be increased or decreased from time to time by amendment to, or in the manner provided in, the articles or the by-laws, subject to any limiting provision adopted pursuant to law, such as an agreed requirement for a unanimous vote by directors for any such change or a requirement that amendments to the by-laws be made by shareholder vote. Similarly, under section 53, the incorporation may be effected by a single incorporator or by more as may be desired.

(8) By section 37 directors may be classified. While this relates to directors classified in such manner that the term of office of a specified proportion terminates in each year, the Model Act does not forbid the election of separate directors by separate classes of stock.

(9) Section 40 permits the articles or the by-laws to require more than a majority of the directors to constitute a quorum for the transaction of business and also permits the articles or by-laws to require the act of a greater number than a majority of those present at a meeting where a quorum is present before any specified business may be transacted. Or a unanimous vote of all directors may be required. This may be utilized to confer a right of veto on any designated class in order to protect its special interests.

(10) By section 50 the authority and duties of the respective officers and agents of the corporation may be tailored and prescribed in the by-laws, or consistently with the by-laws, in such manner as the needs of the shareholders may indicate.

(11) By section 54 the articles may include any desired provision for the regulation of the internal affairs of the corporation, including, in particular, "any provision restricting the transfer of shares." This expressly validates agreements for prior offering of shares to the corporation or other shareholders. All such restrictions must, of course, be clearly shown on the stock certificate as required by the Uniform Commercial Code. A similarly broad provision for the contents of the by-laws is contained in section 27.

(12) By sections 60, 73 and 79, respectively, a class vote may be required for an amendment to the articles, for any merger or consolidation or for a sale of assets other than in the regular course of business.

(13) Section 143 permits the articles to require, for any particular action by the shareholders, the vote or concurrence of the holders of a greater proportion of the shares, or of any class or series thereof, than the Model Act itself requires.

(14) Section 44 permits action by directors without a meeting and section 145 permits the same for shareholders, while section 144 contains a broad provision on waiver of notice. Thus the formality of meetings may, where desired, be eliminated in whole or in part, except for the annual meeting required by section 28.

Under these provisions protection may be afforded for a great diversity of interests. By way of illustration, the shares may be divided into different classes with different voting rights and each class may be permitted to elect a different director. Or some classes may be permitted to vote on certain transactions, but not all.

Even more drastically, some classes may be denied all voting rights whatever. Thus a family could provide for equal participation in the profits of the venture, but restrict the power of management to selected members. The advantages of having a known group of business associates may be safeguarded by restrictions on the transfer of shares. Most commonly this takes the form of a requirement for *pro rata* offering to the other shareholders before selling to an outsider. Or the other shareholders may be given an option, in the event of death or a proposed transfer, to buy the stock *pro rata*. The same option may be given to the corporation. The purchase price may be fixed by any agreed formula, such as adjusted book value or some multiple of recent earnings. Or stockholder agreements may be used to assure that, at least for a limited number of years, all shares will be voted for certain directors and officers, or in a certain way on other corporate matters. Cumulative voting may be provided for, by which each shareholder has a number of votes equal to the number of his shares multiplied by the number of directors to be elected, with the privilege of casting all of his votes for a single candidate, or dividing them as he may wish. This helps minorities obtain representation on the board of directors. Thus the holder of one-fourth of the shares voting, plus one share, is sure of electing one of three directors. The preemptive right is another important protection in the case of close corporations, since it assures each stockholder a right to maintain his proportionate interest. Still more definite protection is afforded by provisions in the articles that prohibit particular transactions except with the assent of a specified percentage of all outstanding shares or of each class of shares. Much the same protection can sometimes be obtained by requiring a specially large quorum for the election of directors, or a specially large vote, or even unanimous vote, by directors for the authorization of particular transactions. Quite the opposite situation exists if one of the participants is to be an inactive investor, for whom non-voting preferred stock, with its prior right to a return from earnings, may be sufficient. But even here he may require a veto power over major transactions, such as the issuance of debt, the issuance of additional preferred shares or mergers or consolidations. Or the preferred shareholders may be given as a class the right to elect one or more of the directors, particularly in the event that dividends should be in arrears.

These possibilities are listed merely as illustrations and not in any sense as exhausting the variations permissible under the Model Act.

The Uniform Partnership Act

(Adopted in 49 States [all of the states except Louisiana], the District of Columbia, the Virgin Islands, and Guam. The adoptions by Alabama and Nebraska do not follow the official text in every respect, but are substantially similar, with local variations.)

The Act consists of 7 Parts as follows:

I. Preliminary Provisions
II. Nature of Partnership
III. Relations of Partners to Persons Dealing with the Partnership
IV. Relations of Partners to One Another
V. Property Rights of a Partner
VI. Dissolution and Winding Up
VII. Miscellaneous Provisions

An Act to make uniform the Law of Partnerships Be it enacted, etc.:

PART I
PRELIMINARY PROVISIONS
§ 1. Name of Act
This act may be cited as Uniform Partnership Act.

§ 2. Definition of Terms
In this act, "Court" includes every court and judge having jurisdiction in the case.

"Business" includes every trade, occupation, or profession.

"Person" includes individuals, partnerships, corporations, and other associations.

"Bankrupt" includes bankrupt under the Federal Bankruptcy Act or insolvent under any state insolvent act.

"Conveyance" includes every assignment, lease, mortgage, or encumbrance.

"Real property" includes land and any interest or estate in land.

§ 3. Interpretation of Knowledge and Notice
(1) A person has "knowledge" of a fact within the meaning of this act not only when he has actual knowledge thereof, but also when he has knowledge of such other facts as in the circumstances shows bad faith.
(2) A person has "notice" of a fact within the meaning of this act when the person who claims the benefit of the notice:

(a) States the fact to such person, or
(b) Delivers through the mail, or by other means of communication, a written statement of the fact to such person or to a proper person at his place of business or residence.

§ 4. Rules of Construction
(1) The rule that statutes in derogation of the common law are to be strictly construed shall have no application to this act.
(2) The law of estoppel shall apply under this act.
(3) The law of agency shall apply under this act.
(4) This act shall be so interpreted and construed as to effect its general purpose to make uniform the law of those states which enact it.
(5) This act shall not be construed so as to impair the obligations of any contract existing when the act goes into effect, nor to affect any action or proceedings begun or right accrued before this act takes effect.

§ 5. Rules for Cases Not Provided for in this Act.
In any case not provided for in this act the rules of law and equity, including the law merchant, shall govern.

PART II
NATURE OF PARTNERSHIP
§ 6. Partnership Defined

(1) A partnership is an association of two or more persons to carry on as co-owners a business for profit.

(2) But any association formed under any other statute of this state, or any statute adopted by authority, other than the authority of this state, is not a partnership under this act, unless such association would have been a partnership in this state prior to the adoption of this act; but this act shall apply to limited partnerships except in so far as the statutes relating to such partnerships are inconsistent herewith.

§ 7. Rules for Determining the Existence of a Partnership

In determining whether a partnership exists, these rules shall apply:

(1) Except as provided by Section 16 persons who are not partners as to each other are not partners as to third persons.

(2) Joint tenancy, tenancy in common, tenancy by the entireties, joint property, common property, or part ownership does not of itself establish a partnership, whether such co-owners do or do not share any profits made by the use of the property.

(3) The sharing of gross returns does not of itself establish a partnership, whether or not the persons sharing them have a joint or common right or interest in any property from which the returns are derived.

(4) The receipt by a person of a share of the profits of a business is prima facie evidence that he is a partner in the business, but no such inference shall be drawn if such profits were received in payment:

    (a) As a debt by installments or otherwise,

    (b) As wages of an employee or rent to a landlord,

    (c) As an annuity to a widow or representative of a deceased partner,

    (d) As interest on a loan, though the amount of payment varies with the profits of the business.

    (e) As the consideration for the sale of a good-will of a business or other property by installments or otherwise.

§ 8. Partnership Property

(1) All property originally brought into the partnership stock or subsequently acquired by purchase or otherwise, on account of the partnership, is partnership property.

(2) Unless the contrary intention appears, property acquired with partnership funds is partnership property.

(3) Any estate in real property may be acquired in the partnership name. Title so acquired can be conveyed only in the partnership name.

(4) A conveyance to a partnership in the partnership name, though without words of inheritance, passes the entire estate of the grantor unless a contrary intent appears.

PART III
RELATIONS OF PARTNERS TO PERSONS DEALING WITH THE PARTNERSHIP
§ 9. Partner Agent of Partnership as to Partnership Business

(1) Every partner is an agent of the partnership for the purpose of its business, and the act of every partner, including the execution in the partnership name of any instrument, for apparently carrying on in the usual way the business of the partnership of which he is a member binds the partnership, unless the partner so acting has in fact no authority to act for the partnership in the particular matter, and the person with whom he is dealing has knowledge of the fact that he has no such authority.

(2) An act of a partner which is not apparently for the carrying on of the business of the partnership in the usual way does not bind the partnership unless authorized by the other partners.

(3) Unless authorized by the other partners or unless they have abandoned the business, one or more but less than all the partners have no authority to:

    (a) Assign the partnership property in trust for creditors or on the assignee's promise to pay the debts of the partnership,

    (b) Dispose of the good-will of the business,

    (c) Do any other act which would make it impossible to carry on the ordinary business of a partnership,

    (d) Confess a judgment,

(e)   Submit a partnership claim or liability to arbitration or reference.

(4)   No act of a partner in contravention of a restriction on authority shall bind the partnership to persons having knowledge of the restriction.

§ 10. Conveyance of Real Property of the Partnership

(1)   Where title to real property is in the partnership name, any partner may convey title to such property by a conveyance executed in the partnership name; but the partnership may recover such property unless the partner's act binds the partnership under the provisions of paragraph (1) of section 9, or unless such property has been conveyed by the grantee or a person claiming through such grantee to a holder for value without knowledge that the partner, in making the conveyance, has exceeded his authority.

(2)   Where title to real property is in the name of the partnership, a conveyance executed by a partner, in his own name, passes the equitable interest of the partnership, provided the act is one within the authority of the partner under the provisions of paragraph (1) of section 9.

(3)   Where title to real property is in the name of one or more but not all the partners, and the record does not disclose the right of the partnership, the partners in whose name the title stands may convey title to such property, but the partnership may recover such property if the partners' act does not bind the partnership under the provisions of paragraph (1) of section 9, unless the purchaser or his assignee, is a holder for value, without knowledge.

(4)   Where the title to real property is in the name of one or more or all the partners, or in a third person in trust for the partnership, a conveyance executed by a partner in the partnership name, or in his own name, passes the equitable interest of the partnership, provided the act is one within the authority of the partner under the provisions of paragraph (1) of section 9.

(5)   Where the title to real property is in the names of all the partners a conveyance executed by all the partners passes all their rights in such property.

§ 11. Partnership Bound by Admission of Partner

An admission or representation made by any partner concerning partnership affairs within the scope of his authority as conferred by this act is evidence against the partnership.

§ 12. Partnership Charged with Knowledge of or Notice to Partner

Notice to any partner of any matter relating to partnership affairs, and the knowledge of the partner acting in the particular matter, acquired while a partner or then present to his mind, and the knowledge of any other partner who reasonably could and should have communicated it to the acting partner, operate as notice to or knowledge of the partnership, except in the case of a fraud on the partnership committed by or with the consent of that partner.

§ 13. Partnership Bound by Partner's Wrongful Act

Where, by any wrongful act or omission of any partner acting in the ordinary course of the business of the partnership or with the authority of his co-partners, loss or injury is caused to any person, not being a partner in the partnership, or any penalty is incurred, the partnership is liable therefor to the same extent as the partner so acting or omitting to act.

§ 14. Partnership Bound by Partner's Breach of Trust

The partnership is bound to make good the loss:

(a)   Where one partner acting within the scope of his apparent authority receives money or property of a third person and misapplies it; and

(b)   Where the partnership in the course of its business receives money or property of a third person and the money or property so received is misapplied by any partner while it is in the custody of the partnership.

§ 15. Nature of Partner's Liability

All partners are liable

(a)   Jointly and severally for everything chargeable to the partnership under sections 13 and 14.

(b) Jointly for all other debts and obligations of the partnership; but any partner may enter into a separate obligation to perform a partnership contract.

§ 16. Partner by Estoppel

(1) When a person, by words spoken or written or by conduct, represents himself, or consents to another representing him to any one, as a partner in an existing partnership or with one or more persons not actual partners, he is liable to any such person to whom such representation has been made, who has, on the faith of such representation, given credit to the actual or apparent partnership, and if he has made such representation or consented to its being made in a public manner he is liable to such person, whether the representation has or has not been made or communicated to such person so giving credit by or with the knowledge of the apparent partner making the representation or consenting to its being made.

(a) When a partnership liability results, he is liable as though he were an actual member of the partnership.
(b) When no partnership liability results, he is liable jointly with the other persons, if any, so consenting to the contract or representation as to incur liability, otherwise separately.

(2) When a person has been thus represented to be a partner in an existing partnership, or with one or more persons not actual partners, he is an agent of the persons consenting to such representation to bind them to the same extent and in the same manner as though he were a partner in fact, with respect to persons who rely upon the representation. Where all the members of the existing partnership consent to the representation, a partnership act or obligation results; but in all other cases it is the joint act or obligation of the person acting and the persons consenting to the representation.

§ 17. Liability of Incoming Partner

A person admitted as a partner into an existing partnership is liable for all the obligations of the partnership arising before his admission as though he had been a partner when such obligations were incurred, except that this liability shall be satisfied only out of partnership property.

PART IV
RELATIONS OF PARTNERS TO ONE ANOTHER
§ 18. Rules Determining Rights and Duties of Partners

The rights and duties of the partners in relation to the partnership shall be determined, subject to any agreement between them, by the following rules:

(a) Each partner shall be repaid his contributions, whether by way of capital or advances to the partnership property and share equally in the profits and surplus remaining after all liabilities, including those to partners, are satisfied; and must contribute towards the losses, whether of capital or otherwise, sustained by the partnership according to his share in the profits.

(b) The partnership must indemnify every partner in respect of payments made and personal liabilities reasonably incurred by him in the ordinary and proper conduct of its business, or for the preservation of its business or property.

(c) A partner, who in aid of the partnership makes any payment or advance beyond the amount of capital which he agreed to contribute, shall be paid interest from the date of the payment or advance.

(d) A partner shall receive interest on the capital contributed by him only from the date when repayment should be made.

(e) All partners have equal rights in the management and conduct of the partnership business.

(f) No partner is entitled to remuneration for acting in the partnership business, except that a surviving partner is entitled to reasonable compensation for his services in winding up the partnership affairs.

(g) No person can become a member of a partnership without the consent of all the partners.
(h) Any difference arising as to ordinary matters connected with the partnership business may be decided by a majority of the partners; but no act in contravention of any agreement between the partners may be done rightfully without the consent of all the partners.

§ 19. Partnership Books

The partnership books shall be kept, subject to any agreement between the partners, at the principal place of business of the partnership, and every partner shall at all times have access to and may inspect and copy any of them.

§ 20. Duty of Partners to Render Information

Partners shall render on demand true and full information of all things affecting the partnership to any partner or the legal representative of any deceased partner or partner under legal disability.

§ 21. Partner Accountable as a Fiduciary

(1) Every partner must account to the partnership for any benefit, and hold as trustee for it any profits derived by him without the consent of the other partners from any transaction connected with the formation, conduct, or liquidation of the partnership or from any use by him of its property.

(2) This section applies also to the representatives of a deceased partner engaged in the liquidation of the affairs of the partnership as the personal representatives of the last surviving partner.

§ 22. Right to an Account

Any partner shall have the right to a formal account as to partnership affairs:

(a) If he is wrongfully excluded from the partnership business or possession of its property by his co-partners,

(b) If the right exists under the terms of any agreement,

(c) As provided by section 21,

(d) Whenever other circumstances render it just and reasonable.

§ 23. Continuation of Partnership Beyond Fixed Term

(1) When a partnership for a fixed term or particular undertaking is continued after the termination of such term or particular undertaking without any express agreement, the rights and duties of the partners remain the same as they were at such termination, so far as is consistent with a partnership at will.

(2) A continuation of the business by the partners or such of them as habitually acted therein during the term, without any settlement or liquidation of the partnership affairs, is prima facie evidence of a continuation of the partnership.

PART V
PROPERTY RIGHTS OF A PARTNER

§ 24. Extent of Property Rights of a Partner

The property rights of a partner are (1) his rights in specific partnership property, (2) his interest in the partnership, and (3) his right to participate in the management.

§ 25. Nature of a Partner's Right in Specific Partnership Property

(1) A partner is co-owner with his partners of specific partnership property holding as a tenant in partnership.

(2) The incidents of this tenancy are such that:

(a) A partner, subject to the provisions of this act and to any agreement between the partners, has an equal right with his partners to possess specific partnership property for partnership purposes; but he has no right to possess such property for any other purpose without the consent of his partners.

(b) A partner's right in specific partnership property is not assignable except in connection with the assignment of rights of all the partners in the same property.

(c) A partner's right in specific partnership property is not subject to attachment or execution, except on a claim against the partnership. When partnership property is attached for a partnership debt the partners, or any of them, or the representatives of a deceased partner, cannot claim any right under the homestead or exemption laws.

(d) On the death of a partner his right in specific partnership property vests in the surviving partner or partners, except where the deceased was the last surviving partner, when his right in such property vests in his legal representative. Such surviving partner or partners, or the legal representative of the last surviving partner, has no right to possess the partnership property for any but a partnership purpose.

(e) A partner's right in specific partnership property is not subject to dower, curtesy, or allowances to widows, heirs, or next of kin.

§ 26. Nature of Partner's Interest in the Partnership

A partner's interest in the partnership is his share of the profits and surplus, and the same is personal property.

§ 27. Assignment of Partner's Interest

(1) A conveyance by a partner of his interest in the partnership does not of itself dissolve the partnership, nor, as against the other partners in the absence of agreement, entitle the assignee, during the continuance of the partnership, to interfere in the management or administration of the partnership business or affairs, or to require any information or account of partnership transactions, or to inspect the partnership books; but it merely entitles the assignee to receive in accordance with his contract the profits to which the assigning partner would otherwise be entitled.

(2) In case of a dissolution of the partnership, the assignee is entitled to receive his assignor's interest and may require an account from the date only of the last account agreed to by all the partners.

§ 28. Partner's Interest Subject to Charging Order

(1) On due application to a competent court by any judgment creditor of a partner, the court which entered the judgment, order, or decree, or any other court, may charge the interest of the debtor partner with payment of the unsatisfied amount of such judgment debt with interest thereon; and may then or later appoint a receiver of his share of the profits, and of any other money due or to fall due to him in respect of the partnership, and make all other orders, directions, accounts and inquiries which the debtor partner might have made, or which the circumstances of the case may require.

(2) The interest charged may be redeemed at any time before foreclosure, or in case of a sale being directed by the court may be purchased without thereby causing a dissolution:

(a) With separate property, by any one or more of the partners, or

(b) With partnership property, by any one or more of the partners with the consent of all the partners whose interests are not so charged or sold.

(3) Nothing in this act shall be held to deprive a partner of his right, if any, under the exemption laws, as regards his interest in the partnership.

PART VI
DISSOLUTION AND WINDING UP
§ 29. Dissolution Defined

The dissolution of a partnership is the change in the relation of the partners caused by any partner ceasing to be associated in the carrying on as distinguished from the winding up of the business.

§ 30. Partnership not Terminated by Dissolution

On dissolution the partnership is not terminated, but continues until the winding up of partnership affairs is completed.

§ 31. Causes of Dissolution

Dissolution is caused:

(1) Without violation of the agreement between the partners,

(a) By the termination of the definite term or particular undertaking specified in the agreement,

(b) By the express will of any partner when no definite term or particular undertaking is specified,

(c) By the express will of all the partners who have not assigned their interests or suffered them to be charged for their separate debts, either before or after the termination of any specified term or particular undertaking,

(d) By the expulsion of any partner from the business bona fide in accordance with such a power conferred by the agreement between the partners;

(2) In contravention of the agreement between the partners, where the circumstances do not permit a dissolution under any other provision of this section, by the express will of any partner at any time;

(3) By any event which makes it unlawful for the business of the partnership to be carried on or for the members to carry it on in partnership;

(4) By the death of any partner;

(5) By the bankruptcy of any partner or the partnership;

(6) By decree of court under section 32.

§ 32. Dissolution by Decree of Court

(1) On application by or for a partner the court shall decree a dissolution whenever:

(a) A partner has been declared a lunatic in any judicial proceeding or is shown to be of unsound mind,

(b) A partner becomes in any other way incapable of performing his part of the partnership contract,

(c) A partner has been guilty of such conduct as tends to affect prejudicially the carrying on of the business,

(d) A partner wilfully or persistently commits a breach of the partnership agreement, or otherwise so conducts himself in matters relating to the partnership business that it is not reasonably practicable to carry on the business in partnership with him,

(e) The business of the partnership can only be carried on at a loss,

(f) Other circumstances render a dissolution equitable.

(2) On the application of the purchaser of a partner's interest under sections 28 or 29 [should read 27 or 28];

(a) After the termination of the specified term or particular undertaking,

(b) At any time if the partnership was a partnership at will when the interest was assigned or when the charging order was issued.

§ 33. General Effect of Dissolution on Authority of Partner

Except so far as may be necessary to wind up partnership affairs or to complete transactions begun but not then finished, dissolution terminates all authority of any partner to act for the partnership,

(1) With respect to the partners,

(a) When the dissolution is not by the act, bankruptcy or death of a partner; or

(b) When the dissolution is by such act, bankruptcy or death of a partner, in cases where section 34 so requires.

(2) With respect to persons not partners, as declared in section 35.

§ 34. Rights of Partner to Contribution from Co-partners After Dissolution

Where the dissolution is caused by the act, death or bankruptcy of a partner, each partner is liable to his copartners for his share of any liability created by any partner acting for the partnership as if the partnership had not been dissolved unless

(a) The dissolution being by act of any partner, the partner acting for the partnership had knowledge of the dissolution, or

(b) The dissolution being by the death or bankruptcy of a partner, the partner acting for the partnership had knowledge or notice of the death or bankruptcy.

§ 35. Power of Partner to Bind Partnership to Third Persons After Dissolution

(1) After dissolution a partner can bind the partnership except as provided in Paragraph (3).

(a) By any act appropriate for winding up partnership affairs or completing transactions unfinished at dissolution;

(b) By any transaction which would bind the partnership if dissolution had not taken place, provided the other party to the transaction

(I) Had extended credit to the partnership prior to dissolution and had no knowledge or notice of the dissolution; or

(II) Though he had not so extended credit, had nevertheless known of the partnership prior to dissolution, and, having no knowledge or notice of dissolution, the fact of dissolution had not been advertised in a newspaper of general circulation in the place (or in each place if more than one) at which the partnership business was regularly carried on.

(2) The liability of a partner under paragraph (1b) shall be satisfied out of partnership assets alone when such partner had been prior to dissolution

(a) Unknown as a partner to the person with whom the contract is made; and

(b) So far unknown and inactive in partnership affairs that the business reputation of the partnership could not be said to have been in any degree due to his connection with it.

(3) The partnership is in no case bound by any act of a partner after dissolution

(a) Where the partnership is dissolved because it is unlawful to carry on the business, unless the act is appropriate for winding up partnership affairs; or

(b) Where the partner has become bankrupt; or

(c) Where the partner has no authority to wind up partnership affairs; except by a transaction with one who

(I) Had extended credit to the partnership prior to dissolution and had no knowledge or notice of his want of authority; or

(II) Had not extended credit to the partnership prior to dissolution, and, having no knowledge or notice of his want of authority, the fact of his want of authority has not been advertised in the manner provided for advertising the fact of dissolution in paragraph (1bII).

(4) Nothing in this section shall affect the liability under Section 16 of any person who after dissolution represents himself or consents to another representing him as a partner in a partnership engaged in carrying on business.

§ 36. Effect of Dissolution on Partner's Existing Liability

(1) The dissolution of the partnership does not of itself discharge the existing liability of any partner.

(2) A partner is discharged from any existing liability upon dissolution of the partnership by an agreement to that effect between himself, the partnership creditor and the person or partnership continuing the business; and such agreement may be inferred from the course of dealing between the creditor having knowledge of the dissolution and the person or partnership continuing the business.

(3) Where a person agrees to assume the existing obligations of a dissolved partnership, the partners whose obligations have been assumed shall be discharged from any liability to any creditor of the partnership who, knowing of the agreement, consents to a material alteration in the nature or time of payment of such obligations.

(4) The individual property of a deceased partner shall be liable for all obligations of the partnership incurred while he was a partner but subject to the prior payment of his separate debts.

§ 37. Right to Wind Up

Unless otherwise agreed the partners who have not wrongfully dissolved the partnership or the legal representative of the last surviving partner, not bankrupt, has the right to wind up the partnership affairs; provided, however, that any partner, his legal representative or his assignee, upon cause shown, may obtain winding up by the court.

§ 38. Rights of Partners to Application of Partnership Property

(1) When dissolution is caused in any way, except in contravention of the partnership agreement, each partner, as against his co-partners and all persons claiming through them in respect of their interests in the partnership, unless otherwise agreed, may have the partnership property applied to discharge its liabilities, and the surplus applied to pay in cash the net amount owing to the respective partners. But if dissolution is caused by expulsion of a partner, bona fide under the partnership agreement and if the expelled partner is discharged from all partnership liabilities, either by payment or agreement under section 36(2), he shall receive in cash only the net amount due him from the partnership.

(2) When dissolution is caused in contravention of the partnership agreement the rights of the partners shall be as follows:

(a) Each partner who has not caused dissolution wrongfully shall have,

(I) All the rights specified in paragraph (1) of this section, and

(II) The right, as against each partner who has caused the dissolution wrongfully, to damages for breach of the agreement.

(b) The partners who have not caused the dissolution wrongfully, if they all desire to continue the business in the same name, either by themselves or jointly with others, may do so, during the agreed term for the partnership and for that purpose may possess the partnership property, provided they secure the payment by bond approved by the court, or pay to any partner who has caused the dissolution wrongfully, the value of his interest in the partnership at the dissolution, less any damages recoverable under clause (2a II) of the section, and in like manner indemnify him against all present or future partnership liabilities.

(c)   A partner who has caused the dissolution wrongfully shall have:

(I)   If the business is not continued under the provisions of paragraph (2b) all the rights of a partner under paragraph (1), subject to clause (2aII), of this section,

(II)   If the business is continued under paragraph (2b) of this section the right as against his co-partners and all claiming through them in respect of their interests in the partnership, to have the value of his interest in the partnership, less any damages caused to his co-partners by the dissolution, ascertained and paid to him in cash, or the payment secured by bond approved by the court, and to be released from all existing liabilities of the partnership; but in ascertaining the value of the partner's interest the value of the good-will of the business shall not be considered.

§ 39. Rights Where Partnership is Dissolved for Fraud or Misrepresentation

Where a partnership contract is rescinded on the ground of the fraud or misrepresentation of one of the parties thereto, the party entitled to rescind is, without prejudice to any other right, entitled,

(a)   To a lien on, or right of retention of, the surplus of the partnership property after satisfying the partnership liabilities to third persons for any sum of money paid by him for the purchase of an interest in the partnership and for any capital or advances contributed by him; and

(b)   To stand, after all liabilities to third persons have been satisfied, in the place of the creditors of the partnership for any payments made by him in respect of the partnership liabilities; and

(c)   To be indemnified by the person guilty of the fraud or making the representation against all debts and liabilities of the partnership.

§ 40. Rules for Distribution

In settling accounts between the partners after dissolution, the following rules shall be observed, subject to any agreement to the contrary:

(a)   The assets of the partnership are:

(I)   The partnership property,
(II)   The contributions of the partners necessary for the payment of all the liabilities specified in clause (b) of this paragraph.

(b)   The liabilities of the partnership shall rank in order of payment, as follows:

(I)   Those owing to creditors other than partners,
(II)   Those owing to partners other than for capital and profits,
(III)   Those owing to partners in respect of capital,
(IV)   Those owing to partners in respect of profits.

(c)   The assets shall be applied in the order of their declaration in clause (a) of this paragraph to the satisfaction of the liabilities.

(d)   The partners shall contribute, as provided by section 18(a) the amount necessary to satisfy the liabilities; but if any, but not all, of the partners are insolvent, or, not being subject to process, refuse to contribute, the other partners shall contribute their share of the liabilities, and, in the relative proportions in which they share the profits, the additional amount necessary to pay the liabilities.

(e)   An assignee for the benefit of creditors or any person appointed by the court shall have the right to enforce the contributions specified in clause (d) of this paragraph.

(f)   Any partner or his legal representative shall have the right to enforce the contributions specified in clause (d) of this paragraph, to the extent of the amount which he has paid in excess of his share of the liability.

(g)   The individual property of a deceased partner shall be liable for the contributions specified in clause (d) of this paragraph.

(h)   When partnership property and the individual properties of the partners are in possession of a court for distribution, partnership creditors shall have priority on partnership property and separate creditors on individual property, saving the rights of lien or secured creditors as heretofore.

(i)   Where a partner has become bankrupt or his estate is insolvent the claims against his separate property shall rank in the following order:

(I)   Those owing to separate creditors,
(II)   Those owing to partnership creditors,
(III) Those owing to partners by way of contribution.

§ 41. Liability of Persons Continuing the Business in Certain Cases

(1)   When any new partner is admitted into an existing partnership, or when any partner retires and assigns (or the representative of the deceased partner assigns) his rights in partnership property to two or more of the partners, or to one or more of the partners and one or more third persons, if the business is continued without liquidation of the partnership affairs, creditors of the first or dissolved partnership are also creditors of the partnership so continuing the business.

(2)   When all but one partner retire and assign (or the representative of a deceased partner assigns) their rights in partnership property to the remaining partner, who continues the business without liquidation of partnership affairs, either alone or with others, creditors of the dissolved partnership are also creditors of the person or partnership so continuing the business.

(3)   When any partner retires or dies and the business of the dissolved partnership is continued as set forth in paragraphs (1) and (2) of this section, with the consent of the retired partners or the representative of the deceased partner, but without any assignment of his right in partnership property, rights of creditors of the dissolved partnership and of the creditors of the person or partnership continuing the business shall be as if such assignment had been made.

(4)   When all the partners or their representatives assign their rights in partnership property to one or more third persons who promise to pay the debts and who continue the business of the dissolved partnership, creditors of the dissolved partnership are also creditors of the person or partnership continuing the business.

(5)   When any partner wrongfully causes a dissolution and the remaining partners continue the business under the provisions of section 38(2b), either alone or with others, and with-

out liquidation of the partnership affairs, creditors of the dissolved partnership are also creditors of the person or partnership continuing the business.

(6)   When a partner is expelled and the remaining partners continue the business either alone or with others, without liquidation of the partnership affairs, creditors of the dissolved partnership are also creditors of the person or partnership continuing the business.

(7)   The liability of a third person becoming a partner in the partnership continuing the business, under this section, to the creditors of the dissolved partnership shall be satisfied out of partnership property only.

(8)   When the business of a partnership after dissolution is continued under any conditions set forth in this section the creditors of the dissolved partnership, as against the separate creditors of the retiring or deceased partner or the representative of the deceased partner, have a prior right to any claim of the retired partner or the representative of the deceased partner against the person or partnership continuing the business, on account of the retired or deceased partner's interest in the dissolved partnership or on account of any consideration promised for such interest or for his right in partnership property.

(9)   Nothing in this section shall be held to modify any right of creditors to set aside any assignment on the ground of fraud.

(10) The use by the person or partnership continuing the business of the partnership name, or the name of a deceased partner as part thereof, shall not of itself make the individual property of the deceased partner liable for any debts contracted by such person or partnership.

§ 42. Rights of Retiring or Estate of Deceased Partner When the Business is Continued

When any partner retires or dies, and the business is continued under any of the conditions set forth in section 41 (1, 2, 3, 5, 6), or section 38(2b) without any settlement of accounts as between him or his estate and the person or partnership continuing the business, unless otherwise agreed, he or his legal representative as against such persons or partnership may have the value of his interest at the date of dissolution ascertained, and shall receive as an ordinary creditor an amount equal to the value of his interest in the dissolved partnership with interest, or, at his option or at the option of his legal representative, in lieu of interest, the profits attributable to the use of his right in the property of the dissolved partnership; provided that the creditors of the dissolved partnership as against the separate creditors, or the representative of the retired or deceased partner, shall have priority on any claim arising under this section, as provided by section 41(8) of this act.

§ 43. Accrual of Actions

The right to an account of his interest shall accrue to any partner, or his legal representative, as against the winding up partners or the surviving partners or the person or partnership continuing the business, at the date of dissolution, in the absence of any agreement to the contrary.

PART VII
MISCELLANEOUS PROVISIONS
§ 44. When Act Takes Effect

This act shall take effect on the ____ day of ____ one thousand nine hundred and ____.

§ 45. Legislation Repealed

All acts or parts of acts inconsistent with this act are hereby repealed.

The Uniform Limited Partnership Act

*(Adopted August 5, 1976, by the National Conference of Commissioners on Uniform State Laws, it is intended to replace the existing Uniform Limited Partnership Act (Appendix D). It has been adopted in 36 States: Alabama, Arizona, Arkansas, California, Colorado, Connecticut, Delaware, Florida, Idaho, Illinois, Iowa, Kansas, Maryland, Massachusetts, Michigan, Minnesota, Mississippi, Missouri, Montana, Nebraska, Nevada, New Jersey, North Carolina, North Dakota, Ohio, Oklahoma, Oregon, Rhode Island, South Carolina, South Dakota, Texas, Virginia, Washington, West Virginia, Wisconsin, and Wyoming.

The Act consists of 11 Articles as follows:

1. General Provisions
2. Formation; Certificate of Limited Partnership
3. Limited Partners
4. General Partners
5. Finance
6. Distributions and Withdrawal
7. Assignment of Partnership Interests
8. Dissolution
9. Foreign Limited Partnership
10. Derivative Actions
11. Miscellaneous

ARTICLE 1
GENERAL PROVISIONS
§ 101. Definitions

As used in this Act, unless the context otherwise requires:

(1) "Certificate of limited partnership" means the certificate referred to in Section 201, and the certificate as amended or restated.

(2) "Contribution" means any cash, property, services rendered, or a promissory note or other binding obligation to contribute cash or property or to perform services, which a partner contributes to a limited partnership in his capacity as a partner.

(3) "Event of withdrawal of a general partner" means an event that causes a person to cease to be a general partner as provided in Section 402.

(4) "Foreign limited partnership" means a partnership formed under the laws of any state other than this State and having as partners one or more general partners and one or more limited partners.

(5) "General partner" means a person who has been admitted to a limited partnership as a general partner in accordance with the partnership agreement and named in the certificate of limited partnership as a general partner.

(6) "Limited partner" means a person who has been admitted to a limited partnership as a limited partner in accordance with the partnership agreement.

(7) "Limited partnership" and "domestic limited partnership" mean a partnership formed by two or more persons under the laws of this State and having one or more general partners and one or more limited partners.

(8) "Partner" means a limited or general partner.

(9) "Partnership agreement" means any valid agreement, written or oral, of the partners as to the affairs of a limited partnership and the conduct of its business.

(10) "Partnership interest" means a partner's share of the profits and losses of a limited partnership

---

*At its annual conference in August 1985, the National Conference of Commissioners on Uniform State Laws approved amendments to the "Revised Uniform Partnership Act." This printing includes these amendments.

and the right to receive distributions of partner-ship assets.

(11) "Person" means a natural person, partnership, limited partnership (domestic or foreign), trust, estate, association, or corporation.

(12) "State" means a state, territory, or possession of the United States, the District of Columbia, or the Commonwealth of Puerto Rico.

§ 102. Name

The name of each limited partnership as set forth in its certificate of limited partnership:

(1) shall contain without abbreviation the words "limited partnership";

(2) may not contain the name of a limited partner unless (i) it is also the name of a general partner or the corporate name of a corporate general partner, or (ii) the business of the limited part-nership had been carried on under that name before the admission of that limited partner;

(3) may not be the same as, or deceptively similar to, the name of any corporation or limited part-nership organized under the laws of this State or licensed or registered as a foreign corporation or limited partnership in this State; and

(4) may not contain the following words [here insert prohibited words].

§ 103. Reservation of Name

(a) The exclusive right to the use of a name may be reserved by:

(1) any person intending to organize a limited partnership under this Act and to adopt that name;

(2) any domestic limited partnership or any for-eign limited partnership registered in this State which, in either case, intends to adopt that name;

(3) any foreign limited partnership intending to register in this State and adopt that name; and

(4) any person intending to organize a foreign limited partnership and intending to have it register in this State and adopt that name.

(b) The reservation shall be made by filing with the Secretary of State an application, executed by the applicant, to reserve a specified name. If the Secre-tary of State finds that the name is available for use by a domestic or foreign limited partnership, he [or she] shall reserve the name for the exclusive use of the applicant for a period of 120 days. Once having

so reserved a name, the same applicant may not again reserve the same name until more than 60 days after the expiration of the last 120-day period for which that applicant reserved that name. The right to the exclusive use of a reserved name may be transferred to any other person by filing in the office of the Secretary of State a notice of the transfer, executed by the applicant for whom the name was reserved and specifying the name and address of the transferee.

§ 104. Specified Office and Agent

Each limited partnership shall continuously maintain in this State:

(1) an office, which may but need not be a place of its business in this State, at which shall be kept the records required by Section 105 to be main-tained; and

(2) an agent for service of process on the limited partnership, which agent must be an individual resident of this State, a domestic corporation, or a foreign corporation authorized to do business in this State.

§ 105. Records to be Kept

(a) Each limited partnership shall keep at the office referred to in Section 104(1) the following:

(1) a current list of the full name and last known business address of each partner sepa-rately identifying the general partners (in alphabetical order) and the limited partners (in alphabetical order);

(2) a copy of the certificate of limited partner-ship and all certificates of amendment thereto, together with executed copies of any powers of attorney pursuant to which any certificate has been executed;

(3) copies of the limited partnership's federal, state and local income tax returns and reports, if any, for the three most recent years;

(4) copies of any then effective written partner-ship agreements and of any financial statements of the limited partnership for the three most recent years; and

(5) unless contained in a written partnership agreement, a writing setting out:

(i) the amount of cash and a description and statement of the agreed value of the other property or services contributed by each partner and which each partner has agreed to contribute;

(ii) the times at which or events on the happening of which any additional contributions agreed to be made by each partner are to be made;

(iii) any right of a partner to receive, or of a general partner to make, distributions to a partner which include a return of all or any part of the partner's contribution; and

(iv) any events upon the happening of which the limited partnership is to be dissolved and its affairs wound up.

(b) Records kept under this section are subject to inspection and copying at the reasonable request at the expense of any partner during ordinary business hours.

§ 106. Nature of Business

A limited partnership may carry on any business that a partnership without limited partners may carry on except [here designate prohibited activities].

§ 107. Business Transactions of Partner with Partnership

Except as provided in the partnership agreement, a partner may lend money to and transact other business with the limited partnership and, subject to other applicable law, has the same rights and obligations with respect thereto as a person who is not a partner.

ARTICLE 2
FORMATION; CERTIFICATE OF LIMITED PARTNERSHIP
§ 201. Certificate of Limited Partnership

(a) In order to form a limited partnership, a certificate of limited partnership must be executed and filed in the office of the Secretary of State. The certificate shall set forth:

(1) the name of the limited partnership;
(2) the address of the office and the name and address of the agent for service of process required to be maintained by Section 104;
(3) the name and the business address of each general partner;
(4) the latest date upon which the limited partnership is to dissolve; and
(5) any other matters the general partners determine to include therein.

(b) A limited partnership is formed at the time of the filing of the certificate of limited partnership in the office of the Secretary of State or at any later time specified in the certificate of limited partnership if, in either case, there has been substantial compliance with the requirements of this section.

§ 202. Amendment to Certificate

(a) A certificate of limited partnership is amended by filing a certificate of amendment thereto in the office of the Secretary of State. The certificate shall set forth:

(1) the name of the limited partnership;
(2) the date of filing the certificate; and
(3) the amendment to the certificate.

(b) Within 30 days after the happening of any of the following events, an amendment to a certificate of limited partnership reflecting the occurrence of the event or events shall be filed:

(1) the admission of a new general partner;
(2) the withdrawal of a general partner; or
(3) the continuation of the business under Section 801 after an event of withdrawal of a general partner.

(c) A general partner who becomes aware that any statement in a certificate of limited partnership was false when made or that any arrangements or other facts described have changed, making the certificate inaccurate in any respect, shall promptly amend the certificate.

(d) A certificate of limited partnership may be amended at any time for any other proper purpose the general partners determine.

(e) No person has any liability because an amendment to a certificate of limited partnership has not been filed to reflect the occurrence of any event referred to in subsection (b) of this section if the amendment is filed within the 30-day period specified in subsection (b).

(f) A restated certificate of limited partnership may be executed and filed in the same manner as a certificate of amendment.

§ 203. Cancellation of Certificate

A certificate of limited partnership shall be cancelled upon the dissolution and the commencement of winding up of the partnership or at any other time there are no limited partners. A certificate of cancellation shall be filed in the office of the Secretary of State and set forth:

(1) the name of the limited partnership;

(2) the date of filing of its certificate of limited partnership;

(3) the reason for filing the certificate of cancellation;

(4) the effective date (which shall be a date certain) of cancellation if it is not to be effective upon the filing of the certificate; and

(5) any other information the general partners filing the certificate determine.

§ 204. Execution of Certificates

(a) Each certificate required by this Article to be filed in the office of the Secretary of State shall be executed in the following manner:

(1) an original certificate of limited partnership must be signed by all general partners,

(2) a certificate of amendment must be signed by at least one general partner and by each other general partner designated in the certificate as a new general partner; and

(3) a certificate of cancellation must be signed by all general partners.

(b) Any person may sign a certificate by an attorney-in-fact, but a power of attorney to sign a certificate relating to the admission of a general partner must specifically describe the admission.

(c) The execution of a certificate by a general partner constitutes an affirmation under the penalties of perjury that the facts stated therein are true.

§ 205. Execution by Judicial Act

If a person required by Section 204 to execute any certificate fails or refuses to do so, any other person who is adversely affected by the failure or refusal, may petition the [designate the appropriate court] to direct the execution of the certificate. If the court finds that it is proper for the certificate to be executed and that any person so designated has failed or refused to execute the certificate, it shall order the Secretary of State to record an appropriate certificate.

§ 206. Filing in Office of Secretary of State

(a) Two signed copies of the certificate of limited partnership and of any certificates of amendment or cancellation (or of any judicial decree of amendment

or cancellation) shall be delivered to the Secretary of State. A person who executes a certificate as an agent or fiduciary need not exhibit evidence of his [or her] authority as a prerequisite to filing. Unless the Secretary of State finds that any certificate does not conform to law, upon receipt of all filing fees required by law he [or she] shall:

(1) endorse on each duplicate original the word "Filed" and the day, month, and year of the filing thereof;

(2) file one duplicate original in his [or her] office; and

(3) return the other duplicate original to the person who filed it or his [or her] representative.

(b) Upon the filing of a certificate of amendment (or judicial decree of amendment) in the office of the Secretary of State, the certificate of limited partnership shall be amended as set forth therein, and upon the effective date of a certificate of cancellation (or a judicial decree thereof), the certificate of limited partnership is cancelled.

§ 207. Liability for False Statement in Certificate

If any certificate of limited partnership or certificate of amendment or cancellation contains a false statement, one who suffers loss by reliance on the statement may recover damages for the loss from:

(1) any person who executes the certificate, or causes another to execute it on his behalf, and knew, and any general partner who knew or should have known, the statement to be false at the time the certificate was executed; and

(2) any general partner who thereafter knows or should have known that any arrangement or other fact described in the certificate has changed, making the statement inaccurate in any respect within a sufficient time before the statement was relied upon reasonably to have enabled that general partner to cancel or amend the certificate, or to file a petition for its cancellation or amendment under Section 205.

§ 208. Scope of Notice

The fact that a certificate of limited partnership is on file in the office of the Secretary of State is notice that the partnership is a limited partnership and the persons designated therein as general partners are general partners, but it is not notice of any other fact.

ARTICLE 3
LIMITED PARTNERS

§ 301. Admission of Additional Limited Partners

(a)   A person becomes a limited partner:

(1) at the time the limited partnership is formed; or
(2) at any later time specified in the records of the limited partnership for becoming a limited partner.

(b)   After the filing of a limited partnership's original certificate of limited partnership, a person may be admitted as an additional limited partner:

(1) in the case of a person acquiring a partnership interest directly from the limited partnership, upon compliance with the partnership agreement or, if the partnership agreement does not so provide, upon the written consent of all partners; and
(2) in the case of an assignee of a partnership interest of a partner who has the power, as provided in Section 704, to grant the assignee the right to become a limited partner, upon the exercise of that power and compliance with any conditions limiting the grant or exercise of the power.

§ 302. Voting

Subject to Section 303, the partnership agreement may grant to all or to a specified group of the limited partners the right to vote (on a per capita or any other basis) upon any matter.

§ 303. Liability to Third Parties

(a)   Except as provided in subsection (d), a limited partner is not liable for the obligations of a limited partnership unless he [or she] is also a general partner or, in addition to the exercise of his [or her] rights and powers as a limited partner, he [or she] participates in the control of the business. However, if the limited partner participates in the control of the business, he [or she] is liable only to persons who transact business with the limited partnership reasonably believing, based upon the limited partner's conduct, that the limited partner is a general partner.

(b)   A limited partner does not participate in the control of the business within the meaning of subsection (a) solely by doing one or more of the following:

(1)   being a contractor for or an agent or employee of the limited partnership or of a general partner or being an officer, director, or shareholder of a general partner that is a corporation;

(2)   consulting with and advising a general partner with respect to the business of the limited partnership;

(3)   acting as surety for the limited partnership or guaranteeing or assuming one or more specific obligations of the limited partnership;

(4)   taking any action required or permitted by law to bring or pursue a derivative action in the right of the limited partnership;

(5)   requesting or attending a meeting of partners;

(6)   proposing, approving, or disapproving, by voting or otherwise, one or more of the following matters:

(i)   the dissolution and winding up of the limited partnership;
(ii)   the sale, exchange, lease, mortgage, pledge, or other transfer of all or substantially all of the assets of the limited partnership;
(iii) the incurrence of indebtedness by the limited partnership other than in the ordinary course of its business;
(iv)   a change in the nature of the business;
(v)   the admission or removal of a general partner;
(vi)   the admission or removal of a limited partner;
(vii) a transaction involving an actual or potential conflict of interest between a general partner and the limited partnership or the limited partners;
(viii) an amendment to the partnership agreement or certificate of limited partnership; or
(ix)   matters related to the business of the limited partnership not otherwise enumerated in this subsection (b), which the partnership agreement states in writing may be subject to the approval or disapproval of limited partners;

(7)   winding up the limited partnership pursuant to Section 803; or

(8)   exercising any right or power permitted to limited partners under this Act and not specifically enumerated in this subsection (b).

(c)   The enumeration in subsection (b) does not mean that the possession or exercise of any other powers by a limited partner constitutes participation by him [or her] in the business of the limited partnership.

(d)   A limited partner who knowingly permits his [or her] name to be used in the name of the limited partnership, except under circumstances permitted by Section 102(2), is liable to creditors who extend credit to the limited partnership without actual knowledge that the limited partner is not a general partner.

§ 304. Person Erroneously Believing Himself [or Herself] Limited Partner

(a)   Except as provided in subsection (b), a person who makes a contribution to a business enterprise and erroneously but in good faith believes that he [or she] has become a limited partner in the enterprise is not a general partner in the enterprise and is not bound by its obligations by reason of making the contribution, receiving distributions from the enterprise, or exercising any rights of a limited partner, if, on ascertaining the mistake, he [or she]:

> (1) causes an appropriate certificate of limited partnership or a certificate of amendment to be executed and filed; or
> (2) withdraws from future equity participation in the enterprise by executing and filing in the office of the Secretary of State a certificate declaring withdrawal under this section.

(b)   A person who makes a contribution of the kind described in subsection (a) is liable as a general partner to any third party who transacts business with the enterprise (i) before the person withdraws and an appropriate certificate is filed to show withdrawal, or (ii) before an appropriate certificate is filed to show that he [or she] is not a general partner, but in either case only if the third party actually believed in good faith that the person was a general partner at the time of the transaction.

§ 305. Information

Each limited partner has the right to:

(1)   inspect and copy any of the partnership records required to be maintained by Section 105; and
(2)   obtain from the general partners from time to time upon reasonable demand (i) true and full information regarding the state of the business and financial condition of the limited partnership, (ii) promptly after becoming available, a copy of the limited partnership's federal, state,

and local income tax returns for each year, and (iii) other information regarding the affairs of the limited partnership as is just and reasonable.

ARTICLE 4
GENERAL PARTNERS
§ 401. Admission of Additional General Partners

After the filing of a limited partnership's original certificate of limited partnership, additional general partners may be admitted as provided in writing in the partnership agreement or, if the partnership agreement does not provide in writing for the admission of additional general partners, with the written consent of all partners.

§ 402. Events of Withdrawal

Except as approved by the specific written consent of all partners at the time, a person ceases to be a general partner of a limited partnership upon the happening of any of the following events:

(1)   the general partner withdraws from the limited partnership as provided in Section 602;
(2)   the general partner ceases to be a member of the limited partnership as provided in Section 702;
(3)   the general partner is removed as a general partner in accordance with the partnership agreement;
(4)   unless otherwise provided in writing in the partnership agreement, the general partner: (i) makes an assignment for the benefit of creditors; (ii) files a voluntary petition in bankruptcy; (iii) is adjudicated a bankrupt or insolvent; (iv) files a petition or answer seeking for himself [or herself] any reorganization, arrangement, composition, readjustment, liquidation, dissolution or similar relief under any statute, law, or regulation; (v) files an answer or other pleading admitting or failing to contest the material allegations of a petition filed against him [or her] in any proceeding of this nature; or (vi) seeks, consents to, or acquiesces in the appointment of a trustee, receiver, or liquidator of the general partner or of all or any substantial part of his [or her] properties;
(5)   unless otherwise provided in writing in the partnership agreement, [120] days after the commencement of any proceeding against the general partner seeking reorganization, arrangement, composition, readjustment, liquidation, dissolution or similar relief under any statute,

law, or regulation, the proceeding has not been dismissed, or if within [90] days after the appointment without his [or her] consent or acquiescence of a trustee, receiver, or liquidator of the general partner or of all or any substantial part of his [or her] properties, the appointment is not vacated or stayed or within [90] days after the expiration of any such stay, the appointment is not vacated;

(6) in the case of a general partner who is a natural person,

    (i) his [or her] death; or

    (ii) the entry of an order by a court of competent jurisdiction adjudicating him [or her] incompetent to manage his [or her] person or his [or her] estate;

(7) in the case of a general partner who is acting as a general partner by virtue of being a trustee of a trust, the termination of the trust (but not merely the substitution of a new trustee);

(8) in the case of a general partner that is a separate partnership, the dissolution and commencement of winding up of the separate partnership;

(9) in the case of a general partner that is a corporation, the filing of a certificate of dissolution, or its equivalent, for the corporation or the revocation of its charter; or

(10) in the case of an estate, the distribution by the fiduciary of the estate's entire interest in the partnership.

§ 403. General Powers and Liabilities

(a) Except as provided in this Act or in the partnership agreement, a general partner of a limited partnership has the rights and powers and is subject to the restrictions of a partner in a partnership without limited partners.

(b) Except as provided in this Act, a general partner of a limited partnership has the liabilities of a partner in a partnership without limited partners to persons other than the partnership and the other partners. Except as provided in this Act or in the partnership agreement, a general partner of a limited partnership has the liabilities of a partner in a partnership without limited partners to the partnership and to the other partners.

§ 404. Contributions by General Partner

A general partner of a limited partnership may make contributions to the partnership and share in the profits and losses of, and in distributions from, the limited partnership as a general partner. A general partner also may make contributions to and share in profits, losses, and distributions as a limited partner. A person who is both a general partner and a limited partner has the rights and powers, and is subject to the restrictions and liabilities, of a general partner and, except as provided in the partnership agreement, also has the powers, and is subject to the restrictions, of a limited partner to the extent of his [or her] participation in the partnership as a limited partner.

§ 405. Voting

The partnership agreement may grant to all or certain identified general partners the right to vote (on a per capita or any other basis), separately or with all or any class of the limited partners, on any matter.

ARTICLE 5
FINANCE
§ 501. Form of Contribution

The contribution of a partner may be in cash, property, or services rendered, or a promissory note or other obligation to contribute cash or property or to perform services.

§ 502. Liability for Contribution

(a) A promise by a limited partner to contribute to the limited partnership is not enforceable unless set out in a writing signed by the limited partner.

(b) Except as provided in the partnership agreement, a partner is obligated to the limited partnership to perform any enforceable promise to contribute cash or property or to perform services, even if he [or she] is unable to perform because of death, disability, or any other reason. If a partner does not make the required contribution of property or services, he [or she] is obligated at the option of the limited partnership to contribute cash equal to that portion of the value, as stated in the partnership records required to be kept pursuant to Section 105, of the stated contribution which has not been made.

(c) Unless otherwise provided in the partnership agreement, the obligation of a partner to make a contribution or return money or other property paid or distributed in violation of this Act may be compromised only by consent of all partners. Notwithstanding the compromise, a creditor of a limited partnership who extends credit, or otherwise acts in reliance on that obligation after the partner signs a writing which, reflects the obligation, and before the amendment or cancellation thereof to reflect the compromise, may enforce the original obligation.

§ 503. Sharing of Profits and Losses

The profits and losses of a limited partnership shall be allocated among the partners, and among classes of partners, in the manner provided in writing in the partnership agreement. If the partnership agreement does not so provide in writing, profits and losses shall be allocated on the basis of the value, as stated in the partnership records required to be kept pursuant to Section 105, of the contributions made by each partner to the extent they have been received by the partnership and have not been returned.

§ 504. Sharing of Distributions

Distributions of cash or other assets of a limited partnership shall be allocated among the partners and among classes of partners in the manner provided in writing in the partnership agreement. If the partnership agreement does not so provide in writing, distributions shall be made on the basis of the value, as stated in the partnership records required to be kept pursuant to Section 105, of the contributions made by each partner to the extent they have been received by the partnership and have not been returned.

ARTICLE 6
DISTRIBUTIONS AND WITHDRAWAL
§ 601. Interim Distributions

Except as provided in this Article, a partner is entitled to receive distributions from a limited partnership before his [or her] withdrawal from the limited partnership and before the dissolution and winding up thereof to the extent and at the times or upon the happening of the events specified in the partnership agreement.

§ 602. Withdrawal of General Partner

A general partner may withdraw from a limited partnership at any time by giving written notice to the other partners, but if the withdrawal violates the partnership agreement, the limited partnership may recover from the withdrawing general partner damages for breach of the partnership agreement and offset the damages against the amount otherwise distributable to him [or her].

§ 603. Withdrawal of Limited Partner

A limited partner may withdraw from a limited partnership at the time or upon the happening of events specified in writing in the partnership agreement. If the agreement does not specify in writing the time or the events upon the happening of which a limited partner may withdraw or a definite time for the dissolution and winding up of the limited partnership, a limited partner may withdraw upon not less than six months' prior written notice to each general partner at his [or her] address on the books of the limited partnership at its office in this State.

§ 604. Distribution Upon Withdrawal

Except as provided in this Article, upon withdrawal any withdrawing partner is entitled to receive any distribution to which he [or she] is entitled under the partnership agreement and, if not otherwise provided in the agreement, he [or she] is entitled to receive, within a reasonable time after withdrawal, the fair value of his [or her] interest in the limited partnership as of the date of withdrawal based upon his [or her] right to share in distributions from the limited partnership.

§ 605. Distribution in Kind

Except as provided in the partnership agreement, a partner, regardless of the nature of his [or her] contribution, has no right to demand and receive any distribution from a limited partnership in any form other than cash. Except as provided in writing in the partnership agreement, a partner may not be compelled to accept a distribution of any asset in kind from a limited partnership to the extent that the percentage of the asset distributed to him [or her] exceeds a percentage of the asset which is equal to the percentage in which he [or she] shares in distributions from the limited partnership.

§ 606. Right to Distribution

At the time a partner becomes entitled to receive a distribution, he [or she] has the status of, and is entitled to all remedies available to, a creditor of the limited partnership with respect to the distribution.

§ 607. Limitations on Distribution

A partner may not receive a distribution from a limited partnership to the extent that, after giving effect to the distribution, all liabilities of the limited partnership, other than liabilities to partners on account of their partnership interests, exceed the fair value of the partnership assets.

§ 608. Liability Upon Return of Contribution

(a)   If a partner has received the return of any part of his [or her] contribution without violation of the partnership agreement or this Act, he [or she] is liable to the limited partnership for a period of one year thereafter for the amount of the returned contribution, but only to the extent necessary to discharge the limited partnership's liabilities to creditors who extended credit to the limited partnership during the period the contribution was held by the partnership.

(b)   If a partner has received the return of any part of his [or her] contribution in violation of the partnership agreement or this Act, he [or she] is liable to the limited partnership for a period of six years thereafter for the amount of the contribution wrongfully returned.

(c)   A partner receives a return of his [or her] contribution to the extent that a distribution to him [or her] reduces his [or her] share of the fair value of the net assets of the limited partnership below the value, as set forth in the partnership records required to be kept pursuant to Section 105, of his contribution which has not been distributed to him [or her].

ARTICLE 7
ASSIGNMENT OF PARTNERSHIP INTERESTS
§ 701. Nature of Partnership Interest
A partnership interest is personal property.

§ 702. Assignment of Partnership Interest
Except as provided in the partnership agreement, a partnership interest is assignable in whole or in part. An assignment of a partnership interest does not dissolve a limited partnership or entitle the assignee to become or to exercise any rights of a partner. An assignment entitles the assignee to receive, to the extent assigned, only the distribution to which the assignor would be entitled. Except as provided in the partnership agreement, a partner ceases to be a partner upon assignment of all his [or her] partnership interest.

§ 703. Rights of Creditor
On application to a court of competent jurisdiction by any judgment creditor of a partner, the court may charge the partnership interest of the partner with payment of the unsatisfied amount of the judgment with interest. To the extent so charged, the judgment creditor has only the rights of an assignee of the partnership interest. This Act does not deprive any partner of the benefit of any exemption laws applicable to his [or her] partnership interest.

§ 704. Right of Assignee to Become Limited Partner

(a)   An assignee of a partnership interest, including an assignee of a general partner, may become a limited partner if and to the extent that (i) the assignor gives the assignee that right in accordance with authority described in the partnership agreement, or (ii) all other partners consent.

(b)   An assignee who has become a limited partner has, to the extent assigned, the rights and powers, and is subject to the restrictions and liabilities, of a limited partner under the partnership agreement and this Act. An assignee who becomes a limited partner also is liable for the obligations of his [or her] assignor to make and return contributions as provided in Articles 5 and 6. However, the assignee is not obligated for liabilities unknown to the assignee at the time he [or she] became a limited partner.

(c)   If an assignee of a partnership interest becomes a limited partner, the assignor is not released from his [or her] liability to the limited partnership under Sections 207 and 502.

§ 705. Power of Estate of Deceased or Incompetent Partner
If a partner who is an individual dies or a court of competent jurisdiction adjudges him [or her] to be incompetent to manage his [or her] person or his [or her] property, the partner's executor, administrator, guardian, conservator, or other legal representative may exercise all the partner's rights for the purpose of settling his [or her] estate or administering his [or her] property, including any power the partner had to give an assignee the right to become a limited partner. If a partner is a corporation, trust, or other entity and is dissolved or terminated, the powers of that partner may be exercised by its legal representative or successor.

ARTICLE 8

DISSOLUTION

§ 801. Nonjudicial Dissolution

A limited partnership is dissolved and its affairs shall be wound up upon the happening of the first to occur of the following:

(1)   at the time specified in the certificate of limited partnership;

(2)   upon the happening of events specified in writing in the partnership agreement;

(3)   written consent of all partners;

(4)   an event of withdrawal of a general partner unless at the time there is at least one other general partner and the written provisions of the partnership agreement permit the business of the limited partnership to be carried on by the remaining general partner and that partner does so, but the limited partnership is not dissolved and is not required to be wound up by reason of any event of withdrawal, if, within 90 days after the withdrawal, all partners agree in writing to continue the business of the limited partnership and to the appointment of one or more additional general partners if necessary or desired; or

(5)   entry of a decree of judicial dissolution under Section 802.

§ 802. Judicial Dissolution

On application by or for a partner the [designate the appropriate court] court may decree dissolution of a limited partnership whenever it is not reasonably practicable to carry on the business in conformity with the partnership agreement.

§ 803. Winding Up

Except as provided in the partnership agreement, the general partners who have not wrongfully dissolved a limited partnership or, if none, the limited partners, may wind up the limited partnership's affairs; but the [designate the appropriate court] court may wind up the limited partnership's affairs upon application of any partner, his [or her] legal representative, or assignee.

§ 804. Distribution of Assets

Upon the winding up of a limited partnership, the assets shall be distributed as follows:

(1)   to creditors, including partners who are creditors, to the extent permitted by law, in satisfaction of liabilities of the limited partnership other than liabilities for distributions to partners under Section 601 or 604;

(2)   except as provided in the partnership agreement, to partners and former partners in satisfaction of liabilities for distributions under Section 601 or 604; and

(3)   except as provided in the partnership agreement, to partners first for the return of their contributions and secondly respecting their partnership interests, in the proportions in which the partners share in distributions.

ARTICLE 9

FOREIGN LIMITED PARTNERSHIPS

§ 901. Law Governing

Subject to the Constitution of this State, (i) the laws of the state under which a foreign limited partnership is organized govern its organization and internal affairs and the liability of its limited partners, and (ii) a foreign limited partnership may not be denied registration by reason of any difference between those laws and the laws of this State.

§ 902. Registration

Before transacting business in this State, a foreign limited partnership shall register with the Secretary of State. In order to register, a foreign limited partnership shall submit to the Secretary of State, in duplicate, an application for registration as a foreign limited partnership, signed and sworn to by a general partner and setting forth:

(1)   the name of the foreign limited partnership and, if different, the name under which it proposes to register and transact business in this State;

(2)   the State and date of its formation;

(3)   the name and address of any agent for service of process on the foreign limited partnership whom the foreign limited partnership elects to appoint; the agent must be an individual resident of this State, a domestic corporation, or a foreign corporation having a place of business in, and authorized to do business in, this State;

(4)   a statement that the Secretary of State is appointed the agent of the foreign limited partnership for service of process if no agent has been appointed under paragraph (3) or, if appointed, the agent's authority has been revoked or if the agent cannot be found or

served with the exercise of reasonable diligence;

(5) the address of the office required to be maintained in the state of its organization by the laws of that state or, if not so required, of the principal office of the foreign limited partnership;

(6) the name and business address of each general partner; and

(7) the address of the office at which is kept a list of the names and addresses of the limited partners and their capital contributions, together with an undertaking by the foreign limited partnership to keep those records until the foreign limited partnership's registration in this State is cancelled or withdrawn.

§ 903. Issuance of Registration

(a) If the Secretary of State finds that an application for registration conforms to law and all requisite fees have been paid, he [or she] shall:

(1) endorse on the application the word "Filed," and the month, day and year of the filing thereof;
(2) file in his [or her] office a duplicate original of the application; and
(3) issue a certificate of registration to transact business in this State.

(b) The certificate of registration, together with a duplicate original of the application, shall be returned to the person who filed the application or his [or her] representative.

§ 904. Name

A foreign limited partnership may register with the Secretary of State under any name, whether or not it is the name under which it is registered in its state of organization, that includes without abbreviation the words "limited partnership" and that could be registered by a domestic limited partnership.

§ 905. Changes and Amendments

If any statement in the application for registration of a foreign limited partnership was false when made or any arrangements or other facts described have changed, making the application inaccurate in any respect, the foreign limited partnership shall promptly file in the office of the Secretary of State a certificate, signed and sworn to by a general partner, correcting such statement.

§ 906. Cancellation of Registration

A foreign limited partnership may cancel its registration by filing with the Secretary of State a certificate of cancellation signed and sworn to by a general partner. A cancellation does not terminate the authority of the Secretary of State to accept service of process on the foreign limited partnership with respect to [claims for relief] [causes of action] arising out of the transactions of business in this State.

§ 907. Transaction of Business Without Registration

(a) A foreign limited partnership transacting business in this State may not maintain any action, suit, or proceeding in any court of this State until it has registered in this State.

(b) The failure of a foreign limited partnership to register in this State does not impair the validity of any contract or act of the foreign limited partnership or prevent the foreign limited partnership from defending any action, suit, or proceeding in any court of this State.

(c) A limited partner of a foreign limited partnership is not liable as a general partner of the foreign limited partnership solely by reason of having transacted business in this State without registration.

(d) A foreign limited partnership, by transacting business in this State without registration, appoints the Secretary of State as its agent for service of process with respect to [claims for relief] [causes of action] arising out of the transaction of business in this State.

§ 908. Action by [Appropriate Official]

The [designate the appropriate official] may bring an action to restrain a foreign limited partnership from transacting business in this State in violation of this Article.

ARTICLE 10
DERIVATIVE ACTIONS
§ 1001. Right of Action

A limited partner may bring an action in the right of a limited partnership to recover a judgment in its favor if general partners with authority to do so have refused to bring the action or if an effort to cause those general partners to bring the action is not likely to succeed.

§ 1002. Proper Plaintiff

In a derivative action, the plaintiff must be a partner at the time of bringing the action and (i) must have been a partner at the time of the transaction of which he [or she] complains or (ii) his [or her] status as a partner must have devolved upon him [or her] by operation of law or pursuant to the terms of the partnership agreement from a person who was a partner at the time of the transaction.

§ 1003. Pleading

In a derivative action, the complaint shall set forth with particularity the effort of the plaintiff to secure initiation of the action by a general partner or the reasons for not making the effort.

§ 1004. Expenses

If a derivative action is successful, in whole or in part, or if anything is received by the plaintiff as a result of a judgment, compromise or settlement of an action or claim, the court may award the plaintiff reasonable expenses, including reasonable attorney's fees, and shall direct him [or her] to remit to the limited partnership the remainder of those proceeds received by him [or her].

ARTICLE 11
MISCELLANEOUS

§ 1101. Construction and Application

This Act shall be so applied and construed to effectuate its general purpose to make uniform the law with respect to the subject of this Act among states enacting it.

§ 1102. Short Title

This Act may be cited as the Uniform Limited Partnership Act.

§ 1103. Severability

If any provision of this Act or its application to any person or circumstance is held invalid, the invalidity does not affect other provisions or applications of the Act which can be given effect without the invalid provision or application, and to this end the provisions of this Act are severable.

§ 1104. Effective Date, Extended Effective Date and Repeal

Except as set forth below, the effective date of this Act is ____ and the following acts [list existing limited partnership acts] are hereby repealed:

(1) The existing provisions for execution and filing of certificates of limited partnerships and amendments thereunder and cancellations thereof continue in effect until [specify time required to create central filing system], the extended effective date, and Sections 102, 103, 104, 105, 201, 202, 203, 204 and 206 are not effective until the extended effective date.

(2) Section 402, specifying the conditions under which a general partner ceases to be a member of a limited partnership, is not effective until the extended effective date, and the applicable provisions of existing law continue to govern until the extended effective date.

(3) Sections 501, 502 and 608 apply only to contributions and distributions made after the effective date of this Act.

(4) Section 704 applies only to assignments made after the effective date of this Act.

(5) Article 9, dealing with registration of foreign limited partnerships, is not effective until the extended effective date.

(6) Unless otherwise agreed by the partners, the applicable provisions of existing law governing allocation of profits and losses (rather than the provisions of Section 503), distributions to a withdrawing partner (rather than the provisions of Section 604), and distribution of assets upon the winding up of a limited partnership (rather than the provisions of Section 804) govern limited partnerships formed before the effective date of this Act.

§ 1105. Rules for Cases Not Provided for in This Act

In any case not provided for in this Act the provisions of the Uniform Partnership Act govern.

§ 1106. Savings Clause

The repeal of any statutory provision by this Act does not impair, or otherwise affect, the organization or the continued existence of a limited partnership existing at the effective date of this Act, nor does the repeal of any existing statutory provision by this Act impair any contract or affect any right accrued before the effective date of this Act.

NALA Code of Ethics and Professional Responsibility

A legal assistant must adhere strictly to the accepted standards of legal ethics and to the general principles of proper conduct. The performance of the duties of the legal assistant shall be governed by specific canons as defined herein so that justice will be served and goals of the profession attained. (See Model Standards and Guidelines for Utilization of Legal Assistants, Section II.)

The canons of ethics set forth hereafter are adopted by the National Association of Legal Assistants, Inc., as a general guide intended to aid legal assistants and attorneys. The enumeration of these rules does not mean there are not others of equal importance although not specifically mentioned. Court rules, agency rules and statutes must be taken into consideration when interpreting the canons.

Definition: Legal assistants, also known as paralegals, are a distinguishable group of persons who assist attorneys in the delivery of legal services. Through formal education, training and experience, legal assistants have knowledge and expertise regarding the legal system and substantive and procedural law which qualify them to do work of a legal nature under the supervision of an attorney.

Comment

Canon 1

A legal assistant must not perform any of the duties that attorneys only may perform nor take any actions that attorneys may not take.

Canon 2

A legal assistant may perform any task which is properly delegated and supervised by an attorney, as long as the attorney is ultimately responsible to the client, maintains a direct relationship with the client, and assumes professional responsibility for the work product.

Canon 3

A legal assistant must not: (a) engage in, encourage, or contribute to any act which could constitute the unauthorized practice of law; and (b) establish attorney-client relationships, set fees, give legal opinions or advice or represent a client before a court or agency unless so authorized by that court or agency; and (c) engage in conduct or take any action which would assist or involve the attorney in a violation of professional ethics or give the appearance of professional impropriety.

Canon 4

A legal assistant must use discretion and professional judgment commensurate with knowledge and experience but must not render independent legal judgment in place of an attorney. The services of an attorney are essential in the public interest whenever such legal judgment is required.

Canon 5

A legal assistant must disclose his or her status as a legal assistant at the outset of any professional relationship with a client, attorney, a court or administrative agency or personnel thereof, or a member of the general public. A legal assistant must act prudently in determining the extent to which a client may be assisted without the presence of an attorney.

Canon 6

A legal assistant must strive to maintain integrity and a high degree of competency through education and training with respect to professional responsibility, local rules and practice, and through continuing education in substantive areas of law to better assist the legal profession in fulfilling its duty to provide legal service.

Canon 7

A legal assistant must protect the confidences of a client and must not violate any rule or statute now in effect or hereafter enacted controlling the doctrine of privileged communications between a client and an attorney.

Canon 8

A legal assistant must do all other things incidental, necessary, or expedient for the attainment of the ethics and responsibilities as defined by statute or rule of court.

Canon 9

A legal assistant's conduct is guided by bar associations' codes of professional responsibility and rules of professional conduct.

NALA Model Standards and Guidelines for Utilization of Legal Assistants

NALA's study of the professional responsibility and ethical considerations of legal assistants is ongoing. This research led to the development of the NALA Model Standards and Guidelines for Utilization of Legal Assistants. This guide summarizes case law, guidelines and ethical opinions of the various states affecting legal assistants. It provides an outline of minimum qualifications and standards necessary for legal assistant professionals to assure the public and the legal profession that they are, indeed, qualified. The following is a listing of the standards and guidelines.

The annotated version of the Model was revised extensively in 1997. It is on-line — NALA Model Standards and Guidelines — and may be ordered through **NALA Headquarters.**

INTRODUCTION

Proper utilization of the services of legal assistants affects the efficient delivery of legal services. Legal assistants and the legal profession should be assured that some measures exist for identifying legal assistants and their role in assisting attorneys in the delivery of legal services. Therefore, the National Association of Legal Assistants, Inc., hereby adopts these Model Standards and Guidelines as an educational document for the benefit of legal assistants and the legal profession.

Comment-NALA Definition

STANDARDS

A legal assistant should meet certain minimum qualifications. The following standards may be used to determine an individual's qualifications as a legal assistant:

1. Successful completion of the Certified Legal Assistant certifying (CLA) examination of the National Association of Legal Assistants;

2. Graduation from an ABA approved program of study for legal assistants;

3. Graduation from a course of study for legal assistants which is institutionally accredited but not ABA approved, and which requires not less than the equivalent of 60 semester hours of classroom study;

4. Graduation from a course of study for legal assistant, other than those set forth in (2) and (3) above, plus not less than six months of in-house training as a legal assistant.

5. A baccalaureate degree in any field, plus not less than six months in-house training as a legal assistant;

6. A minimum of three years of law-related experience under the supervision of an attorney, including at least six months of in-house training as a legal assistant; or

7. Two years of in-house training as a legal assistant.

For purposes of these Standards, "in-house training as a legal assistant" means attorney education of the employee concerning legal assistant duties and these Guidelines. In addition to review and analysis of assignments the legal assistant should receive a reasonable amount of instruction directly related to the duties and obligations of the legal assistant.

GUIDELINES

These guidelines relating to standards of performance and professional responsibility are intended to aid legal assistants and attorneys. The responsibility rests with an attorney who employs legal assistants to educate them with respect to the duties they are assigned to supervise the manner in which such duties are accomplished.

GUIDELINE 1

Legal assistants should:

1.   Disclose their status as legal assistants at the outset of any professional relationship with a client, other attorneys, a court or administrative agency or personnel thereof, or members of the general public;

2.   Preserve the confidences and secrets of all clients; and

3.   Understand the attorney's Code of Professional Responsibility and these guidelines in order to avoid any action which would involve the attorney in a violation of that Code, or give the appearance of professional impropriety.

GUIDELINE 2

Legal assistants should not:

1.   Establish attorney–client relationships; set legal fees, give legal opinions or advice; or represent a client before a court; nor

2.   Engage in, encourage, or contribute to any act which could constitute the unauthorized practice of law.

GUIDELINE 3

Legal assistants may perform services for an attorney in the representation of a client, provided:

1.   The services performed by the legal assistant do not require the exercise of independent professional legal judgment;

2.   The attorney maintains a direct relationship with the client and maintains control of all client matters;

3.   The attorney supervises the legal assistant;

4.   The attorney remains professionally responsible for all work on behalf of the client, including any actions taken or not taken by the legal assistant in connection therewith; and

5.   The services performed supplement, merge with and become the attorney's work product.

GUIDELINE 4

In the supervision of a legal assistant, consideration should be given to:

1.   Designating work assignments that correspond to the legal assistant's abilities, knowledge, training and experience.

2.   Education and training the legal assistant with respect to professional responsibility, local rules and practices, and firm policies;

3.   Monitoring the work and professional conduct of the legal assistant to ensure that the work is substantively correct and timely performed;

4.   Providing continuing education for the legal assistant in substantive matters through courses, institutes, workshops, seminars and in-house training, and

5.   Encouraging and supporting membership and active participation in professional organizations.

GUIDELINE 5

Except as otherwise provided by statute, court rule or decision, administrative rule or regulation, or the attorney's Code of Professional Responsibility; and within the preceding parameters and proscriptions, a legal assistant may perform any function delegated by an attorney, including but not limited to the following:

1.   Conduct client interviews and maintain general contact with the client after the establishment of the attorney–client relationship, so long as the client is aware of the status and function of the legal assistant, and the client contact is under the supervision of the attorney.

2.   Locate and interview witnesses, so long as the witnesses are aware of the status and function of the legal assistant.

3.   Conduct investigations and statistical and documentary research for review by the attorney.

4.   Conduct legal research for review by the attorney.

5.   Draft legal documents for review by the attorney.

6. Draft correspondence and pleadings for review by and signature of the attorney.

7. Summarize depositions, interrogatories, and testimony for review by the attorney.

8. Attend executions of wills, real estate closings, depositions, court or administrative hearings and trials with the attorney.

9. Author and sign letters provided the legal assistant's status is clearly indicated and the correspondence does not contain independent legal opinions or legal advice.

The notes to accompany the NALA Model Standards and Guidelines for Utilization of Legal Assistants are updated regularly by the NALA Professional Development Committee. The standards and guidelines are adopted by the NALA membership, and changes to these provisions must be brought before NALA members during their annual meeting in July.

National Federation of Paralegal Associations, Inc. Model Code of Ethics and Professional Responsibility and Guidelines for Enforcement

PREAMBLE

The National Federation of Paralegal Associations, Inc. ("NFPA") is a professional organization comprised of paralegal associations and individual paralegals throughout the United States and Canada. Members of NFPA have varying backgrounds, experiences, education and job responsibilities that reflect the diversity of the paralegal profession. NFPA promotes the growth, development and recognition of the paralegal profession as an integral partner in the delivery of legal services.

In May 1993 NFPA adopted its Model Code of Ethics and Professional Responsibility ("Model Code") to delineate the principles for ethics and conduct to which every paralegal should aspire.

Many paralegal associations throughout the United States have endorsed the concept and content of NFPA's Model Code through the adoption of their own ethical codes. In doing so, paralegals have confirmed the profession's commitment to increase the quality and efficiency of legal services, as well as recognized its responsibilities to the public, the legal community, and colleagues.

Paralegals have recognized, and will continue to recognize, that the profession must continue to evolve to enhance their roles in the delivery of legal services. With increased levels of responsibility comes the need to define and enforce mandatory rules of professional conduct. Enforcement of codes of paralegal conduct is a logical and necessary step to enhance and ensure the confidence of the legal community and the public in the integrity and professional responsibility of paralegals.

In April 1997 NFPA adopted the Model Disciplinary Rules ("Model Rules") to make possible the enforcement of the Canons and Ethical Considerations contained in the NFPA Model Code. A concurrent determination was made that the Model Code of Ethics and Professional Responsibility, formerly aspirational in nature, should be recognized as setting forth the enforceable obligations of all paralegals.

The Model Code and Model Rules offer a framework for professional discipline, either voluntarily or through formal regulatory programs.

§ 1. NFPA MODEL DISCIPLINARY RULES AND ETHICAL CONSIDERATIONS

1.1 A Paralegal shall Achieve and Maintain a High Level of Competence

Ethical Considerations

EC-1.1(a)   A paralegal shall achieve competency through education, training, and work experience.

EC-1.1(b)   A paralegal shall aspire to participate in a minimum of twelve (12) hours of continuing legal education, to include at least one (1) hour of ethics education, every two (2) years in order to remain current on developments in the law.

EC-1.1(c)   A paralegal shall perform all assignments promptly and efficiently.

1.2 A Paralegal shall Maintain a High Level of Personal and Professional Integrity

Ethical Considerations

EC-1.2(a)   A paralegal shall not engage in any ex parte communications involving the courts or any other adjudicatory body in an attempt to exert undue influence or to obtain advantage or the benefit of only one party.

EC-1.2(b)   A paralegal shall not communicate, or cause another to communicate, with a party the paralegal knows to be represented by a lawyer in a pending matter without the prior consent of the lawyer representing such other party.

EC-1.2(c)   A paralegal shall ensure that all time-keeping and billing records prepared by the paralegal are thorough, accurate, honest, and complete.

EC-1.2(d)   A paralegal shall not knowingly engage in fraudulent billing practices. Such practices may include, but are not limited to: inflation of hours billed to a client or employer; misrepresentation of the nature of tasks performed; and/or submission of fraudulent expense and disbursement documentation.

EC-1.2(e)   A paralegal shall be scrupulous, thorough and honest in the identification and maintenance of all funds, securities, and other assets of a client and shall provide accurate accounting as appropriate.

EC-1.2(f)   A paralegal shall advise the proper authority of non-confidential knowledge of any dishonest or fraudulent acts by any person pertaining to the handling of the funds, securities or other assets of a client. The authority to whom the report is made shall depend on the nature and circumstances of the possible misconduct, (e.g., ethics committees of law firms, corporations and/or paralegal associations, local or state bar associations, local prosecutors, administrative agencies, etc.). Failure to report such knowledge is in itself misconduct and shall be treated as such under these rules.

1.3 A Paralegal shall Maintain a High Standard of Professional Conduct

Ethical Considerations

EC-1.3(a)   A paralegal shall refrain from engaging in any conduct that offends the dignity and decorum of proceedings before a court or other adjudicatory body and shall be respectful of all rules and procedures.

EC-1.3(b)   A paralegal shall avoid impropriety and the appearance of impropriety and shall not engage in any conduct that would adversely affect his/her fitness to practice. Such conduct may include, but is not limited to: violence, dishonesty, interference with the administration of justice, and/or abuse of a professional position or public office.

EC-1.3(c)   Should a paralegal's fitness to practice be compromised by physical or mental illness, causing that paralegal to commit an act that is in direct violation of the Model Code/Model Rules and/or the rules and/or laws governing the jurisdiction in which the paralegal practices, that paralegal may be protected from sanction upon review of the nature and circumstances of that illness.

EC-1.3(d)   A paralegal shall advise the proper authority of non-confidential knowledge of any action of another legal professional that clearly demonstrates fraud, deceit, dishonesty, or misrepresentation. The authority to whom the report is made shall depend on the nature and circumstances of the possible misconduct, (e.g., ethics committees of law firms, corporations and/or paralegal associations, local or state bar associations, local prosecutors, administrative agencies, etc.). Failure to report such knowledge is in itself misconduct and shall be treated as such under these rules.

EC-1.3(e)   A paralegal shall not knowingly assist any individual with the commission of an act that is in direct violation of the Model Code/Model Rules and/or the rules and/or laws governing the jurisdiction in which the paralegal practices.

EC-1.3(f)   If a paralegal possesses knowledge of future criminal activity, that knowledge must be reported to the appropriate authority immediately.

1.4 A Paralegal shall Serve the Public Interest by Contributing to the Improvement of the Legal System and Delivery of Quality Legal Services, Including Pro Bono Publico Services

Ethical Considerations

EC-1.4(a)   A paralegal shall be sensitive to the legal needs of the public and shall promote the development and implementation of programs that address those needs.

EC-1.4(b)   A paralegal shall support efforts to improve the legal system and access thereto and shall assist in making changes.

EC-1.4(c)   A paralegal shall support and participate in the delivery of Pro Bono Publico services directed toward implementing and improving access to justice, the law, the legal system or the paralegal and legal professions.

EC-1.4(d)   A paralegal should aspire annually to contribute twenty-four (24) hours of Pro Bono Publico services under the supervision of an attorney or as authorized by administrative, statutory or court authority to:
>   1. persons of limited means; or
>   2. charitable, religious, civic, community, governmental and educational organizations in matters that are designed primarily to address the legal needs of persons with limited means; or
>   3. individuals, groups or organizations seeking to secure or protect civil rights, civil liberties or public rights.

1.5 A Paralegal shall Preserve all Confidential Information Provided by the Client or Acquired from other Sources Before, During, and After the Course of the Professional Relationship

Ethical Considerations

EC-1.5(a)   A paralegal shall be aware of and abide by all legal authority governing confidential information in the jurisdiction in which the paralegal practices.

EC-1.5(b)   A paralegal shall not use confidential information to the disadvantage of the client.

EC-1.5(c)   A paralegal shall not use confidential information to the advantage of the paralegal or of a third person.

EC-1.5(d)   A paralegal may reveal confidential information only after full disclosure and with the client's written consent; or, when required by law or court order; or, when necessary to prevent the client from committing an act that could result in death or serious bodily harm.

EC-1.5(e)   A paralegal shall keep those individuals responsible for the legal representation of a client fully informed of any confidential information the paralegal may have pertaining to that client.

EC-1.5(f)   A paralegal shall not engage in any indiscreet communications concerning clients.

1.6 A Paralegal shall Avoid Conflicts of Interest and shall Disclose any Possible Conflict to the Employer or Client, as Well as to the Prospective Employers or Clients

Ethical Considerations

EC-1.6(a)   A paralegal shall act within the bounds of the law, solely for the benefit of the client, and shall be free of compromising influences and loyalties. Neither the paralegal's personal or business interest, nor those of other clients or third persons, should compromise the paralegal's professional judgment and loyalty to the client.

EC-1.6(b)   A paralegal shall avoid conflicts of interest that may arise from previous assignments, whether for a present or past employer or client.

EC-1.6(c)   A paralegal shall avoid conflicts of interest that may arise from family relationships and from personal and business interests.

EC-1.6(d)   In order to be able to determine whether an actual or potential conflict of interest exists a paralegal shall create and maintain an effective recordkeeping system that identifies clients, matters, and parties with which the paralegal has worked.

EC-1.6(e)   A paralegal shall reveal sufficient non-confidential information about a client or former client to reasonably ascertain if an actual or potential conflict of interest exists.

EC-1.6(f)   A paralegal shall not participate in or conduct work on any matter where a conflict of interest has been identified.

EC-1.6(g)   In matters where a conflict of interest has been identified and the client consents to continued representation, a paralegal shall comply fully with the implementation and maintenance of an Ethical Wall.

1.7 A Paralegal's Title shall be Fully Disclosed

Ethical Considerations

EC-1.7(a)   A paralegal's title shall clearly indicate the individual's status and shall be disclosed in all business and professional communications to avoid misunderstandings and misconceptions about the paralegal's role and responsibilities.

EC-1.7(b)   A paralegal's title shall be included if the paralegal's name appears on business cards, letterhead, brochures, directories, and advertisements.

EC-1.7(c)   A paralegal shall not use letterhead, business cards or other promotional materials to create a fraudulent impression of his/her status or ability to practice in the jurisdiction in which the paralegal practices.

EC-1.7(d)   A paralegal shall not practice under color of any record, diploma, or certificate that has been illegally or fraudulently obtained or issued or which is misrepresentative in any way.

EC-1.7(e)   A paralegal shall not participate in the creation, issuance, or dissemination of fraudulent records, diplomas, or certificates.

1.8 A Paralegal shall not Engage in the Unauthorized Practice of Law

Ethical Considerations

EC-1.8(a)   A paralegal shall comply with the applicable legal authority governing the unauthorized practice of law in the jurisdiction in which the paralegal practices.

§ 2. NFPA GUIDELINES FOR THE ENFORCEMENT OF THE MODEL CODE OF ETHICS AND PROFESSIONAL RESPONSIBILITY

2.1 Basis for Discipline

2.1(a)   Disciplinary investigations and proceedings brought under authority of the Rules shall be conducted in accord with obligations imposed on the paralegal professional by the Model Code of Ethics and Professional Responsibility.

2.2 Structure of Disciplinary Committee

2.2(a)   The Disciplinary Committee ("Committee") shall be made up of nine (9) members including the Chair.

2.2(b)   Each member of the Committee, including any temporary replacement members, shall have demonstrated working knowledge of ethics/professional responsibility-related issues and activities.

2.2(c)   The Committee shall represent a cross-section of practice areas and work experience. The following recommendations are made regarding the members of the Committee.
   1) At least one paralegal with one to three years of law-related work experience.
   2) At least one paralegal with five to seven years of law related work experience.
   3) At least one paralegal with over ten years of law related work experience.
   4) One paralegal educator with five to seven years of work experience; preferably in the area of ethics/professional responsibility.
   5) One paralegal manager.
   6) One lawyer with five to seven years of law-related work experience.
   7) One lay member.

2.2(d)   The Chair of the Committee shall be appointed within thirty (30) days of its members' induction. The Chair shall have no fewer than ten (10) years of law-related work experience.

2.2(e)   The terms of all members of the Committee shall be staggered. Of those members initially appointed, a simple majority plus one shall be appointed to a term of one year, and the remaining members shall be appointed to a term of two years.

Thereafter, all members of the Committee shall be appointed to terms of two years.

2.2(f)   If for any reason the terms of a majority of the Committee will expire at the same time, members may be appointed to terms of one year to maintain continuity of the Committee.

2.2(g)   The Committee shall organize from its members a three-tiered structure to investigate, prosecute and/or adjudicate charges of misconduct. The members shall be rotated among the tiers.

2.3 Operation of Committee

2.3(a)   The Committee shall meet on as-needed basis to discuss, investigate, and/or adjudicate alleged violations of the Model Code/Model Rules.

2.3(b)   A majority of the members of the Committee present at a meeting shall constitute a quorum.

2.3(c)   A Recording Secretary shall be designated to maintain complete and accurate minutes of all Committee meetings. All such minutes shall be kept confidential until a decision has been made that the matter will be set for hearing as set forth in Section 6.1 below.

2.3(d)   If any member of the Committee has a conflict of interest with the Charging Party, the Responding Party, or the allegations of misconduct, that member shall not take part in any hearing or deliberations concerning those allegations. If the absence of that member creates a lack of quorum for the Committee; then a temporary replacement for the member shall be appointed.

2.3(e)   Either the Charging Party or the Responding Party may request that, for good cause shown, any member of the Committee not participate in a hearing or deliberation. All such requests shall be honored. If the absence of a Committee member under those circumstances creates a lack of a quorum for the Committee, then a temporary replacement for that member shall be appointed.

2.3(f)   All discussions and correspondence of the Committee shall be kept confidential until a decision has been made that the matter will be set for hearing as set forth in Section 6.1 below.

2.3(g)   All correspondence from the Committee to the Responding Party regarding any charge of misconduct and any decisions made regarding the charge shall be mailed certified mail, return receipt requested, to the Responding Party's last known address and shall be clearly marked with a "Confidential" designation.

2.4 Procedure for the Reporting of Alleged Violations of the Model Code/Disciplinary Rules

2.4(a)   An individual or entity in possession of non-confidential knowledge or information concerning possible instances of misconduct shall make a confidential written report to the Committee within thirty (30) days of obtaining same. This report shall include all details of the alleged misconduct.

2.4(b)   The Committee so notified shall inform the Responding Party of the allegation(s) of misconduct no later than ten (10) business days after receiving the confidential written report from the Charging Party.

2.4(c)   Notification to the Responding Party shall include the identity of the Charging Party, unless, for good cause shown, the Charging Party requests anonymity.

2.4(d)   The Responding Party shall reply to the allegations within ten (10) business days of notification.

2.5 Procedure for the Investigation of a Charge of Misconduct

2.5(a)   Upon receipt of a Charge of Misconduct ("Charge"), or on its own initiative, the Committee shall initiate an investigation.

2.5(b)   If, upon initial or preliminary review, the Committee makes a determination that the charges are either without basis in fact or, if proven, would not constitute professional misconduct, the Committee shall dismiss the allegations of misconduct. If such determination of dismissal cannot be made, a formal investigation shall be initiated.

2.5(c)   Upon the decision to conduct a formal investigation, the Committee shall:

1) mail to the Charging and Responding Parties within three (3) business days of that decision notice of the commencement of a formal investigation. That notification shall be in writing and shall contain a complete explanation of all Charge(s), as well as the reasons for a formal investigation and shall cite the applicable codes and rules;

2) allow the Responding Party thirty (30) days to prepare and submit a confidential response to the

Committee, which response shall address each charge specifically and shall be in writing; and

3) upon receipt of the response to the notification, have thirty (30) days to investigate the Charge(s). If an extension of time is deemed necessary, that extension shall not exceed ninety (90) days.

2.5(d)   Upon conclusion of the investigation, the Committee may:

2) dismiss the Charge upon the finding that it has no basis in fact;

2) dismiss the Charge upon the finding that, if proven, the Charge would not constitute Misconduct;

3) refer the matter for hearing by the Tribunal; or

4) in the case of criminal activity, refer the Charge(s) and all investigation results to the appropriate authority.

2.6 Procedure for a Misconduct Hearing Before a Tribunal

2.6(a)   Upon the decision by the Committee that a matter should be heard, all parties shall be notified and a hearing date shall be set. The hearing shall take place no more than thirty (30) days from the conclusion of the formal investigation.

2.6(b)   The Responding Party shall have the right to counsel. The parties and the Tribunal shall have the right to call any witnesses and introduce any documentation that they believe will lead to the fair and reasonable resolution of the matter.

2.6(c)   Upon completion of the hearing, the Tribunal shall deliberate and present a written decision to the parties in accordance with procedures as set forth by the Tribunal.

2.6(d)   Notice of the decision of the Tribunal shall be appropriately published.

2.7 Sanctions

2.7(a)   Upon a finding of the Tribunal that misconduct has occurred, any of the following sanctions, or others as may be deemed appropriate, may be imposed upon the Responding Party, either singularly or in combination:

1) letter of reprimand to the Responding Party; counseling;

2) attendance at an ethics course approved by the Tribunal; probation;

3) suspension of license/authority to practice; revocation of license/authority to practice;

4) imposition of a fine; assessment of costs; or

5) in the instance of criminal activity, referral to the appropriate authority.

2.7(b)   Upon the expiration of any period of probation, suspension, or revocation, the Responding Party may make application for reinstatement. With the application for reinstatement, the Responding Party must show proof of having complied with all aspects of the sanctions imposed by the Tribunal.

2.8 Appellate Procedures

2.8(a)   The parties shall have the right to appeal the decision of the Tribunal in accordance with the procedures as set forth by the Tribunal.

DEFINITIONS

"Appellate Body" means a body established to adjudicate an appeal to any decision made by a Tribunal or other decision-making body with respect to formally-heard Charges of Misconduct:

"Charge of Misconduct" means a written submission by any individual or entity to an ethics committee, paralegal association, bar association, law enforcement agency, judicial body, government agency, or other appropriate body or entity, that sets forth non-confidential information regarding any instance of alleged misconduct by an individual paralegal or paralegal entity.

"Charging Party" means any individual or entity who submits a Charge of Misconduct against an individual paralegal or paralegal entity.

"Competency" means the demonstration of: diligence, education, skill, and mental, emotional, and physical fitness reasonably necessary for the performance of paralegal services.

"Confidential Information" means information relating to a client, whatever its source, that is not public knowledge nor available to the public. ("Non-Confidential Information" would generally include the name of the client and the identity of the matter for which the paralegal provided services.)

"Disciplinary Hearing" means the confidential proceeding conducted by a committee or other designated body or entity concerning any instance of alleged misconduct by an individual paralegal or paralegal entity.

"Disciplinary Committee" means any committee that has been established by an entity such as a paralegal association, bar association, judicial body, or government agency to: (a) identify, define and investigate general ethical considerations and concerns with respect to paralegal practice; (b) administer and enforce the Model Code and Model Rules and; (c) discipline any individual paralegal or paralegal entity found to be in violation of same.

"Disclose" means communication of information reasonably sufficient to permit identification of the significance of the matter in question.

"Ethical Wall" means the screening method implemented in order to protect a client from a conflict of interest. An Ethical Wall generally includes, but is not limited to, the following elements: (1) prohibit the paralegal from having any connection with the matter; (2) ban discussions with or the transfer of documents to or from the paralegal; (3) restrict access to files; and (4) educate all members of the firm, corporation, or entity as to the separation of the paralegal (both organizationally and physically) from the pending matter. For more information regarding the Ethical Wall, see the NFPA publication entitled "The Ethical Wall — Its Application to Paralegals."

"Ex parte" means actions or communications conducted at the instance and for the benefit of one party only, and without notice to, or contestation by, any person adversely interested.

"Investigation" means the investigation of any charge(s) of misconduct filed against an individual paralegal or paralegal entity by a Committee.

"Letter of Reprimand" means a written notice of formal censure or severe reproof administered to an individual paralegal or paralegal entity for unethical or improper conduct.

"Misconduct" means the knowing or unknowing commission of an act that is in direct violation of those Canons and Ethical Considerations of any and all applicable codes and/or rules of conduct.

"Paralegal" is synonymous with "Legal Assistant" and is defined as a person qualified through education, training, or work experience to perform substantive legal work that requires knowledge of legal concepts and is customarily, but not exclusively performed by a lawyer: This person may be retained or employed by a lawyer, law office, governmental agency, or other entity or may be authorized by administrative, statutory, or court authority to perform this work.

"Pro Bono Publico" means providing or assisting to provide quality legal services in order to enhance access to justice for persons of limited means; charitable, religious, civic, community, governmental and educational organizations in matters that are designed primarily to address the legal needs of persons with limited means; or individuals, groups or organizations seeking to secure or protect civil rights, civil liberties or public rights.

"Proper Authority" means the local paralegal association, the local or state bar association, Committee (s) of the local paralegal or bar association(s), local prosecutor, administrative agency, or other tribunal empowered to investigate or act upon an instance of alleged misconduct.

"Responding Party" means an individual paralegal or paralegal entity against whom a Charge of Misconduct has been submitted.

"Revocation" means the recision of the license, certificate or other authority to practice of an individual paralegal or paralegal entity found in violation of those Canons and Ethical Considerations of any and all applicable codes and/or rules of conduct.

"Suspension" means the suspension of the license, certificate or other authority to practice of an individual paralegal or paralegal entity found in violation of those Canons and Ethical Considerations of any and all applicable codes and/or rules of conduct.

"Tribunal" means the body designated to adjudicate allegations of misconduct.

GLOSSARY

abandoned property   Personal property that has been deliberately left in a location without the intention to retrieve it.

acceptance   Final step necessary to form a legal contract. A demonstration of agreement to all of the terms of the contract that has been offered.

actus reus   Element of physical conduct necessary to commit a criminal act.

administrative agency   Government office enabled by the legislature and overseen by the executive branch. The purpose of such agencies is to apply certain specified laws created by the legislature.

administrative branch   Administrative agencies created pursuant to legislation and overseen by the executive branch to administer and define statutes.

administrative law   Regulations and decisions issued by administrative agencies that explain and detail statutes.

administrative law judge   Judicial officer assigned to preside over cases between individuals or entities and government administrative agencies.

Administrative Procedure Act   Congressional enactment applied to all federal administrative agencies requiring them to follow certain procedures in the issuance of administrative law.

adverse possession   When title to real property is acquired without purchase or voluntary transfer of title. Ordinarily, one who obtains title by adverse possession must openly and continuously exercise possession and control over the entire property inconsistent with the interest of the current owner and all others who claim rights to the property for a period of time specified by statute.

affirm   Approve. When an appellate court affirms the result in the original court, that result is approved and can be enforced.

agency   Relationship in which one party, known as the agent, acts on behalf of another party, known as the principal. In a valid agency relationship, the agent can legally bind the principal; e.g., an agent can enter into a contract on behalf of a principal.

ancillary jurisdiction   Authority of a court over issues in a case subject to the court's authority on grounds unrelated to the issues.

annulment   Legal relationship declared invalid in which the parties to the relationship are treated as if the relationship never existed, e.g., marriage.

antenuptial agreement   Agreement between parties prior to a marriage that states the terms for distribution of assets and liabilities in the event the marriage relationship ends.

appellate jurisdiction   Authority of one court to review the actions in another court for the purpose of identifying an abuse of discretion. See *discretion*.

arraignment   Stage of a criminal proceeding in which the accused is formally charged.

articles of incorporation   Document filed with the state at the time of incorporation to state the purpose of the corporation and define the corporate structure.

assignment   A grant of rights to a third party an original party is entitled to under a contract.

assumption of risk   Defense to negligence on the basis that the plaintiff knew of, appreciated, and voluntarily encountered the danger of the defendant's conduct.

attorney   Individual who has completed the necessary requirements of education and training to receive a license to practice law in a jurisdiction.

bailment   Temporary relinquishment of control over one's personal property to a third party.

bench trial   Trial in which the judge determines which law will be applicable and applies the law to the facts of the case.

bilateral contract   Contractual agreement between two or more persons in which each party promises to deliver performance in exchange for the performance of the other.

bill   Proposed law presented to the legislature for consideration.

bylaws   Document of a corporation that details the methods of operation, such as officers and duties, chain of command, and general corporate procedures.

case law   Law that is created judicially when a legal principle of common law is extended to a similar situation.

cases   Judicial opinions that are common law or case law and that interpret statutory and administrative law.

civil law   Law that governs the private rights of individuals, legal entities, and government. See *criminal law.*

Code of Federal Regulations   Publication that contains all current administrative regulations.

codification   Process of incorporating newly passed legislation into existing publication of statutes.

common law   Judicially created legal principles or standards. The judiciary has the authority to create law in situations where none currently exists.

comparative negligence   Degree of plaintiff's own negligent conduct that was responsible for plaintiff's injury.

compensatory damages   An award of money payable to the injured party for the reasonable cost of the injuries.

complaint   (also known as petition) Document that apprises the court and the defendant of the nature of the cause of action by the plaintiff.

concurrent jurisdiction   When more than one court has authority to hear a case.

contract   Legally binding agreement that obligates two or more parties to do something they were not already obligated to do or refrain from doing something to which the parties were legally entitled.

contractual capacity   Ability to enter into and be bound by a legal contract, which ability has not been diminished by age of minority or adjudicated incompetence.

contributory negligence   Doctrine that maintains that a plaintiff who, in any way, contributes to his/her injury cannot recover from a negligent defendant.

consideration   That which one party provides to another party as inducement to enter into a contractual agreement. The benefit a party receives as the result of entering a contract with another party.

corporation   Entity legally recognized as independent of its owners, known as shareholders. A corporation can sue or be sued in its own name regarding its own rights and liabilities.

criminal law   Law created and enforced by the legislature for the health, welfare, safety, and general good of the public.

criminal procedure   Law created to assist in the fair and efficient enforcement of criminal law.

critical stage   Stage of a criminal proceeding in which the presumed innocence of the accused is in jeopardy and thus the accused is entitled to representation of counsel.

damage   Financial, physical, or emotional injury.

deposition   Written or oral questions submitted to a party or witness in a lawsuit in which the answers are given orally and under oath, then transcribed into writing.

defendant   Party against whom a lawsuit is instituted.

delegation   Transfer of one's contractual obligations to a third person.

delegation doctrine   Principle that Congress may not assign its authority to create statutory law, nor may any other government entity assume such authority.

discovery   Court-supervised exchange of evidence and other relevant information between parties to a lawsuit.

discretion   Limits of authority. Abuse of discretion occurs when one's authority is exceeded or improperly used; e.g., abuse of discretion by a judge or jury is grounds for appeal.

dissolution of marriage   End of a marriage relationship.

diversity of citizenship   Method of achieving federal jurisdiction over a matter. It is necessary that all parties be diverse; i.e., no plaintiff and defendant can be domiciled in the same state. The second requirement of diversity of citizenship is that the amount in dispute between the parties be in excess of the minimum amount stated by federal statute.

double jeopardy   Being placed on trial for the same crime twice.

due process   That which is necessary to fundamental fairness in the American system of justice.

enabling act   Congressional enactment that creates the authority in the executive to organize and oversee an administrative agency.

equity   Functional legal remedy sought when money damages would be inadequate as a method of compensating the injured party. Actions in equity ask the court to order performance or nonperformance of certain acts.

estate   All material assets of an individual or legal entity, including liquid assets (cash or items that can readily be converted to cash) and nonliquid assets.

evidence   Testimony, documentation, or tangible items admissible in court to support a party's claims or defenses in a lawsuit.

exclusive jurisdiction   Authority of a court to hear a case, which authority is superior to all other courts.

excusable behavior   Behavior by one who, under the color of authority, is considered to be innocent of otherwise criminal behavior.

exhaustion of remedies   Requirement that anyone having a dispute with an administrative agency must first follow all available procedures to resolve the dispute within the agency before taking the issue before the judiciary.

federal court   A court that is part of the United States courts.

federal question   Method of achieving jurisdiction of the federal courts over a dispute between parties. It is necessary that a significant part of the dispute arise from the Constitution or a federal law.

fee simple   Absolute ownership of property in American law.

felony   Serious crime punishable by imprisonment in excess of one year and/or other significant penalties.

fixture   Item of personal property that has been so affixed to real property that it cannot be removed without damage to the real property. A fixture is personal property that essentially becomes part of the real property.

forced share   Legal right of a surviving spouse to receive a certain percentage of the estate of the deceased spouse, superior to the terms of a will or other rights of inheritance by heirs.

forum non conveniens   (inconvenient forum) Applied when a court with jurisdiction over a matter determines that another court, which also has jurisdiction, would be the more appropriate forum.

freehold estate   Interest in real property that involves certain rights of ownership. See *non-freehold estate*.

grand jury   A number of individuals (usually more than 20) who review the evidence to determine whether defendant could be convicted of the crime if charged and tried.

in personam jurisdiction   Authority of a court over an individual and all of his/her assets.

in rem jurisdiction   Authority of a court over a person's real or personal property.

intentional tort   Act that the actor knows or should know with substantial certainty will cause harm to another.

interrogatories   Questions submitted by one party in a lawsuit to the opposing party. Said questions must pertain to the dispute between the parties and must be answered within a specific time and under oath. A method of discovery.

intestate succession   Method of distributing an estate of one who died without a valid will.

joint custody   Sharing of responsibility for upbringing of children of the joint custodians. In some cases, joint custody also involves shared physical custody of the children.

joint tenancy   Form of multiple property ownership in which the property owners have fee simple and share four unities. Each owner shares in the right of survivorship.

judge   Judicial officer who presides over cases in litigation within a court system.

judiciary   Appointed or elected officials (judges, magistrates, justices of the peace) who preside in the courts over disputes among citizens and the government.

jurisdiction   (1) Authority of a court over parties and subject of a dispute. (2) Geographical boundaries of the area and citizens over which a court has authority.

justifiable behavior   Behavior by one who, under the circumstances, is considered to be innocent of otherwise criminal behavior.

law clerk   Lawyer, law student, or paralegal who conducts legal research and writing and various other duties but who does not represent individual clients as a licensed attorney.

lawyer   See *attorney.*

legal analysis   Process of examining precedent in detail to predict its effect on future similar circumstances.

legal separation   Legal document that establishes the property rights of the parties without effecting a dissolution of the actual marriage relationship.

legal standard   Law created by one of the three sources of government, including the legislature, executive branch or the judiciary.

legislative branch   Members of a congress elected by the citizens of a jurisdiction to represent their interests, e.g., senator or representative.

liability   Legal responsibility resulting from an act or failure to act when there was a legal obligation to do so.

life estate   Right to possess and use real property for the duration of one's life, with limited ownership rights.

limited partnership   Partnership of two or more persons in which the limited partner can be held liable for partnership debts only to the extent of his or her investment and cannot take part in general management and operation of the partnership business.

lobbyist   Individual representing interested parties who meets with legislators about proposed laws.

long-arm jurisdiction   Authority of the government of one jurisdiction to reach into another jurisdiction for the purpose of exercising control over a particular citizen.

lost property   Property unintentionally left by the owner in a place no longer known to the owner.

maintenance   Financial assistance from a divorced spouse to the other divorced spouse to be used for necessary living expenses and income.

material evidence   Evidence necessary to a fair and informed decision by the trier of fact.

mens rea   Mental state required as an element necessary to commit a criminal act.

misdemeanor   Criminal offense punishable by a fine or imprisonment of less than one year.

mislaid property   Property that was intentionally placed by the owner and later forgotten.

modern balance   Goal of lawmaking authorities to balance the need for consistency and stability against the need for a flexible and adaptive government.

motion   Formal request by a party to a lawsuit for court-ordered action/nonaction.

naturalist theory   Philosophy that all persons know inherently the difference between right and wrong.

negligence   Act or failure to act toward another when (1) a duty was owed to the other person; (2) the act or failure to act was less than a reasonable person would have done under the circumstances; (3) the act or failure to act was the direct cause of injury to the other person; and (4) the injury caused measurable financial, physical, or emotional damage to the other person.

negotiable instrument   Document recognized by law as an exchange for legal tender and that meets all legal requirements, including that the document be (1) written, (2) signed, (3) for a specified amount, (4) payable on a certain date or on demand, (5) written with words that indicate whether the document is payable to a stated person (bearer), (6) required that no additional acts are to be performed before payment.

non-freehold estate   Interest in real property that is limited in duration and involves the right of possession but not ownership. See *freehold estate*.

note   Negotiable instrument that involves two parties: the "payor" promises to pay an amount to the "payee" on a specified date.

offer   A party presents an agreement for acceptance or rejection by a second party, which agreement includes all necessary requirements and elements of a legal contract.

original jurisdiction   Authority of a court to rule in a lawsuit from commencement through the conclusion of trial.

overrule   Judicial action that states that a legal standard previously recognized is no longer effective as law. Distinguished from reversal (see below).

par value   Legal value of stock (percentages of ownership) in a corporation. Par value is determined by the board of directors of the corporation.

paralegal/legal assistant   One who has legal training and education and performs tasks in the law office traditionally performed by the attorney, with the exception of advocacy and giving of legal advice. In some geographical areas, these terms are used interchangeably, while in others, they imply distinct levels of professional ability.

partnership   Agreement of two or more parties to engage in business or enterprise, with profits and losses shared among all parties.

pendant jurisdiction   Occurs when a case involves multiple issues and the court in which the case is filed has actual authority over some but not all of the issues, in which case, the court has the option to exercise authority over those issues it could not ordinarily decide, thus exercising pendant jurisdiction.

per capita   Distribution in equal shares, with each person representing one share.

per stirpes   Distribution in equal shares to one level or class of persons; if a member of this level or class is deceased, the member's heirs divide the share.

permanent injunction   Court order that permanently orders a party to act or refrain from acting in a particular manner.

personal property   Movable items that are not land or permanently affixed to land. Personal property includes tangible (physical) and intangible items, such as rights of ownership in property held by others, e.g., bank accounts, or rights of ownership in legal entities, e.g., stock. It does not include rights to bring legal action against others, commonly known as a chose in action.

positivist theory   Political belief that there should be a superior government entity not subject to question or challenge.

precedent   Existing legal standards that courts look to for guidance when making a determination of a legal issue.

preliminary injunction   Court order that orders a party to act or refrain from acting in a particular manner for a specified period of time.

probable cause   Legal concept of suspicion supported by facts necessary before a search or arrest can be conducted by law enforcement officers.

probate   Process of paying creditors and distributing the estate of one who is deceased. Probate courts also often administer the estates of living persons who are incapable of managing their own affairs.

procedural law   Law used to guide parties fairly and efficiently through the legal system.

promoter   One who is hired as a fiduciary to recruit investors in a proposed corporation.

property settlement agreement   Agreement as to the property rights and obligations of co-owners/co-debtors, such as parties to a marriage.

proximate cause   Direct cause sufficient to produce a result. No other intervening force can occur independently and prior to the result that is also sufficient to produce the result.

quasi in rem jurisdiction   Authority of a court to alter a person's interest and/or ownership in real or personal property.

real property   Land or anything permanently affixed to land and no longer movable.

reasonable conduct   That action or nonaction that is appropriate under the circumstances when all risks and benefits are taken into account.

reasonable man   One similar in age, intelligence, and experience to the party alleged to be at fault who perceives and appreciates all dangers and benefits of action or nonaction and who acts in the most careful manner.

recision   Legal termination of a contract prior to its completion. Cancellation.

relevant evidence   Evidence that tends to establish an essential fact in the dispute.

remand   Action of one court that returns a case to the court where it originated, e.g., following a reversal or improper transfer.

removal   Transfer of a case to federal court that was originally filed in state court.

request for production   Written request from one party in a lawsuit to the opposing party that seeks to copy and/or inspect documentary evidence relevant to the dispute. A method of discovery.

res ipsa loquitur   "The thing speaks for itself." Method of proving negligence when (1) the injury would not ordinarily have occurred without negligence, (2) the instrument causing injury was in the exclusive control of the defendant, and (3) the plaintiff in no way contributed to the injury.

respondeat superior   Liability of an employer for the acts of an employee who caused damage to a third party while acting within the scope of employment.

reverse   The action of an appellate court used to invalidate a decision by a court of original jurisdiction. The parties to the lawsuit are affected accordingly.

right of survivorship   Characteristic associated with multiple property ownership in which the ownership interest transfers automatically to co-owners upon death.

session law   Published statutes passed during a specific session of the legislature.

shareholder   One who owns stock representing an ownership interest in a corporation.

slip law   Individual statute not yet published with other statutes.

slip opinion   Individual court opinion that is not yet published with other opinions.

sociological theory   Doctrine that follows the principle that government should adapt laws to reflect the current needs and beliefs of society.

sole proprietorship   Individual ownership of a business entity. The individual is personally liable for debts of the business.

specific performance   Court order to complete performance as stated in a contract. Allowed in certain cases of equity where the performance is unique and cannot be imitated or compensated by the payment of money.

stare decisis   "Let the decision stand." Method used by the judiciary when applying precedent to current situations.

statute of frauds   Statutory law that specifies what contracts must be in writing before they will be enforced.

statutory law   A statute. Law that is created by the legislature.

strict liability   Liability without fault. Applied in situations where the intention or neglect of the party is immaterial. The mere performance of the act or omission will result in liability.

subject matter jurisdiction   Authority of a court to determine the actual issue between the parties.

substantive law   Law that creates and resolves the issue between the parties. Legal standard that guides conduct and is applied to determine whether or not conduct was legally appropriate.

summary judgment   Determination prior to trial of the rights and obligations of the parties. This is granted only when there is no significant fact left to be decided on the basis of the evidence. The greatest weight of the evidence supports only one result.

temporary restraining order   Court order that orders a party to act or refrain from acting in a particular manner for a short time until the court has the opportunity to consider a more permanent ruling.

tenancy in common   Form of multiple ownership of property in which each tenant (owner) shares with the other(s) an undivided interest in the property.

tenancy by entirety   Form of multiple ownership of property between spouses that includes right of survivorship.

testate succession   Method of distributing the estate of a deceased person in accordance with the terms of a valid will.

third-party beneficiary   One who, as the result of gift or collateral agreement, is entitled to the contractual performance owed another.

tort   Civil wrong by a party, other than breach of contract, that results in injury to the private rights or interests of another party.

traditional balance   Goal of the judiciary to allow maximum personal freedom without detracting from the welfare of the general public.

trial court   Court of original jurisdiction with authority to hear evidence of parties and render a verdict.

unilateral contract   Contractual agreement in which one party makes a promise to perform upon receiving the actual performance of the other party.

venue   Proper individual court within a jurisdiction to determine a dispute between parties.

veto   Presidential power to invalidate law passed by a majority of Congress (two-thirds majority of each house needed to override).

INDEX